SUBJECT MAP

W9-AYH-639

ENGLISH

Grammar and Writing 4
Speaking....................74
How to Study 78
Writing a Research Paper....354
Literature..................388
Preparing a Book Report 436

THE YOUNG READER'S COMPANION

English Composition 32
Writing the AP English
    Essay 1157

FOREIGN LANGUAGE

Review of French Grammar 118
Review of German Grammar
.........................152
Review of Spanish Grammar 182
The Latin Language............217

MATHEMATICS

Mathematics—basic
    arithmetic through
    pre-algebra.....................176

MATH FOR FUN PROJECTS

Mathematics—algebra,
geometry, trigonometry......260
Calculus 372
AP Calculus 841

SCIENCE

Health and Safety.............330
Life Science....................354

Physical Sciences 364
Earth Science 384
Space Science 404

NATURE FOR FUN PROJECTS
SCIENCE FOR FUN EXPERIMENTS

Biology..................192
Chemistry 226
Physics 244
Biology...................478
Chemistry 500
Geology 518
Physics 534
AP Biology 573
Earth and the Universe 9
Life on Earth 87
Science and
    Technology 393

SOCIAL SCIENCES

United States History..........106
The United States Today 134
Flags of the U.S., States,
    and Territories.................154
Display and Care of the
    U.S. Flag 173

GEOGRAPHY FOR FUN PROJECTS

United States Government......4
People of the United States ..54
World History...................78
Countries of the World 138
World Atlas follows 188
Economics 246
History of Western
    Civilization 294
Political Science 342
Psychology 356

WHAT HAPPENED WHEN

AP U.S. History...................33
AP U.S. Government &
    Politics 381
People...................197
History.....................311
Arts and Culture 489
International World 571

SURVIVAL GUIDE

Study Skills 550
Taking Major Tests 586
College Entrance
    Exams 598
Thinking About
    College.......................622
Advancing Your
    Career 646

MISCELLANEOUS

Sports....................430
Music.....................456
Entertainment...................468
Tables..............................743

- HANDBOOK 1
- HANDBOOK 2
- HANDBOOK 3
- HANDBOOK 4
- HANDBOOK 5

STUDENT HANDBOOK

Including
SCIENCE FOR FUN EXPERIMENTS
NATURE FOR FUN PROJECTS
GEOGRAPHY FOR FUN PROJECTS
MATH FOR FUN PROJECTS

Volume 1

Today, our students are overwhelmed with information from an amazing number of sources. The *Volume Library* and *Student Handbooks* are a valuable "oasis" from which students can access accurate and reliable information about virtually any academic discipline. These books are outstanding reference guides for all students who wish to excel academically. Additionally, they serve as an excellent resource for students who need a quick review or for students who simply need extra academic help.

Karen C. Tilton, M.A.
Department of English
Maquoketa High School, Maquoketa, Iowa
past recipient of University of Iowa Teacher of the Year award

Having the *Volume Library* and *Student Handbooks* is like having a full-time tutor at home. They are a great learning resource for the entire family.

Daniel H. Durbin, M.A.
Chair, Department of English
Oakland City University, Oakland, Indiana
past recipient of Indiana State Teacher of the Year award

The *Volume Library* and *Student Handbooks* are uniquely designed to provide a student not only with ready access to information but also with problem-solving techniques and study skill guides that enable the student to utilize that information in the most efficient manner. The effective use of boldface type, frequent highlighting, and ample illustrations make the VL and Handbooks extremely user-friendly. Finally, the VL and Handbooks are kept current and topical to an extent that few if any textbooks or other reference books can match.

Art Echerd, Ph.D.
Department of History
Harpeth Hall School, Nashville, Tennessee
past recipient of Presidential Scholar's Inspirational Teacher Award

Designed to put timely and accurate information at the fingertips of people of all ages, the Southwestern Company's *Volume Library* and *Student Handbooks* have quickly become a strategic resource for our entire family. This invaluable compilation of reference material, ranging from a comprehensive review of core curriculum subjects and research skills to a helpful study skills manual and career resource guide, has made our set a series of books that collect no dust. In fact, they are impossible for me to find around our home. If my children don't have them in their rooms, I can assume that they have been loaned to a neighbor or are serving as reference material in my wife's elementary classroom. She has found these texts to be particularly useful as a guide for science fair projects as well as a reliable addition to her modern U.S. and world geography and current affairs lessons. Our college student would not be without them as a desktop encyclopedia resource in his dorm room, while our youngest son continually refers to them for everything from writing his research papers to enhancing his preparations for Advanced Placement exams. If only I had a set to myself! If you're looking for a flexible educational tool that will ensure higher academic performance and increase motivation for learning in your family, the *Volume Library* and *Student Handbooks* belong on an easy-to-reach shelf in your home. Good luck keeping track of where they were last seen!

Stan Johnston, M.A.
Department of English and Assistant Principal
Los Alamos High School, Los Alamos, New Mexico
past recipient of New Mexico State Teacher of the Year award

STUDENT HANDBOOK

Including
SCIENCE FOR FUN EXPERIMENTS
NATURE FOR FUN PROJECTS
GEOGRAPHY FOR FUN PROJECTS
MATH FOR FUN PROJECTS

Volume **1**

SOUTHWESTERN
Nashville, Tennessee

Geography for Fun Projects
© Aladdin Books Ltd. 2001
Math for Fun Projects
© Aladdin Books Ltd. 1999
Nature for Fun Projects
© Aladdin Books Ltd. 2000
Science for Fun Experiments
© Aladdin Books Ltd. 1996

Designed and produced by
Aladdin Books Ltd.
28 Percy Street
London W1P 0LD

First published in the United States by
Copper Beech Books, an imprint of
The Millbrook Press
2 Old New Milford Road
Brookfield, Connecticut 06804

Advisory Board

Preface

This new edition of the *Student Handbook* is among the most practical and appealing student aids ever published. Consisting of more than 1,100 pages in each volume, it brings together information on the major subjects taught in every elementary, junior high, and high school.

For this new edition, the most important information on each subject has been distilled and presented in a visually interesting and easy-to-use way. Both volumes are filled with tables, informative line drawings, brief dictionaries of terms used in special fields, chronologies showing major national or world events year by year, time lines showing the life spans of important men and women in history, and many other features. All information is up to date.

The *Student Handbook* has been organized to present material usually taught in the fourth to eighth grades in Handbook 1 and material taught in ninth grade or above in Handbook 2. Useful information for all ages will be found in both handbooks, however. Each *Student Handbook* is organized in two major parts. PART ONE includes material designed to help students do better in school. PART TWO features a complete reference work that readers of all ages will find useful and enjoyable.

The major headings in PART ONE of Handbook 1 are:

Study Guide (with special emphasis on grammar and writing)
Social Studies (U.S. history and U.S. geography)
Mathematics and Science (basic arithmetic, pre-algebra, and science)
Sports and Entertainment (sports, music, film, and television)

PART TWO of Handbook 1 contains four great references useful for students: *Geography for Fun Projects, Math for Fun Projects, Nature for Fun Projects,* and *Science for Fun Experiments.* Factual and current, these references help children see that learning really is fun.

The major headings in PART ONE of Handbook 2 are:

Social Studies (world history and geography; U.S. government, including the Constitution and the presidents; and a color atlas of the world)
Science and Mathematics (laboratory sciences and algebra, geometry, etc.)
English and Literature (writing research papers and book reports and understanding poetry, drama, and fiction)

PART TWO of Handbook 2 is *The Young Reader's Companion,* an illustrated A-to-Z guide to books, authors, and subjects of special interest to young people. Its more than 2,000 concise, lively entries are as entertaining as they are informative. The entries are carefully crafted to help young people find the books they will enjoy reading, provide them with useful information that will increase their enjoyment of the books they choose, and encourage them to broaden and deepen their reading experiences.

The two handbooks are designed to complement each other. For example, a reader using the algebra section in Handbook 2 may find it helpful to review parts of arithmetic in Handbook 1. Similarly, a reader who has found basic material in "Physical Sciences" in Handbook 1 will find additional, more advanced material in "Physics" in Handbook 2. The comprehensive Index at the end of each handbook helps locate all major information on a given topic.

In the Math and English chapters, you will note that some text is highlighted in either yellow or green. Text highlighted in yellow contains key definitions or concepts; text highlighted in green indicates helpful hints or tips.

The *Student Handbook* offers students and those out of school essential information on basic skills (reading, writing, mathematics) and a vast collection of easy-to-use data on all major school subjects. We are certain that this set of books will contribute to increased success in school and to the enjoyment of learning.

We are also pleased to offer access to our Web site, www.southwestern.com., where, among other things, you will find listings of additional subject-specific reference materials, post-publication additions and corrections, and notes on using the books effectively. Every effort has been made to ensure that these books are as accurate as possible. If errors or omissions should be discovered, however, we would appreciate hearing from you. Please send comments or suggestions to editor@southwestern.com, or to Editor, Student Handbooks, P.O. Box 305142, Nashville, Tennessee 37230.

—The Editors

Contents

Study Guide 2-103

Grammar and Writing

4-73

- Parts of speech 4
- What are sentences? 36
- Combining sentences 44
- Sentence diagrams 50
- Spelling 52
- Punctuation review 54
- Writing a paper 56
- Synonyms and antonyms 58

Speaking

74-77

- How speaking works 74
- Improving your speech 75
- Preparing a report 77

How to Study

78-103

- Make a plan 78
- Learn to listen 81
- Improve your reading 84
- Improve your test-taking 94
- Guide to good reading 96

Social Studies 104-173

United States History

106-133

- Explorers and colonies 106
- A nation is born 110
- Expansion and Civil War 115
- Growing and changing 122
- Boom, bust, war 125
- Modern America 129

United States Today

134-173

- The land 134
- The people 136
- The West 138
- The Midwest 142
- The South 146
- The Northeast 150
- U.S. territories 152
- U.S. flags 154
- State flags 156
- Display and Care of the United States Flag 173

Mathematics and Science 174-427

Mathematics

176-329

- Arithmetic 176
- Addition 178
- Subtraction 191
- Multiplication 209
- Division 220
- Fractions 230
- Exponents 244
- Decimals 246
- Ratio and percent 274
- Pre-algebra 285
- Symbols 319
- Formulas 320
- Dictionary of mathematics 325

Health and Safety

330-353

- Nutrition 331
- Exercise 336
- Drugs and disease 338
- Human anatomy 340
- Safety 344
- Dictionary of health and safety 352

Life Science

354-363

- Natural resources 354
- The ecosystem 356
- Biomes 358
- Cycles 360
- Succession 361
- Dictionary of life science 362

Physical Sciences

364-383

- The scientific method 364
- The physical sciences 368
- Matter 371
- Energy 374
- Electromagnetism 378
- Wave motion 380
- Dictionary of physical sciences 382

Earth Science
384-403

- Plate tectonics 384
- Rocks and minerals 389
- Glaciers 390
- Climate 392
- Weather 396
- Dictionary of earth science 402

Space Science
404-427

- The solar system 404
- Galaxies 411
- Stars 412
- Other phenomena 414
- Cosmology 415
- Space exploration 416
- Dictionary of space science 424

Sports and Entertainment 428-478

Sports

430-455

- Baseball 430
- Football 434
- Basketball 438
- Hockey 440
- Soccer 442
- Tennis 444
- Golf 446
- Olympics 448
- Other sports 450

Music

456-467

- Mechanics of music 457
- Musical instruments 458
- Materials of music 461
- Kinds of music 463
- Dictionary of music 466

Entertainment

468-478

- Live entertainment 468
- Movies 471
- Broadcasting 473
- Dictionary of entertainment 476

Index following page 478

The Student Handbook

Editorial

Editorial Director
Mary Cummings

Managing Editor
Judy Jackson

Editors
Georgia Brazil
Barbara J. Reed

Research Editors
Ashley Bienvenu
Linda Jones
Molly Kempf
Scott Carlton Larson
Debbie Van Mol
Tanis Westbrook

Copy Editors
Tammy Binford
Amy Green
Alison Nash
Andaleah Silka

Art

Design Director
Steve Newman

Designers
Bill Kersey
Jim Scott

Production Designer
Travis Rader

Illustrators
Lloyd Birmingham
Ric Del Rossi
Leslie Dunlap
Mary Jane Huffines
Phillip Jones
Kathie Kelleher
H. Peter Loewer
Jean Loewer
Joel Snyder
Brian H. Thompson
Betty Whelan

Digital Prepress
Donna Bailey

Composition
Jessie Anglin
Sara Anglin

Production

Production Manager
Tom Norvell

*Senior Production
Coordinator*
Powell Ropp

Schedule Coordinator
Wanda Sawyer

Marketing

*Vice President and
Executive Editor*
Dan Moore

Product Manager
Fiona Greenland

Associate Editors
Sharon Dean
Lisa Fairfax

Sales

Sales Director
Creig Soeder

The original *Student Handbook* text, substantial portions of which are included, was developed by The Hudson Group, Inc., Pleasantville, New York: Gorton Carruth and Eugene Ehrlich, Administrative Editors.

Contributors

Barth, Frances F.
Freelance medical writer

Behrendt, Else
Freelance writer

Browne, Renni
Freelance writer

Bunch, Bryan H.
B.A., Writer and textbook consultant; former editor-in-chief, American Book Company

Burr, Marie F.
M.Ed., Teacher of mathematics and freelance writer

Burrowes, Marietta
Freelance writer

Bye, Delia
Freelance writer

Carruth, Gisele
Freelance writer

Davidson, Nance J.
Freelance writer

Dillon, John
B.A., Freelance writer

Echerd, Arthur R., Jr.
Ph.D., Teacher of history and freelance writer

Friese, Karl
Freelance writer

Golub, Marcia H.
B.A., Freelance writer and editor

Grote, Dale A.
Ph.D., Associate Professor of Classics and Director of Main Liberal Studies, University of North Carolina, Charlotte

Hand, Raymond V.
B.A., Writer and editor

Harrington, John P.
Ph.D., Writer and editor of reference works

Helm, Sylvia
Freelance writer

Heyl, Lawrence, Jr.
Freelance writer

Hicks, Mary
Freelance writer

Isaac, Helene
Freelance writer

Johnston, Stan W.
M.A., Teacher of English and freelance writer

Katz, Naomi
Freelance writer

Levine, Seymour
Freelance writer

Liss, Howard
Freelance writer

Loewer, H. Peter
B.F.A., Author and illustrator

Lorayne, Harry
Author and editor

Lorimer, Donald
B.A., Freelance writer

Lorimer, Lawrence T.
M.A., Author and editorial consultant

Maloney, John
Freelance writer

McHugh, Janet
B.A., Writer and editor of textbooks

Munroe, Antje L.
Freelance writer

O'Connor, Kimberly A.
M.A., Freelance writer

Plummer, Samuel C.
M.B.A., Freelance writer and editor

Rich, Elizabeth
Freelance writer

Siegel, Bertram
Freelance writer

Tesar, Jenny
Freelance writer

Wert, Thaddeus
M.E., Teacher of mathematics and freelance writer

Wetterau, Bruce
Freelance writer and editor

Worth, Richard
Freelance writer

STUDENT HANDBOOK

Including
SCIENCE FOR FUN EXPERIMENTS
NATURE FOR FUN PROJECTS
GEOGRAPHY FOR FUN PROJECTS
MATH FOR FUN PROJECTS

Volume **1**

Study Guide

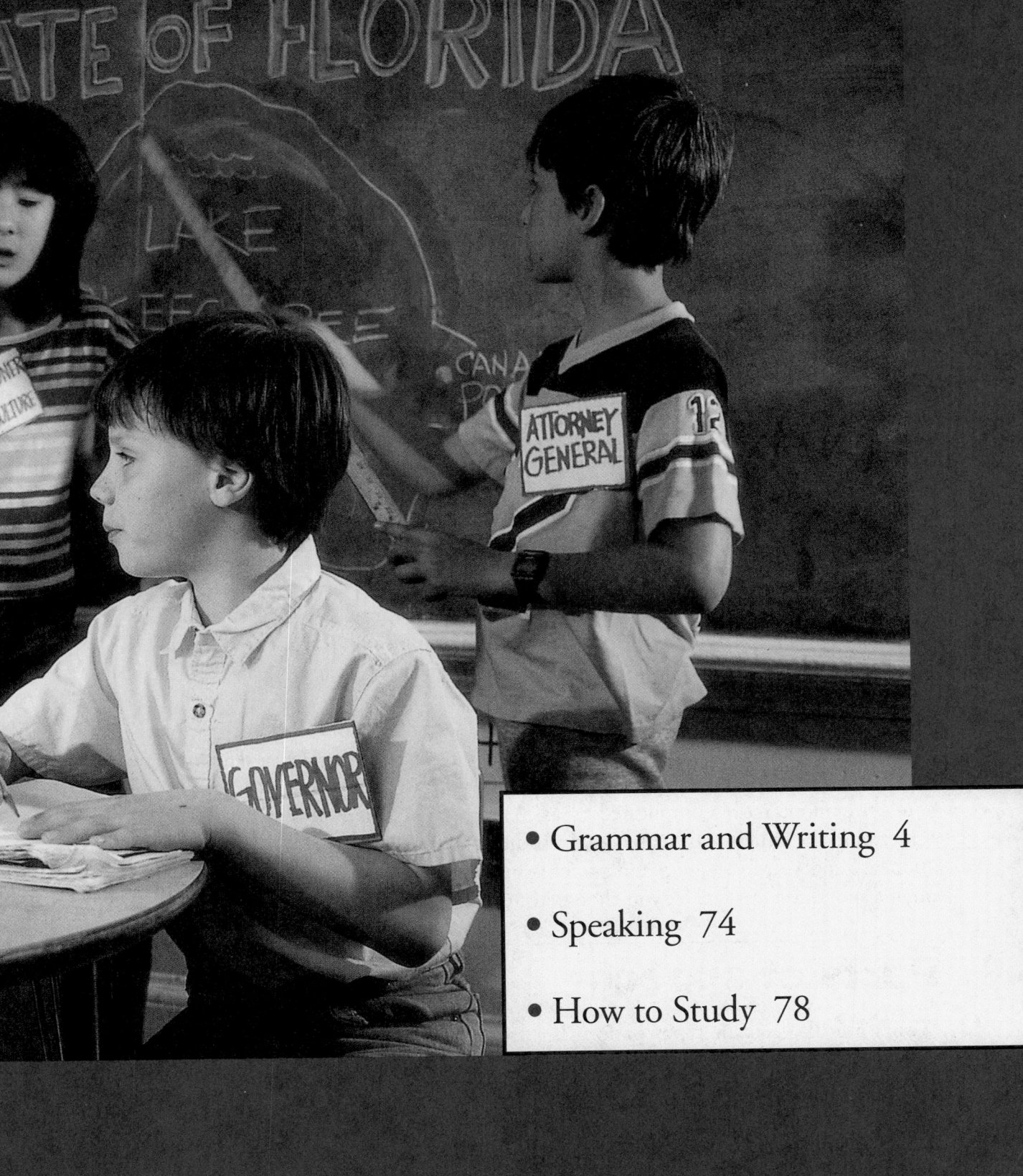

- Grammar and Writing 4

- Speaking 74

- How to Study 78

Parts of speech	**4**
What are sentences?	**36**
Combining sentences	**44**
Sentence Diagrams	**50**
Spelling	**52**
Punctuation Review	**54**
Writing a paper	**56**
Synonyms and antonyms	**58**

Grammar and Writing

Even though the purpose of your writing may change in each assignment you get, the main goal always stays the same: to express ideas clearly and effectively. Unless readers can understand what you write, they will not appreciate your special ideas on a subject. This is where knowing good grammar becomes important. Knowledge of the rules of language helps you to write clearly, express ideas effectively, and avoid being misunderstood.

This section tells about the basics of writing. It begins with an easy-to-use introduction to grammar. Printed in large type and containing many examples, it tells you how words are used to make sentences. The following part on combining sentences will help you write about more complicated ideas. A section on diagramming will help you understand the structure of sentences. In addition, the section on spelling and punctuation will aid you in spelling and punctuating correctly. Finally, a dictionary of synonyms and antonyms will let you choose just the right words for what you want to say.

Parts of speech

Words are like certain types of lizards that change color to fit their surroundings. Words can change their meaning and the job they do, depending on when, where, and how they are used. Because words can be used in so many ways, people have created labels that show how words work in different surroundings. These labels are called *parts of speech*. There are eight parts of speech: nouns, pronouns, verbs, adjectives, adverbs, prepositions, conjunctions, and interjections. Knowing how to identify each part of speech will help you understand the parts of a sentence and write clearly and effectively.

4

Parts of Speech

This box reviews the parts of speech. More detailed coverage appears in the following pages.

A **noun** is a word that names *people, places, things,* or *ideas.*

people	mother, carpenter, Amy	**places**	city, beach, France
things	tree, book, building	**ideas**	honesty, freedom, hope

A **pronoun** is a word that takes the place of a noun, a group of words acting like a noun, or another pronoun.

you, me, their, himself, this, who, any, something

A **verb** is a word that expresses *action* or a *state of being.* It tells what a noun does or helps to tell what or how it is. Some verbs link the subject of a sentence with other verbs; these are called *linking* verbs.

action   run, fly, rest, think, give
being, linking   be, have, appear, smell

An **adjective** is a word that modifies the meaning of a noun or pronoun.

quiet, large, nasty, purple, glorious

An **adverb** is a word that modifies a verb, an adjective, or another adverb by making its meaning more specific. It can answer the questions *when, where, how, how much,* or *to what extent or degree.*

when	now, soon, early, never	**to what extent or degree**	very,
where	here, inside, everywhere		somewhat, not
how	carefully, happily		

A **preposition** is a word that shows the relationship of a noun or a pronoun to some other word in a sentence.

under, before, to, of, with, by, at

A **conjunction** is a word or a group of words that joins single words or sentence parts together.

and, but, or, when, as, wherever, although, however

An **interjection** is a word or a group of words that expresses emotion or exclamation. It has no grammatical connection to other words.

well, ouch, ah, wow

Nouns

A *noun* is one of the most important words used in speaking and writing. It is the word that tells what is being talked about. Nouns name people, places, things, or ideas.

Characteristics of nouns.

Nouns change their form to show the number of people, places, things, or ideas being talked about. They also change form to show ownership.

Number. Nouns can be either singular or plural. A *singular noun* refers to only one person, place, thing, or idea. A *plural noun* refers to more than one. Most plural nouns are formed by adding -s or -es to the singular noun.

SINGULAR

hat   orange   torpedo   gas

PLURAL

hats   oranges   torpedoes   gases

Other nouns become irregular in the plural and do not follow the rules.

SINGULAR

woman   loaf   spacecraft   sheep

PLURAL

women   loaves   spacecraft   sheep

When you are in doubt about the spelling of a plural form of a noun, look it up in the dictionary.

Possessive form. Nouns change form to show possession, or ownership. To form the possessive of a singular noun or a plural noun that does not end in *s*, add -'s.

the astronaut's helmet
the church's steeple

To form the possessive of a plural noun that ends in *s*, add the apostrophe only.

two girls' books
several countries' flags

However, when a person's or place's name (a proper noun) ends in *s*, add -'s.

Mr. Jones's car
Kansas's tornadoes
Davis's raincoat

Possessive nouns are frequently used as modifiers that give additional information about other nouns. Although they often come before the nouns they

> **Tip**
>
> When you are asked to identify a noun, try placing the articles *a, an,* or *the* before the word in question. If the word makes sense with any of these articles, then it is probably a noun.
>
> a boat   the time   an idea

What Is a Noun?

people	places	things	ideas
Ramón	horizon	computer	leadership
mother-in-law	universe	piano	curiosity
Harriet Tubman	village	snow	knowledge
pilot	Sunshine State	dog	hope

modify, they can also appear in other places in the sentence.

Larry's book is on the table.
This book is Larry's.
This book of Larry's is interesting.

Kinds of nouns. Understanding the differences between proper and common nouns, abstract and concrete nouns, general and specific nouns, and compound and collective nouns will help you to write more clearly.

Common and proper nouns. All nouns are either common or proper. *A common noun* refers to a general person, place, thing, or idea. Usually, a common noun is not capitalized unless it begins a sentence. *A proper noun* is the name or title of a specific person, place, thing, or idea. Proper nouns include the names of religions, languages, historical events, documents, days of the week, and months of the year. The first letter of a proper noun is capitalized.

It is much clearer to say, "A chickadee sat on my hand," than it is to say, "A bird sat on my hand."

COMMON NOUNS

scientist	city
cat	actor

PROPER NOUNS

Marie Curie	Denver
Thailand	Robin Williams

Proper nouns help to focus your writing. In the following example, notice how much more information the revised sentence gives you.

ORIGINAL
One day last week the doctor visited a large city.

REVISED
Last Tuesday Dr. Michaels visited Chicago.

General and specific nouns. All nouns are either general or specific. A *general noun* names any person, place, thing, or idea. A *specific noun* names particular people, places, things, or ideas.

GENERAL NOUNS

park	animal
building	flower

SPECIFIC NOUNS

Mellon Park	zebra
Eiffel Tower	rose

Specific nouns create clearer images than general nouns do. Notice how much more you can see in the revised sentence in the following example.

ORIGINAL
The two dogs traveled down the street.

REVISED
The poodle and the cocker spaniel traveled down Oak Street.

Concrete and abstract nouns. All nouns are either concrete or abstract. A *concrete noun* names something that can be experienced through the senses of sight, sound, taste, smell, or touch. *Abstract nouns* name qualities, feelings, conditions, and attitudes. Sometimes abstract nouns seem difficult to identify since they do not refer to things that you can see or touch. Remembering the tip about putting *a, an,* or *the* before a noun will help you be more sure of abstract nouns.

"Statue" is a concrete noun, but this particular statue symbolizes "liberty," an abstract noun.

CONCRETE NOUNS

steak	jeans	waves
noise	garbage	

ABSTRACT NOUNS

truth	freedom	democracy
joy	anger	

Even though abstract nouns may mean different things to different people—for example, most everyone will have a different definition of joy—they are necessary in most forms of writing. If you use abstract nouns along with details and examples that show what they mean to you, your writing will be clearer and more interesting.

Collective nouns. A *collective noun* is a singular noun that names a group of people or things (a collection). These nouns may take a singular or a plural verb, depending on meaning.

bunch	cast	club
committee	herd	family

Compound nouns. A *compound noun* is made up of two or more words used together to form a single noun. One kind of compound noun consists of two or more words joined together.

sunglasses	backpack
spacecraft	sunscreen

Another kind of compound noun has words joined by one or more hyphens.

best-seller	know-it-all
light-year	sister-in-law

A third kind of compound noun consists of two or more words that create a single noun even though they are not joined together in any way.

jet engine	Stars and Stripes
air force	blue jeans

Check a dictionary to make sure you are using the correct form of compound noun.

Pronouns

Pronouns are words that replace nouns, groups of words acting as nouns, or other pronouns. The word or words that a pronoun replaces is called the *antecedent* of that pronoun. Pronouns identify people, places, things, and ideas without renaming or repeating them. As the following two sentences show, pronouns make it possible to eliminate awkward repetition in writing.

AWKWARD

The paper is finished, but the paper must still be typed.

REVISED

The paper is finished, but <u>it</u> must still be typed.

In the above example, *paper* is the antecedent of *it*.

Kinds of pronouns.

There are seven kinds of pronouns: personal, demonstrative, reflexive, intensive, interrogative, relative, and indefinite.

Personal pronouns.

A *personal pronoun* refers to a specific person or thing by indicating the person speaking (the first person), the person being addressed (the second person), or any other person or

You and I will help her study.

First person refers to the person speaking, second person refers to the one spoken to, and third person is the one spoken about.

thing being discussed (the third person). In addition, personal pronouns have forms that indicate possession or ownership. These *possessive pronouns* take the place of possessive nouns (see Pronoun usage on page 11 for more information on possessive pronouns).

Bill called to <u>me</u> just as <u>I</u> opened the door so <u>I</u> waved to <u>him</u>.

Visitors to the museum were disappointed because <u>they</u> could not see the exhibit <u>they</u> had heard so much about.

Personal Pronouns				
			POSSESSIVE	
	SINGULAR	PLURAL	SINGULAR	PLURAL
FIRST PERSON	I, me	we, us	mine	ours
SECOND PERSON	you	you	yours	yours
THIRD PERSON	he, him	they, them	his	theirs
	she, her	they, them	hers	theirs
	it	they, them	its	theirs

Demonstrative pronouns. A *demonstrative pronoun* is used to point out a specific person, place, or thing. It identifies which one or which group is being referred to.

We bought several of <u>those</u>.

<u>This</u> is my favorite pair of boots.

Reflexive pronouns. A *reflexive pronoun* indicates that a person or thing performs actions to, for, or on behalf of herself, himself, or itself. Reflexive pronouns are formed by adding -self or -selves to certain personal pronouns.

She sometimes talks to <u>herself</u> as she works.

They let <u>themselves</u> into the house.

Intensive pronouns. An *intensive pronoun* draws special attention to a noun or pronoun in a sentence. Intensive pronouns are the same words as reflexive pronouns, but they are used for different purposes. You will notice in the following examples that the intensive pronouns could be left out without changing the meaning of the sentences. They simply emphasize their noun antecedents.

The cast <u>itself</u> wrote the play and designed the scenery.

In this example, the intensive pronoun *itself* draws attention to the word *cast*.

We were greeted by the owner of the shop <u>himself</u>.

The intensive pronoun *himself* draws special attention to the word *owner*.

Interrogative pronouns. An interrogative pronoun introduces a question.

<u>What</u> does this word mean?

<u>Who</u> is going with you?

Relative pronouns. A *relative pronoun* introduces an adjective clause, which modifies a noun or pronoun by telling which, what kind, or how many.

The flat tire, <u>which</u> was caused by a nail, took an hour to repair.

Notice that the adjective clause *which was caused by a nail* begins with the relative pronoun *which* and tells which tire took an hour to repair.

Someday we may have personal robots <u>that</u> do our chores.

The adjective clause *that do our chores* begins with the relative pronoun *that* and tells what kind of robots we may have.

Demonstrative Pronouns	
this	that
these	those

Reflexive Pronouns	
FIRST PERSON	myself, ourselves
SECOND PERSON	yourself, yourselves
THIRD PERSON	himself, herself, itself, oneself, themselves

Interrogative Pronouns	
who	whom
which	what
whose	

Relative Pronouns	
who	whom
whose	which
that	

Indefinite pronouns. An *indefinite pronoun* refers to a person, place, or thing in a more general (or indefinite) way than a noun does. Unlike other pronouns, indefinite pronouns have no antecedents. They are used when the appropriate noun is unknown or unspecified.

The Lions Club sent invitations to <u>everyone</u> in the community.

The Denburgs returned from their vacation with <u>plenty</u> of gifts and souvenirs.

Pronoun usage.
Many people make mistakes in using pronouns because some pronouns have a number of different forms. This section will help you learn how and when to use these different forms of pronouns.

Pronoun and antecedent agreement. All pronouns, whether they are personal, demonstrative, reflexive, intensive, interrogative, relative, or indefinite, must agree with their antecedents in number, gender, and person.

"This is one of my favorite books. I'd recommend it to anyone. Most of the books I like best are about horses." In this quotation, the words "one," "anyone," and "Most" are indefinite pronouns.

Agreement in number. Use a singular pronoun to refer to or replace a singular antecedent. Use a plural pronoun to refer to or replace a plural antecedent.

<u>Kameko</u> decided that <u>she</u> would pack a picnic lunch.

Kameko's <u>sisters</u> decided that <u>they</u> would pack a picnic lunch.

Indefinite Pronouns

SINGULAR		PLURAL	SINGULAR OR PLURAL
another	much	both	all
anybody	neither	few	any
anyone	nobody	many	more
anything	no one	others	most
each	nothing	plenty	none
either	one	several	some
enough	other		
everybody	somebody		
everyone	someone		
everything	something		

Use a plural pronoun to refer to or replace two or more singular antecedents joined by *and.* Use a singular pronoun to refer to or to replace two or more singular antecedents joined by *or* or *nor.*

Shannon and Travis have seen their favorite movie six times.

Either Shannon or Travis will bring his photographs to school.

Some indefinite pronouns, such as *all, any, more, most, none,* and *some,* can be either singular or plural. Use either singular or plural pronouns to refer to or replace them, depending on the meaning of the sentence.

All of the color in the painting had lost its glow.

In the example shown above, *All* refers to *color,* which is singular; *its* refers to *all.*

All of the students are required to bring their permission slips.

All refers to *students,* which is plural; *their* refers to *all.*

When an antecedent is a collective noun, you need to determine whether the collective noun is singular or plural in meaning. If it is singular, use a singular pronoun to refer to it or replace it. If it is plural, use a plural pronoun.

The club voted to change its meeting time and location.

The singular is used above because the meeting time and location are for the entire club as one unit.

The city council argued among themselves.

The plural is correct in this example because the individual council members were arguing.

Susan, David, and Mark agreed that they would bring only recyclable packaging with their lunches each day. Susan said that at home she and her family recycle everything. (In these sentences, the pronouns "they" and "she" agree in number and gender with their antecedents, "Susan, David, and Mark" and "Susan.")

Agreement in gender. The gender of a pronoun is either masculine, feminine, or neuter (neither masculine nor feminine).

MASCULINE	he	him	his
FEMININE	she	her	hers
NEUTER	it	it	its

Use a pronoun that agrees in gender with its antecedent.

<u>Dave</u> leaned <u>his</u> bike against the fence.

Occasionally, it is unclear whether the gender of a singular antecedent is masculine or feminine. If a neuter pronoun will not work, use *his or her* or *her or his* to show that the antecedent could be either masculine or feminine. When this kind of sentence becomes awkward, rewrite it so that the antecedent and all words that refer to it are plural.

AWKWARD
A pet owner should care about his or her animal.

REVISED
Pet owners should care about their animals.

Agreement in person. Pronouns are in either the first, second, or third person. Use a pronoun that agrees in person with its antecedent.

FIRST PERSON
I get home before <u>my</u> parents do.

SECOND PERSON
Will you get home before <u>your</u> parents do?

THIRD PERSON
Noel will get home before <u>his</u> parents do.

Agreement of reflexive and intensive pronouns. Reflexive and intensive pronouns must also agree with their antecedents in number, gender, and person. Reflexive and intensive pronouns are always used with antecedents. Do not use them alone to replace a noun or a personal pronoun.

INCORRECT
Dina and I will travel to New Jersey by themselves.

INCORRECT
Dina and myself will travel to New Jersey.

CORRECT
Dina and I will travel to New Jersey by <u>ourselves</u>.

Pronoun case. To show the grammatical use of a pronoun in a sentence, you must use the proper form, or *case.*

Use the *nominative case* when a pronoun acts as a subject or as a complement.

SUBJECT
<u>I</u> am the only one who knows how to get there.

COMPLEMENT
That was <u>she</u> on the telephone.

You will often find that pronouns in the nominative case are not used as complements in casual conversation.

For example, many people say, "It's me" instead of "It is I." You will also hear "That's him" instead of "That is he." Be sure to use pronouns in the nominative case in your own writing for school.

Use the *objective case* when a pronoun acts as a direct object, as an indirect object, or as an object of a preposition.

If a pronoun answers the question *Whom?* after an action verb, it is a direct object.

<u>Whom</u> did I see at the dance?

I saw <u>him</u> at the dance.

A pronoun used as an indirect object comes before the direct object and answers the question *To whom?* or *For whom?*

<u>To whom</u> did Suzette give the credit?

Suzette gave <u>us</u> all the credit.

For more information about direct and indirect objects, see page 38.

Use a pronoun in the objective case when the pronoun is the object of a preposition (*to, in, with,* etc.).

The police officer motioned to <u>them</u> to cross the street.

She has confidence in <u>me</u>.

George went to the store with <u>me</u>.

For more information about prepositions, see page 31.

Use the *possessive case* pronouns *mine, yours, his, hers, its, ours,* and *theirs* to refer to or replace nouns. These pronouns function in the same way as nouns do: as subjects, complements, direct or indirect objects, or objects of prepositions.

Pronoun Case		
	SINGULAR	PLURAL
NOMINATIVE CASE	I	we
	you	you
	he, she, it	they
OBJECTIVE CASE	me	us
	you	you
	him, her, it	them
POSSESSIVE CASE	mine	ours
	yours	yours
	his, hers, its	theirs

Tip

To check the correct case of pronouns in compound direct objects, indirect objects, and objects of the preposition, break the sentence down into parts.

The Norrises' collie always barks at Gwen and (I, me).

The Norrises' collie always barks at Gwen.

The Norrises' collie always barks at me.

The Norrises' collie always barks at Gwen and me.

SUBJECT
<u>Theirs</u> is the party that everyone wants to attend.

COMPLEMENTS
The best short story is <u>his</u>.

DIRECT OBJECT
Although Kate lost her ring almost immediately, Sara wore <u>hers</u> for years.

INDIRECT OBJECT
Despite the rest of the boring speeches, Dwight gave <u>yours</u> his full attention.

OBJECT OF THE PREPOSITION
The twins will be upset that he did not pay attention to <u>theirs</u>.

Determining the case of <u>who</u> and <u>whom</u>. You can use forms of the pronoun *who* either as an interrogative pronoun or as a relative pronoun. The way that you use the pronoun determines the case, or form, that should be chosen.

NOMINATIVE CASE who, whoever
OBJECTIVE CASE whom, whomever
POSSESSIVE CASE whose

Use *who* when an interrogative pronoun acts as a subject or as a predicate nominative. Use *whom* when an interrogative pronoun acts as an object of a verb or as an object of a preposition.

NOMINATIVE
<u>Who</u> is playing the lead in the school play?

Who is the subject of the verb *playing*.

OBJECTIVE
To <u>whom</u> did you speak when you called the doctor's office?

Whom is the object of the preposition *to*.

If the interrogative pronoun *who* or *whom* is followed by a phrase that is not essential to the meaning of the sentence, remove the phrase for a moment to determine the use of the pronoun in the sentence and the form of the pronoun to use.

(Who, Whom) do you think will win the election.

Think: Who will win the election? *Who* is the subject.

Use *who* or *whoever* when a relative pronoun is the subject of a subordinate clause (a dependent clause that functions as a single part of speech). Use *whom* or *whomever* when a relative pronoun is an object within the subordinate clause.

The new student, <u>who</u> has already made a number of friends at our school, has been here little more than a week.

Who is the subject of the clause *who has already made a number of friends at our school.*

The writer, <u>whom</u> many people respect, was honored at the conference.

Whom is the direct object of *respect*.

Pronouns in comparisons. In some comparisons using *than* or *as,* part of the phrase or clause is implied rather than stated. To choose the correct pronoun, think of the missing words to determine how the pronoun is used. In the following examples, you will see how the case of the pronoun used in an incomplete comparison can change the intended meaning.

NOMINATIVE

Gary spends more time with Jeff than I.

Think: *than I spend with Jeff.* I is the subject of the implied clause; therefore, use the nominative form of the pronoun.

OBJECTIVE

Gary spends more time with Jeff than me.

Think: *than he spends with me. Me* is the object of the implied preposition *with;* therefore, use the objective form of the pronoun.

Clear pronoun reference. When you go over something you have written, check to see whether the pronouns are in the correct case and whether there is agreement between pronouns and their antecedents. Also check for pronoun shifts and unclear or missing antecedents. Incorrect pronoun usage will confuse your readers. Do not use a pronoun that can refer to more than one antecedent even if it means repeating the antecedent.

UNCLEAR

Susan chose Lily to be on her team because she knows the game well.

CLEAR

Susan chose Lily to be on her team because Lily knows the game well.

In the first example, we are unsure of which of the two girls knows the game well.

Avoid using the pronouns *it, they, you,* or *your* without a clear antecedent.

UNCLEAR

Before you give the lamb its bottle, be sure to shake it.

"Before you give the lamb its bottle, be sure to shake it." The unclear pronoun reference in this sentence makes for a very silly sentence.

CLEAR

Before you give the lamb its bottle, be sure to shake the bottle.

In the first example, we do not know whether to shake the lamb or the bottle.

Avoid unnecessary pronoun shifts that may change the meaning you intended.

INCORRECT

I like summer best because you can swim in the ocean.

CORRECT

I like summer best because I can swim in the ocean.

Do not use the pronoun *your* in place of an article (*a, an,* or *the*) if possession is not involved.

INCORRECT

Many of your athletes have been training for years.

CORRECT

Many of the athletes have been training for years.

16

Verbs

The *verb* is sometimes considered the part of speech that is at the heart of a sentence, mostly because it affects meaning more than any other element. It determines the number of nouns needed, and it guides the action that takes place. Verbs can indicate a state of being as well as a physical action. They can even focus a reader's attention on a particular part of a sentence.

Kinds of verbs. There are five kinds of verbs that allow you to make a complete statement about something or someone.

Action verbs. An *action verb* describes the behavior, or action, of someone or something. It may express physical action or mental activity.

PHYSICAL

The band <u>marched</u> down Northfield Avenue.

The batter <u>hit</u> the ball to left field.

Louise <u>skates</u> very fast on the smooth ice.

MENTAL

Malcolm <u>thought</u> about his woodworking project.

He <u>believes</u> in working hard.

Linking verbs. A *linking verb* connects a noun or a pronoun with a word or words that identify or describe the noun or pronoun. Forms of the verbs *be* and *have* are the most common linking verbs.

Marnie <u>was</u> the winner of the race.

Was links *winner* with *Marnie; winner* identifies who Marnie is.

My parents <u>were</u> anxious about rush hour traffic.

Were links *anxious* with *parents; anxious* describes the word *parents.*

Mary <u>has</u> chicken pox.

Has links *Mary* with *chicken pox* and *chicken pox* describes Mary's condition.

Babette and Nicole <u>are</u> the twins in school.

Are links *twins* with *Babette* and *Nicole; twins* tell who *Babette* and *Nicole* are.

The verbs in the following list may also be used as linking verbs.

appear	feel	look
seem	sound	taste
become	grow	remain
smell	stay	turn

The first speaker <u>appeared</u> nervous.

All of a sudden Alice <u>became</u> sad.

The long-distance runner <u>looks</u> tired.

The cookies <u>tasted</u> like root beer.

Some verbs can be either action verbs or linking verbs, depending on their use in a sentence.

ACTION

The whistle <u>sounded</u> a warning.

Deborah <u>stayed</u> home from school.

LINKING

His comments <u>sounded</u> really sarcastic.

Robert <u>stayed</u> very still.

Auxiliary verbs. Sometimes a verb needs the help of another verb, called an *auxiliary* or *helping verb.* The verb that it helps is called the *main verb.* The main verb and the helping verb form a *verb phrase.* A verb phrase may have more than one auxiliary verb.

Will you be waiting for me after school?

Waiting is the main verb, *will* and *be* are the helping verbs, and *will be waiting* is the verb phrase.

My sister should have taken that job.

Taken is the main verb, *should* and *have* are the helping verbs, and *should have taken* is the verb phrase.

The teacher is obeyed by her students.

Obeyed is the main verb, *is* is the helping verb, and *is obeyed* is the verb phrase.

Susan ought to study her grammar more.

To study is the main verb, *ought* is the helping verb, and *ought to study* is the verb phrase.

Transitive and intransitive verbs. All action verbs are either transitive or intransitive. A *transitive verb* needs an object, called the *object of the verb,* to complete its meaning. An *intransitive verb* has no object. Linking verbs, such as *be* and *have,* are always intransitive. Some action verbs can be either transitive or intransitive, depending on their meaning and whether an object is necessary.

TRANSITIVE

Mr. Abeed photographed the Great Wall of China.

Great Wall of China is the object of the verb *photographed.*

Li Xiaoshuang gave a fine performance at the 1996 Olympics (a fine performance *is the object of* gave, *so* gave *is a transitive verb*).

Common Auxiliary Verbs		
am	do	must
are	does	ought
be	had	shall
being	has	should
been	have	was
can	is	were
could	may	will
did	might	would

18

Wally <u>painted</u> his house during the summer.

House is the object of the verb *painted*.

INTRANSITIVE

The old house <u>seems</u> haunted.

Seems is a linking verb and therefore has no object.

The blackbird <u>hid</u> in the bushes.

Hid is intransitive because it has no object.

TRANSITIVE

We <u>stopped</u> a stranger on the street to ask for directions.

The object of *stopped* is *stranger*.

*Li Xiaoshuang felt proud to have won a gold medal at the 1996 Olympics (*felt *is a linking verb and has no object and therefore is intransitive).*

Jane <u>smiled</u> a wide, happy grin.

The object of *smiled* is *grin*.

INTRANSITIVE

The subway <u>stopped</u> abruptly.

Stopped has no object.

Jane <u>smiled</u> with pleasure.

Smiled has no object.

How to use verbs.
Verbs have several characteristics, such as tense, that other parts of speech do not. If you understand the forms and tenses of verbs, you will be able to choose the ones that best explain what is going on in your sentences and use them correctly.

Principal parts of verbs.
The four basic forms of a verb are called its *principal parts*. Knowing the principal parts of a verb is important because all the tenses of a verb are formed from them. The principal parts of a verb are the *infinitive*, the *present participle*, the *past*, and the *past participle*. By using these forms alone or with helping (auxiliary) verbs, you can express the various tenses of a verb.

The infinitive and the present participle are formed in the same way for all verbs. The *infinitive* is the basic verb form. The word *to* usually precedes the infinitive in a sentence. The *present participle* is always a combination of the infinitive and -ing. It is used in a sentence with a form of *be* as an auxiliary verb.

INFINITIVE

Five miles is a long way <u>to walk</u> in the snow.

PRESENT PARTICIPLE

Jared <u>is walking</u> home from school.

19

Regular and irregular verbs. Most verbs are *regular verbs.* They form their past and their past participle the same way, by adding -ed or -d to the infinitive. In a sentence, the past participle takes a form of the verb *have* as an auxiliary verb. When certain endings are added to the infinitive, a spelling change may be necessary. Check a dictionary if you are unsure of a particular spelling.

The students rode their bicycles to and from school every day. (Ride is irregular. Its past tense is "rode," not "rided.")

Common Irregular Verbs

INFINITIVE	PAST	PAST PARTICIPLE
awake	awoke	(have) awakened
beat	beat	(have) beat or beaten
become	became	(have) become
begin	began	(have) begun
bite	bit	(have) bitten
bleed	bled	(have) bled
blow	blew	(have) blown
break	broke	(have) broken
bring	brought	(have) brought
build	built	(have) built
buy	bought	(have) bought
catch	caught	(have) caught
choose	chose	(have) chosen
come	came	(have) come
dig	dug	(have) dug
dive	dived or dove	(have) dived
do	did	(have) done
drink	drank	(have) drunk
drive	drove	(have) driven
eat	ate	(have) eaten
fall	fell	(have) fallen
fly	flew	(have) flown
forget	forgot	(have) forgotten
freeze	froze	(have) frozen
get	got	(have) gotten
give	gave	(have) given
go	went	(have) gone

Irregular verbs do not follow the standard rules for forming the past and the past participle. The only way to master the past and past participial forms of irregular verbs is to memorize the main parts of the verbs that you use frequently and check your dictionary for those that you do not use as often. You will find the list of common irregular verbs below useful as an everyday reference.

Verb tense. Various forms of verbs show whether an action or condition takes place in the present, took place in the past, or will take place in the future. The forms of a verb that express time are called *tenses.* There are six different verb tenses: *present; past; future; present perfect; past perfect;* and *future perfect.* To form all but the present and past tenses, combine the principal parts of verbs with auxiliary verbs.

INFINITIVE	PAST	PAST PARTICIPLE
hang	hung	(have) hung
	hanged	(have) hanged
have	had	(have) had
hear	heard	(have) heard
hide	hid	(have) hidden
hurt	hurt	(have) hurt
know	knew	(have) known
lay	laid	(have) laid
lie	lay	(have) lain
lose	lost	(have) lost
make	made	(have) made
pay	paid	(have) paid
prove	proved	(have) proven, (have) proved
ride	rode	(have) ridden
ring	rang	(have) rung
rise	rose	(have) risen
say	said	(have) said
sell	sold	(have) sold
show	showed	(have) shown, (have) showed
sink	sank	(have) sunk
speak	spoke	(have) spoken
take	took	(have) taken
teach	taught	(have) taught
tear	tore	(have) torn
throw	threw	(have) thrown
wear	wore	(have) worn
write	wrote	(have) written

In the following examples, the six tenses of the verb *see* are used to express action at different times.

PRESENT

I <u>see</u> at least one movie a week.

PAST

I <u>saw</u> a good movie two days ago.

FUTURE

I <u>will see</u> the new Disney movie this weekend.

PRESENT PERFECT

I <u>have seen</u> two movies so far this month.

PAST PERFECT

I <u>had</u> not <u>seen</u> many movies before last year.

FUTURE PERFECT

By the end of this year, I <u>will have seen</u> over 50 movies.

To *conjugate* a verb means to list all of

Conjugation of *to fall*

PRINCIPAL PARTS

PRESENT	PRESENT PARTICIPLE	PAST	PAST PARTICIPLE
fall	(is) falling	fell	(have) fallen

	SINGULAR	PLURAL
PRESENT TENSE	I fall	we fall
	you fall	you fall
	he, she, it falls	they fall
PAST TENSE	I fell	we fell
	you fell	you fell
	he, she, it fell	they fell
FUTURE TENSE	I will/shall fall	we will/shall fall
	you will fall	you will fall
	he, she, it will fall	they will fall
PRESENT PERFECT	I have fallen	we have fallen
	you have fallen	you have fallen
	he, she, it has fallen	they have fallen
PAST PERFECT	I had fallen	we had fallen
	you had fallen	you had fallen
	he, she, it had fallen	they had fallen
FUTURE PERFECT	I will/shall have fallen	we will/shall have fallen
	you will have fallen	you will have fallen
	he, she, it will have fallen	they will have fallen

the forms for its six tenses. The conjugation of a verb also shows how the verb forms change for the first person, the second person, and the third person and for the singular and the plural.

To form the *present tense* of a verb, use its infinitive. To form the third person singular, add -s or -es to the infinitive in most cases. Use the present tense to show an action that takes place now, to show an action that is repeated regularly, or to show a condition that is true at any time.

We <u>walk</u> the Livingston High School track.

We <u>walk</u> every day for exercise.

Walking <u>is</u> always good exercise.

Also use the present tense in statements about literary works or other works of art.

This book <u>is</u> about the adventures of a young girl growing up in England.

To form the *past tense* of a regular verb, add -d or -ed to the infinitive. Use the past tense to express action that occurred in the past and was entirely completed.

Yesterday we <u>walked</u> the track.

To form the *future tense,* combine *will* or *shall* with the infinitive form of the main verb. Use the future tense to describe action that will occur in the future.

They <u>will walk</u> with us tomorrow.

The *present perfect tense* is formed by using *has* or *have* with the past participle of the main verb. Use the present perfect tense to describe action that was completed recently or at an indefinite time in the past.

I <u>have walked</u> farther today than I have ever walked before.

To form the *past perfect tense,* use *had* with the past participle of the main verb. The past perfect tense describes an action that was completed by a certain time in the past or before another action was completed.

We <u>had walked</u> the required distance before we realized that we should have stopped to rest.

Form the *future perfect tense* by using *will have* or *shall have* with the past participle of the main verb. Use the future perfect tense to describe an action that will be completed before another action will be.

They <u>will have walked</u> three miles before the rest of the group joins them.

The progressive forms of verbs. Each of the six tenses has an additional form that is used to express continuing action. To form the progressive, use the appropriate tense of the verb *be* with the present participle of the main verb.

PRESENT PROGRESSIVE
We <u>are walking</u> to raise money for charity.

PAST PROGRESSIVE
He <u>was walking</u> faster than we were.

FUTURE PROGRESSIVE
I <u>will be walking</u> for the next 20 minutes.

PRESENT PERFECT PROGRESSIVE

They <u>have been walking</u> all morning.

PAST PERFECT PROGRESSIVE

We <u>had been walking</u> for only a short time when he joined us.

FUTURE PERFECT PROGRESSIVE

By the time they arrive, she <u>will have been walking</u> for an hour.

The emphatic form of verbs. The emphatic form is used to make the present and past tenses of a verb stronger. To use the emphatic form, combine the present or the past tense of the verb *do* with the infinitive form of the main verb.

We <u>do walk</u> every day when the weather is nice.

We <u>did walk</u> during the winter.

Modals. The auxiliary verbs *can, could, may, might, must, will,* and *should* are known as *modals.* These verbs are used with main verbs to add emphasis to a sentence or to provide shades of meaning. Use *can* (present tense) and *could* (past tense) to express the ability to perform the action of the main verb.

We <u>can walk</u> faster if you like.

She <u>could have walked</u> with us yesterday if we had called her.

Use *may* to mean "have permission to" or to express a possibility.

The doctor said my mother <u>may walk</u> now that her ankle has healed.

I <u>may walk</u> this weekend if I have time.

Use *might* (the past tense of *may*) to express a possibility that is less likely than one expressed by *may.*

There is always a chance that the test <u>might be canceled</u>.

Use *must* to show that the action of the main verb is required or to suggest a possible explanation.

Sheila <u>must call</u> her parents immediately.

Gunnar <u>must have been</u> wrong about the date of the meeting.

Use *should* (the past tense of *shall*) to suggest that something ought to happen.

Sheila <u>should call</u> home immediately.

Consistency of tenses. Using verb tenses consistently makes writing clear. A shift in tense often causes confusion and misunderstanding.

When two or more actions take place at the same time, use verbs that are in the same tense.

INCORRECT

Connie <u>collected</u> firewood, and Hugh <u>builds</u> the fire.

CORRECT

Connie <u>collected</u> firewood, and Hugh <u>built</u> the fire.

INCORRECT

Martha's interest in art <u>grows</u> steadily as time <u>went</u> by.

CORRECT

Martha's interest in art <u>grew</u> steadily as time <u>went</u> by.

INCORRECT

The train <u>passed</u> Pleasantville when it <u>is</u> exactly noon.

CORRECT

The train <u>passes</u> Pleasantville when it <u>is</u> exactly noon.

Active and passive voice. In addition to tense, transitive verbs have voice. A verb is in the *active voice* when it has a direct object. A verb is in the *passive voice* when the direct object is converted into the subject.

ACTIVE

The audience <u>applauded</u> the violinist's solo.

The batter <u>hits</u> the ball.

PASSIVE

The violinist's solo <u>was applauded</u> by the audience.

The ball <u>is hit</u> by the batter.

Intransitive verbs are always in the active voice because they do not take objects. As you can see from the examples, when a verb in the active voice is changed to the passive voice, its direct object becomes the subject of the sentence. The subject of the sentence becomes the object of a preposition.

The active voice is generally the more direct and effective way of expressing action. You should use the passive voice only to emphasize the receiver of the action, or when the person or thing performing the action is unknown. Overusing the passive voice makes writing dull.

Choosing effective verbs. In your writing, select the most specific verbs that you can. Strong verbs give your readers precise images.

DULL VERB CHOICE

The puppy <u>walked</u> into the kitchen and <u>lay</u> down.

VIVID VERB CHOICE

The puppy <u>waddled</u> into the kitchen and <u>sprawled</u> on the floor.

Choosing a vivid verb over a dull one will help make your writing more exciting. "The puppy waddled into the kitchen and sprawled on the floor" is a more interesting sentence than "The puppy walked into the kitchen and lay down."

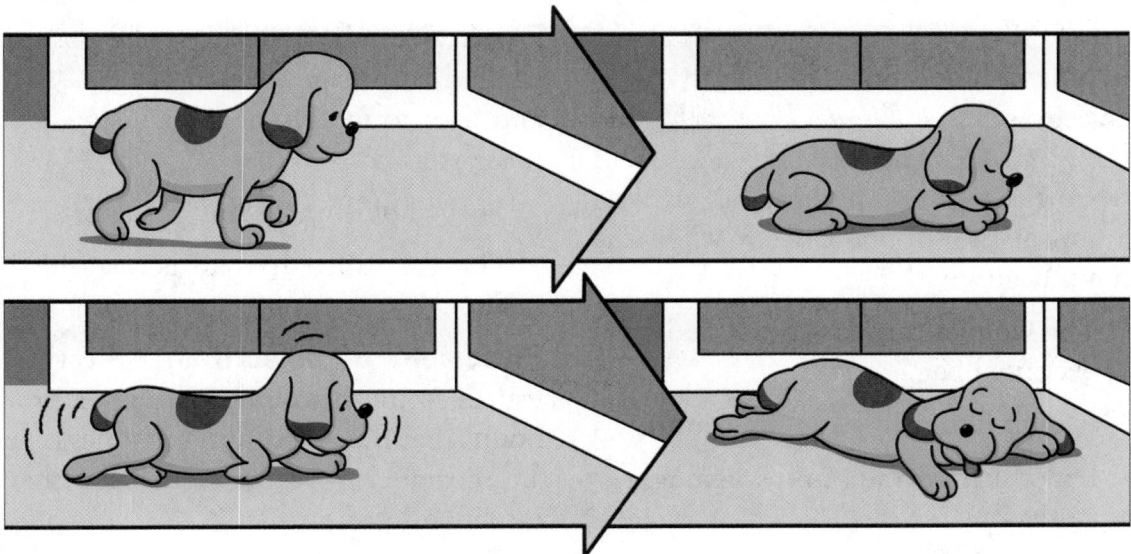

What are modifiers?

Modifiers can change the meaning of nouns, pronouns, and verbs by adding information or limiting a meaning. Adjectives and adverbs, the two most common kinds of modifiers, give color and life to language, helping you to create clearer images in your writing.

Adjectives. An *adjective* is a word that modifies a noun or a pronoun. To modify means to change. An adjective changes the meaning of a noun or a pronoun by describing it or making it more specific. An adjective answers one of three questions: *which? what kind?* or *how many?*

WHICH?

Jodi found a <u>red</u> shoe in front of her <u>gym</u> locker.

WHAT KIND?

We bought <u>fresh</u> vegetables at the <u>farmers'</u> market.

HOW MANY?

<u>Two thousand</u> people attended the concert.

Articles. The most frequently used adjectives are the *definite article (the)* and the *indefinite articles (a* and *an).* Use *a* when the noun it modifies begins with a consonant sound. Use *an* when the noun begins with a vowel sound.

The woman carried <u>a</u> purse and <u>an</u> overnight bag.

It is <u>an</u> honor to serve my country.

Did you find <u>the</u> stamps I bought yesterday?

Proper adjectives. A *proper adjective* is formed from a proper noun. It is always capitalized and can be used to modify a noun or pronoun. The names of products are proper adjectives because the specific name limits the type of general product.

Two sailboats glided into <u>Boston</u> harbor.

Glenda washes her face with <u>Luxury</u> soap.

Nouns used as adjectives. Some nouns function as adjectives without changing form.

The whistle of the <u>freight</u> train interrupted my sleep.

Possessive nouns show ownership, answering the question *which?* When you use them to show possession, change their form by adding 's or just an apostrophe.

<u>Keith's</u> house is at the bottom of the hill.

The <u>cars'</u> headlights bother my eyes.

Possessive adjectives. Use the possessive adjectives *my, your, his, its, our,* and *their* to modify nouns and to show possession.

<u>Their</u> shouts warned us of the fire.

The cat rolled <u>its</u> ball across the floor.

Placement of adjectives. Adjectives usually come before the nouns or pronouns that they modify. Sometimes they are separated from the words that they modify by a comma.

<u>Dull</u> and <u>repetitious</u>, the speech put the audience to sleep.

Dull and *repetitious* modify the noun *speech*.

Adjectives may follow linking verbs, modifying the subject of the sentence.

The cat is <u>frisky</u> and <u>playful</u>.

Sometimes adjectives follow the words that they modify and are separated from them by commas.

The cat, <u>frisky</u> and <u>playful</u>, tore through the house.

Adverbs. Like adjectives, adverbs are modifiers. An *adverb* is a word that modifies a verb, an adjective, or another adverb. An adverb answers one of five questions about the word or phrase that it modifies: *how? when? where? how often?* or *to what extent?*

HOW?
Claus and Yoshio shook hands <u>firmly</u>.

Firmly modifies the verb *shook*.

WHEN?
We will see the Borgese family <u>soon</u>.

Soon modifies the verb *will see*.

WHERE?
Noreen looked <u>everywhere</u> for her lost bracelet.

Everywhere modifies the verb *looked*.

HOW OFTEN?
Their family <u>rarely</u> eats dinner together.

Rarely modifies the verb *eats*.

TO WHAT EXTENT?
Barry was <u>rather</u> doubtful about getting a part in the play.

Rather modifies the adjective *doubtful*.

Placement of adverbs. An adverb does not have to appear next to the verb that it modifies. Notice the different positions of the adverbs *silently* and *slowly* in these sentences.

<u>Silently</u> and <u>slowly</u>, the snow covered the yard.

The snow <u>silently</u> and <u>slowly</u> covered the yard.

The snow covered the yard <u>silently</u> and <u>slowly</u>.

An adverb usually comes directly before the adjective that it modifies.

Josh discovered that the map was <u>fairly</u> easy to read.

Adverbs usually come right before the other adverbs that they modify.

Raisa crossed the balance beam <u>quite</u> slowly.

Common Adverbs

again	just	seldom
almost	later	so
alone	never	soon
already	not	then
also	now	there
always	nowhere	today
away	often	too
even	perhaps	very
ever	quite	yet
here	rather	
indeed	really	

Distinguishing between adjectives and adverbs.

Sometimes it is difficult to tell the difference between an adjective and an adverb. Many adverbs end in -ly, but so do some adjectives.

ADJECTIVE

The <u>daily</u> newspaper has excellent local sports coverage.

ADVERB

Arden delivers the newspaper <u>daily</u>.

How to use modifiers.

Lively modifiers can vastly improve your writing. However, the adjectives and adverbs that you choose must be used correctly to avoid confusing your readers.

Comparison of modifiers.

By using different forms of adjectives and adverbs, you can compare two or more persons or things. The three degrees of comparison are positive, comparative, and superlative.

Use a modifier in the *positive degree* to add some information about a person, a thing, an action, or an idea. Use a modifier in the *comparative degree* to compare a person, a thing, an action, or an idea with another one. Do not use the comparative when more than two things are being compared. Use a modifier in the

> **Tip**
>
> To decide whether a modifier is an adjective or an adverb, figure out the part of speech of the word that it modifies. If the modified word is a noun or a pronoun, the modifier is an adjective. If the modified word is a verb, an adjective, or another adverb, the modifier is an adverb.

"I've looked everywhere for my other running shoe." In this sentence "everywhere" is an adverb, modifying the verb "looked," and "other" and "running" are adjectives modifying "shoe."

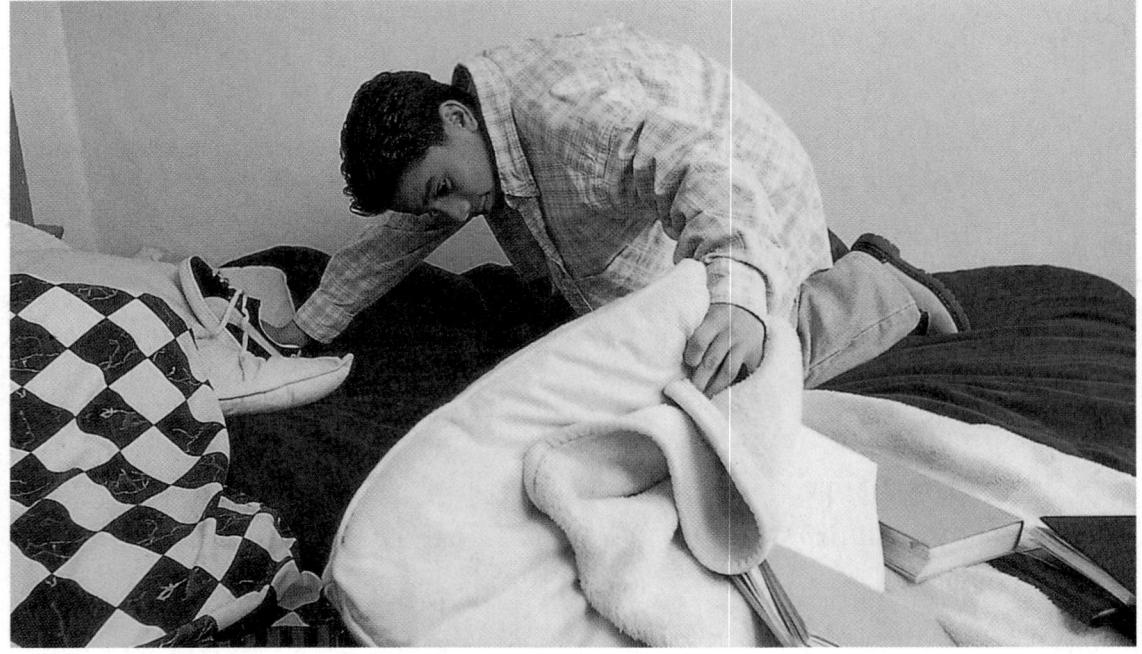

superlative degree to compare a person, a thing, an action, or an idea with at least two others.

ADJECTIVES
POSITIVE
That program was <u>long</u>.

COMPARATIVE
That program was <u>longer</u> than last week's.

SUPERLATIVE
That program was the <u>longest</u> I've seen.

ADVERBS
POSITIVE
Teddy works <u>fast</u>.

COMPARATIVE
Teddy works <u>faster</u> than Eric does.

SUPERLATIVE
Teddy works the <u>fastest</u> of any boy in our grade.

Add -er to form the comparative and -est to form the superlative of modifiers with one or two syllables. In some cases, to form the comparative correctly, you must drop the final *e,* double the final consonant, or change a final *y* to *i* before adding an ending to a word.

clean, cleaner, cleanest
funny, funnier, funniest
old, older, oldest

Use *more* to show the comparative degree and *most* to show the superlative degree in three cases: with all three-syllable words, with two-syllable words that would otherwise be difficult to pronounce, and with adverbs that end in -ly.

serious, more serious, most serious
dreadful, more dreadful, most dreadful
happily, more happily, most happily

Use *less* and *least* to form the comparative and superlative degrees of comparisons showing less.

funny, less funny, least funny
healthy, less healthy, least healthy
hopeful, less hopeful, least hopeful

The comparative and superlative degrees of some modifiers are formed irregularly. Since there are only a few, memorizing them will ensure that you use them correctly.

Certain adjectives, such as *perfect, unique, dead, round, full,* and *empty,* do not have a comparative or superlative degree. These adjectives refer to conditions about which no more can be said. Logically, nothing can be described as

Irregular Comparisons		
POSITIVE	COMPARATIVE	SUPERLATIVE
bad/badly	worse	worst
far	farther/further	farthest/furthest
good/well	better	best
little	less	least
many/much	more	most

"more perfect" or "more empty." You should also avoid double comparisons. Use either the word *more* or *most* or else the correct ending; do not combine the two.

INCORRECT
Which is the <u>most highest</u> mountain?

CORRECT
Which is the <u>highest</u> mountain?

Avoid incomplete comparisons by clearly indicating the things being compared. When you compare one member of a group with the rest of the group, you can avoid being unclear or misleading by using the comparative degree and the word *other* or *else*.

UNCLEAR
Anita plays softball better than anyone in the class.

The sentence above says either that Anita plays softball better than anyone in the class, including herself, or that Anita plays softball better than anyone in a class of which she is not a part.

CLEAR
Anita can play softball better than anyone <u>else</u> in the class.

Now we know that Anita is the best softball player in her class.

Be sure to avoid using double negatives. A *double negative* is the use of two negative words to express only one negative idea. Negative words include *no, none, nothing, not,* and *never.* A contraction ending in *n't* is also a negative word.

INCORRECT
We did <u>not</u> find <u>nothing</u> on the radio worth listening to.

CORRECT
We did <u>not</u> find <u>anything</u> on the radio worth listening to.

CORRECT
We found <u>nothing</u> on the radio worth listening to.

The words *scarcely, hardly,* and *barely* all mean almost not at all. They carry the force of negatives. Therefore, avoid using these words with another negative to express a single idea.

INCORRECT
Connie did <u>not hardly</u> know how to do her math homework.

CORRECT
Connie did <u>not</u> know how to do her math homework.

CORRECT
Connie <u>hardly</u> knew how to do her math homework.

Placement of modifiers. Putting modifiers in the wrong place can create unclear sentences. To avoid misplacing modifiers, put the adjective or adverb as close as possible to the word you wish to modify, while keeping your intended meaning.

UNCLEAR

Strolling by the lake, a family of geese walked in front of Jaime.

In the above example, we do not know who was strolling by the lake.

CLEAR

Strolling by the lake, Jaime noticed a family of geese in front of him.

In this version, Jaime is doing the strolling by the lake.

CLEAR

In front of him, Jaime noticed a family of geese strolling by the lake.

In this version, the family of geese is doing the strolling.

A *dangling modifier* is a phrase or clause that does not clearly or sensibly modify any word in the sentence. To avoid dangling modifiers, provide an antecedent for every modifying phrase or clause.

UNCLEAR

Grilled over charcoal, we particularly enjoy vegetables like zucchini.

Here, the modifying phrase *grilled over charcoal* appears to modify the pronoun *we*.

UNCLEAR

We particularly enjoy vegetables grilled over charcoal like zucchini.

The modifying phrase *like zucchini* seems to modify *charcoal*.

CLEAR

We particularly enjoy vegetables like zucchini grilled over charcoal.

Using effective modifiers. You should practice using precise adjectives and adverbs to create colorful details in your writing. Strong verbs are essential, but even strong verbs often need adverbs to tell more. Your readers will more easily understand what you have to say if your adverbs are specific. When you write, try to avoid using vague adverbs such as *very, really, only, well, hard,* and *often.*

ORIGINAL

She wore a very nice dress.

REVISED

She wore a stylish lace mini dress.

What are connecting words?

In many sentences, special words join or show the connections between other words. Prepositions and conjunctions are these special words.

Prepositions. A *preposition* is a word that shows the relationship between a noun or a pronoun and another word in the sentence. The preposition is usually followed by a noun or a pronoun that is called the *object of the preposition.* Together, the preposition, the object, and the modifiers of that object form a *prepositional phrase.*

Cardinals and robins nest <u>in</u> thickets.

The preposition *in* relates *cardinals* and *robins* to *thickets,* which is the object of the preposition; *in thickets* is the prepositional phrase.

Prepositions usually state direction, time, or position.

The deer are running <u>toward</u> the woods.

The audience became restless <u>during</u> his speech.

Please place the book <u>on</u> that table.

The most common prepositions are *at, by, for, from, in, of, on, to,* and *with.*

A *compound preposition* consists of more than one word.

The Chulaks bought two turkeys <u>instead of</u> just one.

The child is hiding <u>back of</u> the bookcase.

<u>Because of</u> the cold weather, Susie stayed indoors.

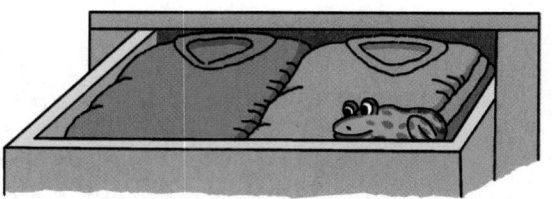

Maria hid her toy frog in her T-shirt drawer. (In this sentence in her T-shirt drawer *is a prepositional phrase.)*

A prepositional phrase functions as an adjective if it modifies a noun or a pronoun. A prepositional phrase functions as an adverb if it modifies a verb, an adjective, or another adverb.

ADJECTIVE

Their housing development has a picnic area <u>for the residents.</u>

In this case, the prepositional phrase *for the residents* modifies the noun *area.*

ADVERB

The exhausted tennis player sat <u>on the grass</u>.

Common Prepositions

aboard	at	but (except)	inside	out	underneath
about	before	by	into	over	until
above	behind	concerning	like	past	up
across	below	down	near	since	upon
after	beneath	during	of	through	via
against	beside	except	off	throughout	with
along	besides	for	on	to	within
among	between	from	onto	toward	without
around	beyond	in	opposite	under	

Common Compound Prepositions

according to	as of	in addition to	instead of
ahead of	back of	in back of	in view of
apart from	because of	in front of	next to
as far as	by means of	in place of	out of
aside from	contrary to	in spite of	prior to

The prepositional phrase *on the grass* modifies the verb *sat*.

Some words can function as prepositions or as adverbs, depending on their use in a sentence. Remember that every preposition must have an object.

PREPOSITION

Hank saw Marilyn <u>outside</u> the theater.

The children are running <u>around</u> the house.

ADVERB

Please don't go <u>outside</u> without your jacket.

The children are somewhere <u>around</u>.

Conjunctions. A *conjunction* is a word that connects words or groups of words. There are three kinds of conjunctions: coordinating, correlative, and subordinating.

Coordinating conjunctions. When you want to connect individual words or groups of words (phrases and clauses) that perform the same function in a sentence, you use a *coordinating conjunction*.

The boys raced across the street <u>and</u> into the house.

The conjunction connects two prepositional phrases.

I remembered his face, <u>but</u> I forgot his name.

The conjunction connects two independent clauses.

You may use a pen <u>or</u> a pencil.

The conjunction connects two words.

Correlative conjunctions. Like coordinating conjunctions, *correlative conjunctions* connect words that perform equal functions in a sentence. Correlative conjunctions consist of two or more words that work together.

Coordinating Conjunctions					
and	but	for	nor	or	yet

Correlative Conjunctions					
both/and	either/or	neither/nor	not only/but also	so/as	whether/or

Subordinating Conjunctions	
TIME	after, as, as long as, as soon as, before, since, until, when, whenever, while
MANNER	as, as if, as though
CAUSE	because
CONDITION	although, as long as, even if, even though, if, provided that, though, unless, while
COMPARISON	as, than
PURPOSE	in order that

We had <u>both</u> snow <u>and</u> sleet during the skiing trip.

The conjunction connects two words.

<u>Not only</u> were we cold, <u>but</u> we were <u>also</u> lost.

The conjunction connects two clauses. Here are some more examples:

Do not become <u>so</u> hungry <u>as</u> to faint.

<u>Either</u> you stay home <u>or</u> you go to school.

You may <u>neither</u> stay home <u>nor</u> go to the movies.

We do not know <u>whether</u> you are going to school or are staying at home.

Subordinating conjunctions. A *subordinating conjunction* introduces a subordinate clause, which is a clause that cannot stand by itself as a complete sentence. A subordinating conjunction connects the subordinate clause to an independent clause, which <u>can</u> stand by itself as a complete sentence. Subordinating conjunctions usually show relationships of time, manner, cause, condition, comparison, or purpose.

<u>Because</u> the sneakers are expensive, we cannot afford to buy them.

The subordinating conjunction *because* introduces the subordinate clause and connects it to the independent clause that follows it.

The stores are extremely crowded with holiday shoppers <u>unless</u> you go first thing in the morning.

The subordinating conjunction *unless* introduces the subordinate clause and connects it to the independent clause that precedes it.

<u>As</u> tall as Adam is, Betty is taller.

The subordinating conjunction *as* introduces the subordinating clause and connects it to the independent clause that follows it.

Conjunctive adverbs. A *conjunctive adverb* functions like a coordinating conjunction because it usually connects independent clauses. A semicolon precedes the conjunctive adverb and a comma usually follows it.

CONJUNCTIVE ADVERB
The races were exciting; <u>therefore</u>, we stayed until the end.

COORDINATING CONJUNCTION
The races were exciting, <u>and</u> we stayed until the end.

More examples of the use of conjunctive adverbs follow:

Frequently Used Conjunctive Adverbs

also	furthermore	later	still
besides	however	moreover	then
consequently	indeed	nevertheless	therefore
finally	instead	otherwise	thus

Charles dislikes vegetables; <u>furthermore</u>, he especially dislikes spinach.

They went swimming in the morning; <u>later</u>, they had lunch on the terrace.

In the afternoon, they walked and read magazines; <u>otherwise</u>, there was nothing else to do.

Interjections

There are a number of words or phrases that are used to express strong feeling or sudden emotion. Words that serve this purpose are called *interjections.* Many interjections stand alone and are followed by exclamation points. Others appear within a sentence and are set off with a comma or commas.

<u>Wow</u>! That taco was really spicy.

<u>Oh</u>, I beg your pardon.

<u>Ouch</u>! You stepped on my toe.

<u>No! No</u>! I won't do it.

Using interjections. Although interjections add variety to writing, you should use them sparingly. The strong feeling in your writing should come from the words you choose, the sentences you construct, and the ideas you express, not just from interjections.

Weak interjections should be avoided.

WEAK
Well, well, what's the use. It won't work.

BETTER
What's the use! It won't work.

Wow! Look at him move! I've never seen someone do that on a skateboard before. (In these sentences, Wow *is an interjection.)*

What are sentences?

When a number of words are put together to express a complete thought, they produce a sentence. By learning the jobs of different kinds of sentences and by understanding their individual parts, you will be able to choose the best ways to express your ideas.

What can a sentence do?

A *sentence* is a group of words that has a subject and a verb and that expresses a complete thought. It describes an action or states something about a person, place, or thing. Even so, some sentences are difficult to define, especially those that consist of only one word: Welcome. Yes. Why? Notice that even these one-word sentences express a complete thought. Two-word sentences are common: Dogs bark. She cried. They sat. You will see, however, that most sentences consist of many words.

There are four types of sentences and each has a different purpose. A *declarative sentence* makes a statement and ends with a period. An *interrogative sentence* asks a question and ends with a question mark. An *exclamatory sentence* shows strong feeling and ends with an exclamation point. An *imperative sentence* gives an order or makes a request. A mild command or request ends with a period, but a strong command or request ends with an exclamation point.

DECLARATIVE	*Xavier's best friend is a talented artist.*
INTERROGATIVE	*Have you decided to enter the essay contest?*
EXCLAMATORY	*What a tragedy that was!*
IMPERATIVE	*Clear the halls at once!* (strong command)
IMPERATIVE	*Please shut the door.* (mild request)

Parts of a sentence.

To express a complete thought, a sentence must have a subject and a verb. However, there are other parts as well that help to provide further information. A sentence may or may not include all the parts of speech described above. These parts of speech can be used in a sentence in many expanded ways. For example, the function of a noun may be modified by several words and the function of a verb may likewise be modified by other words. In order for you to understand how a sentence is put together, you must learn how these larger functions work.

Simple subjects. The *simple subject* of a sentence is the noun or pronoun that names the person, place, thing, or idea that the sentence is about. The simple subject does not include modifiers.

> *Mr. Wong's fried <u>dumplings</u> are the best I've ever tasted.*
> *The <u>stack</u> of dirty dishes in the sink must be washed.*
> *Yesterday <u>they</u> took a boat across Lake Champlain.*
> *Tomorrow <u>he</u> will go alone.*

The simple subject of an imperative sentence is always *you*. Often, *you* is understood rather than stated.

> *Bring your camera to school tomorrow.*

As you can see in the example above, *you* is the understood simple subject of the sentence, as in *you bring your camera.*

> *Wake up!*

Again, *you* is the understood simple subject of the sentence: *You wake up!*

A *compound subject* is a simple subject that has two or more nouns or pronouns of equal rank.

> *<u>Lemonade</u> and <u>iced tea</u> were the only drinks.*
> *The twins <u>John</u> and <u>Mary</u> go to different schools.*
> *The <u>knives</u> and <u>forks</u> are made of silver.*
> *<u>We</u> and <u>you</u> are going to the police station.*

Simple predicates. A *simple predicate* is the verb or verb phrase that describes the action or states something about the subject. The simple predicate does not include modifiers and words that complete the meaning of the verb. It also does not include the adverbs *not* or *never*.

> *Each student <u>collected</u> several kinds of wildflowers.*
> *Lisa and Alan <u>will try</u> to be here on time.*
> *Mary <u>will have received</u> the letter by the time you get there.*

A *compound predicate* is a simple predicate that is made up of two or more verbs or verb phrases of equal importance.

DeVona <u>measured</u> the fabric and then <u>cut</u> out the pieces of the vest.

Mike <u>carried</u> the ball down the football field and <u>crossed</u> the goal line jubilantly.

Dan <u>had worked</u> hard and <u>had saved</u> his money.

Complete subjects and complete predicates. The *complete subject* consists of the simple subject and all the words that modify or identify it.

<u>Union Street, which is in San Francisco</u>, is known for its restaurants and art galleries.

<u>Popular with all their classmates, Len and Lyle, who are identical twins</u>, are the newest students in the school.

<u>High on a mountain, often hidden by clouds, the monastery</u> is rarely visited.

The *complete predicate* consists of the simple predicate and all the words that modify it or complete its meaning.

Union Street, which is in San Francisco, <u>is known for its restaurants and art galleries</u>.

Popular with all their classmates, Len and Lyle, who are identical twins, <u>are the newest students in the school</u>.

High on a mountain, often hidden by clouds, the monastery <u>is rarely visited</u>.

Placement of subjects and predicates. Subjects and predicates may be arranged in a variety of ways in sentences. Where you place the subject and the predicate often depends on the purpose of the sentence. In the examples that follow, the complete subjects are underlined and the complete predicates not underlined.

DECLARATIVE *<u>The giant tortoise, the animal with the longest life span</u>, lives in a pond in the zoo.*

Here, the subject precedes the predicate.

DECLARATIVE *Here are <u>the athletic socks that you ordered from the catalogue</u>.*

The sentence above is written in inverted order; that is, the subject follows the predicate.

DECLARATIVE *Into the street rolled <u>the car</u>.*

This sentence has inverted word order.

DECLARATIVE *Because they had studied Native American jewelry techniques, <u>Paula and Diane, who both love silver and turquoise</u>, were particularly interested in the exhibit.*

In this example, the subject is between the two parts of the predicate.

The simple subject of the sentence "These skiers are going up the hill" is "skiers." The verb "go" supplies the action in the form of the simple predicate, "are going."

INTERROGATIVE *How were you able to fix the plugged drain in the kitchen?*
The subject is between two parts of the predicate.

IMPERATIVE *Try to finish painting the window frames by noon.*
Here, the entire imperative sentence is the complete predicate because the subject, you, is understood.

EXCLAMATORY *The pictures that you took are fantastic!*
The subject precedes the predicate.

EXCLAMATORY *What a fascinating book that was!*
The subject is between two parts of the predicate.

Complements. A *complement* is a word or group of words that completes the meaning of a verb. Complements are always part of the complete predicate. Without complements, the meaning of the following sentences would be incomplete and unclear.

The oranges that the DiNardos brought back from Florida were sweet and juicy.
Soon we must begin chopping wood for the winter.
This winter seems especially cold.

There are three types of complements: direct and indirect objects, objective complements, and subject complements. Sometimes you will have to analyze a sentence carefully to determine which word or words are complements.

A *direct object* is a noun or a pronoun that follows an action verb in the active voice and receives the action of the verb. It answers the question *what?* or *whom?* Verbs that take direct objects are called transitive verbs. (You can learn more about transitive and intransitive verbs under the previous section Verbs. Modifiers are not part of the object.

Mrs. Duryea will visit her great aunt.
This answers the question, will visit *whom?*

Our neighbors have a blower for clearing leaves and snow from their property.
In the example above, the direct object answers the question, have *what?*

The birthday boy ate his cake greedily.
In this example, the question is, the boy ate *what?*

An *indirect object* is a noun or a pronoun that names the person or thing *to* whom or *for* whom something is done. An indirect object follows an action verb in the active voice. In most cases, an indirect object is used with a direct object. The indirect object comes immediately after the verb and before the direct object.

We will show Jared as many historical sites as we have time for.
Think: We will show historical sites *to* Jared.

Her grandmother knitted Sonya a red sweater.
Think: Grandmother knitted a sweater *for* Sonya.

Just as subjects and predicates can be compound, so can objects be compound. A *compound object* consists of two or more objects that complete the same predicate.

COMPOUND DIRECT OBJECT
Jake read several books and articles about icebergs.

COMPOUND INDIRECT OBJECT
Marlene offered Carol and her brother tickets to the game.

An *objective complement* is a noun or an adjective that follows a direct object and explains, identifies, or describes that object. Only certain verbs take an objective complement: *appoint, call, choose, consider, elect, find, make, name, think,* and other verbs that have the same meaning.
The board of trustees has appointed Mr. Gearhart the director of the research department.
Director is the objective complement of the verb *appointed;* it serves to further identify Mr. Gearhart.
We considered the dancer's performance inspiring.
Inspiring is the objective complement of the verb *considered;* it describes the direct object, *performance.*

A *subject complement* is a word that comes after a linking verb and identifies or describes the subject of a sentence or a clause. Subject complements often follow forms of the verb *be* as well as *appear, become, feel, get, grow, look, remain, seem, smell, sound, stay,* and *taste.*

There are two types of subject complements. A *predicate nominative* is a noun or a pronoun that follows a linking verb and identifies the subject of the sentence. The predicate nominative renames the subject.
Owen is a volunteer at the local hospital.

In the last example on page 38, *volunteer* identifies the subject, *Owen*.

> *After working with a trainer, Phineas became an obedient* dog.

Dog renames the subject of the sentence, *Phineas*.

A *predicate adjective* follows a linking verb and modifies the subject of the sentence.

> *The book that I read was* hard *to follow.*

Here, the predicate adjective *hard* modifies the subject, *book*.

> *Micki felt* relaxed *and* sleepy *after reading for only ten minutes.*

The predicate adjectives *relaxed* and *sleepy* modify the subject, *Micki*.

What are phrases?

A *phrase* is a group of related words that functions as a single part of speech. But a phrase is different from a sentence because it lacks a subject, or a predicate, or both. Phrases can add variety to your writing and enable you to use fewer words.

Prepositional phrases. A *prepositional phrase* is made up of a preposition and its object and any modifiers of that object. A prepositional phrase that modifies a noun or a pronoun is called an *adjective phrase*. A prepositional phrase functions as an adverb if it modifies a verb, an adjective, or another adverb. This kind of phrase is sometimes called an *adverb phrase*.

ADJECTIVE PHRASE

> *The newspaper will list the location* of the next meeting.

The prepositional phrase *of the next meeting* modifies the noun *location*.

ADVERB PHRASE

> *Mr. Whiteside will not leave* before dinner.

The prepositional phrase *before dinner* modifies the verb *will not leave*, making it an adverb phrase.

ADVERB PHRASE AND ADJECTIVE PHRASE

> *The entire class was curious* about methods of conserving energy.

Here, the prepositional phrase *about methods* modifies the adjective *curious*; it is an adverb phrase. The prepositional phrase *of conserving energy* modifies the noun *methods*; it is an adjective phrase.

ADVERB PHRASE AND ADJECTIVE PHRASE

> *A boy or girl* with dirty hands *is not welcomed* at the table.

The prepositional phrase *with dirty hands* modifies the nouns *boy* and *girl*; thus, it is an adjective phrase. The prepositional phrase *at the table* modifies the verb *is not welcomed*; it is an adverb phrase.

Appositive phrases. An *appositive* is a noun or a pronoun placed near another noun or pronoun to explain it or identify it. Like an appositive, an *appositive phrase* explains or identifies a noun or a pronoun. It includes all the words or phrases that modify an appositive.

APPOSITIVE

> *The class secretary,* Anton Berrioz, *read the meeting notes aloud.*

The appositive *Anton Berrioz* identifies the class secretary.

APPOSITIVE PHRASE

> *The movie,* a science fiction thriller with special effects, *was exciting.*

The appositive phrase *a science fiction thriller with special effects* further describes the movie.

An *essential appositive phrase* is an appositive that is necessary to the meaning of the sentence. This kind of appositive should *not* be separated from the rest of the sentence with a comma. A *nonessential appositive phrase* is an appositive that is not necessary to the meaning of the sentence. This appositive phrase *should* be separated from the rest of the sentence with a comma or commas.

ESSENTIAL APPOSITIVE PHRASE

> *Edgar Allan Poe's short story "The Telltale Heart" has been recorded many times.*

Poe wrote more than one short story. Therefore, the appositive "The Telltale Heart" is necessary to identify which story has been recorded many times.

NONESSENTIAL APPOSITIVE PHRASE

> *Poe also wrote "The Pit and the Pendulum,"* a story that gives me nightmares every time I read it.

In this case, the appositive is not necessary to identify the story.

The students, searching diligently on the banks of the pond, found many interesting things. (In this sentence searching diligently on the banks of the pond *is a participial phrase.)*

Verbal phrases. *Verbals* are verb forms that function as nouns, adjectives, or adverbs but keep some of the properties of verbs. They express action or a state of being, and may take complements. There are three kinds of verbals: participles, gerunds, and infinitives.

Participial phrases. A *participial phrase* consists of a participle and its modifiers and complements. The participial phrase functions as an adjective to modify a noun or a pronoun. Both present and past participles may be used to form participial phrases.

> *Cooing softly to herself, the baby played with her toes.*

The participial phrase shown above modifies *baby.*

> *The instructions, <u>written in poorly translated Japanese</u>, were impossible to understand.*

The participial phrase modifies *instructions.*

Always place a comma after an introductory participial phrase. If the information in a phrase within a sentence is essential, you do not need to use commas. Essential information identifies a person, place, or thing. If the information in a phrase is nonessential, however, commas are used to separate it from the rest of the sentence. A nonessential phrase contains information that could be removed without changing the basic meaning of the sentence.

ESSENTIAL PARTICIPIAL PHRASE

> *The person talking to the coach is Peter Boland.*

No commas are used because the phrase is needed to identify the person.

NONESSENTIAL PARTICIPIAL PHRASE

> *Peter Boland, talking to the coach, is my friend.*

Commas are needed because the phrase could be removed from the sentence.

Gerunds and gerund phrases. A *gerund* is a verbal that ends in -ing and functions as a noun. It has some of the properties of a verb in that it expresses action or being, and it may take a complement such as a direct object or an indirect object.

SUBJECT   *Pointing is impolite.*

DIRECT OBJECT   *Nell enjoys <u>skating</u> and <u>biking</u>.*

INDIRECT OBJECT

    She gives her <u>practicing</u> one hour a day.

OBJECT OF THE PREPOSITION

    Gil went the whole day without <u>eating</u>.

PREDICATE NOMINATIVE

    Last year my favorite winter sport was <u>skiing</u>.

APPOSITIVE   *Tina has a new interest, <u>sewing</u>.*

A *gerund phrase* is a gerund with its modifiers and complements all working together as a noun.

<u>Singing together</u> is a treat for them.

The Carrs surprised us by <u>visiting for a week</u>.

<u>Painting scenery</u> is Rick's specialty.

The possessive form of a noun or a pronoun is used before a gerund and is considered part of the phrase.

<u>Talia's winning the debate tournament</u> was a shock.

His parents encouraged <u>his studying chemistry</u>.

Infinitives and infinitive phrases. An *infinitive* is a verbal form that consists of the first principal part of the verb. The word *to* usually, though not always, precedes the infinitive. An infinitive may function as a noun, an adjective, or an adverb. Like a participle and a gerund, an infinitive has some of the characteristics of a verb. It expresses action or being, and it may take a complement.

NOUN   *<u>To make</u> a mistake is human.*

    Here the infinitive is the subject.

    Everyone should learn <u>to change</u> a tire.

    The infinitive is a direct object in this instance.

Tip

Because an infinitive begins with the word *to,* it is sometimes confused with a prepositional phrase. An infinitive ends with a verb form, but a prepositional phrase ends with a noun or a pronoun.

ADJECTIVE   *North Caldwell is the team <u>to beat</u>.*

    To beat modifies the noun *team.*

ADVERB   *Young children are quick <u>to learn</u>.*

    To learn modifies the adjective *quick.*

An *infinitive phrase* consists of an infinitive and its modifiers and complements. It can function as a noun, an adjective, or an adverb.

NOUN   *<u>To win at chess</u> requires concentration.*

ADJECTIVE   *The best time <u>to cut flowers</u> is early in the morning.*

ADVERB   *It's fun <u>to try different foods</u> in new restaurants.*

To is sometimes omitted when an infinitive follows such verbs as *dare, feel, hear, help, let, make, need, see,* or *watch.*

Mr. Hussein helped me <u>put up the badminton net</u>.

Think: helped me *to* put up the badminton net.

What are clauses? A *clause* is a group of related words that contains both a subject and a verb. There are two kinds of clauses: independent and subordinate. Understanding clauses and being able to include them in your writing is valuable because clauses show important relationships between ideas. Clauses also let you combine ideas to create clearer sentences.

Independent clauses. An *independent* or *main clause* can stand alone as a sentence because it expresses a complete thought. When an independent clause stands by itself, it is called a *sentence.* When it appears in a sentence with another clause, it is called a clause. In the following example, you will notice how each clause has a subject and a predicate. Each could be a separate sentence.

Janice raked the leaves, and Dwight bagged them.

You can use a comma and a coordinating conjunction like *and* or *but* to join the clauses. *And* is not part of either clause. It coordinates, or connects, the independent clauses. You can also join independent clauses with either a semicolon or a semicolon and a conjunctive adverb.

This sounds like a tall tale, <u>but</u>, believe it or not, it's true.

This sounds like a tall tale; believe it or not, it's true.

This sounds like a tall tale; <u>however</u>, believe it or not, it's true.

41

Dependent clauses. A *dependent* or *subordinate clause* cannot stand alone as a sentence because it does not express a complete thought. Even though it has a subject and a predicate, it depends on the rest of the sentence for meaning.

> *Because we were late*, we missed the kickoff.
> Carly goes to the beach *whenever she has the chance*.

A dependent clause functions as an *adjective clause* if it modifies a noun or a pronoun. Most adjective clauses begin with a relative pronoun: *that, which, who, whom,* or *whose.*

> Teddy wants a pet *that he can play with*.
> Ramona looked for Mrs. Weinstein, *who was holding tryouts in the auditorium*.

Adjective clauses can be either *essential* or *nonessential.* Separate a nonessential clause from the rest of the sentence with a comma or commas, but do not separate an essential adjective clause from its independent clause.

A dependent clause functions as an *adverb clause* when it modifies a verb, an adjective, or another adverb. An adverb clause always begins with a subordinating conjunction, a word that shows the relationship between the dependent clause and the independent clause. Adverb clauses tell *how, when, where, to what extent,* and *why.*

> We will go *whenever you're ready*.
> Alan is taller *than I am*.
> *As long as its chin is being tickled*, the cat will sit quietly.

Place a comma after an introductory adverbial clause. If an adverbial clause interrupts an independent clause, place a comma before and after it.

> *If you win*, will you give your prize money to charity?
> The Senate, *after the President vetoed the bill*, overrode the veto.

A dependent clause functions as a *noun clause* when it is used like a noun: as a subject, a direct object, an indirect object, an object of the preposition, or a predicate nominative. Noun clauses are introduced with interrogative pronouns, subordinating conjunctions, or the relative pronoun *whose.*

SUBJECT   *Whatever you choose is fine with me.*
DIRECT OBJECT   *Did you realize that Lamar won?*
INDIRECT OBJECT   *Give whoever comes to the door the samples.*
OBJECT OF THE PREPOSITION   *Bridget was overwhelmed by what she had heard.*
PREDICATE NOMINATIVE   *Helen's reason for leaving early was that she was sick.*

Subject-verb agreement.

For a sentence to be clear, the subject and its verb must agree. The forms of nouns, pronouns, and verbs can be changed to show whether they are singular or plural. If the subject is singular, the form of the verb should be singular. If the subject is plural, the form of the verb should be plural. This is called making the subject and verb agree in number.

SINGULAR   *Peter lives in a small town near the border of Tennessee.*
PLURAL   *Three of my relatives live in the same town.*

For a verb phrase to agree with its subject, the helping verb must agree in number with the subject.

SINGULAR   *Peter has lived there only since March.*
PLURAL   *My relatives have lived there all their lives.*

Sometimes words and phrases come between a subject and its verb. These words or phrases do not change the number of the subject. Be sure that you make the verb agree in number with the subject of the sentence, not with some other word in another phrase.

SINGULAR   *Lisa, new to the life of babysitters, was unprepared for her lack of free time on weekends.*
PLURAL   *The contestants waiting backstage for a cue were becoming excited and restless.*

Determining the number of the subject. In some sentences, you may find it difficult to determine the number of the subject. These guidelines will help you.

Compound subjects. A *compound subject* is made up of two or more subjects that are connected by a coordinating conjunction. A compound subject may take a singular or a plural verb, depending on which conjunction is used and whether the words in the compound subject are singular or plural. Use a plural verb with most compound subjects connected by *and*.

PLURAL   *The <u>coach</u> and the <u>principal were</u>
          <u>expected</u> to attend the meeting.*

Use a singular verb with a compound subject that refers to one person or one thing, or to something that is generally considered as a unit—plural in form but singular in meaning.

SINGULAR   *This year's most popular <u>player</u>
            <u>and speaker is planning</u> to sign
            autographs.*

The singular is used in the above example because the player and speaker are the same person.

Use a singular verb with a compound subject that has a singular noun or pronoun connected by *or* or *nor*.

SINGULAR   *Either her <u>aunt or</u> her <u>cousin plans</u>
            to attend the concert.*

Use a plural verb with a compound subject that is composed of plural nouns or pronouns connected by *or* or *nor*.

PLURAL   *Neither the old <u>televisions nor</u> the
          broken <u>radios have been fixed.</u>*

When a compound subject is composed of a singular subject and a plural subject connected by *or* or *nor*, use the verb that agrees in number with the subject that is closer to the verb in the sentence.

SINGULAR   *Neither the cellists nor the <u>violinist</u>
            <u>has</u> sheet music.*

PLURAL   *Neither the violinist nor the <u>cellists</u>
          <u>have</u> sheet music.*

Nouns with plural forms. Nouns such as *economics, mathematics, measles,* and *news* are plural in form but singular in meaning. Although they end in <u>s</u>, they refer to a single thing or to a unit and therefore take a singular verb.

SINGULAR   <u>*Physics is*</u> *a challenging branch of
            science.*

Other nouns, such as *clothes, congratulations, pliers, shears,* and *scissors,* end in <u>s</u> but take a plural verb, even though they refer to one thing.

PLURAL   *His garden <u>shears are</u> on the porch.*

Some nouns, such as *athletics, dramatics,* and *politics,* end in <u>s</u> but may be singular or plural depending on their meaning in the sentence. It is important to use your dictionary to find out whether a noun that ends in <u>s</u> takes a singular or a plural verb.

Inverted word order. In some sentences, especially questions or sentences beginning with *Here* or *There,* you may have difficulty locating the subject because the verb comes before it. Rearrange the sentence in its normal subject-verb order to find the subject and make the verb agree with it in number.

SINGULAR   *Beside the building was a tiny park.*
            Think: park *was.*

PLURAL   *There are many caves in those
          mountains.*
          Think: caves *are.*

Sentences with predicate nominatives. Using a predicate nominative can confuse subject-verb agreement when the subject and the predicate nominative differ in number. You should always use a verb that agrees in number with the subject, not the predicate nominative.

INCORRECT   *Roses is one of her favorite flowers.*

CORRECT   *Roses are one of her favorite flowers.*

Every and many a(n). As adjectives, *every* and *many a(n)* emphasize separateness when they modify subjects. *Every* means every single one and *many a(n)* means each item separate from all other items. Therefore, use a singular verb with a single subject or a compound subject modified by *every* or *many a(n).*

Every shirt and vest <u>is</u> on sale this weekend.

Many a cat <u>dislikes</u> milk and fish.

Every man, woman, and child <u>has</u> to be counted.

Many a student <u>prepares</u> thoroughly for tests.

Clothes are fun to shop for. (Clothes is a plural noun and takes a plural verb, are.)

Combining sentences

So far, we have been looking only at simple sentences; yet we all know that not all sentences are simple; they can be highly complex. Writing, indeed, would be very dull if it were nothing but one simple sentence after another after another.

Sentence combining. Simple sentences, of the kinds we have been looking at, can be combined with other simple sentences. The results of these combinations are more complex sentences. In fact, every sentence, no matter how complex, can be thought of as the combining of two or more simple sentences.

There are many ways in which sentences can be combined. In the following pages, we shall look at a number of them. Learning to combine sentences can be of great help in two important ways:

1. Practicing ways of combining sentences will help you learn how the language works: its grammar, its general rules, and its oddities. Start with two simple sentences you have made up. Combine them in as many ways as you can. Although not every pair of sentences can be combined in every way, you will be surprised at how many ways there are to modify the sentences' meanings by combining them. Then try more complex combinations, of three, four, five, and even more sentences. This practice will be a great help in teaching you to write more clearly.

2. Combining sentences can help you clarify your own thinking. When you know what you want to say, but can't get it down on paper, turn to sentence combining. Take the idea that you are having trouble with, and write out its parts in simple sentences. Then try various ways of putting the simple sentences together, being sure that you keep the sentences' main ideas unchanged. Sooner or later (probably sooner than you expect), you will find the right way to say what you want to.

Compounding. The simplest way of combining sentences is called compounding. Compounding combines sentences by joining them together with coordinating conjunctions.

Consider these two simple sentences:
My mother is a dentist.
My father is a writer.
These two sentences can be put together by simply joining them with *and:*
My mother is a dentist, <u>and</u> my father is a writer.
Notice that neither of the original sentences has been changed; they have just been joined together. Notice, too, the comma before *and,* which is important. When two simple sentences are joined in this way, forming what is called a compound sentence, a comma always comes before the word that joins them.

Other conjunctions besides *and* can join sentences in this way:
or, nor, but, for, either/or, neither/nor, both/and, not only/but also
Suppose, for example, that you have these two simple sentences. One of them is true, but you do not know which one it is.
His father is a bus driver.
His uncle is a bus driver.
These sentences can be combined using *either/or:*
<u>Either</u> his father is a bus driver, <u>or</u> his uncle is a bus driver.
Again, notice that the original sentences have not changed; they have just been joined by the conjunctions and the comma.

Now cover the page with a sheet of paper. Write out the combinations of each of these pairs of sentences, using the conjunction given in parentheses after the second sentence. Do not look at the combined versions until you have finished writing your own.

SENTENCES: *Yesterday was beautiful.*
Today is cold and rainy. (but)
COMBINED: *Yesterday was beautiful, <u>but</u> today is cold and rainy.*
SENTENCES: *We took a long walk.*
It was a lovely day. (because)
COMBINED: *We took a long walk, <u>because</u> it was a lovely day.*
SENTENCES: *We shall leave today.*
We shall leave tomorrow. (either/or)
COMBINED: *<u>Either</u> we shall leave today, <u>or</u> we shall leave tomorrow.*

Compounding sentence parts. Take another look at that last pair of sentences. Notice that they are exactly the same except for the adverbs at the end. When two sentences contain some words that are identical, as shown here, the identical words can be crossed out of the second sentence and then the remainder of the sentence can be combined with the first.

> SENTENCES: *We shall leave today.*
> *We shall leave tomorrow.*
> *(either/or)*
> COMBINED: *We shall leave either today or tomorrow.*

This kind of combining can be done with all kinds of sentence parts. Whatever parts are combined in the two sentences are said to be compound. These two sentences, for example,

> *Jerry is ready.*
> *I am ready. (and)*

combine to produce a sentence with a compound subject:

> *Jerry and I are ready.*

(Notice that *Jerry and I,* being two people, require the plural verb *are.*)

Other sentence parts can be compounded:

> VERBS: *The departing guests smiled.*
> *The departing guests waved.*
> *(and)*
> COMBINED: *The departing guests smiled and waved.*
>
> DIRECT OBJECTS: *They will choose Jennifer.*
> *They will choose me. (or)*
> COMBINED: *They will choose Jennifer or me.*
>
> ADJECTIVES: *The day was bright.*
> *The day was sunny.*
> COMBINED: *The day was bright and sunny.*
>
> PREPOSITIONAL PHRASES:
> *She walked across the street.*
> *She walked into the yellow house.*
> COMBINED: *She walked across the street and into the yellow house.*
>
> OBJECTS OF PREPOSITIONS:
> *This gift is for Carol.*
> *This gift is for her husband.*
> COMBINED: *This gift is for Carol and her husband.*

Parallelism. In forming compounds of this kind, it is important that the sentence elements that are compounded be of the same kind. In the following pair of sentences, for example, a compound cannot be correctly formed.

> *He likes tennis.*
> *He likes to swim.*

Tennis and *to swim* are not the same kind of sentence element; they are said to be not parallel. Thus the sentence *He likes tennis and to swim* is incorrect. To combine the sentences, the form of one of them must first be changed.

> SENTENCES: *He likes tennis.*
> *He likes swimming.*
> COMBINED: *He likes tennis and swimming.*

Compounding with semicolons. The two sentences below could be combined using *and:*

> SENTENCES: *Finish your breakfast.*
> *Then we can go.*
> COMBINED: *Finish your breakfast, and then we can go.*

There is, however, another way they can be joined. Simply put them next to each other and join them with a semicolon:

> COMBINED: *Finish your breakfast; then we can go.*

It is important that the punctuation mark be a semicolon. Connecting the sentences with only a comma (or with no punctuation at all) produces a "run-on" sentence and is incorrect.

Series. Supposing that, instead of two sentences with some identical words, you have three:

> *The day was bright.*
> *The day was cold.*
> *The day was windy.*

These three sentences can be combined in exactly the same way as can two sentences:

> *The day was bright and cold and windy.*

Usually, combinations of this kind are taken a step further. First, every conjunction except the last one is taken out; second, commas are inserted after all but the last of the combined elements. This is called a series:

> *The day was bright, cold, and windy.*

Series can be made from any kind of sentence elements so long as the elements are parallel. Just be sure to include the commas.

Complex transformations.

Compounding is the simplest kind of sentence combining. Other ways produce sentences that are more complex.

Relative clauses.
One of the most important ways of combining two sentences is the way that produces a relative clause. A relative clause helps identify or modify a noun. There are two kinds of relative clauses, nonrestrictive and restrictive.

Nonrestrictive clauses. Nonrestrictive clauses modify a noun or a noun phrase without being necessary to identify it. Consider these:

Mr. Johnson is my teacher.
Mr. Johnson is standing on the corner.

The sentences could be combined into a compound sentence:

Mr. Johnson is my teacher, and Mr. Johnson is standing on the corner.

Or, more likely,

Mr. Johnson is my teacher, and he is standing on the corner.

An even more likely way to combine these two sentences is to transform one of them into a relative clause. It's done this way. First, change the part of one sentence that is the same as part of the other sentence—in this case *Mr. Johnson*—to a relative pronoun. The relative pronouns are *who, whom, whose, which,* and *that.* In this case, use *who.* The second sentence of the pair,

Mr. Johnson is standing on the corner.

thus becomes

who is standing on the corner

This group of words can then be inserted into the middle of the first sentence to produce:

Mr. Johnson, who is standing on the corner, is my teacher.

The words *who is standing on the corner* constitute a relative clause. In this case, the relative clause is nonrestrictive; it simply adds the information that he is standing on the corner. Nonrestrictive relative clauses are set off from the rest of the sentence by commas.

Restrictive clauses. A restrictive clause is necessary to identify the particular noun or noun clause it modifies. Start this time with two somewhat different sentences:

The man is my teacher.
The man is standing on the corner.

Here the second sentence can again be transformed into the relative clause,

who is standing on the corner

The relative clause can then be inserted into the first sentence to produce the combined sentence

The man who is standing on the corner is my teacher.

In this case, a restrictive relative clause tells us *which man* we are talking about. It suggests that *the man standing on the corner,* rather than the man walking down the street, is the speaker's teacher. A restrictive relative clause is *not* set off from the rest of the sentence by commas.

Other relative clauses. The relative pronoun *who* is used when it replaces the subject of a sentence, as in the above examples.

When the noun phrase that the relative pronoun replaces is a direct object, use either *whom* or *that.* For example, in the sentences

The woman is my mother.
You saw the woman.

the second of the sentences can be changed to

whom you saw or *that you saw,*

producing either of these combined sentences:

The woman whom you saw is my mother.
The woman that you saw is my mother.

When the relative pronoun replaces the object of a preposition, use *whom* or *which.*

SENTENCES: *The person was grateful.*
You wrote to the person.
COMBINED: *The person to whom you wrote was grateful.*
SENTENCES: *The company is out of business.*
George worked for the company.
COMBINED: *The company for which George worked is out of business.*

In speech it is acceptable to leave the preposition at the end of the relative clause, as in *the company that George worked for,* but such usage is best avoided in writing.

The relative pronoun *that* can be used only in restrictive clauses. Generally, it is best to use *which* only in nonrestrictive clauses. The other relative pronouns—*who, whom,* and *whose*—are correct when used in both restrictive and nonrestrictive clauses.

RESTRICTIVE: *The article that I read was very interesting.*
NONRESTRICTIVE: *The article, which I read, was very interesting.*

Nonrestrictive Clauses

Mr. Johnson, who is on the corner, is my teacher.

Use commas—this part of the sentence could be taken out because we all know Mr. Johnson.

Restrictive Clauses

The man who is on the corner is my teacher.

Do *not* use commas—without "who is on the corner," the sentence would not make sense because we have never met your teacher.

Deletion transformations.

To delete something is to take it out. At certain times it is possible to delete the beginning of a relative clause, producing a number of different kinds of sentence structures. Deletion transformations are only possible when:

1. The relative pronoun is the subject of the relative clause.
2. The word immediately following the relative pronoun is a form of *be;* that is, *am, is, are, was,* or *were.*

Appositives. Look again at these two sentences from the previous page:

Mr. Johnson is standing on the corner.

Mr. Johnson is my teacher.

By changing the second sentence to a relative clause, *who is my teacher,* and inserting it into the first sentence, we produce the combined sentence

Mr. Johnson, who is my teacher, is standing on the corner.

A further change, a deletion transformation, is possible. By deleting *who* and *is,* we can produce:

Mr. Johnson, my teacher, is standing on the corner.

In this last sentence, the noun phrase *my teacher* is what is called an appositive. An appositive is a noun phrase that identifies or renames another noun phrase, which it immediately follows. Notice that the appositive, like the nonrestrictive clause from which it was made, is set off from the rest of the sentence by commas.

Participles. Remember that every verb has two forms called participles. They are the present participle, or *-ing* form *(seeing, showing, looking),* and the past participle *(seen, shown, looked).* As verbs, these forms are used only with auxiliaries. Often the auxiliary is a form of *be.*

Sentences containing participles can be made into relative clauses and combined with other sentences.

SENTENCES: *The boy spoke to me.*

The boy was standing.

The combining of these sentences differs, depending on whether the clause with the participle is restrictive or nonrestrictive.

	RESTRICTIVE	NONRESTRICTIVE
COMBINED:	*The boy who was standing spoke to me.*	*The boy, who was standing, spoke to me.*

Because the relative clause begins with *who was,* those two words can be deleted.

	RESTRICTIVE	NONRESTRICTIVE
DELETION:	*The boy standing spoke to me.*	*The boy, standing, spoke to me.*

Without its auxiliary, the participle in the sentence on the left is now a word by itself, modifying the noun *boy.* It has, in fact, become an adjective. Since it is an adjective, it can be moved (and usually is) to a position before the noun. In the sentence on the right, the participle must continue to be set off by commas, but it can move to the beginning of the sentence.

	RESTRICTIVE	NONRESTRICTIVE
MOVE PARTICIPLE:	*The standing boy spoke to me.*	*Standing, the boy spoke to me.*

The same series of combinations and deletions can be made with a past participle:

	RESTRICTIVE	NONRESTRICTIVE
SENTENCES:	*Our car looked like new.* *That car was washed.*	*Our car looked like new.* *Our car was washed.*
COMBINED:	*Our car that was washed looked like new.*	*Our car, which was washed, looked like new.*
DELETION:	*Our car washed looked like new.*	*Our car, washed, looked like new.*

Participial phrases.

The examples above show how a participle can, by itself, become a noun modifier—an adjective. But participles often are not words by themselves. When they are functioning as verbs in simple sentences, they often have complements.

> The girl is <u>washing the car</u>.
> The man is <u>standing near the door</u>.

In these sentences, *the car* is the direct object of *washing,* and *near the door* is an adverbial complement of *standing.*

Participles with complements can also be made into noun modifiers. As usual, begin with two sentences, and transform one of them into a relative clause.

> SENTENCES: *The girl is my neighbor.*
> *The girl is washing the car.*
> COMBINED: *The girl <u>who is washing the car</u> is my neighbor.*
> DELETION: *The girl <u>washing the car</u> is my neighbor.*

In this sentence, the words *washing the car,* a participle and its complement, are what is called a participial phrase. The phrase follows the noun that it modifies, *girl.* Because the relative clause was restrictive, the participial phrase is also restrictive; there are no commas.

Participial phrases can also be made from nonrestrictive relative clauses:

> SENTENCES: *The small child smiled shyly.*
> *The small child was waving at me.*
> COMBINED: *The small child, <u>who was waving at me</u>, smiled shyly.*
> DELETION: *The small child, <u>waving at me</u>, smiled shyly.*

In the last sentence above, *waving at me* is a participial phrase modifying *child.* Because it was made from a nonrestrictive relative clause, it, too, is nonrestrictive, and so is set off by commas.

A nonrestrictive participial phrase (unlike a restrictive one) can be moved to a position in front of the noun phrase it modifies:

> <u>Waving at me</u>, the young child smiled shyly.

As usual, it is set off by commas.

Gerunds and gerund phrases.

Gerunds are a form of verb used as a noun. Because a gerund, like a participle, uses the *-ing* form of a verb, the two are often confused. But they are not the same thing at all. A gerund is, by itself, the *-ing* form of a verb used as a noun. It can fill any of the noun phrase positions in simple sentences:

> SUBJECT: <u>Cooking</u> *is his hobby.*
> PREDICATE NOMINATIVE: *His hobby is <u>cooking</u>.*
> DIRECT OBJECT: *He enjoys <u>cooking</u>.*
> INDIRECT OBJECT: *He gives <u>cooking</u> all his time.*
> OBJECT OF PREPOSITION: *He takes pride in his <u>cooking</u>.*

Sentences with gerunds are, like other complex sentences, formed by first changing the form of one sentence, and then inserting the transformed sentence into a second sentence. To form the first of the gerund sentences above, for example, begin with these two sentences:

> *Something is his hobby.*
> *He cooks.*

The problem is to transform *he cooks* so that it can take the place of *something* in the first sentence. This is done by changing the verb to its gerund form, *cooking.* The subject of the sentence, *he,* can be transformed to its possessive form, *his.* Thus the sentence *he cooks* has been transformed into the gerund phrase *cooking* or *his cooking,* which can now replace the word *something* in the first sentence:

> *His <u>cooking</u> is his hobby.*
> <u>Cooking</u> *is his hobby.*

When a verb has a complement, the transforming and combining process remains the same:

> SENTENCES: *Something was a pleasant surprise.*
> *Jason won the race.*
> TRANSFORM THE SECOND SENTENCE: *Jason's winning the race . . .*
> AND INSERT IT INTO THE FIRST SENTENCE: *<u>Jason's winning the race</u> was a pleasant surprise.*

Infinitive phrases.

Remember that an infinitive is a verb form that begins with the preposition *to: to see, to have seen, to be seen,* and so on. An infinitive, like a gerund, can fill certain noun phrase positions in a sentence:

> SUBJECT: <u>To sing</u> *is a pleasure.*
> PREDICATE NOMINATIVE: *His greatest pleasure is <u>to sing</u>.*

As with other complex sentences, a sentence with an infinitive is built from two simple sentences.

> SENTENCES: *His greatest pleasure is something.*
> *He sings.*

To make an infinitive phrase of the second sentence, two changes must take place:

1. Change the verb *sings* to the infinitive form *to sing*.
2. Change the subject *he* to the prepositional phrase *for him*. That produces the infinitive phrase *for him to sing*, which can now be inserted into the other sentence:

   His greatest pleasure is <u>for him to sing</u>.

Again, if there is no question as to who is doing the singing, the phrase *for him* can be deleted:

His greatest pleasure is <u>to sing</u>.

Noun clauses.

A noun clause is yet another way to transform a sentence so that it can act as a noun phrase in another sentence. Consider these sentences:

Something is a surprise.

Jan is here.

The second sentence can be transformed into a noun clause simply by adding the word *that* to the beginning of it:

<u>That Jan is here</u> . . .

The resulting noun clause can then be inserted into the first sentence:

<u>That Jan is here</u> is a surprise.

Sometimes a noun clause is introduced by a word like *whoever* or *whomever*:

SENTENCES: *Someone must light the fire.*
Someone arrives first.

Transform the second sentence by changing *someone* to *whoever*:

<u>Whoever</u> arrives first . . .

Insert the noun clause into the first sentence:

<u>Whoever arrives first</u> must light the fire.

Whomever is used when it replaces the direct object in one of the original sentences:

SENTENCES: *Give these books to someone.*
You can find someone.

TRANSFORM: *First: You can find <u>whomever</u> . . .*
Second: <u>Whomever</u> you can find . . .

INSERT: *Give these books to <u>whomever you can find</u>.*

Sometimes a noun clause begins with an adverb like *when* or *where*.

SENTENCES: *I do not know something.*
You got that idea somewhere.

TRANSFORM: *Where you got that idea . . .*

INSERT: *I do not know <u>where you got that idea</u>.*

Adverbial clauses.

When two sentences are joined by a subordinating conjunction (pages 33–34), one of the sentences becomes an adverbial (or subordinate) clause. Look at the following sentences:

We arrived.

The movie had begun.

You can guess that there is some time relationship between the two events that the sentences tell about. A subordinating conjunction such as *after* will make that relationship clear. Adding the subordinating conjunction transforms one sentence into an adverbial clause:

After the movie had begun . . .

This clause can be attached to the first sentence:

We arrived <u>after the movie had begun</u>.

Adverbial clauses usually occupy the adverb slot at the end of a sentence. Like adverbs and adverbial phrases, they can also move to the beginning of a sentence, separated from the rest of the sentence by a comma:

<u>After the movie had begun</u>, we arrived.

Subjunctive mood.

The subjunctive mood is a special verb form that is required in certain adverbial or noun clauses.

The present subjunctive is used in noun clauses that are the direct objects of verbs like *demand, ask,* or *move.* It uses the unmarked form of the verb:

I request that I <u>be</u> allowed to leave.

They demanded that George <u>resign</u>.

The past subjunctive is used in adverbial clauses that begin with such conjunctions as *if* or *as if.* It is used when the statement made in the adverbial clause is clearly contrary to fact:

I would not do that if I <u>were</u> you.

Since I am *not* you, the past subjunctive is used.

For most nouns and pronouns, the past subjunctive is the same as the past tense. Its only difference is that it uses *were* instead of *was* for singular nouns and pronouns as well as for plural.

Note that clauses beginning with *if* do not always have subjunctive verbs:

If he <u>was</u> there, I did not see him.

(Maybe he was there, maybe he wasn't; the subjunctive is not used.)

If he <u>were</u> there, I would have told you.

(He was not there; the subjunctive is used.) Notice, too, that when the past subjunctive is used, the main verb always has the auxiliary *would.*

49

Sentence Diagrams

A sentence diagram has been compared to a map of a sentence. It arranges the words of a sentence on a page in a way that makes it easy to see their relationships. (Caution: a diagram does not necessarily show the word order of the sentence.)

Always begin a diagram with a horizontal line bisected by a vertical line:

Simple sentence: On the left side of the horizontal line, write the simple subject of the sentence. The simple subject is either the main noun in a noun phrase or a pronoun. On the right side of the line, write the verb, including any auxiliaries.

Snow is falling.

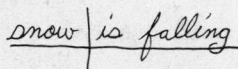

Direct object: When the verb is transitive, draw a vertical line to the right of the verb. The vertical line should meet but not cross the base line. To the right of this line, write the main noun or pronoun of the direct object.

Liz likes me.

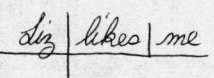

Linking verbs: If the sentence has a linking verb, draw a diagonal line to the right of the verb. The line should meet but not cross the base line. To the right of this line, write the adjective complement or the predicate nominative.

People can be nice.
We are students.

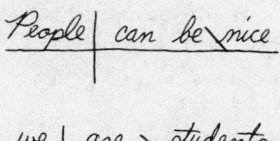

Modifiers: If there are adjectives (including determiners) modifying a noun, put them on a diagonal line beneath the noun. Do the same with adverbs modifying the verb.

A light snow fell softly.

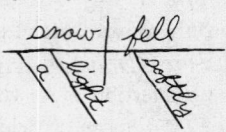

Prepositions: When diagramming a prepositional phrase, write the preposition on a diagonal line beneath the word that the phrase modifies. Then write the noun or pronoun on a horizontal line, and put any adjective modifiers on diagonal lines below.

The woman in the red dress hurried from the room.

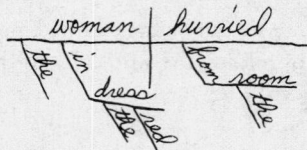

Indirect object: Diagram an indirect object as if it were a prepositional phrase with the preposition *to* understood. Put *to* in parentheses.

The experience taught my friend a hard lesson.

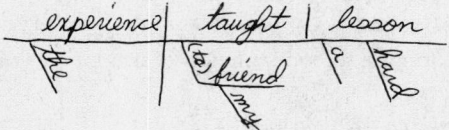

Compound subjects or predicates: To diagram compound sentence elements, place them on parallel lines. Connect the two lines with a dotted vertical line, and write the coordinating conjunction on it.

Ray and Bernice ate lunch together today.
The children washed the dishes and swept the floor.

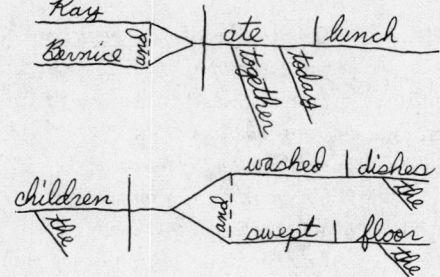

Compound sentences: To diagram a compound sentence—that is, two simple sentences joined by a coordinating conjunction—diagram each of the simple sentences, one above the other. Then connect them with a vertical dotted line, and write the conjunction on that line.

The mail has come, but that letter was not in it.

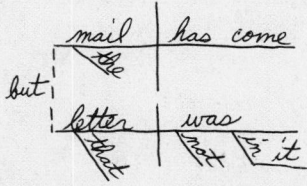

Appositives: To diagram an appositive, put the appositive noun or pronoun in parentheses after the noun that it renames or identifies.

Sam, an old friend of mine, sent this book.

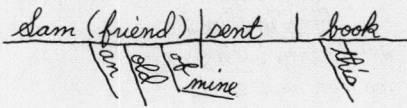

Relative clauses: To diagram a relative clause, diagram the clause on its own line below the main line. With a dotted line, connect the noun that is being modified to the relative pronoun or relative adverb.

Those apples that you sent me were delicious.
This is the place where we saw him last.

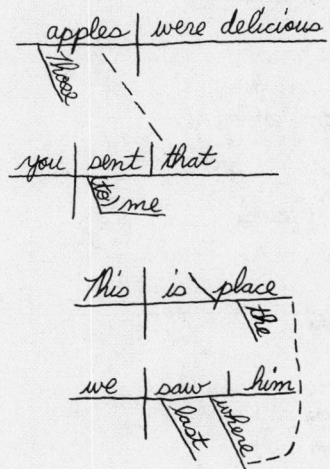

Participles and participial phrases: A participle is diagrammed in a curve along a diagonal and a horizontal line. The complement of the participle, if any, is to the right on the horizontal line.

Laughing, Judy handed me the squirming puppy.
The man scratching his head is your new teacher.

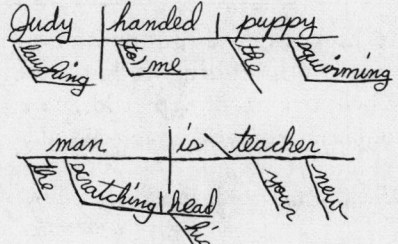

Gerunds: A gerund is diagrammed the same way as a participle, except that it is placed on a pedestal. The bottom of the pedestal rests on the base line in a noun's position.

His being the culprit surprised everyone.

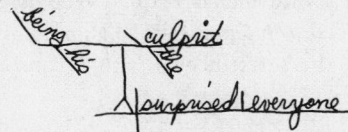

Infinitive phrases: An infinitive phrase occupying a noun position is diagrammed the same way as a gerund.

Nobody wants to leave the game yet.

Adverbial clauses: An adverbial clause is diagrammed on a line below the base line. The subordinating conjunction is written along a diagonal dotted line that connects the word modified to the clause's verb.

If I were you, I would be careful.

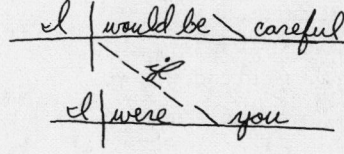

Spelling Rules

Rule 1. Remember this verse:
Use *i* before *e*,
Except after *c*,
Or when sounded like *a*,
As in *neighbor* or *weigh*.

Examples
friend, fiend
piece, tie;
receipt, deceive

Exceptions
ei exceptions:
either, foreign,
forfeit, height,
leisure, neither
ie exceptions:
ancient, efficient

Rule 2. Form the plurals of nouns and the *-s* forms of verbs ending in *y* in these ways:

a. When a noun or verb ends in *y* preceded by a consonant, change the *y* to *i* and add *-es:*

mystery, mysteries;
berry, berries;
carry, carries

b. When a word ends in *y* preceded by a vowel, add *-s:*

boy, boys; key, keys;
pay, pays

c. When a proper noun ends in *y*, add *-s:*

Kennedy, Kennedys

Rule 3. Do the following when adding a suffix to a word that ends in a silent *e:*

a. When the suffix begins with a vowel, drop the silent *e:*

live, living, livable;
bake, baker, baking

b. When a word ends in *ce* or *ge,* keep the silent *e* when it is needed to maintain the soft sound of *c* or *g:*

manage, manageable

c. When the suffix begins with a consonant, keep the final *e:*

care, careful;
aware, awareness

Rule 4. When adding a suffix that begins with a vowel, it sometimes is necessary to double the consonant.

a. When a one-syllable word ends with a consonant preceded by a single vowel, double the consonant: (Applies only when the suffix begins with a vowel.)

hop, hopping;
win, winner;
star, starred

b. When a word of two or more syllables ends in a single consonant preceded by a single vowel, and when the final syllable is accented, double the consonant when adding a suffix:

rebel, rebellious;
control, controlled

c. When a word of two or more syllables does not have the accent on the final syllable, the consonant should not be doubled:

travel, traveler

Rule 5. To form noun plurals and the third-person singular form of present tense verbs

a. In most cases, add *-s:*

pencil, pencils;
jump, jumps

b. When the word ends in *s, sh, ch, x,* or *z,* add *-es:*

brush, brushes;
box, boxes;
watch, watches

Spelling Tables

Homophones. Homophones are words that are pronounced the same but spelled differently. Many spelling errors result from an incorrect choice of homophones. If you are unsure which word is which in a pair, look the word up in a dictionary.

aisle	isle	fair	fare	lead	led	real	reel	stake	steak		
ant	aunt	flea	flee	loan	lone	right	write	rite	stationary	stationery	
ate	eight	flour	flower	made	maid	road	rode	rowed	steal	steel	
bare	bear	foul	fowl	mail	male	role	roll	tail	tale		
be	bee	guest	guessed	meat	meet	sail	sale	their	there	they're	
blew	blue	heal	heel	night	knight	scene	seen	threw	through		
brake	break	hear	here	one	won	sea	see	to	too	two	
buy	by	heir	air	pail	pale	sew	sow	so	vain	vane	vein
capital	capitol	hole	whole	pair	pare	pear	shone	shown	waist	waste	
cell	sell	hour	our	peace	piece	sight	site	cite	wait	weight	
cellar	seller	in	inn	plain	plane	soar	sore	way	weigh		
cent	sent	scent	its	it's	pray	prey	sole	soul	week	weak	
chord	cord	knew	new	principal	principle	some	sum	whose	who's		
dear	deer	knot	not	rain	rein	reign	son	sun	wood	would	
die	dye	know	no	read	red	stair	stare	your	you're		

Commonly misspelled words. The words on the following list are often misspelled. In some cases this list indicates suffixes that can be added without other spelling changes. Thus, for example, the list's *anxious, -ly* indicates the correct spellings of two words, *anxious* and *anxiously*.

absence	awkward	confident	enemy	holiday	marriage	receipt	suit
absolute, -ly	balance	conscience	enough	honor	mileage	receive	surprise
accept, -ance	balloon	control, -led	envelope	huge	mirror	recognize, -d	syllable
accident, -ally	bandage	cooperate	especially	humor	mischief	recommend	symbol, -ize
accurate, -ly	bargain	cough	evidence	hundredth	miserable	refrigerator	synonym
ache	bass	could	exceed, -ed	imagine	missile	relieve	system
achieve	beauty	courage, -ous	excellent, -ly	imitation	muscle	religious	technical
acknowledge	beginning	courtesy	exception	immediate, -ly	necessary	responsibility	temperature
across	behavior	cousin	exercise, -d	importance	necessity	restaurant	temporary
actual	belief	daily	experience	interest	nickel	rhythm	theater
advantage	believe	deceive	explanation	interrupt	niece	ridiculous	therefore
advice	bicycle	decision	familiar	investigate	nuclear	roommate	thief
advise	breath	defense	favorite	invitation	nuisance	sandwich	though
afraid	breathe	definite, -ly	February	island	occur, -red	sanitary	thought
against	brief	definition	federal	jealous	opposite	satellite	tobacco
alcohol	broad	delicious, -ly	foreign, -er	jewelry	parallel	scene	tomorrow
all right	bruise	desert, -ed	forty	journal, -ism	particular	schedule	tongue
already	burglar	design, -ing	forward	journey	peculiar	science	transistor
altogether	bury	dessert	fourth	judgment	peninsula, -r	scissors	truly
among	business	develop, -ed	freight	juicy	perspiration	secretary	tying
ancient	busy	-ment	friend	knowledge	physical	seize	typical
anniversary	captain	diamond	garage	laugh	physician	sense	usual, -ly
answer	celebrate	difference	gasoline	league	picnic, -king	separate	valuable
antenna	cemetery	difficult, -y	generous	length	possession	shoulder, -s	variety
anxiety	certain, -ly	disappear	genuine	liable	possibility	siege	vegetable
anxious, -ly	character	disappoint, -ed	government	library	practice	similar	vicinity
appear, -ance	chief	disease	governor	license	precede	sincere, -ly	view
appetite	chocolate	divide, -d	grammar	lightning	prefer, -red	solemn	villain
appreciate	climate	doctor	grateful	liquid	prejudice, -d	sophomore	visible
approval	climb	doubt	grocery	liquor	probably	specific	Wednesday
arctic	clothe, -s	duplicate	guarantee	literature	procedure	sphere	weight
area	clothing	easily	guess	loneliness	proceed	statue	weird
article	college	effect, -ive	guilt, -y	lonely	psychology	straight	whether
artificial	comfortable	eighth	gymnasium	loose	pursue, -r	strenuous	whose
athlete	competition	either	handkerchief	lose, -r	pursuit	suburb	width
athletic	complexion	electricity	happiness	lovable	qualified	success	witch
attorney	compliment	embarrass, -ing	height	machine	quite	sugar	withhold
audience	confidence	-ment	heroes	magazine	realize	suggestion	yield

Punctuation Review

End punctuation. There are three kinds of end punctuation: the period, the question mark, and the exclamation point. Every sentence must end with one of these marks.

The exclamation point ends an exclamatory sentence (page 36), and the question mark is at the end of a question. All other sentences end with a period.

What a good boy Paul is!
Is Paul a good boy?
Paul is a good boy.

The most common mistake in end punctuation usage is to punctuate as a sentence a group of words that is not a sentence. A sentence must, as a minimum, have a subject and a verb. In addition, it must not have been transformed into an adjective clause by the addition of a subordinate conjunction, nor into a relative clause by the use of a relative pronoun. Such clauses should not be punctuated as separate sentences, but only as parts of some other, longer sentence.

SENTENCE FRAGMENT
Although I like the design.

CORRECTION
(1) *I like the design.*
(2) *Although I like the design, I don't care to use it in a living room.*

Periods. Besides its use at the end of a sentence, the period is used after initials *(T. S. Eliot)* and after many other abbreviations, including those of months *(Feb.)*, countries *(U.S.A.)*, states *(Tenn.)*, and other commonly abbreviated forms *(St., Ave., Dr., Mr.,* and so on).

Commas. The most common mistake in comma usage is to use too many. Limit comma usage to the following situations.

Compound sentences. When two simple sentences are joined together by a coordinating conjunction, put a comma before the conjunction (page 33). (This comma is often omitted when the clauses being joined are especially short.) Do not use commas when only a part of the sentence has been compounded.

She got up to close the window, but he asked her to sit down again.

Series. Use commas after all but the last item in a series (page 45).

Nonrestrictive relative clauses. A nonrestrictive relative clause is set off from the rest of the sentence (page 46). So, too, are expressions that derive from nonrestrictive clauses, such as the appositive (pages 39 and 47) and nonrestrictive participles and participial phrases (pages 47–48).

Mr. Jackson, standing on the makeshift platform, gave a rousing campaign speech.

Adverbial clauses. An adverbial clause at the beginning of a sentence is set off from the rest of the sentence by a comma (page 49). Such a clause at the end of a sentence is not set off.

When we got back from the beach, we were too tired to eat dinner.
We were too tired to eat dinner when we got back from the beach.

Parenthetical expressions. Parenthetical expressions are set off by commas. These include *yes, no,* and mild interjections (those not followed by an exclamation point), such as *well* and *oh.*

Well, it's time to leave.

nouns of address,

How is your garden growing, Mary?

and such expressions as *of course* and *however.*

We will, of course, be ready; others, however, may not be.

Clarity. Sometimes—but very rarely—a comma is needed to avoid confusion and to make a sentence clearer:

To John, Matilda would always be a mystery.

Semicolons. Use a semicolon to join two sentences without using a conjunction (page 45), or when two sentences are joined by such an expression as *therefore* or *however.*

He was ill; however, he worked anyway.

The semicolon is also used to separate the items in a series (page 45) when there are already commas within the series:

He has lived in Moline, Illinois; Boulder, Colorado; and Seattle, Washington.

Colons. The main use of a colon is to introduce a list, an example, a question, or a long quotation:

The question is this: What should we do next?

A colon used in this way should always follow a noun or a pronoun, never a verb or a preposition. It may also come after the expressions *as follows* and *the following*.

Dashes. The dash indicates a sudden break or change of emphasis in a sentence:

I have here a—now, where did I put that thing?

Dashes can also be used to set off an appositive when the appositive is to be emphasized or when it contains commas within it.

Apostrophe. An apostrophe is used to indicate a missing letter in contractions.

She's running for office.

It is also used to show possession.

Peter's father took us to school.
The Smiths' station wagon was damaged.

Parentheses. Parentheses set off material in a sentence that is separate or apart from the main thought.

She traveled through Davenport (a city in which she once lived) and on toward Chicago.

Quotations. A direct quotation—the exact words that someone has said or written—is enclosed in quotation marks. If the quotation is included within another sentence, it is set off from the rest of the sentence by commas:

"I think," he said, "that you are right."

When more than one person is being quoted, as in a conversation, begin a new paragraph for each change of speaker.

Question marks and exclamation points are placed inside the quotation marks as long as they are a part of the quote:

"Who are you?" she asked

and outside if they apply to the sentence as a whole:

Who was it that said, "I shall return"?

Periods and commas are always placed inside quotation marks, while the semicolon and colon are always placed outside, unless they are a part of the quote.

Do not use quotation marks for an indirect quotation, that is, one that does not report someone's exact words:

He said that it was raining.

Italics. Words to be set in italics are indicated in typed or handwritten material by an underline. Italics are used to single out words, phrases, or even sentences for special emphasis. Titles of books, plays, magazines, and newspapers, and the names of ships, trains, and airplanes are italicized. (Shorter works like poems and stories are put in quotation marks.)

The Adventures of Tom Sawyer
Hamlet
National Geographic
the *Titanic*
"Annabel Lee"
"The Masque of the Red Death"

Capitalization. All proper nouns (names of persons, places, or things) are capitalized. In addition, capitalize the first word of every sentence; the first word of a direct quotation embedded in another sentence; the names of groups, associations, and businesses; the letters of some abbreviations; and all historic events, buildings, monuments, and documents. Titles used with proper nouns are capitalized, as are the first, last, and important words in titles of printed texts.

Prepositions, articles, and conjunctions are not capitalized unless they are the first or last word of the title.

General Motors
NASA
World War II
Grant's Tomb
Declaration of Independence
Dr. Brown
Senator Douglas

Writing a paper

Writing a paper is seldom easy. Even the most experienced writers find it hard work. There are, however, some things that can be done to make the work less difficult and to write a better paper at the same time. If you are writing an advanced research paper, see also Handbook 2.

Planning. The first, and perhaps most important, step in writing is to do some good, hard thinking. As you think, keep a sheet of paper in front of you and a pencil in your hand, and make some notes. These notes are just that: notes you are writing to yourself. No one else will ever see them.

Think about the subject of your paper. Think of the various things you could tell about that subject, and make a list of them. Do not worry about the order of things on the list; you can sort that out later. The main point now is not to forget anything that might belong in the paper.

Second, with your list in front of you, think about *why* you are writing the paper. Are you describing someone or something? Are you telling about something amusing that happened, or something that taught you a lesson? Are you arguing for or against something? Are you reporting on something that you have read? As you think about the purpose of your paper, go over your checklist. Look for items on the list that have little or nothing to do with your purpose, and cross them out. Add anything that seems likely to help you carry out the purpose of your paper.

Third, think about the reader of your paper. You are going to write something to be read by *someone.* Think of that person. If, as is likely, there will be more than one reader, think of one individual in that group, and imagine that you are writing the paper for that one reader.

Now go back over your checklist with that reader in mind. Put a (+) by items that you consider it important for that person to know about, and a (-) beside things that you can pass over lightly, probably because your reader knows about them already. Make any other additions to your list, or changes, that come to mind as you think about your reader.

Now you are ready to plan your paper. Rewrite your list in the order that seems best—in terms of

An outline is one way to organize material for a written report. It can help you decide which of your topics are most important (deserving a II or III) and which should be placed under a more important topic (receiving an A or B).

carrying out your purpose and of making things clear to your reader. One of the best ways to organize your list of thoughts is through an outline. An outline encourages you to put related ideas together and to assign levels of importance to each (see box).

Drafting. Write a first draft of your paper. Your purpose in writing this draft is to get what you have to say down on a piece of paper. You should not try to make it perfect or expect it to be perfect. When you cannot think of the best way to say something, write it down anyway as best you can and keep on going.

Keep two things in mind as you write the first draft:

- *Use your own language.* Do not try to be "cute." Do not try to sound like a learned college professor, either. Write as yourself, a person who is telling something interesting to another person, in as clear and uncomplicated way as you can.

- *Think of your reader.* Remember that the reader is the person for whom you are writing in the first place.

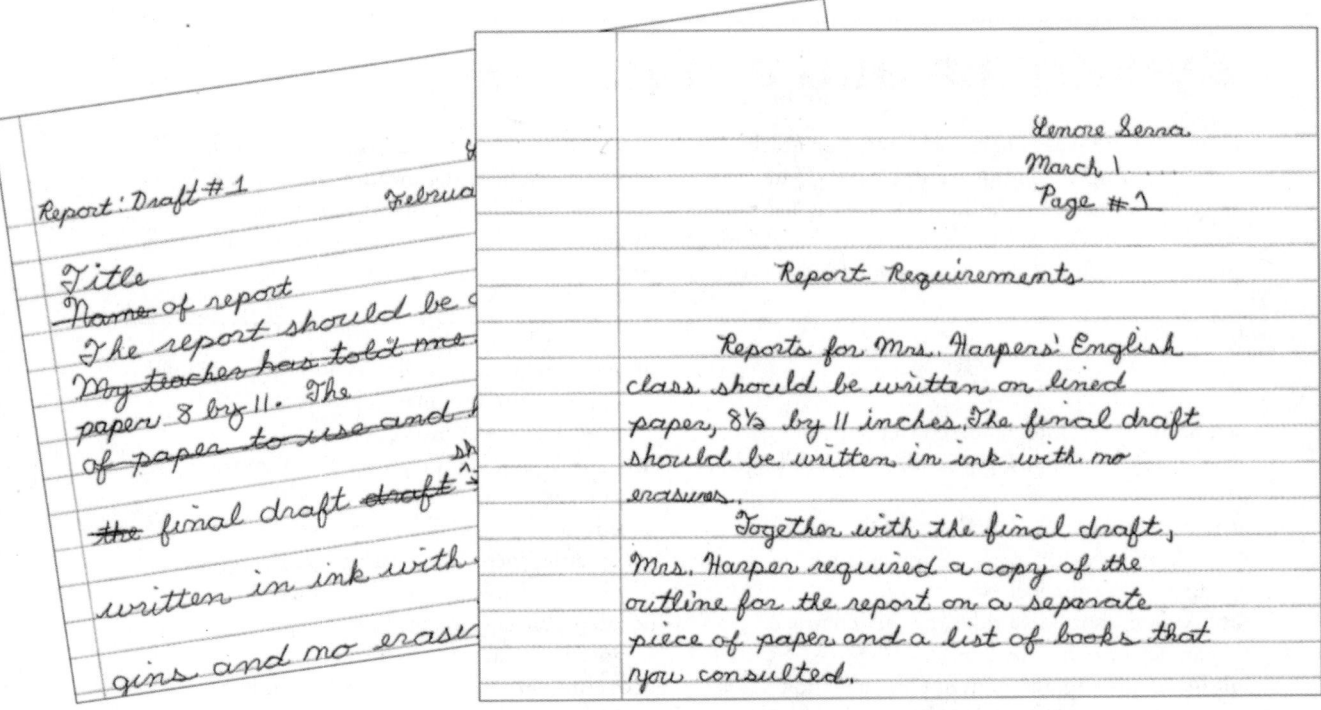

A final draft offers a chance to get your information down on paper. You may rewrite parts of it, making it more specific and easier to understand. If there are many corrections, you may need a second draft before preparing the final draft, which is to be turned in. In addition to following the teacher's requirements, take enough time to make the report neat and readable.

Revising. When you have finished your draft, put it away for a day or two, if possible. Then read the paper aloud to a friendly listener. Usually it is best to read it once straight through. Then read it a second time, asking your listener to point out to you

- parts that are hard to follow and understand;
- parts that leave your listener curious to know more than you have told about; and
- parts that are particularly good: interesting, clear, and complete.

Now go back over the paper yourself. Besides remembering your listener's comments, imagine yourself as your reader and be critical.

Look also at the flow of ideas in your paper. Is it clear how each thing that you are saying relates to what has gone before? Look for places where such expressions as *therefore, however, on the other hand, next,* or *meanwhile* might help your reader follow your train of thought. When you start a new paragraph, use language in the first sentence that ties the new paragraph to what has gone before.

Look, too, for opportunities to say things more clearly and more precisely than in the first draft. Look for words that may be unnecessary, and take them

out. Look for ways to replace several words with one precise, exact one. Look for sentences that can be rewritten so that their relationship to what has gone before and to what follows will be as clear as possible.

Finally, go over your paper for

- *spelling:* check in a dictionary any words about which you are not sure;
- *usage:* check for mistakes in pronoun case forms, irregular verb forms, and the like; and
- *punctuation:* check commas in particular, being sure they are where they belong; be sure that what begins with a capital letter and ends with a period is in fact a sentence.

Remember that a computer spell checker won't flag such things as homophones; a grammar checker's suggestion may not be correct in all circumstances.

Last of all, copy your paper in its final form. Use only one side of the paper, and be sure that your margins are adequate: at least an inch at the sides and bottom, more at the top. Number your pages. If you are writing by hand, write in ink. If you type, be sure to double space. Remember that the neat appearance of your paper may encourage your reader to take you and your ideas seriously.

Synonyms and antonyms

Synonyms are words having the same or nearly the same meaning in one or more senses. Thus, after the entry word **beautiful** in the following list, these words are shown as synonyms: fine, handsome, pretty, bewitching, attractive, comely. The syno-nyms share one characteristic: they all, in one or more senses, have the meaning or nearly the mean-ing of **beautiful**. Antonyms—words with meanings opposite or nearly opposite the entry—follow some of the entries in parentheses.

A

abandon, leave, forsake, desert, renounce, surrender, relinquish, quit, forgo, waive (keep, hold, maintain, cherish)

abate, decrease, ebb, dwindle, subside, moderate, reduce, lessen (increase, revive, enlarge, aggravate, enhance)

abbreviate, shorten, abridge, curtail, contract, condense, reduce (extend)

abdicate, give up, resign, renounce, abandon, forsake, relinquish, quit, forgo

abide, endure, tolerate, bear, continue, wait (avoid, resist, abandon, shun)

ability, capability, talent, faculty, capacity, qualifica-tion, aptitude, aptness, expertness, skill, efficiency, accomplishment, attainment (incompetency)

able, strong, powerful, muscular, stalwart, vigorous, athletic, robust, brawny, skillful, adroit, competent, efficient, capable, clever, qualified, fitted (weak)

abolish, destroy, revoke, cancel, annihilate, nullify, end, remove, repeal (establish, continue, support, sustain, enforce)

abominable, hateful, detestable, odious, vile, execrable (lovable)

about, concerning, regarding, relative to, with regard to, as to, respecting, referring to, around, nearly, approximately

absent, inattentive, abstracted, not present, away, dreamy (present)

absolute, entire, complete, unconditional, unqualified, unrestricted, despotic, arbitrary, tyrannous, imperative, authoritative, imperious, autocratic, positive, unequivocal (limited, conditional, accountable)

absorb, engross, swallow up, engulf, imbibe, consume, merge (eject, exude, emit, disgorge)

absurd, silly, foolish, preposterous, ridiculous, irrational, unreasonable, nonsensical, inconsistent, ludicrous (logical, sensible)

abuse, *n.,* scurrility, ribaldry, contumely, obloquy, opprobrium, foul invective, vituperation, ill-usage (praise, protection)

accelerate, hasten, hurry, expedite, forward, quicken, dispatch (retard)

accept, receive, take, admit (refuse)

acceptable, agreeable, pleasing, gratifying, pleasurable, welcome (displeasing)

accident, casualty, incident, contingency, mishap, adventure, chance

accommodate, serve, oblige, adapt, adjust, fit, suit (disoblige, impede)

accomplice, confederate, accessory, abettor, coadjutor, assistant, ally, associate, helper (adversary)

accomplish, do, effect, finish, execute, achieve, complete, perfect, consummate (fail)

account, narrative, description, relation, detail, recital, reckoning, bill, charge

accountable, punishable, answerable, amenable, responsible, liable

accumulate, bring together, amass, collect, gather (scatter, dissipate)

accurate, correct, exact, precise, nice, truthful (erroneous, careless)

achieve, do, accomplish, effect, fulfill, execute, gain, win

achievement, feat, exploit, accomplishment, attainment, performance, acquirement, gain (failure)

acknowledge, admit, confess, own, avow, grant, recognize, allow, concede (deny)

acquaint, inform, enlighten, apprise, make aware, make known, notify, communicate (deceive)

acquaintance, familiarity, intimacy, cognizance, fellowship, companionship, friendship, knowledge (unfamiliarity)

acquit, pardon, forgive, discharge, set free, clear, absolve (condemn, convict)

act, do, operate, make, perform, play, enact

action, deed, achievement, feat, exploit, accomplishment, battle, engagement, agency, instrumentality

active, lively, sprightly, alert, agile, nimble, brisk, quick, supple, prompt, vigilant, bustling, energetic, busy, laborious, industrious (lazy, idle, inactive, slow, sluggish, indolent, passive)

actual, real, positive, genuine, certain (fictitious)

adapt, accommodate, suit, fit, conform

addition, increase, accession, augmentation, reinforcement (subtraction, separation)

adequate, fit, equal, capable, able, suited, qualified, competent (inferior, unfit, unequal, inadequate, incompetent)

adjourn, defer, postpone

adjust, set right, fit, accommodate, adapt, arrange, settle, regulate, organize (confuse)

admirable, striking, surprising, wonderful, astonishing (detestable)

admire, esteem, love, extol, respect, venerate, honor, adore, approve, enjoy, applaud (abhor, detest, scorn, execrate, dislike, despise, abominate)

admit, allow, permit, suffer, tolerate (deny)

advantageous, beneficial, useful, helpful, valuable (hurtful)

adverse, opposed, unfavorable, inimical, antagonistic, contrary, hostile (helpful, favorable, aiding, assisting, cooperative)

afraid, apprehensive, scared, fearful, timid, alarmed, cautious, anxious (audacious, brave, confident, bold, gallant, heroic, intrepid, valiant, daring, courageous)

agree, accord, acquiesce, concur, harmonize, assent, coincide (contradict, differ, oppose, disagree, dissent)

alarm, fright, panic, terror, fear, dread, dismay, affront (confidence, assurance, calmness, security)

alert, nimble, active, prompt, brisk, lively (dull, inactive, slow, sluggish)

amazement, surprise, awe, wonder, bewilderment, confusion, astonishment (indifference, steadiness, coolness, stoicism, calmness, composure)

amend, improve, correct, better, mend, rectify, repair (impair, harm, spoil, injure)

anger, ire, wrath, indignation, resentment, animosity, displeasure, rage (good nature, amiability)

argue, debate, dispute, reason upon (agree)

artful, disingenuous, sly, tricky, insincere (candid)

association, combination, company, partnership, society (isolation, solitude, separation)

attack, assail, assault, encounter (defend)

austere, rigid, rigorous, severe, stern (dissolute)

aversion, antipathy, dislike, hatred, repugnance (affection)

awe, wonder, amazement, dread, fear, reverence (familiarity)

awkward, clumsy, uncouth, ungainly (graceful, adroit)

B

babble, chatter, prattle, prate, murmur, cackle

bad, wicked, evil (good)

baffle, confound, defeat, disconcert

beautiful, fine, handsome, pretty, bewitching, attractive, comely (homely, ugly, hideous, horrid, unattractive)

becoming, decent, fit, seemly, suitable, befitting, graceful (unbecoming, unsuitable, unfitting, misplaced)

beg, beseech, crave, entreat, implore, solicit, supplicate (give)

behavior, carriage, conduct, deportment, bearing, manner, demeanor

belief, credit, faith, trust (doubt)

benefit, favor, advantage, kindness, civility (injury)

blame, censure, condemn, reprove, reproach, upbraid (praise)

bleak, cheerless, bare, dismal, blank, desolate, waste, unsheltered, dreary (cheery, balmy, sunny, warm, mild)

blemish, defect, disfigurement, imperfection, flaw, speck, spot, stain (ornament)

bold, brave, daring, fearless, intrepid, undaunted (timid)

brave, daring, bold, courageous, adventurous, heroic, intrepid, fearless, valiant, dauntless (afraid, timid, cowardly, fearful)

break, crack, split, smash, bruise, crush, pound

breeze, blast, gale, gust, hurricane, storm, tempest

bright, brilliant, luminous, resplendent, clear, radiant, shining (dull)

C

calm, cool, mild, quiet, peaceful, still, tranquil, composed, placid, serene (stormy, disturbed, agitated, excited, violent, unsettled)

cancel, nullify, abolish, annul, rescind, quash, revoke, repeal (maintain, establish, sustain, uphold, approve)

candid, sincere, honest, truthful, frank, fair, impartial, unbiased (cunning, adroit, crafty, sly, shrewd, tricky, wily, subtle, deceitful, artful)

catch, grasp, grip, capture, clutch, clasp, seize, snatch, secure, take (miss, lose, restore, release)

cause, motive, reason (effect, consequence)

cease, finish, quit, stop, terminate, discontinue, end (continue, begin, inaugurate, start)

certain, secure, sure (doubtful)

chance, fate, fortune (design)

changeable, fickle, inconstant, mutable, variable (unchangeable)

character, reputation, repute, standing

charm, captivate, enchant, enrapture, fascinate (repel, offend)

cheap, inexpensive, inferior, common (dear)

cheerful, gay, merry, sprightly (mournful)

chief, head, leader (subordinate, attendant, follower)

class, degree, order, rank

clear, bright, lucid, vivid (opaque, ambiguous, dim, obscure, vague)

clever, adroit, dexterous, expert, skillful (stupid, awkward, bungling)

command, injunction, order, precept

compassion, sympathy, pity, clemency (cruelty, severity)

compel, force, oblige, necessitate, make, coerce (coax, lead)

complain, lament, murmur, regret, repine (rejoice)

comprehend, comprise, include, embrace, grasp, understand, perceive (exclude, mistake)

conceal, hide, secrete (uncover)

conceive, start, begin, imagine

conclusion, inference, deduction, end (beginning, start)

condemn, censure, blame, disapprove, reprove (justify, exonerate, acquit, approve)

confirm, corroborate, approve, attest (contradict)

conflict, combat, contest, contention, struggle (peace, quiet)

conquer, master, beat, overcome, subdue, surmount, vanquish (defeat, lose, capitulate)

consequence, effect, event, issue, result (cause)

consider, reflect, ponder, weigh (forget, leave out)

consistent, constant, compatible (inconsistent)

console, comfort, solace (harrow, worry)

contaminate, corrupt, defile, pollute, taint

continual, constant, perpetual, incessant (intermittent)

continue, persist, persevere, pursue, prosecute (cease)

contradict, deny, gainsay, oppose (confirm)

contrast, discriminate, differentiate

cowardice, fear, timidity, pusillanimity (courage)

crime, sin, vice, misdemeanor (virtue)

criminal, convict, culprit, felon, malefactor

crooked, bent, curved, oblique (straight)

cruel, barbarous, brutal, inhuman, savage (kind)

custom, fashion, manner, practice

D

danger, hazard, peril (safety)

dark, somber, gloomy, dismal, opaque, obscure, dim (light, bright, clear, radiant)

deadly, fatal, destructive, mortal

deceive, delude, gull, dupe, cheat

decide, determine, settle, adjudicate, resolve

decision, determination, conclusion, resolution, firmness (vacillation)

decrease, diminish, lessen, wane, decline, retrench, curtail, reduce (grow)

dedicate, devote, consecrate, offer, set, apportion

deed, act, commission, achievement, instrument, document

deep, profound, subterranean, submerged (shallow)

deface, mar, spoil, injure, disfigure (beautify)

defect, imperfection, flaw, fault, blemish (beauty, improvement)

defend, guard, protect, justify (attack)

defense, excuse, plea, vindication, bulwark, rampart

defer, delay, postpone, put off, adjourn (force, expedite)

define, fix, settle, determine, limit

delicate, tender, fragile, dainty, refined (coarse)

delicious, sweet, palatable, luscious, savory (bitter, unpalatable)

delight, enjoyment, pleasure, happiness, gladness, rapture, bliss (annoyance)

deliver, liberate, free, rescue, pronounce, give, hand over (retain)

demonstrate, prove, show, exhibit, illustrate

depart, leave, quit, decamp, retire, withdraw, vanish (remain)

describe, delineate, portray, explain, illustrate, define, picture

deserve, merit, earn, justify, win

design, *n.,* delineation, sketch, drawing, cunning, artfulness, contrivance

desirable, expedient, advisable, valuable, acceptable, proper, judicious, beneficial, profitable, good

desire, *n.,* longing, affection, craving, coveting, wish

desolate, bereaved, forlorn, forsaken, deserted, wild, waste, bare, bleak, lonely (pleasant, happy)

desperate, wild, daring, audacious, determined, reckless

destiny, fate, decree, doom, end

destructive, detrimental, hurtful, noxious, injurious, deleterious, baleful, baneful, subversive (creative)

develop, unfold, amplify, expand, enlarge

devoted, attached, fond, absorbed, dedicated

dictate, prompt, suggest, enjoin, order, command

dictatorial, imperative, imperious, domineering, arbitrary, tyrannical, overbearing (submissive)

die, perish, decease, expire, depart, decline, languish, wane, sink, fade, decay (live)

difference, variation, contrast, disparity, separation, disagreement, discord, dissent, estrangement, variety

different, various, manifold, diverse, unlike, separate, distinct (similar)

difficult, severe, arduous, laborious, trying, hard, intricate, involved, perplexing, obscure, unmanageable (easy)

diligence, care, assiduity, attention, heed, industry (negligence)

diminish, lessen, reduce, contract, curtail, retrench (increase)

discipline, order, strictness, training, coercion, punishment, organization (confusion, demoralization)

discover, disclose, detect, make known, find, invent, contrive, expose, reveal

discreet, cautious, prudent, wary, judicious (indiscreet)

disease, illness, unhealthiness, complaint, malady, disorder, ailment, sickness

disgrace, *n.,* disrepute, reproach, dishonor, shame, odium (honor)

disgust, dislike, distaste, loathing, abomination, abhorrence (admiration)

display, show, spread out, exhibit, expose (hide)

dispute, *n.,* argument, debate, controversy, quarrel, disagreement (harmony)

dispute, *v.,* argue, contest, contend, question, impugn (assent)

dissent, disagree, differ, vary (assent)

distinct, clear, plain, obvious, different, separate (obscure, indistinct)

distinguish, perceive, discern, mark out, divide, discriminate

distinguished, famous, glorious, noted, illustrious, eminent, celebrated (obscure, unknown, ordinary)

distribute, allot, share, dispense, apportion, deal (collect)

disturb, agitate, rouse, interrupt, confuse, trouble, annoy, vex, worry (pacify, quiet)

doctrine, tenet, belief, creed, dogma, teaching, conviction

doubt, *n.,* uncertainty, suspense, hesitation, scruple, ambiguity (certainty)

dread, *n.,* fear, horror, terror, alarm, dismay, awe (assurance, calm)

dress, *n.,* clothing, attire, apparel, garments, costume, garb, livery, raiment

drown, inundate, swamp, submerge, overwhelm, engulf

dry, arid, parched, lifeless, dull, tedious (moist, interesting, succulent)

dull, stupid, gloomy, sad, dismal, commonplace (bright)

durable, lasting, permanent, abiding, continuing (ephemeral, perishable)

dwindle, pine, waste, diminish, decrease, fall off (grow)

E

eager, fervent, desirous, hot, ardent, impassioned, forward, impatient (diffident, apathetic, indifferent, unconcerned)

earn, acquire, obtain, win, gain, achieve

easy, light, comfortable, unconstrained (difficult, hard)

economical, sparing, saving, provident, thrifty, frugal, careful, niggardly (wasteful)

effect, consequence, result, issue, event, execution, operation

effective, efficient, operative, serviceable (vain, ineffectual)

efficient, effectual, effective, competent, capable, able, fitted

eliminate, drive out, expel, thrust out, eject, cast out, oust, dislodge, banish, proscribe

embarrass, shame, distress, trouble (assist)

eminent, distinguished, conspicuous, noted, prominent, elevated, renowned, famous, glorious, illustrious (obscure, unknown)

emit, give out, throw out, exhale, discharge

emotion, feeling, sentiment, passion, warmth, excitement

employment, business, vocation, office, trade, profession, occupation, calling

enclose, surround, shut in, fence in, cover, wrap (free)

encourage, countenance, sanction, support, foster, cherish, inspirit, embolden, animate, cheer, incite, urge, impel, stimulate (deter)

endure, last, continue, support, bear, sustain, suffer, brook, submit to, undergo, tolerate (perish, succumb, yield)

enemy, foe, antagonist, adversary, opponent (friend)

energetic, industrious, effectual, efficacious, powerful, binding, forcible, nervous (lazy)

engage, employ, busy, occupy, attract, invite, allure, entertain, engross, take up, enlist

enjoyment, pleasure, gratification (grief, sorrow, sadness)

enlarge, increase, extend, augment, broaden, swell (diminish)

enlighten, illuminate, instruct, inform (befog, becloud)

enormous, gigantic, colossal, huge, vast, immense, prodigious (insignificant)

enroll, enlist, list, register, record

enterprise, undertaking, endeavor, venture, energy

entertain, beguile, amuse, cheer, divert, interest, please (annoy, disturb, tire, bore, weary, distract)

enthusiasm, fervor, warmth, intensity, earnestness, devotion, zeal, ardor (ennui, timidity, wariness, lukewarmness)

entrance, ingress, access, door, approach, inlet, entry, gate, opening, portal (ejection, refusal, expulsion, exit, egress, withdrawal)

equal, even, like, uniform (unequal)

error, blunder, mistake (truth)

especially, chiefly, particularly, principally (generally)

establish, build up, confirm (overthrow)

eternal, perpetual, undying, timeless, unceasing, endless, everlasting (finite)

even, level, plain, smooth (uneven)

event, accident, adventure, incident, occurrence

evil, ill, harm, mischief, misfortune (good)

examination, investigation, inquiry, research, search, scrutiny

exceed, excel, outdo, surpass, transcend (fall short)

exceptional, uncommon, rare, extraordinary (common)

excite, awaken, provoke, rouse, stir up (lull)

execute, fulfill, perform

exhaustive, thorough, complete (cursory)

explain, expound, interpret, illustrate, elucidate

express, declare, signify, utter, tell

extravagant, lavish, profuse, prodigal (parsimonious)

F

face, visage, countenance

fail, fall short, be deficient (accomplish)

faint, weak, irresolute, faltering, feeble, languid (forcible, fresh, hearty, resolute)

fair, equitable, honest, reasonable (unfair)

faith, belief (disbelief)

faithful, staunch, devoted, trusty, true, loyal, constant (faithless, false, untrue)

fall, drop, droop, sink, tumble (rise)

fame, renown, reputation, distinction, eminence

famous, celebrated, renowned, illustrious (obscure)

fast, rapid, quick, fleet, expeditious (slow, sluggish)

fatigue, weariness, lassitude (vigor)

fear, timidity, fright, apprehension, trepidation (bravery)

feeling, sensation, sense

ferocious, fierce, savage, wild, barbarous (mild)

fertile, fruitful, prolific, plenteous, productive (sterile)

feud, bitterness, contest, affray, animosity, brawl, dispute, fray, enmity, riot, quarrel, strife, row, controversy, dissension

firm, constant, solid, steadfast, fixed, stable (weak, flabby)

first, foremost, chief, earliest (last)

fit, accommodate, adapt, adjust, suit

flame, blaze, flare, flash, glare

flat, level, even

flexible, pliable, ductile, supple (inflexible)

flourish, prosper, thrive (decay)

follow, succeed, ensue, imitate, copy, pursue

follower, partisan, disciple, adherent, retainer, pursuer, successor (critic, dissenter)

folly, silliness, foolishness, imbecility, weakness (wisdom)

fond, enamored, attached, affectionate (distant)

foolhardy, venturesome, incautious, hasty, adventurous, rash (cautious)

foolish, simple, silly, irrational, brainless, imbecilic, crazy, absurd, preposterous, ridiculous, nonsensical (discreet, wise)

forecast, forethought, foresight, premeditation, prognostication

foregoing, antecedent, anterior, preceding, previous, prior, former

forerunner, herald, harbinger, precursor, omen

foresight, forethought, forecast, premeditation

forgive, pardon, remit, absolve, acquit, excuse, except (blame)

forlorn, forsaken, abandoned, deserted, desolate, lone, lonesome

form, *n.,* ceremony, solemnity, observance, rite, figure, shape, conformation, fashion, appearance, representation, resemblance

form, *v.,* make, create, produce, constitute, arrange, fashion, mold

formal, ceremonious, precise, exact, stiff, methodical, affected (informal, natural)

former, antecedent, anterior, previous, prior, preceding, foregoing

forsaken, abandoned, forlorn, deserted, desolate, lone, lonesome

fortunate, lucky, happy, auspicious, prosperous, successful (unfortunate)

fortune, chance, fate, luck, doom, destiny, property, possession, riches

fragile, brittle, frail, delicate, feeble (strong)

fragments, pieces, scraps, leavings, chips, remains, remnants

frailty, weakness, failing, foible, imperfection, fault, blemish (strength)

frank, artless, candid, sincere, free, easy, familiar, open, ingenuous, plain (tricky, insincere)

frantic, distracted, mad, furious, raving, frenzied (quiet, subdued)

fraud, deceit, deception, duplicity, guile, cheat (honesty)

free, *adj.,* liberal, generous, bountiful, bounteous, munificent, frank, artless, candid, familiar, open, independent, unconfined, unreserved, unrestricted, exempt, clear, loose, easy, careless (slavish, stingy, artful, costly)

free, *v.,* release, deliver, rescue, liberate, emancipate, exempt (enslave, bind)

freedom, liberty, independence, unrestraint, familiarity, license, franchise, exemption, privilege (slavery)

frequent, often, common, usual, general (rare)

friendly, cordial, fond, companionable, affable, amicable, genial, kind, hearty, neighborly, sociable, social (antagonistic, belligerent, cold, alienated, frigid, hostile, distant, unfriendly, unkind, indifferent)

frugal, provident, economical, saving (wasteful, extravagant)

fruitful, fertile, prolific, productive, abundant, plentiful, plenteous (barren, sterile)

fruitless, vain, useless, idle, abortive, unavailing (productive)

furious, violent, boisterous, vehement, dashing, sweeping, rolling, impetuous, frantic, distracted, stormy, angry, raging, fierce (calm)

G

gain, *n.,* profit, emolument, advantage, benefit, winnings, earnings (loss)

gain, *v.,* get, acquire, obtain, attain, procure, earn, win, achieve, reap, realize, reach (lose)

gallant, brave, bold, courageous, fine, showy, intrepid, heroic, fearless (cowardly)

game, play, diversion, sport, amusement

gang, band, horde, company, troop, crew

gap, breach, chasm, hollow, cavity, cleft, crevice, rift, chink

gather, pick, cull, assemble, muster, infer, collect (scatter)

gaudy, showy, flashy, tawdry, gay, glittering, bespangled (somber)

gaunt, emaciated, scraggy, skinny, meager, lank, attenuated, spare, lean, thin (well-fed)

gay, cheerful, merry, lively, jolly, sprightly, blithe (solemn)

generous, beneficent, noble, honorable, bountiful, liberal, free, magnanimous (niggardly, greedy, miserly, stingy, parsimonious)

gentle, placid, bland, mild, meek, tame, docile (rough, uncouth)

get, obtain, earn, gain, attain, procure, achieve, acquire

gift, donation, benefaction, grant, alms, bequest, present, gratuity, boon, faculty, talent

gigantic, colossal, huge, enormous, vast, prodigious, immense (diminutive)

give, cede, deliver, grant, bestow, confer, yield, impart

glad, pleased, cheerful, joyful, gratified, cheering (sad)

glee, gaiety, merriment, mirth, joviality, joy, hilarity (sorrow)

gloom, cloud, darkness, dimness, blackness, dullness, sadness (light, brightness, joy)

gloomy, lowering, lurid, dim, dusky, sad, glum (bright, clear)

glorify, magnify, celebrate, adore, exalt

glory, honor, fame, renown, splendor, grandeur (infamy)

go, depart, proceed, move, budge, stir

good, *adj.,* virtuous, righteous, upright, just, true (wicked, bad)

good, *n.,* benefit, weal, advantage, profit, boon (evil)

gorgeous, superb, grand, magnificent, splendid (plain, simple)

govern, control, rule, direct, manage, command

government, rule, state, control, sway

graceful, becoming, comely, elegant, beautiful (awkward)

grand, majestic, stately, dignified, lofty, elevated, exalted, splendid, gorgeous, superb, magnificent, sublime, pompous (shabby)

grant, bestow, impart, give, yield, cede, allow, confer, invest

grasp, catch, seize, grip, clasp, grapple

grateful, agreeable, welcome, thankful

grave, *adj.,* serious, sedate, solemn, sober, pressing, heavy (giddy)

grave, *n.,* tomb, sepulcher, vault

great, big, huge, large, majestic, vast, grand, noble, august (small)

grief, affliction, sorrow, trial, woe, tribulation, sadness, melancholy (joy)

grieve, mourn, lament, sorrow, pain, hurt, wound, bewail (rejoice)

grievous, painful, afflicting, heavy, baleful, unhappy

gross, coarse, outrageous, unseemly, shameful, indelicate (delicate)

group, assembly, cluster, collection, clump, order, class

grow, increase, vegetate, expand, advance (decay, diminish)

growl, grumble, snarl, murmur, complain

gruff, rough, rugged, blunt, rude, harsh, surly, bearish (pleasant)

guilty, culpable, sinful, criminal (innocent)

H

habit, custom, practice, fashion, routine, system

happiness, beatitude, blessedness, bliss, felicity, contentment, joy, merriment, rapture, pleasure, enjoyment (unhappiness)

hard, firm, solid, arduous, difficult (soft, easy)

harm, injury, hurt, wrong, affliction (benefit)

harmless, safe, innocuous, innocent (hurtful)

harsh, rough, rigorous, severe (gentle)

harvest, crop, fruit, growth, result, return, yield, proceeds, product, increase

hasten, accelerate, dispatch, expedite, speed (delay)

hasty, hurried, ill-advised (deliberate)

hatred, enmity, ill will, rancor, animosity, hostility, revenge, spite, hate (friendship)

hazard, peril, chance, risk, venture

healthy, hale, vigorous, well, salubrious, salutary, wholesome (unhealthy, diseased, fragile, ill, sick)

hearty, vigorous, cordial, sincere, warm (insincere)

heavy, burdensome, ponderous, weighty (light)

heighten, enhance, exalt, elevate, raise

help, abet, encourage, aid, assist, relieve, succor (hinder, oppose, thwart, discourage)

hesitate, falter, stammer, stutter

hide, cover, disguise, cloak, conceal, bury, veil, suppress, screen, entomb, secrete (confess, admit, divulge, expose, show, reveal, publish, advertise, tell, uncover)

hint, allude, refer, suggest, intimate, insinuate

hold, detain, keep, retain

home, habitation, dwelling, fireside, hearth, house, residence, domicile, abode

homely, plain, ugly, coarse (beautiful)

honesty, integrity, probity, uprightness (dishonesty)

honor, respect, reverence, esteem (dishonor)

hope, confidence, expectation, trust

hot, ardent, burning, fiery (cold)

however, nevertheless, notwithstanding, yet

humble, *adj.,* modest, submissive, plain, unostentatious, simple (haughty)

humble, *v.,* degrade, humiliate, mortify, abase (exalt)

hunt, pursue, search, seek, chase

hypocrite, cheat, deceiver, dissembler, impostor

---

idea, thought, imagination

ideal, imaginary, fancied, perfect (actual, imperfect)

idle, indolent, lazy (industrious)

ignorant, illiterate, uninformed, uneducated (knowing)

illegal, unlawful, illicit, contraband, illegitimate (legal)

illiterate, unlettered, unlearned, untaught, uninstructed (learned, educated)

illusion, fallacy, deception, phantasm

image, likeness, picture, representation, effigy

imaginary, ideal, fanciful, illusory (real)

imagine, conceive, fancy, think, picture, presume

imitate, copy, ape, mimic, mock, counterfeit

immediate, pressing, instant, next, proximate

immediately, instantly, forthwith, directly, presently (later)

immense, vast, enormous, huge, prodigious, monstrous (small)

impartial, just, equitable, unbiased (partial)

imperfection, fault, blemish, defect, vice

importance, significance, avail, consequence, weight, gravity, moment

impressive, stirring, forcible, exciting, affecting, moving

imprison, incarcerate, shut up, immure, confine (liberate)

improve, amend, better, mend, reform, rectify, ameliorate, apply, strengthen (damage, weaken, deteriorate)

impulsive, rash, hasty, forcible, violent (deliberate)

incentive, motive, inducement, impulse

incline, slope, lean, slant, tend, bend, turn, bias, dispose

include, comprise, contain, embrace, take in

incompetent, incapable, unable, inadequate, insufficient (competent)

increase, extend, enlarge, augment, dilate, expand, amplify, raise, enhance, aggravate, magnify, grow (diminish)

indefinite, vague, uncertain, unsettled, loose, lax (definite)

indicate, point out, show, mark

indignation, anger, wrath, ire, resentment

inequality, disparity, disproportion, dissimilarity, unevenness (equality)

infamous, scandalous, shameful, ignominious, opprobrious, disgraceful (honorable)

infinite, eternal, absolute, boundless, countless, limitless, unbounded, numberless, unlimited, unfathomable (brief, bounded, restricted, small, moderate, limited, little, measurable)

inhuman, cruel, brutal, savage, barbarous, ruthless, merciless, ferocious (humane)

injure, damage, hurt, deteriorate, wrong, aggrieve, harm, spoil, mar, sully (benefit)

injustice, wrong, iniquity, grievance, unfairness (right)

innocent, guiltless, inoffensive, innocuous, exemplary, stainless, virtuous (guilty)

inquiry, investigation, examination, research, scrutiny, disquisition, question, query, interrogation

insane, mad, deranged, delirious, demented (sane)

inspire, animate, exhilarate, enliven, cheer, breathe, inhale

instruct, inform, teach, educate, enlighten, initiate

insult, affront, outrage, indignity, blasphemy (honor)

integrity, uprightness, honesty, probity, entirety, completeness, rectitude, purity (dishonesty)

intellect, understanding, sense, mind, intelligence, ability, talent, genius

intense, ardent, earnest, glowing, fervid, burning, vehement

intent, design, purpose, intention, drift, view, aim, purport, meaning

interfere, meddle, interpose

interpret, explain, expound, elucidate, unfold, decipher

intimidate, dishearten, alarm, frighten, scare, appall, daunt, cow, browbeat (encourage)

invasion, incursion, inroad, aggression, raid, fray

invent, devise, contrive, frame, find out, discover, design

investigation, examination, search, inquiry, research, scrutiny

invincible, unconquerable, impregnable, insurmountable

invisible, unseen, imperceptible, impalpable, unperceivable (visible)

invite, ask, call, bid, request, allure, attract, solicit

invoke, call upon, implore, beseech

involve, implicate, entangle, compromise, envelop

irritate, aggravate, worry, embitter, madden, exasperate

issue, emerge, rise, proceed, flow, spring, emanate

J

jarring, conflicting, discordant, inconsonant, inconsistent

jaunt, ramble, excursion, trip

jealousy, suspicion, envy

jeopardy, hazard, peril, danger

jest, joke, sport, divert, make game of

journey, travel, tour, passage, excursion, voyage, trip

joy, happiness, gladness, mirth, delight (grief)

judge, justice, referee, arbitrator, arbiter

judgment, discernment, discrimination, understanding

justice, equity, right: justice is right as established by law, equity according to the circumstances of each particular case (injustice)

K

keep, preserve, save (abandon)

kill, execute, massacre, assassinate, murder, slay, cancel, cross out

knowledge, intelligence, wisdom, comprehension, erudition, learning, science (ignorance, illiteracy, unfamiliarity)

L

labor, toil, work, effort, drudgery (idleness)

lack, need, deficiency, scarcity, insufficiency (plenty)

lament, mourn, grieve, weep (rejoice)

language, dialect, idiom, speech, tongue

large, ample, big, capacious, abundant, coarse, colossal, commodious, enormous, vast, huge, gigantic, great, massive, spacious (little, petty, paltry, scanty, small, tiny, trivial, brief, diminutive, insignificant)

last, final, latest, ultimate (first)

laughable, comical, droll, ludicrous (serious)

leave, quit, relinquish

life, existence, animation, spirit, vivacity (death)

lift, erect, elevate, exalt, raise (lower)

light, clear, bright (dark)

likeness, resemblance, similarity (unlikeness)

linger, lag, loiter, tarry, saunter (hasten)

little, diminutive, small (great)

livelihood, living, maintenance, subsistence, support

lively, jocund, sprightly, vivacious, merry, sportive (slow, languid, sluggish)

long, extended, extensive (short)

look, gaze, discern, behold, glance, see, stare, view, watch, scan, inspect

lose, miss, forfeit (gain)

loss, detriment, damage, deprivation (gain)

loud, clamorous, high-sounding, noisy (low, quiet)

love, fondness, attachment, devotion, affection (hate)

M

mad, crazy, insane, delirious, rabid, violent, frantic (sane, rational, quiet)

make, form, create, produce, build, construct (destroy)

manage, contrive, direct

management, direction, superintendence, care, economy

mania, obsession, madness, insanity, lunacy

manly, masculine, vigorous, courageous, brave, heroic (effeminate)

manner, habit, custom, way, air, look, appearance

mar, spoil, ruin, disfigure (improve)

march, tramp, tread, walk, step

margin, edge, rim, border, brink, verge

marvelous, wondrous, wonderful, amazing, miraculous

masculine, manly, mannish, virile, male, manful, manlike

massive, bulky, heavy, weighty, ponderous, solid, substantial (flimsy)

mastery, dominion, rule, sway, ascendancy, supremacy

matchless, unrivaled, unequaled, unparalleled, peerless, incomparable, inimitable, surpassing (common, ordinary)

meaning, signification, import, acceptation, sense, purport

meek, unassuming, mild, gentle, soft, demure, humble (proud, arrogant, bold, haughty, impudent, presumptuous)

melancholy, low-spirited, dispirited, dreamy, sad (jolly, buoyant)

melodious, tuneful, musical, silver, dulcet, sweet (discordant)

memory, reminiscence, remembrance, recollection

mend, repair, amend, correct, better, ameliorate, improve, rectify (break)

mention, tell, name, communicate, impart, divulge, reveal, disclose, inform, acquaint

merciful, compassionate, lenient, clement, tender, gracious, kind (cruel)

merciless, hard-hearted, cruel, unmerciful, pitiless, remorseless, unrelenting (kind)

mercy, favor, grace, kindness, leniency, pardon, tenderness, pity, compassion, benevolence, clemency, benignity, blessing (revenge, cruelty, harshness, severity, sternness, punishment, implacability, hardness)

merry, cheerful, mirthful, joyous, gay, lively, sprightly, hilarious, jovial, blithe, sportive, jolly (sad)

mimic, imitate, ape, mock

mind, intellect, brain, instinct, reason, sense, soul, thought, understanding, intelligence

mischief, injury, harm, damage, evil, hurt, ill (benefit)

miserable, unhappy, wretched, distressed, afflicted (happy)

misery, wretchedness, woe, destitution, penury, privation, beggary (happiness)

mix, blend, combine, amalgamate, associate, fuse, join, unite, mingle, compound (divide, sift, part, segregate, sort, unravel, disjoin, classify, assort, analyze)

moderate, temperate, abstemious, sober, abstinent (immoderate)

modest, chaste, virtuous, bashful, reserved (immodest)

moist, wet, damp, dank, humid (dry)

monotonous, unvaried, dull, undiversified, tiresome (varied)

monstrous, shocking, dreadful, horrible, huge, immense

monument, memorial, record, remembrance

mood, humor, disposition, vein, temper

mournful, sad, sorrowful, lugubrious, grievous, doleful, heavy (happy)

move, actuate, impel, induce, prompt, instigate, persuade, stir, agitate, propel, push

music, harmony, melody, symphony

musical, tuneful, melodious, harmonious, dulcet, sweet

mute, dumb, silent, speechless

mutual, reciprocal, interchanged, correlative (sole, solitary)

mysterious, dark, obscure, hidden, secret, dim, mystic, enigmatic, unaccountable, inexplicable, abstruse (open, clear)

mystify, confuse, perplex, puzzle (explain)

N

naked, nude, bare, uncovered, rude, unclothed, rough, simple (covered, clad)

narrate, tell, relate, detail, recount, describe, enumerate, rehearse, recite

nation, country, tribe, people, community, realm, state

native, indigenous, inborn, vernacular

neat, natty, nice, orderly, clean, dapper, tidy, trim, prim, spruce (dirty, rough, disorderly, unkempt, soiled, untidy, negligent)

necessary, needful, expedient, essential, requisite, indispensable (useless)

necessity, need, exigency, emergency, urgency, requisite

need, *n.,* necessity, distress, poverty, indigence, want, penury

need, *v.,* require, want, lack

neglect, *n.,* omission, failure, default, negligence, remissness, carelessness, slight

neglect, *v.,* disregard, slight, omit, overlook

neighborhood, environs, vicinity, adjacency, nearness, proximity

nimble, spry, active, brisk, lively, alert, quick, agile, prompt (awkward, slow, clumsy)

notable, plain, evident, remarkable, signal, striking, rare (obscure)

note, token, symbol, mark, sign, indication, remark, comment

notice, *n.,* advice, notification, intelligence, information

notice, *v.,* mark, note, observe, attend to, regard, heed

notify, publish, acquaint, apprise, inform, declare

notorious, conspicuous, open, obvious, ill-famed (unknown)

nourish, nurture, cherish, foster, supply (starve, famish)

nourishment, food, diet, sustenance, nutrition

novel, modern, new, fresh, recent, unused, strange, rare (old)

nutrition, food, diet, nutriment, nourishment

O

obedient, compliant, submissive, dutiful, respectful (obstinate)

obey, conform, comply, submit (rebel, disobey)

object, oppose, except to, contravene, impeach, deprecate (assent)

obnoxious, offensive (agreeable)

obscure, dense, deep, undistinguished, unknown (distinguished)

obsolete, old, rare, ancient, disused, antiquated, archaic

obstruct, block, hinder, clog, bar, arrest, retard, stay, barricade, impede, oppose, interrupt (aid, clear, promote, facilitate, free, advance, accelerate)

offense, affront, misdeed, misdemeanor, transgression, trespass

offensive, insolent, abusive, obnoxious (inoffensive)

old, aged, ancient, antiquated, obsolete, old-fashioned, senile, elderly, venerable (young, new)

open, candid, unreserved, clear, fair (hidden, dark)

opinion, notion, view, judgment, belief, sentiment

oppose, resist, withstand, thwart (give way)

option, choice

origin, cause, occasion, source, beginning, birth (end, conclusion)

overbearing, haughty, proud, arrogant (gentle)

overflow, inundation, deluge

overrule, supersede, suppress

overturn, invert, overthrow, reverse, subvert (establish, fortify)

overwhelm, crush, defeat, vanquish

P

pain, suffering, qualm, pang, agony, anguish, torment, ache, torture (pleasure, delight, rapture)

part, division, portion, share, fraction (whole)

perceive, note, observe, discern, distinguish, comprehend, understand

perfect, ideal, sinless, spotless, stainless, holy, complete, immaculate, unblemished, consummate, correct, faultless (bad, defaced, corrupt, blemished, spoiled, worthless, perverted, inferior, marred, defective, faulty, deficient, imperfect)

peril, danger, pitfall, snare (safety)

permanent, fixed, constant, lasting, perpetual, stable, steadfast, unchanging, imperishable, durable, enduring, changeless

permission, liberty, leave, permit, license, allowance, authority (denial, objection, refusal, prevention)

permit, allow, tolerate (forbid)

perplexity, confusion, doubt, distraction, amazement, astonishment, bewilderment

persuade, coax, convince, urge, allure, entice, prevail upon

physical, corporeal, bodily, material (mental)

picture, engraving, print, representation, illustration, image

pitiful, mournful, pathetic, pitiable, woeful, sorrowful, abject, lamentable, mean, miserable, wretched (glorious, great, grand, mighty, lofty, noble, superb, exalted, commanding, august, superior)

pity, mercy, condolence, compassion, sympathy (cruelty, brutality, harshness, severity, sternness, barbarity)

plain, open, manifest, evident (secret)

play, game, sport, amusement (work)

plead, beseech, ask, beg, entreat, implore, urge, solicit, argue, advocate

plentiful, abundant, ample, copious, plenteous, rich, teeming, luxuriant, full, bountiful, affluent (scarce, deficient, impoverished, scant)

polite, cultured, courtly, elegant, genteel, civil, urbane, gracious, obliging, courteous, accomplished (awkward, coarse, boorish, raw, rude, uncivil, insulting, uncouth, impolite, impudent)

positive, absolute, peremptory, decided, certain (negative)

possessor, owner, proprietor

possible, practical, practicable, likely (impossible)

poverty, penury, indigence, need, want (wealth)

power, authority, force, strength, dominion

praise, acclaim, approbation, commendation, eulogy, plaudit, extol, laud (blame)

prayer, entreaty, petition, request, suit

prevent, obviate, preclude

previous, antecedent, introductory, preparatory, preliminary (subsequent)

pride, haughtiness, arrogance, vanity, conceit (humility)

principal, chief, main, essential

principle, ground, reason, motive, impulse, maxim, rule, rectitude, integrity

privilege, immunity, advantage, favor, prerogative, exemption, right, claim

profession, business, trade, occupation, vocation, office, employment, engagement, avowal

profound, deep, fathomless, penetrating, solemn, abstruse, recondite (shallow)

prohibit, forbid, hinder, prevent, debar, disallow, interdict (permit, license, sanction, allow, tolerate, authorize)

prominent, eminent, marked, important, conspicuous, leading (obscure)

proper, legitimate, right, just, fair, equitable, suitable, decent, becoming, befitting, adapted, pertinent, appropriate (wrong)

prosper, flourish, succeed, grow rich, thrive, advance (fail)

prosperity, well-being, weal, welfare, happiness, good luck (poverty)

prudence, carefulness, judgment, discretion, wisdom (indiscretion)

punctual, exact, precise, nice, particular, prompt, timely (dilatory)

puzzle, perplex, confound, embarrass, bewilder, confuse, pose, mystify (enlighten)

Q

quack, impostor, pretender, charlatan (savant)

quaint, artful, curious, farfetched, fanciful, odd, singular

qualified, competent, fitted, adapted (incompetent)

quality, attribute, rank, distinction

queer, odd, peculiar, singular, quaint, unique, strange, unusual, ridiculous, preposterous, bizarre, curious, eccentric, ludicrous, fantastic, funny (common, natural, usual, normal, ordinary, regular)

question, query, inquiry, interrogatory

quick, lively, brisk, expeditious, impetuous, adroit, fleet, rapid, swift, sweeping, dashing, clever, sharp, ready, prompt, alert, nimble, agile, active (slow)

quote, note, repeat, cite, adduce

R

radiance, splendor, brightness, brilliance, luster, glare (dullness)

rank, order, degree, dignity, nobility, consideration

ransack, rummage, pillage, overhaul, explore, plunder

rare, curious, unique, unusual, strange, peculiar, odd, extraordinary, scarce, singular, uncommon (ordinary)

rascal, scoundrel, rogue, knave, vagabond, scamp

rash, hasty, precipitate, foolhardy, adventurous, heedless, reckless, careless (deliberate)

rate, value, compute, appraise, estimate, chide, abuse

ratify, confirm, establish, substantiate, sanction (protest, oppose)

rational, reasonable, sagacious, judicious, wise, sensible, sound (unreasonable)

ravage, overrun, desolate, despoil, destroy

reach, touch, stretch, attain, gain, arrive at

ready, prepared, ripe, apt, prompt, adroit, handy (slow, dilatory)

real, authentic, actual, literal, practical, positive, certain, genuine, true (unreal)

realize, accomplish, achieve, effect, gain, get, acquire, comprehend

reap, gain, get, acquire, obtain

reason, *n.,* motive, design, end, proof, cause, ground, purpose

reason, *v.,* deduce, draw from, trace, infer, conclude, think

reasonable, rational, wise, honest, fair, right, just (unreasonable)

rebellion, insurrection, revolt

rebellious, mutinous, seditious, refractory, disobedient, ungovernable, insubordinate, contumacious (docile, obedient, yielding, tractable, subservient, compliant, gentle)

recreation, sport, pastime, amusement, play, game, fun

redeem, ransom, recover, rescue, deliver, save, free

reduce, abate, lessen, decrease, lower, shorten, conquer (increase)

refined, polite, courtly, polished, cultured, genteel, purified (boorish)

reflect, consider, meditate, cogitate, think, ponder, muse

reform, amend, correct, better, restore, improve (corrupt)

refute, disprove, falsify (affirm)

regard, mind, heed, notice, behold, view, consider, respect

regret, grief, sorrow, lamentation, repentance, remorse

regular, orderly, uniform, customary, ordinary, stated (irregular)

regulate, methodize, arrange, adjust, organize, govern, rule (disorder)

reliance, trust, hope, dependence, confidence (suspicion)

relief, succor, aid, help, redress, alleviation

relinquish, give up, forsake, resign, surrender, quit, leave, forgo (retain)

remedy, help, relief, redress, cure, reparation

remote, distant, far, secluded, indirect (near)

renounce, disown, recant, refute, reject, retract, revoke, repudiate, recall, discard, deny, abandon, disclaim, disavow (assert, avow, advocate, acknowledge, cherish, claim, uphold, defend, vindicate, proclaim, retain)

report, record, rumor, story, tale, statement, narrative, account, description, recital

reproduce, propagate, imitate, represent, copy

repulsive, forbidding, odious, ugly, disagreeable, revolting (attractive)

reverence, honor, respect, awe, veneration, deference, homage, worship (execration)

revise, review, reconsider

revive, refresh, renew, renovate, animate, resuscitate, vivify, cheer, comfort

rich, wealthy, affluent, opulent, copious, ample, abundant, exuberant, plentiful, fertile, fruitful, superb, gorgeous (poor)

rival, antagonist, opponent, competitor

road, way, highway, route, course, path, pathway

roam, ramble, rove, stray, wander, stroll

robber, bandit, brigand, burglar, pirate, thief, raider, plunderer, pillager, marauder, forager, buccaneer

robust, strong, lusty, vigorous, sinewy, stout, sturdy, stalwart, able-bodied (puny)

rout, beat, defeat, overthrow, scatter

route, road, course, way, path, journey, direction

rude, rugged, rough, uncouth, unpolished, harsh, gruff, impertinent, impudent, saucy, flippant, insolent, churlish (polished, polite)

ruthless, cruel, savage, barbarous, inhuman, merciless, remorseless, relentless (considerate)

S

sacred, holy, hallowed, divine, consecrated, dedicated, devoted (profane)

safe, secure, harmless, trustworthy, reliable (perilous, dangerous)

sane, sober, lucid, sound, rational (crazy)

scandalize, shock, disgust, offend, vilify, revile, malign, traduce, defame, slander

scanty, bare, pinched, insufficient, slender, meager (ample)

scatter, strew, spread, disseminate, disperse, dissipate, dispel (collect)

secret, clandestine, concealed, hidden, sly, underhand, latent, private (open)

send, fling, hurl, emit, drive, dispatch, cast, delegate, throw, launch, project (get, bring, carry, convey, hand, keep, receive, retain, hold)

sense, discernment, appreciation, perception, view, opinion, feeling, sensibility, susceptibility, thought, judgment, import, significance, meaning, purport, wisdom

sensible, wise, intelligent, reasonable, sober, sound, conscious, aware (foolish)

settle, arrange, adjust, regulate, conclude, determine

several, sundry, many, various

severe, austere, inexorable, strict, harsh, stern, stringent, unmitigated, rough, unyielding (lenient, affable, easy, indulgent)

shake, tremble, shudder, shiver, quiver, quake

shallow, superficial, flimsy, slight (deep, thorough)

shame, disgrace, dishonor (honor)

shameless, immodest, impudent, indecent, indelicate, brazen

shape, form, fashion, mold, model

share, portion, lot, division, quantity, quota, contingent

sharp, acute, keen (dull)

shine, glare, glitter, radiate, sparkle

short, brief, concise, succinct, summary (long)

sick, diseased, ill, unhealthy, morbid (healthy)

sickness, illness, indisposition, disease, disorder (health)

significant, expressive, material, important (insignificant)

silent, dumb, mute, speechless (talkative)

simple, single, plain, artless (complex, compound)

sincere, candid, frank, honest, pure, genuine, real (insincere)

situation, condition, plight, predicament, state, position

size, bulk, greatness, magnitude, dimension

slander, defame, detract, revile, vilify, traduce, libel, malign, disparage, decry, calumniate (defend, extol, laud, praise, eulogize)

slavery, servitude, bondage, thralldom (freedom)

sleep, doze, drowse, nap, slumber (wake)

slow, dilatory, tardy, lingering, sluggish (fast)

smell, fragrance, odor, scent, perfume

smooth, even, level, mild (rough)

soak, drench, imbue, steep

social, friendly, communicative (unsocial)

solicit, importune, urge

solitary, sole, only, single

sound, *adj.,* healthy, sane (unsound)

sound, *n.,* tone, noise

sparse, scanty, thin (luxuriant)

speak, converse, talk, say, tell, confer, articulate, express, utter

spend, expend, exhaust, consume, dissipate, waste, squander (save)

spread, disperse, diffuse, expand, disseminate, scatter

stain, soil, discolor, spot, tarnish, color, blot

state, commonwealth, realm

sterile, barren, unfruitful (fertile)

stormy, rough, boisterous, tempestuous (calm)

straight, direct, right (crooked)

stranger, alien, foreigner (friend)

strengthen, fortify, invigorate, encourage (weaken)

strong, robust, sturdy, powerful (weak)

stupid, dull, foolish, obtuse, witless (clever)

subsequent, succeeding, following (previous)

substantial, solid, durable (insubstantial)

suit, accord, agree (disagree)

surrender, cede, give, yield, sacrifice, relinquish, abandon, capitulate, alienate

surround, encircle, encompass, environ

sustain, maintain, support

sympathy, commiseration, compassion, condolence

system, rule, manner, method, plan, order

T

take, accept, receive (give)

talkative, garrulous, communicative, loquacious (silent)

taste, flavor, relish, savor (tastelessness)

tax, custom, duty, impost, excise, toll

tease, taunt, tantalize, torment, vex

temporary, fleeting, transient, transitory (permanent)

term, boundary, limit, period, time

territory, dominion

thankful, grateful, obliged (thankless)

thaw, melt, dissolve, liquefy (freeze)

theatrical, dramatic, showy, ceremonious, meretricious

theft, robbery, depredation, spoliation

theme, subject, topic, text, essay

theory, speculation, scheme, hypothesis, conjecture

therefore, accordingly, consequently, hence

thick, dense, close, compact, solid, coagulated, muddy, turbid, misty, foggy, vaporous (thin)

thin, slim, slender, slight, flimsy, attenuated, lean, scraggy (fat, heavy)

think, cogitate, consider, reflect, ponder, contemplate, meditate, conceive, imagine, apprehend, hold, consider, regard, believe

thorough, accurate, correct, trustworthy, reliable, complete (superficial)

thought, idea, conception, imagination, fancy, conceit, notion, supposition, care, provision, consideration, opinion, view, sentiment, reflection, deliberation

thoughtful, considerate, careful, reflective, cautious, heedful, contemplative, provident, pensive, dreamy (thoughtless)

thoughtless, inconsiderate, rash, improvident, precipitate, heedless

tie, bind, restrain, restrict, oblige, secure, unite, join (loosen)

time, duration, season, period, era, age, date, span, spell

tolerate, allow, admit, receive, suffer, permit, let, endure, abide (oppose)

top, summit, apex, head, crown, surface (bottom, base)

torture, torment, anguish, agony

touching, tender, affecting, moving, pathetic

trade, traffic, commerce, dealing, occupation, employment, office

tranquil, still, unruffled, peaceful, quiet, hushed (noisy, boisterous)

transaction, negotiation, occurrence, proceeding, affair

trash, nonsense, twaddle, trifle

travel, trip, ramble, peregrination, excursion, journey, tour, voyage

treacherous, traitorous, treasonable, disloyal, faithless, false, perfidious, sly (trustworthy, faithful)

trite, stale, old, ordinary, commonplace, hackneyed (novel)

triumph, achievement, ovation, victory, conquest, jubilation (failure, defeat)

trivial, trifling, petty, small, frivolous, unimportant, insignificant (important)

true, genuine, actual, sincere, unaffected, honest, upright, veritable, real, veracious, authentic, exact, accurate, correct (false)

tune, tone, air, melody, strain

type, emblem, symbol, figure, sign, letter, sort, kind

U

ugly, unsightly, plain, homely, ill-favored, hideous (beautiful)

umpire, referee, arbitrator, judge, arbiter

uncertain, doubtful, dubious, questionable, equivocal, ambiguous, indistinct, variable, fluctuating

uncommon, rare, strange, scarce, singular, choice (common, ordinary)

uncouth, strange, odd, clumsy, ungainly (graceful)

under, below, beneath, subordinate, lower, inferior (above)

understanding, knowledge, intellect, intelligence, faculty, comprehension, mind, reason, brains

undertake, engage in, embark on, agree, promise

undo, annul, frustrate, unfasten, destroy

uneasy, restless, disturbed, stiff, awkward (quiet)

unequaled, matchless, unique, novel, new, unheard of

unfortunate, calamitous, ill-fated, unlucky, wretched, unhappy, miserable (fortunate)

uniform, regular, symmetrical, even, equal, alike, unvaried (irregular)

union, junction, combination, alliance, confederacy, league, coalition, agreement, concern (disunion, separation)

unique, unequal, uncommon, rare, choice, matchless (common, ordinary)

unite, join, combine, add, attach, incorporate, embody, clench, merge (separate, disrupt, sunder)

universal, general, all, entire, total, catholic (sectional)

unlimited, absolute, boundless, undefined, infinite (limited)

unreasonable, foolish, silly, absurd (reasonable)

unusual, rare, unwonted, singular, uncommon, remarkable, strange, extraordinary (common)

uphold, maintain, defend, sustain, support, vindicate (desert, abandon)

upright, vertical, perpendicular, just, erect, equitable, fair, pure, honorable (prone, horizontal)

urge, incite, impel, push, drive, instigate, stimulate, press, solicit, induce

urgent, pressing, important, imperative, immediate, serious, wanted (unimportant)

use, n., usage, practice, habit, custom, avail, advantage, utility, benefit, application (disuse, desuetude)

use, v., employ, exercise, occupy, accustom, practice, inure (abuse)

useful, advantageous, serviceable, available, helpful, beneficial, good (useless)

usual, ordinary, common, accustomed, habitual, customary, prevalent, regular (unusual, exceptional, rare, singular, strange)

V

vacant, empty, unfilled, unoccupied, thoughtless, unthinking, void, vacuous (occupied, crowded, full, jammed, packed)

vague, unsettled, undetermined, uncertain, pointless, indefinite (definite)

vain, useless, fruitless, empty, worthless, inflated, proud, conceited, unreal, unavailing, frivolous (effectual, humble, real)

valiant, brave, bold, valorous, courageous, gallant (cowardly)

valid, weighty, strong, powerful, efficient, sound, binding (invalid)

valor, courage, gallantry, boldness, bravery, heroism (cowardice)

value, appraise, assess, reckon, appreciate, estimate, prize, treasure, esteem (despise, condemn)

vanish, disappear, fade, melt, dissolve

vanity, conceit, egotism, affectedness (humility)

variable, changeable, unsteady, shifting, inconstant, wavering, fickle, fitful, restless (constant)

variety, difference, diversity, change, diversification, mixture, medley, miscellany (sameness, monotony)

vast, spacious, boundless, mighty, immense, enormous, colossal, gigantic, huge, prodigious (confined)

verbal, oral, spoken, literal, unwritten (written)

verdict, judgment, finding, decision, answer

vicious, corrupt, depraved, bad, profligate, faulty (virtuous, gentle)

victim, sacrifice, food, prey, sufferer, dupe, gull

view, prospect, survey

violent, destructive, furious (gentle)

virtue, honesty, morality, honor, truth, worth, uprightness, probity, purity, integrity, chastity, goodness, duty, rectitude, faithfulness (vice, viciousness, evil, wrong, wickedness)

W

wander, range, ramble, roam, rove, stroll, stray, deviate

wary, circumspect, cautious (foolhardy)

wash, clean, rinse, wet, moisten, tint, stain

waste, squander, dissipate, lavish, destroy, decay, dwindle, wither

way, method, plan, system, means, manner, mode, form, fashion, course, process, road, route, track, path, habit, practice

wealth, money, pelf, plenty, opulence, means, riches, prosperity, lucre, luxury, assets, abundance, affluence, property (need, destitution, lack, beggary, misery, poverty, privation, want, scarcity)

win, get, obtain, gain, procure, effect, realize, accomplish, achieve (lose)

wisdom, prudence, foresight, sagacity, farsightedness, judiciousness, sense (foolishness, absurdity, idiocy, silliness, stupidity, nonsense)

wit, humor, satire, fun, raillery

wonder, marvel, miracle, prodigy

work, labor, task, toil, occupation, business, employment, exertion (play)

worthless, valueless (valuable)

wrong, injustice, injury (right)

Y

yearn, long for, desire, crave

yell, bellow, cry out, scream

yield, bear, give, afford, impart, communicate, confer, bestow, abdicate, resign, cede, surrender, relinquish, relax, quit (withdraw, withhold, retain, deny, refuse, vindicate)

youthful, young, juvenile, boyish, girlish, puerile, immature, adolescent (aged, mature, decrepit, venerable, antiquated)

Z

zeal, energy, fervor, ardor, earnestness, enthusiasm, eagerness (indifference, apathy, torpor, coldness, carelessness, sluggishness)

zero, nothing, naught, cipher

zest, flavor, appetizer, gusto, pleasure, enjoyment, relish, sharpener, enhancement (distaste, disgust, disrelish)

For Further Reference

Brandt, Sue R.
How to Improve Your Written English
Franklin Watts

Newman, Gerald
How to Write a Report
Franklin Watts

Strunk, William, Jr., and White, E. B.
The Elements of Style
Macmillan

Tchudi, Susan and Tchudi, Stephen
The Young Writer's Handbook
Macmillan

Yates, Elizabeth
Someday You'll Write
E. P. Dutton

- *How speaking works*   **74**
- *Improving your speech*   **75**
- *Preparing a report*   **77**

Speaking

The section on studying, pages 78–103, focuses on the ways that we absorb information in school. The most important ways are through listening and through reading. This section and the prior section concentrate on the way we express ourselves—how we communicate what we have learned to others. The two main ways are by speaking and by writing. This section is on speaking, especially in school situations.

Almost everyone knows how to speak. We say our first words when we are less than a year old, and by the time we reach four, we can form sentences and let people know about our needs and feelings without much trouble. At the same time, however, we do not always know how to speak well. When students give class reports, some mumble and stumble over their words. Others speak too loudly or have irritating mannerisms. This section takes a look at speaking and offers some pointers on how you can become a more effective speaker. It also shows how you can make sure that your listeners hear what you have to say.

How speaking works

The first thing we need to know is how we make the noises that result in speech. Even though we all speak all the time, we are not always aware of how we do so. Following are the four main components in producing spoken sounds.

Breathing. As we are drawing breath into our lungs, we cannot speak—although it is possible for us to make odd ghostly sounds. Speaking is possible when we are pushing air out of our lungs. We force the air to pass through the noise-making part of our throats called the *larynx* or *voice box.*

Once in a while we become aware of how important breath is to speaking. If you have just run half a mile and are out of breath, you will find it difficult to speak because you are breathing too rapidly. If you are bending down to tie your shoe, your lungs and breathing muscles are cramped, and you cannot speak very loudly or clearly.

Many speakers could improve their speech just by remembering the importance of breathing. If you stand in front of the class slouched down or hunched over a lectern or desk, your breathing muscles are cramped, and you cannot use them properly to push air through your larynx. If you stand up straight, and breathe deeply before you start speaking, your words will be much more clear and forceful.

Vibration. The second element in speaking is the actual creation of sound in the larynx, or voice box. When you start to speak, you unconsciously pull your two vocal cords tight and push air from your lungs between them. The air causes them to vibrate in much the same way that a bow causes the string on a violin to vibrate. You control the loudness of your voice by controlling the amount of air you push between the cords. You control the pitch of your voice (shrill, deep, or in between) by controlling how tightly the cords are stretched.

You can actually feel your vocal cords in action by feeling your throat as you make a continuous sound of "ah." If you make a deep sound, then a shrill sound, you will feel the muscles that pull the cords tight and that allow you to change pitch.

Resonance. The third component in speaking may surprise you: it is your head. Just as a violin has a wooden case that gives resonance to the sound of vibrating string, so the nasal passages, mouth, and throat, and the upper chest are resonators for the vibrating vocal cords. The resonators help make the sound of your voice both louder and more pleasing than it would otherwise be. You can feel how they vibrate if you make a loud "mmm" sound and feel your chest, throat, and head. When a person has a bad cold, all the nasal passages are shut, so the voice sounds hollow and weak.

Articulation. The last element in speaking is articulation—the many different ways in which you can vary the sound of your vocal cords to form words. Some sounds (*t* and *p*, for example) do not even require vocal sound. When vocal sound is used, *t* becomes *d*, and *p* becomes *b*. Most of our vocal sounds are used on vowels (a, e, i, o, u), although some consonants (m, n, r) are also sounded.

One of the most common speech problems is lazy articulation. Words get slurred together, and sometimes meanings can be lost altogether. Lazy speech is not usually a problem in informal conversation, but it can be a serious problem when a person is speaking to more than one or two others. When lazy speech is printed out, it looks odd on the page, but we are all used to hearing it. For example: I dough wancha t'go.

I don't want you to go.

Improving your speech

When students in a class give an oral book report, teachers and students alike notice that some have read their books more carefully than others and some have more interesting things to say about their books. But there are always a few who speak so badly that it is difficult to know how carefully they have read or how much they have to say. Even the best students will not be recognized unless they can communicate their knowledge and opinions effectively.

Like listening skills, speaking skills are often ignored because it seems that everyone knows how to listen and speak. But a wise student will put some time and energy into considering basic speaking skills, which can be as important to success in school as the writing skills described in the next section. The following paragraphs will list some of the important things to consider when preparing and giving an oral report in front of the class.

Nonverbal speech. Much of the success of a good speaker may not even be in the words. Listeners are alert not only for what is said but for the way the speaker stands and how the words are delivered.

Many students are nervous about giving a report, and they let the audience know this before they speak a word. They may slouch, sway back and forth, crack their knuckles, or keep their eyes down on their notes to avoid looking at anyone. Mannerisms of this kind detract greatly from a speech. They say to the audience, "I don't even know that you're here, and I do not really have anything I want to tell you." If you are in the audience when someone does this, you probably have the same negative reaction.

Even good speakers are normally a little nervous when they get up in front of a group. But they learn to use their nervousness to advantage. They come to the front of the class, put their notes on the lectern, and look perhaps toward a particular friend in the class, waiting until the class is paying attention before beginning.

Even if you are reading from notes, look up at the audience once in a while. Your glance tells the audience that you are thinking about them. You may also notice some reaction that will tell you how you are doing. If half the class is yawning, perhaps you have gone on too long. If people look puzzled, perhaps there is some important fact you have left out or not explained clearly. With your eyes, you can stay in contact with your listeners and can encourage them to stay in contact with you.

There is a wrong way (left) *and a right way* (right) *to give an oral report. Which speaker would you rather listen to?*

Gestures are another important tool. For a class report, throwing your arms around and jumping up and down may not be appropriate, but if there is something visual in your report that you want to explain—a spiral staircase, the size of the fish you caught—use your hands to help. In some cases, you may be able to demonstrate by walking from one side of the room to another or by showing something you have brought. An audience often listens better when it also has something to watch.

Your face is the most expressive part of your body, and listeners will be watching for expressions that will help them understand what you are explaining. For example, if you are reporting on a funny book you have read, a solemn, slow recital of the plot with no hint of a smile and no twinkle in the eye will probably not be very effective. If you are telling a suspenseful story, your expressions help reflect the growing excitement.

Finally, your voice itself is a very expressive tool. Listeners will try to understand what you are saying partly by the pitch, the tone, and the cadence of your voice. If you always speak at the same pitch and never vary the tone or the cadence (speed), your listeners will soon be lulled to sleep.

In telling about a book or a personal experience, think about what parts should be told slowly and what parts more rapidly. If there is suspense, you might speak more and more softly. If there is a surprise, a sudden change of tone can make it more surprising.

There are many good examples of the way good speakers use their bodies, faces, and tones of voice to help get their messages across. Television announcers, advertisers, politicians, and ministers are often expert in the use of nonverbal communication. Watch them and listen carefully to them, and you may find new things that will work for you.

Preparing a report

In many ways, speaking is easier than writing because you needn't worry about all the mechanics of writing: spelling, punctuation, etc. But a good oral report does require planning.

The first planning step is to consider any requirements—in a book report, you may be asked to begin with the title and author, then tell about the book, then evaluate it. A second step is to decide how to balance the report—about how much time do you want to spend on each of the major topics? Speakers who get up without a plan often waste all their time on one topic and do not have time to finish.

A third step is to consider your audience. For example, if you are reporting on a new home computer, you should consider what others in the class are likely to know about computers in general. If you start at a level that is too advanced, they will not be able to understand you; if you start at a level that is too elementary, they will be bored or even resentful.

Organization. Once you have your general presentation in mind, sit down and write out its main points. Many speakers prefer to use outline form. Like a written report, an oral report often has three main parts: I. Introduction

   II. Body

   III. Conclusion

For a book report, the introduction might consist of the name and author of the book and a brief description of its type—mystery, science fiction, historical fiction, biography, etc. An introduction also may include a general statement of your point of view. For example: "I thought this was the best mystery I had ever read until I came to the last ten pages. Then I changed my mind because the ending was not believable." This helps your listeners know where your report is going and makes it easier to follow.

The body of the report may deal with some aspect of the topic. Unless you have a great deal of time, you probably will not be able to consider all aspects. With a book report, for example, you may have time to consider the plot (it may be the most important item in a mystery), or the characters (they may be most important in a historical novel or a biography), or the mood and style. Pick an aspect and concentrate on it.

Some experience at giving reports will help you judge how much material you can cover in the time you are allowed. Try to isolate the important points so that you do not get bogged down in trying to tell too much. In order to report clearly, you will have to simplify, leaving out the less important topics. Otherwise your listeners may be hopelessly confused.

The conclusion of the report may be the place where you give your personal reactions. Or you may come back to the statement you made in the introduction—illustrating, for example, why the end of the mystery was not believable. Another kind of conclusion summarizes the body of the report in a sentence or two. Always have the introductory material and the conclusion well in mind (or even written down). Do not be like the legendary minister who had at least three conclusions in every sermon.

Practice. Perhaps the most important part of preparing for an oral report is to practice it out loud. Go into a room and start to give the report, listening to the way it sounds. The first time, you are likely to stumble from one point to the next. The second time through, time yourself—if the report is too long, go back and find places where it can be shortened. One of the most useful tools for practicing is a cassette recorder. If you have (or can borrow) one, record your second or third practice run, then listen as if you were sitting in the audience. Where does the report work, and where does it fall down? Experiment with varying your tone of voice and the speed of your delivery. Also listen for signs of lazy speech, such as words or phrases that get lost.

For Further Reference

Detz, Joan
  You Mean I Have to Stand Up and Say Something?
  Atheneum
Monroe, Alan and Ehninger, Douglas
  Principles of Speech Communication
  Scott, Foresman & Co.
Otfinoski, Steven
  Speaking Up, Speaking Out
  Millbrook Press
Silverstein, Alvin and Silverstein, Virginia
  Wonders of Speech
  William Morrow

- *Make a plan*   **78**
- *Learn to listen*   **81**
- *Improve your reading*   **84**
- *Improve your test-taking*   **94**
- *Guide to good reading*   **96**

How to Study

Schools are set up to teach many subjects and many skills. But one skill is important as a beginning—knowing *how to learn.* A serious student soon discovers that he needs to master a few basic skills in order to take advantage of time spent in school. Most important are the skills of planning, listening, reading, and test-taking. With these skills a student can absorb most of what school has to offer. In fact, these basic study skills will be useful all through life, because learning does not end when school ends. The ability to take in new information, digest it, and then use it is the most important skill in a wide variety of occupations and jobs. In school, these same skills can make the difference between being happy and successful and being fearful and unsuccessful. If you know how to study, you are much more likely to succeed and to enjoy your school years. The *Student Handbook*s are filled with information on a wide variety of subjects, but pointers on how to study are equally important because they lay the groundwork for effective learning.

Make a plan

All students want to do their best in school, but many do not succeed. Is it just that others are smarter? Is it that others spend every hour of every day on homework and never have any fun? Some students do pick up and store information more easily than others, and some students do spend huge amounts of time studying; but the real difference between a good student and a bad one comes down to one thing: planning.

Men and women in many professions have learned that they must know how to plan in order to succeed. Many regret that they did not learn this lesson sooner so that they could have profited more from their years in school. Regardless of career, the difference between success and failure is often planning.

Making a good plan is hard work, but it needn't take very long. The most important advantage of a plan is that it helps you to make the best use of your time. Often it may save you hours or days of needless study and worry. When you do study, you learn to do so efficiently and rapidly; then, when the studying is done, you are free to enjoy yourself.

There are six important steps to good planning. They are:
1. Know what you want to accomplish.
2. Decide what steps are necessary to accomplish it.
3. Gather necessary material.
4. Organize your time.
5. Coordinate your plan with other activities.
6. Stick to your plan.

To illustrate how planning works, consider a family planning a trip to a distant town by car. First, they decide where they want to go. This may involve deciding whether there is time for a side trip to visit a friend or to accomplish some other business. Second, they decide on their route. No sensible traveler sets out to stop at each crossroad to decide which way to turn, but instead finds out ahead of time how far the destination is and what roads must be taken to get there. Third, the family gathers the necessary materials for the trip. This may involve being sure that the car is in good working order, filling it with gas, and packing a lunch to eat on the way. Fourth, the travelers plan their time. They estimate how long the trip will take, how far along they should be by midday, and how many stops they can afford to make along the way. Fifth, they coordinate their trip with other plans. Perhaps there is a store along the way where they want to buy clothes or there is a business associate to meet with. Finally, the family sets out. They are more relaxed because they know where they are going and how they will get there. They stick to their plan unless something occurs outside of their control. If the car breaks down, for example, they will revise their schedule—make a new plan that will work in the changed situation.

A plan for a trip that will take place over a few days is simpler than a plan for a whole school year, but it is really not so very different. How does this planning method work for a student?

What do you want to accomplish? Answering this question is the most important step. Like the travelers, you must know the direction in which you want to go, or there will be no reason for a plan. Perhaps your objective is to improve your grades in each subject or to get your highest grade in social studies. Thinking about what you most want to do must come first. A good plan should be ambitious—every student can find lots of room to improve. At the same time, however, you should aim at a realistic goal. If you failed in math last year, planning to become the top student this year may be unrealistic. Set your sights on a goal that is challenging but reachable.

How will you get there? Perhaps you think that if your aim is a higher grade in a class, the best plan is to study harder. But a real plan requires more detailed thinking. What steps will you take? Perhaps you should start with your knowledge about the class. When will the tests be given? What will you be expected to know at the end of the first month? How will you be sure that you are ready by then? Must you do a special report? When is it due, and what steps will you take to do it well and complete it on time?

What materials do you need? Now that you have a basic idea of your plan, you may have some preparations to make. The materials you need may be simple supplies like paper and pencils. For an art project, you will need paints or special paper. For a research report, you may need particular books. Make a list of needed materials and begin to gather them.

A balanced study plan should set aside plenty of time for both study and play. Studying in a group turns learning into a team effort that sharpens your learning skills and increases your knowledge, just as playing a team sport improves your athletic skills and strengthens your body. Physical exercise and other enjoyable activities also help refresh your mind and sharpen your ability to learn.

MY SCHEDULE

Date	School	outside	home
Monday	study period 2:00 Math	Library on way home from school	Make bed [every day]
Tuesday	MATH TEST	Scouts 4:00	Late Supper
Wednesday	Clubs [study period]		Judy's Club [close door]
Thursday	French quiz [study period] 2:00 Book Report	Dave after school Piano lesson 7:00	Finish Book Report
Friday	Book REPORT DUE		
Saturday		[Dan here] 2:00 football	CHORES
Sunday			[Church] check scout project

How will you budget your time? This question is often the hardest one for students to answer. Not all study assignments are pleasant, and it is human to want to postpone dull or difficult assignments. When such things are postponed, time always seems to run out before they are done.

If you really want to accomplish a goal and are willing to make some sacrifices to do so, you must budget time for it. The best way is to do it *first* and to devote the time left over to other enjoyable but less important activities. Although it will be difficult to start with study, you will have more fun after your work is done because you know that you have already made the necessary progress toward your goal. Many students seem worried even when supposedly enjoying themselves because they have left important projects undone.

How does your plan fit with other activities? In planning your time, you might sit down and list all the activities in which you are engaged. Your goal may be a better grade in social studies, but social studies is only a part of your schoolwork; perhaps you also practice a musical instrument, and want to try out for the basketball team.

Once you have listed all your activities, put a number beside each one: "1" for the most important, "2" for the next most important, and so on. This is called setting priorities, and it is a very important part of planning. Both students and adults often find that they must choose between two or more activities because there just is not time or energy for all. If you know ahead of time what is most important, and you pay attention to that activity first, chances are you will succeed in accomplishing your aims.

If you choose an ambitious study goal, you will soon discover that it will have to be high on your list of priorities if it is to be reached. If study is always left until last, and if it gets left out altogether when time is short, then no amount of planning is likely to help you reach your goal.

Can you stick to your plan? There are two kinds of planners: the first likes to make a plan on paper but never follows through; the second makes plans that can be accomplished. The first kind of planner usually ends up disappointed in herself or himself or looking for someone to blame. The second kind knows that a plan is no better than its execution. The successful planner is the one who actually sticks to the plan and reaches the goal.

Talent and success.
Thomas Edison, inventor of the electric light, the phonograph, and many other modern devices, was often called a genius. But Edison himself always insisted that "genius is one percent inspiration and ninety-nine percent perspiration." "Perspiration," or hard work, is often a matter of planning—approaching a task in an orderly way—and concentration—sticking to the plan. Anyone who can master the arts of planning and concentration can realize his or her full potential, both in school and in other pursuits.

Learn to listen

Of all the skills important to students, listening may be the most valuable. It is surprising that schools themselves spend much time and money on teaching reading but scarcely anything on teaching listening.

Of course, everyone has ears, and listening isn't exactly like reading. There is no alphabet to learn, no special process of sounding out words, recognizing punctuation, and so on. But just because we all have ears does not mean that we are all good listeners. In school and in everyday situations, all of us miss words spoken to us because we are not paying attention; or we hear the words but immediately forget them. Even when we hear and remember, we can often get the information confused. Fortunately, however, with a little work, anyone can improve listening skills. For a student, this can mean improving performance in school not by spending hours doing extra work but simply by making better use of class time.

Basic listening. The first important fact about listening is that it is *not* all done with the ears. Understanding spoken language can be greatly improved by watching as well. A teacher may tell a great deal about his subject by posture, facial expression, gestures, and eye contact. Sensitive students get to know their teachers and to understand this language of *visual cues.* It helps students to understand precisely what the teacher is saying and to remember not only the words but the mood or the tone surrounding a particular piece of information. When studying for a test, a student may remember an important phrase by first recalling the teacher's excitement when mentioning it.

A second fact about listening is that it is *not* all a matter of understanding words. Teachers and others communicate a great deal by the loudness, pace, and tone of their voices. For example, one teacher may stress an important point by speaking more loudly and more slowly than normal. Another may stress a point by speaking very quietly, requiring the class to listen intently.

If you listen only to the words, you may mistake the meaning altogether. Many speakers use *irony* or *sarcasm,* employing a tone of voice that tells listeners that they mean exactly the opposite of what they are saying. For example, a student spills milk on the teacher's desk and says, "I hope you are not angry." The teacher replies, "Of course I'm not angry." If she says this in a calm, quiet tone, she means what she says; but if she says it loudly, with her fists clenched and her eyes flashing, she is probably sarcastic and means, "I am not angry—I am furious!"

A third fact about listening is that a good listener must be almost as alert and active as the person being listened to. The listener must note words, tone of voice, and visual cues, and make sense of them as a whole. Many teachers encourage their students to be alert by frequently asking questions. This requires the listener to keep track of more than one speaker and sometimes for the listener to speak, to give an answer or an opinion. Most students could save themselves time spent studying outside of class by listening more closely in class. Good listening takes energy and attention.

Gestures and facial expressions

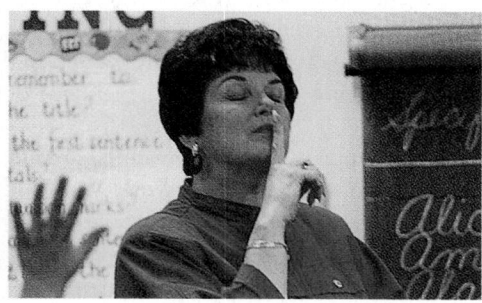

Gestures, such as this teacher's motion for quiet in her classroom (left), *and signs of emotion, such as this girl's expression of surprise and joy* (right), *are good ways to communicate without using words.*

Get the assignment in writing so you won't have to wonder what you are supposed to do.

Different kinds of teachers.

Every student has two different jobs in a classroom. One is to understand and master the material being taught—history, spelling, math, and so on. The other is to understand the teacher—how he or she teaches and what the teacher requires of a student. One teacher may place great emphasis on learning basic principles of a subject. Another may require the mastery of a large body of small facts. Still another may be most interested in encouraging students to think for themselves or to solve problems themselves.

All of these approaches are valid, and it is the responsibility of the student to adapt to each of them. By listening carefully, you can usually understand which approach a teacher is following so that on tests, papers, and other assignments you can meet his or her expectations. This does not mean that you must always say or do exactly what pleases a teacher, but that there is usually room for individual differences within a teacher's general approach.

Listening skills also help a student to find out how he is doing in the teacher's estimation. Whether in a classroom or in a teacher conference, an attentive student uses all her or his listening skills. These include "listening" for what is *not* said as well as for what is said. For example, a teacher might say, "You have a great aptitude for math," in a way that also suggests a criticism: "but you are too careless in your computations."

Getting the facts.
Important as all the general listening skills are, many students fall down on the most basic skill of all—getting the facts. In most classrooms, assignments are given out every day, and every day one or more of the students manage not to hear or to hear wrong.

For specific assignments, use a pencil and paper to assist your memory. In early grades, teachers often require students to write down assignments. But even if the teacher does not require this, do it anyway. You cannot do a good job on an assignment you have forgotten or misunderstood. If you do not understand the assignment, ask questions. Chances are that someone else in the class also does not understand.

Taking notes.
Probably the best way to improve your listening is to get into the habit of taking notes. Note-taking will become more and more important as you progress in school, and learning how to do it early on can be very helpful.

If your teacher is presenting new material, you will be taking "lecture notes." The secret of lecture notes is that you must first work hard to *understand* what the teacher is saying. Unless you can take shorthand, you cannot copy down even half of what is said. Even if you could, the results would probably not be worthwhile. Instead, you must get a sense of how the teacher's material is organized.

Getting the organization. A presentation on history might be organized *chronologically,* moving from one event to a later event, and so on. If so, your notes should be organized accordingly, with dates or the names of major events down the left side of the page.

Another presentation might be organized around people—for example, the leaders of World War II. If so, the main headings in your notes would be the names of these people.

Scientific presentations may follow a step-by-step process. An English lesson may be planned to illus-

> 11/17   History
>
> About Abraham Lincoln
>   President 1861
>   born 1809 Kentucky
>   moved to Indiana
>   moved to Illinois
>   occupations, he had many
>   odd jobs on farms
>   clerk in store
>   law clerk (really a student of law)
>   became a lawyer by studying on his own

Notes from a teacher's presentation may look like an informal outline—with each thought or topic on a new line.

trate all the uses of a comma or all the forms of a verb. These would then become main headings.

Listening at the beginning of a teacher's presentation is especially important, because often he or she will introduce the subject by describing the organization to be used. Even without such an introduction, however, a note-taker can almost always find the organizational pattern in the first few minutes.

Nearly all school presentations have some sort of basic structure, and it is the job of the note-taker to get that structure down on paper. At first, you may have trouble deciding what is important and what is not. Teachers often enliven their presentations with little stories or anecdotes to illustrate or demonstrate a point. If the basic point is a difficult one, they may use several illustrations. You may have time to get some of the illustrations down, but it is most important that you get down the *main points,* even if you miss some of the detail.

How should the notes look? The teacher is the one who sets the organization of your notes, but you are the one who must learn how best to get the information down on paper. Usually, the only person you have to please in note-taking is yourself. If the finished notes recall the teacher's presentation, their purpose has been served. Only you will ever read and evaluate them.

You may want to adopt some personal code to help distinguish between important and less important points. For example, the most important might be written all in capitals. Many note-takers prefer to work in outline form—they may even pretend that they are trying to reproduce the teacher's outline for the presentation. Space is not a serious concern, so you may want to skip lines between the end of one topic and the beginning of another so that when you read through the notes later the breaks will be easily spotted.

In a complicated presentation, you may even want to distinguish between several kinds of notes. For a very important phrase, you might take down the teacher's exact words and put them in quotation marks to remind yourself. Sometimes you might try to rephrase an idea in your own words and underline it as a reminder. There may also be times when you put down your reactions to the teacher's point (disagreement, questions, approval); these might best be put in parentheses so that you do not later confuse your ideas with your teacher's. Even drawings or diagrams can help and save writing time. Many note-takers use arrows, boxes, and other such devices to set off certain material.

As in all listening skills, the important part of note-taking is to remain active—alert for the important points, framing questions about the material, and trying to make connections. If you merely write down an odd part of what you hear now and then, your notes will almost certainly be useless.

At their best, notes can be one of the most worthwhile study aids. You may be reading similar material in your textbook, but your notes are your own—you took them down and they bring back to you information that you have absorbed, whether you are studying for an examination, writing a paper, or preparing for an oral report. Notes can preserve the things you have learned because of your listening skills.

Improve your reading

Your reading will improve if you find a place to read with no distractions.

Listening is one way to gain information in school. As we have seen, students can improve their listening skills with a little practice and attention. The other major way to gain information is through reading. Unlike listening, reading is not a natural skill. Beginning in the early grades, a student must learn to read.

Nearly all students learn the basics of reading in the early grades. Slowly they recognize words that occur often, such as "dog," "cat," and "house." At the same time, students are learning the sound of each letter in the alphabet so that they can sound out unfamiliar words. By third or fourth grade, most students can read simple passages and understand them.

But learning the basic skills is not the end. Many students never go further, however, and for them reading is always a slow, difficult procedure. As they progress in school, they may fall further and further behind because they cannot read well enough. Reading becomes a more and more impor-

tant learning tool. To be a good student, you must be a good reader.

Using your equipment.
If you are having trouble with reading, your first step should be to check out the equipment you use. The most obvious equipment for reading is your eyes. If you have trouble focusing as you read, or if a few minutes of reading gives you a headache or makes your eyes water or burn, you should have your eyes checked by an ophthalmologist without delay. Nearly all common sight problems can be corrected, and it may surprise you how much easier reading can be with correctly prescribed glasses.

Another important tool for good reading is good hearing. This may seem surprising, but studies of reading difficulties have discovered that a sizable number of students with reading problems have hearing problems. Learning to read is a process of translating symbols on a page (visual information)

For Reluctant Readers

There are some people who cannot read. There are many more who know how to read but almost never do. Some of them think that reading is too hard. Others think that reading is not worth the time. Still others are embarrassed to read.

You can learn a great deal without reading, but there are many things that are very hard to learn if you do not read. There are many jobs for which you cannot qualify, and many kinds of enjoyment that you may never know.

Still hate to read? The following suggestions may help.

1. **List your interests.** Make a list of the three subjects in which you are most interested. There are magazines and books available on almost every conceivable subject.
2. **Look for reading material on your interests.** If you like mystery stories, look for mysteries in comic book form, in magazines, or in books. If you want to know more about cars, look for magazines and easy books on this subject. Ask a librarian or a friend who is interested in the same field for recommendations.
3. **Read every day.** Take 20 minutes each day just for reading. You can read almost anywhere, anytime. Take a magazine to read on the bus or in the car; put a book by your bed and read before going to sleep. Once you get the habit, you will not want to stop.
4. **Find a friend with the same interests.** Friends who are reading about the same subject have lots to talk about. Your friends may know of books you would be sure to like.

Is reading worth the trouble? Most people say yes. It will help you do well in school or prepare for a job. Most important, it will help you find out what *you* want to know.

into sounds (aural information). This translation is difficult for those who do not hear well.

A third piece of equipment necessary for good reading is a sound processing center in the brain. Modern reading researchers have found that some students see and hear well enough but have some problem in *processing* the information they see on the printed page. For example, they may see letters in reverse order or be tempted to read some lines from right to left. Such processing problems are known as *dyslexia,* a term that simply means "problems learning to read." Reading specialists have developed special programs of instruction to help those who are *dyslexic.*

There is also the possibility that trouble with reading may have emotional causes. A good reader knows how to concentrate. But someone who is extremely sad or angry cannot concentrate very well on such a demanding task as reading. His or her mind may constantly wander to personal problems or feelings; as a result, the reader may lose track of a sentence in the middle or forget an important fact within moments of having read it. Even good readers have trouble concentrating sometimes. But if you have had trouble concentrating or have had trouble

remembering what you read for weeks or months, you should consider asking for help in solving the problem.

Finally, reading difficulties can be caused by a person's surroundings. One student may grow up in a home where everyone reads—for information, for pleasure, and for learning. Such a student will develop the habit of reading at an early age, and it will seem a natural activity. Another student may grow up in a home where reading is less common. As a result, this student does not develop a reading habit and may come to see reading as unpleasant and seek to do as little of it as possible. In order to become a better reader, such a student must exercise some self-discipline and set aside some time each day—at home, at school, or at a library—to read.

Physical surroundings can also play a part in discouraging reading. Noise and activity in the same room distract many readers. Poor lighting can make reading an unpleasant chore. Other conditions, including extreme heat and cold and poor ventilation, can also slow down even a good reader. For many students, a proper reading environment would increase reading skills without any further effort.

Reviewing basic skills.

One common cause for reading difficulties is a gap in some important part of the process of learning to read. The student may have been sick and missed the important lessons, or may have been too young to fully understand them. If this is the case, it is always possible to go back and relearn or review these lessons—and the result may be a dramatic improvement in reading.

Sounds. The first step in reading is to translate a group of written symbols into a word. Simple words may be easy to recognize, but longer words probably need to be sounded out, especially if they are unfamiliar. If students have never thoroughly learned the sounds of all the letters, they may not be able to sound out such words. This job would be simpler if all letters always had the same sound. But in English, many letters have quite different sounds in different situations. Some letter combinations have a sound quite different from the sound of either of the letters standing alone. For example, the letters *c* and *h* each have their own sounds when used alone. Yet when they are together, they have still another sound, as in *children* or *chief*. The vowel sounds—a, e, i, o, and u—have a still wider variety of sounds, depending on their position in a word and on various combinations. One example is the combination *ai* in *pair* and *wait*.

If the sounds of letters are sometimes confusing to you, you may feel embarrassed about this problem, since letter sounds are taught mainly in the early grades. But you can review the letter sounds all by yourself. The table on this page shows some of the most common sound changes. Dictionaries contain much more information. If you have trouble telling what a word is from its letters, this kind of review may be a first step toward better reading.

Sentence meaning. A second problem for many who find reading difficult is making sense of a group of words strung together. As long as a reader only moves along one word at a time, the meaning of a sentence can get lost. For example, a beginning reader might group words together like this:

Jack . . . and . . .
Jill . . . went . . .
up . . . the . . . hill . . . to . . .
fetch . . . a . . .
pail . . . of . . .
water. . . .

In order to keep track of the meaning, every word must be remembered because the words are not grouped in a reasonable way.

Vowel Sounds

Sound	Letters that can make this sound (example)
a as in cat	**a,** ai (plaid)
a as in cake	**a,** ai (paid), ea (break), ey (obey), ay (say)
a as in care	**a + r,** ai + r (fair), ea + r (wear), e + r (there)
a as in father	**a,** o (stop)
a as in saw	**a,** au (caught), oa (broad), ou (fought)
e as in bed	**e,** ea (heavy), ie (friend), ai (said)
e as in we	**e,** ei (receive), ey (key), ie (field)
i as in it	**i,** ee (been), u (busy), ui (build), y (hymn)
i as in kite	**i,** ie (tie), ei (height), ey (eye), uy (buy), y (fly)
o as in go	**o,** oa (goat), oe (toe), ou (soul), ew (sew), ow (grow)
oo as in tool	**oo,** ue (blue), ui (fruit), ew (threw), ough (through)
oo as in book	**oo,** o (wolf), ou (would), u (pull)
ow as in now	**ow,** ou (out), ough (bough)
oy as in boy	**oy,** oi (toil)
u as in cuff	**u,** o (son), oo (flood), oe (does), ou (double)
u as in hurt	**u + r,** ea + r (heard), i + r (bird), o + r (worry), ou + r (courage)
u as in fuse	**u,** ue (cue), eau (beauty), ew (few), iew (view), yu (yule), you (youth)
ə (an unaccented *uh* sound)	**a** (asleep), e (voted), o (confession), u (focus), etc.

A more skilled reader would naturally group the words in her or his mind:

Jack and Jill	(who?)
went up the hill	(did what?)
to fetch a pail of water	(why?)

Good readers learn to see words in clusters. If you read word for word, and sometimes lose track of a sentence's meaning, try some exercises in seeing clusters of words together. At the beginning, read a simple paragraph word for word. Then go back and read it again, putting the words in groups that help them make sense. When you have done this several times, try reading a new paragraph by clusters the first time—without going through it word for word. Reading words in clusters becomes more important as you begin to read passages with longer, more complicated sentences.

Word meaning. Many readers begin to have trouble when they start to read passages about unfamiliar subjects. These readers may be able to recognize or pronounce all the words and they may be able to see how the words cluster in a sentence, but they cannot tell what a sentence means because they do not know the meaning of an essential word.

For such readers, an important step toward improving their reading is to increase their vocabulary. The box on the following pages provides a basic understanding of the way in which many long words are put together; this can help in learning new words. There are also other ways to increase your knowledge of the meanings of words. The most important are the following:

Learn from context. Readers can often learn a great deal about the meaning of a word simply by paying attention to what the rest of the passage says. Consider the word *perambulator* in the following paragraph, for example.

In the mornings, our nurse would take us to the playground in Central Park. I tagged along, holding onto her skirts, and she pushed my brother along in a great old-fashioned perambulator. It was much bigger and more luxurious than the baby carriages other nannies pushed, and nurse seemed proud of it. She only complained when we went up the big hill, when she used to mutter over and over, "Too heavy! Too heavy!"

A reader who does not know the meaning of *perambulator* can learn a great deal about it from this paragraph. It is compared with other baby carriages, so it must be a thing of that kind. This perambulator is larger and heavy, so it may be that in general perambulators are heavier than baby carriages. There is also the suggestion that a perambulator is an old-fashioned kind of baby carriage.

There are many other cases where the context will help define an unfamiliar word. Schoolbooks are often particularly careful to help a reader with unfamiliar terms.

Use a dictionary. Many students do not understand why teachers stress using a dictionary. It is the one quickest way for students to increase their vocabulary. Even if you can gain the basic meaning of a word from context, it is often wise to look the word up to be sure that you have the correct meaning.

If you look up *obstruction* in a dictionary, you may see that the word just before *obstruction* is *obstruct,* which means "to fill and block," or "to stand or be in the way of." You can guess from this that an *obstruction* is something that blocks or stands in the way of something else. The entries for both words may also present sample sentences to help you understand what the words mean.

Most people use dictionaries to look up long, difficult words. It is worth remembering that a dictionary may also be useful for looking up everyday words that are used in unfamiliar ways. For example, a reader may be confused by this sentence:

She greeted us warmly at the door, but we had the feeling she felt *put upon.*

Under the entry *put* in the dictionary, you can learn that *put upon* means to "take advantage of," so you can conclude that the woman depicted in the sentence above felt that her guests had taken advantage of her.

Write down new words. A fast way to increase your word power is to keep a set of index cards or slips of paper. Each time you hear or read a word that you do not know, write the word down on a card. On the back of the card, write down its definition. Often, just writing the word and definition are enough to make it stick in your memory. If you keep the cards, you can go back through them later and review the new words and meanings.

Increasing Your Vocabulary

Few people have trouble learning everyday words such as *house, man, dog, run.* The ones that give trouble are less common words that are long and that often refer to *abstract* ideas and pursuits.

These long words are often made up of smaller pieces whose meanings are easy to learn. These parts are *roots, prefixes,* and *suffixes.*

For example, consider the word *transportation.* Its root is *port,* a word that comes to English from Latin and that means "to carry." Its prefix is *trans-,* which also comes from Latin and which means "across." Its suffix, *-ation,* tells us that the word is a noun. If we had to "translate" *transportation* into other English words, we might suggest "across-carrying," which is close to the usual meaning of the word, "a carrying of things or people from one place to another."

Once you learn some of the common roots, prefixes, and suffixes, you can reason about the meanings of many other unfamiliar words.

Using the root. Knowing the one root *port,* you can probably think of other words of which port is a part: *import, export, deport, report.* This shows that there are several other common prefixes that can be used with this root. There are also suffixes such as the *-er* in *porter, importer, exporter, reporter.*

Using the prefix. A prefix like *trans-* can be used with many roots: *transatlantic, transcribe, translate, transmit,* and so on. The prefix table gives many of the more common prefixes, their basic meanings, and examples.

Using the suffix. A suffix like *-ation* or *-tion* also has many uses with other roots. It always tells us that the word it is part of is a noun. If *translate* means to change from one language to another, *translation* is the result or the process of translating. The suffix table shows how other suffixes change words from one part of speech to another.

Common English Roots

Root	Meaning	Examples
act	do, drive	act, action, actor, react, reaction, reactor
aud	hear	audio, audience, auditorium, audition
cap (cip, cept, ceiv, ceit)	seize, hold	capture, anticipate, accept, receive, reception, deceit, deception
ced (ceed, cess)	yield, go	secede, recede, proceed, process, procession, recess, recession
clude (clus)	close, shut	conclude, conclusion, seclude, include, recluse
dict	say, speak	dictate, dictation, predict, diction, dictionary
fac (fic, fact, fect)	make, do	manufacture, factory, efficient, perfect, affect
grad (gress)	step	grade, graduate, progress, progression, progressive
jac (ject)	throw	adjacent, inject, reject, subject
mit (miss)	send	transmit, emit, mission, missionary
pel, puls	push	propel, repel, compel, propellant, repulsion, compulsion
pend	hang	pendant, depend, dependent, append, appendix
port	carry	transportation, porter, portable
posit (pos)	put, place	deposit, repose, depose, exposure
scrib (script)	write	describe, subscribe, scripture, manuscript
spec, spic	look	inspect, suspect, spectacle, conspicuous
ven (vent)	come	convene, convent, convention, invent, intervene
vid (vis)	see	video, vision, provide
voc (vok)	call	vocal, vocation, advocate, invoke

Common English Prefixes

Prefix	Meaning	Examples
ab-	away (from)	abnormal, abstract
ad-, ac-, af-, ap-, as-	to, toward	admonish, accept, affect, appear, assign
com-, con-, col-, cor-	with, together	companion, communication, conclude, collect, correct
de-	down, away from	decay, defect, default
ex-, e-, ef-	out (from)	exhale, exhaust, eject, effervescent
in-, im-, en-, em-	in, into	include, inspect, immigrate, enact, emboss
in-, im-, ir-	not	inoffensive, imbalance, irreligious
inter-	between	intercept, intercede, intervene
non-	not	nonsense, nonentity
per-	through	perceive, permit, perseverance
post-	after	postscript, postpone
pre-	before	prescribe, precede, predict
pro-	forward	proceed, progress, project, propose, provide, provoke
sub-, suc-, suf-, sup-	under	submarine, substitute, succeed, suffer, suppose
trans-	across, over	transact, transgress, transmit, transcribe

Common English Suffixes

Purpose	Suffix	Examples
to make a noun from a verb	**-ation, -ion**	transportation, suspension
	-ment	judgment, agreement
to make a noun from a verb, showing who or what is the *doer*	**-or, -er**	actor, porter, transmitter
	-ent, -ant	superintendent, commandant
to make a noun from an adjective	**-ness**	goodness, blackness
	-ence, -ance	independence, radiance
to make a verb from a noun	**-ize**	criticize
to make a verb from an adjective	**-en**	lighten, redden
to make an adjective from a verb	**-y**	scary, runny
to make an adjective from a verb,	**-ical**	practical
showing possibility	**-able, -ible**	breakable, edible
to make an adjective from a noun	**-ary**	revolutionary, fragmentary
	-en	wooden, golden
	-ious, -ous	mysterious, gracious, grievous
	-ic	harmonic, graphic
to make an adverb from an adjective	**-ly, -ally**	slowly, comically

Basic Reading Skills
1. *Review - did I miss something when*
I learned to read?
2. *Sounds - Sounding out words helps*
to recognize them.
(Table: shows many different
combinations of letters that
can make the same sound.
I knew most of them but
there were a few surprises.)
3. *Sentences - Group of words together.*

These are a student's notes about pages 86 and following in this book. The note-taker has recorded his reactions as well as the content.

Reading strategies.

If you have reviewed the basics of reading and do not seem to have any trouble with them, but are still only a fair reader, your next step should be to consider the way you go about reading. Perhaps you are using a wrong approach—reading schoolbooks too fast, for example, or reading simpler material too slowly.

There are several kinds of reading, and each has its place. The important thing is to use the right method at the right time.

Reading for fun.

If you are reading for fun, of course you can read at any speed that suits you. This kind of reading offers you a good chance to experiment at reading faster, trying to see words in larger clusters, seeing if you can guess the meaning of an unfamiliar word by its context. Usually reading for pleasure is comfortable and easy, and it goes faster than reading a history book or a math textbook.

Recreational reading is most important for the practice it gives. Like swimming or playing a musical instrument, reading is a skill that improves with use—the more you do it, the better you are likely to be. Like other skills, reading gradually comes to seem natural and easy.

School texts.

Much of the reading you do for school is for the purpose of extracting information. Some schoolbooks—those on mathematics or on English grammar, for example—are very *dense*. They are not meant to be read through quickly. Often you read only a page or two at a time. For this kind of reading, speed is not important. You may read some sentences several times to be sure you understand them. You may want to do written exercises or answer review questions as you go, making sure you understand one step before going on to the next.

Book reports.

Another kind of informational reading is the kind you do for a book report. With this kind of assignment, you can save time by taking a few minutes before starting the first chapter to examine the book and see what it covers. The box on the next page suggests seven steps to follow in previewing a book.

Reference reading.

Still other informational reading may have a particular aim. For example, you may be preparing a report on the architecture of the Aztecs. Many of the books you find will tell also about Aztec history, society, customs, and other topics. In this case, it is even more important to preview the book. If you just start reading, you may have to go through dozens of pages before you reach any information about architecture. If you check the table of contents, however, you may find that there is one chapter about your subject. The index may show you where there are references to particular buildings. Leafing through the book may reveal a collection of architectural illustrations.

When you are gathering information for a report, you will want to make notes. It is always best to read a whole passage or chapter first before writing anything down, so that you understand what the writer is saying. After reading the whole passage, go back and summarize it in your mind. Put down this summary in your notes. Then, if there is particular information—a date, a name, or a specific idea—write it down afterward. Be sure that each note has the name of the book and the pages you read so that you can find the passage again.

How to Preview a Book

You will be able to understand the material in a book much more quickly if you examine it before you actually start to read. Here are some suggested steps and questions to answer.

1. **Look at the jacket.** If the book has a jacket, its illustration may help you to understand the mood or content of the book. On the *flaps*—the parts that fold inside the front and back covers—there is often a brief description of the book and a brief sketch of the author.

2. **Look at the title page.** The title page has the full, official name of the book. Often there is a subtitle that is not on the jacket or on the cover of the book. The title page will also tell the publisher of the book and the date of publication.

3. **Look at the copyright page.** The copyright notice almost always appears on the back of the title page. It will tell you when the book was originally published. This might be very important if you are looking up the latest information on astronomy, for example. If the book was first published in 1945, it will not have up-to-date information. The copyright page may also have information on where the book's illustrations came from and where it was prepared and published. This might be important, too. A British dictionary would not be a good source for everyday language usage in the United States because British English differs from American English in many small ways.

4. **Study the table of contents.** The table of contents is the framework of most books. A few minutes spent studying it will show you how the book is put together. It will often show you where the material you are looking for can be found. If you are doing research for a report and only need a few facts, the contents can help lead you straight to your material.

5. **Look for a foreword or introduction.** Writers of books often put important information in an introduction. They may tell you how to use the book, or that they have left out certain topics—perhaps even the one you are most interested in. Especially if the introduction is short, it is a good idea to read it.

6. **Page through the book quickly.** Starting at the front, turn the pages, getting yourself familiar with the look and "feel" of the volume. Pay special attention to chapter headings and to other headings in the text—they will help you see how the material is organized. Look for illustrations. Sometimes they fall on the same page as the text on your subject, but sometimes they are all in one place, bound into the middle of the book, for example. If you see illustrations that are particularly interesting, note their page numbers so that you can find them again easily. Also note the pages of any chapters or headings that you want to go back to read.

7. **Check the back of the book.** Several kinds of information are often found in the back of a book. Sometimes there are notes that include valuable information. Often there is a *bibliography*, a list of other books on related topics. In most nonfiction books there is an index. The index can be especially helpful if you are looking for specific information. It can direct you to the page where the information is discussed and even to specific illustrations.

After you have followed these steps, you will be able to decide how to use the book. If you plan to read it through, you already have a kind of road map—you know where the book starts and where it is going. If you are using the book for reference, you may not start at the beginning. Instead, you may go directly to the chapter or page that interests you.

This job of previewing a book, which should only take between ten minutes and half an hour, can save you hours of unnecessary time and add to your enjoyment of each book.

Reading tests. Most students are tested at least once a year for reading comprehension. These tests usually consist of short passages on various subjects and a set of multiple-choice questions on each passage. Many students find it helpful to read such a passage twice—once very quickly to get the general idea, then a second time more slowly to get more detailed information. When answering the questions, read them carefully and be sure you understand them. Even if you understood the reading passage, you will do poorly if you misunderstand the questions.

Reading fiction. Most fiction has been written to entertain the reader as well as to provide information. The great pleasure of many stories is to find out what happens next. Many young readers prefer action stories, where the plot moves along quickly and keeps the reader in suspense.

Fiction from other eras can be more difficult than modern fiction to understand. Stories from long ago can show how people in other times and places felt and thought. Many famous short stories and novels were written many years ago, and they may contain unfamiliar words or ideas, and word-pictures.

The most important skill a reader needs for enjoying fiction is the skill of imagining—of picturing along with the author the time, the place, the emotions of the characters. The reader must provide the picture, the voices, and even the sound effects for himself and be ready to travel anywhere—even into the mind of a character.

Reading fiction is a good way to improve general reading skills. The passage in the box on the next page is the opening of a story by Edgar Allan Poe. At first it may seem difficult, but the readers who master it will find that it raises many questions and makes them want to read on.

Sample Reading Comprehension Test

It might be best to let sleeping sea lions lie. At least this is what Mr. Snow, an explorer, thinks.

One July during the breeding season, he rowed up to an Arctic island through schools of sea lions. They showed no fright and no desire to fight. When he landed he came near the animals and called, "Come on there, you! Come on!"

A sudden roar and a great sea lion was hurtling toward him, his white tusks gleaming. Mr. Snow ran. This big fellow followed. It seemed easy to keep out of reach of the awkward animal. But straight ahead lay a cow with a young one! Mr. Snow knew that he was trapped. He struck frantically at the cow's head with a boat hook. She caught it out of the air and wrenched it from his hand. There was a great crunching and grinding. She was chewing the boat hook to splinters!

Now was Mr. Snow's chance to run. The bull was after him again, but he kept dodging round and round until the sea lion was tired out by the chase. The explorer finally returned to the boat, a wiser man.

1. **The selection is chiefly about**   a. a boat hook   b. a young sea lion   c. a mother   d. an explorer
2. **At first the sea lions were**   a. afraid   b. angry   c. peaceful   d. playful
3. **Which is most probable? The sea lion**   a. did not like the sound of the man's voice   b. was afraid of the man   c. knew he could trap the man   d. liked to fight
4. **Most probably the mother was angry because**   a. she wanted to protect her baby   b. she was a sea lion   c. she lay in the path   d. she did not like the explorer
5. **Sea lions have very strong**   a. tusks   b. tails   c. flippers   d. babies
6. **Sea lions move**   a. gracefully   b. clumsily   c. swiftly   d. crunching and grinding
7. **We may infer from the selection that the mother sea lion**   a. liked to eat wood   b. was playing with the explorer   c. wanted to keep Mr. Snow away   d. was showing one of her tricks
8. **As a result of Mr. Snow's narrow escape he was a**   a. jollier man   b. wiser man   c. more energetic man   d. kinder man

d c a a a b c b

Reading poetry. Poetry is language that has been condensed and that often uses special effects of sound and appearance to make an emotional impression on the reader. Much early poetry was set to music, and even modern poetry sometimes is particularly musical. Most poetry is meant to be *heard,* even when it is read silently, so it should be read slowly. Since its meanings may be very condensed, poetry usually must be read over several times before its full impact is felt.

Often the meanings of poetry are difficult to put into other words because the poetry appeals to the reader's emotions as well as to the mind. Emotions and feelings are personal matters for every reader of poetry. This is why readers will often disagree about the meaning of a poem.

The box on this page lists some of the special uses of language favored by poets. These uses may also be found in some kinds of prose.

Special Language in Poetry

alliteration. Deliberate repetition of sounds.
The fair breeze blew, the white foam flew,
The furrow followed free. . . .

hyperbole. Obvious and deliberate exaggeration, used to emphasize but not deceive.
It rained all night the day I left,
The weather it was dry,
It was so cold I froze to death,
Susanna don't you cry.

metaphor. A figure of speech in which a word or phrase is applied to an object, idea, or person to which it is not literally related.
Tiger! Tiger! burning bright
In the forests of the night . . .

onomatopoeia. Use of words that suggest by their sounds the object or idea being named; for example, *sizzle, twitter, buzz, hiss, coo, roar.*

personification. A figure of speech giving human qualities to animals, objects, or ideas.
His life was so gentle, and the elements
So mix'd in him, that Nature might stand up
And say to all the world, This was a man!

simile. A metaphor employing *like* or *as.*
My love is like a red, red rose . . .
I wandered lonely as a cloud . . .

Edgar Allan Poe "Ligeia"

I cannot, for my soul, remember how, when, or even precisely where, I first became acquainted with the lady Ligeia. Long years have since elapsed, and my memory is feeble through much suffering. Or, perhaps, I cannot *now* bring these points to mind, because, in truth, the character of my beloved, her rare learning, her singular yet placid cast of beauty, and the thrilling and enthralling eloquence of her low musical language, made their way into my heart by paces so steadily and stealthily progressive that they have been unnoticed and unknown. Yet I believe that I met her first and most frequently in some large, old, decaying city near the Rhine. Of her family—I have surely heard her speak. That it is of a remotely ancient date cannot be doubted. Ligeia! Ligeia! Buried in studies of a nature more than all else adapted to deaden impressions of the outward world, it is by that sweet word alone—by Ligeia—that I bring before mine eyes in fancy the image of her who is no more.

Emily Dickinson (A train)

I like to see it lap the miles,
And lick the valleys up,
And stop to feed itself at tanks;
And then, prodigious, step
Around a pile of mountains,
And, supercilious, peer
In shanties by the sides of roads;
And then a quarry pare
To fit its sides
And crawl between
Complaining all the while
In horrid, hooting stanza;
Then chase itself down hill
And neigh like Boanerges;
Then punctual as a star,
Stop—docile and omnipotent—
At its own stable door.

Improve your test-taking

Some students learn more than they are ever able to show on school tests because they are "test-shy." They may actually perform more poorly than students who know less than they do. Everyone wants to do as well as possible on tests, and good test-takers often have an advantage over classmates who do not test well. For these reasons, it is worthwhile to learn about tests and to become "test-wise."

Attitude. The first big step in improving your test-taking is to adopt the right attitude. Tests are designed to *measure* your mastery of a skill or your knowledge of a subject. They are not designed to embarrass you, fool you, or terrify you. In a sense, taking a test should be no harder than taking your temperature or measuring your feet for a new pair of shoes.

Forget about the students around you—what they do is of no concern. Forget about the teacher, about the plans you have for after school, and about anything else that may be on your mind. Until the test is over, the only two things that are important are you and the subject of the test. With this single-minded attitude, you are ready to concentrate and to do your very best. You may feel keyed up, like an athlete before a game. This can make you more alert and ready, but you should not feel anxious or worried.

Preparation. There are two kinds of preparation for any test. The first is study of the subject matter. If you do not know the subject matter, nothing else will help. Some students do study, but do not seem to master the material. They may read a chapter over and over, desperately trying to memorize hundreds of facts, or they may run in circles, trying over and over again to master a new kind of problem without having understood it first.

If the test is on subject matter from a book, try a different approach. Instead of reading the material over and over, read it once, then spend some time organizing it on a piece of paper. What are the two or three major facts or themes of the material? What are the important names or dates or other facts—those necessary to understanding the whole? Many of the other names and dates may be less important—in fact, some of them probably needn't be committed to memory at all.

A good breakfast on the day of a test will help give you the energy you need to do well.

If you are learning a skill, go back to an example—either in the book or in your notes—and follow it step by step, making sure that you see how the right answer was arrived at. Then take a new problem and follow exactly the same steps. If you still do not understand, ask for help from a classmate or teacher.

If you are having trouble, it is important that you start preparing for your test early. Otherwise, there will not be time to ask for help. Starting early is a good idea in any case. Especially when learning vocabulary in a foreign language or basic facts such as the multiplication table, your mind needs time and many repetitions to fix the information firmly. No amount of cramming the night before the test is likely to make up for work not done ahead of time. Even if you do manage to remember part of the material for the test, you will forget it soon afterward.

The second kind of preparation for any test has nothing at all to do with subject matter. It consists of making sure that you are ready physically and mentally to do well. One important factor is a good night's sleep. The day before a test, remember to take a few minutes now and then to relax. Finish your studying early so that you can get to bed and be ready to sleep on time. In the morning, eat a good breakfast. At the same time, train yourself to put aside any other worries or excitements for the few hours until the test is over. You need all your concentration skills for it.

How to Take a Test

There are many kinds of tests, and each requires a slightly different technique. There are a few tips, though, that apply to nearly all tests:

1. **Take a moment or two to look through the whole test.** Read all instructions carefully. Notice how many questions there are altogether, and try to get a sense of how much time you will have for each question. If one part is multiple choice, and a second part is an essay question, decide how much time you will spend on each part.

2. **Read each question carefully.** If you misunderstand the question, you will answer it wrong, no matter how much you know about the subject. Some tests have questions with tricky wording just to test your understanding. Especially if the question is complicated, read it a second time just to be sure.

3. **Skip questions you are not sure about.** It is best to answer all the questions that seem easy first; then you can use the remaining time to consider the more difficult questions. This will keep you from getting a mental block and will assure that you answer everything you know best before time runs out.

4. **Take the last two or three minutes to read through your answers.** This is especially important on essay tests. When you write quickly, you may leave out an important word, leaving a sentence or paragraph that makes no sense. In multiple-choice tests, be sure that you have put your answers in the right space or column and (if there is time) that each answer seems reasonable.

Kinds of tests.

The two main kinds of tests are multiple choice and essay tests.

Multiple choice tests. Multiple choice tests are most often used to test your mastery of facts. Be sure to read the question and each possible answer carefully. Sometimes, more than one answer may seem to be correct; in that case, choose the one that seems most accurate.

On short multiple-choice tests, you usually are graded on the number of right answers. This means that if you do not know the answer to a question, you can guess at the answer without being penalized.

On long multiple-choice tests—especially standardized reading, math, and other such tests—you are penalized for guessing. In this kind of test, you *should not* guess at an answer if you have no idea what the answer is. You *should* guess if you can eliminate one or more of the possible answers as being wrong.

Essay tests. Essay tests require you to put your ideas down on paper clearly. If there are several essay ques-

tions, it is important that you budget your time so that you will finish them all. Do not try to be the one who writes the most: quality is usually better than quantity. Take a few moments to organize your answers before you start to write. Then write slowly enough so that your handwriting is legible.

Learning from results.

In one sense, the test is over the moment you turn it in. But if you want to improve your test-taking, it's not really over until you get the test back. Then is the time to go over the results carefully to see just what errors or mistakes you may have made. Did you misunderstand one of the questions? Did you make any careless error? If there are more wrong answers toward the end, did you run out of time or energy?

If you can determine what you did wrong, you will be able to work on that particular aspect of test-taking and improve accordingly. As you do better, you will also begin to relax and to concentrate until you learn to do your very best in all testing situations.

Guide to good reading

One of the best ways to improve your reading is to take up reading as a hobby. Books are not just for study: millions find them a source of great entertainment as well. In fact, a well-written book can entertain and inform at the same time. It can be the most painless way to learn.

The following lists suggest over 100 books on a wide variety of subjects. No reader will find all of them interesting, but almost every reader will find some to his or her liking. The first (and longest) list is of fiction. Then come two shorter lists—one of poetry and folk tales and the second of books of nonfiction.

The reading level of the books varies—from intermediate (suitable for fourth or fifth grade) to difficult (suitable for ninth grade and above). No reading level markings have been given, however, because interest

often dictates reading level. You may read at a fourth grade level if a subject is boring to you, then read on an eighth grade level when the book's subject is one you really care about. If you find that a book on this list is too difficult, ask a teacher or librarian to recommend a less difficult book.

Many of the books listed here are easily available for purchase. Children's classics are often published in many editions. Some books, however—especially those on the nonfiction list—may be available only in libraries. If you are eager to find a particular book, try the library first. If you want to know whether a book can be purchased, ask a librarian to help you look it up in *Books in Print,* a huge catalog published each year that lists all books currently available.

For more ideas on good reading, see the section on Literature in Handbook 2.

Fiction. Most good fiction is entertaining while at the same time offering food for thought. Some stories help a reader understand the way people think and feel today. Others give a glimpse into the thoughts and feelings of people who lived in other times and places. Many of the books on this list are classics—stories that have been read

and loved by generations of young readers. A few represent newer books about contemporary life. If they are good enough, these new books may also become classics someday. Good books seem to grow better with age. Mediocre books, on the other hand, soon seem dated and are forgotten by later generations.

Alcott, Louisa May
Little Women
A classic American novel about four sisters growing up during the 1860s in New England. Other books by Alcott include *Eight Cousins* and *Little Men.*

Alexander, Lloyd
The High King
Newbery Award winner, the last of five fantasy novels about an imaginary kingdom that resembles ancient Wales.

Armstrong, William
Sounder
A black sharecropper must steal to support his family and his dog Sounder. His son is trying to understand his father's choices.

Asimov, Isaac
The Best New Thing
Science fiction about two children who live on a different planet.

Barrie, Sir James
Peter Pan and Wendy
Classic story about a flight to Never-Never Land with Peter Pan, the boy who refuses ever to grow up.

Baum, Lyman Frank
The Wizard of Oz
Fantasy about Dorothy, who is carried off by a tornado from Kansas to the Land of Oz; subject of a famous movie version. Baum wrote many sequels.

Blume, Judy
Are You There, God?
It's Me, Margaret
A contemporary story about the hopes and fears of an eleven-year-old girl. First of many books by a popular author for young readers.

Blume, Judy
It's Not the End of the World
How three children react when they learn that their parents are about to be divorced.

The Mad Hatter, Dormouse, and March Hare, from the Alice Window, a memorial to Lewis Carroll.

Wizard of Oz *characters opening the Kansas State Fair.*

Boston, Lucy M.
The Children of Green Knowe
First of a series about an old house where present-day children can meet children of the past.

Burnford, Sheila
The Incredible Journey
The epic travels of two dogs and a cat in search of their masters.

Byars, Betsy
The Summer of the Swans
A girl searches for her lost brother, who is mentally retarded. A Newbery Award book.

Carroll, Lewis
Alice's Adventures in Wonderland
Classic fantasy about a girl's adventures in a strange and illogical land.

Chew, Ruth
The Wednesday Witch
A witch rides a flying vacuum cleaner instead of a broom and meets mystery and adventure.

Cleary, Beverly
Ramona the Brave
A popular writer tells about the terrors of being in first grade.

Dahl, Roald
Charlie and the Chocolate Factory
Charlie discovers the amazing factory of Willie Wonka in a modern fantasy classic.

Defoe, Daniel
Robinson Crusoe
The adventures of a man cast ashore on a desert island. Among the most popular books in English for more than 250 years.

Dixon, Franklin W.
The Hardy Boys
This huge series of detective stories has appealed to readers for decades. Frank and Joe Hardy catch the imagination at first, but their adventures become repetitious.

Dodge, Mary Mapes
Hans Brinker, or The Silver Skates
Classic story about a Dutch family and Hans's wonderful ice skates.

Edmonds, Walter D.
The Matchlock Gun
A suspense-packed story about how a boy and his mother fight off Indians on the American frontier.

Farley, Walter
The Black Stallion
First of a series of appealing horse stories; subject of a prize-winning movie.

Fitzhugh, Louise
Harriet the Spy
The diary of a sharp-tongued eleven-year-old falls into the wrong hands.

Forbes, Esther
Johnny Tremain
An apprentice to a silversmith becomes a courier in the American Revolution.

Gipson, Fred
Old Yeller
A stray dog adopts a Texas family in the 1860s and defends them against all dangers.

Grahame, Kenneth
The Wind in the Willows
Classic fantasy about animals who live like human beings and have human problems.

Heinlein, Robert
Podkayne of Mars
Adventures of a 16-year-old girl on Mars by a master of science fiction.

Hitchcock, Alfred, editor
Alfred Hitchcock's Daring Detectives
One of several Hitchcock anthologies of great detective stories.

Juster, Norton
The Phantom Tollbooth
Milo discovers a fantasy land filled with odd creatures and questions about language.

Keene, Carolyn
Nancy Drew
A huge series about a girl detective. Interesting at first, but her adventures become repetitious.

Knight, Eric
Lassie Come Home
A classic dog story about Lassie's long journey in search of her master.

Konigsburg, E. L.
From the Mixed-Up Files of Mrs. Basil T. Frankweiler
Claudia and her younger brother run away and hide in the Metropolitan Museum of Art in New York. A Newbery Award winner.

Lawson, Robert
Ben and Me
A humorous look at the life of Ben Franklin, told by his resident mouse.

LeGuin, Ursula
A Wizard of Earthsea
First of five books about the land of Earthsea by an important science fiction writer.

L'Engle, Madeleine
A Wrinkle in Time
A sister and brother travel to the far reaches of the universe. First book of a trilogy.

Lewis, C. S.
The Chronicles of Narnia
A seven-book series about the mystical land of Narnia, popular both for its adventure and for its serious moral quest. The first book is *The Lion, The Witch, and the Wardrobe.*

Lindgren, Astrid
Pippi Longstocking
Pippi is a girl who lives with a monkey and a horse. Together they create fun and excitement wherever they go.

Lofting, Hugh
The Story of Doctor Dolittle
Delightful fantasy about an amazing—and magical—doctor. First of a series.

London, Jack
Call of the Wild
Classic story of a dog named Buck who returns to the wild to join a pack of wolves in Alaska.

Milne, A. A.
Winnie the Pooh
Whimsical stories about the stuffed bear Pooh and his friends, including the boy Christopher Robin.

North, Sterling
Rascal
The story of a boy and his pet raccoon.

Norton, Mary
The Borrowers
First of six volumes on a family of tiny people who live in the nooks and crannies of big people's houses.

O'Dell, Scott
Island of the Blue Dolphins
An Indian girl is cast away on an island off California, where she lives for 18 years.

Rawlings, Marjorie Kinnan
The Yearling
A classic story about a boy and his pet fawn.

Rogers, Mary
Freaky Friday
A 13-year-old girl suddenly becomes her own mother and must deal with adult problems.

Tom Sawyer whitewashing the fence.

Winnie the Pooh, Tigger, Piglet, and Eeyore at "The Tigger Movie" premiere.

Sobol, Donald
Encyclopedia Brown Saves the Day
First of a series about a boy detective.

Spyri, Johanna
Heidi
A young Swiss girl is uprooted from her mountain home, but succeeds in making friends wherever she goes.

Steinbeck, John
The Red Pony
The story of a boy and a horse by one of America's great writers.

Stevenson, Robert Louis
Treasure Island
A boy's adventures among pirates, the most popular of Stevenson's many adventure stories.

Swift, Jonathan
Gulliver's Travels
Famous satire about Gulliver's visits to strange lands; it is available in many editions for all ages.

Thurber, James
The Thirteen Clocks
A tale by America's great humorist about a wicked duke, a beautiful princess, and a handsome prince.

Tolkien, J. R. R.
The Hobbit
A fanciful creature must find a treasure guarded by a dragon. Tolkien's three-volume fantasy *Lord of the Rings* is also popular.

Travers, P. L.
Mary Poppins
Adventures of an English nursemaid who can fly. The first of a series.

Twain, Mark
The Adventures of Huckleberry Finn
Classic American novel about a footloose boy, son of the town drunk, who runs away on a raft down the Mississippi River with Jim, a runaway slave.

Twain, Mark
The Adventures of Tom Sawyer
Mischievous Tom is growing up in a small Missouri town in the mid-1800s. Filled with humor and adventure.

Verne, Jules
20,000 Leagues Under the Sea
This adventure story imagined submarines before one had ever been built.

White, E. B.
Charlotte's Web
A story of the friendship between a girl, her prize pig, and a spider named Charlotte. Also by White: *Stuart Little* and *Trumpet of the Swan.*

Wilder, Laura Ingalls
Little House in the Big Woods
First of a classic series of "Little House" books following the travels of a pioneer family in the 1870s and 1880s. The books were the basis of a popular television series.

Poetry and folk tales.

The earliest literature that came down to us was in poetic form. Before the advent of writing, the rhythm of poetic lines helped singers and storytellers remember the words. Often, this early literature told of great heroes of the past, preserving the memories for a tribe or a people. Many modern writers and poets have imitated the approach of folk literature, so the style is familiar even today. Folklore continues to survive and to be read and enjoyed all over the world. In fact, familiar stories and themes continue to reappear in new versions. Many of the world's cultures have a story like Cinderella, for example.

The books listed here are the works of both ancient and modern writers. Some are collections of poetry. Others are retellings in prose of the stories of old poems and legends. Still others are modern imitations of folklore.

Amusement park characters Hansel and Gretel at the Gingerbread Castle.

Aesop
Aesop's Fables
Famous animal fables from ancient Greece with morals that still make sense today.

Andersen, Hans Christian
Fairy Tales and Stories
Written by Andersen in the 1800s in the style of traditional fairy tales, these stories are filled with humor and pathos. Among the most popular are "The Ugly Duckling" and "The Emperor's New Clothes."

Arbuthnot, May Hill, and Sheldon L. Root, Jr., editors
Time for Poetry
Poems and verse from the time of Mother Goose to the present.

Bernos de Gasztold, Carmen
Prayers from the Ark
Amusing, often moving prayers of 26 animals on Noah's ark, translated by Rumer Godden.

Cole, William, editor
The Birds and the Beasts Were There: A Book of Nature Poems
One of several appealing anthologies compiled by this editor.

Colum, Padraic
The Children's Homer
A prose version of the great stories told by the Greek poet Homer in the *Iliad* and the *Odyssey*, telling of the war at Troy and of the legendary heroes and gods who fought there.

Colum, Padraic, editor
The Arabian Nights
Colum's retelling of tales from the Middle East. Includes stories of Aladdin, Sinbad the Sailor, and others. Many other editions.

Felton, Harold W.
Pecos Bill and the Mustang
American tall tales about a Southwestern cowboy legend. Felton's other books tell about Mike Fink, John Henry, and other legendary heroes.

Frost, Robert
You Come Too
A selection by the great American poet of his own poetry for young readers.

Grimm, Jakob and Wilhelm
Grimm's Fairy Tales
These very old stories and fables were collected in Germany by the Grimm brothers around 1800. They include "Hansel and Gretel," "Snow White," and many other dramatic and amusing tales.

Harris, Joel Chandler
Nights with Uncle Remus
Classic stories from black American folklore about Br'er Rabbit, Br'er Fox, and other animal heroes.

Kipling, Rudyard
Just So Stories
Humorous explanations of natural facts: how the camel got its hump and others.

From The Emperor's New Clothes

La Fontaine, Jean de
Fables

The great verse fables by this French writer are available in verse translation by American poet Marianne Moore.

Lang, Andrew, editor
The Blue Fairy Book

One of a series of tales collected by Lang from many parts of the world. Other collections have other colors: red, yellow, etc.

Larrick, Nancy, editor
I Heard a Scream in the Street

Poems by—and for—city kids.

Larrick, Nancy, editor
Piper, Pipe That Song Again

A much admired anthology of poetry for all ages.

Lear, Edward
The Complete Nonsense Book

Story poems, limericks, and nonsense from a great humorist of the 1800s.

Malory, Sir Thomas (Sidney Lanier, editor)
The Boy's King Arthur

A modern adaptation of Malory's telling of the legend of King Arthur and his Knights of the Round Table. Many other adaptations are available.

McCord, David
All Day Long: Fifty Rhymes of the Never Was and Always Is

Modern verses, both amusing and serious.

Merriam, Eve
There Is No Rhyme for Silver

One of several volumes of lively free verse by this writer.

Milne, A. A.
Now We Are Six

Whimsical verse about Pooh Bear and Christopher Robin. Appeals to readers older than six.

Perrault, Charles
Perrault's Complete Fairy Tales

The standard versions of many classic tales, collected 300 years ago by Perrault.

Pyle, Howard
The Merry Adventures of Robin Hood

One retelling of the great legends of Robin Hood's adventures in Sherwood Forest as an outlaw hero.

St. Exupery, Antoine
The Little Prince

A whimsical fable that appeals to all ages, by a famous French writer and aviator.

Stevenson, Robert Louis
A Child's Garden of Verses

The classic collection of poems by the gifted turn-of-the-century writer. Available in many editions.

White, Ann Terry
The Golden Treasury of Myths and Legends

Legends from Greece, Scandinavia, and other parts of the world.

Nonfiction.

The range of books on real people, places, and things is huge. Readers who are interested in a particular subject should learn to use a library, where books are carefully arranged by subject category for easy reference.

This list can give only a sampling of the richness of nonfiction books, ranging from science to art and music, from biography to ancient history.

Asimov, Isaac
Asimov's Guide to Science
A survey by a well-known science writer.

Asimov, Isaac
The Egyptians
The lives, beliefs, and activities of the residents of ancient Egypt.

Betterbury, Ariane and Michael
The Pantheon Story of American Art for Young People
A historical survey of the visual arts in the United States; heavily illustrated.

Bliven, Bruce, Jr.
The American Revolution
An exciting account of America's war for independence.

Bliven, Bruce, Jr.
The Story of D-Day: June 6, 1944
The story of the Allied landing in France during World War II.

Britten, Benjamin, and Imogen Holst
The Wonderful World of Music
Musical history and language, explained by a great modern composer.

Carson, Rachel
Silent Spring
Classic explanation of the effects of pollution and pesticides on plant and animal life.

Carson, Rachel
The Sea Around Us
A moving yet scientific look at the importance of the sea to world ecology.

Clayton, Ed
Martin Luther King: The Peaceful Warrior
Biography of the Nobel Prize winner and his struggle for civil rights.

Cohen, Robert
The Color of Man
What determines the skin and hair color and how racial prejudices have evolved.

Coit, Margaret
Andrew Jackson
Biography of a colorful and courageous President.

Coolidge, Olivia
Women's Rights: The Suffrage Movement in America 1840–1920
An account of women's long struggle to receive the right to vote.

Elting, Mary
All Aboard: The Trains That Built America
A lively account of the construction of the railroads and their colorful history.

Emrich, Duncan
The Hodge-Podge Book
An entertaining collection of folk wisdom, riddles, puzzles, verses, and nonsense.

Foster, Genevieve
George Washington's World
How people lived and what they believed in during Washington's lifetime.

Frank, Anne
The Diary of a Young Girl
The moving account of a Jewish family hiding from the Nazis during World War II.

Fritz, Jean
And Then What Happened, Paul Revere?
An amusing but accurate biography.

Gidal, Sonia
My Village in Hungary
One of a series of books on villages in many parts of the world. All are attractively illustrated.

Graham, Frank, Jr.
Since Silent Spring
A sequel to Rachel Carson's book *Silent Spring*, reporting on man's efforts to end water and air pollution.

Gutman, Bill
Duke Ellington
Biography of the great jazz performer and composer.

Anne Frank, The Diary of a Young Girl

Women's suffrage headquarters in Cleveland, Ohio, 1912.

Kelly, Regina Z.
John F. Kennedy
Biography of a President who especially appealed to young people.

Krementz, Jill
A Very Young Dancer
A photographic account of the rigorous life of a young ballet student.

Lorimer, Lawrence, editor
Breaking In
First-person accounts by nine well-known athletes, telling of their early struggles to succeed.

Macauley, David
Cathedral
An illustrated description of the way a medieval cathedral was built. Also by this author, similar books on an Egyptian pyramid and a skyscraper.

McHargue, Georgess
Meet the Werewolf
A look at the lore and superstition about werewolves.

McNeer, Mary
The California Gold Rush
An exciting account of a colorful period in American history.

McWhirter, Norris and Ross
The Guinness Book of World Records
A vast compendium of useful and not-so-useful facts. There are many shorter Guinness collections for young readers.

Renault, Mary
The Lion in the Gateway
The story of the great ancient war between the Greeks and the Persians by a famous novelist.

Sarnoff, Jane, and Reynolds Ruffins
The Code and Cipher Book
Explanations and examples of secret writing.

Savage, Katharine
The Story of World Religion
How the major religions began and grew, and what they believe and practice today.

Shaw, Arnold
The Rock Revolution
The story of the growth of rock music in the 1950s and 1960s.

For Further Reference

Fry, Ronald W.
 How to Study
 Career Press
Gilbert, Sara
 How to Take Tests
 William Morrow
James, Elizabeth and Doty, Roy
 How to Be School Smart
 Lothrop, Lee & Shepard
Kornhauser, Arthur William
 How to Study
 University of Chicago Press
Wikler, Janet
 How to Study and Learn
 Franklin Watts

Social Studies

• United States History 106

• United States Today 134

- *Explorers and colonies*   **106**
- *A nation is born*   **110**
- *Expansion and Civil War*   **115**
- *Growing and changing*   **122**
- *Boom, bust, war*   **125**
- *Modern America*   **129**

United States History

The United States of America has a shorter history than that of the countries of Europe or Asia. The land was discovered less than 1,000 years ago. Settlement began less than 500 years ago, and the country itself has been independent barely 225 years. But in that time, it has grown rapidly in population, power, and influence.

The following pages provide a brief outline of U.S. history, beginning with the earliest explorers and ending at the present day. For more information about the government and people of the United States, see Handbook 2. For more information about the events of September 11, 2001, and their aftermath, see the World History section in Handbook 2.

Explorers and colonies

The early history of the North American continent is lost in time. Descendants of the Native Americans arrived in North America perhaps 10,000 years ago from Asia. By 1500, there were some 1.5 million of them in North America. They were divided into hundreds of tribes, spoke many different languages, and kept no written records.

In the late 1400s, the kingdoms of Europe were seeking to expand. They explored both land and sea in search of treasure, trade, and new possessions. In seeking a better route to the Orient, they discovered the Americas. But for 100 years, they sent only explorers to North America.

Then, beginning in 1587, the English began serious attempts to send colonists to the new lands. Within 200 years, there were nearly 4 million Europeans along the Atlantic coast, forming the nucleus of what was soon to become the United States.

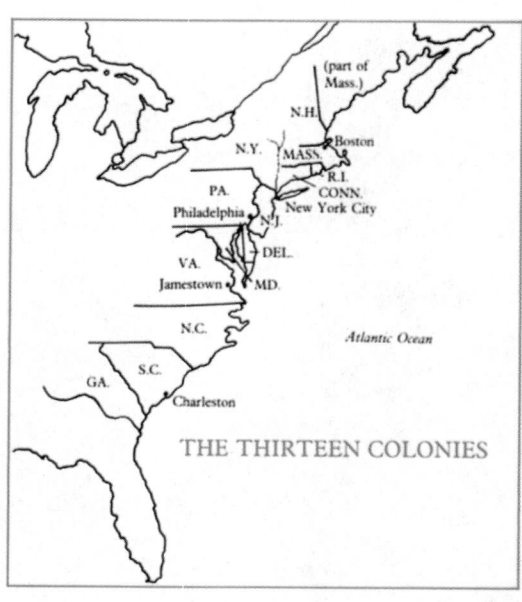

THE THIRTEEN COLONIES

Date	Event
c 1000	**The Vikings,** sailing under the leadership of Leif Ericsson, reach the continent of North America. They make landfalls in Labrador and Newfoundland.
1492–1502	**Christopher Columbus,** searching for a water route to Asia to the west, makes four voyages to the Western Hemisphere. He reaches the islands of the Caribbean and the Central and South American coasts. He claims the newly found lands for Spain, under whose flag he sails.
1497–1498	**John Cabot,** sailing for England, explores the coast of North America in search of a water route across North America to Asia. He claims the land for England.
1513	**Ponce de León,** having already found gold in Puerto Rico, explores Florida in search of the legendary "fountain of youth."
1524	**Giovanni da Verrazano,** sailing for France, explores the North American coast while searching for a waterway west. Because of his explorations, France claims North America.
1534–1536	**Jacques Cartier** penetrates the North American continent by traveling southward and westward along the St. Lawrence River.
1539–1542	**Hernando De Soto,** searching for gold, explores from Florida westward to Oklahoma.
1540–1542	**Francisco Coronado** leads an expedition in search of the legendary "Seven Cities of Gold" through the Southwest. In his travels, he comes upon the Grand Canyon.
1565	**The Spanish establish the first permanent settlement** in what will become the United States, at St. Augustine in Florida.
1587	**The English establish a settlement on Roanoke Island** off the coast of North Carolina. It fails and its inhabitants disappear, including the first child born of English parents in North America, Virginia Dare.
1607	**The English establish their first permanent settlement in America,** at Jamestown in Virginia. Captain John Smith is its leader.
1608	**Samuel de Champlain** establishes a French settlement at Quebec on the St. Lawrence River.
1609	**Henry Hudson,** sailing for the Dutch East India Company, explores the Chesapeake, Delaware, and New York bays and sails up the Hudson River, claiming the region for the Dutch.
	The Spanish establish a settlement at Santa Fe in New Mexico to serve as the center of Spanish government in northern Mexico.
1619	**The House of Burgesses** is established in Virginia. It is North America's first colonial legislature.
	The first blacks arrive in America, as indentured servants. Within a few years, blacks are brought to North America as slaves.
1620	**The Pilgrims,** seeking religious freedom they do not have in England, land on the coast of Massachusetts. Led by William Bradford, they draw up a plan of government, the Mayflower Compact, and found the settlement of Plymouth.

Date	Event

Left, *a replica of the* Mayflower. Right, *Peter Minuit buys Manhattan Island from the Indians.*

1626

Peter Minuit, acting for the Dutch, buys the island of Manhattan from the Indians for $24 worth of goods. The Dutch establish the settlement of New Amsterdam there and found other settlements in New Netherland, an area extending from Delaware Bay in the south northward up the Hudson River.

1628–1630

The Puritans, also seeking the religious freedom denied them in England, establish the Massachusetts Bay Colony under the leadership of John Winthrop.

1634

George Calvert, Lord Baltimore, an English Catholic, founds the colony of Maryland, where Catholics find religious freedom.

1636

Roger Williams, who disagrees with the religious practices of the Puritans in the Massachusetts Bay Colony, is driven out of the colony and founds the colony of Rhode Island.

Thomas Hooker, also in disagreement with Massachusetts Puritans, leaves and founds the colony of Connecticut.

Harvard College is founded, the first college in the English colonies in North America.

1639

The Fundamental Orders of Connecticut, considered the first written constitution in America, are drawn up to govern the colony.

1647

In Massachusetts, the first laws providing for the establishment of **public schools** are passed.

1649

The Maryland Toleration Act grants religious freedom to all Christians who settle in the colony.

1660, 1663

England passes the Navigation Acts, which place restrictions on colonial trade. The acts make it necessary to transport goods only in English-owned ships, to pay taxes to England on colonial goods, and to ship certain goods only to Britain.

1664

The English gain control of New Netherland by ousting the Dutch governor, Peter Stuyvesant. New Amsterdam is renamed New York.

1673

Father Jacques Marquette and Louis Jolliet, sailing for France, travel up the St. Lawrence River, through the Great Lakes, and down the Mississippi to the Gulf of Mexico.

1676

Bacon's Rebellion begins as Nathaniel Bacon leads a small group of farmers to rise up against the English governor of Virginia. The farmers claim that they are not adequately represented in the colony's government, that their taxes are too high, and that they are not protected by the government from Indian attacks.

Date	*Event*
1682	**Robert de La Salle** follows a route similar to Marquette's and Jolliet's and claims the Mississippi River valley for France. He names it Louisiana after the French King Louis XIV.
	William Penn, a wealthy English Quaker, establishes the colony of Pennsylvania, where Quakers, as well as other Protestants, Catholics, and Jews can enjoy religious freedom.
1699	**The French begin to establish trading posts** along the Mississippi River and the Gulf coast. They also begin moving into the valley of the Ohio River.
1712	Twelve wealthy British proprietors establish **North and South Carolina.**
1732	**James Oglethorpe** establishes the colony of Georgia as a place where people imprisoned for debt in Great Britain can settle and start life anew.
1733	**The British pass the Molasses Act** in an attempt to force the colonists to buy molasses only from the British West Indies.
1735	**John Peter Zenger,** a newspaper publisher, is placed on trial for printing articles criticizing the British governor of New York. He is acquitted and the principle of freedom of the press is established in the colonies.
1754	**Several colonies send representatives to Albany** in New York to try to adopt a plan to unite the 13 colonies under one central government. The colonial governments reject the Albany Plan of Union, first proposed by Benjamin Franklin.

1754–1763	**THE FRENCH AND INDIAN WAR.** Britain and France, longtime enemies, wage war in both Europe and North America; each claims ownership of the same territory. From 1754 to 1763, the British and the colonists fight the French and their Indian allies in North America in battles that come to be called the French and Indian War.
1754	A force of Virginia militia, under the command of 22-year-old George Washington, builds Fort Necessity, near the French Fort Duquesne (the site of present-day Pittsburgh) to establish a British presence in the Ohio River valley. The French attack and defeat Washington near Fort Necessity.
1755	General Edward Braddock, in command of 2,500 British redcoats, marches on Fort Duquesne to attack the French. French and Indian troops defeat them soundly, killing Braddock and nearly half his force.
1758	Generals Jeffrey Amherst and James Wolfe capture Louisbourg, a French fortress in Canada. General James Forbes captures Fort Duquesne and drives the French out.
1759	General James Wolfe attacks the French city of Quebec, defended by Louis Joseph de Montcalm. Both commanders are killed, but the British are victorious and capture Quebec.
1763	The Treaty of Paris ends the war and grants Britain control of Canada and lands east of the Mississippi River.

A nation is born

Disagreements between the British government and its colonies in America grew serious in the 1760s. The British saw the colonies as possessions. The colonists, however, sought to govern themselves. The arguments led to war in 1775, and on July 4, 1776, the colonies declared their independence. Five years later, the British were defeated and soon recognized the United States.

The new nation then turned its attention to its two major jobs. The first was to form a lasting government. In 1787, a new Constitution was drawn up, providing a stronger central government. The second job was to develop the vast American lands. By 1814, the United States controlled more than half the continent and had gained new respect among world nations.

Date

Event

1763	**Britain's Proclamation of 1763** prohibits American settlers from moving west of the Appalachian Mountains because British soldiers cannot protect them from unfriendly Indians there. This is the first of several British acts that will anger the American colonists and turn them against Britain.
1764–1765	**Parliament passes the Grenville Acts**—the Sugar, Currency, Quartering, and Stamp acts. The acts call for new duties and taxes from the colonists, forbid colonists from issuing paper money, and force them to house British soldiers.
1766	**Parliament repeals the Stamp Act** after colonists resist paying the taxes it calls for and threaten tax collectors with violence.
1767	**Parliament passes the Townshend Acts,** imposing new duties on colonists for tea and other goods and giving British troops the right to search any colonist's property.
1769–1782	**Father Junípero Serra** and other Franciscan friars establish 21 missions in California.
1770	**The Boston Massacre** erupts as Bostonians, angry at British acts, taunt British soldiers and are fired upon. Five colonists are killed.
	All the Townshend Acts are repealed except for the tax on tea. The British leave that tax to show that they still claim the right to tax the colonists.

Above, *the stamp Britain required colonists to buy to put on all newspapers and documents (1765).* Right, *the Boston Tea Party (1773).*

Date	Event
1773	**The Boston Tea Party** takes place as 50 American patriots dressed as Indians board three ships in Boston Harbor. Angry over a new Tea Act that forces them to buy British tea, they throw all the tea the ships carry overboard into the harbor.
1774	**Parliament passes the Coercive, or Intolerable, Acts,** closing Boston Harbor to shipping, placing Massachusetts under military rule, and forcing Massachusetts colonists to house British soldiers sent to carry out the acts.
	The First Continental Congress meets in Philadelphia as twelve colonies send representatives to protest British actions and to urge the formation of a Massachusetts militia.
1775	**The first military conflicts** between the British and Americans occur at Lexington and Concord in Massachusetts as British soldiers attempt to capture a storehouse of American weapons.
	The Second Continental Congress meets in Philadelphia and names George Washington to command American troops fighting around Boston, which the British have under siege. Before he arrives, British and American troops clash at Breed's Hill and Bunker Hill.
1776	**Thomas Paine,** a writer recently arrived from Britain, publishes *Common Sense,* a pamphlet that urges the American colonies to throw off British rule.
	The Declaration of Independence is signed in Philadelphia after the Second Continental Congress decides that the colonies must break away from British rule.

Declaration of Independence

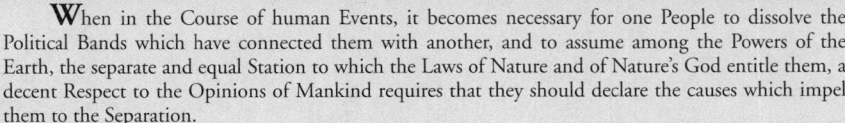

When in the Course of human Events, it becomes necessary for one People to dissolve the Political Bands which have connected them with another, and to assume among the Powers of the Earth, the separate and equal Station to which the Laws of Nature and of Nature's God entitle them, a decent Respect to the Opinions of Mankind requires that they should declare the causes which impel them to the Separation.

We hold these Truths to be self-evident, that all Men are created equal, that they are endowed by their Creator with certain unalienable Rights, that among these are Life, Liberty, and the Pursuit of Happiness—That to secure these Rights, Governments are instituted among Men, deriving their just Powers from the Consent of the Governed, that whenever any Form of Government becomes destructive of these Ends, it is the Right of the People to alter or to abolish it, and to institute new Government, laying its Foundation on such Principles, and organizing its Powers in such Form, as to them shall seem most likely to effect their Safety and Happiness. Prudence, indeed, will dictate that Governments long established should not be changed for light and transient Causes; and accordingly all Experience hath shewn, that Mankind are more disposed to suffer, while Evils are sufferable, than to right themselves by abolishing the Forms to which they are accustomed. But when a long Train of Abuses and Usurpations, pursuing invariably the same Object, evinces a Design to reduce them under absolute Despotism, it is their Right, it is their Duty, to throw off such Government, and to provide new Guards for their future Security. Such has been the patient Sufferance of these Colonies; and such is now the Necessity which constrains them to alter their former Systems of Government.

(Here follows a list of specific complaints against the King and the British government.)

We, therefore, the Representatives of the UNITED STATES OF AMERICA, in GENERAL CONGRESS, Assembled, appealing to the Supreme Judge of the World for the Rectitude of our Intentions, do, in the Name, and by Authority of the good People of these Colonies, solemnly Publish and Declare, That these United Colonies are, and of Right ought to be, FREE AND INDEPENDENT STATES; that they are absolved from all Allegiance to the British Crown, and that all political Connection between them and the State of Great-Britain, is and ought to be totally dissolved; and that as FREE AND INDEPENDENT STATES, they have full Power to levy War, conclude Peace, contract Alliances, establish Commerce, and to do all other Acts and Things which INDEPENDENT STATES may of right do. And for the support of this Declaration, with a firm Reliance on the Protection of divine Providence, we mutually pledge to each other our Lives, our Fortunes, and our sacred Honor.

Date	Event
Date	*Event*
1775–1783	**THE AMERICAN REVOLUTION.** Even before the Declaration of Independence was signed, British troops began arriving to put down the rebellion. They would not leave for another five years.
1776	The British finally leave Boston, but they capture New York City after fighting General Washington and his troops. The Americans retreat to Pennsylvania.
1776–1777	In a surprise move on the British and their Hessian mercenaries, Washington captures British garrisons at Trenton and Princeton, New Jersey, taking weapons and ammunition.
	American troops defeat combined forces of the British at Saratoga, New York. A turning point in the war, this victory strengthens American morale and convinces the French to send military aid and supplies to the Americans.
1777–1778	During the bitter winter, American soldiers face starvation and disease at Valley Forge, Pennsylvania. However, they also receive solid military training and come out a stronger army.
1778	The war moves south as the British capture the port city of Savannah, Georgia.
1779	The most famous naval battle of the war is fought as the American ship *Bonhomme Richard,* under Captain John Paul Jones, defeats and captures the British ship *Serapis.*
1780	The British capture a second major port city in the South, Charleston, South Carolina.
1780–1781	In a series of running battles in the Carolinas at Camden, King's Mountain, Cowpens, and Guilford Court House, the British withdraw to the Atlantic coast.
1781	British troops are trapped at Yorktown, Virginia, as the French fleet cuts off any resupply or escape and as American armies surround them. The British surrender, convincing the British government to end the long and costly war.
1783	The Treaty of Paris, drawn up by the British and American representatives Benjamin Franklin, John Adams, and John Jay, is signed. Through it, the British recognize American independence and cede rights to the rich Ohio valley to the new nation.

Washington visits his troops during the winter at Valley Forge.

Date	Event
1781	**The Articles of Confederation** are adopted by the Continental Congress. They unite the new states and organize a central government.
1785	**The Land Ordinance** is passed by Congress. It tells how the lands to the west of the 13 states will be settled and governed.
1786	**Shays's Rebellion** erupts as Daniel Shays, a Massachusetts farmer, leads other farmers in an armed revolt against the Massachusetts legislature, protesting heavy taxes. The state militia puts down the rebellion.
1787	**The Northwest Ordinance** is passed. It creates the Northwest Territory, made up of part of the Ohio and Mississippi valleys, and provides that it will be divided into several states (eventually Ohio, Indiana, Illinois, Michigan, and Wisconsin).
	A Constitutional Convention is called in Philadelphia when it becomes clear that the government set up by the Articles of Confederation cannot deal adequately with the nation's problems. Fifty-five delegates from twelve states attend, and George Washington serves as president of the convention. In September, the delegates adopt the Constitution, but the states must ratify it.
	The Federalist begins publication. It is a series of essays written by Alexander Hamilton, James Madison, and John Jay in support of the Constitution.
1788	**The Constitution** is ratified by three-fourths of the states and becomes the law of the land.
1789	**George Washington** is elected the first President of the United States and takes the oath of office in the temporary national capital at New York City.
1791	**The Bill of Rights** is ratified and becomes the first ten amendments to the Constitution.
	The Bank of the United States receives its first government charter, to run until 1811.
	Two political parties emerge—Federalists and Democratic-Republicans.
1793	**Eli Whitney** invents the cotton gin. It makes raising cotton highly profitable and causes a demand for more and more slaves, as new southern lands are planted with cotton.
	War between Britain and France leads to their harassment of American shipping and to British impressment of sailors from American ships. A period of crisis among the countries arises.
1794	**The Whiskey Rebellion** erupts in western Pennsylvania as whiskey-producing frontier people protest a new whiskey tax. A federal militia puts down the rebellion with no loss of life.
	The Jay Treaty, negotiated by John Jay with the British, fails to end British impressment of American sailors but does extract a promise to clear British troops out of the Northwest Territory, where many of them are still stationed.
1795	**The Pinckney Treaty,** negotiated by Charles C. Pinckney with Spain, gives Americans free use of the Mississippi River and allows them to set up warehouses for American goods in New Orleans.

Date	Event
Date	*Event*
1797	**The XYZ Affair** occurs when three agents of the French government (referred to as X, Y, and Z) demand huge bribes from the United States in return for peaceful relations between the French and American nations.
1798	**The Alien and Sedition Acts** are passed as President John Adams and other Federalists attempt to quiet criticism of their administration with new laws. Kentucky and Virginia pass resolutions saying that such laws are null and void.
1800	**Thomas Jefferson,** a Democratic-Republican, defeats John Adams for the Presidency in a very close vote. Aaron Burr is Jefferson's Vice President.
1801	**John Marshall** becomes chief justice of the Supreme Court, a post he will hold for the next 34 years, during which many important and lasting decisions will be made. In 1803, Marshall's decision in ***Marbury v. Madison*** establishes the principle that the Supreme Court has the right to decide whether laws passed by Congress are constitutional.
1803	**The Louisiana Purchase** is made when President Jefferson buys the Louisiana Territory from France for $15 million. The purchase doubles the nation's size.
1804–1806	On instructions from President Jefferson, **Meriwether Lewis and William Clark** lead a party of 30 to explore the Louisiana Territory. They travel beyond it, to the Pacific.
1807	**Congress passes the Embargo Act,** forbidding American ships to call on any foreign port after France and Britain both interfere with American shipping.
	Robert Fulton develops the first successful steamboat, inaugurating an era of steamboat shipping and travel on the nation's rivers, lakes, and coastal waterways.
1812–1814	**THE WAR OF 1812.** Continued British interference with American shipping, as well as British encouragement of Indians to attack American frontier settlements, finally causes President Madison and Congress to declare war. Britain, involved in war with France, can spare few troops to fight the war.
1812	A three-pronged American attack on British-held Canada fails.
	The USS *Constitution* ("Old Ironsides") defeats the British *Guerriere* in sea battle.
1813	Captain Oliver Hazard Perry scores a naval victory on Lake Erie and forces the British to leave Detroit.
	General William Henry Harrison attacks British troops retreating from Detroit and the Indian allies. The Indian leader Tecumseh is killed, and the Indians desert the British cause.
1814	The British attack Washington, D.C., and burn the White House.
	The British bombard Fort McHenry near Baltimore, and Francis Scott Key writes "The Star-Spangled Banner" after witnessing the bombardment.
	The Treaty of Ghent is signed in Belgium, ending the War of 1812.
	General Andrew Jackson defeats a British attack on New Orleans. Neither side knows that the war has already been ended by the Treaty of Ghent.

Expansion and Civil War

The period from 1815 to 1880 was one of amazing growth for the United States. Huge parts of the continent were settled; millions of new immigrants arrived from Ireland, Germany, and a great many other countries. The nation became increasingly connected by new roads, canals, railroads, and telegraph wires. By 1880, the United States had acquired all its present territory except Hawaii.

At the same time, the country suffered its most disastrous war. The great Civil War was fought over the issue of black slavery and over many political and economic disagreements between North and South. For four years, the nation was divided, and brother fought against brother. Finally the North won, and the country was reunited, but scars of the war took decades to heal.

Date	Event
1816	**The Tariff of 1816** is passed by Congress to encourage the manufacture of American goods.
	The Second Bank of the United States is chartered.
	The Era of Good Feelings begins as James Monroe is elected to the Presidency.
1816–1817	**The American Colonization Society** is founded to transport free slaves back to a newly founded country in Africa called Liberia. It is an early attempt to abolish slavery.
1818	The United States and Great Britain agree to joint occupation of the **Oregon Territory.**
1819	In *McCulloch v. Madison,* the Supreme Court determines that the Second Bank of the United States is constitutional.
	Through the Adams-Onis Treaty, the United States gains Florida from Spain for $5 million.

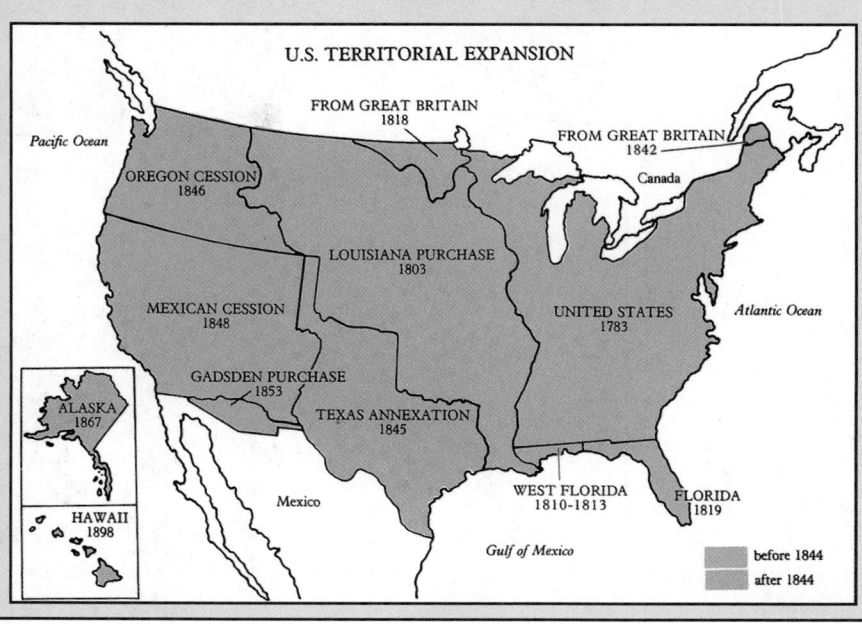

U.S. TERRITORIAL EXPANSION

Date	Event
1820	**The Missouri Compromise,** proposed in Congress by Henry Clay of Kentucky, is reached, maintaining the balance between northern and southern states in Congress by admitting Maine as a free state and Missouri as a slave state. The compromise also states that slavery will not be allowed in any other territory that is part of the Louisiana Purchase.
1821	**Stephen Austin** establishes an American colony in Texas, a part of Mexico. **Emma Willard** opens the Troy Female Seminary, offering collegiate education to American women for the first time.
1823	**The Monroe Doctrine** is proclaimed. President Monroe declares that there shall be no more conquest or colonization in the Western Hemisphere by European nations.
1825	**John Quincy Adams** is elected President by the House of Representatives after the electoral college is unable to provide a clear winner. **The Erie Canal,** linking the Hudson River to the Great Lakes, is completed.

The Erie Canal as it passes through Rochester, New York.

Date	Event
1828	**Andrew Jackson** is elected President and the Democratic Party emerges in the two-party system.
1830	**Peter Cooper** develops the steam locomotive *Tom Thumb*, capable of going 10 miles an hour. **Nat Turner,** a Virginia slave preacher, leads his followers in a rebellion against their slave masters. After the deaths of over 50 whites, Turner is captured and executed. **The Webster-Hayne debates** take place on the floor of Congress as Daniel Webster of Massachusetts and Robert Y. Hayne of South Carolina debate states' rights and whether any state has the right to nullify a federal law. *The Liberator,* a newspaper that demands the abolition of slavery, is founded by William Lloyd Garrison. It strengthens the abolition movement.

Date	Event
Date	*Event*
1832	**The forcible removal of Indians from their homes** in Georgia to lands in the West is ordered by President Jackson, defying a Supreme Court decision.
1833	**President Jackson smashes the Second Bank of the United States,** which leads to the strengthening of Democratic-owned state banks, soon called "pet banks."
1834	**Cyrus McCormick** patents the mechanical reaper, which will soon increase farm production.
1836	**The Whig Party** emerges in the two-party system.
	Texas declares itself independent of Mexico, fights the Battle of the Alamo against Mexican troops, and forms the Texas, or Lone Star, Republic.
1837	**John Deere** introduces the steel plow, which at last makes it possible to farm the Great Plains.
	The Panic of 1837 begins when a boom in land speculation and easy credit ends in depression.
1839	**The Liberty Party** is founded to foster antislavery movements.
	Charles Goodyear develops the vulcanization process that will start a thriving rubber industry.
1842	**The Webster-Ashburton Treaty** settles a dispute with Britain over Maine's boundaries.
1844	**Samuel F. B. Morse** puts the telegraph into operation between Washington, D.C., and Baltimore, Maryland.
1845	**Texas** is added to the Union.
1846	**The Oregon Treaty** divides Oregon between Britain and the United States along the 49th parallel.

1846–1848	**THE MEXICAN WAR.** Eager to see the nation stretch across the continent, several American Presidents offer to buy the Mexican lands of the West and Southwest, but Mexico does not want to sell. To many, war seems the way to get the lands once and for all.
1846	American troops are sent to Texas when a border dispute erupts with Mexico over Texas's rightful boundaries. Mexican troops cross the Rio Grande and attack the American troops. Congress declares war on Mexico and Mexico replies in kind.
	The Bear Flag Revolt erupts in California, a part of Mexico, as American settlers there proclaim their independence from Mexican rule.
1847	General Zachary Taylor and his American troops capture the Mexican cities of Matamoras and Monterrey. General Winfield Scott and his troops take the city of Veracruz and begin a march toward the capital, Mexico City. After defeating Mexican troops under General Antonio Santa Anna, they capture the capital.
1848	The Treaty of Guadalupe Hidalgo ends the war. Mexico cedes the entire Southwest to the United States, for $15 million.

Date	Event
Date	*Event*
1846	**The Wilmot Proviso** is declared on the floor of Congress, stating that "neither slavery nor involuntary servitude shall ever exist" in lands acquired from Mexico.
1847	**The Mormons** end their long trek westward when they reach the Great Salt Lake in Utah.
	Elias Howe patents the sewing machine.
1848	**The Seneca Falls Convention** meets in New York to demand equal rights for women, including the right to vote.
	Gold is discovered at Sutter's mill near Sacramento, California, touching off a gold rush.

Gold miners in California

1850	**The Compromise of 1850,** proposed by Henry Clay, is reached when California tries to enter the Union as a free state. To maintain the North-South balance in the Senate, California is allowed in, but New Mexico and Utah are allowed to choose for themselves whether they want slavery. A tough new Fugitive Slave Law is passed to help slave owners recapture their slaves who have escaped to the North.
1851	**Congress adopts the first reservation policy for Indians,** setting off certain lands for them.
1851–1856	**Henry Bessemer and William Kelly** each discover the same process for producing large quantities of steel. The development of a giant steel industry begins.
1852	*Uncle Tom's Cabin,* a novel by Harriet Beecher Stowe about the cruelties of slavery, is published. It triggers a great new surge of antislavery feeling in the North.
	Elisha Otis develops the electric elevator, which will make skyscrapers possible.
1853	**The Gadsden Purchase** is approved by Congress. Fifteen million dollars is paid to Mexico for a piece of land that will become part of Arizona and New Mexico.

Date	Event
1854	**The Kansas-Nebraska Act** is passed, a compromise between slavery and antislavery forces. It creates two new territories—Kansas and Nebraska—and says that the territories can decide for themselves whether to have slavery.
	The Republican Party is formed as antislavery forces from both the Whigs and Democrats unite.
1856	**"Bleeding Kansas"** begins as proslavery and antislavery forces battle each other in bloody ambushes and attacks in the Kansas Territory.
1857	**In the *Dred Scott* decision,** the Supreme Court rules that slaves are not citizens of the United States, that living in free states does not free slaves, and that the Missouri Compromise was unconstitutional because Congress did not have the right to exclude slavery.
1858	**Abraham Lincoln and Stephen A. Douglas,** running for Congress from Illinois, hold a series of debates in which matters related to slavery figure importantly. The debates give Lincoln a national reputation.
1859	**John Brown,** an antislavery fighter from "Bleeding Kansas," leads a raid on a federal arsenal at Harpers Ferry, Virginia, to seize guns and ammunition for a slave revolt. U.S. Army troops under Colonel Robert E. Lee capture Brown and his followers. Brown is executed for his actions.
	Edwin Drake builds the nation's first oil derrick in Titusville, Pennsylvania, signaling the beginning of the American oil industry.
1860	**Abraham Lincoln,** running as the candidate of the Republican Party, is elected President.
1860–1861	**South Carolina secedes** from the Union and all the other states of the lower South—Mississippi, Florida, Alabama, Georgia, Louisiana, and Texas—follow suit.
1861	Representatives of the seven states that seceded meet in Montgomery, Alabama, to form a new nation, **the Confederate States of America,** with Jefferson Davis of Mississippi as President.
Confederate flag	**The Confederates attack federally held Fort Sumter** in the harbor of Charleston, South Carolina, triggering the Civil War. Virginia, Tennessee, Arkansas, and North Carolina join the Confederacy. The Confederate capital moves from Montgomery, Alabama, to Richmond, Virginia (see next page).
1862	**The Homestead Act** is passed; the government will grant 160 acres of public land to anyone who pays a small registration fee and lives on the homestead for five years. This measure helped settle the plains states.
	The Morrill Act is passed. The government grants the states large tracts of land for them to sell and utilize the proceeds for agricultural and industrial education.
1863	**The Emancipation Proclamation** is signed by President Lincoln, granting freedom to all slaves living in states still involved in rebellion.
1864	**George M. Pullman** develops a sleeping car for the railroads.

Date	Event
1861–1865	**THE CIVIL WAR.** Slavery is one point of disagreement between the North and the South, but there are others. There are quarrels over tariffs and over the rights that states have as part of the Union, as well as differences between the highly industrial North and the highly agricultural South. With secession and the attack on Fort Sumter, the disagreements finally bring on war.
1861	The first battle of Bull Run begins as Union forces marching from Washington, D.C., clash with Confederate troops at Manassas Junction in Virginia. The Union army is forced to retreat.
1862	At Shiloh, Tennessee, a Confederate attack on General Ulysses S. Grant and his Union army fails, and the Confederate troops withdraw after two days of bloody fighting.
	The second battle of Bull Run takes place as Union troops, trying to capture the Confederate capital at Richmond, Virginia, are defeated by Confederate troops under General Robert E. Lee.
	A Union fleet defeats a Confederate fleet on the Mississippi River near Memphis, takes Memphis, and gains control of the entire upper Mississippi.
	At Antietam Creek in Maryland, Confederate troops marching to attack Pennsylvania are stopped by Union troops under General George B. McClellan. They retreat to Virginia.
	At Fredericksburg, Virginia, Union forces are defeated again as they try for Richmond.
1863	At Chancellorsville, Virginia, another Union attempt on Richmond is defeated by Lee's troops.
	At Gettysburg, Lee is again defeated in his march on Pennsylvania and he retreats to Virginia.
	Vicksburg, Mississippi, falls to Union forces. This puts the entire Mississippi River under Union control.
1863–1864	"Sherman's March to the Sea" begins as Union troops under the command of General William T. Sherman march from Chickamauga, Georgia, to Atlanta to Savannah, cutting a path of destruction as they march.
1864–1865	Union troops under Grant repeatedly engage Confederate troops under Lee in Virginia at the Wilderness, Spotsylvania, Cold Harbor, and Petersburg.
1865	Lee surrenders to Grant at Appomattox Courthouse in Virginia and the Civil War ends.

Civil War cemetery, Shiloh National Military Park, at Savannah, Tennessee.

Date	Event
Date	*Event*
1865	**The Freedmen's Bureau** is established by Congress to help recently freed slaves to start life anew.
	President Lincoln is assassinated at Ford's Theater in Washington, D.C., by an actor and Confederate sympathizer, John Wilkes Booth. Andrew Johnson succeeds Lincoln.
	The 13th Amendment is ratified, abolishing slavery in the United States.
1865–1877	The defeated South goes through a period of **Reconstruction** as Congress decides when the states will be readmitted to national government. Federal troops occupy the South.
1866	**Cyrus Field** lays a cable under the Atlantic extending to Europe, making it possible to send messages between the continents in minutes rather than days or weeks.
1867	**The United States buys Alaska** from Russia for over $7 million.
	Christopher Sholes develops the typewriter, which will revolutionize office work before the turn of the century.
	The Grange Movement is founded by farmers who want to better their lives and gain more sympathetic treatment from the government.
1868	**The 14th Amendment** is ratified, granting citizenship to former slaves and to anyone else born in the United States.
	President Johnson is impeached and stands trial in the U.S. Senate. He is acquitted of the "high crimes and misdemeanors" of which some members of Congress accuse him.
1869	**The first transcontinental railroad** is completed at Promontory Point, Utah. It links railroads in the East with the Central and Pacific railroads, stretching from Omaha, Nebraska, to Sacramento, California.
	George Westinghouse patents the air brake, replacing the harder to use railroad hand brake.
	The Knights of Labor is formed in an attempt to bring workers together in a union.
1870	**The 15th Amendment** is ratified, granting black adult males the right to vote.
1871	**The Chicago fire** destroys one-third of the city and kills at least 300 people.
1876	**The United States celebrates the Centennial** of its independence with a lavish exhibition in Philadelphia.
	Alexander Graham Bell applies for a patent for the telephone.
	The Battle of Little Big Horn—Custer's last stand—is fought. The Sioux and Cheyenne, angered over railroad building through their land, wipe out General George Custer and his men.
1878	**Thomas Alva Edison** develops the first practical incandescent light bulb. He had patented the phonograph the year before and would patent many other inventions in the years following.

Growing and changing

Between 1890 and 1920, the United States changed from a pioneer nation to a world power. Huge industrial empires produced coal, steel, and oil. Inventors perfected the use of electricity, and such conveniences as the telephone, the phonograph, the automobile, and the airplane. The government began assembling an empire of possessions in Asia and the Caribbean.

At the same time, these changes caused serious growing pains. Labor unions were organized to demand fair pay and better working conditions. Farmers protested low prices. And the United States was reluctantly drawn into world politics. In 1917, millions of American troops fought in Europe for the first time, helping to bring victory to the Allied powers.

Date	Event
1880–1881	**James A. Garfield** is elected President. Four months after taking office, he is assassinated by Charles J. Guiteau, a mentally unbalanced and disappointed seeker of a government job. Chester A. Arthur succeeds Garfield.
1881	**Tuskegee Institute** in Alabama is founded by Booker T. Washington. Its aim is to provide education for young black men and women for immediate and practical application.
	Clara Barton, a Civil War nurse called "the Angel of the Battlefield," founds the American Red Cross and remains its president until 1904.
1883	**The Civil Service Reform Act,** or Pendelton Act, is passed to assure that many government jobs are given out on the basis of competitive examination rather than political appointment.
1886	**The American Federation of Labor** is founded in Columbus, Ohio. It quickly replaces the Knights of Labor as the leading American labor organization.
	The Haymarket Riot erupts in Chicago as 1,500 workers demonstrate for an eight-hour workday. A bomb explodes and seven police officers and four others are killed; 100 are wounded.
1887	**The Interstate Commerce Act** is passed to stop railroads from engaging in monopolistic practices that give large corporations advantages over smaller ones.
	The Dawes Act is passed in an attempt to "Americanize" the Indians by granting them small tracts of land and eventually ending the reservation system.
1888	**George Eastman** invents a small, inexpensive camera for popular use.
1889	**Jane Addams** opens Hull House in Chicago in an early attempt to provide recreational and educational opportunities for slum dwellers in the nation's growing cities.
1890	**The Sherman Antitrust Act** is passed to protect the public against monopolies and other business abuses.
	Jacob Riis, a New York City reporter, publishes *How the Other Half Lives,* a description of the wretched conditions in which slum dwellers live. It brings cries for reform.
1892	**The Populist Party** is formed by farm and labor groups who demand reforms to give citizens a larger and more direct voice in government.

Date	Event
	The Homestead strike occurs near Pittsburgh as 3,800 workers walk out. Fighting with company police results in the deaths of 12 men. The state militia defeats the strike.
1893	**The Panic of 1893** begins, causing business failures and unemployment.
1894	**"Coxey's Army,"** led by General Jacob S. Coxey of Ohio, marches on Washington, D.C., to demand a huge federal railroad building program to provide jobs for the unemployed. Coxey is arrested.
1896	**William Jennings Bryan** of Nebraska, a Populist hero, is nominated for President but loses to Republican William A. McKinley.
1898	**Hawaii** is annexed by the United States at the request of Americans living there.
1898	**THE SPANISH-AMERICAN WAR.** Like other Western countries, America seeks an empire, eyeing especially the Spanish possessions in the Caribbean and the Pacific. The battleship USS *Maine,* sent to Havana, Cuba, to protect American citizens there, is blown up in the harbor. Two months later, Congress declares war on Spain, after Spain refuses to relinquish Cuba. American forces attack the Spanish fleet in the Philippines and land in Cuba. U.S. Navy ships destroy the Spanish fleet and bombard Santiago. The Spanish surrender. Americans occupy Puerto Rico, another Spanish possession. Spain gives up Cuba and Puerto Rico and sells the Philippine Islands to the United States for $20 million.
1901	**President McKinley is assassinated** by Leon Czolgosz, a crazed anarchist. Theodore Roosevelt succeeds McKinley.
	The United States Steel Corporation is formed by financier J. Pierpont Morgan. It is the world's first billion-dollar corporation.
1902	**President Roosevelt** intervenes in a coal strike in Pennsylvania in support of the labor unions.
1903	**Orville and Wilbur Wright,** from Ohio, accomplish the first heavier-than-air flight in a motor-powered plane, at Kitty Hawk, North Carolina.

The first airplane at Kitty Hawk

Date	Event
1904–1914	**The Panama Canal** is constructed to link the Atlantic and Pacific oceans between North and South America.
1906	*The Jungle,* a novel written by Upton Sinclair that depicts unsanitary conditions in Chicago meat-packing houses, brings reforms in food-processing plants.

Date	Event
Date	*Event*
1909	**The National Association for the Advancement of Colored People** (NAACP) is organized to eliminate segregation and secure civil rights for blacks through legislation and court action.
1912	**Democrat Woodrow Wilson** is elected President when Republican votes are split between Taft and Roosevelt.
1913	**The 16th Amendment** is ratified, giving Congress the power to tax individual incomes.
1914	**The Clayton Antitrust Act** protects the right of labor unions to organize and negotiate.
	World War I breaks out in Europe as Archduke Francis Ferdinand of Austria-Hungary is assassinated. This spark sets off a war between rival alliances: the Allies, led by Britain, France, and Russia; and the Central Powers, led by Germany and Austria-Hungary.
1915	**The *Lusitania,*** a British passenger liner, is sunk off the Irish coast by a German submarine. Among passengers lost are 128 Americans, but Germany pledges to restrict its submarine warfare and stop sinking passenger ships.
	The Ku Klux Klan is organized in Georgia and begins to terrorize immigrants, Catholics, Jews, and especially blacks.
1917	**Germany** resumes unrestricted submarine warfare.
	Communists overthrow the Russian government, and Russia withdraws from the war against Germany.
	The Zimmermann note, suggesting that Germany is encouraging Mexico to go to war against the United States, is revealed.

Date	Event
1917–1918	**THE UNITED STATES IN WORLD WAR I.** In April 1917, President Wilson asks Congress for a declaration of war against Germany, and Congress responds.
1917	The Selective Service Act is passed, providing for the eventual draft of 3 million men. General John J. Pershing is named to command the American Expeditionary Forces (A.E.F.). President Wilson presents his Fourteen Point plan for world peace. The points advocate open diplomacy, freedom of the seas, removal of tariffs, arms reduction, and a league of nations.
1918	At Cantigny, France, American troops achieve the first clear-cut American victory. At Chateau-Thierry, Americans help block a German advance. At Belleau Wood, they drive the Germans out of an important position. In the Battle of the Marne, American and French troops drive the Germans far back, marking the turning point of the war. At St. Mihiel, American troops mount the first distinctly American offensive and capture the town.
	In the Meuse-Argonne offensive, more than a million American troops join British and French troops. They defeat the enemy and the Germans surrender. An armistice is signed, ending the war on November 11, 1918. In 1919, the Treaty of Versailles is signed, providing for the creation of the League of Nations, but Congress opposes American membership. The League of Nations is formed, but the United States never joins it.

Boom, bust, war

Between 1920 and 1954, the United States grew into the most prosperous land on Earth. During the 1920s, the country turned away from world affairs and found excitement at home—the popular entertainment of radio and the movies, jazz, and the promise of ever greater prosperity.

The excitement ended suddenly in the early 1930s, however. A Great Depression wrecked the economy and millions lost their jobs. Even before recovery was complete, the country faced another world war, successfully defending against the aggression of Germany and Japan.

Peace was short-lived, however. The United States was soon competing with the Soviet Union for world dominance, and still another war broke out in Korea within five years.

Date	Event
1919	**The 18th Amendment** is ratified, prohibiting the manufacture and sale of alcoholic beverages. It will be repealed by the 21st Amendment in 1933.
	The "Red scare" erupts as antigovernment bombings occur in the United States. The bombings are blamed on Communist influences. The "Palmer raids," ordered by the attorney general, bring about the arrest and deportation of suspected radicals. The scare dies down.
1920	**The 19th Amendment** is ratified, giving adult women the right to vote. In the first Presidential election in which they vote, Warren G. Harding is elected.
	The nation's first radio station, KDKA in Pittsburgh, goes into operation.
1921–1922	**The Washington Naval Conference** is held. The United States, Britain, and Japan seek to limit naval armaments.
1921–1929	**Congress begins passing laws to restrict immigration,** including the Emergency Quota Act of 1921 and the Immigration Act of 1924. Immigration shrinks to 150,000 a year by 1929.
1923	**President Harding dies** and Calvin Coolidge succeeds him.
1924	**The Teapot Dome** scandal comes to light as the American people learn that several members of the Harding administration are guilty of corruption. Among their crimes is taking bribes to rent government oil-producing land at Teapot Dome, Wyoming, and Elk Hills, California, to private oil interests.

Left, *police watch as illegal liquor is dumped.* Right, *a cartoonist's view of the 1920s dance craze, the Charleston.*

Date	Event
Date	*Event*
1924	**Indians are granted American citizenship,** partly in recognition of Indian wartime service.
1927	**The first talking picture** is released, *The Jazz Singer,* starring Al Jolson.
	Charles A. Lindbergh becomes the first person to fly across the Atlantic alone. His plane, *The Spirit of St. Louis,* makes the trip from New York to Paris in 33 hours.
1929	**The stock market crashes** as sellers find no buyers for their highly overpriced stocks. Falling farm prices, an oversupply of manufactured goods, and a loss of foreign trade also help to bring on the Great Depression, the worst in U.S. history.
1929–1932	**Farm income shrinks** by 50 percent; industry drops to one-half production; 85,000 businesses fail; thousands of banks close after losing their depositors' money; unemployment reaches $12^1/_2$ million, one-quarter of the nation's workforce.
1932	**The "Bonus Army"** marches on Washington. Ten thousand World War I veterans demand the $1,000 bonuses the government has promised them, although the bonuses are not yet due. U.S. Army troops drive them away under orders of President Herbert Hoover.
	Democrat Franklin Delano Roosevelt runs against Hoover for the Presidency, promising the American people a "New Deal" that will bring relief and recovery from the Great Depression. Roosevelt wins by a landslide.
1933	**Roosevelt is inaugurated** and immediately declares a "bank holiday," closing banks temporarily to determine which are sound enough to handle depositors' money.
1933–1938	**The New Deal** begins as Congress passes an amazing number of programs during Roosevelt's first hundred days in office, including the Emergency Banking Relief Act, the Agricultural Adjustment Act, the Tennessee Valley Act, and the National Industrial Recovery Act. Later legislation includes the Social Security Act and the Fair Labor Standards Act.
1939	**World War II begins in Europe** as Adolf Hitler, fascist dictator of Germany, sends troops into Poland, part of an Allied alliance led by Britain and France. Hitler's partners in the Axis alliance, Italy and Japan, also commit aggressive acts—Italy in Africa and Japan in China.
1940	**The Selective Service Act** is passed, the first peacetime draft in American history.
1941	**The Lend-Lease Act** is passed to supply Britain with guns, tanks, ships, and planes.
	The nation's first commercial television broadcasting begins, in New York City.
	The Japanese attack the U.S. Navy Pacific fleet at Pearl Harbor in Hawaii on December 7, sinking or badly damaging 19 ships and killing 2,300 Americans. Congress declares war on Japan, and Germany and Italy declare war on the United States.

Date	Event
1941–1945	**THE UNITED STATES IN WORLD WAR II.** When the United States enters the war, Allied powers Britain and Russia are fighting Axis powers Germany and Italy in Europe and Africa. (France had fallen to Germany in 1940.) In Asia, Axis power Japan is fighting in China and is conquering Southeast Asia and the Pacific. The United States faces war in both Europe and the Pacific.
1942	Wartime agencies are established to mobilize for war. They include the War Production Board and the Office of War Mobilization.
	The draft is extended, eventually helping to raise a military force of 16 million.
	All people in the United States of Japanese ancestry are sent to relocation camps.
	War in Europe and North Africa
1942–1943	The Allies battle the Germans and Italians in North Africa and drive them out.
1943	The Allies invade Italy. After several bloody campaigns, Italy surrenders.
1943–1944	The Russians drive the Germans out of the Soviet Union and back into Poland.
1944	The Allies begin the D-Day invasion of Europe and drive nearly to the German border.
1945	The Allies invade Germany and Germany surrenders on V-E (Victory-Europe) Day.
	War in the Pacific
1942	Manila, Bataan, and Corregidor all fall to the Japanese, and the Philippines are lost. But the U.S. Navy wins the battle of the Coral Sea and of Midway and prevents the capture of Guadalcanal.
1943–1945	American forces drive the Japanese from the Aleutian Islands and begin recapturing other Pacific islands—the Solomons, the Gilberts, the Marshalls, New Guinea, Saipan, Guam, and the Philippines.
1945	American forces begin the invasion of Japan, capturing Iwo Jima and Okinawa. Atomic bombs are dropped on Hiroshima and Nagasaki, and Japan surrenders on V-J (Victory-Japan) Day.

American troops come ashore on Normandy beach, 1944.

Date	Event
1944	**The GI Bill of Rights** is passed, offering government aid and loans to veterans for education, housing, and business ventures.
1945	**President Roosevelt dies** and is succeeded by Harry S. Truman.
	The United Nations is founded in San Francisco. It begins with 50 member nations.
1947	**A "Cold War"** develops between the Soviet Union, which is seeking to spread Communism, and anti–Communist nations led by the United States. The Truman Doctrine is announced, offering American economic and military aid to any nation threatened by Communist takeover. The Marshall Plan follows, offering economic aid to help war-torn countries of Europe.
	The Taft-Hartley Act is passed. It seeks more control over labor unions in a response to the great number of labor strikes since the end of the war.
1948–1949	**The Berlin blockade** begins as the Soviet Union tries to drive Britain, France, and the United States out of Berlin, which the four powers jointly occupy. The Western powers fly in enough supplies to maintain their parts of the city. The Russians finally end the blockade.
1949	**NATO,** the North Atlantic Treaty Organization, is founded to thwart Communist moves against the Western nations. The United States, Canada, Britain, and France are some of the members.
1950–1953	**WAR IN KOREA.** In 1949, after a long civil war, Communist forces finally succeed in winning China. Americans grow fearful that other areas of Asia will also fall to communism. In 1950, China's neighbor, Communist North Korea, invades non-Communist South Korea. President Truman asks the United Nations to send a force to repel the North Koreans. American troops make up most of the force.
1950	U.S. forces attack at Inchon, throwing the North Korean troops back over the South Korean border and almost as far back as North Korea's border with China.
1950–1951	Chinese troops cross their border and drive UN forces south of the South Korean border. UN forces fight their way to back near the border.
1951–1953	Truce talks begin, but the fighting drags on with great loss of life.
1953	An armistice is reached, leaving the border through Korea as it was before the war.
1950–1954	**McCarthyism** is rampant as American fears of communism create fears of possible Communist traitors within the country. Senator Joseph McCarthy of Wisconsin accuses many people of "un-Americanism." He is finally censured by the Congress and McCarthyism fades away.
1952	**Dwight D. Eisenhower is elected President** on the Republican ticket. He serves two terms, presiding over a period of general prosperity. During his first years in office, the Korean War is ended by negotiation and McCarthyism weakens and dies. At the same time, new problems arise.

Modern America

From 1954 to the present, the United States has remained a world power. At the same time, it has struggled to solve many serious problems of its own. The civil rights campaigns of the 1950s and 1960s sought to follow through on promises made to black Americans after the Civil War. In the 1960s and 1970s, citizens debated how best to help the poor; how far the country should involve itself in the long war in Vietnam; and just what a country could expect of its leaders.

While the Cold War with the Soviet Union was giving way to friendlier relations, attention shifted to crises prompted by smaller countries, such as the oil crisis brought on by Arab nations in the Middle East, the hostage crisis in Iran, the Gulf War in Iraq, and, dramatically, the terrorist attacks of September 11, 2001.

Date	Event
1954–1955	**The black civil rights struggle** begins as the Supreme Court decides in *Brown v. Board of Education of Topeka* that school segregation must end. The next year, a bus boycott in Montgomery, Alabama, led by Rev. Martin Luther King, leads to bus desegregation there. Sit-ins lead to desegregation of public places. "Freedom riders" bring on desegregation of interstate buses.
1958	**The National Defense Education Act** is passed, giving federal aid to schools to strengthen their science and math programs in an effort to maintain U.S. technological supremacy.
1961	**The Peace Corps,** to send Americans to help in developing countries, and the Alliance for Progress, offering $10 billion in aid for developing Latin American countries, are inaugurated by President John F. Kennedy.
	The Bay of Pigs invasion takes place as exiled Cubans, driven from their country by the Communist government of Fidel Castro, land in Cuba to overthrow Castro. The American-trained and supplied army of exiles is quickly defeated, and Cuban-American relations grow worse.

President Kennedy

1962	**The Cuban missile crisis** occurs as Soviet-built missiles are discovered in Cuba. President Kennedy demands that the Soviet Union remove the missiles and threatens to turn back any other weapons-carrying Soviet ship headed for Cuba. After a few tense days, the Soviet Union agrees to remove the missiles.
1963	**A march on Washington** is staged by more than 200,000 civil rights supporters, who demand that Congress pass civil rights legislation.
	President Kennedy is assassinated in Dallas, Texas, by Lee Harvey Oswald, an alleged Cuban sympathizer. Lyndon B. Johnson succeeds to the Presidency.
1964–1965	**"Great Society"** legislation is passed as President Johnson declares a "War on Poverty." The Economic Opportunity Act creates the Office of Economic Opportunity, which provides job training; VISTA, a domestic Peace Corps; and Head Start programs for children. The Elementary and Secondary Education Act provides federal grants for schools in low-income districts. The Medicare Act provides federal health benefits for those over 65.
1964–1968	**The Civil Rights Act of 1964** is passed to outlaw racial discrimination in employment and public accommodations. The Voting Rights Act of 1965 follows, to protect black people's right to vote. The Civil Rights Act of 1968 aims to guarantee blacks open housing.

Date	Event
1964–1975	**WAR IN VIETNAM.** Communist North Vietnam fights to take over non-Communist South Vietnam. Presidents Eisenhower and Kennedy send military advisers and supplies to help South Vietnam, but the South keeps losing. President Johnson decides to increase American involvement.
1964	The Gulf of Tonkin Resolution is passed by Congress, giving the President expanded powers to commit American troops and supplies to South Vietnam.
1965–1968	American planes begin flying regular bombing missions over North Vietnam. By the end of 1968, 536,000 American troops have been sent to Vietnam and 25,000 have been killed. The Communist Tet offensive in February 1968 shows how unsuccessful American involvement has been.
1968–1969	Anti-Vietnam War protest gathers strength. A national moratorium is held in October 1968, demanding an end to American involvement.
1969–1972	President Richard M. Nixon takes office and promises to have the Vietnamese take over more of the fighting and thus reduce American involvement. By 1972 American troops in Vietnam are down to 60,000.
1973	"An Agreement on Ending the War and Restoring Peace in Vietnam" is signed, providing for a cease-fire and the withdrawal of all American troops.
1975	The last American troops withdraw from South Vietnam; it is soon overrun by the North.

Left, *a medical evacuation during the Vietnam War.* Right, *an antiwar protest in the United States.*

Date	Event
1966	**The National Organization for Women (NOW)** is founded, signaling the start of a new women's movement to gain equal social, political, and economic rights.
1968	**Martin Luther King** is assassinated in Memphis, Tennessee, by James Earl Ray.
	Robert Kennedy, brother of John F. Kennedy and a Presidential candidate, is assassinated in Los Angeles by Sirhan Sirhan, an Arab nationalist.
1969	U.S. astronauts Neil Armstrong, Edwin Aldrin, and Michael Collins succeed in making **the first manned landing on the moon,** the aim of a space program begun in 1961 by President Kennedy.
1970	**An Ohio National Guard unit** kills four students and wounds nine others during antiwar demonstrations at Kent State University.
1972	**President Nixon visits China,** ending a 20-year period of separation between China and the United States. He and Chinese leaders agree to allow scientific and

Date	Event

cultural ties and to foster trade between their countries. Three months later, Nixon visits the Soviet Union to ease tensions. He and Soviet leaders sign an arms control agreement and agree to more international cooperation.

1972–1974

The Watergate crisis is brought on when Democratic National Headquarters in the Watergate complex in Washington, D.C., are broken into. The intruders are later connected with the White House and the Committee to Re-elect the President. President Nixon denies any involvement, but congressional and judicial investigations find proof of Nixon's participation.

1973

Vice President Spiro Agnew is forced to resign after pleading no-contest to a charge of tax evasion. Gerald R. Ford, member of Congress from Michigan, is selected as Vice President.

An oil crisis erupts as several Arab oil-producing nations refuse to ship oil to the United States. Oil shortages continue even after Arabs start shipping oil again. Oil prices rise, fueling worldwide inflation and threatening the health of the American and world economies.

Roe v. Wade, a Supreme Court ruling, bans state restrictions on abortions.

A common sight during the 1973 oil crisis

1974

Nixon resigns from the Presidency after the House Judiciary Committee approves articles of impeachment. Gerald Ford succeeds him as President. One of Ford's first acts is to pardon Nixon.

1976

The United States celebrates its Bicentennial with events across the country, including a parade of tall ships from all over the world up the Hudson River.

1978

The Panama Canal Treaty is ratified by Congress, providing for the turnover of control of the canal to Panama by the year 2000.

1979

The Camp David accords are reached after President Jimmy Carter calls the leaders of Israel and Egypt together and they agree to a framework for arriving at peace between their nations.

Date	Event
1979–1981	**Iranians take 53 American Embassy personnel hostage** in Teheran and hold them for 444 days in retaliation for American protection of the overthrown Iranian leader Shah Pahlevi.
1980	**Mount Saint Helens,** a volcano in Washington State, erupts, killing 26 people and spreading volcanic ash over 120 square miles.
1981	**President Reagan is shot** by John W. Hinckley, Jr., who is found innocent by reason of insanity. Reagan recovers and returns to work.
	Sandra Day O'Connor becomes the first woman named to the Supreme Court.
1981–1998	**Acquired immune deficiency syndrome (AIDS)** is first reported in the United States in 1981. The virus that causes AIDS is finally discovered in 1986. In the 17 years following the discovery of the syndrome, more than 660,000 people are diagnosed in the United States. Of these cases, about 400,000 deaths are reported.
1982	**Strategic Arms Reduction Talks (START)** begin in Geneva, Switzerland, and attempt to limit the number of nuclear warheads in the world.
1983	**Sally K. Ride** becomes the first American woman in space as a member of the crew of the space shuttle *Challenger.*
	A terrorist bomb at the headquarters of the U.S. peacekeeping force in Beirut, Lebanon, kills 241 American servicemen.
1986	**The space shuttle *Challenger* explodes** on takeoff, killing all aboard, including schoolteacher Christa McAuliffe.
1987	**The Iran-Contra congressional hearings** expose a plot by U.S. government officials to sell arms to Iran in an effort to obtain the release of hostages and to use the money received to support the Contra rebels in Nicaragua.
1988	**A terrorist bomb** explodes aboard a Pan American Boeing 747 jumbo jet flying over Lockerbie, Scotland, killing all 259 passengers and crew and 11 people on the ground below.
1989	**An earthquake** measuring 6.9 on the Richter scale hits the San Francisco area, causing 67 deaths and considerable damage.
	U.S. troops invade Panama in order to install a democratically elected government and to apprehend dictator Manuel Noriega, indicted in the United States on drug-related charges.
	The Exxon *Valdez* supertanker spills more than 11 million gallons of crude oil into Prince William Sound, Alaska.
1990–1991	**The United States responds to the Iraqi invasion of Kuwait** by leading a military coalition of some 527,000 soldiers from 30 nations against Iraq. On January 16, 1991, coalition forces launch a six-week military campaign that decimates Iraq and forces its troops out of Kuwait.

Date	*Event*
1992	**A relief mission to Somalia,** under UN auspices, is led by U.S. forces to help deliver relief supplies and restore order to the war-torn country.
1993	**The worst floods in a century** strike the Mississippi and Missouri river basins, causing some $12 billion in damage and leaving tens of thousands homeless.
1994	**A major earthquake,** measuring 6.6 on the Richter scale, devastates the Los Angeles, California, area, destroying or damaging thousands of buildings, buckling freeways, and leaving some 51 dead and tens of thousands homeless.
1996	**Bill Clinton** becomes the first Democratic president to gain reelection to a second term since Franklin D. Roosevelt in 1936. The Republicans, who gained control of Congress in 1994 for the first time in 40 years, retain majorities in both houses.
1997	**The U.S. economy booms.** In May, unemployment drops below 5 percent for the first time in 24 years, and in July the Dow Jones industrial average rises above 8,000 for the first time.
1998–1999	**Impeachment.** In December 1998, the House of Representatives votes two articles of impeachment against Bill Clinton, charging him with perjury and obstructing justice relating to testimony regarding an extramarital affair. In February 1999, the Senate acquits Clinton on both counts.
2000	**George W. Bush** is elected president in one of the closest U.S. elections ever. For only the second time in history, a son follows his father to the White House.
2001	**On September 11, terrorists simultaneously hijack four American airliners,** crashing one plane into the Pentagon and two into the World Trade Center Towers in New York. The fourth plane crashed in a Pennsylvania field.
2002	**President Bush** signed an act establishing the Department of Homeland Security. This resulted in the most dramatic reshaping of the federal government in more than 50 years, moving the operations of multiple agencies to the new department. The department's mission is to prevent terrorist attacks in the U.S. and reduce the U.S.'s vulnerability to terrorism.
2003	**War in Iraq.** U.S. and British troops entered Iraq in March, making their way to Baghdad, with the intent of toppling the regime of Saddam Hussein. After initially eluding capture, Saddam was eventually apprehended in December.
2004	**President Bush reelected.** After a vigorously contested race in which public opinion was widely expressed and both parties rallied aggressively to register voters, President Bush was reelected, winning both the electoral vote and 51 percent of the popular vote.

For Further Reference

Grun, Bernard
   The Timetables of History: A Historical Linkage of Peoples and Events
   Simon & Schuster
Kirkler, Bernard
   A Reader's Guide to Contemporary History
   Quadrangle

McNeill, William H.
   A World History
   Oxford University Press
Wetterau, Bruce
   The Macmillan Concise Dictionary of World History
   Macmillan

- *The land*   **134**
- *The people*   **136**
- *The West*   **138**
- *The Midwest*   **142**
- *The South*   **146**
- *The Northeast*   **150**
- *U.S. territories*   **152**
- *U.S. flags*   **154**
- *State flags*   **156**

United States Today

The United States today is made up of 50 states. Of these, 48 make up a central band across the continent of North America between Mexico and Canada. The other two states are Alaska, in the northwest corner of the continent, and Hawaii, a chain of islands in the Pacific Ocean some 2,200 miles west and south of the American mainland. This section briefly describes the land and people of the United States. It then presents information on each of the states in the Union by region, beginning with the West and ending with the Northeast. Following that is a section on the history of the U.S. flag and information on the care and display of the flag. There is also information on the flags of the U.S. states and possessions.

The land

The land of the continental United States is divided into major land regions by its mountain chains. The largest and most important of these are the Rocky Mountains, which run from north to south through the Western states from Montana to Alaska. A second major chain is the Appalachian Mountains, which run through the Northeastern states and into the South, from Maine to Alabama. Smaller mountain ranges include the Coastal Mountains, which run parallel to the Pacific coast in Washington, Oregon, and California; and an isolated highland region called the Ozark-Ouachitas, mainly in Arkansas and Missouri.

Between the Coastal Ranges and the Rockies lies the great Basin and Range region of the Far West. It is a generally dry and barren area of high plateaus. Between the Rockies and the Appalachians lies the Great Plains region, covering almost all of the Midwest from the Dakotas to Ohio. The Plains region is drained by the largest U.S. river system, which includes the great Mississippi and its tributaries, especially the Missouri and the Ohio. The region is one of the richest farming areas in the world, producing huge crops of corn, wheat, and other grains and millions of beef cattle and hogs each year. East of the Appalachians and following the seacoast from Maine to Texas are the Coastal Plains. These lowlands were the site of many early American settlements, and today they have many large cities and much fertile farmland.

Along the eastern half of the country, the northern border with Canada is formed by the Great Lakes, five of the largest freshwater lakes in the world. Four of them—Superior, Huron, Erie, and Ontario—are shared with Canada. The fifth lake, Michigan, is the largest body of freshwater wholly in the United States.

Alaska is a vast wilderness bordering Canada on

U.S. landforms

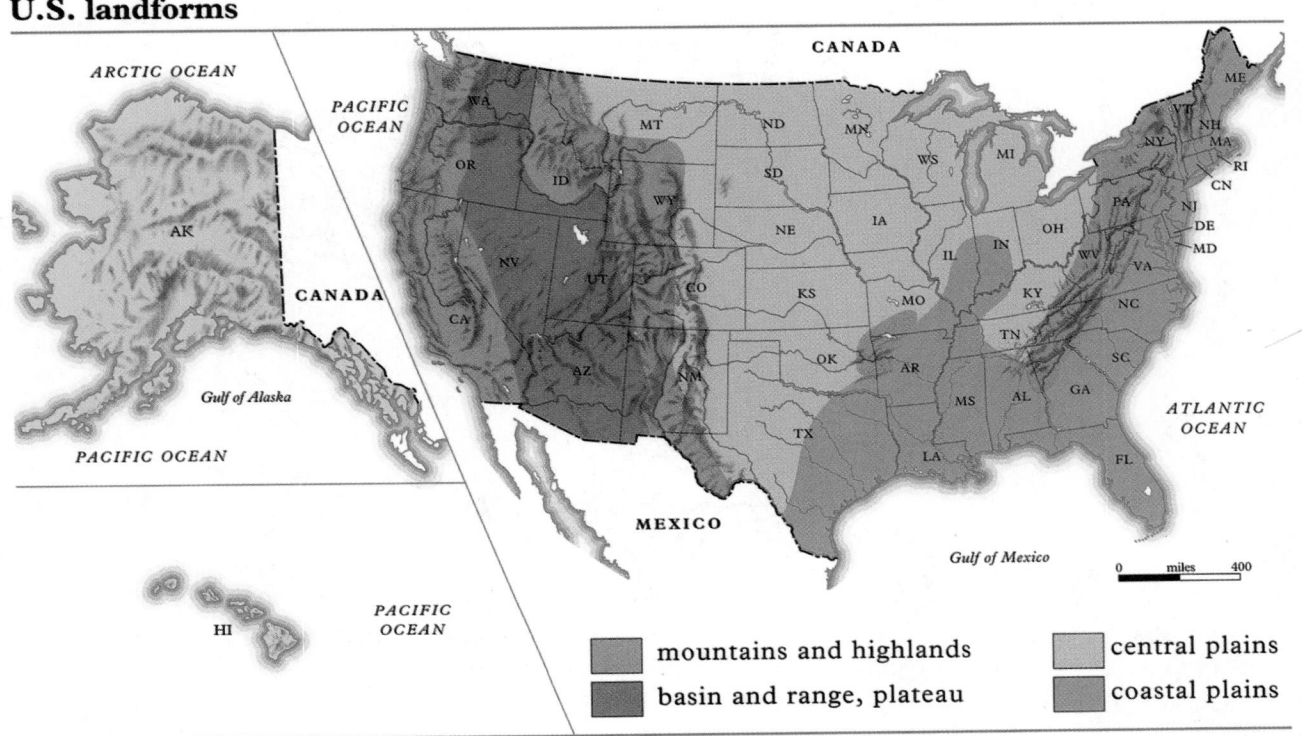

	mountains and highlands		central plains
	basin and range, plateau		coastal plains

the east and facing the Pacific and Arctic oceans and the Bering Sea on its other sides. It includes Mt. McKinley, the highest point in North America. Hawaii is a chain of small volcanic islands, featuring both warm, sandy beaches and snow-capped volcanic peaks.

The climate of the United States is generally *temperate*—neither extremely hot nor extremely cold. The warmest places are in the South—in Florida, Texas, Arizona, California, and Hawaii. The coldest places are in the North—in Minnesota, the Dakotas, and, of course, Alaska. The highest rainfall occurs along the Pacific coast of Washington and in the Southeast. The driest regions are the deserts of the Southwest.

Area. In area, the United States is the fourth largest country in the world, behind Russia, Canada, and China. The continental United States averages 2,500 miles from east to west and some 1,200 miles from north to south.

The Western region is the largest by far, containing more than 2 million square miles and all of the ten largest states. It is larger than all the rest of the country combined. The largest state, Alaska, has

570,374 square miles and is more than twice as large as the second largest state, Texas. The smallest state is Rhode Island, with 1,045 square miles. Alaska is 500 times as large as Rhode Island.

U.S. Area *(in square miles)*		
Regions	West	2,082,068
	Midwest	750,520
	South	540,517
	Northeast	162,274
Largest states	1. Alaska	570,374
	2. Texas	261,914
	3. California	155,973
	4. Montana	145,556
	5. New Mexico	121,364
Smallest states	50. Rhode Island	1,045
	49. Delaware	1,995
	48. Connecticut	4,845
	47. Hawaii	6,423
	46. New Jersey	7,419

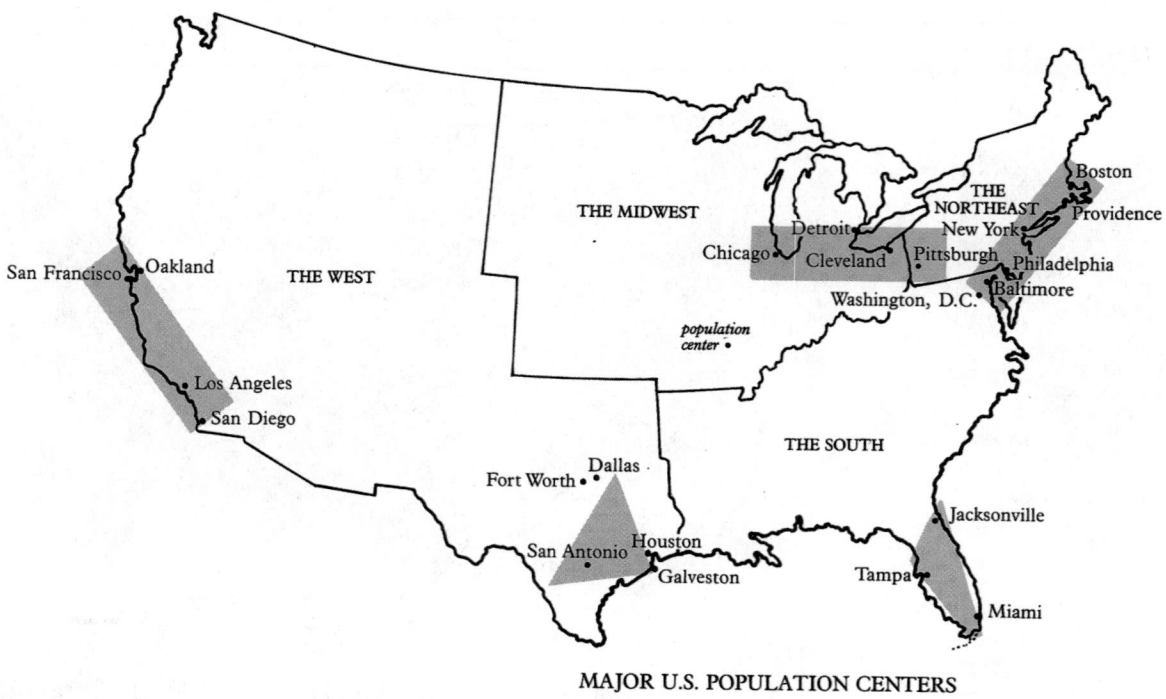

MAJOR U.S. POPULATION CENTERS

The people

The United States is the third largest country in the world in population, behind China and India. According to the 2000 census, there are 281 million Americans, distributed fairly evenly among the four great regions. The West led with 87 million, followed closely by the South and Midwest and trailed by the Northeast.

Because of differences in area, however, far more people live on less land in the Northeast. This can be measured by calculating how many people there are per square mile in each region:

Region	Persons per square mile
Northeast	330
South	140
Midwest	86
West	42

The table shows that there are about eight times as many people per square mile in the Northeast as there are in the West. The most densely populated state, New Jersey, has 1,135 people per square mile.

The most populous state in the United States is California, with almost 34 million people. One person out of eight in the country is a Californian. Other large states are New York; Texas, whose population has passed that of New York; Florida; and Pennsylvania. The two least populous states, Wyoming and Vermont, each have fewer than 650,000 people. For every Alaskan, there are 54 Californians. The average population of a state is about 5.5 million. Fourteen states have between 3 and 5 million residents, and twelve more have between 5 and 9 million.

The people of the United States are a rich, diverse group made up of many races and nationalities. Individuals whose roots lie on every continent are included in the group we call Americans. While English is the language used most commonly, a large percentage of the population speaks Spanish. In any American city, one is likely to hear many languages (Russian, French, and German among them) spoken by American citizens.

U.S. Population
(2000 census)

U.S. total		281,421,906
Regions	West	87,500,000
	Midwest	64,393,000
	South	75,934,000
	Northeast	53,594,000
Largest states	1. California	33,871,648
	2. Texas	20,851,820
	3. New York	18,976,457
	4. Florida	15,982,378
	5. Illinois	12,419,293
Smallest states	50. Wyoming	493,782
	49. Vermont	608,827
	48. Alaska	626,932
	47. North Dakota	642,200
	46. South Dakota	754,844

Largest Cities
(2000 census)

1. New York, NY	8,008,000
2. Los Angeles, CA	3,695,000
3. Chicago, IL	2,896,000
4. Houston, TX	1,954,000
5. Philadelphia, PA	1,518,000
6. Phoenix, AZ	1,321,000
7. San Diego, CA	1,223,000
8. Dallas, TX	1,189,000
9. San Antonio, TX	1,145,000
10. Detroit, MI	951,000
11. San Jose, CA	895,000
12. Indianapolis, IN	792,000
13. San Francisco, CA	777,000
14. Jacksonville, FL	736,000
15. Columbus, OH	711,000
16. Austin, TX	657,000
17. Baltimore, MD	651,000
18. Memphis, TN	650,000
19. Milwaukee, WI	597,000
20. Boston, MA	589,000

Cities.

For nearly 200 years, more and more people have been living in cities. Today, nearly 80 percent of the U.S. population lives in a metropolitan area—a city or a suburb near a large city. Many of the large urban areas are close together in one of three corridors of population.

- BOS-WASH stretches from Boston, Massachusetts, to Washington, D.C., along the Atlantic coast. It includes such major cities as Providence, New York, Philadelphia, and Baltimore.
- CHI-PITTS stretches from Chicago, Illinois, to Pittsburgh, Pennsylvania, along the southern shores of the Great Lakes. It includes Detroit and Cleveland.
- SAN-SAN runs along California's Pacific coast from San Francisco to San Diego. It includes the sprawling Los Angeles region, which is made up of several metropolitan areas.

Another cluster of large cities is growing up in Texas in a triangle whose corners are Houston-Galveston, Dallas-Fort Worth, and San Antonio. There are also three metropolitan areas in Florida with a million or more people. Other large cities such as St. Louis, Minneapolis-St. Paul, and Atlanta serve as important regional capitals.

There are 50 metropolitan areas in the United States with populations of more than 1 million. The three largest are New York, Los Angeles, and Chicago.

Index to the States

State/Page	State/Page
Alabama 146	**Missouri** 144
Alaska 138	**Montana** 138
Arizona 138	**Nebraska** 144
Arkansas 146	**Nevada** 140
California 138	**New Hampshire** 150
Colorado 138	**New Jersey** 150
Connecticut 150	**New Mexico** 140
Delaware 146	**New York** 150
District of	**North Carolina** 148
Columbia 148	**North Dakota** 144
Florida 146	**Ohio** 144
Georgia 146	**Oklahoma** 140
Hawaii 138	**Oregon** 140
Idaho 138	**Pennsylvania** 152
Illinois 142	**Rhode Island** 152
Indiana 142	**South Carolina** 148
Iowa 142	**South Dakota** 144
Kansas 142	**Tennessee** 148
Kentucky 146	**Texas** 140
Louisiana 146	**Utah** 140
Maine 150	**Vermont** 152
Maryland 148	**Virginia** 148
Massachusetts 150	**Washington** 140
Michigan 142	**West Virginia** 148
Minnesota 144	**Wisconsin** 144
Mississippi 148	**Wyoming** 140

The West

The Western United States consists of 13 states in the main continental region, stretching from Texas in the Southeast to Washington in the Northwest. In addition, the region includes the two states that are separated from the other 48—Alaska and Hawaii.

The Western region was scarcely known in 1776 when the United States was formed. The only European settlements were Spanish missions in present-day California and New Mexico. As late as 1900, this huge region had only about 8.3 million people. By 1980, it was the most populous of the four regions, with more than 60 million people. California and Texas are by far the most populous Western states. Nearly two-thirds of all Westerners—about 55 million—live in these two states.

The Western states include vast areas of mountain and desert wasteland. But they also include most of the oil and natural gas deposits in the United States and immense treasures in timber. California is the most important and most diversified agricultural state in the country. Light manufacturing is of growing importance.

The Western region is growing at a faster rate than any other region, especially along its southern half. Between 1990 and 2000, California gained more new residents than any other state, and Nevada and Arizona had the highest percentage increases.

State name Date entered Union	Area 2000 Population	Capital Principal cities	Bird Flower Tree
Alaska Jan. 3, 1959 (49th)	570,374 sq. mi. 626,932	★Juneau, Anchorage	Willow ptarmigan Forget-me-not Sitka spruce
Arizona Feb. 14, 1912 (48th)	113,642 sq. mi. 5,130,632	★Phoenix, Tucson, Mesa, Tempe	Cactus wren Saguaro cactus blossom Palo verde
California Sept. 9, 1850 (31st)	155,973 sq. mi. 33,871,648	★Sacramento, Los Angeles, San Francisco, San Diego, San Jose	California quail California poppy California redwood
Colorado Aug. 1, 1876 (38th)	103,730 sq. mi. 4,301,261	★Denver, Colorado Springs, Aurora	Lark bunting White and lavender columbine Colorado blue spruce
Hawaii Aug. 21, 1959 (50th)	6,423 sq. mi. 1,211,537	★Honolulu, Hilo	Hawaiian goose Yellow hibiscus Kukui (candlenut)
Idaho July 3, 1890 (43rd)	82,751 sq. mi. 1,293,953	★Boise, Pocatello, Idaho Falls	Mountain bluebird Syringa Western white pine
Montana Nov. 8, 1889 (41st)	145,556 sq. mi. 902,195	★Helena, Billings, Great Falls	Western meadowlark Bitterroot Ponderosa pine

Land/Climate	Economy
Southern coastal ranges, extensive interior plateau, and northern mountains to Arctic slope; arctic north and mild summers in south	Drilling of oil and natural gas; limited agriculture, commercial fishing, and tourism
Central mountain highlands with northeast plateau and southwest desert basin; hot and dry at low elevations and milder in highlands	Manufacturing of electrical, metal, and aircraft products; tourism; mining of copper, gold, and silver; cattle and sheep ranching
Coastal ranges, central valley, inland Sierra Nevada Mountains, southern desert; rainfall and temperature variation increasing toward north	Leader in manufacturing, with machinery, electric, and food goods; also leading farm state, with both livestock and varied crop yields; tourism
Eastern plains, central spine of Rocky Mountains, western plateau; mild and dry except in mountains; peaks are snow-covered all year	Manufacturing of food goods and electronic equipment; oil, natural gas, molybdenum; tourism; cattle ranching and wheat
Chain of volcanic islands with sandy beaches broken by coastal cliffs; coastal areas warm year-round, inland areas wetter and cooler	Tourism; crops of pineapple and sugar cane; cattle ranches; manufactures based on food processing
Rocky Mountains in northern half, plains in southern half; dry continental climate of cold winters and warm summers	Agriculture based on potato crop and cattle; manufacturing of processed foods and lumber products; tourism
Rocky Mountains in west and Great Plains over eastern two-thirds; dry, with severe winters and hot summers	Agriculture based on wheat, cattle, and feed crops; mining of copper and coal; timber; tourism

Colorado mountains

Hollywood Boulevard, Los Angeles

State name Date entered Union	Area 2000 Population	Capital Principal cities	Bird Flower Tree
Nevada Oct. 31, 1864 (36th)	109,806 sq. mi. 1,998,257	★Carson City, Las Vegas, Reno	Mountain bluebird Sagebrush Single-leaf piñon
New Mexico Jan. 6, 1912 (47th)	121,364 sq. mi. 1,819,046	★Santa Fe, Albuquerque, Las Cruces	Roadrunner Yucca Piñon
Oklahoma Nov. 16, 1907 (46th)	68,679 sq. mi. 3,450,654	★Oklahoma City, Tulsa	Scissor-tailed flycatcher Mistletoe Redbud
Oregon Feb. 14, 1859 (33rd)	96,002 sq. mi. 3,421,399	★Salem, Portland, Eugene	Western meadowlark Oregon grape Douglas fir
Texas Dec. 29, 1845 (28th)	261,914 sq. mi. 20,851,820	★Austin, Houston, Dallas, San Antonio, El Paso	Mockingbird Bluebonnet Pecan
Utah Jan. 4, 1896 (45th)	82,168 sq. mi. 2,233,169	★Salt Lake City, Ogden, Provo	California seagull Sego lily Blue spruce
Washington Nov. 11, 1889 (42nd)	66,581 sq. mi. 5,894,121	★Olympia, Seattle, Spokane, Tacoma	American goldfinch Coast rhododendron Western hemlock
Wyoming July 10, 1890 (44th)	97,105 sq. mi. 493,782	★Cheyenne, Casper, Laramie	Meadowlark Indian paintbrush Plains cottonwood

State capitol grounds, Olympia, Washington

Sandstone buttes, Monument Valley, Utah

Land/Climate	Economy
Predominantly desert basin with low ranges of hills running north-south; arid climate of hot days and cool nights	Tourism; mining of ores including copper and gold; cattle ranches; electronic and chemical manufactures
Mountains in north, Great Plains in east, arid plateau in west; dry and sunny, with warm days and cool nights throughout the year	Oil, natural gas, and mining of specialized ores including uranium; cattle ranching; tourism; manufacture of food goods and electrical parts
Central lowland, with high plains to west and hilly plateau to east; moderate climate, with rainfall greater in east than west	Drilling of oil and natural gas, with related refining industries; extensive farmland devoted to livestock and feed grains
Coastal ranges and Cascade Mountains in west, with elevated plateau in east; mild and rainy near coast, with drier continental climate inland	Wheat, potatoes, cattle, and sheep; lumber; tourism; mining of nickel ore
Complex topography surrounding southern Gulf Plain and central high plains; warm and rainy near coast, cooler and drier inland	Oil and natural gas; mineral refining and diversified manufacturing; U.S. leader in beef cattle, sheep, and cotton
Mountains in northeast, plateau in southeast, arid basin in west; extremely dry, with mild winters and hot summers	Manufacture of transportation and aerospace equipment, and food goods; copper, oil, and coal mining; dairy livestock and sheep; tourism
Coastal ranges and central Cascade Mountains with eastern plateau; mild and rainy in west, with drier continental climate in east	Manufacture of aircraft and transportation equipment, and lumber products; wheat crops and livestock; tourism; timber
Central mountains, southwest arid basin, eastern plains; generally cool and dry, with variations with elevation	Drilling of oil and natural gas and mining of ores; cattle ranching; tourism; wheat

The Midwest

The Midwestern region encompasses 12 states that stretch from the edge of the Rocky Mountains in the west to the Appalachians in the east. The half of the region west of the Mississippi River is mainly devoted to agriculture, while the half to the east is a major industrial region. These states, clustering around the Great Lakes, were all part of the Northwest Territories, which became part of the United States in the settlement ending the Revolutionary War. The lands west of the Mississippi were part of the Louisiana Purchase and were bought from France in 1803.

The three most populous Midwestern states are Illinois, Ohio, and Michigan. These three are the industrial giants of the region. They are the homes of several major steel companies and of the major U.S. automobile manufacturers. The less densely populated western states constitute the greatest food-producing region in the country and one of the most productive in the world. The major crops include wheat, corn, hogs, and cattle. The northern parts of Minnesota, Wisconsin, and Michigan are heavily wooded and filled with small lakes. The only mountains in the region are the Ozarks, which cover the southern half of Missouri and extend south into Arkansas.

In area, the Midwest is about a third the size of the Western region. In population, with about 64 million, it is three-fourths as large. The people in the Midwest are concentrated especially around such large cities as Chicago, Detroit, Cleveland, St. Louis, and Minneapolis-St. Paul. Between 1970 and 2000, however, the region's industries lost out to foreign competition and laid off thousands of workers. As a result, the region has lost millions of its residents to migration. These migrants have moved to the South and Southwest, leaving the Midwest with only a very small population increase from the excess of births over deaths and migration.

The northern reaches of the Midwest have the most severe cold in the country outside of the interior of Alaska. The Dakotas and northern Minnesota often register the coldest temperatures in the nation. The states west of the Mississippi are accustomed to occasional violent weather: tornadoes and thunderstorms in the warm months and blizzards in the winter.

State name Date entered Union	Area 2000 Population	Capital Principal cities	Bird Flower Tree
Illinois Dec. 3, 1818 (21st)	55,593 sq. mi. 12,419,293	★Springfield, Chicago, Peoria, Rockford	Cardinal Purple violet White oak
Indiana Dec. 11, 1816 (19th)	35,870 sq. mi. 6,080,485	★Indianapolis, Gary, Evansville, South Bend	Cardinal Peony Tulip poplar
Iowa Dec. 28, 1846 (29th)	55,875 sq. mi. 2,926,324	★Des Moines, Cedar Rapids, Davenport	Eastern goldfinch Wild rose Oak
Kansas Jan. 29, 1861 (34th)	81,823 sq. mi. 2,688,418	★Topeka, Kansas City, Wichita	Western meadowlark Wild native sunflower Cottonwood
Michigan Jan. 26, 1837 (26th)	55,809 sq. mi. 9,938,444	★Lansing, Detroit, Flint, Grand Rapids	American robin Apple blossom White pine

CANADA

NORTH DAKOTA

Bismarck ★   Fargo

MINNESOTA   Duluth

St. Paul

Minneapolis   WISCONSIN   MICHIGAN

SOUTH DAKOTA

Pierre ★

Rapid City   Sioux Falls   Madison ★   Milwaukee   Flint
                                              Lansing ★
                              Racine   Grand   Detroit
IOWA   Rapids
NEBRASKA   Cedar Rapids   Rockford   Chicago   Cleveland

              Davenport   Gary   South   Toledo
Omaha   Des Moines   Bend   OHIO
                                                          Columbus
Lincoln ★   Peoria   INDIANA   ★
                                                          Dayton
                              ILLINOIS   Indianapolis ★   Cincinnati

Kansas City   Kansas City   Springfield ★

KANSAS   Topeka ★   St.   Evansville
Jefferson   Louis
Wichita   City

MISSOURI

0   miles   200

Land/Climate	Economy
Predominantly rolling plains with elevations rising toward south; temperate climate of hot summers and cold, snowy winters	Major manufacturer of food and machine products; large corn harvest and extensive dairy farming; mining of coal, oil, natural gas
Central lowland plateau with Great Lakes Plain in north; long, hot summers and cold snowy winters	Manufacturing of primary metal, electrical, and food products; corn crops and hog farms; tourism; mineral fuels and stone quarrying
Uniform plain breaking into rolling lands in east; humid continental climate with long warm summers	Leading agricultural state with largest U.S. yield of corn and hogs; manufacturing sector based on farm machinery and meatpacking
Plains throughout, with higher elevations at east and west extremes; variable continental climate notable for sudden changes	Major agricultural state, with largest U.S. wheat crop; manufacturing of food goods and aircraft; mining of natural gas
Upper peninsula of mountains and uplands and lower peninsula of lowland plains; warm summers and cold winters, most severe in north	Manufacturing of automobiles, machinery, chemicals; orchard crops and dairy farming; tourism; mining of iron ore, stone, natural gas

Clouds over Lake Three, Minnesota

A piping plover, Nebraska

State name Date entered Union	Area 2000 Population	Capital Principal cities	Bird Flower Tree
Minnesota May 11, 1858 (32nd)	79,617 sq. mi. 4,919,479	★St. Paul, Minneapolis, Duluth	Common loon Pink and white lady slipper Red pine
Missouri Aug. 10, 1821 (24th)	68,898 sq. mi. 5,595,211	★Jefferson City, St. Louis, Kansas City	Bluebird Hawthorn Dogwood
Nebraska March 1, 1867 (37th)	76,878 sq. mi. 1,711,263	★Lincoln, Omaha	Western meadowlark Goldenrod Cottonwood
North Dakota Nov. 2, 1889 (39th)	68,994 sq. mi. 642,200	★Bismarck, Fargo	Western meadowlark Wild prairie rose American elm
Ohio March 1, 1803 (17th)	40,953 sq. mi. 11,353,140	★Columbus, Cleveland, Cincinnati, Toledo, Dayton	Cardinal Scarlet carnation Buckeye
South Dakota Nov. 2, 1889 (40th)	75,896 sq. mi. 754,844	★Pierre, Sioux Falls, Rapid City	Chinese ring-necked pheasant Pasque Black Hills spruce
Wisconsin May 29, 1848 (30th)	54,314 sq. mi. 5,363,675	★Madison, Milwaukee, Racine	Robin Wood violet Sugar maple

Automobile assembly line, Michigan

Mt. Rushmore, South Dakota

Land/Climate	*Economy*
Hill and lake region with plain to northwest and mountainous uplands to northeast; cold and dry climate, most severe in north	Extensive dairy farming and largest U.S. oat crop; iron ore mining in northeast Mesabi range; food processing; tourism
Plains and rolling hills in north, rugged Ozark Plateau in south; cold winters and long, hot summers with rain heaviest in north	Agricultural state with northern corn crop, southern cotton crop, cattle and dairy livestock throughout; manufacturing; zinc mining
Great Plains over 80 percent of state area, with central lowlands to the east; dry climate with long, warm summers and severe winters	Major agricultural state, second only to Texas in beef cattle; grower of large corn and wheat harvests; manufacturing of food goods
Eastern river lowland rising to central prairie and western plateau; dry continental climate with cool summer nights and severe winters	95 percent of state farmland devoted to livestock and feed crops; coal and oil fuels; mineral refining
Rolling plains of central lowland with Great Lakes Plain in north; temperate climate with hot, humid summers and cold winters	Manufacturing of steel, machinery, transportation equipment; dairy farming; tourism; mining of fuels and stone
Predominantly Great Plains, with Black Hills in west and Prairie-plains in east; dry climate of dramatic seasonal temperature extremes	Farms principally devoted to livestock, wheat, and corn for feed; manufacturing based on food processing; first in United States in gold mining
Northern rolling uplands and southern lowland plains; long, cold winters with heavy snows and short, warm summers	Manufacturing of machinery, foods, and paper goods; dairy farms and corn and oat crops; tourism; lumber

The South

The South consists of 14 states and the District of Columbia, and occupies the southeastern part of the United States. It is bordered on two sides by water: the Atlantic Ocean is to the east and the Gulf of Mexico is to the south. Most of its northern border is defined by the Ohio River. The region is divided into eastern and western sections by the crest of the Appalachian Mountains.

Six of the Southern states were among the original thirteen states—Delaware, Maryland, Virginia, North Carolina, South Carolina, and Georgia. Important battles of the Revolutionary War were fought in North and South Carolina, and the final surrender of British troops took place at Yorktown, Virginia.

Less than 100 years later, most of the Southern states seceded from the Union to form the Confederate States of America, setting in motion the Civil War. After the defeat of the Confederacy, in 1865, the Southern states joined the Union once again.

The most populous state in the South today is Florida, followed by Georgia, North Carolina, and Virginia. These states grew rapidly between 1970 and 2000, attracting many new residents from the Northeast and Midwest. The region's total population is almost 76 million, about 11 million more than that of the Midwest. The region's largest cities include Baltimore, Maryland; Memphis, Tennessee; Washington, D.C.; New Orleans, Louisiana; and Atlanta, Georgia.

State name / Date entered Union	Area / 2000 Population	Capital / Principal cities	Bird / Flower / Tree
Alabama Dec. 14, 1819 (22nd)	50,750 sq. mi. 4,447,100	★Montgomery, Birmingham, Mobile, Huntsville	Yellowhammer Camellia Southern longleaf pine
Arkansas June 15, 1836 (25th)	52,075 sq. mi. 2,673,400	★Little Rock, Pine Bluff, Hot Springs	Mockingbird Apple blossom Pine
Delaware Dec. 7, 1787 (1st)	1,995 sq. mi. 783,600	★Dover, Wilmington, Newark	Blue hen chicken Peach blossom American holly
Florida March 3, 1845 (27th)	53,997 sq. mi. 15,982,378	★Tallahassee, Miami, Tampa, Jacksonville	Mockingbird Orange blossom Sabal palm
Georgia Jan. 2, 1788 (4th)	57,919 sq. mi. 8,186,453	★Atlanta, Columbus, Savannah, Macon	Brown thrasher Cherokee rose Live oak
Kentucky June 1, 1792 (15th)	39,732 sq. mi. 4,041,769	★Frankfort, Louisville, Lexington	Cardinal Goldenrod Tulip poplar
Louisiana April 30, 1812 (18th)	43,566 sq. mi. 4,468,976	★Baton Rouge, New Orleans, Shreveport	Eastern brown pelican Magnolia Cypress

Land/Climate	Economy
Appalachian Highlands in northeast and Gulf Coastal Plain elsewhere; subtropical in south and milder continental climate in north	Mineral refining and manufacture of steel products; dairy and poultry farms and feed crops; timber; tourism
Gulf Coastal Plain in east and south and highlands in west and north; long, hot summers and mild winters, with ample rainfall	Manufacturing of food, forest, textile, and metal goods; poultry farming; mining of mineral ores and fuels
Sandy coastal plain over most of area, with small northern fringe of forested hills; moderate climate, warmest on coast	Chemical products and food processing; poultry and truck farming; tourism
Atlantic Coastal Plain and sandy beaches on peninsula with hills in panhandle; warm and sunny throughout year except in north	Tourism; citrus fruits; manufacturing of food and electronic products; mining of phosphate rock
Mountains in northwest, central plateau, coastal lowlands; warm and rainy southern climate with mild winters	Manufacturing of textiles, forest products, and transportation equipment; poultry farms and peanut, tobacco, orchard crops; tourism
Eastern mountains, central lowland plateaus, western river plain; moderate climate cooler in mountains with plentiful rain throughout	Food product manufacturing and mineral refining; livestock and crops of tobacco and feed grains; coal mining
Low Gulf Coastal Plain rising into low hills in north; subtropical climate with heavy rainfall	Oil and natural gas drilling and refining; tourism; field crops and poultry farming

Jazz band, New Orleans

Crab fishing boats, Maryland

State name Date entered Union	Area 2000 Population	Capital Principal cities	Bird Flower Tree
Maryland April 28, 1788 (7th)	9,775 sq. mi. 5,296,486	★Annapolis, Baltimore, Rockville	Baltimore oriole Black-eyed Susan White oak
Mississippi Dec. 10, 1817 (20th)	46,914 sq. mi. 2,844,658	★Jackson, Biloxi, Meridian	Mockingbird Magnolia Magnolia
North Carolina Nov. 21, 1789 (12th)	48,718 sq. mi. 8,049,313	★Raleigh, Charlotte, Greensboro, Winston-Salem, Durham	Northern cardinal Flowering dogwood Pine
South Carolina May 23, 1788 (8th)	30,111 sq. mi. 4,012,012	★Columbia, Charleston, Greenville	Carolina wren Yellow jessamine Palmetto
Tennessee June 1, 1796 (16th)	41,219 sq. mi. 5,689,283	★Nashville, Memphis, Knoxville, Chattanooga	Mockingbird Iris Tulip poplar
Virginia June 25, 1788 (10th)	39,598 sq. mi. 7,078,515	★Richmond, Norfolk, Roanoke	Cardinal American dogwood American dogwood
West Virginia June 20, 1863 (35th)	24,087 sq. mi. 1,808,344	★Charleston, Huntington, Wheeling	Cardinal Rhododendron Sugar maple
Washington, D.C.	61 sq. mi. 572,059		Wood thrush American beauty rose Scarlet oak

Blue Ridge Mountains, Virginia

Million Man March, Washington, D.C.

Land/Climate	*Economy*
Coastal plain surrounding bay, with western plateau and mountains; mild climate near bay and colder farther inland	Manufacturing of processed foods and refined minerals; poultry and dairy farms; tourism
Fertile floodplain along Mississippi River, and higher Gulf Coastal Plain over rest of area; warm temperatures and heavy rainfall	Manufacturing of textile, food, wood, and electrical goods; soybean crop and dairy farming; oil and natural gas drilling
Mountains in northwest declining to Piedmont Plateau and Atlantic Coastal Plain; warm southeast climate, drier and cooler inland	Manufacturing of farm products and processing of crops; largest U.S. tobacco harvest; corn, peanuts, poultry farms; tourism
Northwestern mountains declining to central plateau and coastal plain; warm, humid summers and short, mild winters	Manufacturing of textiles, plastics, and paper products; tobacco, orchard crops, and poultry; tourism; timber
Rugged mountains in east, central lowland plateau, plain and river bottomland in west; humid, temperate climate throughout	Manufacturing of chemical, ore, and electrical products; mining of coal, zinc, phosphate; cattle grazing and large tobacco crop
Western mountain and valley region, central plateau, coastal plain; mild seasonal temperature variation, with heaviest rain on coast	Diversified manufacturing of chemical products, farm yield, and textile goods; tobacco crop, poultry, and dairy farming; tourism
Hilly to mountainous throughout, with elevations declining east and west of central Allegheny Mountains; humid with mild winters	Mining of coal, natural gas, and crude oil; mineral refining and related manufacturing; orchard crops and dairy farming
Level shore of Potomac River; warm, humid summers and mild winters without significant snow	Tourism; government services

The Northeast

The Northeast is the smallest of the four U.S. regions, both in area and population. Its nine states take up an area just slightly larger than that of California. Although it is smaller in population than the other regions, its 54 million people are more densely settled than those in other regions. The Northeast has nearly 20 percent of the country's people on less than 5 percent of its land.

The Atlantic shores of the Northeast were settled in the 1600s, mostly by English colonists. Seven of its states were among the original 13. The Declaration of Independence was proclaimed in Philadelphia, and the Revolutionary War began near Boston. During the Civil War, all the Northeastern states were part of the Union. The only major battle of that war fought in the Northeast was the battle of Gettysburg in Pennsylvania.

Before and after the Civil War, the Northeast became the settling place for millions of immigrants from Europe. Even today, the region claims a large proportion of descendants from Ireland, Italy, Germany, and Eastern Europe.

The most populous state in the region is New York. Other populous states are Pennsylvania, New Jersey, and Massachusetts. New Jersey is the most densely populated state in the Union, with about 1,100 residents per square mile. New York and Rhode Island both lost population during the years between 1970 and 1980. All of the states gained population during the years between 1980 and 2000. New Hampshire and Vermont had the highest percentage of gains.

The region's most important city is New York, which is the largest in the United States. Most of its other large cities lie in a corridor that stretches from New York north to Boston and south to Philadelphia and Washington, D.C. Important cities to the west include Pittsburgh and Buffalo.

State name Date entered Union	Area 2000 Population	Capital Principal cities	Bird Flower Tree
Connecticut Jan. 9, 1788 (5th)	4,845 sq. mi. 3,405,565	★Hartford, Bridgeport, New Haven	American robin Mountain laurel White oak
Maine March 15, 1820 (23rd)	30,865 sq. mi. 1,274,923	★Augusta, Portland, Lewiston, Bangor	Chickadee White pine cone and tassel White pine
Massachusetts Feb. 6, 1788 (6th)	7,838 sq. mi. 6,349,097	★Boston, Springfield, Worcester, Lowell	Black-capped chickadee Mayflower American elm
New Hampshire June 21, 1788 (9th)	8,969 sq. mi. 1,235,786	★Concord, Manchester, Nashua, Portsmouth	Purple finch Purple lilac White birch
New Jersey Dec. 18, 1787 (3rd)	7,419 sq. mi. 8,414,350	★Trenton, Newark, Camden, Paterson	Eastern goldfinch Violet Red oak
New York July 26, 1788 (11th)	47,224 sq. mi. 18,976,457	★Albany, New York, Buffalo, Rochester, Syracuse	Bluebird Rose Sugar maple

Land/Climate	Economy
New England Uplands to east and west of central river valley; moderate climate, coldest in northwest areas	Diversified manufactures, including aircraft engines; national insurance companies; dairy farming; tourism
Northeast uplands, central White Mountains, southeast coastal lowlands; cold winters with heavy snows inland and cool summers	Manufacturing of wood pulp, leather, and textile goods; tourism; dairy farming and potato crop
New England Uplands in interior and sandy seaboard lowlands along eastern coast; temperate in east and colder and drier inland	Manufacturer of electrical, textile, machine, and printing goods; tourism; dairy farms and greenhouse vegetables
All hilly uplands surrounding White Mountains except for coastal lowland; severe winters in uplands, with moderate temperatures on coast	Manufacturing of leather, wood pulp, and electronic equipment; tourism; dairy farming
Hilly, forested northern half and flat, sandy south; moderate northeastern climate	Diversified manufacturing notable for chemical products; tourism at coastal beaches; truck farming in south
Appalachian Plateau and mountains over most of area, with Great Lakes Plain to north; moderate climate southeast, colder inland	Second only to California in diversified manufactures; tourism; dairy livestock with orchard, vineyard, and greenhouse crops

Theater, New York City

Sterling Memorial Library, Yale University, New Haven, Connec

| State name
Date entered Union | Area
2000 Population | Capital
Principal cities | Bird
Flower
Tree |
|---|---|---|---|
| **Pennsylvania**
Dec. 12, 1787 (2nd) | 44,820 sq. mi.
12,281,054 | ★Harrisburg,
Philadelphia,
Pittsburgh,
Scranton, Erie | Ruffed grouse
Mountain laurel
Hemlock |
| **Rhode Island**
May 29, 1790 (13th) | 1,045 sq. mi.
1,048,319 | ★Providence,
Warwick,
Pawtucket | Rhode Island Red chicken
Violet
Red maple |
| **Vermont**
March 4, 1791 (14th) | 9,249 sq. mi.
608,827 | ★Montpelier,
Burlington,
Rutland | Hermit thrush
Red clover
Sugar maple |

U.S. territories

The United States held numerous overseas possessions early in the 1900s. Today, however, it retains possession of only a few. The largest by far is the Caribbean island of Puerto Rico. Near Puerto Rico are the U.S. Virgin Islands.

The remainder of U.S. territories are in the Pacific Ocean. The largest of these is the western Pacific island of Guam.

| Official name | Location | Area/Population
2002 |
|---|---|---|
| **American Samoa** | In south Pacific 2,500 miles east of Australia | 76 sq. mi.; 69,000 |
| **Guam** | In west Pacific 1,200 miles east of the Philippines | 212 sq. mi.; 161,000 |

Liberty Bell, Philadelphia

Vermont village

Land/Climate	Economy
Central Allegheny Mountains with rugged plateau north and west and plain to southeast; moderate climate in east and colder in western interior	Manufacturing ranging from heavy coal industries in west to food and electronic products in east; dairy livestock; tourism
Sandy seaboard lowlands rising to hill and lake region in northwest; moderate climate influenced by inland bay	Manufactures include machinery, textiles, and electronics; tourism; truck and dairy farming
Hilly throughout with central spine of Green Mountains; short, warm summers and long winters with heavy snowfall	Manufacturing of machine tools and electronic equipment; tourism; dairy farms and maple syrup

Official name	Location	Area/Population 2002
Midway Islands	In Pacific Ocean 1,000 miles northwest of Hawaii	2.5 sq. mi.; 150
Puerto Rico	Caribbean island east of Dominican Republic	3,514 sq. mi.; 3,863,000
Virgin Islands	Caribbean islands 40 miles east of Puerto Rico	134 sq. mi.; 123,000
Wake Island	In Pacific Ocean 2,000 miles west of Hawaii	2.4 sq. mi.; 124

Flags of the United States and Its States and Possessions

The design of the United States flag evolved over a period of roughly 200 years. Today, every American easily recognizes the "stars and bars." Thirteen stripes, which symbolize the thirteen original colonies, lie horizontally; seven are colored red, and six are white. In the upper corner nearest the staff, there is a rectangular blue field (called a "canton"), which holds the 50 stars that represent all the states of the Union. Congress has defined the symbolic values of the colors as follows: white represents purity and innocence; red symbolizes hardiness, valor, and courage; blue signifies vigilance, perseverance, and justice.

Most Americans are familiar with the legend that accords Betsy Ross the distinction of being the first person to produce the American flag. According to the popular

Population: 281,421,906
Capital: Washington, D.C.
Highest point: Mt. McKinley 20,320 ft. (6,194 m)
Monetary unit: U.S. dollar

myth, which originated with the testimony of William Canby (Ms. Ross's grandson), General George Washington arrived on the doorstep of her Philadelphia home in the summer of 1776. He requested that the seamstress sew the first flag with the aid of a sketch he brought along. Ms. Ross supposedly followed his design exactly, with only a slight modification—she reduced the number of points on the stars from six to five.

The legend of Betsy Ross remains widely believed, but it is almost assuredly untrue. General Washington was in Philadelphia at the alleged time, but he was on urgent military business, making the visit an unlikely possibility. Historians have attributed the design to other individuals several times without any success. Now, it is widely held that the first flag was designed and produced as a group effort, rather than being the brainchild of a single person.

While the origin of the first flag's design and production is unclear, it is known that Congress passed the First Flag Act on June 14, 1777, shortly after the Declaration of Independence was ratified. It specified that the flag should have 13 stripes, alternately red and white in color, as well as a blue field containing 13 stars to represent a "new constellation." The arrangement of the design, however, was not explicitly worded. Important pieces of information, such as proportions of the elements and the direction of the stripes, were not included. This ambiguity regarding the design's layout resulted in considerable diversity among the first flags. The stars appeared in a number of different arrangements, including rows, circles, and stars. The number of points on the stars varied. Although there was no definitive design, the lack of uniformity was not a pressing issue because flags were usually reserved for use on ships.

Of course, the United States grew from the original 13 states that originally formed the Union. As more areas gained statehood, a debate regarding the appropriate number of stripes for the flag ensued. Many people believed that the number of stripes should reflect the number of states, while others argued that the change was superfluous and an unnecessary expense. The controversy officially ended May 1, 1795, when Congress passed the Second Flag Act, which called for 15 stripes and 15 stars to reflect the recent additions of Vermont and Kentucky. This was the second official version of the national flag, but flags continued to be produced differently; uniformity in design was lacking. Incidentally, this design inspired Francis Scott Key to write the "Star-Spangled Banner," which became the national anthem in 1931.

February 4, 1783, marked the end of the Revolutionary War, and the United States flag gained recognition throughout the world, lending it a new importance. The Union continued to grow, and the old debate regarding the number of stars and stripes resurfaced. As states joined the Union, flag designs varied even more widely. Eventually, it became obvious that the stripe-to-state ratio was becoming unmanageable; the stripes were becoming so thin that they were difficult to distinguish, even from a short distance. In 1818, President James Monroe passed the Third Flag Act, which settled the dispute and has directed the flag's design ever since. The new legislation set the number of stripes at the original 13. Additionally, the second section of the Act allowed for the addition of a new star each time a state was admitted to the Union. It also stipulated that the change in number would always take effect on the July 4 following admittance. Unfortunately, the text did not specify the arrangement of the stars; therefore, the United States flag still lacked a definitive design.

At the time of the Third Flag Act, there were 20 stars. The following year, another star was added to signify the admittance of Illinois. July 4, 1820, saw two more additions, representing Alabama and Maine. The 24th star, representing Missouri, was added 2 years later. It wasn't until 1836 that another, symbolizing the statehood of Arkansas, was added, followed by another star in 1837 for Michigan. In 1845, a star was added for Florida; in 1846, another was added for Texas. The additions of Iowa and Wisconsin came in 1847 and 1848, respectively. California gained a star in 1851. Minnesota assumed statehood in 1858, and Oregon became the 33rd star in 1859.

Kansas, West Virginia, and Nevada gained stars in 1861, 1863, and 1865, respectively. The year 1865 also marked the end of the Civil War; notably, despite the secession of a number of states, the quantity of stars on the official design was not altered. The start of the Reconstruction era saw admittance of Nebraska in 1867. A star was added for Colorado in 1877. Five stars, symbolizing North Dakota, South Dakota, Washington, Idaho, and Montana, were added in 1890, bringing the total to 43. The 44th star, belonging to Wyoming, was added in 1891, and Utah was added in 1896.

The addition of Oklahoma occurred in 1908, and two stars, representing New Mexico and Arizona, were added in 1912. That year also marked the year that the flag finally gained specifications for its design. President William Taft issued an executive order June 24, 1912, that set the flag's width and length, as well as the measurements of all of the design's elements. His order led to a much-needed uniformity in design.

In 1959, Alaska was added. Hawaii, the last state to join the Union, added the 50th star in 1960. The result was the 27th, and most current, flag design. Today, many institutions and individuals display the 27th version of the flag to show their patriotic devotion and love for America.

Several traditions and customs surround the United States flag; the definitive guidelines were established when Congress created the Flag Code in 1942 (see page 173 for some of these guidelines). It detailed the conventions for proper display and handling. Generally, the flag should be displayed from sunrise to sunset; if it flies in the dark, appropriate lighting should be provided. The code also stated that the flag should be raised briskly and lowered ceremoniously. In addition, it specified that the flag should not be used for advertising purposes and that it should not be embroidered on anything disposable or inappropriate (e.g., handkerchiefs or cushions). Finally, the Flag Code provided comprehensive instructions for the flag's display in a variety of scenarios involving the presence of other flags.

Perhaps the most familiar tradition associated with the flag is the Pledge of Allegiance. Francis Bellamy authored the Pledge in 1892; it was written to be repeated by schoolchildren on Columbus Day. It first appeared in a publication called *The Youth's Companion* and was officially recognized by Congress in 1942, with only slight modifications.

Flag Day, another tradition related to the flag, marks the anniversary of the First Flag Act. It was first celebrated in Connecticut June 14, 1861. The first nationwide celebration was in 1877, but it was a centennial celebration. Flag Day became an annual tradition in 1949, when June 14 was made a national, legally observed holiday.

The original design of the American flag, representing the 13 colonies.

This flag was secretly sewn by an American prisoner-of-war while he was being held at the "Hanoi Hilton" during the Vietnam War.

ALABAMA

Alabama's flag was created under the administration of Governor William Oates on February 16, 1895. The design is simple, yet striking; vibrantly colored red bars form a cross on a pure white background. The Spanish, who once ruled in that area, may have influenced the design.

The flag was specifically designed to resemble the Confederate flag; the red "X" shape recalls St. Andrew's cross, a prominent feature of the Southern battle flag in the Civil War. This deliberate Confederate allusion is a fairly common practice; as a result, Alabama's flag bears many similarities to the flags of other Southern states, such as Florida.

Population: 4,447,100
Capital: Montgomery
Largest city: Birmingham

Highest point: Cheaha Mtn. 2,407 ft. (734 m)
Settled in: 1702
Popular name: Heart of Dixie; Cotton State; Yellowhammer State

ALASKA

Alaska's flag was adopted May 2, 1927. Benny Benson, a 13-year-old orphan, conceived the design, which was chosen as the winning entry of a statewide contest. (The seventh grader's prize was an engraved watch and $1,000.) The background is a vibrant blue, which represents both the sky and the forget-me-not (the state flower, which was also chosen by the young designer).

Eight gold stars illuminate the vast azure backdrop of the night sky. The largest luminary, located in the upper right-hand corner, represents the North Star; it serves as a reference to Alaska's status as the northernmost state of the Union. The other stars form the well-known constellation called the Big Dipper. The Great Bear, the astrological formation's alternate name, more aptly represents its symbolic significance, which is strength.

Population: 626,932
Capital: Juneau
Largest city: Anchorage

Highest point: Mt. McKinley 20,320 ft. (6,194 m)
Settled in: 1801
Popular name: Great Land; Last Frontier

ARIZONA

The lively, colorful flag of Arizona was adopted February 27, 1917. A five-pointed copper-colored star lies at the center of the flag; it symbolizes Arizona's status as the largest copper producer in the United States. Thirteen rays (alternately colored red and yellow) shine out from the top of the star. The rays represent the thirteen original colonies and the setting sun.

The bottom half of the flag is occupied by an unspotted royal blue field. The color scheme was chosen carefully to reflect state, national, and international heritage: blue and yellow are the official state colors, the red and blue shades are identical to the hues on the national flag, and red and yellow represent the Spanish Conquistadors.

Population: 5,130,632
Capital: Phoenix
Largest city: Phoenix

Highest point: Humphreys Pk. 12,633 ft. (3,851 m)
Settled in: 1752
Popular name: Grand Canyon State

ARKANSAS

The flag of Arkansas was adopted February 23, 1933. Its red, white, and blue design was chosen from a pool of 65 entries (ranging from simple crayon drawings to elaborate silk miniatures) in a statewide contest. Miss Willie Hocker, an Arkansas native, conceived the winning design, which features a diamond centered on a red background.

The diamond represents Arkansas' status as the only diamond mining state of the Union. The blue border surrounding it contains twenty-five white stars; they represent Arkansas' position as twenty-fifth state to join the United States. The middle of the diamond is white and features the state's name surrounded by four blue stars.

The three stars located below the print are symbolically significant in three ways. First, they represent the three countries (France, Spain, and the United States) that owned the state prior to its admittance to the Union. They also allude to 1803, the date of the Louisiana Purchase. Finally, they reference the fact that Arkansas was the third state formed as a result of the Louisiana Purchase. The fourth star, located above the print, commemorates the Confederacy.

Population: 2,673,400
Capital: Little Rock
Largest city: Little Rock

Highest point: Magazine Mtn. 2,753 ft. (839 m)
Settled in: 1685
Popular name: Land of Opportunity

CALIFORNIA

California adopted its state flag on February 3, 1911. The design was conceived by a group of American frontiersmen who stormed a small California town under Mexican rule. Shortly after their victory, they hastily created the first "Bear Flag," which has been modified only slightly in the years since its creation in 1846. The phrase "California Republic" appears in bold, black letters toward the bottom of the flag. It refers to the same event by referencing the words of one of the American victors, William Idle; upon taking a Mexican soldier prisoner, he called California an independent republic.

The design features a bold motif that is juxtaposed against a stark white background. A grizzly bear walks menacingly toward the left; the ferocious beast symbolizes courage and is also the official state animal. One of the bear's eyes seems to gaze at the viewer observantly. A small plot of green grass lies below him. A five-pointed star, colored red, is in the upper left-hand corner. The origin of its symbolism is unknown, but it may refer to the lone star on the Texan flag. A coordinating red stripe forms the border for the bottom of the flag.

Population: 33,871,648
Capital: Sacramento
Largest city: Los Angeles

Highest point: Mt. Whitney 14,494 ft. (4,418 m)
Settled in: 1769
Popular name: Golden State

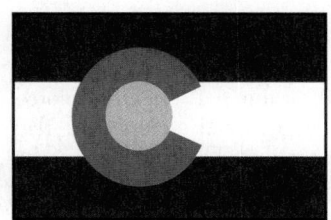

COLORADO

The flag of Colorado, which was designed by Andrew Carlisle Johnson, was adopted June 5, 1911. Its bold design is relatively simple but visually dramatic. The background comprises three horizontal panels; the top and bottom fields are blue, while the middle panel is white. A large, red letter "C" is positioned toward the left. The center of the letter is filled with a gold circle.

The color scheme was carefully chosen to symbolize several features of Colorado's landscape. Blue represents its clear skies. White stands for its snowcapped mountains. Red signifies the color of the earth, or soil. Finally, the gold represents the sun, an oft-enjoyed aspect of Colorado's weather.

Population: 4,301,261
Capital: Denver
Largest city: Denver

Highest point: Mt. Elbert 14,433 ft. (4,399 m)
Settled in: 1858
Popular name: Centennial State

CONNECTICUT

The Connecticut state flag was adopted on June 9, 1897; an American Revolution memorial inspired its design. The flag is made of silk and features a white shield centered on a blue background. The shield's design is simple and classical; it is primarily white, with cloisters of yellow fruit and green leaves around the border. Three naturally colored grapevines climb wooden stakes across the shield; they refer to the copious number of wild grape vines that grow

throughout the Connecticut area. They also symbolize the colony that was brought from Europe and transplanted into the New World.

Reinforcing this theme is the state motto, "Qui Transtulit Sustinet" (a Latin phrase that translates as "He Who Transplanted Still Sustains"), which is written in blue across a billowing white banner located just below the shield. The motto's origin is uncertain, but some believe it was adapted from the 80th Psalm of the Bible, which reads, "Thou hast brought a vine out of Egypt: thou cast out the heathen, and planted it."

Population: 3,405,565
Capital: Hartford
Largest city: Bridgeport

Highest point: Mt. Frissell (S. Slope) 2,380 ft. (725 m)
Settled in: 1635
Popular name: Constitution State; Nutmeg State

DELAWARE

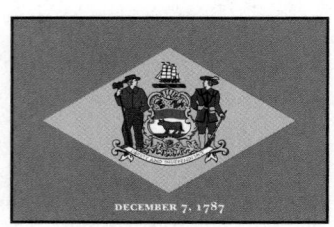

The Delaware state flag, which was adopted on July 24, 1913, features images vibrant in color and rich with symbolism. The colonial blue background and the buff shade of the diamond are the flag's predominant colors; they represent General George Washington's uniform during the Revolutionary War. The state shield, centered within the diamond, pictures a sheaf of wheat, an ear of corn, and an ox. These images function as symbols of Delaware's agricultural prosperity and also represent the state's three counties (New Castle, Kent, and Sussex). Toward the bottom of the flag, the words "December 7, 1787" are printed in white. This date is of special significance, as it was when Delaware became the first state to ratify the United States Constitution.

The ship located above the shield represents both the state's successful ship-building industry and flourishing coastal commerce. A man stands to either side of the shield; the farmer on the left recognizes the important contribution of the farming industry to the state's wealth, while the solider on the right symbolizes Delaware's commitment to fight for freedom. The scroll under the shield, which bears the state motto, "Liberty and Independence," enforces this dedication to freedom and acknowledges the important role that Delaware played during the formation of the United States.

Population: 783,600
Capital: Dover
Largest city: Wilmington

Highest point: Ebright Road 442 ft. (135 m)
Settled in: 1627
Popular name: First State; Diamond State

FLORIDA

The state flag of Florida, adopted in 1900, features a brightly colored design. The red X-shaped cross that is emblazoned across the flag provides a striking contrast to the stark white background. The symbolism of the cross is ambiguous; some people believe it is modeled on the Confederate war flag, while others contend it is based on the Spanish military's "Cross of Burgundy," which was a standard used in the southeastern United States.

A vibrant yellow band borders the state seal, which is positioned at the center of the red cross. The words "Great Seal of the State of Florida" are printed in red across the top; spanning the bottom is the state motto, "In God We Trust." The inner circle depicts a sandy scene that features a Native American woman sprinkling flowers on the beach. She is clothed in traditional Seminole garb, representing a tribe native to the region. A beautiful Florida landscape surrounds her: a boat sails on brilliantly blue water, palm trees are scattered across the beach, and the sun shines brightly in the distance.

Population: 15,982,378
Capital: Tallahassee
Largest city: Jacksonville

Highest point: (Walton County) 345 ft. (105 m)
Settled in: 1565
Popular name: Sunshine State; Peninsula State

GEORGIA

The current state flag of Georgia was adopted on May 8, 2003. It features one band of white between two bands of red. The state coat of arms is in a blue canton in the upper left corner. Thirteen stars encircle the coat of arms, representing Georgia as one of the original colonies. The state seal depicts three pillars supporting an arch; these pillars represent the legislative, judicial, and executive branches of government. Also shown is a man with sword drawn to defend the constitution. The year 1776 and the words "In God We Trust" also appear on the seal.

This current design was confirmed subsequent to a referendum on March 4, 2004. This referendum was to determine whether this design should stand or be replaced by a previous 2001 design. The 2001 design was itself a replacement of a controversial 1956 design, which prominently incorporated the Confederate battle flag. Because the 2001 design also depicted the Confederate battle flag, the governor called for a referendum and the outcome provided for the current design to remain.

Population: 8,186,453
Capital: Atlanta
Largest city: Atlanta

Highest point: Brasstown Bald 4,784 ft. (1,458 m)
Settled in: 1733
Popular name: Empire State of the South; Peach State

HAWAII

The flag of Hawaii was adopted in May of 1845. King Kamehameha I originally commissioned it when Hawaii was still an independent kingdom. It holds the unique distinction of being the only state flag to have flown over a kingdom, territory, republic, and state. The design combines aspects of the flags of the United States and Great Britain in order to acknowledge Hawaii's friendship with both nations.

Eight horizontal stripes (alternating white, red, and blue) occupy the majority of the flag. The number of stripes represents the eight islands that make up Hawaii. The upper left-hand corner of the flag houses a Union Jack (the symbol featured on the flag of the United Kingdom); it was included in order to please British merchants. It is the only state flag that bears such a prominent reference to another country.

Population: 1,211,537
Capital: Honolulu
Largest city: Honolulu

Highest point: Mauna Kea 13,796 ft. (4,205 m)
Settled in: ————
Popular name: Aloha State

IDAHO

Idaho adopted its flag March 12, 1907; it features the state seal centered on a deep blue background. A yellow band with a braided border surrounds the seal. Below the seal, a red stylized banner reading "State of Idaho" appears. The center of the seal depicts a visually busy scene. A woman clothed in classical robes stands on the viewer's left; she personifies liberty and justice. She holds a staff topped with a white liberty cap in her right hand; she grips balanced scales in her left hand. Shafts of wheat and the state flower (syringa) grow to her right, and a man holding a pickaxe and a shovel stands to her left. He represents mining, which was the eminent industry when the seal was designed.

A shield depicting a peaceful Idaho landscape separates the woman and the man. The Shoshone River winds through a wooded area that represents the state's timber industry, and a plowman represents the agricultural industry. In the distance, one can just make out a stamp mill among the mountains. The crest of the shield is the head of an elk; just above him a banner reading "Esto Perpetua" flies. (The state's Latin motto translates as "It Is Forever" or "It Is Perpetuated.") The two overflowing cornucopias that lie just under the shield symbolize prosperity.

Population: 1,293,953
Capital: Boise
Largest city: Boise

Highest point: Borah Pk. 12,662 ft. (3,859 m)
Settled in: 1842
Popular name: Gem State

ILLINOIS

The flag of Illinois was adopted July 6, 1915. It features the state seal against a plain white background. An American eagle, wings outspread, stands proudly in the flag's center; he clutches a shield in his talons. The gold-rimmed protective device has a stars-and-stripes motif that recalls the national flag's design. The upper portion of the shield has a blue background and contains thirteen white stars, which symbolize the original colonies. A leafy green laurel lies just underneath it.

The national bird stands on a rock inscribed with two dates: 1868 and 1818. The state seal was adopted in 1868, while 1818 was the year Illinois became the twenty-first state of the Union. Streaming from the eagle's beak are two red banners; together they form the state motto, "State Sovereignty, National Union." A blazing sun burns over a body of water in the distance. The state's name appears in bold blue letters at the bottom of the flag.

Population: 12,419,293
Capital: Springfield
Largest city: Chicago

Highest point: Charles Mound 1,236 ft. (376 m)
Settled in: 1720
Popular name: Prairie State; Land of Lincoln

INDIANA

Indiana's flag, which was adopted May 31, 1917, features a yellow design printed on a deep blue background. A flaming torch that symbolizes liberty is prominently displayed in the middle. Rays emit from the torch and stretch toward a cluster of nineteen stars that surround it in a circular formation; they reference Indiana's status as the nineteenth state to join the Union.

Thirteen of the stars form the outer rim of the circle; these honor the original thirteen states. The five stars that form the inner semicircle represent the next five states to join; the final (and largest) star is positioned directly over the torch. It represents Indiana, as signified by the state's name, which appears at the top.

Population: 6,080,485
Capital: Indianapolis
Largest city: Indianapolis

Highest point: (Wayne County) 1,257 ft. (383 m)
Settled in: 1730
Popular name: Hoosier State

IOWA

Iowa's flag was adopted March 29, 1921. The primary colors are red, white, and blue; each shade appears in a vertically aligned panel of equal proportion. These hues are of double significance; they honor the colors of France (which ruled the area twice before Iowa became a state) and the United States (which received Iowa as part of the Louisiana Purchase).

The center panel is white; it features an image of an American eagle in flight. The national bird is a symbol of protection. Its beak grips a streaming blue banner printed with the state's motto, "Our Liberties We Prize and Our Rights We Will Maintain," in white block letters. Toward the bottom, the state's name appears in large red letters. A plain blue panel is on the left, and an unadorned red panel appears on the right.

Population: 2,926,324
Capital: Des Moines
Largest city: Des Moines

Highest point: (Osceola County) 1,670 ft. (509 m)
Settled in: 1788
Popular name: Hawkeye State

KANSAS

The state flag of Kansas was adopted March 23, 1927. This colorful flag features the state seal centered on a vast blue background. The seal, a circle with a golden braided border, depicts an idyllic Kansas landscape. Toward the front, a man plows a field with a pair of horses. Just behind him, two covered wagons are pulled through a green landscape. To the right, the chimney of a small log cabin smokes peacefully. In the distance, just beside the water, two hunters on horseback pursue five buffalo.

In the background, an old-fashioned steamboat floats along the Kansas River. Mountains and the rising sun provide a serene backdrop. The unclouded sky features thirty-four silver stars; they represent Kansas' position as the thirty-fourth state to join the Union. An orange banner that arches rainbow-like through the sky is printed with the state's motto, "Ad Astra Per Aspera." (This translates as "To the Stars Through Difficulties.") The crest above the seal is a sunflower, and the state's name is printed in yellow block letters at the bottom.

Population: 2,688,418
Capital: Topeka
Largest city: Wichita

Highest point: Mt. Sunflower 4,039 ft. (1,231 m)
Settled in: 1831
Popular name: Sunflower State

KENTUCKY

The flag of Kentucky was adopted March 26, 1918. The simple design features the state seal centered on a deep blue background. The seal, which is white and banded with gold, depicts two men shaking hands amiably. The person on the left is dressed in traditional garb; his rural clothing recalls the pioneers. The man on the right is a gentleman; his formal attire indicates that he represents the urban population.

Their friendly exchange is an apt illustration for the state motto, which is "United We Stand, Divided We Fall." Appropriately, "United We Stand" is printed above the men's heads, while "Divided We Fall" appears below their feet. The state flower, goldenrod, forms the border outside the bottom half of the seal, and the words "Commonwealth of Kentucky" border the upper half.

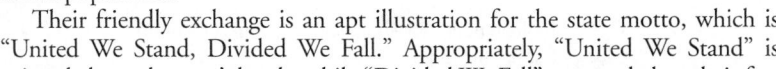

Population: 4,041,769
Capital: Frankfort
Largest city: Louisville

Highest point: Black Mtn. 4,145 ft. (1,263 m)
Settled in: 1774
Popular name: Bluegrass State

LOUISIANA

Louisiana's flag was adopted July 1, 1912. It features the state emblem centered on a deep cobalt background. A brown pelican, the state bird, is pictured spread-winged over her nest, which contains three of her offspring. Their beaks are upturned, indicating their hunger. The pelican is depicted tearing her own flesh in order to feed her young. Although this act of motherly love might seem gruesome to some, the faint-of-heart needn't worry. This behavior is only the stuff of legends; the myth originated from the red-tipped beaks of certain types of pelicans. The mother's self-sacrificing act symbolizes Louisiana's commitment to boundless giving. The state motto, "Union, Justice, and Confidence," appears on a white banner below this scene.

Population: 4,468,976
Capital: Baton Rouge
Largest city: New Orleans

Highest point: Driskill Mtn. 535 ft. (163 m)
Settled in: 1699
Popular name: Pelican State

MAINE

Maine's state flag was adopted February 24, 1909; the background color (as required by state law) is the same shade of blue as found on the United States flag. The coat of arms appears in the middle of the flag and features a large white pine tree (the official state tree) towering over many smaller trees in the distance. In the foreground, a moose rests by a lake. This idyllic pastoral appears with considerable variation from flag to flag, as there are no official colors specified in the state's legislation.

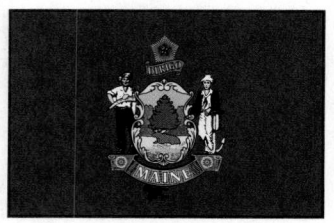

Two men support the shield; a farmer, representing land, rests on a scythe. A sailor, who rests on an anchor on the right, represents the sea. Both men stand on a blue banner with "Maine" printed in bold white letters. The North Star glows brightly over this scene; this crest was chosen when Maine was the northernmost state (its claim to this title has since been usurped by Alaska). The state motto, "Dirigo" (translation: "I Direct or Guide"), appears on the scroll gracing the bottom of the crest.

Population: 1,274,923
Capital: Augusta
Largest city: Portland

Highest point: Mt. Katahdin 5,268 ft. (1,606 m)
Settled in: 1624
Popular name: Pine Tree State

MARYLAND

The flag of Maryland was adopted March 9, 1904. Its unique, quartered design features the coat of arms for the two founding families of Maryland, the Calverts and the Crosslands. The second Lord Baltimore (a Calvert) founded Maryland in 1634; his family is represented by the black and gold-checkered design featured in the first and fourth quartiles of the flag. "Crossland" was the family name of the first Lord Baltimore's mother; the second and third quartiles honor her family. These panels feature a lively color scheme of red and white quadrangles, and a Greek fleur-de-lis cross is formed with contrasting colors in the center.

Population: 5,296,486
Capital: Annapolis
Largest city: Baltimore

Highest point: Backbone Mtn. 3,360 ft. (1,024 m)
Settled in: 1634
Popular name: Old Line State; Free State

MASSACHUSETTS

The Massachusetts state flag was adopted March 18, 1908. It is one of the few two-sided state flags. The reverse side of the flag formerly featured a green pine tree (which symbolized Massachusetts' plentiful forests and the industry they inspired), but it was modified in 1971 as it became increasingly expensive to manufacture. The front consists of the state coat of arms centered on a white background. The three-sided shield is primarily blue with yellow accents. It depicts a native American who clutches an arrow in his left hand and a bow in his right. He represents peace, as his bow is pointed downward. A white star is located just above the bow; it symbolizes Massachusetts.

A streaming blue banner is located just outside the bottom two-thirds of the shield; it reads, "Ense Petit Placidam Sub Libertate Quietem" in yellow. The state's motto translates as "By the Sword We Seek Peace, but Peace Only Under Liberty." The crest reinforces the motto; just above the shield, an arm holding a sword is raised over a blue and yellow wreath.

Population: 6,349,097
Capital: Boston
Largest city: Boston

Highest point: Mt. Greylock 3,491 ft. (1,064 m)
Settled in: 1620
Popular name: Bay State; Old Colony

MICHIGAN

Michigan's flag, which was adopted August 1, 1911, features the state seal centered on a deep cobalt background. The blue shield depicts a frontiersman standing on a green peninsula; his left hand grips a rifle, his right hand is raised in greeting. A body of water surrounds the peninsula, and the sun is rising in the distance. "Tuebor" (translation: "I will defend") appears at the top of the shield. The shield is balanced on two green fronds, and below a white banner reads "Si Quaeris Peninsulam Amoenam Circumspice." The state motto, which references the state's position between the Great Lakes, translates as "If You Seek a Pleasant Peninsula, Look About You."

An American eagle spreads his wings above the shield; he clutches three arrows in his left claw and an olive branch in the right. The thirteen olives on the branch symbolize the original colonies. A red streamer is printed with the United States' motto, "E Pluribus Unum," which means "From Many, One." Two animals rear on their hind legs toward the shield; the beast on the viewer's left is a buck elk, and the one on the right is a moose.

Population: 9,938,444
Capital: Lansing
Largest city: Detroit

Highest point: Mt. Curwood 1,980 ft. (604 m)
Settled in: 1650
Popular name: Wolverine State

MINNESOTA

Minnesota's lively and colorful state flag was adopted February 28, 1893. The background is a deep, vibrant blue. The state seal is centered within a gold-banded white circle toward the middle of the flag. Yellow circles surround the seal, and five clusters of stars appear at intervals around the outside of the dotted border. This formation lends the appearance of the seal being centered on a large star. Four of the clusters contain four stars, while the fifth cluster (at the apex) contains three stars. Altogether there are nineteen stars, which acknowledges Minnesota's position as the nineteenth state to enter the Union.

The seal references three dates. The year the first colonial settlers came to the area, 1819, appears at the top. The year Minnesota gained statehood, 1858, appears toward the left. Finally, 1893, the year the flag was adopted, appears toward the right. The center of the seal depicts a farmer plowing a field and a Native American on horseback. A red banner reading "L'Etoile du Nord" flies over them; it is the state's motto, which translates as "The Star of the North." A wreath of pink and white lady slippers, the state flower, surrounds the seal.

Population: 4,919,479
Capital: St. Paul
Largest city: Minneapolis

Highest point: Eagle Mtn. 2,301 ft. (701 m)
Settled in: 1805
Popular name: North Star State; Gopher State

MISSISSIPPI

The flag of Mississippi, which was adopted February 7, 1894, honors United States heritage and displays Southern pride simultaneously. Its color scheme of red, white, and blue is the same as that of the national flag. The upper left-hand corner contains a reproduction of the Confederate flag, which was used by the Southern United States during the Civil War. A blue "X," outlined in white, is displayed against a red background; the cross contains thirteen white stars that represent the original colonies. The remainder of the state flag comprises three colored bars, or panels. The uppermost panel is blue; the central panel is white. The bottom panel, colored red, is the only one that extends across the entire flag.

Population: 2,844,658
Capital: Jackson
Largest city: Jackson

Highest point: Woodall Mtn. 806 ft. (246 m)
Settled in: 1716
Popular name: Magnolia State

MISSOURI

Missouri's flag was adopted March 22, 1913. The background consists of red, white, and blue panels running horizontally. The coat of arms is centered on the national colors; it is a white circle bordered with a blue ring. The ring is home to twenty-four white stars that represent Missouri's status as the twenty-fourth state to enter the Union.

The seal depicts a large brown bear standing to either side of a shield; the two intimidating animals support it proudly. The shield features a half circle on the right, and two quarter circles on the left. The semicircle depicts a golden American eagle on a white background. The upper left-hand quarter is blue with a crescent moon, representing the night sky. The lower quarter contains a bear on a red and white striped background. The shield is inscribed with the phrase "United We Stand, Divided We Fall." The crest is a knight's helmet.

Twenty-four stars are located just above the crest; the largest star represents Missouri. Toward the bottom, a large banner is printed with the Latin phrase, "Salus Populi Suprema Lex Esto," which translates as "Let the Good of the People Be the Supreme Law." "MDCCCXX" appears below the scroll; these Roman numerals signify 1820, the year of the Missouri Compromise.

Population: 5,595,211
Capital: Jefferson City
Largest city: St. Louis

Highest point: Taum Sauk Mtn. 1,772 ft. (540 m)
Settled in: 1764
Popular name: Show Me State

MONTANA

The flag of Montana was adopted February 27, 1905. The design is based on a flag made for the Montana infantry during the Spanish-American War. It features the state seal, which is bordered in gold fringe, centered on a deep azure background. The seal depicts a serene Montana landscape. Trees are scattered through a grassy green area; various colonial tools, including a pickaxe, a shovel, and a plow, are prominently displayed. They represent agricultural pursuits of the pioneers, such as mining and farming. The Great Falls of the Missouri River flow toward the right, and the sun shines brightly against a backdrop of glorious mountains. Across the bottom, a beige banner inscribed with brown letters waves. It reads "Oro Y Plata," which is Spanish for "Gold and Silver." The motto reflects the state's nickname, "The Treasure State." Above the seal, yellow block letters proclaim the state's name.

Population: 902,195
Capital: Helena
Largest city: Billings

Highest point: Granite Pk. 12,799 ft. (3,901 m)
Settled in: 1809
Popular name: Treasure State; Big Sky Country

NEBRASKA

The flag of Nebraska was adopted March 28, 1925. (Nebraska was one of the last states to approve an official flag.) It prominently displays the state seal against a royal blue background. A silver band surrounds the seal, which is otherwise gold. The seal is surrounded with the words "Great Seal of the State of Nebraska," and the date March 1, 1867, referencing the date Nebraska obtained statehood.

A steamboat ascending the Missouri River is pictured toward the right of the seal. On land, a blacksmith uses an anvil and a hammer. Bundles of wheat and cornstalks are beside him; along with a colonial cabin, they represent the agricultural element. In the distance, a speeding train heads west toward the Rocky Mountains. A banner is suspended in the sky; it is printed with the state motto, "Equality Before the Law."

Population: 1,711,263
Capital: Lincoln
Largest city: Omaha

Highest point: (Kimball County) 5,246 ft. (1,654 m)
Settled in: 1847
Popular name: Cornhusker State

NEVADA

The flag of Nevada was adopted March 26, 1929. It is very simple, as the majority of the flag consists of a deep, unbroken cobalt blue. A relatively small emblem fills the upper left-hand side of the flag. The center of the crest is a silver star; surrounding it are yellow letters that spell "Nevada." Two branches of sagebrush are crossed beneath the star; sagebrush is the state flower and it also is the source of Nevada's nickname, "The Sagebrush State." A yellow banner bearing the words "Battle Born" flies over the star, referencing the numerous struggles staged in the area during the War of Mexico.

Population: 1,998,257
Capital: Carson City
Largest city: Las Vegas

Highest point: Boundary Pk. 13,143 ft. (4,006 m)
Settled in: 1850
Popular name: Silver State; Sagebrush State

NEW HAMPSHIRE

The state flag of New Hampshire was adopted February 24, 1909. It carries the state seal in the middle of a vast blue background. It depicts a boat, the frigate *Raleigh*, propped proudly on the shore. A granite boulder signifying the state nickname ("The Granite State") also occupies the beach. The sea gleams in the background, and the sun peeks over the horizon in the distance.

The scene is framed with a wreath of green laurel; it is dotted with red berries. The words "Seal of the State of New Hampshire" arch around the seal, and the date 1776 (referencing the formation of the United States) appears sandwiched between two stars at the bottom. Another laurel wreath surrounds the gold, double-banded border of the seal. Nine stars are interspersed with the leaves and berries; they symbolize New Hampshire's position as the ninth state to enter the Union.

Population: 1,235,786
Capital: Concord
Largest city: Manchester

Highest point: Mt. Washington 6,288 ft. (1,917 m)
Settled in: 1623
Popular name: Granite State

NEW JERSEY

The flag of New Jersey, which was adopted on March 26, 1896, features the state seal on an unadorned, buff-colored background. Buff was chosen to memorialize members of the Colonial military who fought in the Revolutionary War. The state seal features a simple blue shield depicting three old-fashioned ploughs, which are agricultural symbols. Just above the shield is a knight's helmet, signifying sovereignty. Elaborate blue and silver scrolls surround the helmet; above it, another agricultural symbol, the head of a horse, can be found. A banner reading "Liberty and Prosperity" (the state motto) runs across the bottom of the seal. Note that 1776, the year that the Declaration of Independence was signed, is featured in the middle of the scroll.

Two female figures stand on top of the banner; they personify the "Liberty and Prosperity" motto. Liberty is a goddess-like figure dressed in classical robes of white and beige. She stands to the viewer's left; in her right hand, she holds a staff topped with a red, white, and blue colored cap that represents liberty. Prosperity, who stands to the right of the shield, is embodied as the Roman goddess of agriculture, Ceres. She is also draped in classical clothing; she holds a cornucopia filled with fruit and vegetables, meant to represent the abundance of the land.

Population: 8,414,350
Capital: Trenton
Largest city: Newark

Highest point: High Point 1,803 ft. (550 m)
Settled in: 1617
Popular name: Garden State

NEW MEXICO

New Mexico's flag was adopted March 19, 1925. It features a red symbol centered on a yellow background. The simple yet striking color scheme harks back to Europe; Spanish explorers visited the area in 1540. The red figure is an ancient symbol used by the Zia Pueblo Native Americans; it represents the sun. It has a circular center from which four sunbursts protrude at right angles. Each sunburst consists of four rays of varied lengths.

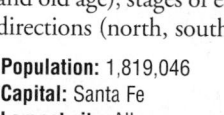

The four sunbursts symbolize gifts the Zia people attributed to their divine maker. These gifts were presented in groups of four: the four seasons (spring, summer, fall, and winter); the four stages of life (childhood, youth, middle age, and old age); stages of each day (sunrise, noon, evening, and night); and the four directions (north, south, east, and west).

Population: 1,819,046
Capital: Santa Fe
Largest city: Albuquerque

Highest point: Wheeler Pk. 13,161 ft. (4,011 m)
Settled in: 1605
Popular name: Land of Enchantment

NEW YORK

The New York state flag was adopted in 1901. Originally, the background was buff, but the color has since been changed to blue. The state seal appears in the middle of the flag; a shield lies at the seal's center. It depicts a sunny landscape containing the Hudson River and its grassy shore. Purple mountains create a majestic background for two ships gliding across the river. An eagle is perched on a globe above the shield.

A woman representing Liberty stands to the viewer's left; she is dressed in colorful robes and holds a staff topped with a Liberty Cap. A crown lies at her feet, symbolizing America's independence from England. A female figure representing Justice stands on the right. She holds balanced scales and a sword, which have long been symbols of justice. Both figures stand on a white banner reading "Excelsior," which is the state motto. It translates "Ever Upward," signifying New York's commitment to ongoing self-improvement.

Population: 18,976,457
Capital: Albany
Largest city: New York

Highest point: Mt. Marcy 5,344 ft. (1,629 m)
Settled in: 1614
Popular name: Empire State

NORTH CAROLINA

The flag of North Carolina was adopted March 9, 1885. The layout of the design is quite simple, and the three national colors are represented. A royal blue panel occupies the left side of the flag, and two horizontal panels (red on top, white on the bottom) fill the remaining space. A white star shines from the middle of the blue field; it symbolizes North Carolina and is sandwiched between the state's initials.

The blue panel also contains two gold banners emblazoned with dates important to the state's history. The top banner references the Mecklenberg Declaration, which occurred May 20, 1775. This was when a North Carolina county declared its independence from Great Britain. The lower banner references the Halifax Resolve, which occurred April 12, 1776. This was when North Carolina sent representatives supporting national independence to Congress.

Population: 8,049,313
Capital: Raleigh
Largest city: Charlotte

Highest point: Mt. Mitchell 6,684 ft. (2,037 m)
Settled in: 1650
Popular name: Tarheel State

NORTH DAKOTA

North Dakota's flag was adopted March 3, 1911. It is two-sided, but it features identical designs on the front and back. The design's focal point is an American eagle on a blue background. One claw clutches an olive branch laden with red berries; its other talon holds a bundle of arrows. A shield decorated with traditionally colored stars and stripes guards his breast. A red banner streams from his parted beak; it is inscribed with the Latin phrase "E Pluribus Unum," which translates as "From Many, One." Thirteen stars, representing the first thirteen states, shine just above the eagle's head. A sunburst with seven points explodes toward the top. Toward the bottom, a red scroll with ornate, gold-colored handles declares the state's name.

Population: 642,200
Capital: Bismarck
Largest city: Fargo

Highest point: White Butte 3,506 ft. (1,069 m)
Settled in: 1780
Popular name: Flickertail State; Sioux State

OHIO

Ohio's flag, adopted on May 9, 1902, is the only state flag with a swallow-tailed, or forked, design. (This design is called a burgee.) Ohio's flag echoes the design of the national flag in many ways; it has red and white stripes and a blue field with white stars. The stripes symbolize the state's roads and waterways, while the blue represents hills and valleys.

The blue field also contains a large "O" (white with a red center); it represents the first letter of the state's name, as well as referencing Ohio's nickname ("The Buckeye State") and official tree (the buckeye tree). Seventeen stars appear around the buckeye; they allude to Ohio's position as the seventeenth state to enter the Union.

Population: 11,353,140
Capital: Columbus
Largest city: Cleveland

Highest point: Campbell Hill 1,550 ft. (472 m)
Settled in: 1788
Popular name: Buckeye State

OKLAHOMA

The flag of Oklahoma was adopted April 2, 1925. The background is sky blue, rather than the darker blue featured on most of the other state flags. In its center lies a Native American war shield made of tan buckskin. Six painted crosses appear on the shield; they represent the tribal symbol for stars. Seven eagle feathers, which are white with colored tips, hang from the bottom of the shield. An Indian peace pipe (called a calumet) and a green olive branch (a traditional symbol for peace) form a cross across the shield. These represent good will between Native Americans and settlers. Toward the bottom of the flag, large white letters proclaim the state name.

Population: 3,450,654
Capital: Oklahoma City
Largest city: Oklahoma City

Highest point: Black Mesa 4,973 ft. (1,516 m)
Settled in: 1889
Popular name: Sooner State

OREGON

Oregon's flag, adopted February 26, 1925, has a unique, two-sided design. Both sides have a simple color scheme of deep blue and vibrant gold. The design on the back of the flag is relatively plain—the profile of a lone beaver (the state animal) stands atop a log that is centered on a field of blue. The front of the flag features the state shield on a plain azure background; it is surrounded by thirty-three yellow stars, representing Oregon's status as the thirty-third state admitted to the Union.

The shield's foreground contains a covered wagon pulled by a team of oxen. In the background, the sun shines on the vast Pacific Ocean; in the distance are two ships, one British and one American, representing trade. A cluster of fir trees and an elk stand proudly on the eastern shore. "The Union" is printed across the bottom, and tools representing farming and mining are piled underneath. An American eagle spreads its wings over the shield, representing protection and unity. The state's name is printed across the top, and the date the state entered the Union, 1859, is printed across the bottom.

Population: 3,421,399
Capital: Salem
Largest city: Portland

Highest point: Mt. Hood 11,239 ft. (3,426 m)
Settled in: 1810
Popular name: Beaver State

PENNSYLVANIA

The Pennsylvania flag was adopted June 13, 1907. The rich azure color of the flag's background matches the vibrant blue found on the national flag; in fact, state law dictates that the shades be identical. The state coat of arms, a shield with three panels, is the focal point of the design. The green panel at the bottom of the shield pictures three bundles of wheat, representing the state's abundant agriculture. The middle panel, colored yellow, features another agricultural symbol, an old-fashioned plow. The blue panel at the top shows a large ship, representing industry and commerce.

A bald eagle, America's national bird and a well-known symbol of freedom, rests on top of the shield, and two plants (a cornstalk and an olive branch) are crossed beneath it. Two lively black stallions rear up to support the shield, one on either side. They stand on an elaborate golden base. A red banner featuring the state's motto, "Virtue, Liberty, and Independence," is draped across the bottom. State legislation requires that the flag be displayed outside of every state-owned building and flown from all buildings open to the public.

Population: 12,281,054
Capital: Harrisburg
Largest city: Philadelphia

Highest point: Mt. Davis 3,213 ft. (979 m)
Settled in: 1682
Popular name: Keystone State

RHODE ISLAND

Rhode Island's flag was adopted May 19, 1897. A gold anchor in the center of the flag represents the Atlantic Ocean, which has played a vital role in the state's history. The anchor is the state symbol; it acknowledges the many contributions the Atlantic has made to the beauty of the state's landscape and to the vitality of its economy.

A deep blue banner lies beneath the anchor; the word "Hope" (the state's official motto) is printed in block letters. Thirteen gold stars, which symbolize the original colonies, form a ring around the anchor. The flag's vast white background provides a bright backdrop for the vivid illustration.

Population: 1,048,319
Capital: Providence
Largest city: Providence

Highest point: Jerimoth Hill 812 ft. (247 m)
Settled in: 1636
Popular name: Little Rhody; Ocean State

SOUTH CAROLINA

The flag of South Carolina was adopted January 28, 1861. Colonel William Moultrie, an important military figure in the late 1700s, conceived the original design. A committee asked him to create a flag to represent South Carolina's troops in the Revolutionary War. The royal blue background is the same color as the uniforms of South Carolinian troops. A crescent moon appears in the upper left-hand corner; it is a reproduction of the silver emblem that appeared on his soldiers' caps. The center of the flag features a palmetto tree; it represents the colonel's successful defense of a palmetto log fort on Sullivan's Island, which he guarded from British attack in June 1776.

Population: 4,012,012
Capital: Columbia
Largest city: Columbia

Highest point: Sassafras Mtn. 3,560 ft. (1,085 m)
Settled in: 1670
Popular name: Palmetto State

SOUTH DAKOTA

The South Dakota flag was adopted March 8, 1909. It features the state seal centered on a sky blue background. The seal, which consists of blue embroidery on a circular field of white, depicts an outdoor scene of a farmer plowing a field. The surrounding fields contain a herd of cattle and a smoking chimney, and a steamboat floats across a river. Hills appear in the distance, and the state motto, "Under God the People Rule," appears on a banner toward the top. A jagged yellow border surrounds the seal, giving the impression that the sun lies behind it. The state's nickname was changed from "The Sunshine State" to "The Mount Rushmore State" in the late 1980s to differentiate it from Florida. The flag was modified to reflect the change in 1992. Large yellow letters arching over the seal proclaim the state's name, and the nickname appears below it.

Population: 754,844
Capital: Pierre
Largest city: Sioux Falls

Highest point: Harney Pk. 7,242 ft. (2,207 m)
Settled in: 1856
Popular name: Coyote State; Mount Rushmore State

TENNESSEE

The Tennessee flag was adopted on April 17, 1905. Its simple color scheme of red, white, and blue can also be found on the national flag. Its minimalist design features a circle centered on a crimson-colored background; on this flag, red (which is widely held to symbolize courage and memorialize bloodshed) honors Tennessee volunteers in the War of 1812. Notably, this is also the source from which Tennessee's nickname, "The Volunteer State," is derived. Three white stars are prominently displayed in a circle of blue in the middle of the flag; each represents a geographic division of the state (West and Middle Tennessee are divided by the

Tennessee River, and East Tennessee is separated from Middle Tennessee by the Cumberland Plateau). The white band circling the stars binds them in what the designer, a captain in the Tennessee infantry, called an "indissoluble trinity."

Population: 5,689,283
Capital: Nashville
Largest city: Memphis

Highest point: Clingmans Dome 6,643 ft. (2,025 m)
Settled in: 1757
Popular name: Volunteer State

TEXAS

Texas adopted its state flag on January 25, 1839. The simple design comprises three rectangles of equal size. The blue rectangle on the left stands vertically, while the others lie horizontally. A large white star is centered on the blue area; it acts as a visualization of Texas' nickname, "The Lone Star State." The color scheme exactly matches the shades found on the national flag. Blue represents loyalty, white symbolizes purity, and red represents bravery.

Population: 20,851,820
Capital: Austin
Largest city: Houston

Highest point: Guadalupe Pk. 8,749 ft. (2,667 m)
Settled in: 1686
Popular name: Lone Star State

UTAH

The flag of Utah, adopted on March 11, 1913, features the state seal centered on a royal blue background. A yellow beehive draws the eye to the center of the shield; the habitat of bees, insects well known for their hard-working nature, is an apt symbol for the state motto, "Industry," which is printed in white letters directly above the hive. Surrounding the beehive are the state's official flowers, sego lilies, representing peace. Two flags that bear the stars-and-stripes motif of the national flag border the shield; they symbolize unity and protection. The flags' shapes mirror the symmetry of the American eagle's spread wings; the magnificent bird is perched on six arrows that form a bridge between the flags. Toward the bottom, two dates appear in white. The first, 1847, acknowledges

the year that Utah's founder, Brigham Young, led his Mormon followers to Salt Lake Valley to establish a settlement. The second, 1896, recognizes the year that Utah became the forty-fifth addition to the United States.

Population: 2,233,169
Capital: Salt Lake City
Largest city: Salt Lake City

Highest point: Kings Pk. 13,528 ft. (4,123 m)
Settled in: 1847
Popular name: Beehive State

VERMONT

The Vermont state flag was adopted April 26, 1923. The state coat of arms serves as its focal point; it is centered on a vast, dazzling blue background. A peaceful New England landscape is pictured on the shield, which is appropriate considering the plentiful and diverse offerings of Vermont's outdoors.

A pine tree, a popular and sweet-smelling native plant, stands tall in the center of the shield's pastoral picture. A brown cow, a reference to Vermont's booming dairy industry, stands in the shade to the tree's right. Three bundles of grain, representing agricultural prosperity, are positioned to the tree's left. In the distance, purple-colored mountains are silhouetted against the bright sky.

A proud stag's head hovers above the shield; it represents Vermont's sizeable wildlife population. Two pine branches, another reference to the state's abundant greenery, are crossed beneath the shield. The state motto, "Vermont, Freedom and Unity," is on the red banner adorning the bottom.

Population: 608,827
Capital: Montpelier
Largest city: Burlington

Highest point: Mt. Mansfield 4,393 ft. (1,339 m)
Settled in: 1764
Popular name: Green Mountain State

VIRGINIA

The flag of Virginia was adopted April 30, 1861. The design comprises the state's coat of arms centered on a deep blue background. The white circle depicts the result of a battle between two figures that personify the concepts of virtue and tyranny. Virtue appears as a woman clothed in blue robes and a Greek helmet; she holds a sword in her left arm and a spear in her right hand. She stands barefoot on top of the prone figure of Tyranny, who wears red battle clothing. The broken chain in his left hand and the crown that lies behind his head symbolize that he has been defeated.

The state motto, printed under the prostrate form of Tyranny, ties in with the scene by commenting on Tyranny's defeat. "Sic Semper Tyrannis," Latin for "Thus Always to Tyrants," acknowledges that the virtuous will always overcome the tyrannical. (Notably, the coat of arms was adopted in 1776, the year the United States gained independence.) The state name arches over the figures' heads. The seal is bordered with red flowers on green vines.

Population: 7,078,515
Capital: Richmond
Largest city: Norfolk

Highest point: Mt. Rogers 5,729 ft. (1,746 m)
Settled in: 1607
Popular name: Old Dominion

WASHINGTON

The state flag of Washington was adopted January 2, 1923. It holds the distinction of being the only United States flag with a green background (blue is the most common color). The state seal, which is the focal point of the design, is centered on the electric green field and it features a portrait of George Washington, America's first president. A band of gold borders it; it contains the words "The State Seal of Washington," which are printed in black. The year that Washington became the forty-second state of the Union, 1889, is also printed within the gold band.

Population: 5,894,121
Capital: Olympia
Largest city: Seattle

Highest point: Mt. Ranier 14,410 ft. (4,392 m)
Settled in: 1811
Popular name: Evergreen State

WEST VIRGINIA

West Virginia's flag was adopted March 7, 1929. The background is white with thick, royal blue edging. The focal point is the state seal, which is bordered with an ornate gold scroll. The shield pictures two men, a farmer (representing the state's agricultural industry) and a miner (representing its mining industry). The farmer, who stands on the viewer's left, holds a woodman's axe and stands beside a bundle of wheat and a plow. The miner, who stands on the right, holds a pick-axe and stands over lumps of various minerals, barrels, and an anvil. A large gray rock stands between the two figures; it is inscribed with "June 20, 1863," the date that West Virginia gained statehood. Under the men's feet are two crossed rifles topped with a Liberty Cap. A red banner at the bottom of the shield reads, "Montani Semper Liberi," which translates as "Mountaineers Are Always Free Men." This is the motto of West Virginia, which is also known as "The Mountain State." Two branches of rhododendron, the state flower, are joined with a red ribbon just below the shield, and a red banner proclaiming the state's name flies just above it.

Population: 1,808,344
Capital: Charleston
Largest city: Charleston

Highest point: Spruce Knob 4,863 ft. (1,482 m)
Settled in: 1774
Popular name: Mountain State

WISCONSIN

The flag of Wisconsin was adopted April 26, 1913. It features the state coat of arms centered on a blue background; it consists of two men supporting the Wisconsin shield. The man on the viewer's left is a sailor; he grips a coil of rope in his right hand. The other figure is a miner holding a pickaxe.

The shield comprises four quarters, each representing a Wisconsin economic pursuit. The plow in the first quarter signifies agriculture. The second quarter houses a pick and shovel, representing mining. The third quarter features an arm holding a hammer, to symbolize industrial activity. Finally, an anchor, symbolizing navigation, lies in the fourth quarter. An American shield lies in a circle at the center and serves to join the four quarters. A band reading "E Pluribus Unum" ("From Many, One") circles the inner shield. The shield stands on a filled cornucopia and a pyramid made from pig lead. Below the gold scrollwork, there is a blue banner with thirteen stars. The crest is a badger, the state animal. Above it, a banner inscribed with the state motto, "Forward," flies proudly.

Population: 5,363,675
Capital: Madison
Largest city: Milwaukee

Highest point: Timms Hill 1,951 ft. (595 m)
Settled in: 1670
Popular name: Badger State

WYOMING

The flag of Wyoming, which was designed by Verna Keyes, was adopted January 31, 1917. It features the white silhouette of a bison (an animal native to the state) contrasted against a large field of royal blue. The blue rectangle has a thin white edging surrounded by a red border. The state seal, which is blue, is printed in the center of the bison. Its position symbolizes the western custom of branding cattle.

The seal depicts a banner printed with the state's motto, "Equal Rights," which appears behind the figure of a woman situated between two pillars. The pillars are each topped with a lamp (representing knowledge); they are printed with the words "Livestock," "Grain," "Oil," and "Mines," which all represent the state's wealth. A miner and a cowboy stand beside the pillars; between them, an American eagle is perched on a shield embossed with the number forty-four, which acknowledges that Wyoming was the forty-fourth state to enter the Union. The year Wyoming became a territory (1869) is printed to the left, and the year it gained statehood (1890) appears on the right.

Population: 493,782
Capital: Cheyenne
Largest city: Casper

Highest point: Gannett Pk. 13,804 ft. (4,207 m)
Settled in: 1834
Popular name: Equality State

AMERICAN SAMOA

The flag of American Samoa features colors representative of both the United States and Samoa. The design consists of a white triangle on a blue background. The triangle has a red border and bears a naturally colored American eagle. The bird clutches traditional Samoan symbols of power—a uatogi, or war club, and a fue, or ritual staff. The symbolism of the eagle, which is the national bird of the United States, clutching traditional Samoan items is clear; it signifies the protection and partnership offered by the United States.

Population: 69,000
Capital/largest city: Pago Pago
Location: South Pacific Ocean

Climate: Tropical marine
Monetary unit: U.S. dollar
Language: Samoan; English

GUAM

The flag of Guam was adopted in 1917. Mrs. Helen L. Paul, the wife of an American naval officer, conceived the design, which consists of the territorial seal centered on a deep blue background. A red border to represent courage surrounds the blue. The blue represents the Pacific Ocean, which borders the American dependency.

The seal's oval shape recalls a slingstone used by the Chamorro people. The focal point of the seal is a tall coconut tree growing from a sandy beach; it represents Guam's ability to prosper under any conditions. The seal also depicts a canoe, called a flying proa, which was used to navigate the sea. The flying proa signifies the early Chamorros' seafaring skills and courage.

Population: 161,000
Capital/largest city: Agana
Location: North Pacific Ocean

Climate: Tropical marine
Monetary unit: U.S. dollar
Language: English; Chamorro; Japanese

PUERTO RICO

The flag of Puerto Rico was designed in 1895 and adopted in 1952. The design features five stripes (three red and two white). A blue triangle protrudes from the left side; its center holds a single white star. The flag strongly resembles the Cuban flag, which can be attributed to Puerto Rican and Cuban opposition to Spanish rule in the late 1890s, when the design was conceived.

The flag's symbolism has changed considerably since its creation; in 1952, legislation approved its official symbolism. The red stripes symbolize the three branches of the government—Legislative, Executive, and Judiciary. The white stripes signify individual freedom and the rights that protect it. The blue triangle represents the government, and the star symbolizes Puerto Rico.

Population: 3,863,000
Capital/largest city: San Juan
Location: Caribbean Sea

Climate: Tropical marine
Monetary unit: U.S. dollar
Language: Spanish; English

VIRGIN ISLANDS

The flag of the Virgin Islands of the United States was adopted May 17, 1917. It features a simplified version of the United States coat of arms centered on a white background. A yellow-colored American eagle, wings outspread, grips a sprig of green laurel in his right talon and three blue arrows in his left claw. The arrows represent the three major islands, which are St. Croix, St. John, and St. Thomas. (Several nearby islets also belong to the dependency, but they are not represented on the flag.) An American shield, which features a red, white, and blue stars-and-stripes motif, protects the eagle's breast. The eagle appears between the territory's initials, which are written in large blue letters.

Population: 123,000
Capital/largest city: Charlotte Amalie
Location: Caribbean Sea

Climate: Subtropical
Monetary unit: U.S. dollar
Language: English; Spanish; Creole

Display and Care of the United States Flag

Folding the Flag

Fold the flag in half width-wise twice. Beginning at the striped end, fold up a triangle and repeat until only the end of the union (the blue field of stars) shows. Tuck the last bit into the other folds to secure it. The final folded flag resembles a cocked hat, with only white stars on a blue field showing.

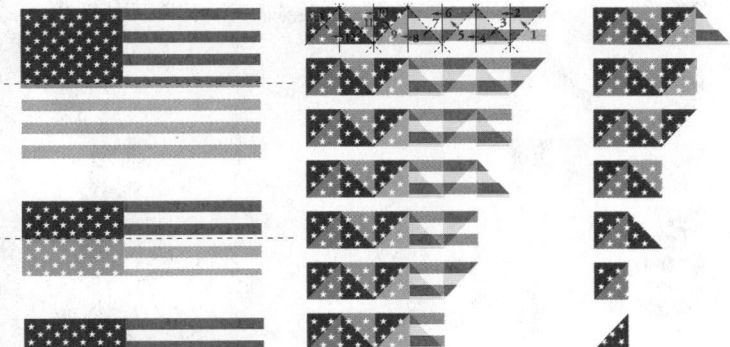

Displaying the Flag

(1) The U.S. flag is flown upside down only as a distress signal. (2) When suspended over a street, the flag should be vertical, with the union to the north in an east-west street or to the east in a north-south street. (3) When displayed in a window, the union should be to the left of an outside observer. (4) When used to cover a casket, the union should be at the head and over the left shoulder. Remove the flag before lowering the casket into the grave.

(5) When flown at half-staff, the flag should be raised to the peak for an instant, then lowered to half-staff. The flag should again be raised to the peak briefly before it is lowered for the day.

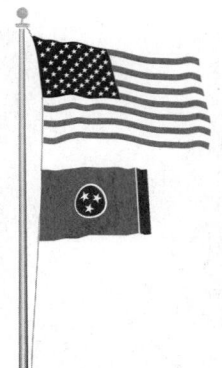

(6) When flags or pennants of states, cities, or societies are flown with the U.S. flag on the same halyard, the U.S. flag should fly at the peak, above all others. If flown from adjacent staffs, the U.S. flag is to be hoisted first and lowered last.

(7) When the U.S. flag and the flags of a number of states, cities, or societies are grouped and displayed from staffs, the U.S. flag should be at the center and at the highest point of the grouping.

(8) When displayed at an angle from a windowsill, balcony, or building, the union should be placed at the peak (unless the flag is at half-staff).

Caring for the Flag

(1) When the flag is lowered, no part of it should touch the ground or any other object. (2) Be sure the flag is dry before storing it. Outdoor flags should be correctly folded and sealed inside moisture-proof plastic bags and then stored in a cool, dry place. (3) Iron-on patches may be used to repair small tears and holes. The patches are available in many fabric departments. (4) A flag that is worn beyond repair should be burned, beyond recognition as a flag, in a modest but blazing fire. This should be done with dignity and respect. Most American Legion posts regularly conduct dignified flag-burning ceremonies, often on Flag Day (June 14).

Mathematics &

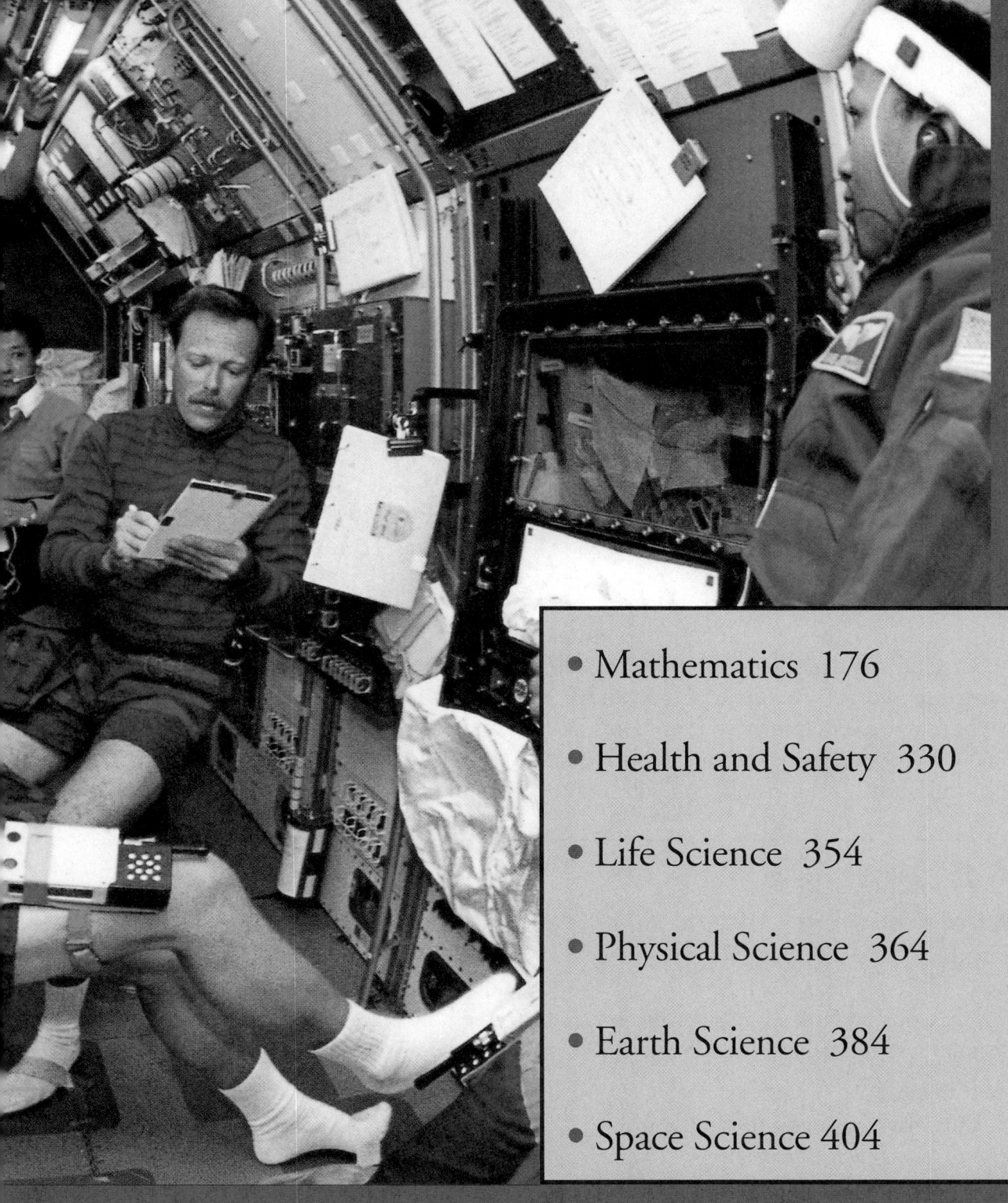

- Mathematics 176

- Health and Safety 330

- Life Science 354

- Physical Science 364

- Earth Science 384

- Space Science 404

Science

- *Arithmetic*   176
- *Addition*   178
- *Subtraction*   191
- *Multiplication*   209
- *Division*   220
- *Fractions*   230
- *Exponents*   244
- *Decimals*   246
- *Ratio and percent* 274
- *Pre-algebra*   285
- *Symbols*   319
- *Formulas*   320
- *Dictionary of mathematics* 325

Mathematics

As you learn mathematics in school, you may find that it takes longer and longer to understand some problems. Or you may forget how to do a certain problem. Or you may need another way to work a problem. You will find the help you need in these pages. There are examples and problems like the ones you have in school, all worked out. When you need help in memorizing the basic facts of addition, subtraction, multiplication, and division, you will find that help in these pages as well.

Arithmetic

Whole numbers. When you do arithmetic, you use ten digits, or numerals: 0, 1, 2, 3, 4, 5, 6, 7, 8, and 9. So we say that our system of numbering is a decimal system—a base-ten system.

Place value. A number like 5 is read 5. But what happens to that number when you write a 1 before it, or a 0 after it? Its value changes. The value of a digit or numeral, or its place value, depends on its place in a number. So the 1 before 5 becomes 15, with 5 in the ones place. Writing 0 after 5 makes it 50, with the 5 in the tens place. As you can see, a number's position makes quite a difference.

In order to add, subtract, multiply, and divide numbers correctly, you must pay careful attention to place value.

To see how place value works, look at the number 37.

$$37 = 3 \text{ tens} + 7 \text{ ones}$$
$$= 30 + 7$$

tens	ones
3	7

The place, or position, of the 7 tells you that its value is seven ones—or 7. The position of the 3 tells you that its value is three tens—or 30. The 7 is in the ones place or ones column and the 3 is in the tens place or tens column.

In a three-digit number like 204, the position of the 2 tells you that its value is two hundreds. The position of the 0 is that of a place holder, meaning that there are no tens in this number. The value of 4 is four ones.

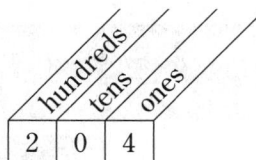

In a four-digit number like 4932, the position of the 4 tells you that its value is four thousands, the position of the 9 tells you that its value is nine hundreds, the position of the 3 tells you that its value is three tens, and 2 is in the ones place.

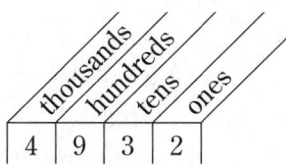

Using place value in renaming numbers. Renaming numbers is just another way of breaking them down into smaller parts, or expanding them. Knowing how to write a number in expanded form or expanded notation will help you to add, subtract, multiply, and divide. For example, 37 in expanded notation would look like this:

$$30 + 7.$$

The three-digit number 204 is 200 + 0 + 4 in expanded notation. And 4932 would look like this:

$$4000 + 900 + 30 + 2.$$

Using place value in rounding numbers. You round numbers to remember them more easily. For example, 400 is

easier to remember than 378. Numbers can be rounded to the nearest tens place, hundreds place, thousands place, ten thousands place, and so on. You use place value by finding the number's position on the chart.

Example 1: Round 23 to the nearest ten.

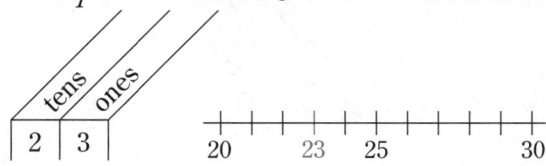

The number to the right of 2 is 3, and 3 is less than 5. Replace 3 with 0. 23 rounded to the nearest ten becomes 20.

Example 2: Round 27 to the nearest ten.

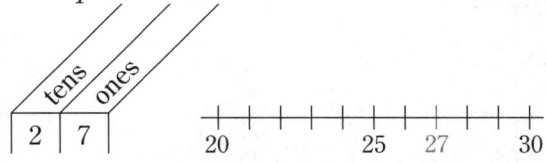

The number to the right of 2 is 7, and 7 is more than 4. The rounded number is 30.

In each of these examples, find the place in the number to which you are rounding. In 23 and 27, 2 is in the tens place. Look one place to the right, or to the ones place in the examples above. If the digit or number in that place is less than 5, *round down*. To round down, replace the digit to the right of the place you found in the first step with 0. The 0 means that there are no ones. So 23 is rounded down to 20.

In 27, the 2 is in the tens place, and the 7 at the right is greater than 5. In that case, *round up*. To round up, increase the digit in the tens place, or 2 in this example, to 3 and replace the digit to the right with 0. So 27 rounded up becomes 30.

These rules for rounding apply to all numbers and whatever places they are rounded to. More examples are shown below:

Example 3: Round 7245 to the nearest ten.

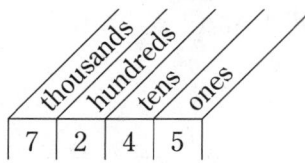

Four is in the tens place, and the number to the right of 4 is 5. You must round up, so 7245 becomes 7250.

Example 4: Round 843 to the nearest hundred.

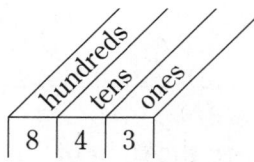

Four is in the tens place, and the number to the right of 4 is 3. Since both 3 and 4 are less than 5, you must round down. So 843 is rounded to 800.

Visualize it this way: 843 is between 800 and 900.

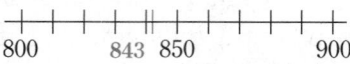

850 is halfway between 800 and 900. 843 is closer to 800.

Rounding Numbers with Your Calculator

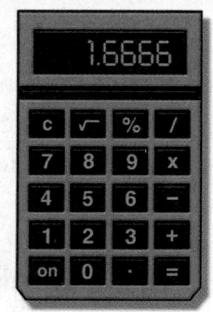

Most calculators do not round numbers. If you divide 10 by 6, the answer will be given as 1.666666. In some cases, you can correct the calculator's rounding to improve accuracy. Most of the time, however, you can use one less place and round the answer that is shown on the calculator. For example, change 1.666666 to 1.66667.

Addition

Everyday addition. You use addition when you find out how much several gifts cost altogether. You also add to find the number of hours you studied in one week. If you are a member of a team, you must add to find the total number of points of your team's score. If you wish to place a border around your garden, you must add the length of each side of the plot of land to find the perimeter. As you can see, addition is used in many ways.

Adding whole numbers. Addition is a binary operation, which means that you can add only two numbers at a time. These numbers tell the size of a group and are called addends. Your answer is called a sum or total. This number tells you how many or how much you have altogether.

Addition is based on a set of basic facts that you should memorize. If you forget a fact, you can still find the answer. Here are some hints:

1. **Use doubles or near doubles.** You may find facts such as 2 + 2 = 4 or 8 + 8 = 16 easy to remember. These facts are known as doubles. Facts such as 6 + 7 and 7 + 9 are near doubles. To find sums such as 6 + 7, think of 6 + 6 = 12, so 6 + 7 = 13. Even 7 + 9 is easy to remember when you start with 7 + 7 = 14. Then add 2 and you will have the answer, 16. So 7 + 9 = 16. To understand how this works, try other doubles, such as 4 + 4 = 8. In an example like 4 + 5 = 9, you count one more. In 4 + 6 = 10, you count two more.

2. **Use tens.** To add 8 + 5, think 8 + 2 = 10 and 5 = 2 + 3, so 8 + 5 = 10 + 3, or 13.

3. **Count if you have to.** Addition is based on counting. For example, add 7 + 4 by counting to the answer: 8, 9, 10, 11.

4. **Switch addends.** If you have forgotten the answer to 6 + 4, all you have to do is turn this problem around to 4 + 6. You can change the order of the addends and still get the same sum.

Basic Addition Facts										
+	0	1	2	3	4	5	6	7	8	9
0	0	1	2	3	4	5	6	7	8	9
1	1	2	3	4	5	6	7	8	9	10
2	2	3	4	5	6	7	8	9	10	11
3	3	4	5	6	7	8	9	10	11	12
4	4	5	6	7	8	9	10	11	12	13
5	5	6	7	8	9	10	11	12	13	14
6	6	7	8	9	10	11	12	13	14	15
7	7	8	9	10	11	12	13	14	15	16
8	8	9	10	11	12	13	14	15	16	17
9	9	10	11	12	13	14	15	16	17	18

5. **Use the table.** *Example:*

$$\begin{array}{r} 5 \\ +3 \\ \hline \end{array}$$

You can solve this problem by using the table of basic addition facts. Read down to row 5 (see the arrow on the side of the table) and across to column 3 (see the arrow at the top of the table). Row 5 and column 3 meet at the number 8, which is the answer.

$$\begin{array}{r} 5 \\ +3 \\ \hline 8 \end{array}$$

A baseball scoreboard is an example of simple addition. Add the number of runs for each inning to get the final score.

Memorizing the basic addition facts.
In order to do addition problems quickly, you should memorize the basic addition facts. These facts are 1 + 1 = 2, 1 + 2 = 3, 1 + 3 = 4, and so on. All of them appear in the table of basic addition facts on page 179.

The best way to memorize the addition facts is by using them as much as possible.

Example:

$$\begin{array}{r} 4 \\ 3 \\ +6 \end{array}$$

You can use the table of basic addition facts to solve this problem if you break it up into two steps.

Add one pair of numbers.

$$\left.\begin{array}{r} 4 \\ 3 \end{array}\right\}7$$
$$+6$$

Add this sum to the third number.

$$\begin{array}{r} 7 \\ +6 \\ \hline 13 \end{array}$$

Adding two-digit numbers.
To add two-digit numbers, such as 27, to other numbers, you can use counters. They often help you understand how whole numbers are used:

■ stands for, or represents, one unit

▮ stands for, or represents, ten units.

A number, such as 23, can be shown as

You can use counters to add 23 to other numbers.

Example:

$$\begin{array}{r} 23 \\ +5 \\ \hline \end{array}$$

First show 23 as two ten units and three one units, and place five units on the other side:

23   5

Count the smaller units, or ones, first, and get 8 as the answer. The number of ten units is still 2. The answer to this problem is 28.

Often, you will be adding two larger numbers, such as the numbers below:

$$\begin{array}{r} 23 \\ +12 \\ \hline \end{array}$$

Show 23 as two ten units and three one units. Then show 12 as one ten unit and two one units.

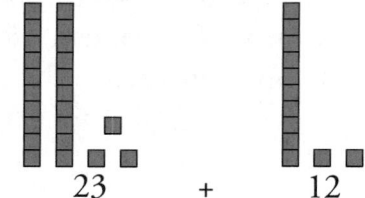

23   +   12

Add the single units first.

$$\begin{array}{r} 23 \\ +12 \\ \hline 5 \end{array}$$

3 + 2

Next, combine and add the tens units. There are three tens units. The answer to this problem is 35.

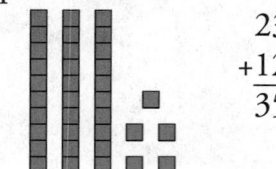

$$\begin{array}{r} 23 \\ +12 \\ \hline 35 \end{array}$$

Ten Hints on Memorizing Addition Facts

1. Do not try to memorize all of the facts at one time. Doing this makes it too hard to remember them later.

2. Do memorize a few at a time, say, five or ten facts in a week.

3. Do remember that changing the order of the numbers you add will not change the answer. For example, 2 + 4 is the same problem as 4 + 2. If you know that 2 + 4 equals 6, you also know that 4 + 2 equals 6. Now you only have half as many facts to remember.

4. Learn with a friend. Let your friend answer your questions on the facts. Then switch turns. How many facts does your friend know? How many do you know?

5. Make an addition table and fill it in. But do not stop there. Look at it more closely and you will see patterns.

6. Play games of addition by yourself. For example, toss two dice and add the dots that come up. Make or buy addition facts bingo to play with a friend. Let each game won be worth seven or twelve points. At the end of three or four games, you and the other player can add up your scores.

7. Make an addition diary. How did you use addition today? How did you see addition used by your family, friends, and teachers? Were large numbers used? In what other ways could the same answer have been obtained?

8. Use things to help you practice. On separate 3 × 5 cards, copy one fact without the answer. On the other side of each card, write the answer. Now mix up the cards and place them on a table facedown. Look at each card and write the answer to the fact. After you have used all of the cards, compare your answers. Then practice only those facts you answered incorrectly.

9. Use your clock. Work with one number at a time. For example, start with 2, add 3 and get 5. Start with 3, add 4 and get 7.

10. Begin practicing using difficult facts. Instead of studying what you probably know, such as 1 + 2 = 3, begin with facts such as 7 + 6 = 13.

23
+ 4

A. Add the numbers in the ones column. Then write the 7 at the bottom of the ones column.

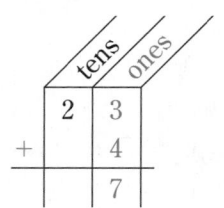

B. Add the numbers in the tens column.

```
  2 tens
+ 0 tens
  2 tens
```

C. Write the 2 at the bottom of the tens column. Your answer is 27.

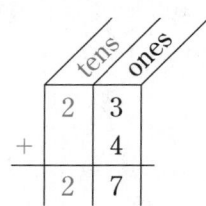

27
+ 9

A. Add the ones.

```
   7
 + 9
  16
```

B. Rename 16 as one ten and six ones. Write the 6 at the bottom of the ones column and the one at the top of the tens column.

C. Add the tens.

```
  2 tens
+ 1 tens
  3 tens
```

D. Write the 3 at the bottom of the tens column. Your answer is 36.

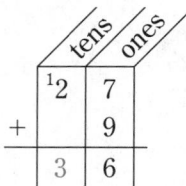

Another way of adding this problem is counting nine numbers up from 27: 28, 29, 30, 31, 32, 33, 34, 35, 36.

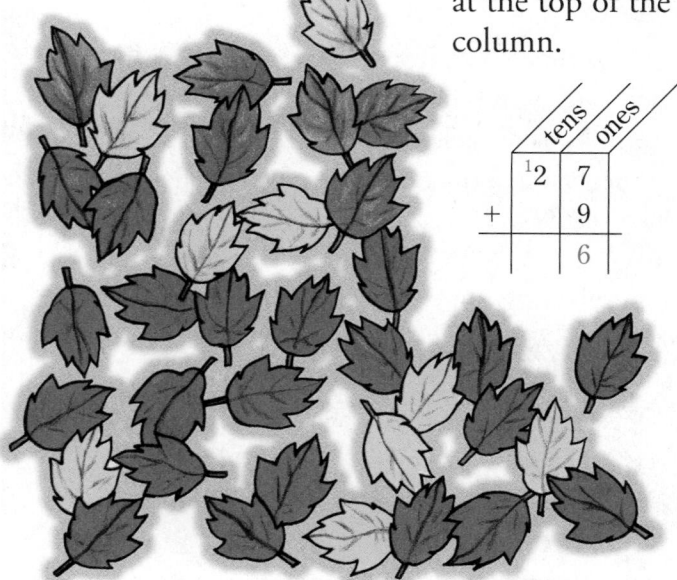

182

Special Help with Carrying in Addition

In many addition problems, you will have to bring a digit into the next value place. For example, if you are adding a column of numbers in the ones place and get 29 as the answer, write this answer with 9 in the ones place and bring, or "carry," 2 to the tens place. Once you have done this, you can add the column of numbers in the tens place.

Suppose you have to add

$$11$$
$$+19$$

Begin adding in the ones place. Your answer will be 10. If you write the whole number 10 as shown, it will be wrong.

$$11$$
$$+19$$
$$10$$

This is incorrect because 10 means one ten and zero ones. The 1 belongs in the tens place column:

This is the one ⟶ you carried

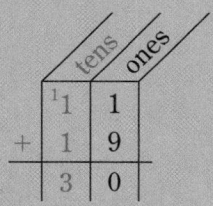

Now add the numbers in the tens column. Do not forget to add the one you carried to the tens place! The problem is done.

Using Base Ten Blocks in Addition

Some textbooks no longer use the term *carrying* in addition. They might use the instruction *regroup* instead of *rename*. Some books suggest a more hands-on approach by using base ten blocks in addition. This is how they would describe the procedure in 11 + 19.

Use base ten blocks and place value to find the sum.

1. Use 1 tens block and 1 ones block to show 11. Use 1 tens block and 9 ones blocks to show 19.

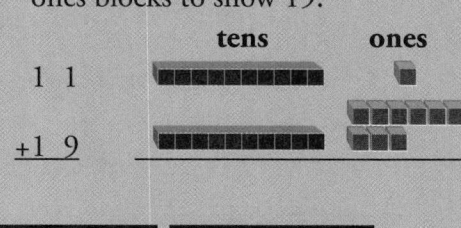

| 1 One Block = 1 | 1 Ten Block = 10 |

2. Add the ones. 1 + 9 = 10 ones blocks. Regroup 10 ones as 1 ten block and 0 ones blocks.

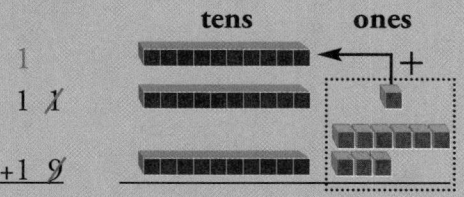

3. Add the tens. 1 + 1 + 1 = 3 You now have 3 tens blocks and 0 ones blocks.

13
+44

A. Add the numbers in the ones column.

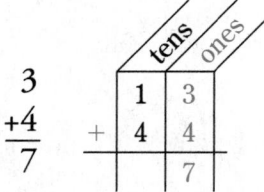

$$\begin{array}{r} 3 \\ +4 \\ \hline 7 \end{array}$$

B. Add the numbers in the tens column.

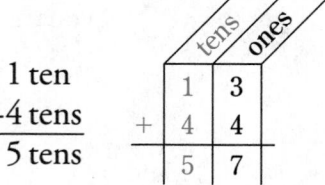

1 ten
+4 tens
5 tens

Write the 5 at the bottom of the tens column. Your answer is 57.

68
+17

A. Add the numbers in the ones column.

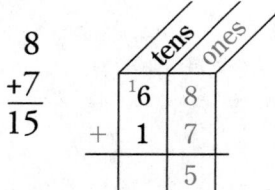

$$\begin{array}{r} 8 \\ +7 \\ \hline 15 \end{array}$$

Rename 15 as one ten and five ones with the 5 at the bottom of the ones column. Write the 1 at the top of the tens column.

B. Add the numbers in the tens column.

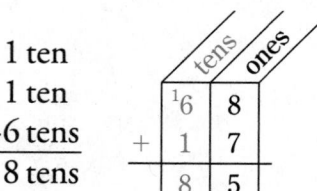

1 ten
1 ten
+6 tens
8 tens

Write the 8 at the bottom of the tens column. Your answer is 85.

$$37 \atop +26$$

A. Add the numbers in the ones column.

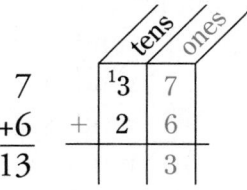

$$7 \atop +6 \above 1pt 13$$

Rename 13 as one ten and three ones. With the 3 at the bottom of the ones column, write the 1 at the top of the tens column.

B. Add the numbers in the tens column.

1 ten
3 tens
+2 tens
6 tens

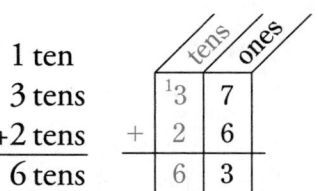

Write the 6 at the bottom of the tens column.

$$57 \atop +88$$

A. Add the numbers in the ones column.

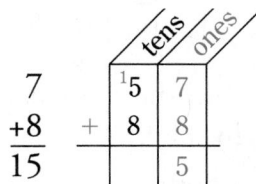

$$7 \atop +8 \above 1pt 15$$

Rename 15 as one ten and five ones. Write the 5 at the bottom of the ones column and the 1 at the top of the tens column.

B. Add the numbers in the tens column.

1 ten
5 tens
+8 tens
14 tens

Rename 14 tens (or 140) as one hundred and four tens. Write the 4 at the bottom of the tens column and write the 1 at the top of the hundreds column.

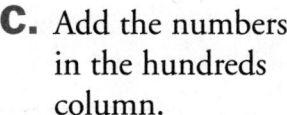

C. Add the numbers in the hundreds column.

1 hundred
+0 hundred
1 hundred

Write the 1 at the bottom of the hundreds column.

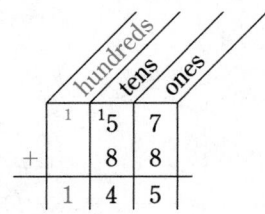

$$731$$
$$+569$$

A. Add the numbers in the ones column.

$$
\begin{array}{r}
1 \\
+9 \\
\hline
10
\end{array}
$$

Write the 0 at the bottom of the ones column and the 1 at the top of the tens column.

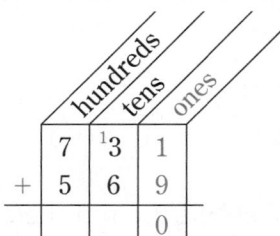

B. Add the numbers in the tens column.

$$
\begin{array}{r}
1 \text{ ten} \\
3 \text{ tens} \\
+6 \text{ tens} \\
\hline
10 \text{ tens}
\end{array}
$$

Write the 0 at the bottom of the tens column and the 1 at the top of the hundreds column.

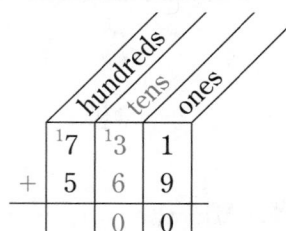

C. Add the numbers in the hundreds column.

$$
\begin{array}{r}
1 \text{ hundred} \\
7 \text{ hundreds} \\
+5 \text{ hundreds} \\
\hline
13 \text{ hundreds}
\end{array}
$$

Write the 3 at the bottom of the hundreds column and the 1 at the top of the thousands column.

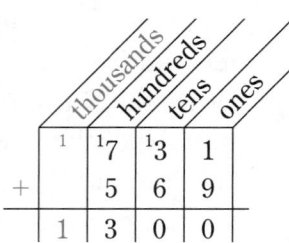

D. Add the numbers in the thousands column.

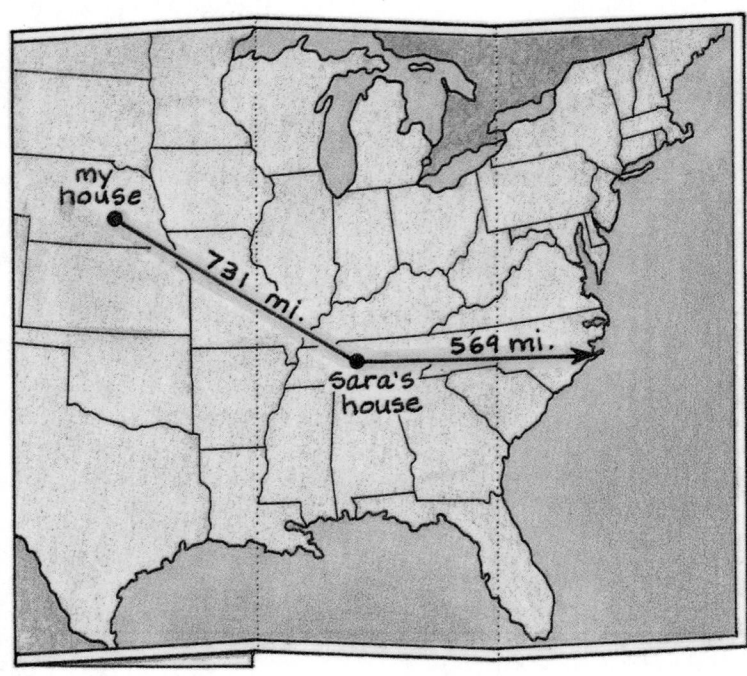

Column addition: Remember, you are still adding two numbers at a time. This means that you will always get the same answer no matter the order in which you add a group of addends.

Add   3
      4
    +6
    ___

To add this column, group any two numbers at a time.

1.   3 ⎱
       4 ⎰ 7
    +6
    ___
    13

2.   3
       4 ⎱
    +6 ⎰ 10
    ___
    13

$$768$$
$$395$$
$$+288$$

A. Add the numbers in the ones column.

    8 ones
    5 ones
    8 ones
   ___
   21 ones

Rename 21 as two tens and one 1. Write the one in the ones column.

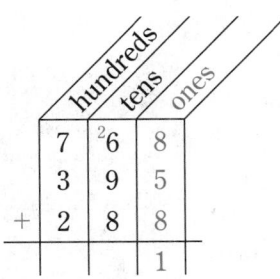

B. Add the numbers in the tens column.

    2 tens
    6 tens
    9 tens
    8 tens
   ___
   25 tens

Rename 25 as two tens and five ones. Write the 5 in the tens column.

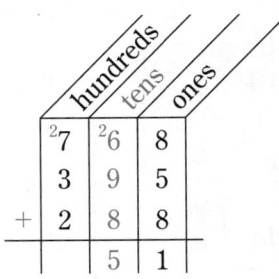

C. Add the numbers in the hundreds column.

    2 hundreds
    7 hundreds
    3 hundreds
    2 hundreds
   ___
  14 hundreds

Write the 4 in the hundreds place and the 1 in the thousands place.

187

Other Ways to Add

1. If you do not have time to find the exact sum, yet need an idea of the answer, round off and add the addends to get an estimate.

   Example: Round each number to the hundreds place. Find the hundreds place in each number and look at the digit to the right.

   2893
   532
   + 1539

Estimating is a way to count when an approximate sum is close enough, as, for instance, when counting the number of apples on the branches of a tree.

   Rounds to hundreds. Becomes

   2900
   500
   + 1500
   4900

2. Adding long columns of large numbers is not so hard when you add one column at a time and do not carry digits to the next place.

Example:

   3462
   1048
   9367
   5290
   + 4738

25	the sum of the ones
28	the sum of the tens
16	the sum of the hundreds
22	the sum of the thousands
23905	sum

Checking Answers

If you are adding a column of numbers, start at the top of the first column and add down. To check your work, start at the bottom of the first column and add up. Or, if you began adding at the bottom originally, check your work by starting to add at the top of the first column and adding down.

Use estimation by rounding off numbers. Use a calculator.

Using Your Calculator to Check Your Work

Begin by pressing the first number, or addend, then the + button, then the next addend, and so on, until you have added the column. To get the answer, press the = symbol.

The answer will appear in the display. Compare it with your written answer.

Solving addition word problems. In word problems, you are asked to use your knowledge of addition in various situations. To solve these problems, read each problem carefully. Then look at the problem's question. What is it asking you to find? If it asks you to tell how many there are in all, or the sum or total, you must add to find the answer.

José borrowed three books from the library on Wednesday and two books on Friday. How many books did he borrow in all?

In this problem, you are asked to find the total of all the books José borrowed from the library in two days. To find this number, add up the number of books.

3 books + 2 books = 5 books

One addend is 18. The sum is 46. Find the missing addend.

A. In this problem, you are given only one addend, 18, and the answer, or sum of 46. Show this information in the following way:

$18 + \square = 46$

B. To find the missing addend, you could count to 46 from 18 to find out how much more would be needed to get the sum. The answer is 28.

In some problems, you are told that someone has 18 cents and wants to buy an item that costs 46 cents. How much more money does he need? Or someone has traveled 18 miles on a trip that is 46 miles long. How many more miles does this person have to travel? To find the answer, write the problem in the same way as the one shown above and solve. Then check your answer by adding the addends and comparing your findings to the total given.

Kerry sold 140 tickets to the local trading card show on Monday, 215 tickets on Tuesday, 134 tickets on Wednesday, 322 tickets on Thursday, and 277 tickets on Friday. How many tickets did he sell in all?

A. In this problem, you are given all of the addends. You must simply add them to find the total number of tickets.

B. $140 + 215 + 134 + 322 + 277 = ?$ The answer is 1088.

Donna and Kim made up and played a dice game. On Donna's first turn, she scored 18 points, on her second turn, 10 points, and on her last turn, 24 points. When Kim played, she scored 15 points on her first turn, 30 points on her second turn, and 12 points on her third turn. How many points did Donna score in all? What was Kim's total score? Who would you say is winning the dice game?

A. This problem has more than one part. It first asks you to find Donna's total score. Remember that the word "total" means addition. So for the first part of this problem, add Donna's scores:
18 + 10 + 24 = 52

B. In the second part of this problem, you are asked to find Kim's total score. Again, this means add:
15 + 30 + 12 = 57

C. Finally, you are asked to compare the two total scores and decide who is winning so far. Kim has more points than Donna.

A sponsor of rock concerts estimated that at least 50,000 tickets would be sold the next year. During that year, the rock star performed in six concerts. The number of tickets sold were 14,320, 26,089, 18,159, 17,763, 10,842, and 20,611. Was the sponsor's estimate correct?

A. One way of solving this problem is by rounding each number of tickets and adding these amounts. You will not get an exact number, but an estimate. The rounded amounts are:
14,000 + 26,000 + 18,000 + 18,000 + 11,000 + 21,000 = 108,000 estimated number of tickets sold.

B. If you compare the sponsor's estimate to the rounded total, you will see that the sponsor's estimate was well under the actual total. To find out the *exact* number of tickets sold, add the amounts.
14,320 + 26,089 + 18,159 + 17,763 + 10,842 + 20,611 = 107,784 actual number of tickets sold.

C. The problem only asked you if the sponsor was correct, not how many tickets were actually sold. All you needed to do was round off the number of tickets and add. The sponsor's estimate was actually very much under the estimated number of tickets sold.

In a spelling bee, Mark spelled 56 words, JoAnn spelled 58 words, Carrie spelled 42 words, Eddie spelled 63 words, Bob spelled 39 words, and Sue spelled 25 words. How many words were spelled altogether?

A. In this problem, the word "altogether" is an addition word. To do this problem, add up all of the words spelled by all of the children named to get the total number of words spelled by all of the children.

B. Mark's words + JoAnn's words + Carrie's words + Eddie's words + Bob's words + Sue's words = total number of words spelled. 56 + 58 + 42 + 63 + 39 + 25 = 283 words spelled altogether.

For a homework assignment, Rodney kept a record of the length of a number of commercials. His record is 20 seconds, 35 seconds, 19 seconds, 42 seconds, and 31 seconds. What was the total number of seconds of these commercials?

The word "total" is also an addition word. You must add to find the total amount: 20 + 35 + 19 + 42 + 31 = 147 seconds.

Subtraction

Everyday subtraction. When you take away an item from a larger group, a smaller number of items is left. If you take a book from a shelf, there is one less book on the shelf. If you pay for a 29-cent item with a dollar bill, you will receive change of 71 cents. When your teacher subtracts 3 points for an incorrect answer from a total score of 100, you are left with 97. You use subtraction every day.

Subtracting whole numbers. The number you subtract from, such as the shelf of books, is called the *minuend*. The number of books you remove is the *subtrahend*. The answer is called the *difference or the remainder*.

In order not to get a ticket, a driver must subtract the time away from the car from the total time paid for on the parking meter.

Subtraction, like addition, is based on a set of basic facts that should be memorized. If you have forgotten one of the basic subtraction facts, there are a number of different ways to remember or relearn the fact.

1. **Count back.** Like all arithmetic, subtraction is based on counting. If you cannot remember what a fact such as $9 - 2$ is, start with the larger number, 9, and count back as many steps as the smaller number: 9, 8, (1 step), 7 (2 steps); the fact is $9 - 2 = 7$.

2. **Compare subtraction with addition.** If you cannot remember what $17 - 9$ is, try to remember the related addition fact: $9 + \square = 17$. What number added to 9 is 17? If you remember the addition fact, you can find that $9 + 8 = 17$, so the subtraction fact is $17 - 9 = 8$.

3. **Use tens.** There are a number of ways to use tens in subtraction. In $17 - 9$, for example, you can think $17 - 7 = 10$; $9 = 7 + 2$, so $17 - 9$ is the same as $10 - 2$, or 8. In a problem like $11 - 6$, 11 is 1 more than ten, so $11 - 6$ is 1 more than $10 - 6$. Since $10 - 6 = 4$, $11 - 6$ is 5.

4. **Use doubles.** Another way to solve $11 - 6$ is to think, two 6s are 12, one 6 and 6 less 1 are 11. The fact is $11 - 6 = 5$.

5. **Use a number line.** You can find the answer to $8 - 5$ by drawing a number line diagram similar to the one below:

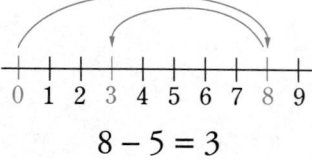

$$8 - 5 = 3$$

6. **Use the table of basic subtraction facts.** To find the answer to a problem such as $8 - 5$, read down the left side of the table to row 8 and across to column 5. Row 8 and column 5 meet at the number 3, so $8 - 5 = 3$.

You will see that some boxes in the chart are blank. These blank boxes show that some subtraction problems, such as $5 - 8$, do not have an answer in whole numbers. The table also shows that such problems as $18 - 5 = 13$ are not basic facts.

Basic Subtraction Facts

−	0	1	2	3	4	5	6	7	8	9
0	0									
1	1	0								
2	2	1	0							
3	3	2	1	0						
4	4	3	2	1	0					
5	5	4	3	2	1	0				
6	6	5	4	3	2	1	0			
7	7	6	5	4	3	2	1	0		
8	8	7	6	5	4	3	2	1	0	
9	9	8	7	6	5	4	3	2	1	0
10	10	9	8	7	6	5	4	3	2	1
11	11	10	9	8	7	6	5	4	3	2
12	12	11	10	9	8	7	6	5	4	3
13	13	12	11	10	9	8	7	6	5	4
14	14	13	12	11	10	9	8	7	6	5
15	15	14	13	12	11	10	9	8	7	6
16	16	15	14	13	12	11	10	9	8	7
17	17	16	15	14	13	12	11	10	9	8
18	18	17	16	15	14	13	12	11	10	9

Memorizing the basic subtraction facts. You will learn the basic subtraction facts by figuring answers to them first. Later on, you will save time by memorizing these facts. The best way to remember subtraction facts is by using them as much as possible.

Ten Hints on Memorizing Subtraction Facts

1. Do not try to memorize all of the facts at one time.

2. Choose a few subtraction facts to memorize, such as five or ten in a week.

3. Remember that you cannot change the order of numbers to be subtracted and still get the same answer. For example, $12 - 5$ will not give you the same answer as $5 - 12$.

4. Write the subtraction facts on a sheet of paper and cover the answers. Then write the answers without looking. Time yourself. Try this activity again. Were you able to get the right answer in less time?

5. Try to see the fact. What does 6 subtracted from 10 look like? Use pennies or buttons to find out. Or draw 10 things and cross out 6.

6. Play with patterns. Do the following examples in the order shown. What did you notice about the answers?

$$
\begin{array}{cccccccccc}
10 & 10 & 10 & 10 & 10 & 10 & 10 & 10 & 10 & 10 \\
-9 & -8 & -7 & -6 & -5 & -4 & -3 & -2 & -1 & -0
\end{array}
$$

   What other patterns can you find or make?

7. Play subtraction pick-up sticks. Use pick-up sticks for this activity. How many sticks do you have now? Play the game. How many sticks were left when you were finished playing? Play the game again. Are more or fewer sticks left this time?

8. Try calendar subtraction. Use any month and circle a special day, such as a friend's birthday or a holiday. If that day is the 17th, for example, cover two days. How many days are left? Cover three days. Remember to write the combination, such as $17 - 2$, and the answer.

9. Count down. Begin with a number, such as 22. Starting with this number, count down to zero. For a challenge, skip count by twos to zero.

10. Play subtraction rummy. Write a number on separate 3 × 5 cards. Shuffle and place all of the cards facedown. Pick up the first card and the card underneath. Does the second card have a lower number than the first? Subtract to find the answer. Use this answer as your score.

Help with Borrowing in Subtraction

In many examples, you will not be able to subtract the numbers in the problem as they are written. You will have to rename those numbers. For example, 330 becomes three hundreds, three tens, and zero ones.

Borrowing is not hard if you understand how place value works. Remember that each number, no matter how large or small, has its own place. When you borrow, you are putting numbers in their right places before subtracting.

Suppose you have this problem:

$$\begin{array}{r} 21 \\ -\ 8 \\ \hline \end{array}$$

Before you subtract, write each number in the problem in its right place as shown:

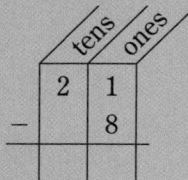

Now look at the ones place. You cannot subtract 8 from 1 in whole numbers. Think about it. If you have one pencil in your hand, there is no way you can take away, or subtract, eight pencils from it. To subtract, you must do something about the 1 in the ones place. This means you will have to go to the tens place for one 10. One 10 can be changed to 10 ones.

Adding these 10 ones to the 1 gives you 11. You can write a small 1 to show 11.

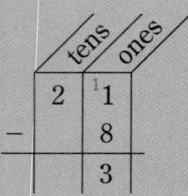

So far, you have renamed the 10 to ones. You can subtract 8 from 11. The answer is 3.

Now look at the tens column. After taking a 10 from it in this problem, you will have only one 10 left. You can write this in the shorthand shown below and finish subtracting.

You have transferred a 10 from the tens place and added it to the 1 in the ones place. You have 11.

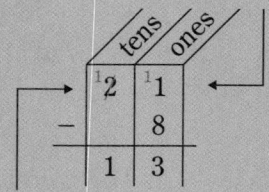

You have one 10 left. Cross out the 2 and write a 1.

Using Base Ten Blocks in Subtraction

Some textbooks no longer use the term *borrowing* in subtraction. They might use the instruction *regroup* instead of *rename*. Some books suggest a more hands-on approach by using base ten blocks in subtraction. This is how they would describe the procedure in $21 - 8$.

Use base ten blocks to find the difference.

1. Use 2 tens blocks and 1 ones block to show 21. Use 8 ones blocks to show 8.

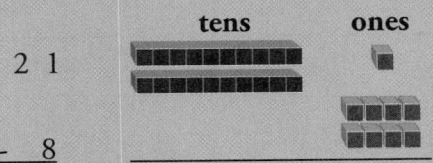

2. Because $8 > 1$, you cannot subtract these numbers. Regroup 2 tens blocks as 1 ten block and 10 ones blocks. Add the ten ones to the 1 already in the ones place to get 11.

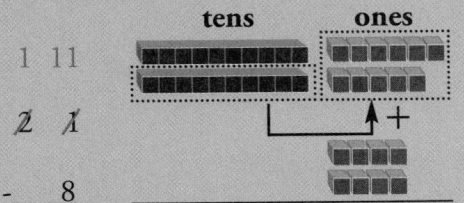

3. Subtract the ones. $11 - 8 = 3$. Since there is no tens digit in the second number, it is like subtracting nothing, so the difference is 1.

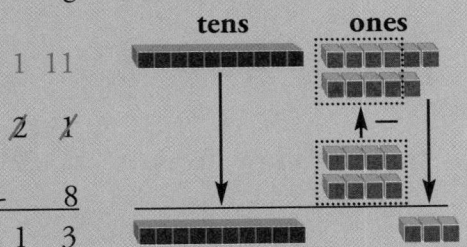

When Do You Need To Regroup?

You need to regroup in addition any time the sum of the addends with the same place value is equal to or greater than 10.

You need to regroup in subtraction any time the value of the subtrahend (the number on the bottom) is greater than the minuend (the number on the top).

Do you need to regroup? Why or why not?

47
+32
No, because $7 + 2 < 10$.

49
+31
Yes, because $9 + 1 = 10$ in the ones place.

58
+24
Yes, because $8 + 4 > 10$ in the ones place.

182
+235
Yes, because $8 + 3 > 10$ in the tens place.

42
-28
Yes, because $8 > 2$ in the ones place.

30
-12
Yes, because $2 > 0$ in the ones place.

67
-34
No, because $4 < 7$ in the ones place and $3 < 6$ in the tens place.

425
- 172
Yes, because $7 > 2$ in the tens place.

$$17$$
$$-\ 8$$

Using the table of basic subtraction facts:

A. Although you cannot subtract 8 from 7, 17 − 8 is in the table.

B. Read down the left side of the table to row 17.

C. Read across the row to column 8. The answer is 9.

Another way to find the answer is by counting down from 17 to 8 on the number line.

$$47$$
$$-\ 5$$

Using a place value chart:

A. Subtract in the ones column.

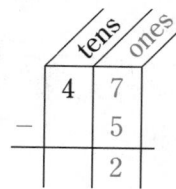

Write the 2 at the bottom of the ones column.

B. Subtract in the tens column.

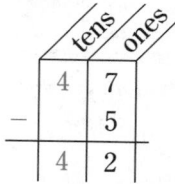

Write the 4 at the bottom of the tens column.

Using counters:

Show the larger number first. Then cross out the counters for the smaller number.

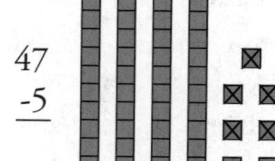

47
-5

Using Your Calculator to Subtract

Press the number to the minuend first, then the − button, and the number of the subtrahend. Then press the = button. The number appearing on the display will be your answer, or the difference.

$$\begin{array}{r} 37 \\ -\ 9 \\ \hline \end{array}$$

Using a place value chart:

A. Before subtracting in the ones column, you must do some borrowing, since 9 cannot be subtracted from 7. Rename the three as two tens and ten ones. This gives you 17 ones in the ones column.
37 = 3 tens + 7 ones
37 = 2 tens + 17 ones

B. Now you can subtract in the ones column.

$$\begin{array}{r} 17 \\ -9 \\ \hline 8 \end{array}$$

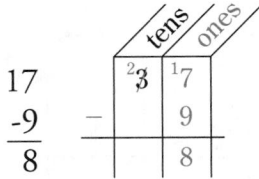

C. Subtract in the tens column.

2 tens
-0 tens
2 tens

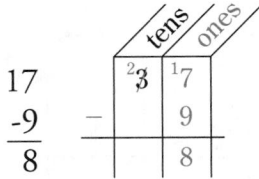

Using counters:

If you have to rename with counters, rename a ten counter as ten ones.

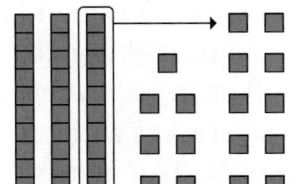

$$\begin{array}{r} 68 \\ -52 \\ \hline \end{array}$$

Using a place value chart:

A. Subtract in the ones column.

$$\begin{array}{r} 8 \\ -2 \\ \hline 6 \end{array}$$

B. Subtract in the tens column.

6 tens
-5 tens
1 tens

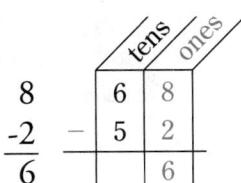

68 snacks...
52 kids want an ⬤...
how many want an 🍎?

$$\begin{array}{r} 70 \\ -45 \\ \hline \end{array}$$

Using a place value chart:

A. Before subtracting in the ones column, you must rename because 5 cannot be subtracted from 0. Rename seven tens as six tens and ten ones. This gives you ten ones in the ones column.

70 = 7 tens + 0 ones
70 = 6 tens + 10 ones

B. Now you can subtract in the ones column.

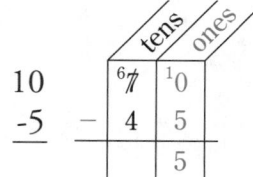

10
−5

C. Subtract in the tens column.

6 tens
−4 tens
2 tens

Using base ten blocks:

A. Use 7 tens blocks to show 70.

70

Use 4 tens blocks and 5 ones blocks to show 45.

45

B. Because 5 > 0, regroup 70 as 6 tens blocks and 10 ones blocks.

70

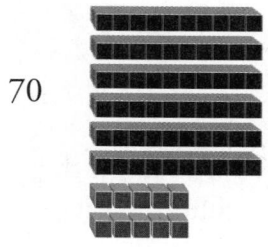

C. Subtract the ones.
10 − 5 = 5

10
−5
5

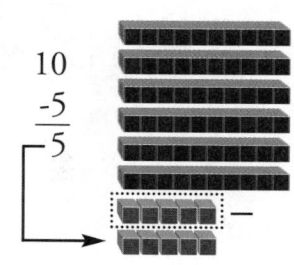

D. Subtract the tens.
6 − 4 = 2

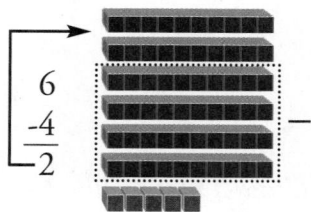

6
−4
2

70 − 45 = 25

682
– 47

Using a place value chart:

A. Before subtracting in the ones column, rename eight tens as seven tens and ten ones. This gives you twelve ones in the ones column. Now you can subtract.

```
 12
 -7
 ─
  5
```

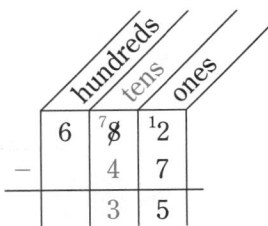

B. Subtract in the tens column.

```
 7 tens
-4 tens
 ──────
 3 tens
```

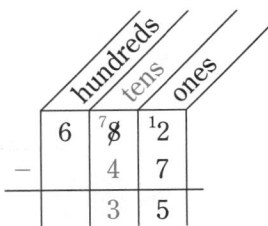

C. Subtract in the hundreds column.

```
 6 hundreds
-0 hundreds
 ──────────
 6 hundreds
```

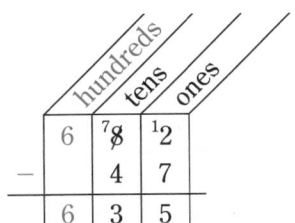

Using base ten blocks:

A. Use 6 one hundreds blocks, 8 tens blocks, and 2 ones blocks to show 682.

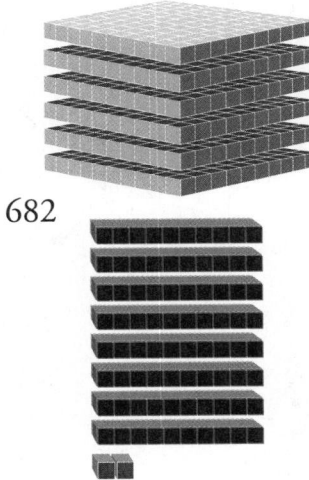

682

Use 4 tens blocks and 7 ones blocks to show 47.

47

1 Hundred Block = 100

B. Because 7 > 2, regroup 80 as 7 tens blocks and 10 ones blocks. Add the 10 ones blocks and the 2 ones blocks to get 12 ones blocks.

```
 7 12
 6 8 2
-  4 7
```

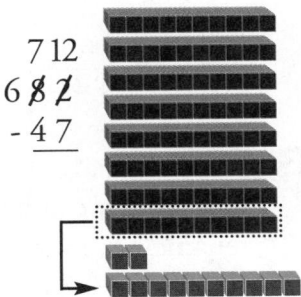

continued on next page

C. Subtract the ones.
$12 - 7 = 5$

$$\begin{array}{r} 12 \\ \cancel{2} \\ -7 \\ \hline 5 \end{array}$$

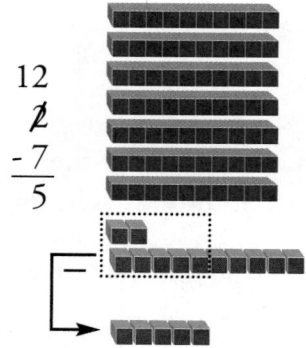

D. Subtract the tens.
$7 - 4 = 3$

$$\begin{array}{r} 7 \\ \cancel{8} \\ -4 \\ \hline 3 \end{array}$$

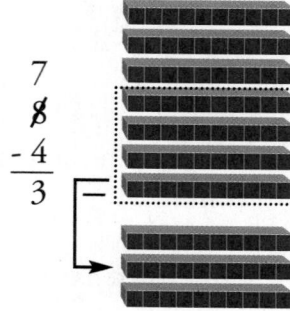

E. Subtract the one hundreds.
$6 - \text{nothing} = 6$

$$\begin{array}{r} 6 \\ - \\ \hline 6 \end{array}$$

F. $682 - 47 = 635$

$$\begin{array}{r} 503 \\ -\ 46 \\ \hline \end{array}$$

Using a place value chart:

A. Before subtracting in the ones column, rename by going to the hundreds column. Rename the five hundreds as four hundreds and ten tens.

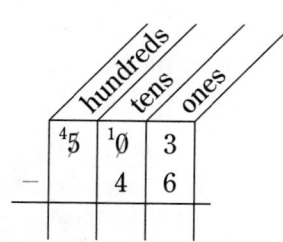

B. Now you have ten tens, which can be renamed as nine tens and ten ones. Subtract.

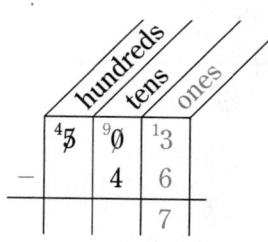

C. Subtract in the tens column.

$$\begin{array}{r} 9 \text{ tens} \\ -4 \text{ tens} \\ \hline 5 \text{ tens} \end{array}$$

Write the 5 at the bottom of the tens column.

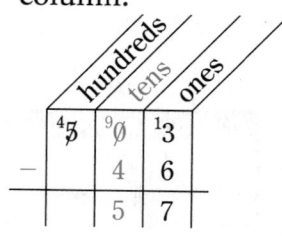

D. Subtract in the hundreds column.

$$\begin{array}{r} 4 \text{ hundreds} \\ -0 \text{ hundreds} \\ \hline 4 \text{ hundreds} \end{array}$$

Write the 4 at the bottom of the hundreds column.

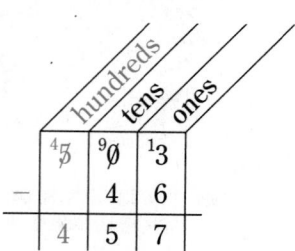

Using base ten blocks:

A. Use base ten blocks to show 503 – 46. Use 5 one hundreds blocks and 3 ones blocks to show 503.

Use 4 tens blocks and 6 ones blocks to show 46.

B. Because 6 > 3, regroup 503 as 4 one hundreds blocks, 10 tens blocks, and 3 ones blocks.

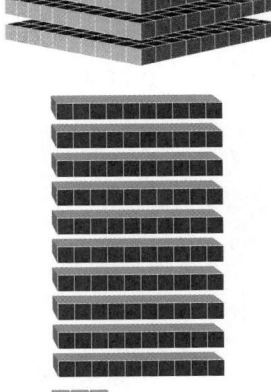

Regroup the 10 tens blocks as 9 tens

blocks and 10 ones blocks.

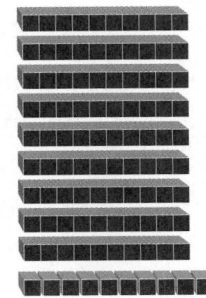

Add the 3 ones blocks and the 10 ones to get 13 ones blocks.

C. Subtract the ones. 13 – 6 = 7

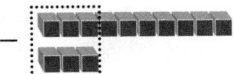

D. Subtract the tens. 9 – 4 = 5

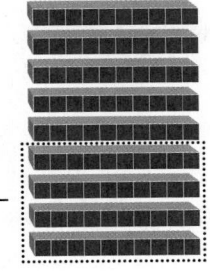

E. Subtract the one hundreds. 4 – nothing = 4

F. 503 – 46 = 457

Checking Answers

To see if your answers are correct, add the difference, or answer, to the subtrahend (number being subtracted). If this number is the same as the minuend, your answer is correct.

```
        791  minuend
      – 398  subtrahend
        393  difference, or remainder

Check:  393  difference
      + 398  subtrahend
        791
```

$$\begin{array}{r} 45 \\ -\ 27 \\ \hline \end{array}$$

Using a place value chart:

A. Before subtracting in the ones column, you must borrow, since 7 > 5.

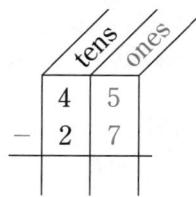

Rename the 4 as 3 tens and 10 ones.

10 + 5 gives you 15 ones in the ones column.

45 = 4 tens + 5 ones
45 = 3 tens + 15 ones

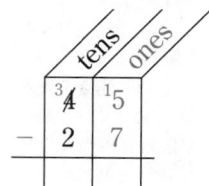

B. Subtract the ones.
15 − 7 = 8

Subtract the tens.
3 − 2 = 1
45 − 27 = 18

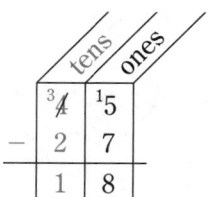

Using base ten blocks and place value:

A. Use 4 tens blocks and 5 ones blocks to show 45.

Use 2 tens blocks and 7 ones blocks to show 27.

B. Because 7 > 5, you cannot subtract these numbers in the ones place.

Regroup 4 tens blocks and 5 ones blocks as 3 tens blocks and 15 ones blocks.

C. Subtract the ones.
15 − 7 = 8

D. Subtract the tens.
3 − 2 = 1

E. 45 − 27 = 18

$$\begin{array}{r} 327 \\ -144 \\ \hline \end{array}$$

Using a place value chart:

A. Subtract in the ones column.

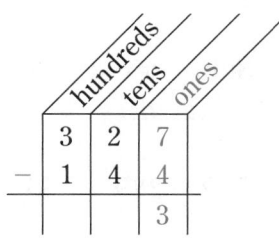

B. Before subtracting in the tens column, you must borrow, since 4 > 2.

Rename the 3 as 2 hundreds and 10 tens. 10 + 2 gives you 12 in the tens column. 327 = 3 hundreds, 2 tens, and 7 ones 327 = 2 hundreds, 12 tens, and 7 ones

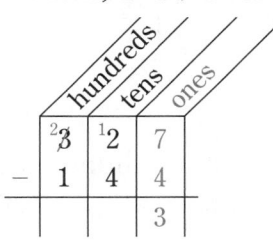

C. Subtract the tens. 12 − 4 = 8

Subtract the hundreds. 2 − 1 = 1

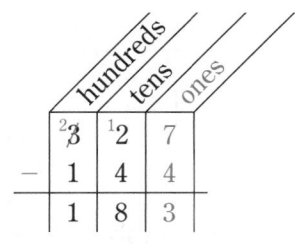

327 − 144 = 183

Using base ten blocks and place value:

A. Use 3 hundreds blocks, 2 tens blocks, and 7 ones blocks to show 327.

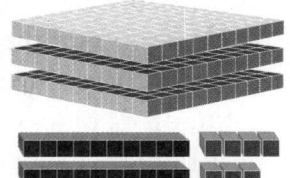

Use 1 hundred block, 4 tens blocks, and 4 ones blocks to show 144.

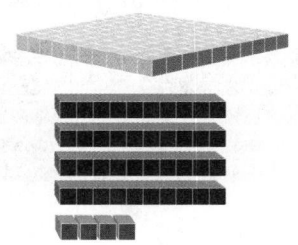

B. Subtract the ones. 7 − 4 = 3

C. Because 4 > 2, you cannot subtract these numbers. Regroup 3 hundreds blocks as 2 hundreds and 10 tens.

Rename 2 tens blocks and 10 tens blocks as

12 tens.

D. Subtract the tens. 12 − 4 = 8

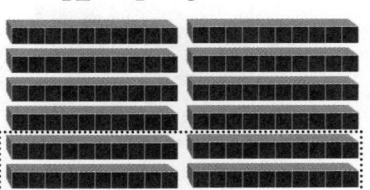

E. Subtract the hundreds. 2 − 1 = 1

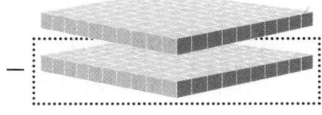

F. 327 − 144 = 183

$$\begin{array}{r} 539 \\ - \underline{289} \end{array}$$

Using a place value chart:

A. Subtract in the ones column.
$9 - 9 = 0$

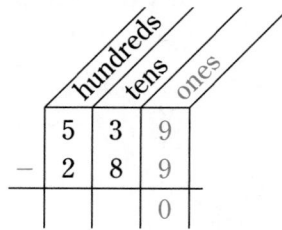

B. Before subtracting in the tens column, you must borrow, since $8 > 3$.

Rename the 5 as 4 hundreds and 10 tens. $10 + 3$ gives you 13 in the tens column.

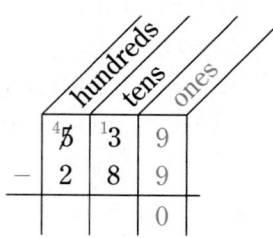

$539 = 5$ hundreds, 3 tens, and 9 ones

$289 = 2$ hundreds, 8 tens, and 9 ones

C. Subtract the tens.
$13 - 8 = 5$

Subtract the hundreds.

$539 - 289 = 250$

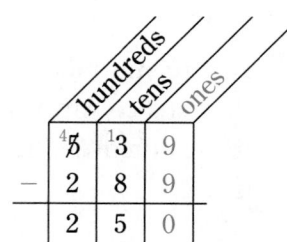

Using base ten blocks and place value:

A. Use 5 hundreds blocks, 3 tens blocks, and 9 ones blocks to show 539.

Use 2 hundreds blocks, 8 tens blocks, and 9 ones blocks to show 289.

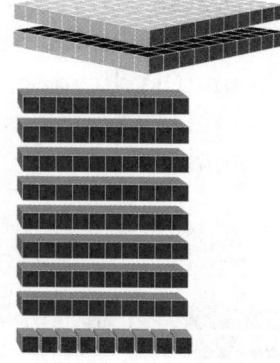

B. Subtract the ones.
$9 - 9 = 0$

C. Because $8 > 3$, you cannot subtract these numbers. Regroup 5 hundreds blocks as 4 hundreds blocks and 10 tens.

continued on next page

Rename 3 tens and 10 tens blocks as 13 tens blocks.

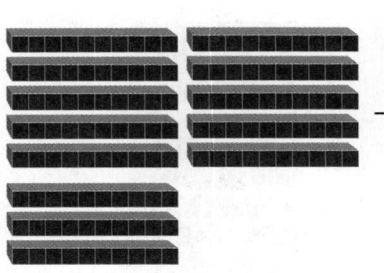

D. Subtract the tens.
13 − 8 = 5

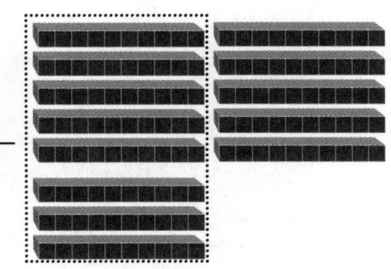

E. Subtract the hundreds.
4 − 2 = 2

F. 539 − 289 = 250

$$
\begin{array}{r}
600 \\
-\ 327 \\
\end{array}
$$

Using a place value chart:

A. Because 7 > 0, and 2 > 0 you must borrow in the ones and tens places.

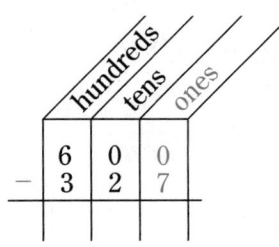

B. Rename the 6 hundreds as 5 hundreds and 10 tens.

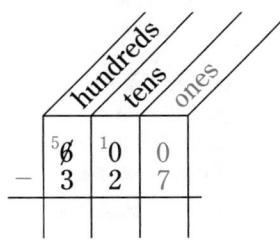

C. Rename the 10 tens as 9 tens and 10 ones.

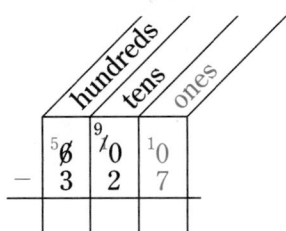

D. Subtract the ones.
10 − 7 = 3

Subtract the tens.
9 − 2 = 7

Subtract the hundreds.
5 − 3 = 2

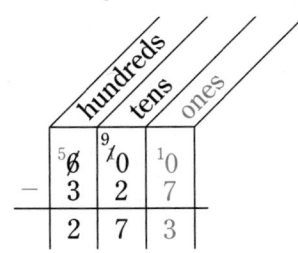

E. 600 − 327 = 273

continued on next page

Using base ten blocks and place value:

A. Use 6 hundreds blocks to show 600.

Use 3 hundreds blocks, 2 tens blocks, and 7 ones blocks to show 327.

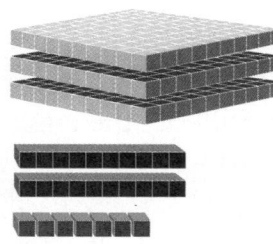

B. Because 7 > 0 in the ones place, you cannot subtract these numbers. Because 2 > 0 in the tens place, you cannot subtract these numbers.

Regroup 6 hundreds blocks as 5 hundreds blocks and 10 tens blocks.

C. Regroup 10 tens blocks as 9 tens blocks and 10 ones.

D. Subtract the ones. 10 − 7 = 3

E. Subtract the tens. 9 − 2 = 7

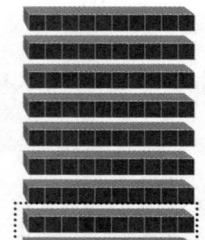

F. Subtract the hundreds. 5 − 3 = 2

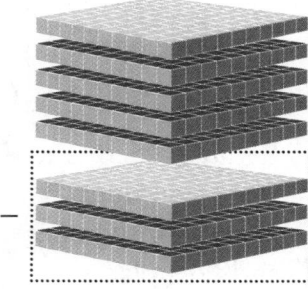

G. 600 − 327 = 273

How to solve subtraction word problems. You must first read the problem carefully, then find out what is being asked for. If you see terms such as *difference, remainder, less,* or a question asking how many are left, you will need to subtract. But be careful here! Sometimes the problem will ask you to find the difference between the two numbers and sometimes you may be given the difference and asked to find the subtrahend.

Tom is 14 years old and Laura is 8. How many years older is Tom than Laura?

In this problem, you are given the ages of two youngsters. You have to find the difference in their ages. This problem asks you to compare by finding the number of years that separate Tom's age from Laura's.

Tom's age – Laura's age = difference in ages
14 – 8 = 6 years
Tom is 6 years older than Laura.

At a local animal shelter 144 animals were adopted in July. 24 were cats. The remaining animals were dogs. How many dogs were adopted?

This problem asks you to find out how many dogs were adopted. To do this, subtract the number of cats from the total number of animals.

Total number of animals – number of cats = number of remaining animals, or dogs.
144 – 24 = 120 dogs were adopted.

Tanya's coat has ten buttons altogether. If she loses three buttons the first time she wears the coat, and two more buttons the next time, how many buttons will be left on her coat?

This problem involves more than one step. You can do this problem in two ways:

1. Write 10 – 3 = number of buttons left after the first time Tanya wears the coat, or 7 buttons. Use the new answer, 7, to figure that 7 – 2 = 5 buttons left after the next time.

2. First add to get the total number of lost buttons, or 3 + 2 = 5. Then subtract this number from the ten buttons that used to be on Tanya's coat: 10 – 5 = 5.

A delivery man carried a crate of 24 bottles of seltzer water to a deli. He lost his balance at the door. The crate tipped and 6 bottles fell out and broke on the sidewalk. How many bottles were actually delivered?

In this problem, 24 bottles of seltzer were supposed to reach the deli. Despite the accident, most of the bottles were safely delivered. The question is, how many bottles were left?

To do this problem, you must subtract. The number of bottles before the accident − number of bottles broken = number of bottles left.
24 bottles − 6 bottles = 18 bottles left.

6540 people paid to enter a popular amusement park. At closing time, only 4692 people had left the park. How many people were still in the amusement park at closing time?

In this problem, you are given the number of people who entered the park. At closing time, not all of the people who came had left the park. You are asked to find the number of people who did not leave.

The total number of people entering the park − number of people who left by closing time = number of people left. 6540 people − 4692 people who left at closing time = 1848 people still in the park.

Relating Addition and Subtraction

When you add two groups together, you will get a sum, or total, as your answer. If you subtract either number, minuend or subtrahend, from this total, you will get one of the numbers in the problem, never a different number. The following shows how this works:

$$12$$
$$+38$$
$$50$$

Subtract 12 from the answer

$$50$$
$$-12$$
$$38$$

Subtract 38 from the total

$$50$$
$$-38$$
$$12$$

As you can see, there are no other numbers than 12, 38, or 50. Since no other numbers are possible, you can say that this so-called "family" has closure in the set of whole numbers. Addition increases, or builds up, numbers, and subtraction decreases, or breaks down, numbers. Addition and subtraction may seem like two different operations, but they are not.

Multiplication

Everyday multiplication. People use multiplication as a shortcut. If a person travels 18 miles for 4 days, he can find the total number of miles traveled by multiplying 18 × 4. The number of miles traveled is 72. Since multiplication is repeated addition, the traveler could have added 18 + 18 + 18 + 18 to get 72. But this is a longer calculation. Multiplication is also useful for finding out the number of all possible combinations of items. For example, if you have three kinds of bread and four sandwich fillings, how many different sandwiches could you make for a family outing? Instead of adding four three times, multiply 3 × 4 and you will find that there are twelve possible sandwich combinations.

Multiplying whole numbers. In multiplication, you are finding the total amount of groups of items. For example, a classroom has six large tables and six chairs at each table. How many students can sit at these tables? The long way to find the answer to this problem is by adding 6 + 6 + 6 + 6 + 6 + 6. To save time, write 6 tables × 6 chairs = total number of students, or 36.

In multiplication, the two numbers that are combined are called *factors*. The two sixes that were multiplied in the problem above are factors. The answer to a multiplication problem, or in this case, 36, is called the *product*.

Sometimes, you will see the terms "multiplicand" and "multiplier." When you multiply 361 × 22, the 361 is the

Multiplication is used in everyday activities like purchasing stamps. This sheet contains four rows of five, or 20, stamps.

multiplicand, or number to be multiplied by another, and the 22 is the *multiplier,* or number by which another is multiplied. The answer is called the *product.*

Just as you memorized the addition and subtraction facts, you also should memorize the multiplication facts. Memorizing these facts may seem like a lot of work now, but you will save time later. You will be able to recall these facts and do problems faster. If you do have trouble trying to remember, here are some hints that do not involve using a table or repeated addition.

1. **Add to a fact that you know.** To find 6 × 7, you can think 6 × 6 is 36, so 6 × 7 is 36 + 6, or 42.

2. **Subtract from a fact that you know.** To find 8 × 9, you can think ten 8's are 80, so nine 8's are 80 − 8 = 72.

3. **Change the order of factors.** As in addition, in multiplication it does not matter whether you multiply 2×8 or 8×2. Both of these problems have the same answer, or product, 16.

4. **Use the patterns in products.** This means the answer, or product, will be even when multiplied by 2, 4, 6, and 8. It also means a factor, such as 3 or 5, multiplied by another number can be divided evenly by 3 or 5. A factor can also divide a number evenly.

Factor of 2: Product is even; for example, $2 \times 1 = 2$, $2 \times 2 = 4$, $2 \times 3 = 6$, $2 \times 4 = 8$; 2, 4, 6, and 8 are even.

Factor of 3: Digits can be added by 3; $3 \times 1 = 3$, $3 \times 2 = 6$, $3 \times 3 = 9$, $3 \times 4 = 12$.

Factor of 4: Product is even; for example, $4 \times 1 = 4$, $4 \times 2 = 8$, $4 \times 3 = 12$.

Factor of 5: Last digit is either 0 or 5; for example, $5 \times 1 = 5$, $5 \times 2 = 10$, $5 \times 3 = 15$, $5 \times 4 = 20$.

Factor of 6: Product is even and digits can be added by 6; $6 \times 1 = 6$, $6 \times 2 = 12$, $6 \times 3 = 18$, $6 \times 4 = 24$.

Factor of 8: Product is even; $8 \times 1 = 8$, $8 \times 2 = 16$, $8 \times 3 = 24$, $8 \times 4 = 32$.

Factor of 9: Digits can be added by 9; $9 \times 1 = 9$, $9 \times 2 = 18$, $9 \times 3 = 27$, $9 \times 4 = 36$.

There is no easy way to recognize products that have a factor of 7.

Memorizing the basic multiplication facts.

As you learn multiplication, you will probably use repeated addition and other ways to figure out answers. Multiplication facts such as 2×2 are easy. Perhaps you have some of them memorized already. Write out all the facts and try to memorize them. Remember that the best way to memorize them is by using them.
Example:

$$\begin{array}{r} 4 \\ \times 3 \\ \hline \end{array}$$

A. You can solve this by using the table of basic multiplication facts. Read down to row 4 and across to column 3. Row 4 and column 3 meet at the number 12, which is the answer.

Basic Multiplication Facts

×	0	1	2	3	4	5	6	7	8	9
0	0	0	0	0	0	0	0	0	0	0
1	0	1	2	3	4	5	6	7	8	9
2	0	2	4	6	8	10	12	14	16	18
3	0	3	6	9	12	15	18	21	24	27
4	0	4	8	12	16	20	24	28	32	36
5	0	5	10	15	20	25	30	35	40	45
6	0	6	12	18	24	30	36	42	48	54
7	0	7	14	21	28	35	42	49	56	63
8	0	8	16	24	32	40	48	56	64	72
9	0	9	18	27	36	45	54	63	72	81

B. You can also find the answer by adding three fours or by counting the elements of three sets of four.

$$\begin{array}{r} 4 \\ 4 \\ +4 \\ \hline 12 \end{array}$$

12 elements

C. Or you can use a number line.

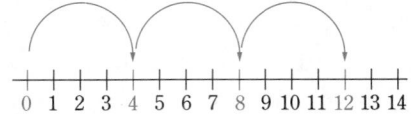

0 1 2 3 4 5 6 7 8 9 10 11 12 13 14

MATHEMATICS

Tests for Divisibility

Divisible by	Test
2	The number in the ones place is an even digit: 0, 2, 4, 6, or 8.
3	The sum of the digits is a multiple of 3.
4	The number formed by the last two digits is divisible by 4.
5	The digit in the ones place is 0 or 5.
6	The number is divisible by both 2 and 3.
8	The number formed by the last three digits is divisible by 8.
9	The sum of the digits is divisible by 9.
10	The digit in the ones place is 0.

Examples:

Is 342 divisible by 2?	*Yes, the digit in the ones place is even.*
Is 342 divisible by 3?	*Yes, the sum of the digits is 3 + 4 + 2 = 9. Nine is divisible by 3.*
Is 342 divisible by 6?	*Yes, both 2 and 3 are factors.*
Is 207 divisible by 5?	*No, the digit in the ones place is neither 0 nor 5.*
Is 5256 divisible by 8?	*Yes, the last three digits, 256, are divisible by 8.*
Is 3463 divisible by 9?	*No, the sum of the digits is 3 + 4 + 6 + 3 = 16. Sixteen is not divisible by 9.*

Combine the rules:

Tell which of the digits 2, 3, 4, 5, 6, 8, 9, or 10 are factors of 35712.

Two is a factor because the digit in the ones place is even.

Three is a factor because the sum of the digits is 3 + 5 + 7 + 1 + 2 = 18. Three is a factor of 18.

Four is a factor because the number formed by the last two digits is 12. Twelve is divisible by 4.

Five is not a factor because the digit in the ones place is not 0 or 5.

Six is a factor because both 2 and 3 are factors.

Eight is a factor because the number formed by the last three digits is 712. 712 is divisible by 8.

Nine is a factor because the sum of the digits is 18. 9 is a factor of 18.

Ten is not a factor because the digit in the ones place is not zero.

With your knowledge of multiplication facts as well as the rules for divisibility, list all the factors of each number.

35: 1, 5, 7, 35

24: 1, 2, 3, 4, 6, 8, 12, 24

56: 1, 2, 4, 7, 8, 14, 28, 56

37: 1, 37

Use 2, 3, 4, 5, 6, 8, 9, and 10 and see which are divisors of the following:

105

The number in the ones place is not even, so 2 is not a factor.	2̸
The sum of the digits is a multiple of 3, so 3 is a factor.	3
Four does not divide into the last two digits, so 4 is not a factor.	4̸
The number ends in 5, so 5 is a factor.	5
Two is not a factor, so 6 is not a factor.	6̸
If 4 is not a factor, 8 will not be a factor.	8̸
The sum of the digits is not a multiple of 9, so 9 is not a factor.	9̸
The number does not have a zero in the ones place, so 10 is not a factor.	1̸0̸

continued on next page

211

Tests for Divisibility (continued)

532

The number in the ones place is even, so 2 is a factor.	2
The sum of the digits is 10, not a multiple of 3, so 3 is not a factor.	3̸
Four divides evenly into the last two digits, so 4 is a factor.	4
The number does not end in 5 or 0, so 5 is not a factor.	5̸
Since 3 is not a factor, 6 is not a factor.	6̸
Eight is not a factor of 532	8̸
The sum of the digits is 11, not a multiple of 9, so 9 is not a factor.	9̸
The number does not end in 0, so 10 is not a factor.	1̸0̸

4050

The number in the ones place is even, so 2 is a factor.	2
The sum of the digits is 9, a multiple of 3, so 3 is a factor.	3
Four is not a factor of the last two digits, so 4 is not a factor.	4̸
The number ends in 0, so 5 is a factor.	5
The number is divisible by 2 and 3, so 6 is a factor.	6
The number 050 is not divisible by 8, so 8 is not a factor.	8̸
The sum of the digits is 9, so 9 is a factor.	9
The number ends in a 0, so 10 is a factor.	10

Identify the missing digit or digits of the first number if the second number is a factor.

24__; 9 is a factor.
The sum of the digits must be a multiple of 9. $2 + 4 + $ __ $ = 9$.
The missing digit is 3. The three-digit number is 243.

24__; 2 is a factor.
The digit in the ones place must be an even number, so 0, 2, 4, 6, and 8 work.
The three-digit numbers are 240, 242, 244, 246, and 248.

Identify the missing digit or digits of the first number if the other two numbers are factors.

25__; 2 and 5 are factors.
If 5 is a factor, the missing digit must be 0 or 5.
If 2 is a factor, the missing digit must be even, therefore 0.
The first number is 250.

46__; 2 and 3 are factors.
If 2 is a factor, the missing digit must be 0, 2, 4, 6, or 8.
If three is a factor, the sum of the digits must be a multiple of 3.
$$4 + 6 + 0 = 10 \qquad \text{0 will not work.}$$
$$4 + 6 + 2 = 12 \qquad \text{2 will work.}$$
$$4 + 6 + 4 = 14 \qquad \text{4 will not work.}$$
$$4 + 6 + 6 = 16 \qquad \text{6 will not work.}$$
$$4 + 6 + 8 = 18 \qquad \text{8 will work.}$$
The missing digits are 2 and 8.
The three-digit numbers are 462 and 468.

Ten Hints on Memorizing Multiplication Facts

1. Do not try to memorize all of the facts at one time.

2. Do memorize one set of tables at a time before moving on to others. For example, begin with the six or seven times tables.

3. Do practice multiplication every day. For example, use multiplication to find the total number of an array of stamps.

4. Do let a change in the order of factors help you. For example, 6×8 and 8×6 both have the same answer, 48. If you know the answer to 6×8, you know the answer to 8×6. So now you only have half as many—or 50—facts to memorize.

5. Double the fun by counting by twos, threes, fives. For example, 2 groups of 2 can be written as 2×2. Three groups of two look like 3×2. Write down the combinations you use, such as $3 \times 7 = 21$.

6. Copy the playing board at the right. Taking turns with a partner, toss a paper clip on the board and write the number it lands on. Toss the clip again and multiply the two numbers. This number is your score.

14	2	10	8
3	0	4	6
7	1	9	11
28	5	0	4
12	8	9	7

7. Write the multiplication facts on a piece of paper with the right answers. Cover the answers and try to fill in the correct ones. How many do you have correct? Time yourself. Can you beat your own record?

8. Fold or rule off a piece of paper to look like the one at right. How many boxes do you have at the top and on one side? Multiply these two numbers. Now try folding this paper so that you have more boxes. Again, count one row and one column of boxes. Multiply these two numbers. Can you fold this paper again so that you have more boxes?

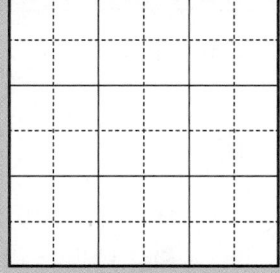

9. Select a partner for a game. Pick any number and tell your partner to multiply it by another number, say, 6. For example, you can pick 3, and tell your partner to multiply it by 6. In the example, 18 ($6 \times 3 = 18$) is one score. You can make this game as easy or as hard as you wish.

10. Glue two toothpicks at a time on heavy paper or cardboard to design a building or invention. Count how many pairs of toothpicks you used after you have completed the project. Then count how many single toothpicks you used altogether.

$$26 \times 3$$

The number 26 does not appear in the table of basic multiplication facts. But 2 and 6 do. You can solve this problem by multiplying ones and tens separately.

A. Multiply ones by three ones.

$$\begin{array}{r} 6 \\ \times 3 \\ \hline 18 \end{array}$$

Write the partial product.

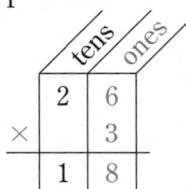

B. Multiply tens by three ones.

$$\begin{array}{r} 2 \text{ tens} \\ \times 3 \text{ ones} \\ \hline 6 \text{ tens} = 60 \end{array}$$

Write the partial product.

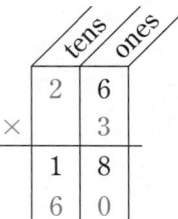

Note that two tens × three ones is six tens—not six ones.

C. Add the partial products.

$$\begin{array}{r} 18 \\ +60 \\ \hline 78 \end{array}$$

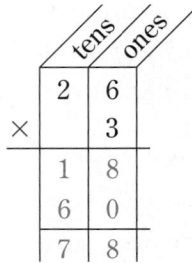

You will find the following method faster.

A. Multiply ones by ones.

$$\begin{array}{r} 6 \\ \times 3 \\ \hline 18 \end{array} = \text{one ten and eight ones}$$

Write the 8 at the bottom of the ones column and write the 1 in the tens column.

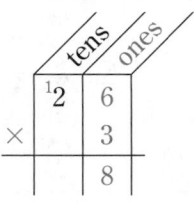

B. Multiply tens by ones.

$$\begin{array}{r} 20 \\ \times 3 \\ \hline 60 \end{array}$$

C. Now add the 10 shown by the small 1 in the tens column.

$$\begin{array}{r} 60 \\ +10 \\ \hline 70 \end{array} = 7 \text{ tens}$$

Write the 7 in the tens column.

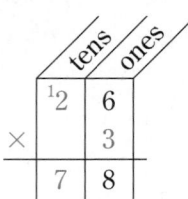

Commutative Law

Multiplication and addition are *commutative.* The order in which one multiplies or adds does not make any difference in the answer. Therefore, since 3 × 26 = 78, it is also true that 26 × 3 = 78.

45
×23

A. Multiply ones by ones.

5
×3
15 = 1 ten and 5 ones

Write the 5 at the bottom of the ones column, and the 1 in the tens column.

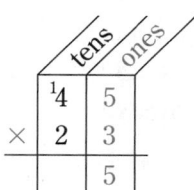

B. Multiply tens by ones.

4 tens
× 3 ones
12 tens

Now add to this the 10 shown by the small 1 in the tens column:

120
+ 10
130 = 1 hundred and 3 tens

Write the 1 in the hundreds column and the 3 in the tens column.

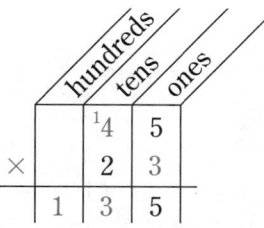

C. Multiply ones by tens.

5 ones
× 2 tens
10 tens

Write a 0 in the tens column and a 1 at the top of the hundreds column.

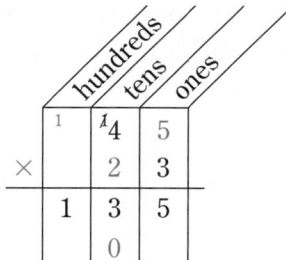

D. Multiply tens by tens.

4 tens
× 2 tens
8 hundreds

Add to this the hundred shown by the small 1.

8 hundreds
+ 1 hundred
9 hundreds

Write the 9 in the hundreds column.

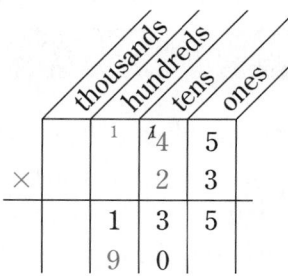

E. Add the columns together.

215

Using counters in multiplication. Counters may be used to show how renaming in multiplication works.

$$\begin{array}{r} 26 \\ \times\, 3 \end{array}$$

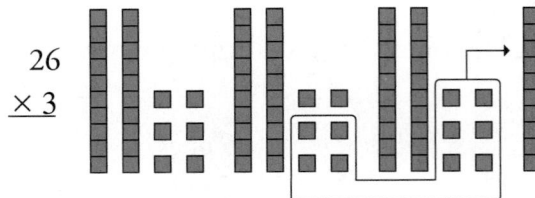

This example shows three groups of 26. To add them together, take 10 of the ones counters (■) and combine them in a tens counter. You end up with 7 tens counters and 8 ones counters. Add the tens counters together (10+10+10+10+10+10+10) to get 70. Then add the remaining 8 ones counters to 70 to get 78.

$$\begin{array}{r} 319 \\ \times 524 \end{array}$$

A. Multiply ones, tens, and hundreds by ones.

$$\begin{array}{r} 319 \\ \times 524 \\ \hline 1276 \end{array}$$

B. Then multiply by tens.

$$\begin{array}{r} 319 \\ \times 524 \\ \hline 1276 \\ 638 \end{array}$$

C. Finally, multiply ones, tens, and hundreds by hundreds.

$$\begin{array}{r} 319 \\ \times 524 \\ \hline 1276 \\ 638 \\ 1595 \end{array}$$

D. Add partial products.

$$\begin{array}{r} 319 \\ \times 524 \\ \hline 1276 \\ 638 \\ 1595 \\ \hline 167156 \end{array}$$

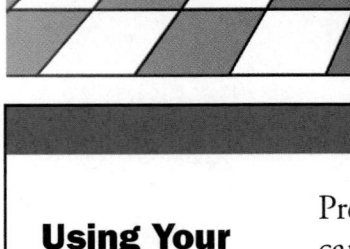

Using Your Calculator to Multiply

Press the number of the multiplicand, the × sign, the number of the multiplier, and the = sign. Your answer should match the answer shown in the display.

How to solve multiplication word problems. You will use the basic multiplication facts as well as the information given to you in the problem. Read the problem and question carefully. In some problems, you may find words that mean multiply, such as *times, how many, how much,* and *product.*

Maria's new garden will have 12 rows of plants on one side and 36 columns of plants on the other. How many plants will be in Maria's garden altogether?

A. Sometimes drawing a picture will help you to solve the problem. In this problem, you are given the number of plants for two sides of the garden. You are asked to find how many plants there are in all.

B. To find the number of plants, multiply 12 × 36. Your product will be 432.

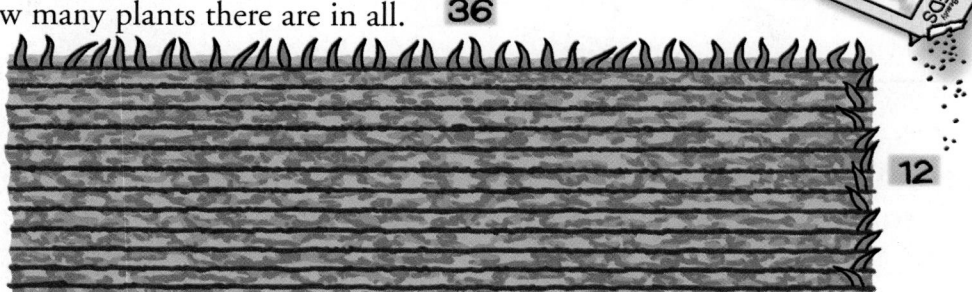

George wanted to multiply 7 × 3 on his calculator, but lost track of the number of three's he pressed. When he pressed the = sign, he was surprised to see 567 on the display. What answer should George have seen on the calculator's display? What problem did George actually solve when he lost count?

A. In the first part of this problem, all you have to do is multiply 7 × 3. If you forgot what 7 × 3 is, switch the factors and write 3 × 7. You will still get 21, which is the answer, or product, to the first part of this problem.

B. The second part of this problem asks you to write the problem George solved instead. The question here is how many extra threes did George press to get 567?

7 × 3 × 3 × 3 × 3

21   × 3 × 3 × 3

C. Press 21 on your calculator, the × sign, and 3. You will get 63. Press the × sign and 3 again and you will get 189. Press the × sign and 3 once more and you will get 567.

Dana is helping to unpack six cartons of new books. Each carton has twelve books inside. How many new books will Dana have to unpack and place on the shelves?

In this problem, you are asked to find the total number of books in all of the cartons. To solve this problem, write:

6 cartons × 12 books = 72 books

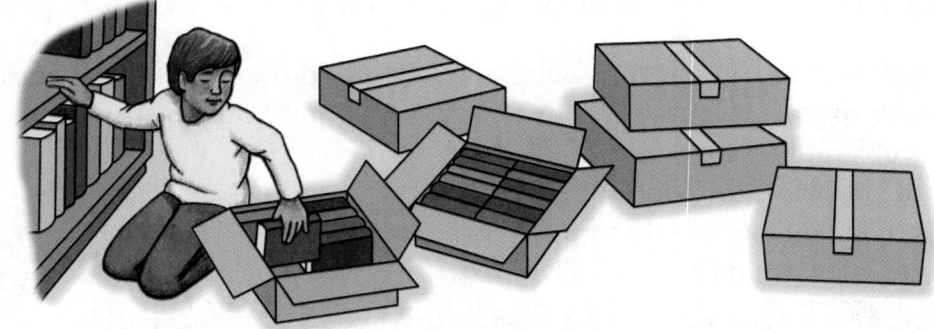

A go-cart for a popular ride can hold an average weight of 510 pounds. Three men weighing 160 pounds each get into the cart. In the meantime, a friend decides to ride, too. This man weighs 130 pounds. Will all of these men be able to ride in the cart together?

A. This is a two-step problem. You are given the number of pounds that the cart can hold and have to find out whether the total weight of the men is under or over this limit. If the men's weight is over this limit, one of the men will have to leave or ride in another cart. So the first step in this problem is to find out how much the first three men weigh together.

Since they each weigh 160 pounds, you need only to multiply to find the answer.

160 pounds, or the weight of one of the men × 3 men = total weight of the three men.

160 × 3 = 480 pounds.

This is the total weight of the first three men. So far, they can all ride in the cart.

B. Now you have to add the last man's weight to the 480 pounds to get the weight of the four men.

480 + 130 = 610 pounds.

This is the total weight of the four men. Not all of these men will be able to ride in the cart together. 610 pounds is over the cart's weight limit of 510 pounds.

Checking Answers

There are several ways to check multiplication. In the first, *reverse the order of the factors.* If you do not remember the product of 9 × 6, try 6 × 9. Either way, you will get 54.

Another way is to *estimate the product* before or after doing the problem. You will not get an exact answer, but a reasonable guess.

Estimating. To estimate in multiplication, round each factor to the place of its first, or leading, digit.

$$5983 \qquad\qquad 6000$$
$$\underline{\times\ 236} \quad \text{rounds to} \quad \underline{\times\ 200}$$

Multiply using the rounded factors.

$$6000$$
$$\underline{\times\ 200}$$
$$1200000$$

The estimated product of 1,200,000 is fairly close to the actual product, which is 1,411,988. This is enough information to be able to tell whether a product obtained on a calculator is likely to be free of mistakes.

One way to get a closer estimate is to include a second estimate as a "correction factor." Estimate the effect of the part of the problem that was lost in rounding.

$$236$$
$$\underline{-\ 200}$$
$$36$$

Round 36 to 40.

$$6000$$
$$\underline{\times\ 40}$$
$$240000$$

Add or subtract the correction factor to or from your previous estimate to obtain a closer estimate.

$$1,200,000$$
$$\underline{+\ 240,000}$$
$$1,440,000$$

The estimate of 1,440,000 is close enough to the true answer of 1,411,988 for most purposes that do not require a computed answer.

For a quick estimate, just multiply the leading digits and write the correct number of zeros. Since 5 × 2 = 10, the quick estimate tells you that the answer will be greater than 1,000,000. You can improve that estimate by rounding both numbers up. If you round 5983 up to 6000 and 236 up to 300, then multiplying the leading digits will give you an estimate of 1,800,000. Now you know that the actual answer will be between 1,000,000 and 1,800,000.

Factors. Factors can also be used to check your work. Factor the multiplier, then multiply using the factors.

Example:
$$24$$
$$\underline{\times\ 12}$$
$$48$$
$$\underline{+24}$$
$$288$$

12 can be factored into 4 × 3, therefore:

$$24$$
$$\underline{\times\ 4}$$
$$96$$
$$\underline{\times\ 3}$$
$$288$$

Division

Everyday division. Whenever you cut a slice of pizza or a piece of cake, or any whole item into one or more parts, you are dividing. You are also using division when you place separate items in two or more containers in equal amounts.

Dividing numbers. In division, the number you are dividing by is called the *divisor,* the number you are dividing into is called the *dividend,* and the answer is called the *quotient.*

There are only 90 division facts because division by zero is not possible (see the basic division table on page 221). Because there are fewer facts, you might suppose that division facts would be easier to learn than those of addition, subtraction, or multiplication (there are 100 facts for each of those operations). But many people have difficulty estimating in division, or guessing how many times a number "goes into" another number. Division also involves addition, subtraction, and multiplication.

To be able to divide easily, you will need to memorize the facts. But if you are unable to remember a fact, there are various tips you can use.

1. **Relate division to multiplication.** For example, if you cannot recall the answer to $3\overline{)9}$, you can ask, 3 times what number equals 9? Or how many sets of 3 are in 9?

    Since $3 \times 3 = 9$, then

    $$3\overline{)9}^{\;3}$$

    is the correct fact.

Even simple everyday things like pouring equal shares of milk from a jug into glasses are a kind of division.

2. **Use the number line.** To find the answer to $4\overline{)12}$, you can draw a picture that is just like a multiplication line except that the jumps go in the other direction.

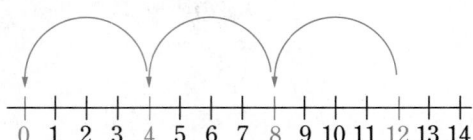

In this case, the answer is the number of jumps it takes to get to 0. Therefore,

$$4\overline{)12}^{\;3}$$

3. **Use an array.** If you want to find the answer to $7\overline{)28}$, you can draw rows of 7 dots until you have 28 dots in all. This may be more work than memorizing the fact.

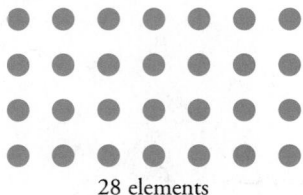

28 elements

The array shows that 28 divided by 7 is 4.

Use the basic division table. The easiest kind of division table to use is just a multiplication table with one column deleted. The 0 column is deleted to show that you cannot divide by 0.

Basic Division Table								
×	1	2	3	4	5	6	7	8	9
0	0	0	0	0	0	0	0	0	0
1	1	2	3	4	5	6	7	8	9
2	2	4	6	8	10	12	14	16	18
3	3	6	9	12	15	18	21	24	27
4	4	8	12	16	20	24	28	32	36
5	5	10	15	20	25	30	35	40	45
6	6	12	18	24	30	36	42	48	54
7	7	14	21	28	35	42	49	56	63
8	8	16	24	32	40	48	56	64	72
9	9	18	27	36	45	54	63	72	81

To find the answer to a problem such as $8\overline{)56}$ using this table, first locate the divisor, 8, at the top of the table. Go down the column headed 8 until you find the dividend, 56, in the body of the table. It is in row number 7. Therefore,

$$8\overline{)56}^{\,7}$$

Memorizing the basic division facts. Like addition, subtraction, and multiplication basic facts, division facts are learned—and memorized—better by using them often. You will save much time if you can just look at a fact and know the answer to it. There are many ways to memorize facts. Using division facts in different ways will help you to memorize them faster.

$$6\overline{)39}$$

A. Use the division table if you do not remember the division facts when the divisor is 6. There is no division fact for $6\overline{)39}$, but it is between two division facts.

$$6\overline{)36}^{\,6} \quad and \quad 6\overline{)42}^{\,7}$$

B. Subtract the lesser dividend from the dividend in the original problem.

$$
\begin{array}{r}
6 \\
6\overline{)39} \\
\underline{36} \\
3
\end{array}
$$

C. Write the result as a quotient with a *remainder,* shown by writing R. A remainder is the number left over after the last subtraction.

$$
\begin{array}{r}
6R3 \\
6\overline{)39} \\
\underline{36} \\
3
\end{array}
$$

This means that $(6 \times 6) + 3 = 39$.

221

Ten Hints on Memorizing Basic Division Facts

1. Do not try to memorize all of the division facts at the same time.

2. Do memorize a few facts at a time, then move on to others. Look for ways that one set of facts is related to another in division.

3. Do remember that $16 \div 4$ and $4 \div 16$ give two different quotients!

4. Practice using division. Pick a number, any number. Can you divide it evenly by 2, 3, 4, 5, 6, 7, 8, or 9? Try dividing other numbers. Does the same thing happen?

5. Another way to practice is to spill a pile of beans or buttons on the table. Count how many there are. Take turns making groups of 2, 3, 4, etc. Did you have any beans or buttons left over each time? Why or why not?

6. Find a book you will enjoy reading, such as a mystery. Write down the number of pages in the whole book. Read the book. How many days did it take you to finish it? Divide this number into the total number of pages. You will get the average number of pages you read each day.

7. Write down the division facts on a piece of paper with the answers. Cover the answers and try to write the correct answers in the shortest amount of time, say five minutes. Try this again tomorrow and see if you can beat your own record.

8. Try to share something when you have four items, such as four pieces of fruit, and two friends. Or four containers for 20 eggs. Think of other situations and practice them on your friends. Then try to help with your friends' division dilemmas.

9. Find examples of the ways people use division every day. Begin by asking your friends and family how they use division. Ask them to show you an example, if possible. If you have a favorite sport, find out if division can be used to figure records of scores and other information.

10. Try using averages. You get an average by first adding, say, six things and dividing this total number by six. To start, keep a record of the time you watch television for five days. Try to use even numbers, such as 30, 60, or 90 minutes. At the end of five days, add up these times. Then divide your answer by five. You will get the *average* time spent watching television. What other ways are averages used?

$$2\overline{)80}$$

A. One approach is to think of the dividend as 8 tens.

$$\begin{array}{r} 4 \text{ tens} = 40 \\ 2\overline{)8 \text{ tens}} \\ \underline{8 \text{ tens}} \\ 0 \text{ tens} \end{array}$$

In effect, if you can solve the problem $2\overline{)8}$, you can solve any of the following problems:

$$2\overline{)800} = \begin{array}{r} 4 \text{ hundreds} = 400 \\ 2\overline{)8 \text{ hundreds}} \\ \underline{8 \text{ hundreds}} \\ 0 \end{array}$$

B. Place value can be used to write the same procedure in a more familiar way.

$$\begin{array}{r} 40 \\ 2\overline{)80} \\ \underline{8} \\ 0 \end{array}$$

$$2\overline{)800} = \begin{array}{r} 4 \text{ hundreds} = 400 \\ 2\overline{)8 \text{ hundreds}} \\ \underline{8 \text{ hundreds}} \\ 0 \end{array}$$

and so on. This fact makes it possible to attack division problems digit by digit.

$$2\overline{)88}$$

A. The problem can be rewritten as follows:

$$2\overline{)8 \text{ tens} + 8 \text{ ones}}$$

B. Divide the tens.

$$\begin{array}{r} 4 \text{ tens} \\ 2\overline{)8 \text{ tens} + 8 \text{ ones}} \\ \underline{8 \text{ tens}} \\ 0 \end{array}$$

C. Divide the ones.

$$\begin{array}{r} 4 \text{ tens} + 4 \text{ ones} = 44 \\ 2\overline{)8 \text{ tens} + 8 \text{ ones}} \\ \underline{8 \text{ tens}} \quad \underline{8 \text{ ones}} \\ 0 \qquad 0 \end{array}$$

D. You can write the problem using place value instead of the words "tens" and "ones."

$$\begin{array}{r} 4 \\ 2\overline{)88} \\ \underline{8} \\ 8 \end{array}$$

E. Note that there is really nothing new in this. The first 8 merely shows that you are subtracting 8 tens from the 88.

The second 8 is a remainder—you have not yet taken away as many twos as you can.

$$\begin{array}{r} 44 \\ 2\overline{)88} \\ \underline{8} \\ 8 \\ \underline{8} \\ 0 \end{array}$$

Using counters in division. When using counters in division, ring each group that is being removed and then count the rings. For example, to divide 88 by 2, remove groups of 2.

The first step is shown in removing groups of two tens. There are four such groups. The second step is shown as removing groups of two ones. There are also four groups of two ones. Therefore, the quotient, when you divide 88 by 2, is four tens and four ones, or 44.

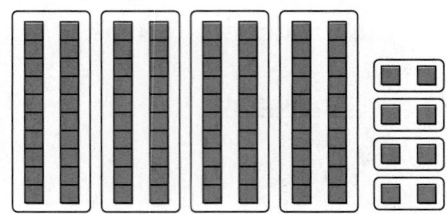

$$3\overline{)78}$$

A. This sort of problem can be attacked by dividing each digit separately.

Divide the tens.

$$
\begin{array}{r}
2 \\
3\overline{)78} \\
60 \\
\hline
18
\end{array}
$$

B. Divide the remainder.

$$
\begin{array}{r}
26 \\
3\overline{)78} \\
60 \\
\hline
18 \\
18 \\
\hline
0
\end{array}
$$

$$3\overline{)528}$$

A. Divide the first digit.

$$
\begin{array}{r}
1 \\
3\overline{)528} \\
3 \\
\hline
2
\end{array}
$$

Here, we write only a 3 to note that we have subtracted three hundreds. We write the remainder as 2, although the remainder at this point is actually 228.

B. Bring down the second digit.

$$
\begin{array}{r}
1 \\
3\overline{)528} \\
3 \\
\hline
22
\end{array}
$$

C. Divide the 22 by 3.

$$
\begin{array}{r}
17 \\
3\overline{)528} \\
3 \\
\hline
22 \\
21 \\
\hline
1
\end{array}
$$

D. Bring down the third digit.

$$
\begin{array}{r}
17 \\
3\overline{)528} \\
3 \\
\hline
22 \\
21 \\
\hline
18
\end{array}
$$

E. Divide the 18 by 3.

$$
\begin{array}{r}
176 \\
3\overline{)528} \\
3 \\
\hline
22 \\
21 \\
\hline
18 \\
18 \\
\hline
0
\end{array}
$$

$$24\overline{)294}$$

A. In this case, there is a two-digit divisor, making it a much more complicated division problem than one with a one-digit divisor. The first step is to estimate what the first partial quotient will be. It is easiest to round the divisor to 20 to make such an estimate. Think:

$$20\overline{)294}^{?}$$

Since 20 will divide into 29 once, the first partial quotient is 1.

B. The next part of the problem is to determine where the partial quotient of 1 should be written. Think: Will the answer be more than 1? More than 10? More than 100? You can look at the related multiplication facts.

$$1 \times 24 = 24$$
$$10 \times 24 = 240$$
$$100 \times 24 = 2400$$

The first digit will be in the tens place.

$$24\overline{)294}^{\;1}$$

C. Now multiply the divisor by the first partial quotient.

$$\begin{array}{r} 24 \\ \times\; 1 \\ \hline 24 \end{array}$$

Write the product under the first two digits of 294.

$$\begin{array}{r} 1 \\ 24\overline{)294} \\ 24 \end{array}$$

D. Subtract the product from the dividend. Remember that the 1 showing as a partial quotient is really one ten—which is shown by its place value in the quotient.

$$\begin{array}{r} 1 \\ 24\overline{)294} \\ \underline{24} \\ 5 \end{array}$$

E. Bring down the next digit of the dividend, in this case the 4 in 294.

$$\begin{array}{r} 1 \\ 24\overline{)294} \\ \underline{24} \\ 54 \end{array}$$

F. Use the rounded version of 24 to estimate how many 24s there are in 54. Since there are two 20s in 50, make 2 the next estimate of a digit in the quotient.

$$\begin{array}{r} 12 \\ 24\overline{)294} \\ \underline{24} \\ 54 \end{array}$$

continued on next page

G. Again multiply the partial quotient by the divisor.

$$\begin{array}{r} 24 \\ \times\ 2 \\ \hline 48 \end{array}$$

Write the product under the earlier difference, 54.

$$\begin{array}{r} 12 \\ 24\overline{)294} \\ 24 \\ \hline 54 \\ 48 \end{array}$$

H. Subtract the product from the remainder.

$$\begin{array}{r} 12 \\ 24\overline{)294} \\ 24 \\ \hline 54 \\ 48 \\ \hline 6 \end{array}$$

I. Since 6 is less than 24, the division cannot continue, so write the quotient with a remainder of 6.

$$\begin{array}{r} 12\ R6 \\ 24\overline{)294} \\ 24 \\ \hline 54 \\ 48 \\ \hline 6 \end{array}$$

The answer to the problem is 12 remainder 6.

How to solve division word problems. When you are trying to solve word problems it helps to follow certain steps:

• Read the problem carefully.

• Read the question and write a math sentence for it.

• Look out for words that will give you a hint meaning divide. Some of these words are *per, average,* and *part of.*

During January, Vanessa tried to lose weight. In the first week, she weighed 130 pounds; in the second, 128 pounds; in the third, 131; and in the fourth, 131. What was Vanessa's average weight in January?

A. This is a two-step problem. Begin solving this problem by adding all of Vanessa's weights. You can write a math sentence as follows: 130 + 128 + 131 + 131 = 520 pounds, total weight.

B. To find the average weight, count the weeks Vanessa weighed herself, which is four, and divide:

$$\begin{array}{r} 130 \\ 4\overline{)520} \\ 4 \\ \hline 12 \\ 12 \\ \hline 0 \end{array}$$

Vanessa's average weight in January was 130 pounds.

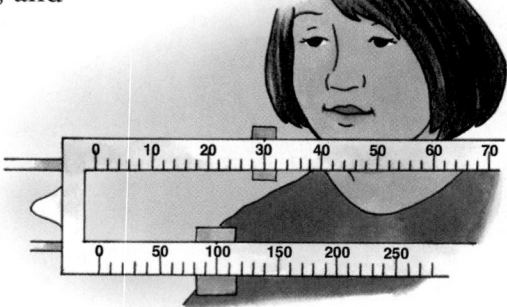

Darryl bought three pizzas for a class party. Each pizza had eight slices. There are 15 students in Darryl's class. According to Darryl, each student will be able to have two slices of pizza. Is he right?

A. This is a multistep problem. First you have to find how many pizza slices there are altogether:
3 pizzas × 8 slices = 24 slices.
There are 24 slices of pizza to be shared among the students.

B. Darryl thinks each student will be able to get exactly two slices of pizza and that there are 15 students, including Darryl. Write this information this way:

$$24 \div 15 \quad or \quad 15\overline{)24}$$
$$\underline{15}$$
$$9$$

with quotient 1.

C. The quotient shows that each student will certainly get one slice of pizza. Since there is a remainder, it is possible that some students will get two slices of pizza, but not all, as Darryl supposed.

Sally traveled 237 miles in three days to a business convention in another state. How many miles did she travel per day?

This problem gives you the total number of miles Sally traveled and asks you to find the number of miles she traveled each day.

To solve this problem, you must divide. You can write the following math sentence:
237 ÷ 3 = number of miles traveled per day.

$$3\overline{)237}$$
$$\underline{21}$$
$$27$$
$$27$$

quotient 79.

A salesman spoke to 1350 customers in ten business days, or two weeks. How many customers did he speak to per day?

In this problem you have to use the total number of customers, or 1350. If you do not read this problem carefully, you might use the two weeks as the divisor. You have to find how many customers were spoken to in a single day.

So if you divided 1350 by the two weeks, your answer would be 675 customers, which is much too large. Besides, such a large number would not make a lot of sense.

Instead, you have to divide 1350 by 10. 1350 customers ÷ 10 days = number of customers the salesman spoke to in one day.
1350 ÷ 10 = 135

Estimating. Estimating in division has more roles than it does in any other part of arithmetic. First, you must estimate to determine where the first digit of the quotient should be shown. Next, you must estimate trial quotients when the divisor has more than one digit. Finally, you may need to estimate the answer to check a calculation on a calculator, or simply because you do not have the time or the need to find the actual answer. Often, the best way to begin estimating in division is to find how many digits will be in the quotient. You can do this by multiplying the divisor by 10, 100, 1000, and so forth. The product can then be compared with the dividend.

For example, to find how many digits are in the quotient of 528 divided by 3, think 3×10 is 30;

528 is greater than 30;
3×100 is 300;
528 is greater than 300;
3×1000 is 3000;
528 is less than 3000,

so the quotient is between 100 and 1000. It will have three digits. The quotient is 176.

Relating Multiplication and Division

When you multiply two numbers, or factors, you will get a product as your answer.

If you divide the product by either factor, you will get one of the numbers in the problem, never a different number. The following shows how this works.

Example: $8 \times 2 = 16$.
Now divide 16 by 2.

$$2\overline{)16}^{8}$$

Now divide 16 by 8.

$$8\overline{)16}^{2}$$

There are no other numbers than 8, 2, and 16. Also, you have probably noticed that multiplication increases, or builds up, numbers, and division decreases, or breaks down, numbers. Multiplication and division may seem like two different operations, but they are not.

Using Your Calculator to Divide

To divide, press the number of the dividend, the ÷ sign, and the number of the divisor on your calculator. Press the = sign. The calculator will display the quotient, or answer.

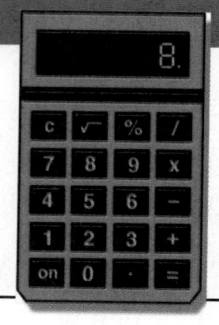

Checking Answers

Even after you have completed a division problem, you should be able to check its accuracy. The following ways show you how to do this.

Example 1:   To check this example, multiply the quotient, 12, by the divisor, 12.

$$12\overline{)144}$$

$$\begin{array}{r} 12 \\ 12\overline{)144} \\ \underline{12} \\ 24 \\ 24 \end{array}$$

Check:

$$\begin{array}{r} 12 \\ \times\ 12 \\ \hline 24 \\ \underline{12} \\ 144 \end{array}$$

Example 2:   To check a division problem with a remainder, multiply the quotient by the divisor, then add the remainder to your answer.

$$\begin{array}{r} 12\ R2 \\ 12\overline{)146} \\ \underline{12} \\ 26 \\ \underline{24} \\ 2 \end{array}$$

Check:

$$\begin{array}{r} 12 \\ \times\ 12 \\ \hline 24 \\ \underline{12} \\ 144 \\ +\ \ 2 \quad \text{remainder} \\ \hline 146 \end{array}$$

You can also check answers by finding factors of the divisor and dividing each factor separately.

Example:

$$\begin{array}{r} 12 \\ 12\overline{)144} \\ \underline{12} \\ 24 \\ 24 \end{array}$$

The divisor, 12, can be factored as 3×4.

First use 4 as a divisor: $4\overline{)144}$

Then use 3 as a divisor: $3\overline{)36}$ the quotient to $144 \div 4$

                             12   the quotient to $36 \div 3$, which matches the quotient in the original problem!

The last answer you got dividing by 3 was 12, which is the answer shown in the original example. Since these answers match, they are correct.

Fractions

Fractions are the quotients of whole numbers (division by zero is, of course, excluded). Instead of writing $4\overline{)3}$, however, a fraction is written as $\frac{3}{4}$. The bottom number in a fraction, the denominator, tells how many parts are being considered in all. The top number, the numerator, specifies some of those parts. For example, $\frac{3}{4}$ could refer to 3 pieces of a pie that had been divided into 4 parts. Operations with fractions are made easier by factoring the numerators and denominators.

Factoring. To *factor* a number, you find its factors: the whole numbers that can be multiplied together to give the number. For many purposes, it is most useful to find the factors that are *prime*—those numbers such as 2, 3, 5, 7, 11, 13, 17, and so forth that have only themselves and 1 as factors. For example, 12 has factors of 1, 2, 3, 4, 6, and 12, but only 2 and 3 are prime factors. When you factor 12, the factor 2 must be included twice: $12 = 2 \times 2 \times 3$.

Which are prime numbers? 2, 6, 17, 51

PRIME

$2 = 2 \times 1$ or 1×2

COMPOSITE

$6 = 6 \times 1$ or 1×6
$ = 2 \times 3$ or 3×2

(A *composite* number is any whole number, greater than 1, that is not prime.)

PRIME

$17 = 17 \times 1$ or 1×17

COMPOSITE

$51 = 51 \times 1$ or 1×51
$ = 3 \times 17$ or 17×3

Factor 60 into primes.

A. Start with the least prime. Work up through the primes. The least prime is 2. Since $\frac{60}{2}$ = 30, 2 is a factor of 60. (The symbol $\frac{60}{2}$ means "60 divided by 2.")

B. Now look at 30, the quotient. Since $\frac{30}{2}$ = 15, 2 is a factor of 60 twice. The quotient, 15, cannot be divided evenly by 2, so look at the next higher prime, 3, as a divisor.

C. Since $\frac{15}{3}$ = 5, 3 is also a prime factor of 60. The quotient, 5, is prime; therefore, the answer is
$60 = 2 \times 2 \times 3 \times 5$.

Factor 30.

A. Successive division by prime numbers, starting with the smallest and working up, is a sure method of finding all the prime factors. Divide 30 by the smallest prime, 2.

$$\frac{15}{2\overline{)30}}$$

In factoring, it is easier to turn the division upside down.

$$2\overline{)30}$$
$$15$$

B. Continue with either 2 again or the next higher prime. Since 15 is not divisible by 2, use 3.

$$2\overline{)30}$$
$$3\overline{)15}$$
$$5$$

C. Since 5 is a prime number, you can stop. You read the factors from the left-hand side of the division (and include the last quotient) to get the factored form.
$30 = 2 \times 3 \times 5$.

Factor 735.

A.   2)735
?

2 is not a factor of 735, since 735 is an odd number. Try the next higher prime, 3.

B.   3)735
245

C. Since 2 was not a factor of 735, it cannot be a factor of 245, so try 3 again.

3)735
3)245
?

3 is not a factor of 245 because the sum of the digits is 11, which is not a multiple of 3.

D.

3)735
5)245
49

E. You should recognize that 5 is not a factor of 49. Try 7.

3)735
5)245
7) 49
7

F. You can stop because the quotient is a prime number. Reading the divisors and the last quotient gives the factored form.

$$735 = 3 \times 5 \times 7 \times 7$$

Simplifying

Reduce $\dfrac{12}{16}$.

A. Factor the numerator and the denominator.

$$\frac{12}{16} = \frac{2 \times 2 \times 3}{2 \times 2 \times 2 \times 2}$$

B. For each like factor in both the numerator and denominator, cross out and replace with a 1.

$$\frac{12}{16} = \frac{\cancel{2} \times \cancel{2} \times 3}{\cancel{2} \times \cancel{2} \times 2 \times 2}$$

C. Rewrite.

$$\frac{12}{16} = \frac{1 \times 1 \times 3}{1 \times 1 \times 2 \times 2} = \frac{3}{4}$$

Reduce $\dfrac{105}{110}$.

A. Factor the numerator and the denominator.

$$\frac{105}{110} = \frac{3 \times 7 \times 5}{2 \times 5 \times 11}$$

B. For each like factor in both the numerator and denominator, cross out and replace with a 1.

$$\frac{105}{110} = \frac{3 \times 7 \times \cancel{5}}{2 \times \cancel{5} \times 11}$$

C. Rewrite.

$$\frac{105}{110} = \frac{3 \times 7 \times 1}{2 \times 1 \times 11} = \frac{21}{22}$$

Reduce $\dfrac{4}{4}$.

It might seem from the earlier problems that the answer would be

$$\frac{4}{4} = \frac{2 \times 2}{2 \times 2} =$$

since the common factors all cancel out.

If all the factors are canceled, a factor of 1 always remains, so

$$\frac{4}{4} = \frac{1}{1}$$

The form $\frac{1}{1}$ is not considered the simplest form, however. Notice that if you divide any number by itself, the result is 1. Since fractions are another way of writing division, the simplest form is

$$\frac{4}{4} = 1 \,.$$

Reduce $\dfrac{127}{8}$.

Whenever the numerator is larger than the denominator, you can use the definition of a fraction as division to simplify. The simplified form will be either a whole number or a *mixed number*, such as $1\frac{1}{2}$, which is a way of writing $1 + \frac{1}{2}$ without using a + sign.

A. Divide the numerator by the denominator.

$$\begin{array}{r} 15 \\ 8\overline{)127} \\ \underline{8} \\ 47 \\ \underline{40} \\ 7 \end{array}$$

This takes care of 120 of the 127 eighths, since 8×15 is 120. The remainder is 7 eighths.

B. Write the whole number and the fractional remainder.

$$\frac{127}{8} = 15\frac{7}{8}$$

Finding the least common multiple (LCM)

You need to be able to find the *least common multiple* of two numbers. The multiples of a number are the products of that number and each of the whole numbers. For example, multiples of 2 are 0, 2, 4, 6, 8, 10, 12, and so forth, and multiples of 3 are 0, 3, 6, 9, 12, and so forth.

Common multiples of 2 and 3 are those that are in both lists: 0, 6, 12, and so forth. By definition, the least common multiple does not include 0 (since 0 is a common multiple of every pair of numbers), so the least common multiple (LCM) of 2 and 3 is 6.

Find the LCM of 4 and 6.

A. List the nonzero multiples of both numbers.
Multiples of 4: 4, 8, 12, 16, 20
Multiples of 6: 6, 12, 18, 24, 30

B. Find the LCM.
Multiples of 4: 4, 8, 12, 16, 20
Multiples of 6: 6, 12, 18, 24, 30

The LCM of 4 and 6 is 12. This method can be used to find the LCM of any two numbers.

Find the LCM of 56 and 42.

A. These numbers are much larger than the 4 and 6 in the previous example. Listing the multiples is very tedious. So list the prime factors of each.
$$56 = 2 \times 2 \times 2 \times 7$$
$$42 = 2 \times 3 \times 7$$

B. The LCM must contain all of the different factors. Use the larger number of each. The different primes are 2, 3, and 7. There are three 2's in 56. If a prime factor appears once in each set, it will be shown only once in the LCM.

C. The LCM is
$$2 \times 2 \times 2 \times 3 \times 7 = 168.$$
Always list the prime factors in increasing order.

Finding the least common denominator (LCD)

The least common multiple of the denominators of two or more fractions is known as the *least common* *denominator* (LCD) of the fractions. The LCD is used in addition.

Find the LCD for $\frac{1}{6}$ and $\frac{3}{4}$.

METHOD 1

Find the least common multiple of the denominators.

Multiples of 6: 6, 12, 18
Multiples of 4: 4, 8, 12

The least common multiple of 6 and 4 is 12. Therefore, the LCD is 12.

METHOD 2

A. Factor each of the denominators.

$$6 = 2 \times 3$$
$$4 = 2 \times 2$$

B. The LCD must contain all of the factors of the two denominators as many times as they occur in the denominator in which each factor occurs the most.

C. The factor 3 occurs the most (1 time) in 6; the factor 2 occurs the most (2 times) in 4. Therefore, the LCD is

$$2 \times 2 \times 3 = 12$$

Multiplying Fractions by 1

When you multiply any number by 1, the product is the same as the original number. This is as true of fractions as it is of whole numbers. With fractions, however, you can change the meaning of the fraction by multiplying by 1 without changing the value of the fraction.

The fraction $\frac{2}{3}$ is shown on the left. On the right, the same diagram is shown with each of the thirds separated into two pieces. Now there are 4 parts shaded, and 6 parts in all, but the same amount of the square is shaded. In other words, if you multiply the numerator of the fraction by the same nonzero number as you multiply the denominator by—in this case,

$$\frac{2 \times 2}{3 \times 2}$$

the result has the same value as the original fraction.

Renaming

$$\frac{2}{3} = \frac{?}{6}$$

To add or subtract fractions, you often have to rename one or both as a fraction with a different denominator. You do this by multiplying the fraction by some fraction equal to 1.

Because 1 is the identity element for multiplication, multiplying a number by 1 does not change its value.

$$\frac{2}{2} \times \frac{2}{3} = \frac{2 \times 2}{2 \times 3} = \frac{4}{6}$$

Multiplying $\frac{2}{3}$ by $\frac{2}{2}$ changes its denominator to 6; but it does not change its value, because $\frac{2}{2}$ is simply a name for 1.

$$\frac{3}{5} = \frac{?}{20}$$

The following fractions are equal to 1.

$$\frac{2}{2}, \frac{3}{3}, \frac{4}{4}, \frac{5}{5}, \frac{6}{6}, \frac{7}{7}, \ldots$$

One of them can be used to change $\frac{3}{5}$ to a fraction with a denominator of 20.

$$\frac{\boxed{?}}{\boxed{?}} \times \frac{3}{5} = \frac{?}{20}$$

Therefore $\frac{4}{4}$ is the fraction we must use to change $\frac{3}{5}$ to a fraction with a denominator of 20.

$$\frac{4}{4} \times \frac{3}{5} = \frac{4 \times 3}{4 \times 5} = \frac{12}{20}$$

We see it must be $\frac{4}{4}$, since $4 \times 5 = 20$. We could also reach this by division:

$$20 \div 5 = 4$$

$$\frac{4}{9} = \frac{?}{45}$$

A. Divide 45 by 9.

$$45 \div 9 = 5$$

B. Write a fraction equal to 1 that has the denominator 5.

$$1 = \frac{5}{5}$$

C. Multiply $\frac{4}{9}$ by $\frac{5}{5}$.

$$\frac{5}{5} \times \frac{4}{9} = \frac{5 \times 4}{5 \times 9} = \frac{20}{45}$$

$$4 = \frac{?}{3}$$

A. Rename 4 as a fraction with the denominator 1.

$$4 = \frac{4}{1}$$

B. Rename $\frac{4}{1}$ as thirds.

$$\frac{3}{3} \times \frac{4}{1} = \frac{12}{3}$$

Improper Fractions

If the numerator is greater than or equal to the denominator in a fraction, it is an *improper fraction*. You can think of the improper fraction $\frac{12}{3}$ as 4 objects, each of which has been divided into 3 parts. Clearly, the number of parts will be 3×4, or 12.

$$257 = \frac{?}{4}$$

A. Rename 257 as a fraction with the denominator 1.

$$257 = \frac{257}{1}$$

B. Rename $\frac{257}{1}$ as fourths.

$$\frac{4}{4} \times \frac{257}{1} = \frac{1028}{4}$$

$$2\frac{1}{3} = \frac{?}{3}$$

A. Rename 2 as a fraction with the denominator 3.

$$\frac{3}{3} \times \frac{2}{1} = \frac{6}{3}$$

B. Add $\frac{6}{3}$ to $\frac{1}{3}$.

$$\frac{6}{3} + \frac{1}{3} = \frac{6+1}{3} = \frac{7}{3}$$

$$4\frac{2}{7} = \frac{?}{7}$$

A. Rename 4 as a fraction with the denominator 7.

$$\frac{7}{7} \times \frac{4}{1} = \frac{28}{7}$$

B. Add $\frac{28}{7}$ to $\frac{2}{7}$.

$$\frac{28}{7} + \frac{2}{7} = \frac{28+2}{7} = \frac{30}{7}$$

A Shortcut

Here is an easy way to rename a mixed number as an improper fraction. Multiply the whole-number part of the mixed number by the denominator of the fraction. Add the product to the numerator of the fraction part of the mixed number. The sum is the numerator of the improper fraction. For example, to rewrite $2\frac{1}{3}$ as a fraction, think $(2 \times 3) + 1 = 7$, so $2\frac{1}{3} = \frac{7}{3}$. Similarly, to rewrite $4\frac{2}{7}$ as a number of sevenths, think $(4 \times 7) + 2 = 30$, so $4\frac{2}{7} = \frac{30}{7}$. The same shortcut will work for changing a whole number to an improper fraction. In that case, the number to be added to the product is 0.

Sets of Numbers

There are several sets of numbers that are used in arithmetic. Here is a summary of the types used in this section:

Counting numbers or natural numbers
The numbers you use to count with: 1, 2, 3, 4, 5, and so forth.

Whole numbers
The counting numbers and 0: 0, 1, 2, 3, 4, and so forth. The whole numbers are the numbers that tell how many members are in a set.

Rational numbers
Rational numbers are fractions, numbers of the form $\frac{a}{b}$ with b not equal to zero. Fractions are numbers formed when any number is divided by any number other than zero. These numbers can be used to describe the relation of part of a set to a whole set. They also can be used to measure quantities that cannot be measured with whole numbers.

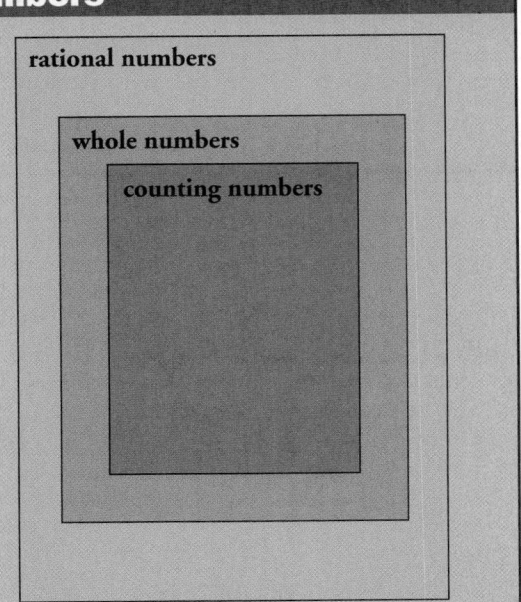

rational numbers

whole numbers

counting numbers

Addition of fractions

$$\frac{1}{5} + \frac{3}{5}$$

Adding fractions that have a common denominator is very simple.

A. Rewrite the numerator addends over the common denominator.

$$\frac{1}{5} + \frac{3}{5} = \frac{1+3}{5}$$

B. Add the numerators.

$$\frac{1+3}{5} = \frac{4}{5}$$

$$\frac{3}{8} + \frac{2}{8}$$

A. Rewrite the numerator addends over the common denominator.

$$\frac{3}{8} + \frac{2}{8} = \frac{3+2}{8}$$

B. Add the numerators.

$$\frac{3+2}{8} = \frac{5}{8}$$

$$\frac{1}{3} + \frac{1}{2}$$

Before adding two fractions with different denominators, you must rewrite them as fractions with a common denominator.

A. Find the least common denominator for $\frac{1}{3}$ and $\frac{1}{2}$. The least common denominator for $\frac{1}{3}$ and $\frac{1}{2}$ is 6.

B. Rename $\frac{1}{3}$ and $\frac{1}{2}$ as sixths.

$$\frac{2}{2} \times \frac{1}{3} = \frac{2}{6} \text{ and } \frac{3}{3} \times \frac{1}{2} = \frac{3}{6}$$

C. Add $\frac{2}{6}$ and $\frac{3}{6}$.

$$\frac{2}{6} + \frac{3}{6} = \frac{2+3}{6} = \frac{5}{6}$$

$$\frac{2}{5} + \frac{3}{7}$$

A. Find the least common denominator for $\frac{2}{5}$ and $\frac{3}{7}$. The least common denominator for $\frac{2}{5}$ and $\frac{3}{7}$ is 35.

B. Rename $\frac{2}{5}$ and $\frac{3}{7}$ as thirty-fifths.

$$\frac{7}{7} \times \frac{2}{5} = \frac{14}{35} \text{ and } \frac{5}{5} \times \frac{3}{7} = \frac{15}{35}$$

C. Add $\frac{14}{35}$ and $\frac{15}{35}$.

$$\frac{14}{35} + \frac{15}{35} = \frac{14+15}{35} = \frac{29}{35}$$

Any two fractions with unlike denominators can be added in this way.

$$2\frac{1}{9} + \frac{4}{9}$$

METHOD 1

Adding a mixed number and a fraction is easy once you have renamed the mixed number as a fraction.

A. Rename $2\frac{1}{9}$ as a fraction.

$$2\frac{1}{9} + \frac{4}{9} = \frac{19}{9} + \frac{4}{9}$$

B. Add.

$$\frac{19}{9} + \frac{4}{9} = \frac{23}{9}$$

C. Simplify.

$$\frac{23}{9} = 2\frac{5}{9}$$

METHOD 2

A. Write in vertical form as you do for the addition of whole numbers.

$$\begin{array}{r} 2\frac{1}{9} \\ +\ \frac{4}{9} \\ \hline \end{array}$$

B. Add the fractions.

$$\begin{array}{r} 2\frac{1}{9} \\ +\ \frac{4}{9} \\ \hline \frac{5}{9} \end{array}$$

C. Add the whole numbers.

$$\begin{array}{r} 2\frac{1}{9} \\ +\ \frac{4}{9} \\ \hline 2\frac{5}{9} \end{array}$$

The fraction part of the mixed number is in lowest terms. If not, reduce.

$$2\frac{1}{9} + 16\frac{4}{9}$$

METHOD 1

A. Rename both addends as fractions.

$$2\frac{1}{9} + 16\frac{4}{9} = \frac{19}{9} + \frac{148}{9}$$

B. Add.

$$\frac{19}{9} + \frac{148}{9} = \frac{19 + 148}{9} = \frac{167}{9}$$

C. Simplify.

$$\frac{167}{9} = 18\frac{5}{9}$$

METHOD 2

A. Add in vertical form.

$$\begin{array}{r} 2\frac{1}{9} \\ +16\frac{4}{9} \\ \hline \end{array}$$

B. Add the fractions.

$$\begin{array}{r} 2\frac{1}{9} \\ +16\frac{4}{9} \\ \hline \frac{5}{9} \end{array}$$

C. Add the whole numbers.

$$\begin{array}{r} 2\frac{1}{9} \\ +16\frac{4}{9} \\ \hline 18\frac{5}{9} \end{array}$$

Picturing Addition of Fractions

If you picture the addition of fractions, you can see why the least common denominator is needed.

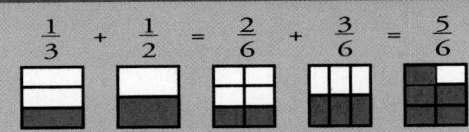

$$\frac{1}{3} + \frac{1}{2} = \frac{2}{6} + \frac{3}{6} = \frac{5}{6}$$

$$3\frac{1}{8} + 6\frac{2}{5}$$

METHOD 1

A. Rename both addends as fractions.

$$3\frac{1}{8} + 6\frac{2}{5} = \frac{25}{8} + \frac{32}{5}$$

B. Rewrite as fractions with a common denominator.

$$\frac{25}{8} + \frac{32}{5} = \frac{125}{40} + \frac{256}{40}$$

C. Add.

$$\frac{125}{40} + \frac{256}{40} = \frac{125 + 256}{40} = \frac{381}{40}$$

D. Simplify. $\dfrac{381}{40} = 9\dfrac{21}{40}$

METHOD 2

A. Write in vertical form as you do for the addition of whole numbers.

$$3\frac{1}{8}$$
$$+6\frac{2}{5}$$

B. Add the fractions.

$$3\frac{1}{8} = 3\frac{5}{40}$$
$$+6\frac{2}{5} = +6\frac{16}{40}$$
$$\frac{21}{40}$$

C. Add the whole numbers.

$$3\frac{1}{8}$$
$$+6\frac{2}{5}$$
$$9\frac{21}{40}$$

$$2\frac{3}{5} + 5\frac{7}{8}$$

A. Add in vertical form.

$$2\frac{3}{5}$$
$$+5\frac{7}{8}$$

B. First rewrite the fractions with the lowest common denominator and add.

$$2\frac{24}{40}$$
$$+5\frac{35}{40}$$
$$7\frac{59}{40}$$

C. The fraction part is improper. Change it to a mixed number and add the whole number part to 7.

$$7\frac{59}{40} = 7 + 1\frac{19}{40} = 8\frac{19}{40}$$

$$2\frac{3}{4} + 1\frac{7}{8}$$

METHOD 1

A. Change the mixed numbers to fractions.

$$2\frac{3}{4} + 1\frac{7}{8} = \frac{11}{4} + \frac{15}{8}$$

B. Use the least common multiple of the denominators as a new denominator—the *lowest common denominator,* or *LCD.*

$$\frac{11}{4} + \frac{15}{8} = \frac{22}{8} + \frac{15}{8}$$

C. Add the numerators and change to a mixed number.

$$\frac{22}{8} + \frac{15}{8} = \frac{37}{8} = 4\frac{5}{8}$$

METHOD 2

A. Write the problem in vertical form.

$$2\frac{3}{4}$$
$$+1\frac{7}{8}$$

B. Rewrite the fractions with a common denominator. Add.

$$2\frac{3}{4} = 2\frac{6}{8}$$
$$+1\frac{7}{8} = 1\frac{7}{8}$$
$$3\frac{13}{8}$$

C. Change the fraction to a mixed number. Since $\frac{13}{8} = 1\frac{5}{8}$ the sum is $4\frac{5}{8}$.

Mixed numbers and the calculator

Mixed numbers and improper fractions

The sum of an integer (whole number) and a fraction, when shown without a + sign, is a *mixed number*.

Examples

$3\frac{1}{2}$ means $3 + \frac{1}{2}$ $5\frac{7}{8}$ means $5 + \frac{7}{8}$

Mixed numbers can also be shown as *improper fractions;* that is, fractions in which the numerator is greater than the denominator.

$3\frac{1}{2} = \frac{7}{2}$ $5\frac{7}{8} = \frac{47}{8}$

Changing mixed numbers to fractions with the calculator

Examples

$3\frac{1}{2}$ $5\frac{7}{8}$

A. Whole number $\times$ denominator. $3\boxtimes2\boxminus6$ $5\boxtimes8\boxminus40$

B. Product (step A) $\boxplus$ numerator. $6\boxplus1\boxminus7$ $40\boxplus7\boxminus47$

C. Sum (step B) is numerator of improper fraction. $3\frac{1}{2} = \frac{7}{}$ $5\frac{7}{8} = \frac{47}{}$

D. Original denominator is also new denominator. $3\frac{1}{2} = \frac{7}{2}$ $5\frac{7}{8} = \frac{47}{8}$

Changing improper fractions to mixed numbers with the calculator

Examples

$\frac{11}{4}$ $\frac{28}{6}$

A. Numerator ÷ denominator. $11\boxdiv4\boxminus2.75$ $28\boxdiv6\boxminus4.666666$

B. Take whole part of decimal and ignore any digits after the decimal point.   2 (ignore .75)   4 (ignore .666666)

C. Whole part (step B) × denominator. $2\boxtimes4\boxminus8$ $4\boxtimes6\boxminus24$

D. Numerator − product (step C). $11\boxminus8\boxminus3$ $28\boxminus24\boxminus4$

E. Whole part (step B) is the whole number. $\frac{11}{4} = 2$- $\frac{28}{6} = 4$-

F. Difference (step D) is the numerator. $\frac{11}{4} = 2\frac{3}{}$ $\frac{28}{6} = 4\frac{4}{}$

G. Original denominator is also the new denominator. $\frac{11}{4} = 2\frac{3}{4}$ $\frac{28}{6} = 4\frac{4}{6}$

H. Fraction may need to be put in simplest form.   Not needed $\frac{28}{6} = 4\frac{2}{3}$

Subtraction of fractions
$$\frac{1}{2} - \frac{1}{3}$$

A. Find the least common denominator for $\frac{1}{2}$ and $\frac{1}{3}$. The least common denominator for $\frac{1}{2}$ and $\frac{1}{3}$ is 6.

B. Rename $\frac{1}{2}$ and $\frac{1}{3}$ as sixths.

$$\frac{3}{3} \times \frac{1}{2} = \frac{3}{6}$$
$$\frac{2}{2} \times \frac{1}{3} = \frac{2}{6}$$

C. Subtract the numerators and write them over the common denominator.

$$\frac{3}{6} - \frac{2}{6} = \frac{3-2}{6} = \frac{1}{6}$$

$$\frac{30}{7} - 3\frac{3}{7}$$

METHOD 1

A. Rewrite $3\frac{3}{7}$ as a fraction.

$$\frac{30}{7} - 3\frac{3}{7} = \frac{30}{7} - \frac{24}{7}$$

B. Subtract.

$$\frac{30}{7} - \frac{24}{7} = \frac{30-24}{7} = \frac{6}{7}$$

METHOD 2

A. Write $\frac{30}{7}$ as a mixed number.

$$\frac{30}{7} = 4\frac{2}{7}$$

B. Write in vertical form.

$$4\frac{2}{7}$$
$$-\,3\frac{3}{7}$$
_____

C. Borrow $\frac{7}{7}$ from the 4, leaving $3\frac{7}{7}$ and $\frac{2}{7}$.

D. Add $\frac{7}{7}$ and $\frac{2}{7}$ to get $3\frac{9}{7}$.

E. Subtract the fractions.

$$3\frac{9}{7}$$
$$-\,3\frac{3}{7}$$
_____
$$\frac{6}{7}$$

F. Since $3 - 3 = 0$, the answer is $\frac{6}{7}$

$$2\frac{5}{8} - 1\frac{1}{3}$$

METHOD 1

A. Rename both mixed numbers as fractions.

$$2\frac{5}{8} - 1\frac{1}{3} = \frac{21}{8} - \frac{4}{3}$$

B. Rewrite as fractions with a common denominator.

$$\frac{21}{8} - \frac{4}{3} = \frac{63}{24} - \frac{32}{24}$$

C. Subtract.

$$\frac{63}{24} - \frac{32}{24} = \frac{63-32}{24} = \frac{31}{24} \text{ or } 1\frac{7}{24}$$

METHOD 2

A. Write in vertical form as you do for whole numbers.

$$2\frac{5}{8}$$
$$-\,1\frac{1}{3}$$
_____

B. Rename the fraction parts and subtract the fractions.

$$2\frac{15}{24}$$
$$-\,1\frac{8}{24}$$
_____
$$\frac{7}{24}$$

C. Subtract the whole numbers.

$$2\frac{15}{24}$$
$$-\,1\frac{8}{24}$$
_____
$$1\frac{7}{24}$$

$$2\frac{5}{8} - 1\frac{2}{3}$$

A. Write in vertical form and rename.

$$2\frac{5}{8} = \quad 2\frac{15}{24}$$
$$-\,1\frac{2}{3} = \quad -1\frac{16}{24}$$
_____

However, you cannot subtract $\frac{16}{24}$ from $\frac{15}{24}$ because 16 is greater than 15.

B. Rename $2\frac{15}{24}$ as follows:

$$1 + \left(1 + \frac{15}{24}\right) = 1\frac{24+15}{24}$$
$$= 1\frac{39}{24}$$

C. Now subtract the fractions first and then the whole numbers.

$$1\frac{39}{24}$$
$$-\,1\frac{16}{24}$$
_____
$$\frac{23}{24}$$

$$5\frac{1}{6} - 3\frac{1}{2}$$

A. Rewrite in vertical form with common denominators.

$$
\begin{array}{rcl}
5\frac{1}{6} &=& 5\frac{1}{6} \\[4pt]
-3\frac{1}{2} &=& 3\frac{3}{6}
\end{array}
$$

B. "Borrow" $1 = \frac{6}{6}$ from 5; that is, rename $5\frac{1}{6}$ as $4\frac{7}{6}$. Subtract.

$$
\begin{array}{rcl}
5\frac{1}{6} &=& 4\frac{7}{6} \\[4pt]
-3\frac{1}{2} &=& 3\frac{3}{6} \\[2pt]
\hline
&& 1\frac{4}{6}
\end{array}
$$

C. Rename $\frac{4}{6}$ as $\frac{2}{3}$. The answer is $1\frac{2}{3}$.

Multiplication of fractions

Multiplication of fractions is a very simple process:
You simply multiply numerators and denominators.

$$\frac{2}{9} \times \frac{6}{7}$$

A. Multiply numerators and denominators.

$$\frac{2}{9} \times \frac{6}{7} = \frac{2 \times 6}{9 \times 7} = \frac{12}{63}$$

B. Simplify.

$$\frac{12}{63} = \frac{4}{21}$$

$$6 \times \frac{3}{8}$$

A. To multiply a whole number by a fraction, you can rewrite the whole number as a fraction.

$$6 = \frac{6}{1}$$

B. Then go on to multiply and simplify.

$$\frac{6}{1} \times \frac{3}{8} = \frac{18}{8} = 2\frac{2}{8} = 2\frac{1}{4}$$

Fractions and Whole Numbers

You may have learned to find $\frac{1}{3}$ of 6 this way: Divide 6 by 3. The quotient is 2, so $\frac{1}{3}$ of 6 is 2. That method is correct, but $\frac{1}{3}$ of 6 also means $\frac{1}{3} \times 6$. Therefore, you can also find $\frac{1}{3}$ of 6 by rewriting 6 as the fraction $\frac{6}{1}$ and multiplying:

$$\frac{1}{3} \times \frac{6}{1} = \frac{6}{3} = 2$$

The multiplication method is more general because you can also use it to find $\frac{1}{3}$ of $\frac{1}{2}$ more easily than by the division method. Furthermore, the division method is not effective for finding $\frac{2}{3}$ of 6.

$$2\frac{3}{7} \times 9$$

A. Rename both factors as fractions.

$$2\frac{3}{7} \times 9 = \frac{17}{7} \times \frac{9}{1}$$

B. Multiply.

$$\frac{17}{7} \times \frac{9}{1} = \frac{17 \times 9}{7} = \frac{153}{7}$$

C. Simplify.

$$\frac{153}{7} = 21\frac{6}{7}$$

$$5\frac{2}{13} \times 2\frac{3}{9}$$

A. Rename both factors as fractions.

$$5\frac{2}{13} \times 2\frac{3}{9} = \frac{67}{13} \times \frac{21}{9}$$

B. Multiply.

$$\frac{67}{13} \times \frac{21}{9} = \frac{67 \times 21}{13 \times 9} = \frac{1407}{117}$$

C. Simplify.

$$\frac{1407}{117} = 12\frac{3}{117}$$

$$\frac{3}{4} \times \frac{2}{3}$$

METHOD 1

A. Multiply the numerators (top numbers in fractions).

$$\frac{3}{4} \times \frac{2}{3} = \frac{6}{}$$

B. Multiply the denominators (bottom numbers).

$$\frac{3}{4} \times \frac{2}{3} = \frac{6}{12}$$

C. Eliminate common factors in the numerator and denominator of the product. The prime factors of 6 are shown as 2 × 3, while the prime factors of 12 are shown as 2 × 2 × 3. *Canceling* is crossing out matching prime factors in the numerator and denominator and indicating that a factor of 1 is left.

$$\frac{3}{4} \times \frac{2}{3} = \frac{\overset{1}{\cancel{2}} \times \overset{1}{\cancel{3}}}{2 \times \underset{1}{\cancel{2}} \times \underset{1}{\cancel{3}}}$$

Multiply the 1's and any numbers not crossed out to get the "reduced" form of the product.

$$\frac{3}{4} \times \frac{2}{3} = \frac{1}{2}$$

METHOD 2

A. Cancel before you multiply.

$$\frac{3}{4} \times \frac{2}{3} = \frac{\overset{1}{\cancel{3}}}{2 \times \underset{1}{\cancel{2}}} \times \frac{\overset{1}{\cancel{2}}}{\underset{1}{\cancel{3}}}$$

Remember that factors in the numerators must be matched with factors in the denominators.

B. Multiply any factors remaining.

$$\frac{3}{4} \times \frac{2}{3} = \frac{\overset{1}{\cancel{3}}}{2 \times \underset{1}{\cancel{2}}} \times \frac{\overset{1}{\cancel{2}}}{\underset{1}{\cancel{3}}} = \frac{1}{2}$$

The Size of the Answer

Pam found $\frac{1}{2}$ of a pizza in the refrigerator. She ate $\frac{1}{3}$ of it for lunch. How much of a whole pizza did she eat?

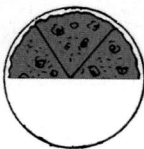

Experience with whole numbers suggests that the answer to multiplication should be *greater* than any of the numbers in the problem. When both of the factors are less than 1, as in this problem, however, the answer will be *less* than either number in the problem. The answer is $\frac{1}{6}$.

Division of fractions

$$\frac{1}{2} \div \frac{2}{3}$$

It is useful to know that dividing by a fraction gives the same result as multiplying by its *reciprocal*.

The reciprocal of $\frac{2}{3}$ is $\frac{3}{2}$. Therefore,

$$\frac{1}{2} \div \frac{2}{3} = \frac{1}{2} \times \frac{3}{2}$$

Dividing fractional numbers then becomes a simple problem of multiplication.

$$\frac{1}{2} \times \frac{3}{2} = \frac{1 \times 3}{2 \times 2} = \frac{3}{4}$$

$$\frac{2}{3} \div \frac{4}{7}$$

A. Rewrite as a multiplication problem.

$$\frac{2}{3} \div \frac{4}{7} = \frac{2}{3} \times \frac{7}{4}$$

B. Multiply.

$$\frac{2}{3} \times \frac{7}{4} = \frac{14}{12}$$

C. Simplify.

$$\frac{14}{12} = 1\frac{2}{12} = 1\frac{1}{6}$$

$$\frac{7}{8} \div \frac{5}{6}$$

A. Invert the divisor to change to multiplication.

$$\frac{7}{8} \times \frac{6}{5}$$

B. Cancel any common factors.

$$\frac{7}{8} \times \frac{6}{5} = \frac{7}{\cancel{2} \times 2 \times 2} \times \frac{\overset{1}{\cancel{2}} \times 3}{5}$$

C. Multiply the remaining numerators and denominators.

$$\frac{7}{\underset{1}{\cancel{2}} \times 2 \times 2} \times \frac{\overset{1}{\cancel{2}} \times 3}{5} = \frac{21}{20} = 1\frac{1}{20}$$

Estimation: Fractions and Mixed Numbers

Close estimates for operations with fractions are generally not needed. Often, it is just as easy to compute the answer to multiplication or division of fractions as it is to estimate. For checking purposes, the most important rules are:

- When adding or dividing two fractions, the answer will be *greater* than either of the fractions.
- When subtracting fractions, the answer will be *less* than the greatest number in the problem.
- When multiplying two fractions, the answer will be *less* than either number in the problem.

For mixed numbers, the best strategy is to estimate by rounding each number in the problem to the nearest whole number. Thus, $5\frac{1}{3} + 2\frac{1}{2}$ is about 8 (rounding $2\frac{1}{2}$ up to 3), $8\frac{1}{4} - 3\frac{7}{8}$ is about 4, $2\frac{1}{6} \times 3\frac{1}{8}$ is about 6, and $5\frac{3}{4} \div 2\frac{5}{6}$ is about $\frac{6}{3}$, or 2.

$$2\frac{5}{8} \div 3$$

A. Rename $2\frac{5}{8}$ and 3 as fractions.

$$2\frac{5}{8} \div 3 = \frac{21}{8} \div \frac{3}{1}$$

B. Rewrite as a multiplication problem.

$$\frac{21}{8} \div \frac{3}{1} = \frac{21}{8} \times \frac{1}{3}$$

C. Multiply.

$$\frac{21}{8} \times \frac{1}{3} = \frac{21 \times 1}{8 \times 3} = \frac{21}{24}$$

D. Simplify.

$$\frac{21}{24} = \frac{7}{8}$$

$$1\frac{5}{6} \div 4\frac{2}{7}$$

A. Rename $1\frac{5}{6}$ and $4\frac{2}{7}$ as fractions.

$$1\frac{5}{6} \div 4\frac{2}{7} = \frac{11}{6} \div \frac{30}{7}$$

B. Rewrite as a multiplication problem.

$$\frac{11}{6} \div \frac{30}{7} = \frac{11}{6} \times \frac{7}{30}$$

C. Multiply.

$$\frac{11}{6} \times \frac{7}{30} = \frac{11 \times 7}{6 \times 30} = \frac{77}{180}$$

Exponents

Powers of ten. An exponent is used to show how many times a number is used as a factor.

Examples $3^2 = 3 \times 3 = 9$;
9 is the *second power* of 3.
$10^4 = 10 \times 10 \times 10 \times 10 = 10,000$;
10,000 is the *fourth power* of 10.

NEGATIVE AND ZERO EXPONENTS
When a minus sign (−) is placed in front of an exponent, the power becomes the denominator of a fraction whose numerator is 1.

Examples $3^{-2} = \frac{1}{3 \times 3} = \frac{1}{9}$;
$\frac{1}{9}$ is 3 raised to the *negative two* power.

$10^{-4} = \frac{1}{10 \times 10 \times 10 \times 10} = \frac{1}{10,000}$;
$\frac{1}{10,000}$ is 10 raised to the *negative four* power.

The exponent 0 always gives the value 1 to the power (except that 0^0 is not defined).

Examples
$3^0 = 1$
$10^0 = 1$

Rules for Exponents

The examples on this page suggest general rules for operating with exponents. If a represents a number, and m and n are whole numbers greater than 1, then

$$a^m \times a^n = a^{m+n}$$
$$a^m \div a^n = a^{m-n}$$
$$\left(a^m\right)^n = a^{m \times n}$$

Find the value of 4^3.

A. Rewrite 4^3 as a multiplication problem.

$4^3 = 4 \times 4 \times 4$

B. Multiply.

$4 \times 4 \times 4 = 64$

Simplify $2^4 \times 2^5$.

A. Rewrite 2^4 and 2^5 as multiplication problems.

$2^4 = 2 \times 2 \times 2 \times 2$

$2^5 = 2 \times 2 \times 2 \times 2 \times 2$

B. Multiply.

$2^4 \times 2^5 = \left(2 \times 2 \times 2 \times 2\right) \times \left(2 \times 2 \times 2 \times 2 \times 2\right)$

C. Count how many twos are being multiplied together. There are 4 twos, then 5 twos being multiplied together.

$2^{4+5} = 2^9$

This could be written as

$2^4 \times 2^5 = 2^{4+5} = 2^9$

Powers of Ten

The number 10 has the special property that the number of times the digit 0 is used in the power is the same as the value of the exponent. For negative exponents, this property holds true for the denominators of powers of 10 in fraction form, but it is only true for powers of 10 in decimal form if a 0 is always written in the ones place (just in front of the decimal point). Counting all the zeros then gives the negative power.

POSITIVE EXPONENTS		ZERO AND NEGATIVE EXPONENTS
	(0 zeros)	$10^0 = 1$, or one
$10^1 = 10$, or ten	(1 zero)	$10^{-1} = \frac{1}{10} = 0.1$, or one tenth
$10^2 = 100$, or one hundred	(2 zeros)	$10^{-2} = \frac{1}{100} = 0.01$, or one hundredth
$10^3 = 1000$, or one thousand	(3 zeros)	$10^{-3} = \frac{1}{1000} = 0.001$, or one thousandth
$10^4 = 10,000$, or ten thousand	(4 zeros)	$10^{-4} = \frac{1}{10,000} = 0.0001$, or one ten thousandth
$10^5 = 100,000$, or one hundred thousand	(5 zeros)	$10^{-5} = \frac{1}{100,000} = 0.00001$, or one hundred thousandth
$10^6 = 1,000,000$, or one million	(6 zeros)	$10^{-6} = \frac{1}{1,000,000} = 0.000001$, or one millionth
$10^7 = 10,000,000$, or ten million	(7 zeros)	$10^{-7} = \frac{1}{10,000,000} = 0.0000001$, or one ten millionth
$10^8 = 100,000,000$, or one hundred million	(8 zeros)	$10^{-8} = \frac{1}{100,000,000} = 0.00000001$, or one hundred millionth
$10^9 = 1,000,000,000$, or one billion	(9 zeros)	$10^{-9} = \frac{1}{1,000,000,000} = 0.000000001$, or one billionth

Simplify $3^7 \div 3^4$.

A. Rewrite 3^7 and 3^4 as multiplication problems.

$3^7 = 3 \times 3 \times 3 \times 3 \times 3 \times 3 \times 3$

$3^4 = 3 \times 3 \times 3 \times 3$

B. Divide.

$$\frac{3^7}{3^4} = \frac{\cancel{3} \times \cancel{3} \times \cancel{3} \times \cancel{3} \times 3 \times 3 \times 3}{\cancel{3} \times \cancel{3} \times \cancel{3} \times \cancel{3}}$$

C. Count how many threes are left. There are 3 threes.

$$3 \times 3 \times 3 = 3^{7-4} = 3^3$$

This could be written as

$$3^7 \div 3^4 = 3^{7-4} = 3^3$$

Simplify $(5^3)^2$.

A. Rewrite 5^3 as a multiplication problem.

$5^3 = 5 \times 5 \times 5$

B. Rewrite as $(5 \times 5 \times 5)^2$.

$$\left(5 \times 5 \times 5\right) \times \left(5 \times 5 \times 5\right)$$

C. Count how many fives are being multiplied together. There are six fives.

$$\left(5 \times 5 \times 5\right) \times \left(5 \times 5 \times 5\right) = 5^{3 \times 2} = 5^6$$

This could be written as

$$\left(5^3\right)^2 = 5^{3 \times 2} = 5^6$$

Decimals

Decimals are another way of writing fractions. The decimal point means that the denominator will be a power of 10. The particular power of 10 is indicated by the number of places to the right of the decimal point. For example, 0.3 has 1 place to the right of the decimal point, so $0.3 = \frac{3}{10^1}$, or $\frac{3}{10}$. The decimal 0.123 has 3 places to the right of the decimal point, so $0.123 = \frac{123}{10^3}$, or $\frac{123}{1000}$.

Decimals are *decimal fractions,* but they are also an extension of the numeration system used for whole numbers. Therefore, both 24 and 1.6 are decimal numerals because each is based on the number 10. The decimal point marks the ones place. A digit to the left of the point means ones, while a digit to the right means tenths.

One way to read decimals is by saying the power of 10 with a *-th* attached after reading the number. Using that system, 0.123 would be read as "one hundred twenty-three thousandths." Another way to read decimals is by reading each digit in order, saying "point" for the decimal point. Using that method, 0.123 would be read as "zero point one two three." If a decimal is greater than 1, the "point" method can still be used as before, but the *-th* method needs to be modified. You must say "and" between the whole-number part and the decimal part. Therefore, 3.14 would be read as either "three point one four" or as "three and fourteen hundredths."

$$11.6$$
$$+ \ 3.34$$

Using a place value chart is a good way of solving problems like this.

A. Add the numbers in the four columns, as before. Insert a decimal point below the column of points. Write the answer at the bottom.

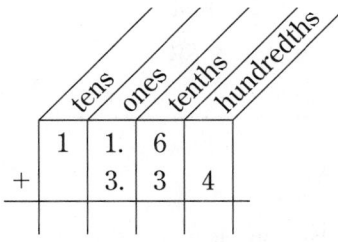

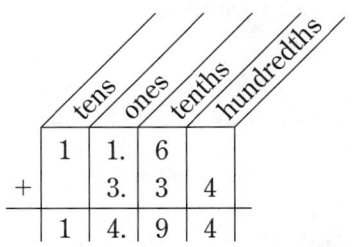

$$6.14$$
$$- 2.05$$

A. Rename the 1 tenths as 10 hundredths. Add the 10 hundredths and the 4 hundredths to get 14 hundredths. Subtract the numbers in the three columns, as before. Insert a decimal point below the column of points.

Write the answer at the bottom.

$$6.\overset{0}{\cancel{1}}\overset{1}{4}$$
$$- 2.05$$
$$\overline{4.09}$$

Checking Answers

To see if your decimal subtraction answers are correct, add the difference (the answer) to the subtrahend (number being subtracted). If this number is the same as the minuend, your answer is correct. This is the same procedure you used for whole numbers.

$$20.$$
$$- \ 0.37$$

A. Enter two zeros to the right of the decimal in the first number. This does not change the value of the number since

$$20. = 20.00$$

B. Rename the 2 tens as 1 ten and 10 ones. Rename the 10 ones as 9 ones and 10 tenths. Rename the 10 tenths as 9 tenths and 10 hundredths.

Subtract the numbers in the four columns, as before. Write the answer at the bottom. Insert a decimal point below the column of points.

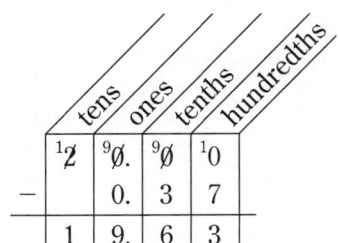

You may have noticed that we entered a zero in the ones column in the number 0.37. This was done to emphasize the location of the decimal. The 0 in the ones place is the format of most numbers in the electronic age of computers. (Sports averages are among the few exceptions.)

$3.04 + 5.6 + 0.04$

A. Write in vertical form, being careful to keep the decimal points lined up.

$$
\begin{array}{r}
3.04 \\
5.6 \\
+\ 0.04 \\
\hline
\end{array}
$$

B. Add as you would for whole numbers, inserting a decimal point below the column of points. Some people prefer to write in extra zeros to make the right align.

This does not change the value of the decimals.

$$
\begin{array}{r}
3.04 \\
5.60 \\
+\ 0.04 \\
\hline
8.68
\end{array}
$$

$3.89 - 2.647$

A. Write in vertical form, keeping the decimal points lined up. Most people find filling out the zeros to be helpful.

$$
\begin{array}{r}
3.890 \\
-\ 2.647 \\
\hline
\end{array}
$$

B. Subtract as with whole numbers, lining up the decimal point in the difference with the ones above it.

$$
\begin{array}{r}
3.890 \\
-\ 2.647 \\
\hline
1.243
\end{array}
$$

Notice that it is necessary to "borrow" 1 from the 9 when you begin to subtract; that is, you must rename 9 hundredths as 8 hundredths and 10 thousandths.

Many people find it easier to show this by writing a 1, the "helping number," just before the 0. They also cross out the 9 and write in a small 8 as another helping number.

$$
\begin{array}{r}
3.8\overset{8\ 1}{9}0 \\
-\ 2.647 \\
\hline
1.243
\end{array}
$$

Subtracting is sometimes more difficult when it is necessary to borrow across zeros.

$7.006 - 4.798$

METHOD 1

A. Write in vertical form. Insert a decimal point below the column of points. Since you cannot borrow from the first 0, or from the second 0, proceed to the 7 to borrow 1. Then the problem, using helping numbers, looks like this:

$$
\begin{array}{r}
\overset{6\ 1}{7}.006 \\
-\ 4.798 \\
\hline
\end{array}
$$

B. Now you can borrow from the 10. Repeat the process until you reach the 6.

$$
\begin{array}{r}
\overset{9\ 9}{6\ \cancel{X}\ \cancel{X}\ 1}{7}.\cancel{0}\cancel{0}6 \\
-\ 4.798 \\
\hline
2.208
\end{array}
$$

METHOD 2

A. Write in vertical form, being careful to line up the decimal points. A place value chart can be helpful.

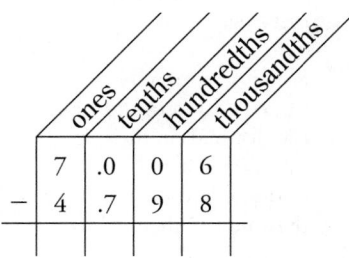

B. Since each digit in the subtrahead in the tenths, hundredths, and thousandths places is greater than the corresponding digit in the minuend, you cannot subtract until you rename.

Rename the 7 ones as 6 ones and 10 tenths.

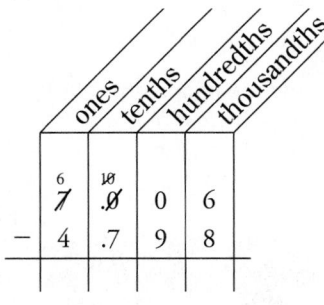

Rename the 10 tenths as 9 tenths and 10 hundreths.

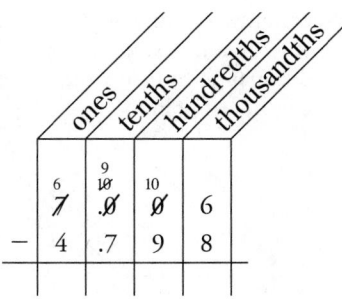

Rename the 10 hundreths as 9 hundredths and 10 thousandths.

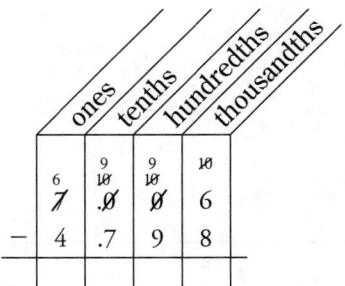

Combine those thousandths with the 6 thousandths to get 16 thousandths.

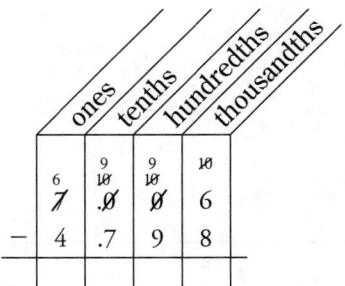

C. Subtract:
7.006 − 4.798 = 2.208

Place Value Chart

hundreds	tens	ones	.	tenths	hundredths	thousandths	ten thousandths
9	8	7	•	6	5	4	3

42.16 + 3.5 + 7

METHOD 1

A. Write in vertical form, being careful to line up the decimal points. Remember that the decimal point always goes to the right of a whole number, so it goes to the right of the 7 in the problem.

A place value chart can be helpful.

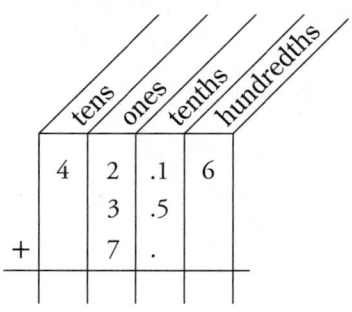

B. Add the numbers in the four columns as you would for whole numbers, inserting a decimal point below the column of points.

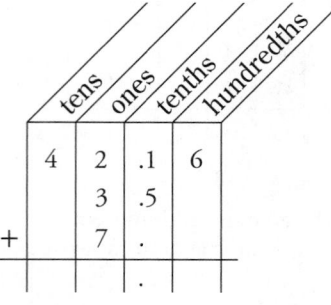

Rename the 12 in the ones column as 1 ten and 2 ones. Some books refer to this as carrying.

Some people prefer to write in extra zeros to the right of the decimal point to make the right align. This is optional and does not change the value of the decimals.

	tens	ones	tenths	hundredths
	$^1\!\!\!4$	2	.1	6
		3	.5	0
+		7	.0	0
	5	2	.6	6

Using base ten blocks:

METHOD 2

A. Use 4 tens blocks, 2 ones blocks, 1 tenths block, and 6 hundredths blocks to show 42.16.

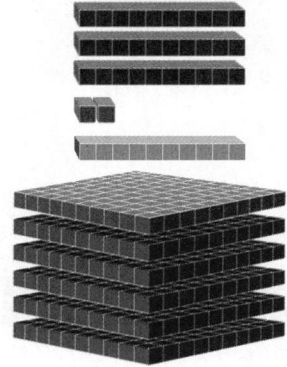

Use 3 ones blocks and 5 tenths blocks to show 3.5.

Use 7 ones blocks to show 7.

B. Add the hundredths blocks. Since there is only one 6 in that place, there are 6 blocks in the answer.

Add the tenths blocks. 5 + 1 = 6 tenths blocks.

continued on next page

Add the ones blocks.
2 + 3 + 7 = 12 ones blocks.

C. Add the tens blocks.
4 + 1 = 5 tens blocks.

D. 42.16 + 3.5 + 7 = 52.66

Regroup the 12 ones as 1 ten
block and 2 ones blocks.

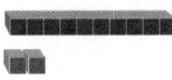

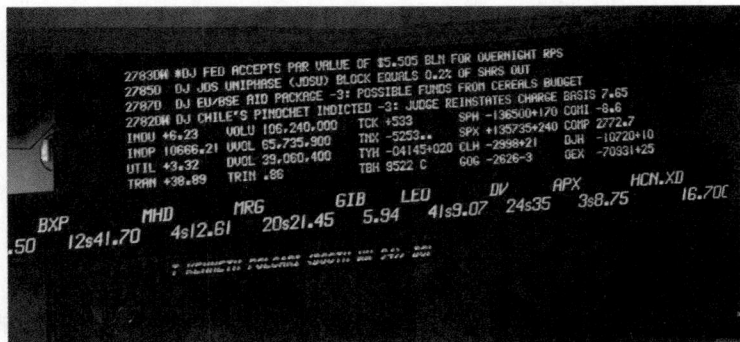

The New York Stock Exchange has switched from fractions to decimals.

Counting Decimals with Base Ten Blocks

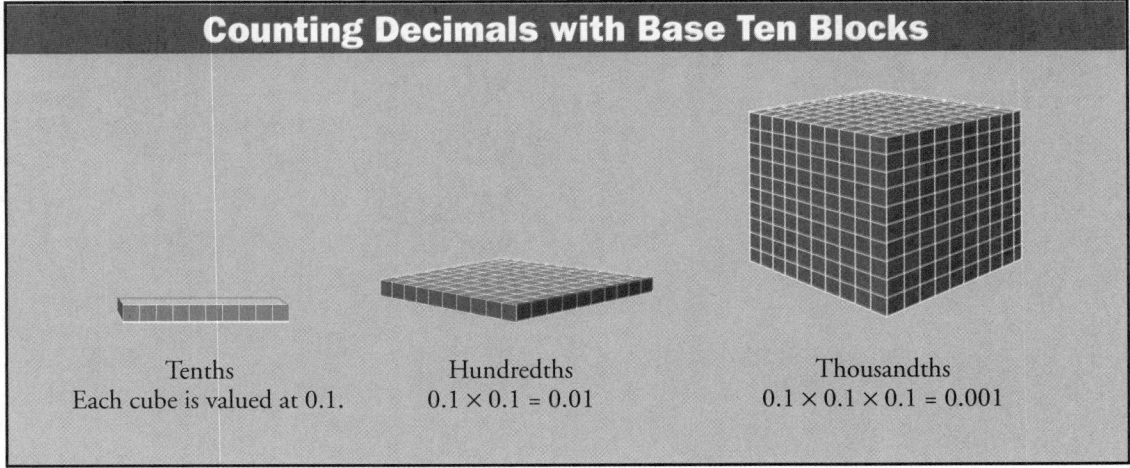

Tenths
Each cube is valued at 0.1.

Hundredths
0.1 × 0.1 = 0.01

Thousandths
0.1 × 0.1 × 0.1 = 0.001

$$4.56$$
$$+\ \ 36.78$$

METHOD 1

A. Add the numbers in the four columns, inserting a decimal point below the column of points.

Rename the 14 in the hundredths place as 1 tenth and 4 hundredths.

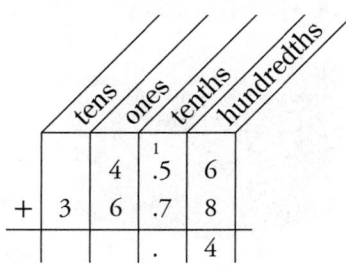

tens		ones	tenths	hundredths
		4	¹.5	6
+	3	6	.7	8
			.	4

Rename the 13 in the tenths place as 1 ones and 3 tenths.

tens		ones	tenths	hundredths
		¹4	¹.5	6
+	3	6	.7	8
			.3	4

Rename the 11 in the ones place as 1 tens and 1 ones.

tens		ones	tenths	hundredths
¹		¹4	¹.5	6
+	3	6	.7	8
	4	1	.3	4

METHOD 2

A. Use 4 ones blocks, 5 tenths blocks, and 6 hundredths blocks to show 4.56.

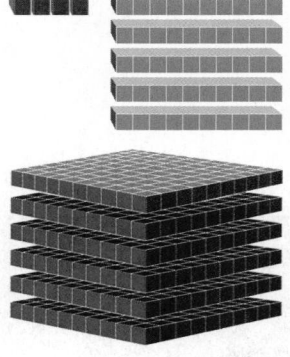

Use 3 tens blocks, 6 ones blocks, 7 tenths blocks, and 8 hundredths blocks to show 36.78.

B. Add the hundredths blocks. $6 + 8 = 14$ hundredths blocks.

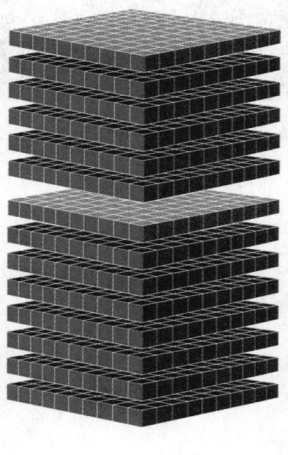

continued on next page

Regroup 14 hundredths blocks as 1 tenths block and 4 hundredths blocks.

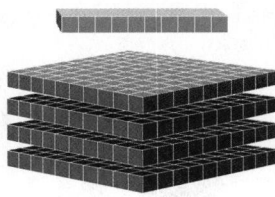

C. Add the tenths blocks.
1 + 5 + 7 = 13 tenths blocks.

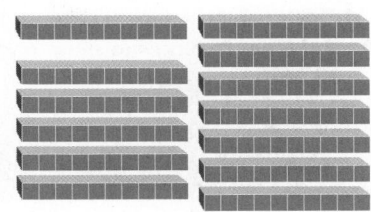

Regroup 13 tenths blocks as 1 ones block and 3 tenths blocks.

D. Add the ones blocks.
1 + 4 + 6 = 11 ones blocks.

Regroup the 11 ones blocks as 1 tens block and 1 ones block.

E. Add the tens blocks.
1 + 3 = 4 tens blocks.

F. 4.56 + 36.78 = 41.34

$$6.35 + 16.1 + 125.6$$

METHOD 1

A. Write in vertical form, being careful to line up the decimal points. A place value chart can be helpful.

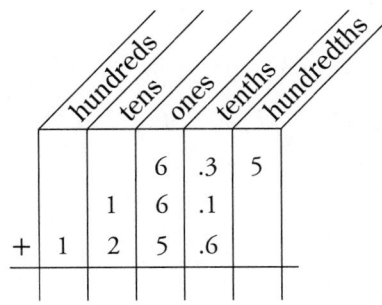

B. Add the numbers in the five columns as you would for whole numbers, inserting a decimal point below the column of points. Rename the 10 tenths as 1 one.

Rename the 18 ones as 1 ten and 8 ones. You may write in extra zeros to the right of the decimal point to make the right align. Remember, this is optional and does not change the value of the decimals.

hundreds	tens	ones	tenths	hundredths
	1	1		
		6	.3	5
	1	6	.1	0
+ 1	2	5	.6	0
1	4	8	.0	5

METHOD 2

A. Use 6 ones blocks, 3 tenths blocks, and 5 hundredths blocks to show 6.35.

Use 1 tens block, 6 ones blocks, and 1 tenths block to show 16.1.

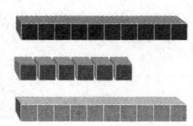

Use one hundreds block, 2 tens blocks, 5 ones blocks, and 6 tenths blocks to show 125.6.

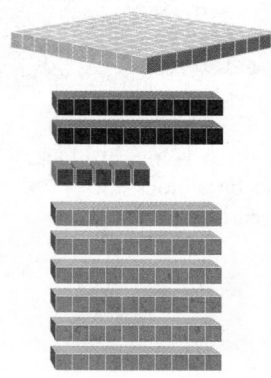

B. Add the hundredths blocks. 5 + nothing = 5 hundredths blocks.

Add the tenths blocks. 3 + 1 + 6 = 10 tenths blocks.

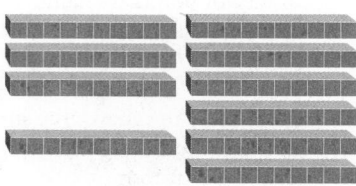

Regroup the 10 tenths blocks as 1 ones block and no tenths blocks.

C. Add the ones blocks. 1 + 6 + 6 + 5 = 18 ones blocks. Regroup the 18 ones blocks as 1 tens block and 8 ones blocks.

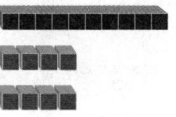

D. Add the tens blocks. 1 + 1 + 2 = 4 tens blocks.

Add the hundreds blocks. 1 + nothing = 1 hundreds block.

E. 6.35 + 16.1 + 125.6 = 148.05

68.45 − 25.3

METHOD 1

A. Write in vertical form, being careful to line up the decimal points. A place value chart can be helpful.

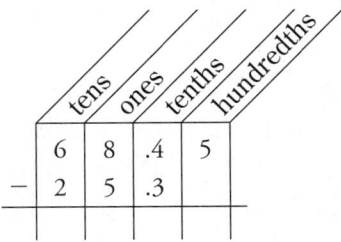

B. Since no number in the subtrahend is > than its counterpart in the minuend, it is not necessary to rename (or borrow). Subtract.

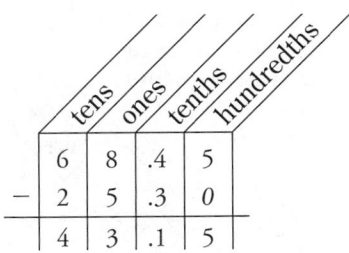

You may write in extra zeros to the right of the decimal point to make the right align. Remember, this is optional and does not change the value of the decimals.

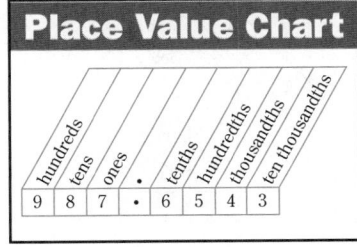

METHOD 2

A. Use 6 tens blocks, 8 ones blocks, 4 tenths blocks, and 5 hundredths blocks to show 68.45.

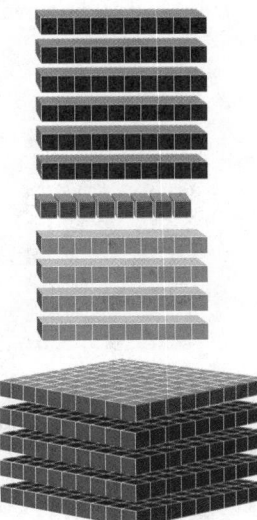

Use 2 tens blocks, 5 ones blocks, and 3 tenths blocks to show 25.3

B. Subtract the hundredths blocks.
5 − nothing = 5 hundredths blocks.

Subtract the tenths blocks.
4 − 3 = 1 tenths block.

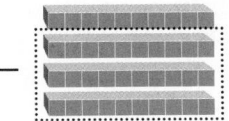

Subtract the ones blocks.
8 − 5 = 3 ones blocks.

Subtract the tens blocks.
6 − 2 = 4 tens blocks.

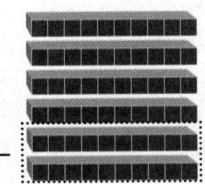

C. 68.45 − 25.3 = 43.15

41 – 0.56

METHOD 1

A. Write in vertical form, being careful to line up the decimal points. Remember that the decimal point always goes to the right of a whole number, so it goes to the right of the 1 in 41. A place value chart can be helpful.

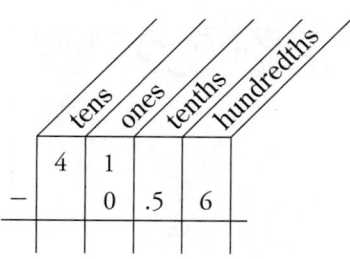

B. Enter two zeros to the right of the decimal in 41. Remember, this does not change its value. Because 5 > 0 in the tenths place, you cannot subtract these numbers. Rename 1 ones as 10 tenths. (Some texts use the instruction: borrow.)

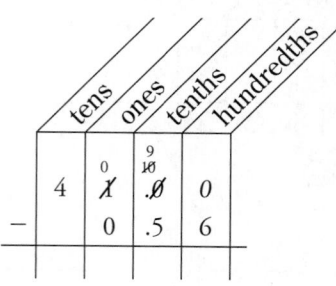

C. Because 6 > 0 in the hundredths place, you cannot subtract these numbers. Rename 10 tenths as 9 tenths and 10 hundredths. (Borrow.)

Subtract.

Insert a decimal point below the column of points.

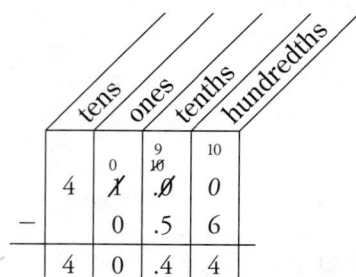

METHOD 2

A. Use 4 tens blocks and 1 ones block to show 41.

Use 5 tenths blocks and 6 hundredths blocks to show 0.56.

B. Because 6 > 0 in the hundredths place, you cannot subtract these numbers. Because 5 > 0 in the tenths place, you cannot subtract these numbers.

Regroup 1 ones block as 0 ones blocks and 10 tenths blocks.

C. Regroup 10 tenths blocks as 9 tenths and 10 hundredths blocks.

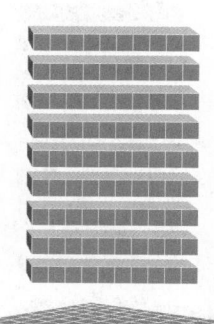

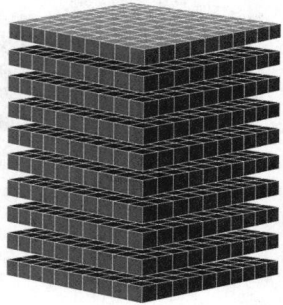

continued on next page

D. Subtract the hundredths blocks.
10 − 6 = 4 hundredths blocks.

E. Subtract the tenths blocks.
9 − 5 = 4 tenths blocks.

F. Subtract the ones blocks.
0 − 0 = 0 ones blocks.

Subtract the tens blocks
4 − 0 = 4 tens blocks.

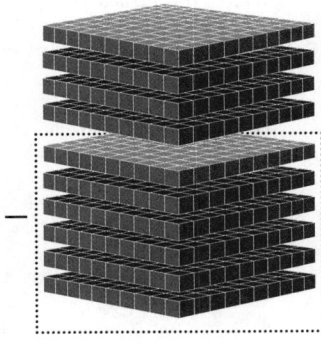

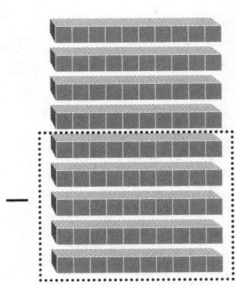

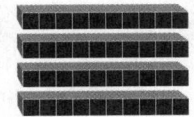

G. 41 − 0.56 = 40.44

---

300 − 1.82

METHOD 1

A. Write in vertical form, being careful to line up the decimal points. Remember that the decimal point always goes to the right of a whole number, so it goes to the right of the 0 in the ones place in the 300.

A place value chart can be helpful.

C. Because 8 > 0 in the tenths place, you cannot subtract these numbers.

Rename the 10 in the tens place as 9 tens and 10 ones.

E. Rename 10 tenths as 9 tenths and 10 hundredths.

F. Subtract.

Insert a decimal point below the column of points.

B. Enter 2 zeros to the right of the 0 in the ones place of 300. Remember, this does not change its value. Because 2 > 0 in the hundredths place, you cannot subtract these numbers.

Rename the 3 in the hundreds place as 2 hundreds and 10 tens.

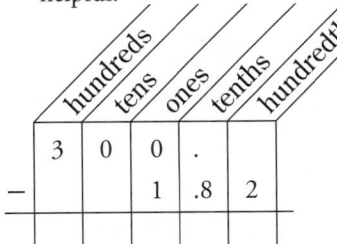

D. Rename the 10 ones as 9 ones and 10 tenths.

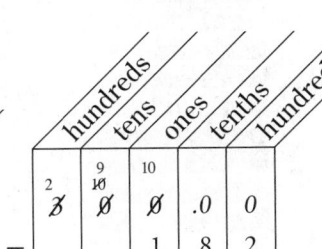

METHOD 2

A. Use 3 hundreds blocks to show 300.

Use 1 ones block, 8 tenths blocks, and 2 hundredths blocks to show 1.82.

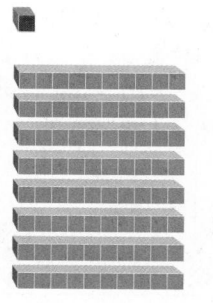

B. Because 2 > 0, 8 > 0, and 1 > 0, you cannot subtract these numbers.

Regroup 3 hundreds as 2 hundreds and 10 tens.

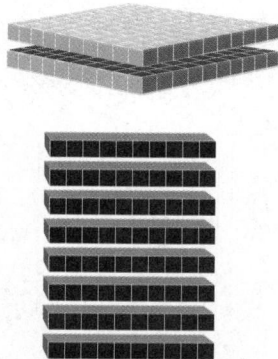

C. Regroup 10 tens as 9 tens and 10 ones.

D. Regroup 10 ones as 9 ones and 10 tenths.

E. Regroup 10 tenths as 9 tenths and 10 hundredths.

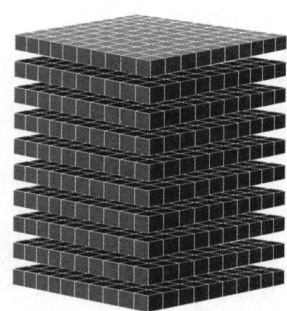

continued on next page

F. Subtract the hundredths.
10 − 2 = 8

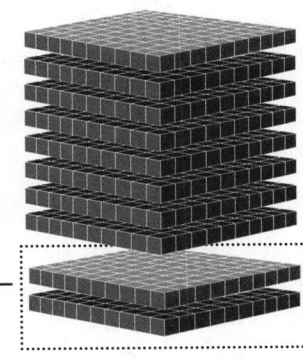

G. Subtract the tenths.
9 − 8 = 1

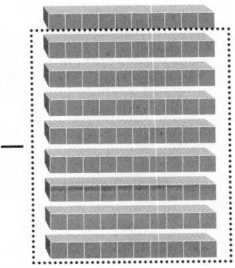

H. Subtract the ones.
9 − 1 = 8

I. Subtract the tens.
9 − nothing = 9

J. Subtract the hundreds.
2 − nothing = 2

K. 300 − 1.82 = 298.18

457.62 + 42.38

METHOD 1

A. Write in vertical form, being careful to line up the decimal points.

A place value chart can be helpful.

B. Add the numbers in the five columns.

Rename the 10 in the hundredths place as 1 tenths.

Rename the 10 in the tenths place as 1 ones.

Rename the 10 in the ones place as 1 tens.

Rename the 10 in the tens place as 1 hundreds.

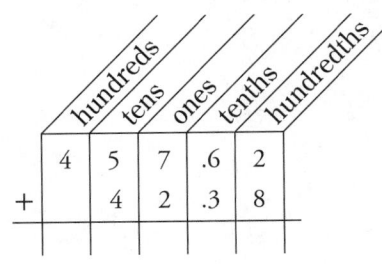

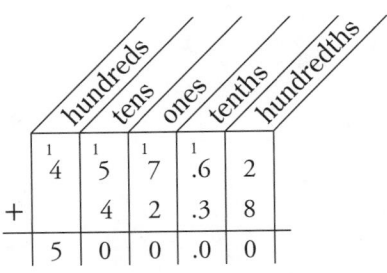

continued on next page

METHOD 2

A. Use 4 hundreds blocks, 5 tens blocks, 7 ones blocks, 6 tenths blocks, and 2 hundredths blocks to show 457.62.

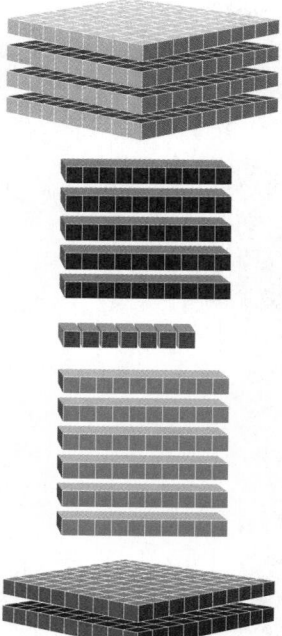

Use 4 tens blocks, 2 ones blocks, 3 tenths blocks, and 8 hundredths blocks to show 42.38.

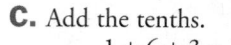

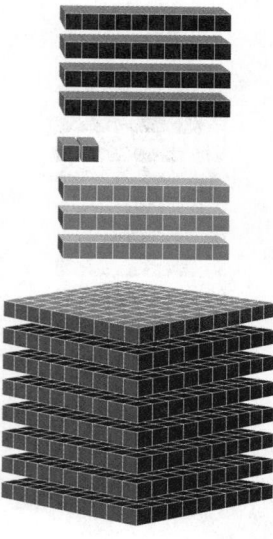

B. Add the hundredths.
2 + 8 = 10 hundredths blocks.

Regroup 10 hundredths blocks as 1 tenths block and 0 hundredths blocks.

C. Add the tenths.
1 + 6 + 3 = 10

Regroup 10 tenths blocks as 1 ones block and 0 tenths blocks.

D. Add the ones.
1 + 7 + 2 = 10

Regroup 10 ones blocks as 1 tens block and 0 ones blocks.

E. Add the tens.
1 + 5 + 4 = 10

Regroup the 10 tens blocks as 1 hundreds block and 0 tens blocks.

F. Add the hundreds.
1 + 4 = 5

G. 457.62 + 42.38 = 500.00

Multiplying by powers of 10

The key to working with decimals is understanding how powers of 10 work, since decimals are based upon powers of 10. The rules for multiplying and dividing by powers of 10 are also useful in solving many problems with whole numbers. You can memorize rules for powers of ten that are based upon counting zeros or on "moving the decimal point" to a different location to get the numeral for a different number. These rules are based on the properties of the numeration system we use.

To start with, make sure that you know the powers of 10 themselves. These are given in the table on page 245. Each positive or negative power of 10 is related in a simple way to the number of zeros shown when the number is written out in the decimal numeration system.

Whole numbers

Notice the pattern.

$3 \times 10^1 = 3 \times 10 = 30$ (1 zero)
$3 \times 10^2 = 3 \times 100 = 300$ (2 zeros)
$3 \times 10^3 = 3 \times 1000 = 3000$ (3 zeros)
$3 \times 10^4 = 3 \times 10000 = 30000$ (4 zeros)

Rule

To multiply a whole number by a non-negative power of 10, write the whole number with the same number of zeros after it as in the power of 10.
(NOTE: This will not work for negative powers.)

Examples

$7 \times 100,000 = 7 \times 10^5 = 700,000$
$40 \times 1000 = 40 \times 10^3 = 40,000$
(NOTE: Keep the 0 from the 40.)

Decimals

$3.455192 \times 10^0 = 3.455192 \times 1 = 3.455192$ (decimal point in same place)
$3.455192 \times 10^1 = 3.455192 \times 10 = 34.55192$ (decimal point 1 place to the right)
$3.455192 \times 10^2 = 3.455192 \times 100 = 345.5192$ (decimal point 2 places to the right)
$3.455192 \times 10^3 = 3.455192 \times 1000 = 3455.192$ (decimal point 3 places to the right)
$3.455192 \times 10^4 = 3.455192 \times 10000 = 34551.92$ (decimal point 4 places to the right)

Rule

To multiply a decimal by a non-negative power of 10, rewrite the decimal with the decimal point the same number of places to the right as the power of 10.

Examples

$27.349 \times 100 = 27.349 \times 10^2 = 2734.9$
$3.82 \times 100 = 3.82 \times 10^2 = 382. = 382$
(You need not show point.)
$3.501 \times 10,000 = 3.501 \times 10^4 = 35,010$
(You may need to write 0s.)
$57 \times 1000 = 57 \times 10^3 = 57. \times 10^3 = 57,000$
(The decimal rule also works for whole numbers.)

Negative exponents

$392.422 \times 10^{-1} = 392.422 \times 0.1 = 39.2422$ (decimal point 1 place to the left)
$392.422 \times 10^{-2} = 392.422 \times 0.01 = 3.92422$ (decimal point 2 places to the left)
$392.422 \times 10^{-3} = 392.422 \times 0.001 = 0.392422$ (decimal point 3 places to the left)
$392.422 \times 10^{-4} = 392.422 \times 0.0001 = 0.0392422$ (decimal point 4 places to the left)

Rule

To multiply a decimal by a negative power of 10, rewrite the decimal with the decimal point the same number of places to the left as the power of 10, ignoring the negative sign.

Examples

$495.3 \times 0.01 = 495.3 \times 10^{-2} = 4.953$
$7534.02 \times 0.0001 = 7534.02 \times 10^{-4} = 0.753402$
$37.5 \times 0.001 = 37.5 \times 10^{-3} = 0.0375$
(You may need to write more zeros to get the decimal point where you want it.)
$5028 \times 0.1 = 5028 \times 10^{-1} = 5028. \times 10^{-1} = 502.8$
(The decimal rule also works for whole numbers.)

$$12.96$$
$$\times \quad 1.8$$

The number 12.96 is close to 13 and the number 1.8 is close to 2 so the product of these two numbers should be close to 13 × 2 = 26. This method of estimating can be used to check on the final location of the decimal point.

A. Multiply the numbers, temporarily forgetting the decimal points.

$$\begin{array}{r} 1296 \\ \times \quad 18 \\ \hline 10368 \\ 1296 \\ \hline 23328 \end{array}$$

B. Count the number of places that are used to the right of the decimal point.

12.96 (two places)
1.8 (one place)

C. Add the number of places.
12.96 (two places)
1.8 + (one place)
(three places)

D. Enter a decimal point in the product so that the number of places on the right of the decimal point is the same as that found in step C.

23.328

23.328 has three places to the right of the decimal. Notice that 23.328 is near the approximate product of 26, which we found earlier.

$$6.1\overline{)43.31}$$

METHOD 1
The number 6.1 is close to 6 and the number 43.31 is close to 42. The quotient of these two numbers should be close to 42 ÷ 6 = 7.

A. Divide the numbers as you would have done earlier, by temporarily forgetting the decimal points.

$$\begin{array}{r} 71 \\ 61\overline{)4331} \\ \underline{427} \\ 61 \\ \underline{61} \\ 0 \end{array}$$

B. Count the number of places that are used to the right of the decimal point in each number.

43.31 (two places)
6.1 (one place)

C. Subtract the number of places in the divisor from the number of places in the dividend.
43.31 (two places) (dividend)
6.1 − (one place) (divisor)
(one place)

D. Enter a decimal point in the quotient so that it has the same number of places to the right of the decimal point as found in step C. This gives us the quotient 7.1.

7.1 has one place to the right of the decimal. Notice that 7.1 is near the approximate quotient of 7, which we found earlier.

Decimals and Place Value

Exponents can be used to make the meaning of decimals clearer. For whole numbers, the powers of 10 descend from left to right when you look at expanded form.
$$60{,}419 = 6 \times 10^4 + 0 \times 10^3 + 4 \times 10^2 + 1 \times 10 + 9$$
For decimals, the part to the left of the decimal point is just like a whole number, but the part to the right uses powers of 1/10; also, the exponents *increase* as you read from left to right.
$$5.287 = 5 + 2 \times (1/10) + 8 \times (1/10)^2 + 7 \times (1/10)^3$$

METHOD 2

A. You need to have the decimal point in the divisor to the right of the last digit, after the one in the tenths place. Since the problem also means $\frac{43.31}{6.1}$, multiply the fraction by $\frac{10}{10}$.

B. $\frac{43.31}{6.1} \times \frac{10}{10} = \frac{433.1}{61}$

C. Divide the numbers as you would have done with whole numbers, but keep the decimal point in the dividend, (433.1), and place the decimal point in the answer above it.

$$61\overline{)433.1}$$

D. Show the answer.

$$\begin{array}{r} 7.1 \\ 61\overline{)433.1} \end{array}$$

To check, multiply 61 by 7.1 to get 433.1. If you multiply 6.1 by 7.1, you will get 43.31, the original dividend.

NOTE: If there are 2 decimals in the divisor, the fraction you will use to multiply by the dividend over the divisor is $\frac{100}{100}$.

$1.44\overline{)57.6}$ would be

$$\frac{57.6}{1.44} \times \frac{100}{100} = \frac{5760}{144}$$

Now divide to get 40.

5.9×2.3

A. Rewrite in vertical form and multiply as if you were dealing with whole numbers.

$$\begin{array}{r} 2.3 \\ \times\ 5.9 \\ \hline 207 \\ 115\ \ \\ \hline 1357 \end{array}$$

B. Count the number of decimal places in the problem as originally posed. The first factor, 2.3, has 1 decimal place. The second factor, 5.9, also has 1 digit to the right of the decimal point. Add the number of decimal places. 1 + 1 = 2.

C. Mark off 2 decimal places in the product.

$$\begin{array}{r} 2.3 \\ \times\ 5.9 \\ \hline 207 \\ 115\ \ \\ \hline 13.57 \end{array}$$

You use the sum of the decimal places in the problem as the number of decimal places in the product because decimals are just fractions that have powers of 10 as their denominators. When you multiply fractions, you multiply the denominators. Using the rule for multiplying by a power of 10 (see box on page 261), the product of the denominators is the sum of the exponents of the powers of 10. 4.7 is another way of writing $\frac{47}{10^1}$ and 3.954 is another way of writing $\frac{3954}{10^3}$. The product has a numerator that is 47×3954. The product also has a denominator of $10^1 \times 10^3$, which is equal to 10^{1+3}. The answer will have 4 decimal places.

0.07×0.005

A. Rewrite in vertical form. Most people ignore lining up the decimal points.

$$\begin{array}{r} 0.005 \\ \times\ 0.07 \\ \hline \end{array}$$

B. Multiply as if the problem had only the whole numbers 5 and 7 shown.

$$\begin{array}{r} 0.005 \\ \times\ 0.07 \\ \hline 35 \end{array}$$

C. Count the number of decimal places in each of the factors: 0.005 has 3 decimal places and 0.07 has 2 decimal places. The number of decimal places in the product is 3 + 2 = 5.

D. The number 35, however, has only 2 digits. Additional zeros must be written in front of 35.

Three additional decimal places are needed, so 3 zeros must be added.

$$\begin{array}{r} 0.005 \\ \times\ \ \ 0.07 \\ \hline 0.00035 \end{array}$$

24.1 × 0.32

METHOD 1

The decimal number 24.1 can be approximated to the whole number 24. The decimal 0.32 is approximately the fraction 1/3. The product of the two is 8. This will help check the final answer and location of the decimal point.

A. Write in vertical form and multiply as if these were whole numbers. Remember, there is no need to line up the decimal points in multiplication.

$$
\begin{array}{r}
24.1 \\
\times\ 0.32 \\
\hline
482 \\
723 \\
\hline
7712
\end{array}
$$

B. Count the number of places to the right of each decimal point in each factor.

24.1   (one place)
0.32   (two places)

C. Add the number of places.

24.1   (one place)
0.32 + (two places)
─────────────────
       (three places)

D. Enter a decimal point in the product so that the number of places to the right of the decimal point is the same as that found in step C.
7.712

Notice that 7.712 is near the approximate product of 8, which we found earlier.

Keeping the decimal point in the factors using base ten blocks

METHOD 2

A. Use 2 tens blocks, 4 ones blocks and 1 tenths block to show 24.1.

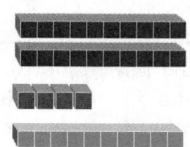

Use 3 tenths blocks and 2 hundredths blocks to show 0.32.

B. Multiply 2 hundredths blocks by 1 tenths block, 4 ones blocks, and 2 tens blocks, to get 4 tenths blocks, 8 hundredths blocks, and 2 thousandths blocks.

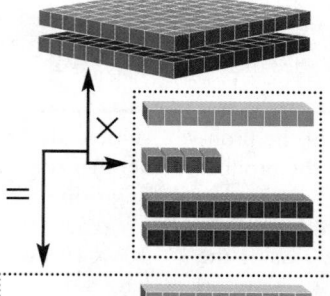

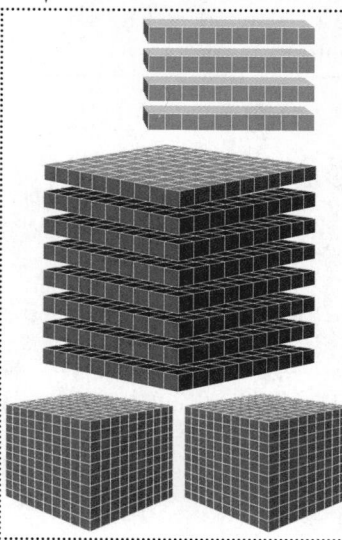

C. Multiply 3 tenths blocks by 1 tenths block, 4 ones blocks, and 2 tens blocks to get 3 hundredths blocks, 12 tenths blocks, and 6 ones blocks.

D. Regroup as 7 ones blocks, 2 tenths blocks, and 3 hundredths blocks.

E. Add the thousandths blocks.
2 + nothing = 2
Add the hundredths blocks.
8 + 3 = 11
Regroup 11 hundredths blocks as 1 tenths block and 1 hundredths block.

F. Add the tenths blocks.
1 + 4 + 2 = 7
Add the ones blocks.
7 + nothing = 7

G. Show this product.
24.1 x 0.32 = 7.712

METHOD 3

You can check the position of the decimal point: Count the number of decimal places in the 2 factors, 24.1×0.32. $1 + 2 = 3$

Place the decimal point 3 places from the last number on the right.
$241 \times 32 = 7712$, so $24.1 \times 0.32 = 7.712$

A. Show the factor as whole numbers 241×32. Count the number of decimal points in the 2 original factors, 24.1×0.32
$1 + 2 = 3$

There will be 3 decimal places in the final answer.

B. Use 2 hundreds blocks, 4 tens blocks, and 1 ones block to show 241. Use 3 tens blocks and 2 ones blocks to show 32.

C. Multiply 2 ones blocks by 1 ones block, 4 tens blocks, and 2 hundreds blocks to get 2 ones blocks, 8 tens blocks, and 4 hundreds blocks.
$2 \times 241 = 482$

D. Multiply 3 tens blocks by 1 ones block, 4 tens blocks, and 2 hundreds blocks to get 6 thousands blocks, 12 hundreds, and 3 tens blocks.

E. Regroup as $6 + 1 = 7$ thousands blocks, 2 hundreds blocks, and 3 tens blocks.
$30 \times 241 = 7230$

F. Add the two products: 4 hundreds blocks, 8 tens blocks, and 2 ones blocks + 7 thousands blocks, 2 hundreds blocks, and 3 tens blocks to get 7 thousands blocks, 6 hundreds blocks, 11 tens blocks, and 2 ones blocks.

G. Regroup as 7 thousands blocks, $6 + 1 = 7$ hundreds blocks, 1 tens block, and 2 ones blocks.

H. $241 \times 32 = 7712$

I. In step A, it was determined that there would be 3 decimal places in the final answer.
$24.1 \times 0.32 = 7.712$

0.08×0.054

METHOD 1

The number 0.08 can be approximated as 0.08 or 8/100. The number 0.054 can be approximated as 0.05 or 5/100. The product of the 2 numbers is 40/10,000 which reduces to 4/1000 or 0.004. This method of estimating can be used to check on the final location of the decimal point.

A. Write in vertical form and multiply as if these were whole numbers. Do not intentionally align the decimal points. Put the number with the largest number of digits on top.

$$\begin{array}{r} 0.054 \\ \times\ 0.08 \\ \hline 432 \end{array}$$

B. Count the number of places to the right of each decimal point.

0.054   (three places)
0.08   (two places)

C. Add the number of places.

0.054   (three places)
0.08   + (two places)
‾‾‾‾‾‾‾‾‾‾‾‾‾‾‾‾‾‾
          (five places)

D. Enter a decimal point in the product so that the number of places to the right of the decimal point is the same as that found in step.C.

Since you need five places and there are only 3 digits in 432, you must write additional zeros in front of (to the left of) 432. You must also have a zero in the ones place.
00432

Place the decimal point to the left of the first zero.
0.00432

Notice that 0.00432 is near the approximate product of 0.004, which we found earlier.

continued on next page

METHOD 2

Keeping the decimal point in the factors using base ten blocks

A. Use 8 hundredths blocks to show 0.08. Use 5 hundredths blocks and 4 thousandths to show 0.054.

B. Multiply 8 hundredths blocks by 4 thousandths blocks to get 3 ten-thousandths blocks and 2 hundred-thousandths blocks

$$0.08 \times 0.004 = 0.00032$$

C. Multiply 8 hundredths blocks by 5 hundredths blocks to get 40 ten-thousandths blocks, and 32 hundred-thousandths blocks.

$$0.08 \times 0.05 = 0.0040$$

D. Regroup 40 ten-thousandths blocks as 4 thousandths blocks and 0 ten-thousandths blocks. Regroup 32 hundred-thousandths blocks as 3 ten-thousandths blocks and 2 hundred-thousandths blocks.

E. Add the two products: 4 thousandths blocks and 0 ten-thousandths blocks + 3 ten-thousandths blocks and 2 hundred-thousandths blocks = 4 thousandths blocks, 3 ten-thousandths blocks, and 2 hundred-thousandths blocks.

F. $0.08 \times 0.054 = 0.00432$

METHOD 3

Showing the factors as whole numbers, using base ten blocks, and positioning the decimal later

A. Show the factors as whole numbers:

$$8 \times 54.$$

Count the number of decimal points in the 2 original factors, 0.08×0.054

$$2 + 3 = 5$$

There will be 5 decimal places in the final answer.

B. Use 8 ones blocks to show 8. Use 5 tens blocks and 4 ones blocks to show 54.

C. Multiply 8 ones blocks by 4 ones blocks to get 32 ones blocks. Multiply 8 ones blocks by 5 tens blocks to get 40 tens blocks.

D. Regroup 32 ones blocks as 3 tens blocks and 2 ones blocks.

Regroup 40 tens blocks as 4 hundreds blocks and 0 tens blocks.

E. Add the two products. 3 tens blocks and 2 ones blocks + 4 hundreds blocks to get 4 hundreds blocks, 3 tens blocks, and 2 ones blocks.

F. $8 \times 54 = 432$

G. In step A, it was determined that there would be 5 decimal places in the final answer.
$$0.08 \times 0.054 = 0.00432$$

4.125×0.98

METHOD 1

The number 4.125 is approximately 4. The number 0.98 is approximately 1. The product of the two is 4.

A. Write in vertical form and multiply as if these were whole numbers. Do not intentionally align the decimal points.

$$
\begin{array}{r}
4.125 \\
\times\ 0.98 \\
\hline
33000 \\
37125 \\
\hline
404250
\end{array}
$$

B. Count the number of places to the right of each decimal point.

4.125 (three places)
0.98   (two places)

C. Add the number of places.

4.125 (three places)
0.98 + (two places)
———————
(five places)

D. Enter a decimal point in the product so that the number of places to the right of the decimal point is the same as that found in step C.

4.04250

Notice that 4.04250 (which can also be written as 4.0425) is near the approximation of 4, which we found earlier.

Showing the factors as whole numbers, using base ten blocks, and positioning the decimal later

METHOD 2

Showing the factors as whole numbers, using base ten blocks, and positioning the decimal later

A. Show the factors as whole numbers 4125 × 98. Count the number of decimal points in the 2 original factors, 4.125 × 0.98
2 + 3 = 5

There will be 5 decimal places in the final answer.

B. Use 4 thousands blocks, 1 hundreds block, 2 tens blocks, and 5 ones blocks to show 4125.

Use 9 tens blocks and 8 ones blocks to show 98.

C. Multiply 8 ones blocks by 4 thousands blocks, 1 hundreds block, 2 tens blocks, and 5 ones blocks to get 32 thousands blocks, 8 hundreds blocks, 16 tens blocks, and 40 ones blocks.

D. Regroup 32 thousands blocks as 3 ten-thousands blocks and 2 thousands blocks.

Regroup 16 tens blocks as 1 hundreds block and 6 tens blocks.

Regroup 40 ones blocks as 4 tens blocks and 0 ones blocks.

E. Add 3 ten-thousands blocks, 2 thousands blocks, 8 hundreds blocks, 1 hundreds block, 6 tens blocks, and 4 tens blocks to get 3 ten-thousands blocks, 2 thousands blocks, 9 hundreds blocks, and 10 tens blocks.

F. Regroup 10 tens blocks as 1 hundreds block and 0 tens blocks.

G. Add the hundreds blocks again: 9 hundreds blocks + 1 hundreds block = 10 hundreds blocks.

H. Regroup 10 hundreds blocks as 1 thousands block and 0 hundreds blocks.

I. Add the thousands blocks again: 1 thousands block + 2 thousands blocks = 3 thousands blocks.

J. 4125 × 8 = 3 ten-thousands blocks and 3 thousands blocks.

K. Multiply 9 tens blocks by 4 thousands blocks, 1 hundreds block, 2 tens blocks, and 5 ones blocks to get 36 ten-thousands blocks, 9 thousands blocks, 18 hundreds blocks, and 45 tens blocks.

L. Regroup 36 ten-thousands blocks as 3 hundred-thousands blocks and 6 ten-thousands blocks.

Regroup 18 hundreds blocks as 1 thousands block and 8 hundreds blocks.

Regroup 45 tens blocks as 4 hundreds blocks and 5 tens blocks.

M. Add 3 hundred-thousands blocks, 6 ten-thousands blocks, 9 thousands blocks, 1 thousands block, 8 hundreds blocks, 4 hundreds blocks, and 5 tens blocks to get 3 hundred-thousands blocks, 6 ten-thousands blocks, 10 thousands blocks, 12 hundreds blocks and 5 tens blocks.

N. Regroup 10 thousands blocks as 1 ten-thousands block and 0 thousands blocks.

Regroup 12 hundreds blocks as 1 thousands block and 2 hundreds blocks.

O. Rename the product as 3 hundred-thousands blocks, 6 + 1 = 7 ten-thousands blocks, 1 thousands block, 2 hundreds blocks, and 5 tens blocks.
90 × 4125 = 371,250

P. Add 3 ten-thousands blocks, 3 thousands blocks to 3 hundred-thousands blocks, 7 ten-thousands blocks, 1 thousands block, 2 hundreds blocks, 5 tens blocks to get 4 hundred-thousands blocks, 0 ten-thousands blocks, 4 thousands blocks, 2 hundreds blocks, 5 tens blocks, and 0 ones blocks.

Q. In step A, it was determined that there would be 5 decimal places in the product.
4125 × 98 = 404,250
4.125 × 0.98 = 4.04250

7.39 × 52.8

The number 7.39 can be approximated as 7. The number 52.8 can be approximated as 50. The product of the two numbers is 350.

A. Write in vertical form and multiply as if these were whole numbers. Do not intentionally align the decimal points.

$$\begin{array}{r} 7.39 \\ \times\ 52.8 \\ \hline 5912 \\ 1478 \\ 3695 \\ \hline 390192 \end{array}$$

B. Count the number of places to the right of each decimal point.

7.39   (two places)
52.8   (one place)

C. Add the number of places.

7.39   (two places)
52.8 + (one place)
─────────────
(three places)

D. Enter a decimal point in the product so that the number of places to the right of the decimal point is the same as that found in step C.

390.192

Notice that 390.192 is near the approximate value of 350, which we found earlier.

Dividing by powers of 10

Non-negative exponents

Notice the pattern.

$872.384 \div 10^1 = 872.384 \div 10 = 87.2384$
$872.384 \div 10^2 = 872.384 \div 100 = 8.72384$
$872.384 \div 10^3 = 872.384 \div 1000 = 0.872384$

Rule

To divide a number by a non-negative power of 10, rewrite the number with the decimal point the same number of places to the left as the power of 10.

Examples

$29837.4 \div 10,000 = 29837.4 \div 10^4 = 2.98374$
$5.9 \div 1000 = 5.9 \div 10^3 = 0.0059$
    (You may need to write more 0s.)
$293 \div 1000 = 293 \div 10^3 = 293. \div 10^3 = 0.293$

Negative exponents

$872.384 \div 10^{-1} = 872.384 \div 0.1 = 8723.84$
$872.384 \div 10^{-2} = 872.384 \div 0.01 = 87238.4$
$872.384 \div 10^{-3} = 872.384 \div 0.001 = 872,384$

Rule

To divide a number by a negative power of 10, rewrite the number with the decimal point the same number of places to the right as the power of 10, ignoring the negative sign.

Examples

$2957.395 \div 0.01 = 2957.395 \div 10^{-2} = 295,739.5$
$3.14 \div 0.0001 = 3.14 \div 10^{-4} = 31,400$
    (You may need to write more zeros.)
$85 \div 0.1 = 85 \div 10^{-1} = 850$

Sam bought three lemons for $0.20 each and four grapefruit for $0.65 each. He gave the clerk a $10.00 bill. How much change did he receive?

A. Multiply 3 by $0.20.
$3 \times 0.20 = \$0.60$

Multiply 4 by $0.65.
$4 \times 0.65 = \$2.60$

B. Add the two products.
$\$0.60 + \$2.60 = \$3.20$

C. Subtract the sum, $3.20, from $10.00.
$\$10.00 - \$3.20 = \$6.80$ in change

Ashley is making a picnic table. The total length of the boards used on the tabletop is 39 feet. There are six boards in the top. How long is each board?

A. Divide 39 ft. by 6.

$6 \overline{)39}$

B. Place the decimal point after the 9. Place a zero in the tenths place.

$6 \overline{)39.0}$

C. Divide.
6.5 feet long

$6 \overline{)39.0}$ = 6.5

Lindsey is making a macramé plant holder. She needs four pieces of cord, each 12 feet long, and two pieces, each 1.5 feet long. She has 50 feet of cord. Is this enough to make the holder?

A. Multiply 4 by 12 feet.
$4 \times 12 = 48$ feet

Multiply 2 by 1.5 feet.
$2 \times 1.5 = 3$ feet

B. Add the two products.
48 feet + 3 feet = 51 feet needed

C. Compare the amount of cord needed, 51 feet, with the amount Lindsey already has, 50 feet. She has less than the amount needed, so, no, she does not have enough cord.

Miss Ahern is making a dish called Cowboy Caviar. She has purchased two cans of black-eyed peas for $0.65 each, one can of yellow corn for $0.49, one can of vegetable juice for $0.55, and a red bell pepper for $0.90. What was the cost of these items?

A. Multiply 2 by $0.65.
$2 \times \$0.65 = \$1.30$

B. Add all the expenses together.
$\$1.30 + \$0.49 + \$0.55 + \$0.90 = \$3.24$ spent

Sam has $2.15 in coins: nickels, dimes, and quarters. He has four nickels. He has three times as many dimes as nickels. If the rest of the coins are quarters, how many dimes and quarters does he have?

A. Multiply the number of nickels, 4, by 3.
$4 \times 3 = 12$ dimes

B. Multiply the number of nickels by $0.05
$4 \times \$0.05 = \$0.20$ in nickels

Multiply the number of dimes by $0.10
$12 \times \$0.10 = \$1.20$ in dimes

C. Add the value of the nickels and the value of the dimes.
$\$0.20 + \$1.20 = \$1.40$

D. Subtract the value of the nickels and dimes, $1.40, from the total amount, $2.15.
$\$2.15 - \$1.40 = \$0.75$ in quarters.

E. Divide the difference, $0.75 by the value of one quarter, $0.25.
$\$0.25 \overline{)\$.75} = 3$ quarters

There are 12 dimes and 3 quarters.

Jason has a watermelon that has a mass of 7.3 kg. If 0.92 of the mass is water, what is the mass of the water? How many kg are not water?

METHOD 1

A. Determine the number of kg that are water. Multiply 7.3 kg by 0.92.
$7.3 \text{kg} \times 0.92 = 6.716$ kg of the watermelon are water.

B. Subtract the mass of the water from the total mass.
$7.3 \text{kg} - 6.716 \text{kg} = 0.584$ kg that are not water.

METHOD 2

A. Determine the number of kg that are water. Multiply 7.3 kg by 0.92.
$7.3 \text{kg} \times 0.92 = 6.716$ kg of the watermelon are water.

B. If 0.92 of the mass is water, then 1.00, the entire watermelon, $- 0.92$ is the mass of the watermelon that is not water.
$1.00 - 0.92 = 0.08$ is the part that is not water.

C. Multiply 7.3kg by 0.08.
$7.3 \times 0.08 = 0.584$ kg that are not water.

Reggie made a long-distance phone call that cost $3.00 for the first minute and $0.35 for each additional minute. He talked for four minutes. What was the cost of the call?

A. Subtract the first minute from the total of four minutes to determine how many minutes will be charged at the $0.35 per minute rate.
4 minutes − 1 minute = 3 minutes.

B. Multiply the first minute by $3.00
$1 \times \$3.00 = \$3.00$

Multiply the other three minutes by $0.35
$3 \times \$0.35 = \$1.05$

C. Add the two products.
$\$3.00 + \$1.05 = \$4.05$ for the call.

Lilly bought a Diva doll for $12.95. The sales tax was $0.08 on each dollar. How much sales tax did she pay? What was the total cost of the doll + tax?

METHOD 1

A. Multiply the doll's price by 0.08.
$\$12.95 \times 0.08 = \$1.036$

B. Round the product to two decimal places.
$1.036 rounds to $1.04, the sales tax.

C. Add the price and the tax.
$\$12.95 + \$1.04 = \$13.99$, the total cost.

METHOD 2

A. Since the tax is $0.08 on each dollar of cost, the total price is $1.08 on each dollar.

B. Multiply $12.95 by 1.08.
$\$12.95 \times 1.08 = \$13.9860$

C. Round to the hundredths place.
$13.9860 rounds to $13.99, the total cost.

Decimals and fractions.

All fractions can be rewritten as decimals. There are, however, two kinds of decimals that result.

If the denominator of the fraction, when written in reduced form, can divide exactly into 10 or a power of 10 (i.e., 100, 1000, 10,000,...), then the decimal will end. If the denominator of the fraction, when written in reduced form, cannot divide exactly into 10 or a power of 10, then the decimal will continue without end and the numbers to the right of the decimal will repeat. The following problems show examples of each kind.

Decimals into fractions

To change a decimal to a fraction, write the decimal as a fraction that has a whole-number (omitting the decimal point) numerator over a denominator of the proper power of 10; then simplify if possible.

NOTE: Decimals greater than 1 may be written as mixed numbers by taking the whole-number part of the decimal as the whole-number part of the mixed number. Treat the fraction part as in the general rule.

Examples

$$0.12 = \frac{12}{100} = \frac{12 \div 4}{100 \div 4} = \frac{3}{25}$$

$$2.314 = \frac{2314}{1000} = 2\frac{314}{1000}$$

Example

$$5.02 = 5\frac{2}{100} = 5\frac{1}{50}$$

Fractions into decimals

To change a fraction to a decimal, divide the numerator by the denominator.

NOTE: For mixed numbers, you may take the whole-number part of the mixed number as the whole-number part of the decimal. Treat the fraction part as in the general rule.

Examples

$$\frac{5}{8} = 5 \div 8$$

$$
\begin{array}{r}
0.625 \\
8\overline{)5.000} \\
\underline{4\ 8} \\
20 \\
\underline{16} \\
40 \\
\underline{40}
\end{array}
$$

$$\frac{11}{4} = 11 \div 4$$

$$
\begin{array}{r}
2.75 \\
4\overline{)11.00} \\
\underline{8} \\
3\ 0 \\
\underline{2\ 8} \\
20 \\
20
\end{array}
$$

Example

$$4\frac{1}{2} = 4 + \left(1 \div 2\right)$$

$$
\begin{array}{r}
0.5 \\
2\overline{)1.0} \\
\underline{1\ 0}
\end{array}
$$

$$4\frac{1}{2} = 4.5$$

Repeating decimals

If the same remainder is encountered more than once after you begin to "bring down" zeros, the decimal will repeat the same pattern of digits over and over. This may be indicated by putting a bar over the digits that repeat.

HINT: All fractions with whole-number numerators and denominators either terminate (the remainder when you divide is zero) or repeat a set of digits. The fraction will *always* terminate if the denominator of the fraction has only the prime factors 2 and 5—so fractions with denominators of 2, 10, 4, 8, 20, 25, and so forth terminate. Otherwise the fraction will repeat with a period (the number of digits that repeat) that is less than the denominator.

Examples

The denominator of $\frac{1}{3}$ has the prime factor 3, so it repeats with a period less than 3 (its actual period is 1).

The denominator of $\frac{11}{40}$ has the factors $2^3 \times 5$, so it terminates.

The denominator of $\frac{2}{7}$ has the prime factor 7, so it repeats with a period less than 7 (its actual period is 6).

The denominator of $\frac{5}{9}$ has the prime factors 3^2, so it repeats with a period less than 9 (its actual period is 1).

Examples

$$\frac{1}{3} = 1 \div 3 \qquad \frac{3}{11} = 3 \div 11 \qquad \frac{2}{7} = 2 \div 7$$

$$
\begin{array}{r}
0.3\overline{3} \\
3\overline{)1.00} \\
\underline{9} \\
10 \\
\underline{9} \\
1
\end{array}
$$

$0.3\overline{3}$ means
0.333333...

$$
\begin{array}{r}
0.2\overline{72} \\
11\overline{)3.0000} \\
\underline{2\ 2} \\
80 \\
\underline{77} \\
30 \\
\underline{22} \\
80 \\
\underline{77} \\
3
\end{array}
$$

$0.2\overline{72}$ or $0.\overline{27}$ means
0.27272727...

$$
\begin{array}{r}
0.\overline{285714} \\
7\overline{)2.00000} \\
\underline{1\ 4} \\
60 \\
\underline{56} \\
40 \\
\underline{35} \\
50 \\
\underline{49} \\
10 \\
\underline{7} \\
30 \\
\underline{28} \\
2
\end{array}
$$

$0.\overline{285714}$ means
0.285714285714285714...

Write $\dfrac{21}{56}$ as a decimal.

A. Reduce the fraction.

$$\dfrac{21}{56} = \dfrac{3}{8}$$

B. Divide the denominator, 8, into 10 or one of its powers. Since 8 divides exactly into 1000, the decimal will end.

C. Divide the denominator into the numerator. Add zeros to the right of the decimal point in the dividend, as needed.

$$
\begin{array}{r}
375 \\
8\overline{)3.000} \\
\underline{2\,4} \\
60 \\
\underline{56} \\
40 \\
\underline{40}
\end{array}
$$

D. Position the decimal point. There are three places in the dividend and no places in the divisor. Therefore, there will be three places in the quotient.

$$\dfrac{21}{56} = 0.375$$

Write $\dfrac{10}{12}$ as a decimal.

A. Reduce the fraction.

$$\dfrac{10}{12} = \dfrac{5}{6}$$

B. Divide the denominator into 10 or one of its powers. Since 6 will not divide exactly into 10, 100, 1000, ..., the decimal will not end.

C. Divide the denominator into the numerator. Add zeros to the right of the decimal point in the dividend, until the decimal begins to repeat.

$$
\begin{array}{r}
833... \\
6\overline{)5.000} \\
\underline{4\,8} \\
20 \\
\underline{18} \\
20 \\
\underline{18} \\
2
\end{array}
$$

D. Position the decimal point. We can use approximation to check on the final location of the decimal point. $5 \div 6$ is close to $6 \div 6$, which is 1. Our answer should be close to 1, which it is.

$$\dfrac{10}{12} = 0.833...$$

The 3 repeats. It is called the repetend. Placing a bar over the repetend indicates that it repeats. So, $\dfrac{10}{12} = 0.8\overline{3}$.

Fraction-Decimal Equivalents

$\frac{1}{16} = 0.0625$	$\frac{1}{3} = 0.\overline{3}$	$\frac{2}{3} = 0.\overline{6}$	$\frac{15}{16} = 0.9375$	$\frac{3}{5} = 0.6$
$\frac{1}{8} = 0.125$	$\frac{3}{8} = 0.375$	$\frac{11}{16} = 0.6875$	$\frac{1}{10} = 0.1$	$\frac{7}{10} = 0.7$
$\frac{1}{6} = 0.1\overline{6}$	$\frac{7}{16} = 0.4375$	$\frac{3}{4} = 0.75$	$\frac{1}{5} = 0.2$	$\frac{4}{5} = 0.8$
$\frac{3}{16} = 0.1875$	$\frac{1}{2} = 0.5$	$\frac{13}{16} = 0.8125$	$\frac{3}{10} = 0.3$	$\frac{9}{10} = 0.9$
$\frac{1}{4} = 0.25$	$\frac{9}{16} = 0.5625$	$\frac{5}{6} = 0.8\overline{3}$	$\frac{2}{5} = 0.4$	$\frac{10}{10} = 1.0$
$\frac{5}{16} = 0.3125$	$\frac{5}{8} = 0.625$	$\frac{7}{8} = 0.875$	$\frac{1}{2} = 0.5$	

Write 2.56 as a fraction.

METHOD 1

A. Expand the decimal.

2.56 = 2 ones + 5 tenths + 6 hundredths

$$2.56 = 2 + \frac{5}{10} + \frac{6}{100}$$

B. Add the numbers.

$$2 + \frac{5}{10} + \frac{6}{100} = \frac{200}{100} + \frac{50}{100} + \frac{6}{100} = \frac{256}{100}$$

C. Reduce the fraction.

$$\frac{256}{100} = \frac{64}{25}$$

METHOD 2

A. Say the decimal aloud: two and fifty-six hundredths.

B. Write as a mixed number:

$$2\frac{56}{100}$$

C. Write as an improper fraction:

$$\frac{256}{100} = \frac{64}{25}$$

D. Reduce the fraction.

$$\frac{256}{100} = \frac{64}{25}$$

Write $1.376376\ldots$ as a fraction.

A. Count the number of places in the part of the decimal that repeats. Since 376 repeats, there are 3 places.

B. Multiply the decimal by 10 raised to that power. 3 places means 10^3 or $10 \times 10 \times 10$.
$1.376376\ldots \times 10 \times 10 \times 10 = 1376.376\ldots$

C. Subtract the smaller decimal from the larger.

$$\begin{array}{r} 1376.376\ldots \\ - \quad 1.376376\ldots \\ \hline 1375. \end{array}$$

D. Divide the result by the power of 10 used in step B (10^3) minus one.

$$\left(10 \times 10 \times 10\right) - 1 = 999$$

$$1375 \div 999 = \frac{1375}{999}$$

$\dfrac{16.1}{2.3}$

A. Division problems are easier to do by hand if they are written in the form that corresponds to vertical form for addition, subtraction, and multiplication. This is sometimes called "example form." Rewrite the problem in example form.

$$2.3\overline{)16.1}$$

B. Division by a whole number is accomplished by dividing as if both the *divisor* (the number that is being divided by) and the *dividend* (the number that is being divided into) are whole numbers. The decimal point in the quotient then lines up with the decimal point in the dividend. The quotient will not change if both the divisor and the dividend are multiplied by the same number. Multiply each number by the power of 10 required to move the decimal point to the right of the divisor. For 2.3 the power is 10^1.

$$2.3\overline{)16.1}$$

C. In this problem, both the divisor and the dividend are changed to whole numbers by multiplication, so the division is completed in the same way as for whole numbers.

$$\begin{array}{r} 7 \\ 2.3\overline{)16.1} \\ \underline{16\ 1} \end{array}$$

In this case, there is no remainder. Had there been a remainder of 3, for instance, it could *not* have been written with the quotient as "R3." Instead, one would need to insert more zeros after the dividend and continue dividing.

$$\frac{23.4}{0.32}$$

A. Rewrite in example form.

$$0.32\overline{)23.4}$$

B. There are 2 decimal places in the divisor, so both the divisor and the dividend must be multiplied by 10^2. This has the effect of "moving the decimal points" each 2 places to the right. Since there is only 1 decimal place in the dividend, however, it is necessary to insert a zero to locate the "new" decimal point.

$$0.\underset{\smile}{32}.\overline{)23.40}.$$

C. Now divide as with whole numbers.

$$\begin{array}{r} 73 \\ 0.\underset{\smile}{32}.\overline{)23.40}. \\ \underline{22\,4} \\ 1\,00 \\ \underline{96} \\ 4 \end{array}$$

Since there is a remainder, it is necessary to insert zeros and keep dividing until (1) you do not require any greater precision; that is, you have as many decimal places as you need; (2) the division terminates because the remainder is 0; or (3) you

reach the same remainder for the second time, which indicates that you have found all of the digits that repeat.

$$\begin{array}{r} 73.125 \\ 0.\underset{\smile}{32}.\overline{)23.40}.000 \\ \underline{22\,4} \\ 1\,00 \\ \underline{96} \\ 4\,0 \\ \underline{3\,2} \\ 80 \\ \underline{64} \\ 160 \\ \underline{160} \end{array}$$

Ratio and percent

Ratio. A *ratio* is a comparison of two quantities by division; frequently, a ratio is also a rate, such as miles per gallon. If you get 37 miles per gallon, then for each gallon of gasoline you use, you can expect to drive 37 miles. Such a ratio is often written as a fraction.

$$\frac{\text{number of mi.}}{\text{number of gal.}} = \frac{37}{1} \text{ or } \frac{\text{number of gal.}}{\text{number of mi.}} = \frac{1}{37}$$

When two ratios are equal, the statement of that equality is a *proportion*. For example, if you can buy 4 apples for a dollar and 1 apple for a quarter, this can be shown by a proportion.

$$\frac{\text{apples}}{\text{cost}} = \frac{4}{1.00} = \frac{1}{0.25} \text{ or } \frac{\text{cost}}{\text{apples}} = \frac{1.00}{4} = \frac{0.25}{1}$$

Proportions are often useful in problem-solving situations.

$$\frac{3}{4} = \frac{6}{?}$$

METHOD 1

A. Rename $\frac{3}{4}$ by multiplying by a fraction form for 1.

B. Since the numerator of the renamed fraction must be 6, the fraction form needed for 1 is $\frac{2}{2}$.

C. $\frac{3}{4} \times \frac{2}{2} = \frac{6}{8}$ so $\frac{3}{4} = \frac{6}{8}$

METHOD 2

A. In a proportion, the product of the numerator of one ratio and the denominator of the other is equal to the product of the denominator of the first with the numerator of the second.

B. Therefore, $3 \times ? = 4 \times 6$
$$= 24$$

C. If 3 times some number is 24, determine the unknown number by dividing 24 by 3. The answer is $\frac{3}{4} = \frac{6}{8}$.

William can go 385 miles on 1 tank of gasoline. If his tank holds 11 gallons, how many gallons of gasoline will he use on a trip of 595 miles?

A. Write the problem as a *proportion*. A proportion is a statement that two *ratios* are equal. A ratio is one way to compare two amounts by division. Each ratio is a number of miles to a number of gallons. The first ratio is the number of miles per tank to the number of gallons per tank, or $\frac{385}{11}$. The second ratio is the number of miles on the trip to an unknown number of gallons. The unknown number is N. Thus, the proportion is

$$\frac{385}{11} = \frac{595}{N}$$

B. Solve the proportion. The easiest way to solve a proportion is to use the *cross-product rule:* In a proportion, the product of the numerator of the first ratio and the denominator of the second ratio is equal to the product of the denominator of the first ratio and the numerator of the second ratio. Accordingly, you can rewrite the proportion as

$$385 \times N = 11 \times 595$$

C. Carry out any multiplication that you can.

$$385 \times N = 6545$$

D. If $385 \times N = 6545$, then

$$N = \frac{6545}{385} = 17$$

The answer is 17 gallons of gasoline.

Percent. A *percent* is a ratio of some quantity to 100. Percents are usually written with a percent sign, %, instead of as fractions. A percent is also equivalent to hundredths, since hundredths are a way of writing fractions with denominators of 100.

Write 37% as a fraction and as a decimal.

A. The numerator of the fraction is 37 and the denominator is 100.

$$37\% = \frac{37}{100}$$

B. 37% is the same as 37 hundredths.

$$37\% = 0.37$$

Find 40% of 150.

METHOD 1

A. Rewrite 40% as a fraction.

$$40\% = \frac{40}{100}$$

B. Simplify.

$$\frac{40}{100} = \frac{2}{5}$$

C. Multiply.

$$\frac{2}{5} \times 150 = \frac{300}{5} = 60$$

METHOD 2

A. Rewrite 40% as hundredths.

$$40\% = 0.40$$

B. Multiply.

$$\begin{array}{r} 150 \\ \times\, 0.40 \\ \hline 60.00 \end{array}$$

METHOD 3

A. A percent problem can always be rewritten as a proportion.

$$\frac{40}{100} = \frac{?}{150}$$

B. Rewrite the proportion as a multiplication problem.

$$40 \times 150 = 100 \times ?$$
$$\text{or } 100 \times ? = 6000$$

C. Solve by dividing 6000 by 100. The quotient is 60.

What percent is 40 of 64?

METHOD 1

A. Use the proportion idea.

$$\frac{40}{64} = \frac{?}{100}$$

B. Rewrite as

$$40 \times 100 = 64 \times ?$$
or $64 \times ? = 4000$.

C. Divide by 64.

$$4000 \div 64 = 62.5$$

40 is 62.5% of 64.

METHOD 2

A. Think of the unknown percent as a decimal.

$$? \times 64 = 40$$

B. Divide 40 by 64.

$$64\overline{)40.000} \quad 0.625$$

C. Rewrite the quotient as a percent. The answer is 62.5%.

18 is 24% of what number?

A. Write a proportion.

$$\frac{18}{?} = \frac{24}{100}$$

B. Rewrite as a multiplication problem.

$$18 \times 100 = ? \times 24$$
or $? \times 24 = 1800$

C. Divide by 24. The quotient is 75. Therefore, 18 is 24% of 75.

Find 37% of 250.

A. A *percent* is a ratio of a whole number to 100, so 37% is the ratio $\frac{37}{100}$. Percent problems can be solved in many ways. You may use decimals, for example, to rewrite this problem as 0.37×250.

The examples here will use the proportion method for solution because it is a useful way to solve practical problems. Think not only of 37% as a ratio, but also of 250 as a ratio.

In this context, the problem "find 37% of 250" may be solved by thinking "37 is to 100 as what number (N) is to 250?"

$$\frac{37}{100} = \frac{N}{250}$$

B. Rewrite using the cross-product rule and complete any multiplication that you can.

$$37 \times 250 = 100 \times N$$
$$9250 = 100 \times N$$

C. Divide by 100 to find N.

$$N = \frac{9250}{100} = 92.5$$

The answer is 92.5.

Notice that this method involves multiplication by whole numbers only. Also, division by 100 is simple.

What percent of 400 is 260?

A. Set up a proportion.

$$\frac{260}{400} = \frac{N}{100}$$

The ratio $\frac{N}{100}$ is the same as N%.

B. Use the cross-product rule.

$$260 \times 100 = 400 \times N$$
$$26000 = 400 \times N$$

C. Divide by 400.

$$N = \frac{26000}{400} = 65$$

The answer is 65%.

52.5 is 35% of what number?

A. Set up a proportion.

$$\frac{52.5}{N} = \frac{35}{100}$$

B. Use the cross-product rule.

$$52.5 \times 100 = N \times 35$$
$$5250 = N \times 35$$

C. Divide by 35.

$$N = \frac{5250}{35} = 150$$

The answer is 150.

Problem solving with percents

A shirt that normally sells for $18 is offered at a 15% discount. How much will you have to pay?

METHOD 1

A. Find 15% of 18 by one of the methods shown earlier. Here conversion to a decimal and multiplication will be used.

$$\begin{array}{r} 18 \\ \times\, 0.15 \\ \hline 2.7 \end{array}$$

B. The answer is the amount of the discount: $2.70. A discount is a *percent of decrease*, which means that the *percentage* (the amount that is a percent of a number) must be

subtracted from the original amount.

$$\begin{array}{r} 18.00 \\ -\, 2.70 \\ \hline 15.30 \end{array}$$

The amount that you will pay is $15.30.

METHOD 2

A. A percent of decrease may be subtracted from 100% before calculating the amount after the decrease. This is often easier to do than subtracting the percentage of decrease from the original amount, since, for example, most people can subtract 15 from 100 in their heads to get 85.

B. Find 85% of 18 by any of the methods used earlier. Here, for comparison, the proportion method will be used instead of the multiplication method that was used in Method 1.

$$\frac{85}{100} = \frac{?}{18}$$

C. Complete the solution.
$$85 \times 18 = 100 \times ?$$
or $100 \times ? = 1530$
Dividing by 100 can be accomplished by "moving the decimal point" to the left 2 places, so the answer is $15.30.

In a state where sales tax is 5¼%, what total must you pay on a purchase of $16.50?

METHOD 1

A. Find the percentage. Here the proportion method is used.

$$\frac{5.25}{100} = \frac{?}{16.5}$$
$$100 \times ? = 86.625$$
$$? = 0.86625$$

B. Since this is a money problem, the percentage must be rounded up to the next higher cent. The percentage is $0.87.

C. A sales tax is a *percent of increase*, so the percentage must be *added* to the original amount to get the answer.

$$\begin{array}{r} 16.50 \\ +\, 0.87 \\ \hline 17.37 \end{array}$$

METHOD 2

A. For a percent of increase, you can add the percent to 100% before you begin to compute. This is easy to do in your head. Therefore, you can compute the final amount by using $105\frac{1}{4}\%$.

B. A percent greater than 100 percent may be written as a decimal that is greater than 1. For example, $105\frac{1}{4}\%$ is equivalent to 1.0525.

C. Complete the solution by finding $105\frac{1}{4}\%$ of $16.50.

$$\begin{array}{r} 16.5 \\ \times\, 1.0525 \\ \hline 17.36625 \end{array}$$

The answer is $17.37.

Interest problems

Find the amount of interest on $1500 at a rate of 9% for 6 months.

METHOD 1

A. The interest formula is $i = prt$ where i is the interest in dollars, p is the amount of money on which interest is being paid (the *principal*), r is the rate expressed as a percent, and t is the time in years. Since t is in months, convert 6 months to years.
$$\frac{6}{12} = \frac{1}{2}$$
The time is $\frac{1}{2}$ year.

B. Substitute into the formula, using the ratio form of percent.
$$i = 1500 \times \frac{9}{100} \times \frac{1}{2}$$

C. Cancel any factors you can and multiply.
$$i = 15 \times 9 \times \frac{1}{2} = \frac{135}{2} = 67\frac{1}{2}$$
The answer is $67.50.

METHOD 2

A. If you are using a calculator it will be easier to work with decimals than with ratios. Use 0.09 for 9% and 0.5 for $\frac{1}{2}$.

B. Use the formula and multiply.
$$i = 1500 \times 0.09 \times 0.5 = 67.5$$
The interest is $67.50.

Find the rate of interest if the interest is $55, the principal is $1000, and the time is 11 months.

METHOD 1

A. The interest formula can be rewritten in several ways by dividing both sides of the formula by one of the factors on the right side.
$$r = \frac{i}{p \times t}$$
$$p = \frac{i}{r \times t}$$
$$t = \frac{i}{p \times r}$$
The most useful form for this problem is the first,
$$r = \frac{i}{p \times t}$$

B. Convert the time to years and substitute into the formula.
$$t = \frac{11}{12}$$
$$r = \frac{55}{1000 \times \frac{11}{12}}$$

C. Multiply and rewrite the fraction as a ratio of some number to 100.
$$r = \frac{6}{100}$$
The answer is 6%.

METHOD 2

A. If you have a calculator it is easier to work with
$$t = \frac{i}{p \times r}$$
which avoids the problem of having to convert $\frac{11}{12}$ to a decimal.
$$\frac{11}{12} = \frac{55}{1000 \times r}$$

B. Use the cross-product rule.
$$11 \times \left(1000 \times r\right) = 12 \times 55$$
$$11000 \times r = 660$$

C. Divide by 11000.
$$r = 0.06$$
The answer is 6%.

Find the amount of money that will result from investing $2500 for 9 months at 10% when the interest is computed every 3 months and left in the account.

A. When interest is collected on the interest, it is known as *compound interest*. While you can calculate compound interest by repeatedly calculating the amount for each period, it is easier to use the *compound interest formula:*
$$A = p \times \left(1 + i\right)^n$$
where A is the amount (principal plus interest), p is the original principal, i is interest rate per period of compounding, and n is the number of periods. To use the formula, convert the interest rate, which is given per year, to a per period ratio. Since the period is 3 months, the per period rate is $\frac{3}{12} \times \frac{10}{100} = \frac{25}{1000} = 2.5\%$. In 9 months, there are 3 3-month periods.

B. Substitute into the formula.
$$A = 2500 \times \left(1 + 0.025\right)^3$$
$$= 2500 \times 1.0768906$$
$$= 2692.2265$$

The amount is $2692.23.

Discounts and taxes

How much does a dress cost if its original price was $80 but it is now on sale at a discount of 20%?

METHOD 1

A. Find 20% of 80.

20% of 80 = 16

B. Subtract 16 from 80.

80 − 16 = 64

The dress will cost $64.

METHOD 2

A. A discount is always a *percent of decrease.* You can solve percent-of-decrease problems in one step by subtracting the percent discount from 100% and then multiplying.

100% − 20% = 80%

B. Multiply.

80 × 0.80 = 64

The dress will cost $64.

Find the total amount for a $50 purchase if the sales tax is $5\frac{1}{2}$%.

A. A sales tax is a *percent of increase,* so the rate of the tax may be added to 100%.

$100\% + 5\frac{1}{2}\% = 105\frac{1}{2}\%$

B. Convert $105\frac{1}{2}$% to a decimal and multiply.

50 × 1.055 = 52.75

The answer is $52.75.

Measurement

What is the precision of a measurement of 5 centimeters when the measurement is made with a ruler that shows only centimeters and millimeters?

A. The *precision* of any measurement is the smallest unit used in making the measurement. In this case it is 1 millimeter.

B. The number of *significant digits* should be the same as the total number of units used. There are two significant digits in 50 mm.

In cm, the measurement should be shown as 5.0. The result can also be expressed in scientific notation (see box on page 283) as 5.0×10^0.

What is the greatest possible error in a measurement of 28.57 meters?

A. Determine the precision of the measurement. Since the measurement is written as 28.57 meters, it was made by measuring to the nearest 0.01 meter.

B. The *greatest possible error* is one-half the precision (the measurement is closer to 0.57 than to 0.56 or 0.58). One-half of 0.01 meter is 0.005 meter, so that is the greatest possible error.

What is the relative error in a measurement of 29 centimeters?

A. Determine the greatest possible error. Since the measurement is expressed to the nearest centimeter, the greatest possible error is one-half of 1 centimeter, or 0.5 cm.

B. The *relative error* is the greatest possible error divided by the measurement. Therefore, the relative error is

$$\frac{0.5}{29} = \frac{1}{58}$$

Handheld calculators

Calculators are useful in many different situations. Most people use one at least sometimes in the home, and many schools now permit students to use calculators to help them with their homework and during exams.

Handheld calculators are so inexpensive that most families and many schools now have them. These calculators make problems with addition, subtraction, multiplication, and division of whole numbers very easy. Calculators can also be used to solve problems involving decimals and percents, but special techniques must be employed to solve problems involving fractions.

Although no two calculators are exactly alike, all have some characteristics in common. For example, on all calculators, problems involving decimals are solved in the same way as problems involving whole numbers. The only difference is that the decimal point key must be depressed when needed.

Simple addition, subtraction, multiplication, and division problems are solved by depressing the correct keys for the numbers, operations, or symbols. Often a more complicated problem must be broken down into a series of simpler problems, but in many cases problems can be solved more easily by attacking the complicated problem in the proper manner. Some methods are detailed on the two pages that follow.

Here are some specific things to look for on the calculator you are using.

Does it have a percent key? Most calculators have a percent key that permits percents to be entered as whole numbers in multiplication. If your calculator has a percent key, you can find the percent of a number by entering the number, entering ×, entering the amount of the percent, and then using the

percent key instead of =. To find 25% of 60, you would enter

$$6 \quad 0 \quad \times \quad 2 \quad 5 \quad \% \, .$$

If your calculator does not have a percent key, you must convert the percent to a decimal, enter the number, the ×, the decimal, and the =.

$$6 \quad 0 \quad \times \quad . \quad 2 \quad 5 \quad =$$

Which key causes the calculator to keep repeating an operation? All calculators have a key that will cause the same number to be added, subtracted, multiplied, or divided over and over, but the key that does this varies from calculator to calculator. The most common key for this is =. You can check to see if this works on your calculator by pressing

$$2 \quad \times \quad 3 \quad = \quad = \quad =$$

If = is the *accumulator key,* the display panel should show

$$2 \quad 3 \quad 6 \quad 12 \quad 24.$$

Notice that on most calculators, the number that is held constant is the *first* number entered, not the second. If the second number entered had been held constant, the display would have been

$$2 \quad 3 \quad 6 \quad 18 \quad 54.$$

Does your calculator use a floating decimal point display for large numbers? On more expensive calculators, an answer may surprise you by being written in a different notation from the familiar one. In that case, the calculator has gone into a "floating-point" notation because it does not have enough room on the display to give the answer. If a calculator has the ability to display up to eight digits, which is common, it will give a floating-point answer for any product greater than 9999 × 10,000. For example, try

$$\boxed{1}\boxed{0}\boxed{0}\boxed{0}\boxed{0}\boxed{\times}\boxed{1}\boxed{0}\boxed{0}\boxed{0}\boxed{0}\boxed{=}.$$

In the floating-point system, the display will read something like

1. × 10 08 or 1. E 8.

If the calculator is not a floating-point calculator and has room to display only eight digits, an error message will appear, for example E, along with a decimal such as 1.000000; or the calculator may be unable to provide an answer.

Using your calculator.

Reading floating-point notation. The first number in a floating-point system is a factor. The number after the × 10 or the E is an exponent. The base of the exponent is always 10. Thus the number 1. E 8 means 1 times 10^8. The number 10^8 is written as 1 followed by 8 zeros, so

1. E 8 = 100,000,000.

A number such as 2.8374 E 10 means

2.8374 × 10,000,000,000 = 28,374,000,000.

Understanding about rounding. The calculator has only a limited space to display answers, so infinite decimals and all of the digits of a floating-point factor cannot be displayed. Most calculators do not round, however. If you divide 10 by 6, the answer will be given as 1.6666666, although the answer to the nearest ten millionth is actually 1.6666667. Similarly, if you multiply 13,131,131 by 20 in a floating-point system, the answer will be shown as 2.6262 E 8, although the correct answer to the nearest ten thousand is 262,630,000. In some cases, you will want to correct the calculator's rounding to improve accuracy. Most of the time, however, it is satisfactory to use one less place and round the answer that is shown on the calculator; in other words, change 1.6666666 to 1.6666667 or 2.6262 E 8 to 262,600,000. Notice that in a series of calculations, the errors produced by dropping digits will all tend to be in the same direction, while rounded subcalculations will sometimes be too great and sometimes be too small, tending to average out the error.

WARNING
You get out what you put in

The most common errors are the result of one of two mistakes.
1. You may punch the wrong key accidentally. These errors can be minimized by using as few keys as possible and by always checking your result by estimating the answer in your head as you do the problem.
2. You may set up the problem the wrong way. Make sure that the answer you get is reasonable for the problem situation. For example, determine in advance whether the answer will be larger or smaller than the largest number in the problem.

Adding columns. Adding on a calculator is more accurate and faster if you can punch in fewer numbers. You can perform easy operations mentally as you go along. For example, here is a way to group an addition problem.

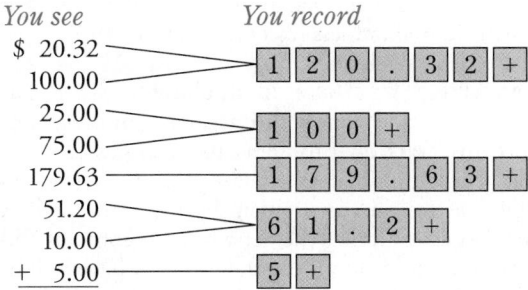

The display should show 466.15, the correct answer. Note that you do not need to enter decimal points and zeros if there are only zeros after the decimal point.
Using the distributive property. The product of a sum is equal to the sum of the products. For example,

$$(3 \times 2) + (3 \times 5) = 3 \times (2 + 5)$$
$$6 \quad + \quad 15 \quad = 3 \times \quad 7$$
$$21 = 21$$

Technically, this is known as *the distributive property of multiplication over addition*. It also applies for multiplication over subtraction.

$$(4 \times 6) - (4 \times 1) = 4 \times (6 - 1)$$
$$24 \quad - \quad 4 \quad = 4 \times \quad 5$$
$$20 = 20$$

Here is an example of how this property can save time and work. Suppose you know the daily amount 5 persons earned in a small business:

Harold	$ 9
Marianne	$31
Dale	$21
Al	$27
Kathy	$25

You need to calculate the total amount paid by the company for a 5-day workweek. The most obvious way is to multiply each daily salary by 5 and then add the totals:

$$5 \times \$\ 9 = \$\ 45$$
$$5 \times \$31 = \$155$$
$$5 \times \$21 = \$105$$
$$5 \times \$27 = \$135$$
$$5 \times \$25 = \underline{\$125}$$
$$\$565$$

Since all the daily income figures are to be multiplied by the same factor, however, you can add the daily salary figures and then multiply the total by 5. Enter:

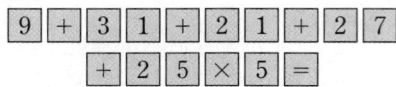

The display should show 565, which means $565. Both ways give the same result, but the second is much shorter and less likely to produce errors, especially on a calculator.

Converting fractions to decimals. Since calculators do not work with fractions, you must convert any fraction problems to decimals. This is easily accomplished by dividing the numerator of each fraction in the problem by the denominator. In most cases (unless the denominator contains factors of 2 and 5 only), the fraction will have a nonterminating decimal expansion and the calculator will drop all digits after the seventh or eighth. Therefore, your answer will be approximate instead of exact.

$$\frac{3}{4} \times \frac{2}{3} = .75 \times 0.6666666 = 0.4999999$$

If you need a more accurate answer, however, you can save the conversion to decimals to the end of the problem. For example, the more accurate way to multiply $\frac{2}{3}$ by $\frac{3}{4}$ is to punch in

record the answer and punch in

and record the answer, then divide the first

answer by the second. In this case, however, you can probably perform the first operations in your head and proceed directly to punch in

which will give a display of 0.5. This answer is the exact one.

Using percents of increase and decrease. When a percentage is to be added to an amount (as in a sales-tax situation), it is a *percent of increase*. When a percentage is to be subtracted from an amount (as in a discount situation), it is a *percent of decrease*. In both cases, it is generally better to solve problems by first adding the given percent to 100% or subtracting it from 100% before performing the calculation. For example, if you want to find the amount of a purchase when the sales tax is $5\frac{1}{4}$%, multiply the amount before the tax by 105.25 and then press the % key (if you do not have a % key, multiply by 1.0525 and press the = key). The result is the same as multiplying by $5\frac{1}{4}$% and then adding the result to the original amount, but the calculation is much easier. Similarly, to find the amount of a purchase after a discount of 20%, it is easier to first subtract 20% from 100% to get 80% (which you can do in your head). Then multiply the amount of the purchase by 80 and press the % key (or multiply the amount of the purchase by .8 and press the = key).

Learning to use the calculator's memory. Almost all handheld calculators have a memory feature, but surveys have shown that most people do not use it. The memory features of calculators usually differ. Use the instructions that come with the calculator. Here is an example of how one calculator works. To calculate $(47 \times 12) + (58 \div 4) - (69 \times 8)$, first clear the memory and then press the following keys:

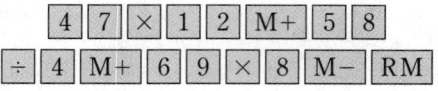

The advantage of using the memory over working without it is in what you see displayed on the screen. After you press M+ for the first time, you will see 564, which is the product of 47 and 12; the second time you press M+ you will see the quotient of 58 divided by 4, 14.5; when you press M− you will see the product of 69 and 8, 552. Only when you press RM will the final answer, 26.5, appear.

Scientific notation and calculators

Scientists and engineers regularly use *scientific notation* to show large and small numbers. Scientific notation may also be used to show the number of significant digits in a number. In scientific notation, a number is shown as a product. One factor is a number between 1 and 10, called the *mantissa*. The other factor is a power of 10. If the number shown is exactly a power of 10, the mantissa of 1 is omitted.

Ordinary notation	Scientific notation
5000	5×10^3
4978	4.978×10^3
49,780	4.978×10^4
49,78<u>0</u>	4.9780×10^4

(NOTE: The line under the 0 in 4.9780 means that the zero is significant. The same information is provided by showing the zero in scientific notation.)

5,000,000,000	5×10^9
10,000,000,000	10^{10}
1	10^0
0.1	10^{-1}
0.20	2.0×10^{-1}
0.0000007	7×10^{-7}
0.00000073	7.3×10^{-7}

Because scientific notation is a compact way to express large numbers, a form of it is used in many handheld calculators and in some computer languages. The displays of calculators and computers cannot indicate exponents as raised numerals, however, so the system is modified to allow for all the characters to be shown on the same line. In this form, scientific notation is often called *floating-point notation*. In the floating-point system, the exponent is shown with the letter E and the times sign may be omitted (although some calculators include the times sign). Often, the sign of the number, positive or negative, is shown.

Ordinary notation	Scientific notation	Floating point
5,000,000,000	5×10^9	+ 5 E+9
3,892,405,000	3.892405×10^9	+ 3.892405 E+9
0.0000957	9.57×10^{-5}	+ 9.57 E−5
−3,028	-3.028×10^3	−3.028 E+3
−0.000054	-5.4×10^{-5}	−5.4 E−5

(NOTE: A handheld calculator will automatically round a number to the number of places that can be shown on its display. Also, many handheld calculators will automatically show very large or small numbers in floating-point notation. Therefore, an answer of 3,892,405,000 may be shown on the calculator as 3.8924 E+9 instead of + 3.892405 E+9.)

Multiplication and division in scientific notation

To multiply
Multiply the mantissas; add the exponents. You may have to adjust the mantissa of the product to get it between 1 and 10 again.
(NOTE: If significant digits are important, the mantissa of the product should be rounded to show only the number of significant digits in the factor with the least number of significant digits.)
$(4.30 \times 10^{-7}) \times (5.329 \times 10^3) = (4.30 \times 5.329) \times 10^{-7+3}$
$= 22.9147 \times 10^{-4}$
$= 2.29147 \times 10^{-3}$,
which rounds to 2.29×10^{-3}.

Examples
$(5.83 \times 10^7) \times (3.07 \times 10^5)$ $= (5.83 \times 3.07) \times 10^{7+5}$
$= 17.8981 \times 10^{12}$
$= 1.78981 \times 10^{13}$

$(2.04 \times 10^{-3}) \times (3.12 \times 10^{-4}) = (2.04 \times 3.12) \times 10^{-3+(-4)}$
$= 6.3648 \times 10^{-7}$

$(7.59 \times 10^4) \times (8.27 \times 10^{-3})$ $= (7.59 \times 8.27) \times 10^{4+(-3)}$
$= 62.7693 \times 10$
$= 6.27693 \times 10^2$

To divide
Divide the mantissa; subtract the exponents. You may have to adjust the mantissa of the quotient to get it between 1 and 10 again.

Examples
$(8.214 \times 10^8) \div (2.24 \times 10^3)$ $= (8.214 \div 2.24) \times 10^{8-3}$
$= 3.67 \times 10^5$ (rounded to two places)

$(5.19 \times 10^5) \div (4.5 \times 10^{-2})$ $= (5.19 \div 4.5) \times 10^{5-(-2)}$
$= 1.2 \times 10^7$ (rounded to one place)

$(7.35 \times 10^{-3}) \div (9.323 \times 10^{-7}) = (7.35 \div 9.323) \times 10^{-3-(-7)}$
$= 0.788 \times 10^4$ (rounded to three places)
$= 7.88 \times 10^3$.

Square roots and the Pythagorean theorem

The two sides of a right triangle that make up the right angle measure 9 centimeters and 40 centimeters. What is the length of the side opposite the right angle (the *hypotenuse*)?

A. This problem can be solved by using *the Pythagorean theorem,* which states that in a right triangle the square of the hypotenuse is equal to the sum of the squares of the two sides.

Therefore, if you call the length of the hypotenuse c, the following relationship is true:

$$c^2 = 9^2 + 40^2$$
$$= 81 + 1600$$
$$= 1681$$

B. Find the square root of 1681. This is most easily accomplished on a calculator. The result is 41.

Find the square root of 30,679 to the nearest tenth without using the square root key on a calculator.

A. Estimate the square root. Since 100×100 is 10,000, the square root will be larger than 100. Use 150 as an estimate.

B. Divide the original number by your estimate.

$$\frac{30679}{150} = 204.52666$$

C. Average the quotient and your estimate. Find the average to 1 significant digit more than your original estimate. Since your estimate of 150 has 2 significant digits, find the average to 3 significant digits.

$$\frac{(150 + 204.5)}{2} = 177.25,$$
which rounds to 177.

D. Use the average as a new estimate and repeat steps A, B, and C.

$$\frac{30679}{177} = 173.32768$$

$$\frac{(177 + 173.33)}{2} = 175.165,$$
which rounds to 175.2.

E. Use that result as a new average and keep repeating steps, A, B, C, and D until the average has "settled down" in the hundredths place. Notice that the tens place, 7, has already "settled down," so the square root of 30,679 to the nearest hundred is 200.

$$\frac{30679}{175.2} = 175.10844$$
$$\frac{(175.2 + 175.108)}{2} = 175.15$$
which rounds to 175.15.
$$\frac{30679}{175.15} = 175.15843$$

Since the hundredths place in 175.15 and in 175.15843 is the same, you have established that the square root to the nearest tenth is 175.2, which is 175.15 rounded to the nearest tenth.

Note that this method, which is called the *method of iteration* (repetition), is considerably easier to remember than the traditional square-root algorithm. Because this method gets you close to the correct answer very quickly, the closeness of the original estimate to the actual square root is not very important. Suppose that your original estimate had been 100:

$$\frac{30679}{100} = 306.79$$
$$\frac{(100 + 306)}{2} = 203$$
$$\frac{30679}{200} = 153.395$$
$$\frac{(200 + 153.4)}{2} = 176.7$$
$$\frac{30679}{177} = 173.32768$$

This is, of course, the same point as was reached in step D, so the calculations proceed exactly as in step E. It only took one more iteration starting with a poor guess than it did starting with a good one.

Pre-algebra

The algebra that is studied in secondary schools has as its goals the ability to manipulate expressions containing variables; the ability to use equations and inequalities to solve problems; and the development of an introductory understanding of the different functions of a variable.

A *variable* is a letter or other sign used to represent any one of a set of numbers; thus, the variable x typically can represent any positive or negative number that can be expressed as a decimal, including infinite decimals such as π. (Although Greek letters are sometimes used as variables, π is a number, not a variable.)

Equations state that two expressions are equal. For example, $2x + 5 = 17$. *Inequalities* use signs such as < ("is less than") or > ("is greater than") to make statements. A *function* is a rule connecting the members of 2 sets. In algebra, most functions are expressed as equations in two variables, such as $y = 3x - 7$. Special notation for one of the variables is often used to indicate its functional nature, most commonly in expressions such as $f(x) = 3x - 7$, where $f(x)$, which is read f of x or f at x, means the same as y in the previous equation.

In algebra, multiplication is shown differently from the familiar × sign of arithmetic. Most commonly, the product of a number and a variable, or two variables, is shown by writing the two adjacent to each other, so $5a$ means $5 \times a$ and ab means $a \times b$. Sometimes a raised dot, •, is used to show multiplication.

Multiplication is also indicated simply by writing two numbers adjacent to each other in parentheses, as $(2)(3) = 6$, for example.

The laws of numbers

For any real numbers a, b, and c:

Closure
$a + b$ is a real number
$a \bullet b$ is a real number

Commutative law
$a + b = b + a$
$a \bullet b = b \bullet a$

Associative law
$a + (b + c) = (a + b) + c$
$a \bullet (b \bullet c) = (a \bullet b) \bullet c$

Identity elements
$a + 0 = a$
$a \bullet 1 = a$

Distributive law
$a \bullet (b + c) = a \bullet b + a \bullet c$

Laws of equality
Reflexive law $a = a$
Symmetric law   If $a = b$, then $b = a$
Transitive law   If $a = b$ and $b = c$, then $a = c$

Laws of equations
Addition   If $a = b$, then $a + c = b + c$
Subtraction   If $a = b$, then $a - c = b - c$
Multiplication   If $a = b$, then $a \bullet c = b \bullet c$
Division   If $a = b$, then $\dfrac{a}{c} = \dfrac{b}{c}$ unless $c = 0$

Inverse elements
For each a there exists a number $- a$ such that $a + (-a) = 0$
For each a (except 0) there exists a number $\dfrac{1}{a}$ such that $a \bullet \dfrac{1}{a} = 1$

Evaluate the expression k + 24 when k = 3.

A. Substitute 3 for k where k occurs in the expression.
$$3 + 24$$

B. Follow the correct order of operations.
$$3 + 24 = 27$$

Evaluate the expression 3m + 5 when m = 7.

A. Substitute 7 for m where m occurs in the expression.

$$3 \times 7 + 5$$

B. Follow the correct order of operations.

$$3 \times 7 + 5$$
$$21 + 5$$
$$26$$

The order of operations

Compute $\left(3 \cdot 4 + \dfrac{8}{2} - \left(\dfrac{3+7}{5} + \sqrt{10-1}\right)\right)^2 + 2 \cdot 8$

First:	Do everything in parentheses following the order of operations. If parentheses are nested (one set inside another), work from the inside set of parentheses to the outside set.	$\left(3 \cdot 4 + \dfrac{8}{2} - \left(\dfrac{10}{5} + \sqrt{9}\right)\right)^2 + 2 \cdot 8$
Second:	Treat the horizontal line in a fraction or in the square root symbol the same as another set of parentheses.	$\left(3 \cdot 4 + \dfrac{8}{2} - \left(2 + 3\right)\right)^2 + 2 \cdot 8$ $\left(3 \cdot 4 + \dfrac{8}{2} - 5\right)^2 + 2 \cdot 8$
Third:	Compute all powers as soon as possible.	$\left(12 + 4 - 5\right)^2 + 16$
Fourth:	Multiply and divide from left to right.	$11^2 + 16$
Fifth:	Add and subtract from left to right.	$121 + 16$ 137

Signed numbers. Algebra makes full use of the complex number system (see Handbook 2), but most secondary-school algebra is confined to real numbers (see box on next page). Operations with real numbers are more difficult than operations with whole numbers because numbers can be both positive and negative. A number on the number line is always less than any number to the right of it, so -3 is less than -1, for example. The *absolute value* of a real number is its distance from 0. Thus, the absolute value of -5 is 5 and the absolute value of $+7$ is 7. Absolute value is indicated by a pair of parallel lines | | that enclose the number. Therefore, $|-4|$ is the same as 4, $|+6|$ is the same as 6, and $|0|$ is the same as 0.

5 + (−2)

A. To add numbers with unlike signs, subtract the absolute value of the lesser number from the absolute value of the greater number.

$$|5| - |-2|$$
$$5 - 2$$
$$3$$

B. Affix the sign of the number with the greater absolute value. The answer is + 3.

Sets of numbers

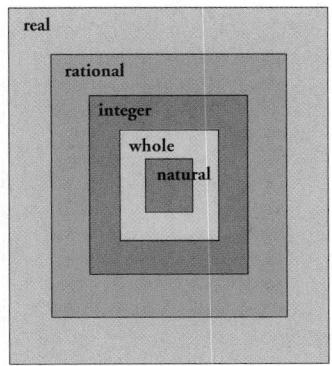

In algebra, mathematicians work with several different sets of numbers. Each set of numbers includes all the numbers in each of the sets above it.

Symbol	Name and description	Examples
N	**Natural numbers** (often called counting numbers): The numbers with which you count; the number of members in a nonempty set.	1, 2, 3, . . .
W	**Whole numbers** (sometimes called natural numbers): The natural numbers and 0; the number of members in any set.	0, 1, 2, . . .
I	**Integers:** Whole numbers and their opposites (or negatives).	. . . , −3, −2, −1, 0, 1, 2, 3, . . .
Q	**Rational numbers:** The quotients of any two integers (with the exception that dividing by 0 is not allowed).	$0, 3, \frac{1}{2}, \frac{3}{4}, 3.2, -\frac{7}{8}, -57,$ $-0.00001, -6\frac{2}{3}, 1,000,001$
R	**Real numbers:** Any numbers that can be represented by an infinite decimal (or equivalently, by a point on a line).	$0, 5, -8, \frac{3}{7}, \pi, \sqrt{2},$ $1.01001000100001...,$ $-\sqrt{137}$

$-4 + (-7)$

A. To add numbers with like signs, add the absolute values.

$$\left|-4\right| + \left|-7\right| = 11$$

B. Affix the sign of the numbers.

$$-4 + \left(-7\right) = -11$$

$5 - 9$

A. To subtract real numbers, replace the number to be subtracted with its *opposite* and add. The opposite of a real number is the number on the other side of 0 on the number line that has the same absolute value (the opposite of 0 is 0). Thus, the opposite of 9 is −9.

$$5 - 9 = 5 + \left(-9\right)$$

B.
$$5 + \left(-9\right) = -4$$

$$5(-3)$$

A. To multiply two real numbers, find the product of their absolute values.

$$|5| \cdot |-3| = 5 \cdot 3 = 15$$

B. If the signs of the numbers are different, the product is negative.

$$5(-3) = -15$$

$-\times-=+$

Filling a tank at $+3$ gal./min.

Five min. from now
$(+5)(+3) = +15$

$$(-8)(-4)$$

A.
$$|-8| \cdot |-4| = 8 \cdot 4 = 32$$

B. If the signs of the factors are the same, the product is positive.
$$(-8)(-4) = +32$$

Emptying a tank at -3 gal./min.

Five min. ago
$(-5)(-3) = +15$

$$(-5)(0)$$

The product of any real number and 0 is 0.

$$(-5)(0) = 0$$

$$\frac{-10}{5}$$

METHOD 1

A. To divide one real number by another, replace the number you are dividing with the inverse for multiplication (1 divided by the number) and multiply.

The multiplicative inverse is the same as the reciprocal.

$$(-10)/5 = -10 \cdot 1/5$$

$\frac{-10}{5}$ is often written as $(-10)/5$ in algebra.

B.
$$|-10| \cdot |1/5| = 2$$

C.
$$|-10| \cdot 1/5 = -2$$

METHOD 2

The fraction bar tells you to divide.

A. Divide -10 by 5.

B. $-10/5 = -2$

$$\frac{-35}{-7}$$

METHOD 1

A. $-35/-7 = -35 \cdot (-1/7)$

B. $|-35| \cdot |-1/7| = 5$

C. $-35 \cdot (-1/7) = +5$

METHOD 2

The fraction bar tells you to divide.

A. Divide -35 by -7.

B. $-35/-7 = 5$

Terms. In the expression 7 + m, 7 and m are called the terms of the expression because they are separated by an addition or subtraction sign. In 4x − 5 the terms are 4x and 5.

Like terms. Two terms are called like terms if their variable parts are the same. 2a and 3a are like terms. 2a and 3ab are not like terms because the variable parts of the values do not contain the same variables.

Simplify 3k + 4 + 2k

A. Combine like terms.

3k + 2k + 4

5k + 4

Simplify 3k − 5m − k − 2m

A. Combine like terms.

3k − k + (−5m − 2m)

2k + (−7m)

2k − 7m

Simplify 4k − 3 + 5k

A. Combine like terms.

4k + 5k − 3

9k − 3

Simplify 5k + 6m + 3k − 4m

A. Combine like terms.

5k + 3k + 6m − 4m

8k + 2m

Simplify 12k − 7 + 4 − 4k

A. Combine like terms.

12k − 4k − 7 + 4

8k − 3

Operations using order of operations, signed numbers, and absolute value

Evaluate expressions using multiplication and division before addition and subtraction from left to right.

2 − 4 × 3 = 2 − 12 = 2 + −12 = −10

3 × −2 + 6 = −6 + 6 = 0

If there are parentheses, brackets, and/or braces, evaluate them from the inside out using the rules for addition, subtraction, multiplication, and division.

These parentheses, brackets, and braces are called grouping symbols; they help you know what operations to use.

5 + (4 − −3 × 5)

5 + (4 − −3 × 5) = 5 + (4 − −15) =

5 + (4 + 15), so 5 + 19 = 23

Simplify $4 - (-2)(-1) + 7$

A. Perform the multiplication.
$$(-2)(-1) = 2$$
so
$$4 - 2 + 7$$

B. Perform the addition and subtraction from left to right.
$$4 - 2 + 7 = 2 + 7 = 9$$

Simplify $|-1|(-2) - 4$

A. Evaluate the absolute value.
$$|-1| = 1$$
so
$$1(-2) - 4$$

B. Perform the multiplication.
$$1(-2) = -2$$
so
$$-2 - 4$$

C. Perform the subtraction.
$$-2 - 4 = -2 + -4 = -6$$

Simplify $-6 - (-2)(-1)$

A. Perform the multiplication.
$$(-2)(-1) = 2$$
so
$$-6 - 2$$

B. Perform the subtraction.
$$-6 - 2 = -6 + -2 = -8$$

Simplify $8 - 2(-4 + 6)$

A. Evaluate the parentheses.
$$-4 + 6 = 2$$
so
$$8 - 2(2)$$

B. Perform the multiplication.
$$2(2) = 4$$
so
$$8 - 4$$

C. Perform the subtraction.
$$8 - 4 = 4$$

Simplify $6 - \left[(-4 + 3) \times 2\right]$

A. Evaluate the inner parentheses.
$$-4 + 3 = -1$$
so
$$6 - [-1 \times 2]$$

B. Evaluate the brackets.
$$-1 \times 2 = -2$$
so
$$6 - -2$$

C. Perform the subtraction.
$$6 - -2 = 6 + 2 = 8$$

Simplify $4 - \left[|-2|(-1) - (4 \times 2)\right]$

A. Evaluate the parentheses.
$$(4 \times 2) = 8$$
so
$$4 - \left[|-2|(-1) - 8\right]$$

B. Evaluate the absolute value of -2 and multiply by -1.
$$2(-1) = -2$$
so
$$4 - \left[-2 - 8\right]$$

C. Evaluate the brackets.
$$-2 - 8 = -2 + -8 = -10$$
so
$$4 - -10$$

D. Perform the subtraction.
$$4 - -10 = 4 + 10 = 14$$

Simplify $5(3)^2 - (-2)(-4)$

A. Evaluate the exponential phrase.
$$(3)^2 = 9$$
so
$$5 \times 9 - (-2)(-4)$$

B. Perform the multiplication from left to right.
$$45 - 8$$

C. Perform the subtraction.
$$37$$

Simplify $3 - \left[(2 \times 3) - (4^2)\right]$

A. Evaluate the parentheses.
$$2 \times 3 = 6$$
so
$$3 - [6 - (4^2)]$$

B. Evaluate the exponential phrase.
$$4^2 = 16$$
so
$$3 - [6 - 16]$$

C. Evaluate the brackets.
$$6 - 16 = 6 + -16 = -10$$
so
$$3 - -10$$

D. Perform the subtraction.
$$3 - -10 = 3 + 10 = 13$$

Simplify $\left\{3 + \left[2 - (4 - 5 \times 2)\right]\right\}$

A. Evaluate the inner parentheses. Do multiplication first.
$$4 - 10$$

B. Perform the subtraction.
$$4 - 10 = 4 + -10 = -6$$

C. Evaluate the brackets.
$$2 - -6 = 2 + 6 = 8$$

D. Evaluate the braces.
$$\{3 + 8\} = 11$$

Solving equations

Use laws of numbers to solve equations. Use the opposite operation from what is happening to the variable. Your goal in each problem is to isolate the variable—to have it apart from any numbers.

To check your answer, substitute the value you find for the variable into the original equation. Your answer is correct if the two sides of the equation are equal.

Example
$$n + 3 = -8$$
Subtract 3 from each side.
$$n + 3 - 3 = -8 - 3$$
Combine like terms on both the left and the right.
$$n = -11$$
Check
Substitute -11 for n in the original equation.
$$-11 + 3 = -8$$
Since $-11 + 3 = -8$, both sides $= -8$ and the problem checks.

Solve and check $m - 7 = 10$

A. Since 7 is subtracted from m, add 7 to both sides.
$$m - 7 + 7 = 10 + 7$$

B. Combine the constants on the left-hand side.
$$m - 7 + 7 = m - 0 \text{ or just } m$$

C. Perform the addition on the right.
$$10 + 7 = 17$$
so
$$m = 17$$

D. Check by substituting 17 for m.
$$17 - 7 \text{ does} = 10, \text{ so } 10 = 10$$

Solve and check m + 6 = −12

A. Since 6 is added to m, subtract 6 from both sides.
$$m + 6 - \mathbf{6} = -12 - \mathbf{6}$$

B. Combine the constants on the left.
$$m + 6 - 6 = m + 0$$
$$\text{or just } m$$

C. Perform the subtraction on the right.
$$-12 - 6 = -12 + -6$$
$$\text{so}$$
$$m = -18$$

D. Check by substituting −18 for m.
$$-18 + 6 \text{ does} = -12$$
$$\text{so}$$
$$-12 = -12$$

Solve and check k + 8 = 4 + 3

A. Combine the like terms on the right.
$$4 + 3 = 7$$
$$\text{so}$$
$$k + 8 = 7$$

B. Undo the 8 that is added to k by subtracting 8 from both sides.
$$k + 8 - \mathbf{8} = 7 - \mathbf{8}$$

C. Combine the constants on the left.
$$k = 7 - 8$$

D. Perform the subtraction on the right.
$$7 + -8 = -1$$
$$\text{so}$$
$$k = -1$$

E. Check by substituting −1 for k.
$$-1 \text{ does} = 7 - 8$$
$$\text{so}$$
$$-1 = -1$$

Solve and check 2 + n − 3 = 8

A. Reorder the left side as
$$2 - 3 + n = 8$$

B. Combine like terms on the left.
$$2 - 3 = 2 + -3 = -1,$$
$$\text{so } n - 1 = 8$$

C. Undo the subtraction by adding 1.
$$n - 1 + \mathbf{1} = 8 + \mathbf{1}$$

D. Perform the addition.
$$n = 9$$

E. Check by substituting 9 for n.
$$2 + 9 - 3 = 8$$
$$2 + 9 - 3 \text{ does} = 8,$$
$$\text{so it checks.}$$

Solve and check 25 − k = 42

METHOD 1

A. Rewrite the equation as
$$25 + -k = 42$$

B. Subtract 25 from both sides.
$$25 + -k - \mathbf{25} = 42 - \mathbf{25}$$

C. Perform the subtraction.
$$42 - 25 = 17,$$
$$\text{so } -k = 17$$

D. Multiply both sides by −1.
$$-k(\mathbf{-1}) = 17(\mathbf{-1}),$$
$$\text{so } k = -17$$

E. Check by substituting −17 for k.
$$25 - -17 = 42$$
$$25 + 17 \text{ does} = 42,$$
$$\text{so it checks.}$$

METHOD 2

A. Add k to both sides.
$$25 - k + \mathbf{k} = 42 + \mathbf{k}$$

B. Subtract 42 from both sides.
$$25 - 42 = 42 + k - 42,$$
$$\text{so } -17 = k \text{ or } k = -17$$

C. Check as in Method 1.

Solve and check $4m = -12$

A. Divide both sides by 4, the coefficient of the variable.

$$\frac{4m}{4} = \frac{-12}{4}$$

B. Evaluate the division.

$$\frac{-12}{4} = -3$$

so

$$m = -3$$

C. Check by substituting -3 for m.

4×-3 does $= -12$, so it checks.

Solve and check $\frac{-k}{3} = 4$

METHOD 1

A. Multiply both sides by 3.

$$\frac{-k}{3}(3) = 4(3)$$

B. Evaluate the multiplication.

$$-k = 12$$

C. Multiply both sides by -1.

$$-k(-1) = 12(-1)$$

so

$$k = -12$$

D. Check by substituting 12 for k.

$\frac{--12}{3}$ does $= 4$,

so it checks.

METHOD 2

A. Put a 1 under the 4 to make a proportion.

$$\frac{-k}{3} = \frac{4}{1}$$

B. Solve the proportion by finding the diagonal cross product.

$(1)(-k) = (4)(3)$ so $-k = 12$

C. Multiply both sides by -1.

$-k(-1) = 12(-1)$,

so $k = -12$

D. Check as in Method 1.

Solve and check $\frac{n}{1.2} = 8$

METHOD 1

A. Multiply both sides by 1.2

$$\frac{n}{1.2}(1.2) = 8(1.2)$$

so

$$n = 9.6$$

B. Check by substituting 9.6 for n.

$\frac{9.6}{1.2}$ does $= 8$,

so it checks.

METHOD 2

A. Put a 1 under the 8 to make a proportion.

$$\frac{n}{1.2} = \frac{8}{1}$$

B. Solve the proportion by finding the diagonal cross product.

$(1)(n) = (1.2)(8)$

so

$$n = 9.6$$

C. Check as in Method 1.

Solve and check $\dfrac{4n}{5} = -24$

METHOD 1

Any time you have a fractional coefficient of the variable, you can transform the equation by multiplying by the reciprocal of the coefficient on both sides of the equation.

The coefficient of n is $\frac{4}{5}$. The reciprocal is $\frac{5}{4}$.

A. Multiply both sides by $\frac{5}{4}$.
$$\frac{5}{4} \times \frac{4n}{5} = -24 \times \frac{5}{4},$$
so n = −30

B. Check: Substitute −30 in place of n.
$$\frac{4}{5} \times -30 = -24$$
$$-24 = -24,$$
so it checks.

METHOD 2

A. Divide both sides by the coefficient of n, $\frac{4}{5}$.
$$\frac{4n}{5} = -24$$
$$\frac{\frac{4}{5}}{} \quad \frac{4}{5}$$

B. Change division to multiplication and invert the fraction.
$$n = -24 \times \frac{5}{4},$$
so n = −30

C. Check as in Method 1.

Solving problems with more than one transformation

Rules

1. Simplify both sides of the equation by combining like terms.
2. Undo addition or subtraction by using the opposite operation.
3. Undo multiplication or division by using the opposite operation.

Solve and check $3k - 2 = 16$

A. Add 2 to both sides.
$$3k - 2 + \mathbf{2} = 16 + \mathbf{2},$$
so
$$3k = 18$$

B. Divide both sides by 3.
$$\frac{3k}{\mathbf{3}} = \frac{18}{\mathbf{3}},$$
so
$$k = 6$$

C. Check:
Substitute 6 for k.
$$3 \times 6 - 2 = 16$$
Simplify.
$$18 - 2 = 16$$
$$16 = 16,$$
so it checks.

Solve and check $\dfrac{1n}{3} + 2 = -3$

A. Subtract 2 from both sides.
$$\frac{1n}{3} + 2 - \mathbf{2} = -3 - \mathbf{2},$$
so
$$\frac{1n}{3} = -5$$

B. Multiply both sides by $\frac{3}{1}$, the reciprocal of the coefficient of n.
$$\frac{3}{1} \times \frac{1n}{3} = -5 \times \frac{3}{1},$$
so
$$n = -15$$

C. Check:
Substitute −15 for n.
$$\frac{1}{3} \times -15 + 2 = -3$$
Simplify.
$$-5 + 2$$
$$-3 = -3,$$
so it checks.

Solve and check $4k + 6 = 17 + 13$

A. Combine like terms on the right.
$$4k + 6 = 30$$

B. Subtract 6 from both sides.
$$4k + 6 - \mathbf{6} = 30 - \mathbf{6},$$
so
$$4k = 24$$

C. Divide both sides by 4.
$$\frac{4k}{4} = \frac{24}{4},$$
so
$$k = 6$$

D. Check:
Substitute 6 for k.
$$4 \times 6 + 6 = 17 + 13$$
Simplify.
$$24 + 6 = 30$$
$$30 = 30,$$
so it checks.

Solve and check $\frac{4}{3}n + \frac{1}{2} = \frac{3}{4}$

A. Subtract $\frac{1}{2}$ from both sides.
$$\frac{4}{3}n + \frac{1}{2} - \frac{\mathbf{1}}{\mathbf{2}} = \frac{3}{4} - \frac{\mathbf{1}}{\mathbf{2}}$$

B. Get a common denominator
for $\frac{3}{4} - \frac{1}{2} = \frac{3}{4} - \frac{2}{4},$
so
$$\frac{4}{3}n = \frac{1}{4}$$

C. Multiply both sides by the reciprocal of $\frac{4}{3}$, which is $\frac{3}{4}$.
$$\frac{3}{4} \times \frac{4}{3}n = \frac{1}{4} \times \frac{3}{4},$$
so
$$n = \frac{3}{16}$$

D. Check:
Substitute $\frac{3}{16}$ in the original equation.
$$\frac{4}{3} \times \frac{3}{16} + \frac{1}{2} = \frac{3}{4}$$
Simplify.
$$\frac{12}{48} + \frac{1}{2} = \frac{3}{4}$$
$$\frac{1}{4} + \frac{1}{2} = \frac{3}{4}$$
$$\frac{1}{4} + \frac{2}{4} = \frac{3}{4},$$

so $\frac{3}{4} = \frac{3}{4}$, and it checks.

Using the distributive property to simplify variable expressions that have parentheses

$$a(b + c) = a \times b + a \times c = ab + ac$$
and
$$4(3 + 2) = 4 \times 3 + 4 \times 2 = 12 + 8 = 20$$

Simplify the following problems.

Simplify $4(k + 3)$

A. Use the distributive property to multiply 4 by k and add the product of 4×3.
$$4 \times k + 4 \times 3 = 4k + 12$$

B. Since 4k and 12 are not like terms, they cannot be combined.

Simplify $3(m - 2) - 6m$

A. Use the distributive property to simplify $3(m - 2)$.
$$3 \times m - 3 \times 2 =$$
$$3m - 6$$

B. Combine like terms.
$$3m - 6 - 6m =$$
$$3m - 6m - 6 =$$
$$-3m - 6$$

C. Since $-3m$ and 6 are not like terms, they cannot be simplified.

Simplify $-3(n + 3) + 6n$

A. Use the distributive property to simplify $-3(n + 3)$.

$-3 \times n + -3 \times 3 =$

$-3n + -9$ or

$-3n - 9$

B. Combine like terms.

$-3n - 9 + 6n = 3n - 9$

Simplify $16 - 2(k - 2)$

A. Use the distributive property to multiply -2 by $(k - 2)$.

$-2 \times k - -2 \times 2 =$

$-2k + 4$

B. Simplify $16 - 2k + 4$.

$16 - 2k + 4 =$

$16 + 4 - 2k =$

$20 - 2k$ or

$-2k + 20$

Simplify $2(m + 4) - 4(m - 3)$

A. Use the distributive property to multiply 2 by $(m + 4)$ and -4 by $(m - 3)$.

$2 \times m + 2 \times 4 - 4 \times m$

$- 4 \times -3 =$

$2m + 8 - 4m - -12$ or $+12$

B. Combine like terms.

$2m + 8 - 4m + 12 =$

$2m - 4m + 8 + 12 =$

$-2m + 20$

Solve the following equations.

First, combine like terms on both sides of the equation.   Third, undo multiplication or division.

Second, undo addition or subtraction.

Solve $3k + 7k = -5$

A. Combine like terms.

$3k + 7k = 10k$

so

$10k = -5$

B. Divide both sides by 10.

$$\frac{10k}{10} = \frac{-5}{10}$$

so

$$k = -\frac{1}{2}$$

or -0.5

C. Check:

Substitute -0.5 for k in the original problem.

$3(-0.5) + 7(-0.5) = -5$

Simplify.

$-1.5 + -3.5 =$

$- 5 = -5$

so it checks.

Solve $5 = m - 5m + 9$

A. Combine like terms.

$m - 5m = -4m$

so

$5 = -4m + 9$

B. Subtract 9 from both sides.

$5 - 9 = -4m + 9 - 9$

so

$-4 = -4m$

C. Divide both sides by -4.

$$\frac{-4}{-4} = \frac{-4m}{-4}$$

so

$m = 1$

D. Check:

Substitute $m = 1$ into

$5 = m - 5m + 9$

Simplify.

$5 = 1 - 5(1) + 9$

$= 10 - 5$

$5 = 5$

so it checks.

Solve $5(2n - 1) = 15$

A. Use the distributive property to multiply 5 by $(2n - 1)$.
$$5(2n - 1) =$$
$$5 \times 2n - 5 \times 1 =$$
$$10n - 5$$

B. Add 5 to both sides.
$$10n - 5 + \mathbf{5} = 15 + \mathbf{5}$$

C. Divide both sides by 10.
$$\frac{10n}{\mathbf{10}} = \frac{20}{\mathbf{10}},$$
so
$$n = 2$$

D. Check:
Substitute 2 for n in the original equation and simplify.
$$5(2 \times 2 - 1) = 15$$
$$5(4 - 1) =$$
$$5 \times 3 =$$
$$15 = 15,$$
so it checks.

Solve $3(k + 2) = -5$

A. Use the distributive property to multiply 3 by $(k + 2)$.
$$3(k + 2) =$$
$$3 \times k + 3 \times 2 =$$
$$3k + 6$$

B. Subtract 6 from both sides.
$$3k + 6 - \mathbf{6} = -5 - \mathbf{6}$$

C. Divide both sides by 3.
$$\frac{3k}{\mathbf{3}} = \frac{-11}{\mathbf{3}},$$
so
$$k = \frac{-11}{3}$$

D. Check:
Substitute $\frac{-11}{3}$ for k in the original equation.
$$3\left(\frac{-11}{3} + 2\right) = -5$$
$$3\left(\frac{-11}{3} + \frac{6}{3}\right)$$
$$3\left(\frac{-5}{3}\right)$$
$$-5 = -5,$$
so it checks.

$7k = 3k - 8$

A. Subtract 3k from both sides.
$$7k - \mathbf{3k} = 3k - \mathbf{3k} - 8,$$
$$\text{so } 4k = -8$$

B. Divide both sides by 4.
$$\frac{4k}{\mathbf{4}} = \frac{-8}{\mathbf{4}},$$
$$\text{so } k = -2$$

Check: Substitute −2 for k in the original equation.
$$7(-2) = 3(-2) - 8$$
$$-14 = -6 - 8$$
$$-14 = -14,$$
so it checks.

$2(k - 3) - 5(k + 6) = -27$

A. Use the distributive property.
$$2k - 6 - 5k - 30 = -27$$

B. Combine like terms on the left.
$$-3k - 36 = -27$$

C. Add 36 to both sides.
$$-3k - 36 + \mathbf{36} = -27 + \mathbf{36},$$
$$\text{so } -3k = 9$$

D. Divide both sides by −3.
$$\frac{-3k}{\mathbf{-3}} = \frac{9}{\mathbf{-3}},$$
$$\text{so } k = -3$$

Check: Substitute −3 for k in the original equation.
$$2(-3 - 3) - 5(-3 + 6) = -27$$
$$2(-6) - 5(3) = -27$$
$$-12 - 15 = -27$$
$$-27 = -27,$$
so it checks.

$$-3k + 2 = 5k$$

METHOD 1

Use this method if you want the coefficient to be positive.

A. Add 3k to both sides.
$-3k + \mathbf{3k} + 2 = 5k + \mathbf{3k}$,
so $2 = 8k$

B. In an equation, you can swap the locations of the right and left side. Do that here.
$8k = 2$

C. Divide both sides by 8.

$\frac{8k}{8} = \frac{2}{8}$, so $k = \frac{2}{8}$,

which reduces to $\frac{1}{4}$, or 0.25

Check: Substitute $\frac{1}{4}$ for k in the original equation.

$-3\left(\frac{1}{4}\right) + 2 = 5\left(\frac{1}{4}\right)$

$-\frac{3}{4} + 2 = \frac{5}{4}$

$-\frac{3}{4} + \frac{8}{4} = \frac{5}{4}$

$\frac{5}{4} = \frac{5}{4}$

and

$-3(0.25) + 2 = 5(0.25)$
$-0.75 + 2 = 1.25$
$1.25 = 1.25$,

so it checks for either answer.

METHOD 2

Use this method if you want the variable on the left.

A. Subtract 5k from both sides.
$-3k - \mathbf{5k} + 2 = 5k - \mathbf{5k}$,
so $-8k + 2 = 0$
Be very careful here. Many students make errors when they have the zero on the right.

B. Subtract 2 from both sides.
$-8k + 2 - \mathbf{2} = 0 - \mathbf{2}$,
so $-8k = -2$

C. Divide both sides by −8.

$\frac{-8k}{-8} = \frac{-2}{-8}$, $k = \frac{2}{8}$,

which reduces to $\frac{1}{4}$, or 0.25

Check: Same as for Method 1

METHOD 3

Use this method if you want the variable on the left and do not want to have a zero on the right.

A. Subtract 2 from both sides.
$-3k + 2 - \mathbf{2} = 5k - \mathbf{2}$,
so $-3k = 5k - 2$

Students sometimes want to subtract 2 from 5 and get 3k, but that is not possible, because they are not like terms.

B. Subtract 5k from both sides.
$-3k - \mathbf{5k} = -2 + 5k - \mathbf{5k}$,
so $-8k = -2$

C. Divide both sides by −8.

$\frac{-8k}{-8} = \frac{-2}{-8}$, so $k = \frac{2}{8}$,

which reduces to $\frac{1}{4}$, or 0.25

Check: Same as for Method 1

$$2m - 3 + m = 2 + 5m - 7$$

METHOD 1

A. Combine like terms on both sides.
$$3m - 3 = 5m - 5$$

B. Subtract 3m from both sides.
$$3m - \mathbf{3m} - 3 = 5m - \mathbf{3m} - 5,$$
$$\text{so } -3 = 2m - 5$$

C. Add 5 to both sides.
$$-3 + \mathbf{5} = 2m - 5 + \mathbf{5},$$
$$\text{so } 2 = 2m$$

D. Divide both sides by 2.
$$\frac{2}{\mathbf{2}} = \frac{2m}{\mathbf{2}} \text{, so } 1 = m, \text{ which is}$$
the same as m = 1

Check: Substitute 1 for m in the original equation.
$$2(1) - 3 + 1 = 2 + 5(1) - 7$$
$$2 - 3 + 1 = 2 + 5 - 7$$
$$0 = 0,$$
so it checks.

METHOD 2

A. Combine like terms on both sides.
$$3m - 3 = 5m - 5$$

B. Subtract 5m from both sides.
$$3m - \mathbf{5m} - 3 = 5m - \mathbf{5m} - 5,$$
$$\text{so } -2m - 3 = -5$$

C. Add 3 to both sides.
$$-2m - 3 + \mathbf{3} = -5 + \mathbf{3},$$
$$\text{so } -2m = -2$$

D. Divide both sides by –2.
$$\frac{-2m}{\mathbf{-2}} = \frac{-2}{\mathbf{-2}} \text{, so } m = 1$$

Check: Same as for Method 1

$$-4(n - 3) - 5n = 5 - 2n + 7$$

METHOD 1

A. Use the distributive property.
$$-4n + 12 - 5n = 5 - 2n + 7$$

B. Combine like terms on both sides.
$$-9n + 12 = -2n + 12$$

Move the variable to the right to keep the coefficient positive.

C. Add 9n to both sides.
$$-9n + \mathbf{9n} + 12 = -2n + \mathbf{9n} + 12,$$
$$\text{so } 12 = 7n + 12$$

D. Subtract 12 from both sides.
$$12 - \mathbf{12} = 7n + 12 - \mathbf{12},$$
$$\text{so } 0 = 7n$$

E. Divide both sides by 7.
$$\frac{0}{7} = \frac{7n}{7},$$
$$\text{so } n = 0$$

Check: Substitute 0 for n in the original equation.
$$-4(0 - 3) - 5(0) = 5 - 2(0) + 7$$
$$-4(-3) - 0 = 5 - 0 + 7$$
$$12 - 0 = 12 - 0$$
$$12 = 12,$$
so it checks.

METHOD 2

A. Use the distributive property.
$$-4n + 12 - 5n = 5 - 2n + 7$$

B. Combine like terms on both sides.
$$-9n + 12 = -2n + 12$$

Move the variable to the left-hand side of the equation.

C. Add 2n to both sides.
$$-9n + 12 + \mathbf{2n} = -2n + \mathbf{2n} + 12,$$
$$\text{so } -7n + 12 = 12$$

D. Subtract 12 from both sides.
$$-7n + 12 - \mathbf{12} = 12 - \mathbf{12},$$
$$\text{so } -7n = 0$$

E. Divide both sides by –7.
$$\frac{-7n}{-7} = \frac{0}{-7},$$
$$\text{so } n = 0$$

Check: Same as for Method 1

$$\frac{4}{k} = -3$$

METHOD 1

A. Place a 1 under the −3 to make a proportion.

$$\frac{4}{k} = \frac{-3}{1}$$

B. Perform a diagonal product to solve the proportion.
$(-3)(k) = (4)(1)$,
so $-3k = 4$

C. Divide both sides by −3.

$$\frac{-3k}{-3} = \frac{4}{-3},$$

so $k = -\frac{4}{3}$ or $\frac{-4}{3}$ or $-1\frac{1}{3}$

Check: Substitute $\frac{-4}{3}$ for k in the original equation.

$$\frac{4}{-4/3} = -3$$

Place a 1 under the −3.

$$\frac{4}{-4/3} = -\frac{3}{1}$$

Solve as a proportion.

$$(4)(1) = \left(-\frac{4}{3}\right)(-3)$$

$4 = 4$,
so it checks.

METHOD 2

A. Multiply both sides by k.

$$\frac{4(k)}{k} = -3(k),$$

so $4 = -3k$

B. Divide both sides by −3.

$$\frac{4}{-3} = \frac{-3k}{-3},$$

so $\frac{-4}{3} = k$ or $k = \frac{-4}{3}$ or $-1\frac{1}{3}$

Check: Same as for Method 1

$$\frac{-2k + 4}{4} = 6$$

METHOD 1

A. Place a 1 under the 6 to make a proportion.

$$\frac{-2k + 4}{4} = \frac{6}{1}$$

B. Perform a diagonal product.
$(-2k + 4)(1) = (4)(6)$,
so $-2k + 4 = 24$

C. Subtract 4 from both sides.
$-2k + 4 - 4 = 24 - 4$,
so $-2k = 20$

D. Divide both sides by −2.
$$\frac{-2k}{-2} = \frac{20}{-2},$$
so $k = -10$

Check: Substitute −10 for k in the original equation.

$$\frac{-2(-10) + 4}{4} = 6$$

$$\frac{20 + 4}{4} = 6$$

$$\frac{24}{4} = 6$$

$6 = 6$,
so it checks.

METHOD 2

A. Multiply both sides by 4.

$$\frac{(-2k + 4)}{4}(4) = 6(4),$$

so $-2k + 4 = 24$

B. Subtract 4 from both sides.
$-2k + 4 - 4 = 24 - 4$,
so $-2k = 20$

C. Divide both sides by −2.
$$\frac{-2k}{-2} = \frac{20}{-2},$$
so $k = 10$

Check: Same as for Method 1

Inequalities. Mathematical sentences showing that one side of the sentence is greater than the other side are called **inequalities**.

The smaller amount should always be on the left-hand side of the inequality. If two inequality signs are in a statement, they should both be $<$ or both be $>$.

Here are some inequalities that have been written from word sentences.

Inequalities	*Solutions*
(1) 5 is less than 9.	(1) Since 5 is less than 9, place 5 on the left.................. 5
	Use the less than sign, $<$, after the 5...................... $5 <$
	Place 9 on the right-hand side................................. $5 < 9$
(2) A number *k* is between 4 and 7.	(2) Since 4 is less than 7, place 4 on the left.................. 4
	Use the less than sign, $<$, after the 4...................... $4 <$
	Since 7 is greater than 4, 7 goes on the right. .... $4 < 7$
	Since *k* is between the two numbers, it is in
	the middle with a $<$ before and after the *k*........... $4 < k < 7$
	Because there are two inequality signs in this statement, it is called a compound inequality.
(3) 3 more than *m* is greater than 8.	(3) 3 more than *m* is written with the variable first........ $m + 3$
	Since 3 more than *m* is greater than 8 that means
	8 is less than 3 more than *m*. Place 8 on the left.... 8
	Use the less than sign, $<$, after the 8...................... $8 <$
	Since $m + 3$ is the greater amount, place it on
	the right.. $8 < m + 3$

Write an inequality for each of the following:

Nine is less than twelve.

A. Since 9 is the smaller quantity, it goes on the left 9
B. Use the less than sign, $<$, after the 9.. $9 <$
C. Since 12 is greater than 9, 12 goes on the right... $9 < 12$

A number *k* is greater than a number *m*.

A. Since *k* is greater, *m* is the smaller; *m* goes on the left .... *m*
B. Since *m* is the smaller, use the less than sign after the *m*. .... $m <$
C. Since *k* is greater than *m*, *k* goes on the right... $m < k$

On a number line, 3*k* is between 5 and 12.

A. Since 5 is less than 12, 5 goes on the left.. 5
B. Use the less than sign, $<$, after the 5.. $5 <$
C. Since 12 is the greater value, place 12 after the $<$ .... $5 < 12$
D. Since 3*k* is between the two values, it goes in the middle with a $<$ before and after the 3*k* ...... $5 < 3k < 12$

On a number line, 5*m* is between *a* and *b*, and *b* is greater than *a*.

A. Since *b* is greater than *a*, *a* is less than *b*; *a* goes on the left .... *a*
B. Use the less than sign, $<$, after the *a* .... $a <$
C. Since *b* is the greater value, place *b* after the $<$ .... $a < b$
D. Since 5*m* is between the two values, it goes in the middle with a $<$ before and after the 5*m*.... $a < 5m < b$

Solving inequalities.

To solve inequalities, we use transformations very similar to those used to solve equations.

1. First, simplify any numerical and variable expressions.
2. Use addition or subtraction on both sides to move terms in the inequality so the term with the variable is on the left.
3. Use multiplication or division to eliminate the coefficient of the variable.
4. If you multiply or divide both sides of the inequality by the same negative number, you must reverse the direction of the inequality sign.
5. When the variable is isolated on the right-hand side, after you have completed all other steps, place the variable on the left and change the direction of the inequality sign.

Numbers 4 and 5 are the only rules that differ from those used in solving equations.

The directions will tell you if the answers are to be **integers**, such as:

$k < 8$, k would be any integer less than 8, such as 7, 6, …

and

$m > -2$, m would be any integer greater than −2, such as −1, 0, 1, …

or

if the answers are to be **rational numbers**, such as decimals or fractions, such as:

$k < 8$, k could be any value less than 8, such as 7.1, $7\frac{1}{2}$, or 7.

Solve and check these inequalities. Give the answers as integers.

$a + 7 < 10$

A. Subtract 7 from both sides.
$a + 7 - 7 < 10 - 7$,
so $a < 3$

Check: Select any integer less than 3 and substitute into the original inequality.

If you choose $a = 2$, the check will be as follows:
$2 + 7 < 10$
9 is less than 10, so it checks.

$-12 < k - 8$

A. Add 8 to both sides.
$-12 + 8 < k - 8 + 8$,
so $-4 < k$

B. Rearrange the order of the inequality, keeping the open side toward the k, which should be on the left.
$k > -4$

Check: Select any integer greater than −4 and substitute into the original inequality.

If you choose $k = -3$, the check will be as follows:
$-12 < -3 - 8$
−12 is less than −11, so it checks.

$8m < 32$

A. Divide both sides by 8.
$\frac{8m}{8} < \frac{32}{8}$,
so $m < 4$

Check: Select any integer less than 4 and substitute into the original inequality.

If you choose $m = 3$, the check will be as follows:
$8(3) < 32$
24 is less than 32, so it checks.

$-7k < 21$

A. Divide both sides by −7.
$\frac{-7k}{-7} < \frac{21}{-7}$

B. Change the direction of the inequality sign because you divided both sides by a negative number.
$k > -3$

Check: Select any integer greater than −3 and substitute into the original inequality.

If you choose $k = -2$, the check will be as follows:
$-7(-2) < 21$
14 is less than 21, so it checks.

$$35 > 5k$$

A. Divide both sides by 5.
$$\frac{35}{5} > \frac{5k}{5},$$
so $7 > k$

B. Rearrange the order of the inequality, keeping the closed side toward the k, which should be on the left.
$$k < 7$$

Check: Select any integer less than 7 and substitute into the original inequality.

If you choose k = 6, the check will be as follows:
$$35 > 5(6)$$
35 is greater than 30, so it checks.

$$\frac{m}{-3} < 7$$

A. Multiply both sides by −3.
$$\frac{(-3)m}{-3} < 7(-3)$$
B. Change the direction of the inequality sign because you multiplied by a negative number.
$$m > -21$$

Check: Select any integer greater than −21 and substitute into the original inequality.

If you choose m = −20, the check will be as follows:
$$\frac{-20}{-3} < 7$$
$\frac{20}{3}$ is less than 7, so it checks.

$$2m - 3 < -7$$

A. Add 3 to both sides.
$$2m - 3 + 3 < -7 + 3,$$
so $2m < -4$

B. Divide both sides by 2.
$$\frac{2m}{2} < \frac{-4}{2},$$
so $m < -2$

Check: Select any integer less than −2 and substitute into the original inequality.

If you choose m = −3, the check will be as follows:
$$2(-3) - 3 < -7$$
$$-6 - 3 < -7$$
−9 is less than −7, so it checks.

$$5(k + 3) > -25$$

A. Use the distributive property.
$$(5)(k) + (5)(3) > -25,$$
so $5k + 15 > -25$

B. Subtract 15 from both sides.
$$5k + 15 - 15 > -25 - 15,$$
so $5k > -40$

C. Divide both sides by 5.
$$\frac{5k}{5} > \frac{-40}{5},$$
so $k > -8$

Check: Select any integer greater than −8 and substitute into the original inequality.

If you choose k = −7, the check will be as follows:
$$5(-7 + 3) < -25$$
$$5(-7) + 5(3) < -25$$
$$-35 + 15 < -25$$
−20 is greater than −25, so it checks.

$$5m - 4 > 3m + 2 - m + 7$$

A. Simplify by combining like terms.
$$5m - 4 > 2m + 9$$

B. Subtract 2m from both sides.
$$5m - 2m - 4 > 2m - 2m + 9,$$
so $3m - 4 > 9$

C. Add 4 to both sides.
$$3m - 4 + 4 > 9 + 4,$$
so $3m > 13$

D. Divide both sides by 3.
$$\frac{3m}{3} > \frac{13}{3},$$ so $m > \frac{13}{3}$

Check: Select any integer greater than $\frac{13}{3}$ and substitute into the original inequality.

If you choose m = 5, the check will be as follows:
$$5(5) - 4 > 3(5) + 2 - 5 + 7$$
$$25 - 4 > 15 + 2 - 5 + 7$$
$$21 > 19$$
21 is greater than 19, so it checks.

Word problems

In solving a word problem, the plan is to:

A. Let n = the number you are trying to find. (You may use whatever variable you prefer.)

B. Write an equation that describes the sentence. (The "is" in the word sentence is represented by the = sign.)

C. Calculate the answer and label, if indicated.

Three times a number n plus 3 is 24. Find the number.

A. Let n = the missing number.

B. Write an equation.
$$3n + 3 = 24$$

C. Solve the equation. Subtract 3 from both sides.
$$3n + 3 - 3 = 24 - 3,$$
$$\text{so } 3n = 21$$

Divide both sides by 3.
$$3n \div 3 = 21 \div 3,$$
$$\text{so } n = 21$$

Find the number m that works in the sentence: The quotient when the sum of m and 5 is divided by three is 14.

A. Let m = the number.

B. Write an equation. (Be careful to use parentheses.)
$$(m + 5) \div 3 = 14$$

C. Solve the equation. Multiply both sides by 3.
$$(m + 5) \div 3 \times 3 = 14 \times 3,$$
$$\text{so } m + 5 = 42$$

Subtract 5 from both sides.
$$m + 5 - 5 = 42 - 5,$$
$$\text{so } m = 37$$

The sum of three consecutive integers is 51. Find the integers.

A. Let n = the first integer.
Let n + 1 = the second integer.
Let n + 2 = the third integer.

B. Write an equation.
$$n + n + 1 + n + 2 = 51$$

C. Solve the equation. Combine like terms.
$$3n + 3 = 51$$

Subtract 3 from both sides.
$$3n + 3 - 3 = 51 - 3,$$
$$\text{so } 3n = 48$$

Divide both sides by 3.
$$3n \div 3 = 48 \div 3,$$
so n = 16 = the first integer
n + 1 = 17 = the second integer
n + 2 = 18 = the third integer

In Friendly Hollow, Tennessee, the high temperature in January was 42°F. The low temperature was −12°F. What was the difference in the two temperatures?

A. Let n = the difference in the temperatures.

B. Write an equation.
$$42 - {-12} = n$$
(Always subtract high minus low.)

C. Solve the equation. Simplify.
$$42 - {-12} = n,$$
$$\text{so } 42 + 12 = n,$$
$$\text{and } n = 54°$$

At the end of the holiday sale, there were 72 televisions remaining out of a shipment of 165. How many televisions were sold during the sale?

A. Let k = the number of televisions sold.

B. Write an equation.
$$165 - k = 72$$

C. Solve the equation. Add k to both sides.
$$165 - k + \mathbf{k} = 72 + k,$$
$$\text{so } 165 = 72 + \mathbf{k}$$

Subtract 72 from both sides.
$$165 - \mathbf{72} = 72 - \mathbf{72} + k,$$
$$\text{so } 93 = k,$$
93 televisions sold

In the 7th grade, $\frac{3}{4}$ of the students played soccer. A total of 36 students played soccer. How many students are there in the 7th grade? ("$\frac{3}{4}$ of" means to multiply by $\frac{3}{4}$.)

A. Let n = the number of students in the 7th grade.

B. Write an equation.
$$\frac{3}{4}k = 36$$

C. Solve the equation. Multiply both sides by the reciprocal, $\frac{4}{3}$.
$$\frac{\mathbf{4}}{\mathbf{3}} \times \frac{3}{4}k = 36 \times \frac{\mathbf{4}}{\mathbf{3}},$$
so k = 48 students in the 7th grade

The difference between three times a number and fifteen is 60. Find the number.

A. Let k = the number.

B. Write an equation. (Since the phrase "three times a number" occurs before "fifteen," the phrase will go before "fifteen.")
$$3k - 15 = 60$$

C. Solve the equation. Add 15 to both sides.
$$3k - 15 + \mathbf{15} = 60 + \mathbf{15},$$
$$\text{so } 3k = 75.$$

Divide both sides by 3.
$$3k \div \mathbf{3} = 75 \div \mathbf{3}, \text{ so } k = 25$$

The difference between 15 and three times a number is 60.

A. Let n = the number.

B. Write an equation. (Since the position of "15" and "three times a number" are reversed in this problem, write the "15" first.)
$$15 - 3n = 60$$

C. Solve the equation. Add 3n to both sides.
$$15 - 3n + \mathbf{3n} = 60 + \mathbf{3n},$$
$$\text{so } 15 = 60 + 3n$$

Subtract 60 from both sides.
$$15 - \mathbf{60} = 60 - \mathbf{60} + 3n,$$
$$\text{so } -45 = 3n$$

Divide both sides by 3.
$$-45 \div \mathbf{3} = 3n \div \mathbf{3},$$
$$\text{so } -15 = n$$

Notice that you will have two different answers depending on how you arrange the equation. Each answer will check for its equation. Sometimes the instruction will say that the answer should be an integer. In that case, the answer n = −15 is not appropriate.
Read each problem carefully.

$\frac{4}{5}$ **of the PE class wanted to play dodge ball. After two more students joined in the game, there were 26 playing. How many students were in the class in all?**

A. Let m = the total number of students in the PE class.

B. Write an equation.
$$\frac{4}{5}m + 2 = 26$$

C. Solve the equation. Subtract 2 from both sides.
$$\frac{4}{5}m + 2 - 2 = 26 - 2,$$
so $\frac{4}{5}m = 24$

Multiply both sides by the reciprocal of $\frac{4}{5}$, $\frac{5}{4}$.
$$\frac{5}{4} \times \frac{4}{5}m = 24 \times \frac{5}{4},$$
so m = 30 students in the class

Kim used $\frac{5}{6}$ of the bag of grass seed on her lawn. She gave 5 pounds to Paula. If Kim had 15 pounds left, how many pounds were in the bag at first?

A. Let n = the number of pounds of grass seed in the bag.

B. Write an equation.
$$\frac{5}{6}n - 5 = 15$$

C. Solve the equation. Add 5 to both sides.
$$\frac{5}{6}n - 5 + 5 = 15 + 5,$$
so $\frac{5}{6}n = 20$

Multiply both sides by the reciprocal of $\frac{5}{6}$, $\frac{6}{5}$.
$$\frac{6}{5} \times \frac{5}{6}n = 20 \times \frac{6}{5},$$
so n = 24 pounds of seed

The sum of two integers is 42. One number is 12 less than the other. Find the numbers.

A. Let k = the smaller number.
k + 12 = the larger number.

B. Write an equation. If k is the smaller number, then k + 12 is the larger. (If you let the variable stand for the bigger number, then k − 12 will be the smaller.

More errors occur in solving problems with subtraction than in problems with addition.)
k + k + 12 = 42

C. Solve the equation. Combine like terms.
k + k + 12 = 42,
so 2k + 12 = 42

Subtract 12 from both sides.
2k + 12 − 12 = 42 − 12,
so 2k = 30

Divide both sides by 2.
2k ÷ 2 = 30 ÷ 2,
so k = 15 = smaller #
k + 12 = 27 = larger #

The sum of 4 consecutive integers is −50. What are the 4 integers?

A. Let n = the 1st integer
n + 1 = the 2nd integer
n + 2 = the 3rd integer
n + 3 = the 4th integer

B. Write an equation.
n + n + 1 + n + 2 + n + 3 = −50

C. Solve the equation. Combine like terms.
4n + 6 = −50

Subtract 6 from both sides.
4n + 6 − 6 = −50 − 6,
so 4n = −56

Divide both sides by 4.
4n ÷ 4 = −56 ÷ 4,
so n = −14
n + 1 = −13
n + 2 = −12
n + 3 = −11

The perimeter of a rectangle is 40 cm. The length is three times the width. Find the length and the width.

A. Let n = the width
3n = the length

B. Write an equation. Use the formula:
2 × length + 2 × width = perimeter
2n + 2(3n) = 40

C. Solve the equation. Simplify 2(3n).
2(3n) = 6n,
so 2n + 2(3n) = 40 is
2n + 6n = 40

Combine like terms.
2n + 6n = 40,
so 8n = 40

Divide both sides by 8.
8n ÷ 8 = 40 ÷ 8,
so n = 5 cm, the width
3n = 15 cm, the length

Naomi is 6 years older than Amy. Five years ago, Naomi was three times Amy's age. How old is each now?

A. Let n = Amy, the younger, now
n + 6 = Naomi, the older, now

B. Make a chart to help you with the information to write the equation.

	Ages now	Ages 5 years ago	
Amy	n	n − 5	The equation is based on the information 5 years ago.
Naomi	n + 6	n + 6 − 5 = n + 1	Naomi's age = 3 × Amy's age $n + 1 = 3(n − 5)$

C. Solve the equation. Use distributive property.
$n + 1 = 3(n − 5)$,
so n + 1 = 3n − 15

Subtract n from both sides.
n − **n** + 1 = 3n − **n** − 15,
so 1 = 2n −15

Add 15 to both sides.
1 + **15** = 2n −15 + **15**,
so 16 = 2n

Divide both sides by 2.
16 ÷ **2** = 2n ÷ **2**,
so 8 = n or n = 8 years for Amy now
n + 6 = 14 years for Naomi now

Jim is 11 and George is 13. How long ago was George twice Jim's age?

A. Let n = the number of years ago that George was twice Jim's age.

B. Make a chart to help you with the information to write the equation.

	Ages now	Ages n years from now	
Jim	11	11 − n	The equation is based on the information n years ago.
George	13	13 − n	George's age = 2 × Jim's age $13 − n = 2(11 − n)$

C. Solve the equation. Use the distributive property.
$13 − n = 2(11 − n)$,
so 13 − n = 22 − 2n

Add 2n to both sides.
13 − n + **2n** = 22 − 2n + **2n**,
so 13 + n = 22

Subtract 13 from both sides.
13 − **13** + n = 22 − **13**,
so n = 9 years ago

A DVD that regularly sells for $98.20 is on sale for 20% off. What is the sale price?

METHOD 1
Calculate from the discount.
Subtract from the original price.

A. Let m = the sale price

B. Multiply the % discount times the original price to get the amount of discount. Then subtract from the original price.
98.20 × 0.20 = discount,
so discount is $19.64

C. Solve. Subtract the discount from the original price.
98.20 − 19.64 = m,
so m = $78.56, the sale price

METHOD 2

Multiply the sale price % that you pay by the original price.

A. Let m = the sale price

B. Subtract the % discount, 20%, from 100%, the original price.
$$100\% - 20\% = 80\%$$

You pay 80% of the original price.
$$m = 80\% \text{ of } \$98.20$$

C. Solve the equation.
$$m = 0.80 \times 98.20 = \$78.56,$$
the discount price

METHOD 3

Set up a proportion comparing percents and dollars.

A. Let m = the sale price. (You will pay 80% and save 20%.)

B. Write an equation:
(sale price)   (original price)
$$\frac{80\%}{m} = \frac{100\%}{\$98.20}$$
Change percents to decimals.
$$\frac{0.80}{m} = \frac{1.00}{98.20}$$

C. Solve. Take the diagonal cross product.
$$1 \times m = 0.80 \times 98.20,$$
so m = \$78.56, the sale price

The markup (the increase in the price of an item to the price it is marked at the store) on a bike is 60%. The amount of markup is $20.97. Find the price before markup. Brandon wants to buy the bike, but does not know how much it will cost.

METHOD 1

Write an equation.

A. Let k = the price of the bike before markup.

B. Write an equation.
$$0.60 \times k = 20.97$$

C. Solve. Divide both sides by 0.60.
$$0.60 \div 0.60 \times k =$$
$$\$20.97 \div 0.60,$$
so k = \$34.95, the price before markup

METHOD 2

Set up a proportion comparing percents and dollars.

A. Let k = the price of the bike before markup.

B. Write an equation.
(% markup)   (original price)
$$\frac{60\%}{\$20.97} = \frac{100\%}{k}$$
Change percents to decimals.
$$\frac{0.60}{20.97} = \frac{1.00}{k}$$

C. Solve. Take the diagonal cross product.
$$0.06 \times k = 1.00 \times 20.97,$$
so 0.60k = 20.97

Divide both sides by 0.6.
$$0.60k \div 0.6 = 20.97 \div 0.6,$$
so k = \$34.95, the price before markup

Use the same information as on the previous page, but this time find the marked-up, or new, price.

METHOD 1

Add markup to the original price.

A. Let n = the marked-up price.

B. Write an equation.
$$34.95 + 20.97 = n$$

C. Solve.
$$34.95 + 20.97 = n,$$
so n = $55.92,
the marked-up price

METHOD 2

Set up a proportion.

A. Let n = the marked-up price.

B. Write an equation.
$$\frac{100\%}{\$34.94} = \frac{160\%}{n}$$

C. Solve. Change the percents to decimals.
$$\frac{1}{34.94} = \frac{1.6}{n}$$
Take the diagonal cross product.
$$1n = 1.6 \times 34.94,$$
so n = $55.92,
the marked-up price

Renee is looking for a dress. She found a purple one on sale for 40% off the original price. If the discount is $16.64, what is the sale price?

METHOD 1

Write equations. Calculate the original price; then subtract the discount.

A. Let m = the sale price.

B. Write equations.
40% × original price = 16.64.
original price − 16.64 = m

C. Solve.
0.40 × original price = 16.64

Divide both sides by 0.40.
0.40 × original price ÷ 0.40 =
16.64 ÷ 0.40,
so original price = $41.60

Subtract the discount from the original price.
41.60 − 16.64 = m, $24.96,
the sale price

METHOD 2

Set up a proportion.

A. Let m = the sale price.

B. Write an equation.
(Remember, if Renee saves 40%, she pays 60%.)
$$\frac{40\%}{\$16.64} = \frac{60\%}{m},$$
so $\frac{0.40}{16.64} = \frac{.60}{m}$

C. Solve. Take the diagonal cross product.
0.40 m = 0.60 × 16.64

Simplify:
0.40 m = 9.984

Divide both sides by 0.4.
0.40m ÷ 0.4 = 9.984 ÷ 0.4,
so m = $24.96, the sale price

Janine purchased 120 shares of stock in Your Best Cosmetics for $16.24 a share. During the next few days her stock declined $1.20 a share, increased $1.05 a share, and declined $1.45 a share. What was the value of her one share of her stock then?

A. Let n = the value of one share of Janine's stock.

B. Write an equation.
$16.24 − 1.20 + 1.05 − 1.45 = n

(You do not have to use the number of shares.)

C. Solve. Combine like terms.
n = $14.64

Gary chose a different stock: Grays Athletic Supply. He bought 80 shares at 12.25 each. His stock rose $1.35, fell $1.50, and rose $2.05. What was the value of all his stock?

A. Let k = the value of all his shares.

B. Write an equation.
80(12.25 + 1.35 − 1.50 + 2.05) = k

C. Solve. Add and subtract in the parentheses.
80(14.15) = k

Multiply.
n = $1132 worth of stock

The gas tank in Mike's mom's SUV holds $30\frac{1}{4}$ gallons. If there are $12\frac{3}{4}$ gallons left, how much has been used?

A. Let m = number of gallons used

B. Write an equation.
$30\frac{1}{4} − m = 12\frac{3}{4}$

C. Solve. Add m to both sides.
$30\frac{1}{4} − m + \mathbf{m} = 12\frac{3}{4} + \mathbf{m}$,
so $30\frac{1}{4} = 12\frac{3}{4} + m$

Subtract $12\frac{3}{4}$ from both sides.
$30\frac{1}{4} − \mathbf{12\frac{3}{4}} = 12\frac{3}{4} + m − \mathbf{12\frac{3}{4}}$,
so $30\frac{1}{4} − 12\frac{3}{4} = m$

Subtract the mixed numbers. (Borrow.)
$29\frac{5}{4} − 12\frac{3}{4} = m$,
so m = $17\frac{2}{4} = 17\frac{1}{2}$ gal.

$\frac{1}{2}$ of the class wanted to go in-line skating, $\frac{1}{3}$ wanted to go ice-skating, and the rest wanted to go roller-skating. What fraction wanted to go roller-skating?

A. Let k = the fractional part of the class that wants to go roller-skating.

B. Write an equation. Represent the entire class with the numeral, like 100%.
$k = 1 − \frac{1}{3} − \frac{1}{2}$

C. Solve. Get a common denominator.
$k = \frac{6}{6} − \frac{2}{6} − \frac{3}{6}$,
so $\frac{1}{6}$ of the class wants to go roller-skating.

A small rectangle, $4\frac{1}{2}$ in. by $5\frac{1}{4}$ in., sits within a larger rectangle, 8 in. by $9\frac{1}{2}$ in. What is the area of the space between the smaller rectangle and the larger one?

A. Let n = the area.

B. Write an equation. (Subtract the area of the smaller rectangle from the area of the larger rectangle.)

$$n = 8 \times 9\frac{1}{2} - 4\frac{1}{2} \times 5\frac{1}{4}$$

C. Solve. Complete the multiplication.

$$n = 76 - 23.625, \text{ or}$$
$$n = 76 - 23\frac{5}{8}$$

Do the subtraction.

$$n = 52.375, \text{ or}$$
$$52\frac{3}{8}, \text{ square miles}$$

The quotient when the sum of 5 and a number is divided by 3 is 17. What is the number?

A. Let m = the number.

B. Write an equation.
$$(5 + m) \div 3 = 17$$

C. Solve the equation. Multiply both sides by 3.
$$(5 + m) \div 3 \times \mathbf{3} = 17 \times \mathbf{3},$$
$$\text{so } 5 + m = 51$$

Subtract 5 from both sides.
$$5 + m - 5 = 51 - 5,$$
$$\text{so } m = 46$$

The speedy French train traveled 560 km in 4 hours. Use a proportion to find out how many km could be covered in 5 hours.

A. Let k = the number of kilometers covered in five hours

B. Write an equation.
$$\frac{560}{4} = \frac{k}{5}$$

C. Solve. Take the diagonal cross product.
$$4k = 5 \times 560$$

Multiply 5 by 560.
$$4k = 2800$$

Divide both sides by 4.
$$4k \div \mathbf{4} = 2800 \div \mathbf{4},$$
$$\text{so } k = 700 \text{ km in 5 hours}$$

The Panthers basketball team started the season with 6 wins and 5 losses. If the team continues to win in the same ratio, how many games will they have won after a total of 33 games? (A proportion will work well.)

A. Let n = the total number of games they would have won.

B. Write an equation.
$$\frac{6 \text{ wins}}{11 \text{ games}} = \frac{n \text{ wins}}{33 \text{ total games}}$$

C. Solve. Take the diagonal cross product.
$$11n = 6 \times 33$$

Multiply 6 by 32.
$$11n = 198$$

Divide both sides by 11.
$$11n \div \mathbf{11} = 198 \div \mathbf{11},$$
$$\text{so } n = 18 \text{ wins}$$

The perimeter of a rectangle is 32 cm. The length is 3 times the width. Find the width and the length.

A. Let k = the width
$$3k = \text{the length}$$

B. Write an equation.
$$k + k + 3k + 3k = 32$$

C. Solve. Combine like terms.
$$8k = 32$$

Divide both sides by 8.
$$8k \div \mathbf{8} = 32 \div \mathbf{8},$$
$$\text{so } k = 4 \text{ cm, the width}$$
$$3k = 12 \text{ cm, the length}$$

Probability and Statistics

How to identify an outcome.

Toss a game cube with the following numbers: 1, 2, 3, 4, 5, 6. There are 6 possible outcomes. Each result is equally likely.

Toss a game cube with the following numbers: 1, 2, 3, 1, 2, 2. There are 3 possible outcomes. Since there are not the same number of the numbers, the outcomes are not equally likely.

Consider a spinner divided into 4 equal parts with the numbers 1, 2, 3, 4. There are 4 possible outcomes. Each result is equally likely.

Can an outcome be a number greater than 5? No, the only outcomes are 1, 2, 3, 4.

Can an outcome be a number less than 5? Yes, all outcomes are less than 5.

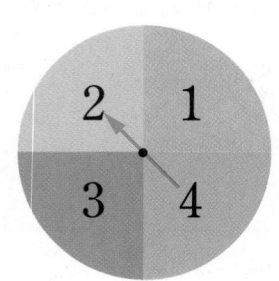

Tree diagrams. Tree diagrams are diagrams that show all the possible outcomes of one or more events. The arrows are like the branches of a tree, hence the name.

I toss a coin 2 times.

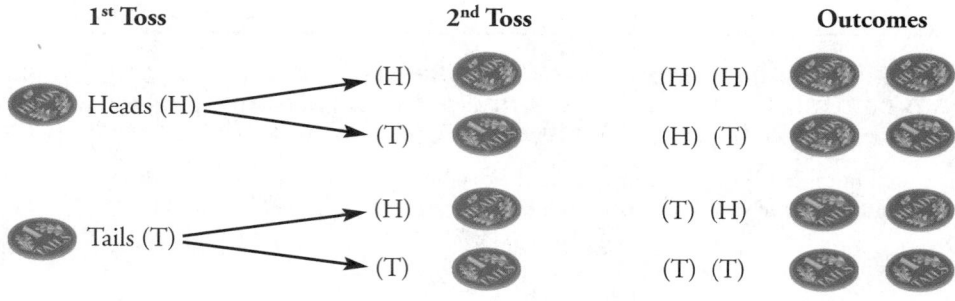

| 1st Toss | 2nd Toss | Outcomes |

Look at the column to the right. There are 4 possible outcomes.

A box contains 3 blue balls, 4 red balls, and 1 white ball. I select 1 ball.

How many outcomes are there?
3 outcomes: blue, red, and white

Are they equally likely?
No, there are unequal numbers of each color.

Which is most likely to be selected? Why?
Red; there are more reds than blues or whites.

Is it possible to have a green outcome?
No, there is no green ball.

Finding probability.

Probability is shown as (P): the number that tells the chance or likelihood that an event (E) will occur.

P(E): the probability of one event: the ratio of the number of favorable outcomes to the total number of possible outcomes *if each is equally likely.*

$$P(E): \frac{\text{The number of favorable outcomes}}{\text{The number of possible outcomes}}$$

I have 4 cards that have the numbers 5, 6, 7, and 8.

What is the probability of selecting a 6?

$$P(6) = \frac{\text{There is 1 chance of selecting a 6}}{\text{There are 4 possible outcomes}} = \frac{1}{4}$$

| 5 | 6 | 7 | 8 |

If the probability of selecting a 6 is 1/4, what is the probability of not selecting a 6?

$$P(\text{not } 6) = \frac{\text{There are 3 chances of not selecting a 6}}{\text{There are 4 possible outcomes}} = \frac{3}{4}$$

$$P(\text{all values}) = \frac{\text{There are 4 different values to select}}{\text{There are 4 possible outcomes}} = \frac{4}{4}, \text{which} = 1$$

$$P(2) = \frac{\text{There are no chances of selecting a 2}}{\text{There are 4 possible outcomes}} = \frac{0}{4}, \text{which} = 0$$

All certain events have a probability of 1.
All impossible events have a possibility of 0.

There is a set of cards: 6, 7, 8, 7, 9, 8, 7, 9. Select one card. Find the probability. Reduce if necessary.

$$P(8) = \frac{\text{There are 2 eights}}{\text{There are 8 possible outcomes}} = \frac{2}{8} = \frac{1}{4}$$

| 6 | 7 | 8 | 7 |
| 9 | 8 | 7 | 9 |

$$P(\text{even}) = \frac{\text{There are 3 even numbers}}{\text{There are 8 possible outcomes}} = \frac{3}{8} = \frac{3}{8}$$

$$P(\text{not } 7) = \textbf{A.} \ \frac{\text{There are 5 numbers not = to 7}}{\text{There are 8 possible outcomes}} = \frac{5}{8}$$

$$\textbf{B.} \ \frac{8 \text{ numbers}}{8 \text{ outcomes}} - \frac{3 \text{ sevens}}{8 \text{ outcomes}} = \frac{8}{8} - \frac{3}{8} = \frac{5}{8}$$

$$P(<10) = \frac{\text{All 8 numbers are less than 10}}{\text{There are 8 possible outcomes}} = \frac{8}{8} = \frac{1}{1} = 1$$

$$P(6 \text{ or } 7) = \frac{\text{There is 1 six} + 3 \text{ sevens}}{\text{There are 8 possible outcomes}} = \frac{4}{8} = \frac{1}{2}$$

$$P(>9) = \frac{\text{There are no numbers greater than 9}}{\text{There are 8 possible outcomes}} = \frac{0}{8} = 0$$

Everyday Math

Addition
Partial-Sums Algorithm

```
  2 5   becomes
+ 4 7
```

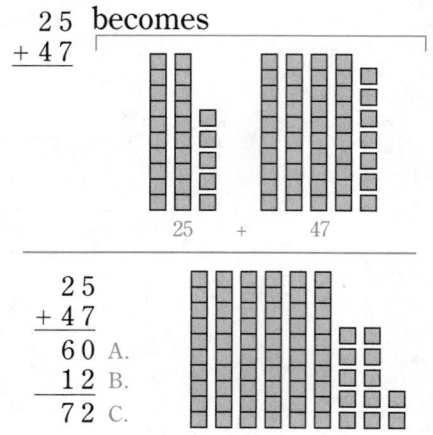

$$25 \quad + \quad 47$$

```
  2 5
+ 4 7
-----
  6 0  A.
  1 2  B.
-----
  7 2  C.
```

A. Add tens.* (2 tens + 4 tens = 6 tens, or 60)

B. Add ones. (5 ones + 7 ones = 12 ones, or 12)

C. Add partial-sums together for the answer.

*can start with tens or ones.

```
  5 8 2
+ 1 5 3
-------
  6 0 0  A.
  1 3 0  B.
      5  C.
-------
  7 3 5  D.
```

A. Start with hundreds. (5 hundreds + 1 hundred = 6 hundreds, or 600)

B. Then add tens. (8 tens + 5 tens = 13 tens, or 130)

C. Then add ones. (2 ones + 3 ones = 5 ones, or 5)

D. Add together.

Subtraction
Trade-First Algorithm

```
  4 9 3
- 3 6 1
```

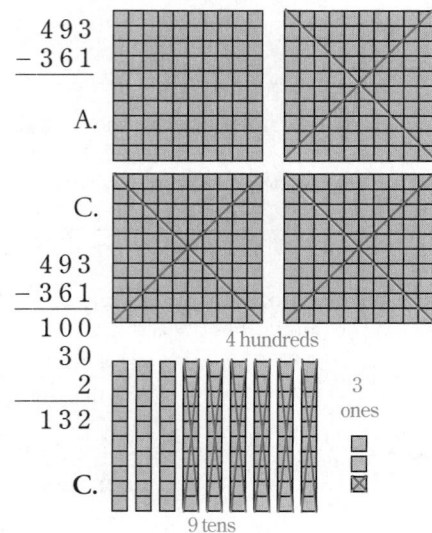

A.

C.

```
  4 9 3
- 3 6 1
-------
  1 0 0
    3 0
       2
-------
  1 3 2
```

4 hundreds

3 ones

9 tens

C.

A. Draw hundreds, tens, and ones.

B. Are there enough hundreds, tens, and ones to take away 3 hundreds, 6 tens, and 1 one? Yes.

C. Mark out or erase.

D. 4 hundreds minus 3 hundreds = 1 hundred. 9 tens minus 6 tens = 3 tens. 3 ones take away 1 one = 2 ones.

E. 1 hundred and 3 tens and 2 ones = 132.

```
  3 5 2
- 1 7 1
```

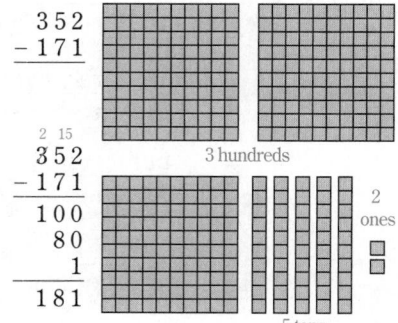

```
      2  15
  3 5 2
- 1 7 1
-------
  1 0 0
    8 0
       1
-------
  1 8 1
```

3 hundreds

2 ones

5 tens

A. Draw hundreds, tens, and ones.

B. Are there enough hundreds, tens, and ones to take away 1 hundred, 7 tens, and 1 one? No.

C. There are not enough tens. I need 7 and there are only 5, but I can trade a hundred for 10 tens. Make the trade.

D. Now there are 2 hundreds and 15 tens. Can I make the trade? Yes.

E. Subtract: 2 hundreds minus 1 hundred = 1 hundred. 15 tens minus 7 tens = 8 tens. 2 ones minus 1 one = 1 one.

F. 1 hundred and 8 tens and 1 one is 181.

Multiplication

There are several ways to work this problem: 432×3.

First, recall arrays.

$4 \times 3 = 12$
$3 \times 4 = 12$

Recall working with problems with 1 or 0.

$$1 \times 8 = 8 \qquad 0 \times 2 = 0$$
$$8 \times 1 = 8 \qquad 2 \times 0 = 0$$

Recall multiplication/division fact families.

$$4 \times 5 = 20 \qquad 20 \div 5 = 4$$
$$5 \times 4 = 20 \qquad 20 \div 4 = 5$$

Recall extended facts: Multiplying 1 digit numbers by 10, 100, or 1,000.

$$5 \times 4 = 20$$
$$5 \times 40 = 200$$
$$5 \times 400 = 2,000$$
$$5 \times 4,000 = 20,000$$

Partial-Products Method

Think of 432 as $400 + 30 + 2$. Multiply starting with hundreds, then tens, then ones. Add partial-products.

$$
\begin{array}{r}
432 \\
\times \quad 3 \\
\hline
1,200 \\
90 \\
6 \\
\hline
1,296
\end{array}
$$

Think of 432 as

$$
\begin{array}{rr}
400 \times 3 = & 1,200 \\
30 \times 3 = & 90 \\
2 \times 3 = & 6 \\
\hline
& 1,296
\end{array}
$$

	100s	10s	1s
	4	3	2
$\times$			3
	1 2	0	0
		9	0
			6
	1, 2	9	6

Division

Partial-Quotients Division

$$4\overline{)14}$$

This strategy uses making as many equal groups as possible, such as 2s, 5s, 10s, dozens, and so forth.

For this problem, let's use 2s because they are well known, and they are easy to work with.

There are at least two 4s because I know $2 \times 4 = 8$. I see there is another group of 4 in 6, so there are three 4s with a remainder of 2.

$$
\begin{array}{r}
3 \\
4\overline{)14} \\
8 \\
\hline
6 \\
4 \\
\hline
2
\end{array}
\quad
\begin{array}{l}
2 \times 4 \\
\\
1 \times 4 \\
\\
\overline{3}
\end{array}
$$

$$14 \div 4 = 3 \text{ R2}$$

These are some of the ways that Everyday Math works these problems. Students are encouraged to use whatever method is easiest for them as long as that method produces the correct answer.

How to Read a Mathematics Textbook

Reading a mathematics textbook is different from reading any other kind of book. You cannot merely sit down and start reading; you must be an *active reader*. Being an active reader means that you have to actively work, think, and learn while you read.

When you get ready to read your math text, make sure you have a good place to study. You should have a table or work surface where you can spread out your notes, textbook, and calculator, yet still have room to work problems. You should have good lighting, and the area in which you plan to study should be free of distractions such as television or loud music.

You need to have paper, a pencil (with a good eraser!), and a calculator (if required). Many math topics do not require a calculator, so ask your teacher if you are allowed to use one for a particular assignment.

When you first receive your math text, spend a little time looking at how it is organized. Many texts place important formulas, graphs, and math facts such as conversion factors at the very front or at the very back. Every text should have a glossary of terms, an index, or both. If you come across a word or term you do not understand, try looking it up in the glossary or index. Solutions to odd-numbered practice problems are often included at the back of the book, so you can check your work as you complete assignments.

Most mathematics textbooks are divided into chapters, and each chapter is divided into sections. Each section will have one or more *objectives*, or goals. For example, in a geometry text, the objective of a section might be to "State and use theorems about perpendicular lines." Sometimes the objective is actually written out at the beginning of the section or chapter, and sometimes it is not. It is up to you to make sure you have accomplished the objective.

Every section will probably also have definitions of new and/or important terms. Look for words that are in *italics* or are in **boldface** type. For example, in an algebra textbook, if you saw a sentence like this—"The **slope** of a line is the ratio of the difference in y to the difference in x"—you would know the definition of slope. Make sure you understand what all the terms in the definition mean and how they define the new concept.

Properties, postulates, theorems, or major definitions may be set apart in their own box or in an area that is a different color from the rest of the page. For example, in a Precalculus text, you might see a box like the one below.

Equations of Circles

The standard form of an equation of a circle with center
(h, k) and radius r is of the form:
$$(x - h)^2 + (y - k)^2 = r^2$$
The general form of an equation of a circle is of the form:
$$ax^2 + by^2 + cx + dy + f = 0$$
where a, b, c, d, and f are real numbers, and a and b are not equal to zero.

If it is important enough that the author has set it apart in a box, then it certainly is important enough for you to memorize and understand!

Each section will also have several examples that illustrate the objective being taught. Here is where your paper and pencil are useful. *When you come to an example in a math text, try to work the example out on your paper alongside the steps that are written out in the book.* It is not enough for you to merely read through the examples and tell yourself that you understand them! Spending a little extra time actually working out the examples with pencil and paper can save you many hours of frustration when it is time to do your homework. As you take more advanced mathematics courses, more and more steps will be left out of the examples in the text. Filling in the missing steps is an important part of mastering a mathematical concept.

Most sections end with a selection of problems for practice and reinforcement of the objective. Even if it seems as if you understand how to solve all the problems after working through the first few, be sure to complete your entire assignment. In math, more so than in any other subject, the old adage "practice makes perfect" holds true. Repetition of a particular type of problem helps you remember how to solve it at a later date when you see it on a chapter test, semester exam, or in real life. *As you work on your assigned problems, pay close attention to the directions given.* Many mistakes can be avoided simply by being aware of what you are asked to do. If you have finished all the assigned problems but are still having trouble with a certain type of problem, then work some more of that type. Many math teachers' assignments are "recommended minimum requirements" for students to fully master a concept.

Successful math students preview sections before their math instructor teaches them. That way, the material is not completely new, and they are better able to understand the teacher's presentation. When you are ready to do your homework, review your class notes, read through the section carefully (working out the examples), and then attempt the homework. Finally, when you are preparing for a chapter test, it is better to spread your studying out over a period of time rather than trying to "cram" everything the night before the test. Learning mathematics does not have to be a frustrating experience; following the steps we have described can make math a lot easier and more fun.

The steps described above may help you turn a poor grade into a better one.

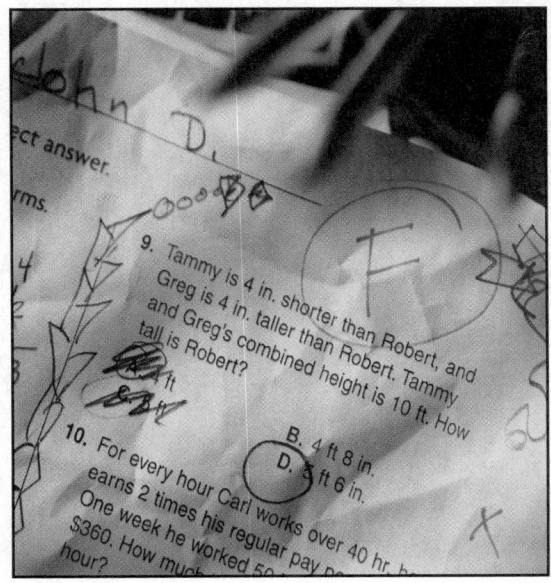
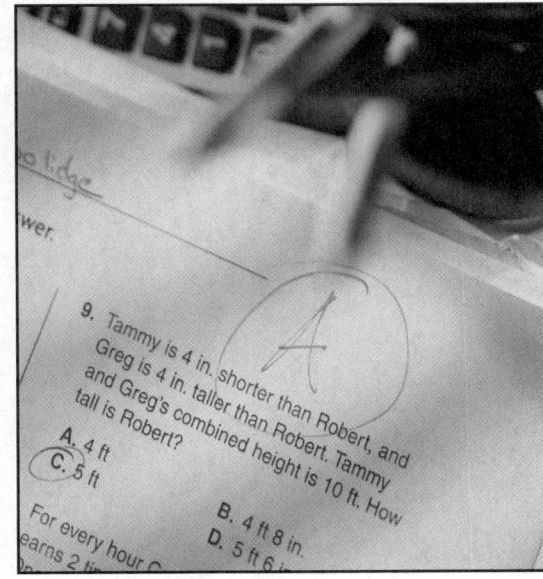

Basic Math Facts

BASIC ADDITION FACTS

0 + 0 = 0	1 + 0 = 1	2 + 0 = 2	3 + 0 = 3	4 + 0 = 4	5 + 0 = 5	6 + 0 = 6	7 + 0 = 7	8 + 0 = 8	9 + 0 = 9
0 + 1 = 1	1 + 1 = 2	2 + 1 = 3	3 + 1 = 4	4 + 1 = 5	5 + 1 = 6	6 + 1 = 7	7 + 1 = 8	8 + 1 = 9	9 + 1 =10
0 + 2 = 2	1 + 2 = 3	2 + 2 = 4	3 + 2 = 5	4 + 2 = 6	5 + 2 = 7	6 + 2 = 8	7 + 2 = 9	8 + 2 =10	9 + 2 =11
0 + 3 = 3	1 + 3 = 4	2 + 3 = 5	3 + 3 = 6	4 + 3 = 7	5 + 3 = 8	6 + 3 = 9	7 + 3 =10	8 + 3 =11	9 + 3 =12
0 + 4 = 4	1 + 4 = 5	2 + 4 = 6	3 + 4 = 7	4 + 4 = 8	5 + 4 = 9	6 + 4 =10	7 + 4 =11	8 + 4 =12	9 + 4 =13
0 + 5 = 5	1 + 5 = 6	2 + 5 = 7	3 + 5 = 8	4 + 5 = 9	5 + 5 =10	6 + 5 =11	7 + 5 =12	8 + 5 =13	9 + 5 =14
0 + 6 = 6	1 + 6 = 7	2 + 6 = 8	3 + 6 = 9	4 + 6 =10	5 + 6 =11	6 + 6 =12	7 + 6 =13	8 + 6 =14	9 + 6 =15
0 + 7 = 7	1 + 7 = 8	2 + 7 = 9	3 + 7 =10	4 + 7 =11	5 + 7 =12	6 + 7 =13	7 + 7 =14	8 + 7 =15	9 + 7 =16
0 + 8 = 8	1 + 8 = 9	2 + 8 =10	3 + 8 =11	4 + 8 =12	5 + 8 =13	6 + 8 =14	7 + 8 =15	8 + 8 =16	9 + 8 =17
0 + 9 = 9	1 + 9 =10	2 + 9 =11	3 + 9 =12	4 + 9 =13	5 + 9 =14	6 + 9 =15	7 + 9 =16	8 + 9 =17	9 + 9 =18

BASIC SUBTRACTION FACTS

0 − 0 = 0									
1 − 0 = 1	1 − 1 = 0								
2 − 0 = 2	2 − 1 = 1	2 − 2 = 0							
3 − 0 = 3	3 − 1 = 2	3 − 2 = 1	3 − 3 = 0						
4 − 0 = 4	4 − 1 = 3	4 − 2 = 2	4 − 3 = 1	4 − 4 = 0					
5 − 0 = 5	5 − 1 = 4	5 − 2 = 3	5 − 3 = 2	5 − 4 = 1	5 − 5 = 0				
6 − 0 = 6	6 − 1 = 5	6 − 2 = 4	6 − 3 = 3	6 − 4 = 2	6 − 5 = 1	6 − 6 = 0			
7 − 0 = 7	7 − 1 = 6	7 − 2 = 5	7 − 3 = 4	7 − 4 = 3	7 − 5 = 2	7 − 6 = 1	7 − 7 = 0		
8 − 0 = 8	8 − 1 = 7	8 − 2 = 6	8 − 3 = 5	8 − 4 = 4	8 − 5 = 3	8 − 6 = 2	8 − 7 = 1	8 − 8 = 0	
9 − 0 = 9	9 − 1 = 8	9 − 2 = 7	9 − 3 = 6	9 − 4 = 5	9 − 5 = 4	9 − 6 = 3	9 − 7 = 2	9 − 8 = 1	9 − 9 = 0
	10 − 1 = 9	10 − 2 = 8	10 − 3 = 7	10 − 4 = 6	10 − 5 = 5	10 − 6 = 4	10 − 7 = 3	10 − 8 = 2	10 − 9 = 1
		11 − 2 = 9	11 − 3 = 8	11 − 4 = 7	11 − 5 = 6	11 − 6 = 5	11 − 7 = 4	11 − 8 = 3	11 − 9 = 2
			12 − 3 = 9	12 − 4 = 8	12 − 5 = 7	12 − 6 = 6	12 − 7 = 5	12 − 8 = 4	12 − 9 = 3
				13 − 4 = 9	13 − 5 = 8	13 − 6 = 7	13 − 7 = 6	13 − 8 = 5	13 − 9 = 4
					14 − 5 = 9	14 − 6 = 8	14 − 7 = 7	14 − 8 = 6	14 − 9 = 5
						15 − 6 = 9	15 − 7 = 8	15 − 8 = 7	15 − 9 = 6
							16 − 7 = 9	16 − 8 = 8	16 − 9 = 7
								17 − 8 = 9	17 − 9 = 8
									18 − 9 = 9

BASIC MULTIPLICATION FACTS

zeros	0 × 0 = 0	1 × 0 = 0	2 × 0 = 0	3 × 0 = 0	4 × 0 = 0	5 × 0 = 0	6 × 0 = 0	7 × 0 = 0	8 × 0 = 0	9 × 0 = 0
ones	0 × 1 = 0	1 × 1 = 1	2 × 1 = 2	3 × 1 = 3	4 × 1 = 4	5 × 1 = 5	6 × 1 = 6	7 × 1 = 7	8 × 1 = 8	9 × 1 = 9
twos	0 × 2 = 0	1 × 2 = 2	2 × 2 = 4	3 × 2 = 6	4 × 2 = 8	5 × 2 = 10	6 × 2 = 12	7 × 2 = 14	8 × 2 = 16	9 × 2 = 18
threes	0 × 3 = 0	1 × 3 = 3	2 × 3 = 6	3 × 3 = 9	4 × 3 = 12	5 × 3 = 15	6 × 3 = 18	7 × 3 = 21	8 × 3 = 24	9 × 3 = 27
fours	0 × 4 = 0	1 × 4 = 4	2 × 4 = 8	3 × 4 = 12	4 × 4 = 16	5 × 4 = 20	6 × 4 = 24	7 × 4 = 28	8 × 4 = 32	9 × 4 = 36
fives	0 × 5 = 0	1 × 5 = 5	2 × 5 = 10	3 × 5 = 15	4 × 5 = 20	5 × 5 = 25	6 × 5 = 30	7 × 5 = 35	8 × 5 = 40	9 × 5 = 45
sixes	0 × 6 = 0	1 × 6 = 6	2 × 6 = 12	3 × 6 = 18	4 × 6 = 24	5 × 6 = 30	6 × 6 = 36	7 × 6 = 42	8 × 6 = 48	9 × 6 = 54
sevens	0 × 7 = 0	1 × 7 = 7	2 × 7 = 14	3 × 7 = 21	4 × 7 = 28	5 × 7 = 35	6 × 7 = 42	7 × 7 = 49	8 × 7 = 56	9 × 7 = 63
eights	0 × 8 = 0	1 × 8 = 8	2 × 8 = 16	3 × 8 = 24	4 × 8 = 32	5 × 8 = 40	6 × 8 = 48	7 × 8 = 56	8 × 8 = 64	9 × 8 = 72
nines	0 × 9 = 0	1 × 9 = 9	2 × 9 = 18	3 × 9 = 27	4 × 9 = 36	5 × 9 = 45	6 × 9 = 54	7 × 9 = 63	8 × 9 = 72	9 × 9 = 81

BASIC DIVISION FACTS

ones	0 ÷ 1 = 0	1 ÷ 1 = 1	2 ÷ 1 = 2	3 ÷ 1 = 3	4 ÷ 1 = 4	5 ÷ 1 = 5	6 ÷ 1 = 6	7 ÷ 1 = 7	8 ÷ 1 = 8	9 ÷ 1 = 9
twos	0 ÷ 2 = 0	2 ÷ 2 = 1	4 ÷ 2 = 2	6 ÷ 2 = 3	8 ÷ 2 = 4	10 ÷ 2 = 5	12 ÷ 2 = 6	14 ÷ 2 = 7	16 ÷ 2 = 8	18 ÷ 2 = 9
threes	0 ÷ 3 = 0	3 ÷ 3 = 1	6 ÷ 3 = 2	9 ÷ 3 = 3	12 ÷ 3 = 4	15 ÷ 3 = 5	18 ÷ 3 = 6	21 ÷ 3 = 7	24 ÷ 3 = 8	27 ÷ 3 = 9
fours	0 ÷ 4 = 0	4 ÷ 4 = 1	8 ÷ 4 = 2	12 ÷ 4 = 3	16 ÷ 4 = 4	20 ÷ 4 = 5	24 ÷ 4 = 6	28 ÷ 4 = 7	32 ÷ 4 = 8	36 ÷ 4 = 9
fives	0 ÷ 5 = 0	5 ÷ 5 = 1	10 ÷ 5 = 2	15 ÷ 5 = 3	20 ÷ 5 = 4	25 ÷ 5 = 5	30 ÷ 5 = 6	35 ÷ 5 = 7	40 ÷ 5 = 8	45 ÷ 5 = 9
sixes	0 ÷ 6 = 0	6 ÷ 6 = 1	12 ÷ 6 = 2	18 ÷ 6 = 3	24 ÷ 6 = 4	30 ÷ 6 = 5	36 ÷ 6 = 6	42 ÷ 6 = 7	48 ÷ 6 = 8	54 ÷ 6 = 9
sevens	0 ÷ 7 = 0	7 ÷ 7 = 1	14 ÷ 7 = 2	21 ÷ 7 = 3	28 ÷ 7 = 4	35 ÷ 7 = 5	42 ÷ 7 = 6	49 ÷ 7 = 7	56 ÷ 7 = 8	63 ÷ 7 = 9
eights	0 ÷ 8 = 0	8 ÷ 8 = 1	16 ÷ 8 = 2	24 ÷ 8 = 3	32 ÷ 8 = 4	40 ÷ 8 = 5	48 ÷ 8 = 6	56 ÷ 8 = 7	64 ÷ 8 = 8	72 ÷ 8 = 9
nines	0 ÷ 9 = 0	9 ÷ 9 = 1	18 ÷ 9 = 2	27 ÷ 9 = 3	36 ÷ 9 = 4	45 ÷ 9 = 5	54 ÷ 9 = 6	63 ÷ 9 = 7	72 ÷ 9 = 8	81 ÷ 9 = 9

List of symbols

Arithmetic

$\cdot$	decimal point
$\div$	divided by
$)$	divided into
$=$	equals
$(\ )$	grouping
$-$	minus
$\times$	multiplied by or times
$\%$	percent
$+$	plus

Geometry

$\angle$	angle
$\odot$	circle
$\cong$	congruent
$\overleftrightarrow{AB}$	line AB
$\overline{AB}$	line segment AB
$\mathbf{m}\ (\angle A)$	measure of angle A
$\|\ \|$	parallel to
$\perp$	perpendicular to
π	pi (about 3.14159)
$\overrightarrow{AB}$	ray AB
$\sim$	similar to
$\therefore$	therefore
$\triangle$	triangle

Algebra

$\|a\|$	absolute value of a
$\approx$	approximately equal to
3	cubed
$>$	greater than
$\geq$	greater than or equal to
$<$	less than
$\leq$	less than or equal to
$\neq$	not equal to
-3	negative 3
$\cdots$	not all members shown
$\pm$	plus or minus
$+3$	positive 3
$'$	prime (changes the meaning of a variable)
$\sqrt{\ }$	square root
2	squared

Sets

$\varnothing$	empty (or null) set
$\cap$	intersection
$\subset$	(proper) subset of
$\in$	member of
$\{\ \}$	set
$\cup$	union

Formulas used in Mathematics

General $d=rt$ where d is distance $\quad$ $p=br$ where p is percent $\quad$ $i=prt$ where i is interest
r is rate $\qquad$ b is base $\qquad$ p is percent
t is time $\qquad$ r is time $\qquad$ r is rate
$\qquad\qquad\qquad\qquad$ t is time

Length $p=a+b+c$ where p is perimeter of a *triangle*
a, b, and c are the lengths of the sides

$p=2l+2w$ where p is perimeter of a *rectangle*
l is length
w is width

$p=4s$ where p is perimeter of a *square*
s is length of a side

$C=\pi d$ where C is circumference of a *circle*
π is pi, a number that is about 3.14 or $\frac{22}{7}$
d is the length of the diameter

$C=2\pi r$ where C is the circumference of a *circle*
π is pi, a number that is about 3.14 or $\frac{22}{7}$
r is the length of the radius

Area $A=lw$ where A is area of a *rectangle*
l is length
w is width

$A=s^2$ where A is area of a *square*
s is length of a side

$A=bh$ where A is area of a *parallelogram*
b is length of the base
h is height

$A=\frac{1}{2}bh$ where A is area of a *triangle*
b is length of the base
h is height

$A=\frac{1}{2}h(B+b)$ where A is area of a *trapezoid*
h is height
B is length of one parallel side
b is length of the other parallel side

$A=\frac{1}{2}Dd$ where A is area of a *kite*
D is length of one diagonal
d is length of the other diagonal

$A=\frac{1}{2}ab$ where A is area of a *right triangle*
a is length of one leg
b is length of the other leg

$A=\frac{s^2}{4}\sqrt{3}$ where A is area of an *equilateral triangle*
s is length of one of the sides

$A=\frac{1}{2}ap$ where A is area of a *regular polygon*
a is length of an apothem
p is perimeter of the polygon

p = perimeter

	$A=\pi r^2$	where A is area of a *circle* π is pi, a number that is about 3.14 or $\frac{22}{7}$ r is length of the radius	
	$A=\sqrt{s(s-a)(s-b)(s-c)}$	where A is area of a *triangle* s is semiperimeter of the triangle; $(s=\frac{a+b+c}{2})$ $a,b,$ and c are the lengths of the sides	*perimeter = 2s*
	$A=2(\pi rh+\pi r^2)$ or $A=2\pi r(h+r)$	where A is total area of a *right circular cylinder* π is pi, a number that is about 3.14 or $\frac{22}{7}$ r is length of the radius of the base h is height of the cylinder	
	$A=\pi rl+\pi r^2$ or $A=\pi r(l+r)$	where A is total area of a *right circular cone* π is pi, a number that is about 3.14 or $\frac{22}{7}$ r is length of the radius of the base l is slant height of the cone	
	$A=4\pi r^2$	where A is area of a *sphere* π is pi, a number that is about 3.14 or $\frac{22}{7}$ r is length of the radius of the sphere	
Volume	$V=lwh$	where V is volume of a *right rectangular prism* l is length w is width h is height	
	$V=e^3$	where V is volume of a *cube* e is length of an edge of the cube	
	$V=Bh$	where V is volume of a *prism* B is area of the base h is height of the prism	*B = area of base*
	$V=\pi r^2 h$	where V is volume of a *circular cylinder* π is pi, a number that is about 3.14 or $\frac{22}{7}$ r is length of the radius of the base h is height of the cylinder	
	$V=\frac{1}{3}\pi r^2 h$	where V is volume of a *circular cone* π is pi, a number that is about 3.14 or $\frac{22}{7}$ r is length of the radius of the base h is height of the cylinder	
	$V=\frac{1}{3}Bh$	where V is volume of a *pyramid* B is area of the base of the pyramid h is height of the pyramid	*B = area of base*
	$V=\frac{4}{3}\pi r^3$	where V is volume of a *sphere* π is pi, a number that is about 3.14 or $\frac{22}{7}$ r is length of the radius of the sphere	

Mathematics Reference Tables

Laws of Exponents

If a and b are not zero

$$a^n a^m = a^{n+m}$$
$$(a^n)^m = a^{mn}$$
$$a^n/a^m = a^{m-n}$$

$$a^n b^n = (ab)^n$$
$$a^n/b^n = (a/b)^n$$
$$a^{-n} = 1/a^n$$

Powers of Ten

The number 10 has the special property that the number of times the digit 0 is used in the power is the same as the value of the exponent. For negative exponents, this property holds true for the denominators of powers of 10 in fraction form, but it is only true for powers of 10 in decimal form if a 0 is always written in the ones place (just in front of the decimal point). Counting all the zeros then gives the negative power.

POSITIVE EXPONENTS		ZERO AND NEGATIVE EXPONENTS
	(0 zeros)	$10^0 = 1$, or one
$10^1 = 10$, or ten	(1 zero)	$10^{-1} = \frac{1}{10} = 0.1$, or one tenth
$10^2 = 100$, or one hundred	(2 zeros)	$10^{-2} = \frac{1}{100} = 0.01$, or one hundredth
$10^3 = 1000$, or one thousand	(3 zeros)	$10^{-3} = \frac{1}{1000} = 0.001$, or one thousandth
$10^4 = 10,000$, or ten thousand	(4 zeros)	$10^{-4} = \frac{1}{10,000} = 0.0001$, or one ten thousandth
$10^5 = 100,000$, or one hundred thousand	(5 zeros)	$10^{-5} = \frac{1}{100,000} = 0.00001$, or one hundred thousandth
$10^6 = 1,000,000$, or one million	(6 zeros)	$10^{-6} = \frac{1}{1,000,000} = 0.000001$, or one millionth
$10^7 = 10,000,000$, or ten million	(7 zeros)	$10^{-7} = \frac{1}{10,000,000} = 0.0000001$, or one ten millionth
$10^8 = 100,000,000$, or one hundred million	(8 zeros)	$10^{-8} = \frac{1}{100,000,000} = 0.00000001$, or one hundred millionth
$10^9 = 1,000,000,000$, or one billion	(9 zeros)	$10^{-9} = \frac{1}{1,000,000,000} = 0.000000001$, or one billionth

Decimals and Place Value

Exponents can be used to make the meaning of decimals clearer. For whole numbers, the powers of 10 descend from left to right when you look at expanded form.

$$60,419 = 6 \times 10^4 + 0 \times 10^3 + 4 \times 10^2 + 1 \times 10 + 9$$

For decimals, the part to the left of the decimal point is just like a whole number, but the part to the right uses powers of 1/10; also, the exponents *increase* as you read from left to right.

$$5.287 = 5 + 2 \times (1/10) + 8 \times (1/10)^2 + 7 \times (1/10)^3$$

Equivalents

1 acre = 43,560 square feet = 4840 square yards
1 bushel (U.S.) = 2150.42 cubic inches
= 32 quarts
1 cord = 128 cubic feet
1 cubic centimeter = 0.061 cubic inch
1 cubic foot = 7.481 gallons = 1728 cubic inches
1 cubic inch = 0.554 fluid ounce
= 16.387 cubic centimeters
1 cubic meter = 1.308 cubic yards
1 cubic yard = 0.765 cubic meter = 27 cubic feet
1 cup = 8 fluid ounces = 0.5 liquid pint
1 gallon (U.S.) = 231 cubic inches
= 128 U.S. fluid ounces
= 4 liquid quarts
1 liter = 1.057 liquid quarts
1 meter = 39.37 inches = 1.094 yards
1 micron = 0.001 millimeter = 0.00003937 inch
1 mile, nautical = 1.852 kilometers
= 1.151 statute miles
= 6076.1155 feet
1 milliliter = 0.061 cubic inch
1 pint, dry = 33.600 cubic inches = 0.551 liter
1 pint, liquid = 28.875 inches = 0.473 liter
= 2 cups = 16 ounces
1 pound, avoirdupois = 7000 grains = 16 ounces
= 453.59237 grams
1 quart, dry (U.S.) = 67.201 cubic inches
= 1.101 liters
1 quart, liquid (U.S.) = 57.75 cubic inches
= 0.946 liter
= 2 pints = 32 ounces
1 square foot = 929 square centimeters
= 144 square inches
1 square inch = 6.45 square centimeters
1 square kilometer = 0.386 square miles
= 247.105 acres
1 square meter = 1.196 square yards
= 10.764 square feet
1 square mile = 640 acres
1 square yard = 0.836 square meter
= 9 square feet
= 1296 square inches
1 tablespoon = 3 teaspoons = 0.5 fluid ounce
1 ton, metric = 2204.623 pounds
= 1.102 net tons
1 ton, net or short = 2000 pounds
= 0.907 metric ton
1 yard = 0.9144 meter = 3 feet = 36 inches

Conversions

To convert	into	multiply by
angstroms	microns	0.0001
centimeters	feet	0.03281
centimeters	inches	0.3937
cubic cm	cubic inches	0.06102
cubic feet	cubic meters	0.02832
days	seconds	86,400.0
degrees (angle)	radians	0.01745
fathoms	feet	6.0
feet	centimeters	30.48
feet	meters	0.3048
feet/min.	cm/sec.	0.5080
feet/sec.	knots	0.5921
feet/sec.	statute mi./hr.	0.6818
furlongs/hr.	statute mi./hr.	0.125
furlongs	feet	660.0
gallons (liq.)	liters	3.785
gal. of water	pounds of water	8.3453
grams	oz. (avoirdupois)	0.03527
grams	pounds	0.002205
hours	days	0.04167
hours	weeks	0.005952
inches	centimeters	2.540
kilograms	pounds	2.205
kilometers	feet	3280.8
kilometers	mi. (statute)	0.6214
knots	feet/hr.	6080.0
knots	nautical mi./hr.	1.0
knots	statute mi./hr.	1.151
liters	gallons (liq.)	0.2642
liters	pints (liq.)	2.113
meters	feet	3.281
meters	mi. (nautical)	0.0005396
meters	mi. (statute)	0.0006214
microns	meters	0.000001
mi. (nautical)	feet	6076.115
mi. (statute)	feet	5280.0
mi. (nautical)	kilometers	1.852
mi. (statute)	kilometers	1.609
mi. (nautical)	mi. (statute)	1.1508
mi. (statute)	mi. (nautical)	0.8684
mi. (statute)/hr.	feet/min.	88.0
millimeters	inches	0.03937
oz. (avoirdupois)	grams	28.3495
oz. (avoirdupois)	lb. (avoirdupois)	0.0625
pints (liq.)	gallons (liq.)	0.125
pints (liq.)	quarts (liq.)	0.5
lb. (avoirdupois)	kilograms	0.4536

Principal Units of Measurement

The customary system of length

1 mile = 1760 yards = 5280 feet

1 yard = 3 feet = 36 inches

1 foot = 12 inches

The metric system of length

kilometer	km	1000 meters	$1000 \times$ meter
meter	m	1 meter	—
centimeter	cm	0.01 meter	$\frac{1}{100}$ meter
millimeter	mm	0.001 meter	$\frac{1}{1000}$ meter

Metric units of liquid volume

kiloliter	kl	1000 liters	$1000 \times$ liter
liter	l	1.0 liter	—
centiliter	cl	0.01 liter	$\frac{1}{100}$ liter
milliliter	ml	0.001 liter	$\frac{1}{1000}$ liter

Metric units of mass

kilogram	kg	1000 grams	$1000 \times$ gram
gram	g	1.0 gram	—
centigram	cg	0.01 gram	$\frac{1}{100}$ gram
milligram	mg	0.001 gram	$\frac{1}{1000}$ gram

Fraction-Decimal Equivalents

$\frac{1}{16} = 0.0625$

$\frac{1}{12} = 0.0833...$

$\frac{1}{10} = 0.1$

$\frac{1}{9} = 0.1111...$

$\frac{2}{16}, \frac{1}{8} = 0.125$

$\frac{1}{7} = 0.142857...$

$\frac{2}{16}, \frac{1}{6} = 0.1666...$

$\frac{3}{16} = 0.1875$

$\frac{2}{10}, \frac{1}{5} = 0.2$

$\frac{2}{9} = 0.2222...$

$\frac{4}{16}, \frac{3}{12}, \frac{2}{8}, \frac{1}{4} = 0.25$

$\frac{2}{7} = 0.285714...$

$\frac{3}{10} = 0.3$

$\frac{5}{16} = 0.3125$

$\frac{4}{12}, \frac{3}{9}, \frac{2}{6}, \frac{1}{3} = 0.3333...$

$\frac{6}{16}, \frac{3}{8} = 0.375$

$\frac{4}{10}, \frac{2}{5} = 0.4$

$\frac{5}{12} = 0.4166...$

$\frac{3}{7} = 0.428571...$

$\frac{7}{16} = 0.4375$

$\frac{4}{9} = 0.4444...$

$\frac{8}{16}, \frac{6}{12}, \frac{5}{10}, \frac{4}{8}, \frac{3}{6}, \frac{2}{4}, \frac{1}{2} = 0.5$

$\frac{5}{9} = 0.5555...$

$\frac{9}{16} = 0.5625$

$\frac{4}{7} = 0.571428...$

$\frac{7}{12} = 0.5833...$

$\frac{6}{10}, \frac{3}{5} = 0.6$

$\frac{10}{16}, \frac{5}{8} = 0.625$

$\frac{8}{12}, \frac{6}{9}, \frac{4}{6}, \frac{2}{3} = 0.6666...$

$\frac{11}{16} = 0.6875$

$\frac{7}{10} = 0.7$

$\frac{5}{7} = 0.714285...$

$\frac{12}{16}, \frac{9}{12}, \frac{6}{8}, \frac{3}{4} = 0.75$

$\frac{7}{9} = 0.7777...$

$\frac{8}{10}, \frac{4}{5} = 0.8$

$\frac{13}{16} = 0.8125$

$\frac{10}{12}, \frac{5}{6} = 0.8333...$

$\frac{6}{7} = 0.857142...$

$\frac{14}{16}, \frac{7}{8} = 0.875$

$\frac{8}{9} = 0.8888...$

$\frac{9}{10} = 0.9$

$\frac{11}{12} = 0.9166...$

$\frac{15}{16} = 0.9375$

abscissa. Directed distance of a point from the *y* axis. In a pair of coordinates, the first member.

absolute value. The distance on the number line from zero.

acute. An angle with a measure of less than 90° or a triangle with three acute angles.

addend. Any one of a set of numbers that are being added.

addition. Process of finding the number of members in two or more sets that have been combined.

additive identity element. A number *z* such that for any number in a set, *z* added to it gives the original number. For the real numbers, the additive identity element is 0.

additive inverse. A number that can be added to another number to produce the additive identity element is the additive inverse of the second number. For the real numbers, the additive inverse of *x* is −*x*, because $x + (-x) = 0$, and 0 is the additive identity element.

algorithm. Any formal method for performing a computation.

amplitude. For a trigonometric function, the largest value of the function.

angle. Union of two rays with a common endpoint.

arc cosine. The inverse of the cosine function; that is, the angle that has a particular value of the cosine. Abbreviated either arc cos or $\cos^{-1}$.

arc sine. The inverse of the sine function; that is, the angle that has a particular value of the sine. Abbreviated either arc sin or $\sin^{-1}$.

arc tangent. The inverse of the tangent function; that is, the angle that has a particular value of the tangent. Abbreviated either arc tan or $\tan^{-1}$.

area. Two-dimensional measure of the surface inside a plane (flat) geometric figure.

arithmetic mean. The average; that is, the quotient formed when the numbers in a set are added and then divided by the number of numbers in the set.

arithmetic sequence. The sequence formed by adding the same amount to a given number over and over.

arithmetic series. Series formed as the indicated sum of an arithmetic sequence.

associative law. When three numbers are added (or multiplied), the sum (product) is the same when the sum (product) of the last two numbers is added to (multiplied by) the first as when the sum (product) of the first two numbers is added to (multiplied by) the last.

average. The arithmetic mean.

axiom. A statement that is accepted without proof and then used as the basis of a system of proofs.

base. When an exponent is used, the number to which the exponent is applied.

basic fact. For addition, subtraction, multiplication, and division of whole numbers, the sums, differences, products, and quotients formed when two numbers less than 10 are added or multiplied, or when a subtrahend and difference are both less than 10, or when a divisor and quotient are less than 10.

binomial. Polynomial that has two terms.

bisect. Separate into two congruent parts.

circle. Plane figure that is the set of points equidistant from a given point.

common denominator. For two or more fractions, a denominator with which each fraction may be shown.

commutative law. When two numbers are added (or multiplied), the sum (product) is the same no matter which

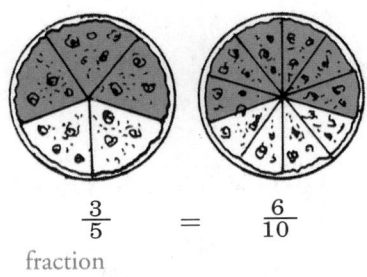

$$\frac{3}{5} = \frac{6}{10}$$

fraction

Dictionary of mathematics

Roman Numerals

The ancient Romans used seven letters in their number system. The letters and their values are:

I	V	X	L	C	D	M
1	5	10	50	100	500	1000

In Roman numerals, a number is written from left to right, with the symbols added together to determine the value of the number. For example, the value 56 in Roman numerals is LVI (50 + 5 + 1). When a smaller numeral is to the left of a larger one, the smaller is subtracted from the larger. For example, the number 90 is written as XC (10 *subtracted* from 100).

order they are added (multi-plied) in.

complement. For sets, the elements of a set with respect to another set that are not included in the first set.

complex number. A number that is the sum of a real number and an imaginary number.

composite number. A composite number is a number with more than two whole number factors. The whole numbers zero and one are considered neither prime nor composite.

conditional equation. Any equation that is true for some values or the variable(s) and false for others. In trigonometry, a conditional equation involving one or more trigonometric functions is called a trigonometric equation.

constant. In algebra, a quantity that does not vary in a given situation.

coordinate plane. A set of points that can be located by two numbers in an ordered pair. Most often the coordinate plane is determined by two intersecting perpendicular lines, commonly the x axis and the y axis.

cosecant. A trigonometric function that is defined as the distance of a point on a particular ray from the origin divided by the ordinate of the point on the ray. It is a constant for the angle that the ray makes with the positive horizontal axis.

cosine. A trigonometric function defined as the abscissa of a point on a particular ray from the origin divided by the distance of that point from the origin. It is a constant for the angle the ray makes with the positive horizontal axis.

cotangent. A trigonometric function that is defined as the abscissa of a point on a particular ray divided by the ordinate of the point. It is a constant for the angle that the

ray makes with the positive horizontal axis.

counting number. One of the numbers 1, 2, 3, ... that are used to count with; also called a natural number.

cross-product rule. In a proportion, the rule that the product of the numerator of one ratio with the denominator of the other ratio is always equal to the product of the denominator of the first ratio with the numerator of the second ratio.

cube. In geometry, a figure in three dimensions that has six congruent squares as faces.

cubed. Taken as a factor three times.

decimal. Number shown using a decimal point to indicate fractions whose denominators are powers of 10.

denominator. In a fraction, the number that tells the number of parts into which something has been divided.

dependent system of equations. System in two or more variables in which each equation has the same solution.

dependent variable. The variable that represents the value of the function.

difference. In subtraction, the answer, sometimes called the remainder. A distinction is maintained between subtraction used to show comparison (when difference is used) and subtraction to show part of a set taken away (when remainder is used).

digit. Whole number less than 10.

distributive law. The product of a number and a sum is equal to the sum of the product of the number with each of the addends.

dividend. In division, the quantity that is to be divided.

division. Operation that can be either treated as repeated sub-

traction or as the inverse (opposite operation) of multiplication.

divisor. Quantity by which the dividend is divided.

element. Another name for a member of a set.

empty set. A set that is a subset of every set and that contains no members; often symbolized by ∅.

equilateral. For a triangle, having all sides congruent.

event. In probability, a set or sentence that describes the outcomes that will be considered successful.

expanded form. Method of writing a number as the sum of powers of 10, either with or without using exponents.

exponent. Small numeral (superscript) written above and to the right of a number. Exponents that represent counting numbers tell how many times the number is used as a factor.

factor. In multiplication, any one of the numbers to be multiplied to form a product.

factoring. Process of finding the counting numbers that when multiplied will form a given number.

fraction. Number formed by dividing a whole number by a counting number.

function. A rule that connects two sets of numbers in such a way that a member of the second set is completely specified by choosing a member of the first set.

greatest common factor. Number that is the largest factor shared by two or more numbers.

geometric mean. For two numbers, the positive square root of their product.

geometric sequence. The sequence formed by multiplying a given number by the same factor over and over.

geometric series. Indicated sum of a geometric sequence.

greatest common factor. Largest factor that is common to two or more numbers.

harmonic mean. For two numbers, the multiplicative inverse of the mean (average) of their multiplicative inverses.

harmonic sequence. A sequence formed by the multiplicative inverses of the terms of an arithmetic sequence.

harmonic series. Indicated sum of a harmonic sequence.

heptagon. Seven-sided polygon.

hexagon. Polygon with six sides.

i. Symbol used to denote the square root of -1; when multiplied by any real number (except 0), it forms an imaginary number.

identity. Any equation that is true for all values of the variable or variables.

imaginary number. The product of any real number (except 0) and *i*, the square root of -1.

inconsistent system of equations. System of equations with no solution to the system.

independent variable. For a function, the variable over which the function is defined; that is, the variable representing the set that is the domain of the function.

inequality. Sentence containing one of the following relations: greater than, less than, not equal, greater than or equal, less than or equal.

infinite sequence. Sequence for which the domain is the entire set of natural numbers.

infinite series. Indicated sum of an infinite sequence.

infinity. Various related mathematical ideas, of which the most common is an indication that a sequence of numbers continues indefinitely. Also indicates size of a set that can be matched with all the natur-al numbers or all the real numbers.

integer. Number that is either whole or the negative of a whole.

intercept. For graphs, either the point at which the graph crosses one of the axes or the distance of that point from the origin.

intersection. For sets, the set that contains all the members common to two or more sets.

inverse function. A function formed by interchanging the two variables, such as x and y. In general, the inverse of a function $f(x)$ is labeled as $f^1(x)$, although inverse trigonometric functions are more commonly indicated by the prefix arc, as in arc sin x.

inverse operation. An operation that undoes the effect of a given operation; for example, addition is the inverse of subtraction.

irrational number. Real number that is not also a rational number.

isosceles. A triangle that has two congruent sides.

kite. Polygon that has two pairs of adjacent congruent sides.

least common denominator. Least common multiple of the denominators of a set of fractions.

least common multiple. Smallest nonzero number that is a multiple of all numbers in a set of numbers.

mean proportional. A number that is both the denominator of one ratio and the numerator of the other.

member. For sets or for ordered pairs, one of the individual parts of the set or pair.

minuend. In subtraction, the number from which you subtract or the larger of two amounts being compared by subtraction.

mixed number. Sum of a whole number and a fraction that is written by adjoining the numeral for the fraction to the numeral for the whole number.

monomial. Product of a number and one or more variables.

multiple. Product of a given number and a whole number.

multiplicand. Number that you are multiplying; when multiplication is viewed as repeated addition, the addend that is repeated.

multiplication. Operation that for counting numbers may be viewed as repeated addition.

multiplicative identity element. A number I such that for any number in a set, I times the number gives the original number. For real numbers, the element is 1.

multiplicative inverse. Number such that the product of that number and a given number is 1.

multiplier. Number by which you are multiplying; when multiplication is viewed as repeated addition, the number that indicates how many times the repeated addend will be used.

natural number. Number that is 1 or formed by starting with 1 and adding 1 more each time.

negative number. Number to the left of 0 on the number line.

null set. Set with no members; the empty set.

number line. Line on which a scale of numbers is indicated.

numeral. Written symbol for a number.

numerator. In a fraction, the number of parts represented by the fraction.

oblique. A triangle that does not contain a right angle.

obtuse. An angle greater than 90° and less than 180°.

octagon. Eight-sided polygon.

opposite. Number that is equal in value but opposite in sign to a given number.

ordinate. For a point in the coordinate plane, the directed distance from the *x* axis; the second member of the coordinates of the points.

outcome. In probability, the result of a trial.

parallel. For lines, two or more lines in a plane that do not meet.

parallelogram. Quadrilateral for which both pairs of opposite sides are parallel.

pentagon. Five-sided polygon.

percent. Ratio of a number to 100 that is shown as a whole number or mixed number with a percent sign.

percent of decrease. Percent used to indicate that the percentage must be subtracted from the original amount.

percent of increase. Percent used to indicate that the percentage must be added to the original amount.

percentage. Quantity found by taking a percent of a number.

perimeter. Distance around a plane figure (usually called the circumference if the figure is a circle).

period. For trigonometric functions, the size of the interval before the values of the function begin to repeat exactly. For trigonometric functions other than the tangent and cotangent, the period is 360°, or 2π, but for the tangent and cotangent it is 180°, or π.

perpendicular. For lines or line segments, two lines (segments) that meet at right angles.

pi. A Greek letter. Its lowercase form, π, is used for the ratio of the circumference of a circle to its diameter. Although pi cannot be expressed exactly as a decimal, it is 3.14159 to six decimal places.

place value. System of representing numbers in which the place a digit has in a numeral indicates the value of the digit.

plane. Flat surface extending infinitely in all directions.

point of inflection. A point at which a curve changes from being convex to concave.

polygon. A closed plane figure formed by three or more primes linked in pairs by line segments that do not cross each other.

polynomial. A monomial or the sum of any finite number of monomials.

positive number. Number to the right of 0 on the number line.

power. Number formed by using the same number as a factor more than once; more generally, any number indicated by an exponent.

prime. For natural numbers, a number that has only itself and 1 as factors.

prime factorization. The process of writing a number as the product of its primes. $140 = 2 \times 2 \times 5 \times 7$.

prime number. A whole number, greater than 1, with only two factors: 1 and the number itself.

probability. Number that describes the chance that a given event will take place.

product. The answer in multiplication.

proportion. Statement that two ratios are equal.

Pythagorean theorem. For right triangles, the statement that the area of a square that has one side on the side of the triangle opposite the right angle is equal to the sum of the areas of the squares on the other two sides of the triangle.

quadrant. On the coordinate plane, one of the four regions into which the plane is separated by the axes.

quadratic equation. An equation in one variable for which the highest power of the variable is the second and all the powers of the variable are whole numbers.

quadrilateral. Four-sided polygon.

quotient. Answer in division.

radian measure. System for measuring general angles based on a unit defined so that π radians is a straight angle, or 180°.

radical. Sign used to indicate that a square root of a number (or, combined with an index, another root of the number) is to be taken.

radicand. Number or expression under a radical.

ratio. Comparison of two quantities by division, often expressed as a rate.

rational number. The ratio of an integer to a natural number.

real number. Any positive or negative number that can be shown on a number line.

reciprocal. For a given number, the number formed by dividing the given number into 1.

rectangle. Parallelogram that contains a right angle.

relation. Any rule connecting the members of two sets.

relative maximum. Greatest value of a function in an interval.

relative minimum. The least value of a function in an interval

remainder. In division, the whole number left over in addition to the quotient. Sometimes used to name the answer in subtraction.

rhombus. Parallelogram with adjacent sides congruent.

right angle. When two lines intersect to form four equal angles, one of the four angles.

right triangle. Triangle that contains a right angle.

root. A number such that the product of the number repeated two or more times is a given number.

sample space. In probability, the set of all outcomes of a given experiment.

scalene. Triangle in which no two sides are equal.

secant. (1) A trigonometric function that is defined as the distance of a point on a particular ray from the origin divided by the abscissa of the point on the ray. It is a constant for the angle that the ray makes with the horizontal axis. (2) A line that intersects a circle in two planes.

sequence. The ordered values of a function over the natural numbers.

series. Indicated sum of a sequence.

set. Any collection of objects or ideas such that you can tell whether a given object or idea is a member of the collection.

signed number. Number written with a positive or negative sign.

similar figures. Geometric figures that have the same shape but not necessarily the same size.

sine. A trigonometric function that is defined as the ordinate of a point on a particular ray from the origin divided by the distance of that point from the origin. It is a constant for the angle that the ray makes with the positive horizontal axis.

slope. The quotient of rate of change of the ordinates on a line divided by the rate of change of the abscissas.

solution. In algebra, an equation that states the value of a variable that will make another given equation true.

square. Plane figure formed of four equal line segments that share endpoints and also make four right angles.

squared. Taken as a factor two times.

straight angle. Angle that measures 180° or π radians.

subtraction. Operation that can be viewed as finding the number when objects are taken away from a set or as a comparison to determine how much greater one amount is than another; the inverse (opposite) of addition.

subtrahend. Either the number

that is taken away in subtraction or the smaller of two amounts being compared.

sum. Answer in addition.

system of equations. Set of two or more equations in two or more variables to be solved for the intersection of the solutions of the equations in the set.

tangent. (1) Trigonometric function that is defined as the ordinate of a point on a particular ray divided by the abscissa of that point. It is a constant for the angle that the ray makes with the positive horizontal axis. (2) A line that intersects a circle at one and only one point.

tetrahedron. Four-sided solid whose faces are all triangles.

theorem. Statement that has been derived from a set of axioms according to the rules of logic.

transformations. Changes made in an equation to isolate the variable from the other numerals in the equation.

triangle. Plane figure formed from three different line segments that share endpoints.

trigonometric function. Function whose independent variable is an angle and whose value is defined as a quotient of one pair from the following:
  abscissa
  ordinate
  distance from origin of a

point on a ray that makes the given angle with the positive *x* axis.

trinomial. Polynomial that has three terms.

union. For two sets, the set that contains all the members of both sets.

variable. Letter or other symbol that can represent any one of a specified set of numbers.

vertical angles. Two angles formed by intersecting lines so that the angles do not have a ray in common.

whole number. Either a counting number or zero.

zero. A number that tells the number of members in a set that is empty (a set that has no members).

hexagon

For Further Reference

Hogben, Lancelot
Mathematics for the Million
W. W. Norton
Prindle, Anthony and Prindle, Katie
Math the Easy Way
Barron's

Sperling, Abraham P. and Levison, Samuel D.
Arithmetic Made Simple
Doubleday
Trivieri, Lawrence A.
Basic Mathematics
HarperCollins

- *Nutrition* **331**
- *Exercise* **336**
- *Drugs and disease* **338**
- *Human anatomy* **340**
- *Safety* **344**
- *Dictionary of health and safety* **352**

Health and Safety

A healthier and happier lifestyle is within reach of everyone who understands and follows sensible health practices. To enjoy a high level of "wellness," it is essential to eat sufficient nutritional foods; obtain enough rest and relaxation; exercise sensibly; attend to personal grooming; and cultivate a positive outlook on life. You should also learn to avoid dangerous situations and know the proper procedures to follow in an emergency.

It is equally important to be aware of potential threats to good health (such as persistent pain or bleeding), and to report promptly such distress signals to your physician. Regular medical checkups, as recommended by your family physician, provide the best possible method of detecting medical problems as they arise.

Common Distress Signals

*If any of the following conditions arise and are persistent, severe, or unexplained,
check with your physician without delay.*

Pain (the foremost danger signal, especially when the cause is not known)

Fatigue (without obvious cause)

Weight change (gain or loss)

Headache (especially if it recurs)

Fever (almost always a sign of infection)

Hemorrhage (bleeding)

Indigestion (especially if it recurs often)

Insomnia (sleeplessness)

Skin changes (rashes or ulcers)

Personality changes (abnormal restlessness or aggression)

Vision changes (seeing double or poorly)

Edema (swelling)

Lumps or growths (especially if they get larger)

Breathlessness (especially after slight exertion)

Coughing and hoarseness (if continued for a period of time)

Sore throat (if not relieved within a few days)

Loss of appetite (or difficulty in swallowing)

Excessive thirst (especially if there is excessive or painful urination)

Dizziness, giddiness, or vertigo

Bowel-habit changes (especially unaccustomed constipation or diarrhea)

Nutrition

The human body requires adequate amounts of basic foods together with their nutrients to keep it functioning properly and to stay healthy and strong. Some foods are needed to supply energy or growth, while others are necessary to regulate body processes. There are also some foods whose use should be restricted.

Because no one food contains all the nutrients (proteins, carbohydrates, fats, vitamins, and minerals) needed for good health, it is important that you select the right amounts and combinations of foods. Proper nutrition consists of eating well-balanced meals that include daily servings from each of five major food groups.

The United States Department of Agriculture (USDA) has developed the Food Guide Pyramid, which illustrates the five major food groups and identifies the number of servings from each that you need for a healthful, well-balanced diet. No single food group is more important than another—all are needed to achieve a balanced diet.

The Food Guide Pyramid is also a good guide to limiting the amount of fat in your diet. The top of the pyramid represents fats, oils, and sweets, items that add calories and little else to the diet. These have so little nutritional value that you should eat them sparingly.

The base of the pyramid represents low-fat, high-energy foods that come from grains. Above this are the food groups for fruits and vegetables, also low-fat foods that are important for vitamins and minerals and for dietary fiber. Above these are the food groups for milk, yogurt, and cheese and for meat, poultry, fish, beans, and nuts. Both are higher in fat but are good sources of protein and such minerals as calcium, zinc, and iron.

The USDA Food Guide Pyramid

The pyramid shape reflects the relative number of servings you need from each food group daily. Eat more cereals, grains, vegetables, and fruits, less dairy foods and meat. Limit fat and sweets.

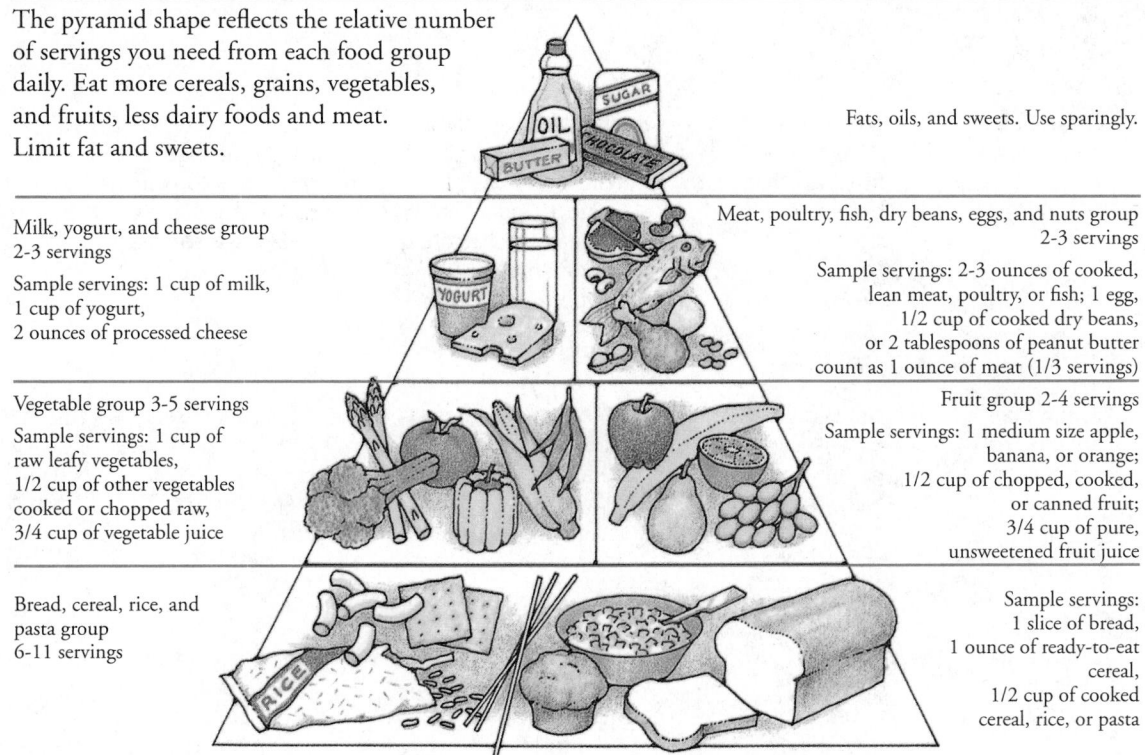

Fats, oils, and sweets. Use sparingly.

Milk, yogurt, and cheese group
2-3 servings

Sample servings: 1 cup of milk,
1 cup of yogurt,
2 ounces of processed cheese

Meat, poultry, fish, dry beans, eggs, and nuts group
2-3 servings

Sample servings: 2-3 ounces of cooked, lean meat, poultry, or fish; 1 egg, 1/2 cup of cooked dry beans, or 2 tablespoons of peanut butter count as 1 ounce of meat (1/3 servings)

Vegetable group 3-5 servings

Sample servings: 1 cup of raw leafy vegetables, 1/2 cup of other vegetables cooked or chopped raw, 3/4 cup of vegetable juice

Fruit group 2-4 servings

Sample servings: 1 medium size apple, banana, or orange; 1/2 cup of chopped, cooked, or canned fruit; 3/4 cup of pure, unsweetened fruit juice

Bread, cereal, rice, and pasta group
6-11 servings

Sample servings:
1 slice of bread,
1 ounce of ready-to-eat cereal,
1/2 cup of cooked cereal, rice, or pasta

Vitamins and nutrition.

In themselves, vitamins are not sources of energy but they help to process carbohydrates, fats, and proteins so that they can be turned into energy or be used in the body to build cells and restore tissues. Vitamins are divided into two groups, depending on whether they can dissolve in fat (fat-soluble) or in water (water-soluble). The water-

Vitamins			

Fat-soluble vitamins

Vitamin	Good sources	Recommended daily allowances*	Average serving in some foods
Vitamin A	butter, cheese, whole milk liver green leafy and yellow vegetables apricots, peaches, persimmons	infants and children: 375 to 700 mcg RE** males and females: 800 to 1000 mcg RE pregnant and lactating women: 800 to 1300 mcg RE	$1/2$ cup raw, or 1 cup cooked carrots 1 apricot or peach 1 large egg 1 cup whole milk 3 oz. Cheddar cheese 1 cup dandelion or turnip greens
Vitamin D	cod-liver or other fish-liver oils dairy products	infants and children: 300 to 400 I.U. males and females: 200 to 400 I.U. pregnant and lactating women: 400 I.U.	4 8-oz. glasses whole milk 14 tbsp. butter 12 large egg yolks
Vitamin E alpha-tocopherol	green leafy vegetables fish and other oils butter rice	infants and children: 3 to 7 mg alpha -TE** males and females: 8 to 10 mg alpha-TE pregnant and lactating women: 10 to 12 mg alpha-TE	9 to 15 tbsp. olive oil 2 tbsp. safflower oil $3/4$ lb. beet top greens 5 to 6 large stalks broccoli 18 Brussels sprouts $2/3$ lb. spinach

Water-soluble vitamins

Vitamin	Good sources	Recommended daily allowances*	Average serving in some foods
Thiamine vitamin B$_1$	whole grain cereals peas, beans many fruits and vegetables brewer's yeast liver, kidney	infants and children: 0.3 to 1.0 mg males and females: 1.0 to 1.5 mg pregnant and lactating women: 1.5 to 1.6 mg	$2^1/2$ cups cooked peas 1 tbsp. brewer's yeast 10 stalks broccoli 5 large oranges 3 oz. liver, calf
Riboflavin vitamin B$_2$	enriched foods green leafy vegetables liver, kidney lean meat eggs, milk wheat germ, yeast	infants and children: 0.4 to 1.2 mg males and females: 1.2 to 1.8 mg pregnant and lactating women: 1.6 to 1.8 mg	$2^2/3$ cups whole milk 3 cups low-fat yogurt 2 cups cottage cheese $3/4$ cup broccoli 4 oz. liver, calf $1/4$ cup peanut butter

soluble vitamins, unlike the fat-soluble vitamins, are not stored effectively in the body and must be obtained from the daily diet. The fat-soluble vitamins can cause disease if taken in excessive amounts. When taking vitamin supplements, it is wise to check with your physician regarding your special needs. Each average serving meets the daily allowance.

Vitamins

Water-soluble vitamins (cont.)

Vitamin	Good sources	Recommended daily allowances*	Average serving in some foods
Niacin nicotinic acid	beefsteak, liver fish legumes whole grain cereals peanuts, soybeans	infants and children: 5 to 13 mg males and females: 13 to 20 mg pregnant and lactating women: 17 to 20 mg	3 cups fresh peas 3 cups cooked lentils 2 cups cottage cheese 3 cups soybeans, uncooked $1/2$ cup bran or oatmeal $1/4$ cup peanuts
Vitamin B$_{12}$* cyanocobalamin	liver, kidney dairy products brewer's yeast fish eggs	infants and children: 0.3 to 1.4 mcg males and females: 2.0 mcg pregnant and lactating women: 2.2 to 2.6 mcg	3 cups whole or skim milk $1 1/2$ cups cottage cheese 3 eggs 12 oz. Cheddar cheese 6 oz. Swiss or cream cheese
Vitamin C ascorbic acid	most fruits and vegetables, especially citrus fruits and juices	infants and children: 30 to 45 mg males and females: 50 to 60 mg pregnant and lactating women: 70 to 95 mg	1 apple or orange $1/2$ cantaloupe or grapefruit $1/2$ cup collards, raw or cooked 2 tomatoes 2 boiled potatoes with jackets 2 cups raw spinach
Vitamin B$_6$ pyridoxine	blackstrap molasses liver, kidney, heart whole grains wheat germ	infants and children: 0.3 to 1.4 mg males and females: 1.4 to 2.0 mg pregnant and lactating women: 2.1 to 2.2 mg	$2 1/2$ lbs. raw spinach 1 cup peas 2 cups dry lentils 1 medium baked potato 1 tbsp. molasses 4 oz. liver, beef
Folic acid folate	liver, kidney brewer's yeast green leafy vegetables legumes	infants and children: 25 to 100 mcg males and females: 150 to 200 mcg pregnant and lactating women: 260 to 400 mcg	6 stalks broccoli 15 large Brussels sprouts 9 beets $1/2$ lb. spinach $1 3/4$ cups dry chickpeas or kidney beans

*The average requirements shown are taken from *Recommended Daily Dietary Allowances* (revised 1989), Food and Nutrition Board, National Academy of Sciences. These allowance levels are estimated to be adequate for practically all healthy people in the United States.
**Synthetic vitamins are measured by weight, with the main weight measurement called a gram (about 1/28 of an ounce). The vitamins shown here are recommended in a certain number (I.U.), or by weight in grams or parts of grams (milligrams or micrograms).
    I.U.—International Unit (amount of vitamin necessary to produce the identifying action of the vitamin).
    mg—milligram (one-thousandth of a gram).   RE—retinol equivalent (I mcg retinol or 6 mcg beta-carotene).
    mcg—microgram (one-thousandth of a milligram).   alpha-TE—alpha-tocopherol equivalent.
***Note that there are no vegetable sources of Vitamin B$_{12}$. Strict vegetarians should take B$_{12}$ supplements.

Faulty food habits. It is well recognized and a cause of concern that many Americans eat far too many "empty calories" (calories that are found in refined flour, highly milled rice, refined sugar, and alcohol) in their daily diets. Nutritionists recommend that such foods as these be either avoided or greatly limited, especially in the diets of growing children and in those of adults who may have severe nutritional problems (for example, alcoholics and the aging). In the United States today, the emphasis on good nutrition has shifted from the problem of getting enough of the right nutrients to problems resulting from getting too much of some ingredients.

NUTRITION INFORMATION PER SERVING

SERVING SIZE . . . . . (8 OZ. AS PREPARED—226 G)
CALORIES 75
PROTEIN (GRAMS) 3
TOTAL CARBOHYDRATES (GRAMS) 8
FAT (GRAMS) 4
SODIUM . . . . 960 MG/SERVING

INGREDIENTS: CHICKEN STOCK, CHICKEN, POTATOES, WATER, SALT, PEPPER, CARROTS, CELERY, PEAS, CORN STARCH, MONOSODIUM GLUTAMATE, CHICKEN FAT, DEHYDRATED ONIONS, YEAST EXTRACT AND PLANT PROTEIN.

By law, ingredients are listed in order of the amount used, so there is more salt than carrots in this soup. Monosodium glutamate also adds to the sodium content.

Hard facts about sugar and salt (sodium)

Sugar

- Foods containing white sugar, white flour, or refined cereals account for more than 50 percent of the calories in the average American diet.
- Refined sugar is 100 percent carbohydrate. It supplies nothing more than "empty calories." It has no proteins, vitamins, or minerals.
- Refined sugar is truly a starvation food. At first, it satisfies the call for food and causes the blood sugar level to rise very rapidly. Then, however, this level drops far below normal limits, resulting in hypoglycemia (abnormally low blood sugar), which is frequently accompanied by extreme fatigue.
- Refined sugar is hidden in many popular and processed foods such as bakery products, cereals, soups, salad dressings, jams and jellies, and soft drinks.
- Bacteria that thrive on refined white sugar create acids that are chiefly responsible for tooth decay. Dentists recommend not eating sweets between meals and rinsing the mouth after eating or drinking to remove anything sweet from the teeth.
- The names given sugars end in "-ose." Fructose (fruit sugar), glucose (found in honey and corn syrup), dextrose (bread sugar), and lactose (milk sugar) are sugars found in food. Sucrose (a molecular combination of fructose and glucose) is table sugar. Check product labels to see the amount of sugar content in processed foods.

Salt (sodium)

- Sodium salts are necessary to perform various functions in the body. It takes about 230 milligrams of sodium every day to maintain a healthy balance of water and minerals. The U.S. Surgeon General has established 2,000 milligrams as the daily allowance; this is slightly more than nine times actual body needs.
- Most Americans consume at least 5,000 milligrams of sodium every day. This amounts to 20 times actual body needs and is at least 2½ times the recommended daily sodium intake.
- Since World War II, Americans have relied more and more on processed and fast foods. Such foods are often greatly overloaded with sodium. For example, one tablespoon of canned peas contains as much salt as 5½ pounds of fresh peas. A McDonald's Big Mac contains 962 milligrams of sodium, just about half the recommended daily allowance.
- The greatest source of sodium in the American diet today can be found in cereals and breads, cakes, pies, and cookies, baking powder, and baking soda. This is reason enough to not use salt in cooking or at the table. Yet many people habitually reach for the salt shaker before even tasting the food they are about to eat.
- In checking product labels, it is important to recognize sodium in its various forms: sodium chloride (table salt); monosodium glutamate (a flavor enhancer); and sodium benzoate and sodium nitrate (preservatives).

Hard facts about fats and alcohol

Fats

- Like carbohydrates and proteins, fats are energy-producing foods. In addition, fats have various other important functions, such as heat insulation under the skin and protective support to various parts of the body. Fats also serve as a vehicle for fat-soluble vitamins.
- There are three principal dietary sources of fat supply: animal fats, dairy products, and plant oils. Fat contains over twice as many calories as an equal amount of protein or carbohydrate. In a good diet, fats should constitute only about 25 percent of the body's total caloric needs.
- Excessive amounts of fat stored in the body cause people to be overweight. This overworks the heart and circulatory system. The strain is tremendous; it takes 4,000 feet of blood vessels to nourish every pound of extra fat.
- Animal fats (beef, pork, lamb, dairy products) are high in saturated fatty acids. Vegetable fats (vegetable oils, fish, poultry) contain large amounts of polyunsaturated acids.
- While the matter of polyunsaturated (soft) fats versus unsaturated (hard) fats in preventing heart disease has not yet been completely resolved, there is general agreement that total fat intake should be limited. The American Heart Association suggests that animal fats be limited to 10 percent of daily caloric intake, and that vegetable fats constitute 10 to 15 percent of daily caloric intake.

Alcohol

- There are an estimated 10 million alcoholics in the United States; these people affect the lives of more than 40 million nonalcoholics. Almost half of all alcoholics are women; men in their early 20s make up the largest number of problem drinkers.
- Alcohol is absorbed directly into the bloodstream without digestion. The body oxidizes alcohol slowly, only ½ ounce an hour. If too much alcohol is taken too quickly, intoxication results. A blood alcohol level of 80 mg per 100 ml (0.08 percent) can be expected when a man of average weight drinks two double whiskeys or two pints of beer. At this level, driving may be seriously impaired.
- Alcohol is alcohol, no matter what the form. There are equal amounts of alcohol in 12 ounces of beer, 4 ounces of wine, and 1½ ounces of whiskey.
- Alcoholism is a sickness and a social problem. It is well to learn in young adulthood that alcohol is not a necessity of life, nor does it add to one's total social acceptability. For some people drinking is no problem, but for others it can result in serious harm.
- The longer alcoholism continues untreated, the greater the risk of damage to the liver, heart, and brain. A number of special problems of chronic alcoholism are related to nutritional deficiencies caused by the ability of alcohol to supply calories and depress the appetite without supplying needed vitamins or amino acids.

A chicken leg has about 260 calories fried, but only 230 stewed. Most of the fat is in the skin; without the skin, the same chicken leg has only about 190 calories.

There is about the same amount of alcohol in a can of beer, a glass of wine, and a highball. Two of any of them can become the cause of impaired driving.

Good nutrition and healthy teeth

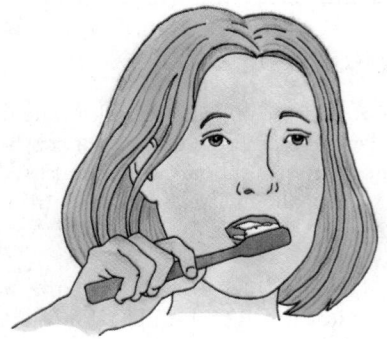 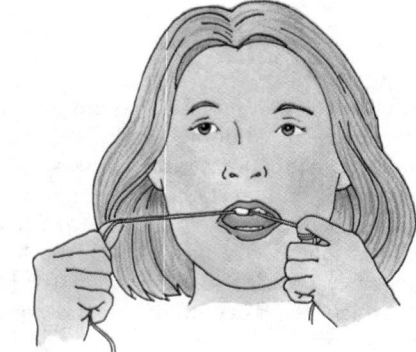

Both brushing up-and-down thoroughly and flossing are needed after each meal.

It is not known exactly how dental caries (tooth decay) are caused, but dental authorities agree that the best way to prevent dental problems is with twice daily cleaning of the teeth (using a brush and floss), attention to diet, and twice-a-year visits to the dentist. Decayed teeth interfere with proper chewing of food and may contribute to digestive disorders.

The purpose of brushing the teeth is to remove fermentable debris (especially carbohydrates such as sugar) on which acid-forming bacteria flourish. Toothpastes or powders (used only to aid the brush) are a matter of choice, but the toothbrush must be of a suitable design and construction to permit proper cleaning of the teeth.

A sufficient intake of calcium and vitamins, especially in infancy and childhood, will help the normal development of teeth and jaws. Regular visits to the dentist should start early in life, especially to correct the overcrowding of teeth or improper growth.

Exercise

Every healthy person needs regular exercise to keep physically fit and enjoy robust health. The benefits of even a fair amount of exercise are many: improved digestion and blood circulation; more efficient functioning of the lungs and heart; increased muscle tone; and an easing of tension.

Keeping physically fit does not mean having to join an expensive health spa or buy special equipment. The benefits of exercise can be obtained just by pursuing your favorite sport, by taking an exercise break instead of a coffee break, or by doing ordinary chores in and about the home. When sweeping, dusting, making beds, or gardening, make a conscious effort to bend and stretch. Break up your day with a brisk walk. Walking uses most of the vital muscles, and it can be done anytime, anywhere, in almost any kind of weather.

Whatever the sport or exercise program chosen, your age, weight, and physical condition are important factors to consider. Start slowly and build up your exercises as your endurance increases. Ease into an exercise period with some simple warm-up exercises (stretching and bending) and cool down the same way at the end of an exercise period. In general, aerobic exercises provide the most benefits.

Weight control. Regular exercise can help the body to burn up unnecessary fat and should be a part of any weight-control process. It is the combination of improved eating habits (notably, cutting out empty calories) and regular exercise that will make for the success and permanent value of a weight-reduction program.

Eating less of high-fat meats, sauces, and pastries, and substituting more cereal products, vegetables, and fruits, will not only reduce the number of calories but will afford the body needed vitamins and minerals. To be safe, an exercise and diet program should be approved by your physician.

Exercise does more than merely burn off calories. Studies have shown that regular exercise helps moderate the appetite by changing the levels of hormones in the body. As a result, lost weight is not regained the way it often is when a weight-loss diet ends.

Varieties of Exercise

Type		Example	Effects
Aerobic		walking jogging cycling swimming aerobic dancing	This type of activity helps the lungs process more air, which in turn strengthens the heart and builds up endurance.
Anerobic	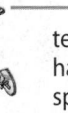	tennis handball sprinting	Activity of short, intense duration, followed by a period of rest, places a sudden high demand on the heart and lungs. These sports also have an aerobic effect.
Isometric		hand, arm, or leg pulls and presses principle involves pitting one muscle group against another, or against an object that does not move, for about 10 to 15 seconds	These exercises, having very little or no movement connected with them, are intended to increase the strength of the muscles exercised.
Isotonic		calisthenics, such as toe touches, jumping jacks, sit-ups, leg lifts, push-ups	This form of exercise permits considerable free body movement.

Energy Costs for Different Kinds of Activities

Home Activities	Calories spent per minute	Sports and hobbies	Calories spent per minute
bringing in laundry	3.2	basketball	8.6
hanging laundry	4.7	bowling	8.1
ironing clothes	4.2	cycling	8.0
machine sewing	1.5	fencing	4.0
making beds	5.3	golfing	5.5
mopping floors	5.3	horseback riding	3.0
peeling vegetables	2.0	jogging	up to 17.0
scrubbing floors	6.0	Ping-Pong	4.8
stirring, mixing foods	3.0	swimming	12.1
sweeping floors	1.7	tennis	7.0
washing clothes	2.9	walking outdoors	6.1

Drug Abuse

Drug group	Drugs	Effects of occasional use	Effects of chronic use
CNS (central nervous system) general depressant	**Alcohol**	Slurred speech, hangover; impaired coordination and judgment; increased tolerance.	Addiction; loss of responsibility; tremors; shakes; depression; seizures; delirium; possible liver damage.
	Barbiturates Called downers, yellow jackets, red or blue devils; swallowed or injected.	Sluggishness; impaired thinking and speech; poor memory and judgment; personality changes.	Anxiety; nausea; weakness and insomnia; possible convulsions; delirium; hallucinations; death from overdose.
	Inhalants (aerosols/volatile hydrocarbons)	Lowered pulse and respiration; exhilaration; confusion; delirium; coma; heart failure.	Weight loss; fatigue; brain, kidney, and liver damage.
CNS (central nervous system) general stimulant	**Amphetamines** Called speed or uppers; swallowed or injected.	Elevated mood; sense of ability and energy; nervousness; less need for food and sleep.	Fatigue; depression; loss of appetite; paranoia; convulsions; death from overdose.
	Cocaine Inhaled, smoked, or injected; crack, a crystalline form, is smoked.	Short-term high followed by depression; restlessness; irritability; loss of appetite; less need for sleep; anxiety.	Psychological dependence; sleeplessness; loss of appetite; nasal passage damage.
	Nicotine Smoked, snuffed, or chewed.	Tobacco smell; increased heart rate; stained teeth and hands.	Addiction; respiratory problems; lung and heart disease; cancer.
Hallucinogen	**LSD** (lysergic acid diethylamide) Called acid; swallowed or injected.	Hallucinations; mood swings; enhanced senses; time distortion; bad trips can be terrifying.	Psychological dependence; time distortion; flashbacks; lapses in sense of reality; panic reactions.
	Marijuana Called pot, grass, or joints; smoked or eaten.	Relaxed feeling; enhanced senses; anxiety; paranoia; time distortion.	Psychological dependence; memory impairment; lack of motivation; respiratory problems; chromosome damage.
	Ecstasy (MDMA) Swallowed.	Hallucinations; sense of well-being; euphoria; nervousness; increased blood pressure and heartbeat; sweating; insomnia.	Possible brain damage; other long-term effects not determined.
Narcotic analgesic (pain-relieving medicine)	**Heroin, Morphine Methadone** Swallowed, smoked, or injected.	Drowsiness; changes in mood; mental clouding; unrealistic sense of well-being, or the opposite.	Addiction; suppression of pain, hunger, aggression, and sexual drive; coma or death from overdose.
Dissociative anesthetic (block all bodily sensations)	**PCP Special K** (phencyclidine hydrochloride) Swallowed, smoked, injected, or snuffed.	Blockage of bodily sensations, particularly sense of pain; clouded thinking; delusions; aggression; mood swings; nausea; coma.	Interference with normal growth; inhibition of cognitive abilities and learning; psychological dependence.

Communicable diseases.

Infection can only be conveyed by contact with the infecting organism.

Direct contact means actually touching, or being touched by, the person having the infection or the natural source of the infection. Such contact also includes breathing in air exhaled by the person within a range of 3 feet or less.

Indirect contact occurs mainly by means of contaminated vehicles of infection (food, clothing, etc.), air convection, and insects or animals.

Suggested Vaccination Schedule

Age	Vaccine
Birth–2 months	Hepatitis B shot
2 months	DTP (diphtheria, tetanus, pertussis) shot Hib (H. influenzae type b) shot IPV (inactivated polio virus) shot
2–4 months	Hepatitis B shot
4 months	DTP shot Hib shot IPV shot
6 months	DTP shot Hib shot* OPV (oral polio vaccine) dose
6–18 months	Hepatitis B shot
12–15 months	Hib shot MMR (measles, mumps, rubella) shot
12–18 months	DTP; or DTaP (diphtheria and tetanus toxoids and acellular pertussis vaccine) at 15 months VZV (varicella zoster virus) shot
18 months	OPV dose
4–6 years	DTP or DTaP shot
4–6 years or 11–12 years	MMR shot (consistent with state immunization requirements)
11–12 years	Hepatitis B series (for those who have not already received three doses)
11–16 years	Tetanus-diphtheria booster
13 years	VZV (for those who have not already received the vaccine)

*May not be required, depending on the type of vaccine administered

Source: Public Health Service, Centers for Disease Control and Prevention, Atlanta, Georgia 30333

Some Communicable Diseases

Method of transfer	Disease
By respiratory discharges (droplet infection and/or contact)	chicken pox common cold diphtheria German measles (rubella) mumps pneumonia/influenza streptococcal sore throat tuberculosis whooping cough
By discharges from intestinal tract (therefore, often by contaminated soil or water)	cholera dysentery (amoebic and bacillary) hookworm paratyphoid fever typhoid fever
By contaminated food or milk	botulism cholera food infections (salmonellosis) intestinal worms streptococcal infections tuberculosis typhoid fever undulant fever
By association with animals	anthrax plague (e.g., from rats) tularemia (e.g., from rabbits) undulant fever (e.g., from cows)
By insects (usually the bite of an insect)	sleeping sickness (tsetse fly) dengue fever (mosquito) malaria (mosquito) plague (rat-flea) typhus (louse) yellow fever (mosquito)
By intimate contact or, usually, by sexual intercourse	gonorrhea syphilis herpes (genital) AIDS

Human anatomy

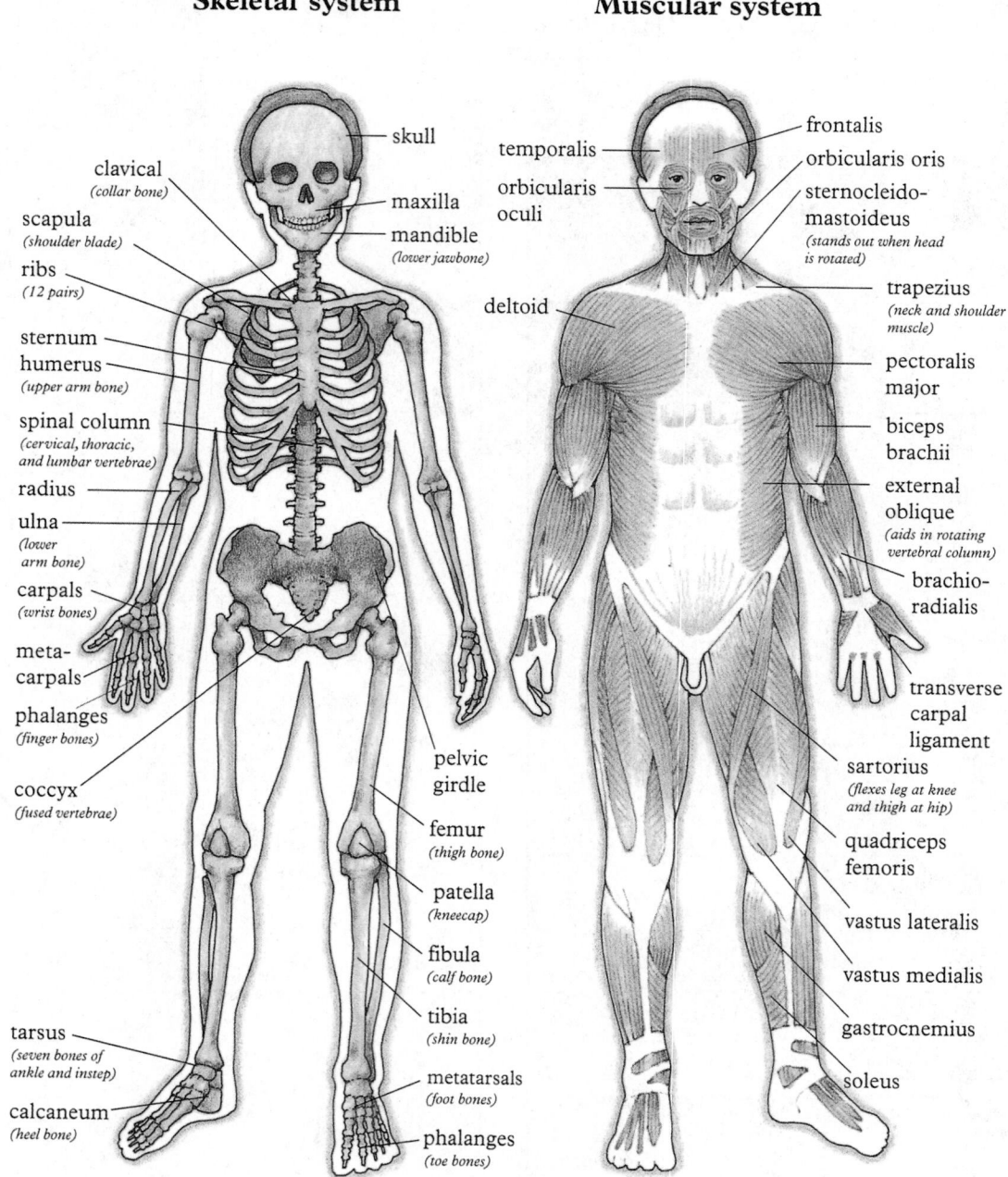

Skeletal system

skull

clavical
(collar bone)

maxilla

mandible
(lower jawbone)

scapula
(shoulder blade)

ribs
(12 pairs)

sternum

humerus
(upper arm bone)

spinal column
*(cervical, thoracic,
and lumbar vertebrae)*

radius

ulna
*(lower
arm bone)*

carpals
(wrist bones)

meta-
carpals

phalanges
(finger bones)

coccyx
(fused vertebrae)

pelvic
girdle

femur
(thigh bone)

patella
(kneecap)

fibula
(calf bone)

tibia
(shin bone)

tarsus
*(seven bones of
ankle and instep)*

calcaneum
(heel bone)

metatarsals
(foot bones)

phalanges
(toe bones)

Muscular system

frontalis

temporalis

orbicularis oris

orbicularis
oculi

sternocleido-
mastoideus
*(stands out when head
is rotated)*

trapezius
*(neck and shoulder
muscle)*

deltoid

pectoralis
major

biceps
brachii

external
oblique
*(aids in rotating
vertebral column)*

brachio-
radialis

transverse
carpal
ligament

sartorius
*(flexes leg at knee
and thigh at hip)*

quadriceps
femoris

vastus lateralis

vastus medialis

gastrocnemius

soleus

Respiratory system

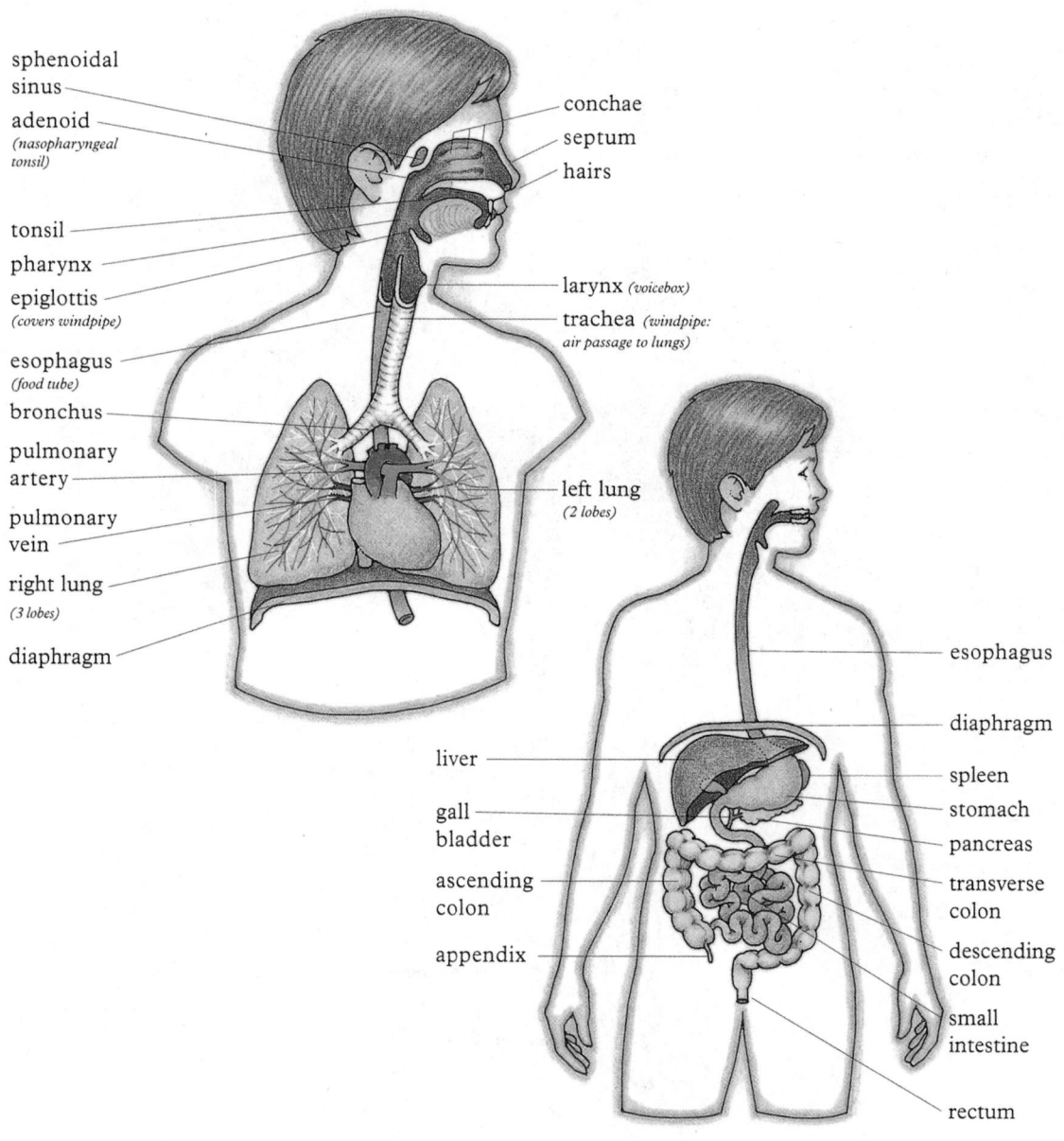

sphenoidal sinus

adenoid
(nasopharyngeal tonsil)

conchae

septum

hairs

tonsil

pharynx

epiglottis
(covers windpipe)

esophagus
(food tube)

bronchus

pulmonary artery

pulmonary vein

right lung
(3 lobes)

diaphragm

larynx *(voicebox)*

trachea *(windpipe: air passage to lungs)*

left lung
(2 lobes)

liver

gall bladder

ascending colon

appendix

esophagus

diaphragm

spleen

stomach

pancreas

transverse colon

descending colon

small intestine

rectum

Digestive system

Nervous System

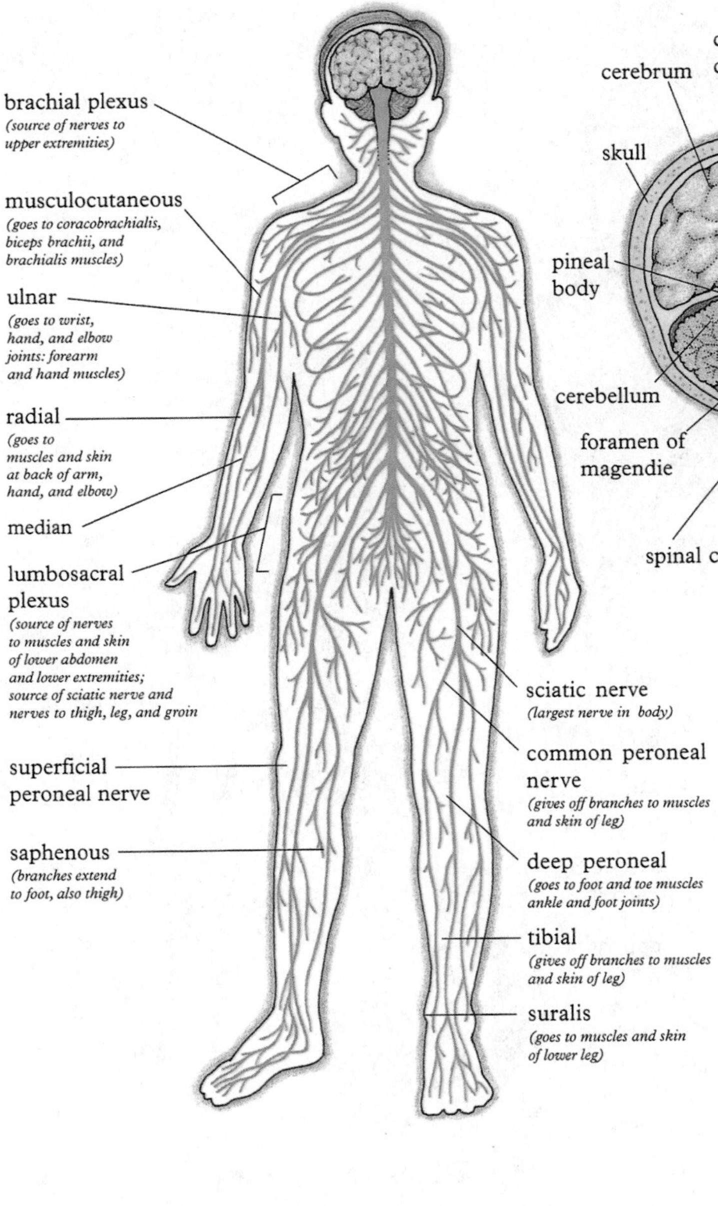

brachial plexus
(source of nerves to upper extremities)

musculocutaneous
(goes to coracobrachialis, biceps brachii, and brachialis muscles)

ulnar
(goes to wrist, hand, and elbow joints: forearm and hand muscles)

radial
(goes to muscles and skin at back of arm, hand, and elbow)

median

lumbosacral plexus
(source of nerves to muscles and skin of lower abdomen and lower extremities; source of sciatic nerve and nerves to thigh, leg, and groin

superficial peroneal nerve

saphenous
(branches extend to foot, also thigh)

sciatic nerve
(largest nerve in body)

common peroneal nerve
(gives off branches to muscles and skin of leg)

deep peroneal
(goes to foot and toe muscles ankle and foot joints)

tibial
(gives off branches to muscles and skin of leg)

suralis
(goes to muscles and skin of lower leg)

Human brain

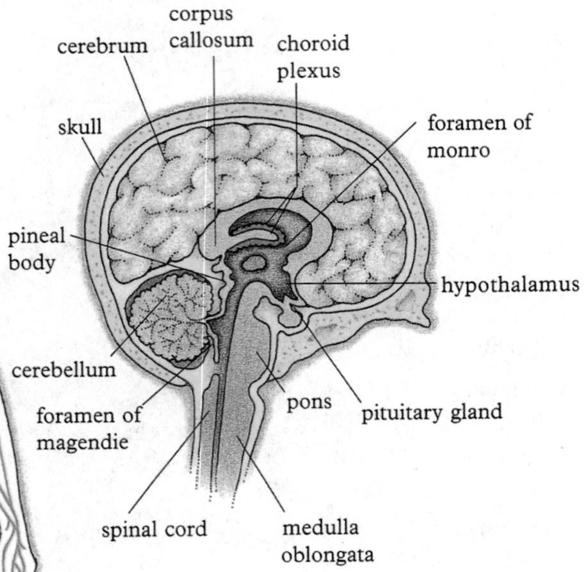

cerebrum

corpus callosum

choroid plexus

skull

foramen of monro

pineal body

hypothalamus

cerebellum

foramen of magendie

pons

pituitary gland

spinal cord

medulla oblongata

Circulatory System

Human heart

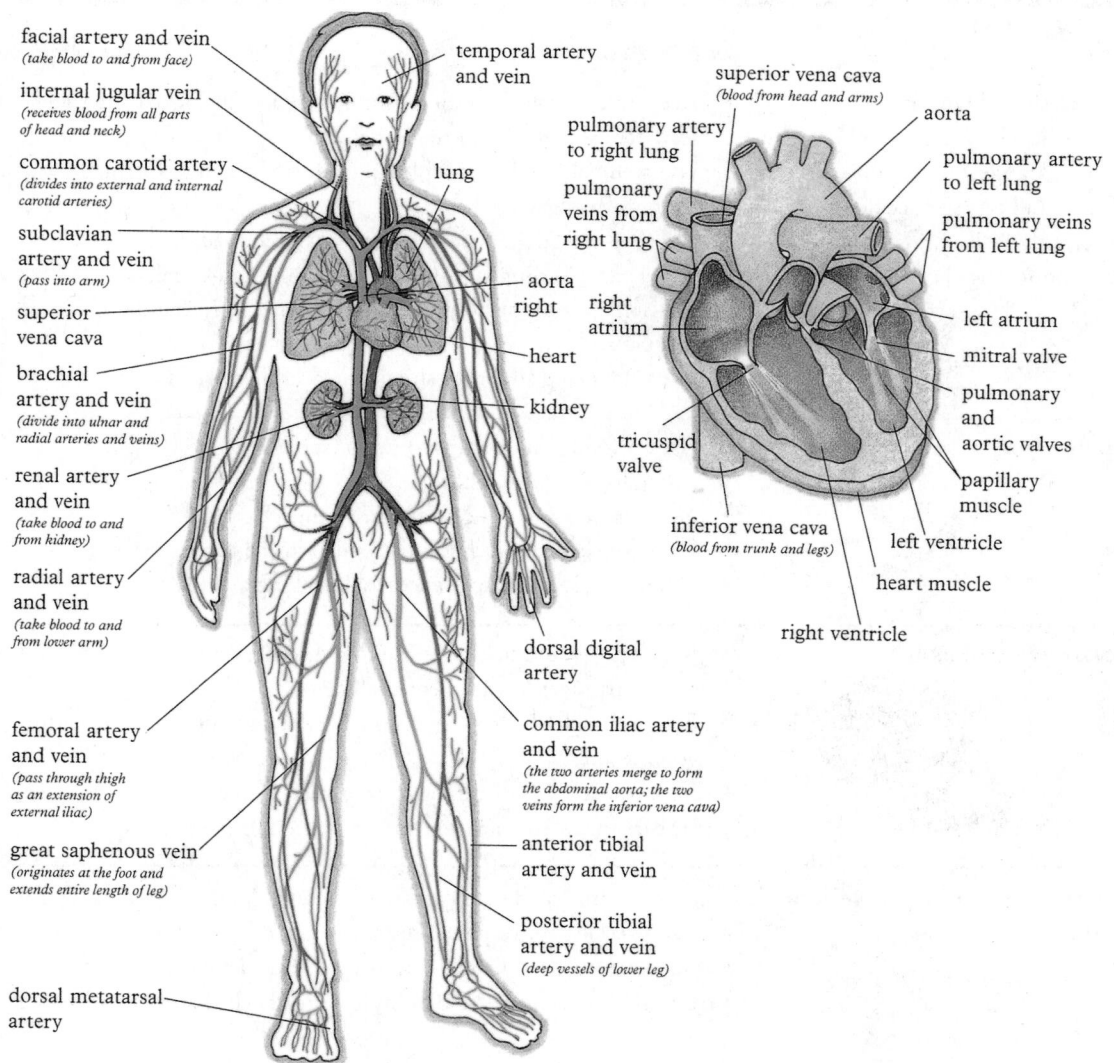

facial artery and vein
(take blood to and from face)

internal jugular vein
(receives blood from all parts of head and neck)

common carotid artery
(divides into external and internal carotid arteries)

subclavian artery and vein
(pass into arm)

superior vena cava

brachial artery and vein
(divide into ulnar and radial arteries and veins)

renal artery and vein
(take blood to and from kidney)

radial artery and vein
(take blood to and from lower arm)

femoral artery and vein
(pass through thigh as an extension of external iliac)

great saphenous vein
(originates at the foot and extends entire length of leg)

dorsal metatarsal artery

temporal artery and vein

lung

aorta

right

heart

kidney

dorsal digital artery

common iliac artery and vein
(the two arteries merge to form the abdominal aorta; the two veins form the inferior vena cava)

anterior tibial artery and vein

posterior tibial artery and vein
(deep vessels of lower leg)

superior vena cava
(blood from head and arms)

pulmonary artery to right lung

pulmonary veins from right lung

right atrium

tricuspid valve

inferior vena cava
(blood from trunk and legs)

right ventricle

aorta

pulmonary artery to left lung

pulmonary veins from left lung

left atrium

mitral valve

pulmonary and aortic valves

papillary muscle

left ventricle

heart muscle

Safety

Everyone is aware of the great numbers of serious and fatal accidents on the highway, but not everyone realizes that many more accidents happen at home. Most often, children under five years of age and adults over 65 are involved. Much can be done to prevent accidents in the home: it is usually just a matter of combining common sense and good housekeeping.

Safety at Home

Area	*Safety precautions*
Kitchen and laundry (The kitchen may well be the most dangerous room in the house. All types of accidents occur there: e.g., falls, burns, explosions, and poisonings.) 	• Keep lye, bleach, and all cleaning supplies in locked, or tightly secured, cabinets out of the reach of children and away from food. • Use well-balanced pots and pans, and keep handles turned away from stove edges. • Wipe up spilled grease, water, and bits of food at once. • Never mix cleaning aids. Dangerous fumes can be released. • Use well-made pot-holders, not dish towels, to handle hot pots and pans. • Use sturdy stepladders or stools to reach high places.
Bathroom 	• Use nonskid mat or strips in tub or shower. • Install handrails on bathtub. • Never leave a tub of hot water unattended. • Never leave a young child unattended in the tub. • Never use electrical appliances while taking a bath.
Stairways and halls 	• Keep well-lit and litter-free (no toys or other objects strewn about) so that passageways are clear at all times. • Be sure handrails or banisters on all stairways are adequate and in good repair. • Be sure stair pads or carpeting is securely fastened. • Be sure throw rugs are nonskid or secured to the floor.
Basement, attic, garage, and other storage areas 	• Store flammable liquids, charcoals, paints, and poisons in tightly covered, labeled, original containers out of the reach of children. • Keep area free of oily rags and combustible litter. • Be sure furnace, flue, and chimneys are checked and cleaned once a year.
Electrical 	• Be sure there are enough outlets and circuits for all lighting and appliances without dangerous overload. • Keep unused outlets covered by dummy plugs, or block access with furniture. • Be sure major electrical appliances are grounded. • Follow the manufacturer's recommendations on all lighting equipment and appliances. Use only where specifically stated.

Fire Emergencies

Solid fuel fires

Solid fuel fires can usually be put out with water or a multipurpose extinguisher.

Clothing on fire. DO NOT RUN. Drop to the floor. Roll over and over. If a heavy blanket or rug is at hand, wrap yourself in it in order to smother the flames.

Mattress on fire. Saturate with water. Call the fire department and have them remove it. If the mattress is in flames, leave the premises and call the fire department.

Oven or broiler fire. Turn off the heat. Close the oven door and keep it closed.

Pan-on-the-stove fire. Turn off the heat. Cover the pan with a lid, or throw salt or baking soda at the *base* of the flames in the pan. Do *not* pick up or move the pan, or throw water on it.

Fireplace or wood-burning stove fire. Do not close the damper (located in the flue). Leave the premises at once and call the fire department.

Liquid fires

Liquid fires are either flammable or combustible (gasoline, solvents, paints, cooking oil, grease). If such fires spread, you must leave the premises at once and call the fire department.

Grease fire (deep-fat fryer or pan). Do *not* move the appliance or pan. Turn off the heat. Cover with a metal lid; if flames are too high, throw baking soda or salt into the pan. Cover with a lid after flames have died down.

Gasoline, acetone, benzene fire. Do *not* try to put out such fires. Leave the premises at once and call the fire department. Take off any clothing that has come into contact with gasoline.

Charcoal lighter fluid (used in barbecues) fire. If fire is confined to barbecue, try to cover with a large metal lid, or throw sand or dirt on the barbecue.

Lacquer thinner, alcohol, turpentine fire. If fire has not spread, smother it with baking soda, sand, or a multipurpose extinguisher.

Kerosene heater or lamp fire. Use sand, baking soda, or a multipurpose extinguisher to smother.

Electrical fires

Electrical fires are doubly difficult to control because it is imperative to avoid electric shock while putting out the fire. Do *not* throw water on an electrical appliance until it is unplugged.

Television smoking. Keep away from the TV set as the picture tube may burst. Shut off power to the circuit from a switch or the fuse box and call the fire department.

Faulty wiring. If switch outlets and plugs feel warm to the touch, disconnect all electricity. Call the fire department.

Shock from an electrical appliance. This could be from a defective plug or loose wiring in the outlet or the appliance. Unplug at once, or shut off power to the circuit from a switch or from the fuse box, as continued use of the appliance may result in fire.

345

Shock.

Shock is brought on by a sudden and dangerous drop in blood pressure. It may be caused by a variety of conditions: bleeding, infection, injuries, drug reaction, poisoning, and heart damage. No matter what the cause, shock demands prompt treatment. If shock is not treated, it may prove fatal. *When present, stoppage of breathing, severe bleeding, or poisoning must be treated first.*

Signs
- The skin is pale and cold and clammy.
- Lips and fingernails may have a bluish-gray tinge.
- Breathing is rapid and weak; the pulse is fast and faint.
- The victim may be restless or drowsy, partly or totally unconscious, and there may be internal bleeding.

Treatment
- *A physician should be called at once.*
- Do not let victim sit, walk, or stand.
- Keep victim lying down and prop up legs about 12 inches (except in case of broken leg or possible head injury).
- Do not move victim unless necessary.
- Keep victim warm but apply no heat of any kind.
- Give nothing by mouth.
- Stay calm and attentive.

Electric shock.

This happens when a person has been in contact with electricity (including lightning).
- Do *not* touch the person, but turn off power at source if possible. It may be necessary to call the power company.
- Call an ambulance or doctor.
- After person is clear of contact, assistance may be given, if needed, for unconsciousness and lack of breathing or heartbeat.
- If possible, free person from electrical contact with dry nonconducting material such as wood or cloth. Be certain not to use metal.

How to Treat for Shock

1. Call a physician before beginning treatment if possible.
2. Free shock victim from electric contact if necessary.

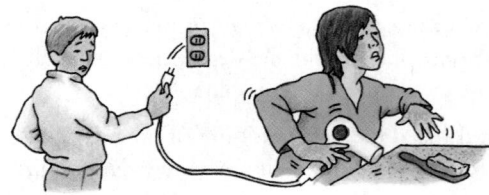 

3. Treat stoppage of breathing or bleeding before treating shock.

 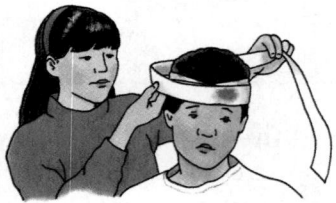

4. Keep victim lying down, with feet elevated, and warm.

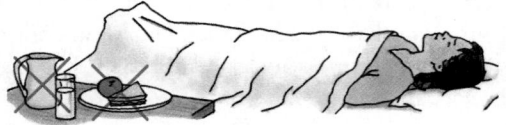 

Choking.

A person who is choking on food cannot speak or make any noise (that is, groan, wheeze, or move air) and his or her face turns blue. The person may then collapse.

First Aid for Choking

When standing

1. Give victim four sharp blows on the back. (Omit this step for children.)
2. Stand behind the choking victim and wrap your arms around the victim's waist.
3. Place a fist against the victim's abdomen between the navel and the breastbone. Grasp the fist with other hand.
4. *Press your fist in and upward* sharply into the victim's abdomen.

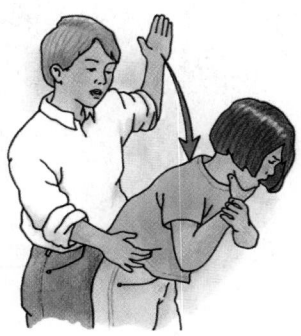  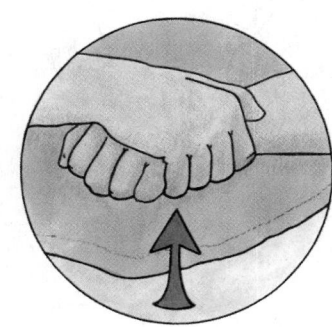

When sitting

Stand behind the chair, and follow the same procedure outlined above.

When lying down

1. Place the victim on his back with head turned. Straddle victim's legs and face him.
2. Put one hand on top of the other with the heel of your bottom hand placed slightly above the victim's navel and just below the rib cage.
3. Press your hand into the victim's abdomen with a *quick upward push*. Repeat the procedure several times, if necessary.

 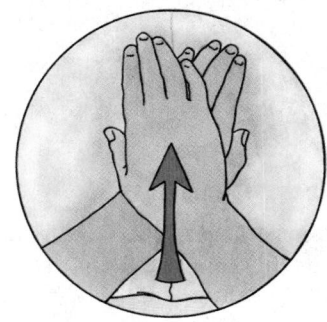

347

Restoring breathing.

When a person has stopped breathing (from drowning, electric shock, carbon monoxide or other gaseous poisoning, or disease), start artificial respiration to restore breathing as quickly as possible. Check for someone with CPR training first.

Mouth-to-Mouth (or Nose) Method

1. Lay the victim on his back. Wipe or remove foreign matter from his mouth.

2. Tilt head backward; chin up. To keep tongue out of air passage, lift the chin with one hand and use other hand to push back on forehead.

3. Take hand placed on forehead and pinch the nose shut. Or press your cheek against the nose to close it.

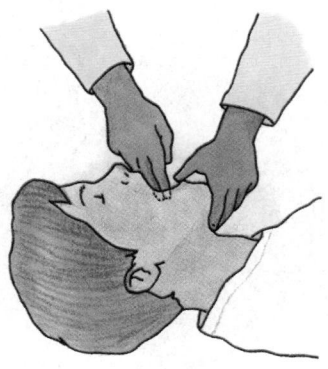 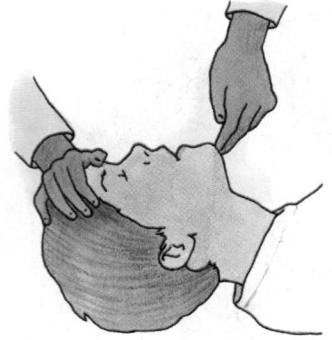 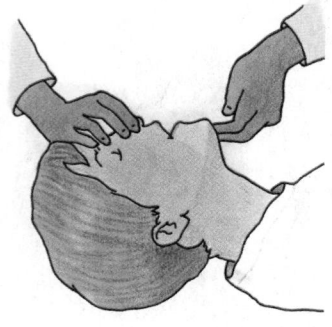

4. Open your mouth wide and take a deep breath. Cover victim's mouth with yours and give four deep quick breaths. Take your mouth away after each breath.

5. When victim's chest has expanded, stop blowing and listen for exhalation. Watch to see that chest falls. Repeat the blowing cycle.

6. For mouth-to-nose method, tilt head back as before but close mouth with other hand. Open your mouth wide, seal it around victim's nose, and blow.

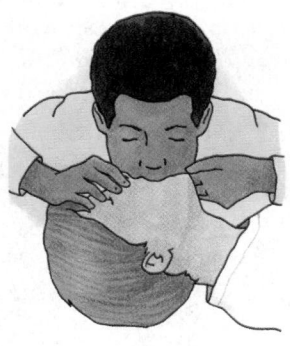  

Learning about CPR. Cardio-Pulmonary Resuscitation (CPR) must be given to someone who is unconscious and in whom the heart and/or breathing may have stopped. However, CPR can only be done properly by a trained person, or damage may be caused by the technique.

CPR courses are widely available and, depending upon the community, may be given at hospitals, fire departments, or colleges. Generally, the local office of the American Heart Association or the American Red Cross can tell you where to enroll in a well-taught CPR course.

Poisoning.

The symptoms of poisoning vary with the type of poison. Most suspected poisonings do not require hospitalization.

1. Look for poison, medication, or liquid swallowed or its container.
2. Note if there are any marks or odors on the person. Corrosives may leave marks on face or clothes. Gasoline and other petroleum products have a characteristic odor.
3. Call Poison Control Center or hospital emergency room.
4. Give all available information: the name and the ingredients of the poison, the amount swallowed, how long ago, the condition of the victim.
5. Follow instructions given. You may be guided to treat the poisoning at home, but if you go to the hospital, be sure to take the poison container with you.
6. Do *not* give antidotes or induce vomiting unless so instructed by a medical professional. Causing vomiting after ingesting acid, lye or other corrosives, or petroleum products such as lighter fluid would only do more harm.
7. Do *not* give salt solution. It can prove dangerous to the victim.
8. Do *not* dilute the poison by giving lots of milk or water. It may make things worse by speeding up the rate at which the poison is absorbed by the body.

Poison control centers. There are many Poison Control Centers throughout the country. Check your local telephone book for a listing of these centers under Poison Control Center (in the white pages), Emergency Numbers, or Community Service Numbers, or dial 911 and have the emergency operator assist you. Check your local hospital listings for Emergency Room numbers. Note these numbers with other emergency numbers and keep them readily available.

  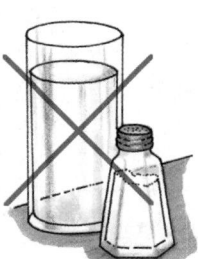

Poisoning by Plants and Animals

Poison ivy, poison oak, poison sumac dermatitis	If there has been known exposure to any of these plants, a thorough washing of the skin with soap and water, and a complete change of clothing is advisable. If the skin inflammation is mild, applying a soothing lotion is usually sufficient. In more severe cases, cool wet dressings or baths may help give relief. Check with a physician to see if medication is needed.
Snakebite, scorpion stings, and spider stings	Have person lie down. Wipe away from the bite area any venom on the skin. Wash area with soap and water. Pat dry. Do not rub. Apply clean dressing. Watch breathing. Get person to hospital immediately. Do *not* suck wound area, cut into area, or apply tourniquet or chemicals.

First aid. A first-aid kit will help you be ready to deal with emergency situations when they happen. First-aid kits may be purchased at your local pharmacy or put together on your own. A good-sized metal box, brightly colored to make it quickly visible on a shelf, is suitable. Keep the kit in one place at all times. Here are suggested supplies for your kit:

Bandages and dressings. Include assorted sizes of adhesive and sterile vaseline gauze bandages; 1″

First Aid Remedies

Animal bites	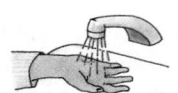	Wash the wound freely with water (under a running tap for a few minutes, if possible). Cover with sterile gauze dressing or compress. Get to a physician or to a hospital emergency room without delay. The offending animal should be caught and tested for rabies.
Blisters		Do not puncture blister. Apply a sterile dressing and bandage. If the blister is broken, clean the wound with soap and water. Blot dry with clean towel. Cover with sterile dressing and bandage.
Bruises		Apply cold cloths or icebag for about 25 minutes. If the injury is severe, have it examined by a physician.
Burns		DO NOT APPLY BUTTER, GREASE, OR OINTMENTS. *First-degree burns* (like sunburn, red and painful): submerge burned part in cold water or apply cold-water bottle. *Second-degree burns* (red and painful with blisters): submerge burned part in cold water. Put cold, wet dressings on burn, using clean, freshly pressed cloths if possible. Get medical help. *Third-degree burns* (skin destroyed, white or charred): do not remove clothing on burn area or apply wet packs. Elevate burned limbs to keep burn higher than heart. Get medical help quickly.
Cuts or scrapes	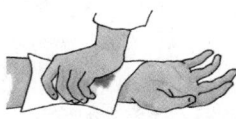	For minor injuries with no bleeding, sponge off area gently. Blot dry and cover with a simple bandage. In deeper cuts, apply direct constant pressure on the wound to stop the bleeding. Use a sterile pad and press down with your hand. If blood seeps through, place more padding over the first pad and continue pressure. If the bleeding persists or the wound is severe, call a doctor.
Fainting		If a person feels faint, have the person sit down and lower the head between the knees or, preferably, lie down with head lower than the body. If the person has already fainted, lay him or her flat on the back, tilt head back, and elevate feet. Loosen tight clothing around neck and waist. Person should be seen by a doctor to determine the cause of fainting.
Foreign bodies	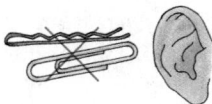	*Ear.* If there is an insect in the ear, lay person on side and pour a little warm water or oil into the ear. This will allow the insect to float out. However, if there is any chance that eardrum is perforated, do not put fluid into ear. Do not attempt to remove any other object. Call a doctor.

adhesive tape; cotton-tipped swabs; gauze bandage rolls (1″ × 4″ wide), and triangular bandages (37″ × 37″) cut or folded diagonally.

Medicine. Include hydrogen peroxide, aspirin or acetaminophen tablets, and children's aspirin; anes-thetic ointment and antibiotic ointment; ipecac syrup and/or activated charcoal.

Other aids. The kit should also contain a thermometer, a tourniquet, safety pins, tweezers, and scissors.

Foreign bodies

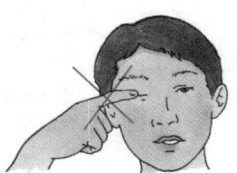

Eye. Do not let person rub eye. Seat person in good light and, if object can be seen, try to remove it by touching it *gently* with a dry corner of a handkerchief. If it does not come out with the first try, or cannot be seen, cover eye with a clean pad or compress and take person to a physician or hospital emergency room.

Nose. Have person blow nose carefully, but not hard. If this does not remove the object, call doctor. Do not try to poke the object loose.

Frostbite

Frostbite usually begins as patches of white or grayish-yellow skin after exposure to extreme cold. Rewarm person slowly in air at room temperature. Gently cover frozen part with hand, or place in warm (not hot) water. Do not apply heat or expose person to heat from stove. Do not rub (especially not with snow or ice). Warm drinks may be given (tea, coffee, or beef tea), but no alcohol.

Heat exhaustion

Help person lie down in cool place, loosen clothes, and apply cool, wet cloths. Keep in lying position with head low. Give salt water to drink (1 teaspoon of salt to a pint of water) in small amounts at frequent intervals, and large amounts of fruit juices.

Heatstroke or sunstroke

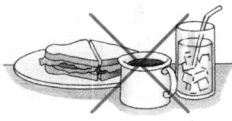

Heatstroke is characterized by an extremely high body temperature (106° F) and a lack of sweating to relieve temperature. Remove person to cool place and remove most clothing. Reduce temperature by covering skin with cold cloths or towels, changing frequently. Place person in tub of cold water, keeping head above water. Give nothing by mouth.

Insect bites and stings

If swelling is severe, or person has allergic reaction (pallor, collapse), get medical help at once. Allergic reactions to insect bites can be fatal. Generally, the sting is not serious. If stinger is embedded in skin, remove with tweezers and then apply a soothing cream or a paste made of baking soda and water.

Embedded ticks. Kill the tick with a few drops of turpentine, or touch it with a hot needle to make it release its hold. Then carefully remove tick with tweezers, being careful not to crush the insect or only half pull it out.

Sprains

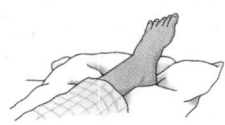

If the victim's leg or foot is sprained, do not allow walking. Elevate the joint (ankle, wrist, finger, knee) and apply cold compresses. Give firm support by using thick pads and then firm bandaging (elastic bandage).

AIDS

Dictionary of health and safety

minerals

plague

poison ivy

acquired immune deficiency syndrome (AIDS). Caused by a retrovirus that attacks the immune system and so enables life-threatening diseases to flourish. AIDS is transmitted primarily through sexual activity and sharing of needles by drug users.

anthrax. Acute infectious disease that usually attacks cattle and sheep. Humans contract it by handling contaminated animal hair or hides, or through inhalation of anthrax spores.

bacteria. One-celled microorganisms without nuclei that may cause such diseases as cholera, syphilis, and typhoid fever.

botulism (food poisoning). The growth of pathogenic organisms in food itself causes the poisoning, while the toxins produced by the organisms result in the illness. It may be hours after contaminated food is eaten before abdominal pain, vomiting, and diarrhea appear.

chancroid. Infectious venereal disease that begins as a pustule or ulcer and spreads.

chicken pox (varicella). Highly contagious but mild infectious disease occurring mostly in children. There is slight fever, and a sparse red rash develops that becomes blistery and finally crusts. Itching may be intense.

cholera. Acute epidemic infectious disease that is marked by profuse watery diarrhea.

cholesterol. Sterol (fatlike substance) widely found in animal tissues and occurring in egg yolk, various oils, fats, and nerve tissue.

germ. Common name for agents of disease, including bacteria, viruses, and protozoans.

herpes simplex (Type I and Type II). Virus that causes cold sores or fever blisters, but which may also cause many other complications. Type I is usually found on the upper half of the body, where it is most common around the mouth. Type II (genital herpes) is more common on the lower part of the body. Both types can be sexually transmitted.

lymphogranuloma venereum. Venereal disease that is caused by a virus and is readily transmitted by sexual contact.

measles (rubeola). Highly contagious disease in which there is fever, catarrhal symptoms, and a typical skin eruption. It usually occurs before adolescence. German measles (rubella) resembles measles but its course is short, fever is slight, and there are no aftereffects.

minerals. Inorganic elements (calcium, phosphorus, iron, sodium, etc.) that in general are the regulators of the metabolic processes.

mumps. Acute, contagious, and feverish disease in which there is inflammation of the parotid (below the ear) glands and other salivary glands.

nutrients. Food components that supply the body with necessary elements. Some nutrients (carbohydrates, fats, proteins) provide energy; others (water, minerals, vitamins) are needed for regulatory processes.

plague (Black Death). Bubonic plague is primarily transmitted to humans by the bite of fleas that have fed on infected animals.

pneumonia. Characterized by cough, chest pain, and fever, pneumonia is an acute illness resulting from inflammation or infection of the lungs, either bacterial or viral.

poison ivy. A climbing vine, *Rhus toxidendrom,* causes a severe form of skin inflammation on contact.

proteins. Essential for growth and repair of body tissues; of the utmost importance in body functioning.

protozoans. One-celled animals. Some cause such diseases as malaria, sleeping sickness, and dysentery.

sleeping sickness (African trypanosomiasis). Endemic disease caused by the bite of a tsetse fly. The main symptoms are an increasing tendency to drowse or sleep, tremors, fever, wasting, and weakness.

smallpox. Contagious disease caused by a virus found in the oral and nasal secretions and skin lesions of infected persons. Smallpox had been virtually eliminated all over the world, with the only known remaining viruses being kept in a few research laboratories. In response to the escalating threat of terrorism, many countries are reevaluating their vaccination policies.

stroke (apoplexy). There is a sudden loss of consciousness (coma) followed by paralysis, usually of the side of the body opposite the side of the brain affected.

syphilis. Infectious venereal disease that can result in destructive lesions almost anywhere in the body. When fully developed, soft tissue tumors appear and there is damage to the heart, brain, and blood vessels.

tetanus. Disease marked by painful muscular contractions. At first, there is an inability to move the jaw (lockjaw); this is followed by tetanic spasm, another characteristic of the disease.

tuberculosis. Infectious disease caused by the tubercle bacillus. It may affect almost any body tissue or organ, but it occurs most commonly in the lungs.

tularemia (rabbit fever, deer fly fever). Humans acquire the disease from rodents through the bite of an infected tick or other blood-sucking insect, by handling of infected animal tissues, or by eating undercooked meat or drinking contaminated water.

typhoid fever. This illness, caused by the bacillus *Salmonella typhosa,* is marked by continued fever, the eruption of rose-colored spots on the chest and abdomen, and an enlarged spleen.

typhus (epidemic and endemic). One of a group of rickettsial infectious diseases marked by high fever, severe prostration and headache, and a generalized rash.

undulant fever. An infectious disease in which fever rises to 104° or 105° F (40° to 40.6° C) in the evening, gradually returning to normal by morning. Other symptoms include weakness, sweating, chills, anorexia, malaise, and nervousness.

viruses. Microorganisms smaller than cells that cause such diseases as herpes, measles, and colds.

vitamins. These organic substances perform a specific metabolic function, depending upon the vitamin, and are essential to the diet.

whooping cough. Acute infectious disease marked by a peculiar recurrent spasm of coughing that ends in whooping.

yellow fever. Acute infectious disease that is marked by jaundice, tenderness in the pit of the stomach, vomiting, hemorrhage, and recurrent fever. It is transmitted by the bite of a female mosquito.

For Further Reference

American Red Cross
The American Red Cross First Aid and Safety Handbook
Little, Brown

Bosco, Dominick
The People's Guide to Vitamins and Minerals, From A to Zinc
Contemporary Books

Consumer Guide Editors
Emergency First Aid for Your Child
Publications International

Dunne, Lavon J.
Nutrition Almanac
McGraw-Hill

Madison, Arnold
Drugs and You
Julian Messner

Nardo, Don
Vitamins and Minerals
Chelsea House

Null, Gary
The Complete Guide to Health and Nutrition
Delacorte

Peavy, Linda S. and Smith, Ursula
Food, Nutrition and You
Scribner's

- *Natural resources*   **354**
- *The ecosystem*   **356**
- *Biomes*   **358**
- *Cycles*   **360**
- *Succession*   **361**
- *Dictionary of life science*   **362**

Life Science

Life sciences have become both better understood and more relevant in the past few years, after decades dominated by the physical sciences. Since the 1960s it has become increasingly clear that the environment is in danger and that we must maintain the other living creatures in our environment to maintain both our health and a sound economy. In this brief article, the focus is on the environment; other important topics in life science are treated in that context. One major focus is the different natural environmental regions that comprise North America. Another is natural recycling. Understanding the environment requires knowledge of how such natural resources as air and water are recycled by nature. This process involves several steps. So does the process by which part of an environment that has been destroyed restores itself.

The relationship of living things to their environment is one of the basic ways that life science can be approached. In Handbook 2, the biology article takes another one of the basic approaches, starting with the cell and working up to the organism in its environment.

Natural resources

Wildlife. Among our planet's most valuable natural resources is its great variety of wildlife—plants and animals. Unfortunately, some types of wildlife are threatened with extinction, and they have been declared *endangered species*. An endangered species is any type of plant or animal that is protected by law from being killed. It is protected so that it will not become *extinct* (cease to exist as a living species). Endangered species in North America include the California condor, the whooping crane, the star cactus, the manatee, and the Steller sea-lion.

It is important to preserve as many species of wildlife as possible because of the species' potential use to the human race. Wild varieties of plants or animals often have useful properties that can be bred into domestic plants or animals.

Land and forests. Productive farmland contains a substantial layer of fertile topsoil that is rich in the vital nutrients needed by plants to grow. Many years are necessary to build up this topsoil. According to the U.S. Department of Agriculture, about five tons of topsoil per acre per year are being lost in the United States from erosion caused by poor farming practices.

To reduce erosion, farmers often resort to *strip cropping,* in which different types of crops are planted in alternate strips. Typically, corn alternates with grass, which cuts down on water runoff. Some farmers also build *terraces*—platforms with plants growing on them. These terraces catch the water and prevent erosion.

Planting wheat or corn in the same field each year removes vital nutrients from the topsoil and makes the land less productive. In *crop rotation,* the crop is changed from year to year.

National and state forests are another vital land resource. These precious lands are carefully administered so they can fulfill a variety of important functions:

- Provide a habitat for wildlife.
- Protect important watershed areas.
- Prevent soil erosion.
- Serve as recreation areas.
- Provide timber for building and other purposes.

Timber can be removed from forests in different ways, depending on the species of trees involved. *Clear-cutting* removes large blocks of trees, but this method disrupts the natural beauty of the forest and can lead to soil erosion. *Selection cutting* is used for species that can thrive in shade. In selection cutting, older trees are cut down while younger ones are left to grow taller.

Air.

The quality of our air is affected by pollution, which creates a variety of problems. *Hydrocarbons,* which are released when coal or oil is burned as fuel, have been linked to cancer. Pollutants have also been cited as a cause of such lung diseases as emphysema.

Another type of pollution, which often blankets cities like Los Angeles, is called *smog.* Smog is a yellowish haze produced by the reaction of oxygen, hydrocarbons, and other pollutants in sunlight. One of the elements in smog is *ozone,* a type of oxygen with a pungent odor. Ozone causes coughing and eye irritation in humans and damages plants.

A serious problem created by air pollution is *acid rain.* Pollutants, especially those released by coal-burning power plants in the Midwest, mix with moisture in the air to produce nitric and sulfuric acids. These fall as acid rain or snow, destroying vegetation, polluting waterways, and killing fish. At present, many lakes in New York, New England, and Canada have been polluted by acid rain.

Over the past few years, progress has been made in reducing air pollution through legislation such as the Clean Air Act and the efforts of the Environmental Protection Agency. Pollution control devices on automobiles are one example of this progress.

Water.

Fresh, clean water is essential for residential use, agriculture, and industry, but the water quality in many lakes and rivers has been destroyed by pollution. The Great Lakes, for example, were polluted by industries dumping chemicals and heavy metals into them. A massive cleanup program was initiated to save the lakes and to restore the quality of their water. Similar programs have been started in other parts of the country, as on Ohio's Cuyahoga River and along the Maine coast.

In some of the Western states the problem is not so much pollution as it is the threat of water shortages. Limited amounts of rainfall in that part of the U.S. are insufficient to fill all the needs of an expanding population.

Vast quantities of water are necessary to irrigate dry areas in the West for agriculture. Although irrigation ditches are commonly used to transport water, some of the water is lost through seepage and evaporation. An alternate method of irrigation, called the *drip system,* brings water to plants through pipes and reduces waste.

Sources of Air and Water Pollution		Average Water Consumption
Air	**Water**	residential 60
Transportation (cars, etc.)	Industrial wastes	
Fuel combustion for heating	Fertilizers and pesticides	industrial 50
Industrial pollutants	Oil spills	
Dust from land	Sewage	commercial 20
Volcanic eruptions	Nuclear wastes	public 10
Burning solid wastes	Heat from power stations	leakage 10
Forest fires	Strip mining	

150 gallons per person per day

The ecosystem

Survival of all living things depends on a carefully balanced system called an *ecosystem.* All life needs energy, and the original source of energy in an ecosystem is the sun. Green plants, called *producer organisms,* use the sun's energy to make their food. Animals, which get their energy by eating plants or other animals, are called *consumers.* There are different kinds of consumers. A rabbit, which eats plant material, is called a *primary* consumer. An eagle is called a *secondary* consumer when it gets its energy from eating animals that eat plants. A snake is also called a secondary consumer because it eats animals that eat plants. When an eagle eats a snake, the eagle is called a *tertiary* consumer. There are other organisms in an ecosystem, such as bacteria that decompose dead animals and plant material. Such organisms, called *decomposers,* return minerals and organic material to the air and soil. They are not shown here.

Green plants are the producers because only they can manufacture their own food by a process called *photosynthesis.* The raw materials of photosynthesis are carbon dioxide, water, and sunlight, all of which are absorbed by the plants. Inside plant cells is a pigment called *chlorophyll* that gives green plants their color. Chlorophyll also captures the sun's energy and plays

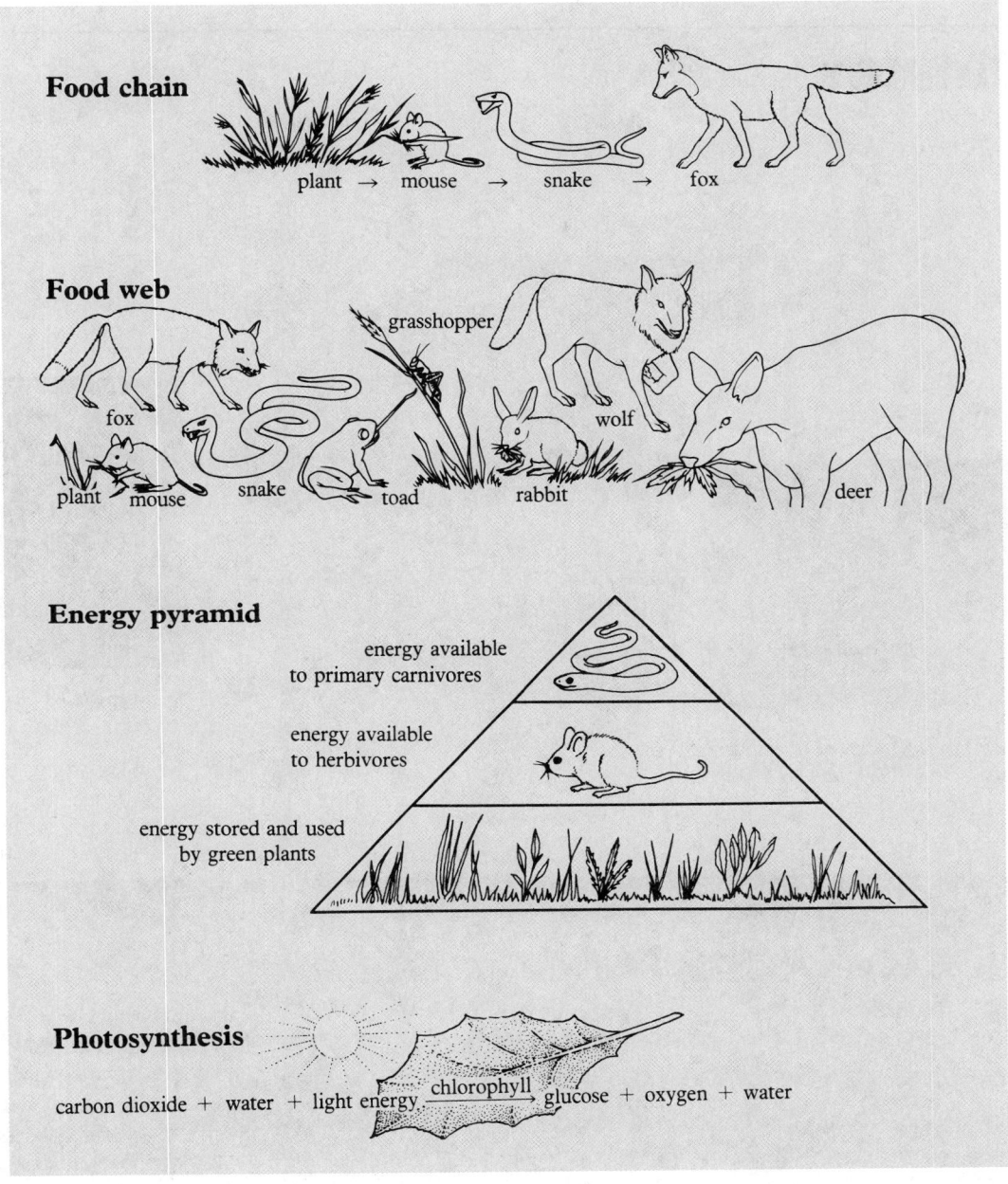

Food chain

plant → mouse → snake → fox

Food web

grasshopper

fox

wolf

plant mouse snake toad rabbit deer

Energy pyramid

energy available to primary carnivores

energy available to herbivores

energy stored and used by green plants

Photosynthesis

carbon dioxide + water + light energy $\xrightarrow{\text{chlorophyll}}$ glucose + oxygen + water

an essential role in the chemical reactions that occur during photosynthesis. These reactions produce a sugar called *glucose* and release oxygen and water.

Glucose is a food that provides energy necessary to sustain life. Plants use some of the glucose for their own life functions and store the rest. When plants are eaten by primary consumers, the consumers obtain the stored glucose and their cells convert it into energy.

In the ecosystem, the relationship between producers and consumers is often illustrated by a *food chain* such as the one shown at the top of this page. But the relationship between living organisms is often far more intricate than a chain suggests. For example, plants are eaten by other animals besides mice. Snakes prey not only on mice, but on toads and prairie dogs as well. A fox's diet consists of more than just snakes. The complex feeding pattern linking organisms together is called a *food web.*

In food webs and food chains, energy is transferred from one living thing to the next. However, only about 10 percent of the energy contained in a plant ever reaches a primary consumer. An even smaller amount is eventually passed on to secondary and tertiary consumers. This transfer of energy is called the *energy pyramid.*

Biomes

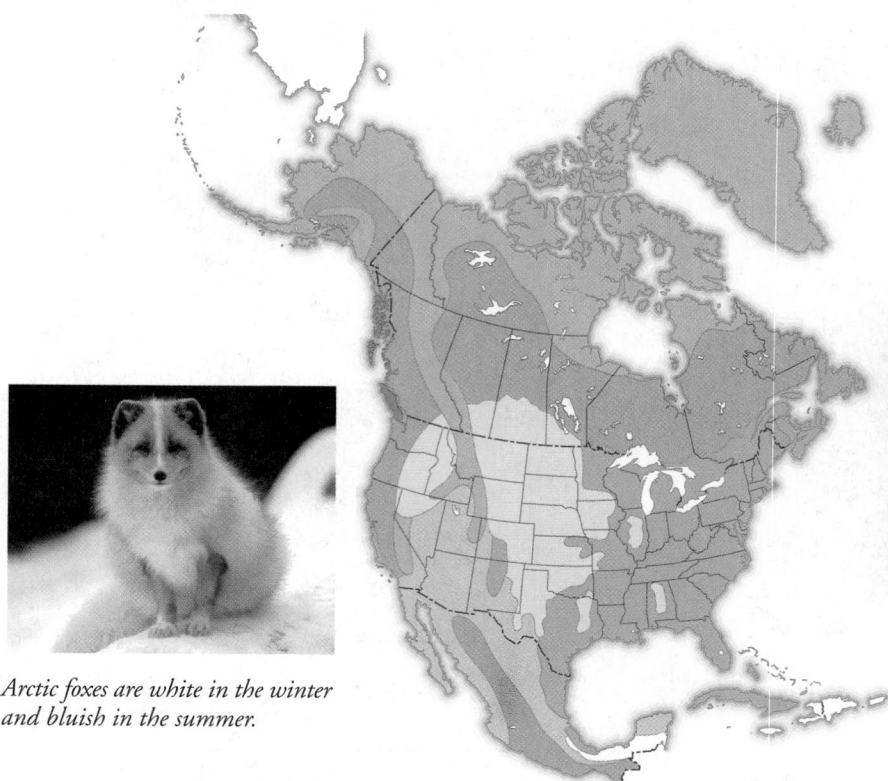

Arctic foxes are white in the winter and bluish in the summer.

Snowshoe hares live in the taiga.

Biomes of North America

		Plant life	Animal life
	Tundra cold and dry	lichens	caribou; wolves; foxes; lemmings; ptarmigan; ducks and geese (summer only)
	Taiga cool and less dry than tundra	pines; spruces; firs; cedars; redwoods; wood sorrel; sphagnum moss	moose; mule deer; bobcats; lynx; snowshoe hare; red crossbill
	Temperate-deciduous forest moderate temperatures and wet	oak; elm; maple; birch; mountain laurel; ferns; aspen	chipmunks; rabbits; bears; squirrels; deer; raccoons
	Grasslands moderate temperatures and less wet than forests	big bluestem grasses; cordgrass; little bluestem; psoralea; clover	bison; pronghorn antelope; prairie dogs; prairie chickens; mice
	Desert moderate to hot and very dry	cactus; yucca; sagebrush; desert palms; mesquite; desert dandelions	jackrabbits; owls; snakes; kangaroo rats; lizards; roadrunners

A *biome* is an ecological unit that has a certain general type of vegetation. Many of the natural biomes of North America have been changed by the process of civilization. Without the interference of human beings, biomes are determined by temperature, moisture, and soil. There are five large natural biomes in America north of Mexico. In the southern part of North America is a sixth biome, the rain forest (not discussed here).

Tundra.
The North American series of six biomes begins in the Arctic region with the *tundra*. The tundra is a cold plain where average temperatures remain below freezing. During the short summer, however, the tundra becomes warmer, allowing ponds and marshes to thaw. Here water fowl such as ducks and geese reside before migrating south for the long winter.

Rainfall is sparse in the tundra, and only hardy plants such as mosses and lichens, which require little water, can survive.

An unusual type of bird found in the tundra is the ptarmigan. The ptarmigan is brown in summer but white in winter, allowing it to blend with its snowy environment. Other animals found in the tundra region include caribou, reindeer, musk ox, arctic hare, and lemming.

Taiga.
South of the tundra is the coniferous forest, or *taiga*. The beginning of this biome is marked by the timber line, the point at which trees begin to grow. Average temperatures are higher than in the tundra and there is more rainfall, so certain species of trees can thrive. The coniferous forest takes its name from the word *conifer,* meaning "cone-bearing," which describes the trees of this biome.

The conifers have needlelike leaves, and most are evergreen. This means that only part of the leaves fall at any one time, so the trees always remain green. Conifers include pines, spruces, firs, and cedars. Along the west coast is another species of conifer—the giant redwood. Some redwood trees are thousands of years old.

Among the animals that inhabit the taiga are herbivores (plant eaters) such as deer and beaver. Carnivores (meat eaters) include wolves and bobcats. There are also varieties of birds and insects.

Forest.
In the eastern United States is the *temperate-deciduous forest*. This biome receives large amounts of precipitation, and temperatures are generally moderate. These conditions allow many species of wildlife to flourish.

Throughout the year the deciduous forest changes dramatically. In autumn the leaves turn color; in winter the leaves drop to expose bare limbs; in spring new leaves return.

Many types of flowering plants can be found in the deciduous forest. The rich flora provide food for vast numbers of herbivores. These, in turn, support a large population of higher level consumers such as foxes and owls.

Grasslands.
In the central part of the United States, rainfall begins to decrease, and we enter the biome known as *grasslands*. In the eastern part of the grasslands, where there is the most moisture, tall bluestem grasses grow. These are sometimes eight feet high with very deep roots. Farther west, where there is less precipitation, the grasses are shorter. These grasses include little bluestem, western wheatgrass, and short blue gramma. The grasses provide food for grazing animals such as white-tailed deer.

A variety of animals in the grasslands make their homes underground. These include gophers, moles, and prairie dogs. The prairie dogs live in large communities, or "towns," with huge populations. Many prairie animals are endangered by the replacement of grasses by crops.

Desert.
A biome that receives very little precipitation is called a *desert*. Perhaps the most familiar type of desert plant is the cactus, which adapted itself to survive in dry conditions. The Giant Desert Cactus, for example, has no leaves; this reduces the amount of water that the cactus loses through evaporation. It has a wide root system so that it can absorb the small amounts of rain that do fall. The cactus also has the ability to store water for quite long periods of time.

Desert temperatures are very hot during the day because there is little moisture to reflect the sunlight. At night temperatures drop rapidly because there are few clouds to prevent the heat from leaving the earth. As a result of the extreme daytime heat, many desert animals are *nocturnal*—active mainly at night.

Some of the animals that live in the desert include the desert fox and the kangaroo rat. One of the most common desert species is the jackrabbit, which plays an important role in the food web.

Cycles

Water cycle

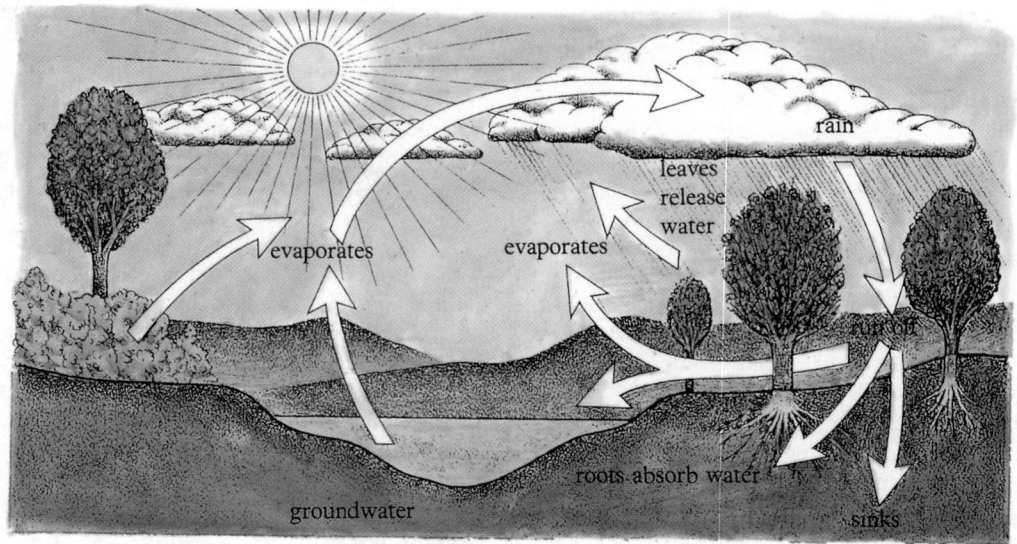

In the water cycle, water is evaporated into the atmosphere by the sun's energy. The water vapor is then carried by the wind, condenses, and forms clouds. Eventually, the water falls as precipitation—rain or snow. Some of the water is absorbed by plants; some sinks into the ground or flows as runoff into lakes and streams. Evaporation occurs again, and the cycle continues.

Oxygen-carbon dioxide cycle

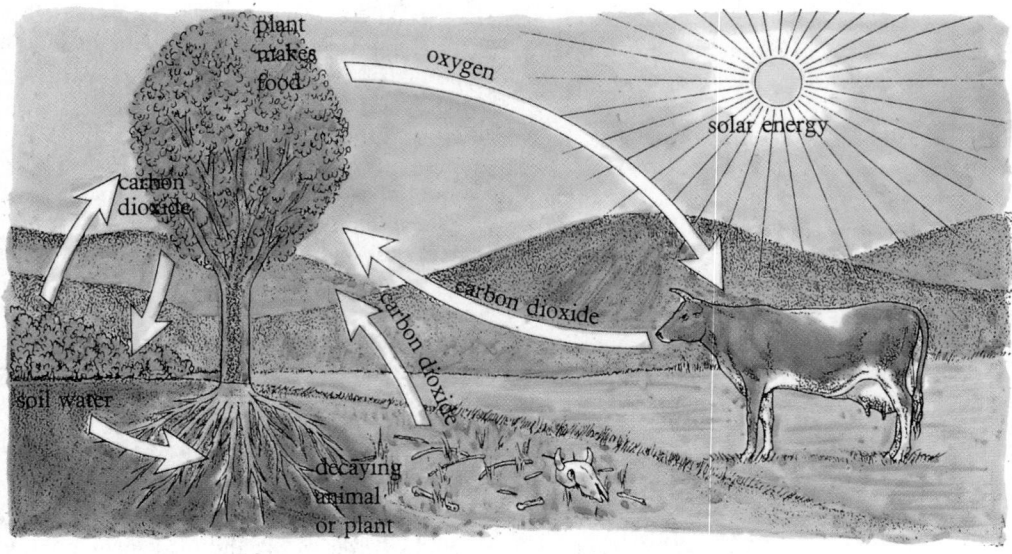

Green plants absorb carbon dioxide (CO_2) and release oxygen in the process of photosynthesis. Oxygen is used by both plant and animal cells during respiration, and carbon dioxide is released in the process. Carbon dioxide also enters the atmosphere from decaying organic material.

Succession

When an ecosystem has been destroyed by fire, glacier, wind, volcano, or human intervention, the pattern of life that existed before the destruction is not immediately restored. Instead, a step-by-step process gradually follows. This process is called *succession*. Here are a few examples of succession in different settings. Each example leads to a *climax* forest, one that is stable.

A Glacial Lake

1. After a glacier melts, it leaves behind lakes of various depths that are devoid of life.

2. Shallow parts of the lake are soon invaded by plants that grow completely under water.

3. Debris from plant remains and silt allows water lilies to grow. These shade out underwater plants.

4. A marsh forms, allowing cattails, reeds, and other marsh plants to grow in the muddy soil.

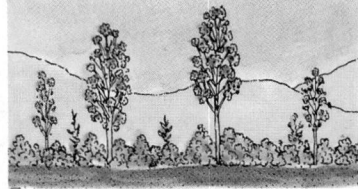

5. The plants take water from the mud and release it to the air. As the soil becomes drier, trees begin to grow.

A Cleared Field

1. When farmland is no longer plowed, seeds of annual plants left in the soil begin to grow.

2. Gradually, plants that live for several years establish themselves and crowd out the annuals.

3. Larger perennial plants become bushes in time. Small trees such as thorns or sumac take hold.

4. Fast-growing pine trees may take over the field for many years, although a few hardwoods grow among the pines.

5. After many years, larger hardwoods shade out the pines, forming a forest that perpetuates itself.

A Lava Flow

1. When lava first cools, it is pure rock that contains no life of any kind.

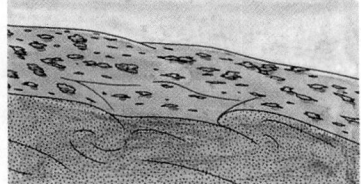

2. Lichens, a combination of algae and fungi growing together, can live on rock surfaces.

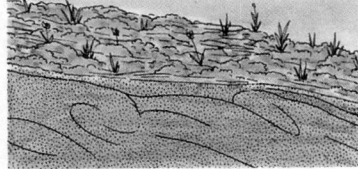

3. Chemicals produced by lichens and weathering produce patches of sandy soil that support mosses and other small plants.

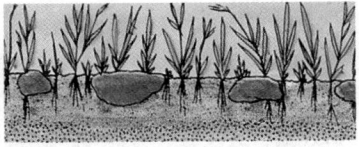

4. Decaying plant materials mix into the sand, improving the soil so that it can support small herbs and grasses. Their roots help break up the rock and hold the soil in place.

5. Bushes and small trees take hold. Sun-loving small plants are replaced by plants that thrive in partial shade.

fossil
reveals fern from the past

Dictionary of life science

instinct
shapes the wasps' nest

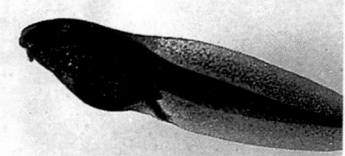

metamorphosis
of tadpole into frog

symbiosis
red-billed oxpeckers and warthog

abiotic. Parts of the environment that are not living.

acquired characteristic. Physical trait of an organism that is brought about by its environment.

adaptations. Features of structure and function that make an organism better suited for living and reproducing in a particular environment.

algae. Simple plants that carry on photosynthesis. Most are single-celled.

anatomy. Study of the structure of organisms.

angiosperms. Plants that form true flowers as their structures of reproduction. The seeds of angiosperms are enclosed in structures of the parent plant. These structures are usually called fruits.

antibiotic. Substance produced by one organism that is used to kill another organism. Penicillin was the first antibiotic to be discovered.

asexual reproduction. Reproduction from one parent organism without the union of germ cells.

bacteria. Microscopic organisms found throughout the environment. They are neither plants nor animals.

balance of nature. Natural condition in which plant and animal communities continue unchanged in either numbers or composition.

biogeography. Study of the plants and animals found in various climatic and geographic zones.

biome. Largest ecological unit. A biome includes all of the plants and animals of a particular region of Earth.

carnivore. Organism that eats meat.

cell. Smallest unit of living matter, usually composed of a nucleus, cytoplasm, and a membrane or wall.

cell membrane. Thin outer layer of animal cells.

cell wall. Outer layer of plant cells.

chlorophyll. Green pigment in plants that transforms sunlight into usable energy for the process of photosynthesis.

chloroplast. Cellular structure in plants that contains chlorophyll.

conifer. Cone-bearing shrub or tree.

conjugation. Form of sexual reproduction in which two cells join and transfer genetic material. Conjugation is usually associated with single-celled organisms.

consumer. Organism that survives by eating other organisms.

cytoplasm. Semifluid material surrounding the nucleus of a cell and enclosed by the cell membrane.

deciduous. Type of plant that sheds all its leaves after a growing season.

ecology. Study of organisms in relation to each other and to their environment.

ecosystem. Living community that contains an energy source, abiotic chemicals, and organisms that function as producers, consumers, and decomposers.

environment. Total surroundings of a living thing.

evolution. Genetic change in a species that, over a period of time, better adapts it to its environment.

food web. Feeding pattern of organisms in the ecosystem.

fossil. Organism's remains or the traces that have been preserved.

genus. Group of related species.

gymnosperm. Seed plant that has exposed ovules. Gymnosperms are often referred to as conifers or evergreens.

habitat. Natural home of an animal or plant.

herbivore. Plant-eating organism.

heredity. Traits that are genetically passed from parent to offspring; biological inheritance.

hermaphrodite. Animal or plant possessing both male and female reproductive organs.

hybrid. Cross between different species.

instinct. Type of behavior that is inborn.

invertebrate. Organism that lacks a backbone.

lichen. Alga and a fungus living together and depending on each other for survival.

mammal. Vertebrate with milk-producing (mammary) glands, such as a dog or cat.

meiosis. Special kind of cell division in organisms that have sexual reproduction. Meiosis reduces the chromosome number in the mature germ cells by half.

metabolism. Set of interrelated chemical processes characteristic of life.

metamorphosis. Radical changes in the development of some animals as they mature. Metamorphosis is usually associated with insects and amphibians.

mitosis. Cell division in which two daughter cells have the same genetic material as the parent cell.

morphology. Study of the form and structure of living things.

mutation. Inheritable change in a chromosome or gene.

niche. Organism's role in the ecosystem.

nucleus. Inner body in a cell that contains the cell's hereditary material (chromosomes, genes, and DNA) and controls the activity of the cytoplasm.

omnivore. Organism that consumes both plants and animals. Humans are omnivores.

parasite. Organism that takes its food from another living organism.

photosynthesis. Process by which green plants manufacture food (glucose) from carbon dioxide, water, and light.

predator. Animal that feeds on other animals.

protoplasm. All the material in a living cell.

respiration. Chemical reactions in a cell that release energy.

sexual reproduction. Reproduction that requires the combination of genetic material from the germ cells of two individuals.

species. Particular group of plants or animals that maintains its distinctness over many generations.

spontaneous generation. Living things emerging from nonliving material.

spore. Single-celled reproductive body.

succession. Gradual replacement of plant and animal species at a given site in a regular pattern after removal of an existing ecosystem at the site by a disaster such as fire, flood, or removal of the ecosystem by human beings. Succession also occurs at new sites, such as lakes, which gradually change to bogs and then to land.

symbiosis. Relationship in which two dissimilar organisms live together and benefit each other.

taxonomy. Classification of plants and animals according to evolutionary relationships.

transpiration. Process by which plants lose water through evaporation.

vertebrate. Animal having a segmented spinal column, a skull surrounding the brain, and an internal skeleton.

zygote. Egg cell at the moment of fertilization.

For Further Reference

Allen, Durward
The Life of Prairies and Plains
McGraw-Hill
Attenborough, David
Life on Earth
Little, Brown
Clement, Roland C.
Nature Atlas of America
Hammond

Peck, Robert McCracken
Land of the Eagle: A Natural History of North America
Summit Books
Teal, John and Teal, Mildred
Life and Death of the Salt Marsh
Ballantine Books
Wagner, Frederic H.
Wildlife of the Deserts
Harry N. Abrams

- *The scientific method*   **364**
- *The physical sciences*   **368**
- *Matter*   **371**
- *Energy*   **374**
- *Electromagnetism*   **378**
- *Wave motion*   **380**
- *Dictionary of physical sciences*   **382**

Physical Sciences

Although knowledge about nature can be divided into the life sciences and the physical sciences, it is common to define the expression *physical science* as the combined study of topics in physics and chemistry. This convention is adopted here.

You will learn how scientists work, the principal units of measurement, the basic meaning of matter and energy, the way that energy can be changed by machines or transmitted by waves, and how waves can be modified. And you will find the answers to many often-asked questions, such as: What is the difference between heat and temperature? What causes rainbows? And why is the sky blue? See also the sections on Chemistry and Physics in Handbook 2.

The scientific method

What is science?

Science is one of the branches of knowledge that requires systematic study and method. In an attempt to answer questions about the nature of things, scientists ask "what" and "how" questions. *What* questions are usually answered by a description. "What kind of animals live in that pond?" Answer: "Frogs, fish, and reptiles." *How* questions often require the study of a particular natural phenomenon. "How is energy conducted?" The answer, "Energy is transferred from atom to atom in a conductor," requires the study of a number of different substances. Many substances have to be compared and measurements taken.

Measurement is extremely important in science. Questions of how much and how fast can only be answered by measurement. Measurement allows scientists to compare the results of their experiments. Measurement has been called the "language of science."

Science and scientists, in an attempt to explain nature, use facts to formulate laws and theories. *Facts* are particular pieces of information. *Laws* describe regular natural occurrences; they are records of what happens. *Theories* use facts in an organized way to explain both laws and facts, and to predict what will occur in similar situations. In order for a theory to be acceptable, it must predict correctly how something will react before it happens. If a theory does not predict properly, it must be changed or a new theory must take its place. Science is cumulative and self-correcting.

How scientists work.

Scientists test theories by performing experiments and making their results known so that other scientists can view the results and repeat the experiments. This system is called *the scientific method.*

The scientific method has been divided into a series of steps, a blueprint for action; but not all scientists follow this blueprint all of the time. There is no single method or way that scientists work, but the scientific method has helped many people.

What is an experiment?

An experiment is a controlled procedure carried out to test or discover something. It is the process of making something happen under conditions controlled by the observer. The key word for a scientific experiment is *controlled.*

Let us assume we wish to answer the question, "Do seeds need water to germinate?" We buy a package of seeds and place one in a bottle that has some dry soil in it. We allow it to stand for several days without watering. We observe that the seed did not germinate (sprout). However, we cannot tell why the seed did not sprout. Perhaps it needed water; perhaps the seed was dead; perhaps the soil was poor; perhaps the bottle was inadequate; perhaps it was too hot or cold or too light or dark. All of these are possible answers to why the seed did not germinate. There were too many *variables* in this experiment.

Now let us design another experiment to answer the same question, only this time we will attempt to eliminate as many variables as possible. This time we take two identical, clean bottles and put the same amount of soil from the same location in each one. Next we plant a seed from the same package in each bottle. For convenience, we label one bottle A and the other B. We place both bottles in the same place and water the soil in bottle A, but not in bottle B. Bottle A is our control. After several days, the seed in bottle A germinates, but not the one in bottle B. By using a control, we have eliminated the variables of the bottle, soil, temperature, and light. The possibility that the particular seed in bottle B was dead still exists, however. This last variable can be eliminated by using many seeds and bottles in both the control and experimental setups. After several days we can compare the number of seeds that germinated in each group. All experiments must be planned and controlled to eliminate variables so that the results provide only one answer to the question being asked.

A scientific experiment is not performed in a vacuum, however. First the scientist must learn enough about a subject to identify a problem and to find out what others have done to solve the problem. If the problem has not been solved, or if the scientist thinks there is a better solution for the problem, then the scientist can work on a possible solution for the problem in a form that can be tested by experiment. A solution is not considered "scientific" unless an experiment can be devised to test it.

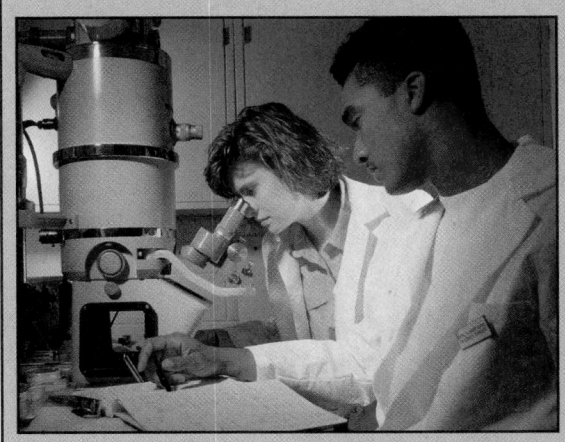

The Scientific Method

1. **Identify** or state the problem.

2. **Analyze** the problem: gather information, find out what is known about the problem. It may have been solved.

3. **Form a hypothesis:** make an "educated guess" as to what the answer may be. This can be based on a hunch or past experience.

4. **Test the hypothesis:** design and carry out an experiment or experiments.

5. **Record** observations and measurements, interpret them, and form conclusions.

6. **Revise** the hypothesis based on data.

High school students take notes of their observations through a microscope in the science lab.

Measurement.

Scientists constantly compare things. It may be easy to say that one object is bigger or heavier than another; or that a place is farther away than another without measuring them. But to answer questions like "How big?"; "How much bigger?"; "How heavy?" requires measuring—a more exact way of comparing. The measurements scientists gather must be available to other scientists so that they can repeat the experiment or use the information in their own work. The units of measurement must be standard, that is, they must mean the same everywhere. There are two standard systems in use today. We commonly use the customary system (also known as the English system). In the customary system, the *yard* is the basic unit of length. You know this system and probably use it quite easily. However, it was difficult to learn because the units within the system are not related.

Metric system. The *metric system* is in common use in most countries and by scientists all over the world. This system of measurement is a decimal system. Each unit is related by a factor of 10. The basic unit of length is the *meter*. All other units are 10, 100, or 1000 times larger than the meter or ⅒, ¹⁄₁₀₀, or ¹⁄₁₀₀₀ of a meter.

The units of 10 meters (dekameter), 100 meters (hectometer), and ⅒ meter (decimeter) are not commonly used. The key to using the metric system is understanding the prefixes used to designate the decimal fractions. "Kilo-" means 1000 times the basic unit; "cent-" means 0.01 or ¹⁄₁₀₀ of the basic unit; and "milli-" means 0.001 or ¹⁄₁₀₀₀ of the basic unit. The basic unit of liquid volume in the metric system is the *liter* and the basic unit of mass is the *gram*.

Temperature. Temperature is measured on the Fahrenheit or Celsius scales. On the Fahrenheit scale, water freezes at 32 degrees and boils at 212 degrees. The Celsius (formerly the centigrade scale) is used in scientific work. On this scale, water freezes at 0 degrees and boils at 100 degrees. There are 180 degrees between boiling and freezing on a Fahrenheit thermometer, and 100 degrees between the same points on a Celsius thermometer. To convert a Fahrenheit value to the Celsius, subtract 32 from the Fahrenheit value and multiply by ⅝. $C = \frac{5}{9}(F - 32)$. To convert a Celsius temperature to Fahrenheit, multiply the Celsius value by ⁹⁄₅ and add 32 to it. $F = \frac{9}{5}C + 32$.

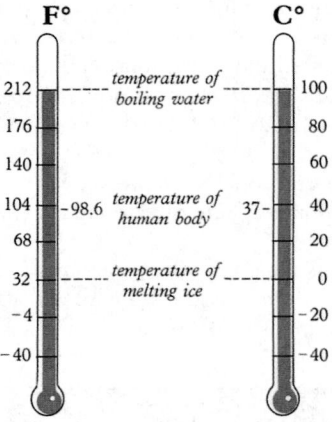

Principal Units of Measurement

The customary system of length		
1 mile =	1760 yards =	5280 feet
1 yard =	3 feet =	36 inches
	1 foot =	12 inches

The metric system of length			
kilometer	km	1000 meters	1000 × meter
meter	m	1 meter	—
centimeter	cm	0.01 meter	$\frac{1}{100}$ meter
millimeter	mm	0.001 meter	$\frac{1}{1000}$ meter

Metric units of liquid volume			
kiloliter	kl	1000 liters	1000 × liter
liter	l	1.0 liter	—
centiliter	cl	0.01 liter	$\frac{1}{100}$ liter
milliliter	ml	0.001 liter	$\frac{1}{1000}$ liter

Metric units of mass			
kilogram	kg	1000 grams	1000 × gram
gram	g	1.0 gram	—
centigram	cg	0.01 gram	$\frac{1}{100}$ gram
milligram	mg	0.001 gram	$\frac{1}{1000}$ gram

Equivalents

1 acre = 43,560 square feet = 4840 square yards
1 bushel (U.S.) = 2150.42 cubic inches
= 32 quarts
1 cord = 128 cubic feet
1 cubic centimeter = 0.061 cubic inch
1 cubic foot = 7.481 gallons = 1728 cubic inches
1 cubic inch = 0.554 fluid ounce
= 16.387 cubic centimeters
1 cubic meter = 1.308 cubic yards
1 cubic yard = 0.765 cubic meter = 27 cubic feet
1 cup = 8 fluid ounces = 0.5 liquid pint
1 gallon (U.S.) = 231 cubic inches
= 128 U.S. fluid ounces
= 4 liquid quarts
1 liter = 1.057 liquid quarts
1 meter = 39.37 inches = 1.094 yards
1 micron = 0.001 millimeter = 0.00003937 inch
1 mile, nautical = 1.852 kilometers
= 1.151 statute miles
= 6076.1155 feet
1 milliliter = 0.061 cubic inch
1 pint, dry = 33.600 cubic inches = 0.551 liter
1 pint, liquid = 28.875 inches = 0.473 liter
= 2 cups = 16 ounces
1 pound, avoirdupois = 7000 grains = 16 ounces
= 453.59237 grams
1 quart, dry (U.S.) = 67.201 cubic inches
= 1.101 liters
1 quart, liquid (U.S.) = 57.75 cubic inches
= 0.946 liter
= 2 pints = 32 ounces
1 square foot = 929 square centimeters
= 144 square inches
1 square inch = 6.45 square centimeters
1 square kilometer = 0.386 square miles
= 247.105 acres
1 square meter = 1.196 square yards
= 10.764 square feet
1 square mile = 640 acres
1 square yard = 0.836 square meter
= 9 square feet
= 1296 square inches
1 tablespoon = 3 teaspoons = 0.5 fluid ounce
1 ton, metric = 2204.623 pounds
= 1.102 net tons
1 ton, net or short = 2000 pounds
= 0.907 metric ton
1 yard = 0.9144 meter = 3 feet = 36 inches

Conversions

To convert	into	multiply by
angstroms	microns	0.0001
centimeters	feet	0.03281
centimeters	inches	0.3937
cubic cm	cubic inches	0.06102
cubic feet	cubic meters	0.02832
days	seconds	86,400.0
degrees (angle)	radians	0.01745
fathoms	feet	6.0
feet	centimeters	30.48
feet	meters	0.3048
feet/min.	cm/sec.	0.5080
feet/sec.	knots	0.5921
feet/sec.	statute mi./hr.	0.6818
furlongs/hr.	statute mi./hr.	0.125
furlongs	feet	660.0
gallons (liq.)	liters	3.785
gal. of water	pounds of water	8.3453
grams	oz. (avoirdupois)	0.03527
grams	pounds	0.002205
hours	days	0.04167
hours	weeks	0.005952
inches	centimeters	2.540
kilograms	pounds	2.205
kilometers	feet	3280.8
kilometers	mi. (statute)	0.6214
knots	feet/hr.	6080.0
knots	nautical mi./hr.	1.0
knots	statute mi./hr.	1.151
liters	gallons (liq.)	0.2642
liters	pints (liq.)	2.113
meters	feet	3.281
meters	mi. (nautical)	0.0005396
meters	mi. (statute)	0.0006214
microns	meters	0.000001
mi. (nautical)	feet	6076.115
mi. (statute)	feet	5280.0
mi. (nautical)	kilometers	1.852
mi. (statute)	kilometers	1.609
mi. (nautical)	mi. (statute)	1.1508
mi. (statute)	mi. (nautical)	0.8684
mi. (statute)/hr.	feet/min.	88.0
millimeters	inches	0.03937
oz. (avoirdupois)	grams	28.3495
oz. (avoirdupois)	lb. (avoirdupois)	0.0625
pints (liq.)	gallons (liq.)	0.125
pints (liq.)	quarts (liq.)	0.5
lb. (avoirdupois)	kilograms	0.4536

The physical sciences

The word "science" comes from the Latin word *scire,* which means "to know." The attempt "to know" the universe involves the study of many different subjects. For this reason, science is divided into different branches. The *physical sciences* form one of these major branches. The word "physical" comes from the Greek word *physika,* meaning "natural things." Today the physical sciences involve the study of matter and energy. There are two main branches of the physical sciences. *Chemistry* is the study of the substances found in nature and the ways new substances can be formed. *Physics* deals with energy and the way it changes from one form to another. Physics also studies the basic nature of the physical world.

Both chemistry and physics study *matter* from different points of view. Matter is anything that takes up space, that has volume and weight. Both volume and weight are measurements. Weight is the measure of the force of gravity on an object. The gravitational force on an object depends on the quantity of matter that makes up the object. The quantity of matter is called *mass.* All matter has mass.

Different kinds of matter are often described in terms of their properties. Properties are characteristics or qualities that allow us to put substances into groups, to identify them, and to predict how the substances will act under certain conditions. There are two kinds of properties. A *physical* property of a substance can be determined without changing that substance into another. The temperatures at which substances freeze and boil are physical properties. The *phase* of a substance is another common

Melting and Boiling Points of Some Substances

Substance	Melting point (°C)	Boiling point (°C)
Neon	-248.0	-246
Ethyl alcohol	-117.3	+ 78.5
Chlorine	-101	- 34.6
Water	0	100
Sodium	98	882.9
Sodium chloride	801	1413
Silver	961.9	2212
Copper	1083	2567
Iron	1535	2750

property. Phase is the form that a substance normally exists in at room temperature. There are three common phases of matter—solid, liquid, and gas. A solid has a definite shape and a definite volume; a liquid has a definite volume but no definite shape; a gas has neither a definite shape nor a definite volume. Liquids and gases are fluids—they take the shape of their container.

Another physical property is the *solubility* of a substance; that is, the ability of that substance to dissolve in water or other liquids.

The *density* of a substance is an important physical property because it allows us to compare equal volumes of different substances. Density is the mass of a definite volume of a substance. It is usually measured in grams (units of mass) per cubic

Densities of Some Common Substances (in grams per cubic centimeter)

balsa wood	0.11 to 0.14	alcohol	0.791	marble	2.6 to 2.84
cork	0.22 to 0.26	kerosene	0.82	granite	2.64 to 2.76
oak	0.60 to 0.80	paraffin	0.87 to 0.91	aluminum	2.70
walnut	0.64 to 0.70	ice	0.917	diamond	3.01 to 3.52
ash	0.65 to 0.85	water	1.00	steel	7.6 to 7.8
gasoline	0.66 to 0.69	sea water	1.025	iron	7.85
cardboard	0.69	milk	1.028 to 1.035	brass	8.2 to 8.7
beech	0.70 to 0.90	rubber	1.19	copper	8.89
paper	0.7 to 1.15	sugar	1.59	lead	11.3
ether	0.736	clay	1.8 to 2.6	mercury	13.6
dogwood	0.76	glass	2.4 to 2.8	gold	19.3

centimeter or per milliliter (both units of volume). The density of water under normal pressure at room temperature is 1.0g/cc.

Chemical properties describe how a substance reacts with other substances. Iron will rust when it combines with oxygen. The metal iron has changed into a new substance, iron oxide.

Types of matter.

Scientists have learned that matter can be divided into three different groups. *Elements* are substances that cannot be divided into any other substance. Ninety occur naturally, and scientists have created 26 others in the laboratory for a total of 116 elements (including 6 yet-unnamed elements). Most elements are solids at room temperature. Hydrogen, helium, oxygen, and a few others are gases. Mercury and bromine are the only elements that are liquids at normal room temperature. Each named element has been given a symbol or abbreviation that is related to its English, Greek, or Latin name. (For more information about chemical elements, see the Chemistry section in Handbook 2.)

Many kinds of matter are made up of two or more elements that are chemically combined. Water is one example. It is made up of hydrogen and oxygen. Sugar is made up of carbon, hydrogen, and oxygen. Salt is composed of sodium and chlorine. A substance that is made up of two or more elements that have been chemically combined is a *compound*. A chemical change occurs when elements combine to form a compound. The elements lose their identity and a new substance is formed. Each compound

A miner uses the different densities of substances in the mixture that is sand and gravel to separate the very heavy element gold from the lighter compounds of silicon that form most of the mixture.

has its own chemical formula that uses the symbols of the elements forming it.

Mixtures are a third kind of matter. A mixture is made up of two or more elements or compounds that are mixed together. No chemical change takes place, so the individual components do not lose their identity and can be separated from each other physically. Soil and air are mixtures. Soil is mostly a mixture of compounds, while air is mostly a mixture of elements.

Some common compounds

The number of elements is small compared to the vast number of compounds that can be made from them. Here are four very different compounds formed out of only five elements: sodium (Na), hydrogen (H), carbon (C), oxygen (O), and nitrogen (N).

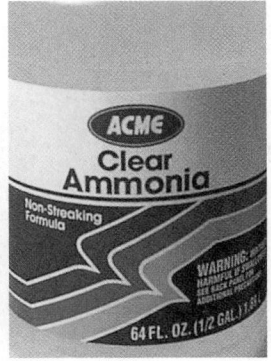

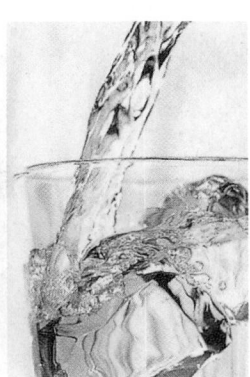

$NaHCO_3$ baking soda $C_{12}H_{22}O_{11}$ sugar NH_4OH ammonia H_2O water

The particle theory.

In order to explain the different kinds of matter and how matter changes, scientists assume that all matter is made up of tiny particles. Elements are made up of *atoms*. An atom is the smallest particle of an element that still has the properties of that element. When elements combine chemically to form a compound, their atoms usually become bonded together. Atoms of elements bonded together may form *molecules* of compounds. A molecule is made up of two or more atoms bonded together. A molecule is the smallest particle of a compound that has all the properties of that compound. When two atoms of hydrogen, H, combine with one atom of oxygen, O, one molecule of water, H_2O, is formed. Some compounds are formed without molecules, strictly speaking. In ionic compounds such as table salt, NaCl, the particles of sodium, Na, and chlorine, Cl, are loosely bonded when dissolved in water.

In addition to assuming that all matter is made up of particles, scientists also state that these particles are constantly moving and that there are spaces between the particles. These three statements allow us to offer an explanation for the differences between the phases of matter, how substances boil and melt, how substances change phase, and other basic questions about matter.

Although scientists cannot see individual atoms, they use mental models of what atoms are like to predict their behavior. A picture of such a mental model of the helium atom shows four heavy particles at the atom's center—two protons and two neutrons. Two much lighter particles—electrons—are thought of as moving in regions outside the heavy center.

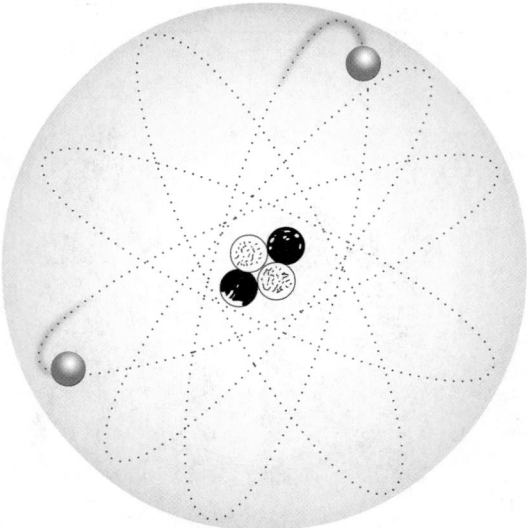

How to Read a Chemical Equation

Chemical equations provide a compact way to represent the reactions that occur when two compounds are combined. A typical chemical equation is

$$SO_2 + H_2O \rightarrow H_2SO_3$$

The + sign means that the two compounds are combined. The $\rightarrow$ means "yields." This equation, then, means sulfur dioxide (SO_2) combined with water (H_2O) yields sulfurous acid (H_2SO_3).

Frequently, the amount of one compound that enters into the combination is different from the amount of the other compound. In that case, the chemical equation is "balanced" by writing numbers indicating the amounts involved before the symbol for the compound.

$$P_4 + 5\,O_2 \rightarrow 2\,P_2O_5$$

In this equation, one part of phosphorus, which occurs as a molecule of four phosphorus atoms, is combined with five parts of oxygen, which occurs as a molecule of two oxygen atoms, to yield two parts of a compound named phosphorus pentoxide. Often you see arrows pointing up or down in chemical equations. Arrows pointing up indicate that the substance is formed as a gas, while arrows pointing down mean that the substance is formed as a solid when two liquids are combined. For example,

$$AgNO_3 + NaCl \rightarrow AgCl \downarrow + NaNO_3$$

means that when silver nitrate ($AgNO_3$) in solution is added to salt (NaCl) in solution the silver chloride (AgCl) is formed as a solid that collects at the bottom of the mixture. The sodium nitrate ($NaNO_3$) that also forms stays in solution. Similarly,

$$3NO_2 + H_2O \rightarrow 2HNO_3 + NO \uparrow$$

means that three parts of nitrogen dioxide (NO_2) dissolved in one part of water yields two parts of nitric acid (HNO_3) and one part of the gas nitric oxide (NO).

A small triangle written over the "yields" arrow means that the chemicals must be heated for the reaction to occur. Similarly, a small "D.C." over the arrow means that direct current (electricity) must be applied.

Matter

The smaller particles that make up atoms are called electrons, protons, and neutrons. The simplest kind of atom is the hydrogen atom, which is built from just one proton and one electron. One might expect that the next simplest atom would consist of a pair of protons and a pair of electrons, but the forces in the central part of the atom, called the nucleus, do not permit this atom to exist. In fact, the next-most-complicated atom is another form of hydrogen, called heavy hydrogen or deuterium. Its atoms each contain one proton, one neutron, and one electron. A third form of hydrogen, called tritium, can also exist; it has two neutrons, a proton, and an electron.

The type of element is normally given by the number of electrons. Only electrons enter into chemical reactions. However, the number of electrons in an atom may be easily changed, while the number of protons is more constant. Therefore, physical scientists say that the element is determined by the number of protons.

When the elements are arranged in order by the number of protons, called the *atomic number,* there is an element for each whole number of protons. Hydrogen has the atomic number 1, helium has the atomic number 2, carbon has the atomic number 6, oxygen has the atomic number 8, and so forth, up to uranium, the last naturally occurring element, which has the atomic number 92. But 24 elements, with atomic numbers between 93 and 116, have been created, as have 2 others.

Neutrons occur in all atomic nuclei heavier than hydrogen. The number of protons and neutrons, which are both much heavier than electrons, gives the *mass number* of each element. Deuterium has a mass number of 2, tritium of 3, and helium of 4. From this information (helium's atomic number of 2 and mass number of 4), one can determine that helium must consist of two protons, two neutrons, and two electrons.

Most elements found in nature are a mixture of atoms that all have the same number of protons, but have different numbers of neutrons. Such different versions of the same element are called *isotopes.* For example, the most common isotope of carbon is the one with a mass number of 12, which is called carbon 12. Since the atomic number of carbon is 6, carbon 12 has six protons, six neutrons, and six electrons. There exist in nature, however, small amounts of both carbon 13 and carbon 14. Carbon 13 has seven neutrons and carbon 14 has eight.

Elements with smaller atomic masses tend to be very light. Helium, the element with the second lowest atomic mass, is used in modern blimps to make them lighter than the air they displace.

When the mass of an atom is adjusted for small differences in the mass of the proton and neutron, for the mass of the electrons in the atom, and for the relative abundance of isotopes, a number close to—but not equal to—the mass number results. Since this number, called the *atomic mass,* can be measured directly, the atomic mass is often used by chemists or physicists instead of the mass number. (The mass number cannot be directly measured.) For example, the atomic mass of carbon, which reflects the amount of carbon 13 and carbon 14, is 12.01115.

Although the only forms of matter that we normally experience are elements, compounds, and mixtures, the individual particles that make up atoms are considered matter as well. In addition to electrons, protons, and neutrons, matter also includes such particles as muons, pions, kaons, and many other *subatomic* particles. Most subatomic particles are very short-lived, however. After tiny fractions of a second, they change into other particles or into energy.

Some Important Elements

A *mass number* is the mass of the atom compared with carbon 12, an isotope of carbon whose mass has been assigned the value 12. The *atomic mass* is the average mass number of the different forms of the element.

The *atomic number* is the number of protons in the nucleus of the atom. Atomic number is the most important factor in determining the chemical properties of the element.

Element	Symbol	Atomic mass	Atomic number	Properties, uses
aluminum	Al	26.9815	13	White metal, used in construction where light weight is important. As oxide, used as abrasive.
bismuth	Bi	208.98	83	Brittle metal used in electric fuses, fire sprinkler systems, safety valves.
bromine	Br	79.909	35	Red corrosive liquid used to make organic compounds, medicines, photographic film.
cadmium	Cd	112.40	48	Blue-white metal used in electroplating, bearings, batteries, atomic reactors.
calcium	Ca	40.08	20	Silvery, active metal. Compounds used in mortar, plaster, cement, agriculture.
carbon	C	12.011	6	Black or transparent nonmetal. As diamond, used in jewelry, abrasives; as graphite, in lubricants. Forms innumerable compounds. Basis of all life.
chlorine	Cl	35.453	17	Green corrosive gas. Used in bleach, germicides, drugs, manufacture of organic chemicals.
copper	Cu	63.54	29	Reddish metal used as electrical conductor, to make brass, bronze, other alloys. Compounds used in water purification.
fluorine	F	18.9984	9	Yellow gas, very corrosive. Used to make refrigerants, plastics. As hydrofluoric acid, etches glass.
gold	Au	196.97	79	Yellow metal, used in coins, jewelry, dentistry.
helium	He	4.003	2	Inert gas, used in balloons.
hydrogen	H	1.008	1	Gas used for heat, to make ammonia, many chemical processes.
iodine	I	126.90	53	Black solid, used as germicide, for organic chemicals, photography.
iron	Fe	55.85	26	White, hard metal. Chief component of steel. Compounds used in medicine, blueprints.
lead	Pb	207.21	82	White metal used in plumbing, solder, type metal, batteries. Compounds used as pigments.
lithium	Li	6.940	3	Light, very active metal. Salts used in medicine, fireworks.

Element	Symbol	Atomic mass	Atomic number	Properties, uses
magnesium	Mg	24.32	12	Light, white metal, used to make light alloys for airplanes. Salts used in medicine.
manganese	Mn	54.938	25	Gray-white, brittle metal. Used in stainless steel, other alloys.
mercury	Hg	200.59	80	Liquid, silvery metal, used in thermometers, barometers, other instruments.
neon	Ne	20.183	10	Inert gas used in electric signs.
nitrogen	N	14.007	7	Colorless gas, used to make ammonia, nitric acid, many organic compounds.
oxygen	O	15.999	8	Colorless gas, essential for life, used in oxyacetylene flames, aid to respiration.
phosphorus	P	30.98	15	Yellow, waxy form; red, crystalline form. Compounds used in fertilizer, detergents.
platinum	Pt	195.09	78	Silvery metal used in jewelry, instruments, laboratory ware, catalysts.
potassium	K	39.096	19	Soft, silvery, very active metal. Salts used in fertilizers, medicine.
radium	Ra	226.05	88	Radioactive metal, used in medicine, to make luminous watch dials.
silicon	Si	28.086	14	Brown nonmetal. Compounds used in glass, cement, ceramics, photoelectric cells.
silver	Ag	107.870	47	White metal used in jewelry, coins, tableware, photography, medicine, electroplating.
sodium	Na	22.9898	11	Silvery, very active metal. Salts used in seasoning, fertilizers, detergents.
sulfur	S	32.064	16	Yellow solid, used to vulcanize rubber, make sulfuric acid; sulfur dioxide used as fumigant, bleach.
tin	Sn	118.70	50	White metal, used to plate steel, make pewter, solder, bronze, type metal. Salts used in textiles.
titanium	Ti	47.90	22	Lustrous white metal used in alloys. Oxide used as paint pigment.
uranium	U	238.029	92	White, dense metal, radioactive, used in glass and china, source of atomic energy.
zinc	Zn	65.37	30	Blue-white metal used in brass, many other alloys, metal plating. Compounds used in paints, antiseptics.

Energy

Physics is the branch of physical science that deals with energy, its forms, and the way it changes. In science, energy is the ability to do work. There are several types of energy and each type can be transformed into another. A common example can be found in the automobile. The source of energy is the gasoline used as fuel. The gasoline is burned in the engine. The chemical energy of the fuel is transformed into heat. The heat energy causes other parts to move, causing the car to move. The heat energy is converted or transformed into mechanical energy.

Many different experiments performed over many years have shown scientists that energy can neither be created nor destroyed by chemical or mechanical methods, but it can be transformed from one type to another.

Energy is the ability to do work. For work to be done, an object must move or be moved over a distance. A *force* is required to move or lift an object. A force is a push or pull. There are several kinds of forces. You can exert force on a wall by pushing on it, but no work will be done if the wall does not move. More work is done when you lift a pencil than when you push on a wall! The amount of work that is done by a force depends on two factors: the weight of the object to be lifted or moved and the distance it is lifted or moved. The amount of work done (W) is equal to the force (F) required to lift or move an object multiplied by the distance (d) through which the force is exerted. The relationship between work done, force, and distance is expressed by the formula $W = F \times d$.

Forms of energy. Each type of energy can exist in two different *forms*. Electrical energy can be stored in a cell. A bicycle at the top of a hill has stored energy to coast down. Food has energy stored within the molecules that make it up. The cell, bicycle, and food have energy that is stored up owing to the composition of the material or the position of the object. This energy is called *potential energy*. Potential energy is commonly called energy of position. A hammer that has been raised to hit a nail has potential energy. When you drop the hammer, it has the energy of motion. The potential energy has become *kinetic* energy. Kinetic energy is the energy of motion. Since both potential and kinetic energy are associated with motion, they are often considered as kinds of mechanical energy.

Energy conversions

Energy can be changed from one form to another. The energy of the sun, stored by green plants millions of years ago in what has become coal or oil, is recaptured in part by burning. The heat energy released is used to produce steam, which turns the blades of a turbine, converting the heat energy into mechanical energy. The turbine drives a generator, which converts the mechanical energy into electrical energy. The electrical energy can then be converted by machines, tools, or appliances into heat, light, or mechanical energy.

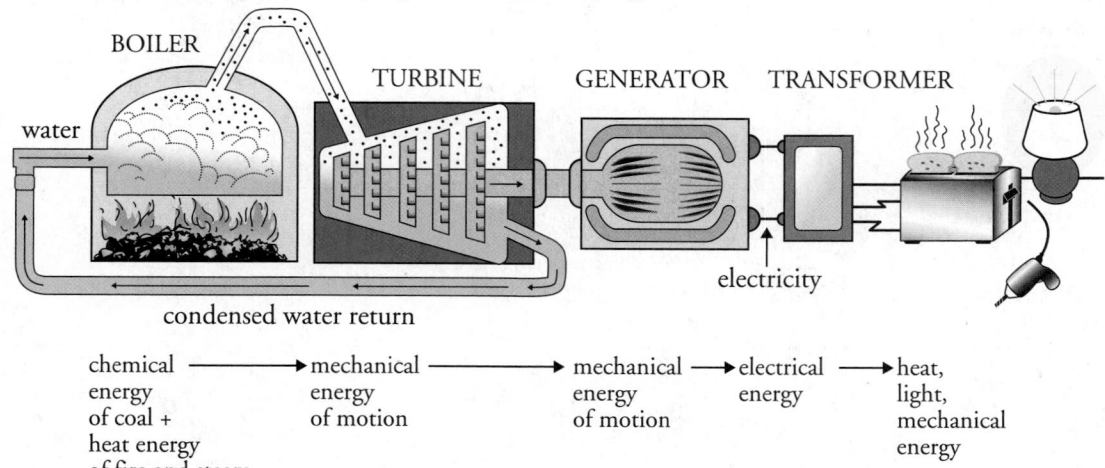

BOILER   TURBINE   GENERATOR   TRANSFORMER

water

condensed water return

electricity

| chemical energy of coal + heat energy of fire and steam | → | mechanical energy of motion | → | mechanical energy of motion | → | electrical energy | → | heat, light, mechanical energy |

Heat energy.

According to the particle theory, all matter is made up of particles that are always moving. All matter has this internal kinetic energy called *heat energy*. The amount of heat an object contains is measured in either of two units, the *calorie* or the *British thermal unit* (Btu). The calorie is the amount of heat required to raise the temperature of 1 gram of water 1 degree Celsius. The Btu is used in heating and air-conditioning systems. One Btu is the amount of heat required to raise the temperature of 1 pound of water 1 Fahrenheit degree.

Temperature is a measurement of how hot something is, not how much heat something contains. The amount of heat something contains will vary with the mass of the object. A bathtub full of water will melt more ice than a cup full of water at the same temperature. Temperature is a measurement of the average kinetic energy of the particles in an object. When the average kinetic energy increases, the temperature will increase. A thermometer usually is made up of a glass tube from which the air has been removed and partially replaced with a small amount of alcohol or mercury. When a thermometer is placed in hot water, it absorbs energy from the water. The particles of the alcohol or mercury begin to move faster and move away from each other. The mercury or alcohol expands up the tube.

In addition to the Celsius and Fahrenheit temperature scales, the Kelvin scale is used to measure very high or low temperatures. The Kelvin, or absolute, scale is based on the assumption that there is a temperature at which all particle motion stops. At this temperature there is no heat. This temperature has been calculated to be about 273 degrees below zero on the Celsius scale and is called *absolute zero*. Absolute zero equals −273.16° C. Water freezes at 273.16° Kelvin (K) and boils at 373.16° K.

Heat energy always moves from a substance with a higher temperature to a substance with a lower one. Heat can be transferred in three different ways: *conduction, convection,* and *radiation.*

In *conduction,* an object must be in direct contact with another. Heat energy will be transferred, or conducted, from the hotter object to the cooler.

Heat is transferred through liquids or gases by *convection.* When water is heated in a pan, the water at the bottom is heated first. It expands and becomes less dense. Cooler, denser water sinks and replaces the warmer water. Convection currents of rising warm water and settling cooler water are set up. This movement of the fluid will continue until the entire container of water is equally heated.

Both conduction and convection involve particles of matter. *Radiation* does not. Heat can be transferred through space in the form of waves that move at the speed of light. When these waves are absorbed by an object, they are converted to heat energy.

Heat transfer

The hot water or steam produced in a boiler transfers heat to a radiator through conduction, *then flows back to the boiler for reheating. The radiator warms the air around it through* convection. *The warm air rises and cooler air sinks, producing* convection currents. *The radiator also heats the air and objects in a room through* radiation, *by which energy waves emitted by the radiator directly heat the molecules they strike.*

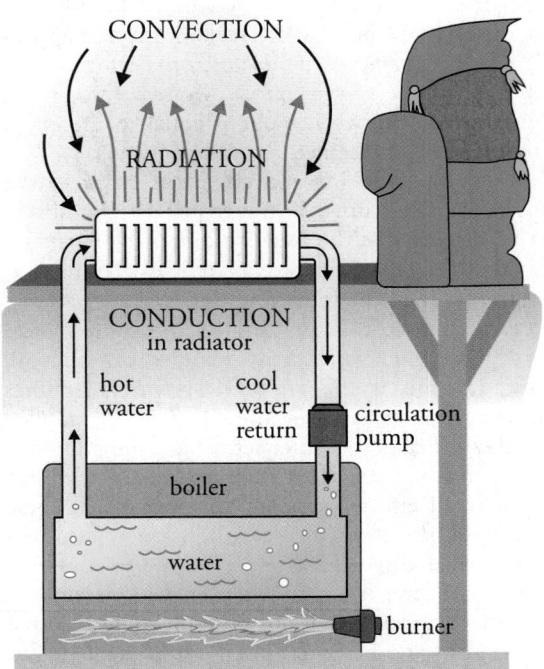

CONVECTION

RADIATION

CONDUCTION
in radiator

hot
water

cool
water
return

circulation
pump

boiler

water

burner

Machines.

Mechanical energy is the energy an object has from its position or motion. The moving parts of an automobile engine are an example of mechanical energy. A hammer hitting a nail also has mechanical energy.

When you think of mechanical energy and machines, you may think of motors and engines, such as the engine in an automobile. The actions of such motors, however, are based in part on fundamental arrangements that transfer mechanical energy. These arrangements are known as *simple machines*.

People have always sought ways to make the work they do easier or faster, or both. Simple machines can make work easier or faster, but they cannot increase the amount of work done. The operator of a simple machine must do work in order to operate it. This work is called the *input* or *work input*. The work the machine does is the *output* or *work output*. The output is never greater than the input. In fact, the input work is usually greater than the output work. Some of the input is used to overcome *friction*. Friction is a force that resists movement between two surfaces. Friction converts mechanical energy into heat energy as parts of machines rub against each other, in the same way that heat is generated when a person's hands are rubbed together.

There are six simple machines: levers, pulleys, wheels and axles, inclined planes, wedges, and screws. These machines help us do work by multiplying the force we put into them or by changing the direction of that force. With any machine, the user must apply a force to overcome the resistance of the object being moved. The force the user applies is called the *effort*. The distance the effort moves through is the *effort distance*. Work is force times distance, so the work input is equal to the effort times the effort distance.

The object being moved exerts a force, the *resistance,* that must be overcome by the effort. The distance that the machine moves the resistance is the *resistance distance*. The work output is the product of the force of the resistance times the resistance distance. If friction and other resistances are ignored, the work input should equal the work output. This is the *law of machines*. Machines can increase or multiply the effort that is applied to them, making work easier. This is usually done by increasing the effort distance. The work done by a small effort over a large distance will equal the work done when a large resistance is moved over a small distance.

Levers. A lever is a simple machine consisting of a bar that is supported at one position while a force is applied at another position. The place where the lever is supported is the *fulcrum*. There are three classes of levers, depending on the positions of the effort, fulcrum, and resistance.

1st class levers: the fulcrum is between the effort and resistance. These levers multiply effort.

2nd class levers: the resistance is between the fulcrum and the effort. These levers also multiply the effort applied to them.

3rd class levers: the effort is between the fulcrum and the resistance. This arrangement multiplies the effort distance.

Pulleys. A pulley is a grooved wheel supported in a frame with a rope placed in the groove of the wheel. The simplest pulley is one that is fixed. This machine does not increase the force applied but does allow a change in the direction of the force. If the pulley is fixed to a ceiling or bar, one can pull down on the rope to lift a resistance. Movable pulleys, where a pulley or combination of pulleys is attached to the resistance, allow us to decrease the force applied to produce the same force on the resistance.

Wheels and axles. These simple machines are made up of a large wheel attached to a smaller wheel, the *axle,* so that both wheels turn together. A small effort applied to the large wheel can overcome a large resistance on the axle. However, the effort must move through a greater distance. The steering wheel of a car is a wheel and axle, as is a screwdriver attached to the head of a screw.

Inclined planes. It is easier to push an object up a gradual slope than to lift it directly. It might take three men to lift a 400-pound object to the back of a truck that is 3 feet high. One man can raise the object to that height by rolling it along a 10-foot ramp.

Wedges. A wedge is an inclined plane that moves into or under a resistance. A small ax or wedge can be used to split a large log. The thin side of the wedge inserted into a small lengthwise split in a log will cause the log to separate over the entire length when the wedge is driven deeper into the split by strikes from a mallet. A thin, gently tapering wedge is more effective (and requires less force to be exerted with each mallet strike) than a wide, sharply tapering wedge. Wedges are also used to raise loads over a short distance, such as in leveling furniture and appliances. Carpenters make frequent use of thin wedges, referred to as shims, in forcing wood pieces to position together snugly to expedite fastening.

Screws. A screw is often described as an inclined plane wrapped around a post. The ridges of a screw are called the *threads* and the distance between threads is the *pitch*. The smaller the pitch of a screw, the more times it must be turned to fasten it in place. The number of turns equals the effort distance.

Simple Machines

levers

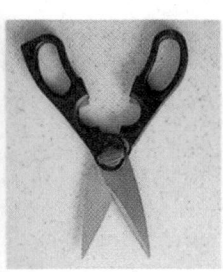
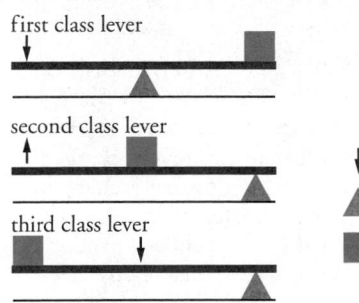

first class lever

second class lever

third class lever

↓ effort

▲ fulcrum

■ resistance

The fulcrum of a bottle opener rests atop the cap. The fulcrum of a scissors is where the two halves are connected.

pulleys

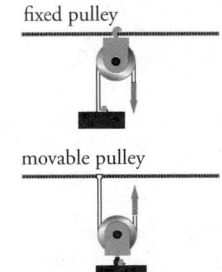

fixed pulley

movable pulley

pulley system

A system of pulleys enables the winch on this tow truck to lift the weight of an automobile.

wheels and axles

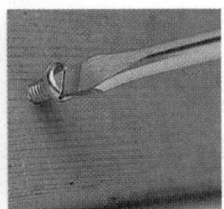
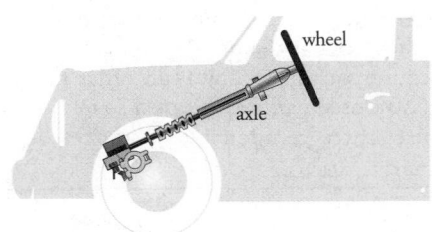

wheel

axle

Doorknobs and screwdrivers are both combinations of axles (the shafts) and wheels (the handles).

inclined planes   ## screws   ## wedges

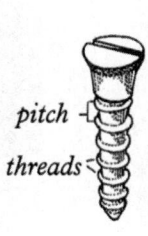

pitch

threads

It is much easier to roll an automobile up a ramp—an inclined plane—than to lift it up and carry it forward.

A screw is an inclined plane around a cylinder.

A drill bit tip is a wedge, and its threaded shaft is an inclined plane. A wedge separates objects or splits material apart.

377

Electromagnetism

Static electricity.
Another form of energy is electromagnetism. One kind of electromagnetism is *static electricity*. Atoms have no electric charge since the number of negatively charged electrons equals the number of positively charged protons. Electrons can be transferred to or from certain substances when they are rubbed, producing static electricity. A substance that gains electrons becomes negatively charged. It has more electrons than protons. A substance that loses electrons becomes positively charged since it now has more protons than electrons. Experiments have shown that substances that have like charges will repel each other.

Some substances can become electrically charged when they touch a charged object. Those substances that allow electrons to move freely, such as metals, are *conductors*. Materials that do not allow electric charges to move easily, such as glass, are *insulators*.

Electric circuits.
When a stream of electrons can be made to move through a device that uses their energy, useful work can be done by the moving charges. Electric charges in motion produce *current*. The force or push required to move electrons through a conductor is called *voltage*. The higher the voltage (the greater the number of volts), the more work the electrons can do.

Electrons require a closed pathway in order for them to flow. This closed pathway is called a *circuit*. A circuit requires three components: a source of electrons, a conducting pathway, and a device that will use the energy of the moving electrons. The device that uses the energy is called the *load* or *resistance*.

Two or more resistances can be connected so that there is only one path for the electric energy. This is known as a *series circuit*. Since there is only a single pathway, a break anywhere in the circuit will open the entire circuit. If lightbulbs in a house were to be connected in series, the loosening or burning out of one bulb would cause all the bulbs in the house to go out. In a *parallel circuit* there is more than one path for electrical energy to follow. Each pathway can operate a different appliance or room in a house.

Electromagnetism.
A *magnet* is a substance that attracts iron. Some materials are natural magnets. Others can become magnetized when they are stroked several times in the same direction with a magnet. Magnets can attract objects without touching them. A magnetic field extends around each magnet. When a bar magnet is suspended freely and allowed to come to rest, it will point in a north-south direction. This happens because Earth itself has a magnetic field. The end pointing north is the north-seeking or north pole. The opposite end is the south-seeking or south pole. When two bar magnets are brought near each other, unlike poles will attract each other while like poles will repel each other.

Electrical circuits

Series

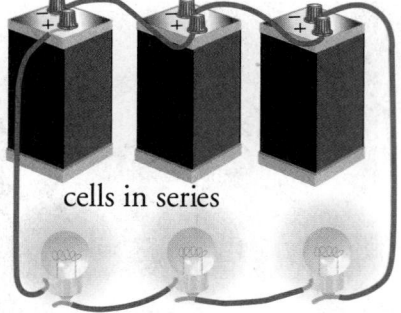

cells in series

resistances in series

Parallel

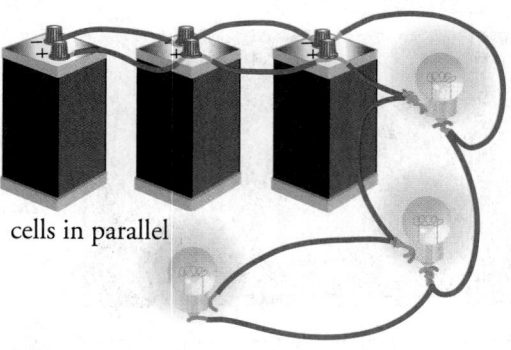

cells in parallel

resistances in parallel

When a compass is placed parallel to a wire conducting an electric current, the compass needle, a small bar magnet, will move sideways. This indicates that there is a magnetic field around a wire conducting electricity. The direction of the magnetic field depends on the direction in which the current is flowing in the conductor.

When a conducting wire is formed into a coil, the strength of the magnetic field is increased. This electromagnetic effect can be made even stronger if a piece of iron is placed inside the coil of wire. Electromagnets are used to lift heavy metal objects, in telephones, electric motors, and electric generators.

Electric motors convert electrical energy into mechanical energy. A motor is made up of a moving electromagnet and a fixed magnet. The electromagnet spins on an axle. This magnet and axle are called the *armature*. When current flows through the electromagnet, the armature is attracted to and turns toward the opposite pole of the fixed magnet. As the armature moves toward the opposite pole, the direction of current flowing in it is reversed. This causes the magnetic field to be reversed. Instead of being attracted to the pole of the fixed magnet, the armature is now repelled by it. The armature is kept spinning by alternating the direction of the current flowing through the electromagnet.

Just as an electric current produces a magnetic field, a magnetic field can produce an electric

A magnet such as the bar magnet shown at the left produces a magnetic field around it, a field that can be shown as lines of force. When the north pole of one magnet is placed near the north pole of another, the lines of force interfere with each other, causing the magnets to repel one another. When the north pole of one magnet is placed near the south pole of another, however, the lines of force work together to make the two magnets attract each other.

current. An electric current can be *induced* in a conductor when the conducting wire is moved within a magnetic field. A *generator* uses this principle to convert mechanical energy into electrical energy. In a generator, a coil of wire is made to turn within the magnetic field of a U-shaped magnet. When the coils cut across the lines of force in the field, a current is induced to flow in the coil. As the coil continues to turn, it again cuts across the lines of force, but the induced current flows in the opposite direction. Such generators produce the *alternating current* we use in our homes, industries, and schools.

Electrical generators

When the field of a magnet moves with respect to a loop of conducting wire (1), an electric current is produced in the wire. This effect can be enhanced by using a coil of wire, since the more times the wire cuts the magnetic lines of force, the greater will be the electric current (2). The direction of motion controls the direction of the current in the wire.

By mounting a coil of wires on an axle inside a magnet (3), a generator can be produced. As the axle is turned by an engine or by waterpower, the wire continually cuts across the lines of magnetic force, first in one direction, then in the other. The same principle, but reversed, is used in electric motors.

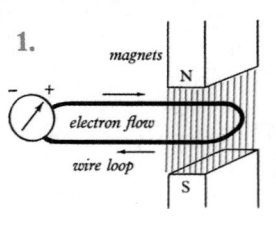

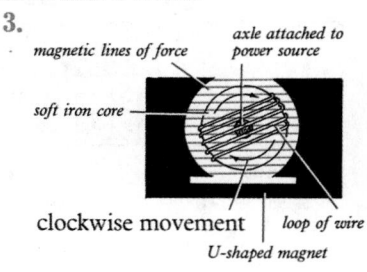

Wave motion

Energy is often transmitted or transferred in the form of waves. A *wave* is a series of back and forth or up and down vibrations. The energy in a wave travels but the material that the wave travels through only vibrates. A boat bobs up and down as waves pass. The boat moves at right angles to the direction of the waves. This is an example of *transverse waves*. Light, television, radio, and x-rays are transverse waves. Sound is an example of a *longitudinal wave*. In longitudinal waves, the material that the wave is traveling through vibrates parallel to the direction of the wave.

Sound energy. Sound is produced when an object is made to vibrate (move rapidly back and forth). We perceive these vibrations as sounds when they are transmitted by our ears to our brains.

Sound requires a *medium;* that is, a substance to carry the energy. A medium can be a solid, liquid, or gas. Sound is transmitted when the vibrating object disturbs the particles that make up the medium. When an object is made to vibrate, it collides with the particles of the medium. These particles receive energy from the vibrating object and pass the energy to the particles with which they collide. The energy of the vibrating object is transferred to particles around it with each back and forth movement. In this way, sound is transmitted in all directions.

The speed of sound depends on the density of the medium through which it is traveling. In general, sound has a greater velocity in solids than in liquids or gases.

The rate at which vibrations of an object are produced is called the *frequency* of that sound. Frequency is the number of *cycles* per second. A cycle is one sound wave. One *hertz* is equal to one cycle per second.

The human ear can detect sounds from about 20 hertz to 20,000 hertz. Sounds with a greater frequency than 20,000 hertz are called *ultrasonic*. *Pitch* is the highness or lowness of a sound. Pitch is related to frequency in that the greater the frequency, the higher the pitch produced.

Wavelength is also related to the pitch. The wavelength is the length of one cycle. Greater frequency means a shorter wavelength and a higher pitch of the sound produced. The *amplitude* of a sound wave is the distance that the particles of the medium were displaced. Greater amplitude means a greater intensity, or loudness, of the sound produced.

Types of wave motion

Longitudinal

Transverse

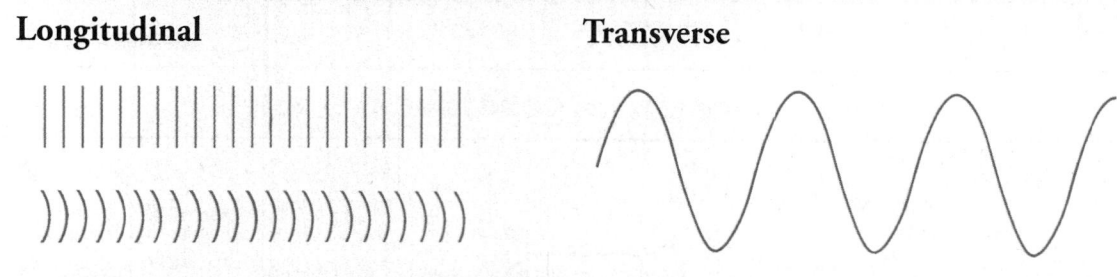

Sound

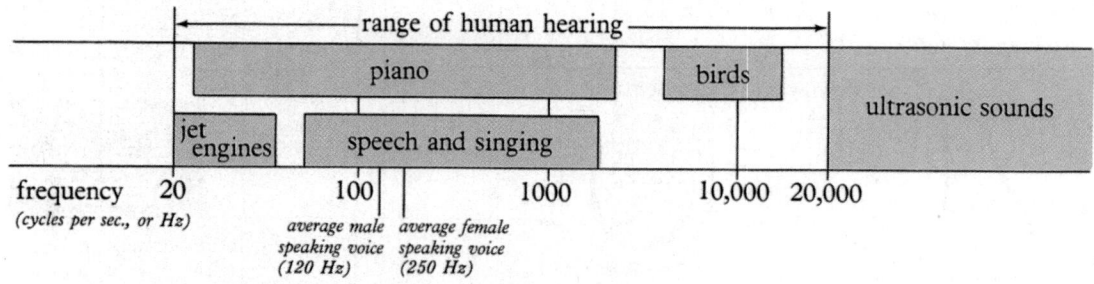

Light energy. The speed of light is accepted today as approximately 300,000 kilometers per second in a vacuum. This is equal to about 186,000 miles per second. In a more dense medium, such as glass, light will slow down, causing a change in the direction of the wave. This change of direction of waves as they pass in a slanted path from one medium to another is called *refraction.*

Refraction enables us to bend and focus light, making telescopes, cameras, and microscopes possible. Prisms allow us to separate visible light in the various wavelengths we see as colors.

Color. White light is actually a group of wavelengths and frequencies. Each frequency is refracted differently as it passes from air into glass and from glass into air again. The higher frequencies are refracted more than the lower ones. Violet is refracted most, followed by blue, green, yellow, orange, and red.

Rainbows are caused by the refraction of sunlight by raindrops. Rainbows are usually visible when the sun and rain are opposite each other and the sun is low in the sky. Usually, we must be facing the falling rain with the sun behind us to see a rainbow. In addition, the raindrops must be of a certain size to act as tiny prisms.

The color that an object appears to be depends on the frequency of the light that reaches the eye from the object. A red apple appears red because to our eyes it reflects only red light. It absorbs all other colors of light. If the same apple were placed in green light, it would appear black to us. The apple would absorb the green light; since there would be no red light to reflect, it would appear black. This is true for all *opaque* objects. Opaque objects do not allow light to pass through.

Transparent objects, such as glass, do allow light to pass through. They appear to be the color of the wavelength of light that passes through them. Green glass transmits or sends through light in the green frequency range and absorbs or filters out other colors.

The sky appears blue to our eyes when the particles of dust and gas in the atmosphere scatter the wavelengths of blue light. During midday, when the sun is most directly overhead, its light passes through a minimum of atmosphere. The light we receive appears white. The sun is close to the horizon in the evening and morning. Its light passes through more atmosphere. Dust particles in the air block off or scatter the shorter (blue) wavelengths of light and the sky around the sun appears to be orange or red.

Light

Lenses

nearsightedness
*image formed
in front of retina*

*correction
concave lens*

farsightedness
*image blurred
on retina*

*correction
convex lens*

Rainbows

sunlight

Why sky is blue

sunlight

*scattering by
air molecules*

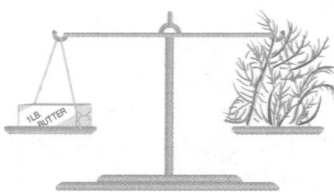

density

Dictionary of physical sciences

physical change

pitch

refraction

ampere. Unit of measurement used to describe the rate of flow of current in an electric circuit.

amplitude. Height of a crest of a wave; the maximum displacement of the medium through which a wave is traveling.

atom. Smallest particle of an element that retains the properties of that element.

atomic mass. Average of the mass numbers of an element for forms found in nature.

atomic number. Number of protons in the nucleus of an atom.

chemical change. Change in which the substances involved lose their identities to form different substances with different properties.

compound. Substance consisting of two or more elements that are chemically combined by weight in definite proportions.

concave. Surface (lens or mirror) that is hollowed inward like a bowl, thicker at the edges than in the center.

conservation of mass-energy, law of. In any change, the sum of the amount of matter and the amount of energy remains constant.

control. Part of an experiment for which all conditions except the one being tested are kept the same as in the experimental setup; that condition, which is the one being changed in the experiment, is left unchanged in the control.

convex. Surface (lens or mirror) that is thicker in the center than at its edges.

density. Mass of a definite volume of a substance, usually expressed in grams per cubic centimeter.

effort. Force put into a machine in order for it to do useful work.

effort arm. In a lever, the distance the effort must act over to provide the input work.

electromagnetic waves. Transverse waves produced by vibrations of electric charges. Electromagnetic waves travel at the speed of light and do not need a medium to travel through.

element. One of 116 substances that are composed of only one kind of atom.

energy. Ability to perform work.

force. Push or pull that will cause an object to change its motion or direction.

frequency. Number of cycles of a wave per unit time.

friction. Force that resists motion between two surfaces.

heat. Energy transferred from one place to another owing to differences in temperature; the kinetic energy of the particles of a substance owing to their random motion.

hypothesis. Possible solution to a scientific problem that can be tested by an experiment.

image, real. Image formed when light passes from an object through a convex lens. The image is on the opposite side of the lens from the object, is always inverted, and can be projected on a screen.

incident ray. Incoming light ray that strikes a surface.

isotope. Form of an element with the same atomic number but a different mass number.

law. In science, laws describe naturally occurring events. They are records of what happens.

lens. Transparent material designed to cause light to converge or diverge when passing through it.

longitudinal waves. Waves in which the vibration of the moving particles is parallel to the wave direction; that is, sound.

magnetic field. Area around a magnet in which the effects of its magnetism can be detected.

mass. Amount of matter in a body. It is a measure of the inertia of an object.

mass number. Weight of an atom compared with the weight of an atom of carbon that has been assigned the value of 12.

matter. Anything that has mass and occupies space.

mixture. Two or more elements or compounds that have been mixed together. The components of a mixture retain their properties and no chemical change takes place.

nucleus. Central, positively charged portion of an atom, made up of protons and neutrons.

Ohm's law. Electric current is equal to the ratio of voltage and resistance.

phase. Form that a substance normally exists in at room temperature; that is, solid, liquid, gas.

physical change. Change in a substance that does not change its chemical characteristics or composition.

pitch. Frequency of a sound wave.

power. Rate at which work is done.

prism. Device used to separate visible light into different wavelengths.

radioactivity. Spontaneous breakdown of atomic nuclei.

reflection, law of. Angle between an incident ray of light and the normal is always equal to the angle between the reflected ray and the normal.

refraction, law of. When light passes at an oblique angle from one medium into another of greater density, the velocity of light decreases and is bent toward the normal.

resistance. Opposition offered to the flow of electric current by a substance through which it is passing; an opposing force.

simple machine. Any one of the six basic devices used to change the direction, intensity, or distance traveled of a force.

sound waves. Compressional waves of audible frequencies move through an elastic medium by compressions and rarefactions of the particles.

spectrum. Continuous series of wavelengths.

subatomic particle. Any of the particles of matter that are smaller than an atom such as electrons, protons, neutrons, photons, or mesons.

telescope. Arrangement of lenses or mirrors used to see distant objects.

temperature. Condition of a substance that determines the direction of heat flow from one object to another; a measurement of the kinetic energy of the particles of a substance.

theory. General explanation that describes the results of many confirmed hypotheses.

transverse waves. Waves in which the particles move perpendicular to the direction of the wave; that is, light.

ultrasonic. Sound waves having a frequency of more than 20,000 hertz.

wave. Cyclic disturbance traveling through a medium.

wavelength. Distance between adjacent peaks of a wave.

weight. Measure of the pull of the force of gravity on a body.

work. Product of a force and the displacement of an object in the direction of the force.

For Further Reference

Adler, Irving
  The Story of Light
  Harvey House
Clark, John
  Matter and Energy: Physics in Action
  Oxford University Press
Newton, David E.
  The Chemical Elements
  Franklin Watts

Sobel, Michael I.
  Light
  University of Chicago Press
Stevens, S. S. and Warshofsky, Fred
  Sound and Hearing
  Time-Life Books
Trefil, James
  From Atoms to Quarks: An Introduction to the Strange World of Particle Physics
  Doubleday

- *Plate tectonics* **384**
- *Rocks and minerals* **389**
- *Glaciers* **390**
- *Climate* **392**
- *Weather* **396**
- *Dictionary of earth science* **402**

Earth Science

Over the past few decades, science has changed our perceptions and expanded our horizons. Astronauts have walked on the surface of the moon. Satellites hover above Earth sending back photographs that aid in weather forecasting. Other satellites travel through the solar system, transmitting photographs of Venus, Jupiter, and Saturn. Oceanographers have mapped the sea floor and discovered huge deposits of valuable minerals. Scientists have theorized about the forces that set Earth's surface in motion, unleashing the awesome power of earthquakes and volcanoes. What scientific discoveries will revolutionize our world in the future?

Plate tectonics

Continental drift. By looking at a map of the world, you will notice that Africa and South America seem to fit together. Fossil remains of the same animals have been found on both continents, and both share the same rock formations. Is this just coincidence?

A German scientist named Alfred Wegener did not think so. In 1912 he proposed his theory of continental drift. According to Wegener, about 200 million years ago all the land on Earth was one large continent that he called Pangaea. Approximately 180 million years ago, Pangaea began to break apart to form three separate continents. The large block to the north (which later became Europe, Asia, North America, and Greenland) is called Laurasia. It broke away from the other two land masses, which together are called Gondwanaland.

The northern block of Gondwanaland was to become South America and Africa; the southern block would become Antarctica, Australia, and New Zealand. A small piece broke away between the northern and southern parts of Gondwanaland and began moving northward. This would be India.

These land masses continued to drift. About 65 million years ago, the continents began to look as they do today. South America and Africa had drifted apart, and soon North America and Greenland would break away from Laurasia. India was about to collide with Asia. The southern block of Gondwanaland would soon break apart into separate pieces, forming Antarctica, Australia, and New Zealand.

Although Wegener's theory of continental drift was disbelieved at first, eventually it came to be accepted in a modified form. Increasingly, geologists found geological, fossil, and magnetic evidence that the continents were no longer in the same relationship to each other as before. More recently, evidence has turned up to show that the continents themselves have been built in part from large islands that have drifted and stuck to the continents' shorelines.

Continental drift

200 million years ago

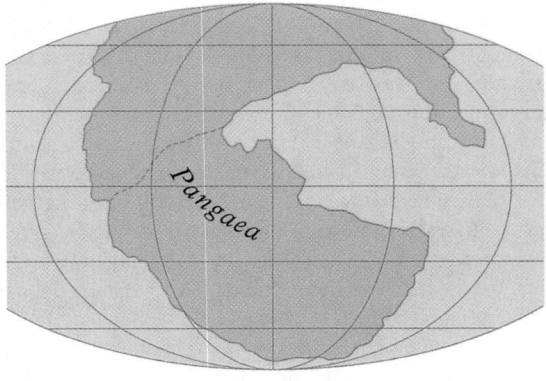

135 million years ago

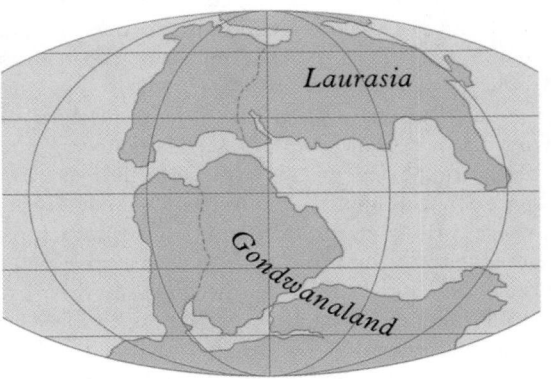

65 million years ago

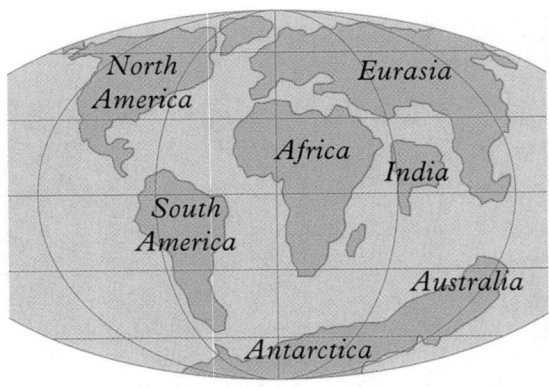

today

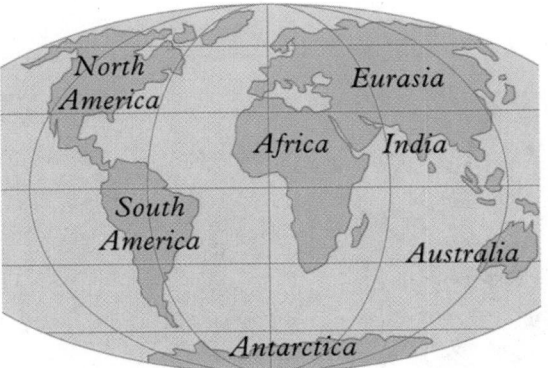

The moving crust.

Today Earth's surface continues to be in motion. According to the *plate tectonics theory*, Earth's surface—or *crust*—is broken into pieces called plates. A crustal plate may carry only ocean floor, only continent, or some combination of both. Some plates are huge, such as the Pacific Plate, which carries most of the Pacific Ocean. Others are much smaller, like the Nazca Plate, which lies off the west coast of South America. These plates move around on a layer of molten rock beneath Earth's surface much as a boat floats on water.

Plates are involved in three different types of movement. On the floor of the Atlantic Ocean, the plates are moving apart in a process called *sea-floor spreading*. The amount of movement is about 2 inches a year, which means that the Atlantic is constantly growing wider, and Europe is moving farther away from the United States. As the plates move apart, molten rock wells up from beneath the surface to form new ocean floor.

Sea-floor spreading in the Atlantic occurs along a huge underwater mountain range called the *mid-ocean ridge*. Within the ridge is an opening called a *rift valley*, through which the molten rock pours out. Rift valleys can be found in other parts of the world too. In East Africa a large rift valley has formed; it may indicate that the African continent is beginning to break apart. The Red Sea may have appeared as a result of the Arabian Peninsula separating from Africa.

In some parts of the world, crustal plates are converging. Here crust is being destroyed, offsetting the new crust being formed in other regions, thereby keeping the size of Earth's surface constant. When a plate carrying oceanic crust collides with a plate carrying continental crust, the sea floor sinks beneath the continent, forming a deep ocean trench. Such trenches are found along Japan and the Aleutian Islands. In these areas volcanoes are common. For example, the volcanic Andes Mountains in South America and the deep trench in the nearby Pacific may have been produced when two plates converged.

The collision of two plates carrying continental crust may also lead to the formation of huge mountain ranges. An example is the Himalayas, which were created when India collided with Asia millions of years ago.

When two plates carrying oceanic crust converge, one is forced beneath the other. This results in the formation of an ocean trench accompanied by undersea volcanic activity and earthquakes.

Instead of separating or coming together, two plates may simply move past each other. This type of movement is occurring along the San Andreas fault in California.

Theory of plate tectonics

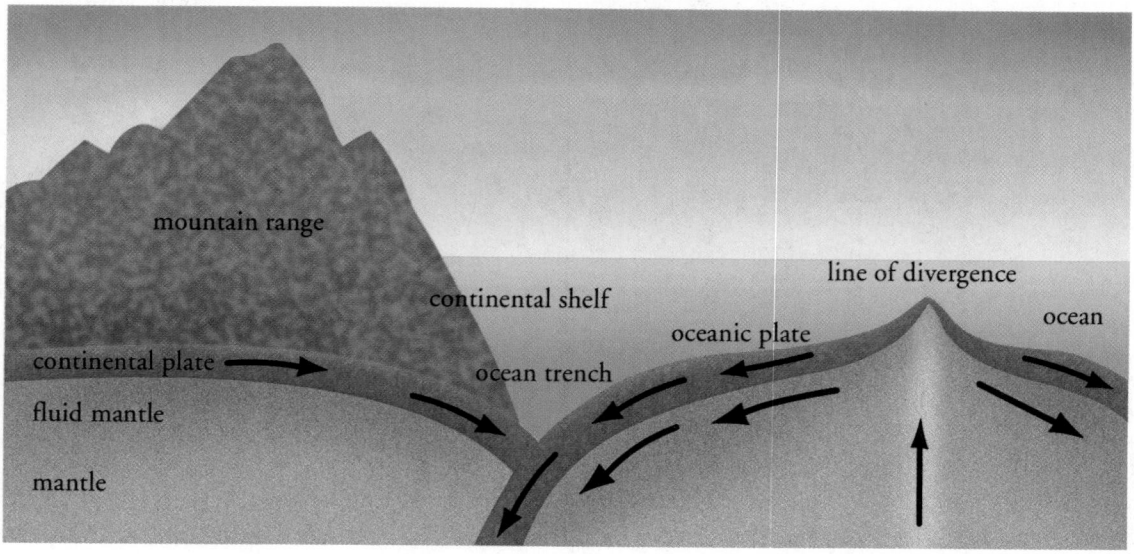

Earthquakes.

An earthquake is a sudden trembling of Earth's crust. Earthquakes generally occur as a result of the movement of crustal plates. The crust cracks along a line called a *fault,* such as the San Andreas fault, which is at the boundary between two plates. As the crust moves apart, rocks on either side bend until they finally break, creating the vibrations that are called an earthquake.

A particularly powerful earthquake struck Alaska on March 27, 1964, causing the death of 114 people. Many died as a result of the *tsunami,* or giant wave, created when the sea floor moved during the earthquake. Tsunamis can travel across the ocean at speeds of 600 mph and reach heights of 100 feet as they crash into coastal towns and cities. Earthquakes also produce landslides and fires that cause enormous damage.

The spot under Earth's surface where an earthquake originates is called the *focus.* The *epicenter* is the point on the surface directly above the focus. When a quake occurs, waves radiate out from the focus. There are several types of waves. **P** (primary) waves are longitudinal, or push-pull, waves that travel through the earth. They can penetrate solid and liquid material. **S** (secondary) waves are transverse, or shake, waves. They also travel through the earth, but cannot penetrate liquids very well. **L** waves travel along the surface and do the most damage.

Earthquake waves are recorded on an instrument called a *seismograph.* Since **S** waves travel more slowly than **P** waves, we can tell how far away an earthquake occurred by computing the difference in time it takes for the two waves to arrive at the seismograph. Using seismographs at three or more locations enables scientists to calculate where an earthquake has occurred.

The strength of an earthquake is indicated on a scale called the *Richter scale,* which is based on the magnitude of the waves recorded by the seismograph. A magnitude of 2.5 is enough to be recorded but not felt; 6.0 may cause great damage; a very large earthquake registers over 8.0. The Alaska earthquake registered 8.4 to 8.6 on the Richter scale.

Earth's interior.

By studying **S** and **P** waves, scientists have learned about the structure of Earth's interior. For example, they have concluded that Earth's *outer core* is liquid material, because **S** waves cannot travel through it very well. The outer core is thought to be iron and nickel, which is kept in a liquid state because of the enormous heat inside Earth. The *inner core,* also made up of nickel and

The inner Earth

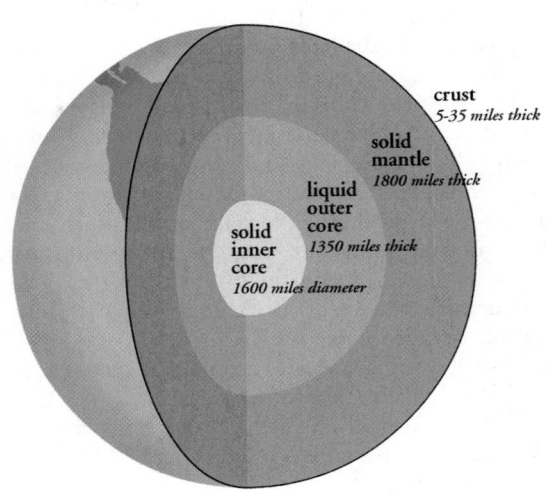

crust
5-35 miles thick

solid mantle
1800 miles thick

liquid outer core
1350 miles thick

solid inner core
1600 miles diameter

Earthquake belts

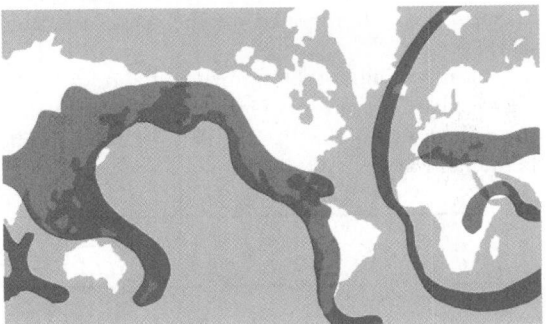

Movements of the crustal plates cause most earthquakes. Consequently, belts of earthquake activity can be found near the edges of the plates.

iron, is solid as a result of the enormous pressure on Earth's interior.

Above the core is a mostly solid layer called the *mantle.* It consists of rocks containing iron, magnesium, and silicon. The upper layer of mantle is partially molten, and it is in this material that the crustal plates "float." Convection currents set up within the liquid part of the mantle are thought to be the force that moves the plates. Above the mantle is Earth's *crust.* The crust is the part of Earth that can be directly observed as rock and soil.

Volcanoes. Volcanic activity occurs along the boundaries between plates, just as earthquakes do. In fact, surrounding the Pacific Ocean, in the same area as the earthquake belt is a circle of volcanoes that is called the "Ring of Fire."

When crustal plates come together, one plate often sinks, forming a deep ocean trench. The material in this plate is heated by the high temperatures found within Earth's interior and transformed into a molten substance. This molten substance is called *magma.* Pressure exerted on the magma from above may force it up through a chamber. Eventually the magma may pour out through an opening, or *vent,* in the earth and flow onto the surface. As the magma pours out, it changes and becomes a substance called *lava.*

The flow of lava creates a cone that grows larger and that may rise above the surface of the water. In this way island chains, such as Japan and the Aleutians, were created adjacent to the deep ocean trenches.

Volcanoes also appear where crustal plates are separating, such as at the mid-ocean ridge. As the lava pours out through openings, it forms new sea floor and may build up into huge cones. Sometimes a cone above the mid-ocean ridge also breaks the water's surface, thereby forming an island such as Surtsey, which appeared off the coast of Iceland in 1963.

Volcanoes can also be formed in the middle of a crustal plate. Perhaps the most famous examples are the volcanoes in the Pacific Plate that form the Hawaiian Islands.

There are different types of volcanic eruptions, resulting in various kinds of volcanic cones. Sometimes the lava flows quietly along the surface, creating a *shield cone.* An example of a shield cone is Mauna Loa on the island of Hawaii. This huge volcano is over 27,000 feet in height. The island of Hawaii is composed of five shield volcanoes.

Magma does not always flow easily, and it can plug up an opening to the surface. If gases from the magma build up, they may eventually force it through the opening with a violent explosion. Volcanic materials can then be seen shooting into the sky creating a spectacular display. These materials include cinders, ash, and larger fragments called bombs. They build up around the volcanic opening forming a *cinder cone.* An example of a cinder cone is Parícutin, which erupted outside of Mexico City in 1943.

A third type of volcanic cone is a combination of lava and cinders. It is called a *composite cone.* Two composite cones found in North America are Mt. Rainier and Mt. Hood.

At the top of a volcano is a depression called a *crater.* When a volcano becomes inactive, the crater may fill with water, forming a lake. Crater Lake in Oregon was created in this way. Wizard Island, which is found in the lake, is part of a volcanic cone.

In the United States, active volcanoes are found in Hawaii, Alaska, and along the Pacific coast. Mount St. Helens in the state of Washington began erupting on May 18, 1980, and continues to erupt frequently.

Volcanoes

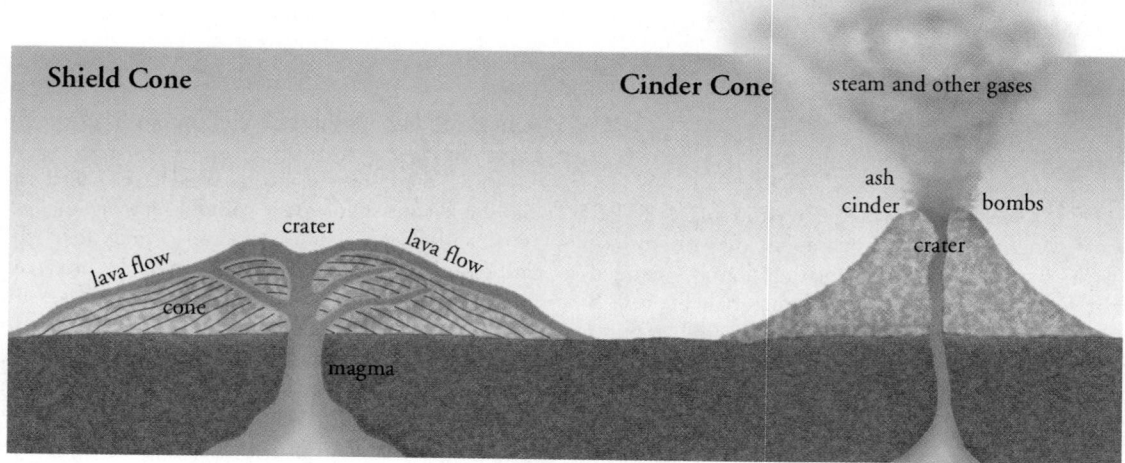

Rocks and minerals

The rock cycle. The rock cycle shows the relationship between the three types of rocks. *Igneous* rocks are formed when magma or lava cools and solidifies. Common igneous rocks are granite, pumice, and obsidian. When igneous rocks are broken down, they form sediments. After these sediments are compacted under pressure or cemented together by dissolved minerals, they form *sedimentary* rocks. These include sandstone, shale, and limestone. Some sedimentary rocks are also formed almost entirely from the remains of living organisms. Coal is a well-known example. The action of pressure, heat, and chemicals in the environment can transform igneous and sedimentary rocks into *metamorphic* rocks. Common metamorphic rocks are marble and slate.

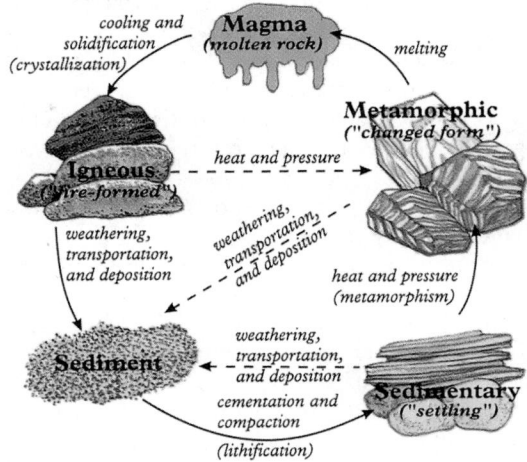

Common Minerals

Group	Member	Formula	Description/use
Silicates	Feldspar (orthoclase)	$KAlS_{13}O_8$	most common mineral
	Quartz	S_1O_2	used in radios, clocks, etc.
	Garnet	$Mg_3Al_2S_{13}O_{12}$	jewelry
Carbonates	Calcite	$CaCO_3$	chief minerals in limestone
	Dolomite	$CaMg(CO_3)_2$	found in limestone and marble
Oxides	Hematite	Fe_2O_3	ore of iron
	Magnetite	Fe_3O_4	ore of iron
	Corundum	Al_2O_3	used as an abrasive
	Ice	H_2O	solid form of water
Sulfides	Galena	PbS	ore of lead
	Sphalerite	ZnS	ore of zinc
	Pyrite	FeS_2	fool's gold
	Chalcopyrite	$CuFeS_2$	ore of copper
Sulfates	Gypsum	$CaSO_4 \cdot 2\,(H_2O)$	used for plaster
	Anhydrite	$CaSO_4$	used for plaster
Native elements	Gold	Au	
	Copper	Cu	
	Diamond	C	
	Sulfur	S	
	Graphite	C	
Halides	Halite	$NaCl$	common salt
	Fluorite	CaF_2	used in steel making, chemicals, ceramics

Glaciers

Approximately 2 million years ago, during the Pleistocene epoch, vast sheets of ice called *glaciers* advanced southward covering large parts of North America and Northern Europe. The glaciers alternately advanced and retreated, creating a series of ice ages. These ice ages apparently ended between 10,000 and 15,000 years ago, when the glaciers began to recede. Many scientists believe, however, that the ice may yet return.

Glaciers occur where temperatures are low enough to permit a large and lasting snow accumulation. As pressure builds up on the lower layers of snow, the layers turn to ice and eventually begin to move.

There are two types of glaciers. Huge *continental glaciers,* like those of the ice ages, still cover Antarctica and most of Greenland. The Antarctic glacier stretches for about 8 million miles and contains 80 percent of the world's ice. Continental glaciers can move as fast as 100 feet a day.

Much more common are *Alpine glaciers,* which are found in mountainous regions. These glaciers are smaller and move more slowly, generally only a few inches a day. Glaciers begin to retreat when more ice starts to melt than is accumulated.

All glaciers cause erosion. At its head, a glacier may carve out a basin called a *cirque.* Sometimes a few cirques may cut into the side of a mountain, creating a sharp peak. This is known as a *horn,* or matterhorn, like the spectacular mountain in Switzerland called the Matterhorn.

When a glacier moves along, it picks up pieces of rock and other material and carries these pieces forward. Thus, a glacier can have the effect of broadening and deepening a narrow valley. When the glacier recedes, a wide glacial trough, or U-shaped valley, remains. Waterfalls often can be seen tumbling into a glacial trough from shallower valleys above.

A particular type of glacial trough found near the sea is a *fjord.* The fjords were created during the ice ages. As the ice retreated and sea level rose, the fjords filled with water to form deep ocean inlets.

Glaciers deposit the rocks and other material they accumulate as *till.* When a glacier retreats, it leaves behind layers of till called *moraine.* On the side of

Glacial formations

the moraine away from the ice is a relatively level area called an *outwash plain*. This is composed of fine material washed away from the moraine by glacial meltwater. Found in the moraine and outwash plain are pits called *kettle holes*. These are formed by the melting of buried blocks of ice. Lakes, created when the kettle holes fill with water, can be seen in New York and New England.

Continental glaciers also form groups of hills called *drumlins*, which are composed of till. Drumlins may be as high as 200 feet. They occur in New York, Wisconsin, and other areas. Ridges of till, called *eskers*, are found along the Mississippi River valley.

Pleistocene ice ages.

There have been many ice ages in the remote past, such as 200 million and 600 million years ago. About 1 million years ago, another series of advances and retreats of the continental ice sheets began. Geologists equate the first advance of the ice with the beginning of the Pleistocene epoch, the epoch that saw the development of modern human beings. In between the first four advances, there were long warm periods, which led to retreat of the ice. These times are known as interglacial periods. It is not known whether the present is the early part of an interglacial period or a temporary retreat during a glacial period.

Area covered by ice during last ice age

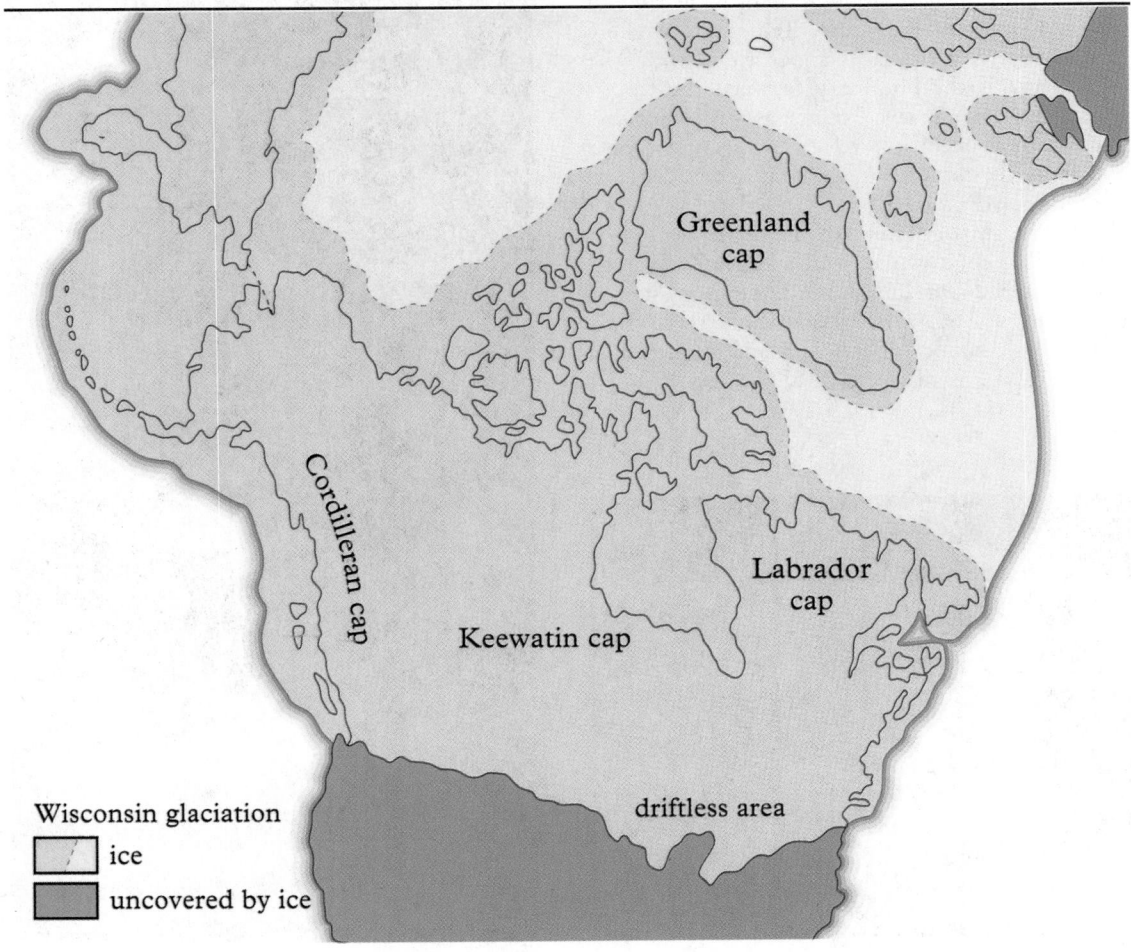

Greenland cap

Labrador cap

Cordilleran cap

Keewatin cap

driftless area

Wisconsin glaciation
- ice
- uncovered by ice

Climate

The planet Earth is surrounded by a layer of air that is called the *atmosphere*. This is largely composed of two gases—*nitrogen* and *oxygen*. But other vital substances are found in the atmosphere as well. *Carbon dioxide,* for example, absorbs heat that leaves Earth's surface. This helps to keep the atmosphere warm. *Ozone,* which is found mainly in the higher reaches of the atmosphere, absorbs the sun's ultraviolet rays and prevents most of them from reaching Earth. The small amounts of *water vapor* found in the atmosphere are extremely important because they are the source of precipitation. And *dust particles* serve as the nuclei around which raindrops form. In fact, the atmosphere is where Earth's climate and weather actually happen. Therefore, the place to begin to understand climate and weather is by taking a tour of the atmosphere.

The atmosphere is divided into a series of layers separated by differences in temperature. Nearest Earth is the *troposphere*. This is the zone in which our weather occurs. Temperatures here drop at about 3.5 degrees F per 1,000 feet. The tropopause is the boundary between the troposphere and the next layer, known as the *stratosphere*. Temperatures begin to level off in the stratosphere and gradually start to rise. The stratosphere contains the ozone layer.

At a height of about 40 miles, the *ionosphere* begins. This zone is filled with electrically charged particles called *ions*. Ions aid in the transmission of radio waves. The waves, which only travel in a straight line, bounce off the ions and are deflected over much greater distances.

Elements in the Atmosphere

Component	Symbol	Percent
Nitrogen	N_2	78.08
Oxygen	O_2	20.95
Argon	A	0.93
Carbon dioxide	CO_2	0.03
All others		variable

neon Ne, water vapor H_2O, helium He, dust, ozone O_3

Earth's atmosphere

400 miles
exosphere

Satellite

Space shuttle: 200 mi.

Landsat: 200 mi.

thermosphere

Highest manned aircraft: 60 mi.

50 mesosphere
ionosphere

Highest manned balloon: 21.5 mi.

30

stratosphere

Ozone layer: 12 mi.

Highest mountain: 5.5 mi.

10 troposphere

Seasons

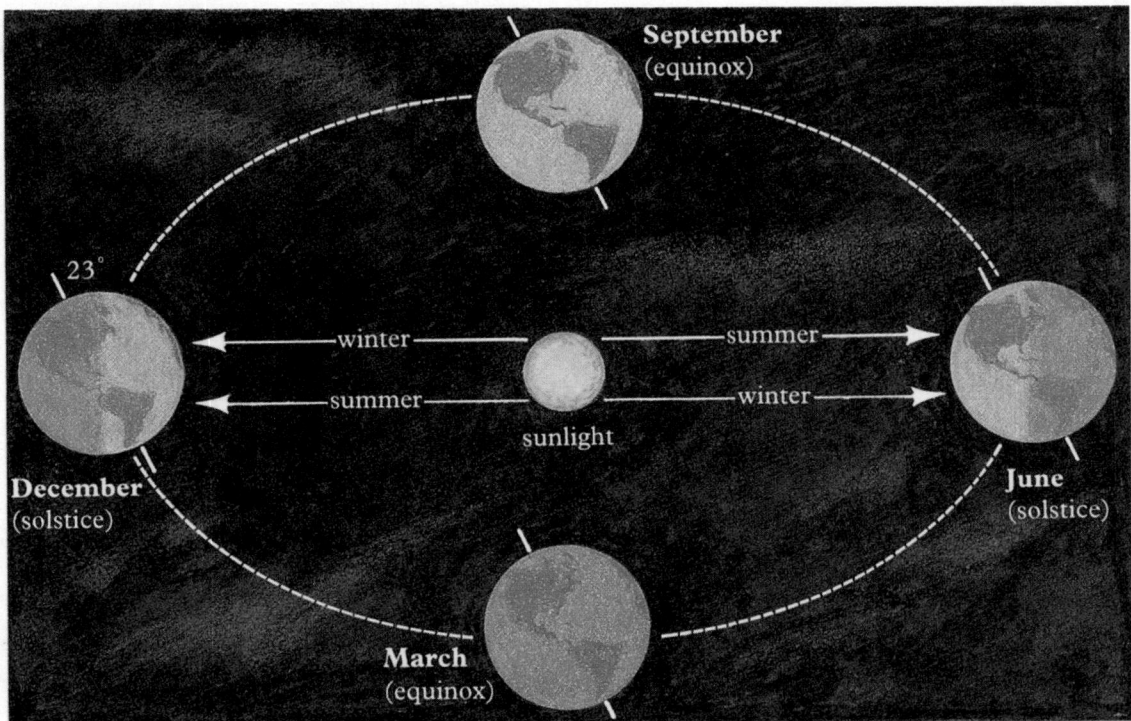

The seasons. The climate over much of Earth is characterized by seasons. In some parts of the world these are summer, fall, winter, and spring; in other parts, these are simply a wet, or rainy, season and a dry season. Each year at a particular place on the surface of Earth the seasons change much as they did the year before. But these changes are different in different parts of the world. When it is summer in New York City, it is winter in Buenos Aires, Argentina. In fact, the pattern of the seasons is reversed completely on the different sides of the equator. At the equator itself, and in the region on both sides of the equator that is called the *tropics*, there is almost no seasonal change. Seasonal changes in weather occur outside the tropics for two reasons. First, the Earth tilts on its axis at 23 degrees. Second, Earth revolves around the sun. As a result, most areas of Earth receive different amounts of sunlight throughout the year. During summer, the northern hemisphere is tilted toward the sun and receives longer periods of light. The sun's rays also strike more directly, producing more heat. During winter, opposite conditions prevail.

The reverse conditions occur in the southern hemisphere, of course. When the northern hemisphere is tilted toward the sun, the southern hemisphere is tilted away from it. The positions are shown in the diagram above.

Many people assume that winter is colder because Earth is farther from the sun during the winter. A little thought would show that that cannot be the case because if it were, winter would occur all over Earth at the same time. In fact, Earth is closest to the sun around January 1, a time when most of the northern hemisphere experiences some of its coldest weather.

Other seasonal changes are caused in part by the tilt of Earth with respect to the sun. If Earth did not tilt, each place would have the same season all year long.

U.S. climate zones.

Climate refers to the average weather conditions of a region over a long period of time. These conditions include temperature, precipitation, and humidity. A variety of factors affect the climatic conditions of a particular region. One of these is latitude, or distance from the equator. Regions lying closer to the equator receive more of the sun's direct rays for longer periods of time, and their average temperatures are generally higher than regions farther away. Another factor is altitude. A city perched high in the mountains usually has lower average temperatures than another one lying in a valley, even if both are located at the same latitude. Other factors affecting climate are prevailing winds, mountain ranges, and oceans.

The United States experiences different types of climate in various parts of the country. Since the southern part of the United States lies closest to the equator, average temperatures tend to be warmer here than in other areas. The climate in the southern region is called *humid subtropical.* The climate is a variation of the hot, rainy conditions found in the tropics. Air masses traveling in from the Gulf of Mexico and the Atlantic Ocean bring humid weather and high precipitation. Summers are hot, and winters tend to be relatively mild.

Around the city of San Francisco, California, and northward into Oregon and Washington, is a climate zone known as *marine west-coast.* This zone is characterized by mild summers and winters because of the prevailing westerlies—winds that blow inland from the Pacific Ocean. The westerlies bring large amounts of precipitation to the Pacific Northwest, allowing huge coniferous forests to flourish there.

In southern California, winters are mild, but summers are hotter and drier. The climate here, called *Mediterranean,* after similar climatic areas in Europe, results from seasonal shifts in the winds.

East of the Sierra Nevada mountain range lie the deserts of southern California, Nevada, and Arizona.

Climate zones of the continental United States

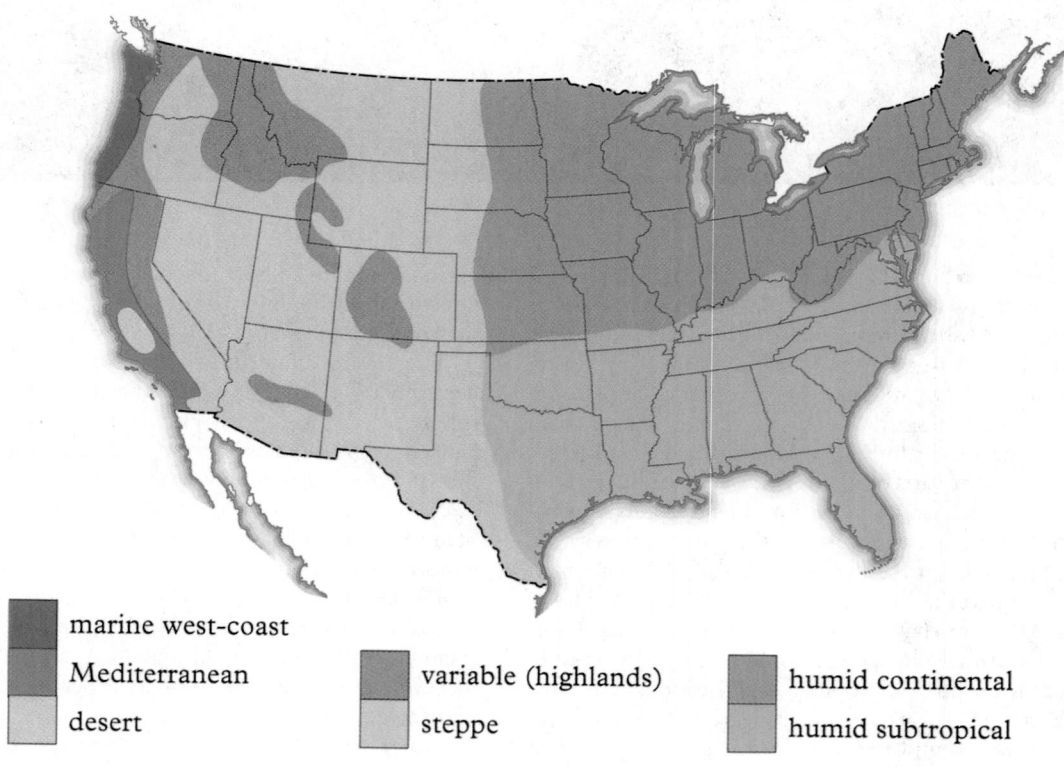

marine west-coast
Mediterranean
desert

variable (highlands)
steppe

humid continental
humid subtropical

As the westerlies rise over the mountains, they lose their moisture. Regions on the other side of the mountains are said to be in the "rain shadow," receiving little or no precipitation. Winds blowing off the mountains are hot and dry, absorbing any moisture that may be found in the atmosphere.

Northward is a climate zone called the *steppe,* after the vast plains of central Europe. It includes parts of Utah, Colorado, Kansas, and all the states north to the Canadian border. Although this region receives more rain than desert regions, it is still quite dry because the huge Rocky Mountains act as a barrier to rainfall. This is an area of vast grasslands for grazing cattle and other animals.

The rest of the country experiences a *continental climate.* Frigid air masses from the north bring cold winters and high accumulations of snow. Warm air masses from the south bring hot, muggy weather during summer.

Winds.
Winds result from differences in pressure owing to the unequal heating of Earth's atmosphere by the sun. The direction of wind flow is always from an area of high pressure to an area of low pressure. Giant wind systems, powered by the sun, travel across the globe and influence our weather.

Along the equator, the sun's rays shine directly from above for longer periods of time than they do farther north or south. Here the air is heated and begins to rise, creating an area of low pressure. The warm air travels north and south to a latitude of about 30 degrees, where, after being cooled, it begins to descend. These areas of high pressure, called *horse latitudes,* often have very little wind.

Air flows along the surface from the areas of high pressure at the horse latitudes to the areas of low pressure along the equator. This air flow is called the *trade winds.* Instead of flowing directly to the equator in a straight line, the winds are deflected to the right in the northern hemisphere and to the left in the southern hemisphere. This phenomenon, which is caused by Earth's rotation, is called the *Coriolis force.*

Some of the air descending in the horse latitudes flows away from the equator. This flow of air is known as the *prevailing westerlies,* because the winds come from a general westerly direction. Winds are always named for the direction from which they flow.

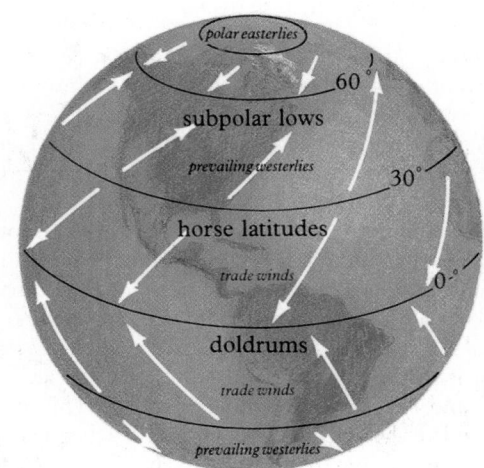

Wind belts of Earth

The third great wind system, called the *polar easterlies,* consists of cool air blowing from the polar regions. The easterlies meet the westerlies at about 60 degrees N and S latitude.

High above Earth's surface flow the *jet streams.* These are high-velocity winds that circle the globe in both hemispheres. Jet streams over North America often change position, dipping into the southern part of the United States, and then receding northward. Such changes may lead to storms in various parts of the country.

Local winds operate according to the same principles as the world's great wind systems. One example is a land-sea breeze. During the day, the sun's rays heat the land more rapidly than a nearby body of water. Warm air rises over the land, creating a low pressure area, and cool air flows inland from the sea. At night the flow of air is reversed as the land cools more rapidly than the water.

The *monsoon* is a giant land-sea breeze that occurs in the Indian subcontinent as well as other areas of the world. During summer the land heats up faster than the ocean. Monsoon winds blow inland, bringing torrential rains.

Local winds are also created in mountainous regions. During the day the exposed slopes of a mountain are heated faster than the surrounding valley. Warm air along the slopes rises, and cool air pushes up from the valley below. At night the flow of air is down the mountain.

Weather

Rain, snow, and dew.
Water is constantly circulating throughout the atmosphere in a cycle that involves evaporation, condensation, and precipitation. This is called the *water cycle*. The energy that runs the water cycle comes from the sun.

When heat from the sun is applied to the molecules of water found in a lake or stream, the molecules begin to move more rapidly. Eventually some of these molecules evaporate; that is, they enter the air as a gas called *water vapor*. Evaporation is a cooling process. Heat is absorbed by the water molecules that evaporate, and the water remaining is cooled. This same principle of heating and cooling applies when perspiration is evaporated from the skin, a process that makes one's body cooler.

The amount of water vapor in the air is known as its *humidity*. During a weather report, one generally hears the forecaster refer to *relative humidity*. This is a percentage that compares the amount of water vapor actually in the air at a particular temperature with the amount of water the air could hold if it were filled to capacity. When the temperature is high and the relative humidity is over 90 percent, most people feel very uncomfortable. This is because the air is almost filled to capacity with water vapor and cannot absorb much perspiration. When the air reaches capacity, it is said to be *saturated*.

Relative humidity is measured by a device called a *psychrometer*. It consists of two thermometers called a wet-bulb and a dry-bulb. The wet-bulb thermometer is covered with a water-soaked cloth. As air passes over, it absorbs some of the water. Cooling occurs, lowering the temperature on the wet-bulb thermometer. When the air is dry, it can absorb more water, creating a greater temperature difference between the wet-bulb and dry-bulb thermometers. (The dry-bulb simply records air temperature.) This difference in temperature is correlated with relative humidity by using a chart.

How much water vapor can be contained in a volume of air? This depends on the air temperature. The warmer the air, the more water vapor it can hold. The temperature at which the air becomes saturated is called the *dew point*. If any more water vapor enters the air, the vapor will begin to condense, forming a liquid. If the temperature of the air lowers, so that its holding capacity is reduced, condensation will occur.

Dew and frost.
During the night, as the land cools, the temperature of the air near the surface may fall below the dew point. In the morning, moisture appears on the grass in the form of *dew*. If the temperature of the grass drops below freezing, *frost* occurs.

Fogs.
When warm, saturated air passes over a cool surface, the air temperature may fall beneath the dew point. Then the water vapor condenses to form *fog*. This type of fog is *advection fog*. During the winter months, as warm, moist air from the Gulf of Mexico is blown over the cold ground of the Midwest, advection fogs occur frequently. Another type of fog is common in river valleys. This type of fog is produced by the cooling of a moist layer of air just above Earth's surface.

Clouds.
As a parcel of warm, moist air rises into the atmosphere, the air expands and cools. Eventually the temperature of the air may drop below the dew point. Then the water vapor condenses as cloud droplets. These water droplets are so small and light that they can float through the air.

Rain and snow.
Precipitation occurs when cloud droplets become large and heavy enough to fall. To explain this process, scientists have proposed two different theories. In some high clouds, the droplets are *supercooled*. This means that their temperature falls below freezing without the droplets turning to ice. Sometimes an ice crystal is present in the cloud, and the supercooled droplets may attach themselves to it. When the droplets strike this colder surface, they freeze. Gradually, the ice crystal grows larger and begins to fall. Sometimes the crystal breaks apart, creating surfaces to which other droplets can attach themselves. If temperatures near Earth's surface are cold enough, ice crystals will land as snow. Otherwise, the crystals will melt and fall as rain.

In lower-level clouds, precipitation is formed differently. Droplets often coalesce around particles of dust or grains of salt called *condensation nuclei*. As the droplets coalesce and grow larger, they begin to fall, picking up more droplets along the way. These reach the ground as rain.

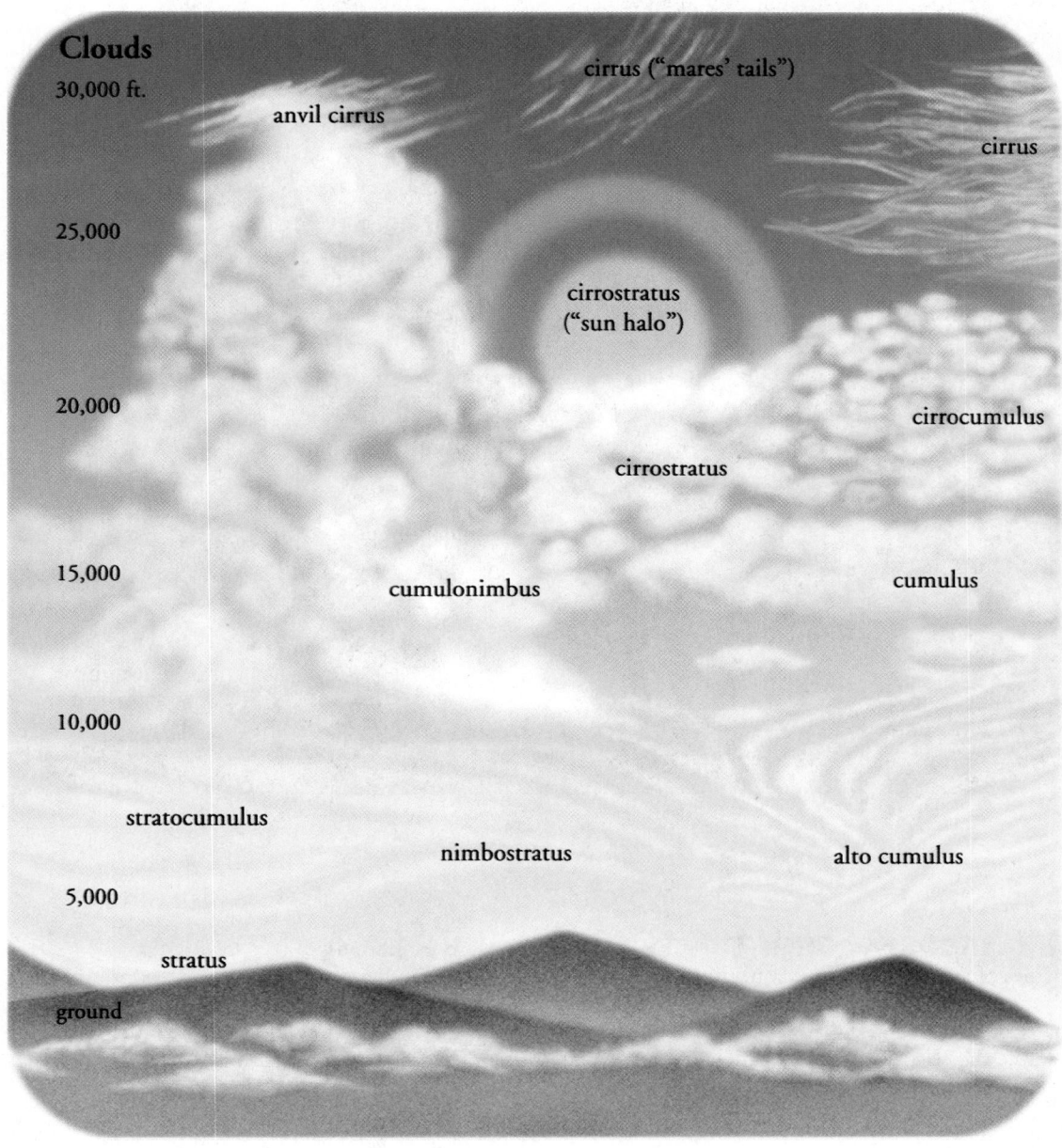

Clouds

30,000 ft.

cirrus ("mares' tails")

anvil cirrus

cirrus

25,000

cirrostratus
("sun halo")

20,000

cirrocumulus

cirrostratus

15,000

cumulonimbus

cumulus

10,000

stratocumulus

nimbostratus

alto cumulus

5,000

stratus

ground

Hail and sleet. Two other common types of precipitation are *hail* and *sleet.* Hailstones are ice pellets. They are created from supercooled water that freezes inside huge cumulonimbus clouds. The frozen drops are carried repeatedly through-out the cloud, picking up more ice and growing larger.

Sleet occurs when rain passes through a layer of air that is below freezing. The rain is turned to ice before reaching the ground.

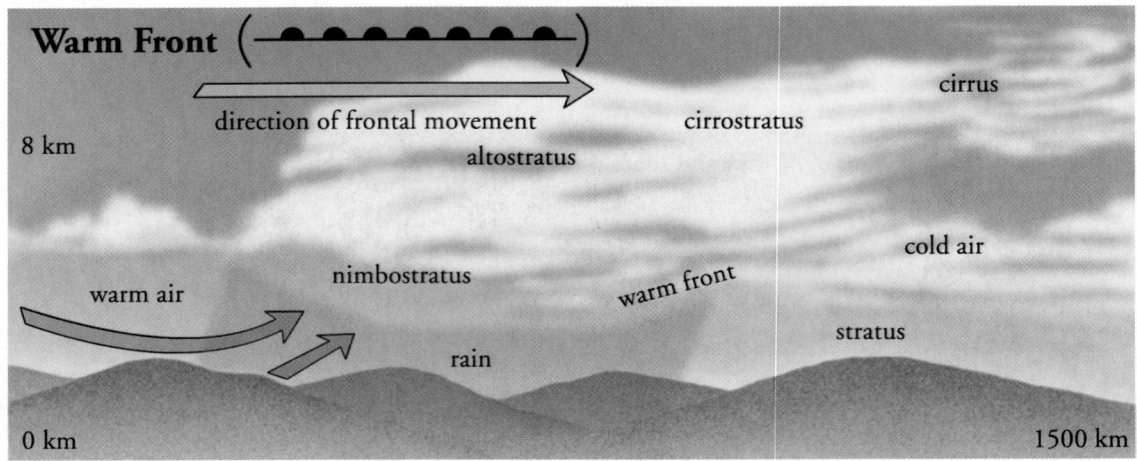

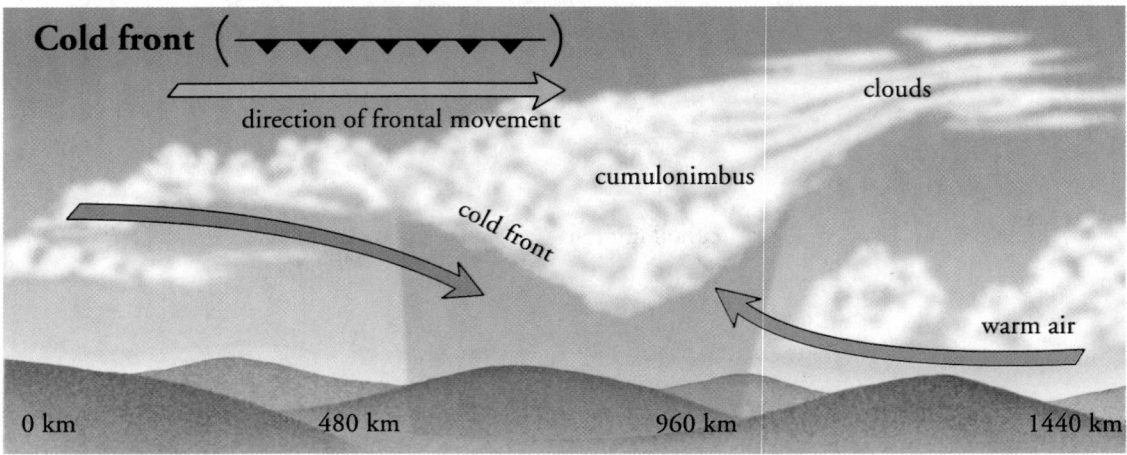

Air masses and fronts.

Large bodies of air with uniform temperature and humidity are called *air masses*. Air masses form over a particular surface area—either land or ocean—and assume the characteristics of that area. Thus, an air mass that forms over the Arctic tundra will be cooler and drier than one that originates in the Gulf of Mexico.

Weather conditions in North America are influenced by several types of air masses. *Continental polar* air forms over the frigid landscape of Canada and Alaska. This cool, dry air mass is carried southward by the polar easterlies. It brings clear, crisp weather to the eastern United States during the winter, and relief from the hot spells of summer.

Continental tropical air masses originate in Mexico. They are blown by the westerlies into the southwestern United States, creating hot, dry weather conditions.

Maritime tropical air masses form over the Caribbean Sea and the Atlantic Ocean. They absorb moisture from the sea and carry it to the southeastern United States. Maritime tropical air brings humid weather and precipitation to the South, the Atlantic coastal states, and farther inland.

Maritime polar air masses can be found over the northern Pacific Ocean and the icy north Atlantic. A polar air mass may be blown inland by the easterlies, creating a heavy storm called a *northeaster*.

As air masses move across North America, they frequently bump into each other. The boundary line between two different air masses is called a *front*.

Warm fronts. When a cold air mass is being replaced by a warm air mass, its leading edge is called a *warm front*. As the warm air gradually rises over the cold air, clouds begin to appear. *Cirrus* clouds foretell the approach of the front. These are followed by *cirro-stratus* and *altostratus* clouds. Eventually, the low *nimbostratus* clouds appear, followed by periods of rain or snow. As the warm air mass settles in a region, the weather clears, temperatures rise, and the winds shift to the southwest.

Cold fronts. When warm air is replaced by a cold air mass, its leading edge is called a *cold front.* A cold front travels rapidly. Owing to friction, the air travels more slowly along Earth's surface than in the atmosphere. As a result, the cold front takes on a very steep slope. Moist air is pushed high into the atmosphere, forming huge *cumulonimbus* clouds. These bring a short period of heavy thunderstorms accompanied by brisk winds. As cold air settles in a region, temperatures drop and wind direction changes to the north or northwest.

Stationary fronts. Sometimes two air masses remain in a region for some time without either one replacing the other. The boundary line between them is called a *stationary front.*

LOWS. In the United States, air masses often meet along a boundary known as the *polar front.* This front extends worldwide in the middle latitudes. Typically, tropical air from the south meets polar air from the north, with the wind in each air mass blowing in a different direction.

Eventually, a wave may develop along the front. Cold air begins pushing into warm air, creating a cold front. The warm air mass tries to displace the cold air mass, producing a warm front. As the warm air rises, it creates an area of low pressure. This gives the entire weather system its name—a *low.*

When a low enters a region, weather conditions change rapidly. A storm will begin with the rainy weather generally associated with a warm front. This will be followed by clearing and higher temperatures. Soon a cold front will arrive, bringing more rain. Then skies will clear.

As moist air ascends along the fronts and water condenses to form precipitation, large amounts of heat are released. This deepens the low-pressure area. The winds flowing into this area increase, and the storm grows in intensity. A satellite photo of the storm system would show that the winds are spiraling in a counterclockwise rotation. For this reason, the low is called a *cyclone.*

The faster moving cold front often overtakes the warm front, lifting it off the ground. This creates an *occluded front.* As the warm air rises, more heat is released. Winds are especially strong in this area, and the storm is intense. Eventually, the low will run its course, and the polar front will return to its original condition.

Storm systems generally originate in the south or west and move toward the northeast. Their speeds vary, making the task of predicting the arrival time of a storm especially difficult.

Developing Low

The four diagrams here show a "weather-map" picture of a low developing and beginning to disperse; that is, you are looking at the map as the low moves eastward (toward the right of the page). In the first diagram, there is no low. In the second and third diagrams, the low develops rapidly and begins to move east. The cold front moves faster than the warm front. In the last diagram, the air from the cold front has begun to mix with the air from the warm front, dissipating the low.

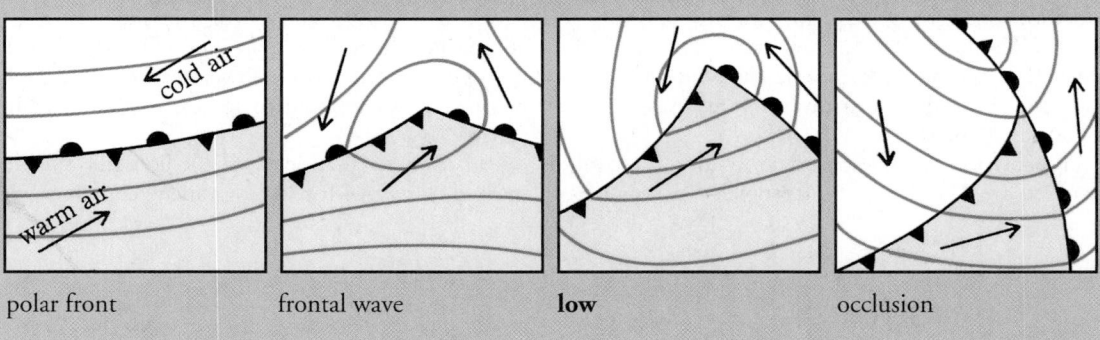

polar front   frontal wave   **low**   occlusion

Storms.

The large cumulonimbus clouds that accompany cold fronts often produce *thunderstorms.* These types of storms are short-lived, generally lasting for no more than an hour. Perhaps the most spectacular aspect associated with a thunderstorm is *lightning.* This is the result of a discharge of electricity within a cloud, between clouds, or between a cloud and Earth.

Although scientists cannot fully explain how lightning occurs, they believe that two areas of oppositely charged particles are created within a cumulonimbus cloud. Positively charged ions are gathered at the top of the cloud; at the bottom of the cloud are mostly negatively charged ions. When these charges build up to a certain point, a stroke of lightning will then pass between them. A similar process occurs when lightning strikes Earth.

A discharge of lightning creates enough heat to expand the air in an explosive way. This sends out sound waves that are heard as *thunder.* Since light travels much faster than sound, the lightning is seen before the thunder is heard. To determine the distance of a storm from a given location, you can count the number of seconds between the flash of lightning and the sound of the thunder. For every 5-second interval, the storm is about 1 mile away.

Tornadoes. The *tornado* is a funnel-shaped storm that is characterized by rapidly twisting winds. For this reason it is often called a "twister." Wind speeds in a tornado may exceed 400 miles per hour. The winds swirl around an area of extremely low pressure created at the center of the storm. The storm's dark cloud is due to the condensation of moisture inside it.

When tornadoes strike, they can cause enormous damage. This damage results in part from the high velocity of the winds. The destruction is also due to the low pressure area inside the funnel. As the funnel passes over a building, the difference in pressure inside the structure and outside causes the walls to explode.

Tornadoes can move very rapidly, sometimes at speeds of 70 miles per hour, although they generally travel more slowly than that. The diameter of the funnel averages anywhere from 500 to 2,000 feet. Tornadoes occur most frequently during the springtime. While they may strike any part of the United States, they are most common in the South and the Midwest. The leading tornado states are Texas, Oklahoma, and Nebraska.

Probably the most destructive tornado on record occurred in March 1925. It traveled along the ground for more than 200 miles through the states of Missouri, Illinois, and Indiana. In the tornado's wake, the storm left 695 people dead, and over 2,000 were injured.

Hurricanes. A *hurricane* is a large tropical storm that originates in the ocean. Hurricanes that strike the United States start in the Atlantic Ocean near the Caribbean Sea. These tropical storms are most common in the summer during the months of August and September.

Hurricanes form around a low-pressure area. Within a hurricane, large amounts of water vapor are condensing and releasing heat. This causes air to rise, reducing the already low pressure even further. More moist air rushes into the storm, giving it a constant supply of heat. At the hurricane's center is an area of calm that is called the "eye." From a satellite photo, winds can be seen whirling about the hurricane's eye in a counterclockwise direction typical of a cyclone. Wind speeds in a hurricane are 75 miles per hour or more.

Hurricanes move at speeds of 10 to 20 miles per hour. They are carried from their point of origin by the trade winds. Eventually a hurricane in the Atlantic Ocean may strike the islands of the Caribbean or the mainland of the United States. Some hurricanes follow a path that takes them from Florida northward along the Atlantic coast and on into the New England states. The strong winds, high sea waves, and flooding that accompany the storm wreak tremendous damage on both property and lives.

Weather prediction.

A meteorologist relies on a variety of instruments to predict the weather. A *barometer* is an instrument used to measure air pressure. Perhaps you have heard a weather forecaster say that the barometric pressure is 30.62 inches and steady. This pressure reading refers to the height of a column of mercury. In a mercury barometer, air pushes down on liquid mercury that is in a dish, forcing it up a glass tube. The height of the column in the tube corresponds to the amount of pressure exerted by the air. At sea level, the standard air pressure is 29.92 inches of mercury. If a low approaches the area, the pressure will drop and the barometer will record a lower reading. Thus, the barometer can be used to forecast an approaching storm.

A barometer that does not use liquid is called an *aneroid barometer.* It relies on a metal container with

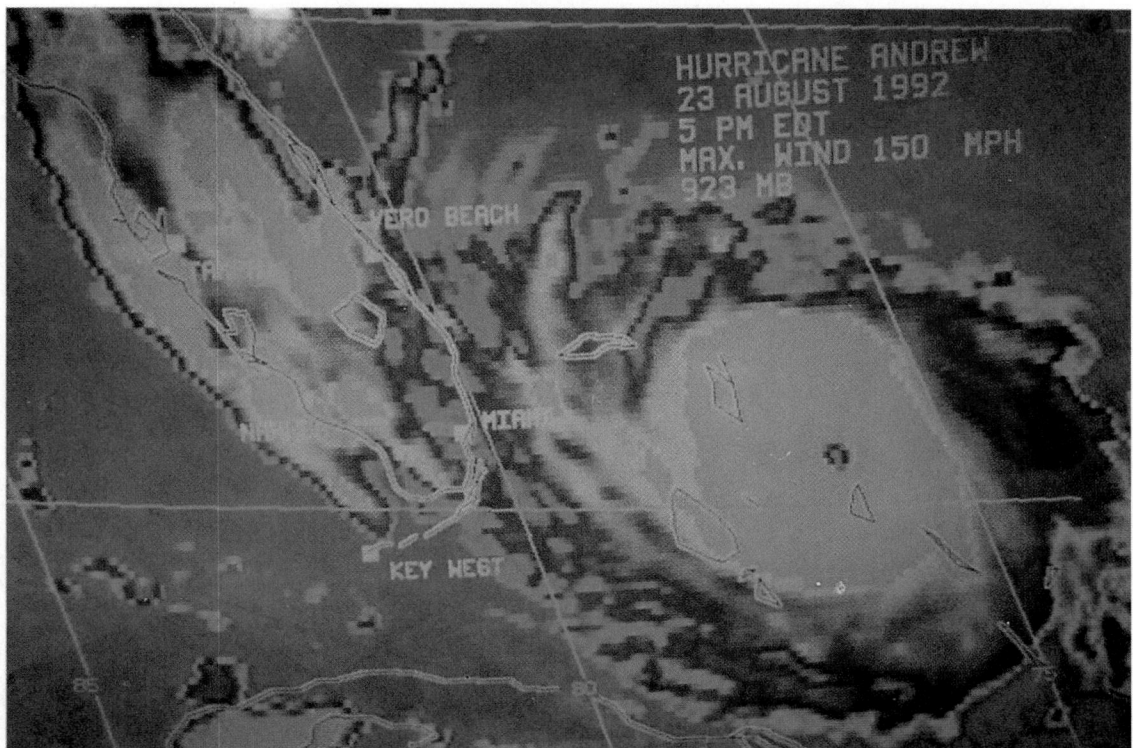

Meteorologists today have at their disposal a great deal of information collected from ground stations and satellites alike. All of this information is combined to produce computerized weather maps such as this one, which shows the devastating hurricane Andrew approaching Florida in August 1992.

most of the air removed. This container is very sensitive to changes in air pressure. A *barograph* consists of an aneroid barometer attached to a recording device. It provides a continuous written record of barometric changes.

The *rain gauge* measures levels of precipitation. A *wind vane* indicates wind direction. The most common wind vane is an arrow with a large tail. This arrow rotates freely on a fixed base and points into the wind in the direction from which the wind is blowing.

An instrument used to measure wind speed is called an *anemometer.* The cup anemometer is made up of three of four hollow cups attached to horizontal arms extending from a vertical axis. The force of the wind on the cups causes the apparatus to turn on the axis; the higher the wind speed, the faster the cups turn. The spinning apparatus is linked to a pointer that moves over a scale and indicates wind speed in knots or in miles per hour.

Another device is the *thermograph,* a metal thermometer that keeps a written record of temperature changes. During a weather forecast, you may hear temperature given according to two scales, Fahren-

heit and Celsius. Freezing is 32 degrees on the Fahrenheit scale and 0 degrees on the Celsius scale.

Located throughout the country are weather stations that record local conditions on their instruments. To determine conditions in the atmosphere, the stations launch weather balloons that contain thermometers and barometers.

Each station records such things as wind conditions, temperature, the amount of cloud cover, dew point, and precipitation. This information is then transmitted to the National Meteorological Center in Maryland, run by the National Weather Service. The Weather Service also relies on satellite pictures and radar. Satellite pictures show the movement of entire weather systems. All the information is analyzed with the aid of computers. The data are then used to design a weather map for the entire country.

Lines called *isobars* are drawn to connect areas with the same barometric pressure. *Isotherms* are drawn to connect points with the same temperature. The map shows the location of any fronts, storm systems, and high pressure zones (areas of clear, dry weather).

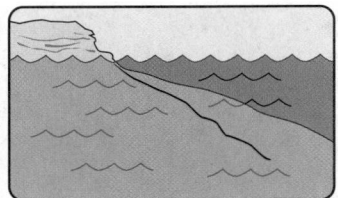

continental shelf

Dictionary of earth science

fjord

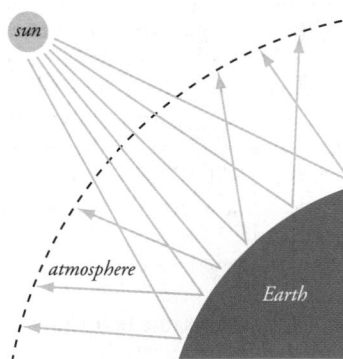

greenhouse effect

absolute humidity. Weight of water vapor in a specific amount of air.

adiabatic change. Temperature change of air when it expands or is compressed without any heat being added from outside sources.

advection fog. Fog created when warm, moist air moves over a cool surface.

air mass. Large body of air with uniform temperature and humidity.

alluvial plain. Fan-shaped plain formed by materials deposited from a river.

altimeter. Instrument that measures altitude.

anemometer. Device that measures the velocity of wind.

aneroid barometer. Barometer that does not contain a liquid.

anticline. Upfolded region of layers of rock.

aquifer. Rock structure that contains groundwater.

arête. Sharp divide between glacial cirques.

barometer. Device used to measure air pressure.

caldera. Large crater in a volcano.

chinook. Warm wind that blows down the eastern slope of the Rocky Mountains.

cinder cone. Steep cone formed by the cinders from an explosive volcanic eruption.

cirque. Basin found at the head of a glacier.

cirrus clouds. High, feathery clouds.

climate. Average weather conditions in a region over a long period of time.

cold front. Leading edge of a cold air mass that is displacing a warm air mass.

composite cone. Cone produced by a combination of lava and cinders.

condensation. Change from a gas to a liquid.

continental drift. Movement of the continents on pieces of Earth's crust called plates.

continental shelf. Gently sloping part of a continent that extends under the sea to the continental slope.

continental slope. Steep slope that extends from the continental shelf to the ocean bottom.

core (inner). Solid layer inside the earth composed of iron and nickel.

core (outer). Liquid layer outside the inner core.

Coriolis force. Force caused by Earth's rotation.

crater. Depression found at the top of a volcano.

crevasse. Large and deep crack in a glacier.

cyclone. Area of low pressure in which winds rotate in a counterclockwise direction.

delta. Sediment deposited where a river enters a lake or ocean.

density. Weight per unit volume.

dew point. Temperature at which the air can hold no more water.

dike. Region in which magma has forced itself into vertical cracks in the crustal rock.

epicenter. Spot on Earth's surface directly above the focus of an earthquake.

esker. Long ridge composed of till.

evaporation. Conversion of liquid to gas.

eye of the hurricane. Area of calm in the center of a hurricane.

fault. Crack in rock along which movement has occurred.

firn. Grainy snow or ice in a glacier.

fjord. Valley that has been created by a glacier and later filled by the sea.

focus. Point under Earth's surface where an earthquake originates.

front. Boundary line between two different air masses.

glacier. Large sheet of ice.

greenhouse effect. Process of trapping heat waves radiated from Earth.

hail. Lumps of ice.

high. Area of high air pressure.

horn. Sharp peak created by a series of cirques.

horse latitudes. Areas of high pressure located at 30 degrees N and S latitude.

hurricane. Tropical storm with very high winds that begins in the Atlantic Ocean near the Caribbean Sea.

hygrometer. Device used to measure relative humidity.

igneous rock. Rock formed when magma or lava cools.

ionosphere. That part of the atmosphere that contains many ions.

isobar. Line on a map that connects points with the same atmospheric pressure.

jet streams. Upper atmosphere winds that move at very high velocity.

joint. Large crack in crustal rock.

kettle holes. Pits created by the melting of buried blocks of ice deposited by glaciers.

lava. Magma that has flowed onto Earth's surface.

low. Storm center that is characterized by an area of low pressure.

magma. Molten rock found beneath Earth's surface.

mantle. Layer of earth found just beneath the crust in Earth's interior.

metamorphic rock. Rock that has been changed by pressure, heat, or chemicals.

mineral. Crystalline substance occurring naturally in the environment.

monsoon. Huge land-sea breeze found in India and other areas of the world.

moraine. Layers of till.

occluded front. Front created when a warm front is lifted by a cold front.

plate tectonics. Theory that continents and oceans are contained in crustal plates that move continually.

polar easterlies. Cold winds that blow from the poles.

polar front. Boundary line between warm air masses and cold air masses.

prevailing westerlies. Winds that blow out of the west in the mid latitudes.

psychrometer. Device that measures relative humidity.

relative humidity. Percent that expresses the relationship between the amount of water vapor contained in a volume of air and the amount the air can hold when saturated.

Richter scale. Measure of earthquake intensity.

seismograph. Device that records earthquake waves.

shield cone. Volcanic cone created by lava flow.

stationary front. Boundary between two air masses that are not moving.

subpolar lows. Low pressure areas located at about 60 degrees N and S latitude.

syncline. Layers of rock folded into a U-shape.

till. Rocks and other material carried or deposited by glaciers.

tornado. Violent, twisting wind that forms a funnel cloud.

trade winds. Winds that blow from a general easterly direction from the horse latitudes to the equator.

troposphere. Lower part of Earth's atmosphere.

tsunami. Giant wave produced by an earthquake or other force that affects the sea floor.

warm front. Leading edge of a warm air mass that is displacing a cold air mass.

water table. Part of the upper level of earth that is saturated with groundwater.

weathering. Process by which rocks are broken down by natural forces in the environment.

wind vane. Device that indicates wind direction.

For Further Reference

Burroughs, William James
Weather
Time-Life Books
National Geographic Society
Powers of Nature

Sullivan, Walter
Continents in Motion
McGraw-Hill
Williams, Jack
The Weather Book
Vintage Books

- *The solar system* **404**
- *Galaxies* **411**
- *Stars* **412**
- *Other phenomena* **414**
- *Cosmology* **415**
- *Space exploration* **416**
- *Dictionary of space science* **424**

Space Science

It is astonishing that people have learned so much about stars and galaxies that are so far away that we see them as tiny points of light. Today scientists can often tell how far away a star or galaxy is, the elements from which it is made, its true brightness, its mass, and even its history over several million years merely by examining the light. In fact, all that we know about distant stars and galaxies has been learned from the record of electromagnetic waves. These waves are often millions of years old when they reach Earth.

Closer to home, the sun and six of the nine planets (counting Earth) can be seen with the naked eye, although the planets, too, are millions of miles from us. What is more, we have been able to reach out to the planets with space probes that have landed on Mars and Venus and also provided close-up views of all the planets visible without a telescope. These close-up pictures have dramatically changed our knowledge of the solar system.

The solar system

Earth is one of nine planets that revolve around a star we call the sun. There are also more than 125 moons that revolve around the various planets. In addition, there are asteroids, meteors, comets, dust, and gas. Taken together, these make up the *solar system.*

The sun. The sun is the power center of the solar system. Its gravitational pull keeps the planets in their orbits. Its energy provides heat and light to the planets. According to one estimate, the sun produces more energy in a single second than the human race has used in its entire existence.

How is this energy created? The sun is made up largely of hydrogen atoms. Under the high temperatures that exist on the sun, these atoms move very rapidly. The nuclei of four hydrogen atoms come together, or fuse, to form one atom of an element called helium. This process is known as *nuclear fusion.* The helium atom contains less mass than did the original four hydrogen atoms. According to Einstein's well-known equation $E = mc^2$, the mass that is lost during fusion is converted into energy.

The sun is a fiery ball of hot gases. On the yellow surface, or *photosphere,* temperatures average about 10,000 degrees F. Although the photosphere may appear uniform, closer observation reveals many bright spots. These spots are caused by hotter gases emerging from inside the sun. Temperatures in the solar interior are thought to reach as high as 27,000 degrees F.

Dark spots are also found on the sun's surface. Such dark spots, which are more easily seen than bright spots, are called *sunspots.* The sunspots are areas of cooler temperatures. The number of sunspots varies according to an eleven-year cycle. Explosions on the sun's surface, called *solar flares,* occur in conjunction with the sunspots. During these explosions, a glow may appear in the sky at Earth's poles. This glow is called an *aurora.* The colorful night sky of the aurora borealis, or northern lights, can be seen from Canada and the United States. The northern aurora is called the *aurora borealis.*

The sun's surface is enveloped by the solar atmosphere. The lower part of the atmosphere—called the *chromosphere*—appears red because of the hydrogen set aglow there by the high temperatures. The upper atmosphere, or *corona,* is the white halo seen during a solar eclipse. Electrically charged particles are emitted by the corona and travel rapidly into the solar system. These particles, known as *solar winds,* blow across our moon, scarring its landscape.

The sun is by far the largest part of our solar system. The mass of the sun is about 700 times as large as the rest of the solar system. Its diameter is so large that 110 Earths could be strung along the disk we see at its widest point. Its volume is more than 1 million times that of Earth.

The planets.

Mercury, Venus, Earth, and Mars are called the *inner planets.* Mercury, the smallest planet, is the one closest to the sun. This nearness to the sun, combined with Mercury's long days, produces very high temperatures on the planet's surface. Mercury has an extremely thin atmosphere that may have been created by the solar winds. Thus, meteors encounter little resistance and bombard the surface, producing huge craters.

In contrast to Mercury, the planet Venus has a thick atmosphere comprised mainly of carbon dioxide (CO_2). This creates a "greenhouse effect," so-called because of the similarity to what happens inside a greenhouse. The sun radiates shortwave energy that passes through the CO_2 and heats the surface of the planet. But the heat is radiated back from the surface in longer waves, which are trapped by the CO_2 layer, creating tremendously high temperatures.

During the 1970s and 1980s, the Soviet Venera satellites landed on Venus. They photographed a parched, rocky surface filled with many rounded and sharp boulders.

The solar system

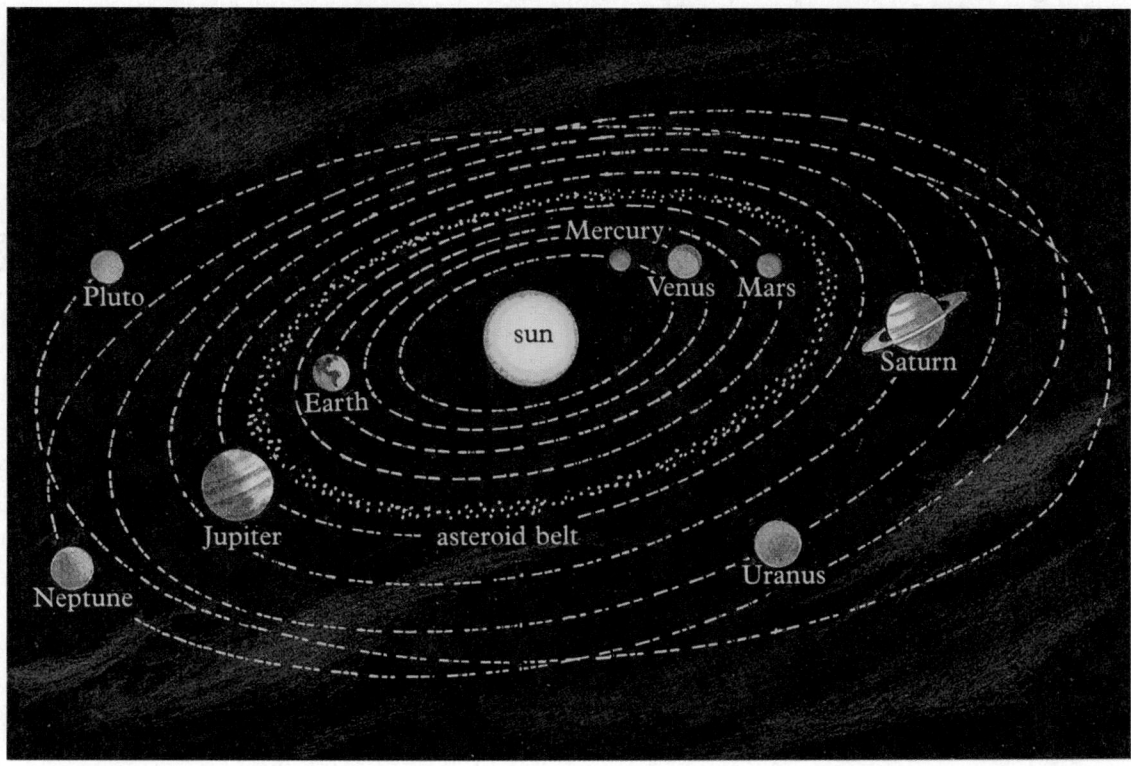

405

In some ways the planet Mars resembles Earth. Its day lasts just over 24 hours. The planet inclines on its axis at 24 degrees, creating a change in seasons, although the seasons are about double Earth's in length. At each of the poles is a huge ice cap that grows during the winter and recedes in the summer. These ice caps are comprised largely of frozen carbon dioxide.

Photographs taken during the Viking and Mariner space missions launched by the United States in the 1970s revealed many features of the Martian surface. Some areas have large craters, much like those on the planet Mercury. In other areas are huge volcanoes similar to the shield cones found on Earth. One cone, called Olympus Mons, is over 360 miles wide. Mars also shows signs of erosion from wind and water, although no water presently flows on the surface. Photographs of the planet's surface sent back by rovers *Spirit* and *Opportunity* in 2004 seem to confirm the previous presence of water.

The *outer planets* include Jupiter, Saturn, Uranus, Neptune, and Pluto. Jupiter is the largest of the planets of the solar system, with a greater mass than the combined total of all the others. Encircling Jupiter are bands of clouds that contain the planet's most prominent feature—the Great Red Spot. Sci-

Facts About the Solar System

Mars, the red planet

Venus, taken by the Magellan probe

Earth, seen from space

	Mercury	Venus	Earth	Mars
Distance from sun	36,000,000 mi.	67,000,000 mi.	93,000,000 mi.	142,000,000 mi.
Length of year	87.96 days	224.70 days	365.26 days	687 days
Diameter	3000 mi.	7500 mi.	8000 mi.	4200 mi.
Length of day	58.65 Earth days	about 243 Earth days	23 hr., 56 min.	24 hr., 37 min.
Mass relative to Earth	0.056	0.815	1.00	0.108
Surface temperature (average)	332°F	750°F	59°F	-67°F
Atmosphere	solar wind	carbon dioxide, nitrogen	nitrogen, oxygen, carbon dioxide, argon	carbon dioxide, argon, nitrogen, water
Weight of 150 lbs.	58 lbs.	130 lbs.	150 lbs.	58 lbs.
Number of moons	none	none	1	2

entists are still uncertain about its cause but the Spot seems to be a storm that has persisted for hundreds of years.

Jupiter has 63 known satellites. On Ganymede, enormous craters pit the surface. Volcanoes have been observed on Io, while extensive fractures break up the landscape of Europa.

Beyond Jupiter is the planet Saturn, which is distinguished by its extensive ring system. Photographs from the Voyager space probes showed that the system is composed of almost 1,000 small rings. Vast numbers of tiny particles comprise the rings, which are about 10 miles thick. In 2004 the Cassini-Huygens spacecraft and probe began to expand on information gleaned from the Voyager mission. This included information that indicated the moon Titan's atmosphere is similar to that of early Earth.

The planet Uranus appears as a greenish-blue disk. In 1977 scientists discovered that Uranus is encircled by rings.

In 1989 Neptune was visited by *Voyager 2*. It was learned that Neptune also has rings, that it is swept by violent storms, and that it apparently generates part of its own internal heat. To date, little is known about Pluto.

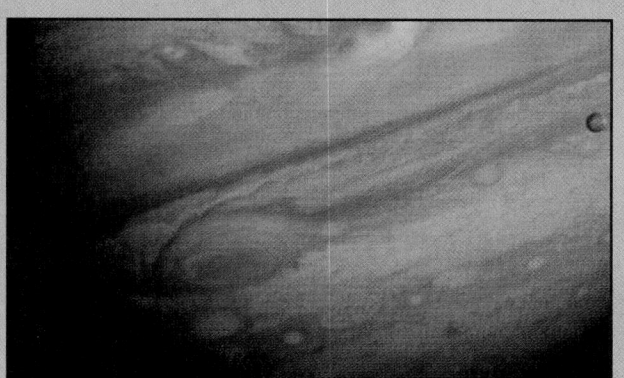

Jupiter and the Great Red Spot

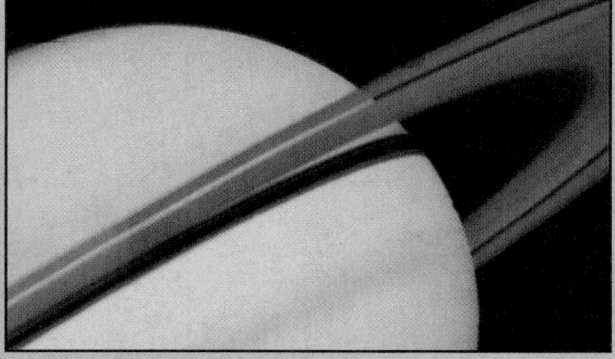

Saturn and its rings

Jupiter	Saturn	Uranus	Neptune	Pluto	Sun
484,000,000 mi.	887,000,000 mi.	1,800,000,000 mi.	2,800,000,000 mi.	3,700,000,000 mi.	
11.86 yr.	29.46 yr.	84.01 yr.	164.79 yr.	247.7 yr.	200 million yr.
89,000 mi.	75,000 mi.	32,000 mi.	31,000 mi.	1500 mi.	860,000 mi.
9 hr., 50 min.	10 hr., 39 min.	16 hr., 20 min.	16 hr., 3 min.	6.39 Earth days	25 days
317.9	95.2	14.6	17.2	0.2	333,000
-128°F*	-148°F*	-344°F	-365°F	-355°F	10,000°F
hydrogen, helium, methane, ammonia, water	hydrogen, helium, methane, ammonia	hydrogen, helium	hydrogen, helium, methane	methane (trace)	hydrogen, helium
380 lbs.	160 lbs.	155 lbs.	210 lbs.	24 lbs.	
63 known	33 known	27 known	13 known	1	

*Effective temperature, a measure of the amount of energy given off by the planet

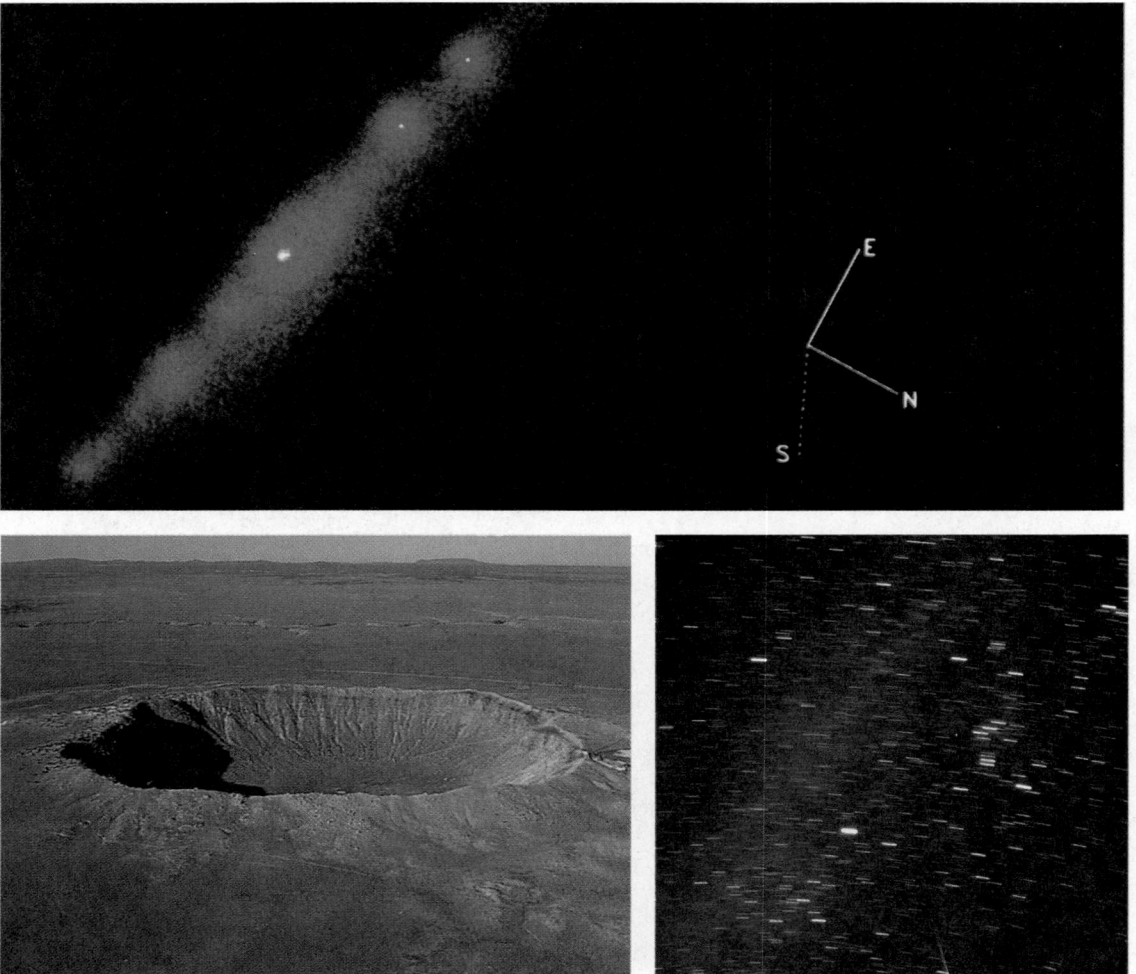

A comet, such as the one shown in the top photograph (Shoemaker-Levy 9, the "String of Pearls" comet), is one of the most spectacular sights in the heavens. Visitors from space, in the form of meteorites, sometimes bombard Earth, as Meteor Crater in Arizona demonstrates. Most meteors, such as those shown in the shower (lower right), burn up in the atmosphere and do not reach Earth.

The minor planets.

Asteroids are the minor planets of our solar system. Most of them can be found orbiting the sun in a zone between Mars and Jupiter. The vast majority of asteroids are small, measuring less than a mile in diameter. But the largest, Ceres, is approximately 500 miles across. Asteroids may have resulted from the destruction of larger bodies.

In 1986 a bright light was seen shooting across the sky. This was Halley's comet, which has appeared at regular intervals for centuries. A *comet* consists of tiny particles of frozen gases. As a comet approaches the sun, these particles melt and begin to glow, creating the bright head known as a *coma.* Some of the particles escape the coma and flow outward, producing the comet's *tail.* Each time a comet approaches the sun and returns to space, it loses some of its mass; eventually it will totally disintegrate.

Meteoroids are tiny particles traveling through space. Sometimes they enter our atmosphere, where they are set aglow by friction. These glowing particles are called *meteors* or, more popularly, "shooting stars." A vast number of meteors, called a meteor shower, may be created from the remains of a passing comet. Generally, meteoroids are quite small and disintegrate in the atmosphere, but a few may be large enough to reach the surface of Earth. These are called *meteorites.* When they strike the surface, meteorites can produce enormous craters such as the one found in Arizona that is approximately 4,000 feet wide.

The moon. Earth's only natural satellite is called the *moon*. The moon is an average distance of 238,857 miles from Earth. The moon orbits Earth once every 27⅓ days; during that time it makes a single rotation on its axis. This means that the same side of the moon is always facing Earth.

From our position on Earth, the moon appears as a patchwork of light and dark areas. The light areas are created by sunlight reflecting off the craggy lunar mountains. Some of the mountains are over 5 miles high. The lunar surface is also deeply pitted with craters that result from the impact of numerous meteors. Since there is no atmosphere on the moon, meteors have been able to reach the surface easily. One crater, called Clavius, is about 148 miles in diameter.

The dark areas are the lunar seas, or *maria*. These are not actual bodies of water, for no water exists on the moon's surface. The maria were created by volcanic activity that occurred millions of years ago. As lava flowed onto the surface, it solidified into dark rock. The maria have been given names such as the Sea of Rains, the Sea of Tears, and the Sea of Serenity.

Various types of rocks were found on the moon during the lunar landings. The maria are comprised of dark basalts. The highlands contain other types of igneous rock such as breccia.

Because of its orbit, the moon is constantly changing position with respect to Earth and the sun. Consequently, the amount of sunlight reflected by the moon to Earth changes. This creates the *phases of the moon.* For example, at new moon, half of the lunar surface is lighted by the sun, but the moon appears dark to us because of its position between Earth and the sun. The moon *waxes* as it reflects more light to Earth, and *wanes* as the amount of light diminishes. An entire cycle (new moon to new moon) takes 29½ days, which is two days longer than the period of the moon's revolution. The reason for this time difference is that Earth has been moving in its orbit.

The moon

The moon and its changes have always fascinated people on Earth. Although there are many myths to explain the phases of the moon, the ancient Greeks had long ago found the true explanation: the changes are caused by the motions of the sun, Earth, and moon. Now, men have walked on the moon's surface.

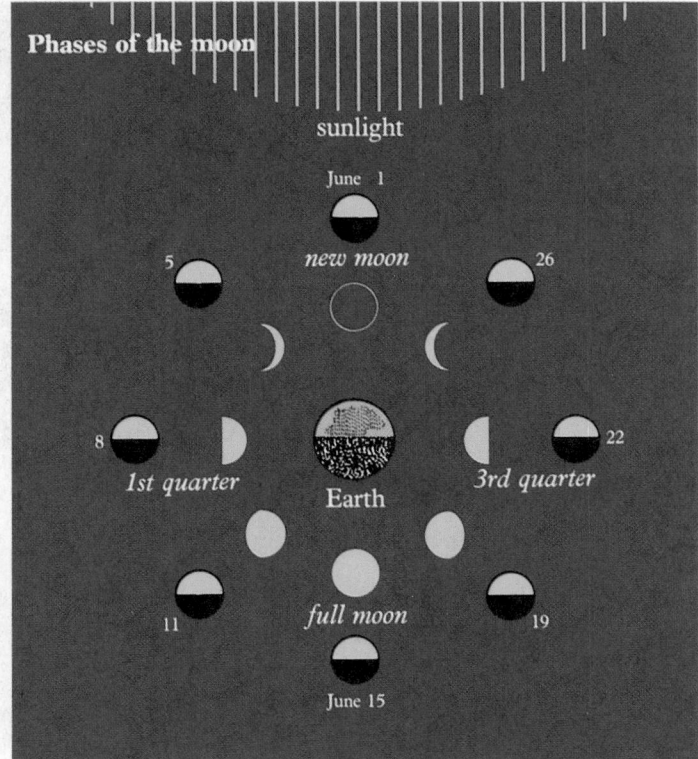

Phases of the moon

sunlight

June 1

new moon

5

26

8

1st quarter

22

3rd quarter

Earth

11

full moon

19

June 15

Eclipses.

A celestial body casts a shadow into space when it is lighted from one side. The light usually comes from a sun. If another celestial body passes into this shadow, it is eclipsed. For example, when Earth passes between the sun and the moon, a lunar *eclipse* occurs. When the moon passes between the sun and Earth, a solar eclipse occurs.

The shadow that is cast by Earth or the moon is really of two different darknesses. The inner shadow, which is very dark, is called the *umbra*. Outside the umbra is a shadow of semidarkness called the *penumbra*.

A lunar eclipse can only occur during a full moon, when sun, Earth, and moon are in a straight line. Most of the time, the moon's orbit takes it out of Earth's shadow. When Earth's umbra covers the moon's surface, a total eclipse of the moon can be seen from an entire hemisphere on Earth.

A solar eclipse occurs when sun, moon, and Earth are in a straight line. Because of the sun's size compared with the moon's, the umbra cast by the moon is small, covering an area about 167 miles wide. The penumbra covers an area about 2,000 miles wide. People in the area where the umbra falls see a total solar eclipse. Those in the area of the penumbra see a partial solar eclipse. Solar eclipses happen less often than lunar eclipses and are over more quickly.

Eclipses

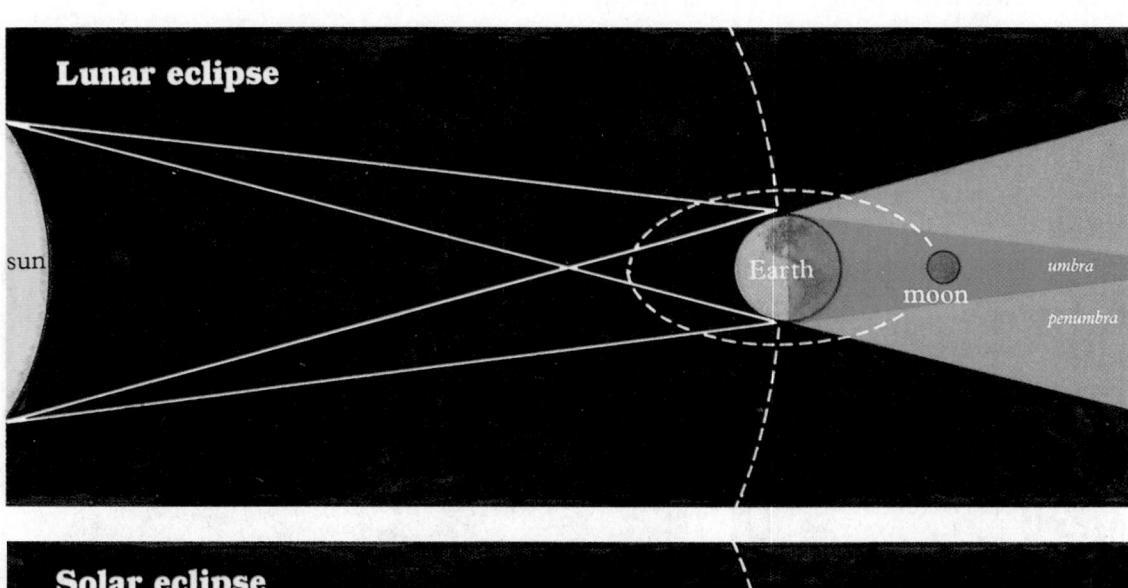

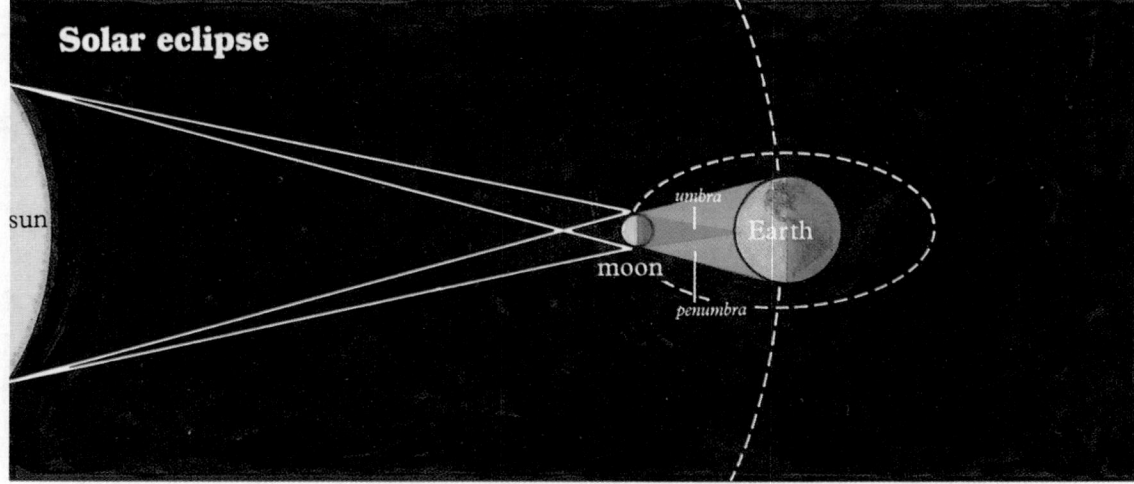

Galaxies

Our solar system is a small part of a *galaxy*. A galaxy is a very large collection of stars, gas, dust, and other objects traveling through space as a unit. Our galaxy is called the *Milky Way* because we see millions of stars whose light gives a milky haze when we look at the night sky. The Milky Way is relatively thin and flat, something like a wristwatch, but it also has spiral arms, something like a pinwheel. Our sun is located in one of these arms, far from the center of the galaxy.

The universe consists of many galaxies. Some, like Andromeda, are spiral-shaped. Andromeda is visible to the naked eye, but it is very faint because of its great distance. Many galaxies have an elliptical shape, while others appear formless and are called irregular galaxies. These include the Large and Small Magellanic Clouds, which are the galaxies located closest to the Milky Way.

Distances in astronomy are so great that the unit of measurement most often used is the *light-year*. A light-year is the distance that light travels in a year, or about 6 trillion miles. Another unit is the *parsec*, which is 3.26 light-years. The Milky Way has a diameter of about 100,000 light-years and is believed to be about 10,000 light-years thick. It contains about 100 billion stars, as well as huge amounts of dust and gas. The entire galaxy rotates very slowly, taking about 200 million years to complete one revolution.

The distance to a nearby star can be determined

The Milky Way galaxy is a disk with spiral arms, representing one of the more common types of galaxies.

by using a method known as *parallax*. This refers to the apparent shift in a star's position when viewed from two different locations. Astronomers observe a star at an interval of six months, when Earth is at two different locations in its orbit. Using trigonometry, they then calculate a star's distance. The nearest star is Alpha Centauri, about 4.3 light-years away.

In the galaxy M100, in this photograph made by the Hubble Space Telescope, spiral arms are prominent. The Horsehead Nebula is a cloud of dust and gas.

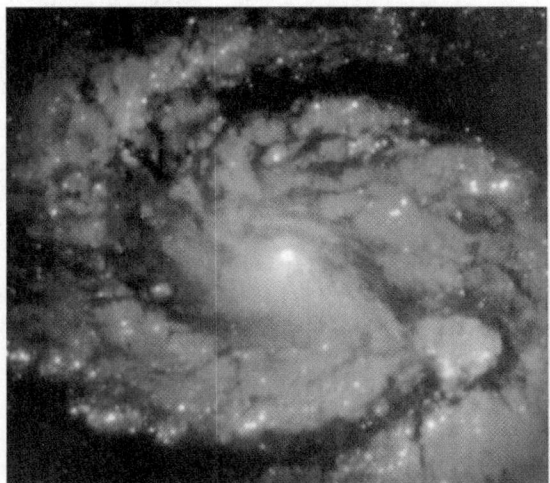

Stars

Stars are born in a rotating cloud of gas and dust called a *nebula*. The laws of physics predict that such a cloud will break up into many smaller clouds under the influence of gravity, and that gravity will also cause the smaller clouds to contract. As the hydrogen atoms in such a cloud fall faster and faster toward the center, the cloud becomes hot and starts to glow. Finally it becomes so hot at the core that a nuclear reaction begins: hydrogen atoms are fused to form helium. This is the same reaction that occurs in the sun, producing huge amounts of energy. The energy exerts an outward pressure that balances the force of gravity; at this point the gas cloud stops contracting. This is how stars are created. New stars are still being born from the nebulas in our galaxy.

Luminosity. One of the most important facts about a star is its brightness, or *luminosity.* Luminosity is the rate at which a star radiates energy. Astronomers generally use the term *magnitude* to express the brightness of a star. There are two kinds of magnitude. *Apparent magnitude* is the brightness as it appears to us, without corrections for the distance of the star from Earth. *Absolute magnitude* is brightness after allowing for the fact that stars are at different distances from us. The bright stars are given a magnitude of one and are first-magnitude stars. A first-magnitude star is about 2.5 times as bright as a second-magnitude star and $2.5 \times 2.5 = 6.25$ times as bright as a third-magnitude star, and so on. The human eye can see stars down to the sixth apparent magnitude, which is about 100 times fainter than the first magnitude. Some stars are brighter than first magnitude; these stars are given a negative magnitude. Apparent magnitudes range from -26.5 for the sun to about $+20$, which can be detected only by the largest telescopes.

To calculate absolute magnitude, one must correct for the different distances of the stars. One star may look much fainter than another although it is actually putting out far more energy. It appears fainter because it is farther away. The apparent brightness of a star is inversely proportional to the square of its distance. That is, the farther away a star is, the less its apparent brightness. The absolute magnitude is the value one would measure if the star or other celestial object were at a distance of 10 parsecs (32.6 light-years). On this scale, the stars show a magnitude range of -10 to $+20$. Our sun is somewhere in the middle with $+5$. It is an average star.

Constellations

Although the origin of the names for the constellations goes back to the dawn of recorded time, astronomers still use these handy apparent groupings of stars as a means of locating objects in the sky. Modern lists of constellations are defined so that all stars are included in one group.

Orion

Cancer

Leo

Stars: H–R diagram

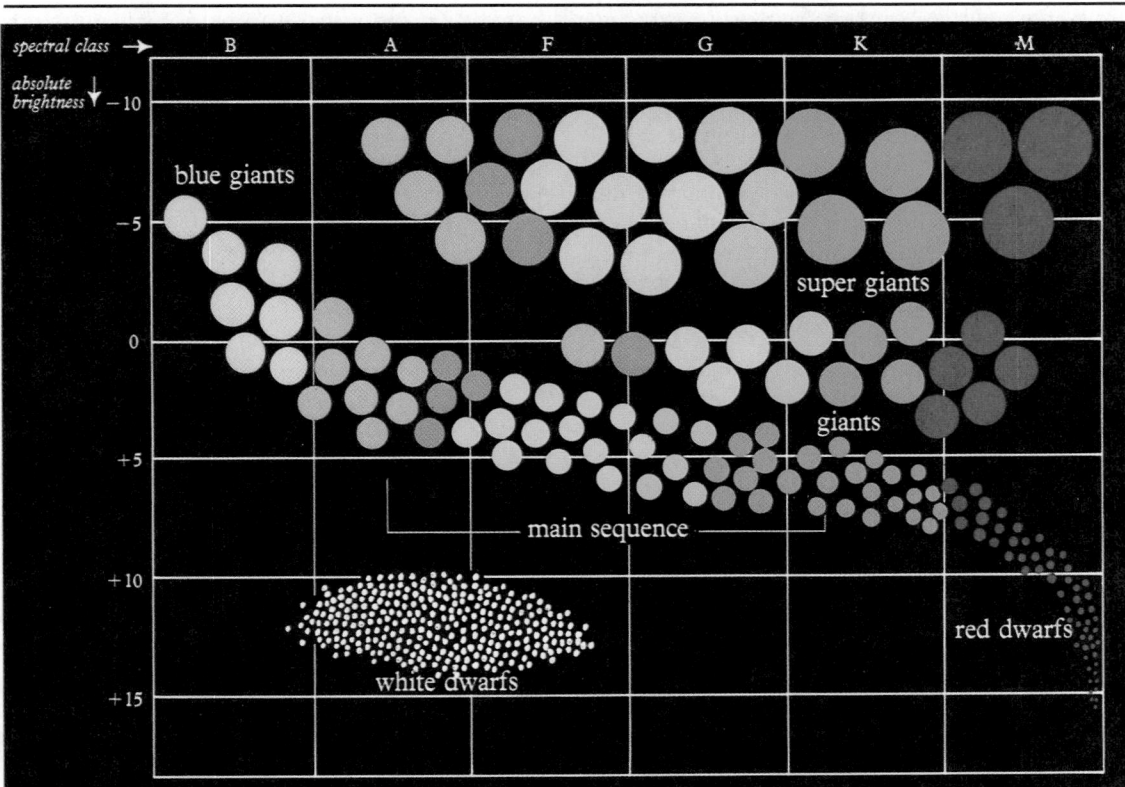

Classification of stars.

Stars appear to us as luminous dots that "twinkle." This is due to their distance from Earth and to the effect of our atmosphere on the light that they emit. Stars glow in various colors of the spectrum depending on their surface temperatures. The hottest stars glow a brilliant blue-white; others glow yellow; while the coolest stars glow red. A spectroscope is a device that breaks down the light coming from a star and helps scientists obtain a fairly accurate measure of a star's surface temperature. Scientists have used letters to classify stars into the following spectral groups based on temperature:

O 50,000 C	G 5,500 C
B 20,000 C	K 4,500 C
A 10,000 C	M 3,000 C
F 7,500 C	

Each major group is further subdivided. Our sun is class G_2, temperature 6000 degrees C.

The astronomers Ejnar Hertzsprung and Henry Russell plotted the absolute magnitude (brightness) of many stars and compared it to the stars' spectral classes (surface temperatures). This resulted in the *H-R diagram*. Most stars fall into a regular order known as the *main sequence*. It was found that a star's position along the main sequence depends on its mass. The very massive stars have a high temperature and appear blue, whereas the smaller stars have lower temperatures and appear yellow or red.

Life cycle of a star.

The H-R diagram provides an effective way to chart the life cycle of a star. After a star is born and becomes stable, it eventually enters the main sequence. Massive stars, such as Vega and Sirius, show up on the left. An average-size star, such as our sun, can be found near the center of the main sequence. Smaller stars join at the right.

The length of time that a star remains stable is a function of its mass. The more massive stars consume their hydrogen faster. Those similar to our sun burn much more slowly.

As a star begins to run out of hydrogen, it becomes unstable. Its surface cools, and its size may grow enormously. A massive star may expand to become one of the supergiants shown in the upper part of the H-R diagram. These stars glow very brightly because of their enormous surface area. An example of a supergiant is the star Betelgeuse, which is found in the constellation Orion.

An average-size star, such as our sun, will not expand so much as the supergiants; it will become a giant. In time the giant sun will use up all its energy and begin to contract. Finally, the sun will enter its last stage and become a cold star that emits only a faint glow. Such a star is called a *white dwarf*.

The end of a supergiant can occur in different ways. The supergiant may explode and become very bright, forming a spectacular *supernova*. In 1054, Chinese astronomers observed such a supernova in our galaxy; today we can still see the cloud of expanding gas that remains from the explosion. It forms the Crab nebula in the constellation Taurus. A more recent supernova occurred in our galaxy in 1604.

Following the explosion of a supernova, the remains of the star that exploded may collapse. Its protons and electrons may be pushed so closely together that they fuse to produce neutrons. Such a star is called a *neutron star,* and it is very small in size. For example, if the planet Earth were to become a neutron star, it would be only 100 yards in diameter.

Some neutron stars emit bursts, or pulses, of radio waves. These stars are called *pulsars.* In the Crab nebula, astronomers have found a pulsar that gives off radio waves and flashes of light. Other pulsars emit x-rays.

After its explosion as a supernova, a large part of a star—perhaps three times or more as massive as our sun—may still remain and begin to collapse. Eventually it may become even smaller than a neutron star and have a gravitational force so strong that light cannot escape from its surface. As a result, the star will simply disappear. The result is a *black hole.* Of course, black holes cannot be observed directly, but their existence can be inferred from the way they affect visible stars nearby. The gravitational attraction of a black hole makes its visible neighbor move abnormally. Astronomers believe a black hole may be present in the constellation Cygnus, although it is difficult to prove that black holes exist.

Other phenomena

The heavens include many different types of phenomena. Astronomers have observed that two stars often revolve around each other because of their gravitational attraction. These stars are called *binary* stars. If more than two are involved, they are called *multiple* stars.

Stars known as *cepheid variables* glow lighter and darker according to a definite pattern. The cepheids have been helpful in calculating the distances to stars that are too far away to allow for the use of the parallax method. Astronomers have discovered that the absolute magnitude of a cepheid is directly related to the time interval between its bright and dark periods. By comparing absolute magnitude to apparent magnitude, they can calculate the distance to a cepheid, or to a galaxy with a cepheid. The distance to the Andromeda galaxy was determined in this way.

During the 1960s, astronomers observed faint stars that emitted radio waves. They called these star-like objects *quasars,* short for quasi-stellar radio sources. Astronomers estimate that quasars are bil-lions of light-years away. Since they still appear to us as faint stars even at this distance, it must mean that they are many times brighter than our sun. As yet there is no accepted theory to explain quasars. A quasar may be the center of a dense galaxy, or it may have giant stars.

Astronomers are still puzzled by quasars, but they think that pulsars are neutron stars. The pulses of the first one discovered were so regular that some astronomers thought at first that they were signals sent by intelligent life-forms millions of years away.

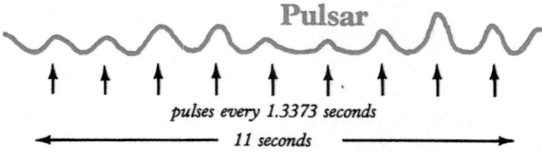

Pulsar

pulses every 1.3373 seconds

11 seconds

Cosmology

Cosmology is the study of the way the universe as a whole is organized, how it began, and what will eventually happen to it. One of the most important events in the history of cosmology occurred during the 1920s. The American astronomer Edwin Hubble discovered that the universe is expanding. Evidence for this was provided by the so-called *red shift*. Stars moving away from us appear to emit longer waves of light. In other words, the light is shifted toward the red end of the spectrum. Stars approaching us seem to give off shorter waves of light.

Hubble observed that light from distant galaxies is shifted in its wavelength toward the red; the farther away the galaxy, the greater the shift. Apparently, the galaxies—including our own—are receding from one another, and those most distant from us are traveling the fastest. The situation can be likened to the effect of inflating a ball. As the ball expands, all the points on it move farther apart.

How did the expansion of the universe begin? Some astronomers theorize that all matter was concentrated in a huge ball that exploded. This idea is called the *big-bang* theory. It postulates that the explosion is still occurring, which accounts for the continuous expansion of the universe that Hubble observed.

As a result of evidence discovered over the past two decades, the big-bang theory is now widely accepted. Calculations show that the universe is 15 to 20 billion years old. In 1965, scientists working at Bell Laboratories discovered a type of radiation coming from the universe. This is exactly the form of radiation that would remain following a giant explosion to form the universe.

Origins of solar system.
For centuries scientists have speculated about the origins of our solar system. One theory, formulated during the eighteenth century, was called the *nebular hypothesis*. This stated that the sun was originally a nebula of gases whirling in space. As the nebula condensed, it spun more and more rapidly, becoming a flat disk. Eventually the disk began to discharge rings of material that condensed to become the planets. If this theory were accurate, we might expect the sun to be still revolving at very high velocities. But it is not. In addition, the rings of gaseous material would expand, not contract. Consequently, this theory was rejected.

As the universe expands, the galaxies become farther apart, like points on a vast inflating balloon.

Other scientists proposed the *close-encounter* theory. They speculated that at some point in the past, the sun had encountered another huge body and created enormous turbulence within the gaseous material that constitutes the sun. They further speculated that some of the material was ejected and later condensed to become the planets. A major flaw in the theory is that the material could not have been pulled out with enough force to produce planets at such great distances from the sun as Pluto.

The currently accepted theory about the origins of the solar system is a variation of the nebular hypothesis. Scientists now believe that a huge nebula contracted and slowly started to rotate. A large whirlpool inside the nebula eventually condensed and became the sun. Smaller whirlpools, known as protoplanets, formed and broke away. These contracted to produce the planets. A planet's gravitational force might be strong enough to hold tiny eddies around it in place. These eddies condensed to form the satellites.

Space exploration

Many people think that the age of space exploration began with the launch of the first space vehicles in the 1950s and 1960s. In fact, astronomers, using only the naked eye or a telescope, had been exploring the universe long before the beginning of space flight. To this day, telescopes are still the primary means of learning more about the universe, its galaxies, and our solar system.

Telescopes. Galileo constructed the first optical telescope used for astronomy in 1609. Since then, astronomical telescopes have grown much larger and more complex. Still, there are only two basic types of optical telescopes: refracting and reflecting.

Refracting telescopes. This type of telescope is generally a long tube with an objective lens at one end and an eyepiece at the other. The objective lens gathers light and focuses an image in front of the eyepiece at a point called the focus. The eyepiece acts like a magnifying glass, enlarging the image at the focus for the eye to see.

Reflecting telescopes. A reflecting telescope uses mirrors to capture and magnify an image. Light passes down a tube to the mirror, which gathers the light and focuses it to form an image. The image is often reflected on another mirror to an eyepiece on the side of the tube.

Until the end of the 19th century, the largest telescopes were the refracting type. However, there is a practical limit to the size of an objective lens. Above a diameter of about 40 inches, the glass becomes very thick, and the thickness begins to limit the amount of light that passes through the lens.

Therefore, the largest optical telescopes today are reflecting. Not only can mirrors be made larger without loss of image, but several mirrors can be combined to create an even more powerful telescope.

Astronomers can learn much from direct observation of stars and planets. Details of the surfaces of the closest celestial objects, the planets, can be discerned using powerful optical telescopes. Astronomers can also track the movement of stars and planets, plotting their positions and determining their effects on one another.

A great deal can also be learned about the sun and the stars by analyzing the light a star emits. The light that reaches Earth from a star is made up of a spectrum of light of different colors. (See page 381 for a more complete discussion of the light spectrum.) Different patterns in the spectrum of a star can provide information about its chemical compo-

Telescopes

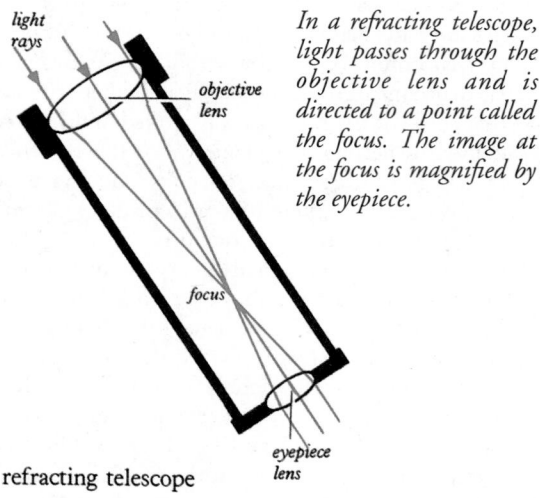

In a refracting telescope, light passes through the objective lens and is directed to a point called the focus. The image at the focus is magnified by the eyepiece.

refracting telescope

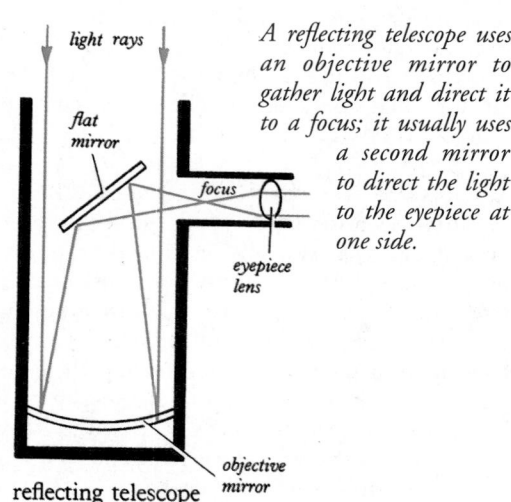

A reflecting telescope uses an objective mirror to gather light and direct it to a focus; it usually uses a second mirror to direct the light to the eyepiece at one side.

reflecting telescope

sition, and shifts in the colors in the spectrum can indicate the velocity and direction of the movement of a star.

Radio telescopes. These telescopes are used to detect radio waves. Radio waves are given off naturally by many different bodies in the universe. By studying the waves, astronomers have made important discoveries about stars, distant galaxies, quasars, pulsars, and other mysteries of the universe.

There are many different kinds of radio telescopes. One of the most common is similar to, though much larger than, the satellite dishes that people use to receive television signals. Often, astronomers will connect many such dishes together in a long line, or even in different parts of the world, in order to achieve images of greater detail and precision.

Telescopes in space. Earth's atmosphere causes distortion in the images received by telescopes on the ground. Placing telescopes in orbit aboard satellites eliminates the interference that the atmosphere causes. The most famous orbiting telescope is the Hubble Space Telescope, which was placed into orbit in 1990. After a 1993 space shuttle mission repaired flaws in the telescope's main mirror that had greatly reduced its effectiveness, the Hubble telescope began providing the best images ever made of deep-space objects.

In 1993 the Hubble Space Telescope was repaired by the crew of the space shuttle Endeavour, *greatly improving the quality of its images.*

Scientists have also learned a great deal about the universe by using orbiting telescopes that detect infrared waves, X-rays, and gamma rays.

The two most common types of telescopes used by astronomers are optical and radio. These dish antennae are part of the Very Large Array radio telescope in New Mexico.

Planetary space probes.

Much has also been learned about the solar system and its planets from the information returned to Earth by interplanetary probes. Probes are unmanned space capsules that carry photographic and sensing equipment as well as equipment that transmits information back to Earth.

From the beginning of the space age, both the United States and the Soviet Union were active in the exploration of the solar system using probes. Indeed, the competition between the two countries was a spur to both their space programs, since neither wanted the other to be first in the accomplishment of space feats.

The moon. The United States sent four different series of probes to the moon. The first, four Pioneer probes launched in 1958 and 1959, was not notably successful in returning information about the moon. The remaining three programs were designed to return information that would be useful to the manned Apollo lunar missions.

Nine Ranger probes were launched from 1961 to 1965. They were designed to return photographs of the surface of the moon during the few minutes before the probe would crash into the surface. The first six Ranger missions were unsuccessful; however, *Ranger 7, 8,* and *9* returned thousands of photos of the moon's surface.

The five Lunar Orbiter probes were designed to remain in orbit around the moon and photograph its surface, focusing particularly on areas of interest to the Apollo program. In all, the Orbiter craft were able to map about 95 percent of the surface of the moon.

Surveyor, a series of seven missions launched from 1966 to 1968, was the first U.S. probe designed to soft-land on the moon. Although two of the missions were unsuccessful, the others sent back thousands of photos and performed tests of the soil, temperature, and the effects of the sun's radiation on the moon's surface.

During this time the Soviet Union was also sending probes to the moon. The Luna series of 24 missions lasted from 1959 until 1976. Many of the early milestones in lunar exploration were first achieved by Luna craft. They were the first to pass near the moon, impact on it, return photographs of it, soft-land on it, and take soil samples and return them to Earth.

Venus. Both the Soviet Union and the United States have sent many probes to Venus. The first Venus probe was the Soviet *Venera 1;* however, the probe missed the planet, and radio contact was lost. The first probe to reach the planet was *Mariner 2,* launched by the United States in 1962. It con-

firmed the planet's high surface temperature and established that Venus has no magnetic field or radiation belt.

In all, the Soviet Union sent 13 Venera probes to Venus, beginning in 1961 and ending in 1983. Some of these craft were orbiters and some landed on the surface. In 1985 the Halley's comet probes *Vega 1* and *Vega 2* dropped a total of four probes, two landers and two atmospheric balloons, during a flyby of Venus.

Two more Mariner missions visited Venus, *Mariner 5* in 1967 and *Mariner 10* in 1974. They provided information about the planet's atmosphere. Two Pioneer Venus craft reached Venus in 1978, orbiting the planet and sending probes to the surface. The Magellan probe, which reached the planet in 1990, used radar to map the entire planet.

Mars. The Mariner program also sent four missions to Mars. *Mariner 4, 6,* and *7* were flyby visits designed to take and transmit photographs back to Earth. *Mariner 9* became the first probe to orbit another planet when it reached Mars in 1971. The probe took thousands of pictures and mapped the entire surface of the planet. From 1971 to 1973 the Soviet Union sent a series of Mars probes to the planet, but they were not particularly successful in sending back information to Earth.

The most successful missions to Mars were the *Viking 1* and *2* orbiter-lander combinations. The landers set down on the surface in 1976 and continued to transmit data for 6 and 4 years, respectively. They analyzed soil and atmosphere, monitored the weather, tested for the presence of life, and returned images of the surface. The orbiters returned over 50,000 photographs of the planet.

Two Mars rovers, *Spirit* and *Opportunity,* launched in 2003, landed on the planet's surface in January 2004. The rovers sent back geologic data and dramatic photographs which indicated to scientists the probability of the presence of water previously. The mission was extended several times.

The outer planets. Two pairs of very important probes have taught us a great deal about the planets beyond the asteroid belt. *Pioneer 10,* launched in 1972, and *Pioneer 11,* launched in 1973, became the first interplanetary craft to visit one of the outer planets. *Pioneer 10* returned hundreds of images of Jupiter and its moons and carried instruments to study cosmic radiation and other phenomena. *Pioneer 10* passed beyond Jupiter and in 1984 became the first man-made object to leave the solar system. *Pioneer 11,* after transmitting images of Jupiter, traveled on to become the first probe to visit Saturn.

But even these two hugely successful missions were dwarfed by the success of the next two Voyager missions. Both probes encountered Jupiter in 1979; *Voyager 1* went on to fly by Saturn in 1980. *Voyager 2* passed Saturn in 1981 and went on to encounter Uranus in 1986 and Neptune in 1989. The astonishingly clear images of these planets and their satellites captured the imaginations of scientists and amateur astronomers the world over.

In 1989 the U.S. launched Galileo, which took up orbit around Jupiter in 1995. Galileo's mission ended in 2003, after being extended multiple times, orbiting Jupiter 35 times, and transmitting more than 14,000 images of Jupiter and its moons.

In 2004 the U.S. orbiter Cassini delivered the Huygens probe, provided by the European Space Agency, to Titan, a moon of Saturn. It continued its orbit of Saturn, returning spectacular photos of the planet's rings and moons. Two new moons were identified.

Highlights of Unmanned Space Probes

The Voyager space probe (above right) *visited Jupiter, Saturn, Uranus, and Neptune and sent back valuable information. The Viking lander missions sent back images of the surface of Mars* (above).

1964	**Ranger 7** (U.S.). Photographs the moon.
	Mariner 4 (U.S.). Photographs Mars from 6,000 miles away.
1965	**A-1 Diamant** (France). First French satellite is in orbit.
1967	**Mariner 5** (U.S.). Passes within 2,500 miles of Venus.
1969	**Mariner 6** (U.S.). Passes within 2,000 miles of Mars.
1970	**Ohsumi** (Japan). Satellite is placed in orbit.
1971	**Mariner 9** (U.S.). Orbits Mars.
1972	**Pioneer 10** (U.S.). Passes Jupiter; becomes the first man-made object to leave the solar system.
1973	**Mariner 10** (U.S.). Reaches Mercury.
1976	**Viking 1** (U.S.). Lands on the surface of Mars.
1977	**Voyager 1** (U.S.). Passes Jupiter and then Saturn.
	Voyager 2 (U.S.). Passes Jupiter, Saturn, and Uranus.
1978	**Pioneer Venus 1** (U.S.). Enters orbit of Venus.
	Pioneer Venus 2 (U.S.). Probes reach the surface of Venus.
1984	**Ariane 3** (European Space Agency). Launch vehicle developed by French scientist deploys two satellites.
1985	**Giotto** (European Space Agency). Passes within 335 miles of Halley's comet's nucleus.
1990	**Hubble Space Telescope** (U.S., European Space Agency). Greatly enhances the resolution for viewing stars.
	Magellan (U.S.). Orbits Venus, provides detailed radar mapping of the planet's surface.
	Ulysses (U.S., European Space Agency). Launched to study the sun's poles in 1994 and 1995.
1995	**Galileo** (U.S.). Enters orbit of Jupiter to study the planet's atmosphere and moons.
1997	**Mars Pathfinder** (U.S.). Sends back soil analyses and 16,000 photos of Martian surface.
2000	**Image** (U.S.). Launched to study Earth's magnetosphere's response to changes in solar wind.
2004	**Spirit/Opportunity** (U.S.). Mars rovers landed to study planet's geology, sending back data and photographs.
	Cassini (U.S.). Enters orbit of Saturn and begins providing dramatic photos of its rings and moons.

Manned space flights.

The first manned flight took place on April 12, 1961, when Yuri Gagarin went into orbit in the Soviet *Vostok 1* spacecraft. Gagarin made one revolution of Earth; his total flight time was 1 hour, 48 minutes.

On May 5, 1961, the United States sent up its first astronaut, Alan B. Shepard, Jr. In a Mercury capsule boosted by a Redstone launch vehicle, Shepard made a suborbital, 15-minute flight that took him to an altitude of 117 miles.

Vostok (U.S.S.R.). Vostok was a cylindrical spacecraft weighing slightly more than 5 tons. It was an elementary one-man vehicle designed to prove man's survivability in space. It was lowered to Earth by parachute after reentry. The cosmonaut ejected at a low altitude and parachuted separately. The Vostok program consisted of six flights between 1961 and 1963, including the first manned flight, the first missions of more than 24 hours in space *(Vostok 2)*, and the first piloted by a woman *(Vostok 6)*.

Mercury (U.S.). Like Vostok, Mercury was an elementary spacecraft designed only for the initial steps of manned spaceflight. Mercury was a bell-shaped capsule. Its weight was about 3,000 pounds, varying slightly with each mission. The small capsules used parachutes during their descent inside the atmosphere before splashing down in the ocean, where the astronaut and capsule were recovered by U.S. ships and helicopters. The program consisted of six flights between 1961 and 1963, two of them suborbital and the rest orbital. The program included the first U.S. orbital flight *(Mercury-Atlas 6)* and the first flight of more than 24 hours by a U.S. spacecraft *(Mercury-Atlas 9)*.

Voskhod (U.S.S.R.). The second-generation Soviet manned spacecraft Voskhod made only two flights (1964–1965), but it represented a considerable advance over its predecessor. Voskhod's first flight, on October 12, 1964, marked the first multiman space mission. A crew of three made the 24-hour flight. The second flight, on March 18 and 19, 1965, was notable because the copilot, Alexei Leonov, became the first space walker. He spent 10 minutes outside the spacecraft in a special multi-layered extravehicular suit.

Gemini (U.S.). The United States' second-generation manned spacecraft Gemini offered a great many improvements over Mercury. Among the most important, it was a two-man craft and was maneuverable. All previous manned spacecraft had been unable to change course.

The first Gemini was launched March 23, 1965, and the program continued through ten manned flights; the last was launched November 11, 1966. The program included a number of highlights: the

The Gemini spacecraft were a great improvement over the earlier Mercury craft.

first orbital maneuvering by a manned spacecraft *(Gemini 3)*; the first U.S. multiman flight *(Gemini 3)*; the first U.S. space walk *(Gemini 4)*; a flight of exceptionally long duration—330 hours and 30 minutes—for that time *(Gemini 7)*; the first rendezvous between two spacecraft *(Gemini 6 and 7)*; the first docking in space *(Gemini 8)*.

Soyuz (U.S.S.R.). In 1967 the Soviet Union introduced its third-generation manned spacecraft, Soyuz. The first flight, on April 23 of that year, ended tragically when the parachute descent system failed, killing Vladimir Komarov, the first man to die during a space mission. Soyuz was the first Soviet manned spacecraft capable of maneuvering, rendezvousing, and docking. It is also capable of almost unlimited time in space. Among the highlights of the Soyuz program are the first Soviet rendezvous and docking (the manned *Soyuz 3* docked with an unmanned *Soyuz 2*); the first transfer of men from one spacecraft in orbit to another *(Soyuz 4 and 5)*; and the first triple launch and rendezvous of manned spacecraft *(Soyuz 6, 7, and 8)*.

International space station

During a space walk in December 1998, astronauts Jerry Ross and Jim Newman worked on the Russian-made module Zarya. *The linking of the Russian module with the* U.S. Unity *module* (lower left) *marked the beginning of the station's construction, which was scheduled to continue for 5 years. Twelve other countries, including Japan, Canada, and the member nations of the European Space Agency, worked with the United States and Russia to build the station.*

Soyuz 11 was part of a three-spacecraft experiment in space station development. The first segment, a prototype space laboratory called *Salyut 1,* was sent into orbit unmanned on April 19, 1971. *Soyuz 10,* launched April 22 and carrying a three-man crew, docked with *Salyut* and the cosmonauts transferred to the laboratory, where they conducted experiments for almost 2 days. They returned to Earth in *Soyuz 10.* On June 7, *Soyuz 11* docked with *Salyut.* Its three astronauts worked in the laboratory for 23 days, but they died during their return flight to Earth.

In later Soyuz flights, the Soviets continued docking maneuvers with Salyut space stations and conducting experiments. During 1984, Russian astronauts sent aloft in a Soyuz mission set a then record of 237 days for space endurance.

In the 1980s the Soviet space program was centered on the development of a permanently manned space station. The *Mir* space station was launched in 1986 and continued to function into 2000, well past its planned life span. With six docking ports, *Mir* had a much greater capacity for expansion than the Salyut stations.

In 1988 the Soviet Union completed *Buran,* a craft similar to the U.S. space shuttle. *Buran* made one unmanned orbital flight but funding cuts halted the program permanently.

Apollo (U.S.). Apollo, the third generation of U.S. manned spacecraft, represented a great advance, as demonstrated in repeated lunar landings. Apollo included a command module; the reentry capsule, which also served as crew quarters and command post; the lunar module, in which two of the three astronauts descended to the lunar surface; and the service module, a jettisonable segment that contained much of the fuel, expendables, and other equipment. The lunar module had separate descent and ascent engines for its trip to the lunar surface.

The first manned Apollo mission *(Apollo 7),* an 11-day Earth-orbital flight, was flown October 11–21, 1968. The highlight of the program was the first manned lunar landing, on July 20, 1969. *Apollo 11* astronauts Neil A. Armstrong and Edwin A. (Buzz) Aldrin were the first men to set foot on the moon. There were six Apollo landings on the moon before the program was concluded.

Skylab (U.S.). Skylab used modified Apollo hardware to create a prototype manned space station. Skylab was a large orbital laboratory weighing close to 85 tons. Its major elements were a large workshop with laboratory and living quarters, an astronomical observatory, and a docking port for manned spacecraft.

Skylab was launched on May 14, 1973, as a single unmanned unit. On May 25, 1973, the *Skylab 1* astronauts—Charles Conrad, Jr., Joseph P. Kerwin, and Paul J. Wertz—were launched to the space station for a 28-day stay in space.

On July 28, 1973, the *Skylab 2* astronauts— Alan L. Bean, Jack R. Lousma, and Owen K. Garriott—set out to link up with the station. After being in space for 59 days, they returned on September 25, 1973. The astronauts brought back 77,600 pictures of the sun's corona, 14,000 pictures of Earth, and 18 miles of magnetic tape data.

Space shuttle (U.S.). On April 12, 1981, the space shuttle *Columbia* was launched from Cape Canaveral, Florida, on its first journey into space. Two astronauts, John Young and Robert Crippin, piloted the vehicle through 36 orbits of Earth at 200 miles above the surface. After 54 hours, *Columbia* touched down safely on a runway at Edwards Air Force base in California.

The space shuttle is about the size of a DC-9 airplane, 122 feet long with a wingspan of 78 feet. The plane is linked to an external fuel tank and two solid-fuel booster rockets. On launch, the boosters provide 2,650,000 pounds of thrust for 2 minutes. Afterward, the booster rockets fall away into the ocean, from which they are recovered and reused. The shuttle receives liquid fuel from the external tank until the tank is ejected about 8 minutes into the flight. After the shuttle finishes orbiting Earth and reenters the atmosphere, it glides downward toward the surface. When its journey is complete, the vehicle can be refueled and prepared for another trip.

The space shuttle has been designed for a variety of uses. With its large cargo hold, it can carry a satellite and place it in space. In fact, over the years, a primary purpose of the shuttle has been to place communications satellites in orbit around Earth.

Following the explosion of the space shuttle *Challenger* in 1986, the program's schedule was delayed pending a thorough investigation. The program was resumed with a successful launching in September 1988. Eighty-seven successful shuttle missions were completed between 1988 and the end of 2002. Space shuttle crews began assembling the new International Space Station at the end of 1998.

Fifteen of the subsequent nineteen shuttle missions were in support of the space station, primarily through assembly assistance. In January 2003 the program suffered another loss when the space shuttle *Columbia* exploded on reentry after a 16-day mission. Further shuttle missions were suspended until safety and program deficiencies, determined by a subsequent investigation, could be addressed.

Shenzhou (China). On October 14, 2003, China launched its first manned spacecraft, which orbited Earth 14 times during a voyage that lasted approximately 21 hours. Though not ground-breaking, this accomplishment fulfilled the country's program of manned space flight that began in the early 1970s but was abandoned until the early 1990s.

Space shuttle

A large part of a space shuttle's length is taken up by its 60-foot payload bay. The payload bay can carry satellites to be placed in orbit, a special module containing a laboratory in which astronauts can perform experiments, or other cargo. At the front of the ship is the cockpit from which the shuttle is controlled; on the lower level are the crew quarters.

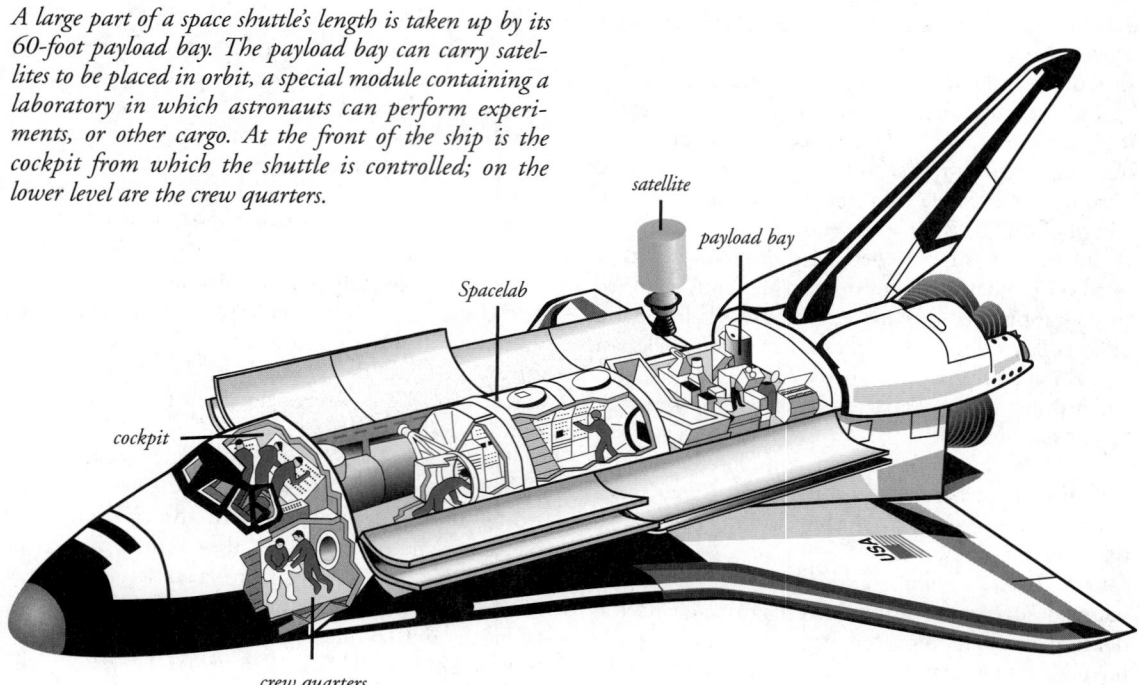

satellite

payload bay

Spacelab

cockpit

crew quarters

Memorable Moments of Manned Space Missions

The Apollo moon landings, during which astronauts walked on the surface of the moon, are considered by many to be the most important achievement in the history of space exploration.

1961   Vostok 1 (U.S.S.R.). Yuri Gagarin is the first to orbit the Earth.
           Mercury 3 (U.S.). Alan Shepard becomes the first American in space.
1962   Mercury 6 (U.S.). John Glenn is the first American to orbit Earth.
1963   Vostok 6 (U.S.S.R.). Valentina Tereshkova becomes the first woman in space.
1965   Voskhod 2 (U.S.S.R.). A cosmonaut is the first to leave a spacecraft for a space walk.
           Gemini 3 (U.S.). Becomes first manned spacecraft to maneuver out of its regular orbital path.
1967   Apollo 1 (U.S.). Launchpad fire kills Virgil Grissom, Edward White, and Roger Chafee.
           Soyuz 1 (U.S.S.R.). Cosmonaut is killed when parachute fails during reentry.
1968   Apollo 8 (U.S.). First manned flight orbits moon.
1969   Soyuz 5 (U.S.S.R.). Crew members transfer to *Soyuz 4* after space docking.
           Apollo 11 (U.S.). First manned moon landing; Neil Armstrong and Edwin Aldrin walk on moon.
1971   Apollo 14 (U.S.). Astronauts explore the surface of the moon for 9 hours.
           Soyuz 11 (U.S.S.R.). Docks with Salyut space station; craft orbit Earth together for 23 days; crew of three is killed during reentry.
1973   Skylab 2 (U.S.). Mission established Skylab in Earth's orbit; crew conducts experiments aboard Skylab.
1975   Apollo 18 (U.S.) and Soyuz 19 (U.S.S.R.). After docking, U.S. and Soviet crews cooperate in experiments.
1979   Soyuz 34 (U.S.S.R.). Launched unmanned and returns with the crew from the *Salyut 6* space station.
1981   Space shuttle Columbia (U.S.). Reusable spacecraft enters space for first time and returns safely.
1982   Space shuttle Columbia (U.S.). Deploys satellites from its payload.
1983   Space shuttle Challenger (U.S.). Sally Ride becomes the first American woman in space.
           Remote Manipulator Structure (mechanical arm) retrieves a satellite.
1984   Space shuttle Challenger (U.S.). Jet-propelled backpacks allow astronauts to fly free of their spacecraft.
1986   Space shuttle Challenger (U.S.). Explodes shortly after launch, killing crew of seven.
           Soyuz T15 (U.S.S.R.). Launches a new space station, *Mir*, into Earth's orbit.
1988   Space shuttle Discovery (U.S.). Shuttle program resumes with a successful mission.
1989   Space shuttle Atlantis (U.S.). Launches Magellan radar-mapping spacecraft to Venus.
           Space shuttle Atlantis (U.S.). Launches Galileo probe to Jupiter.
1990   Space shuttle Discovery (U.S.). Shuttle places the Hubble Space Telescope in orbit.
1991   Space shuttle Discovery (U.S.). Launches the Gamma Ray Observatory.
1993   Space shuttle Endeavour (U.S.). Repairs Hubble telescope in space.
1995   Space shuttle Atlantis (U.S.). Successfully docks with Russian space station *Mir*, is 100th U.S. manned mission.
2000   Space shuttle Atlantis (U.S.). Successfully launches International Space Station living quarters.
2003   Space shuttle Columbia (U.S.). Explodes during reentry, killing crew of seven.
           Shenzhou 5 (China). Orbits Earth carrying Yang Liwei, making China only the third country to send a human into space.

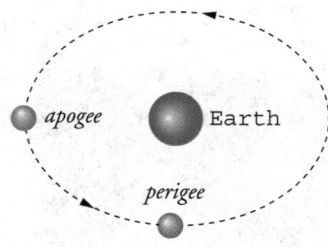

apogee/perigee

Dictionary of space science

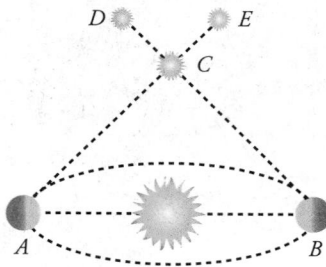

parallax

satellite

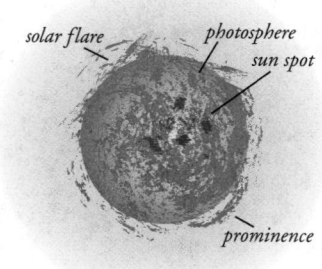

sun

absolute magnitude. Apparent brightness of a star viewed from a distance of 32.6 light-years.

active satellite. Communications satellite that includes equipment to rebroadcast radio or television signals.

albedo. Amount of light reflected by a heavenly body that does not produce its own light.

altitude of a star. Angle of a star above the horizon.

angular resolution. A measure of the sharpness of an image obtained by a telescope.

aperture. Diameter of the objective lens or the primary mirror of a telescope. The larger the aperture, the better its light-gathering power and angular resolution.

aphelion. Point in a planet's orbit when it is at the greatest distance from the sun.

apogee. Point in the orbit of a satellite when it is farthest from Earth.

apparent magnitude. Brightness of a star as it appears to us on Earth.

artificial satellite. Object that is placed into orbit around Earth or some other body in space.

asteroids. Small planetlike bodies that orbit the sun.

astronaut. Name given by the United States to a traveler in a spacecraft.

astronautics. Scientific study of the principles and technology of space travel.

astronomical unit. Unit of measurement equal to the mean distance from the sun to Earth, about 93,000,000 miles.

astrophysics. Study of the physics and evolution of the universe.

aurora. Colorful display of light caused by solar radiation that occurs at the poles.

big-bang theory. Theory stating that the universe was created when a large mass of matter exploded.

binary stars. Two stars that orbit around each other because of their gravitational attraction.

black hole. Very dense object that may form from an exploded star. A black hole does not emit light.

Bode's law. Series of numbers equivalent to the approximate distances of the planets from the sun.

booster. Rocket used to propel a vehicle other than the rocket itself.

capsule. Type of spacecraft that has just enough room for one or two persons.

cepheid variable. Type of pulsating star that glows with varying amounts of intensity.

chromosphere. Lowest level of the sun's atmosphere.

close-encounter theory. Theory that states that the solar system was formed when the sun encountered another huge body. This event caused the sun to eject gaseous material that formed the planets.

cluster. Close grouping of stars of the same age. *Globular clusters* are spherical groupings of stars found in galaxies that contain up to several hundred thousand stars. Large groupings of galaxies are also called clusters.

color index. Number that indicates the color of a star. It is equal to the difference between the magnitude of a star measured in blue light and one measured in yellow light.

coma. Bright head of a comet.

comet. Mass of frozen gases orbiting the sun. On approaching the sun, the comet's material begins to melt and glow.

command module. Part of the Apollo system that remained in orbit around the moon while the lunar module landed.

communications satellite. Satellite used to relay signals from one point on Earth to another.

conjunction. One of two planetary configurations. The *superior conjunction* is the one in which the sun is between Earth and a planet. The *inferior conjunction* occurs when a planet is between Earth and the sun.

constellation. Apparent grouping of stars named after a mythical character.

corona. Outer layer of the sun's atmosphere.

cosmic background radiation. Microwave radiation coming from all directions in the universe. It is believed to be a remnant of the big bang.

cosmic radiation. Vast stream of atomic nuclei and electrons moving at very high speeds that reach Earth from all directions.

cosmology. Study of the general structure, origin, and development of the universe.

cosmonaut. Name given by the Soviet Union to a traveler in a space vehicle.

docking. Linking two spacecraft.

Doppler effect. Apparent change in the wavelength of radiation owing to the motion of the source and the observer.

Doppler tracking. Technique used to chart the progress of space probes. The changing frequency of the radio waves received from a spacecraft is measured to determine the craft's position and velocity in the solar system.

Earthshine. Light seen from Earth that is caused by the reflection of sunlight to the moon from the surface of Earth. It is a faint illumination of the moon's surface most easily seen when the moon is a crescent.

eclipse. Darkening of one celestial body when its light is cut off by another.

ecliptic. Apparent path of the sun among the stars.

ephemeris. Published table of the daily positions of the sun, moon, planets, artificial satellites, and selected stars. It also provides other data necessary for astronomical and navigational observations.

equinox. Two times of the year (March 21 and September 23) when day and night are of equal length.

escape velocity. Velocity required for a spacecraft to overcome the gravity of Earth or any other body in the solar system.

event horizon. Boundary of the region around a black hole from which no light or matter can escape.

extravehicular activity. Activity outside a spacecraft that has left the atmosphere of Earth.

field stars. Stars in our galaxy that are found outside stellar clusters.

free fall. Any condition in which the force of gravity is not opposed by another force. In space, free fall occurs when the propulsion system of a space vehicle is turned off.

galactic halo. Region surrounding a galaxy filled with gas and globular clusters that appears to glow.

galaxy. Giant system of stars, dust, and gas.

geosynchronous orbit. Orbit used for communications satellites in which the satellite stays at the same place over Earth's surface.

Hertzsprung-Russell diagram. Chart that compares a star's absolute magnitude and its spectral class.

interstellar matter. Dust and gas found between the stars.

jet aircraft. Aircraft propelled by heating air to produce a stream of particles that gives the aircraft thrust.

jettison. Release part of a space vehicle so that it does not continue on a mission.

Jovian planets. Planets with orbits beyond that of Mars: Jupiter, Saturn, Uranus, Neptune, and Pluto.

Kepler's law of equal areas. One of the laws of planetary motion that the astronomer Kepler deduced from studying the planets. Kepler found that the path of a planet is such that a line from the sun to the planet sweeps out equal areas in equal times.

Lagrange point. The point between two celestial bodies at which the gravitational pulls of the two bodies on a third body cancel each other out.

launch vehicle. Rocket used to lift a satellite or probe into space.

libration. The oscillation in the motion of a celestial body traveling about another body.

light-year. Distance light travels in a year—about 6 trillion miles.

lunar module. In the Apollo program, the vehicle that landed on the moon.

magnitude. The brightness of a star or other celestial object. *Apparent magnitude* is the brightness of a star as it appears to an observer on

Earth. *Absolute magnitude* is the apparent magnitude that a star would have if it were observed from a distance of 10 parsecs.

mare. Latin word for sea that refers to a dark area on the moon. Plural is maria.

meteor. Light produced by a meteoroid after entering Earth's atmosphere.

meteorite. Meteor that strikes Earth's surface.

meteoroid. Solid particle traveling through space.

meteor shower. Large group of falling meteors.

Milky Way. Galaxy in which our solar system is located.

nebula. Originally thought to be great clouds of dust and gas, but better telescopes revealed that many nebulae were actually vast collections of stars. Today the word "nebula" is generally replaced by "galaxy" for patches in the sky that resolve into stars. Consequently, the old meaning of "nebula" has returned, but sometimes well-known galaxies, such as Andromeda, are still called "nebula."

nebular hypothesis. Theory that states that the solar system was formed from a nebula of gases whirling in space.

neutron star. Very dense star composed of neutrons.

nova. Star that flares from obscurity to great brilliance and then sinks back to obscurity. *See also* **supernova.**

objective lens. Lens mounted at the front end of a telescope. It gathers light from a celestial object and focuses it in front of the eyepiece.

occultation. The hiding of one celestial body by another. Eclipses of a star or planet by the moon are occultations.

orbit. Travel in a closed path around some body in space; the path of a revolving body.

A *heliocentric orbit* is an orbit with the sun as its center.

parallax. Distance an object appears to move when viewed from two different locations.

parsec. Distance equivalent to 3.26 light-years.

passive satellite. Communications satellite from which radio or television signals can be reflected.

penumbra. Part of a shadow that is partly lighted, as during an eclipse.

perigee. Point in the orbit of a satellite when it is nearest Earth.

perihelion. Point in a planet's orbit when it is closest to the sun.

period (of an orbiting body). Amount of time for one orbit.

perturbation. Disturbance in the orbit of a celestial body caused by the gravitational force of another body. Perturbations in the orbit of Uranus led to the discovery of Neptune and Pluto.

photosphere. Surface of the sun.

plasma. Gas that is almost completely ionized, that is, one or more electrons are split off each atom. Most of the matter in the universe, such as that inside stars, is plasma.

primary. Larger object around which a smaller object revolves. In a binary star, the primary is the larger of the two stars.

probe. Unmanned spacecraft that is not put into orbit around Earth.

prominence. Cloudlike structure that appears as a bright flame above the sun.

pulsar. Celestial body that emits pulses of light and radio waves.

quasar. Quasi-stellar radio source; a celestial body similar to a star that is intensely bright.

radiation belt. Zone around a planet that contains high-speed charged particles. The radiation belts around Earth are called *Van Allen belts.*

radio telescope. Device for collecting radio waves emitted from space.

red shift. Shift toward the red end of the spectrum caused by a body moving away from an observer.

reentry. Return to the atmosphere of Earth from space.

remote manipulator system. U.S. space shuttle's mechanical arm. It is used mainly for deploying and retrieving satellites.

retrograde motion. Motion in the opposite direction of Earth's rotation.

revolution. Orbital motion of a planet or satellite about its primary.

Roche's limit. Closest point to which a satellite can approach its primary without being pulled apart by the tidal effects of the gravitational fields of the primary.

rocket. Device that internally generates a stream of gases or particles to propel itself.

rotation. Turning of an object on its axis.

satellite. Small body orbiting a larger one.

scintillation. Irregular variation in the brightness of a star caused by variations in the density of the clouds of gases in Earth's atmosphere. This makes stars appear to twinkle.

solar flare. Explosion on the sun's surface.

solar wind. Electrically charged particles emitted by the corona.

solstices. Two points at which the sun is at its maximum distance from the equator. These two points correspond to the longest and shortest days of the year.

space station. Satellite designed for long-term use by several different teams.

space transportation system. Official name of the space shuttle.

spectroscope. Instrument that breaks down light into its colors.

spectrum. Band of different wavelengths that has been produced by separating the light or other electromagnetic radiation.

suborbital. Space mission that leaves the atmosphere but returns to Earth without going into orbit.

sunspot. Dark area of relatively cool temperatures on the sun's surface.

supercluster. Cluster of clusters of galaxies.

supernova. Exceptionally bright nova caused by the explosion of a star during the final stage of its development.

terrestrial planets. Planets with orbits within the orbit of Jupiter: Mercury, Venus, Earth, and Mars.

trajectory. Path that a rocket or spacecraft takes, especially the path after the propulsion engine has been jettisoned and the spacecraft is in free fall.

transit. Passing of a planet between Earth and the sun so that the planet can be seen crossing the face of the sun.

umbra. Darkest part of a shadow, as in an eclipse.

Van Allen belt. *See* radiation belt.

Vernier engine. Small motor used to steer booster rockets during flight or a spacecraft attempting to land on a planet.

wane. Decrease in brightness.

wax. Increase in brightness.

For Further Reference

Asimov, Isaac
The Universe
Walker and Co.

Chetty, P. R. K.
Satellite Technology and Its Applications
TAB Books

Jastrow, Robert
Red Giants and White Dwarfs
Harper & Row

Pasachoff, Jay M. and Menzel, Donald H.
A Field Guide to the Stars and Planets
Houghton Mifflin

Sagan, Carl
Cosmos
Random House

Shipman, Harry L.
Humans in Space: Twenty-First Century Frontiers
Plenum Press

Smith, Arthur
Planetary Exploration
Patrick Stevens

Spangenburg, Ray and Moser, Diane
Opening the Space Frontier
Facts on File

Sports &

- Sports 430

- Music 445

- Entertainment 468

Entertainment

- *Baseball* **430**
- *Football* **434**
- *Basketball* **438**
- *Hockey* **440**
- *Soccer* **442**
- *Tennis* **444**
- *Golf* **446**
- *Olympics* **448**
- *Other sports* **450**

Sports

Sports has become an important part of modern life. Millions compete in amateur events, and tens of millions keep track of major professional sports. Sports stars are often major public figures, and some have later served with distinction in government and business. This section provides brief introductions to the most popular American games, beginning with the most widely followed team sports and concluding with major individual events. The major sports have sections on the history, the principal rules, and the current major competitions. Where possible, important records have been included. In each case, brief dictionaries of terms used in the sport have been included.

Baseball

Baseball evolved from *rounders,* an old British game in which a ball was hit with a stick. The American Alexander Cartwright wrote the first rules of baseball, sketched the first diamond, and organized the first team, the New York Knickerbockers. The first baseball game was played in 1846 on a picnic field in Hoboken, New Jersey, between the Knickerbockers and a team called the New York Nine. The Knickerbockers lost, 23-1.

In 1869 the Cincinnati Red Stockings became baseball's first professional team. Soon other pro teams were formed. The National League was organized in 1876, and in 1901 the year-old American League began challenging the National League for fans. The first World Series was played in 1903, with Boston of the American League defeating Pittsburgh of the National League, five games to three.

The modern major league baseball season lasts from early April to the beginning of October. There are now 30 teams, 16 in the National League, 14 in the American League. Each league is divided into Eastern, Central, and Western divisions. At the end of the season the leaders of each division and a single "wild card" team hold two playoff rounds to determine the league champion. Then the two league champions play a best-four-out-of-seven World Series to determine the year's national champion.

In July, an All-Star game is played between the two leagues. The starting lineups are determined by the votes of fans. The teams are managed by the managers of the previous season's pennant winners. These managers choose reserve players and the pitching staff for the game.

In addition to the major leagues, there are a number of minor leagues, ranging from Class-A through Class-AAA, the latter for players almost ready for major league competition. High schools and colleges also field varsity teams. Younger players participate in such organized leagues as Little League, Babe Ruth League, American Legion baseball, and others.

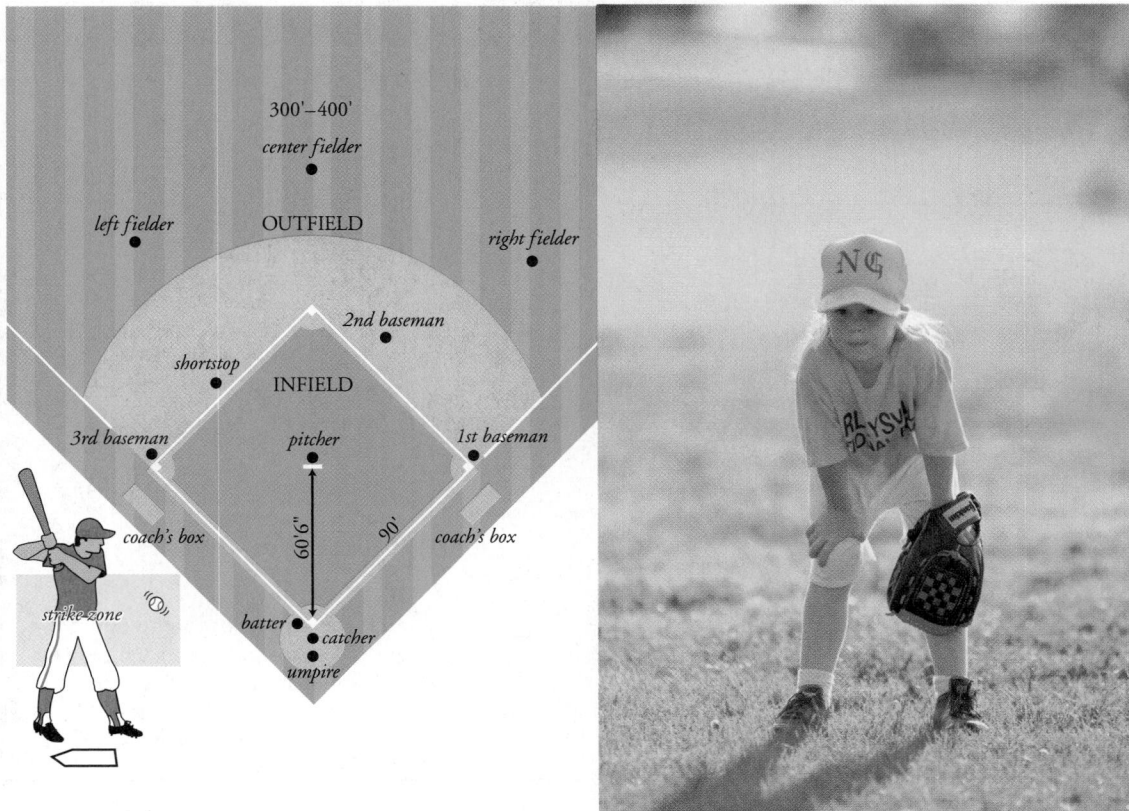

300'–400'
center fielder

left fielder   OUTFIELD   right fielder

2nd baseman

shortstop   INFIELD

3rd baseman   pitcher   1st baseman

60'6"   90'

coach's box   coach's box

batter

strike zone   catcher

umpire

Baseball is one of America's favorite sports, both to watch and to play.

Rules. Baseball teams consist of nine players per side. In the American League, the pitcher does not bat for himself. His turn at the plate is taken by a tenth man, the *designated hitter,* who does not play in the field. The fielders are the pitcher, catcher, first baseman, second baseman, shortstop, third base-man, left fielder, center fielder, and right fielder. They are positioned as shown in the diagram. The bases are fixed 90 feet apart, while the pitching rub-ber is located 60 feet 6 inches from the plate. The outfield area varies from stadium to stadium.

At the beginning of the game, the home team takes the field while the visiting team is at bat. The batter stands in the *batter's box* (left or right side) located alongside home plate. A batter may be *put out* in several ways: if the pitcher delivers three *strikes* (pitched balls that cross some portion of the plate between the knees and armpits) that the batter does not hit or hits foul (out of the playing area); if the batter hits a ball, fair or foul, that is caught before it touches the ground; if the batter hits the ball on the ground and a fielder throws it to first base before the batter reaches the base. Base runners may be put out if they are tagged with the ball when not touching

a base or, in certain circumstances, if the ball is thrown to a fielder touching the base that the runner must reach. If a base runner and a batter are put out on the same play, it is called a *double play.*

A batter may reach first base safely if the pitcher delivers four *balls* (pitches not within the strike zone); if the batter is struck by a pitched ball; or if the batter hits the ball into fair territory (within the foul lines) and it is not caught on the fly or thrown to first base before the batter arrives there. If the ball is hit far enough, the batter can try for more than one base. A ball hit over the fence in fair territory is a *home run.*

When runners are on first and second base, or when the bases are "loaded" (runners on first, second, and third), they must try to advance to the next base when a fair ground ball is hit. However, when a base immediately *behind* a runner is not occupied, the runner is not forced to run to the next base. On fly balls (fair or foul), a base runner returns to the original base but can try to advance after the ball is caught.

Baseball umpires determine whether a pitched ball is a strike or a ball, whether batted balls are fair or foul, and whether a base runner is safe or out.

Reading a Box Score

A surprising amount of information is detailed in a baseball box score. Only a knowledge of baseball abbreviations is necessary in order to read one:

ab	at bat	r	runs scored
h	hit	rbi	runs batted in
avg.	batting average	E	error
DP	double plays	LOB	left on base
2B	two-base hits	3B	three-base hits
HR	home runs	SB	stolen bases
S	sacrifice	IP	innings pitched
ER	earned runs	BB	bases on balls
SO	strikeouts	ERA	earned run average
L	losing pitcher	W	winning pitcher
dh	designated hitter	S	save
	(American League only)		

The symbols after players' names show their position in the field.

The team lineups at the top of the box score show the performance of each player at bat. The paragraph after the lineups gives information about other aspects of the game—fielding, extra-base hits, base running.

VISITORS

	ab	r	h	rbi	avg.
Able—1b	4	0	1	0	.256
Baker—2b	3	1	1	0	.277
Charlie—3b	3	0	0	0	.301
David—ss	4	1	1	2	.321
Easy—lf	4	0	1	0	.250
Fox—cf	4	0	0	0	.226
George—rf	4	1	0	0	.304
Henry—c	4	0	2	1	.282
Inger—dh	4	0	0	0	.223

HOME TEAM

	ab	r	h	rbi	avg.
John—1b	4	1	1	0	.213
King—2b	4	0	0	0	.244
Long—3b	4	1	1	1	.276
Mike—ss	3	0	1	0	.282
Norman—lf	4	0	2	1	.248
Oscar—cf	4	1	1	1	.199
Peter—rf	4	0	0	0	.302
Quick—c	3	1	2	0	.254
Roger—dh	3	0	1	1	.238

E—King. DP—Home Team, 2. LOB—Visitors 5, Home Team, 7. 2B—Henry. 3B—Roger. HR—David. SB—George.

		R	H	E
VISITORS:	200 100 000 =	3	6	0
HOME TEAM:	000 110 02x =	4	9	1

VISITORS:	ip	H	R	ER	BB	SO	ERA
Sugar—L	7 1/3	8	4	4	2	2	4.18
Tommy	2/3	1	0	0	0	0	3.56

HOME TEAM:							
Uncle—W	8	6	3	2	1	4	3.26
Victor—S	1	0	0	0	0	0	2.82

Next comes the line score—the score by inning in condensed form. The last lines give detailed information about the pitchers. This game was played by American League rules, so the pitchers do not appear in the batting lineup.

The Major Leagues

National League

East	*Central*	*West*
Atlanta Braves	Chicago Cubs	Arizona Diamondbacks
Florida Marlins	Cincinnati Reds	Colorado Rockies
New York Mets	Houston Astros	Los Angeles Dodgers
Philadelphia Phillies	Milwaukee Brewers	San Diego Padres
Washington Nationals	Pittsburgh Pirates	San Francisco Giants
	St. Louis Cardinals	

American League

East	*Central*	*West*
Baltimore Orioles	Chicago White Sox	Anaheim Angels
Boston Red Sox	Cleveland Indians	Oakland Athletics
New York Yankees	Detroit Tigers	Seattle Mariners
Tampa Bay Devil Rays	Kansas City Royals	Texas Rangers
Toronto Blue Jays	Minnesota Twins	

Lifetime records

Highest batting average:
Ty Cobb (1905–1928)	.367
Rogers Hornsby (1915–1937)	.358

Most home runs:
Henry Aaron (1954–1976)	755
Babe Ruth (1914–1935)	714

Lowest earned run average:
Ed Walsh (1904–1917)	1.82
Addie Joss (1902–1910)	1.89

Most victories (pitcher):
Cy Young (1890–1911)	511
Walter Johnson (1907–1927)	417

Most consecutive games played:
Cal Ripken, Jr. (1982–1998)	2632
Lou Gehrig (1925–1939)	2130

Season records *(since 1900)*

Highest batting average:
Nap Lajoie (1901)	.426
Rogers Hornsby (1924)	.424

Most home runs:
Barry Bonds (2001)	73
Mark McGwire (1998)	70
Sammy Sosa (1998)	66
Mark McGwire (1999)	65
Sammy Sosa (2001)	64
Sammy Sosa (1999)	63
Roger Maris (1961)	61
Babe Ruth (1927)	60

Lowest earned run average:
Dutch Leonard (1914)	.96
Three-Finger Brown (1906)	1.04

Most victories (pitcher):
Jack Chesbro (1904)	41

Team records *(since 1900)*

Most pennants won:
New York Yankees	39
Brooklyn/Los Angeles Dodgers	18
New York/San Francisco Giants	18

Most World Series won (began 1903)
New York Yankees	26
St. Louis Cardinals	9
Philadelphia/Kansas City/ Oakland A's	9

Manager records

Most pennants won:
Casey Stengel (1934–1965)	10
John McGraw (1899–1932)	10

Barry Bonds

Dictionary of baseball

Randy Johnson

Cal Ripken, Jr.

Sammy Sosa

assist. Fielding help in putting out an opponent. A player who fields a ground ball and throws to first base to put out a batter is credited with an assist.

balk. An illegal move by a pitcher when there are runners on base. All base runners advance one base.

batting average. A decimal obtained by dividing a batter's number of hits by his number of official at bats. A batter getting 3 hits in 10 at-bats is batting .300.

bull pen. Where pitchers warm up before coming in to pitch.

bunt. A ball hit gently into the infield. It is most often used to advance a base runner. *See also* sacrifice.

change-up. A pitch delivered with less speed than a fast ball or slider.

fielder's choice. A situation where a fielder may put out either a base runner or the batter.

force play. A play in which the ball is thrown to a base ahead of a base runner to force out the base runner.

infield fly. If a batter hits a fly to the infield when there are base runners on first and second, or first, second, and third, and not more than one out, the batter is out automatically. Otherwise, an infielder could drop the ball intentionally, then make a double or triple play.

leadoff man. The first batter in the batting order, or in an inning.

passed ball. A pitched ball that gets past the catcher that the catcher could have stopped.

pinch hitter. A batter substituted for the player scheduled to bat. The batter who is being replaced may not reenter the game.

pitchout. A pitch deliberately delivered wide of the plate in order to give the catcher freedom to throw to a base to put out a runner.

pull hitter. A batter who "pulls the ball." A left-handed batter pulls the ball to right field, a right-handed hitter pulls to left field.

run-down. A situation in which a base runner is trapped off base, and two (or more) infielders try to tag the runner out.

sacrifice. A bunt with a runner on base and less than two out in which the runner advances a base but the batter is put out at first.

sacrifice fly. A fly ball with less than two out that allows a runner on third base to tag up after the out and score.

signals. The third base coach uses hand signals to relay the manager's orders. A catcher uses finger signals for various types of pitches to be delivered by the pitcher.

squeeze play. Trying to score a runner from third base by means of a batter's bunt.

switch hitter. A batter who can bat left-handed and right-handed.

utility man. A substitute who can play several positions.

wild pitch. A pitch delivered by a pitcher that is so wide of the plate (high, low, outside, inside) that the catcher has no chance to block it.

windup. The pitcher's motion before throwing the ball.

Football

American football, first played in the 1800s, is a relative of soccer and rugby. Early football was a violent game, with few rules and much pushing, punching, and piling on. Serious injuries were common. Early in the 1900s, President Theodore Roosevelt threatened to ban the game unless the violence was lessened. The forward pass, legalized in 1906, was a step in that direction. Additional rules have since been added to minimize injuries, but they still occur.

College football. The first intercollegiate football game (really more like a violent soccer game) was played between Rutgers and Princeton universities on November 6, 1869. Other schools became interested in the game and it spread throughout the United States. College football today is governed by the National Collegiate Athletic Association (NCAA). Most universities are members of various *conferences,* such as the Ivy League, the Big Ten, the Pacific Ten, the Southeastern Conference, and numerous others. Some schools, such as Notre Dame, elect to remain independent and belong to no conference. The college football season runs from early September to mid-December, with the best teams participating in post-season games.

Professional football. Professional football was born on August 31, 1895, in Latrobe, Pennsylvania, when Latrobe played against the neighboring town of Jeanette. Other pro teams were formed, and in 1920 the National Football League (NFL) was organized. Several rival leagues have merged with the NFL or gone out of business.

The professional football season begins with an exhibition schedule in August. The regular season starts early in September and lasts until mid-December, after which a series of playoffs determine the pro football championship.

Post-season play. At the conclusion of the regular college season, various teams are invited to play in "bowl" games. The oldest of these is the *Rose Bowl,* in Pasadena, California. Others of major importance are the *Sugar Bowl* in New Orleans, Louisiana, the *Orange Bowl* in Miami, Florida, and the *Cotton Bowl* in Dallas, Texas.

At the conclusion of the regular professional season, twelve teams participate in a series of playoff games. They include eight division champions plus two "wild card" teams from each conference—the teams with the next best record. These playoffs determine the champion of each conference, and

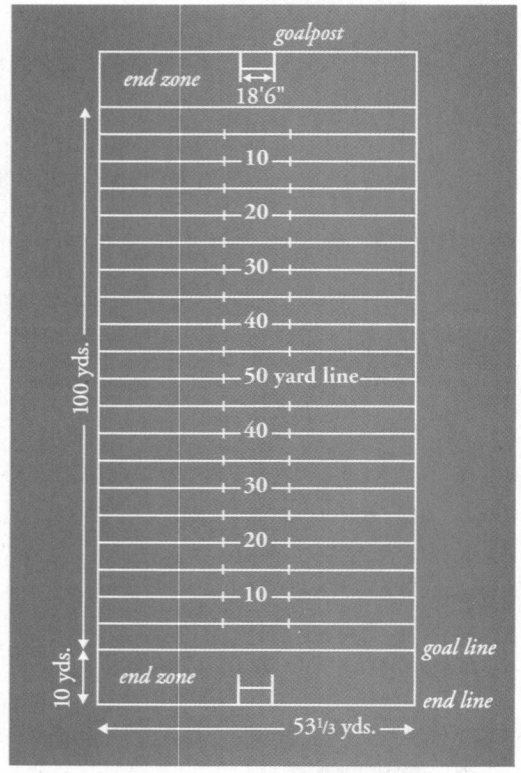

A football field is 120 yards long and 53⅓ yards wide.

the two champions clash in the annual *Super Bowl* to determine the championship of professional football.

Rules.

Football teams are composed of eleven players per side, with frequent substitutions permitted. The modern football is made of grainy plastic material, about 11 inches long from point to point and just over 21 inches in circumference in the middle.

The field measures 120 yards long by 53⅓ yards wide. The actual playing area is 100 yards long, with 10-yard *end zones* at each end. White stripes run across the width of the field at 5-yard intervals. The mid-field line is the 50-yard line, with other lines numbering down toward the *goal lines.* At the back of each end zone is the goalpost, the target for kickers on certain scoring plays.

The game begins with one team kicking the ball to the other, then trying to tackle the ball carrier, who is protected by blockers. The spot where the runner is tackled or steps out of bounds becomes the *scrimmage line.* The team with the ball has four tries (downs) to advance the ball 10 yards or more. Its aim is to move the ball into the opposing team's end zone for a *touchdown,* worth 6 points. Failure to gain at least 10 yards in four tries results in loss of the ball. Usually, when a team has used three downs and has little chance to gain the remaining yards, it will *punt* (kick) the ball away, thus giving up possession to the other team.

A team may advance the ball by running or passing. A team may score via a *placekick* (field goal, worth 3 points); a similar kick after a touchdown has been scored (*conversion,* worth 1 point); running or passing the ball over the goal line following a touchdown (worth 2 points); or grounding an opponent with the ball behind his own goal line (*safety,* worth 2 points). Teams can be penalized yardage for various infractions of rules, including unnecessary roughness and pass interference. Penalties vary from 5 to 15 yards.

College and professional football games are divided into four 15-minute quarters. The clock is stopped when a runner steps out of bounds, a forward pass is incomplete, or a team calls a time out. **Football positions.** The offensive team *must* have a seven-man line at the line of scrimmage: two ends, each eligible to receive a forward pass, two tackles stationed inside the ends, two guards stationed inside the tackles, and a center who snaps the ball to the quarterback. The offensive backfield may use several different formations (straight-T, slot-T, split-T, etc.). Usually, the quarterback is positioned directly behind the center. Behind him are the halfback and the fullback. The flanker back is usually split to one side of the offensive line. All backfielders are eligible to receive a pass.

The defensive team can use various formations, but most often (especially in professional football) there are four linemen, three linebackers, two cornerbacks, and two safety men. The linemen generally rush the ball carrier; backfield men stay back watching for passes.

Football is a popular high school sport.

The lineup for a play from scrimmage

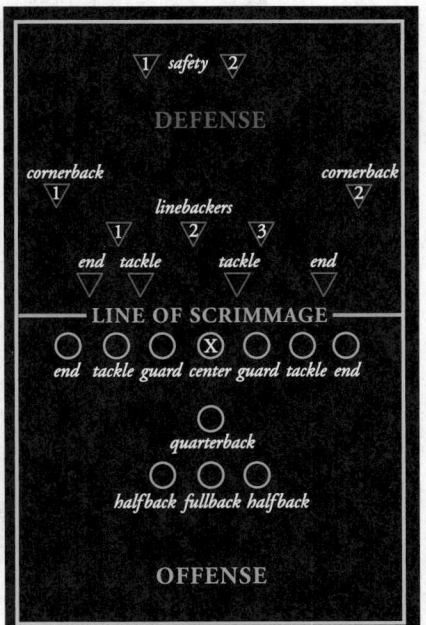

National Football League Roster of Teams

American Conference

Eastern Division	*Northern Division*	*Southern Division*	*Western Division*
Buffalo Bills	Baltimore Ravens	Houston Texans	Denver Broncos
Miami Dolphins	Cincinnati Bengals	Indianapolis Colts	Kansas City Chiefs
New England Patriots	Cleveland Browns	Jacksonville Jaguars	Oakland Raiders
New York Jets	Pittsburgh Steelers	Tennessee Titans	San Diego Chargers

National Conference

Eastern Division	*Northern Division*	*Southern Division*	*Western Division*
Dallas Cowboys	Chicago Bears	Atlanta Falcons	Arizona Cardinals
New York Giants	Detroit Lions	Carolina Panthers	St. Louis Rams
Philadelphia Eagles	Green Bay Packers	New Orleans Saints	San Francisco 49ers
Washington Redskins	Minnesota Vikings	Tampa Bay Buccaneers	Seattle Seahawks

The Green Bay Packers' Brett Favre

Professional Football Records

Super Bowl victories:
5—Dallas Cowboys, 1972, '78, '93, '94, '96
5—San Francisco 49ers, 1982, '85, '89, '90, '95
4—Pittsburgh Steelers, 1975, '76, '79, '80
3—Oakland Raiders, 1977, '81, '84
3—Washington Redskins, 1983, '88, '92
3—Green Bay Packers, 1967, '68, '97
3—New England Patriots, 2002, '04, '05
2—Miami Dolphins, 1973, '74
2—New York Giants, 1987, '91
2—Denver Broncos, 1998, '99
1—New York Jets, 1969
1—Kansas City Chiefs, 1970
1—Baltimore Colts, 1971
1—Chicago Bears, 1986
1—St. Louis Rams, 2000
1—Baltimore Ravens, 2001
1—Tampa Bay Buccaneers, 2003

Yards gained rushing:
1.	Emmitt Smith	17,418
2.	Walter Payton	16,726
3.	Barry Sanders	15,269

Most yards gained rushing, one season:
Eric Dickerson (1984)   2,105

Yards gained passing:
1.	Dan Marino	61,361
2.	John Elway	51,475
3.	Warren Moon	49,325

Most yards gained passing, one season:
Dan Marino (1984)   5,084

Yards gained receiving:
1.	Jerry Rice	22,466
2.	Tim Brown	14,734

Most yards gained receiving, one season:
Jerry Rice (1995)   1,848

Red Grange

Dictionary of football

Coach Vince Lombardi

Dan Marino

Joe Montana

audible. A shouted signal changing an offensive play at the line of scrimmage before the ball is snapped.

blitz. A charge at the ball carrier by members of the defensive backfield.

bootleg. A fake handoff by the quarterback to another running back, in which the quarterback keeps the ball; also called "keeper."

clip. An illegal block in which an offensive player blocks a defensive player from behind.

draw play. A play in which the quarterback drops back as if to pass, then suddenly hands off to a running back who has been pretending to block for him.

endlines. White lines at the rear of both end zones.

end zone. Touchdown area. It runs the width of the field and is 10 yards deep.

extra point. The point after touchdown by placekick.

fair catch. When a team punts or kicks off the ball, the receiver may elect not to attempt to run with the ball but merely to catch it. He raises his arm overhead to signal "fair catch." No tackler may touch him, but if the receiver fumbles the ball, an opponent is permitted to recover it if possible.

fumble. Drop the ball.

hand-off. The handing of the ball from the quarterback to a running back.

huddle. Circle of players ready to receive instructions or signals between plays.

in motion. A running back on the offensive team may run laterally, parallel to the line of scrimmage before the ball is snapped. He is "in motion."

line of scrimmage. An imaginary line, the "no-man's-land" about a foot wide, between the offensive and defensive lines before the ball is snapped.

offside. When an offensive or defensive lineman crosses the line of scrimmage before the ball is snapped. The offender's team is penalized 5 yards.

play-action pass. A fake handoff to a running back by the quarterback, who then passes the ball.

punt. A kick by the offensive team when it has not gained 10 yards in three of its four tries.

roughing. When a kicker has kicked the ball away, or a passer has passed the ball, he cannot be hit. If he is, a penalty for roughing is assessed.

safety. When an offensive player in possession of the ball is tackled behind his own goal line, the defense has scored a safety, worth 2 points.

shotgun. A formation in which the quarterback stands about 5 yards behind his center. It is almost always a passing formation.

touchback. When the ball is grounded by a team in its own end zone on a punt or kickoff reception or on the interception of a pass, a touchback is called: the team takes possession of the ball at its 20-yard line.

zone defense. A strategy in which each defensive backfield player is responsible for a definite area or "zone."

Basketball

Basketball, the most widely played team sport in the world, was invented by Dr. James Naismith, an instructor at the International Young Men's Christian Association Training School (now Springfield College) in Massachusetts in 1891. Naismith fixed peach baskets 10 feet off the ground at both ends of the gym, devised a set of rules, and used a group of students as players.

Today, nearly all American colleges field varsity teams. Men's professional basketball is played under the auspices of the National Basketball Association (NBA), and women's professional basketball is played under the auspices of the Women's National Basketball Association (WNBA). The college sport is governed by the National Collegiate Athletic Association (NCAA).

Post-season play. The most important post-season tournament in college basketball is the NCAA tournament, which includes the best independent and conference teams. Regional eliminations among 64 teams are held in March, and the final four teams play an elimination tournament early in April. The NCAA champion is usually considered the nation's best team.

In NBA basketball, the best teams in each of the divisions compete in a post-season tournament culminating in a championship playoff between the two remaining clubs.

Rules.
The size of a basketball court varies. It can be no larger than 94 by 50 feet and no smaller than 74 by 42 feet. The inflated basketball is made of leather or rubberized plastic material, measures between 29½ and 30 inches in circumference, and weighs between 20 and 22 ounces. Baskets, affixed to a backboard, are 10 feet above the floor.

A basketball team consists of five players: two guards, two forwards, and one center. The object of the game is to score points by throwing the ball through the hoop of the opponent's basket, which counts 2 points. A ball thrown through the hoop from behind the *3-point line* scores 3 points. Foul shots, taken from the *free throw line,* count 1 point each.

The game begins with a center jump as the referee tosses the ball up between the opposing centers at mid-court. They leap, trying to tap the ball to a teammate. The ball is advanced by passing from one player to another or by bouncing the ball on the run (dribbling). Following a score of any

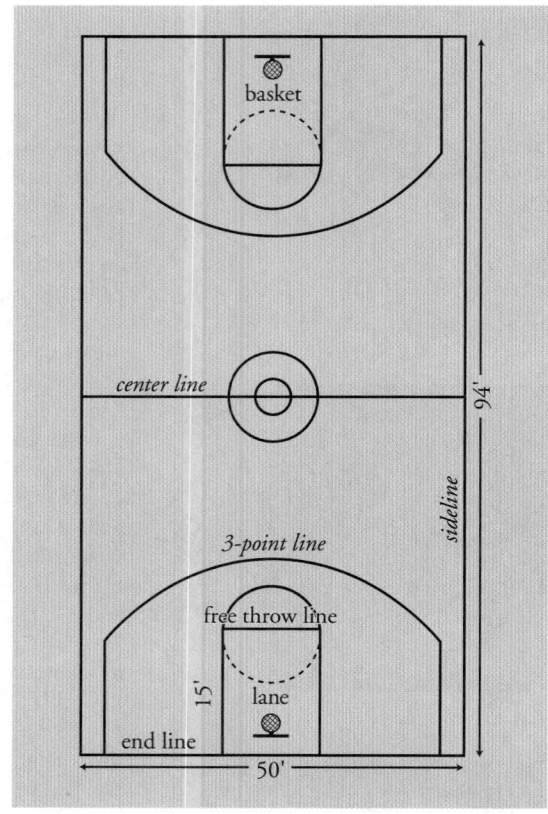

A regulation basketball court.

kind, the opposing team puts the ball in play from behind its own end line.

Free throws are awarded for personal or technical fouls. Personal fouls include pushing, hacking (interfering with an opponent's arm in the act of shooting), and tripping. The fouled player is awarded one or two foul shots depending on the situation. Technical fouls are awarded for unsportsmanlike conduct, delay of a game, or abuse of an official. Technical violations by the offensive team cause the ball to be awarded to the other team. These violations include double dribbling (dribbling, holding the ball, then dribbling again), traveling (running without dribbling), or remaining in an opponent's foul lane too long.

Time of play varies. High-school games consist of four 8-minute periods. College games consist of two 20-minute periods. Professional games consist of four 12-minute periods.

National Basketball Association

Eastern Conference

Atlantic Division	*Central Division*	*Southeast Division*
Boston Celtics	Chicago Bulls	Atlanta Hawks
New Jersey Nets	Cleveland Cavaliers	Charlotte Bobcats
New York Knicks	Detroit Pistons	Miami Heat
Philadelphia 76ers	Indiana Pacers	Orlando Magic
Toronto Raptors	Milwaukee Bucks	Washington Wizards

Western Conference

Southwest Division	*Northwest Division*	*Pacific Division*
Dallas Mavericks	Denver Nuggets	Golden State Warriors
Houston Rockets	Minnesota Timberwolves	Los Angeles Clippers
Memphis Grizzlies	Portland Trailblazers	Los Angeles Lakers
New Orleans Hornets	Seattle SuperSonics	Phoenix Suns
San Antonio Spurs	Utah Jazz	Sacramento Kings

Women's National Basketball Association

Eastern Conference

Charlotte Sting	Indiana Fever
Connecticut Sun	New York Liberty
Detroit Shock	Washington Mystics

Western Conference

Houston Comets	Sacramento Monarchs
Los Angeles Sparks	San Antonio Silver Spurs
Minnesota Lynx	Seattle Storm
Phoenix Mercury	

Dictionary of basketball

Shaquille O'Neal

assist. When a player passes to a teammate who scores, the passer is credited with an assist.

back court. The defensive part of the court for each team.

bonus shot. An extra free throw awarded to a team when its opponents have committed a certain number of fouls in a period of play.

charging. Personal contact by one player who moves against an opponent who is not moving. Usually, it is an offensive foul.

fast break. A quick attack after a score or a rebound.

foul out. After a college player has committed five personal fouls, the player fouls out and must leave the game (six fouls in pro basketball).

goaltending. A defensive violation in which the defender taps a shot from the basket or backboard while the ball is descending toward the basket.

loose ball foul. A foul committed by a player when neither team is in possession of the ball.

press. Playing defense closely against the opposing team.

screen. An offensive play in which one player takes position between the player in possession of the ball and the guarding player.

technical foul. An infraction of the rules that is not a personal foul. Failure to report to the officials when entering the game and abusive language are examples.

tip-in. A leaping tap of an unsuccessful shot, resulting in a score.

twenty-four-second rule. A rule in pro basketball requiring the team in possession to take a shot within 24 seconds or lose possession to the other team.

Hockey

There are hockey leagues for even the youngest players.

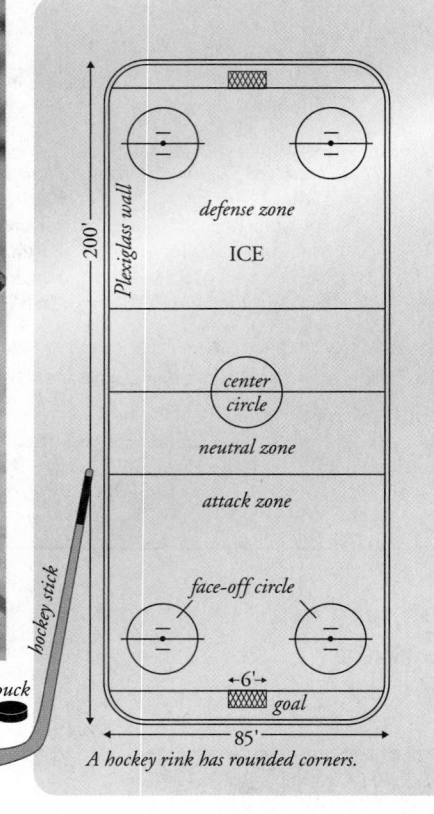

A hockey rink has rounded corners.

Ice hockey in crude form was first played by soldiers of the Royal Canadian Rifles stationed near Kingston, Ontario, Canada, during the 1850s. In 1879, W. F. Robertson and R. F. Smith devised some rules based on field hockey and other goal games. By the 1890s hockey had spread to the northern United States.

In 1917 the National Hockey League (NHL) was formed. The championship trophy of the NHL is the Stanley Cup, first offered in 1893 by Canada's governor-general, Lord Stanley of Preston. Ice hockey is one of the major sports of the winter Olympics.

Rules.
Hockey rinks vary in size, but the average is 200 feet long by 85 feet wide. The rink is surrounded by a 4-foot wall topped by Plexiglas, which allows spectators to see the game while being protected from errant pucks. Ten feet from each end of the rink are goals with nets affixed to them. The goal measures 4 feet high by 6 feet wide. The rink is divided into three zones, the one nearest a team's goal being their defense zone, the middle the neutral zone, and the farthest the attack zone. The puck is

made of hard rubber and is an inch thick by 3 inches in diameter. Sticks are not more than 53 inches long, with a "blade" not more than 14¾ inches wide.

Teams consist of six players: three forwards, two defensemen, and a goalkeeper. Games are divided into three 20-minute periods, with a change of goals after each period. Games can (and often do) end in ties, but in playoff and championship games, the winner is decided in overtime play, with the first team to score winning.

Play begins with a *face-off*. The referee drops the puck at center ice between the two centers. The puck is batted along the ice with the sticks. No players except the goalkeeper may touch the puck with their gloved hands. If a player crosses the blue line ahead of the puck, an offside is called, and a new face-off occurs.

Penalties are assessed for various infractions, such as tripping, high-sticking, spearing, slashing, or other unnecessarily rough play. The player committing the violation must leave the ice for a specified time (2 minutes or more) and that player's team must play "short-handed."

National Hockey League

Eastern Conference

Atlantic Division
New Jersey Devils
New York Islanders
New York Rangers
Philadelphia Flyers
Pittsburgh Penguins

Northeast Division
Boston Bruins
Buffalo Sabres
Montreal Canadiens
Ottawa Senators
Toronto Maple Leafs

Southeast Division
Atlanta Thrashers
Carolina Hurricanes
Florida Panthers
Tampa Bay Lightning
Washington Capitals

Western Conference

Central Division
Chicago Blackhawks
Columbus Blue Jackets
Detroit Red Wings
Nashville Predators
St. Louis Blues

Northwest Division
Calgary Flames
Colorado Avalanche
Edmonton Oilers
Minnesota Wild
Vancouver Canucks

Pacific Division
Anaheim Mighty Ducks
Dallas Stars
Los Angeles Kings
Phoenix Coyotes
San Jose Sharks

Dictionary of hockey

Wayne Gretsky

assist. A player gets an assist upon passing the puck to a teammate who scores. Two or more players can be credited with an assist on the same scoring play.

bench minor penalty. A penalty in which a player must sit in the penalty box even though the player did not commit a foul. If a club official (coach, etc.) uses profanity or otherwise interferes with play, the referee can impose a penalty. The coach can designate a player to serve the penalty.

blue line(s). The line(s) dividing each attack zone from the neutral zone.

change on the fly. While play is going on, a whole new forward line enters the game while the other line returns to the bench.

face-off circle. One of four circles in the corners of the rink where face-offs occur after icing, offside, and other minor violations.

forecheck. To check an opponent in his own defensive zone.

hat trick. A player's scoring of three goals in one game.

icing. Intentionally shooting the puck across the center line and over the opponent's goal line. A face-off results, in a circle near the offending team's goal.

offside. A violation in which a player crosses into his or her team's attack zone ahead of the puck. Play is suspended and a face-off occurs.

penalty shot. A free shot on goal. Only the goalkeeper is permitted to block the shot.

power play. When one team is short-handed, the opposing team sets up special plays to take advantage of its greater numbers.

red line. The line across the rink dividing the playing area in half.

washout. The disallowance of a goal because of a foul or other infraction.

Soccer

Soccer is the most popular spectator sport in the world. Except in America, it is usually known as "football." The Chinese played a crude form of the game about 2,500 years ago, calling it "tsu chu," meaning "kicking a ball with the foot." The Romans called their version of the game "harpastum," and it was played with an inflated pig's bladder. According to legend, in medieval times Danish raiders invaded an English town and the people fought off the Danes until help arrived from London. The Danish leader's head was cut off and kicked through the town. Since the incident occurred on Shrove Tuesday, that event has been celebrated annually with a kicking game.

Soccer was a rough game at first with few rules. In 1846 Cambridge University formulated a set of rules that eliminated some of the rugged aspects, and, in 1863, representatives of eleven clubs met to form the Football Association in England. Not until 1890 did officials take complete control of the game.

Several other kicking games are relatives of soccer, including American football, Gaelic football, Irish hurling, and rugby. International soccer is governed by the *Federation Internationale de Football Association.* Soccer's version of the World Series is the World Cup match, held every four years, which

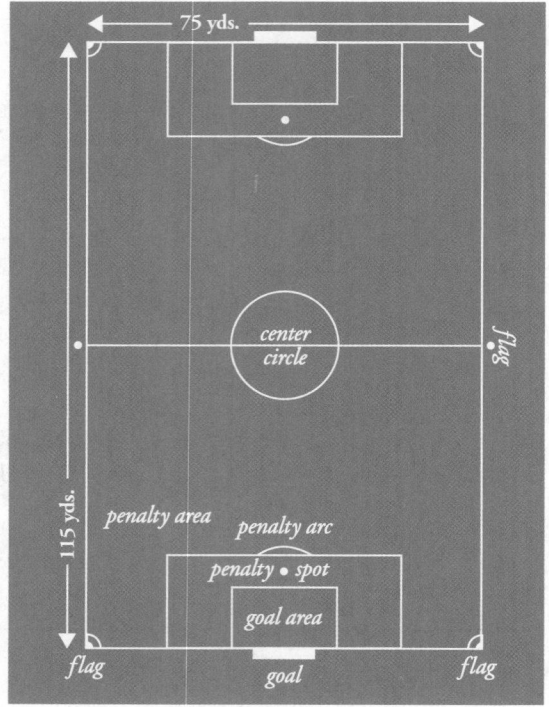

A soccer field is about as long as a football field, but more than 20 yards wider.

pits teams from many nations against each other. The final games of the World Cup Series are watched by more than a billion people on tele-

One of the most popular games around the world, soccer is only recently beginning to attract large numbers of players and fans in the United States.

vision. In 1994 the United States was the site of the Men's World Cup Series, and in 1999 and 2003 it hosted the Women's World Cup Series.

Rules.

A soccer field is 115 yards long by 75 yards wide. The ball is kicked into play from a line at midfield. At each end of the field is a goal backed by a net, 24 feet wide, 8 feet high, and 3 feet deep. The object of the game is to put the ball into the opponent's goal. The soccer ball is 27 to 28 inches in circumference and weighs 14 to 16 ounces. A game lasts 90 minutes, divided into two 45-minute periods.

A soccer team consists of eleven players: five forwards, three halfbacks, two fullbacks, and a goalkeeper. Only the goalkeeper may use his or her hands; the others may control the ball using their feet, knees, torso, or head. Substitutions are usually made only in case of injury.

There are relatively few rules in soccer. An attacking player cannot get between the ball and the opponent's goal unless there are at least two defenders between him or her and the goal. If not, an offside is called and the defensive team gets the ball.

The rule does not apply if the ball was last touched by an opponent.

There are three basic types of "free kicks" in soccer. One is the *indirect* free kick, awarded in cases of offside, intentionally blocking or charging an opponent not in possession of the ball. The indirect free kick is taken at the point at which the infraction occurred, but the ball must be played by a teammate before it is kicked at the goal. A *direct* free kick is awarded for more serious infractions, such as charging from behind, tripping, hitting, holding, etc. The ball may be kicked directly at the goal, defenders must be at the goal, and all defensive players must be at least 10 yards from where the ball is kicked. If a foul is committed inside the penalty area (see diagram), a *penalty* kick is awarded. The ball is placed on the penalty spot and the kicker shoots for the goal with only the goalkeeper defending.

If a game ends in a tie, an overtime period is played in which the first team to score wins. If two overtime periods are played with no scoring, the tie stands. In the North American Soccer League, a "shootout" is held. Each team takes five penalty kicks, and the team with the most goals wins.

Dictionary of soccer

Pelé

corner area. The small arc at the corners of the field from which corner kicks are taken. A corner kick is used to put the ball in play after the ball has gone over the goal line and out of play if it was last touched by a player defending that goal.

dribbling. Advancing the ball with a series of short kicks.

goal kick. When the attacking team kicks the ball over its opponent's goal line, the goalkeeper gets the ball and may kick it far downfield.

half volley. A ball kicked just as it is bouncing up from the ground.

screening. Keeping a player's body between an opponent and the ball.

tackle. Using the feet to try to take the ball away from an opponent.

throw-in. When the ball goes across the touch line, possession is awarded to the opponent of the last player to touch the ball. The throw-in is made with an overhand motion using both hands.

touch line. The sidelines running the length of the field.

trapping. Gaining control of the ball using some part of the body other than the hands or arms.

volley. A ball kicked while it is still in the air.

Tennis

Some crude forms of paddle-and-ball games were played before the Christian era in ancient civilizations such as those in Egypt, Greece, Rome, and Mexico. The French of six centuries ago enjoyed a court game called "Jeu de Paume," and other European countries tried similar games (*see also* Wall and net games on page 454).

During the 1860s and 1870s there was a renewed interest in sports, but most were only for men. People wanted a game both sexes could enjoy. In 1873 Walter C. Wingfield of England devised some rules for a "net game" that was the basis for *lawn tennis*. It spread to France, the United States, and other countries. Many changes were made in Wingfield's rules, including the shape of the court (an hourglass in his rules).

The game dropped "lawn" from its name and gained popularity through the early 1900s. Then during the late 1960s and 1970s the game's popularity increased when television began featuring world-class matches. It was during that time that amateurs and professionals were allowed to compete in the same "open" tournaments. The four great tournaments, constituting a "grand slam of tennis," are Wimbledon (the British Open), the U.S. Open, and the Australian and French championships. Today's professionals play in tournaments that offer huge sums of money to the winner.

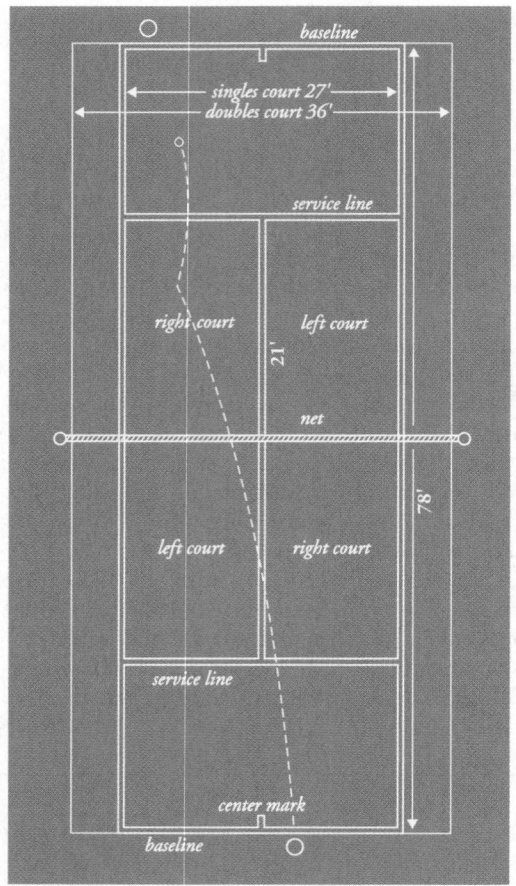

The diagram shows the path of a first serve.

Major Tennis Victories (since 1945)

British Open, men's and women's singles:

Won 9 times:	Martina Navratilova, 1978, '79, '82, '83, '84, '85, '86, '87, '90	Won 3 times:	Maureen Connolly, 1952, '53, '54
Won 7 times:	Steffi Graf, 1988, '89, '91, '92, '93, '95, '96		Maria Bueno, 1959, '60, '64
	Pete Sampras, 1993, '94, '95, '97, '98, '99, 2000		Margaret Smith Court, 1963, '65, '70
Won 6 times:	Billie Jean King, 1966, '67, '68, '72, '73, '75		John Newcombe, 1967, '70, '71
Won 5 times:	Bjorn Borg, 1976, '77, '78, '79, '80		Chris Evert Lloyd, 1974, '76, '81
Won 4 times:	Louis Brough, 1948, '49, '50, '55		John McEnroe, 1981, '83, '84
	Rod Laver, 1961, '62, '68, '69		Boris Becker, 1985, '86, '89

United States Open, men's and women's singles:

Won 6 times:	Chris Evert Lloyd, 1975, '76, '77, '78, '80, '82
Won 5 times:	Margaret Smith Court, 1962, '65, '69, '70, '73
	Jimmy Connors, 1974, '76, '78, '82, '83
	Steffi Graf, 1988, '89, '93, '95, '96
	Pete Sampras, 1990, '93, '95, '96, 2002
Won 4 times:	Maria Bueno, 1959, '63, '64, '66
	Billie Jean King, 1967, '71, '72, '74
	John McEnroe, 1979, '80, '81, '84
Won 3 times:	Margaret Osborne DuPont, 1948, '49, '50
	Maureen Connolly, 1951, '52, '53
	Ivan Lendl, 1985, '86, '87

Steffi Graf

Rules. A tennis ball is an inflated, hollow rubber ball with a tight flannel covering, weighing 2 to 2¹⁄₁₆ ounces and measuring 2½ to 2⅝ inches in diameter. Rackets are oval shaped and strung with nylon or gut. Tennis courts may have surfaces of grass, clay, asphalt, or concrete. Each surface subtly affects the strategy of the game.

The court is rectangular, 78 feet long and 27 feet wide for singles, extending to 36 feet wide for doubles. A net strung across the center of the court is 3 feet 6 inches high (see diagram). A 2-inch white line running parallel to the net 21 feet from it on each side marks off the *service area.*

A match is divided into points, games, and sets. At least 4 points must be won in order to win a game, but it is necessary to win each game by at least 2 points. Three of the points have a determinate number: the first is called "15," the second "30," the third "40." The fourth point is called "game." No points (zero) has a special name—*love.* If a game comes to be tied at 40, the score is "deuce." The next player to win a point has the "advantage." If that player wins the next point, he or she has won the game.

A set is won by the first player to win six games and lead the opponent by at least two games. Until recently, if a set was tied at six games all, a player had to win two games in a row to win the set. One tournament match in the 1940s went to 59-57. Today, most tournaments have a tie-breaker, a special game for use when the set is tied at six all.

In a tie-breaker, players alternate serve. There are two types of tie-breakers. In the 9-point or "sudden death" version, the first player to score 5 points wins the game and the set. The 12-point tie-breaker, used in major tournaments, requires that a player score at least six points and be ahead of the opponent by two points to win. If the game is tied at six, it is at deuce, and continues until one player gains a 2-point advantage.

A match consists of a maximum of three sets in women's and doubles matches (first player to win two wins the match); in major men's tournaments, there are a maximum of five sets (first player to win three).

The game begins when one player, with both feet behind the baseline, serves the ball diagonally into the service area of the opponent. A ball not landing in the proper service court, or one that hits into the net, is called a *fault.* Two consecutive faults loses the point. A ball hitting the net but bouncing into the service court is called a *let* and is served over. After serving from the right, the server serves from the left, and continues alternating until the game is over. The player who hits the ball into the net or outside the confines of the court loses the point.

Dictionary of tennis

Pete Sampras

ace. A serve that an opponent finds impossible to return.

advantage. The point scored after deuce.

backhand. A stroke in which the player who is right-handed hits the ball from the left side (and vice versa for a left-handed player).

break service. When a player wins a game against his opponent's serve.

forehand. A stroke in which a right-handed player hits the ball from the right side (and vice versa for a left-handed player).

ground stroke. A ball hit after it has bounced.

half volley. A ball hit immediately after it has bounced and is on the rise (also called pick-up).

lob. A ball arched high into the air over the opponent's head.

rally. Hitting the ball back and forth across the net until one player loses the point.

smash. A hard overhand stroke.

volley. A stroke, usually made near the net, in which the ball has not bounced.

Golf

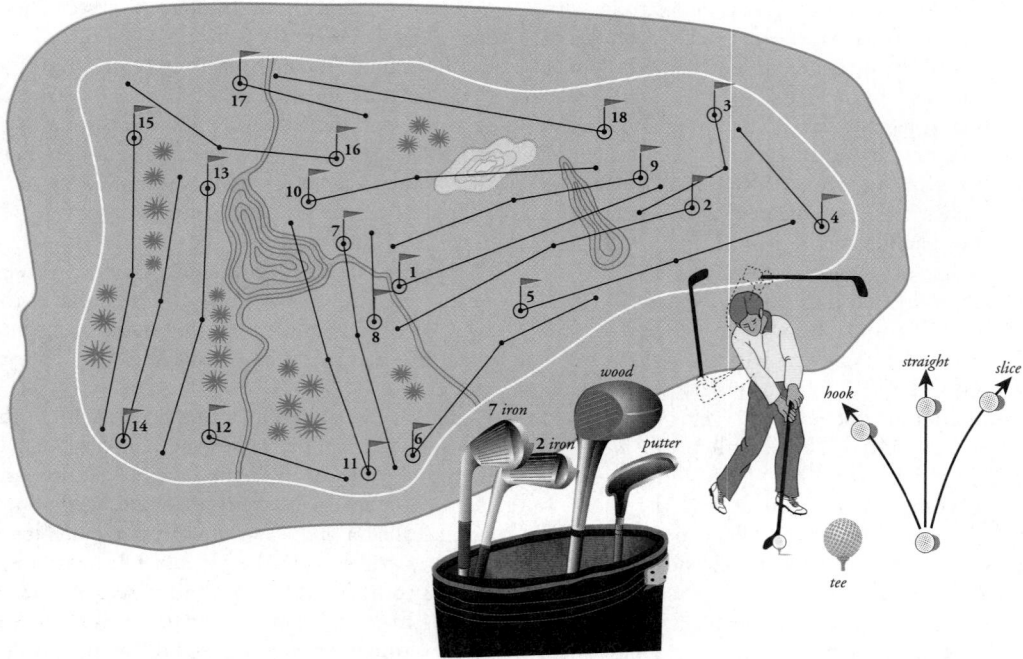

The layout of a typical 18-hole course (left), *representative clubs* (center), *and a diagram showing a hook and a slice, common golfing faults* (right).

Golf probably began as a team field game, called *paganica,* played by the Romans. There is no record as to when the first hole was introduced, but an illustrated book published in the year 1500 shows golfers standing around a hole.

The Scots were the first to formalize the game. In 1754 the St. Andrews Society of Golfers established a set of rules. The United States Golf Association (USGA) was organized in 1894; it offered a national championship tournament, the National Open. The U.S. Amateur tournament and a women's amateur tournament followed shortly.

For many years golf was considered "a rich man's game," but after World War II the game began to boom. Many public courses and less expensive private courses made the game affordable for millions of new players.

Tournament golf is governed in the United States by the USGA, and in England by the Royal Academy of Golf Clubs (St. Andrews, Scotland). The Professional Golfers Association (PGA) was formed in 1916. Although there are many tournaments during a year, the four that make up the "grand slam" of golf are the U.S. Masters Tournament, the PGA, the U.S. Open, and the British Open. In addition, there are important tournaments for women, such as the

Ladies PGA, and team matches, such as the Walker Cup (the United States vs. Great Britain and Ireland) and the Ryder Cup (for professionals of the United States and Great Britain).

Rules. Golf rules are quite uniform, except for size of the ball. By U.S. rules, the ball is 1.68 inches in diameter; the British ball is slightly smaller.

A golf course can be any size, varying from about 7,000 to 7,800 yards from the first tee to the 18th hole. Interspersed over all courses are many *hazards,* such as sand traps, bodies of water, high grass, or clumps of trees. A "round" of golf consists of 18 holes. *Par* for each hole may be three, four, or five strokes, depending on the distance from tee to hole.

A player is permitted a maximum of 14 clubs in his or her bag. Usually they consist of four *woods* (which years ago had wooden heads but now usually have steel heads), nine *irons,* and a *putter,* the last club used, to stroke the ball into the hole.

Different types of penalties add strokes to a golfer's score. Penalties are accrued for replacing a lost ball (often when it drops into a water hazard), moving a ball (even unintentionally), hitting a ball with an object other than a club, etc.

Major Golf Victories (since 1945)

United States Open:		*U.S. Women's Open:*	
Won 4 times:	Ben Hogan, 1948, '50, '51, '53	Won 4 times:	Betsy Rawls, 1951, '53, '57, '60
	Jack Nicklaus, 1962, '67, '72, '80		Mickey Wright, 1958, '59, '61, '64
		Won 3 times:	Babe Zaharias, 1948, '50, '54
PGA Tournament:			Susie Maxwell Berning, 1968, '72, '73
Won 5 times:	Jack Nicklaus, 1963, '71, '73, '75, '80		Hollis Stacy, 1977, '78, '84
		Won 2 times:	Louis Suggs, 1949, '52
U.S. Masters Tournament:			Donna Caponi, 1969, '70
Won 6 times:	Jack Nicklaus, 1963, '65, '66, '72, '75, '86		JoAnne Carner, 1971, '76
Won 4 times:	Arnold Palmer, 1958, '60, '62, '64		Betsy King, 1989, '90
Won 3 times:	Sam Snead, 1949, '52, '54		Meg Mallon, 1991, 2004
	Gary Player, 1961, '74, '78		Patty Sheehan, 1992, '94
	Nick Faldo, 1989, '90, '96		Annika Sorenstam, 1995, '96
	Tiger Woods, 1997, 2001, '02		Juli Inkster, 1999, 2002
			Karrie Webb, 2000, '01

Betsy King

Dictionary of golf

Tiger Woods

ace. A hole-in-one.

address. A player's position when preparing to hit the ball.

approach. A stroke following the drive from the tee, intended to get the ball close to or onto the green putting surface.

birdie. Scoring one stroke under par for a hole.

bogey. Scoring one stroke over par for a hole. Two strokes over par is a double bogey, three is a triple bogey, etc.

bunker. A sand trap.

caddie. The person carrying the golfer's bag of clubs.

chip shot. A short approach shot, toward the green.

divot. A piece of turf torn from the ground by a stroke.

dogleg. A hole with a fairway that turns to the left or right.

duffer. An inept golfer.

eagle. Scoring two strokes under par.

fairway. A corridor between tee and green where the grass is closely cropped. Higher grass on either side is called the rough.

fore. The warning cry called out by a golfer so that others on that fairway know a ball is being hit in their direction.

green. The area of close-cut grass surrounding the hole.

handicap. A system of rating golfers. It is a method of "spotting" less skilled golfers a number of strokes against more skilled golfers.

hook. For a right-handed golfer, a drive that curves from right to left.

lie. The position of the ball after it has been hit and stops rolling.

pitch. A short approach shot.

putt. A stroke made on the putting green with the putter, intended to drop the ball into the hole.

scratch golfer. A skilled golfer who has no handicap.

slice. For a right-handed golfer, a ball that curves from left to right.

tee. A small wooden or plastic peg, inserted into the ground, on which the ball is placed before driving off. Also, the area from which the golfer tees off.

whiff. To swing and miss the ball completely.

Olympics

The first Olympics were held in the Olympic Valley of Greece in 776 B.C. They only lasted a day and consisted of a 200-yard (one *stade*) race. The first champion was Coroebus of Elis, a young cook. The games grew and prospered in the years after 776, but by Roman times they had become a travesty. The emperor Nero was declared the winner of the chariot race, for example, even though he fell out of the cart. "Professional" athletes were entered. At last, in A.D. 394, the games were outlawed by Theodosius I, the Christian emperor of Rome.

Modern games. During the 1800s A.D., German archaeologists uncovered the area in Greece that had been the site of the temples and stadium of the ancient Olympics. A French scholar, Baron Pierre de Coubertin, visited the excavation and was so impressed that he began a campaign to have the Olympics restored. He was successful, and in 1894 the "new" or "modern" Olympiad was held in Athens, Greece. Athletes from 13 nations competed.

The United States' "unofficial" team won nine out of the twelve track and field events held that year. The new Olympics were a success. It was decided that future Olympics should be held in different cities of the world rather than only in Greece.

The Olympics have been held every four years since 1896 with only a few exceptions. A special Olympics was staged in Athens in 1906; all events were canceled in 1916 owing to World War I, and in 1940 and 1944, owing to World War II. The 1980 Olympics were boycotted by the United States and many other nations to protest the invasion of Afghanistan by the Soviet Union.

Over the years the Olympics have changed greatly. Women first competed in 1910, but they were only allowed to compete in golf, an event no longer part of the Olympics. In 1928 they were permitted to take part in track and field. There were no winter Olympics until 1924, when they were first held in Chamonix, France. Many additional events have

Sites of Modern Olympic Games

Year	Summer games	Winter games
1896	Athens, Greece	
1900	Paris, France	
1904	St. Louis, USA	
1906	Athens, Greece	
1908	London, England	
1912	Stockholm, Sweden	
1920	Antwerp, Belgium	
1924	Paris, France	Chamonix, France
1928	Amsterdam, Holland	St. Moritz, Switzerland
1932	Los Angeles, USA	Lake Placid, USA
1936	Berlin, Germany	Garmische-Partenkirchen, Germany
1948	London, England	St. Moritz, Switzerland
1952	Helsinki, Finland	Oslo, Norway
1956	Melbourne, Australia	Cortina d'Ampezzo, Italy
1960	Rome, Italy	Squaw Valley, USA
1964	Tokyo, Japan	Innsbruck, Austria
1968	Mexico City, Mexico	Grenoble, France
1972	Munich, Germany	Sapporo, Japan
1976	Montreal, Canada	Innsbruck, Austria
1980	Moscow, USSR	Lake Placid, USA
1984	Los Angeles, USA	Sarajevo, Yugoslavia
1988	Seoul, S. Korea	Calgary, Canada
1992	Barcelona, Spain	Albertville, France
1994*		Lillehammer, Norway
1996	Atlanta, USA	
1998		Nagano, Japan
2000	Sydney, Australia	
2002		Salt Lake City, USA
2004	Athens, Greece	
2006		Turin, Italy
2008	Beijing, China	
2010		Vancouver, Canada

*Starting in 1994, Olympic summer and winter games were staggered at two-year intervals.

448

Olympic women's hockey, U.S. vs. Canada

Olympic sports. Olympic events fall into two categories, team sports and individual sports. Among the team sports are basketball, field hockey, rowing, soccer, volleyball, and water polo during the summer games; bobsleigh and ice hockey during the winter games. Figure skating can be an individual sport, or the competitors can be a man and woman paired for the event. Bobsleigh can have two or four sledders. Women and men do not compete in all the same sports. For example, women do not box or compete in the decathlon.

been added. Today the Olympics are a major international event, attracting competitors from more than one hundred nations. Cities from around the world seek the honor of playing host.

It is not required that the host nation have all the possible sports; some, in the past, have been dropped and then reinstated. The decathlon, an individual competition in ten track and field events, is an outstanding event in any Olympiad. The most grueling race, the marathon, is the traditional conclusion of the summer games. The race is named for the legendary feat of Phidippides, a Greek warrior who ran from Marathon to Athens with news of victory.

Olympic Events

Summer Games

Men

Archery	Pentathlon	
Badminton	Rowing	
Baseball	Sailing	
Basketball	Shooting	
Boxing	Swimming	
Canoeing/Kayaking	Table Tennis	
Cycling	Taekwondo	
Diving	Tennis	
Equestrian	Track and Field	
Fencing	Triathlon	
Field Hockey	Volleyball	
Football (Soccer)	Water Polo	
Gymnastics	Weight Lifting	
Handball	Wheelchair Events	
Judo	Wrestling	

Women

Archery	Sailing
Badminton	Shooting
Basketball	Softball
Canoeing/Kayaking	Swimming
Cycling	Synchronized Swimming
Diving	Table Tennis
Equestrian	Taekwondo
Fencing	Tennis
Field Hockey	Track and Field
Football (Soccer)	Triathlon
Gymnastics	Volleyball
Handball	Water Polo
Judo	Weight Lifting
Pentathlon	Wheelchair Events
Rowing	Wrestling

Winter Games

Men

Biathlon	Luge
Bobsleigh	Skiing
Skeleton	Ski Jumping
Curling	Snowboarding
Figure Skating	Speed Skating
Ice Hockey	

Women

Biathlon	Ice Hockey
Bobsleigh	Luge
Skeleton	Skiing
Curling	Snowboarding
Figure Skating	Speed Skating

Other sports

Auto racing.

Auto racing began in Europe in 1894 with a series of town-to-town races. In 1895 a group of cars raced between Chicago and Evanston, Illinois. All these were relatively minor events. The first important American race was run in 1903 on a three-mile track at Grosse Pointe, Michigan. The driver was Barney Oldfield; the builder of the car was Henry Ford. Since then, auto racing has become a popular sport throughout the world, with different types of cars competing in various races.

Grand Prix events are staged over courses in Holland, France, England, Italy, Mexico, and other countries. Drivers compete through a special point system for the title of Drivers' World Championship. Only Formula I cars—"pure" racing cars—may compete in these events. The Grand Prix courses are usually several miles long and are irregular in shape, requiring drivers to negotiate a variety of curves and hills. Grand Prix races are governed by the *Federation Internationale de l'Automobile.* The American arm of the body is the Automobile Competition Committee of the United States.

Many races in the United States are held on paved or dirt tracks. The most famous track is the

Action in the Indianapolis 500.

Indianapolis International Speedway, home of the Indianapolis 500. Stock car racing features modified production cars. Stock car events are sponsored by the National Association for Stock Car Auto Races. Other types of racing, as with sports cars, are governed by the Sports Car Club of America and the United States Auto Club.

Bowling.

Bowling was known to exist around 5000 B.C. in Egypt. Modern-type bowling was developed by the Germans about the fourth century A.D. as part of their religious services. The Dutch brought the game to America. A part of Manhattan Island is still called Bowling Green.

Bowlers try to knock down ten pins that are arranged within a 36-inch triangle. The ball travels along a lane of polished wood, 60 feet from foul line to the headpin. The lane is 42 inches wide with gutters on either side. A bowling ball can be no more than 8.59 inches in diameter or 27 inches in circumference and can weigh not more than 16 pounds. Each ball has two or three finger holes. A game consists of ten frames. A perfect score is 300, meaning that the bowler has knocked down all ten pins in each frame with his first ball. The game is under the sanction of the American Bowling Congress.

Bowling scores

A strike *is noted by an* X *in the left small box; no score for that frame is entered until the bowler bowls the next two balls. The bowler receives a score of 10 for the strike* plus *the total pins knocked down on the next two rolls.*

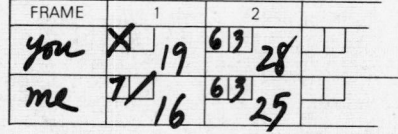

A spare *is noted by a slash (/) in the right small box. A spare earns 10 points plus the pins knocked down on the next roll.*

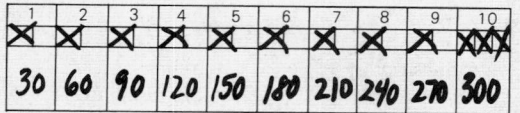

A perfect game consists of 12 strikes in a row; the bowler receives a score of 30 for each frame, for a total of 300.

Boxing and martial arts.

Modern boxing originated in England with the adoption of the Marquess of Queensbury rules in 1867; the rules were intended to eliminate the more brutal aspects of the sport. Essentially the same rules are in effect today. Boxers compete in matches that are divided into 3-minute rounds (2 minutes in some amateur bouts), with a minute of rest between rounds. Bouts last from 3 rounds in the Olympics to 15 rounds in professional championship matches. Certain blows are outlawed, such as rabbit or kidney punches, or those struck below the waist. A bout may terminate through a decision of the judges or by a knockout. Boxers compete according to various weight limitations.

The martial arts are a series of unarmed combat styles originating in Far Eastern cultures. The most popular are karate, judo, jujitsu, and kung fu. Judo is an Olympic event.

Boxing Weight Classifications	
Flyweight:	not over 112 lbs.
Bantamweight:	not over 118 lbs.
Junior featherweight:	not over 122 lbs.
Featherweight:	not over 126 lbs.
Junior lightweight:	not over 130 lbs.
Lightweight:	not over 135 lbs.
Junior welterweight:	not over 140 lbs.
Welterweight:	not over 147 lbs.
Junior middleweight:	not over 154 lbs.
Middleweight:	not over 160 lbs.
Light heavyweight:	not over 175 lbs.
Cruiserweight:	not over 195 lbs.
Heavyweight:	over 195 lbs.

Figure skating.

Figure skating was invented by a ballet teacher named Jackson Haines, an American who went to Vienna in 1863 to escape the Civil War and further his profession. As he watched skaters move about aimlessly, he conceived the idea of setting skating to waltz music and "dancing on ice." The first noted figure skater in America was one of his pupils, Louis Rubinstein of Canada. His exhibitions led to the formation of the Amateur Skating Association of Canada and the Skating Club of the United States.

In Olympic figure skating, skaters perform two programs: a short program, incorporating eight different moves, and a long program, in which

Speed skates (left) *have long straight blades; figure skates are turned up at the toe for sudden starts and stops.*

each skater selects his or her own routine of jumps, spins, or other moves.

Gymnastics.

Gymnastics stems from *gymna-zein,* a word of Greek origin that means to "exercise naked." Although the sport was popular during Greek and Roman days, gymnastics disappeared and did not surface again until late in the 1700s, when Frederick Jahn of Germany introduced some of the equipment now used in the sport. A few years later, gymnastics was introduced in the United States. Today, the U.S. Gymnastics Federation is the governing body, in charge of events featuring side horse, calisthenics, horizontal bars, rings, parallel bars, and long horse. Gymnastics is an Olympic sport.

Competitive gymnastics requires intense physical preparation.

Equestrian sports.

Horse racing can be divided into three types of events: *flat racing* around an oval track (or part of it); *harness racing* for "gaited" horses pulling light two-wheeled carts called "sulkies"; and *steeplechase racing,* in which horses must hurdle hedges and water hazards. Flat racing features *thoroughbred horses,* which are bred and trained only for racing. *Quarter horses,* an American offshoot of this breed, are trained only for short sprints. Harness racing horses are called *standardbreds* and are trained not to gallop. A *trotter* moves its left front leg and and right back leg simultaneously, while a *pacer* uses both legs on the same side of its body in unison. Steeplechase horses are bred and raced in Europe.

In equestrian events, speed is of no importance. Horses are judged on conformation, which includes height, weight, and form, soundness of bone and limb, training, and fitness. Horses compete in jumping events, leaping hurdles of various heights. *Dressage* is an obedience event. Responding to barely perceptible movements by the rider, the horses execute various maneuvers and gaits.

Jumping fences is part of many equestrian events.

Skiing.

Skiing is by far the most popular of all winter sports. Recreational skiing began in Austria toward the end of the 1700s, but competitive skiing started in Norway during the middle of the 1800s. Modern competitive skiing, as sanctioned in the Olympics, consists of Alpine and Nordic events.

Alpine events include the *downhill,* a run down a course in the fastest possible time. Some courses are two miles long. The *slalom* is shorter than the downhill. "Gates"—a set of two flags of the same color—are set in a zigzag pattern down a slope. The skier must pass through the gates in the fastest possible time. The *giant slalom* and the *super-g* are shorter than the downhill but longer than the slalom. A giant slalom race consists of two runs, a super-g one run.

Nordic events include *jumping,* in which the skier zooms down an inclined ramp and off its lip into the air. Jumps are judged for form and distance. *Cross-country* races are run over courses that include level, uphill, and downhill stretches. *Nordic combined* competitions include ski jumping and cross-country racing.

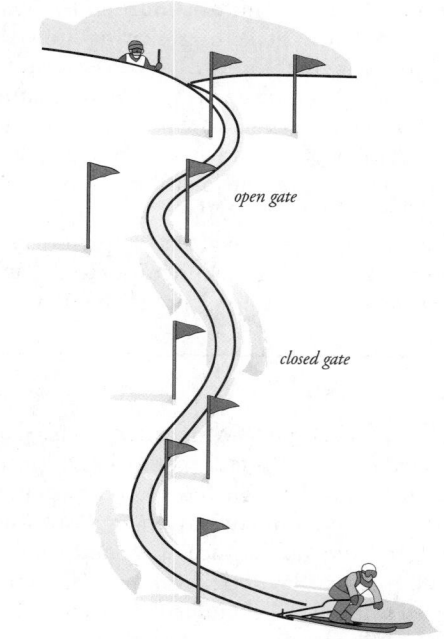

open gate

closed gate

A slalom course: A winning skier must follow the irregular course through the "gates" and finish in the best time.

Swimming and diving.

Although humans have probably always known how to swim, the first nation to take swimming seriously was Japan, where the emperor ordered schools to compete against each other in that sport. However, the English developed swimming on a worldwide basis, beginning in the 1800s. Modern swimming uses four basic strokes in competition: freestyle (usually the Australian crawl), backstroke, breaststroke, and butterfly. In Olympic competition, races vary from 50 to 1,500 meters.

"Fancy" diving began in England in 1905. Modern divers use both a stationary platform and a springboard. There are three classifications of dives: the layout (a swan dive); the pike (a jackknife); and the tuck (contained in somersaulting). Divers are judged on the difficulty and form of their dives.

Three basic diving positions

Track and field.

Track events consist of running various distances, from short sprints (100 meters) to middle distances (400 to 1,500 meters) to the marathon (26 miles, 385 yards). Also included in track events are *hurdles*—races in which runners leap obstacles placed in each running lane at regular intervals. Hurdles vary in height from 2 feet 6 inches to 3 feet 6 inches, according to the length of the race and the sex of the competitors.

Field events include the throwing of the *discus,* a flattened disk made of wood with a metal center and rim. It is thrown with one hand. The *shot put* is a brass or iron ball, which is also thrown with one hand, with a pushing-out motion. The *javelin* is a spear thrown overhand for the greatest distance. Jumping events include the *high jump,* in which the jumper takes a short run at a bar that he or she must clear, and the *long jump,* in which the jumper takes a running start to a set mark and then leaps forward, landing in a sand pit. In the *pole vault,* the jumper takes a running start and uses a flexible pole to vault high up and over a bar. In the *triple jump* (also called hop-skip-and-jump), the athlete gets a running start to a mark, then leaps forward and lands on the takeoff foot, leaps forward again landing on the opposite foot, and leaps ahead a third time landing on both feet.

Track events include the hurdles (above); *field events include the high jump* (below).

Handball is a game popular in many cities. It is played against a wall by two or four players, who hit the ball with the flat of their hands.

Wall and net games.
Wall and net games have a number of similarities. All involve the use of a ball of varying size that is thrown or batted either against a wall or over a net using a racket, a paddle, a kind of basket, or a gloved hand (*see also* Tennis).

Badminton was invented during the 1870s by British army officers. It is a simple game involving light rackets, a shuttlecock (which is mostly cork with feathers stuck into the "head"), and a net. The shuttlecock is batted back and forth over the net until a player fails to return it, allowing the opponent to score a point. Usually, 15 points wins the game.

Handball was invented by the Irish in the 900s. In its modern form, it is played against walls on three sides of the player. The ball is hard rubber, $1\frac{7}{8}$ inches in diameter and weighing 2.3 ounces. Gloves are worn to protect the hands. Only the server can score points. The server puts the ball in play by serving from behind a line; the opponent attempts to return the ball against the wall. Failure to return the serve scores a point for the server. A variation of the game is played in a four-wall court.

Jai alai was invented in the 1600s by the Basques of the Pyrenees Mountains. It has become popular in the Philippines, Mexico, and the United States. The game resembles handball to a great extent. Instead of a glove, players use a curved basket called a cesta. The pelota (ball) is made of rubber with a layer of nylon thread; it rebounds from the wall at extremely high speeds.

Paddle tennis is a smaller form of lawn tennis. The court is smaller and paddles are used instead of rackets. The ball is a deadened tennis ball. Overhand smashes are outlawed. Scoring is the same as in tennis, except that there is no tie-breaker.

Ping-Pong (table tennis) was invented by an American named James Gibb in 1899. As now played, the game involves a table 9 feet 5 inches long, 6 feet wide, and 30 inches high. The ball is made of celluloid, the paddles are wood covered with some kind of stippled or foam rubber. The server hits the ball so that it bounces first on his or her side of the net, then onto the opponent's side. Failure to return gives the opponent a point. Both server and opponent can score points in Ping-Pong. Service is alternated after each 5 points; 21 points wins the game.

Volleyball is played at all levels of skill, from pickup games on the beach and local leagues to the Olympics.

If the score is tied at 20 all, the winner must score 2 additional points.

Racquetball is a combination of tennis and handball. A standard four-wall handball court is used. The racket resembles the one used in tennis except that the handle is shorter. The ball is very lively.

Squash was invented by students at Harrow School, England, during the 1800s. A modern squash court (singles) has walls 32 feet long on the sides and 18½ feet wide to the front. The front wall is 16 feet high. A floor service line is marked 22 feet from the front wall, and a line bisects the back court in half, similar to a tennis court. A front wall service line is marked 6½ feet above the floor, and all serves must hit above it. Returns must hit above a metal strip called the *telltale,* 17 inches above the floor. A score of 15 points usually wins.

Volleyball was invented in 1895 by Dr. William G. Morgan, a YMCA instructor. A volleyball court measures 30 by 60 feet; it is divided by a net 8 feet off the floor. A team consists of six players. It is similar to tennis in that the aim is to hit the ball over the net and to try to force the opposing team to hit the ball into the net or out of bounds. Only the hands or arms may be used to bat the ball, and it may be hit only three times on the same side of the net, never twice by the same player. Only the serving team may score. Game is usually 15 points. World-class volleyball is an extremely demanding sport that is a regular Olympic event, but the game is also enjoyed as a recreation by millions.

For Further Reference

Baker, William
   Sports in the Western World
   Rowman and Littlefield
Diagram Group
   Rules of the Game: Complete Illustrated Encyclopedia of All the Sports in the World
   Paddington
Ritter, Lawrence S.
   The Story of Baseball
   William Morrow
Sullivan, George
   All About Football
   Dodd, Mead

- *Mechanics of music*   **457**
- *Musical instruments*   **458**
- *Materials of music*   **461**
- *Kinds of music*   **463**
- *Dictionary of music*   **466**

Music

Music—along with drama and dance—is one of the performing arts. Its history runs further into the past than written language, but because it was not written down or recorded, nearly all early music is lost to us. We know, for example, that early Greek drama included music and dance as well as spoken words, but only the words have been preserved. Biblical psalms and songs may have been written to be sung with musical accompaniment, but if so, the music has been lost. In the 1500s, musicians began to perfect a means of writing down their compositions, but even these early musical manuscripts are difficult to understand, and we cannot always be certain how they sounded when performed.

Today, music is everywhere. Performers record their music, making sure that they will be remembered as long as there is recording equipment to play back their performances. Great works from the past have been recorded hundreds of times.

No special knowledge is required to listen to music, but much study is required to become a performer. The following section briefly describes the mechanics of music, the elements of musical language and notation, and the major types of music important today. A dictionary of common musical terms is also provided.

Time Line of Music

Classical music		American music
Baroque (1700–1760)	1700	
	1750	
Classical (1760–1790)		
Romantic (1790–1890)	1800	
		Minstrel shows (c 1830–1890)
	1850	
Modern (1890–)		Vaudeville (1890–1925)
Sound recording	1900	Jazz (1900–)
Radio (1922)		Musical comedy (1925–)
Long-play records, high fidelity (1950)	1950	Rock (1955–)
Stereophonic sound (1960)		
Digital recordings (1980)	2000	

Mechanics of music

Music consists of sound; to understand it, one must understand how sound is made.

Vibrations. All sound is made by vibration. If you strike a drum, the drum head vibrates, sending sound waves out through the air. If you pluck a guitar string, it vibrates, sending out similar waves. These waves, which we perceive with our ears, we call sound. When the guitar string is at rest, it looks like this:

When it is plucked, it vibrates in a wave motion, first one way, then the others:

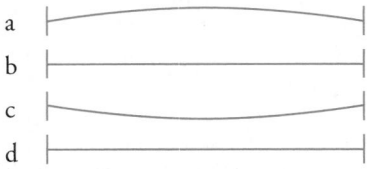

One complete movement through these stages is called a *cycle*.

Frequency. How high or low the guitar's sound is—its *pitch*—depends on its *frequency*, or the number of cycles it goes through in a second. A frequency of 440 cycles per second has the pitch of the A above middle C on the piano; a frequency of 220 cycles per second (half of 440) has the pitch of the A below middle C; and one of 880 cycles per second (twice 440) has the pitch of the second A above middle C.

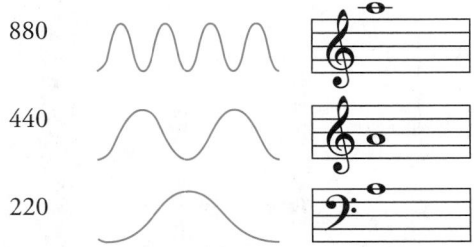

Amplitude. Amplitude is a measure of how far the guitar string (or other vibrating material) moves in a single cycle. If the amplitude is large, the sound is loud. If the amplitude is small, the sound is soft.

= loud
= soft

Some musical sounds, such as that of a trumpet, are steady in loudness. As long as the trumpeter's breath holds out, the sound can be kept at the same level. Other musical sounds, such as those of a guitar or piano, start out loud as the string is plucked or struck, but begin immediatey to die out or *decay:*

Complex sounds. Each sound maker or musical instrument has its own particular sound. The actual vibrations that cause the sounds are much more complex than the simple wave forms illustrated above. These complex vibrations give each sound maker its particular sound quality or *timbre.* Actual wave representations of familiar musical instruments are shown below.

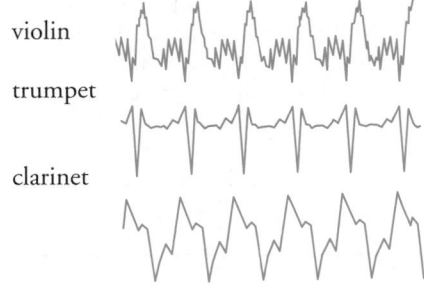

violin

trumpet

clarinet

Familiar noises as sound waves

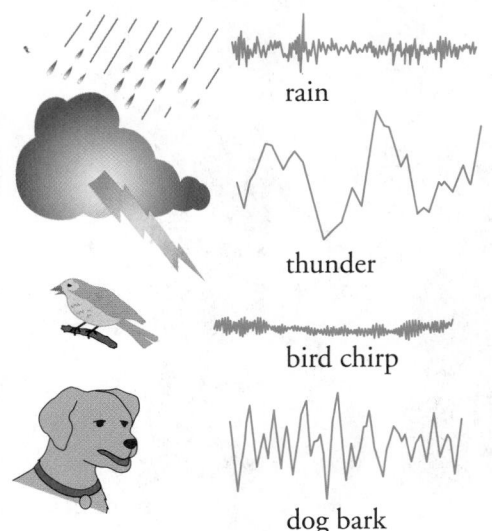

rain

thunder

bird chirp

dog bark

Musical instruments

People have used hundreds of different objects to make musical sounds. The following list considers those most common today: the human voice, the four "families" of orchestral instruments, keyboard instruments, other nonorchestral instruments, and the growing number of electronic and electronically enhanced instruments.

Human voice.

Perhaps the original musical instrument was the human voice. Vocal sound is created by forcing air between the vocal cords. A singer can vary the pitch of the voice by tightening or loosening the cords and can also vary its quality and loudness. The singer's chest and head act as a *resonator,* increasing the volume and affecting the timbre of the sound.

In general, men's voices are of lower pitch than women's. Choral groups are divided into sections by the pitch levels of the singers' voices. Men with the lowest voices are basses; men with higher voices are tenors; women with the highest voices are sopranos; women with lower voices are altos.

Strings.

The strings are the first of the four families of orchestral instruments. They include the violin, viola, cello, and string bass. Each is normally played by drawing a bow over strings of different thickness and tautness, giving a sound of even loudness. The strings can also be plucked like those of a guitar; in that case, the sound decays rapidly. Different pitches on string instruments are produced by shortening the vibrating length of a string with a finger on the fingerboard. The wood sounding case under the strings acts as a resonator, increasing the volume of the sound and helping to give it its distinctive quality. The most valued string instruments were made in Italy in the 1700s—their rich sound has never been equaled by modern instruments. As with voices, string instruments are arranged according to their pitch from the string bass (the lowest) to the violin (the highest).

Woodwinds.

The woodwinds include the bassoon, oboe, clarinet, flute, and piccolo. The flute and piccolo are tubes of metal or wood with small

Orchestral instrument families

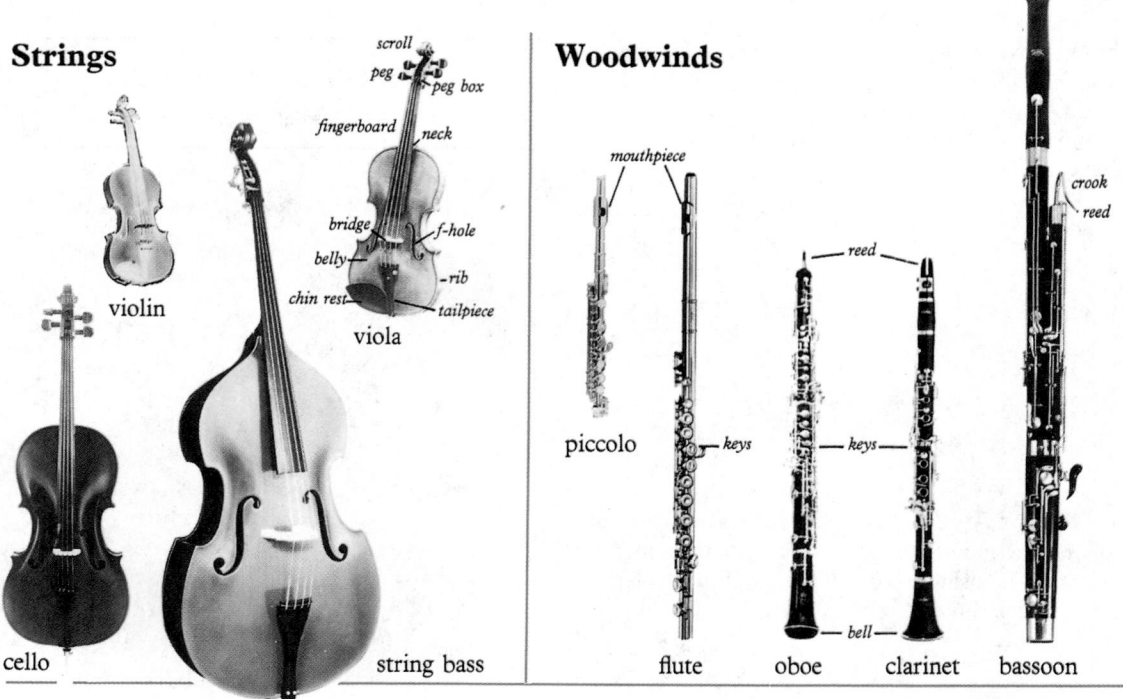

Strings

violin

scroll
peg
peg box
fingerboard
neck
bridge
belly
f-hole
rib
chin rest
tailpiece

viola

cello

string bass

Woodwinds

mouthpiece

reed

reed

crook

reed

piccolo

keys

keys

bell

flute

oboe

clarinet

bassoon

mouthpieces. The performer blows air over the hole in the mouthpiece, causing the air in the tube to vibrate, just as one blows air over the mouth of a bottle to produce a sound. The other woodwinds have mouthpieces with a reed. Performers put the reed between their lips and blow in a way that causes the reed to vibrate. Woodwind players change the pitch of their instruments by working levers that open and close holes along the length of the instruments, changing the length of the column of air inside them. The bassoon is the bass member of the woodwind family. The oboe, clarinet, and flute play in the alto and soprano range, and the piccolo has the highest range of any orchestral instrument.

Brass.

The brass instruments include the trumpet, French horn, trombone, and tuba. Each of these instruments is a long tube of metal with a circular metal mouthpiece. Performers purse their lips and blow into the mouthpiece so that their lips vibrate. These vibrations are amplified by the long tube of air in the instrument.

Brass players change the pitch of their instruments partly by changing the tightness of their lips and partly by pressing valves that change the length of the column of air in the instrument. The trombone has a slide instead of valves to change the length of the column of air—the farther it is extended, the lower the note of the instrument. The brass instruments with the pitch range from the lowest to the highest are the tuba, trombone, French horn, and trumpet.

Percussion.

The percussion section in an orchestra contains a wide variety of instruments that are most often used for rhythmic effect rather than for producing particular pitches or melodies. The section includes various drums, xylophone, cymbals, triangle, and special noisemaking devices such as maracas and castanets. Nearly all percussion instruments are *struck* to make sound. Some percussion instruments have variable pitch (timpani, xylophone), and others do not (cymbals, snare drum). The piano is sometimes considered a percussion instrument.

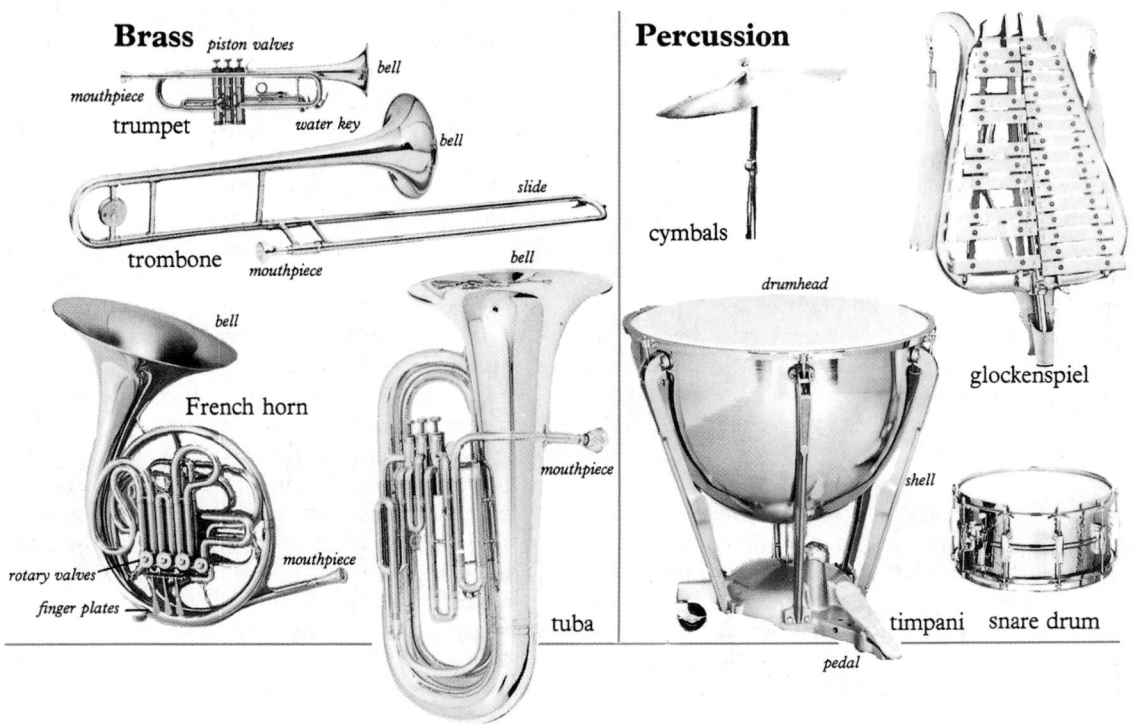

Brass — piston valves, mouthpiece, bell, water key — trumpet — bell — trombone, slide, mouthpiece — bell — French horn, bell, rotary valves, finger plates, mouthpiece — tuba, mouthpiece

Percussion — cymbals — glockenspiel — drumhead, shell, timpani, pedal — snare drum

459

A classic configuration for a jazz combo includes piano, upright bass, saxophone, trumpet, and drums.

Keyboard instruments.

Perhaps the most popular solo instruments are those with a keyboard. The keyboard instruments have a much wider range of pitches than the orchestral instruments, and more than one note can be struck at a time, producing rich harmonies as well as melody.

Keyboard instruments use different methods to produce sound. The organ is a wind instrument related to the woodwinds. Pressing a note on its keyboard releases air into a pipe of a certain length and thickness, creating a woodwind-like sound. Large pipe organs may have hundreds of separate pipes, including many that have the same pitch but different sound qualities. The piano is both a percussion and a string instrument. Pressing a note on its keyboard causes a felt hammer to strike a string inside the piano.

Other instruments.

There are many nonorchestral instruments important in music. They include such popular string instruments as the guitar and banjo, which are played by plucking the strings rather than bowing them; such woodwind instruments as the saxophone, which is widely used in jazz and in bands; and such brass instruments for band as the cornet, baritone, and sousaphone.

Electronic instruments.

The development of electricity has produced a growing number of new musical instruments. Perhaps the most familiar is the electronic organ, which was designed to resemble the pipe organ in sound. When a key is depressed on an electronic organ, a pitch is produced by an oscillator and amplified by a speaker—there are no pipes or wind-producing mechanisms.

Other electronic keyboard instruments have been developed with a wide range of special abilities. These new instruments are called *synthesizers* and they can mimic the sounds of nearly any instrument. In addition, synthesizers can create sound qualities and effects never produced by any natural instrument or group of instruments.

Electronics has also been used to amplify many conventional instruments, creating sounds that are partly old and partly new. The electric guitar has become an important instrument in popular music, and the microphone has allowed singers to achieve new effects that would be impossible without amplification.

Finally, the tape recorder has helped modern musicians create many new musical sounds. A recording may be slowed down, speeded up, played backward, or superimposed to produce many exotic and revolutionary sound effects.

Materials of music

Most music has certain characteristics in common. These characteristics include melody, rhythm, and harmony. The following section explains each of them and illustrates how they are shown in traditional musical notation.

Melody.

Melody consists of a number of pitches in a row. A melody may be long and complex or short and simple, consisting of only two or three notes.

Each pitch is represented in musical notation by a *note* placed on a staff:

The notes of the staff have letter names as shown below. They represent the pitches that can be played by all conventional instruments and are arranged on two *clefs:* the bass clef for lower pitches and the treble clef for higher pitches.

treble clef   bass clef

Any combination of pitches on the staff can create a melody. Those below are the opening pitches of "Three Blind Mice" and "Taps."

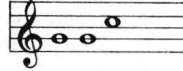

A melody may be performed by itself, or it may have accompaniment, which provides harmonies matching the melody.

Rhythm.

Rhythm consists of several musical notes held for varying amounts of time or separated by silences called *rests.*

The major rhythmic pattern of a piece of music is shown at the beginning of the piece. The top number of the *time signature* shows how many beats there will be in a *measure,* a unit set off in written music by bar lines. The first beat of a measure is often stressed.

Two beats to the measure
Count 1-2 1-2 1-2
May be a march: left-right left-right

Three beats to the measure
Count 1-2-3 1-2-3
May be a waltz:
oom-pah-pah oom-pah-pah

The rhythmic pattern of the notes themselves is shown by the shadings of the notes and by a system of flags (see "Note values" below).

The two melodies shown below are both in ⁴⁄₄ time. The bottom number in the time signature tells what kind of note is to receive one beat. The bottom "4" in this signature says that the *quarter* note gets one count. With time signature and note values, the two melodies look like this:

Pitch names

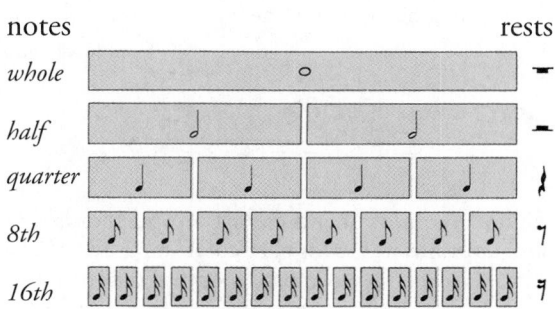

Note Values

461

Rhythm is also affected by the speed at which the music is played—its *tempo*. Some indication of the proper speed is often given in the *tempo marking* at the beginning of the piece. Traditional Italian terms are recognized internationally by musicians. Among the most common are:

>   allegro: fast, lively
>   andante: moderately, at a walking speed
>   adagio: slowly

Some compositions also provide a metronome marking:

♩ = 120

This marking says that the composition should be played so that there are 120 quarter-note counts per minute.

Harmony.

A third element of music is harmony, which consists of the sound of two or more notes played at the same time. For example, one might add a bass line to "Three Blind Mice" to create simple harmony:

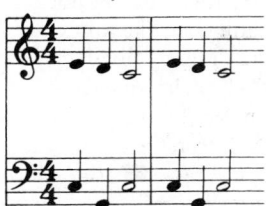

Traditional harmony is based on chords—harmonious combinations of notes. Accompaniments to many simple songs may consist of only three chords:

I IV V

These may be broken up in any way. For example, the following measures are a series of I chords that could accompany the opening measures of a waltz:

Guitar accompaniments consist only of chords that are appropriate to a particular melody. Many pianists learn to accompany popular songs by following the chord patterns rather than by playing the melody.

Other elements of music.

Among other elements of music are key, dynamics, and articulation.

Key. The examples given above have all been given in the key of C major. The C major scale consists of the white notes on a piano, running upward or downward from one C to the next. However, any melody may be written and performed in any of twelve major keys. For example, the opening of "Three Blind Mice" may appear as follows:

key of C   key of G   key of F

In the key of G, the F is always sharped—raised one-half step (to the next highest black note on a piano). In the key of F, the B is always flatted—lowered one-half step (to the next lowest black note on a piano).

Each major key has a *relative minor* key. A minor scale has a different, "sadder" sound. "Three Blind Mice" in the key of C minor would look like this:

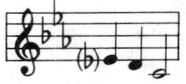

The box below shows the key signatures (number of sharps or flats), key names, and relative minors for each major key.

Sharps and flats may also be used to raise and lower particular notes in a composition. When used this way, they are called *accidentals*. Other accidentals are the natural sign (♮), which tells the performer to use the natural pitch for a note that has been sharped or flatted; the double sharp (𝄪), which calls for a note already sharped to be sharped still

Key signatures

sharp signatures

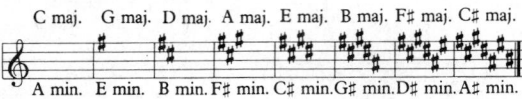

flat signatures

F maj. B♭ maj. E♭ maj. A♭ maj. D♭ maj. G♭ maj. C♭ maj.

D min. G min. C min. F min. B♭ min. E♭ min. A♭ min.

another half step; and the double flat (♭♭), which calls for a note already flatted to be lowered still another half-step. The relation of these accidentals is shown below:

Dynamics. Musical notation has a system of alerting the performer to the loudness or softness desired by the composer or editor of the music. Like tempo markings, dynamic markings are in Italian. They are shown in the following table.

ppp	(pianississimo)	= as soft as possible
pp	(pianissimo)	= very soft
p	(piano)	= soft
mp	(mezzo piano)	= moderately soft
mf	(mezzo forte)	= moderately loud
f	(forte)	= loud
ff	(fortissimo)	= very loud
fff	(fortississimo)	= as loud as possible
————	(crescendo)	= get louder
————	(diminuendo)	= get softer

Articulation. Traditional notation may also have marks suggesting the way in which a note or series of notes should be performed. Among the articulation marks are the following:

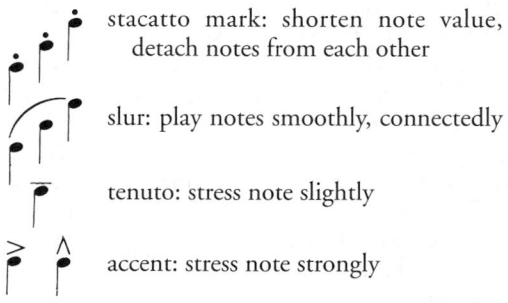

staccato mark: shorten note value, detach notes from each other

slur: play notes smoothly, connectedly

tenuto: stress note slightly

accent: stress note strongly

Traditional notation has been the way of preserving music from the distant past. Since the 1890s, however, music has been even more carefully preserved by recordings. A recording can save not only the notes and the general playing instructions, but an exact performance of a particular piece. By comparison, even the best edition of written music is only a blueprint for a performance. Modern composing synthesizers produce both a printed score and a recording.

Kinds of music

More kinds of music are available to interested listeners today than ever before—on records, on tape, on CDs, and in live performances. There are two major traditions of music, generally known as *classical* and *popular,* although the line between them is not always clear.

Classical music. This term is often used to describe the long tradition of "serious" music from the European Middle Ages to the present. The classics are often associated with orchestral music, but they also include solo music for instruments, opera, and choral music.

Early music. European music grew from the music of the Christian church in the Middle Ages. The church used *chants* in its services—simple music for one voice, intoning words from the psalms or from ancient services of worship. In time, some churches added a second voice, producing a kind of harmony. By 1400, composers were writing music for four or more voices.

By the year 1600, music both for the church and for the courts of kings and nobles was highly developed. During the 1600s the pipe organ was perfected for church use. Court entertainments included the use of other instruments and the production of elaborate musical plays that gradually developed into opera and ballet. Composers wrote many pieces for two or more parts (either voices or instruments) and developed a style of music called *polyphonic,* or many-voiced.

The composer and performer who acted as a bridge between this early style and later, more "modern" styles was Johann Sebastian Bach (1685–1750). He was a great organist and composed many pieces for the organ. As a director of church music, he wrote hundreds of *cantatas* for small orchestra, solo voices, and chorus. For his wealthy patrons he wrote much instrumental music for groups of instruments that were coming to resemble the modern orchestra. The most famous of these are the six *Brandenburg Concertos.*

The other great composer of the age was George Frederick Handel (1685–1759). Although born in Germany, Handel spent most of his life in England. His greatest works were *oratorios,* dramatic works that often told a biblical story for orchestra, solo voices, and chorus. His *Messiah* is the most popular of all oratorios.

Classic and Romantic. By 1750, composers were tired of the complicated many-voiced music of Bach and Handel. They were looking for a simpler musical language. The result was the music of the classical period (about 1760 to 1790): symphonies, concertos for solo instruments with orchestra, and an increasing amount of music for the newly developed *pianoforte.* This instrument is an early version of the modern piano.

The classical period produced two great composers: Franz Joseph Haydn (1732–1809) and Wolfgang Amadeus Mozart (1756–1791). Haydn wrote over a hundred symphonies and scores of works for chamber groups—quartets, trios, and other small groups. Indeed, it is sometimes said that Haydn "invented" the string quartet. The *chamber music* was played in the halls of noblemen for the enjoyment of the players and for a small audience of friends. He also wrote a number of operas.

Mozart was a great musical prodigy who began performing in public at age five and who had written whole symphonies before he was ten. He played for the Austrian empress when he was six. His father, his sister, and he toured Europe as concert musicians until he was 16. In his short life (he died at 35), he wrote symphonies, many great piano concertos, and several operas, including *The Marriage of Figaro,* perhaps the first great modern opera.

By 1790, still another style was beginning to take over from the classical style. Composers were seeking a musical language that would more nearly express their innermost thoughts and feelings. The new style came to be called Romantic, and it influenced serious musicians for more than 100 years.

The first great Romantic composer was Ludwig van Beethoven (1770–1827). His early works owed much to Haydn and Mozart, but he gradually learned to express his own tempestuous and dramatic feelings in his music. His nine symphonies are among the most important orchestral works ever written, and his 32 piano sonatas are the first great works for the modern solo instrument. Early in his career, Beethoven became almost completely deaf; he never really heard many of his great compositions performed except in his own mind.

Among later Romantic composers in Germany were Franz Schubert, whose songs for voice and for the piano are still widely loved and played; Robert Schumann, a great composer for the piano;

Johannes Brahms, a great orchestral composer, was also a pianist.

and Johannes Brahms, whose orchestral works seek to outshine even those of Beethoven. The Polish-French pianist Frédéric Chopin and the Hungarian Franz Liszt wrote challenging new pieces for piano, while the Russian Peter Ilyich Tchaikovsky became a master of the symphony and other orchestral forms. Tchaikovsky's compositions contain highly original melodies, sudden shifts in mood and harmony, and frequent use of folk song material. His ballet scores for *Swan Lake, The Sleeping Beauty,* and *Nutcracker Suite* are world famous.

Meanwhile, opera became the great national music of Italy. Gioacchino Rossini and Giuseppe Verdi made opera perhaps the most satisfying of all musical experiences, combining great music with the color and spectacle of the stage. Late in the 1800s, Richard Wagner developed a form of grand opera in Germany, and his daring compositions greatly influenced modern composers.

Modern period. Since 1900, serious music has undergone rapid changes. Claude Debussy and Maurice Ravel sought to make music more like painting, seeking new "colors" and sounds in the orchestra. Igor Stravinsky's early compositions were so filled with unfamiliar timbres, rhythms, and harmonies that they caused riots in their first performances. Arnold Schoenberg and Alban Berg gave up traditional scales and harmonies and composed in a new musical language. The Hungarian Béla Bartók and others searched for folk themes and used them in new and surprising ways. Among the modern experimenters were Americans Charles Ives and Aaron Copland.

The Beatles began with American rhythm and blues music, then added new influences to rock 'n' roll.

Popular music.
From earliest times, there has been a lively popular music tradition. Early church composers often used popular songs of their day as the basis for their serious compositions. During the late 1700s, musicians in many parts of Europe began to take their national folk music and ballads seriously.

The popular tradition has been especially strong in the United States since the late 1800s. It includes folk music, jazz, and rock.

Folk music. Immigrants to the United States brought folk music from their native countries. For example, English and Scottish folk ballads were kept and developed by isolated communities in the Appalachian Mountains until recent times. Sometimes words were changed to suit new situations, and many new tunes were developed and handed down from one generation to the next. In the 1900s, various folk music traditions contributed to revivals of bluegrass and country-and-western music.

The blacks of the South also developed their own special folk materials. Combining African and Western forms, they created *blues, spirituals,* and a wide variety of music for dancing, from the *ragtime* of the 1890s to the later jazz and rock forms. Perhaps their greatest contribution was the development of jazz.

Jazz. Just how jazz came to be is not clear. By 1900, black musicians playing in clubs and on riverboats around New Orleans had created this new kind of music. It differed from both serious and popular music of the day in its intense rhythm and in its encouragement of *improvisation.* Jazz compositions were not written down; great jazz performers played by ear and improvised, never performing the same tune the same way twice. Fortunately, early efforts at sound recording have preserved some of these early jazz performances.

By the 1920s the popularity of jazz had spread far beyond the black community. European composers were studying and imitating it. George Gershwin, a composer of Broadway musicals, adapted jazz elements for "Rhapsody in Blue." His popular *Porgy and Bess* is a folk opera about black people.

The mainstream of jazz was made up of black performers. Louis Armstrong, who started with an early New Orleans band, became an international celebrity. Duke Ellington, leader of a jazz "big band," gradually became a serious and widely respected composer. Charlie "Bird" Parker developed a new kind of jazz called *bop* in the 1940s. More recent jazz giants include Miles Davis, Thelonius Monk, and Charlie Mingus.

Many jazz students believe that jazz has become a new "classical" music for the United States. At the same time, however, the language of jazz has so influenced popular American music that it is often difficult to tell where jazz ends and other popular forms begin.

Rock 'n' roll. Rock music came to public attention in the 1950s. Its insistent, rhythmic style probably originated in the traditions of black Americans, but a young white singer named Elvis Presley helped make rock a household word. Rock appealed to teenagers and sometimes angered their parents, but it gradually attracted a wide and knowledgeable audience. A British group, the Beatles, adopted rock, then mixed it with musical ideas from other parts of the world. Later "fusion" groups experimented with combinations of rock, jazz, and other popular styles.

Recording. This rapid musical development was all made possible by the art of recording. Until 1900, a musician knew about other musicians in distant places only by reputation or by written copies of their music. Today, widely available recordings allow new musical ideas and styles to spread worldwide within weeks or months. American popular music is becoming a musical tradition with an international following.

chamber music

Dictionary of music

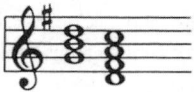

chords

monophonic music

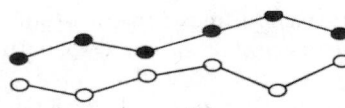

polyphonic music

an octave

synthesizer

accelerando. Tempo marking: speed up.

accidental. Musical sign that instructs the player to alter the pitch of a note. The signs include sharps, flats, and naturals.

adagio. Tempo marking: slowly.

allegro. Tempo marking: quickly, in a lively mood.

alto. Pitch range below soprano and above tenor and bass.

andante. Tempo marking: moderately, at a walking pace.

arpeggio. Method of playing a chord, note after note from the bottom up.

articulation. Class of music instructions telling how notes or phrases should be played.

Baroque. Name for the musical period from 1600 to 1750 that culminated in the music of Bach and Handel.

bass. Lowest pitch range; a singer or instrument in this range.

brass. Family of instruments, including the trumpet, French horn, trombone, and tuba.

cadenza. Difficult, showy passage at the end of a solo or concerto for the soloist.

cantata. Setting of a religious text for soloists, chorus, and instruments.

chamber music. Instrumental music for a small group to be performed in an intimate setting.

chord. Three or more notes sounded at the same time; the basic unit of harmony.

clef. Sign at the beginning of a musical staff showing the pitch levels on that staff.

coda. Final section ending a work or movement.

concerto. Composition in three or four movements for solo instrument and orchestra.

counterpoint. Music in which two or more voices have melodic lines at the same time; polyphonic music.

diatonic scale. Traditional scale (major or minor) consisting of a combination of whole and half steps. There are seven notes between octaves (or eight including the octave); for example, C, D, E, F, G, A, B, (C). *See also* twelve-tone music; whole-tone scale.

dissonance. Chords or melodic intervals that are disagreeable to the ear and that tend to produce tension.

dynamics. Volume level of music, expressed in musical notation by terms such as *forte, piano,* etc.

forte. Dynamic marking: loud.

harmony. Sounding of two or more different tones at the same time; chords that are agreeable to the ear and tend to resolve tension.

interval. Distance between two tones.

key signature. Sharps or flats written at the beginning of a musical staff to show what key the music is in.

largo. Tempo marking: very slowly.

mass. Musical setting of the traditional Christian service of communion.

measure. Rhythmic unit in musical notation. Measures are separated by bar lines.

meter. Organization of beats into measures as dictated by a composition's time signature.

moderato. Tempo marking: in moderate time.

modulation. Changing from one key to another in a piece.

monophonic. Music consisting of one melodic line without accompaniment.

octave. Interval that contains eight steps of the conventional (diatonic) scale.

oratorio. Dramatic composition for soloists, chorus, and orchestra, usually on a religious theme and designed for concert performance.

percussion. Family of instruments that produces sounds by being struck: drums, etc.

pitch. Highness or lowness of a tone that can be measured in cycles per second. Pitch is shown in musical notation by the position of a note on a staff.

presto. Tempo marking: very fast.

quartet. Group of four musicians or music written for such a group. A string quartet consists of two violins, a viola, and a cello.

rest. Sign that corresponds to the value of a musical note and that indicates a similar period of silence.

rondo. Musical form in which a theme section is repeated several times, separated by contrasting sections; often used in the last movement of a sonata, concerto, or symphony.

round. Polyphonic song in which a second voice begins the first line as the first voice begins the second line; for example, "Three Blind Mice."

scale. Arrangement of tones between one note and its octave in ascending or descending order. A diatonic scale (major or minor) includes eight tones from base note to octave; a chromatic scale contains 13 notes from base note to octave.

scherzo. Musical form in lively ¾ or ⅜ tempo, often used as the third of four movements in a symphony, sonata, or string quartet.

sonata. Composition in three or four movements for piano, or for solo instrument and piano; a common form in the classic and Romantic periods.

sonata form. Musical form in which two or more themes are stated, then developed, then repeated in their original form; often used in the first movement of a sonata, concerto, or symphony.

soprano. Highest of the four traditional pitch ranges; a voice or instrument that plays in this range.

strings. Family of instruments including the violin, viola, cello, and string bass.

symphony. Extended composition of three or four movements for full orchestra; a common form in the classic and Romantic periods.

syncopation. Strong rhythmic accents on normally weak beats; important in jazz and other popular forms.

synthesizer. Electronic instrument with an almost unlimited range of sound qualities or timbres.

tempo. Rate of speed of a composition. A general tempo is indicated by tempo markings above the staff (*allegro, andante,* etc.).

tenor. Pitch range above bass and below alto and soprano; a voice or instrument in this range.

timbre. Sound quality of a particular instrument or voice.

time signature. Two numbers placed after the key signature at the beginning of a piece of music showing the rhythmic organization of the piece.

triad. Chord with three notes: key note, third, and fifth.

trill. Rapid alternation between the note printed and the note above it.

twelve-tone music. Music using a chromatic scale with twelve notes between octaves rather than the traditional diatonic scale (which has only seven notes).

whole-tone scale. Scale with only whole-tone intervals consisting of only six notes from octave to octave; for example, C, D, E, F#, G#, A#, (C).

woodwinds. Family of instruments including the piccolo, flute, clarinet, oboe, and bassoon.

For Further Reference

Britten, Benjamin and Holst, Imogene
The Wonderful World of Music
Doubleday

Hurd, Michael and Scholes, Percy
The Oxford Junior Companion to Music
Oxford University Press

Machlis, Joseph
The Enjoyment of Music
W.W. Norton

Miller, Jim
The Rolling Stone Illustrated History of Rock and Roll
Rolling Stone Press

- *Live entertainment*   **468**
- *Movies*   **471**
- *Broadcasting*   **473**
- *Dictionary of entertainment*   **476**

Entertainment

Nearly everyone enjoys entertainment, and some people enjoy even more being entertainers—actors, comedians, dancers, singers. This section takes a brief look at the world of entertainment, from its earliest days to the present. Only in the last hundred years have we been able to record sound and pictures and to broadcast them through wire or air. These improvements have brought entertainment to every corner of the world and into most of our homes. They have also made it possible for us to store our memories. Actors and singers long dead seem to come to life again every time their films or records are played. The world of entertainment has grown tremendously, and it can teach us as well as entertain us. The first part of the section provides a thumbnail history of live entertainment—the only kind that existed until 100 years ago. The second part looks at movies, a new dramatic entertainment that has also become an art form. The third part describes radio and television, the most recent and widespread form of all.

Live entertainment

The beginnings of popular entertainment go back to primitive societies, when dance and music, magic, and storytelling were created to celebrate the societies' rituals and gods. At first, people tried to gain control of their world through the magic of imitation. They believed that if they could create the sound of rain falling, real rain would fall. This belief in the magic of imitation gradually led to the arts of acting, theater, and popular entertainment.

Greece and Rome. The traditions of Western entertainment began in Greece over 2,500 years ago with the development of Greek drama. Festivals were held to worship Dionysus (Bacchus), the Greek god of wine and new life, with song and dance. By the seventh century B.C., poets began to write stories for a large group of performers, known as a chorus, and a lead actor to recite. By 500 B.C.,

Aeschylus added a second actor, making possible dialogue between characters. Within 50 years yet another character was added.

Even now, the plays that were written for ancient Greek theater are among the most powerful known. There were two main forms of classical Greek drama—tragedy and comedy. Tragedy tells the story of a great person who by the end of the story is destroyed by a flaw in his or her own character. Comedies made fun of the shortcomings of individuals and society.

There were other kinds of entertainment, too. "Mimus" presented scenes from common life using stock comic characters who would act out familiar situations by improvising. The humor was often rough and crude. This form of popular entertainment appears again and again throughout history.

The Romans continued the traditions of Greece and developed other forms of entertainment as well. The beginnings of the circus appeared when conquering generals brought to Rome rare animals and strangely dressed captives from the farthest reaches of the Roman Empire. Chariot races were held and gladiators fought to the death in public arenas.

Middle Ages.

After the fall of the Roman Empire, entertainment and drama were considered pagan and sinful by the Christian church. For hundreds of years, there is little evidence of public entertainment of any kind, but by the 1200s drama reappeared. On special occasions the church added dialogues to its service. Gradually these dialogues became more complex and theatrical. They became so popular that they began to interrupt the rest of the service, so these performances were moved out onto the steps of the church.

Trade unions or guilds took on the responsibility of producing these dramas. The themes were always religious. The stories based on the life of Christ were known as mysteries. Miracle plays told of the lives of saints. Morality plays emphasized the error of wicked ways and the triumph of virtue.

Renaissance.

In theater, the Renaissance began in the 1500s. The theater became less religious. Interest in long lost comedies and tragedies of classical Greek and Roman theater were rediscovered and the nobles used them as models for courtly entertainments. But for popular entertainment, nothing could equal the commedia dell'arte, a refinement of the early Greek Mimus. The commedia dell'arte was performed by a traveling group of actors, each of whom played the same standard character throughout his career. The costume of each character was traditional so that the audiences could easily pick out the familiar types. There were about twelve stock characters in all, including a clown, a beggar, a vain young man, a merchant deceived by his wife, and various servants, one cunning, one witty, and one cruel and mean-spirited. There was no script for the actors, only a rough outline of what was to happen—and how the story was to end. The dialogue was made up as the actors performed, filling the story with traditional jokes, speeches, and stories. As long as each actor stayed within the limits of his character, anything was allowed. The commedia was improvised, fast-paced, and unpredictable. The actors usually performed from wooden platforms raised above the street for the general public, but the nobility also built special theaters for private performances.

Golden age of theater.

Before the late 1500s in England, there were small bands of actors who traveled from town to town performing in the courtyards of inns and taverns. These actors offered entertainments, which included plays, songs, and dances, that became so popular that by the 1580s, special theaters resembling inn courtyards were built in London. The building of these theaters was the beginning of the golden age of Elizabethan theater. Among the writers for this theater was William Shakespeare, probably the greatest dramatist in any language. His plays were written for the general public, most of whom were neither cultivated nor learned but wildly enthusiastic nevertheless. Shakespeare created a great dramatic literature, but at the same time he provided his audience with popular entertainment of wide and lasting appeal.

In Spain and France, the 1600s also became a golden age of theater. Thousands of plays were written and performed for both the nobility and the general public. There were fewer tragedies and more comedies, satires, melodramas, and farces. Theater became a main source of diversion for the middle class and a truly popular entertainment while at the same time entering the great tradition of Western literature. For more information on the history of dramatic literature see *Literature* in Handbook 2.

A stock character from commedia dell'arte

American entertainment.

Theater and entertainment were not well regarded in the early years of colonial America. Professional actors were looked upon with suspicion and mistrust and play acting was considered immoral. In New England theater was banned, but the Southern colonies were more tolerant. By 1716 the first theater in America was built in Williamsburg, Virginia. There are few records of theatrical productions before the Revolutionary War. What theater there was, was dominated by English producers and actors. At the outbreak of the war, Congress ordered that the theaters be closed because they were controlled by the English. Some states kept these anti-theatrical laws for many years after the war was over.

During the 1800s, new forms of popular entertainment grew rapidly. Every decade, thousands of immigrants arrived from different countries, all bringing their own ideas about entertainment. Scenes from Shakespearean plays were popular as well as melodramas and sentimental plays such as *Uncle Tom's Cabin.* Plays about firemen and Indians were in vogue during the 1840s and 1850s. Operas were brought from Italy, and circuses began to tour from town to town. Variety shows featured comedy skits, singing, and dancing. Stars brought from Europe were in great demand. They included actors and actresses, opera singers, and variety performers.

Medicine shows. The advent of railroads allowed troupes of actors and musicians to easily travel from place to place, bringing entertainment to more and more people. Productions became larger and more elaborate. At the same time, many prosperous towns built theaters where these entertainments could be performed. In towns that were too small to build a theater, the entertainers would set up a tent outside of town. The traveling entertainers offered music, skits, and comedy routines and often full plays. In the middle of a performance or at the end, a "doctor" or an "Indian" would come on stage and sell patent medicine that was promised to cure almost anything. The shows that came to be called *medicine shows* were a major source of entertainment in small-town America.

Circuses. The circus also started to move across the country by train. There were lion tamers and elephants, high-wire artists and clowns, acrobats and magicians, music, parades, cotton candy, and sideshows. By the end of the 1800s, the circus had become big business and a circus train often had 20 cars or more. The Wild West Show was an American variation of the circus; it featured trick riding, shooting exhibitions, and Indians. The most famous of these shows was the *Buffalo Bill Cody Wild West Show.* Annie Oakley and Sitting Bull often traveled with the show.

Minstrel shows. The minstrel show was a new kind of variety show that made use of music and dance that had been brought to America by black slaves. The performers were all white at first, and much of the humor was at the expense of blacks. The singers and dancers appeared on stage in black-face, dressed in tuxedos and top hats. The central character and comic was called "Mr. Interlocutor." On either side of the stage were the "endmen," who were given standard names like Mr. Bones or Sambo. The comedy routines centered on the dialogue among these three characters. Behind them was the chorus. Minstrel shows reached their height of popularity in the 1880s, when some of the larger shows employed over one hundred performers to tap dance and sing, joke, and fiddle. Some later minstrel shows were made up of all-black performers.

Vaudeville. Before the Civil War, a new kind of variety show was developed for all-male audiences. After 1865, these shows opened their doors to women and children and began to emphasize wholesome family entertainment. Dishes and sewing patterns were offered as door prizes to encourage ladies to attend. This new form came to be known as vaudeville. It consisted of many short acts introduced by a master of ceremonies, and usually included comedy skits, dancing bears, acrobats, black-face entertainers, and music. Almost anything that would keep the audience's attention was allowed on stage, no matter how silly.

Burlesque developed in the late 1860s, when vaudeville became family entertainment. Many familiar forms of American performance prospered in vaudeville, including tap dancing, the soft shoe, and the two-man comedy team. Vaudeville disappeared in the 1930s owing to the popularity of motion pictures. But some great vaudeville performers are still remembered for their later performances in radio, television, or the movies. They include George Burns and Gracie Allen, W. C. Fields, Mae West, and Jack Benny.

Movies

The next big revolution in entertainment came about because of a new invention—the motion picture. Motion pictures made it possible for the first time to *record* a performance for viewing by hundreds or thousands of people.

In the mid-1800s, the still camera was being developed. Almost immediately there were experiments to try to make photographs appear to move. The first man to fully succeed was Thomas Edison, who invented the Kinetoscope, a small coin-operated machine that was cranked by hand and that showed the viewer a few seconds of motion, usually someone falling down or undressing.

In 1896, Edison held the first public showing of motion pictures projected onto a screen in this country. The exhibition caused a sensation. Movie houses called nickelodeons opened across the country, offering short features for a nickel. These shorts were no more than silent scenes from stage plays or vaudeville with subtitles; music was provided by a piano player in the theater. By 1910 the shorts were making more money than vaudeville and live theater together.

Camera language.

The American film director D. W. Griffith was the first to learn how to use the full potential of movies. His *Birth of a Nation* was the first great American screen epic. Griffith developed a technique that allowed him to place the audience into the middle of a story, thereby involving them emotionally. By using three different kinds of camera shots—the long shot, the medium shot, and the close-up—he gave the viewer a feeling of participation. The long shot was used to show the viewer location and situation at the beginning of a scene. The medium shot was then used to follow the action. The close-up could show the subtle emotion on a character's face or an important detail of the action, especially at the climax of a scene. By linking these shots together in a meaningful and rhythmic fashion, Griffith and others learned to increase the emotional pace of the story and show the action from many points of view. The filmmakers learned that, like a novelist, they could choose whether their audience would see all of the action in a scene or see the action only from one character's point of view.

Al Jolson is The Jazz Singer *in the first full-length movie with sound. The enormous success of this pioneering movie signaled the beginning of the end of the era of the silent movie.*

Sound.

The next major advance in movies came in 1927 with the addition of sound. The craft of recording sound had a history of its own, and, by 1927, many American households had simple mechanical phonographs and recordings of popular or classical music. Matching sound to action on film was a difficult problem. Finally, a process was developed of placing recorded sound on movie film itself; when it was run through the projector, the sound could be amplified to match the motion on the screen.

The first major movie to use the sound-on-film process was *The Jazz Singer,* starring Al Jolson. When Jolson sat at a piano and began to sing, the theater was filled with the sound of his music. The new sound films, called "talkies," made movies more popular than ever. Movies began to replace live theater and vaudeville. Moviemakers also began to explore the world of special sound effects. They found they could express the mood of a scene through the sound of birds singing or of hurricane winds. Suspense could be heightened by the intelligent use of sound as well as image.

Color.

The new talkies were more realistic, but they were still only in black and white. Then, in 1939, *Gone With the Wind,* one of the first major movies filmed in color, was released. The beauty and realism of this film amazed audiences. *Gone With the Wind* became the most popular movie of all time. From 1939 on, movie makers learned that color, too, could be used to set a mood or create a special atmosphere.

The golden age.

From the late 1920s until about 1950, movies were the most popular of all American entertainments. The new film industry, centered around Hollywood, California, employed thousands of people. More than half of all Americans went to the movies every week. In towns and cities across the country, movie palaces were built—elaborately decorated theaters focused on a white screen. Other forms of popular entertainment disappeared. Vaudeville and traveling shows could not compete with the emotionally charged stories and musicals that were brought to town every week. Vaudeville comedians, actors, actresses, stunt men, and daredevils went to Hollywood, and many became movie stars.

Since 1950.

The movies continue to be a major form of entertainment, but their popularity began to fall in the 1950s. When television became widespread, people began to stay home. There seemed to be less reason to go out when they could be entertained in their own living rooms. By 1980 only one American out of ten went to the movies in a given week.

At the same time, however, millions of viewers see movies every week on television. Even movies that are 40 years old continue to play on television to enthusiastic audiences. They include such classics as *The Wizard of Oz, Snow White, Gone With the Wind,* and *Casablanca.*

Movies have grown into a serious art form. New films and old by great directors are studied and admired—and often imitated by new filmmakers. The movies have shown that they can move an audience in many of the same ways as a great live drama or a great painting or sculpture. Even as they entertain millions around the world, they have entered the arena of serious artistic concern.

Academy Awards for Best Picture

Year	Film
2003	The Lord of the Rings: The Return of the King *(fantasy/drama)*
2002	Chicago *(musical)*
2001	A Beautiful Mind *(drama)*
2000	Gladiator *(drama)*
1999	American Beauty *(comedy)*
1998	Shakespeare in Love *(comedy/drama)*
1997	Titanic *(drama)*
1996	The English Patient *(drama)*
1995	Braveheart *(drama)*
1994	Forrest Gump *(comedy/drama)*
1993	Schindler's List *(drama)*
1992	Unforgiven *(drama)*
1991	The Silence of the Lambs *(drama)*
1990	Dances with Wolves *(drama)*
1989	Driving Miss Daisy *(comedy/drama)*
1988	Rain Man *(drama)*
1987	The Last Emperor *(drama)*
1986	Platoon *(drama)*
1985	Out of Africa *(drama)*
1984	Amadeus *(drama)*
1983	Terms of Endearment *(drama)*
1982	Gandhi *(drama)*
1981	Chariots of Fire *(drama)*
1980	Ordinary People *(drama)*
1979	Kramer vs. Kramer *(drama)*
1978	The Deer Hunter *(drama)*
1977	Annie Hall *(comedy)*
1976	Rocky *(drama)*
1975	One Flew Over the Cuckoo's Nest *(comedy)*
1974	The Godfather Part II *(drama)*
1973	The Sting *(drama)*
1972	The Godfather *(drama)*
1971	The French Connection *(drama)*
1970	Patton *(drama)*
1969	Midnight Cowboy *(drama)*
1968	Oliver! *(musical)*
1967	In the Heat of the Night *(drama)*
1966	A Man for All Seasons *(drama)*
1965	The Sound of Music *(musical)*
1964	My Fair Lady *(musical)*
1963	Tom Jones *(comedy)*
1962	Lawrence of Arabia *(drama)*
1961	West Side Story *(musical)*
1960	The Apartment *(drama)*

Titanic won the Academy Award for the best picture in 1997.

Broadcasting

Early history. The movie and sound-recording revolution changed popular entertainment in important ways, allowing performances to be preserved and reproduced over and over again. But there was still another revolution to come. Today we call it broadcasting, and it has brought entertainment from public places into the home.

The telegraph was the first invention that allowed the instant transmission of information over long distances. Telegraph communications were in wide use by 1860. In the 1870s, the telephone allowed transmission of voices by wire, making it possible for a household to communicate with any of hundreds of other households. Perhaps some inventor would have found a way to send music and other entertainment into homes by telephone wire; but before that could happen, an even better system was developed.

Radio. Early radio was called "wireless." Sending messages through the air by the broadcast of electromagnetic (or radio) waves was seen as a wonderful tool for communication between ships at sea. At first, only code signals could be sent and received, but soon voice communication was also possible. Radio equipment was greatly improved during World War I (1914–1918). In 1919, a few enterprising Americans got the idea of sending music and other entertainment out over the air waves. At first, the only listeners were a few other radio technicians who had transmitting and receiving equipment. But the general public soon wanted this home entertainment, too, and inexpensive radio receivers were soon on sale.

Between 1920 and 1927, several million radio receivers were sold, and radio stations sprang up across the country. Radio executives set up the first *network,* which sent programs to scores of local stations.

The golden age. Radio's golden age ran from 1927 to about 1950, the same years as the golden age of movies. Radio programs were paid for by sponsors, who advertised their goods and hoped that listeners would respond by buying their products.

Early radio developed important new forms of entertainment: the musical variety show (using many vaudeville stars); the soap opera, a serial about

Actors in an early radio drama surround the magic microphone. Their vast audiences used their imaginations to supply the details of scenery and costume that made radio drama so convincing.

the problems of everyday life that got its name because it was sponsored by soap companies; and the situation comedy, a series in which the same characters appeared each week. In addition, radio brought news and play-by-play accounts of big sports events.

In the 1930s, President Franklin Roosevelt was the first President to use radio regularly as a means of addressing all (or nearly all) Americans at the same time. His broadcasts were not called speeches; instead, he called them "fireside chats," and spoke in a quiet conversational tone. During World War II (1939–1945), radio became a major source of war news.

In the 1930s, still another improvement was being made in radio. A new way of transmitting, called *frequency modulation,* or FM for short, was invented. Beginning in the 1950s, FM transmission brought hundreds of new stations to radio. It was also chosen as the system for transmitting television sound.

The so-called golden age of television in the 1950s produced such great television shows as "The Honeymooners."

Television. The developers of radio were soon supporting research into television—transmitting pictures and sound together. A working electronic television system had been developed in 1926 by a 20-year-old inventor named Philo T. Farnsworth, but the introduction of television to home audiences was slowed first by patent lawsuits, then by World War II. After the war ended, a great television boom began. Between 1946 and 1952, some 7 million sets were sold in the United States alone.

Television borrowed most of its programming from radio or from the movies. Like radio, television broadcasting was paid for by the sale of advertising. Also like radio, television offered musical variety shows, soap operas, and, especially, situation comedies. It also took many radio stars and made them television stars.

From the movies, television borrowed old movies. Old movies were the least expensive way to fill time, and they ran late at night, early in the morning, and at other off hours. Television also borrowed the most popular movie types. Westerns and action dramas were soon being made for television, bringing excitement and adventure to the home screen.

Most important, television "borrowed" radio listeners and moviegoers. At first, it seemed that radio and the movies might disappear. Many movie theaters closed, and radio stations were near bankruptcy. Soon, however, both "old" mediums learned to survive by attracting special audiences. Radio turned to music—helped by the new and improved method of transmission called FM. And filmmakers were free to appeal to adult audiences.

Meanwhile, television developed some new strengths of its own. It learned to broadcast sports events with great skill, even showing important plays over and over again through video recording. Television news became the most important news medium. It covered many historic events, such as a President's funeral or a moon landing, live, as it happened.

In early television, almost all shows were broadcast live. Recording techniques were crude, and filming was too expensive. New video recording made possible not only instant replay for sports, but also a new, inexpensive way to record drama and variety shows.

Television drama also grew into an important entertainment form. Camera language was borrowed

The rise in popularity of cable television over the last decade has revolutionized television watching, providing, among other options, 24-hour news channels.

from the movies, but it was revised to suit a smaller screen. Television was less impressive than movies in long shots showing a huge battlefield or natural panorama, but it was more effective in close-ups. Television stars became almost like friends to many viewers, appearing each week or each evening in the viewers' own homes.

The future. Today, broadcasting is the most important form of popular entertainment. But now it is being challenged by still newer inventions. Video playback and recording equipment make it possible for home viewers to buy or record their favorite shows. Many classic movies are already available for home viewing. This new equipment may encourage many viewers to spend fewer hours watching network offerings of situation comedies and action dramas.

At the same time, cable television may revolutionize viewing habits in another way. Cable companies offer hundreds of channels rather than three or four. They bring their programs directly into the home by cable, offering high-quality sound and picture. Cable television may offer every viewer programs on his or her special interest—sports events played on any given day, news at any

time, music or drama of any style, or special information such as stock market reports, weather, or congressional hearings. Improvements such as high definition television (HDTV) and interactive television will revolutionize broadcasting as well as viewers' habits.

Modern popular entertainment is a combination of ancient performing arts and new technology. Each time the technology changes, performers change with it, providing both pleasure and information in a form that suits the new medium. Many productions appear in many different media at once. For example, a Broadway musical may first appear as a live show in New York, then as a touring show in various cities; its music may be available on disc or tape recording. Then it may appear as a movie or as a made-for-television production. Viewers may see this new form in a movie theater or at home, by way of conventional television, cable TV, or their own videotape or DVD players.

Never in recorded history have the entertainment arts been so important in the lives of so many. Modern inventions have put nearly every person within reach of music and drama all day, every day, at home, and away from home.

animation

Dictionary of entertainment

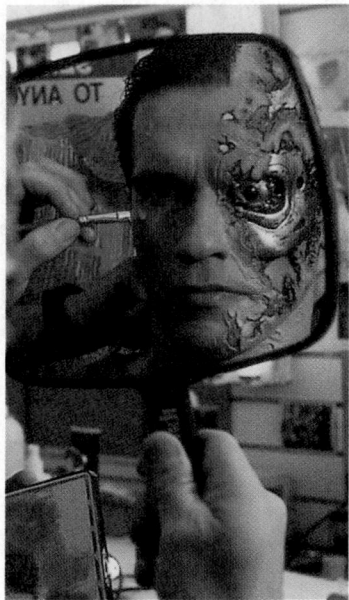
makeup

set design

act. (1) A main division of a play, usually broken down into one or more scenes. Modern plays often have three acts. (2) An individual performance in a variety show.

animation. Drawing objects on each frame of motion picture film so that when the film is run through a projector the objects will seem to move. Walt Disney made many of the best known animated movies, including *Snow White* and *Cinderella*.

audio. (1) The sound portion of television broadcasts. (2) The equipment that plays back sound recordings.

backdrop. The rear curtain of a stage set; it is often painted and lighted so that it appears to be a view of the real world.

backstage. Behind or to the side of the stage. This is where the actors wait to go on stage. It is also where the dressing rooms are and where the stagehands, makeup artists, and lighting technicians work.

ballet. A dance performance that usually tells a story through dance and music alone. The ballet style was developed in the 1800s; it requires a large corps (company) of dancers and features two to eight solo dancers. One famous ballet is the *Nutcracker Suite*.

cable television. Television that is brought into the home by wire (cable). Cable television offers better reception, many channels and programs, and noncommercial broadcasting paid for by the user.

cast. All the actors and actresses in a play, movie, or television show. To *cast* a show is to find and hire the actors and actresses.

character actor. An actor (male or female) who plays supporting roles, portraying people of widely differing ages, backgrounds, and mannerisms.

choreographer. The dance director who invents the dances and teaches them to the dancers by showing them when, where, and how to move.

chorus. The singers and dancers in a show who do not have leading parts. In the theater they are sometimes called gypsies. After the choreographer has taught them the dances, the dance master is in charge of their performance.

cinematographer. The director of photography for a film. With the director, the cinematographer plans how the action in a movie will be photographed, determining the placement of cameras, the length of each shot, and the lighting. During filming, he or she controls the operation and movement of the camera.

comedy. A play, movie, or television show that is written and acted in a light or humorous way and that ends cheerfully.

comic relief. A comic character or situation in a play, movie, or TV show that prevents the audience from being too depressed by the more serious parts of the story.

costume. Special clothing required for a dramatic production. The costume designer selects and designs the clothes. The wardrobe master/mistress makes sure that the costumes are repaired, cleaned, and available on cue. The dresser helps actors change costumes between scenes.

cue. A signal to an actor to begin his or her next line or action. If an actor misses the cue, the other actors may have to ad-lib or make up lines until he or she begins.

curtain. Most theaters have curtains between the stage and the audience. The play starts when the curtain is raised. At the end of the play, the curtain falls, marking the end. The raising of the curtain to allow the cast to accept the audience's applause is called the curtain call.

director. The person responsible for deciding how the story is to be presented, when and how the characters will move on the stage or screen, and how they will read their lines. It is the director's overall idea of the story that guides the cast and stage and film technicians in creating the performance. In the movies, the director also supervises the cinematographer and helps decide how the story will be photographed.

dub. In movies originally made in a foreign language, the actors' lines are recorded again in English. Special attention is given to matching the movement of the actors' lips on screen to the sound of the new language. This is called dubbing or *lip synching*. Dubbing is also used when a singer's voice replaces that of an actor who cannot sing very well.

extra. A person in a play or movie who has no speaking part. Often the extra is a part of a crowd scene.

film editor. Movies are shot on hundreds of separate pieces of film. The job of a film editor is to assemble the movie by attaching the best pieces of film in a pattern that tells the story in the most dramatic and interesting way. If film editing is done poorly, the movie may appear jumpy or confusing.

gaffer. In movies, the chief electrician who designs and sets up the lighting and works closely with the cinematographer.

green room. A room backstage in a theater or television studio where actors and guests wait before going on stage. It is also used as a reception room after performances.

grip. In movies and television, the person in charge of the props.

laughtrack. Prerecorded laughter added to the soundtrack of some television shows. The volume of the laughter is electronically controlled.

lighting designer. In the theater the lighting designer works closely with the set designer and in the movies works closely with the cinematographer. Lighting can focus the audience's attention on specific areas of action, provide realistic atmosphere, and create moods.

location. Movies that are made "on location" are filmed in real places with natural surroundings, not on sets or sound stages.

makeup. In the theater, makeup is often exaggerated so that the expressions on the actors' faces will not wash out in the bright stage lights. In movies and television, makeup is usually less exaggerated. Makeup is an art of illusion. Men can be made into very real looking monsters, and young actresses can age 30 years between the acts of a play.

melodrama. An exaggerated, sentimental, and often emotional story that is neither a comedy nor a tragedy. Many television shows are melodramas.

musical comedy. Movies and plays in which the characters sing and dance and in which musical production numbers are the main attraction.

network. The original national television broadcasting companies, NBC, CBS, and ABC, and, since 1986, Fox Broadcasting. Two additional networks, UPN and WB, began operations in the 1990s.

prime time. The evening hours, when the greatest number of people are watching television. The most popular shows are usually broadcast during this time by the national networks.

producer. The person who chooses a play or screenplay, raises the money, and hires the main people, including the director, set designer, cinematographer, and often the stars. Since he or she has raised the money and is responsible for the show's success, he or she has final say on everything.

prompter. The person who stands backstage in the theater in view of the actors to help them with their lines if they forget them.

props. All of the objects on the stage except the scenery. Stage props include furniture, and hand props include swords or guns. The property manager makes sure that all the props are in place for the performance.

rehearsal. A run-through of a show without an audience. In the theater, the *dress rehearsal* is the last rehearsal; it is performed as if it were a public performance.

repertory theater. A theatrical company that performs several different plays during the same season, alternating them each week or each night. The same actors usually play parts in all or most of the plays.

road show. An entertainment that travels from town to town.

scene. In the theater, a subdivision of an act. Usually each scene takes place at a different time or in a different location from the scene before it. In the movies, a scene usually takes place in one location and shows one complete situation or action. However, movies can switch between two scenes that are taking place at the same time in different places.

screenplay. The script of a movie. The *shooting script* includes the stage directions and camera directions.

set design. A set is the surroundings in which a play or film takes place. The set designer makes drawings of a new set, allowing for the script's requirement for proper entrances, exits, and props, then builds a scale model that must be approved by the director and producer. The sets are built by the master carpenter, then furnished and lighted to create the right atmosphere.

shot. In movies, a single piece of film photographed at one time. The shot is the basic building block of a movie. By connecting shots, the film editor is able to tell a story in a pleasing way. He or she varies the length and rhythm of individual shots and connects them in different ways.

situation comedy. A common type of television show where the character and situation remain the same from week to week. Usually 30 minutes long, it deals with the comic side of family or work life.

soundtrack. The sound portion in movies and television. It is often made of several tracks mixed together: the dialogue, sound effects, and background music.

special effects. Any number of tricks used in moviemaking to produce visual illusion. Some common effects mix animation with real life action, create elaborate robots, and photograph scale models as if they were actual size (a trick especially useful in disaster pictures).

stagehands. The workers backstage who change the scenery, operate the curtain, and, in smaller theaters, control the stage lights during a performance.

stage manager. In the theater, the person who is in charge of everything once the play has opened.

technical director. In television, the person who works the control board and decides which picture out of several will be broadcast.

tragedy. A play or movie that deals with the serious side of life and in which the main character comes to an unhappy end.

understudy. The actor who is prepared to take over a role if the actor who plays the part cannot go on stage.

video. The picture part of a television production.

voice-over. In television, the voice of an announcer who is not seen on the screen. Most often, the voice-over is used in commercials.

For Further Reference

Barnouw, Eric
Tube of Plenty: The Evolution of American Television
Oxford University Press

Brooks, Tim and Marsh, Earle
The Complete Directory to Prime Time Network and Cable TV Shows, 1946 to the Present
Ballantine Books

Halliwell, Leslie
Halliwell's Filmgoer's Companion
Hill and Wang

Lewis, Tom
Empire of the Air
HarperCollins

Monaco, James
How to Read a Film
Oxford University Press

Find It Fast

How to use the index. This index is a quick, easy guide to the information in the *Student Handbooks*. The Find It Fast boxes are a shortcut to locating some of the major entries of, for example, math without having to search the main index. All entries are in alphabetical order, but the descriptive identification in parentheses following entries is not alphabetized. Each entry contains the volume number and page number for locating that topic. For example, the first entry below means that page 325 of Handbook 1 and pages 329 and 348 of Handbook 2 contain information on amplitude as it relates to math. There is a separate entry for amplitude relative to sound, shown in column 2.

amplitude (math) **1:** 325; **2:** 329, 348

amplitude (sound) **1:** 380, 382; **2:** 251, 258; **3:** 540, 548

Names beginning with Mac or Mc are arranged in strict alphabetical order. The abbreviation St. is indexed under St-.

There are no alphabetical priorities for persons of rank, such as kings and emperors. All the firsts (I) are listed together, then the seconds (II), and so forth. Descriptive identification follows in parentheses.

Henry II (Eng.) **2:** 94.
Henry II (Fr.) (Valois) **2:** 100

Few abbreviations have been used in the index; those that have been are standard and readily identifiable.

FIND IT FAST:
DICTIONARIES AND GLOSSARIES

BIOLOGY
see also **LIFE SCIENCE**
❷: 224–225
❸: 498–499
❹: 821–840

CALCULUS
see also **MATHEMATICS**
❸: 475

CHEMISTRY
❷: 242–243
❸: 516–517

EARTH SCIENCE
see also **GEOLOGY**
❶: 402–403

ECONOMICS
❸: 292–293

ENTERTAINMENT
❶: 476–478

GEOLOGY
see also **EARTH SCIENCE**
❸: 532–533

GOVERNMENT U.S. see also **POLITICAL SCIENCE**
❹: 566–571

HEALTH AND SAFETY
❶: 352–353

HISTORY
U.S. ❹: 349–380
Western civilization
❸: 340–341

LIFE SCIENCE
see also **BIOLOGY**
❶: 362–363

MATHEMATICS
see also **CALCULUS**
❶: 325–329
❷: 348–351

MUSIC
❶: 466–467

PHYSICAL SCIENCES see also **PHYSICS, CHEMISTRY**
❶: 382–383

PHYSICS
❷: 258–259
❸: 548–549

POLITICAL SCIENCE see also **GOVERNMENT**
❸: 354–355

PSYCHOLOGY
❸: 370–371

SPACE SCIENCE
❶: 424–427

SPORTS
baseball
❶: 433
basketball
❶: 439
football
❶: 437
golf
❶: 447
hockey
❶: 441
soccer
❶: 443
tennis
❶: 445

SYNONYMS AND ANTONYMS
❶: 58–73

WORD USAGE
❷: 376–387

FIND IT FAST:
MATHEMATICS

ARITHMETIC ❶: 176–284
  addition ❶: 178–191, 314, 318
    base 10 blocks ❶: 183
    basic facts grids
      ❶: 179, 318
    carrying ❶: 183
    checking answers ❶: 188
    Everyday Math ❶: 318
    memorizing basic facts
      ❶: 181
    place value ❶: 176–178
    rounding ❶: 178, 281
  subtraction ❶: 191–208
    base 10 ❶: 195, 198–206
    basic facts grids
      ❶: 192, 318
    borrowing ❶: 194
    checking answers ❶: 201
    memorizing basic facts
      ❶: 193
    place value ❶: 196–206
    regrouping ❶: 195
  multiplication
    basic facts grids
      ❶: 210, 318
    checking answers ❶: 219
    commutative law ❶: 214
    distributive property
      ❶: 281
    divisibility, tests for
      ❶: 211–212
    memorizing basic facts
      ❶: 213
  division
    basic facts grids
      ❶: 221, 318
    checking answers ❶: 229
    memorizing basic facts
      ❶: 222
  exponents ❶: 244–246, 283, 322
    negative ❶: 245, 261, 322
  fractions ❶: 230–244, 271, 272, 324
    decimals ❶: 246–274, 322, 324
  ratio and percent
    ❶: 274–279
  proportion ❶: 274
  square root ❶: 284
  symbols ❶: 319

PRE-ALGEBRA ❶: 285–311
  absolute value ❶: 286
  equations ❶: 291–300, 316; ❷: 264, 266–268
  inequalities ❶: 301–303
  laws of numbers ❶: 285; ❷: 260–261
  like terms ❶: 289, 298
  order of operations
    ❶: 286, 289–291
  probability and statistics
    ❶: 312–313
  set symbols ❶: 319
  signed numbers ❶: 286; ❷: 262
  symbols ❶: 319

ALGEBRA ❷: 260–305
  see also Pre algebra
  algebraic fractions ❷: 278
  binomial expansions
    ❷: 275
  binomial theorem ❷: 277
  conic sections ❷: 283
  determinants ❷: 291
  equations with fractions
    ❷: 300–301
  graphing lines ❷: 279–282
  matrices ❷: 288, 293
  Pascal's triangle
    ❷: 275–276
  quadratic equations
    ❷: 295–298
  symbols ❷: 319

GEOMETRY ❷: 306–323
  angles ❷: 306
  circles ❷: 320–323
  constructions ❷: 307–309
  formulas ❷: 344–345
  polygons ❷: 316
  quadrilaterals ❷: 316
  sample proofs ❷: 311–315
  symbols ❶: 319; ❷: 343
  triangles ❷: 309–310, 319

TRIGONOMETRY ❷: 324–342
  angles ❷: 324, 327, 328
  equations ❷: 333–334
  DeMoivre's theorem
    ❷: 340
  formulas ❷: 335
  graphs ❷: 328
    polar graphs ❷: 337–339
  identities ❷: 331
  radians ❷: 337
  reading tables ❷: 325
  solving triangles
    ❷: 334–336

CALCULUS ❸: 372–475; ❹: 843–1142
  differentiation
    ❸: 388–407; ❹: 945–968
  integration ❸: 408–417; ❹: 1046–1063
  definite integrals
    ❸: 440–453; ❹: 1064–1082, 1121–1133
  functions ❸: 372–387; ❹: 899–938
  fundamental theorems
    ❹: 1068–1071
  antiderivative ❸: 418–439
  derivative applications
    ❹: 1003–1023, 1024–1045
  infinite sequences and
    series ❸: 454–473
  limits and continuity
    ❸: 372–387; ❹: 922–944
  slope ❸: 466–473; ❹: 889–892
  graphing with calculators
    ❹: 986–991
  graphing without
    calculators ❹: 984–986

CALCULATOR TECHNIQUE
  addition ❶: 178, 188, 281
  subtraction ❶: 196
  multiplication ❶: 216
  division ❶: 228
  mixed numbers ❶: 239
  percent ❶: 280
  decimal point ❶: 280–281
  rounding ❶: 281
  fractions to decimals
    ❶: 282
  memory ❶: 282
  scientific notation
    ❶: 283; ❷: 347
  graphing calculators *see*
    specific problems in
    Handbooks 3 and 4
  graphing with calculators
    ❹: 986–991
  graphing without
    calculators ❹: 984–986

FIND IT FAST:
ENGLISH

BOOK REPORTS
fiction reports **❷**: 455–456
nonfiction reports
  ❷: 456–458
oral reports **❷**: 458–460
reading the book
  ❷: 441–443
selecting the book
  ❷: 436–441
the report
  outline **❷**: 445–446
  rough draft **❷**: 446–448
  final draft **❷**: 449–454

ENRICHMENT, AP READING
  SUGGESTIONS **❹**: 1377–1383

GRAMMAR
grammar rules **❸**: 95–98
parts of speech **❶**: 4–35;
  ❸: 84
  adjectives **❶**: 5, 26–31, 45;
    ❸: 84, 86
  adverbs **❶**: 5, 27–31, 49,
    51; **❸**: 84, 86
  articles **❶**: 26
  conjunctions **❶**: 5, 33–35;
    ❸: 84
  interjections **❶**: 5, 35
  nouns **❶**: 5, 6–8, 43; **❸**: 84
  prepositions **❶**: 5, 31–33,
    50; **❸**: 84, 98
  pronouns **❶**: 5, 9–16; **❸**: 84
  verbs **❶**: 5, 17–25;
    ❸: 84, 87–89
sentence structure
  ❶: 36–51; **❸**: 83–84
  clauses **❶**: 41–42, 46–47
  diagrams **❶**: 50–51
  objects **❶**: 38–39, 50; **❸**: 84
  phrases **❶**: 39–41, 51

predicates **❶**: 36–38, 43,
  50 **❸**: 84
subjects **❶**: 36–38, 42–43,
  50–51; **❸**: 84
punctuation **❶**: 45, 54–55;
  ❷: 374–375; **❸**: 89–94, 98

LITERATURE
  ❶: 96–103; **❷**: 388–435;
  ❸: 69–80
drama **❷**: 404–412
  dramatists **❷**: 407–412
  Shakespeare
    ❷: 409, 410–411
  timeline of drama
    ❷: 404–405
fiction **❷**: 413–435
  timeline of fiction
    ❷: 414–415
  writers **❷**: 418–423
masterpieces of literature
    ❷: 424–435
nonfiction **❶**: 102–103
poetry **❶**: 100–101;
    ❷: 390–403; **❸**: 76–80
  poets **❷**: 394–403
  timeline of poetry
    ❷: 392–393

PUNCTUATION REVIEW
  ❶: 54–55

SPEAKING
body language **❶**: 75–76
delivery **❶**: 74–75
organization **❶**: 77
reports **❷**: 458–460

SPELLING HELPS
  ❶: 52–53
capitalization **❶**: 55
italics **❶**: 55; **❸**: 94

SYNONYMS AND ANTONYMS
  ❶: 58–73

USAGE DICTIONARIES
  ❷: 376–387; **❸**: 115–117

WORD STUDY
  ❶: 86–89

WRITING
  ❶: 54–73; **❸**: 32–117
see also Study Skills
book reports **❷**: 436–460
creative writing **❸**: 82
essays **❸**: 81
first draft **❶**: 56; **❸**: 48–63
paper types **❸**: 50–56
planning a paper **❶**: 56;
  ❸: 32–47
proofreaders marks **❸**: 68
punctuation review
  ❶: 54–55
research papers
  ❸: 81, 102–112
revising **❶**: 57; **❸**: 64–68,
  111-112
style **❷**: 366–367;
  ❸: 99–101

WRITING RESEARCH PAPERS
  ❷: 354–387; **❸**: 102–112
footnotes and bibliographies
  ❷: 368–373; **❸**: 110–111
APA style **❷**: 372–373
MLA style **❷**: 370–371
outline **❷**: 362, 364–365
plagiarism **❸**: 109
research methods **❷**: 361;
  ❸: 102–107
research sources
  ❷: 355–360, 363
revising **❷**: 367;
  ❸: 64–68, 111–112
thesis (topic) **❷**: 354–355;
  ❸: 108
writing **❷**: 366–367;
  ❸: 48–63

FIND IT FAST:
TIMELINES

HISTORY
United States
  c 1000 to present
    ❶: 107–133
  colonization **❹**: 103, 111
  revolution
    ❹: 119–120, 130
  new government
    ❹: 139, 148, 157
  growing nation
    ❹: 168–169
  civil war **❹**: 179

reconstruction **❹**: 187
western expansion **❹**: 199
industrial growth
  ❹: 213–214
imperialism **❹**: 224
progressive era
  ❹: 235–236
World War I **❹**: 245–246
1920s **❹**: 259
depression and New Deal
  ❹: 275–276
World War II **❹**: 287–288
Cold War **❹**: 300, 309,
  322–323
to present **❹**: 336–337,
  346

Western civilization
  ancient times **❸**: 294-304
  Middle Ages **❸**: 305
  Crusades **❸**: 313–314
  Renaissance **❸**: 315–319
  modern Europe
    ❸: 325–337
World
  ancient times to present
    ❷: 79–124, 128–137
Literature
  drama **❷**: 404–405
  fiction **❷**: 414–415
  poetry **❷**: 392–393

3

FIND IT FAST:
SOCIAL SCIENCES

ECONOMICS ❸: 246–293
equations and graphs
❸: 248–252
  common abbreviations
  ❸: 252
glossary of economics
❸: 292–293
macroeconomics
❸: 268–286
  balance of trade
  ❸: 284–286
  Consumer Price Index
  ❸: 270–271
  federal fiscal policy
  ❸: 279–286
  Federal Reserve
  ❸: 282–284
  free trade ❸: 286
  GNP/GDP ❸: 268–272
  inflation ❸: 274–276
  unemployment
  ❸: 276–278
microeconomics ❸: 247,
255–267
  competition types ❸: 267
  cost types ❸: 263
  demand (market)
  ❸: 255–259
  market equilibrium
  ❸: 265
  market types ❸: 254
  supply
  (output/production)
  ❸: 260–267

POLITICAL SCIENCE
❸: 342–355
glossary of political science
❸: 354–355
political spectrum ❹: 472
political ideologies
❸: 344–346; ❹: 471
who governs?
❸: 345; ❹: 446–447
international relations
❸: 351–352; ❹: 556–558

**UNITED STATES
GOVERNMENT**
❷: 4–53; ❸: 347–350;
❹: 443–561

Constitution of the United
States ❷: 15–28; ❸: 347,
349; ❹: 452–457, 467–473
Bill of Rights
❷: 22–23; ❸: 347
Federal system ❷: 4, 7–14;
❹: 461–466
executive branch
❷: 4, 10–11, 19–20, 22;
❸: 347, 349; ❹: 519–524
  departments and
  agencies ❷: 11;
  ❹: 522–524, 556–558
  presidential succession
  ❷: 10, 28
legislative branch ❷: 7–9,
11, 15–19; ❹: 505–512
  Senate ❷: 7, 15–16;
  ❸: 347–352
  House of
  Representatives
  ❷: 7, 15, 16;
  ❸: 347–349
judicial branch
❷: 4, 20–21; ❸: 347–349;
❹: 528–534
  landmark Supreme
  Court decisions
  ❷: 12; ❹: 456–457
  how a bill becomes a law
  ❷: 8–9; ❹: 510–511
  state government
  ❷: 6, 21
  local government ❷: 5
  elections ❷: 14, 24
glossary of U.S. government
❹: 566–571
Presidents ❷: 29–53
United Nations
  organization ❷: 13

PSYCHOLOGY
❸: 356–371
glossary of psychology
❸: 370–371
human development
❸: 360–362
learning and cognition
❸: 363–365
personality and disorders
❸: 366–368
philosophy vs. physiology
❸: 356
theory movements ❸: 57
therapy styles ❸: 367

FIND IT FAST:
YOUR FUTURE

**THINKING ABOUT
COLLEGE**
❸: 622–645
your qualifications
❸: 622–626
selecting a college
❸: 627–630
entrance exams
❸: 598–621
admissions ❸: 631–637
applying ❸: 633–637
  application essay
  ❹: 1341–1375
costs and financial aid
❸: 637–644
campus services
❸: 576–579
living arrangements
❸: 645

COLLEGE SUCCESS
Study Skills
❸: 550–585

**ALTERNATIVE JOB
PREPARATION**
❸: 655

ADVANCING YOUR CAREER
❸: 646–681
job opportunities ❸: 647
assessing yourself
❸: 648–649
resumé writing
❸: 656–657
job search ❸: 657–659
interview ❸: 660–663
negotiating terms
❸: 664–665
starting your own business
❸: 673–675
job success and
advancement ❸: 665–668
re-entering the workforce
❸: 671
job classifications
❸: 676–681

FIND IT FAST:
SCIENCES

MEASUREMENT AND CONVERSIONS
1: 366–367; **2:** 244–246;
3: 476–477

SCIENTIFIC METHOD
1: 364–365

SCIENTIFIC NOTATION
3: 477

BIOLOGY
see also **LIFE SCIENCE**
2: 192–225;
3: 478–499
animal systems **2:** 208;
3: 492–496; **4:** 630–637,
804–805
cell functions **2:** 198–200;
3: 481
cell structure **2:** 192–197;
3: 480–482; **4:** 621–627
classification system
2: 210–223; **3:** 487–488;
4: 717–730
dictionary/glossary of
biology **2:** 224–225;
3: 498–499
DNA **2:** 201–202; **3:** 486
ecology **4:** 782–797,
811–812
evolution **4:** 701–716,
808–809
genetics **2:** 206–207;
3: 484–486; **4:** 665–682,
683–700
human physiology
4: 741–761
lab experiments
4: 798–816
plant systems **2:** 208;
3: 489–491; **4:** 641–652,
731–740, 802–804
reproduction **2:** 203–205;
3: 482–483; **4:** 653–664,
665–682, 762–773

CHEMISTRY
2: 226–243;
3: 500–511; **4:** 609–670,
800
atomic structure
2: 228–231; **3:** 501–503
chemical reactions **2:** 232;
3: 508–509, 514
balancing equations
2: 233; **3:** 507–508
lab reports **2:** 233
dictionary/glossary of
chemistry **2:** 242–243;
3: 516–517

GEOLOGY (EARTH SCIENCE)
1: 384–403; **3:** 518–533
climate **1:** 392–401
continental drift
1: 384–385; **3:** 520–521
dictionary/glossary of earth
science/geology
1: 402–403; **3:** 532–533
earthquakes **1:** 387;
3: 525–526
earths structure **3:** 518–520
erosion **3:** 526
geologic time **3:** 527–529
glaciers **1:** 390–391;
3: 526
ice ages **1:** 391
earth resources **3:** 530
rock cycle **1:** 389
volcanos **1:** 388;
3: 523–524

HEALTH AND SAFETY
1: 330–353
communicable diseases
1: 339
dictionary of health and
safety **1:** 352–353
drug abuse **1:** 338
exercise **1:** 336, 337
fire safety **1:** 345
first aid **1:** 346–351
human anatomy
1: 340–343
illness distress signals
1: 330
nutrition **1:** 331–334
safety precautions **1:** 344
vaccination schedule
1: 339
weight control **1:** 336

LIFE SCIENCE
see also **BIOLOGY**
1: 354–363
biomes of North America
1: 358
dictionary of life science
1: 362–363
ecosystems
1: 356–357, 361
natural resources
1: 354–355
water and oxygen cycles
1: 360

PHYSICS
1: 364–383;
2: 244–259; **3:** 534–549
dictionary/glossary of
physics **1:** 382–383;
2: 258–259; **3:** 548–549
electricity **1:** 378–379;
2: 254; **3:** 541–543
electromagnetic radiation
2: 252–253
energy **1:** 374–375;
2: 250
light **1:** 381; **2:** 252–253;
3: 543–544
matter **1:** 368–373
mechanics **3:** 534–537
nuclear physics
2: 256–257; **3:** 546
relativity **2:** 255; **3:** 545
simple machines
1: 376–377
sound **1:** 380; **2:** 251;
3: 540
waves **3:** 539–540

SPACE SCIENCE 1: 404–427
dictionary of space science
1: 424–427
solar system
1: 404–410, 415
space exploration
1: 416–423
stars **1:** 412–414

FIND IT FAST:
SOCIAL STUDIES

GEOGRAPHY
How to read a map
❷: 188
United States
❶: 134–173
Midwest states
❶: 142–145
Northeast states
❶: 150–151
People of the U.S.
❷: 54–77
South states ❶: 146–149
territories ❶: 152–153
West states ❶: 138–141
World ❷: 138–189
★Atlas: 1–24
Africa ❷: 160–173
★Atlas: 12–13
Asia ❷: 144–151
★Atlas: 17, 18, 19, 20
Australasia (Oceania)
❷: 144–151
★Atlas: 22–23, 24
Europe ❷: 152–159
★Atlas: 14-15, 16
Middle East ❷: 160–173
★Atlas: 18
North America
❷: 174–179 ★Atlas: 4–9
South America
❷: 180–183
★Atlas: 10–11
tables of geographical
information
❷: 140–143
territories
❷: 184–187

★Atlas is insert between
❷: 188 and 189

HISTORY
Key events and people
❸: 295, 305, 313, 314, 325
Makers of World History
❷: 128–137
U.S. History.
see also Timelines
Exploration and
colonization
❶: 106–109; ❹: 97–112
a nation is born
(circa 1750–1800)
❶: 110–114; ❹: 113–140
Growth, Civil War
and reunion
(circa 1800–1870)
❶: 115–121; ❹: 141–189
Developing power
(circa 1870–1915)
❶: 122–124;
❹: 190–237
War, boom, bust and war
(circa 1915–1950)
❶: 124–128;
❹: 238–289
Modern America
(circa 1950–present)
❶: 129–133;
❹: 290–347
Presidents of the U.S.
❷: 29–53

World History
Ancient world (circa
2000 B.C.–500 B.C.)
❷: 78–84;
❸: 294–296
Golden age of Greece
(circa 500 B.C.–300 B.C.)
❷: 84–86;
❸: 296–300
Roman Empire (circa
300 B.C.– A.D. 476)
❷: 85–89;
❸: 300–303
Middle Ages
(circa 476–1500)
❷: 90–96;
❸: 305–314
Renaissance
(circa 1500–1750)
❷: 97–103;
❸: 315–324
Modern World
(circa 1750–present)
Revolutions and Empires
❷: 104–124;
❸: 325–332
Invention and change
❷: 108–109;
❸: 327–332
World War I
❷: 110–111;
❸: 332–333
Between the Wars
❷: 112–113;
❸: 333–334
World War II
❷: 114–116;
❸: 334–336
Postwar World
❷: 117–127;
❸: 336–337

FIND IT FAST:
U.S. PRESIDENTS

ADAMS, John ❶: 112, 114;
❷: 30-31, 32, 62
ADAMS, John Quincy
❶: 116; ❷: 32-33, 35, 62
ARTHUR, Chester Alan
❶: 122; ❷: 40-41, 62
BUCHANAN, James
❷: 38-39, 62; ❹: 166
BUSH, George H.
❷: 52-53, 62; ❹: 339-341
BUSH, George W.
❶: 132; ❷: 52-53, 62,
124, 126, 127; ❹: 344
CARTER, Jimmy
❶: 131; ❷: 50-51, 62, 122;
❸: 352; ❹: 331-333
CLEVELAND, Grover
❷: 42-43, 62;
❹: 79, 197, 211, 217
CLINTON, William J.
❶: 132; ❷: 52-53, 62;
❸: 351; ❹: 78, 341-344
COOLIDGE, Calvin ❶: 125;
❷: 46-47, 62; ❹: 251-252
EISENHOWER, Dwight David
❶: 128, 130; ❷: 48-49,
51, 62, 116; ❹: 77, 78,
296-298, 304-306, 317
FILLMORE, Millard
❷: 36-37, 62; ❹: 166
FORD, Gerald R.
❶: 131; ❷: 50-51, 62,
122; ❹: 330-331
GARFIELD, James Abram
❶: 122; ❷: 40-41, 62; ❹: 210
GRANT, Ulysses Simpson
❶: 120; ❷: 40-41, 62;
❹: 177, 185
HARDING, Warren Gamaliel
❶: 125; ❷: 46-47, 62;
❹: 78, 250-251
HARRISON, Benjamin
❷: 42-43, 62
HARRISON, William Henry
❶: 114; ❷: 34-35, 62
HAYES, Rutherford Birchard
❷: 40-41, 62; ❹: 186
HOOVER, Herbert
❶: 126; ❷: 46-47, 62;
❹: 258, 262, 266-267
JACKSON, Andrew
❶: 114, 116, 117;
❷: 34-35, 37, 39, 62;
❹: 154-156, 176
JEFFERSON, Thomas
❶: 114; ❷: 30-31, 61,
62, 134; ❹: 79, 124
JOHNSON, Andrew
❶: 121; ❷: 38-39, 40, 62;
❹: 178, 182, 184-185

JOHNSON, Lyndon Baines
❶: 129, 130; ❷: 48-49,
62, 70, 120; ❹: 79, 313-
314, 318-319
KENNEDY, John Fitzgerald
❶: 129, 130; ❷: 48-49,
51, 62, 70, 119; ❸: 101;
❹: 77, 78, 312-313, 315,
317-318
LINCOLN, Abraham
❶: 119, 121; ❷: 38-39,
60, 62, 64, 67-68, 107,
134, 402; ❹: 166-167,
176-178, 181
MADISON, James
❶: 113, 114; ❷: 32-33, 62
McKINLEY, William
❶: 123; ❷: 42-43, 62;
❹: 219-222
MONROE, James
❶: 115, 116; ❷: 32-33, 62
NIXON, Richard Milhous
❶: 130, 131; ❷: 49, 50-
51, 62, 121, 122, 136;
❸: 325; ❹: 77, 78, 312,
320, 325-330
PIERCE, Franklin
❷: 38-39, 62; ❹: 164-165
POLK, James Knox
❷: 36-37, 62; ❹: 161-162
REAGAN, Ronald
❶: 132; ❷: 50-51, 62,
122, 123; ❹: 333-335
ROOSEVELT, Franklin Delano
❶: 126, 128, 473;
❷: 45, 46-47, 62, 113,
116, 135; ❸: 325, 335,
336; ❹: 76-77, 267-272,
279-280, 282-283, 290
ROOSEVELT, Theodore
❶: 123, 434; ❷: 44-45,
62, 135; ❹: 79, 220, 222-
223, 231-234
TAFT, William Howard
❷: 44-45, 62;
❹: 232-233, 249
TAYLOR, Zachary
❶: 117; ❷: 36-37, 62;
❹: 162-163
TRUMAN, Harry S.
❶: 128; ❷: 48-49, 62, 69,
116; ❹: 76, 284, 291, 304
TYLER, John ❷: 35, 36-37, 62
VAN BUREN, Martin
❷: 33, 34-35, 62
WASHINGTON, George
❶: 111, 112, 113;
❷: 30-31, 59, 62, 109,
134; ❹: 123, 126
WILSON, Woodrow
❶: 124; ❷: 44-45, 62,
111; ❸: 333; ❹: 79, 234,
235, 239-240, 243-244

FIND IT FAST:
STUDY SKILLS

KNOW YOURSELF ❸: 551-352
ROADBLOCKS TO SUCCESS
❸: 552-554
WHY STUDYING PAYS OFF
❸: 553, 561, 563, 564, 569
biology ❸: 482, 491, 483
calculus ❸: 372, 387, 401
chemistry ❸: 503, 510, 512
economics ❸: 246, 259, 277
English ❸: 48, 66, 102, 109
geology ❸: 523, 527, 530
history ❸: 298, 324, 335
physics ❸: 534, 546
political science ❸: 343, 348
psychology ❸: 357, 361, 368
HOW TO STUDY
❸: 564-565, 566-468,
570-571, 572
biology ❸: 497
calculus ❸: 474
chemistry ❸: 514
economics ❸: 288-291
English ❸: 113-114
geology ❸: 531
history ❸: 338-339
physics ❸: 546
political science ❸: 352
psychology ❸: 369
TEST-TAKING STRATEGIES
❶: 94-95, 114;
❸: 571-572, 586-597
fill in the blanks ❸: 289,
339, 352, 531, 585
definitions ❸: 289, 585
matching ❸: 290, 584
multiple choice ❶: 95; ❸: 289,
339, 352, 369, 497, 584
true-false ❸: 584-585
calculation ❸: 474, 514, 546
essays ❶: 95; ❸: 224, 290,
339, 352, 369, 497, 585
PROJECTS AND FIELDWORK
biology ❸: 497
economics ❸: 292
English ❸: 114
geology ❸: 531
history ❸: 338
political science ❸: 352
psychology ❸: 369
LAB REPORTS
❸: 497, 514, 531, 546
CALCULATOR SKILLS
❸: 575-576, 589
COMPUTER LITERACY
❸: 573-575
ORAL REPORTS ❸: 568-569
WRITING ASSIGNMENTS
❸: 569-570 see also
English: Writing research
papers; Book reports

Index

A

a, an (usage) **2:** 376
AARP 3: 349
Abbasid dynasty 2: 91
abbreviations
 economics **3:** 252
 English **3:** 94
 usage **2:** 376
ABCs of studying 3: 572
Abelard, Peter **2:** 131;
 3: 311
abiotic 1: 362
abnormal behavior
 3: 366
abolitionists 2: 67; **4:** 153,
 160
abolition movement
 1: 116; **4:** 349
abortion 1: 131
about, almost (usage)
 2: 376
Absalom, Absalom!
 2: 420
Absalom and Achitophel
 2: 396
abscissa 1: 325; **2:** 279,
 348; **3:** 374
absolute
 advantage (econ.)
 3: 284–285, 292
 convergence (math)
 3: 462
 dating (geol.) **3:** 516,
 528, 532
 humidity (geol.) **1:** 402
 magnitude (astron.)
 1: 412, 424
 maximum (math) **3:** 404
 minimum (math) **3:** 404
 temperature scale
 (physics) **2:** 258
 value (math) **1:** 286,
 325; **2:** 263; **3:** 373;
 4: 893–895
 zero (chem.) **3:** 516
 zero (physics) **1:** 375;
 538
absolutely (usage) **2:** 376
absolutism 3: 343, 344,
 354
abyssal plain 3: 520, 532
Academy Award films
 1: 472
accelerando 1: 466

acceleration 2: 244, 258;
 3: 475, 534, 535–536,
 537, 548
accept, except (usage)
 2: 376; **3:** 115
accessory sex organs
 3: 496
accidental(s) 1: 462, 466
achievement tests 3: 363,
 370
acid(s) 2: 236, 242; **3:** 512,
 516
 and conjugate bases
 3: 512
 strength of **3:** 512
acid rain 1: 355
acquired characteristic
 1: 362
Acquired Immune
 Deficiency
 Syndrome (AIDS)
 1: 132, 352
Acre 3: 313
Acropolis 2: 84
acrostic poems 2: 391
ACT (American College
 Testing Program)
 3: 363, 616
 sample questions
 3:617–618
act (drama) **1:** 476;
 2: 406
actinides 3: 504
Actium, Battle of **3:** 300
activation energy 3: 480,
 514, 516
active
 metals (chem.) **3:** 504
 satellite (astron.) **1:** 424
 site (biol.) **3:** 480, 498
 transport (biol.) **2:** 198;
 3: 480
active/passive voice
 (Eng.) **1:** 25; **3:** 87;
 4: 1324–1326
Acts 3: 308
acute (angle) **1:** 325;
 2: 348
Adages **3:** 318–319
adagio 1: 462, 466
Adam Bede **2:** 419, 421;
 3: 50
Adams, John **1:** 112, 114;
 2: 30–31, 32, 62

Adams, John Quincy
 1: 116; **2:** 32–33,
 35, 62
 Adams-Onis Treaty
 1: 115
adapt, adopt (usage)
 2: 376
adaptation(s) 1: 362;
 2: 224
Addams, Jane **1:** 122
addend 1: 325; **2:** 348
Addison, Joseph **2:** 389;
 4: 1382
addition (chem.) **2:** 238
 reaction **2:** 238, 242
addition (math)
 1: 178–191, 314, 318,
 325; **2:** 266
 facts **1:** 179, 181, 318
additive (math)
 identity element **1:** 325;
 2: 260, 348
 inverse **1:** 325; **2:** 348
Aden, Yemen **2:** 125
adenine (A) **3:** 479
adenosine diphosphate
 (ADP) **3:** 479–480,
 483
adiabatic change 1: 402
adjectives
 English **1:** 5, 26–31;
 3: 84
 usage **2:** 376
 French **3:** 120–125
 German **3:** 157–158
 Latin **3:** 217, 219, 220
 Spanish **3:** 184–186
adolescence 3: 360
Adonais **2:** 400
adopt, adapt (usage)
 2: 376
ADP (adenosine
 diphosphate)
 3: 479–480, 483
adulthood 3: 361
ADVANCING YOUR
 CAREER
 3: 646–681
advection fog 1: 396, 402
Adventures of Sherlock
 Holmes **2:** 417
adverbs
 English **1:** 5, 27–31, 34,
 49; **3:** 84

adverbial clauses
   1: 49, 51, 54; **2:** 374
   usage **2:** 376
   German **3:** 157–158
   Latin **3:** 219
   Spanish **3:** 184–185
advice, advise (usage)
   2: 376
advise, advice (usage)
   2: 376
Aegospotami, Battle of
   2: 84
Aeneas 3: 317–318
Aeneid **2:** 87, 391, 392,
   399, 402, 424, 429;
   3: 300, 317–318
aeolian landforms
   3: 520
aerobic (exercise) **1:** 337
aerobic (respiration)
   2: 199, 224
   processes **3:** 483
Aeschylus 1: 468; **2:** 84,
   128, 404, 406, 407;
   3: 298; **4:** 1380
Aesop 1: 100; **2:** 416
affect, effect (usage)
   2: 376; **3:** 115
affirmative action 4: 566
Afghanistan 2: 122, 125,
   126, 127, 143, 144;
   3: 337
   2: *Atlas* 19
Africa 1: 115, 126; **2:** 98,
   101, 108, 114, 126,
   138, 139, 140, 142,
   160–173; **3:** 295, 332,
   336, 337, 521, 523,
   529
   2: *Atlas* 12–13
   African plate **3:** 529
African-Americans
   2: 65–70
African National
   Congress (ANC)
   2: 123
"After Apple Picking"
   2: 397
After the Fall **2:** 408
Agamemnon **2:** 406, 407;
   3: 298
agenda-setting 4: 566
Age of
   Absolutism **3:** 314
   Enlightenment **3:** 344;
   4: 355
   Revolutions **3:** 327
aggravate (usage) **2:** 376

aggregate
   demand **3:** 272–273,
   275, 292
   supply **3:** 273, 275, 292
aggressive behavior
   3: 368
Agincourt, Battle of
   3: 308, 324
aging 3: 362
Agnew, Spiro **1:** 131; **2:** 51
agree to, agree with
   (usage) **2:** 376
agriculture 1: 121
Agriculture Adjustment
   Act 1: 126
Agriculture, Department
   of **1:** 354; **2:** 11
Ah Bing 2: 72
Ah Nam 2: 71
Ahriman (god) **2:** 83
ain't (usage) **2:** 376; **3:** 115
air mass 1: 398–399, 402
airplane 1: 123; **2:** 109
air pollution 1: 355
Akkadian Empire 2: 79
Alabama 1: 119, 146–147,
   156; **2:** 55, 67
Alamo 1: 117
Alaska 1: 121, 134,
   138–139, 156; 387;
   2: 55
   2: *Atlas* 8
Alastor **2:** 400
Albania 2: 113, 117, 143,
   152
   2: *Atlas* 14–15
Albany, New York **1:** 109
albedo 1: 424
Albee, Edward **2:** 405,
   407
Alcatraz 2: 58
Alchemist, The **2:** 408
alchemy 3: 326
alcohol (chem.) **2:** 237,
   238, 242
alcohol facts 1: 335, 338
Alcott, Louisa May **1:** 96
aldehydes 2: 237, 238
Aldrin, Edwin (Buzz)
   1: 130, 421; **2:** 118
Aleutian Islands 1: 127,
   388
Alexander the Great
   2: 82, 83, 85, 128;
   3: 295, 299, 301
Alexandria 2: 85, 86
Alfred the Great 2: 92,
   130

algae 1: 362; **2:** 214–215;
   3: 487, 489
algebra 2: 260–305
   equations in one variable
   2: 267
   fundamental theorem
   3: 412
   symbols **1:** 319
algebraic
   fractions **2:** 278
   properties of definite
   integrals **3:** 415
Algeria 2: 125, 140, 143,
   160
   2: *Atlas* 12
Algonquin (Indians)
   2: 55
algorithm(s) 1: 314, 325;
   3: 365
Alice's Adventures in
   Wonderland **2:** 417,
   418
Alien and Sedition Acts
   1: 114; **2:** 31; **4:** 138,
   141, 349
alimentary canals
   (digestive tracts)
   3: 493
alkali 2: 242
   alkaline-earth metals
   3: 503
   metal(s) **2:** 235, 242;
   3: 503
alkane/alkene/alkyne
   2: 237, 242
Al-Khwarizmi 2: 130
Allah 3: 304
allegorical morality plays
   2: 404
allegory 4: 1386
allegro 1: 462, 466
allele(s) 2: 206–207, 224;
   3: 485, 498
Allen, Gracie **1:** 470
Alliance for Progress
   1: 129
alliances 2: 13; **3:** 351
Allied v. Axis 1: 127
Allies 1: 124, 127; **2:** 110,
   111, 114, 115, 116
alliteration 4: 1234
   in poetry **1:** 93; **2:** 391
all of, alongside of (usage)
   2: 376
all ready, already (usage)
   2: 376
all right, alright (usage)
   2: 377; **3:** 115

All's Well That Ends Well
2: 411, 424
all the farther, as far as
(usage) 2: 377
all together, altogether
(usage) 2: 377
allude, elude (usage)
2: 377
allusion 3: 75; 4: 1235
**allusion, illusion,
delusion** (usage)
2: 377
alluvial
fan 3: 532
plain 1: 402
almanacs 2: 358
Almond, Gabriel 3: 344
almost, about (usage)
2: 376
almost, most (usage)
2: 377
alongside of, all of (usage)
2: 376
a lot (usage) 2: 377; 3: 115
alpha
decay 2: 241
particle(s) 2: 239, 242,
257, 258; 3: 546
Alpha Centauri 1: 411
alpine glacier(s) 1:
390–391; 3: 526,
532
Alps 2: 86; 3: 311, 315,
529
al Qaeda (The Base)
2: 125, 126, 127
already, all ready (usage)
2: 376
alright, all right (usage)
2: 377; 3: 115
Alsace-Lorraine 3: 330
alternating current(s)
(AC) 1: 379; 2: 252;
3: 548
**alternative job
preparation** 3: 655
although, though (usage)
2: 377
altimeter 1: 402
altitude of a star 1: 424
alto 1: 458, 466
altogether, all together
(usage) 2: 377
altruistic behavior
3: 368
aluminum 1: 372
alumnus (usage) 2: 377
Alvarez, Luis 2: 74

Al-Zawahiri, Ayman
2: 127
Alzheimer's disease
3: 358
AM (amplitude
modulation) 2: 252
Amadeus 2: 409
Amasis I 2: 80
Ambassadors, The 2: 421
amendment(s) 1: 124;
2: 22–28, 45; 4: 566
Amenemhet I 2: 80
Amenhotep IV (Ikhnaton)
2: 80
American
Colonization Society
1: 115; 4: 349
embassy 1: 132
Expeditionary Forces
(AEF) 1: 124; 4: 349
Federation of Labor
(AFL) 1: 122; 4: 349
Indian Movement (AIM)
2: 58; 4: 79, 349
Psychological
Association (APA)
3: 357
bibliography style
2: 372–373
Red Cross 1: 122
Revolution 1: 112; 2: 61,
67, 104; 3: 325;
4: 113–118, 122–129
sailors, impressment of
1: 113
Sign Language 3: 365
**American College
Testing Program**
(ACT) 3: 363, 616
sample questions
3: 617–618
American Dream, The
2: 407
American Samoa 1: 152,
172
2: *Atlas* 22
American, The 2: 421
American Tragedy, An
2: 419
Amherst 2: 46
Amherst, Jeffery 1: 109
amicus curiae brief
4: 566
amino
acids 3: 479, 486, 498
group (NH$_2$) 3: 478
ammonia 3: 493
amnesia 3: 367

**Amnesty Act for
Confederate
veterans** 2: 41
amoeba 3: 487
among, between (usage)
2: 377; 3: 115
Amores 3: 399
amorphous solid 3: 510
amount, number (usage)
2: 377
ampere 1: 382; 2: 254
Ampère, André 3: 542
amphibians class 2: 223
amplitude (math) 1: 325;
2: 329, 348
amplitude (sound) 1: 380,
382; 2: 251, 258;
3: 540, 548
Amundsen, Roald 2: 186
an, a (usage) 2: 376
Anabaptists 3: 319–320
anabolic pathways 3: 483
anaerobic 2: 199–200, 224
Analects 2: 84
analogy 4: 1235, 1236
analysis reactions 2: 236
**analyzing a writing
assignment** 3: 37–39
anapestic 2: 403
anaphase 2: 203; 3: 482,
483, 485
anarchist, anarchy
1: 123; 3: 344, 354
anatomy/physiology
1: 362; 3: 356
ancien régime 3: 340
Ancient Evenings 2: 422
ancient
Greece (map) 3: 297
Middle East (map)
3: 296
world 2: 78–89;
3: 294–304
andante 1: 462, 466
Andersen, Hans Christian
1: 100; 2: 416
Anderson, Sherwood
2: 416
Andes Mountains 1: 386;
2: 180; 3: 522, 529
and etc. (usage) 2: 377
and/or (usage) 2: 377
Andorra 2: 143, 152
Andromache 2: 409
Andromède 2: 408
anemometer 1: 401, 402
anerobic exercise 1: 337
aneroid barometer 1: 402

Angel of the Battlefield
  1: 122
Angelou, Maya **4:** 1382
angiosperms 1: 362;
  2: 219; **3:** 489, 498
angle(s) (math) **1:** 325;
  2: 306, 307–308, 324,
  327, 328, 331, 335,
  348
  defined **2:** 306
  of rotation **2:** 337–338
angle of incidence
  3: 544
Angles (people) **2:** 92
Anglo-Americans
  2: 59–61
Anglo-Saxon(s) 2: 92, 93;
  3: 307, 340
Angola 2: 66, 143, 160
  2: *Atlas* 13
angstrom 2: 251
Anguilla 2: 184
  2: *Atlas* 5
angular (physics)
  displacement **3:** 536,
  537, 548
  momentum **3:** 536
  velocity **3:** 536, 537, 548
angular resolution 1: 424
***Animal Farm* 2:** 417, 424
Animalia (kingdom)
  2: 192, 210, 220–223;
  3: 487–488
animal(s)
  cells **2:** 197; **3:** 481
  learning and behavior
  4: 774–778, 811
  systems **2:** 208; **3:** 492
  tissues **2:** 209
animation 1: 476
anion 3: 501, 516
***Anna Karenina* 2:** 421,
  423
Annapolis 2: 50
***Anschluss* 3:** 334
answer checking (math)
  1: 188, 219, 229, 247
Antarctica 2: 139, 140,
  142, 180, 184, 186;
  3: 523
  Antarctica Treaty **2:** 186
anther 3: 491
anthrax 1: 339, 352
anthropomorphic 3: 295
antibiotic 1: 362; **2:** 112
anti-Christianism 3: 326
anticline 1: 402; **3:** 525,
  532

antiderivative 3: 475
  formulas **3:** 417
  search **3:** 418–440
antidifferentiation 3: 416
Antietam Creek,
  Maryland **1:** 120
Anti-Federalists 4: 566
Antigonus I **3:** 299
Antigua and Barbuda
  2: 143, 174
  2: *Atlas* 5
antimatter 2: 256
antimuon 2: 256
antineutron 2: 256
Antioch 3: 309, 313
antiparticle 2: 256
antiproton 2: 256
anti-theatrical laws
  (U.S.) **1:** 470
antithesis 4: 1236–1237
antitrust laws 2: 45
Anti-Vietnam protests
  1: 130
antiwar demonstration
  1: 130
Antony and Cleopatra
  2: 411, 424
Antony, Marc **2:** 129
anxiety disorders 3: 367,
  370
anxious, eager (usage)
  2: 377
anybody, anyone (usage)
  2: 377
anyone, anybody (usage)
  2: 377
anyway (usage) **2:** 377
anywhere, everywhere,
  nowhere,
  somewhere (usage)
  2: 377
Apache (Indians) **2:** 57
APA style for
  bibliography
  2: 372–373
aperture 1: 424
aphelion 1: 424
apical meristems 3: 491
apogee 1: 424
Apollo 1: 421, 423
apostrophe (poetic device)
  3: 80; **4:** 1238
apostrophes (Eng.) **1:** 55;
  3: 92, 97
Appalachian Mountains
  1: 110, 134; **3:** 529
apparent magnitude
  1: 424

appeals courts 2: 11;
  3: 349
appeasement 2: 113
appellate jurisdiction
  4: 566
application of
  differentiation
  3: 399–407
applications, definite
  integrals **3:** 440–453
Appomattox Courthouse,
  Virginia **1:** 120
apportionment 4: 566
appositive(s) (Eng.) **1:** 41,
  47, 51; **3:** 85
  phrase (Eng.) **1:** 39
appraise, apprise (usage)
  2: 377
Apprenticeship of
  Wilhelm Meister,
  ***The* 2:** 414, 420
apprise, appraise (usage)
  2: 377
appropriations 4: 566
***apse* 3:** 313
aptitude tests 3: 363, 370
aquifer 1: 402
Aquinas, Thomas **2:** 131;
  3: 312, 320
Arab(s) 2: 92, 121; **3:** 304,
  305, 306, 337
  Arab-Israeli War **2:** 118,
  121, 122
  nationalist **1:** 130
  nations **2:** 118
  oil nations **1:** 131
Arabia 2: 91
Arabian peninsula
  3: 523
Arabic (language) **3:** 304,
  312
arachnida class 2: 221
Arafat, Yasser **2:** 125
Aragon 2: 96
arc 2: 320
  cosine **1:** 325; **2:** 348
  length **3:** 451–452
  sine **1:** 325; **2:** 348
  tangent **1:** 325; **2:** 348
Archaean (geol.) **3:** 529
archbishop of
  Canterbury 2: 94
architecture 3: 318
Arctic 2: 186
  Islands **2:** *Atlas* 7
  Ocean **2:** 141, 152, 174,
  186
area 1: 325; **3:** 408–411

and volume
4: 1083–1109
formulas 1: 320–321
surface of revolution
3: 453
areolar tissue 2: 209
arête 1: 402
Argentina 2: 123, 140,
143, 180
2: Atlas 11
Arianism 2: 89
Ariosto, Lodovico 2: 392,
394
aristocrats, aristocracy
3: 340, 344, 345
Aristophanes 2: 84, 404,
406, 407; 3: 297
Aristotle 2: 84, 128, 404;
3: 71, 298–299, 312,
318, 356; 4: 1378
Aristotelian method
3: 312
Aristotelian philosophy
3: 317, 318
arithmetic 1: 176–283
fundamental theorem
3: 412
mean 1: 325; 2: 348
sequence 1: 325; 2: 305,
348
series 1: 325; 2: 305,
348
symbols 1: 319
Arius 2: 129
Arizona 1: 118, 138–139,
156; 2: 55, 58, 72–73
Arkansas 1: 119, 146–147,
156–157; 2: 52, 55,
72–73
Arkansas (Indians) 2: 55
armature 1: 379
Armenia 2: 143, 152
Armies of the Night, The
2: 422
armistice 1: 124; 2: 111
Arms and the Man
2: 409
arms
race 2: 117
reduction 1: 124
Armstrong, Louis 1: 465;
2: 69
Armstrong, Neil A.
1: 130, 421; 2: 118
Armstrong, William 1: 96
Arnold, Matthew 2: 389,
393, 394; 4: 1379,
1382

aromatic 2: 237, 242
around, 'round (usage)
2: 377
arpeggio 1: 466
Arrhenius, Svante 3:512
Arrhenius acid/base/
theory 3: 512
"Ars Poetica" 2: 391
arteries 3: 493
arthropods 2: 221; 3: 498
Arthur, Chester Alan
1: 122; 2: 40–41, 62
Arthur, King (Eng.) 2: 91,
130
Arthurian legend
2: 424–425
articles
English 1: 5, 26
French 3: 118–120
German 3: 152–153
Latin 3: 217
Spanish 3: 183
Articles of Confederation
1: 113; 2: 4;
4: 127–128, 132, 566
articulation (music)
1: 463, 466
artificial
intelligence (psych.)
3: 365
satellite (astron.) 1: 424
transmutation (chem.)
2: 240, 241
artillery 2: 110
as (usage) 2: 377; 3: 115,
116
as, like (usage) 2: 377
as, than (usage) 3: 85
Ascension 2: 187
2: Atlas 13
ascomycetes 2: 216
ascorbic acid (vitamin C)
1: 333
asexual reproduction
1: 362; 2: 224;
3: 490, 498
as far as, all the farther
(usage) 2: 377
Ashurbanipal 2: 82
Ashurnasirpal II 2: 81
Asia 1: 386; 2: 46, 94, 95,
98, 108, 126, 138,
139, 140, 142, 144,
186; 3: 301, 311, 315,
337, 522, 523
2: Atlas 17
Asia and Australasia
2: 144–151

Asia Minor 2: 81, 85, 88,
96
Asian-Americans
2: 71–73
aside (drama) 2: 406
Asimov, Isaac 1: 96, 102;
2: 136, 417
asking questions (comp.)
3: 39, 43–44
Asoka 2: 128
assassination 1: 122;
2: 119
assassins
Booth, John Wilkes
1: 121; 2: 38, 107
Brutus 2: 87
Guiteau, Charles J.
1: 122; 2: 40
Hinckley, John W. Jr.
1: 132
Oswald, Lee Harvey
1: 129
Ray, James Earl 1: 130
Sirhan, Sirhan 1: 130
assembly line 2: 109
Assembly of Nobles
3: 327
assertion 4: 1386
assimilation 2: 224
association (psych.) 3: 370
associative law 1: 285,
325; 2: 260, 348
assure, ensure, insure
(usage) 3: 115
Assyrian Empire 2: 81,
82
Assyrians 3: 296, 299
astenosphere 3: 518, 521,
522, 532
asteroids 1: 408, 424
Astor, John Jacob 2: 62
astronaut(s) 1: 130, 424
Aldrin, Edwin (Buzz)
1: 130, 421; 2: 118
Armstrong, Neil 1: 130;
2: 118
Chaffee, Roger 1: 423
Gagarin, Yuri 1: 420,
423; 2: 118
McAuliffe, Christa
1: 132
Ride, Sally 1: 132, 423
Shepard, Alan 1: 420,
423
Tereshkova, Valentina
1: 423
White, Edward 1: 423
astronautics 1: 424

astronomical unit 1: 424
astronomy 2: 99
astrophysics 1: 424
asymptote 3: 375
As You Like It **2:** 411, 425
at (usage) **2:** 377
Athena 3: 297
Athens 2: 82, 83, 84; **3:** 297–300
   Athenian democracy **2:** 84
Atlanta, Georgia **1:** 120
Atlantic
   cable **1:** 121
   Ocean **2:** 138, 141, 152, 174, 180; **3:** 521, 522, 523, 529
   theater, WWII **2:** 114
Atlantis (space shuttle) **1:** 423
at-large 4: 566
atlases 2: 359
Atlas, following **2:** 188
atmosphere 1: 392; **3:** 518, 532
atom(s) 1: 370–371, 382; **2:** 226, 242; **3:** 478, 498, 501, 516
   models **2:** 229
atomic
   age **2:** 108, 113
   and nuclear physics **3:** 546
   bomb **2:** 49, 116; **3:** 335
   mass **1:** 371–373, 382; **2:** 230, 242
   mass table **2:** 230
   mass unit (amu) **3:** 508, 516
   number **1:** 371–373, 382; **2:** 228, 242, 257; **3:** 501, 503, 516
   particles **2:** 239
   parts **2:** 228
   structure **2:** 228; **3:** 502–504
   theory **2:** 228
   weight **3:** 508, 516
Aton 2: 80
ATP (adenosine triphosphate) **2:** 224; **3:** 479–480, 483, 484, 498
attention 3: 370
Attila 2: 89, 129; **3:** 302
attitudes 3: 368

attraction 3: 368
Attucks, Crispus **2:** 67
Auden, W. H. (Wystan Hugh) **2:** 391, 393, 394; **4:** 1379
audience (comp.) **3:** 33
audio 1: 476
auditory
   cortex **3:** 359
   system **3:** 359, 370
"Audley Court" 2: 401
Augsburg 3: 311
August 1914 **2:** 422
Augustus (Emperor) **2:** 85, 87; **3:** 295, 300
Augustus Caesar 2: 129
aurora 1: 405, 424
   borealis **1:** 405
Austen, Jane **2:** 414, 415, 418
Australia 2: 46, 103, 108, 139, 140, 142, 143, 144, 186; **3:** 523
   2: *Atlas* 24
   territories **2:** 184, 187
Austria 2: 103, 105, 106, 107, 111, 113, 143, 153; **3:** 329–330, 337
   2: *Atlas* 14
Austria-Hungary 1: 124
Austro-Hungarian Empire 2: 110, 111; **3:** 332
Austro-Prussian War 2: 107
authoritarianism 3: 345, 354
authority 3: 343, 354
autobahns 3: 333
autocracy 3: 343
automatic weapons 2: 107
autonomic system 3: 358, 370
auto racing 1: 450
autos sacramentales **2:** 407
autotroph(s) 2: 198, 199, 224; **3:** 479, 498
auxiliary verbs (Eng.) **1:** 18, 24
Avars 2: 91
average 1: 325; **2:** 348
"Average Waves in Unprotected Waters" 3: 90
Averroës (ibn Rushd) **2:** 131

aversion therapy 3: 367, 370
Avicenna 2: 131
Avignon 2: 95, 96; **3:** 314
Avogadro, Amedeo
   Avogadro's law **3:** 510
   Avogadro's number **3:** 508, 516
away (usage) **2:** 377
away, 'way (usage) **2:** 387
awful (usage) **2:** 377
awhile, a while (usage) **2:** 378
axiom(s) 1: 325; **2:** 306, 348
   axiomatic system **2:** 306
Axis powers 1: 126; **2:** 113, 114, 115; **3:** 335
axles 1: 376–377
axon 3: 370, 496
Azerbaijan 2: 143, 153
   2: *Atlas* 18
azimuthal projections 2: 189
Aztecs 2: 99; **3:** 322

B

Baathists 2: 127
  regime (of Hussein)
    2: 126
Babbitt **2:** 425
Babel, Isaac **2:** 416
Babylonia/Babylon 2: 80,
    83; **3:** 295–296
Babylonian(s) 2: 82;
    3: 325
  Captivity **2:** 82, 84
  Captivity of the papacy
    2: 95
  Empire **2:** 82, 84
Bacchae **2:** 408
Bacchus *see* Dionysus
Bach, Johann Sebastian
    1: 463; **2:** 133
bacillus 2: 213, 224
backbone 2: 224
backdrop 1: 476
backstage 1: 476
backward(s), forward(s)
    (usage) **2:** 378
Bacon, Francis **2:** 97;
    4: 1382
Bacon, Nathaniel **1:** 108
Bacon's Rebellion 1: 108
bacteria 1: 352, 362;
    2: 213; **3:** 487, 527
  bacteria/virus
    comparison **2:** 212
  blue-green **2:** 213
bad, badly (usage) **2:** 378;
    3: 115
badly, bad (usage) **2:** 378;
    3: 115
badminton 1: 454
Baez, Joan **2:** 74
Baghdad 2: 89, 91; **3:** 304
Bahamas 2: 98, 143, 174
    2: *Atlas* 5
Bahrain 2: 143, 161
    2: *Atlas* 18
"Bait, The" 2: 396
balance
  of nature **1:** 362
  of trade **3:** 284–285, 292
balanced equation
    (chem.) **3:** 508
balancing
  equations (math) **2:** 233
  redox reactions **3:** 513
Bald Soprano, The
    2: 408
Baldwin, James **4:** 1380
Bali 2: 126

Balkans 2: 96, 110, 111;
    3: 332
ballad 2: 391
ballet 1: 476
Baltic 2: 102
  Sea **3:** 304
Baltimore, Maryland
    1: 114, 117
Balzac, Honoré de **2:** 414,
    415, 418
Bandura, Albert **3:** 364
Bangladesh 2: 140, 143,
    144
    2: *Atlas* 17
bank holiday 1: 126
Bank of the United
    States 1: 113; **2:** 35
baptism 3: 319
Barbados 2: 143, 175
    2: *Atlas* 5
"Barbara Allen" 2: 391
barbarians 2: 86, 90
Barbarossa, Frederick
    2: 131
Bardi
  banks **3:** 311, 315
  family **3:** 315
barely (usage) **2:** 378
Bar Kokba 2: 89
"Barn Burning" 3: 92
barometer 1: 400, 402
Baroque (music) **1:** 456,
    466
baroque architecture
    3: 320
Barrie, Sir James **1:** 96
barter markets 3: 253
Bartholomew Fair **2:** 408
Bartók, Béla **1:** 464
Barton, Clara **1:** 122
baryons 2: 256; **3:** 546
basalt 3: 524
base (chem.) **2:** 236, 242;
    3: 512, 516
base (math) **1:** 325; **2:** 348
  base 10 1: 183, 195,
    198–206
baseball 1: 430–433
  dictionary of **1:** 433
  major league records
    1: 432
  reading a box score
    1: 432
basic
  concepts (chem.)
    3: 500–501
  fact (math) **1:** 325
  needs (human) **3:** 366

basidomycetes 2: 216
basketball 1: 438–439
  dictionary of **1:** 439
  team lists **1:** 439
bass 1: 458, 461, 466
Bastille 2: 104; **3:** 327
Bataan 1: 127; **2:** 116
  Death March **4:** 350
bathroom safety 1: 344
batteries 3: 542
Battle(s)
  of Aegospotami **2:** 84
  of Britain **2:** 115
  of Bull Run **4:** 352
  of Crécy **3:** 308, 324
  of Fredericksburg
    1: 120; **4:** 357
  of Gettysburg **1:** 120;
    4: 357
  of Guadalcanal **1:** 127;
    2: 116; **4:** 359
  of Hastings **2:** 93; **3:** 307
  of Kadesh **2:** 80
  of Legnano **3:** 310, 314
  of Midway **2:** 116
  of Nations **2:** 105
  of Pavia (1525) **3:** 324
  of Sedan (1870) **3:** 330
  of Tanis **2:** 80
  of Tannenberg **2:** 111
  of the Bulge **2:** 116
  of the Marne, first
    2: 111
  of the Marne, second
    2: 110, 111
  of Verdun **2:** 111
  of Waterloo **2:** 105;
    3: 327
  of Ypres, first **2:** 111
  of Ypres, second **2:** 111
  of Zama **2:** 86
Baudelaire, Charles Pierre
    2: 393, 394, 398
Baum, Lyman Frank **1:** 96
Bavaria 2: 91, 92; **3:** 329
Bay of Pigs 1: 129; **2:** 49,
    119; **4:** 350
Bay Psalm Book **2:** 60
Beagle **3:** 331
Bean, Alan L. **1:** 421
Bear Flag Revolt 1: 117;
    4: 350
Beatles 1: 465
beautiful (usage) **2:** 378
Beauvoir, Simone de
    4: 1382
because, reason (usage)
    3: 117

"Because I Could Not Stop for Death/He Kindly Stopped for Me" 2: 396
Becket, St. Thomas à **2:** 131
Beckett, Samuel **2:** 405, 406, 407
Beckford, William **2:** 417
Becquerel, Antoine Henri **2:** 108, 257
Beethoven, Ludwig van **1:** 464; **2:** 134
began, begun (usage) **2:** 378
Begin, Menachem **2:** 122
begun, began (usage) **2:** 378
behavioralism (pol. sci.) **3:** 354
behavioral view (psych.) **3:** 366
behaviorism (psych.) **3:** 357, 370
behavior therapies (psych.) **3:** 367, 370
Beijing 2: 123
Beirut, Lebanon **2:** 123
Belarus 2: 124, 143, 153
2: *Atlas* 15
Belgium 1: 114; **2:** 105, 108, 110, 111, 114, 115, 119, 143, 154; **3:** 332, 337
2: *Atlas* 14
Belize 2: 143, 175
2: *Atlas* 5
Bell, Alexander Graham **1:** 121; **2:** 108, 135
Bell, Ellis *see* Bronte, Emily
Belleau Wood 1: 124
Bellevue Hospital 3: 363
Benedictine(s)
monk **2:** 93
order **2:** 90
Rule **3:** 309, 311
Ben-Gurion, David **2:** 135
Benin 2: 66, 143, 161
2: *Atlas* 12
Benjamin, Judah P. **2:** 64
Bennett, Floyd **2:** 186
Benny, Jack **1:** 470
bent molecule3: 505, 506
benzene 2: 237
Beowulf **2:** 392, 394, 424
Beppo **2:** 395

Berg, Alban **1:** 464
Bergen (Norway) **3:** 311
Bergson, Henri **3:** 71
Bering Sea 1: 135; **2:** 141
Berkeley, George **2:** 133
Berlin 2: 116
blockade **1:** 128; **2:** 117
Wall **2:** 49, 119, 123; **3:** 336, 337; **4:** 351
Bermuda 2: 184
2: *Atlas* 4
Bernard of Clairvaux 2: 131
Bernstein, Leonard **2:** 136
beside, besides (usage) **2:** 378
Bessemer, Henry **1:** 118
best, better (usage) **2:** 378
beta
decay **2:** 241
particle(s) **2:** 239, 242, 257; **3:** 546
rays **2:** 258
Betelguese 1: 414
Bethlehem 2: 88
Betterbury, Ariane and Michael **1:** 102
better, best (usage) **2:** 378
between, among (usage) **2:** 378; **3:** 115
between you and me (usage) **2:** 378
Beyle, Marie Henri *see* Stendhal
Bhopal 2: 123
Bhutan 2: 143, 145
2: *Atlas* 17
Bible 2: 88
bibliographies 2: 359, 361, 369–373
bicameral legislatures 2: 6; **3:** 347; **4:** 351, 566
Bidlake, John *see* Lawrence, D. H.
big-bang theory 1: 415, 424; **3:** 527
Big Sleep, The **2:** 417
bildungsroman **2:** 416
bill(s) 3: 354; **4:** 566
of attainder **4:** 566
Bill of Rights 1: 113; **2:** 12, 22–23; **3:** 347, 350; **4:** 77, 134–135, 351, 566
binary
acids **3:** 507

covalent compound **3:** 507
fission **2:** 224; **3:** 482, 498
stars **1:** 414, 424
Binet, Alfred **3:** 363
bin Laden, Osama **2:** 125, 127
binomial(s) 1: 325; **2:** 272, 275, 277, 348
expansions **2:** 275
theorem **2:** 277
biogeography 1: 362
Biographica Literaria **2:** 396
biography/autobiography 2: 389
BIOLOGY 2: 192–225; **3:** 478–499; **4:** 595–840
biological classification (5 kingdoms) **3:** 487–488
biome(s) 1: 362
of North America **1:** 358–359
biomedical therapies 3: 367, 370
"Birches" 2: 397
birds class 2: 223
Birds, The **2:** 407
Birmingham, Alabama **2:** 70
Birth of a Nation **1:** 471
bisect 1: 325; **2:** 307–308, 348
Bismarck **2:** 115
Bismarck, Otto von **2:** 134; **3:** 325, 330, 332
bismuth 1: 372
black-body radiation 3: 545
Black Boy **2:** 423
Black Death (bubonic plague) **2:** 95, 131–132; **3:** 311, 315
Black Hawk 2: 36
black hole 1: 414, 424
Black Muslims 2: 70
black(s) 1: 107
civil rights (nationalism) **1:** 129; **4:** 351
Black Sea 2: 96, 106; **3:** 294, 304
bladder 3: 493

Blair, Eric **2:** 432
 see also Orwell, George
Blair, Tony **2:** 126
Blake, Eubie **2:** 69
Blake, William **2:** 134,
 393, 394–395, 400;
 4: 1378
blanket primary 4: 566
blank verse 2: 391;
 3: 79–80
Bleak House **2:** 419
"Bleeding Kansas"
 1: 119; **4:** 351
Blenheim 2: 103
"Blessed Damozel, The"
 2: 400
Bliven, Bruce, Jr. **1:** 102
block grant 4: 566
bloodstream 3: 496
bluegrass (music) **1:** 465
blues (music) **1:** 465
Blume, Judy **1:** 96
Boccaccio, Giovanni
 2: 97, 131, 414; **3:**
 315; **4:** 1378
Bode's law 1: 424
Boer War 2: 109
Boethius 2: 130; **3:** 303
Bohemia 2: 101
Bohr, Niels **2:** 228;
 3: 502
boiling point(s) 1: 366,
 368; **2:** 227, 242
Boleyn, Anne **2:** 98
Bolívar, Simón **2:** 105, 134
Bolivia 2: 143, 180
 2: *Atlas* 10
Bologna 3: 311
Bolsheviks 2: 111; **3:** 333,
 340
Bonaparte, Napoleon
 see Napoleon I
bond (chem.)
 angle **3:** 505
 energy **3:** 505
 lengths **3:** 505
bone tissue 2: 209
Bonhomme Richard
 1: 112
Bonus Army 1: 126;
 4: 351
book
 catalogs (library)
 2: 356–358
 how to preview **1:** 91
 reports **2:** 436–460
 fiction **2:** 455–456
 nonfiction **2:** 456–458
 oral **2:** 458–460
 written **2:** 444–454
*Book of American Negro
 Poetry* **2:** 69
Book of the Courtier
 3: 317
booster 1: 424
Booth, John Wilkes **1:** 121;
 2: 38, 107
bop (music) **1:** 465
borrow, lend (usage)
 2: 378
borrowing (math)
 1: 194
Bosnia-Herzegovina
 2: 124, 143, 154;
 3: 337, 351, 352
 2: *Atlas* 14
Boston 1: 110; **2:** 32
 Harbor **1:** 111
 Massacre **1:** 110; **2:** 67;
 4: 351
 Tea Party **1:** 111; **4:** 79,
 351
Boston, Lucy M. **1:** 97
Boswell, James **2:** 389;
 4: 1382
botany 2: 103
Botswana 2: 143, 162
Botticelli, Sandro **2:** 132
botulism (food poisoning)
 1: 339, 352
Bourbon(s) 3: 322
 kings (Fr.) **3:** 326
bourgeois, bourgeoisie
 3: 340
bowling 1: 450
 sample score card **1:** 450
Boxer Rebellion 2: 109
boxing 1: 451
 weight classes **1:** 451
Boyle's law (for gases)
 2: 258; **3:** 510
brackets (Eng.) **3:** 93
Bradbury, Ray **2:** 417
Braddock, General
 Edward **1:** 109
Bradford, William **1:** 107
Brahms, Johannes **1:** 464
brain (human) **1:** 342;
 3: 358
brainstorming (comp.)
 3: 39, 43
brainstorming (psych.)
 3: 365
Brand **2:** 408
Brandenburg Concertos
 1: 463
brass instruments 1: 459,
 466
Braun, Wernher von
 2: 136
Brave New World **2:** 417
Brazil 2: 140, 143, 181
 2: *Atlas* 10–11
Brecht, Bertolt **2:** 405, 407
breeder reactor 2: 240,
 241, 242
Brezhnev, Leonid **2:** 136
brief 4: 566
 orders **4:** 566
bring, take (usage) **3:** 117
Britain 1: 109, 110, 113,
 114, 117, 124, 125,
 126, 127; **2:** 103, 105,
 106, 108, 109, 110,
 111, 114, 119, 123;
 3: 332
Britain, Battle of **2:** 115
Britannicus **2:** 409
British *see also* United
 Kingdom **1:** 109, 112;
 2: 101, 106, 109, 112,
 113, 115, 116; **3:** 332,
 337
 Crown colonies **2:** 109
 Indian Ocean Territory
 2: 184
 Isles **2:** 114
 Parliament **1:** 111
 Raj (empire) **3:** 332
 territories, Africa and
 Asia **2:** 108
 Virgin Islands **2:** 184
**British North America
 Act 2:** 107
British thermal unit
 (Btu) **1:** 375
Britten, Benjamin and
 Imogen Holts **1:** 102
broad money 3: 281–282
Broca, Paul **3:** 356
bromine 1: 372
bronchi, bronchioles
 3: 493
Brønsted, Johannes **3:** 512
 Brønsted acid **3:** 512
 Brønsted base **3:** 512
 Brønsted-Lowry theory
 3: 512
Brontë, Charlotte **2:** 414,
 415, 418; **4:** 1378
Brontë, Emily **2:** 414, 415,
 418
Bronze Age 2: 79, 82
Brooke, Edward **2:** 70

Brooklyn
Bridge **2:** 64
Dodgers **2:** 69
Brothers Karamazov,
The **2:** 415, 419, 425
Brown, John **1:** 119
Brown, Ronald **2:** 70
Browning, Elizabeth
Barrett **2:** 393, 395;
3: 77
Browning, Robert **2:** 391,
393, 395; **4:** 1379
Brown v. Board of
Education of
Topeka **1:** 129; **2:** 12,
69; **4:** 78, 305, 566
Bruce, Robert **2:** 131
Brueghel, Pieter the Elder
2: 97
Bruges 3: 310
Brunei 2: 143, 145
2: *Atlas* 21
Brunelleschi 3: 315
Bruni, Leonardo **3:** 316
Bruno, Giordano **3:** 315
Brutus 2: 87
Bryan, William Jennings
1: 123; **2:** 43; **4:** 211
Bryant, William Cullen
2: 393, 395
bryophytes 2: 217–219;
3: 489
bubonic plague (Black
Death) **2:** 95,
131–132; **3:** 311,
315
Buchanan, James
2: 38–39, 62; **4:** 166
Buddenbrooks **2:** 422
Buddha, Gautama **2:** 128
Buddha Gaya 2: 84
Buddhism 2: 84
Budé, Guillaume **3:** 318
budget
deficit **3:** 280, 292
surplus **3:** 280, 292
Buffalo, New York **2:** 42
Buffalo Bill's Wild West
Show **1:** 470
bulbs (plant) **3:** 490
Bulgaria 2: 117, 143, 154
2: *Atlas* 15
Bull Moose Party
4: 351–352
Bull Run, Battles of **4:** 352
Bunyan, John **2:** 414, 418
Buran (space shuttle)
1: 421

bureaucracy 3: 348;
4: 522–524, 566
bureaucratic theory
4: 566
Burgundians 3: 303, 308
Burgundy (duchy) **2:** 93;
3: 311
Burkina Faso 2: 143, 162
2: *Atlas* 12
burlesque 1: 470
Burma 2: 96, 145,
see also Myanmar
Burnford, Sheila **1:** 97
Burns, George **1:** 470
Burns, Robert **2:** 390;
4: 1378
Burr, Aaron **1:** 114; **2:** 31;
4: 144
Burundi 2: 143, 162
2: *Atlas* 13
Bush, George H. **2:** 52–53,
62; **4:** 339–341
Bush, George W. **1:** 133;
2: 52–53, 62, 124,
126, 127; **4:** 344
business ventures
(GI bill) **1:** 128
but (usage) **2:** 378
Butler, Samuel **2:** 416
Byars, Betsy **1:** 97
Byrd, Richard E. **2:** 186
Byron, George Gordon
2: 393, 395; **4:** 1379
Byzantine(s) 2: 91, 94;
3: 313, 324
Byzantine-Christian-
Islamic world (map)
3: 303
Byzantine Christians
2: 90
Byzantine Empire **2:** 85,
89, 90, 96
Byzantium 3: 303, 304
"Byzantium" 2: 403

C

Cabinet Departments
2: 11; 3: 349; 4: 566
cable television 1: 476
Cabot, John 1: 107;
2: 98
cacophony 4: 1386
cadenza 1: 466
Cadiz 2: 81
cadmium 1: 372; 2: 257
Caesar and Cleopatra
2: 404
Caesar Augustus 3: 301
Caesari 3: 340
Caesaropapism 3: 304
Cage, John 2: 136
Calais, port of 3: 308
calcium 1: 372
calculate, reckon (usage)
2: 378
calculator exercises
(calculus)
3: 374–376, 378,
381–385, 387, 389,
390, 392–394,
399–401, 403–404,
407, 414–416, 419,
421–423, 427,
429–431, 434–435,
437, 445, 450, 452,
454–458, 460–461
calculator skills
3: 575–576
calculator tips 3: 589
calculator use (arith.)
1: 280–283
addition 1: 178, 188,
281
decimal point
1: 280–281
distributive property
1: 281–282
division 1: 228
fractions to decimals
1: 282
memory 1: 282
mixed numbers 1: 239
multiplication 1: 216
percent 1: 280
rounding 1: 281
scientific notation
1: 283; 2: 347
subtraction 1: 196

CALCULUS 3: 325,
372–475;
4: 889–1153

answers to exercises
3: 682–685
first fundamental
theorem 3: 413
second fundamental
theorem 3: 414
caldera 1: 402; 3: 524, 532
Calderón de la Barca
2: 404, 407–408
Calhoun, John C.
4: 163–164
California 1: 110, 117,
118, 121, 138–139,
157; 2: 37, 50, 58,
72–73, 75; 3: 523,
525
caliph 3: 304
Calixtus II (pope)
3: 309
call numbers (lib.)
2: 356
caloric expenditures
1: 337
Calvary, cavalry (usage)
2: 378
Calvert, George (Lord
Baltimore) 1: 108
Calvin, John 2: 99, 132;
3: 317, 319, 320
Calvinist(s) (church)
2: 99, 100, 101;
3: 319–322
calyx 3: 491
Cambodia 2: 143, 145
2: *Atlas* 17
Cambrian Period 3: 529
Camden, South Carolina
1: 112
Camelot 2: 91
camera 1: 122
shots (movies) 1: 471
Cameroon 2: 162
2: *Atlas* 12
Camp David Accords
1: 131; 2: 122; 4: 352
Camp David, Maryland
2: 51, 122
campus services
3: 576–579
Camus, Albert 2: 415,
418; 4: 1380
can, may (usage) 2: 378;
3: 115
Canaan (Lebanon coast)
2: 81
Canada 1: 109, 114, 134,
135, 143; 2: 33, 101,
103, 107, 108, 140,

176; 3: 351
2: *Atlas* 6–7
canceling (math) 1: 242
cancer 2: 224
Cancer Ward, The 2: 422
Candida 2: 406
Candide 2: 416, 417, 425
Cannon-Bard theory
3: 366
cannons 3: 324
cannot 3: 115
can't (usage) 2: 378
cantata(s) 1: 463, 466
Canterbury Tales, The
2: 96, 392–393, 395,
414, 425–426
can't hardly (usage)
2: 378
Cantigny, France 1: 124
Cantos 2: 399
Canute, King (Eng.) 2: 93,
131; 3: 307
capacitance 3: 541, 542,
548
in parallel 3: 542
in series 3: 542
capacitor 3: 541, 542,
543, 548
Cape Canaveral, Florida
1: 421–422
Capet, Hugh 2: 93, 131;
3: 307
Capetian(s) 3: 307
dynasty 2: 93
Cape Verde 2: 143, 163
capillaries 3: 493
capital 3: 253, 262, 292
capital, capitol (usage)
2: 378
capitalism 3: 322, 328
capitalization (Eng.)
1: 55; 2: 375
capitol, capital (usage)
2: 378
capsule 1: 424
carbohydrates 3:
478–479, 484
carbon 1: 372
carbon 14 2: 239
dating 3: 546
dioxide 1: 392
isotopes 3: 501
carbonates 1: 389
Carboniferous Period
3: 529
carbonyl (CO, COOH)
3: 478
carboxyl (COOH) 3: 478

card catalogs (lib.) **2:** 356
cardiac tissues 2: 209
cardiovascular systems
   3: 493
Caribbean
   islands **2:** 101
   Sea **1:** 107; **2:** 141, 174
Carnegie, Andrew
   2: 64
Carnegie Steel Company
   2: 64
carnivore(s) 1: 362;
   3: 492, 498
Carolingian(s) 2: 93;
   3: 306, 340
   dynasty **3:** 305
   Empire **2:** 91, 92; **3:** 307
   period **3:** 327
carpels 3: 491
carpetbaggers 4: 352
Carroll, Lewis **1:** 97;
   2: 415, 417, 418
carrying (math) **1:** 183
Carson, Rachel **1:** 102;
   4: 1383
Carter, Jimmy **1:** 131;
   2: 50–51, 62, 122;
   3: 352; **4:** 331–333
Cartesianism **3:** 326
Carthage 2: 81, 85, 86,
   89; **3:** 295, 300,
   340
Carthaginians 2: 86, 300
Cartier, Jacques **1:** 107
cartilage tissue 2: 209
cartography 2: 188
Casablanca **1:** 472
Casals, Pablo **2:** 74
Casals, Rosemary **2:** 74
Casca 2: 87
case (usage) **2:** 378
cases (Lat.) **3:** 217, 218,
   219, 220, 221
casework (constituent
   service) **3:** 347
"Cask of Amontillado,
   The" 2: 422
Caspian Sea 2: 96, 141,
   153
Cassini probe 1: 419
Cassiodorus 3: 303
cast 1: 476
Castiglione, Baldassare
   3: 317
Castile 2: 96
Castle, The **2:** 421
Castle of Otranto, The
   2: 417

Castro, Fidel **1:** 129;
   2: 76, 119; **3:** 343
catabolic pathways 3: 483
catalog, catalogue (usage)
   2: 378
catalogue, catalog (usage)
   2: 378
catalyst(s) 2: 200; **3:** 480,
   514, 516
Catcher in the Rye, The
   2: 426
Cateau-Cambrésis,
   Treaty of **3:** 321
categorical grant
   4: 566
catharsis (lit.) **3:** 71
Cather, Willa **4:** 1380
Catherine de Medici
   3: 322
Catherine the Great
   2: 103
Catholics 1: 108; **2:** 101,
   102
cation 3: 501, 507, 516
Cato 3: 300
   conspiracy **2:** 67
   the Elder **2:** 128
Catton, Bruce **4:** 1382
Caucasian Chalk Circle,
   The **2:** 407
caucus 4: 566
cause and effect paper
   (comp.) **3:** 56
cavalry 3: 324
cavalry, Calvary (usage)
   2: 378
Cavendish, Henry **2:** 248
Cavour, Camillo di **3:** 331
Caxton, William **2:** 132
Cayman Islands 2: 184
   2: *Atlas* 5
Ceausescu 2: 123
cell 1: 362; **2:** 192, 224;
   3: 480–483;
   4: 621–625
   components and
     functions **3:** 481
   differences **2:** 196
   division **3:** 482–483,
     496; **4:** 653–661,
     801–802
   membrane **1:** 362;
     3: 480, 498
   nucleus **3:** 498
   structure and function
     2: 195
   wall **1:** 362; **2:** 192–193,
     195; **3:** 481, 498

cellular
   phases **3:** 483
   respiration **3:** 482, 483,
     484, 498
cellulose 2: 224
Celsius temperature
   scale 1: 375; **2:** 250,
   258
Cenozoic Era 3: 527,
   529
censer, censor, censure
   (usage) **2:** 378
censor, censure, censer
   (usage) **2:** 378
censorship 3: 323
censure, censer, censor
   (usage) **2:** 378
center around, center on
   (usage) **3:** 115
center on, center around
   (usage) **3:** 115
Central African Republic
   2: 143, 163
   2: *Atlas* 12
Central America 1: 107
Central America and
   West Indies
   2: *Atlas* 2
central
   angle **2:** 320
   nervous system **3:** 358
Central
   Intelligence Agency
     (CIA) **2:** 11, 53, 119
   Pacific Railroad **2:** 71
   Powers **1:** 124; **2:** 110;
     4: 352
centration 3: 370
centrioles 2: 195; **3:** 481,
   482
centromere 3: 482
cepheid variable(s)
   1: 414, 424
cerebellum/cerebrum
   3: 358, 370
Cervantes, Miguel de
   2: 97, 133, 414, 416,
   418–419; **4:** 1378
ceteris paribus **3:** 252,
   292
Cézanne, Paul **2:** 134
Chad 2: 143, 163
   2: *Atlas* 12
Chadwick, J. **3:** 501
Chaffee, Roger **1:** 423
chain reaction 2: 113,
   240, 242, 257
Chairs, The **2:** 408

Chaldea 2: 81
Challenger (space shuttle)
  1: 132, 422, 423
Chalons 2: 89
Chamberlain, Neville
  2: 115
chamber music 1: 464,
  466
Champagne (French
  region) **3:** 308
Champlain, Samuel de
  1: 107
Chancellorsville, Virginia
  1: 120
chancroid 1: 352
Chandler, Raymond
  2: 417
Chandragupta Maurya
  2: 128
changes
  in matter **2:** 228
  of state **3:** 510–511
changing careers
  3: 668–670
chants (music) **1:** 463
character (comp.) **2:** 413;
  4: 1386
character (lit.) **3:** 72–73
character actor 1: 476
charismatic authority
  3: 342
Charlemagne 2: 90, 91,
  92, 130; **3:** 299, 305,
  306, 307, 309
Charles I (Eng.) **2:** 102;
  3: 326
Charles II (Eng.) **2:** 102;
  3: 327
Charles V (Hapsburg Holy
  Roman Emperor)
  2: 99, 132; **3:** 314,
  321
Charles VII (Fr.) **2:** 95;
  3: 308
Charles VIII (Fr.) (Valois)
  3: 321
Charles IX (Fr.) **3:** 322
Charles XII (Swed.)
  2: 102
Charles Martel 2: 91,
  130; **3:** 305, 306
Charles's law (for gases)
  2: 258; **3:** 510
Charleston (dance)
  1: 125
Charleston, South
  Carolina **1:** 112,
  119

Chateau-Thierry 1: 124
Chaucer, Geoffrey **2:** 96,
  132, 392, 395, 414,
  425–426; **4:** 1378
Chavez, Cesar **2:** 75;
  4: 79
Chavez, Dennis **2:** 74
checklist for outlines
  2: 365
checks and balances 2: 8;
  3: 347; **4:** 566
Chekhov, Anton **2:** 405,
  406, 408, 416;
  4: 1378, 1380
chemical
  arithmetic **3:** 507–509
  bond(s) **3:** 505–506, 516
  change **1:** 382; **3:** 501
  equation(s) **1:** 370;
  2: 242; **3:** 507
  equilibrium **3:** 514, 516
  kinetics **3:** 514
  properties of matter
  1: 369; **3:** 501
  reaction(s) **2:** 228, 232,
  242; **3:** 479–480
  symbols **2:** 226
CHEMISTRY 2: 226–243;
  3: 500–517; **4:**
  609–617, 800
Cherokee (Indians) **2:** 55,
  57, 58; **4:** 352
Cherry Orchard, The
  2: 406, 408
Chesapeake Bay 1: 107
Chesterton, G. K. **4:** 1382
Chew, Ruth **1:** 97
Cheyenne (Indians)
  1: 121; **2:** 57
Chiang Kai-shek 2: 117
Chicago 1: 122; **2:** 113
  fire **1:** 121
Chickamauga, Georgia
  1: 120; **2:** 40
chicken pox (varicella)
  1: 339, 352
child development, stages
  of **3:** 360, 361
*Childe Harold's
  Pilgrimage* **2:** 395,
  400
childish, childlike (usage)
  2: 378
childlike, childish (usage)
  2: 378
Chile 2: 143, 181
  2: *Atlas* 10–11
chilopoda class 2: 221

China 1: 126, 128; **2:** 13,
  84, 90, 92, 94, 96,
  102, 106, 109, 117,
  121, 122, 140, 143,
  146; **3:** 311, 314, 324,
  336
  2: *Atlas* 17
  trade **1:** 130
Chinatowns 2: 71
Chinese 2: 92, 109
  Chinese-Americans
  2: 71–72
  Civil War **2:** 117
  Communist Party **2:** 109
  Exclusion Act **2:** 72
  space flight **1:** 422, 423
Ch'ing dynasty 2: 102,
  109
chinook 1: 402
Chippewa (Indians) **2:** 55
Chisholm, Shirley **2:** 70
chivalry, code of **3:** 324
chlorine 1: 372
chlorophyll 1: 356, 362;
  2: 224; **3:** 484, 498
chloroplast(s) 1: 362;
  2: 195, 196, 199;
  3: 481, 482, 484, 498
Choctaw (Indians) **2:** 55
choking treatment 1: 347
cholera 1: 339, 352
cholesterol 1: 352
Chomsky, N. **3:** 357
Chopin, Frédéric **1:** 464
chord(s) (math) **2:** 320
chord(s) (music) **1:** 462,
  466
**chordata (vertebrates)
  phylum 2:** 223
choreographer 1: 476
chorus 1: 476
chorus (drama) **2:** 406
Christ 3: 295
"Christabel" 2: 396
Christianity/Christians
  1: 108; **2:** 83, 88, 89,
  94; **3:** 296, 300–303,
  314
  Eastern and Western
  2: 90
  Old Testament **3:** 308
  Reconquista of Spain
  3: 310
Christie, Agatha **2:** 417
Christmas Carol, A
  2: 426
Christmas Island 2: 184
  2: *Atlas* 23

chromatids **3:** 482
chromatin **2:** 193, 224;
    3: 482, 483
chromoplasts **2:** 196
chromosome(s) **2:** 192,
    193, 195, 205, 224;
    3: 481, 482, 485, 498
   mapping **3:** 485
chromosphere **1:** 405, 424
"Chrysanthemums, The"
    3: 91
Churchill, John (Duke of
    Marlborough) **2:** 103
Churchill, Winston
    2: 115, 135; **4:** 1382
Church of England **2:** 98,
    100, 102
church reform **3:** 311
Cicero **2:** 128; **3:** 316
Cid, Song of the **2:** 395–396
cileophora **2:** 214
cilia **2:** 195, 196, 224;
    3: 481
cinder cone(s) **1:** 388,
    402; **3:** 524
cinematographer **1:** 476
circle(s) **1:** 325; **2:** 283,
    320–323, 327, 348
   definitions **2:** 320
   equations of **1:** 316
circuit(s) **3:** 543, 548
   diagram symbols
    3: 543
circular
   flow (econ.) **3:** 253
   theory of change
    (pol. sci.) **3:** 346
circulatory system
   (human) **1:** 343;
    2: 208; **3:** 493, 494
circumlocution (usage)
    2: 378
circuses **1:** 469, 470
cirque **1:** 390, 402
cirrus clouds **1:** 397, 398,
    402
Cistercians **3:** 311
cite, site, sight (usage)
    2: 378
cities, most populous
    2: 140
citizen **3:** 354
citizen, native (usage)
    2: 383
citizenship **1:** 121
citric acid (Krebs) cycle
    3: 483, 484, 498
city-state **3:** 354

civic
   humanism **3:** 316
   republicanism **3:** 316
civil
   Civil Rights Act of 1866
    4: 352
   Civil Rights Act of 1964
    (employment) **1:** 129;
    4: 352
   Civil Rights Act of 1968
    (housing) **1:** 129
   Civil Service Reform Act
    of 1883 **1:** 122; **2:** 41;
    4: 352
   disturbance **3:** 346
   liberties **2:** 12; **3:** 350;
    4: 537–543, 566
   rights **1:** 129; **2:** 105,
    119; **3:** 346, 350;
    4: 305–306, 314–316,
    543–545, 566
   service **2:** 41; **4:** 210
Civil War (U.S.) **1:** 119,
    120, 122; **2:** 39, 40,
    42, 64, 67–68, 107;
    4: 79, 171–178
Clarissa **2:** 422
Clark, Kenneth **4:** 1382
Clark, William **1:** 114
Clarke, Arthur C. **2:** 417
classes (biol.) **2:** 211
classical
   conditioning **3:** 364
   music **1:** 456,
    463–464
   physics **3:** 534
classification
   examples **2:** 211
   of matter **3:** 500
   of plants and animals
    2: 103
   paper (comp.) **3:** 52
   system (5 kingdoms)
    2: 210–211
clauses (Eng.) **1:** 41–42,
    46–47, 48. 49, 51
Clausius statement
    3: 539
Clay, Henry **1:** 116, 118;
    4: 164
Clayton, Ed **1:** 102
Clayton Antitrust Act
    1: 124; **2:** 45; **4:** 352
clear-cutting **1:** 355
Cleary, Beverly **1:** 97
cleavage (geol.) **3:** 532
clef(s) **1:** 461, 466
Cleisthenes **2:** 84

Clemenceau, Georges
    3: 333
Clemens, Samuel **2:** 415,
    419
   see also Mark Twain
Clement, First Letter of
    3: 308
Clemente, Roberto **2:** 74
Cleopatra **2:** 87, 129;
    3: 299, 300
clergy **3:** 327
Clermont **2:** 62
Cleveland, Grover
    2: 42–43, 62; **4:** 79,
    197, 211, 217
client-centered therapy
    3: 367, 370
climate **1:** 392–401, 402
   changes **3:** 527
   U.S. **1:** 135
   zones, U.S. **1:** 394
Clinton, Hillary Rodham
    2: 52
Clinton, William Jefferson
    (Bill) **1:** 132;
    2: 52–53, 62; **3:** 351;
    4: 78, 341–344
clone(s) **2:** 224; **3:** 496
closed
   circuit **3:** 543
   primary **4:** 566
close-encounter theory
    1: 415, 424
closing (comp.) **3:** 62–63
closure **2:** 260
cloture rule **4:** 567
Clouds, The **3:** 297
cloud types **1:** 396–397
Clovis **2:** 90, 130; **3:** 305,
    306
Cluny (abbey) **3:** 311, 340
cluster **1:** 424
Coalition Provisional
   Authority (Iraq)
    2: 126
cocci **2:** 213
Cocos (Keeling) Islands
    2: 184
coda **1:** 466
code of chivalry **3:** 324
Code of Hammurabi
    3: 296
codon **3:** 486, 498
Cody, Buffalo Bill **1:** 470
coefficients **3:** 507
coelenterates phylum
    2: 220
cognition **3:** 363, 364, 370

cognitive
 processes **3:** 365
 science **3:** 357
 therapies **3:** 367
Cohen, Robert **1:** 102
coherent light 2: 253
coin problems 2: 268
Coit, Margaret **1:** 102
cold front 1: 399, 402
Cold Harbor, Virginia
 1: 120
Cold War 1: 128;
 2: 117, 121; **3:** 336;
 4: 290–298, 317–318,
 352–353
Cole, Nat "King" **2:** 69
Cole (U.S.S.) **2:** 125
Coleridge, Samuel Taylor
 2: 393, 396, 403;
 4: 1379
Colet, John **3:** 318
Colgate, William **2:** 62
college
 application essay
 4: 1341–1375
 placement tests **3:** 552,
 598–621
 subjects **3:** 580–582
**COLLEGE ENTRANCE
 EXAMS 3:** 598–621
Collins, Michael **1:** 130
colloidal suspension
 2: 194
Colombia 2: 143, 182
 2: *Atlas* 10
Colonel Jack **2:** 419
colonies, English **1:** 107;
 2: 60; **4:** 99–102,
 107–110, 113–118
colonies, French **1:** 107;
 4: 98–99
colonies, Spanish **1:** 107;
 2: 60; **4:** 98–99
colons (Eng.) **1:** 55;
 2: 375; **3:** 92
color(s) 3: 501, 544
 index **1:** 424
 movies **1:** 472
Colorado 1: 138–139, 157;
 2: 72–73, 74
Colum, Padraic **1:** 100
Columbia (space shuttle)
 1: 421–422
Columbia Law School
 2: 44, 46
Columbus, Christopher
 1: 107; **2:** 60; 98, 132;
 3: 314, 322

Columbus, Ohio **1:** 122
coma 1: 424
combination reaction
 3: 508, 509
combining sentences
 (Eng.) **1:** 44–46
combustion reaction
 3: 508, 509
Comédie Française 2: 409
comedy (lit.) **1:** 468, 469,
 476; **2:** 404; **3:** 71
 by Shakespeare **2:** 411
Comedy of Errors, The
 2: 410, 411, 426
comet(s) 1: 408, 425
comic relief 1: 476;
 2: 406; **4:** 1386
command
 economy **3:** 254, 292
 module **1:** 425
commas (Eng.) **1:** 45, 54;
 2: 374; **3:** 89–91
Commedia (The Divine
 Comedy) **2:** 396
commedia dell 'arte
 1: 469
commerce department
 2: 11
commercial
 revolution **3:** 310
 television **1:** 126
**Committees of
 Correspondence**
 4: 353
**Committee to Re-elect
 the President 1:** 131
Commodius 2: 89
common
 denominator
 1: 232–233, 325
 minerals **1:** 389
**commonly misspelled
 words** (Eng.) **1:** 53;
 3: 68
Common Market
 (European Union)
 2: 119
commonplace book
 (comp.) **3:** 39, 45
Common Sense **1:** 111;
 2: 61; **4:** 353
**Commonwealth of
 Independent States**
 (CIS) **2:** 124
**communicable disease
 vectors 1:** 339
communications satellite
 1: 425

Communism 1: 124, 125,
 128, 130; **2:** 117;
 3: 344, 345, 346, 354
Communist(s) 2: 107,
 112, 113, 117, 119
 China **2:** 121
 Communist Party
 2: 124; **3:** 337
 North Korea **2:** 118
Communist Manifesto
 2: 107
commutative law 1: 214,
 285, 325–326; **2:** 260,
 348
Comoros 2: 143, 163
compact/contract 3: 344
comparable worth 4: 567
comparative advantage
 3: 284–285, 292
**compare and contrast
 paper** (comp.)
 3: 55–56
**compare to, compare
 with** (usage) **2:** 378
comparison(s) (Eng.)
 1: 28–30
 adverbs (Eng.) **1:** 29–30
competition (econ.)
 3: 266–267
complement(s) (Eng.)
 1: 38
complement(s) (math)
 1: 326; **2:** 348
**complement,
 compliment** (usage)
 2: 378
complementary
 cofunctions **2:** 331
 goods **3:** 256, 257, 292
complex
 number(s) **1:** 326;
 2: 262, 340, 348
 plane **2:** 340
**compliment,
 complement** (usage)
 2: 378
composite
 cone **1:** 388, 402
 number **1:** 230, 326;
 2: 348
 volcano (stratovolcano)
 3: 524
Composition (Eng.)
 1: 56–57; **3:** 32–117
compound 1: 369, 382;
 2: 226, 242; **3:** 500,
 516
 interest (math) **1:** 278

objects (Eng.) **3:** 84
predicates (Eng.) **1:** 50
prepositions (Eng.)
　1: 32
sentences (Eng.) **1:** 51,
　54; **2:** 374
subjects (Eng.) **1:** 42–43,
　50; **3:** 84
comprehensible,
　comprehensive
　(usage) **2:** 379
comprehensive,
　comprehensible
　(usage) **2:** 379
Compromise of 1850
　1: 118; **2:** 37; **4:** 353
computer(s) 2: 118
catalogs (lib.) **2:** 356
literacy **3:** 573–575
sciences **3:** 582
concave 1: 382
concentrated solution
　3: 511
concentration 3: 511, 514
gradient **3:** 480
concerto(s) 1: 463, 464,
　466
concluding the essay
　4: 1327–1337
Concordat of Worms
　2: 93
concrete operations
　period 3: 360, 361
concurrent
jurisdiction **4:** 567
powers **4:** 567
condensation 1: 396, 402;
　3: 510
conditional
equation **1:** 326; **2:** 348
statements (math) **2:** 310
conditioned response
　3: 364
conditioning 3: 370
conducting materials
　3: 542
conduction 1: 375
conductor(s) (physics)
　2: 254; **3:** 541, 548
Confederate 1: 120
Congress **2:** 37
fleet **1:** 120
States of America **1:** 119;
　2: 107; **4:** 353
confederation 3: 354
Confederation, Aticles of
　1: 113; **2:** 4;
　4: 127–128,132, 566

conference committee
　4: 567
Confessions of St.
　Augustine 2: 389
Confessions of Women,
　The **2:** 399
conflict 4: 1386
resolution **3:** 354
conformable rock layers
　3: 528, 532
Confucius 2: 84, 128
Confucianism **2:** 92
Congo, Democratic
　Republic of the
　(formerly Zaire)
　2: 140, 143, 164
　2: *Atlas* 12–13
Congo, Republic of **2:** 143,
　164
　2: *Atlas* 12–13
Congress (gov.)
see also House of
　Representatives;
　Senate **1:** 116, 117,
　121, 126
Congress
of Industrial
　Organizations (CIO)
　2: 69; **4:** 353
of Racial Equality
　(CORE) **2:** 70
of Vienna **2:** 105; **3:** 325
congressional districting
　4: 567
congruent triangles
　2: 310, 317
conic
projection **2:** 189
sections **2:** 283
conifer 1: 362
conjugate acid-base pair
　3: 512, 516
conjugating verbs (Eng.)
　1: 19–24
conjugation (biol.)
　1: 362
conjunctions
English **1:** 5, 33–35
German **3:** 161
conjunctive adverbs
　(Eng.) **1:** 34
Connecticut 1: 108,
　150–151, 157–158;
　2: 52, 55, 60
Connecticut
　Compromise 4: 567
connective tissue(s) 2:
　209; **3:** 492

connotation 4: 1386
connotative literature
　2: 389
connote, denote (usage)
　2: 379
Conossa 2: 93
conquistadors 2: 73–74
Conrad III, emperor of
　Germany **3:** 313
Conrad, Charles Jr. **1:** 421
Conrad, Joseph **2:** 415,
　416, 419; **4:** 1380
conscience, conscious
　(usage) **3:** 115
conscious, conscience
　(usage) **3:** 115
consciousness 3: 359, 370
consecutive number
　problems 2: 268
consensus (usage) **3:** 115
conservation
of energy, law of **3:** 537,
　538, 548
of mass-energy, law of
　1: 382; **2:** 250, 258
of momentum, law of
　2: 249, 258; **3:** 356,
　548
conservatism 3: 345,
　354
conservative 4: 567
conservative liberalism
　3: 344
Constance, Council of
　2: 96
constant (math) **1:** 326;
　2: 348
constant
acceleration (physics)
　3: 534, 536
angular acceleration
　(physics) **3:** 536
slope (econ.) **3:** 251
Constantine I (the Great)
　2: 89, 129; **3:** 295,
　302, 303, 304
Constantinople (Istanbul)
　2: 89, 95, 96; **3:** 295,
　303, 313, 314, 324
constellations 1: 412, 425
constituent 4: 567
constitution 3: 343
Constitution (U.S.)
　1: 113; **2:** 4, 15–28;
　3: 347, 349; **4:** 132–
　134, 452–457, 567
amendments **2:** 22–28;
　3: 350

Constitution (U.S.S.)
("Old Ironsides")
1: 114
Constitutional
Convention 1: 113;
2: 31
constitutional
courts **4:** 567
law **4:** 567
constitutionalism
3: 354
constructive interference
3: 540
consul, council, counsel
(usage) **2:** 379
Consulate 3: 327
Consumer
Price Index (CPI)
3: 270–272, 292
Product Safety
Commission **2:** 11
Publication Catalog
2: 360
consumer(s) (biol.)
1: 356, 362
consumer(s) (econ.)
3: 253, 255–259,
279
contact metamorphism
3: 519
continental
air masses **1:** 398
climate **1:** 395
crust **3:** 518, 522
drift **1:** 384–385, 402
drift theory **3:** 520–521,
532
glacier(s) **1:** 390–391;
3: 526, 532
margin **3:** 520, 532
rise **3:** 520, 532
shelf **1:** 402; **3:** 520, 532
slope **1:** 402; **3:** 520, 532
U.S. regions **1:** 134, 135,
138–152
Continental
Army **2:** 30, 62; **4:** 353
Congress **1:** 111, 113;
2: 31, 61
plates **3:** 522
continent(s)/region(s)
2: 140; **3:** 520
continual(ly),
continuous(ly)
(usage) **2:** 379; **3:** 115
continuity (math) **3:** 475
of a function **3:**
385–387; **4:** 936–938

continuous(ly),
continual(ly) (uage)
2: 379; **3:** 115
contractile vacuoles
2: 196
contractions (Eng.) **3:** 95
control 1: 382
convection 1: 375
convergence and
divergence
3: 456–457
convergent
boundary **3:** 522
thinking **3:** 365, 370
converging
lenses **2:** 252
plates **3:** 522, 523
conversions (math) **1:** 323
convex 1: 382
lenses **2:** 252
Cook Islands 2: 184
2: *Atlas* 22
Cook, James **2:** 103
Coolidge, Calvin **1:** 125;
2: 46–47, 62; **4:**
251–252
Coolidge, Olivia **1:** 102
Cooper, James Fenimore
2: 415, 416, 419
Cooper, Peter **1:** 116;
2: 62
cooperative federalism
4: 567
coordinate plane 1: 326;
2: 279, 348–349
coordinating
conjunctions (Eng.)
1: 33
Copernicanism 3: 326
Copernicus, Nicolaus
2: 97, 99, 132;
3: 325
Copland, Aaron **1:** 464
copper 1: 372
Copperheads 4: 353
Copyright Royalty
Tribune 2: 11
Coral Sea 1: 127
core 3: 518, 532
inner **1:** 402
outer **1:** 388, 402
Corinthians 3: 300
Coriolanus **2:** 411
Coriolis force 1: 395, 402
corms 3: 490
Corneille, Pierre **2:** 404,
405, 406, 408
corona 1: 405, 425

Coronado, Francisco
1: 107
corporatism 3: 354
Corregidor 1: 127
correlation (psych.) **3:** 363
correlative conjunctions
(Eng.) **1:** 33
Corsica 3: 300
Cortés, Hernán **2:** 99, 132
cortex 3: 489
cosecant 1: 326; **2:** 324,
349; **3:** 373
cosine(s) 1: 326; **2:** 324,
335, 349; **3:** 373
law of **2:** 335
cosmic
background radiation
1: 425
"egg" **3:** 527
radiation **1:** 425
cosmology 1: 415, 425
cosmonaut 1: 425
cosmopolitanism 3: 310,
313
Costa Rica 2: 143, 176
2: *Atlas* 5
cost-push inflation 3: 275
costume 1: 476
cotangent 1: 326; **2:** 324,
349; **3:** 373
Côte d'Ivoire 2: 143, 164
2: *Atlas* 12
cottage industry 3: 322
cotton 1: 113
gin **1:** 113; **2:** 67
cotyledons 3: 491, 498
could of (usage) **2:** 379
could've (usage) **2:** 379
coulomb 2: 254
Coulomb's constant
3: 541
Coulomb's law **2:** 258;
3: 541, 542
Council
of Constance **2:** 96
of Economic Advisers
2: 11
of Nicaea **2:** 89; **3:** 295
of Trent (1545–1547)
2: 100; **3:** 320
of Trent (1551–1552)
3: 320
of Trent (1562–1563)
3: 320
council, counsel, consul
(usage) **2:** 379
counsel, consul, council
(usage) **2:** 379

counseling and advising
3: 578
counterpoint 1: 466
Counter-Reformation
2: 100; 3: 319–321
counters (math) 1: 216
counting number 1: 235,
326; 2: 349
countries see also
individual country
names 2: 140, 143
countries
largest 2: 140
most populous 2: 140
COUNTRIES OF THE
WORLD 2: 143–187
see also individual
countries
country-and-western
(music) 1: 465
courtier(house scholar)
3: 318
courtly humanism
3: 317
courts of appeal 4: 567
Cousin Bette 2: 418
covalent
bond(s) 2: 232, 242;
3: 505, 506, 516
bonding 3: 478
crystals 3: 510
Cowpens, South Carolina
1: 112
Coxey, General Jacob S.
1: 123
Coxey's Army 1: 123;
4: 354
Crab nebula 1: 414
craft traditions 3: 322
Crane, Stephen 2: 416;
4: 1379, 1380
Crassus 2: 87
crater 1: 388, 402; 3: 523
Crater Lake, Oregon
1: 388
creativity 3: 370
Crécy 2: 95
Battle of (1346) 3: 308,
324
credible, credulous,
creditable (usage)
2: 379
creditable, credible,
credulous (usage)
2: 379
credulous, creditable,
credible (usage)
2: 379

creeds 3: 308
crest 3: 548
Cretaceous Period 3: 529
Crete 2: 79
crevasse 1: 402
Crick, F. H. C. (Francis)
2: 201; 3: 486
Crime and Punishment
2: 413, 415, 419,
426
Crimea 2: 96, 103
Crimean War 2: 106
Crippen, Robert 1: 422
cristae 2: 194
criteria (usage) 2: 379;
3: 116
critical mass 2: 240, 257,
258
Croatia 2: 124, 143, 154;
3: 337, 351
2: Atlas 14
Croats 2: 124
Cromwell, Oliver 2: 102,
133, 396; 3: 314,
326–327
crop rotation 1: 355
crossbows 3: 324
"Crossing Brooklyn
Ferry" 2: 402
cross
-pollination 3: 491
-product rule 1: 326;
2: 349
Crucible, The 2: 408
cruel and unusual
punishment (Eighth
Amendment) 3: 350
Crusades 2: 94, 131; 3:
305, 310, 314–340;
4: 97
Crusaders 2: 90, 94;
3: 310
Crusader States 2: 94
crust 1: 387; 3: 518,
532
crustacea class 2: 221
crustal deformation
3: 525
Crying of Lot 49, The
2: 422
crystal(s) 2: 242; 3: 510
crystalline solid 3: 510,
516
crystallization 3: 519
Cuba 1: 123, 129; 2: 43,
45, 119, 143, 176;
3: 343, 346
2: Atlas 5

Cuban missile crisis
1: 129; 2: 49, 119;
3: 336; 4: 354
Cubans 2: 76
cube 1: 326; 2: 349
cubed 1: 326
cubic functions 3: 373
cubing (comp.) 3: 39, 41,
43
cue 1: 477
cultural revolution 2: 121
cummings, e e 4: 1380
cumulus clouds 1: 397
cuneiform writing 3: 295
Curie, Marie and Pierre
2: 108, 257
current and resistance
3: 542
curriculum (usage) 2: 379
curtain 1: 477
curve(s)
characteristics of 3: 401
lengths of 3: 451
curved mirrors 2: 252
Custer, George Armstrong
1: 121; 2: 57
customary measurement
(fps) system 1: 366;
2: 244–245
cute (usage) 2: 379
cuticles 2: 195
cuttings 3: 491
cyclical unemployment
3: 277
cyclone 1: 399, 402
Cymbeline 2: 411
Cyprus 2: 164; 3: 351
Cyrillic alphabet 3: 304
Cyrus the Great 2: 83,
84, 128
cytogenetics 3: 485
cytokinesis 3: 483, 485,
498
cytoplasm 1: 362;
2: 192–193, 194, 224;
3: 480, 498
cytoskeleton 3: 482
czar 2: 100
Czar Nicholas II 2: 111
Czechoslovakia 2: 113,
117, 121
Czech Republic 2: 143,
154
2: Atlas 14
Czolgosz, Leon 1: 123;
2: 42

D

Dacia (Rumania) **2:** 89
dactylic 2: 403
da Gama, Vasco *see* Gama, Vasco da
Dagobert I 3: 306
Dahl, Roald **1:** 97
Dahl, Robert **3:** 344
Daisy Miller **2:** 421
Dakota (Indians) **2:** 55
Dallas 2: 119
Dalton, John **2:** 228
  Dalton's law of partial pressure **3:** 510
Damascus 3: 313
Danes 2: 92
dangling modifiers (Eng.) **3:** 97–98
  usage **2:** 379
Danish territories 2: 185
"Danny Deever" 2: 398
Dante Alighieri 2: 94, 97, 131, 392, 396, 426–427
Danube 2: 91
Dare, Virginia **1:** 107
Darius I (the Great) **2:** 83, 128; **3:** 297
Dark Ages 3: 305
dark horse (candidate) **2:** 37, 39; **4:** 354
Darwin, Charles **2:** 107, 134, 414; **3:** 331; **4:** 1383
dashes (Eng.) **1:** 55; **2:** 375; **3:** 92
Das Kapital **2:** 107
data (usage) **2:** 379; **3:** 116
Daugherty, Harry **2:** 47
Dauphin 3: 308
David, King **2:** 81, 128; **3:** 296
David **3:** 318
David Copperfield **2:** 414, 416, 426, 430
da Vinci, Leonardo *see* Leonardo
Davis, Jefferson **1:** 119
Davis, Miles **1:** 465
Dawes Act 1: 122; **4:** 354
Dayton Accord 3: 337
D-Day 1: 127; **2:** 48, 116
Death in Venice **2:** 422
Death of a Salesman **2:** 408, 426
Death of Ivan Ilich, The **2:** 423

de Broglie, Louis **3:** 502
  de Broglie wavelength **3:** 545
Debussy, Claude **1:** 464
decagon 2: 316
Decameron **2:** 414
decay of synthetic radioisotopes 2: 241
decibels 2: 251
deciduous 1: 362
decimal(s) 1: 246–274, 322, 324, 326; **2:** 346
  and place value **1:** 322; **2:** 346
Declaration of Independence (U.S.) **1:** 111; **4:** 123–124, 567
Declaration of the Rights of Man **2:** 104
declensions (Lat.) **3:** 217, 218, 220
decomposition 2: 242
  reaction(s) **2:** 236; **3:** 508, 509
deconstruction 4: 1280
de Coubertin, Pierre **1:** 448
decreasing 3: 475
deduce, deduct (usage) **2:** 379
deduct, deduce (usage) **2:** 379
deductive reasoning 3: 57–60
deep-ocean trench 3: 532
Deere, John **1:** 117
Deer Park, The **2:** 422
Deerslayer, The **2:** 430
Defense, Department of **2:** 10, 11
deferred payment, standard for **3:** 281
deficit 3: 292; **4:** 567
definite integrals 3: 411–412, 415, 475; **4:** 1064–1076, 1121–1133
  applications **3:** 440–453
definitely (usage) **2:** 379
definition paper (comp.) **3:** 50–52
deflation 3: 275
Defoe, Daniel **1:** 97; **2:** 414, 416, 419
De Gaulle, Charles **2** 135
degrees (Lat.) **3:** 219

deism 2: 102; **3:** 340
"Dejection: An Ode" 2: 396, 400
De Klerk, F.W. **2:** 137
Delacroix, Eugène **3:** 329
Delaware 1: 146–147, 158
  Bay **1:** 107
Delay, J. **3:** 367
delegated powers 4: 567
Delicate Balance, A **2:** 407
delta 1: 402; **3:** 532
Delta Wedding **3:** 53
delusion, allusion, illusion (usage) **2:** 377
demand (econ.) **3:** 253, 255–259, 292
  curve **3:** 292
  demand-pull inflation **3:** 275
  schedule **3:** 292
de Maupassant, Guy *see* Maupassant, Guy de
de Medici, Catherine *see* Catherine de Medici
de Medici, Cosimo *see* Medici, Cosimo de
democracy 3: 326, 344, 345, 346, 351, 354; **4:** 567
Democrat(s) 1: 119, 124, 126, 133; **3:** 349
  Democratic Party **1:** 116; **4:** 354
  Democratic-Republicans **1:** 113, 114; **4:** 354
democratic government theories 4: 446–447
  democratic socialism **2:** 107
Democritus 2: 228
DeMoivre's theorem 2: 340
demonstrative pronouns (Eng.) **1:** 10
Demosthenes 2: 128
dendrites 3: 358, 496
Deniker, A. **3:** 367
Denmark 2: 92, 101, 102, 114, 115, 119, 143, 154; **3:** 337
  2: *Atlas* 14
denominator 1: 230–236, 326; **2:** 349
denotation 4: 1386
denotative literature 2: 389

denote, connote (usage)
2: 379
density 1: 368, 382, 402;
3: 501
chart 1: 368
dependent (math)
system of equations
1: 326; 2: 349
variable 1: 326; 2: 349
dependent (usage)
2: 379
dependent clauses (Eng.)
1: 42
deposit feeders 3: 492
deposition 3: 510
Der Ring des Nibelungen
3: 329
Das Rheingold
Die Walküre
Götterdämmerung
Siegfried
derivative(s) 3: 388,
390–391, 394,
397–398; 475
and integrals 3: 428
applications
4: 1003–1013,
1024–1038
of trig functions 3: 394
to investigate functions
and curves
3: 401–407
Descartes, René 2: 102,
133; 3: 326, 356
description paper (comp.)
3: 52–54
desegregation 1: 129
desert(s) 1: 358–359
largest 2: 142
desert, dessert (usage)
2: 379
Desert Storm 3: 351
De Soto, Hernando
1: 107; 2: 73–74
despot 3: 354
dessert, desert (usage)
2: 379
"de-Stalinization" 2: 118
destructive interference
3: 540
d'Etaples, Jacques Lefèvre
3: 318–319, 320
detective fiction 2: 413,
417
détente 2: 51, 121; 4: 354
determinants 2: 291
Detroit, Michigan 1: 114
deuteromycetes 2: 216

development (psych.)
3: 370
developmentalism (hist.)
3: 331
development strategies
(comp.) 3: 50–56
deviance 3: 366
device, devise (usage)
2: 379
devise, device (usage)
2: 379
devolution 4: 567
Devonian Period 3: 529
Dewey Decimal System
2: 358
dew point 1: 396, 402
Diagnostic and
Statistical Manual
of Mental
Disorders, The
(DSM) 3: 367
dialectics 3: 354
dialectical materialism
3: 329, 354
dialog, dialogue (usage)
2: 379
Dialogue on the Two
Great World
Systems 3: 326
Dialogues 3: 298
diameter 2: 320
Diary of Anne Frank
2: 389
Dias, Bartholomeu 2: 98
diatomic molecule 3: 501
diatonic scale 1: 466
Dickens, Charles 2: 134,
404, 414, 415, 416,
419, 426, 427–428;
4: 1380
Dickinson, Emily 1: 93;
2: 393, 396
dicotyledons (dicots)
2: 219, 224; 3: 489,
498
dictator 3: 340
dictatorship 3: 343
diction 4: 1252–1254
dictionary list 2: 360
dictionary
of chemistry 2: 242–243
of earth science
1: 402–403
of entertainment
1: 476–478
of mathematics
1: 325–329; 2:
348–351; 3: 475

of music 1: 466–467
of space science
1: 424–427
use 1: 87
did, done (usage)
2: 379
Diderot, Denis 2: 102
Dido 3: 317–318
Diet of Worms 2: 99
difference 1: 191, 326;
2: 349
difference quotient
3: 390–391
different from, different
than (usage) 2: 379;
3: 116
differentiability and
continuity
3: 394–395
differentiable 3: 390
differential calculus
3: 388–407, 408
differentiation (biol.)
2: 208, 224; 3: 496
differentiation (math)
3: 388–407, 475;
4: 945–962
chain rule 3: 392
Newton's root-finding
method 3: 399–400
rules for 3: 392
differ from, differ with
(usage) 2: 379
diffraction 3: 544, 548
grating 3: 544
diffusion 2: 198, 224;
3: 480, 498
digestion 2: 208, 224;
3: 492–493
digestive system (human)
1: 341; 3: 494
digit (math) 1: 326
problems 2: 268
dike 1: 402
dilute solution 3: 511
diminishing returns
3: 262–263
dinoflagellates 2: 215
Diocletian 2: 89, 129;
3: 295, 303, 304
Dionysus (Bacchus) 2: 84;
3: 297
diploid 2: 206–207, 224
diplomacy 1: 124
diplopoda class 2: 221
dipole
forces 3: 506, 516
molecule 3: 506

direct
combination **2:** 242
combination reactions
2: 236
current (DC) **3:** 548
objects (Eng.) **1:** 38, 50
primary **4:** 567
director 1: 477
Directory (France) **3:** 327
disc method 4: 1102–1106
discontinuous integrands
3: 438–439
discount rate (econ.)
3: 283, 292
discounts (math) **1:** 279
Discourse on the Origins
of Social Inequality,
The **3:** 326
discreet, discrete (usage)
2: 379
discrete, discreet (usage)
2: 379
discretionary spending
4: 567
discrimination, racial
1: 129
discs, volume 3: 443–446
diseconomies of scale
3: 264
disinflation 3: 275
disinterested,
uninterested (usage)
2: 379
dispersion forces 3: 506,
516
displacement 3: 534, 536,
548
dissenting opinion
4: 567
dissociative
disorders **3:** 367, 370
drugs **1:** 338
dissonance 1: 466
distance-rate-time
formulas 2: 268
distributive law 1: 281,
285, 326; **2:** 260,
349
district courts 4: 567
dived, dove (usage) **2:** 379
divergent
boundary **3:** 522
thinking **3:** 365, 370
diverging plates 3: 522
dividend 1: 220, 326;
2: 349
Divine Comedy, The
2: 94, 392, 426–427

divine-right kingship
3: 326–327, 340, 343,
344
diving 1: 453
division (math) **1:** 220–229,
314, 315, 315, 326;
2: 266
facts **1:** 221, 222,
318
divisions (phylum) **3:** 489
divisor 1: 220, 326; **2:** 349
Dixon, Franklin W. **1:** 97
Djibouti 2: 143, 164
2: *Atlas* 12
DNA (dioxyribonucleic
acid) **2:** 192, 193,
200, 201–202, 224;
3: 479, 482, 486, 498
fingerprinting **3:** 486
replication **2:** 201
docking 1: 425
Dr. Faustus **2:** 422
Doctor Faustus **2:** 408
"Doctors of the Church"
3: 309
Doctor Zhivago **2:** 422
doctrine of salvation
3: 319
documenting sources
2: 361, 363, 368–373;
3: 110–111
Dodge, Mary Mapes
1: 97
Dodgson, Charles
Lutwidge *see* Carroll,
Lewis
Doe v. Bolton **2:** 12
doesn't, don't (usage)
2: 379
Doll's House, A **2:** 408
domain 3: 374, 375,
475
dominant trait
2: 206–207, 224;
3: 484, 498
Dominica 2: 143, 176
2: *Atlas* 5
Dominican Republic
2: 143, 177
2: *Atlas* 5
Dominicans 3: 311,
312–313
Donatello 2: 97
done, did (usage)
2: 379
Don Juan **2:** 395, 400
Donne, John **2:** 391, 392,
396

Don Quixote de la
Mancha, The
Ingenious
Gentleman **2:** 414,
416, 419, 427
don't, doesn't (usage)
2: 379
Doppler
effect **1:** 425; **2:** 253,
258
tracking **1:** 425
Dorian invasions 2: 82
Dorsey, Thomas A. **2:** 69
Dostoevski (Dostoevsky),
Feodor (Fyodor)
2: 134, 413, 415, 419;
4: 1378
double
angles **2:** 335
bonds **2:** 237; **3:** 505
double-entry
bookkeeping **3:** 311,
340
helix **2:** 201; **3:** 486
jeopardy **4:** 567
negative (usage) **2:** 379
possessive (usage) **2:** 380
replacement **2:** 242
replacement reaction(s)
2: 236; **3:** 508
doubt but (usage) **2:** 380
Douglas, Stephen A.
1: 119; **2:** 39;
4: 165–167
Douglass, Frederick **2:** 67
dove, dived (usage) **2:** 380
Dow Jones industrial
average 1: 133
Down's syndrome
3: 363
Doyle, Arthur Conan
2: 417
Draco 2: 83
Draconian laws **2:** 83
Dracula **2:** 417
draft 1: 127
Drake, Edwin **1:** 119
Drake, Francis **2:** 133
drama (comp.) **3:** 70
drama (lit.) **2:** 404–412
dramatic
monologue **2:** 391
poetry **2:** 390
drank, drunk, drink
(usage) **2:** 380
dream 3: 370
dreamed, dreamt (usage)
2: 380

dreamt, dreamed (usage)
    2: 380

Dred Scott v. Sandford
    1: 119; **2:** 12, 39;
    4: 166, 355

Dreiser, Theodore **2:** 415,
    419; **4:** 1380

drink, drank, drunk
    (usage) **2:** 380

drive 3: 370

drowned (usage) **2:** 380

drug abuse 1: 338

drumlins 1: 390–391

drunk, drink, drank
    (usage) **2:** 380

Dryden, John **2:** 392, 396

dual federalism 4: 567

dub 1: 477

Dubcek, Alexander **2:** 121

Dubliners **2:** 421

DuBois, W.E.B. **2:** 68

Duchy of Moscow 2: 100

Duino Elegies **2:** 399

Duke William
    (Normandy) **3:** 307

Dunciad, The **2:** 399

Dunkirk 2: 115; **3:** 335

Duquesne, Fort **1:** 109

Dürer, Albrecht **2:** 97, 132

Dutch 1: 107, 108; **2:** 101;
    4: 99

    East India Company
      1: 107

    settlers **2:** 109

Duvalier, Francois "Baby
    Doc" **2:** 123

DVD 1: 475

dynamics (music) **1:** 463,
    466

dyne 2: 245

E

each, everybody, everyone (usage) **2:** 377
eager, anxious (usage) **2:** 377
early literature 2: 388
Earth 1: 404, 405, 406, 408, 409, 411
  core **3:** 527
  crust elements **2:** 227
  resources **3:** 530
  structure **3:** 518–520
EARTH SCIENCE 1: 384–403; **3:** 518–533
earthquake(s) 1: 387; **3:** 525–526
  belts **1:** 387
  recent **2:** 142
Earthshine 1: 425
East
  African rift valleys **3:** 523
  Germany **2:** 119, 123; **3:** 337
  Indies **2:** 101
Eastern
  bloc **3:** 351
  Europe **3:** 318
  Orthodox Church **2:** 93
"Easter 1916" 2: 403
"Easter Wings" 2: 391
Eastman, George **1:** 122
East of Eden **2:** 423
easy (usage) **2:** 380
echinoderms phylum 2: 221
Eckstein, Harry **3:** 344
eclipses, ecliptic 1: 410, 425
Eclogues **2:** 402
ecology 1: 362; **4:** 782–792, 811–812
economic, economical (usage) **2:** 380
economic
  Advisors, Council of **2:** 11
  aid **1:** 128
  Opportunity Act **1:** 129
  rationality **3:** 252
  rights **1:** 130
ECONOMICS 3: 246–293
economies of scale 3: 264, 292
ecosystem 1: 356, 360, 362

Ecuador 2: 143, 182
  2: *Atlas* 10
Edict
  of Milan **2:** 89; **3:** 302
  of Nantes (1598) **2:** 100; **3:** 321
  revocation **2:** 102
Edison, Thomas Alva **1:** 121, 471; **2:** 108, 135
Edmonds, Walter D. **1:** 97
education 1: 116, 128
Education, Department of **2:** 11
Edward III (Eng.) **2:** 95; **3:** 311
Edward the Confessor 2: 131; **3:** 307
EEG (electroencephalogram) **3:** 359
EEOC (Equal Employment Opportunity Commission) **2:** 11
effect, affect (usage) **2:** 376
effort 1: 382
  arm **1:** 382
e.g. (usage) **2:** 380
eggs/ova 3: 496
ego 3: 366, 370
egoism, egotism (usage) **2:** 380
egotism, egoism (usage) **2:** 380
Egypt 1: 131; **2:** 51, 79, 80, 82, 85, 87, 121, 122, 125, 140, 143, 164; **3:** 295–296, 299
  2: *Atlas* 13
  Egyptians **2:** 83
Eighteenth Amendment 1: 125
Eight Men **2:** 423
Einstein, Albert **2:** 65, 109, 135, 255; **3:** 545
Eisenhower, Dwight David **1:** 128, 130; **2:** 48–49, 51, 62, 116; **4:** 77, 78, 296–298, 304–306, 317
  Eisenhower Doctrine **4:** 355
Eisley, Loren **4:** 1383
either (usage) **2:** 380
El Alamein 2: 116
elastic clause 4: 567

elasticity 3: 258–259, 292
Elba 2: 105; **3:** 327
Elbe River 2: 116; **3:** 310
Eleanor of Aquitaine 2: 131; **3:** 307, 314
elections 2: 7, 10, 12, 14; **4:** 485–492
Electoral College 1: 116; **2:** 14; **4:** 355, 567
electoral process 3: 354
electors 3: 307
Electra **2:** 408
electrical
  circuits **1:** 378–379
  fire safety **1:** 345
  generators **1:** 379
  safety **1:** 344
electric
  charge **3:** 541
  current **2:** 254; **3:** 541, 542, 548
  field **3:** 541, 542, 548
  motors **1:** 379
  potential energy **3:** 541
  power **2:** 254
  shock treatment **1:** 346
electricity 2: 108, 254; **3:** 548
  and magnetism **3:** 541–543
electroconvulsive therapy 3: 367
electroencephalogram (EEG) **3:** 359
electromagnetic
  induction **3:** 548
  spectrum **3:** 543, 548
  waves **1:** 378–379, 382, 404; **2:** 251, 252, 258; **3:** 502, 543, 548
electromagnetism 1: 378–379; **3:** 542–543
electromagnets 1: 378–379
electromotive force (emf) **3:** 542, 548
electron(s) 2: 228, 242, 254, 256; **3:** 478, 501, 502, 516, 546
  electron-cloud model **2:** 229
  electron configuration **3:** 503, 516
  electron-shell model **2:** 229
  microscope **2:** 194, 197
  orbits **3:** 502

sharing **2:** 232
shell **3:** 502
structures **2:** 231
spin **3:** 503
transfer **2:** 232
transport **3:** 483
transport chain **3:** 483
volts **2:** 256
electronegativity 3: 505
**electronic instruments
    1:** 460
electronics 3: 546
**electrostatic attraction
    3:** 510
electroweak force 2: 256
Elegies **2:** 391, 396
elegy 2: 391
**"Elegy Written in a
    Country
    Churchyard" 2:** 391
element (math) **1:** 285,
    326; **2:** 260, 349
element (science) **1:** 369,
    382; **2:** 226, 242;
    3: 500, 516
**Elementary and
    Secondary
    Education Act
    1:** 129
**elements of Earth's crust
    2:** 227
elevation 2: 189
elevators 1: 118
El Greco *see* Greco, El
elicit 3: 370
elicit, illicit (usage) **2:** 380
Eliot, George **2:** 415, 419;
    3: 50; **4:** 1380
Eliot, T.S. (Thomas
    Stearns) **2:** 135, 391,
    393, 396; **3:** 80;
    4: 1379
elitist theory 4: 567
Elizabeth I 2: 133; **3:** 322,
    326
**Elizabethan theater
    1:** 469
Elizondo, Hector **2:** 74
Elk Hills, California **1:** 125
Ellington, Duke **1:** 465
ellipse 2: 283
ellipsis (Eng.) **3:** 93
Ellis, Albert **3:** 366, 367
el-Sadat, Anwar *see* Sadat,
    Anwar-el
El Salvador 2: 143, 177
    2: *Atlas* 5
else's (usage) **2:** 380

Elting, Mary **1:** 102
elude, allude (usage)
    2: 377
**Emancipation
    Proclamation
    1:** 119; **2:** 39, 68;
    4: 355
Embargo Act 1: 114;
    2: 31
embryo 2: 224; **3:** 496
embryonic stage 3: 360
Emergency
    Banking Relief **1:** 126
    Quota Act of 1921
    1: 125; **4:** 355
Emerson, Ralph Waldo
    2: 420
emigrant, immigrant
    (usage) **2:** 380
Émile **3:** 326
eminent, imminent
    (usage) **2:** 380
eminent domain 4: 568
Emma **2:** 418
emotion 3: 366, 370
**"Emperor of Ice Cream,
    The" 2:** 401
**empirical formula(s)
    3:** 507, 516
empiricism 3: 356
empty set 1: 326; **2:** 349
Emrich, Duncan **1:** 102
encoding 3: 370
encyclopedia list 2: 358
Encyclopédie **2:** 102;
    3: 326
**endangered species
    1:** 354
Endeavour (space shuttle)
    1: 423
Endgame **2:** 407
endocrine 2: 208, 224
endocrine system 3: 359,
    494, 496
endodermis 3: 489
**endoplasmic reticulum
    2:** 194, 195, 224;
    3: 481, 482, 498
endosperm 3: 491, 498
endothermic
    changes **3:** 501
    processes **3:** 510
    reactions **3:** 509
Enemy of the People, An
    2: 408
energy 1: 374–381, 382;
    2: 246, 247, 255, 258;
    3: 501, 537, 548

conversions **1:** 374
energy-mass relationship
    3: 545
forms **1:** 374–381
levels **3:** 502
pyramid **1:** 357
types **2:** 247
use graph **3:** 530
Energy, Department of
    2: 11
Engel v. Vitale **2:** 12
Engels, Friedrich **2:** 107;
    3: 328–329
England 1: 107; **2:** 92, 93,
    94, 95, 96, 97, 99,
    100, 101, 102, 103,
    105, 131, 133, 186;
    3: 307, 308, 309, 315,
    318
    2: *Atlas* 14
English colonies **1:** 107;
    2: 60; **4:** 99–102,
    107–110, 113–118
English
    –French dictionary
        3: 145–151
    –German dictionary
        3: 176–181
    grammar **1:** 4–55;
        3: 83–91
    –Latin dictionary
        3: 238–244
    Revolution of 1641,
        3: 314, 326
    –Spanish dictionary
        3: 210–215
    system of measurement
        1: 366
ENIAC 2: 118
Enlightenment
    (Age of Reason)
    2: 102, 104; **3:** 326,
    340
ensure, insure, assure
    (usage) **3:** 115
**ENTERTAINMENT
    1:** 468–478
enthalpy 3: 509, 516
enthuse (usage) **2:** 380
**entitlement program
    4:** 568
entrance exam
    acronyms **3:** 598
    preparation **3:** 598–621
entropy 2: 250, 258
environment 1: 362
**environmental impact
    statement 4:** 568

Environmental Protection Agency (EPA) **2:** 11; **3:** 349
enzyme(s) 2: 200, 224; **3:** 480, 498
  enzyme-substrate complex **2:** 200; **3:** 480
Eocene Epoch 3: 529
"Eolian Harp, The" 2: 396
EPA (Environmental Protection Agency) **2:** 11; **3:** 349
ephemeris 1: 425
epic 2: 391
epic, epoch (usage) **2:** 380
epicenter 1: 387, 402; **3:** 525, 532
Epictetus 2: 129
epidermis 2: 224; **3:** 489, 498
epigram 3: 79–80
Epistles (Pauline) **3:** 318
epitaph, epithet (usage) **2:** 380
epithelial tissue(s) 2: 209; **3:** 492
epithelium 2: 224–225
epithet 4: 1239
epithet, epitaph (usage) **2:** 380
epoch, epic (usage) **2:** 380
Equal Employment Opportunity Commission (EEOC) **2:** 11
equality, laws of (math) **1:** 285; **2:** 260
equal protection clause 4: 568
equation abbreviations (chem.) **3:** 508
equations (econ.) **3:** 252
equations (math) **1:** 285; **2:** 260, 266–268, 284–287, 300–301, 333; **3:** 507
  systems of **2:** 284–287
  with fractions **2:** 300–301
equations (physics) **3:** 545
  electricity and magnetism **3:** 542
  laws of **2:** 260
  of motion **3:** 536
  of thermodynamics **3:** 539

Equatorial Guinea 2: 143, 165
  2: *Atlas* 12
equestrian sports 1: 452
equilateral 1: 326; **2:** 349
equilibrium 3: 265, 292, 548
  constant **3:** 512, 514
  factors **3:** 514
  national output **3:** 274
  price level **3:** 274
  quantity **3:** 265
equinox 1: 393, 425
equivalents and conversions (math) **1:** 323
equivalents and conversions (science) **1:** 367
Equus **2:** 409
"Era of Good Feelings" 1: 115; **2:** 33; **4:** 355
Erasmus, Desiderius **2:** 97, 132; **3:** 318–319, 320
erg 2: 246
  erg/second **2:** 246
Erickson, Erik **3:** 360, 361
Ericsson, Leif **1:** 107; **2:** 93, 131
Eric the Red 2: 131
Erie Canal 1: 116
Erie, Lake **1:** 114, 134, 143
Eritrea 2: 143, 165
  2: *Atlas* 12
erosion 3: 526, 532
eruptions 3: 524
Esarhaddon 2: 82
Escalante, Jaime **2:** 74
escape velocity 1: 425
esker 1: 390, 402
especially, specially (usage) **2:** 380
essay(s) 3: 48–49, 81–82, 316
  as literature **3:** 70–71
  body and syntax **4:** 1308–1309
  expectations **4:** 1168–1170
  "prompts" **4:** 1274–1279
Essay on Criticism **2:** 399
"Essay on Man" 3: 79
essential phrase (Eng.) **1:** 39

Estates-General 3: 327, 340
Estefan, Gloria **2:** 74
esterification 2: 238, 243
Estonia 2: 143, 155
  2: *Atlas* 15
etc. (usage) **2:** 380; **3:** 116
Ethelred II, the "Unready" **2:** 131
Ethiopia 2: 140, 143, 165; **3:** 334
  2: *Atlas* 12
Etruria 2: 83
Etruscans 2: 83
EU (European Union) **2:** 126; **3:** 351
Eucharist (communion) **3:** 319
Euclid 2: 86, 128
Eugene Onegin (opera by Tchaikovsky) **2:** 399
euglena 2: 214
eukaryotes 2: 193, 196–197, 225; **3:** 480, 482–483, 487–488, 498
  eukaryotic **2:** 214
Eumenides, The **2:** 407
euphony 4: 1386
Euphrates 3: 294, 295
Eurasian empires 3: 304
Eurasian Mongol empire 2: 94
Euripides 2: 84, 128, 404, 406, 408; **3:** 298; **4:** 1378
euro 3: 337
Europa 1: 407
Europe 1: 127; **2:** 46, 94, 95, 96, 97, 99, 113, 116, 138, 139, 140, 142, 152–159, 186; **3:** 315
  2: *Atlas* 3, 14–15
European-Americans 2: 59–65
European colonies/colonists 2: 56
  see also individual nationalities, colonies
European plate 3: 529
European Union (EU) **2:** 126; **3:** 351
evaluating sources 2: 363
Evangeline **2:** 398
Evans, Mary Ann *see* Eliot, George

evaporation **1:** 402
event (math) **1:** 326;
    2: 349
event horizon **1:** 425
Evers, Medgar **2:** 70
everybody, everyone,
    each (usage) **2:** 377
every day, everyday
    (usage) **2:** 380
every/many (Eng.) (usage)
    1: 43
everyone, each,
    everybody (usage)
    2: 377
everywhere, nowhere,
    somewhere,
    anywhere (usage)
    2: 377
evolution **1:** 362;
    4: 701–712, 808–809
except, accept (usage)
    2: 376; **3:** 115
excess
    demand **3:** 292
    reserves **3:** 292
    supply **3:** 292
exchange rate **3:** 292
excited state **3:** 502, 516
exclamation points (Eng.)
    1: 54; **2:** 374; **3:** 93
excretion **3:** 493
    excretory system **2:** 208
Executioner's Song, The
    2: 422
executive
    branch **2:** 4, 10–11,
      19–20, 22; **3:** 347,
      349; **4:** 516–524
    order **4:** 568
    privilege **4:** 568
exercise **1:** 336–337
Exodus **2:** 80
exothermic
    changes **3:** 501
    reactions **3:** 509
expanded form (math)
    1: 326
expect (usage) **2:** 381
experiment **1:** 365
exploration **3:** 322
exponential functions
    3: 373
exponent(s) **1:** 244–246,
    261, 283, 322, 326;
    2: 349
    laws of **1:** 322; **2:** 272,
    346
    negative **1:** 245, 261, 322

exposition **4:** 1386
ex post facto law **4:** 568
exterior angles **2:** 317
external center of
    similitude **2:** 321
extinction **3:** 370
extra **1:** 477
extradition **4:** 568
extravehicular activity
    1: 425
extrusive (volcanic) rock
    3: 519
"Exultation" **2:** 397
Exxon *Valdez* **1:** 132
eye **3:** 359
eye of the hurricane
    1: 402

F

fables/fairy tales/tales
2: 416
Aesops Fables 1: 100
Arabian Nights, The
1: 100
Blue Fairy Book, The
1: 101
Boy's King Arthur, The
1: 101
Fables 1: 100, 101
Fairy Tales and Stories
1: 100
*Golden Treasury of Myths
and Legends, The*
1: 101
Grimm's Fairy Tales
1: 100
Just So Stories 1: 100
Little Prince, The 1: 101
*Merry Adventures of
Robin Hood* 1: 101
Nights with Uncle Remus
1: 100
*Pecos Bill and the
Mustang* 1: 100
*Perrault's Complete Fairy
Tales* 1: 101
Meet the Werewolf 1: 103
facilitated diffusion
3: 480
fact, the fact that (usage)
2: 381
factor(s) 1: 209, 230, 326;
2: 273, 349
factoring 1: 326;
2: 273–274
factorial 3: 455
factory system 2: 105
Faerie Queen 2: 393, 403
Fahrenheit 451 2: 417
**Fahrenheit temperature
scale** 1: 375; 2: 250,
258
**Fair Labor Standards
Act** 1: 126
fairy tales *see* fables/fairy
tales/tales
falconry 3: 314
Falkland Islands (Islas
Malvinas) 2: 123, 185
2: *Atlas* 11
Fall, Albert B. 2: 47
Fall, The 2: 418
falling body 2: 248
families (scientific
classification) 2: 211

famous, infamous (usage)
2: 381
Faneuil Hall 2: 61
FAO (Food and Agricultural
Organization of the
United Nations) 2: 13
Faraday, Michael 3: 541,
543
Faraday's law 3: 542
Far East 2: *Atlas* 20
Farewell to Arms, A
2: 420
Farley, Walter 1: 97
farm production
1: 117
Farnsworth, Philo T.
1: 474
Faroe Islands 2: 185
2: *Atlas* 14
farther, further (usage)
2: 381
fascism 1: 126; 3: 326,
333, 340, 343, 344,
345, 346, 354
Fascist 2: 113
Party 2: 112
fats, facts 1: 335
fat-soluble vitamins
1: 332
fat tissue 2: 209
Faulkner, William 2: 415,
419–420; 3: 53, 73,
92; 4: 1380
fault 1: 387, 403;
3: 524–525, 532
fault block mountains
3: 525
faulting 3: 525
Faust 2: 397, 427
faze (usage) 2: 381
FCC (Federal
Communications
Commission) 2: 11
FDIC (Federal Deposit
Insurance
Corporation) 2: 11
FDR *see* Roosevelt,
Franklin D.
Fechner, Gustav 3: 356
federal agencies 3: 349
Federal
Communications
Commission (FCC)
2: 11
Federal Deposit
Insurance
Corporation (FDIC)
2: 11

Federal Election
Commission 2: 11
Federal Housing Finance
Board 2: 11
Federal Mediation and
Conciliation Service
2: 11
Federal Open Market
Committee (FOMC)
3: 282
Federal Reserve System
2: 11, 45; 3: 282–284,
292; 4: 356
Federal Trade
Commission (FTC)
2: 11; 4: 79
federal court system
3: 348
district courts 2: 11
federal debt 3: 280–281,
292
federalism 3: 347, 354;
4: 461–466
Federalist, The 1: 113;
2: 33
Federalists 1: 113, 114;
4: 79, 134, 135, 144,
356, 568
**Federal Republic of
Germany** *see* West
Germany
federal system (gov.)
4: 568
feel (usage) 2: 381
feet (poetry) 3: 79–80
Fellowship of the Ring
2: 430
Felton, Harold W. 1: 100
Ferdinand, King (Sp.)
2: 96, 132
fermentation 2: 216;
3: 483
Fermi, Enrico 2: 65, 113
"Fern Hill" 2: 402
ferns 2: 217
fertilization 3: 491, 496,
498
fetal stage 3: 360
feudalism 2: 91, 130;
3: 306, 340
feudal system 3: 305
"Fever, A" 2: 396
fewer, less (usage)
2: 377
fibrous tissue (dense)
2: 209
Ficino, Marsilio 3: 317,
318

fiction 1: 96; **2:** 388, 389, 413–435; **3:** 69–70
  elements of **2:** 413
  good reading suggestions for young people **1:** 96–99
  types of **2:** 416
  writers' brief biographies **2:** 418–423
fief 3: 309, 340
Field, Cyrus **1:** 121
Fielding, Henry **2:** 414, 415, 416, 420; **4:** 1380
Fields, W. C. **1:** 470
field stars 1: 425
Fifteenth Amendment 1: 121; **2:** 41; **4:** 356
figurative
  language **4:** 1387
  poetic devices **2:** 390
figuratively, literally (usage) **2:** 383
figure skating 1: 451
figures of speech (poetry) **3:** 80
Fiji 2: 143, 146
  2: *Atlas* 22
filibuster 4: 568
Filipino-Americans 2: 73
Fillmore, Millard **2:** 36–37, 62; **4:** 166
film editor 1: 477
filter feeders 3: 492
final goods 3: 268
Finland 2: 115, 143, 155; **3:** 337
  2: *Atlas* 15
Finnegans Wake 2: 421
fire safety 1: 345
fireside chats 4: 356
firn 1: 403
first, firstly (usage) **3:** 116
first aid
  assistance **1:** 346–351
  remedies **1:** 350–351
First Bull Run 1: 120
First Circle, The 2: 422
"First Folio" 2: 410
First Letter of Clement 3: 308
firstly, first (usage) **3:** 116
first triumvirate 2: 87
fiscal policy 3: 279–286, 292; **4:** 568
fish class 2: 223
Fisk University 2: 68

fission (reproduction) **2:** 203, 213, 225
fissure 3: 532
Fitzgerald, Ella **2:** 69
Fitzgerald, F. Scott **2:** 415, 420; **4:** 1380
Fitzhugh, Louise **1:** 97
fix (usage) **2:** 381
fixed costs 3: 262–263, 292
fjord 1: 390, 403
flag, U.S., display and care **1:** 173
flagellum(a) 2: 195, 225; **3:** 481
flags
  U.S., history of **1:** 154–155
  U.S. states and territories **1:** 156–172
flammable, inflammable (usage) **2:** 381; **3:** 116
Flanders 3: 310, 311
flashback 4: 1387
flatworms phylum 2: 220
Flaubert, Gustave **2:** 415, 420; **4:** 1380
flaunt, flout (usage) **2:** 381
"Flea, The" 2: 396
flee, fly (usage) **2:** 381
Fleming, Sir Alexander **2:** 112
floating point notation 2: 347
floods 1: 133
Florence 3: 310–311, 315, 317
Flores, Thomas **2:** 74
Florida 1: 107, 115, 119, 146–147, 158; **2:** 33, 73, 74, 76
flout, flaunt (usage) **2:** 381
fluid feeders 3: 492
fluorine 1: 372
fluvial landforms 3: 520
fly, flee (usage) **2:** 381
flying buttresses 3: 313
Flying Dutchman, The 3: 329
FM (frequency modulation) **1:** 473, 474
focal length 2: 252
focus 1: 387, 403
fog 1: 396
folded mountains 3: 525
folding 3: 525
folds 3: 525

folic acid 1: 333
folk
  music **1:** 465
  tales **1:** 100–101
  tales, good reading suggestions for young people **1:** 100–101
FOMC (Federal Open Market Committee) **3:** 282
Food and Agricultural Organization of the United Nations (FAO) **2:** 13
Food and Drug Act 4: 356
food
  chain **1:** 357
  pyramid **1:** 331
  web **1:** 357, 362
football 1: 434–437
  dictionary of **1:** 437
  NFL (National Football League) teams **1:** 436
  records, professional football **1:** 436
Foote, Shelby **4:** 1382
footnotes 2: 368–369
foot-pound 2: 246
foot-pound/second 2: 246
Forbes, Esther **1:** 98
force(s) 1: 374, 376, 382; **2:** 244–245, 258; **3:** 534, 535, 536, 548
Ford, Gerald R. **1:** 131; **2:** 50–51, 62, 122; **4:** 330–331
Ford, Henry **2:** 109, 135
Ford Motor Company 2: 109
Ford's Theater 1: 121; **2:** 38
forebrain 3: 358
foreign policy 2: 13; **4:** 556–558
foreign relations 2: 13
forest 1: 358–359
form (Eng.) **4:** 1387
formalism 3: 354
formally, formerly (usage) **2:** 381
formal operations period 3: 360, 361
format 3: 68
former, latter (usage) **2:** 381
formerly, formally (usage) **2:** 381

forms of government
4: 446
formulas (chem.) 2: 227;
3: 507
formulas (math)
1: 320–321; 2: 268,
335, 344–345
for problem solving
2: 268
trigonometry 2: 335
formula weight 3: 508,
516
Forster, E. M. 4: 1380
Fort
Duquesne
(Pennsylvania) 1: 109
McHenry (Maryland)
1: 114
Necessity (Pennsylvania)
1: 109
Sumter (South Carolina)
1: 119, 120; 4: 356
forte 1: 466
49th parallel 1: 117
forward(s), backward(s)
(usage) 2: 378
For Whom the Bell Tolls
2: 420, 427
fossil 1: 362, 3: 528, 532
Foster, Genevieve 1: 102
Founding Fathers 3: 347,
348
Four Freedoms 2: 47
Fourteen Points 1: 124;
2: 45, 111; 4:
356–357
Fourteenth Amendment
1: 121; 2: 68; 4: 357
fraction(s) 1: 230–244,
271, 272, 324, 326;
2: 300–301
adding 1: 236–239
decimal 1: 246
dividing 1: 243–244
improper 1: 234, 235
multiplying 1: 241–242
renaming 1: 234–235
simplifying 1: 231
subtracting 1: 239–241
fragmentation (biol.)
3: 490
France *see also* French
1: 107, 109, 123, 469;
2: 13, 89, 92, 93, 95,
97, 99, 100, 101, 102,
103, 104, 105, 106,
108, 110, 114, 119,
140, 143, 155; 3: 306,

308, 309, 315, 318,
325, 332, 334, 336,
337
2: *Atlas* 14
Third Republic
3: 330–331
franchise 3: 354
Francis I (Fr.) 3: 314, 324
Francis II (Fr.) (Valois)
3: 321
Franciscans 1: 110;
3: 311, 312–313
Francis Ferdinand,
Archduke 1: 124;
2: 110, 111
Franco, Francisco 2: 113,
135
Franconia 2: 92
Franco-Prussian War
3: 330, 333
Frank, Anne 1: 102, 103
Frankenstein 2: 400, 417
Franklin, Benjamin
1: 109, 112; 2: 31,
103, 133
Franks 2: 91; 3: 303, 305,
306
Fraunhofer diffraction
pattern 3: 544
Frederick I (Barbarossa;
Ger.) 2: 94; 3: 310,
313, 314
Frederick II (Frederick
the Great; Prussia)
2: 103, 133
Frederick II (Holy Roman
Empire) 2: 94; 3: 314
Fredericksburg, Virginia
(Battle of) 1: 120;
4: 357
freedmen 4: 357
Freedmen's Bureau
1: 121
freedom 3: 346, 350, 354
of the press 1: 109
of the seas 1: 124
freedom ride(r)s 1: 129;
2: 70; 4: 357
Freedom's Journal 2: 67
free
fall 1: 425
market 3: 254
state 2: 37
trade 3: 286; 4: 135
verse 3: 79, 80
freewriting (comp.)
3: 39–40, 42
freezing 3: 510

Fremont, John C. 2: 39
French *see also* France
1: 109, 112, 114;
2: 101, 106, 109, 113,
120, 123; 3: 307, 332
and Indian War(s)
1: 109; 2: 103;
4: 113, 357
colonies 1: 107; 4: 98–99
Empire 2: 105
Republic 2: 104
Revolution 2: 104, 134;
3: 325, 327; 4: 136
Second Republic 2: 106
territories 2: 185, 186,
187
Valois 3: 318
French-English
dictionary
3: 140–144
FRENCH GRAMMAR
3: 118–151
French Guiana 2: 185
2: *Atlas* 10
French Indochina 2: 115
French Polynesia 2: 185
2: *Atlas* 23
frequency 1: 380, 382;
2: 251, 255, 258;
3: 540, 548
Fresnel diffraction
pattern 3: 544
Freud, Sigmund 2: 108,
135; 3: 331–332, 357,
366, 367
Freytag's pyramid 3: 72
friction 1: 376, 382; 3: 535
frictional unemployment
3: 277
Friedman, Milton 3: 287
fringes 3: 544
Fritz, Jean 1: 102
frog dissection 2: 222
Frogs, The 2: 406, 407
front 1: 398–399, 403
Frost, Robert 1: 100;
2: 393, 396–397
fruit 3: 491, 498
FTC (Federal Trade
Commission) 2: 11;
4: 79
Fugitive Slave Act 1: 118;
4: 357
fugitive slave laws 2: 37,
40; 4: 76
fulcrum 1: 376, 377
full faith and credit
clause 4: 568

Fulton, Robert **1:** 114,
    2: 62
function(s) (math) **1:** 285,
    326; **2:** 329, 330;
    3: 372–387, 475;
    4: 899–938
    graphs **3:** 373;
    4: 910–918, 969–991
    limits **4:** 922–935
functional group(s)
    2: 243; **3:** 478, 498
functionalism 3: 357
fundamental (frequency)
    3: 540
fundamental identities
    2: 331
Fundamental Orders of
    Connecticut 1: 108
fundamental theorem(s)
    of calculus 3: 413,
    414, 475;
    4: 1068–1071
fungi (kingdom) **2:** 210,
    216; **3:** 487
fungus cells 2: 196–197
funny (usage) **2:** 381
further, farther (usage)
    2: 381
Fust, Johann **3:** 322

G

Gabon 2: 143, 165
Gabrieli, Giovanni **3:** 320
Gadsden Purchase
    1: 118; **2:** 39; **4:** 357
gaffer 1: 477
Gagarin, Yuri A. **1:** 420,
    423; **2:** 118
galactic halo 1: 425
galaxy(s) 1: 411, 425
Galen 2: 129
Galileo, Galilei **2:** 97, 133,
    248; **3:** 325–326
Galileo probe 1: 419
Gallipoli 2: 111
Galton, Sir Francis **3:** 363
Gama, Vasco da **2:** 98,
    132; **3:** 314
Gambia, The 2: 66, 143,
    165
    2: *Atlas* 12
gametes 2: 204, 205;
    3: 496, 499
gamma ray(s) 2: 239,
    243, 251, 252, 257,
    258; **3:** 546
Gandhi, Indira **2:** 123, 136
Gandhi, Mohandas K.
    2: 112, 135; **3:** 342
Gandhi, Rajiv **2:** 123
Ganymede 1: 407
GAO (Government
    Accounting Office)
    2: 11
"Garden, The" 2: 398
Garfield, James A. (Abram)
    1: 122; **2:** 40–41, 62;
    4: 210
Garibaldi, Giuseppe **2:** 107
Garriott, Owen K. **1:** 421
Garrison, William Lloyd
    1: 116
gas(es) 2: 227; **3:** 509–511
    concepts **3:** 500–501
    constant **3:** 510
    mixtures **3:** 510
gastrovascular cavities
    3: 493
Gates, Bill **2:** 137
Gauguin, Paul **3:** 328
Gaul 2: 87, 89, 90; **3:** 295,
    340
Gaza 2: 124, 125
GDP (Gross Domestic
    Product) **3:** 268–272,
    292
    deflator **3:** 292

**GED (General Education
    Development)
    exams 3:** 590–597
Gemini flights 1: 420, 423
**gender of singular
    pronouns** (usage)
    2: 381
genera 2: 211
general
    angle functions
        2: 327–328
    angles (0) **2:** 327
    bibliography list **2:** 359
    depressant drugs **1:** 338
    election(s) **2:** 14; **4:** 568
    stimulant drugs **1:** 338
**General Education
    Development
    (GED) examination
    3:** 590–597
**General Services
    Administration**
    (GSA) **2:** 11
generators 3: 542
genes 3: 484, 499
genetic(s) 2: 206–207;
    3: 484–486
    abnormalities **3:** 363
    code **2:** 202
    engineering **3:** 486
Geneva, Switzerland
    1: 132
Geneva convention 2: 120
Genghis Khan 2: 94, 96,
    131
Genoa 3: 310–311
genome 3: 486
genotype 2: 206; **3:** 484,
    499
genres of fiction 2: 413,
    417
Gentleman **2:** 423
**Gentlemen's Agreement
    of 1907 2:** 72
genus 1: 362; **2:** 225
geologic processes
    3: 523–526
geologic time 3: 527–529
    scale chart **3:** 529
GEOLOGY 3: 518–533
geomagnetism 3: 522
geometric
    constructions **2:** 307–308
    mean **1:** 326; **2:** 349
    sequence **1:** 326; **2:** 305,
        349
    series **1:** 326; **2:** 305,
        349

GEOMETRY 2: 306–323
    formulas **2:** 344–345
    symbols **1:** 319; **2:** 343
Georgia 1: 109, 117, 119,
    120, 124, 146–147,
    159; **2:** 51
Georgia (country) **2:** 143,
    155
    2: *Atlas* 15
Georgics **2:** 402
geosynchronous orbit
    1: 425
germ 1: 352
German(s) 2: 103, 109,
    115, 116; **3:** 332
German-Americans
    2: 61–62, 64
**German Democratic
    Republic** (East
    Germany) **3:** 337
**German-English
    dictionary**
    3: 170–175
**GERMAN GRAMMAR
    3:** 152–181
Germanic (peoples) **2:** 89;
    3: 305
    invaders **2:** 85
    tribes **3:** 303, 304
German-Soviet alliance
    2: 115
Germany see also
    German(s) **2:** 92, 94,
    97, 99, 101, 105, 106,
    107, 108, 110, 111,
    112, 113, 114, 115,
    124, 126, 127, 134;
    2: 140, 143, 155;
    3: 302, 307, 309,
    311, 315, 318, 332,
    334–335, 337
    2: *Atlas* 14
Germany, state formation
    3: 329–330
Germinal **2:** 423
germinal stage 3: 360
germination 3: 491
Geronimo 2: 56
gerrymandering 4: 568
Gershwin, George
    1: 465
gerund(s) (Eng.) **1:** 48,
    51
    phrases **1:** 40–41, 48
Gestalt psychology
    3: 357, 366, 370
gestation 3: 360
get (usage) **2:** 381

Gettysburg, Pennsylvania
(Battle of) **1:** 120;
4: 357
Ghana 2: 66, 143, 165
2: *Atlas* 12
Ghent 3: 310
Treaty of **1:** 114
Ghibellines 2: 94
Ghosts **2:** 408
GI Bill of Rights 1: 128
Gibraltar 2: 185; **3:** 523
Gidal, Sonia **1:** 102
Gilbert Islands 1: 127
Gilded Age 4: 359
Gilgamesh **2:** 392, 397,
424
Gilligan, Carol **3:** 362
Ginsberg, Allen **2:** 393,
397
Giotto 2: 97, 131; **3:** 315
Gipson, Fred **1:** 98
Giuliani, Rudolph **2:** 126
glacier 1: 390–391, 403;
3: 526, 529, 532
glands 3: 496
glasnost (openness) **2:** 124
Glenn, John **1:** 423; **2:** 118
glial cells 3: 496
globes 2: 188
Glorious Revolution
2: 133; **3:** 327, 340
glucose 3: 484
glycolysis 2: 200; **3:** 483,
484, 499
Gnosticism 2: 83
GNP (gross national
product) **3:** 268–272,
292
go, went, gone (usage)
2: 381
Godfrey of Bouillon
3: 313
Godwin, Earl **3:** 307
Godwinson, Harold **3:** 307
Goethe, Johann Wolfgang
von **2:** 134, 393, 397,
409, 414, 420;
4: 1378
Goizueta, Roberto **2:** 74
Golan Heights (Syria)
2: 121
gold 1: 372
Golden Age
of Greece **2:** 82
of Greek drama **2:** 84
Golden Apples, The **3:** 53
gold rush, California
1: 118

gold standard 2: 43;
4: 358
golf 1: 446–447
dictionary of **1:** 447
major victories **1:** 447
Golgi 2: 213
apparatus **2:** 194; **3:** 482
bodies **2:** 194, 195
complex **3:** 481
gonad(s) 3: 496, 499
Gondwanaland
1: 384–385; **3:** 529
gone, go, went (usage)
2: 381
Gone With the Wind
1: 472
good, well (usage) **2:** 381;
3: 116
Goode's projection 2: 189
goods (econ.) **3:** 247
goodwill 3: 262
Good Woman of Setzuan,
The **2:** 407
Goodyear, Charles **1:** 117
Gorbachev, Mikhail S.
2: 123, 124, 137;
3: 325, 336
Gorky, Maxim **2:** 416
Gospels 2: 88; **3:** 308
Gospel of John **3:** 308
Gospel of Luke **3:** 308
Gospel of Mark **3:** 308
Gospel of Matthew
3: 308
Gospel of Thomas
3: 308
got to (usage) **2:** 381
Gothic
architecture **3:** 305, 340
fiction **2:** 413, 417
script **3:** 313
style **3:** 313
Goths 2: 89
Gould, Stephen Jay
4: 1383
government transfer
payments 3: 268
Government, United
States **2:** 4–53;
3: 347–350;
4: 405–571
Accounting Office **2:** 11
Printing Office **2:** 11
Goya 2: 134
Gracchi brothers 3: 300
Graduate Record
Examination (GRE)
3: 586

grafting 3: 490
Graham, Frank, Jr.
1: 102
Grahame, Kenneth
1: 98
gram 2: 245
gram-centimeter/second
2: 246
GRAMMAR (Eng.)
1: 4–55
grammar rules (Eng.)
3: 95–98
GRAMMAR AND
WRITING (Eng.)
1: 4–73
Grand Canyon 1: 107;
2: 74
strata of **3:** 528
Grange (movement)
1: 121; **4:** 358
granite 3: 526
Grant, Ulysses S.
(Simpson) **1:** 120;
2: 40–41, 62; **4:** 177,
185
granules 2: 195
Grapes of Wrath, The
2: 423
graphic scale (maps)
2: 189
graphs (econ.) **3:** 248
reading **3:** 249–251
graphs and graphing
(math) **2:** 328–329
calculators **3:** 372, 374;
4: 986–987
lines **2:** 279–282
without calculators
4: 984–986
grasslands 1: 358–359
grassroots 4: 568
Graves, Robert **4:** 1380
gravitation/gravity
2: 244; **3:** 326, 536,
548
constant **3:** 536
laws of **2:** 248, 249, 258;
3: 326, 536
Gravity's Rainbow
2: 422
Gray, Thomas **2:** 391
GRE (Graduate Record
Examination) **3:** 586
Great
Awakening **4:** 110, 152,
358
Basin **1:** 134
Compromise **4:** 358

Depression **1**: 126; **2**: 47, 69, 75, 113, 136; **3**: 268, 333; **4**: 262–274
Lakes **1**: 108, 116, 134
Migration
African-Americans North **2**: 68; **4**: 358
European immigration **2**: 61
Plains **1**: 134
Powers **3**: 332
Red Spot **1**: 406–407
Salt Lake **1**: 118
Schism **2**: 95, 96
Society **1**: 129; **2**: 49; **4**: 314, 358
Sphinx **3**: 296
Wall of China **2**: 86
Great Britain 1: 109, 115; **2**: 13; **3**: 334
greatest
common factor **1**: 326, 327; **2**: 349
integer functions **3**: 373
Great Expectations **2**: 427–428
Great Gatsby, The **2**: 415, 420, 428
Greco, El **2**: 133
Greco-Roman 3: 315, 317–318
civilization **2**: 85
culture **3**: 316
world **3**: 301
Greece 2: 82, 85, 87, 88, 89, 111, 114, 115, 117, 143, 155; **3**: 301, 302, 337
2: *Atlas* 15
Greek(s) 2: 83; **3**: 325
alphabet **3**: 304, 377
and Roman culture **2**: 90
and Roman theater **2**: 404
city-states **3**: 295, 296–297, 299, 300, 302
drama **1**: 468
fire **3**: 324
philosophers **3**: 343
greenhouse effect 1: 402, 403, 405
Greenland 1: 384; **2**: 93, 185
2: *Atlas* 7
green room 1: 477

Gregorian calendar 2: 100
Gregory I (pope) **2**: 90
Gregory the Great 2: 130; **3**: 308, 309
Gregory VII (pope) **2**: 131
Gregory XI (pope) **2**: 95
Gregory XIII (pope) **2**: 100
Grenada 2: 123, 143, 177
2: *Atlas* 5
Grenville Acts 1: 110
grid system 2: 188
Griffith, D. W. **1**: 471
Grimm, Jakob and Wilhelm **1**: 100; **2**: 416
grip 1: 477
Grissom, Virgil **1**: 423
gross domestic product (GDP) **3**: 268–272, 292
gross national product (GNP) **3**: 268–272, 292
ground meristems 3: 491
ground state 3: 502, 517
ground tissue 3: 489
group behavior 3: 368
groups (elements) **2**: 235
groups/families (chem.) **3**: 503
GSA (General Services Administration) **2**: 11
Guadalcanal (Battle of) **1**: 127; **2**: 116; **4**: 359
Guadeloupe 2: 185
2: *Atlas* 5
Guadaloupe-Hidalgo, Treaty of **1**: 117; **4**: 359
Guam 1: 127, 152, 172; **2**: 43
guanine (G) **3**: 479
Guatemala 2: 143, 177
2: *Atlas* 5
Guelphs 2: 94
Guerriere **1**: 114
Guido of Arezzo 2: 93
Guilford Court House, North Carolina **1**: 112
Guinea 2: 143, 166
2: *Atlas* 12
Guinea-Bissau 2: 143, 166
2: *Atlas* 12
Guises 3: 322

guitar 1: 460
Guiteau, Charles J. **1**: 122; **2**: 40
Gulf of Mexico 1: 108
Gulf of Tonkin Resolution 1: 130
Gulf War 1991 2: 127
Gulliver's Travels **2**: 417, 428
"Gunga Din" 2: 398
gunpowder 2: 92; **3**: 324
gustatory system 3: 359, 370
Gustavus Adolphus (Swed.) **2**: 101
Gutenberg, Johann **2**: 96, 132, 388; **3**: 322–323
Gutman, Bill **1**: 102
Guyana 2: 143, 182
2: *Atlas* 10
gymnastics 1: 451
gymnosperm(s) 1: 362; 489, 499; **2**: 218
Gypsies 3: 334

H

habitat 1: 363
had best, had better
(usage) **2:** 381
had better, had best
(usage) **2:** 381
had of, had've (usage)
2: 381
had ought (usage) **2:** 382
Hadrian 2: 129; **3:** 295,
301, 302
hadrons 3: 546
had've, had of (usage)
2: 381
Hagia Sophia 2: 90;
3: 304
Hahn, Otto **2:** 257
hail 1: 403
Haines, Jackson **1:** 451
Haiti 2: 66, 123, 143,
177
half angles 2: 335
half-life 2: 239, 243, 257,
258; **3:** 546
half-reaction 3: 513
halides 1: 389
Hall, G. Stanley **3:** 357
Halley's comet 1: 408,
418
hallucinations 3: 367, 371
hallucinogenic drugs
1: 338
halogens 2: 235; **3:** 503
Hamas 2: 125
Hamburg, Germany
3: 311
Hamilton, Alexander
1: 113; **2:** 33, 62
Hamlet, Prince of
Denmark **2:** 100,
411, 428
Hammett, Dashiell **2:** 417
Hammurabi 2: 80
Code of **3:** 296
handball 1: 454
Handel, George Frederick
1: 464
Handy, W. C. **2:** 69
hanged, hung (usage)
2: 382
Hanging Gardens of
Babylon 2: 82
Hannibal 2: 86, 128;
3: 300
Hanseatic League 3: 311
haploid 2: 206, 225;
3: 496

Hapsburg(s) 3: 322, 340
Hapsburg (Hispano-
Germanic) **3:** 318
Hapsburg family **2:** 101
Hapsburgs, Spanish
3: 316
Hard Times **2:** 419
Harding, Warren G.
(Gamaliel) **1:** 125;
2: 46–47, 62; **4:** 78,
250–251
hardly (usage) **2:** 382
Hardy, Thomas **2:** 415,
420; **4:** 1380
Harlem and Watts riots
2: 70
Harlem Renaissance
2: 69, 398; **4:** 257,
359
Harlot's Ghost **2:** 422
harmonic
mean **1:** 327; **2:** 349
sequence **1:** 327; **2:** 349
series **1** 327; **2:** 349
wave **3:** 539
harmony 1: 462, 466
Harpers Ferry, Virginia
1: 119
Harris, Joel Chandler
1: 100
Harrison, Benjamin
2: 42–43, 62
Harrison, William Henry
1: 114; **2:** 34–35, 62
Harte, Bret **2:** 416
Harun Al-Rashid 2: 130
Harvard 1: 108; **2:** 40, 44,
46, 48, 52
Hastings, Battle of (1066)
2: 93; **3:** 307
Hatch Act 4: 568
Havana, Cuba **2:** 43
have got (usage) **2:** 382
Havel, Vaclav **2:** 137
Hawaii 1: 123, 134, 135,
138–139, 159; **2:** 71,
73, 103, 114
2: *Atlas* 8
Hawaiian Islands 1: 388;
3: 524
Hawking, Stephen **2:** 137
Hawthorne, Nathaniel
2: 415, 420; **4:** 1378
Haydn, Franz Joseph
1: 464
Hayes, Rutherford B.
(Birchard) **2:** 40–41,
62; **4:** 186

Haymarket (Square)
Riot 1: 122; **4:** 359
Hayne, Robert Y. **1:** 116
HDTV 1: 475
Head Start 1: 129; **4:** 359
Health and Human
Services,
Department of **2:** 10,
11
HEALTH AND SAFETY
1: 330–353
heart (human) **1:** 343
Heart of Darkness
2: 416
heat 1: 375, 382; **2:** 250;
3: 538, 548
capacity **3:** 538, 539,
548–549
energy **1:** 375
of reaction **3:** 509, 517
transfer **1:** 375
Hebb, D. O. **3:** 357
Hebrew(s) 2: 80, 81;
3: 296
Covenant **3:** 295
kingdoms **3:** 295
Hedda Gabler **2:** 408
Hegel, George Wilhelm
Friedrich **3:** 328–329
Hegira 2: 91
Heine, Heinrich **2:** 393,
397
Heinlein, Robert **1:** 98
Heinz, Henry J. **2:** 64
Heisenberg, Werner **2:** 256
Heisenberg uncertainty
principle **3:** 545–546
heliocentric theory 2: 99;
3: 325
helium 1: 372
Hellenistic
Age **2:** 82; **3:** 299, 300,
316
kingdoms **3:** 295
world **3:** 325, 341
Helmholtz, Hermann von
3: 356
Heloïse 3: 311
help but (usage) **2:** 382
Hemingway, Ernest
2: 415, 420; **4:** 1378
hemopoietic tissue 2: 209
Henderson, Fletcher **2:** 69
Henry Esmond **2:** 423
Henry, Joseph **3:** 541
Henry, Patrick **2:** 61
Henry II (Eng.) **2:** 94,
131; **3:** 307, 308, 314

Henry II (Fr.) (Valois) **3:** 321–322
Henry IV (Fr.) **2:** 100; **3:** 309, 322
Henry IV (Holy Roman Empire) **2:** 93; **3:** 309
Henry V (Eng.) **3:** 308
Henry VII (Henry Tudor) (Eng.) **2:** 96, 132
Henry VIII **2:** 98, 132, 133; **3:** 314
Henry IV (Pirandello) (lit.) **2:** 409
Henry IV, Part I (Shakespeare) (lit.) **2:** 410, 411, 428
Henry IV, Part II (Shakespeare) (lit.) **2:** 411, 428
Henry V (Shakespeare) (lit.) **2:** 411, 428
Henry VI (Shakespeare) (lit.) **2:** 410, 411
Henry the Navigator (Port.) **2:** 98
heptagon 1: 327; **2:** 349
Herbert, George **2:** 391
herbivore(s) 1: 363; **3:** 492, 499
heredity 1: 363; **2:** 225; **4:** 665–676, 807–808
heresy 3: 341
Hermann and Dorothea **2:** 397
hermaphrodite 1: 363
Hermitage, The (Tennessee) **2:** 34
Hernandez, Keith **2:** 74
Herod the Great 2: 129
heroic couplet 3: 79–80
Heroic Stanzas **2:** 396
herpes simplex (Type 1 and Type II) **1:** 339, 352
Hershey, Milton **2:** 64
Hershey Chocolate Company **2:** 64
hertz 1: 380
Hertzsprung, Ejnar **1:** 413
Hertzsprung-Russell diagram **1:** 413, 425
Hess, Harry H. **3:** 521
Hesse, Hermann **2:** 415, 420
Hessian mercenaries 1: 112; **4:** 359
heterogeneous matter 3: 500

heterotroph(s) 2: 198, 225; **3:** 480, 487, 499
heterozygote 2: 206
heterozygous 3: 485, 499
heuristic(s) 3: 365, 371
hexagon 1: 327; **2:** 316
hexameter 2: 403
Hezbollah 2: 125
"Hickory Dickory Dock" 2: 391
high 1: 403
higher-degree polynomial functions 3: 373, 374
higher-order derivatives 3: 397–398
high frequency 2: 252
"High-Toned Old Christian Woman, A" 2: 401
Himalaya Mountains 1: 386; **2:** 144; **3:** 522, 529
Hinckley, John W. Jr. **1:** 132
hindbrain 3: 358
Hindus 3: 337
Hippocrates 2: 85, 128
Hippocratic Oath 2: 85
Hiroshima 1: 127; **2:** 49, 114, 116; **3:** 335
Hispanic-Americans 2: 73–76
historical literature 2: 389
historical plays by Shakespeare 2: 411
history of drama 2: 404–405
history of poetry 2: 392–393
HISTORY OF WESTERN CIVILIZATION 3: 294–341
Hitchcock, Alfred **1:** 98
Hitler, Adolf **1:** 126; **2:** 69, 113, 116, 135; **3:** 329, 333–334, 342
Hittites 2: 80; **3:** 296
H. J. Heinz Company 2: 64
Hobbes, Thomas **3:** 344; **4:** 1382
Hobbit, The **2:** 430
Ho Chi Minh 2: 120

hockey 1: 440–441
dictionary of **1:** 441
NHL (National Hockey League) teams **1:** 441
Hohenstaufens 2: 94; **3:** 314
Holbein, Hans the Younger **2:** 97
Holland/Dutch 3: 332
Holocaust 3: 334; **4:** 359
Holocene Epoch 3: 529
holophrases 3: 365
holotrophs 3: 492
Holy Land (Palestine) **2:** 94; **3:** 313
Holy Roman Emperor 2: 101
Henry IV **2:** 93
Holy Roman Empire 2: 92, 94, 99, 100, 101, 103; **3:** 307, 309, 310
Holy Sonnets **2:** 396
Homeland Security, Department of 1: 133; **2:** 11, 126
homeostasis 2: 225; **3:** 492, 499
Homer 1: 100; **2:** 80, 81, 82, 128, 391, 392, 397, 398, 429; **4:** 1378
Homeric Hymns **2:** 391
Homestead Act 1: 119; **4:** 359
Homestead strike 1: 123
homogeneous matter 3: 500
homophones (Eng.) **1:** 53
Homo sapiens 2: 211
homozygous 3: 485
Honduras 2: 143, 178 **2:** *Atlas* 5
Hong Kong 2: 72, 106, 124
Hood, Mt. (Washington) **1:** 388
Hooker, Thomas **1:** 108
Hoover, Herbert **1:** 126; **2:** 46–47, 62; **4:** 258, 262, 266–267
"Hoover commissions" 2: 47
Hoover Institute 2: 47
hopefully (usage) **2:** 382
Hopkins, Gerard Manley **2:** 393, 397
Horace 2: 129

hormones 3: 359, 371, 496, 499
horn 1: 403
horn (music) **1:** 459
horse latitudes 1: 395, 403
horsepower 2: 246
House of Burgesses 1: 107; **2:** 31
House of Life, The **2:** 400
House of Representatives 1: 116, 133; **2:** 7, 15–16, 22, 32; **3:** 347, 349
House Judiciary Committee **1:** 131
House Un-American Activities Committee **4:** 359–360
House of the Seven Gables, The **2:** 420
Houses of York and Lancaster 2: 96
housing (GI bill) **1:** 128
Housing and Urban Development, Department of **2:** 11
Housman, Alfred Edward **2:** 393, 398
How a bill becomes a law 2: 8–9
How the Other Half Lives **1:** 122
How to read a map 2: 188
HOW TO STUDY 1: 78–103
Howard University 2: 68
Howe, Elias **1:** 118
"Howl" 2: 397
Hsüan T'ung 2: 109
Hubble, Edwin **1:** 415
Hubble Space Telescope **1:** 411, 417, 423
Huckleberry Finn, The Adventures of **2:** 415, 419, 421, 428
Hudson Bay 2: 101
Hudson, Henry **1:** 107
Hudson River 1: 107, 108, 116
Hughes, Langston **2:** 69, 393, 398
Hugo, Victor **2:** 414; **4:** 1378
Huguenots 2: 61, 100; **3:** 321–322; **4:** 360
Hull House 1: 122; **4:** 360

human
anatomy **1:** 340–343
body, types of cells **2:** 193
development **3:** 360–362
organism **3:** 358–359
organ systems **3:** 494–495
physiology **4:** 741–757, 810–811
reproduction **4:** 762–770
voice **1:** 458
Human Comedy, The **2:** 414, 418
humanism 3: 316, 317, 325, 357, 371, 580
humanistic
humanist-Platonic ideas **3:** 318
therapy **3:** 367
scholarship **3:** 318
Hume, David **2:** 133
humid continental 1: 394
humidity 1: 396
humid subtropical 1: 394
Hundred Days 2: 105
Hundred Years' War 2: 95, 131; **3:** 308
hung, hanged (usage) **2:** 382
Hungarian revolution 2: 118
Hungary 2: 94, 96, 99, 106, 110, 117, 143, 155
2: *Atlas* 14–15
Huns 2: 89; **3:** 302, 341
Huron, Lake **1:** 134, 143
hurricane 1: 400, 403
eye of **1:** 402
Hus, Jan **3:** 324
Huss, John **2:** 132
Hussein, Saddam **1:** 133; **2:** 124, 126, 127; **3:** 337, 343
Huxley, Aldous **2:** 416, 417; **4:** 1381
Huygens, Christiaan **2:** 255; **3:** 543
hybrid 1: 363; **2:** 225; **3:** 484
hydrocarbon(s) 1: 355; **2:** 237, 243; **3:** 530
structures **2:** 237
hydrogen 1: 372
bonds **3:** 506
isotopes of **2:** 231
hydrophobic 3: 479

hydrosphere 3: 518, 532
hydroxyl (OH) **3:** 478
hygrometer 1: 403
Hyksos 2: 80
hymn 2: 391
"Hymn to God the Father, A" 2: 391
"Hymn to Intellectual Beauty" 2: 391
hyperbola 2: 283
hyperbole 1: 93; **3:** 80; **4:** 1387
Hyperion, The Fall of **2:** 398
hyperpluralism 4: 568
hyphens (Eng.) **3:** 93
hypotenuse 2: 324
hypothalamus 3: 358, 359
hypothesis 3: 371
hypothesis (math) **1:** 382; **2:** 310
hypotonic solution 2: 198

I

i. **1:** 327; **2:** 349
iambic 2: 403
  pentameter **3:** 79
Iberian Peninsula 2: 96
Ibsen, Henrik **2:** 405, 408;
  4: 1378
ice ages 3: 527
Iceland 2: 143, 155
  2: *Atlas* 14
Iceman Cometh, The
  2: 409, 429
"Ichabod" 2: 402
id 3: 366, 371
Idaho 1: 138–139, 159;
  2: 43, 55, 73
ideal gas 3: 509–510,
  517
  equations **3:** 539
  law **3:** 510, 517, 539
identity (math) **1:** 285,
  327; **2:** 260, 331, 349
  elements **1:** 285; **2:** 260
ideology 3: 344, 346, 354
Idiot, The **2:** 419
Idylls of the King, The
  2: 401
i.e. (usage) **2:** 382
igneous rock 1: 389, 403
  3: 519, 532
"I Have a Dream" 3: 59
il Duce *see* Mussolini,
  Benito
Île de France 3: 307
Iliad **2:** 81, 390, 391, 392,
  397, 429; **3:** 300
illicit, elicit (usage) **2:** 380
Illinois 1: 113, 142–143,
  160; **2:** 38, 55
illness distress signals
  1: 330
illusion, delusion,
  allusion (usage)
  2: 377
Il Penseroso **2:** 398
image 4: 1387
image, real 1: 382; **2:** 252,
  258
imagery (lit.) **3:** 75;
  4: 1387
  figurative poetic devices
  2: 390
imaginary number
  1: 327; **2:** 349
IMF (International
  Monetary Fund)
  2: 13

Imitations of Horace
  2: 399
immigrant, emigrant
  (usage) **2:** 380
immigration 1: 125;
  2: 59–65; **4:** 207–208,
  254
Immigration Act of 1924
  1: 125
imminent, eminent
  (usage) **2:** 380
immune system, human
  3: 495
impeachment 1: 121, 131,
  133; **2:** 39, 53; **4:** 568
imperialism 3: 325, 332;
  4: 216–223
implicit differentiation
  3: 396–397
implied powers 4: 568
imply, infer (usage)
  2: 382; **3:** 116
important elements
  1: 372–373
improper integrals
  3: 436–440, 475
improvisation (music)
  1: 465
Inauguration 2: 14
incidence, angle of **3:** 549
incidence, incidents
  (usage) **2:** 382
incident ray 1: 382
incidents, incidence
  (usage) **2:** 382
inclined planes
  1: 376–377
income 3: 256, 292
  tax **1:** 124; **2:** 45
incomplete valence shells
  3: 505
inconsistent system of
  equations 1: 327;
  2: 349
increasing 3: 475
incredible, incredulous
  (usage) **2:** 382
incredulous, incredible
  (usage) **2:** 382
incumbent 4: 569
indefinite integral
  3: 475
  notation **3:** 416
indefinite pronouns
  (Eng.) **1:** 11
indentured servants
  1: 107; **2:** 60–61; **4:**
  100, 360

independent clauses
  (Eng.) **1:** 41
independent government
  agencies 2: 11
independent variable
  1: 327; **2:** 349
indeterminant form
  3: 406
indeterminate growth
  3: 491
indexes, periodical **2:** 359;
  3: 106
index of forbidden books
  3: 321
index of refraction
  (refractive index)
  2: 252; **3:** 544
India 2: 84, 85, 91, 92, 94,
  96, 101, 103, 108,
  112, 127, 140, 143,
  146, 386; **3:** 332, 336,
  337, 351
  2: *Atlas* 19
Indiana 1: 113, 142–143,
  160; **2:** 34
Indian(s) *see also* Native
  Americans; individual
  tribal names **1:** 117;
  2: 99
  citizenship **1:** 126
  Claims Commission
  2: 58
  place names **2:** 54–55
  Reorganization Act of
  1934 **2:** 58
  reservations **1:** 118, 122;
  2: 57–59
  Territory **2:** 35, 46
  wars **2:** 34, 56–57
Indian Ocean 2: 141, 144;
  3: 521, 523
indicative verbs (Eng.)
  3: 88
indirect
  measurement **2:** 325
  objects (Eng.) **1:** 38, 50
individualism 3: 346
Indochina 2: 120; **3:** 336
Indonesia 2: 127, 140,
  143, 146
  2: *Atlas* 21
induced radioactivity
  2: 239
inductive reasoning 3: 57
indulgences 3: 341
industrial development
  (U.S.) **4:** 150–151,
  201–208

Industrial Revolution
2: 104, 105; 3: 325, 327–329
Industrial Workers of the World (IWW) 4: 360
inequalities (math) 4: 894–899
inequality (math) 1: 285, 301, 302, 327; 2: 260, 302–304, 349
inertia 2: 248, 258; 3: 545, 549
infamous, famous (usage) 2: 381
infancy and childhood 3: 360
infant industries 3: 286
infection vectors 1: 339
infer, imply (usage) 2: 382; 3: 116
Inferno 2: 426
infinite
sequence 1: 327; 2: 349; 3: 454–455
sequences and series 3: 454–473
series 1: 327; 2: 349; 3: 458
infinitives (Eng.) 1: 19, 20, 41, 48–49, 51
phrases 1: 40, 41, 48, 51
infinity 1: 327; 2: 349
inflammable, flammable (usage) 2: 381; 3: 116
inflation 3: 274–276, 292
inflection point 3: 475
information processing 3: 371
infrared 2: 252
radiation 2: 258
rays 2: 251
ingenious, ingenuous (usage) 2: 382
ingenuous, ingenious (usage) 2: 382
ingestion 2: 225
In Memorium 2: 401
"In Memory of W.B. Yeats" 2: 391
inner
core 1: 387; 3: 518
planets 1: 405
transition metals 3: 504
Innocent III (pope) 2: 94, 131; 3: 309, 313, 314
innumerable, numerous (usage) 2: 382

inorganic chemistry 2: 236, 243
inorganic compounds, naming 3: 507
inputs 3: 261, 262
Inquisition 3: 321, 326
inscribed angle 2: 320
insecta class 2: 221
insectivorous plant 3: 490
inside, inside of (usage) 2: 382
insight therapies 3: 367, 371
instantaneous acceleration 3: 534
instinct 1: 363
Institutes of the Christian Religion 3: 320
institutions 3: 355
insulator 3: 541, 549
insure, assure, ensure (usage) 3: 115
integer 1: 327; 2: 262, 349
integral
calculus 3: 408–417
evaluation theorem 3: 414
test 3: 459
integrand 3: 475
integration (math) 3: 408–417, 475; 4: 1046–1059
by parts 3: 429–431
integumentary system 2: 208
human 3: 495
intelligence 3: 371
quotient (I.Q.) 3: 363
tests 3: 363
intensity 2: 253
intercept 1: 327; 2: 350; 3: 475
interest group(s) 3: 349, 355; 4: 496–498
interesting (usage) 2: 382
interference 3: 540, 544, 549
Interior, Department of the 2: 11
interjections (Eng.) 1: 5, 35
intermediate goods 3: 268
intermolecular forces 3: 506, 517
internal center of similitude 2: 321

internal energy 3: 538, 539, 549
kinetic 2: 250
International
Conference on Limitations of Armaments 2: 47
Court of Justice 2: 13
Monetary Fund (IMF) 2: 13
international relations 3: 351–352
internment camps 2: 72–73; 4: 360
interphase 2: 203; 3: 482, 483, 485
interpretive (connotative) literature 2: 389
interrogative pronouns (Eng.) 1: 10
interrupted projections 2: 189
intersection 1: 327; 2: 279, 350
Interstate Commerce Act 1: 122; 4: 360
interstellar matter 1: 425
interval (music) 1: 466
interviewing
for college 3: 635
for the job 3: 660–663
intimacy 3: 371
Intolerable (Coercive) Acts 1: 111; 4: 360–361
intransitive/transitive verbs (Eng.) 1: 18–19; 3: 87
intransitive verbs (usage) 2: 382
introductory paragraph 4: 1294–1307
introspection 3: 357
intrusive (plutonic) rock 3: 519, 532
intuitive approach to limits (math) 3: 377
Inuit (Indians) 2: 55, 186
invention strategies (comp.) 3: 39–46
inverse
elements (math) 1: 285; 2: 260
function(s) 1: 327; 2: 330, 350; 3: 475
matrices 2: 293

operation **1:** 327; **2:** 350; **3:** 413

relationship (econ.) **3:** 249

square law **2:** 253, 258–259

trigonometric functions **2:** 330; **3:** 424–426

invertebrate(s) 1: 363; **3:** 499

investiture controversy 2: 93; **3:** 309

invitation, invite (usage) **2:** 382

invite, invitation (usage) **2:** 382

inward(s) (usage) **2:** 378

iodine 1: 372

ion(s) 1: 392; **2:** 227, 243; **3:** 501, 517

Ionesco, Eugene **2:** 405, 408

ionic

bond **2:** 232, 243; **3:** 505, 517

compound **3:** 505, 507, 517

crystals **3:** 510

ionosphere 1: 392, 403

Iowa 1: 142–143, 160; **2:** 46, 55

Iran 2: 126, 127, 140, 143, 166

2: *Atlas* 18

hostage crisis **1:** 132; **2:** 51, 122; **4:** 361

Iran-Contra affair **1:** 132; **2:** 51; **4:** 361

Iran-Iraq War **2:** 122

revolution **2:** 122

Iraq 1: 132; **2:** 122, 123, 124, 126, 127, 143, 166; **3:** 337, 343, 351, 352

2: *Atlas* 18

Iraq War 2: 53, 124

Ireland 1: 124; **2:** 119, 143, 156; **3:** 337

2: *Atlas* 14

Irish potato famine 2: 64

I, Robot **2:** 417

iron 1: 372

"Iron Chancellor" 2: 107

Iron Curtain 2: 123; **4:** 361

irony 4: 1387

Iroquois (Indians) **2:** 55

irrational number 1: 327; **2:** 350

irregardless (usage) **2:** 382; **3:** 116

irregular verbs (Eng.) **1:** 20–21

irrigation 1: 355

Irving, Washington **2:** 416

Islam 2: 91; **3:** 303, 304, 305, 313

Islamists 2: 125, 127

islands, largest **2:** 142

isobar 1: 401, 403

isolationism 4: 361

isometric exercise 1: 337

isosceles 1: 327; **2:** 309, 350

isotherm 1: 401

isotonic

exercise **1:** 337

solution **2:** 198

isotope(s) 1: 371, 383; **2:** 231, 243, 259; **3:** 501, 517, 532

of hydrogen **2:** 231

Israel 1: 131; **2:** 51, 81, 118, 122, 124, 143, 167; **3:** 337

2: *Atlas* 18

Israeli athletes **2:** 121

Israelis **2:** 121, 123

Isthmus of Panama 3: 529

Italian 2: 94, 97, 113, 123

city-states **3:** 310

state system **3:** 314

italics (Eng.) **1:** 55; **2:** 375; **3:** 94

Italy 1: 126, 127; **2:** 85, 87, 89, 90, 93, 97, 105, 106, 107, 108, 111, 112, 113, 114, 115, 116, 119, 143, 156; **3:** 295, 304, 307, 314, 315, 318, 325, 332, 333, 334, 335, 337

2: *Atlas* 14

Risorgimento **3:** 331

iterative method of differentiation 3: 399–400

I, the Jury **2:** 417

its, it's (usage) **2:** 382; **3:** 116

it's I, it's me (usage) **2:** 382

Ivanhoe **2:** 413, 416

Ivan the Great 2: 132

Ivan the Terrible 2: 100, 132

Ives, Charles **1:** 464

Iwo Jima 1: 127

-ize (usage) **2:** 382

J

Jack, or The Submission
2: 408
Jackson, Andrew
1: 114, 116, 117;
2: 34–35, 37, 39, 62;
4: 154–156
Jackson, Jesse **2:** 70
Jackson, Mahalia **2:** 69
Jacksonian Era
4: 153–156
jai alai 1: 454
Jamaica 2: 66, 143, 178
2: *Atlas* 5
James I (Eng.) **3:** 322, 326
James II (Eng.) **3:** 327
James VI (Scot.) **3:** 326
James, Henry **2:** 415, 416,
417, 420–421;
4: 1379, 1381
James, William **3:** 357
James-Lange theory
3: 366
Jamestown 1: 107; **2:** 56,
60
Jane Eyre 2: 414, 418, 429
Japan 1: 125, 126, 127,
388; **2:** 45, 84, 94,
108, 109, 112, 113,
114, 115, 116, 140,
143, 147; **3:** 335
2: *Atlas* 20
Japanese 2: 109, 115, 116,
117
Japanese-Americans
2: 72–73
relocation camps **1:** 127
Jay, John **1:** 112, 113;
2: 33, 62
Jay Treaty **1:** 113; **4:** 361
jazz 1: 465
Jazz Age 4: 256–257, 361
Jazz Singer, The 1: 126,
471
Jefferson, Thomas **1:** 114;
2: 30–31, 61, 62, 134;
4: 79, 124
Jennie Gerhardt 2: 419
Jensen, Arthur **3:** 363
Jericho 2: 124
Jerusalem 2: 395, 400
Jerusalem 2: 81, 84, 88,
89, 94; **3:** 313
Jesuits 3: 321
Jesus Christ 2: 88, 89,
129; **3:** 301, 304, 308
jet aircraft 1: 425

jet streams 1: 395, 403
jettison 1: 425
Jew of Malta, The 2: 408
Jew(s) 2: 88, 89, 113;
3: 334, 337
sacred books **3:** 308
jihad (holy war) **2:** 125,
127
Jim Crow laws 2: 68
Joan of Arc 2: 95, 132;
3: 308
job
classifications
3: 676–681
loss **3:** 670
search **3:** 657–663
success **3:** 665–668
John Bull's Other Island
2: 409
John, Gospel of **3:** 308
John, King (Eng.) **2:** 94;
3: 309
John of Burgundy (Fr.)
3: 308
Johnson, Andrew **1:** 121;
2: 38–39, 41, 62;
4: 178, 182, 184–185
Johnson, James Weldon
2: 69
Johnson, Lyndon B.
(Baines) **1:** 129, 130;
2: 48–49, 62, 70, 120;
4: 79, 313–314,
318–319
Johnson, Samuel **2:** 133,
309, 390, 417; **3:** 36,
101
John Paul II (pope)
2: 122, 136
John the Baptist 2: 88
John XXIII (pope) **2:** 135
joint 1: 403
Joliot-Curie, Irène and
Frédéric **2:** 240
Joliot-Curie experiment
2: 241
Jolliet, Louis **1:** 108, 109
Jolson, Al **1:** 126, 471
Jonathan Wild 2: 416, 420
Jones, John Paul **1:** 112;
2: 62
Jonson, Ben **2:** 404, 406,
408; **3:** 79
Joplin, Scott **2:** 69
Jordan 2: 121, 143, 167
2: *Atlas* 18
Joseph and His Brothers
2: 422

Joseph Andrews 2: 420
joule 2: 246
**Journal of the Plague
Year 2:** 419
Jovian planets 1: 425
Joyce, James **2:** 415, 421,
435; **4:** 1379, 1381
Judaea 2: 86
Judah, Kingdom of **2:** 81
Judaism 3: 296
Judea 2: 88
Judeo-Christian
tradition **3:** 304
Jude the Obscure 2: 420
judicial, judicious (usage)
2: 382
judicial branch 2: 4, 11,
12, 20–21; **3:** 347,
348, 349; **4:** 528–534
judicial review 2: 12;
3: 347, 348; **4:** 569
judicious, judicial (usage)
2: 382
Julian 3: 302
Julian calendar 2: 100
Julius Caesar 2: 411, 429
Julius Caesar 2: 87, 128;
3: 295, 300
Jung, C. G. **3:** 367
Jungle, The 1: 123
Jungle Book, The 2: 398
Juno and the Paycock
2: 406, 409
Jupiter 1: 406–407, 418;
3: 325
Jurassic Period 3: 529
Juster, Norton **1:** 98
justice 3: 355
Justice, Department of
2: 11
Justin I 2: 130
Justinian I 2: 90, 130;
3: 304, 305, 341
Code **2:** 90

K

"Kaddish" **2:** 397
Kadesh, Battle of **2:** 90
Kafka, Franz **2:** 415, 421; **4:** 1379
Kaiser Wilhelm I 3: 329–330, 332–333
kamikaze 2: 94
Kansas 1: 119, 142–143, 161; **2:** 55
Kansas-Nebraska Act of 1854 1: 119; **2:** 39; **4:** 362
Kant, Immanuel **2:** 134
Karzai, Hamid **2:** 126
Kashmir 2: 127
Kazakhstan 2: 143, 147 **2:** *Atlas* 16
KDKA Pittsburgh 1: 125; **2:** 112
Keats, John **2:** 391, 393, 398, 399; **4:** 1379
Keene, Carolyn **1:** 98
Kelly, Regina Z. **1:** 103
Kelly, William **1:** 118
Kelvin-Planck statement 3: 539
Kelvin temperature scale 2: 250, 259
Kennedy (Onassis), Jacqueline Bouvier **2:** 48
Kennedy, John F. (Fitzgerald) **1:** 129, 130; **2:** 48–49, 51, 62, 70, 119, 136; **3:** 101; **4:** 77, 78, 312–313, 315, 317–318
Kennedy, Robert **1:** 130; **4:** 315
Kent State University, Ohio **1:** 130
Kentucky 1: 114, 116, 146–147, 161; **2:** 38, 55
Kenya 2: 125, 143, 167 **2:** *Atlas* 12–13
Kenyatta, Jomo **2:** 135
Kepler, Johannes **3:** 326 Kepler's law of equal areas **1:** 425
Kerwin, Joseph P. **1:** 421
ketone 2: 238, 243
kettle holes 1: 390, 403
keyboard instruments 1: 460
Key, Francis Scott **1:** 114

Keynes, John Maynard **3:** 268, 287
key signature 1: 462, 466
Khan, Abdel Qadeer **2:** 127
Khomeini, Ayatollah **2:** 122, 125; **3:** 342
Khrushchev, Nikita **2:** 118, 119
Khufu (Cheops) **2:** 79
kidneys 3: 493
kilocalorie 2: 246
kilogram 2: 245 kilogram-meter **2:** 246 kilogram-meter/second **2:** 246
kilowatt 2: 246 kilowatt-hour **2:** 246
kind of, sort of (usage) **2:** 382
kinesthetic sense 3: 359
kinetic energy **1:** 374; **2:** 247, **3:** 501, 537, 539, 549 theory of chemical reactions **3:** 514 theory of gases **3:** 509, 538
Kinetoscope 1: 471
kinetosome(s) 2: 195, 196
Kingdom of Judah 2: 81
Kingdom of the Two Sicilies 2: 107; **3:** 331
kingdoms (biol.) **2:** 210; **3:** 487
King Henry VI Part I **2:** 410, 411
King Henry VI Part II **2:** 410, 411
King Henry VI Part III **2:** 410, 411
King John **2:** 411
King Lear **2:** 406, 410, 411, 429
King, Martin Luther, Jr. **1:** 129, 130; **2:** 69–70, 136; **3:** 59, 342
King's Mountain, North Carolina **1:** 112
Kipling, Rudyard **1:** 100; **2:** 393, 398
Kiribati 2: 143, 147 **2:** *Atlas* 22
kitchen and laundry safety 1: 344
kite 1: 327; **2:** 316, 350

Kitty Hawk, North Carolina **1:** 123; **2:** 109
knight(s) 3: 324, 341
Knight, Eric **1:** 98
Knights of Labor 1: 121, 122; **4:** 362
Knossos 2: 80
Know-Nothing Party 4: 362
Kohlberg, Lawrence **3:** 362
Komarov, Vladimir **1:** 420
Konigsburg, E. L. **1:** 98
Koran 3: 304, 305
Korea *see also* North Korea; South Korea **2:** 84, 90, 94, 96, 109 Korean-Americans **2:** 73 Korean War **1:** 128; **2:** 49, 71, 73, 75, 117, 118; **4:** 362 **2:** *Atlas* 20
Kosciusko 2: 61
Krapp's Last Tape **2:** 407
Krebs cycle 2: 200; **3:** 483
Krementz, Jill **1:** 103
Kublai Khan 2: 92, 94, 96, 131; **3:** 311
"Kubla Khan" **2:** 396, 400
Ku Klux Klan 1: 124; **4:** 362
Kurds 2: 127
Kuwait 1: 132; **2:** 53, 123, 126, 143, 167; **3:** 351, 352 **2:** *Atlas* 18
Kyrgyzstan 2: 143, 147 **2:** *Atlas* 19

L

"La Belle Dame sans
    Merci" 2: 391, 398
labor
    labor (econ.) 3: 253, 262
    legislation 2: 105
    unions 1: 124, 128;
        4: 205–206, 362
Labor, Department of
    2: 11, 45
laboratory experiments
    (biol.) 4: 798–812
Labrador 1: 107
lab report format 2: 233
Lackland, John
    3: 307–308
Lady Chatterley's Lover
    2: 421
Lafayette 2: 61
La Fontaine, Jean de
    1: 101
Lagrange point 1: 425
La Guardia, Fiorello 2: 64
laissez-faire economy
    3: 254, 293
"Lake Isle of Innisfree,
    The" 2: 403
Lakes, Great
    Erie 1: 114, 134, 143
    Huron 1: 134, 143
    Michigan 1: 134, 143
    Ontario 1: 134, 143
    Superior 1: 134, 143
lakes *see also* individual lake
        names 2: 141
    largest 2: 141
L'Allegro 2: 398
Lam, Wilfredo 2: 74
land (econ.) 3: 253
landforms 3: 520
    U.S. 1: 135
Land Ordinance 1: 113
language 3: 365, 371
    of poetry 1: 93
lanthanides 3: 504
Laos 2: 143, 147
    2: *Atlas* 21
Lao-tze 2: 84
L'Apres midi d'un faune
    ("Afternoon of a
    Faun") 2: 398
largo 1: 466
larynx 3: 493
La Salle, Robert de 1: 109
laser 2: 253
*Last of the Mohicans,
    The* 2: 430

Last Tycoon, The
    2: 420
late adulthood 3: 362
Latin abbreviations
    (Eng.) 3: 94
Latin American 1: 129
Latin-English dictionary
    3: 231–244
LATIN GRAMMAR
    3: 217–244
latitude 2: 188
latter, former (usage)
    2: 381
Latvia 2: 143, 156
    2: *Atlas* 15
laughtrack 1: 477
launch vehicle 1: 425
Laurasia 1: 384–385;
    3: 523
lava 1: 388, 403; 3: 524
La Vita Nuovo 2: 396
law (math)
    of exponents 1: 322
    of probability 2: 256
law (science) 1: 383
    of conservation of energy
        3: 501
    of conservation of mass
        3: 501
    of machines 1: 376
    of motion and
        gravitation 2: 102
    of reflection 3: 544
Law Code 2: 80
law making process 2: 9;
    4: 510–511
Lawrence, David Herbert
    2: 415, 416, 421;
    4: 1381
Lawson, Robert 1: 98
lay, lie (usage) 2: 383;
    3: 89, 116
Lazarillo de Tormes
    2: 416
lead 1: 372
League of Nations
    1: 124; 2: 45, 47,
    112, 117; 3: 333, 352;
    4: 362–363
Lear, Edward 1: 101
learn, teach (usage)
    2: 382
learning 3: 363, 364,
    371
    labs 3: 577–578
least common
    denominator (LCD)
    1: 233, 327; 2: 350

least common multiple
    (LCM) 1: 232–233,
    327; 2: 350
Leatherstocking Tales
    2: 416, 419, 430
leave, let (usage) 2: 382
leaves 3: 489
Leaves of Grass 2: 393,
    402
Lebanon 2: 125, 143, 167
    2: *Atlas* 18
"Le Bateau Iure" ("The
    Drunken Boat")
    2: 400
*Le Bourgeois
    Gentilhomme (The
    Would-be Gentleman)*
    2: 408
Le Châtelier's principle
    3: 514
Le Cid 2: 406, 408
Lee, Robert E. 1: 119, 120;
    2: 64, 134
*Left Hand of Darkness,
    The* 2: 417
legal/rational authority
    3: 342
legends 2: 189
legislative branch 2: 4, 7,
    11, 15–19; 3: 347,
    349; 4: 505–512
legislative oversight 2: 11
legitimacy (pol. sci.)
    3: 342, 355
Legnano, Battle of (1176)
    3: 310, 314
LeGuin, Ursula 1: 98;
    2: 417
Leibniz, Gottfried Wilhelm
    2: 133; 3: 372
Leipzig 2: 105
leitmotifs 3: 329
Le Misanthrope 2: 408
lend, borrow (usage)
    2: 378
Lend-Lease Act 1: 126;
    4: 363
L'Engle, Madeleine 1:
    98
length formulas 1: 320
lengths of curves 3: 451
Lenin, Vladimir Ilyich
    2: 111, 135; 3: 329,
    333, 345
lens 1: 381, 383; 2: 252;
    3: 359
Leo I (pope) 3: 302
Leo III (pope) 3: 305, 309

Leonardo da Vinci 2: 97, 132

Leonov, Alexei **1:** 420

Lepidus 2: 87

leptons 2: 256; **3:** 546

Les Illuminations **2:** 400

Lesotho 2: 143, 167
  2: *Atlas* 13

less, fewer (usage) **2:** 377

less, lesser (usage) **2:** 383

Lesson, The **2:** 408

let, leave (usage) **2:** 382

let's us (usage) **2:** 383

**"Letter from
  Birmingham Jail"
  3:** 59

letters of credit 3: 311

Letters of John 3: 308

Letters of Paul 3: 308

Letters of Peter 3: 308

letter writing (Ger.) **3:** 162

Leucippus 2: 228

leucoplasts 2: 196

levée en masse **3:** 341

lever(s) 1: 376–377
  formulas **2:** 268

Levinson, Daniel **3:** 361

**Lewis and Clark
  Expedition 2:** 31;
  4: 363

Lewis, C. S. **1:** 98

Lewis diagram(s) 3: 505, 506, 517

Lewis, Matthew **2:** 417

Lewis, Meriwether **1:** 114

Lewis, Sinclair **2:** 425

**L' Hôpital's rule
  3:** 406–407

Libation Bearers, The
  2: 407

liberal 4: 569

liberalism 3: 325, 344, 345, 346, 355

Liberator, The **1:** 116

Liberia 1: 115; **2:** 143, 168
  2: *Atlas* 12

Libertarians 3: 349

liberty 3: 355

*Liberty Leading the
  People* **3:** 329

Liberty Party 1: 117

library, kinds of **2:** 355
  using **2:** 355–360;
  3: 104–107

Library of Congress 2: 11
  classification system
  2: 358

libration 1: 425

Libya 2: 115, 127, 140, 143, 168
  2: *Atlas* 12

lichen(s) 1: 363; **2:** 216

lie, lay (usage) **2:** 383;
  3: 89, 116

Liechtenstein 2: 143, 156
  2: *Atlas* 14

liege-lord 3: 341

*Life and Opinions of
  Tristram Shandy,
  The* **2:** 423

*Life and Times of
  Frederick Douglass*
  2: 67

**life cycle of a star
  1:** 413–414

life forms 3: 527–528

Life Is a Dream **2:** 407

Life of Samuel Johnson
  2: 389

**LIFE SCIENCE
  1:** 354–363

"Ligeia" 1: 93; **2:** 422

light
  and wave optics
  3: 543–544
  bulb **1:** 121; **2:** 108
  -dependent reactions
  3: 484
  energy **1:** 381
  -independent reactions
  3: 484
  ray **3:** 544
  spectrum **1:** 416–417
  speed **2:** 252
  -year **1:** 425

Light in August **2:** 420

lighting designer 1: 477

lightning rod 2: 103

like, as, as if (usage)
  2: 383; **3:** 116

like terms (math) **1:** 289, 298; **2:** 261

limbic system 3: 358, 371

limerick 2: 391

limit(s) 3: 372–385
  calculating **3:** 380–385
  comparison test **3:** 460
  defined **3:** 378
  involving infinity
  3: 383–385
  values **3:** 377

Lincoln, Abraham **1:** 119, 121; **2:** 38–39, 60, 62, 64, 67–68, 107, 134, 402; **4:** 166–167, 176–178, 181

**Lincoln-Douglas debates
  2:** 39

Lindbergh, Charles A.
  1: 126; **2:** 112

Lindgren, Astrid **1:** 98

linear
  bond **3:** 505, 506
  functions **3:** 373
  motion **3:** 534, 536, 549

line item veto 4: 569

**"Lines Composed Above
  Tintern Abbey"
  2:** 400, 402

lines of force (field lines)
  3: 541

line spectra 3: 502, 517

linking ideas (comp.)
  3: 61

linking verbs (Eng.) **1:** 50

Linnaeus Carolus (Carl
  von Linné) **2:** 103, 133, 210; **3:** 487

lipids 2: 192; **3:** 478, 479, 499

Li Po 2: 130

liquid(s) 2: 227; **3:** 510, 511

liquid, concepts of
  3: 500–501

liquid, fire safety **1:** 345

Liszt, Franz **1:** 464

literal equations 2: 268

literally, figuratively
  (usage) **2:** 383

literary
  approaches **2:** 389
  forms **2:** 388–389
  genres **3:** 69–71

literature, elements of
  3: 72–75

LITERATURE (Eng.)
  2: 388–435

lithification 3: 532

lithium 1: 372

lithosphere 3: 518, 521, 532
  lithospheric plates **3:** 521

Lithuania 2: 143, 156
  2: *Atlas* 15

litotes 3: 380; **4:** 1242

Little Big Horn, battle of
  1: 121

Little Rock, Arkansas
  2: 69

liturgy 3: 341

Livingstone, David **3:** 332

Liwei, Yang **1:** 423

Lloyd, Alexander **1:** 96

loan (usage) **3:** 116
lobby 3: 349; **4:** 569
local (math)
    maximum **3:** 404, 475
    minimum **3:** 404, 475
local governments 2: 5;
    3: 347
localism 3: 306
location 1: 477
Locke, John **2:** 102, 133;
    3: 344, 356; **4:** 1383
Lockerbie, Scotland
    1: 132
Lofting, Hugh **1:** 98
logarithmic functions
    3: 373
logic (comp.) **3:** 56–60
logical errors (comp.)
    3: 60
Loire River 3: 306
Lombards 2: 91; **3:** 303,
    306
London 3: 311
London forces 3: 506
London, Jack **1:** 98; **2:** 416
Lone Star Republic
    1: 117
longbow 3: 324
Long Day's Journey into
    Night **2:** 409, 430
Longfellow, Henry
    Wadsworth **2:** 390,
    393, 398
long fiction, kinds of
    2: 416
longitude 2: 188
longitudinal wave(s)
    1: 380, 383; **2:** 251,
    259; **3:** 539, 549
long/short run 3: 260
long-term memory
    3: 363
Look Homeward, Angel
    2: 423, 430
looping (comp) **3:** 39, 42
loose, lose (usage) **2:** 383;
    3: 116
Lopez, Nancy **2:** 74
Lord Jim **2:** 419, 430
Lord of the Ring, The
    2: 430
Lorraine 2: 93
Los Angeles earthquake
    1994 1: 133
lose, loose (usage) **2:** 383;
    3: 116
Lost Worlds of 2001, The
    2: 417

Louis I (the Pious) **2:** 92;
    3: 306
Louis VII (Fr.) **3:** 313
Louis XII (Fr.) (Valois)
    3: 321
Louis XIV (Fr.) **1:** 109;
    2: 102, 103, 104, 133;
    3: 314, 327
Louis XV (Fr.) **2:** 103;
    3: 327
Louis XVI (Fr.) **2:** 104;
    3: 327
Louis, Joe **2:** 69
Louisiana 1: 109, 114,
    119, 146–147, 161;
    2: 68
    Purchase **1:** 114, 115,
    116; **2:** 33; **4:** 143
    Territory **1:** 114
Lousma, Jack R. **1:** 421
lousy, lovely (usage)
    2: 383
lovely, lousy (usage)
    2: 383
Love's Labours Lost
    2: 411
"Love Song of J. Alfred
    Prufrock, The"
    2: 391, 396
low (weather) **1:** 399, 403
Low Countries 3: 310
low frequency 2: 252
Lowry, Thomas **3:** 512
Loyola, Ignatius of **2:** 132;
    3: 321
Lucca 3: 310–311
Lucretius 2: 128
Lue Gim Gong 2: 72
Luke, Gospel of **3:** 308
luminosity 1: 412
lunar module 1: 425
Lunar Orbiter probes
    1: 418
Luna series 1: 418
Lusitania **1:** 124; **2:** 111;
    4: 363–364
Lutheran Church 2: 99;
    3: 319–321
Lutheranism 2: 100
Luther, Martin **2:** 99, 132;
    3: 314, 317, 319, 320,
    323, 324
Luxembourg 2: 111, 114,
    119, 143, 156; **3:** 337
    2: *Atlas* 14
Lyceum 3: 299
Lycidas **2:** 391, 398
Lydia 2: 83

lymphatic system, human
    3: 495
lymphogranuloma
    venereum 1: 352
Lyrical Ballads **2:** 396,
    402
lyric poetry 2: 390; **3:** 79
Lysistrata **3:** 297
lysosomes 2: 194, 195;
    3: 481, 482

M

Maastricht Treaty 3: 337
MacArthur, Douglas
  2: 116, 118; **4:** 283
Macau 2: 186
  2: *Atlas* 17
Macauley, David **1:** 103
Macbeth **2:** 100, 404, 406,
  410, 411, 430
Maccabees 2: 86
Maccabeus, Judas **2:** 86,
  128
Macedonia 2: 85, 143, 156
  2: *Atlas* 15
Machiavelli, Niccoló
  2: 97, 132; **3:** 316,
  343; **4:** 1383
machines 1: 376–377
MacLeish, Archibald
  2: 391
macroeconomics 3: 247,
  268–286, 293
macromolecule(s)
  3: 478–479, 499
  major types of **3:** 479
Madagascar 2: 143, 168
  2: *Atlas* 13
Madame Bovary **2:** 415,
  420
Madison, Dolley **2:** 32
Madison, James **1:** 113,
  114; **2:** 32–33, 62
Magellan, Ferdinand
  2: 98
Magellanic Clouds 1: 411
Magellan probe 1: 418,
  419
Magic Mountain, The
  2: 422
magma 1: 389, 403;
  3: 519, 521, 522, 524,
  532
Magna Carta 2: 94, 131;
  3: 305, 308
magnesium 1: 373
magnetic
  field **1:** 378–379, 383;
  3: 542, 549
  poles (North and South)
  3: 542
magnets 1: 378–379;
  3: 542
magnitude 1: 412,
  425–426
Magyars 2: 92–93
Maid of Orléans (Joan of
  Arc) **2:** 95, 132; **3:** 308

Mailer, Norman **2:** 415,
  421–422; **4:** 1383
Maine 1: 116, 117,
  150–151, 162
Maine (U.S.S.) **1:** 123;
  2: 43
Makers of World History
  2: 128–137
makeup 1: 477
maladaptive behavior
  3: 366
Malawi 2: 143, 168
  2: *Atlas* 13
Malaysia 2: 143, 147
  2: *Atlas* 17
Malcom X 2: 70
Maldives 2: 143, 147
  2: *Atlas* 19
Mali 2: 143, 168
  2: *Atlas* 12
Mallarmé, Stephane
  2: 393, 398
Malory, Sir Thomas
  1: 101
Malta 2: 143, 156
  2: *Atlas* 14
Maltese Falcon, The
  2: 417
mammal 1: 363
  class **2:** 223
Manassas Junction 1: 120
Manchuria 2: 90, 109,
  113; **3:** 335
mandates 4: 569
Mandela, Nelson **2:** 123,
  136
manganese 1: 373
Manhattan Island 1: 108;
  2: 101
Manhattan Project
  2: 113; **4:** 364
Manicheism 2: 83
manifest destiny
  4: 159–168, 190–198,
  217, 364
Manila 1: 127
manned space flights
  1: 420–423; **2:** 49
Mann, Thomas **2:** 415,
  422
manorialism 3: 306
Mansfield Park **2:** 418
mantissa (math) **1:** 283;
  2: 347
mantle 1: 387, 403;
  3: 518, 533
Mao Tse-tung 2: 117, 121
map projection 2: 188

maps *see also* specific
  locations
  Atlas following **2:** 188
Marathon 2: 84
Marbury v. Madison
  1: 114; **2:** 12; **4:** 142,
  364, 456–457, 569
Marc Antony 2: 87, 129
March on Washington
  2: 70; **4:** 364
Marconi, Guglielmo
  2: 112
Marco Polo *see* Polo,
  Marco
Marcos, Ferdinand
  2: 123
Marcus Aurelius
  2: 129; **3:** 301, 302,
  303
Mardi **2:** 422
Marduk 3: 296
mare 1: 426
marginal
  cost **3:** 262–263, 293
  product **3:** 262, 293
  revenue **3:** 264, 293
  utility **3:** 257, 293
maria 1: 409
"Mariana" 2: 401
Mariana Islands 3: 522
Maria Theresa 2: 134
Marie Antoinette 2: 104,
  134; **3:** 327
marine invertebrates
  3: 527
Mariner space missions
  1: 406
Mariner series **1:** 418,
  419
maritime air masses
  1: 398
market (econ.) **3:** 253–254
market
  demand **3:** 265
  equilibrium **3:** 265
  supply **3:** 265
Mark, Gospel of **3:** 308
Marlowe, Christopher
  2: 100, 404, 408, 427
Marquess of Queensbury
  rules 1: 451
Marquette, Father Jacques
  1: 108, 109
Márquez, Gabriel Garcia
  2: 136
marriage 3: 361
Marriage of Figaro, The
  1: 464

Mars 1: 404, 405, 406, 418, 419
  probes **1:** 418, 419
  rovers **1:** 418
Marshall Islands 1: 127; **2:** 143, 147
  2: *Atlas* 22
Marshall, John **1:** 114
Marshall Plan 1: 128; **2:** 49, 117; **4:** 292, 364
marsupials 3: 528
Martel, Charles *See* Charles Martel
martial arts 1: 451
Martin Chuzzlewit **2:** 414
Martin V (pope) **2:** 96
Martinez, Manuel **2:** 74
Martinique 2: 186
  2: *Atlas* 5
Marvell, Andrew **2:** 392, 398
marvelous (usage) **2:** 383
Marx, Karl **2:** 107, 134; **3:** 287, 328–329, 344, 345
  Marxist-Leninism **3:** 333
  Marxist socialism **2:** 107
Mary Stuart **2:** 409
Mary Stuart (Queen of Scotland) **3:** 321–322
Maryland 1: 108, 148–149, 162; **2:** 60
Maryland Toleration Act 1: 108
Masaccio 3: 315
Maslow, Abraham **3:** 357, 366, 367
  Maslow's hierachy of needs **3:** 366
mass (rel.) **1:** 466
mass (science) **1:** 368, 383; **2:** 226, 244–245, 255, 259; **3:** 535, 536, 549
  increase with motion **3:** 545
  number **1:** 371, 383; **3:** 501
  wasting **3:** 526, 533
Massachusetts 1: 107, 108, 111, 116, 150–151, 162; **2:** 46, 49, 52, 55, 60, 70, 102
Massachusetts Bay Colony 1: 108; **2:** 60
"Massachusetts to Virginia" 2: 402

mass media 4: 499–502
mass production 2: 109
masterpieces of literature, plots **2:** 424–435
Masters, Edgar Lee **2:** 393, 398
mastigophora 2: 214
Matamoras, Mexico **1:** 117
MATHEMATICS 1: 176–329; **2:** 260–351
mathematics 1: 129; **3:** 295
  and engineering **3:** 581
  symbols **1:** 319
  textbook, how to read **2:** 264–265
matrix, matrices 2: 288–294
  operations **3:** 434
matter 1: 368, 371, 383; **2:** 226; **3:** 500, 501, 509–511, 517
Matterhorn 1: 390
Matthew, Gospel of **3:** 308
"Maud" 2: 401
Maugham, W. Somerset **2:** 416
Mauna Loa, Hawaii **1:** 388
Maupassant, Guy de **2:** 416
Mauritania 2: 143, 168
  2: *Atlas* 12
Mauritius 2: 143, 169
Maximilian I 2: 132
may, can (usage) **2:** 378; **3:** 116
Mayan empire 2: 99
Mayflower **2:** 60, 102
Mayflower Compact 1: 107
may of, must of, might of (usage) **2:** 383
Mayor of Casterbridge, The **2:** 420
mayors of the palace 3: 341
Mazzini, Giuseppe **3:** 331
McAuliffe, Christa **1:** 132
McCarran-Walter Act 2: 73; **4:** 364
McCarthy, Joseph **1:** 128; **4:** 295–296
McCarthyism 1: 128; **4:** 296, 364

McClellan, General George B. **1:** 120
McCord, David **1:** 101
McCormick, Cyrus **1:** 117; **2:** 62
McCulloch v. Madison **1:** 115; **4:** 569
McHargue, Georgess **1:** 103
McHenry, Fort **1:** 114
McKinley, Mt. **1:** 135
McKinley, William **1:** 123; **2:** 42–43, 62; **4:** 219–222
McNeer, Mary **1:** 103
McWhirter, Norris and Ross **1:** 103
Mead, Margaret **4:** 1383
mean for (usage) **2:** 383
mean proportional 1: 327; **2:** 350
measles (rubeola) **1:** 352
measure 1: 461, 466
Measure for Measure **2:** 406, 411, 430
measurement (math) **1:** 279, 323, 324
measurement (physics) **1:** 366; **2:** 244
meat-packing 1: 123
Mecca 2: 91; **3:** 304
mechanical energy 1: 376; **3:** 537
mechanics (physics) **2:** 248; **3:** 534–537, 549
mechanics of music 1: 457
Medea **2:** 406, 408
Medes 2: 82
media (usage) **3:** 116
median (usage) **2:** 383
medical science 3: 295
Medicare (Act) **1:** 129; **4:** 364
Medicean planets 3: 326
Medici, Catherine de **2:** 132
Medici, Cosimo de **3:** 314, 316–317
Medici family 3: 315, 316, 317, 322
Medici, Lorenzo de **2:** 132
medicine shows 1: 470
Medieval Europe 3: 305–314
Medina 2: 91; **3:** 304

Mediterranean 2: 85, 105, 114; **3:** 295, 300, 305, 311, 315
Mediterranean Sea 2: 141, 152
medium 1: 380
of exchange **3:** 281
medium (usage) **2:** 383
medulla 3: 358
meiosis 1: 363; **2:** 204–205, 225; **3:** 485, 499
divisions **2:** 205
melodrama 1: 477
melody 1: 461
melting 3: 510
melting point(s) 1: 366, 368; **2:** 227, 243
Melville, Herman **2:** 413, 415, 416, 422, 431; **4:** 1381
member (math) **1:** 327; **2:** 350
membrane 2: 192, 195
memory 3: 363–364
Memphis (Egypt) **3:** 295
Memphis, Tennessee **1:** 120, 130
Mencius 2: 84
Mendel, Gregor **3:** 484
Mendelian genetics **2:** 206–207
Mendelian square **2:** 207
Mendeleev, Dmitri **2:** 234; **3:** 503
"Mending Wall" 2: 397
Menes, King (Egypt) **2:** 79
mental retardation 3: 371
mercantilism 3: 314; **4:** 105–106, 135, 364
Mercator, Gerardus **2:** 132, 188
Mercator projection **2:** 188
Merchant of Venice, The **2:** 411, 430–431
mercury 1: 373
Mercury 1: 405, 406
Mercury flights 1: 420, 423
meridians 2: 188, 189
meristem 3: 491, 499
meritocracy 3: 341
Merlin **2:** 400
Merovingians 2: 90; **3:** 306, 341
Merriam, Eve **1:** 101

Merry Wives of Windsor, The **2:** 411, 431
mesons 3: 546
mesophyll 3: 489
Mesopotamia 2: 81, 83; **3:** 294–296
modern Iraq **2:** 79, 80
Mesozoic Era 3: 527, 529
Messiah **1:** 464
messiah 3: 296, 341
metabolism 1: 363; **2:** 225; **3:** 483, 499
metabolic pathways **3:** 483, 499
metal(s) 2: 234, 243; **3:** 504, 517
metallic bonds **3:** 510
metallic crystals **3:** 510
metalloids **3:** 504
metamorphic rock 1: 389, 403; **3:** 519, 533
metamorphism 3: 519, 533
Metamorphoses **2:** 87, 399, 400
metamorphosis 1: 363
"Metamorphosis, The" 2: 421
metaphase 2: 203; **3:** 482, 483, 485
metaphor 1: 93; **3:** 80; **4:** 1242–1244
Metaphysics **3:** 312
meteor(s), meteorites, meteroids 1: 408, 426
shower **1:** 426
meter (music) **1:** 466
meter (poetry) **2:** 403
methodology, educational **3:** 313
metonymy 3: 80; **4:** 1244–1245
metric measurement (cgs/mks) system 2: 244–245
metric measurement system 1: 366
Metternich, Clemens von **2:** 105, 134
Meuse-Argonne 1: 124
Mexican-Americans 2: 74–76
Mexican War 1: 117; **2:** 36, 38, 40, 74; **4:** 160–163

Mexico 1: 117, 118, 124; **2:** 99, 140, 143, 178; **3:** 351, 524
2: *Atlas* 5
Mexico City **1:** 117, 388
Mexico and Central America 2: *Atlas* 5
Michelangelo 2: 97, 132; **3:** 315, 318
Michigan 1: 113, 114, 131, 142–143, 163; **2:** 55
Michigan, Lake **1:** 134, 143
microeconomics 3: 247, 255–267, 293
microfilaments 2: 196; **3:** 482
microfilm, microform, microfiche 2: 360
micron 2: 251
Micronesia 2: 143, 148 **2:** *Atlas* 22
microtubules 2: 196
microwaves 2: 251, 259
Mid-Atlantic Ridge 3: 522
midbrain 3: 358
Middle Ages 1: 469; **2:** 89, 90–96, 129; **3:** 305, 307, 310, 315, 324, 325, 343
Middle East 3: 296, 299, 302, 304, 313, 314, 337
and Africa **2:** 160–173
and U.S. affairs **4:** 331–332, 335, 340–341
2: *Atlas* 18
Middle Passage 4: 364
Middlemarch **2:** 415, 419; **3:** 50
"Midnight Ride of Paul Revere, The" 2: 390
mid-ocean ridge(s) 1: 386; **3:** 520, 521, 533
Midsummer Night's Dream, A **2:** 411, 431
Midway, Battle of **1:** 127
Midway Islands 1: 153
Midwest (U.S.) **1:** 142–145
map **1:** 143
might-makes-right doctrine 3: 343

might of, may of, must of (usage) **2:** 383
mighty (usage) **2:** 383
migration, urban **3:** 328
Milan 2: 103; **3:** 315, 316, 321
  Edict of **2:** 89; **3:** 302
mildews 3: 487
militarists 2: 113
Milky Way 1: 411, 426
Mill, John Stuart **4:** 1382
Millay, Edna St. Vincent **4:** 1380
Miller, Arthur **2:** 405, 408, 426; **4:** 1381
milligram 2: 245
millimicron 2: 251
Mill on the Floss, The **2:** 419; **3:** 50
Milne, A. A. **1:** 98, 101
Milosevic, Slobodan **3:** 337
Milton **2:** 395
Milton, John **2:** 133, 391, 392, 398, 399, 432; **3:** 315
"Mimus" (theater) **1:** 468, 469
mineral(s) 1: 352, 389, 403; **3:** 519, 530, 533
  resources **3:** 530
Ming dynasty 2: 96
Mingus, Charlie **1:** 465
Minh, Ho Chi **2:** 135
miniaturization 2: 118
"Miniver Cheevy" 2: 400
Minnesota 1: 144–145, 163; **2:** 55
Minoans 2: 79, 80
minor planets 1: 408
minstrel shows 1: 470
minuend 1: 191, 327; **2:** 350
Minuit, Peter **1:** 108
Miocene Epoch 3: 529
Mir (space station) **1:** 421, 423
miracle plays 1: 469; **2:** 404
Miranda v. Arizona **4:** 569
Mirandola, Giovanni Pico della **3:** 317
Missi Dominici **3:** 306
Mississippi 1: 119, 120, 148–149, 163; **2:** 55, 67

River **1:** 109, 113, 120, 133, 134
  valley **1:** 113; **2:** 101
Missouri 1: 116, 144–145, 164; **2:** 48, 49, 55
  River **1:** 133, 134
Missouri Compromise 1: 116, 119; **2:** 33; **4:** 76, 147, 163, 365
Mithraism 2: 83
mitochondria 2: 194, 195, 213, 225; **3:** 481, 482, 483
mitosis 1: 363; **2:** 203, 225; **3:** 482, 485, 499
  phases **2:** 203
mixed
  economy **3:** 254
  meter **2:** 403
  number **1:** 327
mixture 1: 369, 383; **2:** 226, 243; **3:** 500, 517
MLA style for bibliography 2: 370–371
MMPI inventory (psych.) **3:** 367
Moby-Dick **2:** 413, 415, 421, 422, 431; **3:** 75
modals (Eng.) **1:** 24
model 3: 293
Model T 2: 109; **4:** 365
moderate (pol. sci.) **4:** 569
moderato 1: 467
Modern Europe 3: 325–337
Modern Language Association (MLA) bibliography style 2: 370–371
modern
  period (music) **1:** 456, 464
  periodic table **3:** 503–504
  physics **2:** 255–257; **3:** 534, 545–546
  poetry **2:** 393
modifier (usage) **2:** 383
modifiers (Eng.) **1:** 26–31, 50; **3:** 97–98
  see also adjectives; adverbs
modulation 1: 467
Mohammed, Khalid Shaikh **2:** 127
Mohican (Indians) **2:** 55

Moho 3: 518, 525, 533
molality 3: 511
molarity 3: 511
molar mass 3: 508
Molasses Act 1: 109; **4:** 365
Moldova 2: 143, 157
  2: *Atlas* 15
molds 2: 216
mole 3: 508, 511, 517
  fraction **3:** 511
molecular
  crystals **3:** 510
  formula(s) **3:** 507, 517
  genetics **4:** 683–695
  geometry **3:** 505, 517
  weight **3:** 508, 517
molecule(s) 2: 227, 243; **3:** 478, 499, 501, 517
Molière 2: 133, 404, 405, 406, 408–409; **4:** 1378
Moll Flanders **2:** 416, 419
mollusks 2: 221
moment of inertia 3: 536, 537, 549
momentum 2: 246, 247, 248, 249, 259; **3:** 536, 549
Monaco 2: 143, 157
  2: *Atlas* 14
monarchy 3: 343, 345, 355
Monera (kingdom) **2:** 192, 210, 213, 225; **3:** 487
monetary policy 3: 281, 293
Mongolia 2: 90, 96, 140, 143, 148
  2: *Atlas* 17
Mongol(s) 2: 91, 92, 94; **3:** 305
  invasions **2:** 100
  Tatars **2:** 100
Monk, The **2:** 417
Monk, Thelonius **1:** 465
monoatomic
  anion compound **3:** 507
  cation compound **3:** 507
monochromatic light 3: 544
monocotyledons (monocots) **2:** 219, 225; **3:** 489, 499
monologue 4: 1387
monomers 3: 478, 499
monomial 1: 327; **2:** 272, 350

monophonic 1: 467
monopoly 1: 22;
    3: 266–267, 293
    monopolistic
      competition
      3: 266–267, 293
monosaccharides
    3: 478–479
monotheism 3: 296, 301,
    341
monotonic sequence
    3: 456
Monroe, H. H. *see* Saki
Monroe, James **1:** 115,
    116; **2:** 32–33, 62
    Monroe Doctrine
      1: 116; **2:** 33; **4:** 151,
      365
monsoon 1: 395, 403
Montaigne, Michel
    Eyquem de **2:** 97,
    389; **3:** 315, 316, 317
Montalban, Ricardo **2:** 74
Montana 1: 138–139, 164;
    2: 74
Montcalm, Louis Joseph
    de **1:** 109
Monte Cassino 2: 90
Monterrey, Mexico **1:** 117
Montesquieu 2: 104
Montezuma 2: 132
Montgomery, Alabama
    1: 119, 129; **2:** 69
Montoya, Carlos **2:** 74
Montoya, Joseph **2:** 74
Montpellier (France)
    3: 311
Mont St. Michel 3: 341
Montserrat 2: 187
    2: *Atlas* 5
mood disorders 3: 367
moon 1: 409, 418, 419
    landing **1:** 130; **2:** 118,
    137
    probes **1:** 418, 419
Moon for the
    Misbegotten, A
    2: 409
moraine 1: 390, 403
moral, morale (usage)
    2: 383
moral development
    3: 362
morale, moral (usage)
    2: 383
morality plays 1: 469
More, Sir Thomas **2:** 97,
    132, 417; **4:** 1382

Moreno, Rita **2:** 74
Morgan, J. Pierpont **1:** 123
Morita, Akio **2:** 136
Mormons 1: 118
Morocco 2: 127, 143, 169;
    3: 332
    2: *Atlas* 12
morphogenesis 3: 496
morphology 1: 363
Morrill (Land Grant) Act
    1: 119; **4:** 365
Morrison, Toni **4:** 1381
Morse, Samuel F. B.
    1: 117; **2:** 62
Morton, John **2:** 61
Mosaic Law 3: 302
Moscow 2: 100, 115
Moseley, Henry **3:** 503
Moses 2: 80; **3:** 295, 296,
    304
moss 2: 217
most, almost (usage)
    2: 377
must of, might of, may
    of (usage) **2:** 383
Mother Courage **2:** 407
Mother Teresa of
    Calcutta 2: 136
"Mother to Son"
    2: 398
motif 4: 1387
motion 3: 534
    Newton's laws of
      2: 248–249, 255, 259;
      3: 535–536, 549
motivation 3: 366, 371
motorized tanks 2: 110
motor neurons 3: 496
mountains, highest **2:** 142
Mount St. Helens,
    Washington **1:** 132,
    388; **2:** 142; **3:** 524
Mourning Becomes
    Electra **2:** 409
mouth-to-mouth
    resuscitation 1: 348
movable type 2: 92, 96
movies 1: 471–472, 474
"Mower Against the
    Garden, The" 2: 398
Mozambique 2: 143, 169
    2: *Atlas* 13
Mozart, Wolfgang
    Amadeus **1:** 464;
    2: 134
"Mr. Flood's Party"
    2: 400
Mrs. Dalloway **2:** 423

Mrs. Warren's Profession
    2: 409
Mt. Hood, Washington
    1: 388
Mt. McKinley 1: 135
Mt. Rainier, Washington
    1: 388
Mt. Sinai 2: 80
Much Ado About Nothing
    2: 406, 411, 431
muckrakers 4: 365
Mugabe, Robert **2:** 124
Muhammad 2: 91, 130;
    3: 304
Muhammad, Elijah **2:** 69
multicellular
    organization 2: 208
multilinear theory of
    change 3: 346
multiple (math) **1:** 327;
    2: 350
multiple personalities
    3: 367
multiple stars 1: 414
multiplication 1:
    209–219, 261, 315,
    318, 327; **2:** 266
    facts **1:** 210, 213, 318
multiplicative
    identity element **1:** 327;
    2: 350
    inverse **1:** 327; **2:** 350
multiplier 1: 209, 327
multiplier effect (econ.)
    3: 280
mumps 1: 339, 352
Munich Olympics
    massacre 2: 121
Munich Pact 2: 113
muons 2: 256; **3:** 546
Murder on the Orient
    Express **2:** 417
muscle tissues 2: 209;
    3: 492
muscular system (human)
    1: 340; **2:** 208; **3:** 495
Musharraf, Pervez **2:** 127
mushrooms 3: 487
MUSIC 1: 456–467. *See*
    also Sound (Physics)
music, popular **1:** 465
musical
    characteristics
      1: 461–463
    comedy **1:** 477
    dynamics **1:** 463
    instruments **1:** 458–460
    notation **2:** 93

Muslim(s) 2: 94, 122, 124, 125; **3:** 304, 314, 337
Turks **2:** 90, 94
Mussolini, Benito **2:** 112, 116, 135; **3:** 333–334, 335
mutant 2: 225
mutation 1: 363; **2:** 225
Myanmar (formerly Burma) **2:** 143, 148
2: *Atlas* 17
Mycenaean civilization 2: 80
My Fair Lady **2:** 409, 412
myofibrils 2: 195
myself (usage) **2:** 383
Mysteries of Udolfo, The **2:** 417
mystery plays 2: 404

N

NAACP (National Association for the Advancement of Colored People) **1:** 124; **2:** 68, 69, 70; **3:** 349; **4:** 365
Nabopolassar 2: 82
NADPH 3: 484
NAFTA (North American Free Trade Agreement) **2:** 53; **3:** 351; **4:** 365, 569
Nagasaki 1: 127; **2:** 49, 114, 116; **3:** 335
Naismith, James **1:** 438
Naked and the Dead, The **2:** 422
Namibia 2: 143, 169
   2: *Atlas* 13
Nana **2:** 415, 423
Nantes, Edict of **2:** 100, 102; **3:** 321
Naples 2: 103; **3:** 315, 316, 321
Napoleon I 2: 104, 105, 134; **3:** 299, 325, 327
   Napoleonic Code **2:** 105
Napoleon III 3: 325, 330
NARA (National Archives and Record Administration) **2:** 11
narcotic drugs 1: 338
narration paper (comp.) **3:** 54
narrative poetry 2: 390; **3:** 79
narrator 4: 1387
NASA (National Aeronautics and Space Administration) **2:** 11; **3:** 349
Nashville, Tennessee **2:** 34, 36
nation 3: 355
National
   Aeronautics and Space Administration (NASA) **2:** 11; **3:** 349
   Archives and Records Administration (NARA) **2:** 11
   Assembly (France) **2:** 104
Association for the Advancement of Colored People (NAACP) **1:** 124; **2:** 68, 69, 70; **3:** 349; **4:** 365
   Congress of American Indians **2:** 58
   Convention (France) **3:** 327
   Defense Education Act **1:** 129
   Equal Rights League **2:** 68
   Foundation on the Arts and the Humanities **2:** 11
   Industrial Recovery Act **1:** 126
   Labor Relations Board (NLRB) **2:** 11; **4:** 366
   Liberation Front (Vietcong) **2:** 120
   Mediation Board **2:** 11
   Organization for Women (NOW) **1:** 130; **4:** 367
   Rifle Association (NRA) **3:** 349
   Science Foundation **2:** 11
   Security Council **2:** 11; **3:** 349
   Transportation Safety Board (NTSB) **2:** 11
   Urban League **2:** 68
national debt 4: 569
nationalism 3: 325
Nationalist China 2: 121
Nationalist Kuomintang Party 2: 109, 117
national security 3: 286
Nations, Battle of **2:** 105
Native Americans 2: 54–59; **4:** 97–99, 151–152, 194–195
   see also Indians; individual tribal names
Native American state names 2: 55
native, citizen (usage) **2:** 383
native elements 1: 389
Native Son **2:** 423
nativism 3: 356
NATO (North Atlantic Treaty Organization) **1:** 128; **2:** 13, 49, 117, 124, 126; **3:** 336, 337, 351; **4:** 366
Nat Turner Rebellion 1: 116; **2:** 67
natural
   laws **2:** 102
   logarithm e^x **3:** 427–429
   numbers **1:** 327; **2:** 262, 350
   radioactivity **2:** 239, 241
   resources **1:** 354–355
   sciences **3:** 581
Nauru 2: 143, 148
   2: *Atlas* 22
Nautilus (U.S.S.) **2:** 186
Navaho (Indians) **2:** 55, 58
nave 3: 313
Navigation Acts 1: 108; **4:** 366
Nazca Plate 1: 386; **3:** 522
Nazi(s) 3: 334
   Party **2:** 113
Nebraska 1: 121, 144–145, 164; **2:** 6, 50, 55
Nebuchadnezzar 2: 82, 128
nebula(e) 1: 412, 426; **3:** 527
   nebular hypothesis **1:** 415, 426
necessary and proper clause 4: 569
Necessity, Fort **1:** 109
negative
   angles **2:** 331
   charge (electrons) **3:** 541
   number **1:** 327; **2:** 350
negotiating for the job 3: 664–665
"Negro Speaks of Rivers, The" 2: 398
Nehru, Jawaharlal **2:** 135
neither, nor (usage) **2:** 383
neon 1: 373
Neoplatonic humanism 3: 318
Nepal 2: 143, 148
   2: *Atlas* 19
Neptune 1: 406, 407, 419
Nero 2: 88, 129; **3:** 295
nerves 3: 371
nervous 2: 208

nervous system, human
1: 342; **3:** 492, 494,
494, 496
tissues **3:** 496
Netherlands 2: 99, 103,
105, 114, 115, 119,
143, 157; **3:** 337
2: *Atlas* 14
Netherlands Antilles
2: 187
2: *Atlas* 5
network
radio **1:** 473
television **1:** 477
neurochemical
abnormalities
3: 367
neurofibrils 2: 195
neuron(s) 2: 225; **3:** 358,
371, 496, 499
neuroscience 3: 357
neurotransmitter 3: 358,
371
neutralization 2: 236
reaction(s) **3:** 508–509
neutrino(s) 2: 256; **3:** 546
neutron(s) 2: 228, 239,
243; **3:** 478, 501, 517,
546
neutron star(s) 1: 414,
426
Nevada 1: 140–141, 165;
2: 74
never, not (usage) **2:** 383
Nevski, Alexander **2:** 131
New
Deal **1:** 126; **2:** 47, 113;
4: 77, 262–274, 366
Frontier **4:** 312–313,
367
Global Crisis,
Understanding a
2: 125
Testament **3:** 304, 308,
318
New Amsterdam 1: 108;
2: 101
New Caledonia 2: 187
2: *Atlas* 22
New England 2: 60–61,
102
Newfoundland 1: 107
New France 2: 101
New Guinea 1: 127
New Hampshire 1:
150–151, 165; **2:** 39
New Jersey 1: 150–151,
165; **2:** 42

New Mexico 1: 107, 118,
140–141, 166; **2:** 58,
74, 75, 116
New Netherland 1: 108;
2: 60
New Orleans, Louisiana
1: 113, 114; **2:** 34,
68
New Sweden 2: 60
newton 2: 245
Newton, Isaac **2:** 102, 133.
248, 256; **3:** 34, 325,
326, 372, 535, 536
laws of motion
2: 248–249, 255, 259;
3: 535–536, 549
root-finding method
3: 399–400, 475
New World 2: 98, 99;
3: 315
New York 1: 108, 109,
150–151, 166; **2:** 36,
40, 41, 45, 46, 58, 60,
61
Bay **1:** 107
City **1:** 112, 113, 126;
2: 31
New Zealand 2: 103, 143,
148
2: *Atlas* 24
territories **2:** 184, 187
niacin 1: 333
Nicaea, Council of 325
3: 308
Nicaragua 1: 132; **2:** 143,
178
2: *Atlas* 5
nice (usage) **2:** 383
Nicene Creed 2: 89
niche 1: 363
Nicholas II, Czar **2:** 111
nickelodeons 1: 471
Niger 2: 140, 143, 169
2: *Atlas* 12
Nigeria 2: 66, 140, 143,
169; **3:** 351
2: *Atlas* 12
Nigger of the Narcissus,
The **2:** 419
Nightingale, Florence
2: 106
Nile River 3: 295–296
Nin, Anaïs **2:** 74
9/11 2: 124, 125
Nineteen Eighty-Four
2: 432
Nineteenth Amendment
1: 125

Ninety-Five Theses **2:** 99;
3: 319, 323
Nineveh 2: 82
nitrogen 1: 373, 392
fixation **2:** 213; **3:** 490,
499
Niue 2: 187
Nixon v. United States.
2: 12
Nixon, Richard Milhous
1: 130, 131; **2:** 49,
50–51, 62, 121, 122,
136; **3:** 325; **4:** 77, 78,
312, 320, 325–330
NLRB (National Labor
Relations Board)
2: 11; **4:** 366
Nobel Peace Prize 2: 45,
50
nobility 3: 327
noble gases 2: 232; **3:** 503
nobody, none, no one
(usage) **2:** 377; **3:** 116
noise 3: 540
nominal GDP 3: 293
Nominalist 3: 312
nonaggression pact
2: 113
none, no one, nobody
(usage) **2:** 377; **3:** 116
nonessential appositive
phrase (Eng.) **1:** 39
nonfiction, good reading
suggestions for young
people **1:** 102–103
nonmetal(s) 2: 234, 243;
3: 504, 517
nonpolar
covalent bond **3:** 505
molecule **3:** 506, 517
nonrenewable resources
3: 530
nonrestrictive
clauses (Eng.) **1:** 46, 54;
2: 374
relative clauses (Eng.)
1: 54; **2:** 374
no one, nobody, none
(usage) **2:** 377; **3:** 116
nor, neither (usage) **2:** 383
Norfolk Island 2: 187
2: *Atlas* 22
Noriega, Manuel **1:** 132
normal (physics) **3:** 549
normal fault 3: 524–525
normal goods 3: 256
Normandy 1: 127; **2:** 92,
93, 114, 116; **3:** 307

Norman(s) 2: 91; **3:** 307
Norman Conquest
2: 131; **3:** 305
Norman invasion **2:** 93
normative economics
3: 248
Norse 2: 93
Norsemen 2: 92
North
American Free Trade
Agreement (NAFTA)
2: 53; **3:** 351; **4:** 365,
569
Atlantic Treaty
Organization (NATO)
1: 128; **2:** 13, 49, 117,
124, 126; **3:** 336, 337,
351; **4:** 366
North (U.S. Civil War)
1: 120
North Africa 2: 89, 91,
96, 114, 115, 116;
3: 300, 303, 304
North America 1: 107;
2: 93, 101, 108, 138,
140, 142, 174–179,
186; **3:** 523, 529
2: *Atlas* 4
North American plate
3: 523
North Carolina 1: 107,
109, 112, 119, 123,
148–149, 166;
2: 58
North Dakota 1: 144–145,
167; **2:** 55
Northeast United States
1: 150–153
map **1:** 151
Northern Ireland 3: 351
North Korea 1: 128; **2:**
127, 143, 148; **3:** 337
North, Sterling **1:** 98
North Vietnam 1: 130;
2: 120
Northwest
Ordinances **1:** 113;
4: 367
Passage **2:** 103, 186
Territory **1:** 113; **2:** 35
Norton, Mary **1:** 98
Norway 2: 93, 114, 115,
143, 157
2: *Atlas* 14
notable, notorious (usage)
2: 383
note cards (comp.) **2:** 361;
3: 107–108

note values (music) **1:** 461
"Not Marble, nor the
Gilded
Monuments" 3: 77
not, never (usage) **2:** 383
notorious, notable (usage)
2: 383
noun clauses (Eng.) **1:** 49
nouns
English **1:** 5, 6–8, 9, 41;
3: 84
German **3:** 153–154
Latin **3:** 217, 218
Spanish **3:** 184
nova 1: 426
novel 2: 416
novella 2: 416
Novello, Antonia **2:** 74
Novgorod (Russia) **3:** 311
NOW (National
Organization for
Women) **1:** 130;
4: 367
nowhere, somewhere,
anywhere,
everywhere (usage)
2: 377
NRA (National Rifle
Association) **3:** 349
nth term test 3: 462
NTSB (National
Transportation Safety
Board) **2:** 11
nuclear
bomb **3:** 337
chemistry **2:** 239–241
chemistry symbols
2: 239
energy **2:** 240
envelope **3:** 482
fission **2:** 240, 241, 243,
257, 259
fusion **2:** 240, 241, 243,
257, 259
fusion (sun) **1:** 404
membrane **2:** 195;
3: 481
particles **2:** 256
physics **2:** 109, 257, 259
reaction **2:** 259
reaction, types **2:** 241
reactor **2:** 241, 243, 257
symbol **3:** 501
warheads **1:** 132; **2:** 123
Nuclear Regulatory
Commission 2: 11
nucleic acids 2: 192;
3: 478, 479, 499

nucleolus 2: 193, 195;
3: 481, 482
nucleotides 2: 201; **3:** 479
nucleus 1: 363, 383;
2: 192, 193, 225, 228;
3: 480, 482, 501, 517
null set 1: 327; **2:** 350
number, amount (usage)
2: 377
number(s) (language)
English **3:** 94
usage **2:** 383
French **3:** 138
German **3:** 368
Latin **3:** 221, 222
Spanish **3:** 202
numbers (math)
laws of **1:** 285;
2: 260–261
line **1:** 192, 210, 220,
327
sets **1:** 287; **2:** 262
numeral 1: 327
numerator 1: 230, 231,
327; **2:** 350
numerous, innumerable
(usage) **2:** 382
Nuremberg 3: 333
war crimes trials **2:** 116
Nutcracker Suite **1:** 464
nutrients 1: 352
see also fats, minerals,
vitamins
nutrition 3: 492

O

OAS (Organization of American States) **2:** 13
o, oh (usage) **2:** 384
Oakley, Annie **1:** 470
objective
  complement (Eng.) **1:** 38
  lens **1:** 426
  pronouns (Eng.) **3:** 84
objects (Eng.) **1:** 38–39, 50; **3:** 84
oblique 1: 327; **2:** 350
  triangles **2:** 334
observational learning 3: 364
obstruction of justice 1: 133
obtuse 1: 327; **2:** 350
O'Casey, Sean **2:** 405, 406, 409
occluded front 1: 399, 403
occultation 1: 426
ocean
  basins **3:** 520
  floor **3:** 520
  oceanic crust **3:** 518, 520
Oceania 2: *Atlas* 22–23
oceans *see also* individual ocean names **2:** 141; **3:** 520
Ochoa, Ellen **2:** 74
Ochoa, Severo **2:** 74
O'Connor, Flannery **2:** 416; **3:** 53
O'Connor, Frank **2:** 416
O'Connor, Sandra Day **1:** 132; **2:** 51
octagon 1: 327; **2:** 316, 350
octahedral bond 3: 505
octave 1: 467
Octavia 2: 87
Octavian 2: 87; **3:** 300
octet rule 3: 503, 517
ode 2: 391
O'Dell, Scott **1:** 98
"Ode: Intimations of Immortality" 2: 391, 400, 402
"Ode on a Grecian Urn" 2: 398, 400
"Ode to a Nightingale" 2: 391, 398, 400

"Ode to the West Wind" 2: 400
Odoacer 2: 89, 129
Odyssey **2:** 81, 391, 392, 397, 429, 432
Oedipus Rex **2:** 406
Oedipus the King **3:** 298
Oersted, Hans **3:** 541, 542
of (usage) **2:** 384
Office of
  Management and Budget (OMB) **2:** 11
  the United Nations High Commissioner for Refugees (UNHCR) **2:** 13
  War Mobilization **1:** 127
Of Mice and Men **2:** 423
Oglethorpe, James **1:** 109
oh, o (usage) **2:** 384
O'Henry 2: 416
Ohio 1: 113, 122, 144–145, 167; **2:** 40, 41, 43, 46, 55
  National Guard **1:** 130
  River **1:** 109, 134
  Valley **1:** 112, 113
ohm 2: 254
  Ohm's law **1:** 383; **2:** 254, 259; **3:** 542
oil 1: 119; **2:** 121
  crisis, 1973 **1:** 131
OK, okay (usage) **2:** 384
Okinawa 1: 127; **2:** 116
Oklahoma 1: 107, 140–141, 167; **2:** 46, 55, 58
  Territory **2:** 43
Oldfield, Barney **1:** 450
"Old Ironsides" 1: 114
Old Testament 3: 302, 304
olfactory system 3: 359, 371
oligarchy 3: 343
Oligocene Epoch 3: 529
oligopeptides 3: 479
oligopoly 3: 267, 293
Oliver Twist **2:** 404, 419, 432
Olmos, Edward James **2:** 74
Olympics 1: 448–449
  ancient **3:** 297, 300
  first **2:** 82
  modern sites **1:** 448

  summer events **1:** 449
  winter events **1:** 449
Omaha (Indians) **2:** 55
Omaha, Nebraska **1:** 121
Oman 2: 143, 170
  2: *Atlas* 18
OMB (Office of Management and Budget) **2:** 11
omnivore 1: 363; **3:** 492, 499
Omoo **2:** 422
on appeal 2: 12
on, onto, on to (usage) **2:** 384
Ondovician Period 3: 529
one (usage) **2:** 384
One Day in the Life of Ivan Denisovich **2:** 422, 432
O'Neill, Eugene **2:** 405, 409, 429, 430; **4:** 1379
One Writer's Beginnings **3:** 52–53
only (usage) **2:** 384; **3:** 117
"On Melancholy" 2: 398
onomatopoeia 1: 93; **4:** 1245
Ontario, Lake **1:** 134, 143
On the Family **3:** 316
On the Interpretation of Dreams **3:** 331–332
On the Revolution of the Heavenly Spheres **3:** 325
On the Two New Sciences **3:** 326
onto, on to, on (usage) **2:** 384
onward(s) (usage) **2:** 378
OPEC (Organization of Petroleum Exporting Countries) **4:** 368
open
  (broken) circuit **3:** 543
  -door policy **4:** 368
  form poetry **3:** 80
  market trading **3:** 284
  primary **4:** 570
openers (comp.) **3:** 49–50
operant conditioning 3: 364, 371
operative 3: 544
opium wars 2: 106
opportunity cost 3: 247, 293
opposite 1: 327; **2:** 350

Optimist's Daughter, The
3: 53
or (usage) **2:** 384
Oration on the Dignity of Man **3:** 317
oratorio(s) 1: 464, 467
orbit(s) (astron.) **1:** 426
orbit (chem.) **3:** 502, 517
   orbital **3:** 517
   orbiting electron atom model **2:** 229
orchestral instruments 1: 458–459
ordered pairs 3: 374
order
   of events (Eng.) **2:** 413
   of operations (math) **2:** 261
orders, scientific classification **2:** 211
ordinate 1: 327–328; **2:** 279, 350; **3:** 374
Oregon 1: 140–141, 167–168; **2:** 55
   Territory **1:** 115
   Treaty **1:** 117; **4:** 368
Oresteia **2:** 407
Orestes trilogy 3: 297–298
organ 2: 208, 225; **3:** 492, 499
organelle(s) 2: 192, 194, 196, 225; **3:** 480, 482, 484, 499
organic
   acid(s) **2:** 237, 238, 243
   chemistry **2:** 237–238, 243
   reaction, types of **2:** 238
organisms, processes of **2:** 192
organization 4: 1261, 1308–1309
Organization of
   American States (OAS) **2:** 13
   Petroleum Exporting Countries (OPEC) **4:** 368
organ systems (human) **3:** 494–495, 499
Origen 2: 129
Origin of Species, On the **2:** 107, 414
origins of solar system 1: 415
Orion 1: 414
Orleáns 2: 95; **3:** 307, 308

orogenesis 3: 524, 533
orthodoxy 3: 341
Ortiz, Carlos **2:** 74
Orwell, George **2:** 417, 424, 432; **3:** 69; **4:** 1381, 1383
Osiris 3: 296
osmosis 2: 198, 225; **3:** 480, 493, 499
   osmotic pressure **3:** 480
Ostrogoths 3: 302, 341
Oswald, Lee Harvey **1:** 129
Othello, the Moor of Venice **2:** 410, 411, 432
Otis, Elisha **1:** 118
Otto I (the Great) (Ger.) **2:** 131
   Holy Roman Empire **2:** 92; **3:** 307
Ottoman
   Empire **2:** 96, 103, 106, 110, 111; **3:** 332
   sultan **3:** 321
   Turks **2:** 96; **3:** 304, 311, 314, 315, 324
ought (usage) **2:** 384
ounce 2: 245
Our Town **2:** 432
outcome (math) **1:** 328; **2:** 350
outer
   core **1:** 387; **3:** 518
   planets **1:** 406–407
outlines, sentence **2:** 364–365
outlining 2: 362–365
Out of the Silent Planet **2:** 417
outside of (usage) **2:** 384
outward(s) (usage) **2:** 378
outwash plane 1: 390–391
ovary 3: 491, 496, 499
overtones 3: 540
Ovid 2: 87, 129, 396, 399, 400
Owens, Jesse **2:** 69
oxidation 3: 513, 517
   and reduction **3:** 513
   number(s) **3:** 513, 517
   of a hydrocarbon **2:** 238
   -reduction reactions **2:** 236; **3:** 509–513
oxides 1: 389
oxyacids 3: 507
oxyanion compound 3: 507

oxygen 1: 373, 392
   -carbon dioxide cycle **1:** 360
oxymoron 4: 1246
Ozark Mountains 1: 134
ozone 1: 355, 392
   layer **3:** 527

P

PAC (political action committee) **3:** 349; **4:** 570
Pacific
islands **1:** 127; **2:** 108
Ocean **2:** 138, 141, 144, 174, 180; **3:** 520, 523
Plate **1:** 386; **3:** 522, 523
Rim **3:** 523
theater, WWII **1:** 127; **2:** 114, 116
Pact of Steel 2: 113
Pahlevi, Shah Mohammed Riza **2:** 122
Paine, Thomas **1:** 111; **2:** 61, 134; **4:** 123
pain-relieving drugs 1: 338
Pakistan 2: 126, 127, 140, 143, 149; **3:** 337
2: *Atlas* 19
Palau 2: 143, 149
2: *Atlas* 22
Paleocene Epoch 3: 529
paleomagnetism 3: 522, 533
paleontology 3: 533
Paleozoic Era 3: 527, 529
Palestine 2: 81, 86, 118, 125; **3:** 337
Liberation Army **2:** 123
Liberation Organization (PLO) **2:** 124, 125; **3:** 337
Palestinian guerillas **2:** 121
Palestrina 3: 320
palisade cells 3: 489
"Palmer raids" 1: 125
Pamela: or Virtue Rewarded **2:** 414, 422
Panama 1: 132; **2:** 53, 143, 178
2: *Atlas* 5
Canal **1:** 123, 131; **2:** 45, 124; **3:** 352; **4:** 222, 368
Canal Corporation **3:** 348
Isthmus of **3:** 529
Pangaea 1: 384–385; **3:** 520, 523, 529, 533

Panic
of 1837 **1:** 117; **2:** 35; **4:** 368
of 1893 **1:** 123; **2:** 43
Pantheon 3: 341
Papago (Indians) **2:** 55
Papal States 2: 91, 107, **3:** 306, 315, 331
paper 2: 89
Papua New Guinea 2: 143, 149
2: *Atlas* 22
parable 4: 1387
parabolas 2: 283
Paradise Lost **2:** 393, 398, 399, 432
paragraphs 3: 48–49
Paraguay 2: 143, 182
2: *Atlas* 11
parallax 1: 411, 426
parallel
circuits **1:** 378–379; **3:** 543
latitudes **2:** 188
play (psych.) **3:** 371
parallel(s) (math) **1:** 328; **2:** 308, 350
parallelism (Eng.) **1:** 45; **3:** 101; **4:** 1247–1248
parallelogram 1: 328; **2:** 316, 350
paraphrasing 2: 361; **3:** 109
parasite 1: 363
pardon 4: 570
parentheses (Eng.) **1:** 55; **2:** 375; **3:** 93
parenthesis (comp.) **4:** 1250
parenthetical expressions (Eng.) **1:** 54; **2:** 374
Parícutin, Mexico **1:** 388; **3:** 524
Paris 2: 90, 116, **3:** 307, 311
Treaty of (1763) **1:** 109
Treaty of (1783) **1:** 112
Treaty of (1856) **2:** 106
Parker, Charlie "Bird" **1:** 465
Parkinson's disease 3: 358
Parks, Rosa **2:** 69
Parliament 1: 110; **2:** 102, 107; **3:** 305, 327, 341
Parliament of Fowls, The **2:** 395
parody 4: 1387

parsec 1: 411, 426
Parthenon 2: 84, 85
partial
fraction decomposition **3:** 434–436
pressure **3:** 510
-quotients division **1:** 315
-sums algorithms **1:** 314
participatory democracy 3: 345, 355
participles (Eng.) **1:** 47, 51
participial phrases **1:** 40, 48, 51
particle
physics **2:** 256
theory **1:** 370
wave behavior of light **3:** 543–544
parts of speech (Eng.) **1:** 5
Pascal, Blaise **2:** 133, 275
Pascal's triangle **2:** 275–276
pass (usage) **2:** 384
passive/active voice (Eng.) **1:** 25
passive satellite 1: 426
Pasternak, Boris **2:** 415, 422
Pasteur, Louis **2:** 134
past participles (Eng.) **1:** 19, 20–21, 47
Paterson **2:** 402
Pathfinder, The **2:** 430
pathos 4: 1387
Paton, Alan **4:** 1381
Pauli exclusion principle 3: 503
Paul of Tarsus 2: 88; **3:** 302, 308
Paul III (pope) **2:** 100
Pavia, Battle of (1525) **3:** 324
Pavlov, Ivan **3:** 357, 364
Pax Romana 3: 295
Paz, Octavio **2:** 136
Peace
accord in the Middle East **2:** 124
Corps **1:** 129; **2:** 11
of Augsburg **2:** 100
of Prague **2:** 101
of Utrecht **2:** 103
of Westphalia **2:** 101; **3:** 314

Pearl Harbor, Hawaii **1:** 126; **2:** 72, 114, 115
Pearl, Daniel **2:** 126
Peary, Robert E. **2:** 186
Peer Gynt **2:** 408
Pei, I. M. **2:** 72
Peking 2: 94, 109, 117
pellicles 2: 195
Peloponnesian War 2: 82, 84, 128; **3:** 297, 299
Peloponnesian War, The **2:** 388
Pena, Federico **2:** 74
Pendleton Act 1: 122
penicillin 2: 112
penicillium molds 3: 487
Penn, William **1:** 109; **2:** 61
Pennsylvania 1: 109, 112, 113, 119, 120, 152–153, 168; **2:** 61
Pennsylvania Dutch 2: 61
Pentagon 1: 133
papers **4:** 79, 368
pentagon 1: 328; **2:** 316, 350
pentameter 2: 403
penumbra 1: 410, 426
PEOPLE OF THE UNITED STATES 2: 54–77
people, persons (usage) **3:** 117
People's Republic of China 2: 117, 121, 124; **3:** 343
Pepin III (the Short) **2:** 91, 130; **3:** 306
peptide bond 3: 486
Pepys, Samuel **2:** 389; **4:** 1382
per, percent (usage) **2:** 384
percent 1: 274–279, 328; **2:** 350
percentage **1:** 328; **2:** 350
by weight **3:** 511
of decrease **1:** 282, 328
of increase **1:** 282, 328
perception 3: 371
perceptual systems 3: 359
percussion 1: 459, 467
Père Goriot **2:** 418
perestroika (restructuring) **2:** 124

perfect competition 3: 266–267, 293
Pericles **2:** 411
Pericles 2: 84, 128; **3:** 297, 299
pericycle 3: 489
perigee 1: 426
perihelion 1: 426
perimeter 1: 328
period(s)
and symmetry **2:** 328–329
astronomy **1:** 426
chemistry **2:** 234, 243
English punctuation **1:** 54; **2:** 374; **3:** 93
math **1:** 328; **2:** 328–329, 350
physics **3:** 540, 549
periodical(s) 2: 358–359
periodical indexes **2:** 359; **3:** 106
periodic
relations **2:** 331
table **2:** 234–235
wave **3:** 539
Peripatetic philosophy, Aristotle's **3:** 299
peripheral nervous system 3: 358
perjury 1: 133
Permian Period 3: 529
Perot, H. Ross **2:** 136
perpendicular 1: 328; **2:** 307–308, 350
Perrault, Charles **1:** 101
Perry, Oliver Hazard **1:** 114
persecute, prosecute (usage) **2:** 384
Pershing, John J. **1:** 124
Persia 2: 85, 92, 94
Persians **2:** 81, 82, 84, 91; **3:** 299, 304
Persian
Empire **2:** 83; **3:** 299
Gulf **2:** 53, 122; **3:** 294
Gulf War **2:** 123
Personae **2:** 399
personal distress 3: 366
personality 3: 366, 371
disorders **3:** 367
personal pronouns (Eng.) **1:** 9
personal, personnel (usage) **2:** 384
personification 1: 93; **3:** 80; **4:** 1246

personnel, personal (usage) **2:** 384
persons, people (usage) **3:** 117
perspective, prospective (usage) **2:** 384
perturbation 1: 426
Peru 2: 140, 143, 183; **2:** *Atlas* 10
Peruzzi
bank **3:** 311, 315
family **3:** 315
Pétain, Henri **2:** 115
petals 3: 491
pet banks 1: 117
Peter III (Russ.) **2:** 103
Peter (the Great) (Russ.) **2:** 133; **3:** 325
Petersburg, Virginia **1:** 120
petiole 3: 489
Petrarch, Francesco **2:** 97, 131; **3:** 79, 305 315, 316
pH 3: 512, 517
phagocyte 2: 225
phalanx 3: 324
pharaohs 2: 79, 80; **3:** 341
Pharsala 2: 87; **3:** 300
pharynx 3: 493
phase(s) 1: 368, 383; **2:** 227, 243, 259
change **3:** 511, 538
-Contrast Microscope **2:** 197
diagram **3:** 511
of the moon **1:** 409
shift **2:** 329
Phèdre **2:** 409
phenomenon (usage) **2:** 384
phenotype 2: 206, 225; **3:** 484, 499
Phidippides 1: 449
Philadelphia, Pennsylvania **1:** 111, 113; **2:** 61, 68
Centennial exhibition **1:** 121
Philip II (Fr.) **3:** 313
Philip II (Hapsburg Spain) **2:** 100, 128; **3:** 321, 322
Philip V (Sp.) **2:** 103
Philip of Macedon(ia) 3: 295, 299
Philippine plate 3: 522

Philippines 1: 123, 127; **2:** 43, 45, 98, 116, 140, 143, 149
   2: *Atlas* 21
Phillip Augustus (Fr.) **3:** 308
philosophes 3: 341
philosophy 3: 356
phloem 3: 489, 499
phobia 3: 371
Phoenicia 2: 85
Phoenicians 2: 81
phoneme 3: 365, 371
   phonemic memory **3:** 363
phonograph 1: 121
phosphate PO_4^{-2} **3:** 478
phospholipids 3: 479
phosphorus 1: 373
photoelectric effect 2: 255, 259
photon 2: 251, 255, 256, 259; **3:** 545, 546
photosphere 1: 404, 426
photosynthesis 1: 356–357, 363; **2:** 199; **3:** 483–484, 489, 490, 499, 527; **4:** 641–649, 802–804
   and respiration **2:** 199
phrases (Eng.) **1:** 39–41, 51
phylum 2: 211, 225
physical
   change **1:** 383; **2:** 228, 243; **3:** 501
   properties of matter **1:** 368; **3:** 501
   states of matter **3:** 500–501
PHYSICAL SCIENCES 1: 364–383
PHYSICS 2: 244–259; **3:** 534–549
   dictionary **2:** 258–259
physiologists 3: 356
physiology, human **4:** 741–757, 810–811
pi 1: 328; **2:** 350
Piaget, Jean **3:** 360, 361, 362
pianoforte 1: 464
Piazza Tales **2:** 416
picaresque fiction 2: 416
Picasso, Pablo **2:** 135
Pickwick Papers, The **2:** 419

pictographs 3: 295, 341
piecewise defined function 3: 373
"Pied Beauty" 2: 397
Pierce, Franklin **2:** 38–39, 62; **4:** 164–165
pikes 3: 324
Pilgrims 1: 107; **2:** 60, 102
Pilgrim's Progress, The **2:** 414, 418, 432
Pinckney, Charles C. **1:** 113
   Pinckney Treaty **1:** 113
Pindar 2: 391
ping pong 1: 454–455
Ping-Pong diplomacy 2: 122
Pinter, Harold **2:** 405
Pioneer (astron.) **1:** 418, 419
Pioneers, The **2:** 430
Pirandello, Luigi **2:** 405, 409
Pirenne, Henri **3:** 305
   Pirenne thesis **3:** 305
pistil 2: 219; **3:** 491, 499
"Pit and the Pendulum, The" 2: 422
Pitcairn Islands 2: 187
pitch
   music **1:** 461, 467; **3:** 540
   screws **1:** 376
   sound **1:** 383; **2:** 251, 259
pitchblende 2: 108
pith 3: 489
Pittsburgh, Pennsylvania **1:** 109, 123
pituitary gland 3: 359, 371
place value 1: 176–178, 196–206, 249, 328; **2:** 346
plagiarism (Eng.) **3:** 100, 109
plague 1: 339
Plague, The **2:** 418
Plains (Indians) **2:** 56
planar bond 3: 505
Planck, Max **2:** 255; **3:** 545, 546
   Planck's constant **2:** 253, 259; **3:** 545
plane(s) 1: 328; **2:** 306, 340
plane geometry 2: 86

planetary
   orbits **3:** 326
   positions **3:** 295
planets of solar system 1: 405–408
plankton 2: 215
plant
   cells **2:** 197; **3:** 481
   systems **2:** 208; **3:** 489–491; **4:** 731–737, 809–810
plantae (kingdom) **2:** 192, 210, 217–219; **3:** 487, 488
plasma 1: 426
plasma membrane 2: 195; **3:** 481
plasmolysis 2: 198, 225
plastids 2: 196
plate (geol.) **3:** 533
   boundaries **3:** 521
   movement **3:** 523
   tectonics **1:** 384–388, 403; **3:** 520–523, 528, 533
platinum 1: 373
Plato 2: 84, 128; **3:** 298–299, 343
   Platonic Academy of Florence **3:** 318
   Platonic philosophy **3:** 299, 317
   Platonism **3:** 299, 317
   Platonistic humanism **3:** 325
Plautus 2: 128, 404
Playboy of the Western World, The **2:** 406, 432–433
plebeians 3: 341
Pleistocene Epoch 1: 391; **3:** 529
plenty (usage) **2:** 384
Plessy v. Ferguson **2:** 12, 68
Pliocene Epoch 3: 529
PLO (Palestine Liberation Organization) **2:** 124, 125; **3:** 337
plot 2: 413, **3:** 72; **4:** 1387
Plough and the Stars, The **2:** 409
Plunkett, Jim **2:** 74
Plutarch 2: 129, 389; **3:** 301
Pluto 1: 406, 407, 415
Plymouth 1: 107; **2:** 56, 60

Plymouth Rock 2: 102
pneumonia 1: 352
Poe, Edgar Allan **1:** 93;
    2: 390, 415, 416, 417,
    422; **3:** 86
poetic devices 2: 390–391
poetry 1: 100–101;
    2: 390–403; **3:** 70,
    76–80
    kinds of **2:** 390
poetry for young readers
    1: 100–102
    All Day Long: Fifty
      Rhymes of the Never
      Was and Always Is
      1: 101
    Birds and the Beasts Were
      There, The: A Book of
      Nature Poems **1:** 100
    Child's Garden of Verses, A
      1: 101
    Complete Nonsense Book,
      The **1:** 101
    I Heard a Scream in the
      Street **1:** 101
    Now We Are Six **1:** 101
    Piper, Pipe That Song
      Again **1:** 101
    There is No Rhyme for
      Silver **1:** 101
    Time for Poetry **1:** 100
    You Come Too **1:** 100
poets, biographies
    2: 394–403
Point Counter Point
    2: 416, 417
pointed arches 3: 313
point
    of inflection **1:** 328;
    2: 350
    of view **3:** 74–75;
    4: 1261–1262
poison control centers
    1: 349
poison gas, use in WWI
    2: 110, 111
poison ivy 1: 349, 353
poisoning, exposures and
    symptoms **1:** 349
Poitiers 2: 95
Poland 1: 126, 127; **2:** 99,
    102, 103, 110, 113,
    114, 115, 117, 122,
    123, 143, 157; **3:** 334,
    337
    2: *Atlas* 14–15
polar
    axis **2:** 337

covalent bond **3:** 505
easterlies **1:** 395, 403
front **1:** 399, 403
graphs **2:** 337–339
molecule **3:** 479, 505,
    506, 517
regions **2:** 186
policy making 4: 552–558
polio 2: 46, 47
polis 3: 341
political
    action committee(s)
      (PAC) **3:** 349; **4:** 570
    adaptability **3:** 346
    development **4:** 469–471
    equality **3:** 355
    ideologies **3:** 344–346
    party, parties **3:** 349,
      355; **4:** 474–480, 570
    rights for women **1:** 130
    spectrum **3:** 344; **4:** 472
    stability **3:** 346
    theory **3:** 342–346
POLITICAL SCIENCE
    3: 342–355
politics 3: 342, 355
politics (usage) **2:** 384
Polk, James Knox
    2: 36–37, 62;
    4: 161–162
pollen 2: 219; **3:** 491, 499
    tube **3:** 491
pollination 3: 491, 499
pollution 1: 355
Polo, Marco **2:** 94, 131
polonium 2: 108
polyatomic
    ion **2:** 227, 243
    molecule **3:** 501
polyconic projection
    2: 189
polygon(s) 1: 328;
    2: 316–319, 350
polymer(s) 3: 478, 499
polynomial 1: 328;
    2: 272–274, 350
polypeptides 2: 202;
    3: 479
polyphonic music 1: 463
polysaccharides 3: 479
polytheists 3: 294
Pompey 2: 87, 128;
    3: 300
Ponce de León, Juan
    1: 107
pons 3: 358
Poor Richard's
    Almanack **2:** 103

Pope, Alexander **2:** 393,
    399; **3:** 79
Pope Calixtus II 3: 309
Pope Gregory I 2: 90
Pope Gregory the Great
    2: 130; **3:** 308, 309
Pope Gregory VII 2: 93
Pope Gregory XI 2: 95
Pope Gregory XIII 2: 100
Pope Innocent III 2: 94,
    131; **3:** 309, 313, 314
Pope John Paul II 2: 122,
    136
Pope John XXIII 2: 135
Pope Leo I 3: 302
Pope Leo III 3: 305, 309
Pope Martin V 2: 96
Pope Paul III 2: 100
Pope Urban II 3: 313
Pope Zacharius 3: 306
Popular Front 2: 113
population *see* specific
    locations **2:** 140
population, U.S.
    1: 136–137
populism 4: 195–198
Populist Party 1: 122, 123
Porgy and Bess **1:** 465
pork barrel legislation
    3: 347; **4:** 570
Port Arthur 2: 109
Porter, William Sidney *see*
    O'Henry
Portrait of a Lady, The
    2: 421
Portrait of the Artist as
    a Young Man, A
    2: 421
Portugal 2: 98, 101, 103,
    105, 143, 158; **3:** 337
    2: *Atlas* 14
positive charge (protons)
    3: 541
positive economics 3: 248
positively (usage) **2:** 384
positive number 1: 328;
    2: 350
positron 2: 239, 243, 256;
    3: 546
possessive nouns (Eng.)
    1: 6, 9, 41
possessive pronouns
    (Eng.) **3:** 84
postal system 2: 41
potassium 1: 373
potential
    difference **3:** 541, 542,
    549

energy **1:** 374; **2:** 247;
  3: 501, 537, 541, 549
  of a point charge **3:** 542
Potsdam 3: 334, 335
  Conference **2:** 116;
  4: 369
pound 2: 245
Pound, Ezra **2:** 393, 396,
  399, 402
Powell, Colin **2:** 70
Powell v. Alabama
  2: 12
power
  physics **1:** 383; **2:** 246,
    247, 259; **3:** 536, 537,
    542, 549
  political science **3:** 342,
    355
power(s) (math) **1:** 261,
  268, 322, 328; **2:** 346,
  350
  see also exponents
  of 10 **1:** 322; **2:** 346
  series **3:** 463
**practicable, practical,
  practically** (usage)
  2: 384
**practical, practically,
  practicable** (usage)
  2: 384
**practically, practicable,
  practical** (usage)
  2: 384
**Prague spring movement
  2:** 121
pre-algebra 1: 285–311
pre-calculus 4: 889–921
Precambrian Era 3: 527,
  529
precede, proceed (usage)
  2: 385; **3:** 117
precedence, precedents
  (usage) **2:** 385
precedents, precedence
  (usage) **2:** 385
precipitate 3: 517
precipitation 1: 396–397
precipitation reaction
  (chem.) **3:** 508–509
predator 1: 363
predicate(s) (Eng.)
  1: 36–38, 43, 50
  adjective **1:** 39
  nominative(s) **1:** 38–39,
    43; **3:** 84
prefixes (Eng.) **1:** 89
prejudice 3: 368
Prelude, The **2:** 400, 402

preoperational stage
  3: 360, 361
prepositional phrase
  (Eng.) **1:** 39
preposition(s)
  English **1:** 5, 31–33, 50;
    3: 84, 98
  at the end of a clause
    (usage) **2:** 385
  German **3:** 156
  Latin **3:** 221
  Spanish **3:** 189
prescribe, proscribe
  (usage) **2:** 385
present participle(s)
  (Eng.) **1:** 19, 47
presently (usage) **2:** 385
president, presidency
  (U.S.) *see also* names
  of presidents **2:** 8–11,
  14, 29–53, 62; **3:** 348,
  349
  duties of **2:** 10; **3:** 348
  elections **2:** 14
  powers **4:** 519–521
  succession **2:** 10, 28
president pro tempore
  4: 570
Presley, Elvis **1:** 465
pressure 3: 514
presto 1: 467
Pretoria 2: 109
pretty (usage) **2:** 385
prevailing westerlies
  1: 395, 403
prewriting 4: 1281–1293
price 3: 256, 260–267
Pride and Prejudice
  2: 418, 421, 433
primary (astron.) **1:** 426
primary sex organs
  3: 496
primary structure (biol.)
  3: 479
prime (math) **1:** 328;
  2: 350
  factorization **1:** 328
  number **1:** 230, 328
prime
  meridian **2:** 188
  time **1:** 477
primogeniture 3: 341
*Prince and the Pauper,
  The* **2:** 419
Prince, The (Il principe)
  3: 316
Princeton, New Jersey
  1: 112; **2:** 32, 44

Prince William Sound,
  Alaska **1:** 132
principal energy levels
  3: 502, 517
principal, principle
  (usage) **2:** 385; **3:** 117
principle
  of superposition **3:** 540
  of uncertainty **2:** 256
  quantum number **3:** 502
principle, principal
  (usage) **2:** 385; **3:** 117
printing 3: 322–324
  press **2:** 132
prism 1: 383; **2:** 252
pro and con thinking
  3: 39, 44–45
probability and statistics
  1: 312–313, 328;
  2: 350
probe(s) (astron.)
  1: 418–419, 426
problem-solving (psych.)
  3: 365
procedural due process
  4: 570
proceed, precede (usage)
  2: 385; **3:** 117
Proclamation of 1763
  1: 110
producer(s)
  (entertainment)
  1: 477
producers (econ.) **3:** 253,
  260–264, 279
product(s) (chem.) **2:** 233,
  243; **3:** 507, 517
product(s) (math) **1:** 209,
  328; **2:** 350
**production of
  radioisotope of
  same element 2:** 241
**production possibilities
  frontier** (econ.)
  3: 247, 293
proficiency tests 3: 363
Profiles in Courage **2:** 48
profit 3: 293
progressive liberalism
  3: 344
progressivism
  4: 227–234, 369
prohibition 1: 125
projectile motion (math)
  2: 298–299
prokaryotes 2: 193, 196,
  213, 225; **3:** 480, 482,
  487, 499

proletariat 3: 322, 341
Prometheus Bound
2: 400, 407
Prometheus Unbound
2: 400
prominence 1: 426
Promontory Point, Utah
1: 121
prompter 1: 477
pronoun(s)
agreement (Eng.) **1:** 13
case (Eng.) **1:** 14
English **1:** 5, 9–16;
3: 84
usage **2:** 385
French **3:** 120–125
German **3:** 154–156
Latin **3:** 224–229
Spanish **3:** 186–188
pronunciation (Lat.)
3: 217, 218
proofreading 3: 67–68
proofreaders marks
3: 68
propagates 3: 539
prophase 2: 203; **3:** 482,
483, 485
prophecy, prophesy
(usage) **2:** 385
prophesy, prophecy
(usage) **2:** 385
proportion 1: 274, 328;
2: 350
proportional
representation
4: 369
props 1: 477
proscribe, prescribe
(usage) **2:** 385
prosecute, persecute
(usage) **2:** 384
prospective, perspective
(usage) **2:** 384
Protectorate 2: 102
Protector of the
Commonwealth
3: 326
protein(s) 1: 353; **2:** 192;
3: 478, 479, 499
synthesis **3:** 486
Proterozoic Period 3: 529
Protestant(s),
Protestantism 2:
100, 101, 102; **3:** 317,
321, 322
-Catholic world (map)
3: 322
Churches **2:** 99

movement **2:** 99; **3:** 321
Reformation **2:** 100;
3: 314, 319–321
protist 2: 196, 214–215,
225
Protista, Kingdom **2:** 192,
210, 214–215; **3:** 487
proton(s) 2: 228, 239,
243, 256; **3:** 478, 501,
517, 546
protoplanets 1: 415
protoplasm 1: 363; **2:** 194
protozoans 1: 353
Proust, Marcel **2:** 415, 422
proved, proven (usage)
2: 385
proven, proved (usage)
2: 385
Prussia 2: 103, 107, 111;
3: 325, 329–330
Psalms (Old Testament)
3: 318
pschoanalytic psychology
3: 357
pseudopodia 2: 195, 196
P, S, L waves 1: 387
psychoanalysis 2: 108;
3: 332, 357, 367
ego **3:** 332
id **3:** 332
superego **3:** 332
psychodynamic view
3: 366
psychological
disorders **3:** 367
tests **3:** 363
PSYCHOLOGY
3: 356–371
psychrometer 1: 396, 403
Ptolemy 2: 129
Ptolemy I 2: 128; **3:** 299
Ptolemy (dynasty) **3:** 299,
300
public
policy **4:** 570
resources **3:** 342
schools, establishment of
1: 108
Pudd'nhead Wilson
2: 419
Pueblo (Indians) **2:** 55
Puerto Ricans 2: 76
Puerto Rico 1: 107, 123,
153, 172; **2:** 43
2: *Atlas* 5
Pugatorio **2:** 426–427
Pulaski 2: 61
pulleys 1: 376–377

Pullman, George M.
1: 119
Pullman Strike, 1894
2: 43
pulsar(s) 1: 414, 426
punctuation (Eng.) **1:** 45,
54–55; **2:** 374–375;
3: 89–94
review (Eng.) **1:** 54–55;
2: 374–375
Punic Wars 2: 85, 86;
3: 295, 300
punishment 3: 371
pupil (eye) **3:** 359
pure substance 3: 500,
517
purines 3: 479
Puritans 1: 108; **2:** 60,
102; **4:** 78, 369
"Purloined Letter, The"
2: 417, 422
Pushkin, Aleksandr **2:** 393,
399
Putin, Vladimir **3:** 337
putting-out system 3: 341
P-waves 3: 525
Pygmalion **2:** 409
Pyle, Howard **1:** 101
Pynchon, Thomas **2:** 415,
422
Pyramids of Giza 2: 79
pyrimidines 3: 479
pyroclastic material
3: 524
pyrrhic foot 2: 403
Pythagoras 2: 128
Pythagorean theorem
1: 284, 328; **2:** 338,
350

Q

Qatar 2: 143, 170
   2: *Atlas* 18
quadrant 1: 328; **2:** 279,
   350
quadratic
   equation(s) **1:** 328;
      2: 295–298, 350
   functions **3:** 373
quadrilateral(s) 1: 328;
      2: 316–319, 350
Quakers 1: 109; **2:** 61, 67
qualitative chemistry
      3: 500
quanta *see also* quantum
      2: 255; **3:** 545
quantitative
   chemistry **3:** 500
   relationships **3:** 507
quantity
   demanded (econ.)
      3: 293
   supplied (econ.) **3:** 293
   usage (Eng.) **2:** 385
quantized electron
      3: 502
quantum *see also* quanta
      2: 259
   -mechanical model
      3: 502
   mechanics **2:** 228;
      3: 545–546
   physics **3:** 545–546
   theory **2:** 255; **3:** 545
   (wave) mechanics **2:** 256
quarks 2: 256
quartet 1: 467
quartz 3: 526
quasar(s) 1: 414, 426
Quaternary Period
      3: 529
Quebec, Canada **1:** 107,
   109
Queen Elizabeth I (Eng.)
      2: 100
Queen Isabella (Sp.) **2:** 96
question mark(s) (Eng.)
      1: 54; **2:** 374; **3:** 93,
      98
Quinn, Anthony **2:** 74
quota (import) **3:** 286, 293
quotation marks (Eng.)
      1: 55; **2:** 375; **3:** 92
quotation, quote (usage)
      2: 385
quote, quotation (usage)
      2: 385

quotient 1: 220, 328;
      2: 350
quoting (comp.) **2:** 361;
      3: 109–110

R

rabbi 3: 341
Rabelais, François **2:** 97
Rabin, Yitzhak **2:** 124
racial discrimination
    1: 129
Racine, Jean **2:** 404, 405, 409; **4:** 1378
racquetball 1: 455
radar 2: 252, 253, 259
Radcliffe, Anne **2:** 417
radian(s) 2: 327
    measure **1:** 328; **2:** 351
radiation 1: 375
    belt **1:** 426
radical (math) **1:** 328; **2:** 305, 351; **4:** 570
    functions **3:** 373
radical (pol. sci.) **3:** 355
radicand 1: 328; **2:** 305, 351
radio 1: 473, 474; **2:** 112
    station, first **1:** 125
    waves **2:** 251
radioactive, radioactivity
    1: 383; **2:** 108, 239, 241, 243, 257, 259; **3:** 546
    decay **2:** 239; **3:** 527
    isotope(s) **2:** 240; **3:** 528, 546
radiocarbon dating
    2: 239, 241
radioisotope 2: 239, 240, 241, 243
    half-lives **2:** 239
    of same element, producing **2:** 241
    particle emission **2:** 239
radiometric dating
    3: 528, 533
radio telescope(s) 1: 417, 426
radium 1: 373; **2:** 108
radius 2: 320, 337–338
    of convergence **3:** 463
ragtime 1: 465
ragtime, blues, jazz, rhythm & blues, rock & roll 2: 68–69
railroad(s) 1: 119, 122; **2:** 107; **3:** 327–328
rain 1: 392
rainbows 1: 381
Rainbow, The **2:** 421
Rainier, Mt. (Washington)
    1: 388

raise, rise (usage) **2:** 385
Ramses II 2: 80
Ramses III 2: 80
range (math) **3:** 374, 475
Ranger (astron.) **1:** 418
Rape of Lucrece, The **2:** 400
Rape of the Lock, The **2:** 399
Raphael 2: 97, 132
rapid eye movement sleep (REM) **3:** 359
rarely ever, seldom ever (usage) **2:** 385
Rasselas **2:** 417
rate
    of change of a function **3:** 388–389
    of reaction **3:** 514
ratio 1: 274–275, 328; **2:** 351
    test **3:** 461
rational
    -emotive therapy **3:** 371
    functions **3:** 373, 383
    number **1:** 235, 328; **2:** 262, 351
rational, rationale, rationalization (usage) **2:** 385
rationale, rationalization, rational (usage) **2:** 385
rationalism 2: 102
rationalization, rational, rationale (usage) **2:** 385
Ravel, Maurice **1:** 464
Rawlings, Marjorie Kinnan **1:** 98
ray (math) 2: 306
Ray, James Earl **1:** 130
Raymond, count of Toulouse **3:** 313
RDA vitamin sources
    1: 332–333
reactant(s) 2: 233, 243; **3:** 507, 517
reactionary 4: 570
reactions (chem.)
    and equilibrium **3:** 514
    types of **3:** 508
read about entertainment
    Duke Ellington **1:** 102
    Rock Revolution, The **1:** 103

    Very Young Dancer, A **1:** 103
    Wonderful World of Music, The **1:** 102
read about science
    Azimov's Guide to Science **1:** 102
    Color of Man, The **1:** 102
    Sea Around Us, The **1:** 102
    Silent Spring **1:** 102
    Since Silent Spring **1:** 102
read about sports
    Breaking In **1:** 103
    Guinness Book of World Records, The **1:** 103
read about U.S. history
    All Aboard: The Trains That Built America **1:** 102
    American Revolution, The **1:** 102
    And Then What Happened, Paul Revere? **1:** 102
    Andrew Jackson **1:** 102
    California Gold Rush, The **1:** 103
    George Washington's World **1:** 102
    John F. Kennedy **1:** 103
    Martin Luther King: The Peaceful Warrior **1:** 102
    Pantheon Story of American Art for Young People, The **1:** 102
    Story of D-Day, The: June 6, 1944 **1:** 102
    Women's Rights: The Suffrage Movement in America 1840–1920 **1:** 102
read about world history
    Cathedral **1:** 103
    Dairy of a Young Girl, The **1:** 102
    Egyptians, The **1:** 102
    Lion in the Gateway, The **1:** 103
    My Village in Hungary **1:** 102
    Story of World Religion, The **1:** 103
read for fun
    Code and Cipher Book, The **1:** 103
    Hodge-Podge Book, The **1:** 102

reading
  comprehension 1: 92
  fiction 1: 92
  for pleasure and
      enrichment
      2: 436–443; 3: 583
  poetry 1: 93
  skills 1: 86–87
  strategies 1: 90, 92–93
  tips 3: 566–568
  trigonometry tables
      2: 325
Reagan, Ronald 1: 132;
      2: 50–51, 62, 122,
      123; 4: 333–335
real
  GDP 3: 293
  image 2: 259
  number 1: 286, 288,
      328; 2: 262, 351
  wealth effect 3: 272–273
real, really (usage) 2: 385
Realist 3: 312
reaper 1: 117
reapportionment 4: 570
reason, because (usage)
      3: 117
recall 4: 370, 570
receptor cells 3: 359, 496
recessive trait 2: 206–207,
      225; 3: 484, 499
reciprocal 1: 243, 328;
      2: 351
  relations 2: 331
reckon, calculate (usage)
      2: 378
Reconquista 3: 341
Reconstruction 1: 121;
      2: 41, 70; 4: 181–186,
      370
rectangle 1: 328; 2: 316,
      351
rectangular coordinate
      system 3: 374
Red and the Black, The
      2: 414, 423
Red Badge of Courage,
      The 2: 433
Red
  Guard (Maoists) 2: 121
  scare 1: 125; 4: 370
  Sea 1: 386; 2: 80, 153;
      3: 523, 529
  shift 1: 426
"red shirts" (Italy) 3: 331
redox reaction 3: 513,
      517
Reds (Bolsheviks) 2: 111

reduction 3: 513, 517
reentry 1: 426
reference
  frame (physics) 3: 545
  tables (math) 1: 322–323
  triangle 2: 327
referendum 4: 570
reflecting telescopes
      1: 416
reflection 3: 544, 549
  angle of 3: 544, 549
  law of 1: 383; 2: 259
reflectors 2: 252
reflexive pronouns (Eng.)
      1: 10
Reformation 2: 99
Reformed Church 2: 99
refracted ray 3: 544
refracting telescopes
      1: 416
refraction 1: 381; 2: 252;
      3: 544, 549
  angle of 3: 544, 549
  index of 3: 549
  law of 1: 383; 2: 259
regardless (usage) 2: 385
regeneration 2: 204, 225
regional metamorphism
      3: 519
regions of the world
      2: 140
regroup (math) 1: 195
regulatory commissions
      3: 349
rehearsal 1: 477
Reign of Terror 2: 104;
      3: 327
reinforcement 3: 364,
      367, 371
related rates of change
      3: 404–405
relating addition and
      subtraction 1: 208
relation 1: 328; 2: 351
relative
  clauses (Eng.) 1: 46, 51
  dating 3: 528, 533
  humidity 1: 396, 403
  maximum 1: 328; 2: 351
  pronouns (Eng.) 1: 10
relativity, theory of 2: 255,
      259; 3: 545
relics 3: 341
religious freedom 1: 109
Religious Peace of
      Augsburg 2: 99, 100
REM (rapid eye movement
      sleep) 3: 359

remainder 1: 191,
      328
Rembrandt 2: 133
Remembrance of Things
      Past 2: 422
remote
  interior angles 2: 317
  manipulator system
      1: 426
Remus 2: 82
Renaissance 1: 469; 2: 90;
      3: 313, 314, 315–319
  Italian 3: 315–316
  northern 3: 318
Renault, Mary 1: 103
renewable resources
      3: 530
repeated derivatives
      3: 398
repertory theater 1: 478
replication (DNA) 3: 486
representative
  democracy 4: 570
  elements 3: 504
reproduction 3: 482–483,
      494, 496; 4: 762–770
  human 3: 482–483, 494,
      496; 4: 762–770
reproductive systems
      2: 208; 3: 494, 496
  human 3: 494
reptiles class (Reptilia)
      2: 223
republic 3: 355
republicanism 3: 355
Republican Party 1: 119,
      128, 133; 2: 39;
      3: 349; 4: 371
research
  methods 2: 361;
      3: 102–107
  paper, types of 2: 365
reserve requirement
      3: 283, 293
reserved powers 4: 570
resignation avoids
      impeachment
      2: 122
resistance 1: 376, 383;
      3: 542, 549
resistor 3: 542, 543, 549
resolved light sources
      3: 544
resolving triangles 2: 332
respectfully, respectively
      (usage) 2: 385
respectively, respectfully
      (usage) 2: 385

respiration **1:** 363;
   2: 198–200, 208, 225;
   4: 630–637, 804–805
respiratory system
   (human) **1:** 341;
   3: 495
respiratory systems
   3: 493
response(s) (psych.)
   3: 357, 371
rest(s) (music) **1:** 461, 467
rest-mass-energy 2: 247
restrictive clauses (Eng.)
   1: 46
resumé writing
   3: 656–657
reticular tissue 2: 209
retina 3: 359
retirement 3: 362
retrograde motion 1: 426
Return of the King, The
   2: 430
Return of the Native, The
   2: 420
Réunion 2: 187
revenue 3: 293
   sharing **4:** 570
reverse fault(s)
   3: 524–525
reverse processes 3: 510
reversible reactions
   3: 514
revise and polish (comp.)
   3: 64
revolution (astron.) **1:** 426
revolution (pol. sci.)
   3: 346, 355
Revolutions of 1848
   2: 106
Reynolds v. Sims **2:** 12
"Rhapsody in Blue"
   1: 465
Rheims 2: 95
   rhetorical
     question **4:** 1249
     writing strategies
       4: 1187–1232,
       1308–1309
Rhine 2: 116
Rhineland 2: 112, 113
rhizoids 2: 217; **3:** 489
rhizomes 3: 490
Rhode Island 1: 108,
   152–153, 168; **2:** 60
Rhodes, Cecil **3:** 332
rhombus 1: 328; **2:** 316,
   351
rhyme (poetry) **2:** 391

rhyolite 3: 524
rhythm 1: 461
   in poetry **2:** 403
riboflavin (vitamin B2)
   1: 332
ribosomes 2: 194, 195,
   202; **3:** 481, 482
Rice, Condoleezza **2:** 70
"Richard Cory" 2: 400
Richard II **2:** 404, 411,
   433
Richard III **2:** 411, 433
Richard I (the Lion-
   Hearted) (Eng.)
   2: 96, 131; **3:** 307,
   313, 314
Richardson, Bill **2:** 74
Richardson, Samuel
   2: 414, 415, 416, 422
Richelieu, Cardinal **2:** 133
Richmond, Virginia
   1: 119, 120
Richter scale 1: 387, 403;
   3: 526, 533
Ride, Sally K. **1:** 132, 423
rider 4: 570
Riders to the Sea
   2: 433–434
Rienzi, Tribune of the
   People **3:** 329
rift(s) 3: 529
rift valley 1: 386
right (math)
   angle **1:** 328; **2:** 351
   right- and-left-hand
     limits **3:** 379
   triangles **1:** 328; **2:** 324
right (pol. sci.)
   to counsel (Sixth
     Amendment) **3:** 350
   to vote **1:** 118, 121
Riis, Jacob **1:** 122
Rilke, Rainer Maria **2:** 393,
   399
Rimbaud, Arthur **2:** 393,
   399–400
"Rime of the Ancient
   Mariner, The"
   2: 400, 403
"ring of fire" (Pacific
   Rim) **3:** 523
Rio Grande 1: 117
rise, raise (usage) **2:** 385
Risorgimento 3: 341
Rivals, The **2:** 406
rivers *see also* individual
   river names **2:** 141
   longest **2:** 141

RNA (ribonucleic acid)
   2: 192, 193, 200, 202,
   225; **3:** 479, 499
   in protein synthesis
   2: 202
road show 1: 478
Roanoke Island 1: 107
Robber Bridegroom, The
   3: 53
Robertson, W. F. **1:** 440
Robespierre, Maximilien
   2: 104
Robinson Crusoe **2:** 414,
   416, 419
Robinson, Edwin
   Arlington **2:** 393, 400
Robinson, Jackie **2:** 69
Rochambeau 2: 61
Roche's limit 1: 426
rock cycle 1: 389; **3:** 533
rock 'n' roll 1: 465
rocket 1: 426
rocks (layers) **3:** 528
Rocky Mountains 1: 134;
   2: 174; **3:** 529
Rodriguez, Chi Chi **2:** 74
Roe v. Wade **1:** 131; **2:** 12;
   4: 317, 371
Roebling, John A. **2:** 64
Rogers, Carl **3:** 357, 366,
   367
Rogers, Mary **1:** 98
roles (psych.) **3:** 368
roman à clef 2: 416
Roman
   Catholic Church **2:** 85,
     90, 93, 94, 98, 99,
     100, 105; **3:** 308,
     319–322
   Catholicism **3:** 327
   conquest **3:** 299
   Empire **2:** 85, 88, 89, 90,
     91, 129; **3:** 295,
     301–303, 304
   numerals **1:** 325
   people **2:** 80, 89, 118;
     3: 306
   Republic **3:** 295, 300
   Senate **3:** 300
romance (lit.) **3:** 71
   fiction **2:** 416
   poetry **2:** 391
Romania *see also* Rumania
   2: 143, 158
Romanov dynasty 2: 101
Romanov, Michael **2:** 101
romanticism 3: 329
   in poetry **2:** 393

romantic
    poets **2:** 400
    style (music) **1:** 456, 464
Rome 2: 83, 85, 86, 87,
    88, 89, 95, 116, 129;
    3: 295, 300–303, 326,
    343
Romeo and Juliet **2:** 100,
    411, 434
Rommel, General Erwin
    2: 115
Romola **3:** 50
Romulus 2: 82
Romulus Augustulus
    2: 89; **3:** 302, 305
rondo 1: 467
Roosevelt Corollary
    4: 371
Roosevelt, Eleanor **2:** 46
Roosevelt, Franklin
    Delano (FDR)
    1: 126, 128, 473;
    2: 46–47, 62, 113,
    135; **3:** 325, 335, 336;
    4: 76–77, 267–272,
    279–280, 282–283,
    290
Roosevelt, Theodore **1:**
    123, 434; **2:** 44–45,
    62, 135; **4:** 79, 220,
    222–223, 231–234
root(s) (bot.)
    fibrous **3:** 489
    hairs **3:** 489
    system **2:** 208
root(s) (math) **1:** 328;
    2: 351; **3:** 475
    test **3:** 461
root words (Eng.) **1:** 88
"Rose for Emily, A" 3: 73
Rossetti, Dante Gabriel
    2: 393, 400
Rossini, Gioacchino **1:** 464
rotation 1: 426
rotational motion 3: 534,
    536–537
Rough Riders 2: 44;
    4: 371
'round, around (usage)
    2: 377
round (music) **1:** 467
rounding numbers (math)
    1: 178, 281
Round Table 2: 91
roundworms 2: 220
Rousseau, Jean Jacques
    2: 104, 133, 414;
    3: 325, 326, 332, 344

Rowling, J. K. **2:** 137
rows/periods 3: 503
Royal Hunt of the Sun,
    The **2:** 409
rubber 1: 117
Rubens, Peter Paul **2:** 133
Rubicon 2: 87
Rubinstein, Louis **1:** 451
Ruffins, Reynolds **1:** 103
rule
    of few **3:** 346
    of many **3:** 346
rules for differentiation
    3: 392
Rumania *see also* Romania
    2: 117, 123
run (usage) **2:** 385
Runnymede 2: 94
Russell, Henry **1:** 413
Russia, Russian(s) 1: 121,
    124; **2:** 13, 45, 94,
    100, 101, 102, 103,
    105, 106, 109, 110,
    111, 116; **3:** 325, 332,
    333, 337
    2: *Atlas* 16
    Federation **2:** 140, 143,
    158
    Republic **2:** 124
    Revolution **2:** 111,
    135–136; **3:** 325
    space flights **1:** 420–421,
    423
    space probes **1:** 418
Russo-Finnish War 2: 115
Russo-Japanese War
    2: 109
Russwurm, John **2:** 67
Rutherford, Ernest **2:** 228,
    240
Rutherford experiment
    2: 241
Rwanda 2: 143, 170
    2: *Atlas* 13

S

Sacramento, California
  1: 118, 121
Sadat, Anwar el- **2:** 122,
  125, 136, 137
Saddam Hussein 2: 124,
  126–127
safety at home 1: 344
Sagan, Carl **4:** 1383
said, same (usage) **2:** 385
St. Ambrose 3: 309
St. Anselm 2: 131
St. Anthony 3: 309
St. Athanasius 2: 129
St. Augustine 2: 129;
  3: 309, 316
St. Augustine, Florida
  1: 107; **2:** 73
St. Benedict 2: 130;
  3: 309
St. Benedict's monastery
  2: 90
St. Bernard of Clairvaux
  3: 311
St. Columba 2: 130
St. Dominic 2: 131;
  3: 311
St. Exupery, Antoine
  1: 101
St. Francis of Assissi
  2: 131; **3:** 311
St. Gregory I 2: 90
St. Helena 2: 187
  2: *Atlas* 13
St. Helens, Mount
  (Washington) **1:** 132,
  388; **2:** 142; **3:** 524
St. Jerome 2: 129; **3:** 309
St. Joan **2:** 406
St. Kitts and Nevis
  2: 143, 179
  2: *Atlas* 5
St. Lawrence River
  1: 107, 108
St.-Lô 2: 116
St. Lucia 2: 143, 179
  2: *Atlas* 5
St. Michael 3: 308
St. Mihiel 1: 124
St. Patrick 2: 129
St. Paul 2: 129; **3:** 312
St. Paul's (London)
  3: 318
St. Peter 3: 308, 320
St. Peter's basilica 3: 319
St. Petersburg (Russia)
  2: 111

St. Pierre and Miquelon
  2: 187
  2: *Atlas* 7
St. Teresa 3: 320
St. Thomas à Becket
  2: 94
St. Thomas Aquinas 2: 94
St. Vincent and the
  Grenadines 2: 143,
  179
  2: *Atlas* 5
Saipan 1: 127
Saki 2: 416
Saladin 3: 313
Salamis 2: 84
Salazar, Alberto **2:** 74
Salerno (Italy) **3:** 311
Salian Franks (Germanic)
  2: 90
Salinger, J. D. **2:** 426
Salonika 2: 111
salt 2: 236, 243
salt (sodium) facts 1: 334
Salutati, Coluccio **3:** 316
Salyut **space stations**
  1: 421
Samarkand 2: 96
same, said (usage) **2:** 385
Samoa 2: 43, 143, 149
  2: *Atlas* 22
sample exam questions
  ACT **3:** 617–618
  GED **3:** 590–596
  SAT I **3:** 610–616
  SAT II **3:** 619, 602–621
  TOEFL **3:** 619
sample geometry proofs
  2: 311–315
sample space 1: 328;
  2: 351
San Andreas fault 1: 386,
  387; **3:** 523
San Francisco, California
  1: 128; **2:** 71, 74
  earthquake (1989)
  1: 132
San Francisco
  Conference 2: 117
San Marino 2: 143, 158
  2: *Atlas* 14
Santa Anna, General
  Antonio **1:** 117
Santa Fe, New Mexico
  1: 107
São Tomé and Príncipe
  2: 143, 170
  2: *Atlas* 13
Saratoga, New York **1:** 112

Sargon (Akkad) **2:** 79
Sargon (Akkad) **II 2:** 82
Sarnoff, David **2:** 112
Sarnoff, Jane **1:** 103
Sarnoff, Reynolds Ruffin
  1: 103
Sartre, Jean-Paul **4:** 1381
SAT I and II 3: 363
SAT/ACT comparison
  3: 600, 603
satellite 1: 426
satire (lit.) **3:** 71; **4:** 1388
satirical fiction 2: 413,
  417
saturated hydrocarbon
  2: 237, 243
Saturn 1: 406, 407, 418,
  419
Saudi Arabia 2: 91, 123,
  125, 127, 140, 143,
  170
  2: *Atlas* 18
Savage, Katharine **1:** 103
Savannah, Georgia **1:** 120
saw, seen, see (usage)
  2: 385
Saxons 2: 92
Saxony 2: 91, 92
SBA (Small Business
  Administration) **2:** 11;
  3: 349
scale 1: 467; **2:** 189
scalene 1: 328; **2:** 351
Scandinavia 2: 94; **3:** 302,
  304, 307, 311
scanning electron
  microscope 2: 197
scarcely (usage) **2:** 385
scarcodina 2: 214
Scarlet Letter, The **2:** 420
scene 1: 478; **2:** 406
Schachter's two-factor
  theory 3: 366
Schenck v. United States
  2: 12
scherzo 1: 467
Schiller, Friedrich von
  2: 405, 409
Schism of 1054 2: 93
schizophrenic disorders
  3: 367, 371
Schliemann, Heinrich
  2: 81
Schoenberg, Arnold
  1: 464
Schöffer, Peter **3:** 322
Scholastic Assessment
  Test (SAT)

sample questions
3: 601–616, 620–621
scholasticism 3: 341
scholastics 3: 318
Schrödinger, Erwin 3: 502
Schrödinger equation
3: 502
Schubert, Franz 1: 464
Schumann, Robert 1: 464
science (Enlightenment)
2: 102
science fiction 2: 413, 417
scientific
method 1: 364–365
notation (math) 1: 283;
2: 347
revolution 3: 325
socialism 3: 328
scintillation 1: 426
Scipio Africanus Major
2: 86
SCLC (Southern Christian
Leadership Council)
2: 69
Scoop 2: 417
Scopes trial 4: 372
Scotland 2: 99
2: Atlas 14
Scott, Robert F. 2: 186
Scott, Walter 2: 413, 416
Scott, Winfield 2: 38, 39
Scotus, Duns 3: 312–313
Scourge of God 2: 89
Screen Actors Guild
(SAG) 2: 50
screenplay 1: 478
screws 1: 376, 377
sea-floor spreading
1: 386; 3: 520, 521
Seagull, The 2: 408
seamount(s) 3: 520, 533
seas 2: 141
see also individual sea
names
largest 2: 141
Seascape 2: 407
seasonal unemployment
3: 277
seasons 1: 393
SEATO (Southeast Asia
Treaty Organization)
3: 351
SEC (Securities and
Exchange
Commission) 2: 11
secant 1: 328–329; 2: 320,
324, 351; 3: 373
secession 1: 120; 4: 372

Second Babylonian
Empire 2: 82
Second Bank of the
United States
(Second National
Bank) 1: 115, 117;
4: 372
Second Bull Run 1: 120
"Second Coming, The"
2: 403
Second Reich 3: 330
second triumvirate 2: 87
Secret Accords 3: 332
Secretariat of the United
Nations 2: 13
Securities and Exchange
Commission (SEC)
2: 11
Security Council of the
UN 2: 118
Sedan, Battle of (1870)
3: 330
sediment 3: 526, 533
sedimentary rock(s)
1: 389; 3: 519, 526,
533
see, saw, seen (usage)
2: 385
seen, see, saw (usage)
2: 385
segmented worms 2: 220
segregation 2: 68, 69
seismic waves 3: 525
seismograph 1: 387, 403;
3: 525–526, 533
seldom ever (usage)
2: 385
Selective Service
Act (draft) 1: 124, 126
System 2: 11
Seleucids 2: 86
Seleucus I 3: 299
self-
assessment for job search
3: 648–655
concept 3: 371
esteem 3: 371
incrimination, protection
against (Fifth
Amendment) 3: 350
interest 3: 344
pollination 3: 491
rule 3: 346
Seljuk Turks 2: 90
semantic memory 3: 363
semantics 3: 365
semicolons (Eng.) 1: 45,
54; 2: 375; 3: 91–92

semiconducting devices
2: 244
semimetals 3: 504
Seminole (Indians) 2: 34,
36
wars 2: 36
semi-permeable
membrane 2: 198
Senate 1: 121, 133; 2: 7,
15–16; 3: 347, 349,
352
Seneca 2: 129, 404; 3: 316
Seneca Falls Convention
1: 118
Senegal 2: 66, 143, 171
2: Atlas 12
senility 3: 362
Sense and Sensibility
2: 418
sensorimotor period
3: 360, 361
sensory
memory 3: 363
neurons 3: 496
sentence(s) 1: 36–51
diagramming (Eng.)
1: 50–51
outlines 2: 364–365
structure (Eng.)
1: 36–51; 3: 83–84
Sentimental Education,
The 2: 420
sepal(s) 3: 491
separation of powers
3: 347; 4: 571
September 11 1:133
sequence(s) (math)
1: 329; 2: 305, 351;
3: 475
formulas 3: 457
Serapis 1: 112
Serbia 2: 110; 3: 337, 351
Serbia and Montenegro
2: 143, 158
2: Atlas 15
Serbs 2: 124; 3: 332
serfs 3: 310
series
circuits 1: 378; 3: 543
English 1: 45, 54; 2: 374
math 1: 329; 2: 305,
351; 3: 475
Serra, Father Junípero
1: 110
services (econ.) 3: 247
set design 1: 478
set, sit (usage) 2: 385;
3: 89

set(s) (math) **1:** 235, 287, 329; **2:** 262, 351
  symbols **1:** 319
setting (lit.) **2:** 413; **3:** 73; **4:** 1388
Seven Against Thebes **2:** 407
Seven Cities of Gold (Cibola) **1:** 107
Seven Years' War **2:** 103
sewing machine **1:** 118
sexagesimal number system **3:** 295, 341
sexist speech (Eng.) **3:** 85–86
sex-linked inheritance **2:** 207
sexual reproduction **1:** 363; **3:** 499
sexual reproduction (plants) **3:** 490, 491
Seychelles **2:** 143, 171
  2: *Atlas* 13
Sforza family **3:** 315
  Francesco **3:** 314
  Ludovico **3:** 316, 321
Shadow of a Gunman, The **2:** 409
Shaffer, Peter **2:** 409
Shah Pahlevi **1:** 132
Shakespeare, William **1:** 469; **2:** 87, 97, 100, 133, 391, 392, 400, 401, 404, 405, 406, 409, 410–411; **3:** 77, 314; **4:** 1378
shall, will (usage) **2:** 386; **3:** 117
Shamela **2:** 420
Shatt-al-Arab (waterway) **2:** 122
Shaw, Arnold **1:** 103
Shaw, George Bernard **2:** 404, 405, 406, 409; **4:** 1381
Shays, Daniel **1:** 113
  Shays's Rebellion **1:** 113; **4:** 129
Sheen, Martin **2:** 74
Shelley, Mary Godwin **2:** 400, 417; **4:** 1381
Shelley, Percy Bysshe **2:** 391, 393, 400; **4:** 1379
shell method (math) **3:** 449–451
shells, volume **3:** 448–451
Shenzhou **1:** 422, 423

Shepard, Alan **1:** 420, 423
Shepheardes Calendar, The **2:** 401
Sheridan, Richard Brinsley **2:** 405, 406, 412
Sherman Antitrust Act **1:** 122; **2:** 43; **4:** 373
Sherman, William T. **1:** 120
  Sherman's "March to the Sea" **1:** 120
shield
  cone **1:** 388, 403
  volcano **3:** 524
Shih Hwang-ti, Emperor (China) **2:** 86
Shiite Muslims **3:** 304
Shiloh **2:** 40
Shiloh, Tennessee **1:** 120
shock, signs and treatment of **1:** 346
Shoemaker-Levy 9 **1:** 408
Sholes, Christopher **1:** 121
shoot system **2:** 208
shortage (econ.) **3:** 293
short
  fiction **2:** 416
  stories **2:** 416
  -term memory **3:** 363
  ton **2:** 245
  wave **2:** 252
Shoshone (Indians) **2:** 55
shot **1:** 478
should of (usage) **2:** 386
should, would (usage) **2:** 386
Shropshire Lad, A **2:** 398
Shuffle Along **2:** 69
Shura Mazda **2:** 83
Siberia **2:** 100
Sicily **2:** 89, 114, 116; **3:** 300, 314
"Sick Rose, The" **2:** 395
Siddhartha **2:** 420
Siddhartha Gautama **2:** 84
Sierra Leone **2:** 66, 143, 171
  2: *Atlas* 12
Sierra Nevada **3:** 525
sight, cite, site (usage) **2:** 378
sigma notation **3:** 409
signed number(s) **1:** 329; **2:** 262, 351
sign patterns (math) **2:** 304
Sikhs **2:** 123

Silas Marner **2:** 419; **3:** 50
silicates **1:** 389
silicon **1:** 373
  chips **2:** 118
Silurian Period **3:** 529
silver **1:** 373
similar figures **1:** 329; **2:** 351
simile **1:** 93; **4:** 1242–1244
Simon, H. **3:** 357
simple machine **1:** 376, 377, 383
Simpson's rule (parabolic approximation) **3:** 423, 475
Sinai, Mt. **2:** 80
Sinai Peninsula **2:** 121
Sinclair, Upton **1:** 123; **4:** 78, 1379
sine(s) **1:** 329; **2:** 324, 335, 351; **3:** 373
  curve **3:** 539
  law of **2:** 335
sing (usage) **2:** 386
Singapore **2:** 143, 149
  2: *Atlas* 17
Singer, Isaac Bashevis **2:** 135
single
  bond(s) **2:** 237; **3:** 505
  replacement **2:** 243
  replacement reaction(s) **2:** 236; **3:** 508
singular pronouns (usage) **2:** 386
sink (usage) **2:** 386
sinusoidal graphs **2:** 329
Sioux (Indians) **1:** 121; **2:** 55, 57, 58; **4:** 373
  Wars **2:** 57
Sir Gawain and the Green Knight **2:** 391, 400, 424
Sirhan, Sirhan **1:** 130
Sirius **1:** 413
Sister Carrie **2:** 419
sit, set (usage) **2:** 385; **3:** 89
site, sight, cite (usage) **2:** 378
sit-ins **1:** 129; **4:** 373
Sitting Bull **1:** 470
situation comedy **1:** 478
Six Characters in Search of an Author **2:** 409
Six Days War **2:** 121
Sixteenth Amendment **1:** 124; **2:** 45

skeletal system **2:** 208
human **1:** 340; **3:** 495
skeletal tissues **2:** 209
Sketches by Boz **2:** 419
skiing **1:** 452
Skinner, B. F. **3:** 357, 364,
366, 367
Skinner box **3:** 364
Skylab 1: 421, 423
skyscrapers **1:** 118
slashes (Eng.) **3:** 93
Slater, Samuel **2:** 62
slave(s), slavery **1:** 107,
115, 116, 118, 119,
120, 121; **2:** 61,
66–68, 107; **4:** 77–78,
106–107, 133, 147,
153, 160, 162–168
emancipation **1:** 121
music **2:** 67
Slavs 2: 90; **3:** 304
sleep **3:** 359
Sleeping Beauty **1:** 464
sleeping sickness (African
trypanosomiasis)
1: 353
slime molds **2:** 216;
3: 487
slope (math) **1:** 329;
2: 351; **3:** 250–251,
293, 389–390;
4: 889–892
Slovakia 2: 143, 158
2: *Atlas* 14–15
Slovenia 2: 124, 143, 159;
3: 351
2: *Atlas* 14
slow(ly) (usage) **2: 386**
slug **2:** 245
slug-foot/second **2:** 246
slums **1:** 122
**Small Business
Administration**
(SBA) **2:** 11; **3:** 349
smallpox **1:** 353
Smith, Adam **3:** 287
Smith, John **1:** 107
Smith, R. F. **1:** 440
smog **1:** 355
SNCC (Student
Nonviolent
Coordinating
Committee) **2:** 70
Snell's law 2: 253; **3:** 544
"Snowbound" 2: 402
"Snow man, The" 2: 401
Snow White **1:** 472
so (usage) **2:** 386

soaring vaults **3:** 313
Sobol, Donald **1:** 99
soccer **1:** 442–443
dictionary of **1:** 443
social
contract **3:** 355
interactions **3:** 368
psychology **3:** 368
rights (for women)
1: 130
sciences **3:** 581
welfare **2:** 105
Social Contract, The
3: 326
Social Darwinism 3: 331;
4: 373
socialism **3:** 344, 345, 355
Socialist Labor party
3: 349
Socialists 2: 112
Social Security 2: 10;
3: 349
Act **4:** 373
Administration **2:** 11
society (-ies) **3:** 342, 346
**Society of American
Indians 2:** 58
Society of Jesus (Jesuits)
3: 321
"society of orders"
3: 327, 341
Socrates 2: 84, 128; **3:** 301
sodium **1:** 373
solar
eclipse **1:** 405
flare(s) **1:** 405, 426
system **1:** 404-410
facts about **1:** 406–407
wind **1:** 426
solenoid **3:** 542–543, 549
solid(s) **2:** 227; **3:** 500,
510, 511
Solidarity 2: 122, 123
solid fuel, fire safety **1:** 345
soliloquy (drama) **2:** 406
solo flight across Atlantic
1: 126
Solomon 2: 81, 128
Solomon Islands 1: 127;
2: 48, 143, 150
2: *Atlas* 22
Solon 2: 83, 128
solstice(s) **1:** 393, 426
solubility **1:** 368; **3:** 511,
517
solute **3:** 511, 517
solution **1:** 329; **2:** 351;
3: 511, 517

solvent **3:** 511, 517
solving triangles
2: 334–336
Solzhenitsyn, Aleksandr
2: 415, 422
Somalia 1: 133; **2:** 143,
171
2: *Atlas* 12
somatic system **3:** 358,
371
somatoform disorders
3: 367
somatosensory cortex
3: 359
somebody, someone
(usage) **2:** 386
someone, somebody
(usage) **2:** 386
somewhere, anywhere,
everywhere,
nowhere (usage)
2: 386
Somme offensive (WWI)
2: 111
sonata(s) **1:** 464, 467
form **1:** 467
"Song of Myself" 2: 402
Song of Roland, The
2: 392, 400–401, 424;
3: 324
Song of the Cid **2:** 392,
424
Songs of Experience
2: 395, 400
Songs of Innocence
2: 395, 400
sonnet **2:** 391; **3:** 77–79,
316
"Sonnet 68," Spenser's
2: 401
"Sonnet 73,"
Shakespeare's **2:** 401
"Sonnet XLIII," Elizabeth
Barrett Browning
3: 77
Sons and Lovers **2:** 421
Sons of Liberty 4: 373
Sophocles 2: 84, 128, 404,
406, 412; **4:** 1378
soprano **1:** 458, 467
*Sorrows of Young
Werther, The* **2:** 397,
414, 420
sort of, kind of (usage)
2: 382
sound **1:** 380
energy **1:** 380
movies **1:** 471

recording **1:** 456, 465
speed **2:** 251
wave(s) **1:** 380, 383;
    2: 251, 259
waves and music
    3: 540
Sound and the Fury, The
    2: 420
soundtrack 1: 478
South (U.S. Civil War)
    1: 120
South (U.S.) **1:** 146–149
South Africa 2: 109, 123,
    143, 171
South America 1: 107;
    2: 99, 101, 105, 138,
    139, 140, 142,
    180–183; **3:** 521, 523
    2: *Atlas* 10–11
South American plate
    3: 522
Southampton 3: 311
South Asia 2: *Atlas* 19
South Carolina 1: 109,
    112, 116, 119,
    148–149, 168
South Dakota 1: 144–145,
    169; **2:** 55
Southeast Asia 1: 127;
    2: 49
    2: *Atlas* 21
**Southeast Asia Treaty
    Organization**
    (SEATO) **3:** 351
**Southern Christian
    Leadership Council**
    (SCLC) **2:** 69
Southern states 1: 147
South Korea 1: 128; **2:** 49,
    118, 143, 150
South Pole 2: 186
South Vietnam 1: 130;
    2: 120
Southwest 1: 117
sovereign, sovereignty
    3: 343, 355
Soviet bloc 2: 119
Soviet(s) 2: 115, 116, 118,
    121, 125
Soviet satellites 1: 405
Soviet Union 1: 127, 128,
    129; **2:** 112, 113, 114,
    115, 116, 117, 118,
    136–137; **3:** 334–335,
    336, 337, 343, 351
Soyuz 1: 420–421, 423
space
    and mass **3:** 500–501

exploration **1:** 416–423;
    2: 117
probes **1:** 418–419
shuttles **1:** 421–422, 423
station **1:** 427
-time-gravity **2:** 109
transportation system
    1: 427
SPACE SCIENCE
    1: 404–427
Spain 1: 107, 113, 115,
    123, 469; **2:** 33, 43,
    86, 89, 91, 94, 96, 97,
    99, 100, 101, 103,
    105, 113, 143, 159;
    3: 300, 304, 318, 337
    2: *Atlas* 14
Spanish
    -American War **1:** 123;
        2: 43, 45; **4:** 218–222,
        374
    Armada **2:** 100, 133;
        3: 314, 322
    Civil War **2:** 113
    colonies **1:** 107; **2:** 60;
        4: 98–99
    Inquisition **2:** 96, 132
    Loyalists **2:** 113
    names of U.S. states
        2: 74
    Nationalists **2:** 113
**Spanish-English
    dictionary**
    3: 204–209
SPANISH GRAMMAR
    3: 182–215
Spanish Netherlands 2:
    103
Sparta 2: 82, 84; **3:** 297,
    299
SPEAKING (Eng.)
    1: 74–77; **2:** 458–460
special collections
    (library) **2:** 360
special effects 1: 478
specially, especially
    (usage) **2:** 380
specie, species (usage)
    2: 386
species 1: 363; **2:** 211, 225
Spectator, The **2:** 389
spectrometer 3: 502
spectroscope 1: 427
spectrum (light) **1:** 383,
    427; **2:** 251, 252, 259;
    3: 502, 544
speed 3: 534, 549
    of light **3:** 544

spelling (Eng.)
    commonly misspelled
        words **1:** 53; **3:** 68
    rules **1:** 52
Spenser, Edmund **2:** 100,
    392, 401
sperm/spermatozoa
    3: 496
Sperry, R. **3:** 357
Spice Islands 2: 98
Spielberg, Steven **2:** 137
Spillane, Mickey **2:** 417;
    3: 35
spinal cord 3: 358
spindle fibers (cells)
    2: 203, 205; **3:** 482
spirilla 2: 213
Spirit of St. Louis, The
    1: 126; **2:** 112
spirituals (music)
    1: 465
split infinitive (usage)
    2: 386
spoils system 2: 35, 41;
    4: 209–212, 374
spondee 2: 403
sponges 2: 220
spontaneous generation
    1: 363
Spoon River Anthology
    2: 398
spore(s) 1: 363; **2:** 204
sporozoa 2: 214
SPORTS 1: 430–455
Spotsylvania, Virginia
    1: 120
Sputnik 2: 118; **4:** 374
Spyri, Johanna **1:** 99
squamous tissues 2: 209
Squanto 2: 60
square 1: 329; **2:** 316, 351
squared 1: 329
square root 1: 284
squash (game) **1:** 455
Sri Lanka 2: 143, 150
    2: *Atlas* 19
stacks (library) **2:** 356
stage
    directions **4:** 1388
    manager **1:** 478
    stagehands **1:** 478
    terms **2:** 406
stagflation 3: 275
stairway and hall safety
    1: 344
Stalin, Josef/Joseph **2:** 112,
    118, 135; **3:** 329, 334,
    335, 336

Stalingrad **2:** 116
Stalwart Republicans
2: 41
stamen **2:** 219; **3:** 491, 499
Stamp Act 1: 110; **2:** 31;
4: 374
standardization **3:** 371
standardized tests **3:** 363
Standard Oil 2: 45
standard temperature
and pressure (STP)
3: 509
Stanford University
2: 46; **3:** 363
Stanley, Henry **3:** 332
Stanley, Lord **1:** 440
Stanton, Edwin M.
2: 39
stanza **4:** 1388
stars **1:** 412–414
classifications **1:** 413
"Star-Spangled Banner,
The" 1: 114
START (Strategic Arms
Reduction Talks)
1: 132
starting your own
business **3:** 673–675
state **3:** 343, 355
State, Department of
2: 11, 13
state government **2:** 6,
21; **3:** 347
state-of-being verbs
(Eng.) **3:** 87
States and Territories
(U.S.) **1:** 134–153
states of matter **3:**
509–511, 517
states' rights **1:** 116, 120;
2: 21
static electricity **1:** 378;
3: 541, 549
stationary front **1:** 399,
403
stationary, stationery
(usage) **2:** 386
stationery, stationary
(usage) **2:** 386
statism **3:** 335
statistics (usage) **2:** 386
stayed, stood (usage)
2: 386
steam engine **3:** 327
steel **1:** 118
Steele, Richard **2:** 389;
4: 1382
Steffens, Lincoln **4:** 1382

Steinbeck, John **1:** 99;
2: 415, 423; **3:** 91;
4: 1381
Stendhal 2: 414, 415,
423
Stephen, count of Blois
3: 313
steppe **1:** 395
Steppenwolf **2:** 420
stereotypes **3:** 368
Sterne, Laurence **2:** 423
steroids **3:** 479
Steuben, Baron von **2:** 62
Stevens, Wallace **2:** 393,
401
Stevenson, Robert Louis
1: 99, 101
stigma **3:** 491, 499
stimulus(i) **3:** 357, 371
stock market crash
(1929) **1:** 126; **2:** 47,
113
stoichiometry **3:** 507, 517
Stoker, Bram **2:** 417
stomata **3:** 489
Stonehenge 3: 295
Stoppard, Tom **2:** 405,
412; **4:** 1381
"Stopping by Woods on
a Snowy Evening"
2: 397
storage area safety **1:** 344
store of value **3:** 281
storms **1:** 400
storyteller **3:** 74
Stowe, Harriet Beecher
1: 118
STP (standard temperature
and pressure) **3:** 509
straight angle **1:** 329;
2: 351
Stranger, The **2:** 418,
434
Strassman, Fritz **2:** 257
strata **3:** 528, 533
Strategic Arms
Reduction Talks
(START) **1:** 132
stratigraphy **3:** 519
stratosphere **1:** 392
stratum (usage) **2:** 386
stratus clouds **1:** 397, 398
Stravinsky, Igor **1:** 464;
2: 135
stream of consciousness
3: 357
Streetcar Named Desire,
A **2:** 434

striations **3:** 533
strict constructionist
4: 571
Stride Toward Freedom
3: 59
strike-slip fault **3:** 525
Strindberg, Johan August
2: 405, 412
string instruments
(music) **1:** 458, 467
strip cropping **1:** 354
stroke (apoplexy) **1:** 353
strong force **2:** 256
structural memory
3: 363
structuralism **3:** 357
structure **4:** 1388
Stuart kings (Eng.)
3: 326, 327
Student Nonviolent
Coordinating
Committee (SNCC)
2: 70
studia humanitatis
3: 316, 318
study, roadblocks to
successful **3:** 552–554
STUDY SKILLS
3: 550–585
stupor mundi **3:** 314
Sturm und Drang **2:** 397,
409
Stuyvesant, Peter
1: 108
style (bot.) **3:** 491
style (comp.) **3:** 66;
4: 1262–1266
subatomic particle(s)
1: 371, 383; **3:** 501,
546
subduction zone **3:** 522,
533
subjective pronouns
(Eng.) **3:** 84
subjectivism **3:** 316
subject(s) (Eng.) **1:** 36–38,
42–43, 50–51; **3:** 84
complement **1:** 38
subject/verb agreement
1: 42–43
subjunctive (Eng.)
mood **1:** 49
verbs **3:** 88
sublevels, atomic **3:** 502
sublimation **3:** 510
submarine(s) **1:** 124;
2: 111
suborbital **1:** 427

subordinating conjunctions (Eng.) **1:** 33, 34
subpolar lows 1: 403
subscripts (chem.) **3:** 507
substitute goods 3: 256, 257, 293
substitution 2: 238, 243
substrate 3: 480, 499
subtraction 1: 191–208, 314, 318, 329; **2:** 266
  facts **1:** 192, 193, 318
subtrahend 1: 191, 329; **2:** 351
succession 1: 363
such (usage) **2:** 386
Sudan 2: 125, 140, 143, 171
  2: *Atlas* 12
Suetonius 2: 389
suffixes (Eng.) **1:** 89
sugar facts 1: 334
sulfates 1: 389
sulfhydryl group (SH) **3:** 478
sulfides 1: 389
sulfur 1: 373
sum 1: 329; **2:** 351
Sumer 2: 79
Summa Theologiae **3:** 312
Sumpter, Fort **1:** 119, 120; **4:** 356
sums and differences of angles 2: 335
Sun 1: 407
Sun Also Rises, The **2:** 420
"Sunday Morning" 2: 401
Sung dynasty 2: 92
Sunni
  Muslims **3:** 304
  Triangle **2:** 127
sunspot 1: 404–405, 427
Sun Yat-sen 2: 109, 117
supercluster 1: 427
supercontinent 3: 520
supercooled droplets 1: 396
superego 3: 332, 366
Superior, Lake **1:** 134, 143
supernova 1: 414, 427
superposition, law of **3:** 528, 533

supply (econ.) **3:** 260–261, 293
  and demand **3:** 248, 265
  curve **3:** 293
  schedule **3:** 293
  -side policies **3:** 280
supremacy clause 4: 571
Supreme Court 1: 114, 115, 119, 131, 132; **2:** 12, 44, 51, 68, 69; **3:** 347, 348, 349; **4:** 529–534
  landmark decisions **2:** 12
sure to (usage) **2:** 386
surface
  revolution, area of a **3:** 453
  tension **3:** 510
  waves **3:** 525
Suriname 2: 143, 183
  2: *Atlas* 10
surplus 3: 265, 293
Surveyor series (astron.) **1:** 418
Sutter's mill 1: 118
Swabia 2: 92
Swan Lake **1:** 464
Swan, Sir Joseph **2:** 108
S-waves 3: 525
Swaziland 2: 143, 172
  2: *Atlas* 13
Sweden 2: 101, 102, 103, 143, 159; **3:** 315, 337
  2: *Atlas* 14–15
Swift, Jonathan **1:** 99; **2:** 389, 417; **4:** 1378
swim (usage) **2:** 386
swimming 1: 453
Switzerland 2: 143, 159
  2: *Atlas* 14
symbiosis 1: 363; **2:** 194
  symbiotic relationships **3:** 490
symbol(s)
  in circuit diagrams **3:** 543
  literature **3:** 75; **4:** 1388
  maps **2:** 189
Symeon the Stylite 3: 309
symphony (-ies) **1:** 464, 467
Symposium **3:** 298
synapse(s) 3: 358, 371, 496, 499
syncline 1: 403; **3:** 525, 533
syncopation 1: 467

synecdoche 3: 80; **4:** 1244–1245
Synge, John Millington **2:** 405, 406, 412, 432–433, 434
syntax 3: 365; **4:** 1255–1258
synthesis
  of new element **2:** 241
  reactions **2:** 236
synthesizer 1: 460, 467
syphilis 1: 339, 353
Syria 2: 80, 121, 143, 172
  2: *Atlas* 18
system of equations 1: 329; **2:** 351
systems (biol.) **2:** 208

T

table of atomic masses
2: 230
table tennis 1: 454–455
"tabula rasa" 3: 356
tabular integration
3: 431, 444
Tacitus 2: 129
tactile system 3: 359, 371
Taft-Hartley Act 1: 128;
4: 375
Taft, William Howard
2: 44–45, 62; 4:
232–233, 249
Tahiti 3: 328
taiga 1: 358, 359
Taiwan 2: 72, , 117, 121,
143, 150
2: *Atlas* 20
Tajikistan 2: 143, 150
2: *Atlas* 19
take, bring (usage) 3: 117
TAKING MAJOR TESTS
3: 586–597
Tale of Two Cities, A
2: 421
tales *see* fables/fairy
tales/tales
Taliban 2: 125
talking motion pictures
1: 126
Tamayo, Rufino 2: 135
Tamburlaine the Great
2: 408
Tamerlane 2: 96, 132
*Taming of the Shrew,
The* 2: 411, 434
Tammany Hall 2: 43, 45;
4: 375
T'ang dynasty 2: 90
tangent(s) 1: 329; 2: 320,
321, 324, 351; 3: 373
lines 3: 389–390, 391
Tanis, Battle of 2: 80
Tannenberg, Battle of
2: 111
Tannhäuser 3: 329
Tanzania 2: 143, 172
taproots 3: 489
tariff(s) 1: 120, 124;
3: 286, 293, 311
Tariff of 1816 1: 115;
4: 375
Tarquin kings (Etruscan)
2: 83, 85
Tartuffe 2: 406, 408
tax cuts 3: 280

taxes (math) 1: 279
taxing powers 2: 5, 6
taxonomy 1: 363
and classification
4: 717–727
Taylor series 3: 463
Taylor, Zachary 2: 36–37,
62, 117; 4: 162–163
Tchaikovsky, Peter Ilyich
1: 464; 2: 134
teach, learn (usage)
2: 382
Teapot Dome scandal
1: 125; 2: 47; 4: 78,
375
technical director 1: 478
techniques of integration
3: 418–423
technology 3: 261
tectonic 3: 520, 533
forces 3: 523
Tecumseh 1: 114; 2: 34
teeth, care of 1: 336
telegraph 1: 117, 473;
2: 107
telegraphic sentences
3: 365
telephone 1: 121; 2: 108
telescope(s) 1: 383,
416–417; 3: 325
television 1: 380,
474–475; 2: 118
"Tell-Tale Heart" 3: 86
telophase 2: 203; 3: 482,
483, 485
temperature 1: 383;
2: 250, 259; 3: 514,
538, 539, 549
comparisons 2: 250
scale conversions 3: 539
Tempest, The 2: 411, 434
tempo 1: 461–462, 467
Ten Commandments
2: 80; 3: 296
Tender Is the Night
2: 420
Tennessee 1: 119, 120,
130, 148–149, 169;
2: 35, 36, 37, 38, 39,
55
Tennessee Valley Act
1: 126
Tennessee Valley
Authority (TVA)
2: 11; 3: 348; 4: 376
tennis 1: 444–445
dictionary of 1: 445
major victories 1: 444

Tennyson, Alfred 2: 393,
401; 4: 1379
tenor 1: 458, 467
ten rules for writing style
2: 367
ten ways to improve test
scores 3: 588
Terence 2: 404
Tereshkova, Valentina
1: 423
Terman, Lewis 3: 363
terrestrial planets 1: 427
terrible, terrific (usage)
2: 386
terrific, terrible (usage)
2: 386
territorial expansion
U.S. 1: 115
territories 2: 184–187
terrorism, terroritsts
1: 132, 133; 2: 53,
121, 124, 125, 126,
127
Tertiary Period 3: 529
Tess of the D'Urbervilles
2: 420
test charge 3: 541
testes 3: 496
test for divergence (math)
3: 459
Test of English as a
Foreign Language
(TOEFL) 3: 589
tests for divisibility
(math) 1: 211, 212
tetanus 1: 353
Tet offensive 1: 130;
4: 376
Tethys Sea 3: 523
tetrad 2: 205
tetrahedral 3: 505
tetrahedron 1: 329; 2: 351
tetrameter 2: 403
Tetzel 3: 319
Texas 1: 117, 119,
140–141, 169; 2: 37,
48, 53, 55, 67, 74–75
Texas Rangers 2: 52
textbooks 3: 565–566
Thackeray, William
Makepeace 2: 415,
423
Thailand 2: 140, 143, 150
2: *Atlas* 21
thalamus 3: 358, 359
than, as (usage) 3: 85
than, then (usage) 2: 386
Thanksgiving 2: 60

that (those) there, this (these) here (usage) **2:** 386
that, which (usage) **2:** 387
Thatcher, Margaret **2:** 136
Thebes 2: 80; **3:** 300
The Four Zoas **2:** 395
their, theirs, there, there's, they're (usage) **2:** 386; **3:** 117
theirselves (usage) **2:** 386
theme 4: 1388
then, than (usage) **2:** 386
Theodoric 2: 130; **3:** 302, 303, 305
Theodosius I 3: 302
theorem(s) 1: 329; **2:** 316–319, 322–323, 351
theory, theories
  of change (pol. sci.) **3:** 346
  of relativity **2:** 109
  physics **1:** 383
  psychology **3:** 371
therapy styles 3: 367
there, there's, they're, their, theirs (usage) **2:** 386; **3:** 117
therefore (usage) **3:** 117
thermal
  contact **3:** 538
  equilibrium **3:** 538
thermodynamics 2: 250, 259; **3:** 538–539, 549
  laws of **2:** 259; **3:** 538–539, 549
  system **3:** 538
thermograph 1: 401
thermometers 3: 538
thermonuclear 2: 259
  reaction **2:** 241, 243
thesis (comp.) **3:** 45–46
  sentences **2:** 362; **3:** 108–109
Thespis 2: 404
The Trial **2:** 421
they're, their, theirs, there, there's (usage) **2:** 386 ; **3:** 117
thiamine (vitamin B1) **1:** 332
THINKING ABOUT COLLEGE 3: 622–645

Third
  Reich **2:** 113
  World **3:** 351
Thirteenth Amendment 1: 121; **2:** 39, 68; **4:** 376
38th parallel 2: 118
Thirty Years' War 2: 99, 101, 102; **3:** 314
this (these) here, that (those) there (usage) **2:** 386
Thomas, Dylan **2:** 393, 401–402; **4:** 1380
Thomas, Gospel of **3:** 308
Thomas, Piri **2:** 74
Thomson, J. J. **3:** 501
Thoreau, Henry David **2:** 134, 420; **4:** 1382
though, although (usage) **2:** 377
three-field method of plowing 3: 310, 341
Threepenny Opera, The **2:** 407
Three Sisters **2:** 408
Through the Looking-Glass **2:** 418
thru (usage) **2:** 386
Thucydides 2: 128, 309
Thurber, James **1:** 99; **2:** 416
Thuringia 2: 92
thymine (T) **3:** 479
Tiananmen Square 2: 123
Tiberius 2: 129; **3:** 295
Tibet 2: 90
Tiglath-pileser III 2: 82
Tigris 3: 294–295
Tikrit 2: 127
Tilden, Samuel J. **2:** 41
till 1: 390, 403
till, until (usage) **2:** 386
timbre 1: 457, 467
time line
  of drama **2:** 404–405
  of fiction **2:** 414–415
  of music **1:** 456
  of poetry **2:** 392–393
  U.S. history **1:** 107–133; **4:** 103, 119–120, 130, 139, 148, 157, 168–169, 179, 187, 199, 213–214, 224, 235, 236, 245–246, 259, 275–176, 287–288, 300, 309,

322–223, 336–337, 346
  World History **2:** 79–124, 128–137; **3:** 295, 305, 313, 314, 325
Time Machine, The **2:** 417
time
  management **3:** 556–563
  signature **1:** 461, 467
Timon of Athens **2:** 411
tin 1: 373
Tippecanoe River (Indiana) **2:** 34
tissue(s) 2: 208, 209, 225; **3:** 489, 492, 499
  culturing **3:** 490
Titan 1: 407
titanium 1: 373
Titian 2: 97; **3:** 315
titles (comp.) **3:** 66–67
Titus Andronicus **2:** 410, 411
Titusville, Pennsylvania **1:** 119
to, too, two (usage) **2:** 386–387
toadstools 3: 487
"To a Skylark" 2: 400
"To Autumn" 2: 398, 400
Tocqueville, Alexis de **4:** 1382
"To Doctor Empiric" 3: 79
TOEFL (Test of English as a Foreign Language) **3:** 589
Togo 2: 66, 143, 172 **2:** *Atlas* 12
To Have and Have Not **2:** 420
"To His Coy Mistress" 2: 398
Tojo, Hideki **2:** 113, 115
Tokelau 2: 187
token economy (reinforcement) **3:** 367
Tolkien, J. R. R. **1:** 99; **2:** 430
Tolstoy, Leo **2:** 134, 415, 423; **4:** 1378
Tom Jones **2:** 414, 420, 434
Tom Sawyer, The Adventures of **2:** 419, 434; **3:** 101

Tom Thumb (locomotive)
1: 116; **2:** 62
"Tommy" 2: 398
tone (lit.) **3:** 73–74;
4: 1258–1261
tone (physics) **3:** 540
Tonga 2: 143, 151
2: *Atlas* 22
too, two, to (usage)
2: 386–387
Topeka, *Brown v. Board of Education of* **1:** 129
topic outlines 2: 364–365
topographic maps 2: 189
tornado 1: 400, 403
torque 3: 536, 537, 549
Torquemada, Tomás de
2: 96
Torres, Jose **2:** 74
total
cost **3:** 262–263
fixed cost **3:** 262–263
revenue **3:** 264
variable cost **3:** 262–263
totalitarianism 2: 113;
3: 334, 343, 345, 346, 355
To the Lighthouse **2:** 423
Tours (France) **3:** 306
toward(s) (usage) **2:** 387
Townshend Acts 1: 110;
4: 79, 376
trachea 3: 493
tracheophytes 3: 489
track and field 1: 453
trade
deficit **3:** 284, 293
-first algorithms (math)
1: 314
routes **3:** 315
surplus **3:** 293
winds **1:** 395, 403
tragedy, tragedies (lit.)
1: 468, 469, 478;
2: 404; **3:** 71
by Shakespeare **2:** 411
Trail of Tears 2: 57; **4:** 376
Trajan 2: 129; **3:** 295, 301, 302
trajectory 1: 427
transactions money (M1)
3: 281–282
transalpine provinces
3: 302
trans-Asian trade 3: 311
transcendental
function(s)
3: 424–429, 475

transcontinental railroad
1: 121
transcription (RNA)
3: 486, 499
transfer payments
3: 279
transformations (math)
1: 329
transform faults 3: 523
transistor(s) 2: 118, 244
transit 1: 427
transition metals 3: 504
transitive/intransitive
verbs (Eng.)
1: 18–19; **3:** 87
transitive verbs (usage)
2: 387
translation 3: 486, 499
transmission electron
microscope 2: 197
transmutation 2: 239, 240, 241, 243, 259
transpiration 1: 363
Transportation,
Department of **2:** 11
transubstantiation 3: 319
transversal (math) **2:** 308, 319
transverse wave(s)
1: 380, 383; **2:** 251, 259; **3:** 539, 549
trapezoid 2: 316
trapezoidal
approximation **3:** 422
trapezoidal rule
3: 421–423
travel vocabulary
French **3:** 133–139
German **3:** 163–169
Spanish **3:** 198–203
Travers, P. L. **1:** 99
Treasury, Department of
2: 11
treaties 2: 13; **3:** 352
Treaty of
Cateau-Cambrésis
3: 321
Ghent (1814) **1:** 114
Guadalupe Hidalgo
1: 117; **4:** 359
Paris (1763) **1:** 109
Paris (1783) **1:** 112
Paris (1856) **2:** 106
Verdun (843) **2:** 92;
3: 306
Versailles (1919) **1:** 124;
2: 45, 110, 111, 112;
3: 334

tree diagrams (math)
1: 312
trench warfare 2: 111
Trent, Councils of
1545–1547 **2:** 100;
3: 320
1551–1552 **3:** 320
1562–1563 **3:** 320
Trenton, New Jersey
1: 112
Trevino, Lee **2:** 74
triad 1: 467
Trial, The **2:** 421
triangle(s) 1: 329;
2: 309–312, 319, 327, 332–336, 351
area of **2:** 335
inequalities **2:** 319
kinds **2:** 309
parts **2:** 309
triangular trade system
4: 377
Triassic Period 3: 529
triglycerides 3: 479
trigonal bipyramidal
bond 3: 505
trigonometry 2: 324–342
trigonometric
equations **2:** 333–334
formulas **2:** 335
function **1:** 329; **2:** 351
graphs **2:** 328
identities **2:** 331
substitution,
integration
3: 432–434
tables, how to read
2: 325
trill 1: 467
Trinidad and Tobago
2: 143, 179
2: *Atlas* 5
trinomials 1: 329; **2:** 272, 351
triple
bonds **3:** 505
point **3:** 511
Tripoli 3: 313
Tristan da Cunha 2: 187
Tristram **2:** 400
trochaic 2: 403
Troilus and Cressida
2: 411
Troilus and Criseyde
2: 395
Trojan War 2: 81
Trojan Women **2:** 408;
3: 298

Trollope, Anthony **3:** 36
tropics 1: 393
troposphere 1: 392,
　　403
Trotsky, Leon **2:** 112
trough 3: 549
Troy 2: 81
Troy Female Seminary
　　1: 116
true-breeding 3: 484
Truman, Harry S. **1:** 128;
　　2: 48–49, 62, 69, 116;
　　4: 76, 284, 291, 304
　　Truman Doctrine
　　　1: 128; **2:** 49, 117;
　　　4: 377
Tse-ung, Mao *see* Mao
　　Tse-tung
tsunami 1: 387, 403
tuberculosis 1: 339, 353
Tubman, Harriet **2:** 67
Tuchman, Barbara **4:** 1382
tularemia (rabbit fever,
　　deer fly fever) **1:** 339,
　　353
tundra 1: 358–359
Tunisia 2: 143, 172
　　2: *Atlas* 12
turbidity current(s)
　　3: 520, 533
Turgenev, Ivan **2:** 416
turgor pressure 2: 198
Turkey 2: 89, 117, 127,
　　140, 143, 172
　　2: *Atlas* 18
Turkistan 2: 90, 96
Turkmenistan 2: 143, 151
　　2: *Atlas* 16
Turks and Caicos Islands
　　2: 187
　　2: *Atlas* 5
Turn of the Screw, The
　　2: 416, 417
Turner, Nat **1:** 116; **2:** 67
Tuskegee Institute,
　　Alabama **1:** 122
Tutankhamen 2: 80
tutoring 3: 577
Tuvalu 2: 143, 151
　　2: *Atlas* 22
TVA (Tennessee Valley
　　Authority) **2:** 11;
　　3: 348; **4:** 376
TV/FM 2: 252
Twain, Mark **1:** 99; **2:** 134,
　　415, 423; **3:** 101;
　　4: 1381
　　see also Clemens, Samuel

Tweed, William Marcy
　　"Boss" **4:** 211–212
Twelfth Night **2:** 411
twelve-tone music 1: 467
twenty largest U.S. cities
　　1: 137
Twenty Thousand
　　Leagues Under the
　　Sea **2:** 417
Twice-Told Tales **2:** 416
two, to, too (usage)
　　2: 386–387
Two Gentlemen of
　　Verona, The **2:** 411,
　　434–435
Two Noble Kinsmen, The
　　2: 411
two-party system 1: 116,
　　117; **3:** 349
Two Towers, The **2:** 430
Tyler, Anne **3:** 90
Tyler, John **2:** 35, 36–37,
　　62
Typee **2:** 422
typewriter 1: 121
typhoid fever 1: 339, 353
typhus (epidemic and
　　endemic) **1:** 339, 353
Tyre 2: 81; **3:** 313

U

Uganda 2: 143, 173
　　2: *Atlas* 12–13
"Ugly Duckling, The"
　　2: 416
UK *see* United Kingdom
Ukraine 2: 124, 143, 159
　　2: *Atlas* 15
Ultramontanes 3: 315
ultrasonic 1: 380, 383
ultrasound 3: 546
ultraviolet 2: 252, 259
　　rays **2:** 251
Ulysses **2:** 421, 435
Umayyad dynasty 2: 91
umbra 1: 410, 427
uncertainty, principle of
　　2: 259
Uncle Tom's Cabin
　　1: 118, 470
Uncle Tom's Children
　　2: 423
Uncle Vanya **2:** 408
unconditioned
　　response **3:** 371
　　stimulus **3:** 371
unconformity (geol.)
　　3: 528, 533
unconscious 2: 108
uncontrolled chain
　　reaction 2: 257
undefined geometry
　　terms 2: 306
underemployed 3: 293
Underground Railroad
　　2: 67
underlining (Eng.) **3:** 94
understatement 4: 1241
understudy 1: 478
undoing algebra
　　equations 2: 266
undulant fever 1: 339,
　　353
unemployed 3: 293
unemployment 1: 123,
　　133; **3:** 276–278
　　rate **3:** 278, 293
UNESCO (United Nations
　　Educational, Scientific
　　and Cultural
　　Organization) **2:** 13
unfair trade practices
　　3: 286
UNHCR (Office of the
　　United Nations High
　　Commissioner for
　　Refugees) **2:** 13

unicameral (one-house)
　　legislature 2: 6;
　　4: 377
UNICEF (United Nations
　　Children's Fund)
　　2: 13
unification movements
　　3: 329
Unification of Italy 2: 107
uniformitariansim 3: 533
unilinear theory of
　　change 3: 346
uninterested,
　　disinterested (usage)
　　2: 379; **3:** 116
Union (U.S. Civil War)
　　1: 118
　　army **1:** 120
　　fleet **1:** 120
union
　　labor **1:** 121
　　math **1:** 329; **2:** 351
Union Carbide 2: 123
unionization 2: 105
unique (usage) **2:** 387;
　　3: 117
unit
　　circle **2:** 327
　　of account **3:** 281
unitary government
　　3: 355
United Arab Emirates
　　2: 143, 173
　　2: *Atlas* 18
United Kingdom 2: 124,
　　143, 159; **3:** 337 *see*
　　also England; Britain;
　　Great Britain
　　2: *Atlas* 14
　　territories **2:** 184, 185,
　　187
United Nations 1: 128;
　　2: 13, 53, 112, 117,
　　118, 143; **3:** 352
　　Charter **2:** 117
　　Children's Fund
　　　　(UNICEF) **2:** 13
　　Conference on Trade
　　　　and Development
　　　　(UNCTAD) **2:** 13
　　Disarmament
　　　　Commission **2:** 13
　　Economic and Social
　　　　Council **2:** 13
　　Educational, Scientific
　　　　and Cultural
　　　　Organization
　　　　(UNESCO) **2:** 13

　　Food and Agricultural
　　　　Organization (FAO)
　　　　2: 13
　　General Assembly **2:** 13
　　High Commissioner for
　　　　Refugees (UNHCR)
　　　　2: 13
　　International Court of
　　　　Justice **2:** 13
　　International Monetary
　　　　Fund (IMF) **2:** 13
　　members **2:** 143
　　organization **2:** 13
　　Relief and Works Agency
　　　　(UNRWA) **2:** 13
　　Secretariat **2:** 13
　　Secretary General **2:** 13
　　Security Council **2:** 13
　　　　permanent members
　　　　(China, France, Great
　　　　Britain, Russia,
　　　　United States) **2:** 13
　　Trusteeship Council
　　　　2: 13
　　World Health
　　　　Organization (WHO)
　　　　2: 13
United Provinces
　　(Netherlands) **2:** 101
United States (U.S.) *see*
　　also locations **1:** 125,
　　127; **2:** 13, 104, 105,
　　108, 110, 112, 113,
　　114, 121, 122, 123,
　　124, 140, 143, 179;
　　3: 332, 337, 351
　　2: *Atlas* 8–9
　　Civil Service
　　　　Commission **2:** 45
　　Constitution **1:** 110;
　　　　2: 104; **3:** 325
　　flag, display and care
　　　　1: 173
　　Geological Survey **2:** 46
　　Information Agency
　　　　2: 11
　　land forms **1:** 135
　　Navy, Pacific fleet **1:** 126
　　Postal Service **2:** 11
　　Senate **2:** 112
　　Southwest **1:** 107
　　space flights **1:** 420,
　　　　421–422, 423
　　state flags **1:** 154–173
　　Steel Corporation **1:** 123
　　Treasury **3:** 282
universities, birth of
　　3: 311–313

University of Wittenberg
2: 99
unless (usage) 2: 387
unmanned space probes
1: 419
unsaturated hydrocarbon
2: 237, 243
until, till (usage) 2: 386
"Upon Appleton House"
2: 398
upwarped mountains
3: 525
uracil (U) 3: 479
uranium 1: 373; 2: 113,
257
Uranus 1: 406, 407,
419
Urban II (pope) 3: 313
ureters 3: 493
urinary system, human
3: 494
Uruguay 2: 143, 183
2: *Atlas* 11
U.S. GOVERNMENT
2: 4–53; 3: 347–350;
4: 405–571
U.S. HISTORY
1: 106–133;
: 122–380
us, we (usage) 3: 85
usage guides (Eng.)
2: 376–387;
3: 115–117
USDA food guide
pyramid 1: 331
use to, used to (usage)
3: 117
used (usage) 2: 387
used to, use to (usage)
3: 117
using the library
2: 355–360;
3: 104–107
USS *Cole* 2: 125
USS Constitution ("Old
Ironsides") 1: 114
USS *Maine* 1: 123
USS *Nautilus* 2: 186
USSR *see* Soviet Union
U.S. Term Limits, Inc. v.
Thornton 2: 12
u-substitution 3: 418–420
Utah 1: 118, 121,
140–141, 169–170;
2: 55, 73
utility 3: 293
Utopia 2: 417
utopian socialism 3: 328

Uzbekistan 2: 143, 151
2: *Atlas* 19

V

vaccination schedule,
suggested **1:** 339
vacuoles 2: 195, 196;
3: 481, 482
valence
electrons **2:** 232, 243;
3: 517
shell **2:** 232; **3:** 503
Valley Forge, Pennsylvania
1: 112
Van Allen belt 1: 427
Van Buren, Martin
2: 34–35, 62
Vandals 2: 89; **3:** 303
Vanity Fair **2:** 414, 423
Vanuatu 2: 143, 151
2: *Atlas* 22
vapor pressure 2: 227,
243
vaporization 3: 510, 511
Varangians 2: 92
variable (math) **1:** 285,
329; **2:** 260, 351
variable (econ.)
costs **3:** 262–263, 293
slope **3:** 251
vascular plants 3: 499
vassal 3: 341
Vathek **2:** 417
Vatican 2: 143, 159
2: *Atlas* 14
vaudeville 1: 470
V-E Day 1: 127
vector(s) 3: 534
and scalars **3:** 535
Vega 1: 413
Vega probes **1:** 418
Vega, Lope de **2:** 404, 405,
412
vegetative reproduction
2: 204; **3:** 490
veins 3: 493
Velásquez, Diego **2:** 133
velocity 2: 244–245;
3: 534, 536, 549
venal, venial (usage)
2: 387
Venera satellites 1: 405
Venera probe **1:** 418, 419
Venerable Bede 2: 130
Venetia 2: 107
Venezuela 2: 143, 183
2: *Atlas* 10
venial, venal (usage)
2: 387
Venice 3: 311, 315

vent 3: 533
Venus 1: 404, 405, 406,
418, 419
probes **1:** 418, 419
Venus and Adonis **2:** 400
verbal scale 2: 189
verbals (Eng.) **1:** 40
verbs
English **1:** 5, 17–25;
3: 84
agreement **3:** 89
tenses **1:** 21–25;
3: 87–88, 96–97
French **3:** 126–132
German **3:** 158–161
Latin **3:** 221–228
Spanish **3:** 190–197
Verdi, Giuseppe **1:** 464
Verdun
Battle of **2:** 111
Treaty of **2:** 92; **3:** 306
Vergil 2: 87, 129, 391, 392,
398, 399, 402, 424;
3: 300, 316, 317–318
Vermeer, Jan **2:** 133
Vermont 1: 152–153, 170;
2: 40, 46
vernacular languages
2: 392
Verne, Jules **1:** 99; **2:** 417
Vernier engine 1: 427
Verrazano, Giovanni da
1: 107
Versailles 2: 102, 104;
3: 327, 330
Treaty of **1:** 124; **2:** 45,
110, 111, 112; **3:** 334
verse forms 2: 391
vertebrate(s) 1: 363;
3: 493, 499
vertex 2: 283
vertical
angles **1:** 329; **2:** 351
files **2:** 360
integration **4:** 378
line test **3:** 374
very (usage) **2:** 387
**Very Large Array radio
telescope 1:** 417
Vespucci, Amerigo **2:** 98
vestibular system 3: 359,
371
Vesuvius (volcano) **3:** 524
Veterans Affairs,
Department of **2:** 11
veto 2: 8–9, 13; **3:** 347
vibrations and waves
3: 539–540

Vicksburg, Mississippi
1: 120
Victor Emmanuel II
(Sardinia) **2:** 107;
3: 331
Victor Emmanuel III (It.)
2: 112
video 1: 478
Vienna 3: 334
Vietnam 2: 51, 96, 140,
143, 151;**3:** 337
2: *Atlas* 17
War **1:** 130; **2:** 49, 71,
73, 120, 135–137;
4: 77, 318–321
Vietnamese-Americans
2: 73
viewing rectangle 3: 374
Viking space mission
1: 406
Viking probes **1:** 418,
419
Vikings 1: 107; **2:** 92, 130,
131; **3:** 304, 305, 306,
307, 341
**"Village Blacksmith,
The" 2:** 398
Vinci, Leonardo da *see*
Leonardo da Vinci
Vineland **2:** 422
Vinland 2: 93
Virgil *see* Vergil
Virgin Islands 1: 153,
172; **2:** 184
2: *Atlas* 5
Virginia 1: 109, 112, 114,
119, 120, 148–149,
170; **2:** 37
militia **1:** 109
virtue, virtuosity (usage)
2: 387
virtuosity, virtue (usage)
2: 387
viruses 1: 353; **2:** 192,
212, 225
visceral tissues 2: 209
Visconti, Gian Galeazzo
3: 316
viscosity 3: 510
visible
light **2:** 251; **3:** 544
spectrum **2:** 252
Visigoths 3: 303
VISTA 1: 129
visual
cortex **3:** 359
system **3:** 359
vitalism 3: 326, 341

vitamins 1: 332–333, 353
   A **1:** 332
   B **1:** 332
   B_6 **1:** 333
   B_{12} **1:** 333
   C **1:** 333
   D **1:** 332
   E **1:** 332
V-J Day 2: 116
Vladimir, Prince of Kiev
      3: 304
vocabulary growth
      1: 87–89
vocation 3: 361
voice 4: 1324–1326
voice-over 1: 478
volcanic eruptions, recent
      2: 142
volcanoes 1: 388; **3:** 523,
      529
   types of **3:** 524
Volkswagen 3: 333
volleyball 1: 455
Volpone **2:** 406, 408
volt 2: 254
Voltaire 2: 133, 416, 417,
      425; **3:** 326; **4:** 1378
volume (chem.) **3:** 514
volume (math) **1:** 321
   of a solid of revolution
      3: 443–451
   washer method
      3: 447–448;
      4: 1107–1109
volume of trade 3: 328
von Steuben, Baron *see*
      Steuben, Baron von
Voshkod flights 1: 420,
      423
Vostok flights 1: 420, 423
voting rights 2: 41
Voting Rights Act of 1965
      1: 129; **2:** 70
vowel sounds 1: 86
Voyager space probes
      1: 407, 419
voyages of exploration
      2: 98
vulcanization 1: 117

W

Wagner, Richard **1:** 464;
2: 134; **3:** 329
wait for, wait on (usage)
2: 387
wait on, wait for (usage)
2: 387
Waiting for Godot **2:** 406,
407
Wake Island 1: 153
Walesa, Lech **2:** 137;
3: 337
Walker, Alice **4:** 1381
Wallenstein **2:** 409
**Wallis and Futuna
Islands 2:** 187
2: *Atlas* 22
Walpole, Horace **2:** 417
Wanamaker, John **2:** 64
wane 1: 427
War and Peace **2:** 415,
423, 435
War(s)
between Britain and
France (1793) **1:** 113
in Europe and North
Africa **1:** 127
in Iraq **1:** 133
of 1812 **1:** 114; **2:** 33,
34, 36, 38; **4:**
144–147
of Austrian Succession
2: 103
of Spanish Succession
2: 103
of the Roses **2:** 96
on Poverty **1:** 129
Production Board **1:** 127
warfare, tactics of **3:** 324
warm front 1: 398–399,
403
warrants before seizures
(Fourth Amendment)
3: 350
Warsaw Pact 2: 121;
3: 351
washer method
3: 447–448;
4: 1107–1109
washers, volume
3: 446–448
Washington (State)
1: 140–141, 170
**Washington Naval
Conference 1:** 125
Washington, Booker T.
1: 122; **2:** 68

Washington, D.C. **1:** 114,
117, 121, 123, 126,
131, 148–149
Washington, George
1: 111, 112, 113;
2: 30–31, 59, 62, 109,
134; **4:** 123, 126
Washoe 3: 365
Waste Land, The **2:** 396;
3: 80
water
consumption, average
1: 355
cycle **1:** 360, 396; **3:** 533
molds **3:** 487
pollution **1:** 355
-soluble vitamins
1: 332–333
table **1:** 403
vapor **1:** 392
waterfalls, highest
2: 141
Watergate affair
1: 131; **2:** 51, 122;
4: 327–330, 379
Waterloo, Battle of **3:** 327
Watson, James **2:** 201;
3: 486
Watson, John **3:** 357
watt 2: 246, 254
Waugh, Evelyn **2:** 417
wave 1: 380, 383; **2:** 259;
3: 539, 549
characteristics **3:** 540
energy **2:** 253
equation **2:** 253
mechanics **3:** 502
motion **1:** 380–381;
2: 251–253; **3:** 539
pulse **3:** 539, 549
train **3:** 539, 549
wavelength 1: 380, 383;
2: 251, 259; **3:** 540,
549
Waves, The **2:** 423
wax 1: 427
'way, away (usage)
2: 387
Way of All Flesh, The
2: 416
we, us (usage) **3:** 85
weak force 2: 256
wealth 3: 256, 293
Weary Blues **2:** 69
weather 1: 396–401
prediction **1:** 400–401
weathering 1: 403; **3:** 526,
533

Weber, E. H. **3:** 356
Webster, Daniel **1:** 116;
2: 37, 402
Webster-Ashburton
Treaty **1:** 117
Webster-Hayne debate
1: 116; **4:** 379
wedges 1: 377
Wegener, Alfred **1:** 384;
3: 520
weight 1: 383; **2:** 244, 259;
3: 549
weight control 1: 336
Weill, Kurt **2:** 407
Weimar Republic 3: 333,
334
Weiss, Peter **2:** 405, 412
well, good (usage) **2:** 381;
3: 116
Wells, H. G. **2:** 417
Welty, Eudora **3:** 52–53;
4: 1382
went, gone, go (usage)
2: 381
Werthheimer, Max **3:** 357
Wertz, Paul J. **1:** 421
Weschler, David **3:** 363
Wessex 2: 92
West (U.S.) **1:** 117,
138–141
West Africa 2: 101
West Bank (Jordan)
2: 121, 124, 125
West Germany 2: 119,
123; **3:** 337
West Indies 2: 99, 101
2: *Atlas* 5
West Point 2: 40, 48
West Virginia 1: 148–149,
171
West, Mae **1:** 470
Western
and Eastern Christian
Church **2:** 93
Hemisphere **1:** 107, 116;
3: 322
Roman Empire **3:** 295
states **1:** 139
trade **2:** 102
**WESTERN
CIVILIZATION,**
History of **3:** 294–341
Westinghouse, George
1: 121
wheels and axles
1: 376–377
"When I Have Fears"
2: 399

"When Lilacs Last in the Dooryard Bloom'd" 2: 402
which, that (usage) 2: 387
which, who (usage) 2: 387
Whig Party 1: 117, 119; 2: 37; 4: 156, 379
while (usage) 2: 387
Whiskey Rebellion 1: 113; 2: 31; 4: 379
White House 1: 114
White, Ann Terry 1: 101
White, E. B. 1: 99; 4: 1382
White, Edward 1: 423
Whites (anti-Bolsheviks) 2: 111
Whitman, Walt 2: 393, 398, 402
Whitney, Eli 1: 113
Whittier, John Greenleaf 2: 393, 402
WHO (World Health Organization) 2: 13
who, which (usage) 2: 387
who, whom (usage) 3: 85
who's, whose (usage) 2: 387; 3: 117
whoever, whomever (usage) 2: 387
whole number 1: 176, 235, 261, 329; 2: 262
whole-tone music 1: 467
whom, who (usage) 3: 85
whomever, whoever (usage) 2: 387
whooping cough 1: 339, 353
Who's Afraid of Virginia Woolf? 2: 407
whose, who's (usage) 2: 387; 3: 117
Why We Can't Wait 3: 59
"Wife of Bath's Tale, The" 2: 395
Wild Duck, The 2: 408
Wilder, Laura Ingalls 1: 99
Wilder, Thornton 2: 432; 4: 1381
Wilderness, the, Virginia 1: 120
Wilhelm I (kaiser) 3: 329–330, 332–333
Wilhelm II (Ger.) 3: 332
Wilkes, Charles 2: 186
will, shall (usage) 2: 386; 3: 117

Willard, Emma 1: 116
William (duke of Normandy) 3: 307
William I (Prussia) 2: 107
William and Mary (Eng.) 3: 327
William and Mary, College of 2: 32, 36
William Tell 2: 409
William the Conqueror 2: 93, 131
Williams, Roger 1: 108; 2: 60
Williams, Tennessee 2: 405, 412, 434; 4: 1381
Williams, William Carlos 2: 393, 402
Williamsburg, Virginia 1: 470
Wilmot Proviso 1: 118; 4: 378
Wilson, Woodrow 1: 124; 2: 44–45, 62, 111; 3: 333; 4: 79, 234, 239–240, 243–244
wind belts 1: 395 vane 1: 403
"Windhover, The" 2: 397
Wingfield, Walter C. 1: 444
Winter of Our Discontent, The 2: 423
Winter's Tale, The 2: 410, 435
Winthrop, John 1: 108; 2: 60
"wireless" 1: 473
wireless telegraphy (radio) 2: 112
Wisconsin 1: 113, 128, 144–145, 171; 2: 55
-wise (usage) 2: 387
without (usage) 2: 387
Wittenberg, University of 2: 99
Wizard of Oz 1: 472
Wolfe, James 1: 109
Wolfe, Thomas 2: 415, 423, 430; 3: 35
Wolfe, Tom 4: 1382
Wolpe, J. 3: 367
Women in Love 2: 421
women's suffrage 1: 125; 4: 230–231

wonderful (usage) 2: 387
"Woodspurge, The" 2: 400
woodwind instruments 1: 458–459, 467
Woolf, Virginia 2: 415, 423; 4: 1381, 1383
word meaning 1: 87–89 order German 3: 162 Latin 3: 217
Wordsworth, William 2: 134, 391, 393, 402; 4: 1379
work 1: 376, 383; 2: 246, 247, 250, 259; 3: 537, 549 formulas 2: 268 -energy 3: 537
working women 3: 672
World 2: 139 2: *Atlas* 2–3
World Health Organization (WHO) 2: 13
WORLD HISTORY 2: 78–137
world population 3: 530
World Trade Center 1: 133; 2: 124, 125
World War I 1: 124, 473; 2: 45, 47, 75, 108, 110, 111, 112, 135, 136; 3: 330, 332–333, 352; 4: 238–244
World War II 1: 126, 127, 473; 2: 47, 48, 49, 50, 58, 73, 75, 113, 114, 115–116, 135–137; 3: 330, 334–335, 351, 352; 4: 278–286 Pacific 1: 127; 2: 71
would, should (usage) 2: 386
Wounded Knee 2: 57
Wright, Frank Lloyd 2: 135
Wright, Orville 1: 123; 2: 109, 135
Wright, Richard 2: 415, 423; 4: 1381
Wright, Wilbur 1: 123; 2: 109, 135
writ of habeas corpus 4: 571

WRITING (Eng.)
    1: 56–73; **2:** 354–387,
    436–460; **3:** 32–117;
    4: 1161–1389
  assignments **3:** 569
  basics **4:** 1179–1186
  materials **3:** 35–36
  style **2:** 366–367;
    3: 95–101
  tips **3:** 36
Wundt, Wilhelm
    3: 356–357
Wuthering Heights
    2: 414, 418, 435
Wycliffe, John **2:** 132
Wyoming 1: 140–141,
    171; **2:** 43, 55, 57

X

Xerxes I 3: 297
x-rays 1: 380; **2:** 251, 252, 259; **3:** 546
xylem 3: 489, 499
XYZ Affair 1: 114

Y

Yahweh 3: 296
Yale 2: 44
Yalta 3: 334
   Conference **4:** 380
Yang Liwei *see* Liwei, Yang
yeasts 3: 487
Yeats, William Butler **2:** 391, 393, 403
yellow
   fever **1:** 339, 353
   journalism **4:** 380
Yeltsin, Boris N. **2:** 124, 137; **3:** 337
Yemen 2: 143, 173
   2: *Atlas* 18
Yorktown, Virginia (Battle of) **1:** 112; **4:** 380
you (usage) **2:** 387
you all (usage) **2:** 387
you and I (usage) **2:** 387
you're, your (usage) **2:** 387; **3:** 117
Young, John **1:** 422
Young, Thomas **3:** 544
your, you're (usage) **2:** 387; **3:** 117
Ypres, first Battle of **2:** 111
Ypres, second Battle of **2:** 111
Yugoslavia 2: 110, 114, 115, 117, 124; **3:** 336, 337, 351

Z

Zacharius (pope) **3:** 306
Zama, Battle of **2:** 86
Zambia 2: 143, 173
   2: *Atlas* 13
Zanghi, governor of Mosul **3:** 313
Zara 3: 313
Zenger, Peter **2:** 61; **4:** 77
zero 1: 329
Zimbabwe 2: 124, 143, 173; **3:** 332
   2: *Atlas* 13
Zimmermann note (telegram) **1:** 124; **4:** 380
zinc 1: 373
Zinger, John Peter **1:** 109
Zola, Émile **2:** 415, 423
***Zoo Story, The* 2:** 407
Zoroastrianism 2: 83
Zwingli, Huldreich **3:** 319
Zwinglian (church) **3:** 319–321
zygote 1: 363; **2:** 206, 225; **3:** 360, 485, 491, 496

SCIENCE
for FUN
EXPERIMENTS

© Aladdin Books Ltd 1998
Designed and produced by
Aladdin Books Ltd
28 Percy Street
London W1P OLD

First published in the United States by
Copper Beech Books,
an imprint of
The Millbrook Press
2 Old New Milford Road
Brookfield, Connecticut 06804

Design: David West Children's Book Design
Illustrator: Tony Kenyon
Photography: Roger Vlitos
Models: David Millea

Library of Congress
Cataloging-in-Publication Data
Gibson, Gary, 1957–
Science for fun experiments / by Gary Gibson; illustrated by Tony Kenyon.
p. cm. Includes index.
Summary: Provides instructions for a selection of hands-on experiments
introducing basic scientific principles,
in such areas as magnetism, electricity, and water.
ISBN 0-7613-0517-3 (pbk.)
1. Science---Experiments---Juvenile
literature. [1. Science--Experiments.
2. Experiments.] I. Kenyon, Tony. Ill. II. Title.
Q164.G524 1996   96-13908
507' .8--dc20   CIP AC

SCIENCE
for FUN

EXPERIMENTS

GARY GIBSON

x

COPPER BEECH BOOKS
Brookfield, Connecticut

CONTENTS

CHAPTER ONE
Light and Color 8-33

CHAPTER TWO
Making Shapes 34-59

CHAPTER THREE
Pushing and Pulling 60-85

CHAPTER FOUR
Making Things Change 86-111

CHAPTER FIVE
Understanding Electricity 112-137

CHAPTER SIX
Making Things Float and Sink 138-163

CHAPTER SEVEN
Playing with Magnets 164-189

CHAPTER EIGHT
Hearing Sounds 190-215

Glossary 216

Index 759

INTRODUCTION

Have you ever wondered what would happen to the Earth if there were no sunlight? Have you thought about where magnetism comes from, or what life would be like without electricity?

You will probably have tried to walk as a weightless astronaut, and come down to Earth with a bump and wondered why that happens. But have you wondered why a submarine can both sink and float? Do you understand how musical instruments make sounds?

For centuries scientists have worked to find out more about these things. They have investigated light and color, shapes, pushing and pulling, and why and how things change. They have also experimented with floating and sinking,

electricity, magnetism, and sound.

Science for Fun Experiments introduces you to some of the fascinating discoveries that have been made about these scientific phenomena. It takes you step-by-step through fun, "hands-on" experiments, giving you a brief explanation of why they work, so you can impress your friends with your scientific knowledge! You will learn how to make useful gadgets – a stethoscope, a banger, a compass, a jet boat, a motor, even 3-D glasses – to name just a few of the exciting projects.

Whenever this symbol appears, adult supervision is required.

CONTENTS

Light for life   10

Day and night   12

Seeing images   14

Bouncing light   16

Up periscope!   18

Moving pictures   20

Splitting light   22

Mixing colors   24

Seeing in three-dimension   26

Separating colors   28

Colored dyes   30

Color changes   32

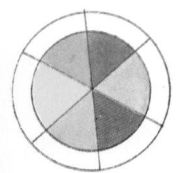

CHAPTER *One*

LIGHT AND COLOR

LIGHT FOR LIFE

Green plants need sunlight to live and grow. They use the light's energy to grow. All animals get their food from plants, either directly or indirectly. Since plants need sunlight to grow, all living things depend on the sun.

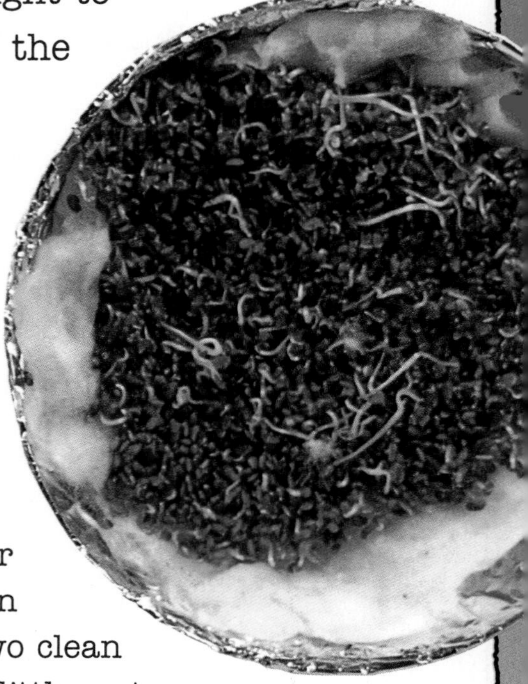

GROWING WATERCRESS

1 Put a layer of cotton in the bottom of two clean dishes. Add a little water. Sprinkle watercress seeds evenly over the cotton.

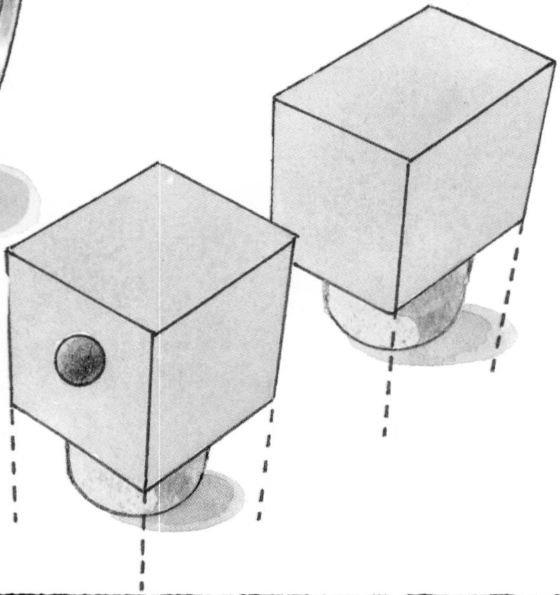

2 Put the dishes on a sunny windowsill and cover each dish with a cardboard box. Make a hole in the side of one box and leave for several days. Check daily that the cotton is damp.

3 The seeds under the box with no hole have grown straight up looking for light. The watercress under the box with the hole has grown toward the light.

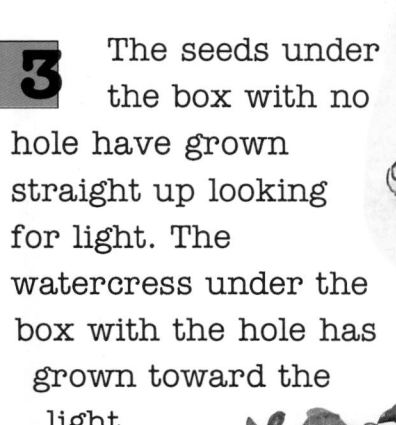

WHY IT WORKS

Green plants contain a chemical called chlorophyll. Chlorophyll traps light, which combines with water and air to help make plants grow. This process is called "photosynthesis." Plants cannot see light but can bend and grow toward where it comes from.

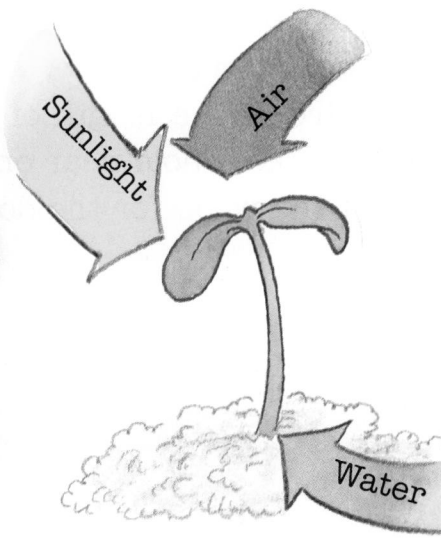

Sunlight

Air

Water

FURTHER IDEAS

Follow step 1 again. Cover one dish with a large, clean glass jar to make a "greenhouse." Compare the growing roots and shoots with the uncovered dish. Which seedlings grow the best?

DAY AND NIGHT

Half the world is in daylight and the other half in darkness. As the Earth spins around, each part takes its turn to face the sun. Parts of the Earth facing away from the sun can be lit only by the moon. Sometimes the moon passes between the sun and the Earth, so the sun's rays are blocked and the sky grows dark. This is called an eclipse.

MAKE A SUNDIAL

1 You need a piece of wood, or thick cardboard, and a length of dowel. Make a hole near one edge of the wood for the dowel.

2 Stand the dowel in the hole (fix with glue if necessary). Decorate using waterproof paints.

3 On a sunny morning put the sundial outside. The dowel casts a shadow; paint along the shadow.

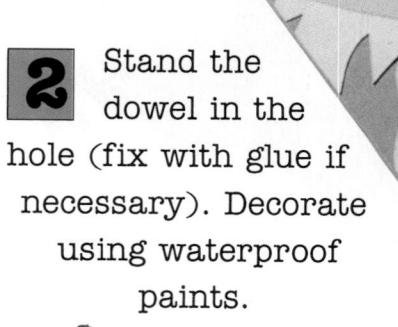

4 Repeat step 3 every hour. Paint the time next to each shadow. The sundial will only work on sunny days. Remember to keep it in the same place, facing the same way.

WHY IT WORKS

The stick blocks the sun and casts a shadow. The shadow's position changes as the sun moves across the sky.

As the Earth spins around, the sun appears to move across the sky.

FURTHER IDEAS

Make a shadow animal with your hands. In a darkened room, get a friend to shine a flashlight onto the wall. Put your hands in front of the flashlight and see if you can make an animal-shaped shadow on the wall.

SEEING IMAGES

An image is a likeness of something or someone. What we see in photographs or a movie are images. A camera is a box that can make an image on photographic film. The film contains chemicals that will keep the image for years.

MAKE A PINHOLE CAMERA

1 Find a small cardboard box that does not let light through. Use a pair of scissors to cut out one side of the box.

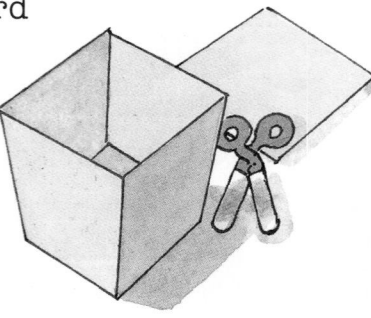

2 Tape a piece of tracing paper over the cutout side of the box. Make sure that the tracing paper is kept as smooth as possible.

3 Make a pinhole in the side of the box opposite the tracing paper. Point the pinhole at a window. Move toward the window until you see its image on the tracing paper.

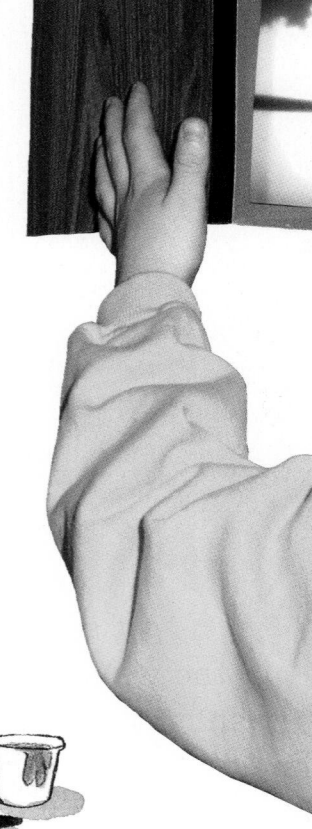

WHY IT WORKS

Light rays in air do not bend or curve; they always travel in straight lines. Rays of light from the window enter the pinhole in straight lines and hit the tracing paper. The light rays from the bottom and the top of the window cross over as they pass through the hole, so the image appears upside down.

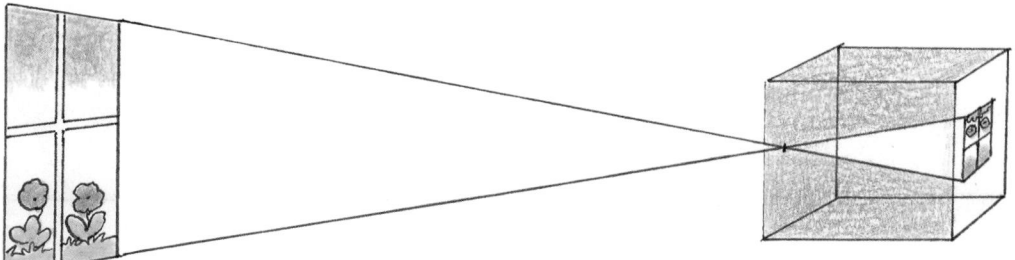

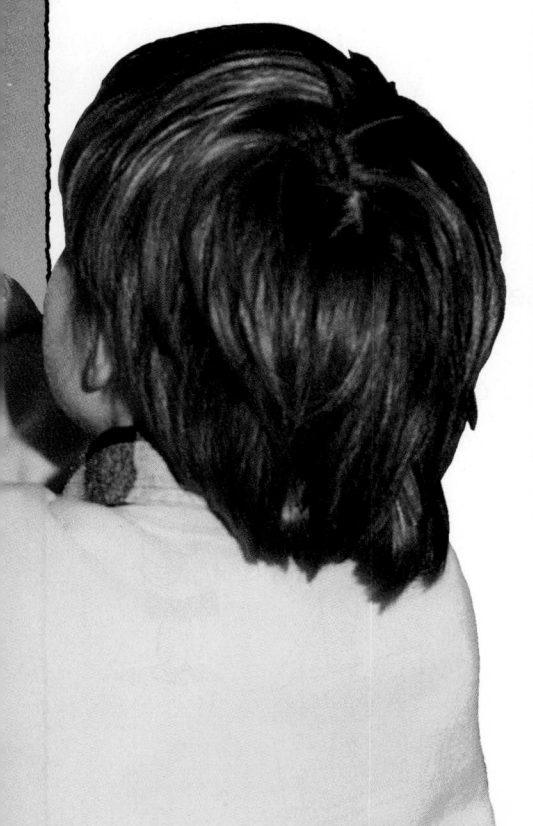

FURTHER IDEAS

Make the pinhole a little bigger so more light enters the camera. The image becomes brighter but less clear. A magnifying glass in front of the pinhole can sharpen the image. The image will be faint, so point the pinhole at a bright object such as a lightbulb.

BOUNCING LIGHT

Rays of light can be bounced off an object like a rubber ball bouncing off a wall. We call this "reflection." Light rays are reflected best by flat, shiny surfaces such as shiny spoons, cans, bottles, or mirrors.

MAKE A KALEIDOSCOPE

1 Carefully tape together three identical-sized small mirrors. Make a triangle-shaped tube with the shiny sides facing inside.

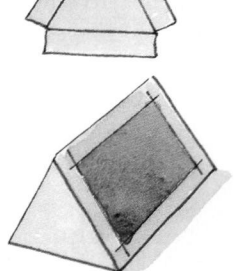

2 Cut out a triangle-shaped piece of paper, allowing for flaps. Tape it over one end of the triangle of mirrors to form a box.

GET AN ADULT TO HELP YOU

3 Cut out small pieces of brightly colored paper from a magazine and drop them into the bottom of the box.

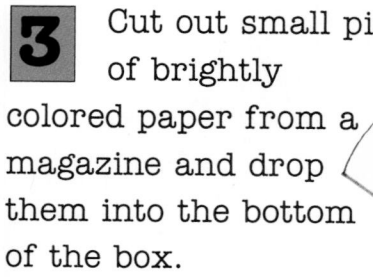

4 Tape another triangle of paper over the other end of the tube. Using a pencil, make a hole to look through. The kaleidoscope is finished.

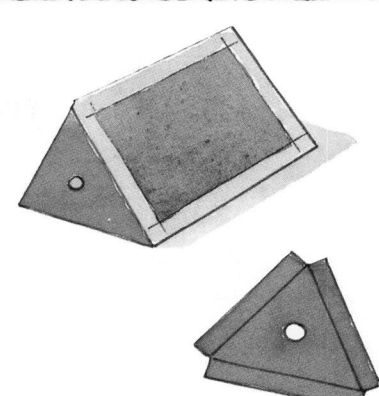

5 Hold the kaleidoscope level, and point it at a bright light. Look at the pattern through the eye piece. Shake and look again.

WHY IT WORKS

Light rays from the colored paper are reflected back and forth between the mirrors. Each image is doubled by the mirrors before the light rays reach your eye.

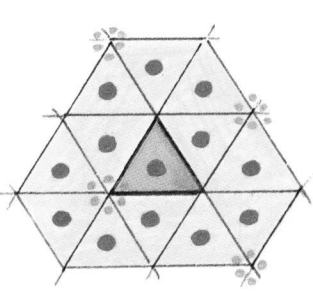

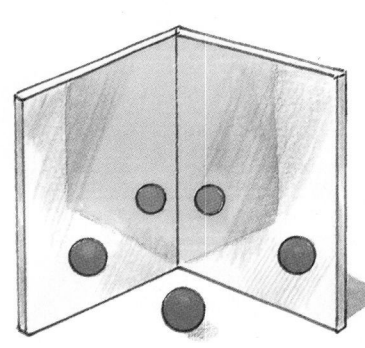

FURTHER IDEAS
Stand two mirrors up at right angles, using modeling clay. Place a marble between the mirrors. How many images can you see?

UP PERISCOPE!

Submarine crews want to know what is going on above the waves without being seen. Instead of rising to the ocean's surface, the submarine raises its periscope. On land you can use periscopes to see over walls and around corners!

MAKE A PERISCOPE

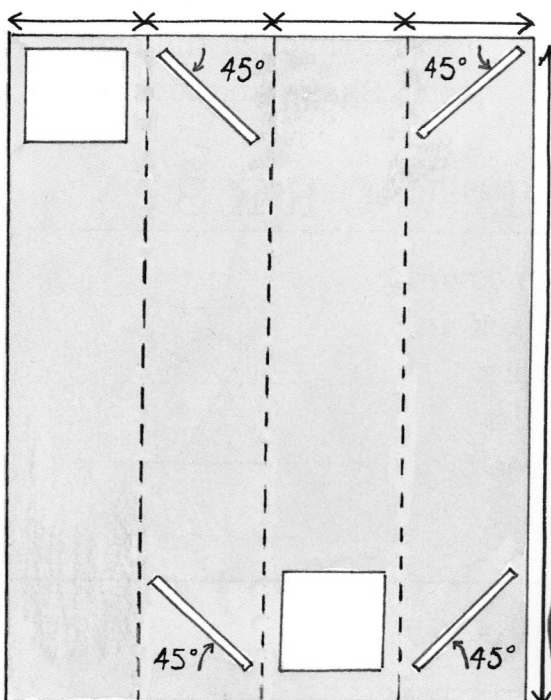

1 Copy the pattern onto cardboard. Cut around the outline. Cut out the slots and squares. Fold on the dotted lines.

2 Tape the edges of the cardboard together to form a box. Make sure that the slots line up. Paint to decorate.

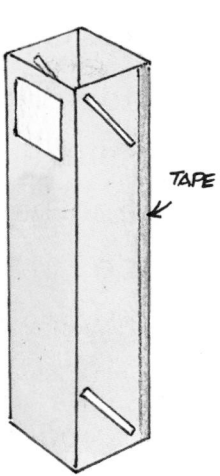

TAPE

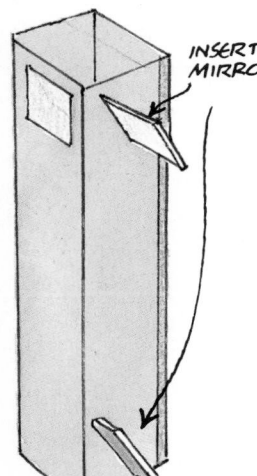

INSERT MIRROR

3 Insert two mirrors into the slots, top mirror facing down, bottom mirror facing up. Look into the lower mirror.

WHY IT WORKS

Light rays above and ahead of you hit the upper mirror. It reflects the rays down to the lower mirror, which in turn reflects the light rays into your eyes.

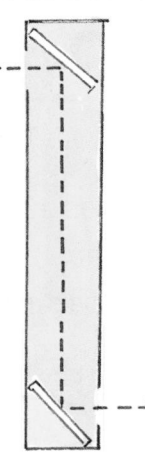

FURTHER IDEAS
Make a periscope to see around corners. Copy the design shown below. Follow instructions 1 and 2 as before. But this time the angles of the mirror slots are different. Make sure the top mirror faces down and the bottom mirror faces up.

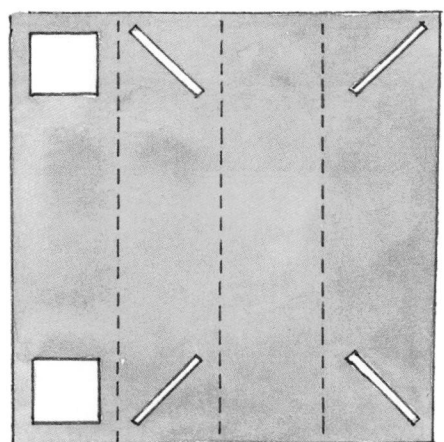

MOVING PICTURES

Cartoon films are made out of many drawings. These are photographed one after another by a movie camera. When the film is projected onto a screen, the images seem to move. If you move your eyes quickly over the pictures on the right, the ball seems to bounce.

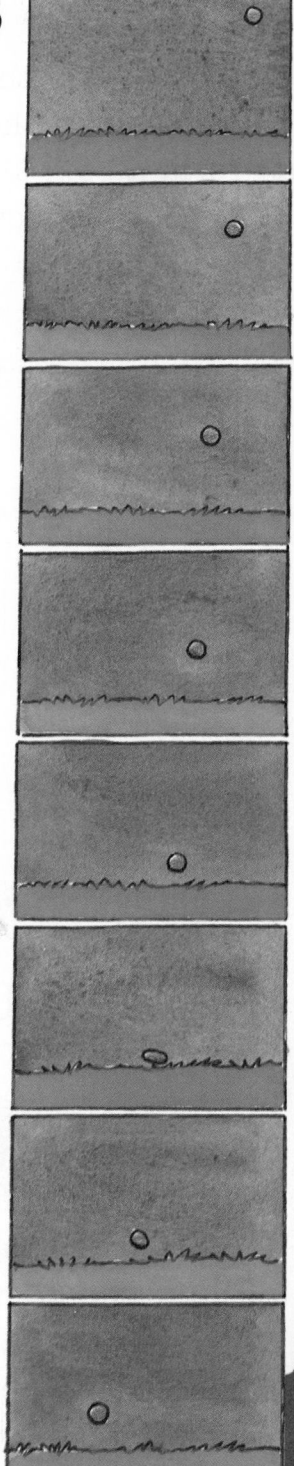

MAKE A FLICK BOOK

1 Draw a background picture. Trace it onto at least 12 pages of the same size. Leave a margin down one side of each drawing.

2 Draw the sun high in the sky on the first page. Draw it slightly lower on the second page. Repeat until the sun has set on the last page.

3 Stack the pages neatly and staple them together with two staples along the edge of the margin.

WHY IT WORKS

Your eyes see each image for a fraction of a second. If the images are shown fast enough, the eye runs the images together. Differences in the separate images appear as movement.

FURTHER IDEAS

Copy the two faces (below) onto two sheets of tracing paper. Staple the two sheets together. Roll the upper sheet tightly around a pencil. Move the pencil up and down to roll and unroll the upper sheet.

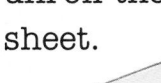

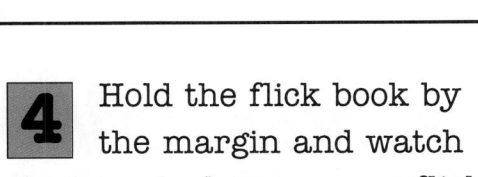

4 Hold the flick book by the margin and watch the sun go down as you flick the pages.

SPLITTING LIGHT

More than 300 years ago, Sir Isaac Newton proved that white light is made from the colors of the rainbow. Newton split white light into a rainbow using a wedge of glass called a prism. We see rainbows in the sky because water droplets in the air split the sunlight before it reaches us.

MAKE A RAINBOW

2 Angle a mirror in a bowl of water. Bend a large piece of white posterboard away from the bowl.

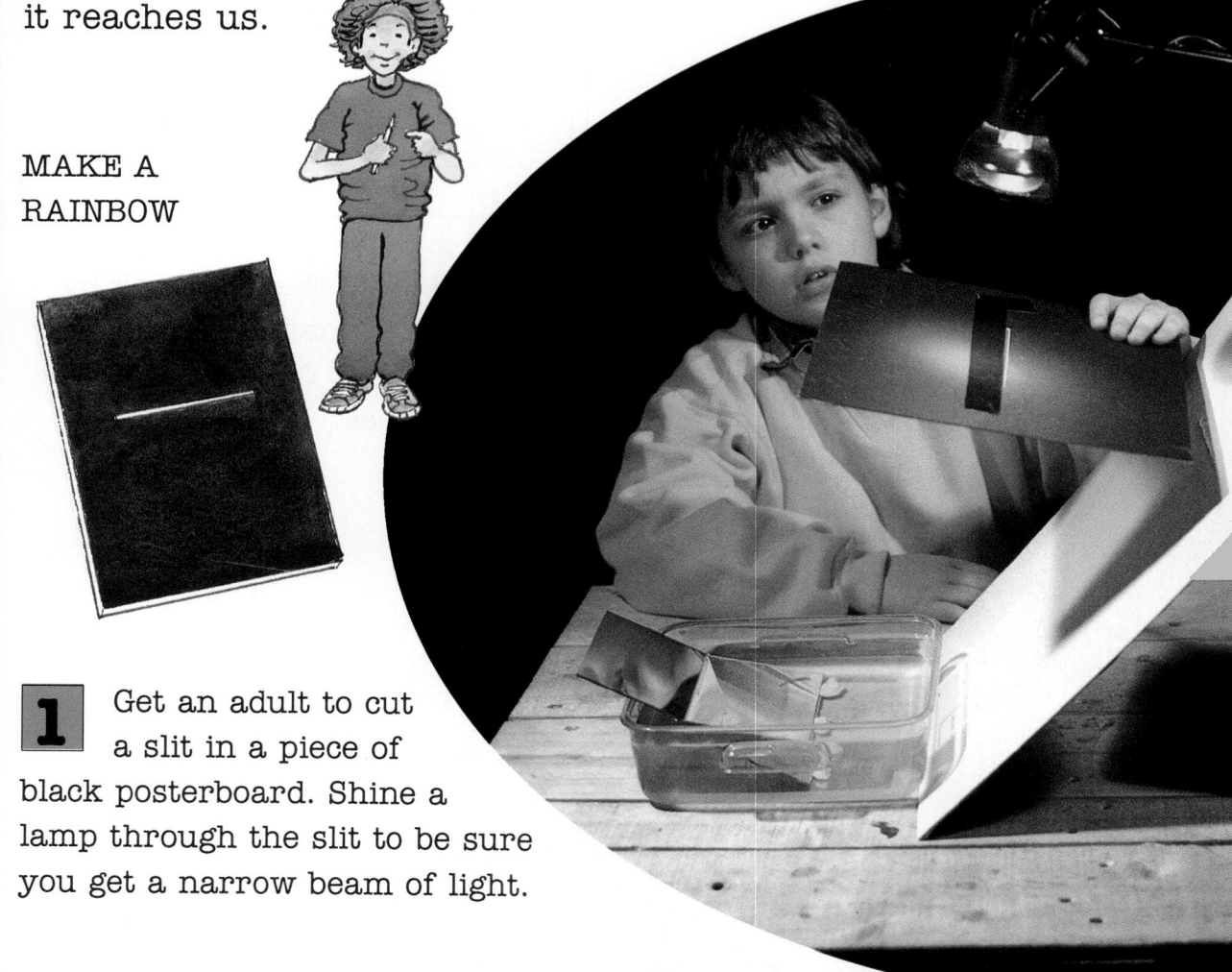

1 Get an adult to cut a slit in a piece of black posterboard. Shine a lamp through the slit to be sure you get a narrow beam of light.

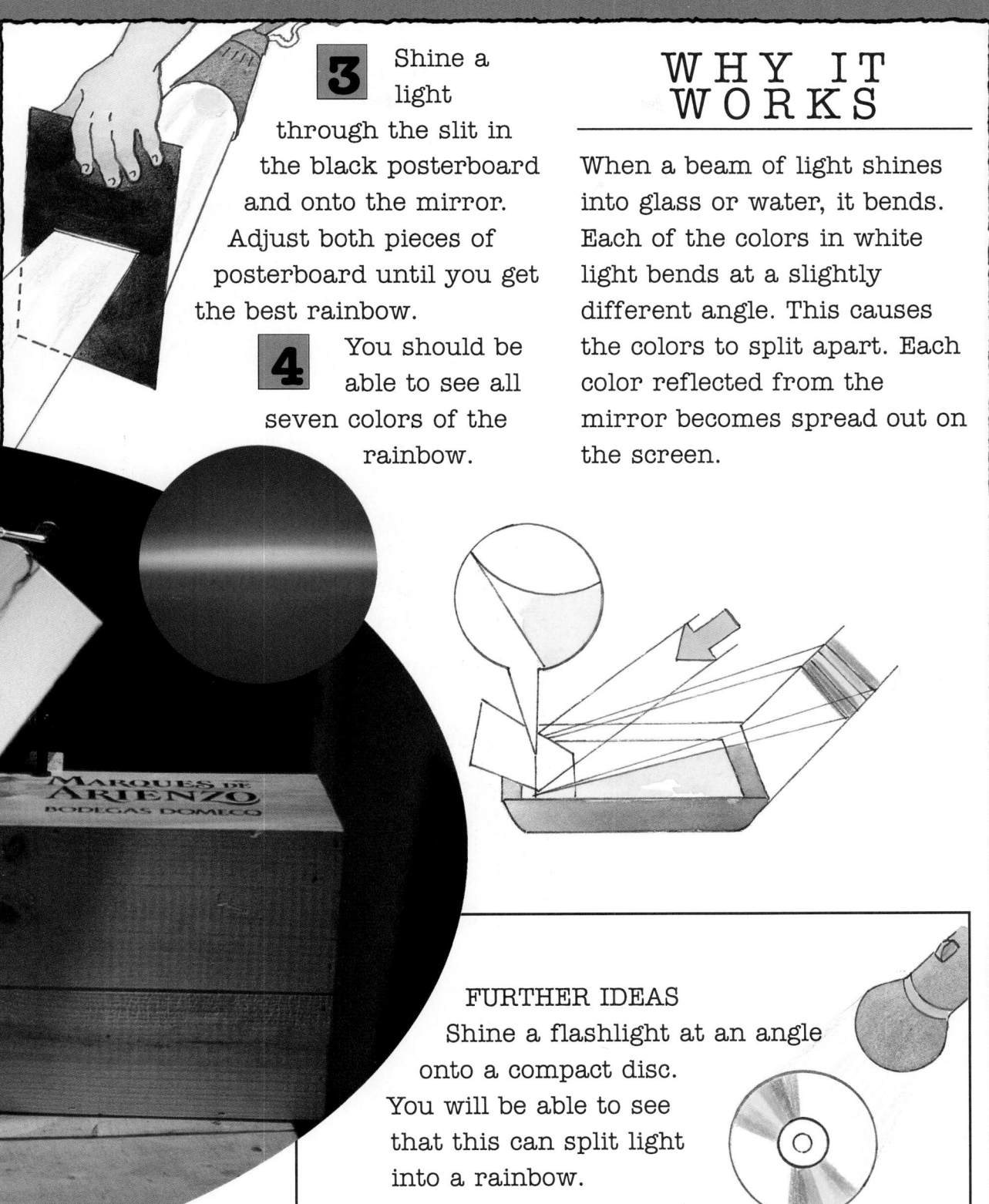

3 Shine a light through the slit in the black posterboard and onto the mirror. Adjust both pieces of posterboard until you get the best rainbow.

4 You should be able to see all seven colors of the rainbow.

WHY IT WORKS

When a beam of light shines into glass or water, it bends. Each of the colors in white light bends at a slightly different angle. This causes the colors to split apart. Each color reflected from the mirror becomes spread out on the screen.

MARQUES DE ARIENZO
BODEGAS DOMECQ

FURTHER IDEAS
Shine a flashlight at an angle onto a compact disc. You will be able to see that this can split light into a rainbow.

MIXING COLORS

Look closely at a color TV or the photographs in this book. The pictures are made up of lots of tiny, colored dots. Because we see books or TV from a distance, the dots seem to mix to make colors.

MAKE A COLOR SPINNER

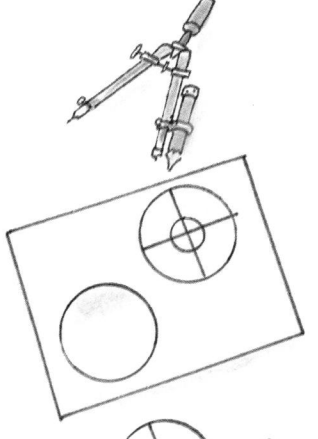

1 Use a pencil and a pair of compasses to draw circles of different sizes onto white posterboard. Cut them out with scissors.

2 Divide the circles into equal sections and decorate each section with different colors. Push a sharp pencil or stick through a hole in the center of each circle.

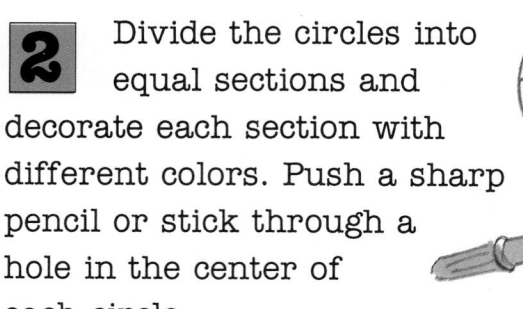

3 Spin the spinner as fast as you can on a tabletop and watch the different colors merge. If you color a spinner with the colors of the rainbow, it may appear white when you spin it.

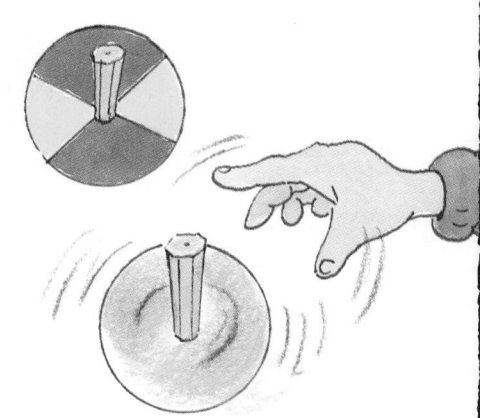

WHY IT WORKS

The spinner is turning so fast that instead of seeing separate colors, our eyes see a mixture. White light is made up of the colors of the rainbow, so a spinner decorated with these colors appears white.

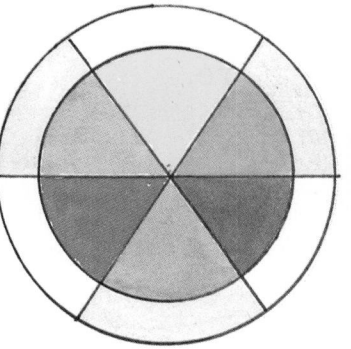

FURTHER IDEAS
Cover three flashlights with red, blue, and green cellophane. Shine them onto white paper (or a white floor). Allow the light beams to overlap. See how many new colors you can make.

SEEING IN THREE-DIMENSION

Animals usually have two eyes. Close one eye and look at an object. Guess how far away it is. Try again with both eyes open. It is much harder to judge distances using only one eye. Having two eyes gives us a sense of depth.

MAKE 3-D GLASSES

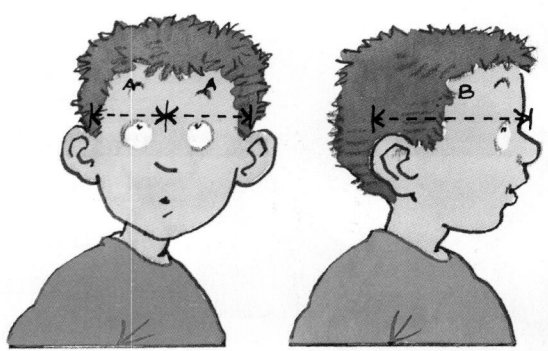

1 Measure the distances A and B around your head with a tape measure.

2 Use the distances to draw out your glasses onto cardboard. Cut out the glasses and fold along the dotted lines.

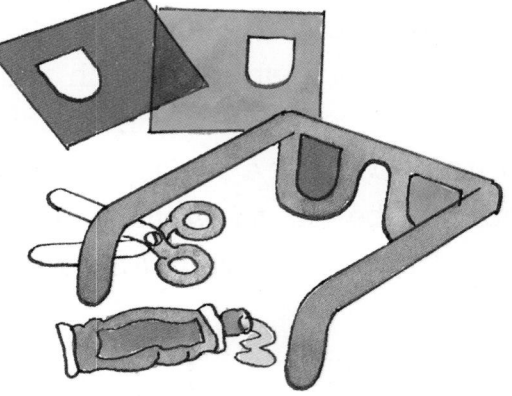

3 Cut out red and green cellophane for the eyeholes. Glue the green over the right eyehole and red over the left. Try on the glasses. Look at the insect picture opposite.

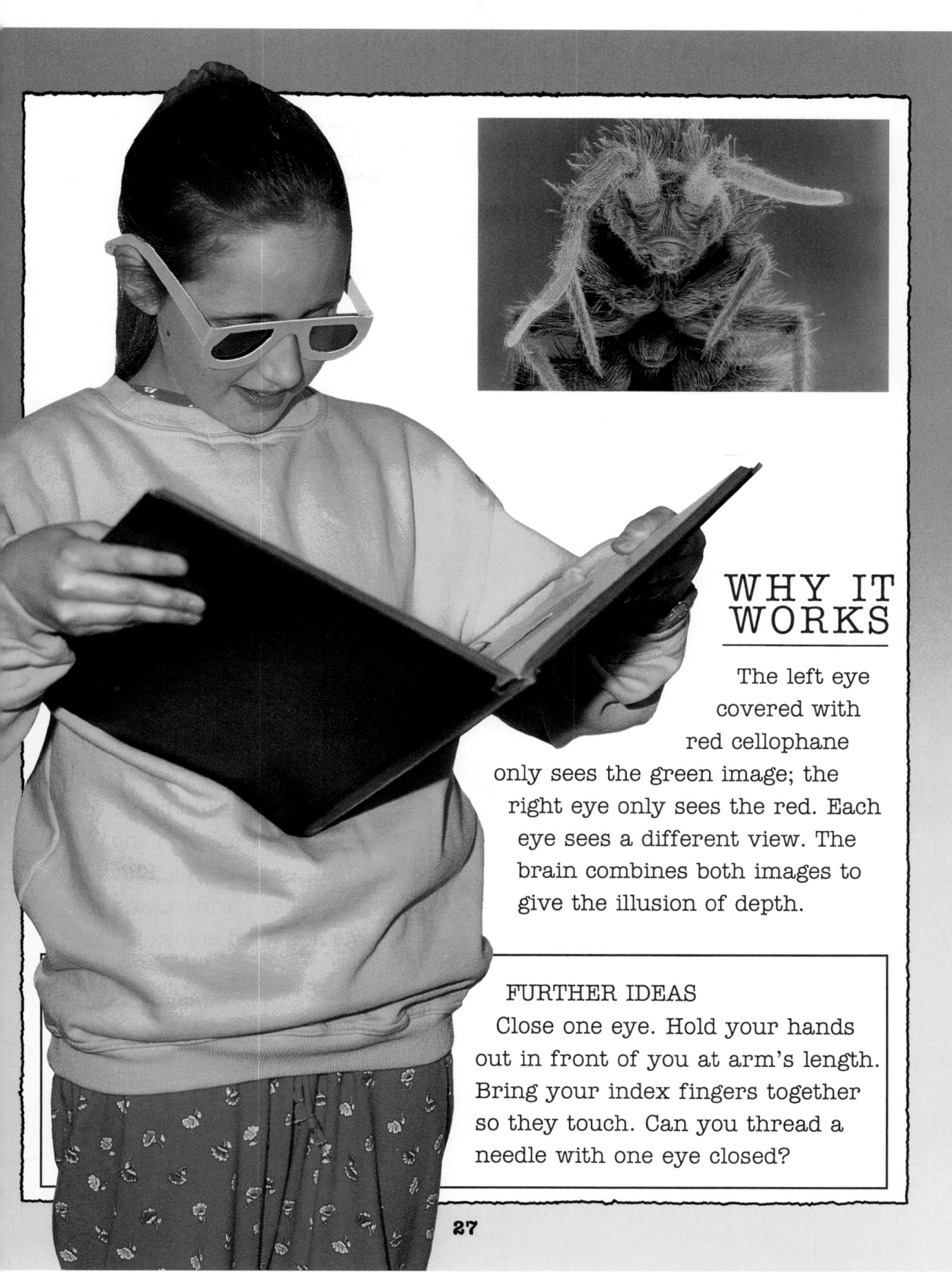

WHY IT WORKS

The left eye covered with red cellophane only sees the green image; the right eye only sees the red. Each eye sees a different view. The brain combines both images to give the illusion of depth.

FURTHER IDEAS

Close one eye. Hold your hands out in front of you at arm's length. Bring your index fingers together so they touch. Can you thread a needle with one eye closed?

27

SEPARATING COLORS

In printing and painting there are three primary colors – red, blue, and yellow. The enormous variety of colored dyes, paints, and inks are made by mixing different amounts of two or more of the primary colors.

FIND THE HIDDEN COLORS

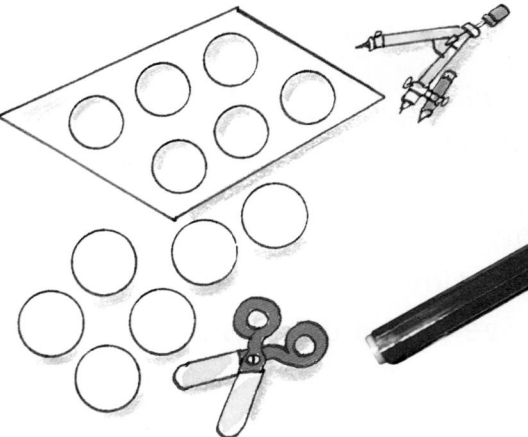

1 With a pair of compasses draw some circles onto paper towels. Cut them out with scissors.

2 Using marker pens, draw a dot of color in the middle of each circle. Black, purple, green, brown, and orange are good colors to use.

3 Place each circle of paper towel over the top of a clean, dry jar.

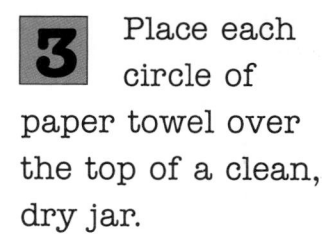

4 Add drops of water to the dot of color. Dip a straw into water. Block the top with your finger. Touch the ink dot with the straw.

WHY IT WORKS

Some inks are made up of several colors. These can separate as the water spreads, carrying the colors at different speeds.

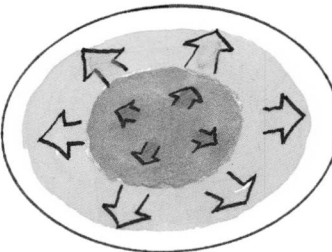

FURTHER IDEAS
Take a long strip of paper towel. Draw a large dot near the bottom. Hang the strip up so the end just dips into a bowl of water. Watch the colors separate as the water rises up the paper.

COLORED DYES

Today we can buy clothes in an enormous variety of colors. These colors come from modern artificial dyes made from oil. Before the nineteenth century, people had always used natural dyes made from plants, animals, or materials in the ground.

TIE–DYE A HANDKERCHIEF

GET AN ADULT TO DO THIS FOR YOU

2 Tie some string around a white cotton handkerchief as tightly as you can.

1 Collect lots of brown onion skins. Ask an adult to boil them in water for 20 minutes.

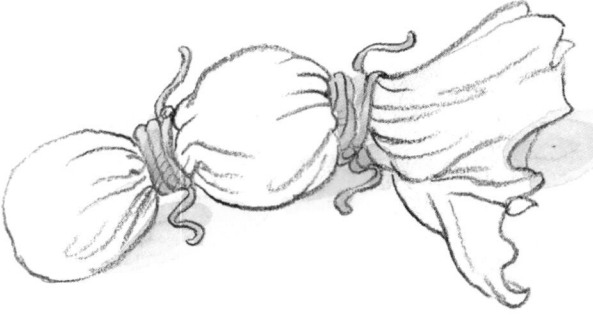

3 Soak the tied handkerchief in the onion skin water for five minutes. Use an oven glove to protect yourself.

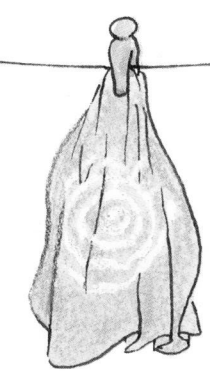

4 Cut the string from the dyed handkerchief when cool. Fasten the handkerchief to a clothesline until it is dry.

FURTHER IDEAS
Many vegetables contain different colored pigments. See what color beet juice or spinach water dyes fabric.

WHY IT WORKS

Onion skins contain a chemical called a pigment. Boiling brings out the pigment, which in onion skin is yellow. Compare how well the pigment dyes fabrics other than cotton.

COLOR CHANGES

Lemons taste sour because they contain acid ("acid" means sour). Hundreds of chemicals are acidic. It would be very dangerous if scientists had to taste chemicals to identify them. Instead they use a chemical that changes color when acid is added.

GET AN ADULT TO DO THIS FOR YOU

TESTING FOR ACIDS

1 Ask an adult to chop up half a red cabbage. Boil the chopped cabbage in a pan of water for about five minutes.

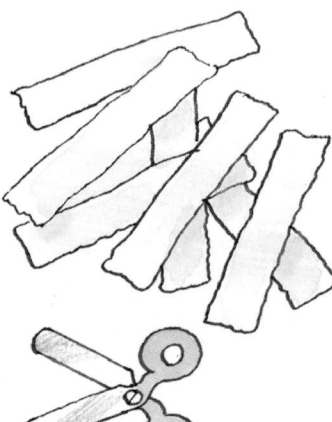

2 Remove the cabbage from the water. Cut paper towels or filter paper into strips.

3 Dip each strip into the cabbage water. Allow the strips to soak the water up.

4 Let the strips dry. When dry, try adding drops of vinegar, lemon, soap, and other harmless substances to each strip.

WHY IT WORKS

Red cabbage contains a chemical called an indicator. Indicators change color when an acid or alkali is added. Red cabbage juice turns red in acids and green in alkalis. Litmus is an important indicator commonly used by scientists.

5 Note the different colors you see on each strip.

FURTHER IDEAS
You can use geranium petals instead of red cabbage. Geranium petals also contain an indicator that changes color when an acid or alkali is added.

CONTENTS

Mysterious shapes 36

Shapes in nature 38

Hanging rocks 40

Shape and strength 42

Hanging around 44

Making materials 46

Filling shapes 48

Elastic materials 50

Shapeless plastics 52

Fibers and threads 54

Fitting it together 56

Bridges 58

CHAPTER
Two

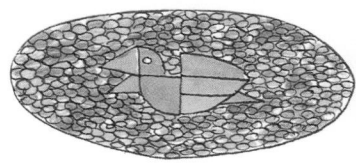

MAKING
SHAPES

MYSTERIOUS SHAPES

We can learn a lot about materials and their shapes from nature. All of these shapes are solids, and have at least two sides. What about a one-sided shape? What special properties does it have?

MAKE A MÖBIUS STRIP

1 Color both sides of three paper strips. Tape together the first strip to make a band.

2 Repeat with the second strip, but twist the strip once before sticking the ends together.

WHY IT WORKS

The first strip will make two new bands, the second a single long band and the third, two linked bands. This is a trick of mathematics. The second and third strips are called *Möbius strips*, after their inventor.

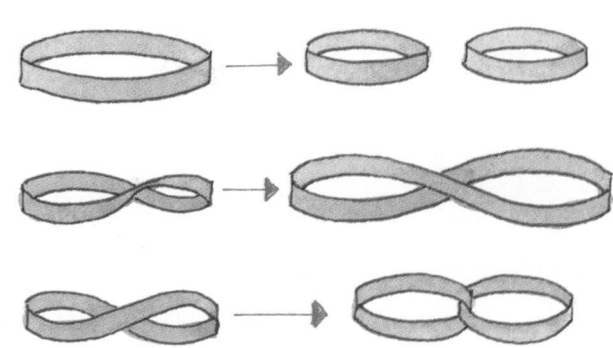

3 Twist the third strip twice before taping the ends together.

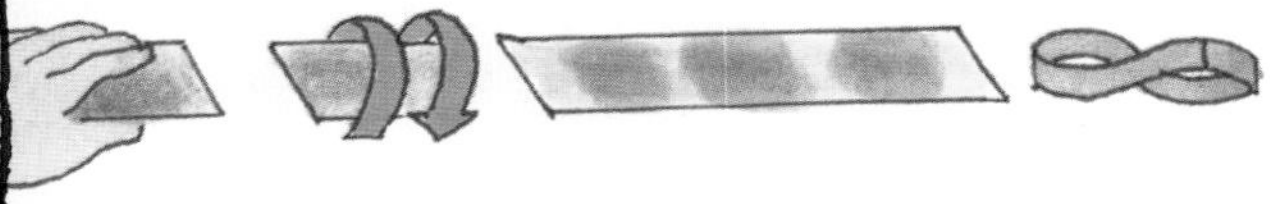

4 Finally, cut each band in half lengthwise.

FURTHER IDEAS
Draw a pencil line along each of the bands. You will find that the line continues along both "sides" of the second band!

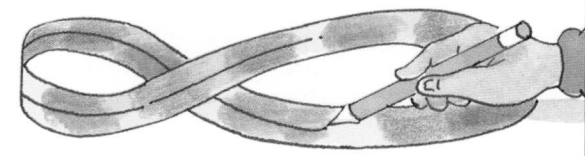

SHAPES IN NATURE

You can find crystals everywhere around you. Gemstones, like emeralds, have always fascinated people. Salt, sand, and sugar are also made from crystals. Then there are the quartz crystals in your watch and the silicon in your computer.

GROW SOME CRYSTALS

1 Pour some hot tap water into a clean glass jar. Stir in one spoonful of potash of alum at a time.

2 Keep adding alum until no more will dissolve. You now have a *saturated solution*. Leave it for two days.

3 Drain the saturated solution through a strainer. Save the water for later and keep the crystals.

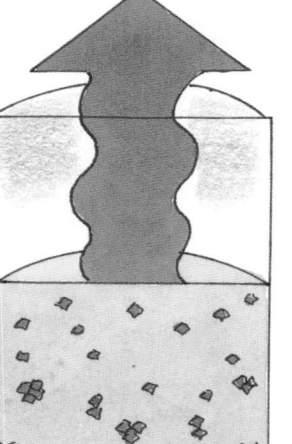

WHY IT WORKS

When the alum dissolved, the particles it was made up of spread out in the water. As the water evaporated, there was not enough water to dissolve the rest of the alum. The particles of alum were forced back together again to make crystals.

4 Look at the crystals with a magnifying glass. They are different sizes. Are they the same shape?

FURTHER IDEAS
Pour the spare saturated solution into a jar. Hang a crystal from a pencil and lower it into the jar. Watch it grow over a few days.

HANGING ROCKS

Rainwater can dissolve some types of solid rock. Sometimes the water drips into an underground cave, leaving a solid behind.

Over time this solid slowly builds up to form columns, which hang down from the roof of the cave, called *stalactites*.

GROW A STALACTITE

1 Make a saturated solution with Epsom salts in a jar of hot water.

2 Fill two glasses with the saturated solution.

3 Attach paper clips to the ends of some wool. Hang the ends in the two glasses.

4 Place a saucer under the wool. Leave in a warm, safe place for one week.

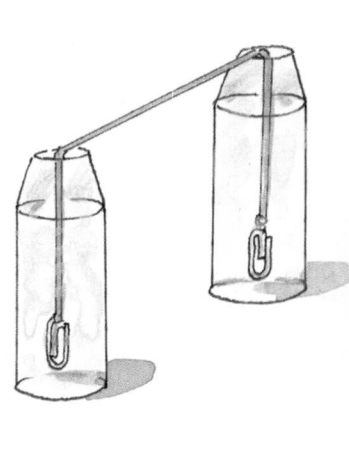

5 Watch as the stalactite grows down from the wool to the saucer, over a number of days.

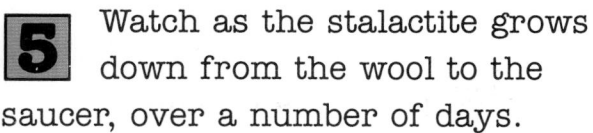

WHY IT WORKS

The saturated solution soaks into the wool and spreads along its length. Some of it drips off the wool and onto the saucer. As it drips, the water evaporates, leaving behind a column of salts.

FURTHER IDEAS

Create your own crystalline sculpture. Make a letter by bending a clean pipe cleaner. Dip it into a jar of saturated solution for a few minutes. Leave it to dry slowly.

41

SHAPE AND STRENGTH

Everybody knows how easy it is to break an egg, because of its very thin shell. However, the egg can also be very strong. It must withstand the impact of falling to the ground when the egg is laid. The egg shape has been produced by nature to be both light and strong.

TEST THE STRENGTH OF AN EGG

1 Find a large tray. Stand up the egg at one side of the tray using clay to hold it in place.

2 At the other side of the tray place two piles of coins exactly the same height as the egg. The egg and two piles should make a triangle.

3 Wrap some books in plastic wrap for protection. Support one book on the coins and egg.

4   Add another book. Watch the egg carefully as you add each book. How many books can the egg help support before it breaks?

WHY IT WORKS

The shape of the egg makes it both hollow and light. It has an arch at each end, a good structure for supporting weight. The egg has a lot of strength lengthwise because the tall arches spread more weight. It is much easier to break when on its side because these arches are weaker.

FURTHER IDEAS

Repeat the test. This time compare the egg's strength to that of some paper shapes, such as a box and a cone.

HANGING AROUND

One of the most important properties of any material is its strength. A material that snaps under the slightest weight is not much use. Nature has made some of the strongest materials around. For example, the silken strands in a spider's web are stronger than steel of the same thickness.

FIND THE STRONGEST STRIP

1 Cut three strips of paper, tissue paper, and plastic from a plastic bag, making them the same length and width.

2 Using tape, fasten a wooden dowel to each end of the strips.

GET AN ADULT TO DO THIS FOR YOU

3 Ask an adult to cut two small holes on each side of the top of three plastic bowls, to make three baskets.

44

4 Attach a basket to one of the wooden dowels. Tie string around the other wooden dowel.

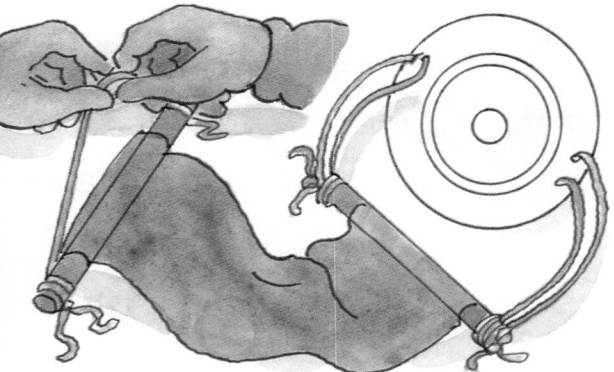

5 Hang each strip from a wall. Slowly add weights to the baskets until each strip breaks.

WHY IT WORKS

Plastic is the strongest because its particles are held together by very strong bonds. Paper is made from densely packed fibers that can be split apart quite easily. Tissue paper fibers are not as densely packed, making it the weakest of the three.

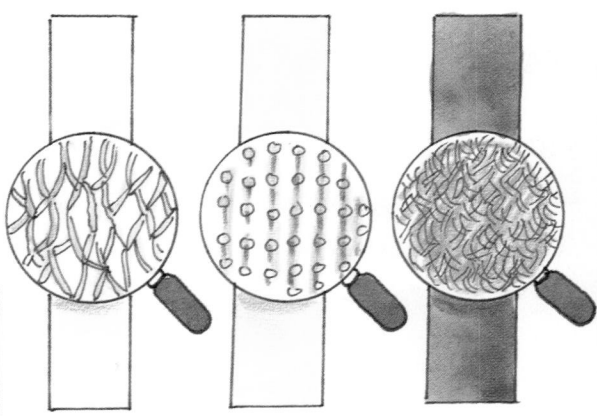

FURTHER IDEAS
Repeat the test with plastic strips of different widths. How does this affect the strength?

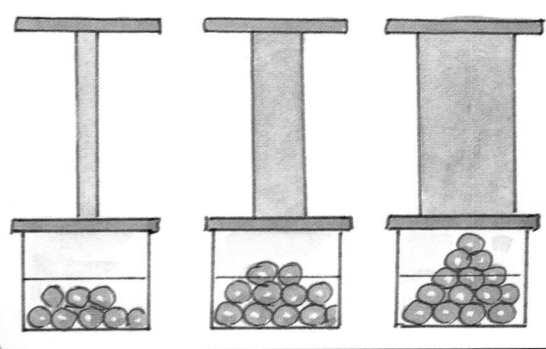

MAKING MATERIALS

The materials we find in nature are called *raw materials*. We use many of these and change them to make other products. Glass is made from sand, and paper from wood. We can usually improve a material by changing its properties.

MAKE A PAPIER-MÂCHÉ BOWL

1 Mix some flour and water in a large plastic bowl, keeping the mixture runny.

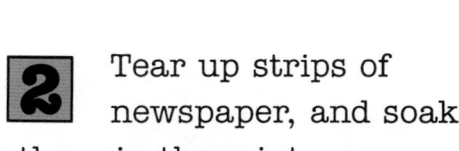

2 Tear up strips of newspaper, and soak them in the mixture.

3 Inflate a balloon. Starting near the balloon's middle, apply the soaked paper in layers.

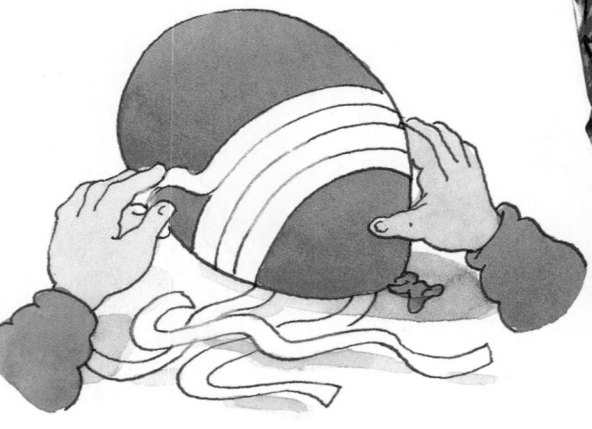

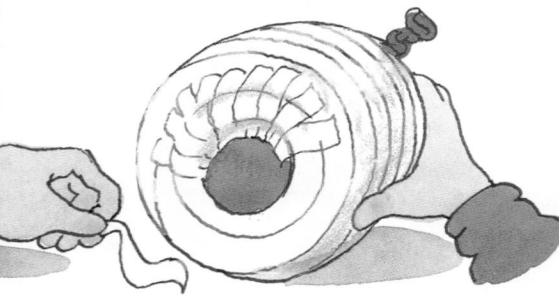

4 To make the bowl's base, sit the balloon on a plastic lid. Cover the lid with more papier-mâché.

5 Leave overnight, then remove the balloon. Paint the finished bowl for decoration. Varnish it for extra protection.

WHY IT WORKS

Paper is made up of thousands of tiny strands of wood fibers. The mixture of flour and water fills the gaps between these fibers. As the mixture dries it becomes hard and makes the paper strong and more rigid. It keeps its new shape until soaked again in water.

FURTHER IDEAS

You can use a real bowl as a mold. Cover the bowl with plastic wrap first to make the papier-mâché easy to remove.

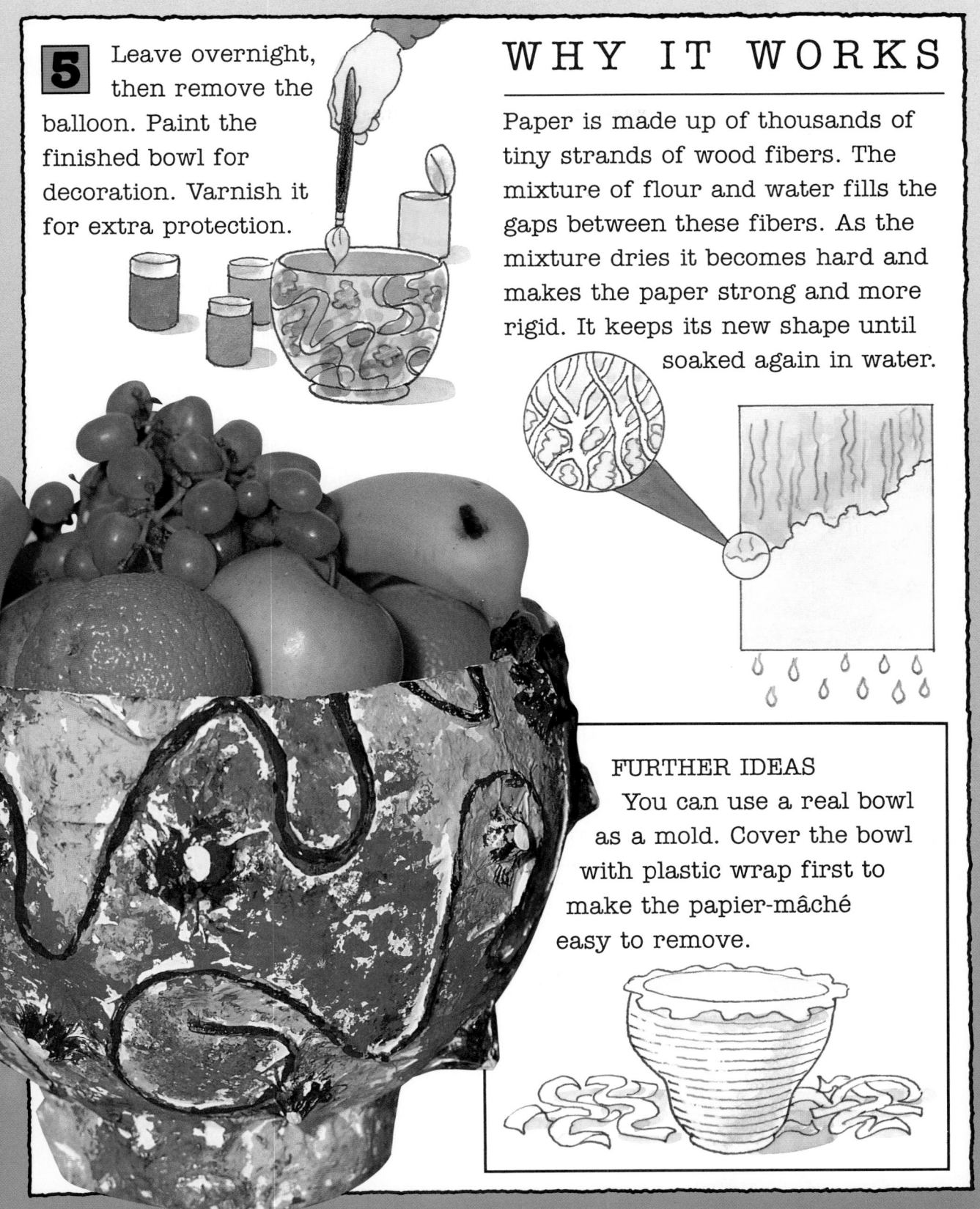

FILLING SHAPES

Like papier-mâché, materials such as cement, plaster, and gypsum alter their form when mixed with water and allowed to dry. Unlike papier-mâché, these substances can be poured into molds and used to form shapes, from small statues to enormous buildings.

PLASTER OF PARIS

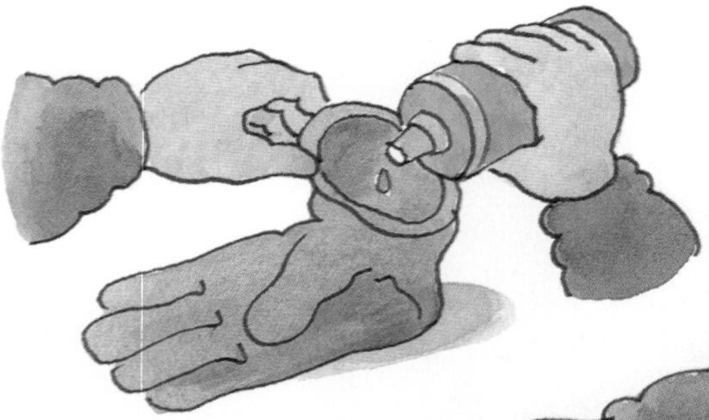

1 Lubricate the inside of a clean, rubber glove with a few drops of liquid soap.

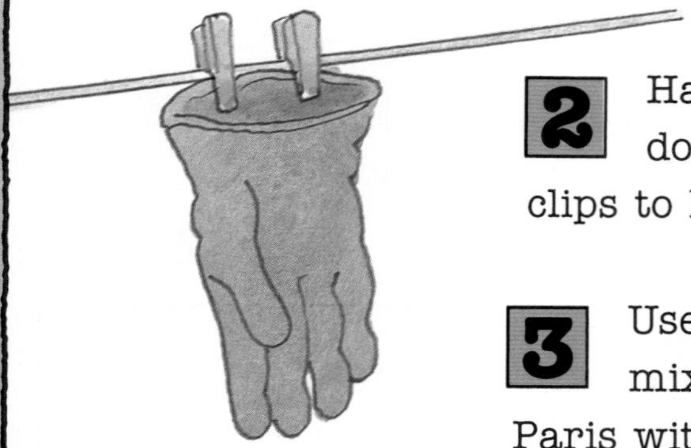

2 Hang the glove upside down with a couple of clips to hold it open.

3 Use a wooden stick to mix some plaster of Paris with cold water in a glass jar. Mix thoroughly until creamy.

4 Pour the mixture into the glove. Make sure it is filled to the top.

5 Leave overnight to dry out. Gently peel off the glove from the plaster underneath. Be careful! The plaster is quite fragile.

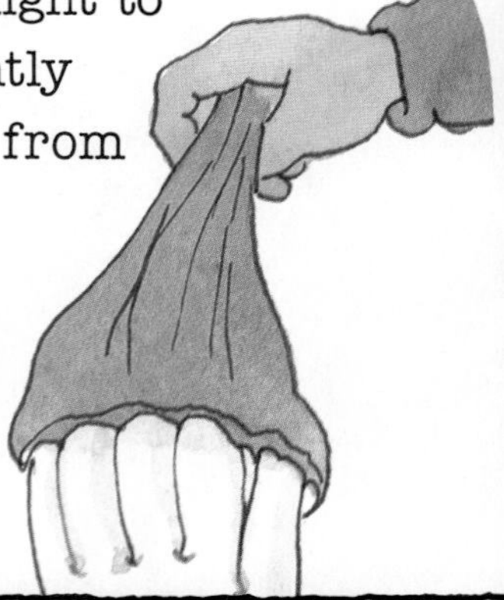

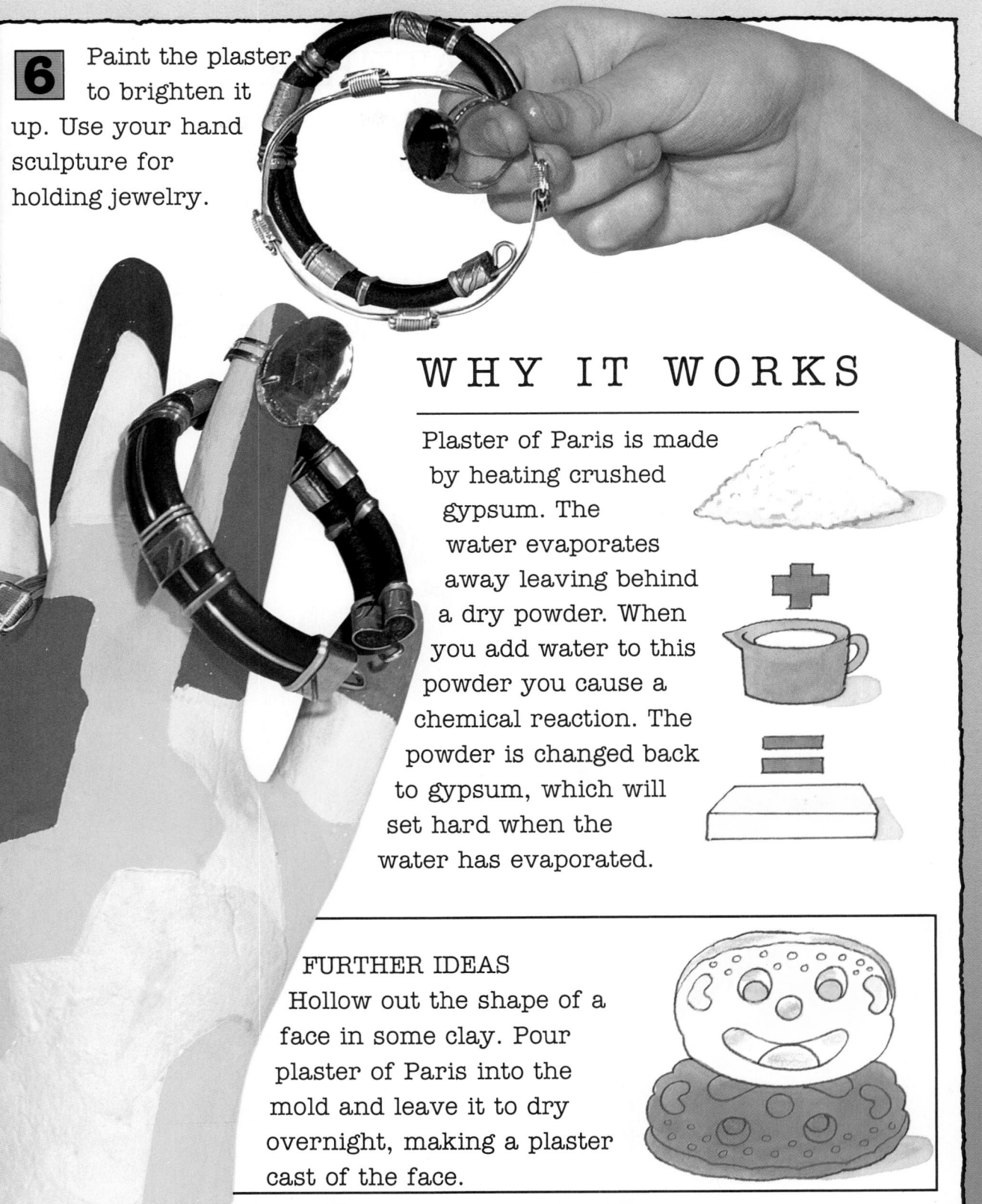

6 Paint the plaster to brighten it up. Use your hand sculpture for holding jewelry.

WHY IT WORKS

Plaster of Paris is made by heating crushed gypsum. The water evaporates away leaving behind a dry powder. When you add water to this powder you cause a chemical reaction. The powder is changed back to gypsum, which will set hard when the water has evaporated.

FURTHER IDEAS

Hollow out the shape of a face in some clay. Pour plaster of Paris into the mold and leave it to dry overnight, making a plaster cast of the face.

ELASTIC MATERIALS

One of the reasons metals are so useful is because of their springiness, or *elasticity*. This means that as you pull the material out of shape it tries to return to that shape. Most things have some springiness, especially elastic bands, which are very strong. Glass is also strong, but instead of being elastic it is brittle and shatters.

MAKE A JACK-IN-THE-BOX

1 Ask an adult to coil a piece of stiff wire around a broom handle to make a spring.

2 Cut the neck from a plastic bottle. Attach the spring to the bottom with tape.

3 Ask an adult to secure a lid with paper fasteners.

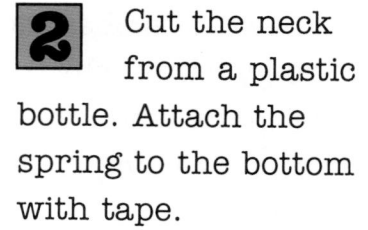

GET AN ADULT TO DO THIS FOR YOU

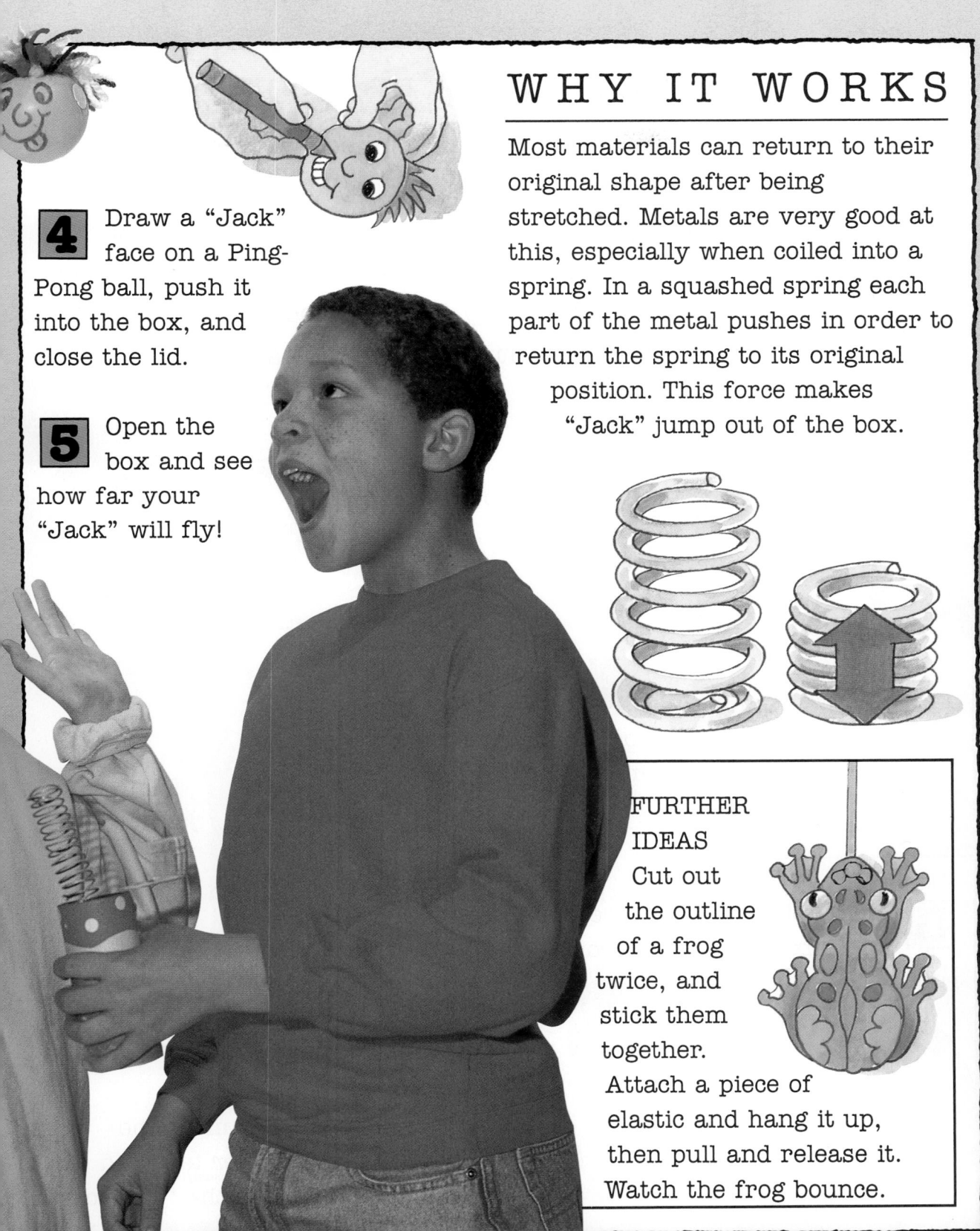

4 Draw a "Jack" face on a Ping-Pong ball, push it into the box, and close the lid.

5 Open the box and see how far your "Jack" will fly!

WHY IT WORKS

Most materials can return to their original shape after being stretched. Metals are very good at this, especially when coiled into a spring. In a squashed spring each part of the metal pushes in order to return the spring to its original position. This force makes "Jack" jump out of the box.

FURTHER IDEAS
Cut out the outline of a frog twice, and stick them together. Attach a piece of elastic and hang it up, then pull and release it. Watch the frog bounce.

SHAPELESS PLASTICS

Some materials can be pulled into new shapes which they then keep. They do not return to their previous shape as an elastic material would. Such materials are called "plastic." For example, wet clay is plastic because you can mold it into any shape you want and it stays that way.

MAKE SOME PLASTIC MILK

1 Ask an adult to warm some milk in a pan.

2 When the milk starts to boil, slowly stir in a little vinegar.

GET AN ADULT TO HELP YOU WITH THESE

3 Keep stirring. Within seconds the mixture should become rubbery.

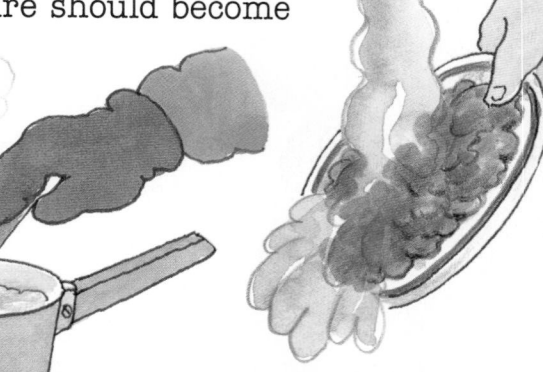

4 Let this rubbery mixture cool. Wash it under the cold water tap, and examine the "plastic."

WHY IT WORKS

Vinegar is a member of the chemical family called *acids*. When it is added to the warm milk, it sets up a chemical reaction which rearranges the particles in the milk. Instead of being "runny" and free to move, they clump together. It is this clump that becomes the lump of "plastic."

FURTHER IDEAS
Put a plastic container in a saucepan. Ask an adult to boil water. Pour the boiling water to cover the container, and watch it lose its shape.

FIBERS AND THREADS

Fibers are long, thin, flexible strands of material like threads. Each of your hairs is a fiber. Natural fibers also include animal fur, cotton, and wool. Fibers can be twisted together to make yarn, which can be woven in turn to make fabrics or cloth.

MAKE A LOOM

1 Cut an odd number of notches along the top and bottom of some cardboard.

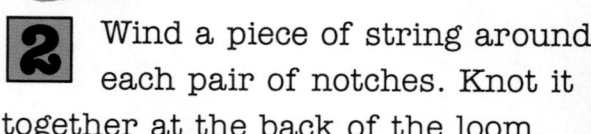

GET AN ADULT TO DO THIS FOR YOU

2 Wind a piece of string around each pair of notches. Knot it together at the back of the loom.

3 Weave some thick wool across the loom, in and out of the string. To change color, tie another strip to the old one.

4 When you have filled the loom, tie off the last strip of fabric. Lift the weaving off the cardboard.

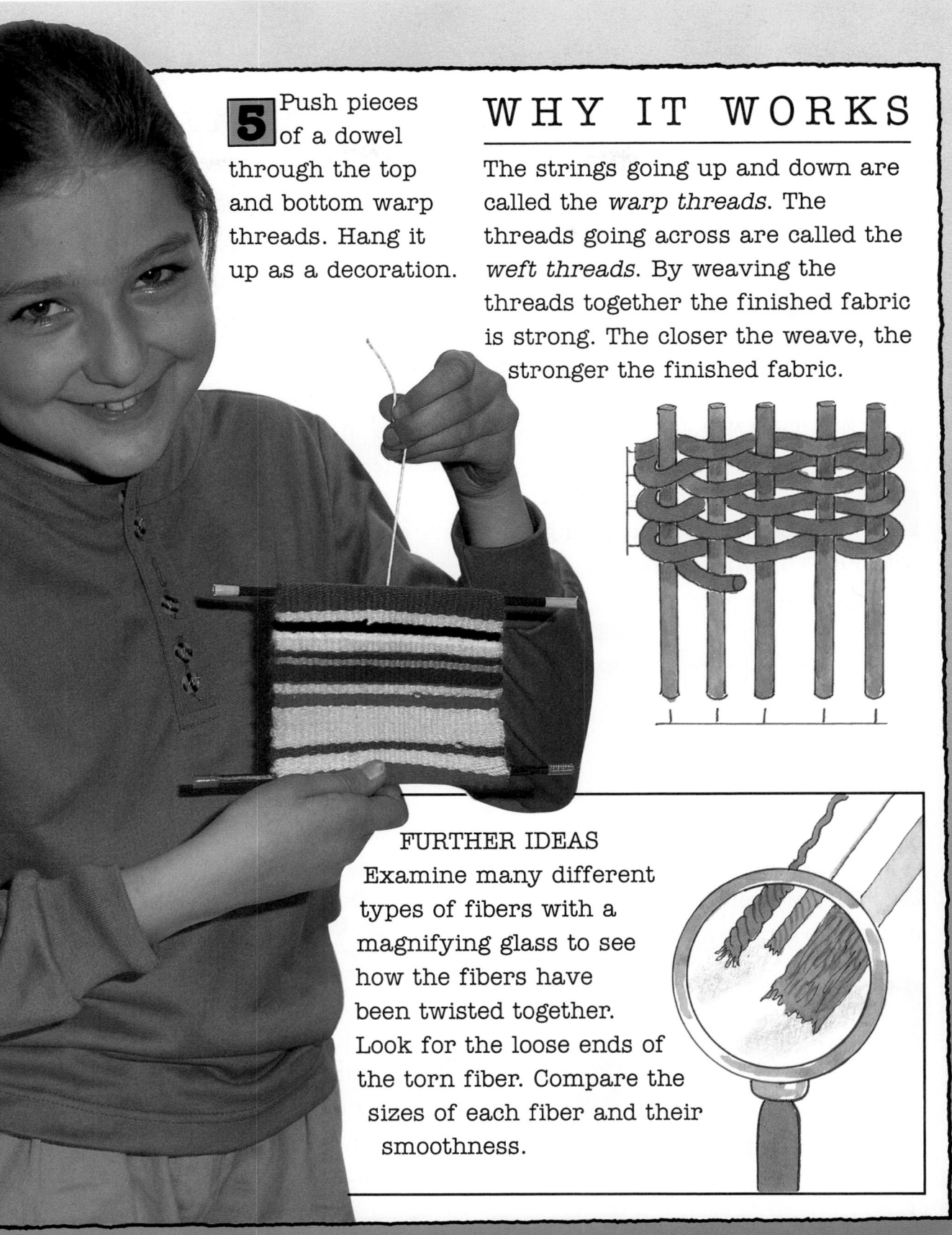

5 Push pieces of a dowel through the top and bottom warp threads. Hang it up as a decoration.

WHY IT WORKS

The strings going up and down are called the *warp threads*. The threads going across are called the *weft threads*. By weaving the threads together the finished fabric is strong. The closer the weave, the stronger the finished fabric.

FURTHER IDEAS

Examine many different types of fibers with a magnifying glass to see how the fibers have been twisted together. Look for the loose ends of the torn fiber. Compare the sizes of each fiber and their smoothness.

FITTING IT TOGETHER

Some shapes fit neatly together to cover an area without overlapping or leaving spaces. This is called *tessellation*. Examples are the bricks in a wall and the squares on a chessboard. An example in nature is the honeycomb in a beehive, where hexagonal cells fit snugly together.

MAKE A TRIANGLE PUZZLE

1 On a large sheet of white cardboard, draw a triangle with sides 12 inches long.

2 Divide the large triangle into nine smaller ones. Each side should be 4 inches long.

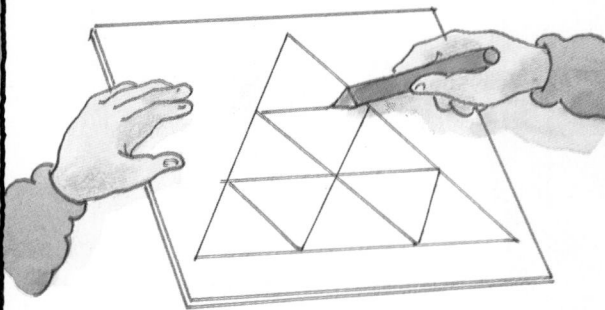

3 On each of the triangles draw a circle, a square, and a triangle as shown.

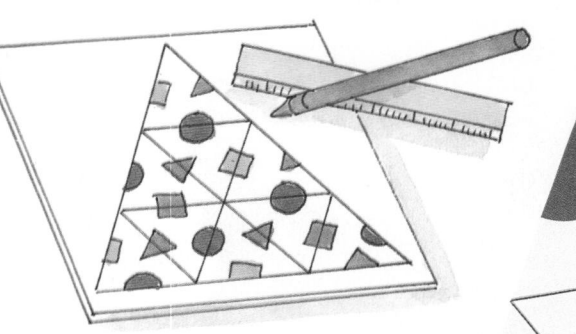

GET AN ADULT TO HELP YOU WITH THIS

4 Use sharp scissors to carefully cut out each of the nine small triangles.

WHY IT WORKS

A tessellated structure, like a beehive, must have no gaps or overlapping shapes. Only certain shapes, such as triangles and hexagons, will tessellate. To cover a surface with circles, which do not tessellate, you would have to overlap the shapes, or leave gaps.

5 Challenge a friend with your triangle puzzle. They should be able to match up the pattern to correctly put the big triangle back together again.

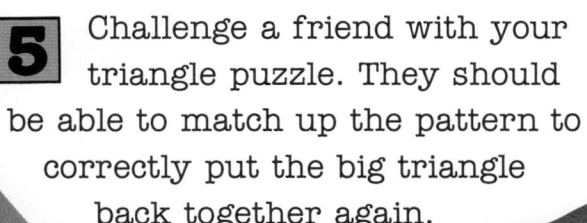

FURTHER IDEAS
A mosaic is like a tessellation, but the shapes that fit together are not the same. Cut out a lot of small cardboard shapes. Glue them down to fit the outline of a drawing on cardboard. Make the gaps as small as possible.

BRIDGES

Since earliest times people have built bridges to cross rivers and other obstacles. The first bridges were probably tree trunks laid across a stream. Later, bridges were built from arches to carry heavier loads. Modern bridges use either steel girders or suspension cables, for support.

BUILD MODEL BRIDGES

1 Find six blocks of wood to make three bridges. Tape pencils to two of the corners on each block.

2 Ask an adult to cut some strips of thick cardboard the same width as the blocks.

GET AN ADULT TO HELP YOU WITH THIS

3 Place a strip of cardboard between two blocks to make a beam bridge. With the second, use an arch as a support.

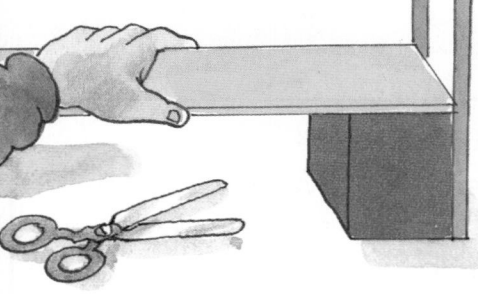

4 On the third, tie string to the pencils, and tape the string to the strip to make a suspension bridge.

5 Draw a river on a sheet of cardboard. Place it under your bridges.

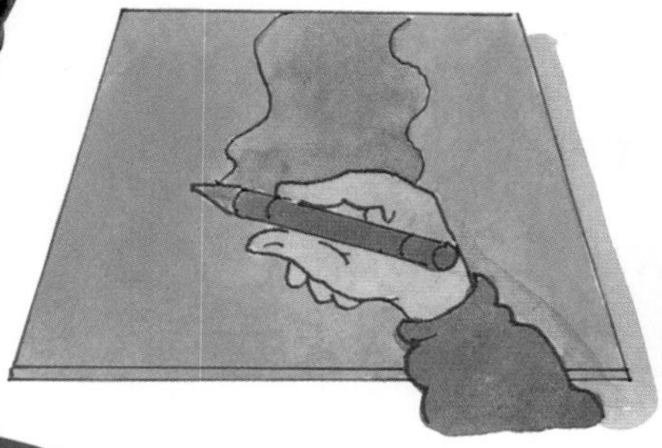

6 Place weights in the middle to test which bridge is the strongest.

WHY IT WORKS

The beam bridge is the weakest because the weight is not spread. The string in the suspension bridge takes some of the weight. The arch is strongest because the weight is spread out over its whole length.

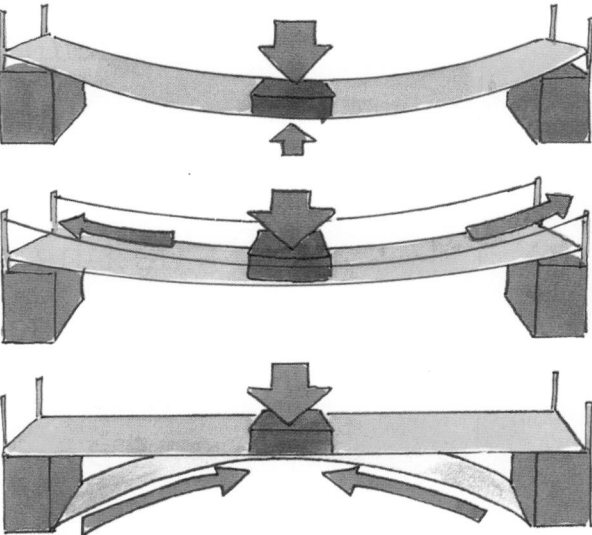

FURTHER IDEAS

Try making a bridge frame out of plastic straws. Join the straws together by pushing the end of one into another.

CONTENTS

What is a force? 62

The pull of gravity 64

Balancing weight 66

Small weights 68

Friction 70

Getting a grip 72

Hydraulic forces 74

What a drag! 76

Pulleys 78

Around and around 80

Transferring forces 82

Equal and opposite 84

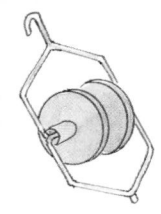

CHAPTER *Three*

PUSHING AND PULLING

WHAT IS A FORCE?

If you want to make anything move you have to give it a push or a pull. Scientists call this push or pull a force. Sir Isaac Newton was inspired to write about the force of gravity after an apple landed on his head. The unit of force is called a newton – roughly the force or weight of one apple!

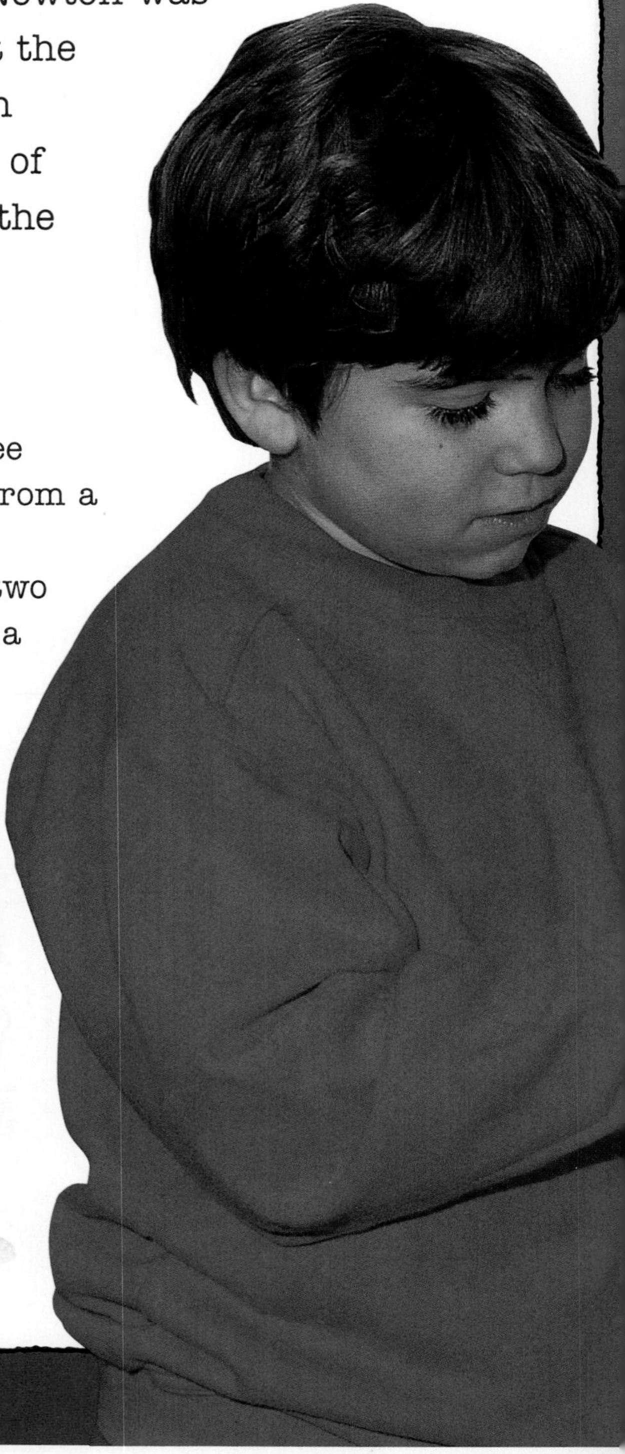

MAKE A FORCE METER

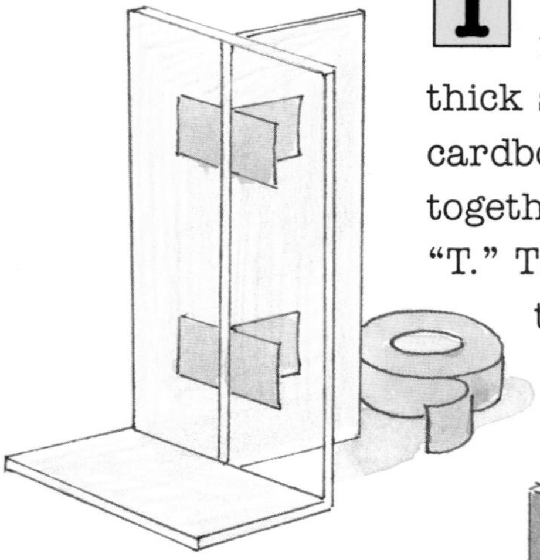

1 Cut out three rectangles from a thick sheet of cardboard. Tape two together to make a "T." Tape the third to support the base.

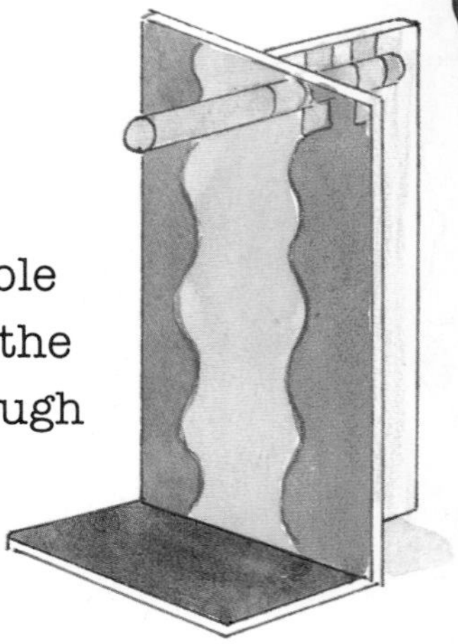

2 Make a small hole near the top of the cardboard. Push through a wooden dowel about six inches long. Secure firmly.

3 Find a circular-shaped box or can. Attach two strong threads to the box. Hang the threads from a paper clip.

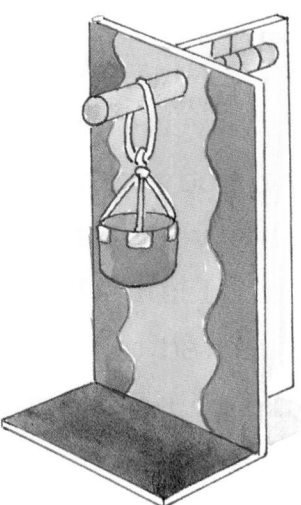

4 Loop a rubber band through the paper clip. Hang the box from the wooden dowel using the rubber band.

5 Place one object at a time in the box. Note how far the rubber band stretches.

WHY IT WORKS

We can measure how big forces are by seeing how far the rubber band stretches each time. The band must return to its original length after each stretch.

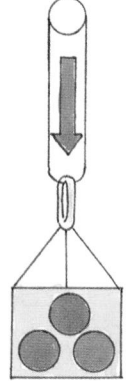
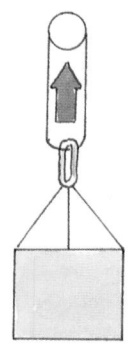

FURTHER IDEAS

Measure the forces made by your own muscles with a set of bathroom scales. Squeeze as hard as you can and check how far the scale goes around. Can you push as hard as your own weight?

THE PULL OF GRAVITY

Gravity is the mysterious force: Everybody knows it is there but it is very difficult to understand. Planet Earth keeps everything attracted to it quite firmly, because of the pull of gravity. When you see pictures of astronauts floating around in space apparently weightless, they are not being subjected to the Earth's pull of gravity.

RACE WITH GRAVITY

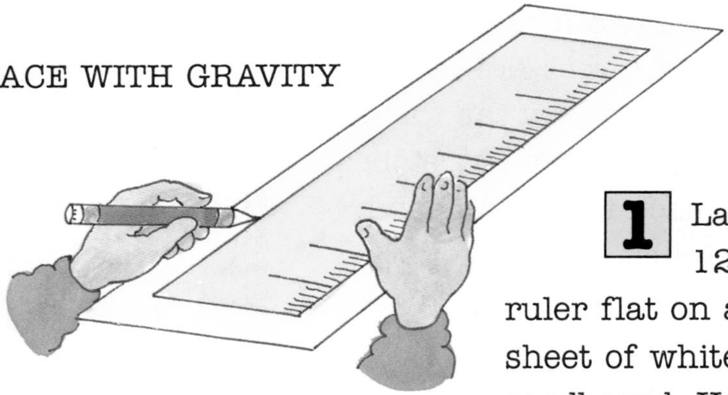

1 Lay a 12-inch ruler flat on a sheet of white cardboard. Use a pencil to draw a line all around the ruler.

2 Use a pair of scissors to carefully cut out the shape from the cardboard.

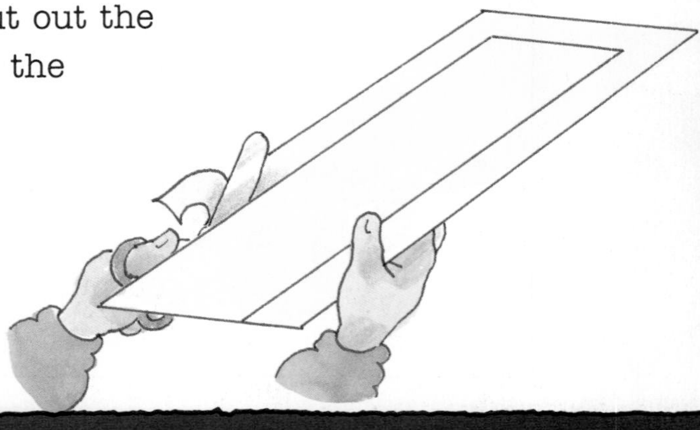

3 Divide the cardboard into six equal parts. Color each part brightly with markers.

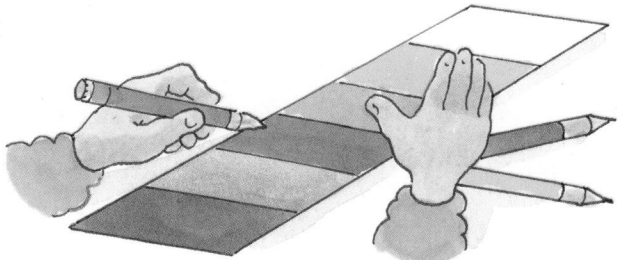

4 Ask a friend to hold the cardboard hanging down just above your outstretched hand. When your friend releases it, try to catch the cardboard as quickly as you can.

WHY IT WORKS

This is a race between gravity and your body. By the time the message has traveled from your brain to your hand, gravity has pulled the cardboard down by many inches.

FURTHER IDEAS
Ask a friend to drop a small (Ping-Pong) ball down a cardboard tube. Hold a ruler ready near the bottom of the tube. You have to swat the ball before it hits the ground.

BALANCING WEIGHT

We take the art of balance for granted once we have learned to walk as babies. Tightrope walkers have only the thin rope keeping them in the air. Everyone marvels as they balance carefully and defy gravity. This takes great skill as well as courage.

MAKE A BALANCING MAN

1 Draw a "man" shape onto some thick white cardboard. Carefully cut out the shape with scissors.

2 Color in the man to make him look more human. Carefully glue a thumbtack to the bottom of the cardboard.

3 Ask an adult to cut off a piece of coat hanger wire. Glue it into place.

4 Make two small clay balls of the same size. Wrap one ball around each end of the wire.

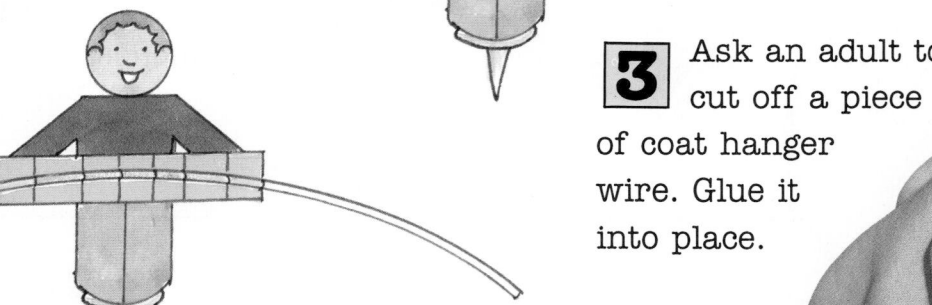

5 Carefully stand the balancing man on top of a bottle. He may wobble slightly but should keep his balance.

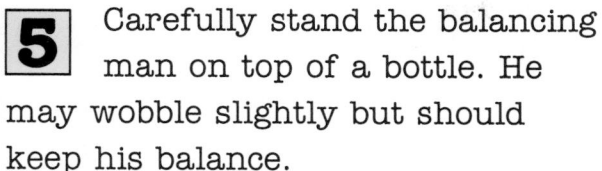

WHY IT WORKS

Gravity keeps everything resting on the ground. In this experiment most of the pulling force of gravity is due to the two heavy balls. It is because these balls are low that the man has a low center of gravity. Any object will balance when its center of gravity is low.

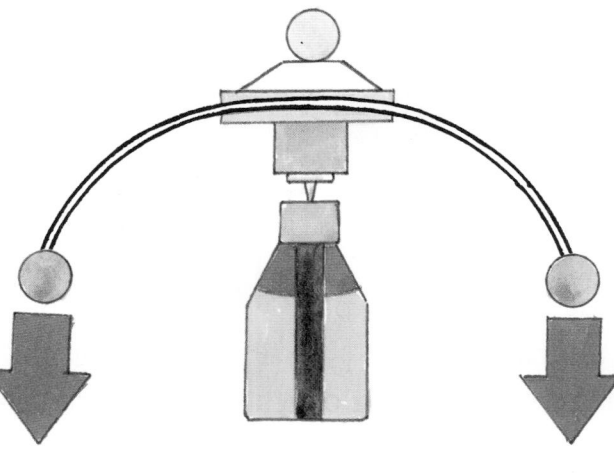

FURTHER IDEAS
You can make a simpler balancing sculpture. Ask an adult to stick a long pin through a cork. Push a fork into each side of the cork. Stand your sculpture on top of a bottle to balance.

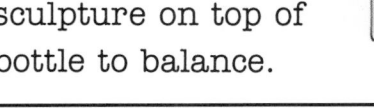

SMALL WEIGHTS

You probably see people weighing goods every time you go shopping. They expect to pay only for what they get. "How much" you have of something is normally measured by its weight. Everything has weight, no matter how small, because of the pull of gravity.

MAKE A MICROBALANCE

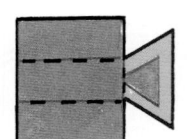

1 Cut some thick cardboard into this diamond shape. Fold along the dotted lines.

2 Cut out this shape (slightly over three times the width of a drinking straw) twice from cardboard. Fold into triangular shapes and slide one over each end of a straw.

3 Fold the thick cardboard diamond into a support. Push a steel pin through the cardboard and straw. Strengthen the base with tape.

4 Glue the triangular shapes to the ends of the straw. Make sure they balance each other.

5 Remove the front of a cardboard box to screen your microbalance from drafts. Compare the weights of small objects like a pea or bean.

WHY IT WORKS

The heavier an object is, the bigger the force of gravity tugging on it. The side of the straw that is pulled harder will tilt down. When the weights on both sides are equal, then the two forces balance out.

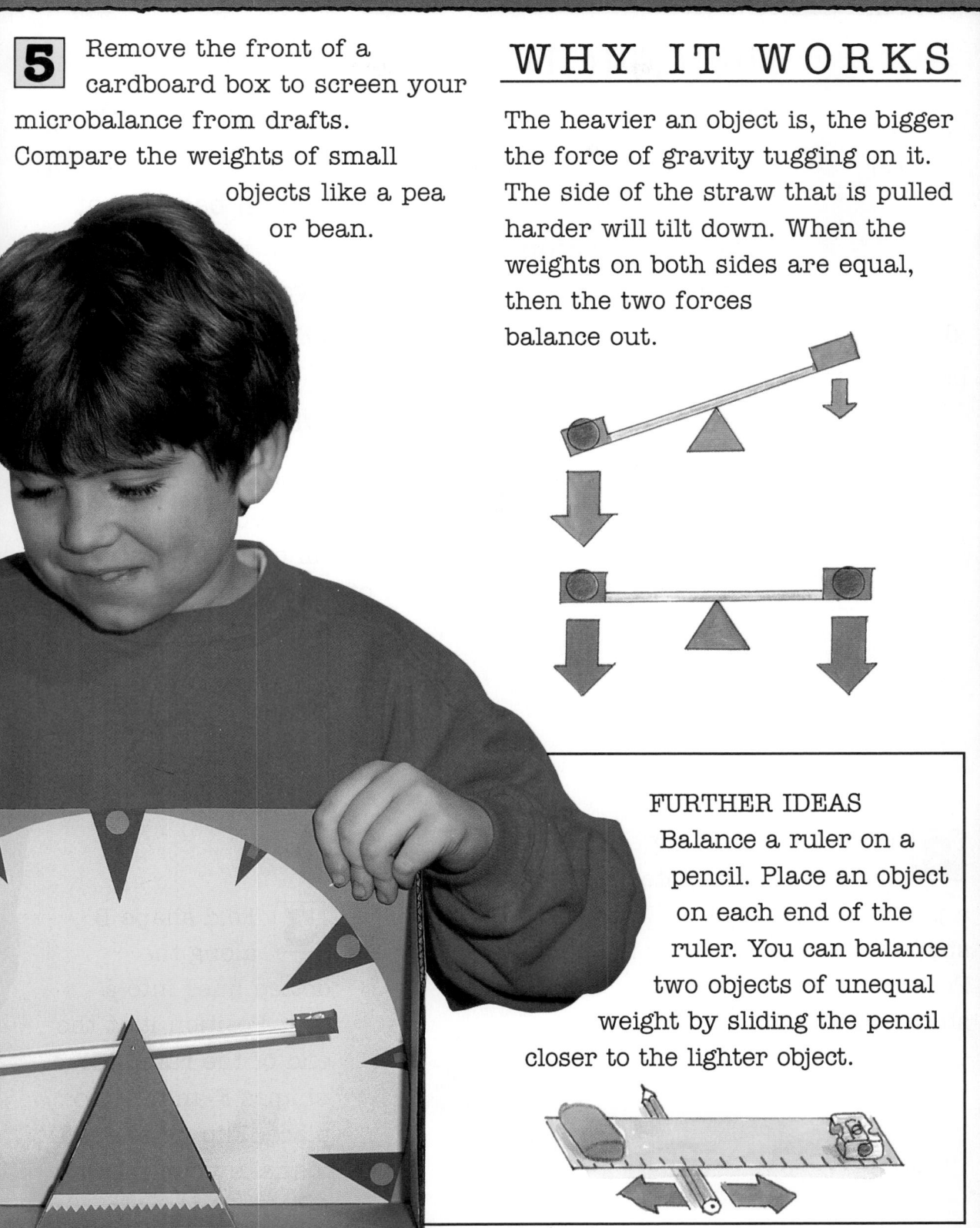

FURTHER IDEAS
Balance a ruler on a pencil. Place an object on each end of the ruler. You can balance two objects of unequal weight by sliding the pencil closer to the lighter object.

FRICTION

Whenever any two things rub against each other, the force of friction tries to stop them. Rubbing your hands together warms them because of friction. Friction is useful because without it there would be no grip! Things would just slip and slide away from each other. Friction can also be a problem because it causes things to overheat.

MEASURING FRICTION

1 Draw the seven shapes A to G on thick cardboard. Carefully cut them out. They will be the parts of your ramp.

2 Fold shape A along the dotted lines into a prism and stand it on shape C. Tape shape E to shape C. Position shape D between shapes A and E.

3 Fold shape B along the dotted lines into a box. Position it at the end of the ramp. Glue shapes F and G into place. Flip up shape D to make your runway (shape E) steeper.

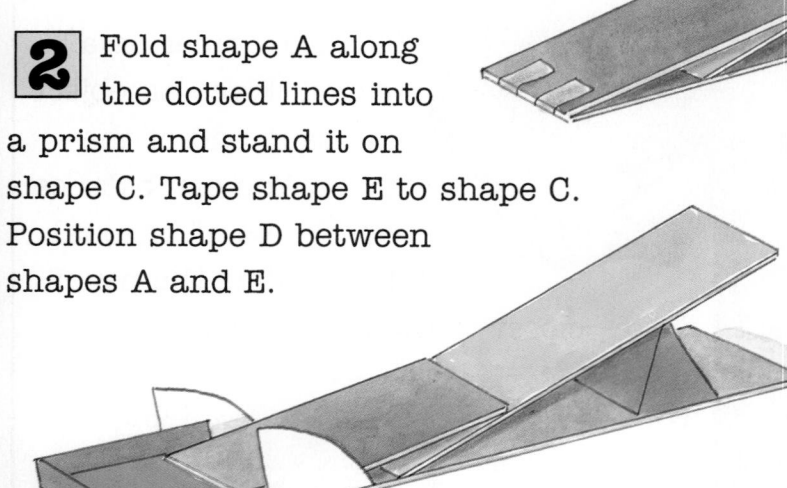

WHY IT WORKS

4 Place a coin at the top of the runway. Slowly make the runway steeper until the coin slides down. Compare with a wooden block, an eraser, and a cork.

There is more friction, or grip, between rough surfaces than between smooth ones. Even though the eraser and the cardboard feel smooth, they have tiny rough edges. Only when the runway is steep enough can this grip between eraser and cardboard be overcome.

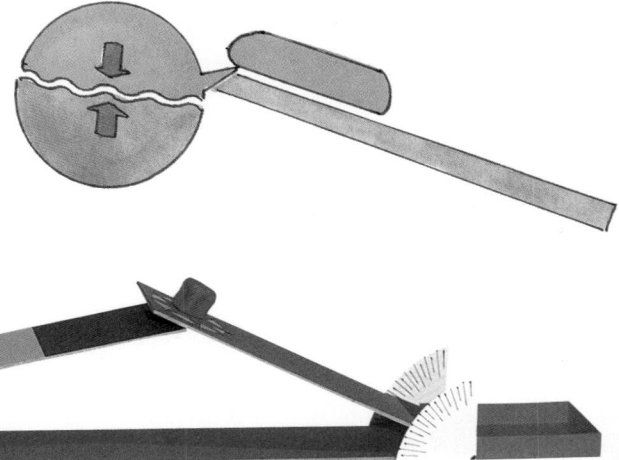

FURTHER IDEAS

Cut out a piece of aluminum foil to fit your runway. Carefully lay it flat and into place. Repeat your tests. Is there more friction from the aluminum compared to the cardboard? Compare other surfaces, such as felt, plastic, or paper. Can you tell which surface has the most friction?

GETTING A GRIP

Grip is very important to drivers. The wheels of a vehicle can slide, especially on slippery surfaces like mud, and may cause an accident. Tractors' wheels are very big and knobbly to increase their grip on muddy fields.

MAKE A SPOOL TRACTOR

1 Ask an adult to remove the wick from a candle and cut off a disc from the end of the candle.

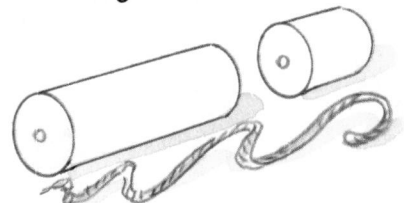

2 Cut out two circles of cardboard to fit the ends of a spool of thread. Make a small hole in the center and tape each into place.

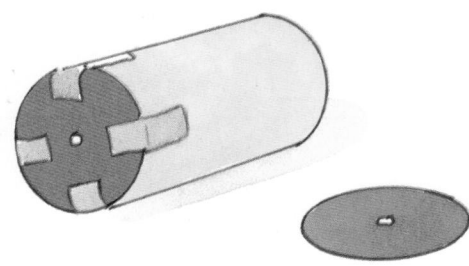

3 Thread a small rubber band through the wax disc. Stop it from going all the way through by looping the end around a pencil.

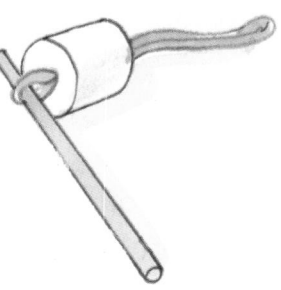

4 Thread the other end of the rubber band through the spool. A straightened paper clip will help with threading. Attach the end of the rubber band to half of a matchstick.

5 Wind up the pencil tightly without breaking the rubber band. Place the tractor on the floor, and let the matchstick push it along.

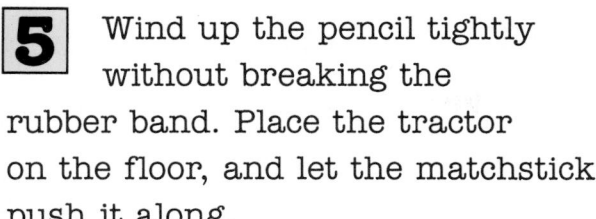

WHY IT WORKS

The wound up rubber band stores energy. As the rubber band starts to unwind, it makes the pencil rotate. The matchstick presses against the ground. Since one end of the matchstick cannot move against the ground, the energy is used up by making the spool of thread rotate instead. This is what pushes the tractor forward.

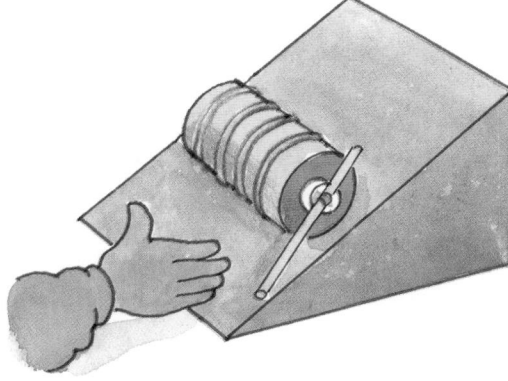

FURTHER IDEAS
Wrap rubber bands around the spool to act as rubber tires and improve the grip. See what is the steepest slope it can climb up. (Use the friction tester on pp 70 and 71).

HYDRAULIC FORCES

Powerful machines like cranes, forklifts, and fire engines use hydraulic forces to lift heavy things quite easily. "Hydro" means water, although in practice these machines use other liquids in their hydraulics.

MAKE A HYDRAULIC FORCE

1 Ask an adult to cut the necks off two large plastic bottles, then to cut a hole near the bottom of each.

2 Thread a plastic tube through the bottles. Tie the neck of a balloon over one end of the tube. Fill the other end of the tube with water.

3 Fill another balloon with water. Tie this balloon to the free end of the tube. Both balloons and the tube must be filled with water.

4 Find two empty cans that just fit into the bottles. Place them above the balloons. Gently push down on one can with the palm of your hand.

5 The second can rises by the same distance that you pressed down the first. You can reverse this by pressing down on the second can.

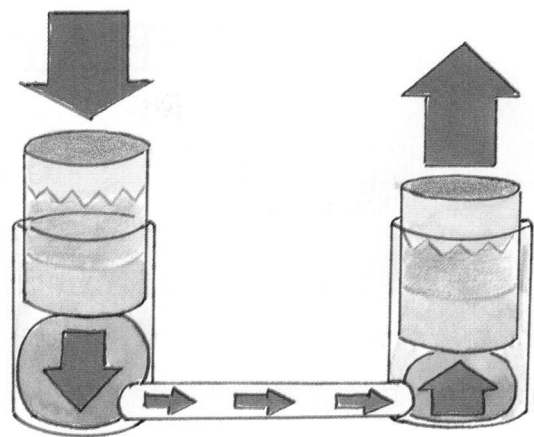

WHY IT WORKS

It is very difficult to squash water. If you squeeze it hard in one place, it will push out just as hard in another place. The water transmits the force from one can to the other. This is the principle used by all hydraulic machines.

FURTHER IDEAS

Glue a small plastic toy to a balloon. Connect the balloon to a plastic syringe with a tube. Lay the balloon flat in a glass tumbler and inflate with the syringe. This pump uses air, which is springy compared to water, to make the balloon inflate.

WHAT A DRAG!

It is quite hard to move quickly under the water. The water gets in your way and before you can move forward you must push it out of the way. The water exerts a special force of friction called "drag." Birds and airplanes have wings designed to reduce "drag" in the air.

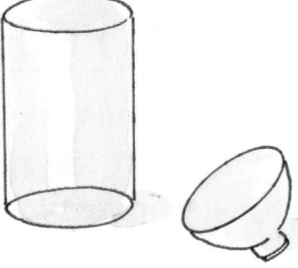

TESTING MOVING SHAPES

1 Find a large plastic bottle and ask an adult to cut off the neck. Otherwise use a long plastic tube.

2 Find a small but sturdy box. Cut a piece of thick cardboard and tape it to the back of the box.

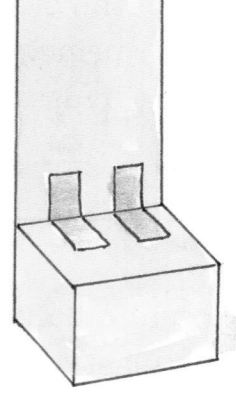

3 Use a funnel to carefully fill the bottle with cooking oil. Stand the bottle on the box.

76

4 Mold the same amount of clay into different shapes. Attach a piece of cotton to each shape.

5 Hold the shapes just above the bottle, release, and start timing. Make sure you hold on to the cotton. Stop timing when the shapes reach the bottom.

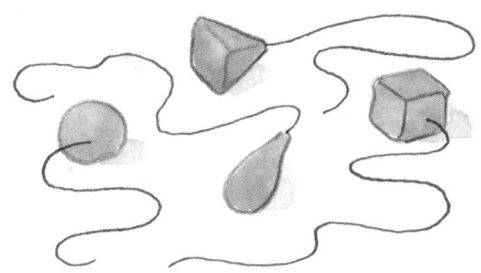

WHY IT WORKS

Cooking oil has more drag than water so it is easier to see how much the shapes are slowed down. A shape has to push the oil out of its path to move forward. Shapes with a rounded front allow liquids to pass around them with little drag.

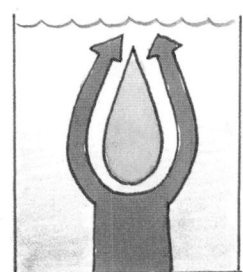 

FURTHER IDEAS

Try some of these shapes. Predict which will move the fastest before you test them. Add a small weight to the front of each shape to stop it from turning around as it falls.

PULLEYS

A pulley is a machine to help you lift very heavy loads. Cranes are useful machines with a system of pulleys that make lifting heavy objects easier. You can see cranes almost everywhere – on building sites, at docks and railroad stations.

MAKE A SIMPLE PULLEY

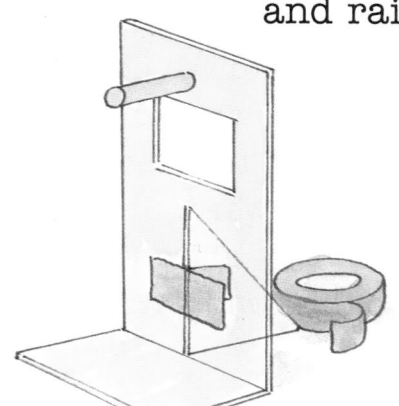

1 Cut out a window from cardboard. Fold it and tape a triangle to the back to help it stand up. Push a short wooden dowel through the top.

3 Bend three pieces of thin wire into shape. Attach the circles to the wire to make one double pulley and one single pulley.

2 Cut four circles of cardboard, each with a hole in the middle. Push a piece of straw through each pair of circles.

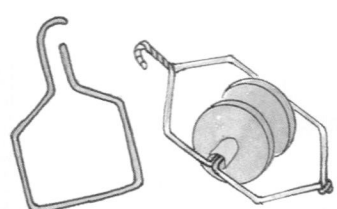

4 Hang the pulleys as shown. Make sure you loop the thread around the lower pulley, back over the top pulley, and out through the window.

5 Hang a small weight from the hook on the lower pulley. Pull the thread from behind the window to lift the weight.

WHY IT WORKS

A pulley system allows a force to be transferred from one place to another. As you pull on the thread, the force is transferred along the thread all the way to the weight. You can lift the weight with half the effort but it only moves half the distance.

FURTHER IDEAS

Make a winch from a cardboard base and clay-filled straw. Hold the straw in place with wire. Wrap thread around the straw, and tie a hook to the other end. Attach weights to the hook and pull them in by winding the winch.

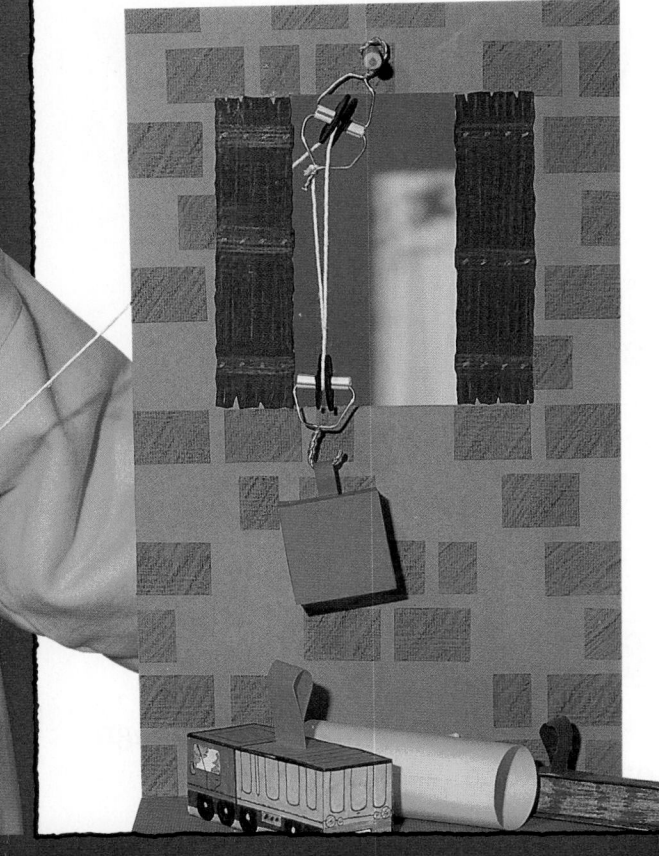

AROUND AND AROUND

Electric mixers, washing machines, and dryers all operate by spinning forces. A gyroscope is a terrific toy that seems to defy gravity while it spins. The spinning force balances out the force of gravity and makes the spinning object hard to push over.

MAKE SPINNING TOPS

1 Find a large sheet of thin white cardboard. Use a pair of compasses to draw some circles of different sizes.

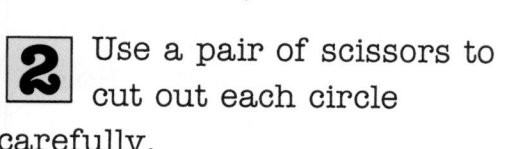

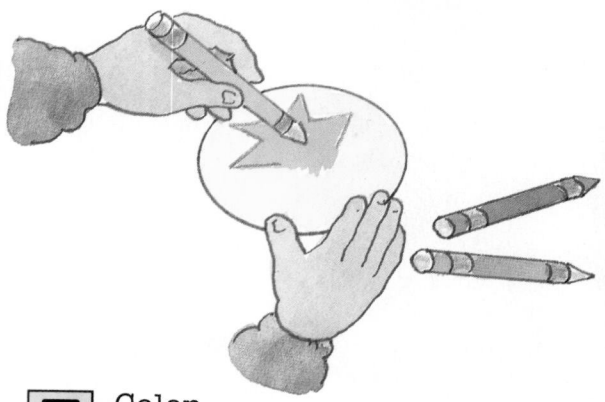

2 Use a pair of scissors to cut out each circle carefully.

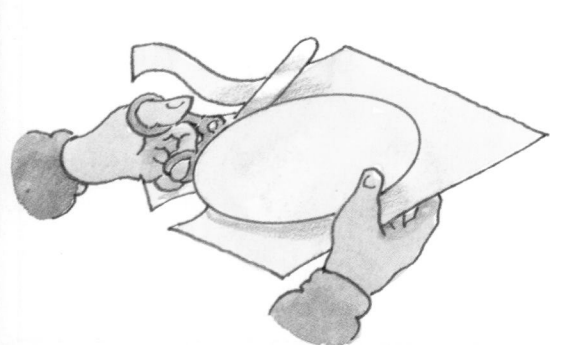

3 Color each circle with bright markers. Create a different design for each one.

4 Make a small hole through the center of each circle. Then push a sharp pencil through each hole.

WHY IT WORKS

When you start the top spinning, you give it a lot of spinning energy. The top spins for minutes before this energy is all used up. The top actually stores some of the energy during this time so that it can go on spinning. The energy you gave it is only gradually released.

5 Hold the top of the pencil between two fingers and spin it as fast as you can. Release it and let it spin on a smooth tabletop.

FURTHER IDEAS
Place an egg on a plate and start it spinning fast. Suddenly grab the egg to stop its spinning. Quickly release it and it will start spinning again all by itself!

TRANSFERRING FORCES

All of the power in a modern car comes from the engine. The forces made by the engine are then transferred to where they are needed – mainly to make the wheels turn. One of the most common ways of transferring forces is through gearwheels.

MAKE MODEL GEARS

1 Draw and cut out four equal circles with teeth all the way around them using thick cardboard. These are your gearwheels.

2 Make a small hole in the middle of each wheel. Add another close to the middle of one wheel. Draw and cut out the other shapes shown here.

3 Use a thumbtack to attach one wheel to a piece of cardboard. Insert an extra piece of cardboard between the cardboard and paper clip for a tight fit.

4 Attach the other wheel to the bar and hammer with a thumbtack. Attach these to the first wheel so that the teeth match.

5 Rotate the upper wheel slowly. Watch how the hammer moves from side to side.

WHY IT WORKS

As you turn the first gearwheel, this turning movement is passed on to the second gearwheel. The bar moves from side to side as the wheel turns and this sets up the sideways movement of the hammer.

FURTHER IDEAS
Try using different-sized wheels in your gear system. Notice how they move at different speeds: The larger gears move more slowly than the smaller gears.

EQUAL AND OPPOSITE

Forces always come in pairs. When a cannon fires a shell, the cannon itself recoils. The force pushing the shell FORWARD has an equal but opposite force.

MAKE A JET ENGINE

1 Cut out these shapes from thin cardboard. Tape the strip into a circle. Attach a drinking straw.

2 Tape together all of the shapes to make up the outline of a rocket like the one illustrated below.

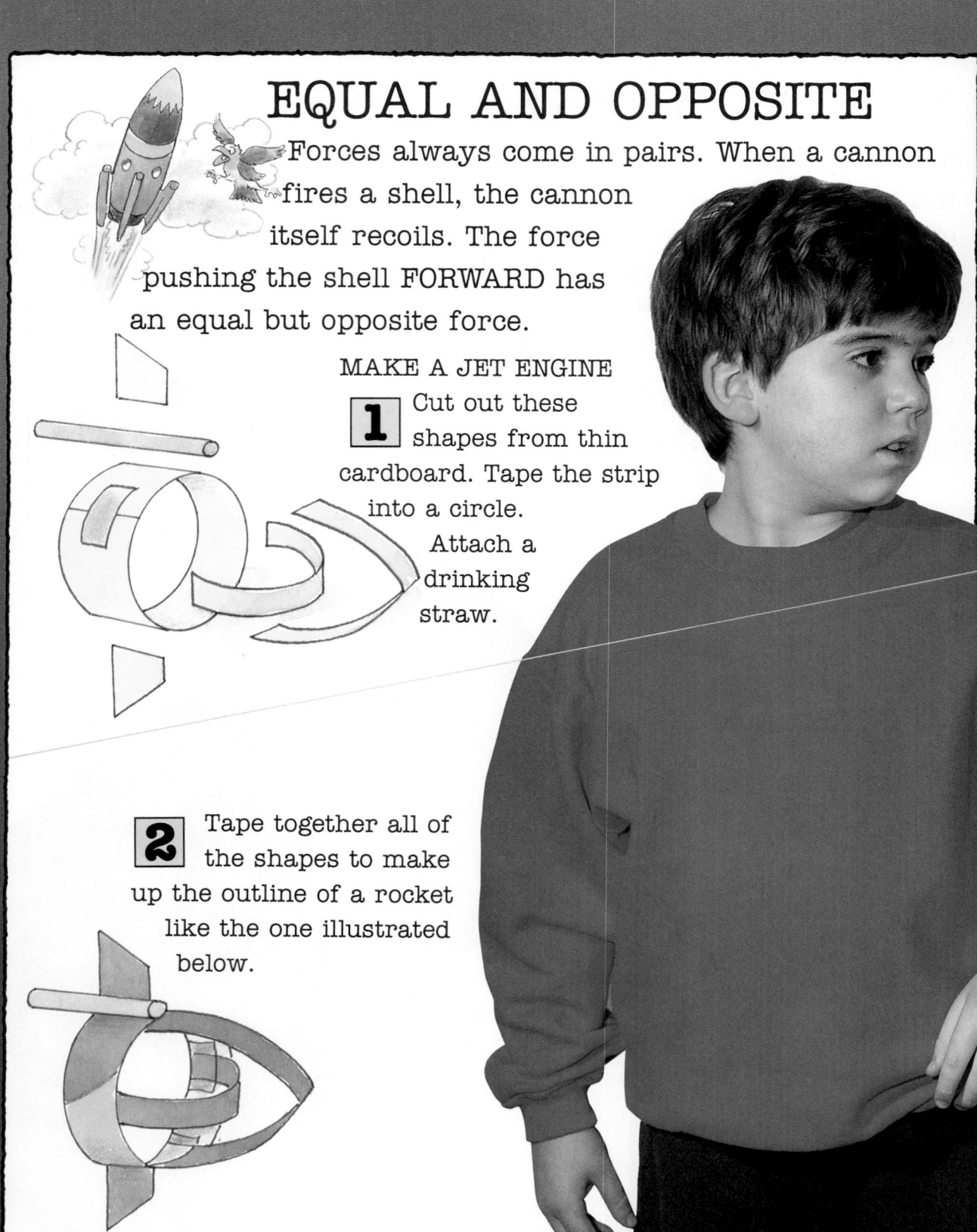

3 Place a balloon in the cardboard. Slowly inflate it until it is a tight fit inside the rocket outline. Keep holding the neck of the balloon.

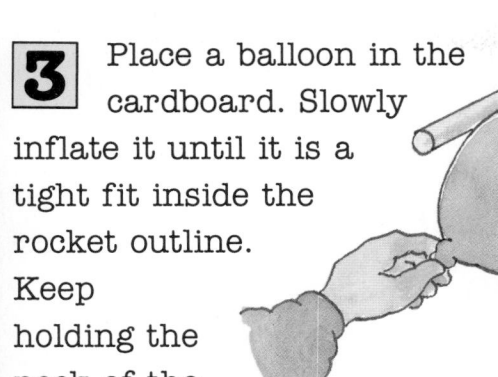

4 Thread string through the straw. Fasten the ends of the string across the room. Release the balloon to be jet-propelled along the string.

WHY IT WORKS

Over 300 years ago, Sir Isaac Newton found that every force has an equal but opposite reaction. As the air rushes out of the back of your balloon in one direction, the balloon itself is pushed forward in the opposite direction. This is the principle on which all jet engines work.

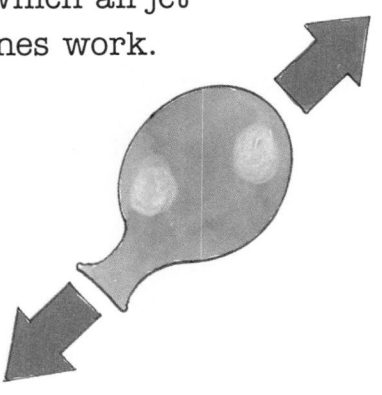

FURTHER IDEAS
Sit in a chair with wheels, and hold a soccerball. Try to throw it without moving. The harder you throw it, the stronger is the opposite force that pushes you backward.

CONTENTS

Freezing and melting 88

The acid test 90

Bubbles and fizz 92

Pretty flowers 94

Flowing currents 96

Rising temperatures 98

Separating mixtures 100

Rust or bust 102

Invisible ink 104

Splitting colors 106

Burning and breathing 108

Living yeast 110

CHAPTER *Four*

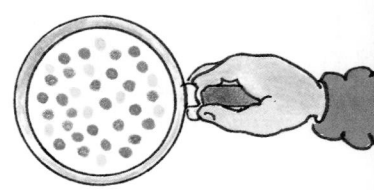

MAKING THINGS CHANGE

FREEZING AND MELTING

When the weather becomes cold, it can change many of the things around us. It can cause water to freeze, or solidify, into ice or snow. This change is easy to reverse; warmed ice will thaw, or melt, back into water.

EXPANDING ICE

1 Find two large empty plastic bottles. Tape a paper marker around each about half way up.

2 Using a large pitcher of water, carefully fill each of the bottles exactly to the mark on the paper.

3 Place one bottle in a warm room and the other in your freezer. Leave them overnight.

4 Take out the frozen bottle and compare the water level in each of them.

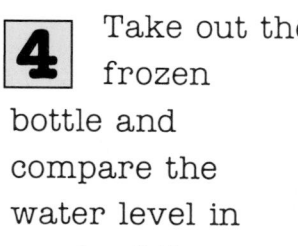

WHY IT WORKS

There seems to be more ice. This is because water expands, gets larger, when it freezes. Pipes sometimes burst in winter because the water inside freezes and expands.

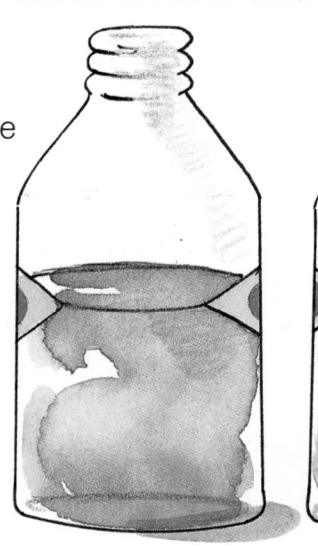

FURTHER IDEAS
Find lumps of chocolate, butter and wax from a candle, about the same size as an ice cube. Place them on a tray. Leave the tray in a warm place to compare how they melt. Place the tray in the freezer to reverse the changes.

THE ACID TEST

Chemicals are split into families of *acids*, *alkalis* or *neutrals*. These chemicals are everywhere – even in soil. The color of the Hydrangea flower depends on the levels of acid or alkali in the soil. Blue flowers mean there is more acid in the soil; pink, more alkali.

MAKE A CHEMICAL INDICATOR

1 Take a red cabbage, tear it into shreds, and place these shreds into a bowl.

GET AN ADULT TO HELP YOU WITH THIS

2 Pour hot water into the bowl. The cabbage color dissolves to make an indicator.

3 Strain the juice, and pour the liquid into three small jars.

4 Add a different liquid to each jar, such as vinegar or liquid soap. Compare the colors.

WHY IT WORKS

A chemical that changes color in acids and alkalis is called an indicator. Red cabbage juice turns red when in acids, like vinegar, and green when in alkalis, like soap.

FURTHER IDEAS
Make indicator paper by soaking blotting paper in the indicator. Then test household items.

BUBBLES AND FIZZ

Carbon dioxide is the gas in carbonated drinks which keeps them full of bubbles. When you shake a carbonated drink, then suddenly release the cap, the gas inside bubbles up and escapes. Carbon dioxide gas is important in other ways. It can be used to put out fires and it also makes cakes rise. Here you can make your own bubbles of gas.

MAKE AN ERUPTING VOLCANO

1 Find a small glass jar. Stand it on a saucer. This will be your volcano.

2 Cover the sides of the jar with clay to make the volcano.

3 Carefully fill half the jar with baking soda. Add a few drops of red food coloring. Then add vinegar, a spoonful at a time.

4 Stand back and watch as the mixture bubbles up and over the sides of the volcano.

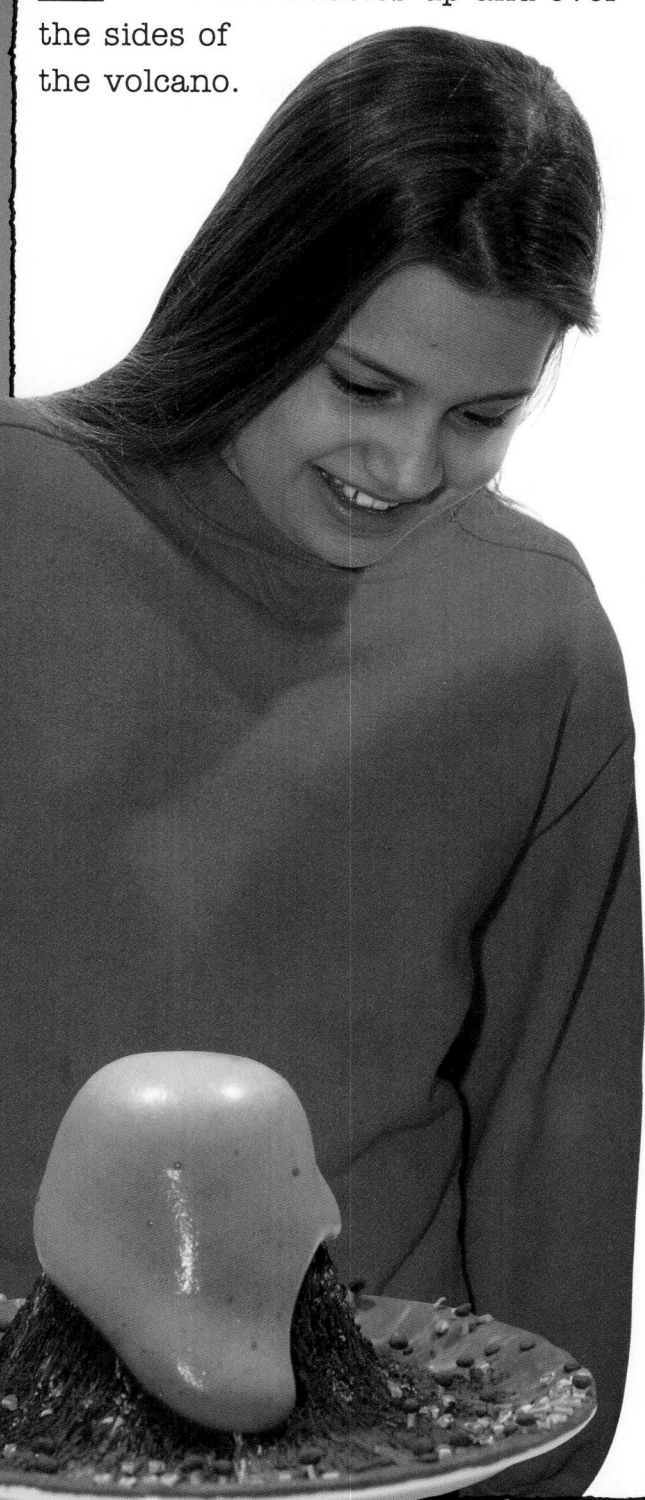

WHY IT WORKS

A mixture of the acid in vinegar and alkali in baking soda makes bubbles of gas. The thousands of bubbles are very light and this causes the mixture to fizz. The eruption of bubbles is similar to lava erupting from a volcano.

FURTHER IDEAS
Fill a glass with vinegar and add a tablespoonful of baking soda. Drop in mothballs. Bubbles of gas make them rise back to the surface.

PRETTY FLOWERS

Plants, like animals, need water to stay alive. The roots of plants are especially good at taking water from the ground. Water moves through the plant in tiny tubes, which are similar to the blood vessels in an animal.

CHANGE FLOWER COLORS

1 Fill three glass bottles with water. Add a few drops of different food coloring to each.

2 Find three freshly cut flowers, preferably white or light-colored.

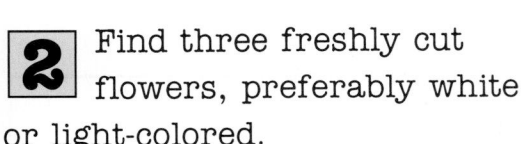

3 Trim the stem of each flower before placing them into the three bottles.

94

4 Leave the flowers overnight. Each becomes the color of the water in which it was placed.

WHY IT WORKS

Water travels up the stem of each flower and spreads to all parts of the plant, including the petals. The water then escapes from the plant into the air by evaporation. Fresh water is continually drawn up to replace the lost water.

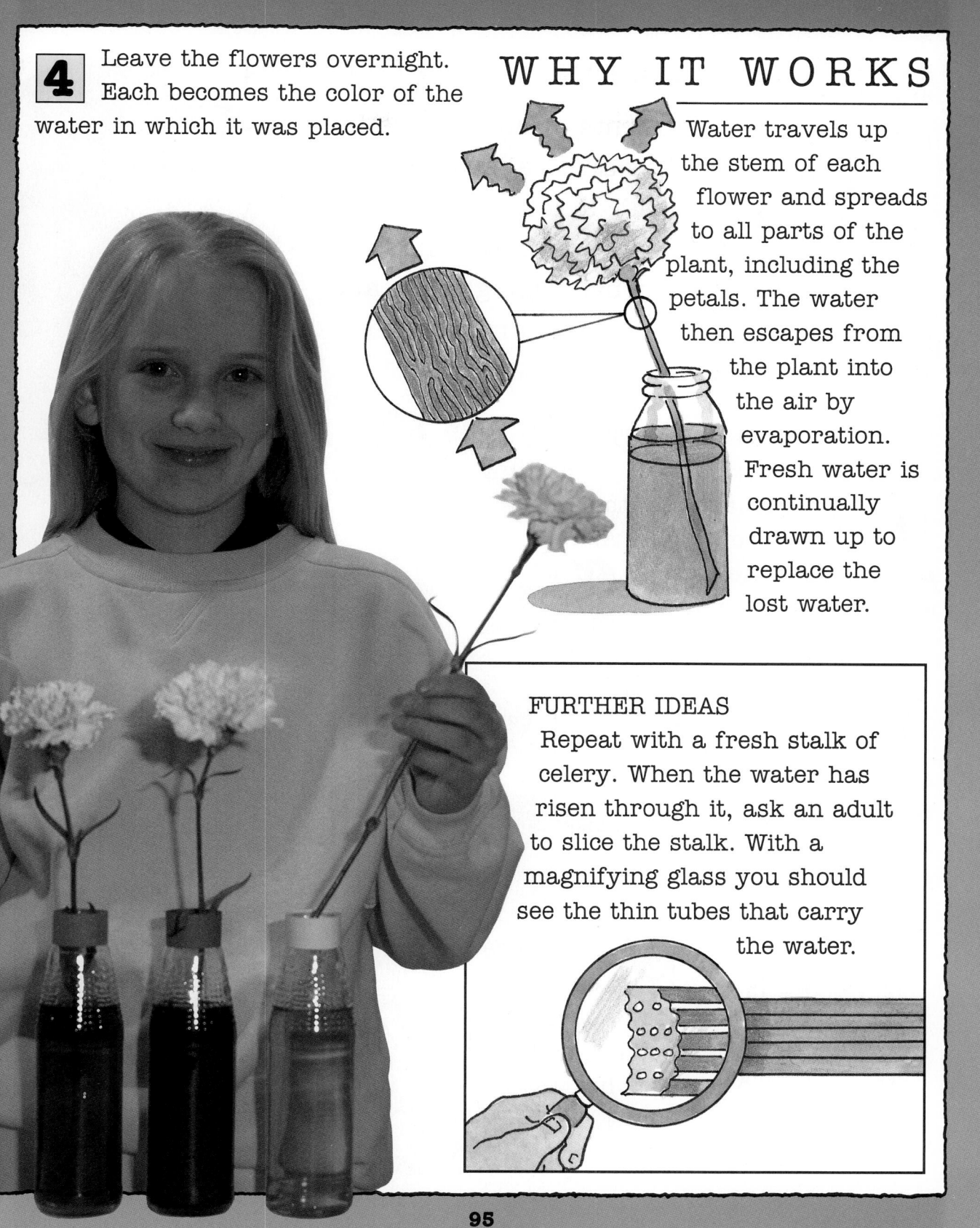

FURTHER IDEAS

Repeat with a fresh stalk of celery. When the water has risen through it, ask an adult to slice the stalk. With a magnifying glass you should see the thin tubes that carry the water.

FLOWING CURRENTS

Currents of hot air rise from warm valleys to the cooler hilltops. These are called *thermals*. They are very useful to hot air balloons, gliders, and even birds. The rising warm air helps to keep them aloft.

SEE HOT WATER CURRENTS

GET AN ADULT TO DO THIS FOR YOU

1 Find a small jar with a metal screw-on lid. Ask an adult to make some small holes in the lid.

2 Tie a piece of string tightly around the neck of the jar. Make sure the string can support the jar.

3 Place a few drops of food coloring in the jar and fill it with hot water. Screw the lid on tightly.

4 Fill a glass jug with cold water. Holding the string, gently lower the jar into the glass jug.

5 Watch as the colored water swirls around in the cold water.

WHY IT WORKS

Hot liquids expand and become less dense than the cold liquid around them. This causes the hot liquid to rise into the jug. Eventually the heat is spread out, and the cooled, denser liquid sinks to the bottom of the pitcher. This movement of the liquid is known as a *convection current.*

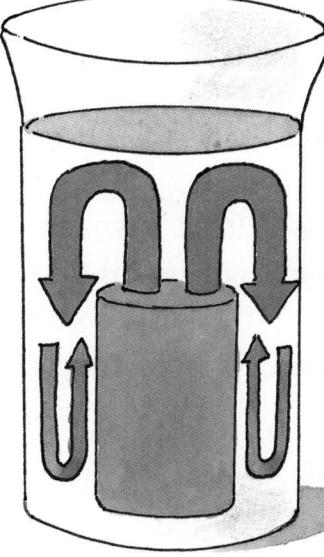

FURTHER IDEAS
Cut out some strips from circles of paper. Hold them above a heater. Rising warm air causes the strips to rotate.

RISING TEMPERATURES

On a hot day, you can see the temperature rise if you watch a thermometer carefully. As the air gets hotter, the liquid inside the thermometer expands up the glass tube. All liquids expand when heated, but usually only by a tiny amount.

MAKE A BOTTLE FOUNTAIN

1 Find a small glass jar with a screw-on lid. Fill the jar half full with cold water. Add a few drops of food coloring.

GET AN ADULT TO HELP YOU WITH THIS

2 Ask an adult to make a hole in the lid just big enough for a thin straw. Seal the straw in place with some clay.

3 Plug the end of the straw with clay. Use a pin to make a tiny hole in the plug.

4 Fill a large bowl with hot tap water. Stand the small jar upside-down in the bowl on some clay, with the straw sticking above the water level.

WHY IT WORKS

The heat from the hot water bowl warms up the air inside the jar, and this air expands. As it does so, it pushes on the water below. The water can only escape one way – by spraying out of the top of the straw.

5 Wait for the small jar to heat up, and stand back to admire the fountain of colored water spraying out of the top.

FURTHER IDEAS

Fill a jar with water. Put a straw through a hole in the lid and seal with clay. Turn the jar upside-down. See how the level in the straw changes when the jar is put in hot water and in a refrigerator.

SEPARATING MIXTURES

Tap water has been filtered many times to remove all impurities before you drink it. Filtering is like straining; it is a way of purifying a liquid by removing any solids that do not dissolve naturally.

MAKE MUDDY WATER CLEAR

1 Mix some mud, clay, or soil with water in a jar. Make a cone shape out of a coffee filter.

2 Carefully place the cone in the neck of a clean glass jar. Slowly pour the muddy mixture through the cone.

3 See how much clearer the filtered water appears. Warning: Do not drink the filtered water – it still contains germs.

WHY IT WORKS

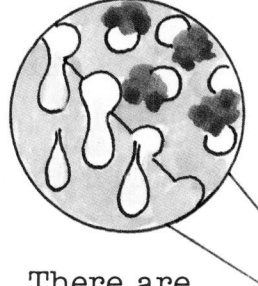

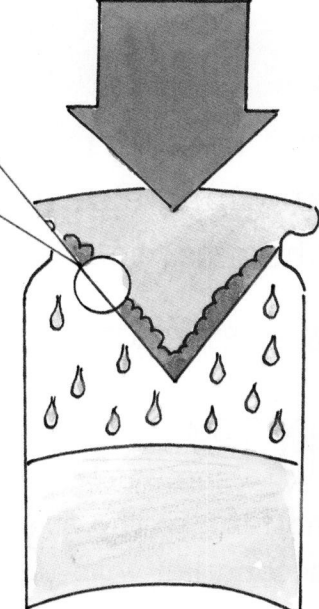

There are tiny holes in the paper that only allow water droplets to squeeze through. The pieces of solid are larger and get trapped.

FURTHER IDEAS

Dissolve some salt in a tall, clean glass of water. Leave it in a warm place for a few days. See how salt is left behind when all the water has evaporated.

RUST OR BUST

Though many metals are strong, tough materials, they do not last forever. When iron is constantly damp it will rust; pieces of iron turn brown and crumble away. Rust can be a terrible problem. It can attack your car, bicycle, or anything else made from iron. The iron is changed into a new chemical that we call *rust*, or "iron oxide."

A RUST RACE

1 Set up five glass jars with some steel wool in each. Add nothing to the first jar. Fill half the second jar with tap water. Fill the third to the brim with boiled water and tighten the lid. In the fourth, put the steel wool on a piece of damp cloth. Put tap water in the last jar, and add a pinch of salt.

2 Leave the jars for at least a week. Regularly examine the steel wool for signs of rust.

WHY IT WORKS

So-called "steel wool" is really made of iron. The steel wool rusts in jars 2 and 4, but especially in jar 5. Iron needs water and air to rust. The air and water particles attach to the iron particles to form iron oxide. Boiled water has no air in it. Salt makes iron rust faster.

FURTHER IDEAS
Scratch away some of the surface of some empty cans. See if the cans rust when damp.

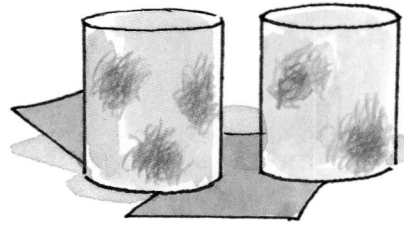

INVISIBLE INK

Have you ever wanted to write a secret message that only you can read? This project lets you write your message on a sheet of paper. When you have finished, the message is invisible – the paper just looks blank. Nobody can read it unless they know the method for making the message visible.

SEND A SECRET MESSAGE

1 Squeeze some lemon juice into a glass.

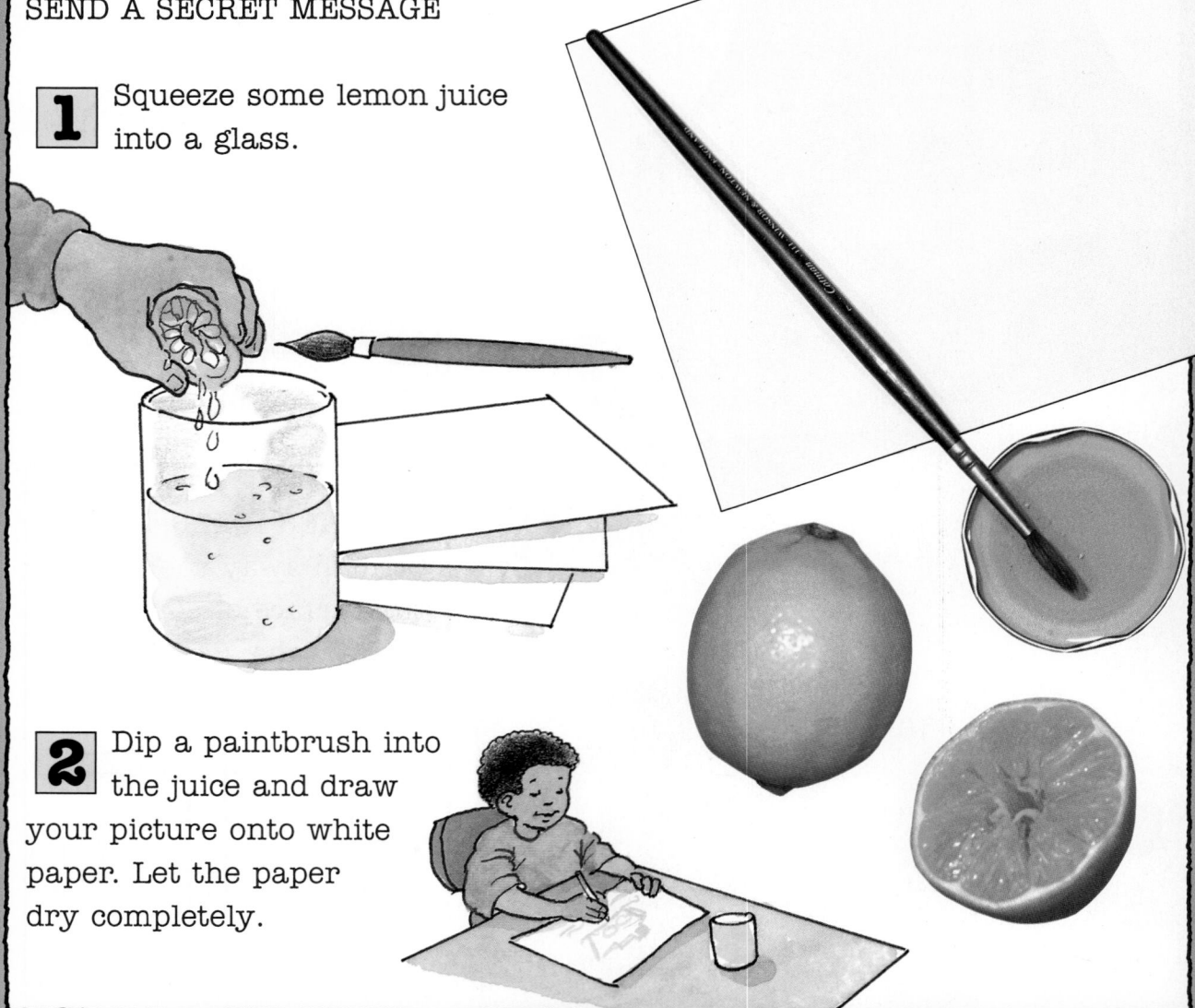

2 Dip a paintbrush into the juice and draw your picture onto white paper. Let the paper dry completely.

3 Ask an adult to place the paper in the oven for a few minutes, and the picture will reappear.

WHY IT WORKS

When the lemon juice is heated, water evaporates away. The compounds that remain combine with oxygen in the air. This turns the juice brown and makes the picture visible.

GET AN ADULT TO DO THIS

FURTHER IDEAS

Draw on white paper using a wax candle. Warm the paper on a radiator until the wax melts and the picture is revealed.

SPLITTING COLORS

If you look very carefully with a magnifying glass at the colored dots that make up the colors in this book, you may notice that there are only four colors. All of the other colors are made by mixing these colors together.

SEPARATE COLORED INKS

1 Cut some blotting paper into strips, 1 inch wide and 6 inches long.

2 Make a large dot just above the bottom of each strip with several different-colored felt-tip pens.

3 Tape the other end of the strips to a string. Hang the string over a bowl with two pencils set in clay. Fill the bowl with water until it touches the strips.

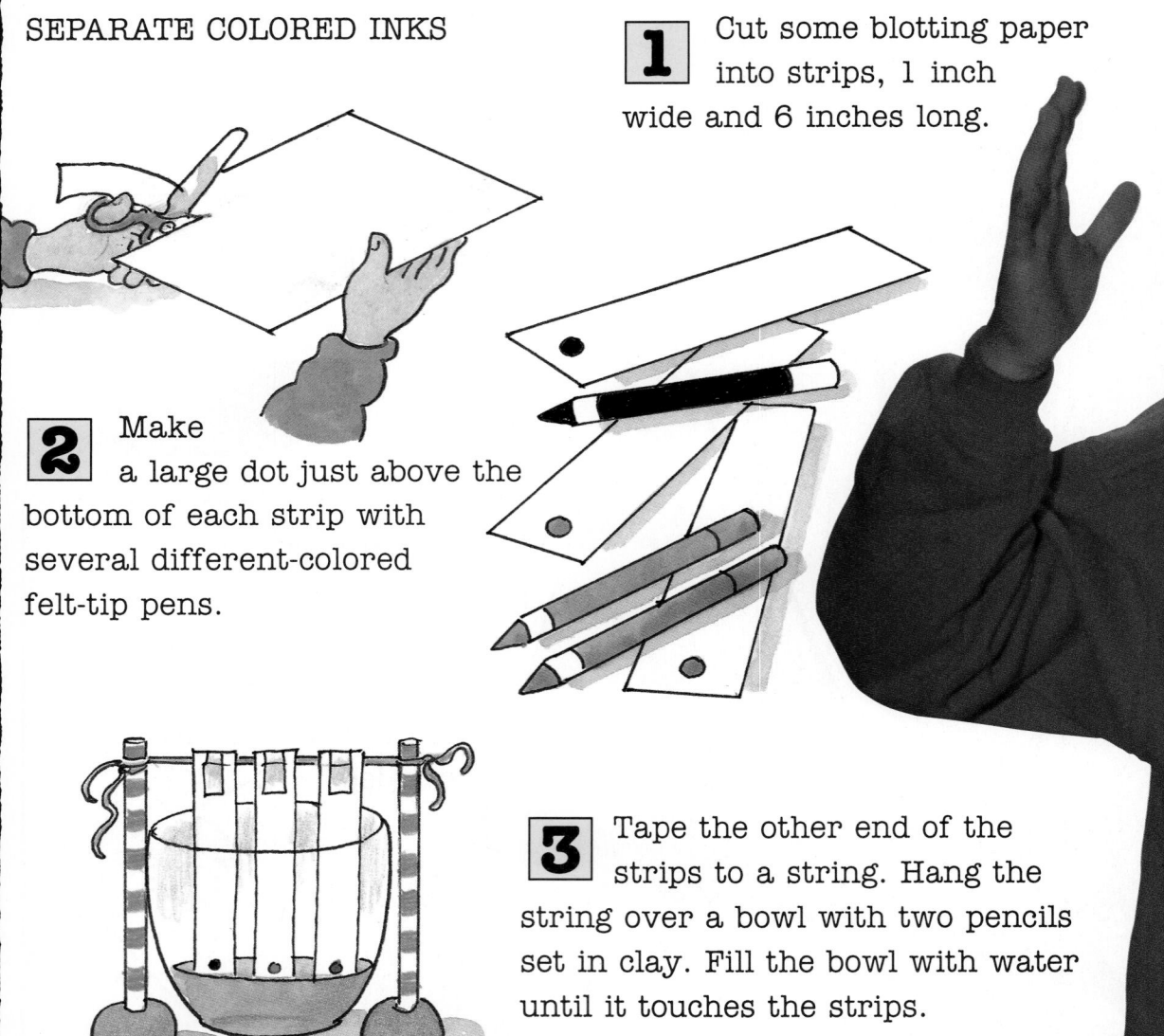

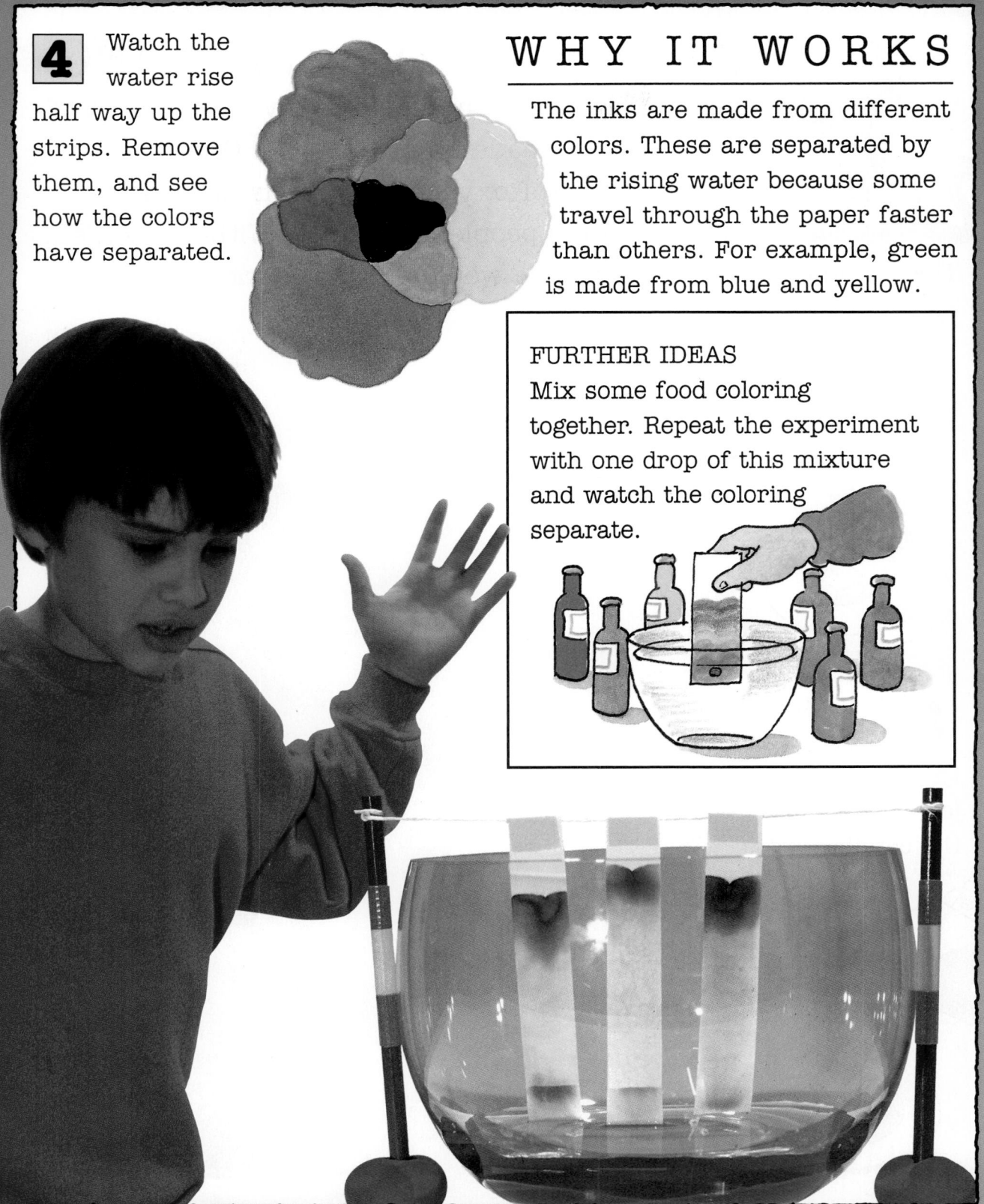

4 Watch the water rise half way up the strips. Remove them, and see how the colors have separated.

WHY IT WORKS

The inks are made from different colors. These are separated by the rising water because some travel through the paper faster than others. For example, green is made from blue and yellow.

FURTHER IDEAS
Mix some food coloring together. Repeat the experiment with one drop of this mixture and watch the coloring separate.

107

BURNING AND BREATHING

Air is really a mixture of many gases. Most of the air is made up of nitrogen. One fifth is made up of oxygen. Oxygen is needed for fires and for people to breathe. Without oxygen, fires wouldn't burn and people would suffocate and die.

INVESTIGATE A BURNING CANDLE

1 Use clay to stand a candle upright in the middle of a small, shallow saucer.

2 Place four piles of coins around the clay so that a jar can sit over the candle.

3 Add a few drops of food coloring to a jug filled with water. Then fill the saucer with the colored water.

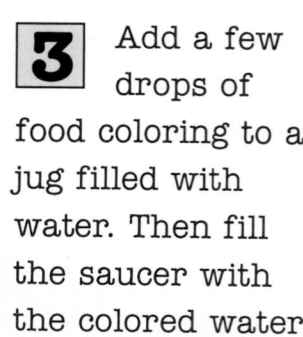

4 Ask an adult to light the candle and lower the jar over it. Watch the water level in the jar rise as the candle goes out.

GET AN ADULT TO DO THIS

WHY IT WORKS

The burning candle flame uses up the particles of oxygen. Water is sucked up into the jar to replace the used oxygen. Water rises about one fifth up the jar. The burning stops when all of the oxygen in the jar has been used up.

FURTHER IDEAS
Compare how long similar candles burn when different jars are placed over them. The longer they burn, the more oxygen is present.

LIVING YEAST

Most germs, or "microbes," are bad for us, because they cause illness and disease. However, some microbes can be useful to us. We use microbes to make yogurt, cheese, bread, and beer. Yeast is a microbe that looks like a yellow powder, but under a microscope you can see that it is made of living cells.

SEE YEAST BREATHING

1 Find a glass bottle and pour in a teaspoonful of sugar and some dried yeast.

2 Pour in some warm water. Swirl the bottle to mix the water, sugar, and yeast.

3 Fit a balloon over the neck of the bottle and make sure it is sealed tightly.

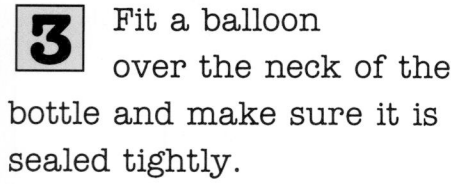

4 Stand the bottle in a large bowl of hot water to keep it warm. Watch the mixture for bubbles of gas. Eventually, the balloon will fill with gas and inflate.

WHY IT WORKS

When you add the warm water, the yeast "wakes up" and feeds on the sugar. As it feeds, it breathes out carbon dioxide and fills the balloon.

FURTHER IDEAS

Stir a spoonful of sugar and dried yeast in warm water. Mix half a pound of flour with half an ounce of butter and a little salt. Add the yeast and water and knead into a dough. Bake the bread for fifteen minutes at 425°F (220°C).

CONTENTS

What is electricity? 114

Static electricity 116

Battery power 118

Simple circuits 120

Conductors and insulators 122

Resistance 124

Open circuits 126

Turned on 128

Bigger circuits 130

House lights 132

Movement from electricity 134

Electroplating 136

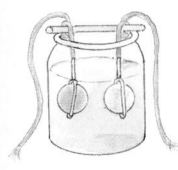

CHAPTER *Five*

UNDERSTANDING ELECTRICITY

WHAT IS ELECTRICITY?

All things are made up of tiny particles called atoms. Atoms are made from even smaller particles, some of which are electrically charged. This charge may be negative or positive. Electricity is a flow of the negatively charged particles. You can see a flow of charge in the form of a spark.

LISTENING TO ELECTRICITY

1 Find a metal tray or a cookie tin lid. Place a lump of clay, large enough to use as a handle, in the middle of the tray.

2 Place the tray on a large plastic bag. Grip the clay firmly with one hand, press down, and rotate the tray vigorously for two minutes on the plastic.

3 Be very careful not to touch the tray with your hands. Lift the tray off the plastic with the clay grip.

4 Pick up a metal fork with your free hand. Touch the edge of the tray with it. Hear the sparks crackle!

WHY IT WORKS

As the tray is rubbed on the plastic, it becomes negatively charged. The fork is positively charged and when it is brought close to the tray it attracts the negative charges. They jump through the air to the fork as a spark.

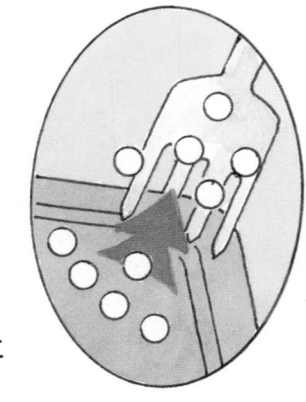

FURTHER IDEAS
Charge up a plastic comb by rubbing it vigorously on a clean, dry cloth. Adjust a faucet to give a thin stream of running water. Bring the comb close to the stream. The comb pulls at the water! Make the water dance by jiggling the comb.

STATIC ELECTRICITY

The ancient Greeks noticed that when amber (fossilized tree resin) is rubbed, it attracts light objects, such as feathers. This is because the amber has become electrically charged. The word *electricity* comes from the Greek word *elektron*, meaning amber. Scientists use an electroscope to check if an object is electrically charged.

MAKE AN ELECTROSCOPE

1 Find a clean jar. Cut a circle of cardboard big enough to fit over the top of a glass jar. Cut two ½ inch-long parallel slots in the middle of the cardboard.

2 Cut out two strips of aluminum foil. They should each be about ½ inch wide and 2 inches long.

3 Insert one strip through each slot so the strips overlap at the top. Tape the cardboard to the top of the jar so the strips hang downward.

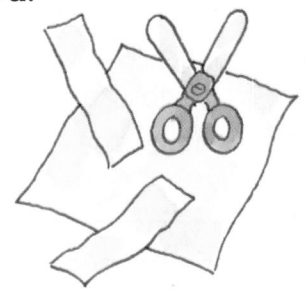

116

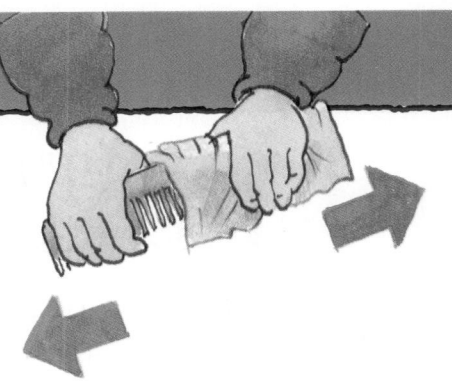

4 Charge up a plastic comb by rubbing it vigorously for a couple of minutes with a clean, dry cloth.

5 Test the comb for charge with your electroscope. Touch the top of the aluminum strips with the comb. Watch what happens to the two strips.

WHY IT WORKS

Electricity cannot move through plastic or amber. But they can hold a *static* (not moving) electric charge. When the comb touches the strips, the electric charge is released because electricity can move through metal. Both strips receive the same kind of charge, and because like charges repel (push away) each other, the strips move apart.

FURTHER IDEAS

Inflate two balloons. Tie a piece of nylon thread to the end of each balloon. Rub each balloon on a wool sweater. Hang both balloons together from their threads. Watch how they repel each other.

BATTERY POWER

Static electricity is not very useful for powering machines, so we use *current* electricity. An electric current is a controlled flow of electric charge. Batteries produce electric currents from chemicals. Alessandro Volta made the first battery in 1800. The volt, a unit of electric measurement, is named after him.

MAKE A BATTERY

1 Find 12 copper coins and zinc washers of similar size. They will need to be stacked. Cut out 12 same-sized circles of blotting paper.

2 Pour vinegar into a glass with a tablespoonful of salt. Soak each piece of blotting paper in the mixture. Stack a coin, then a washer, on a piece of blotting paper. Finish with a washer.

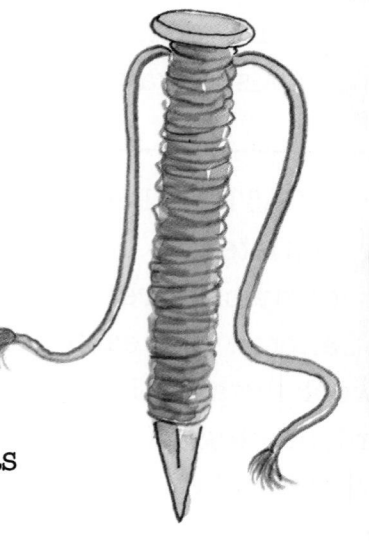

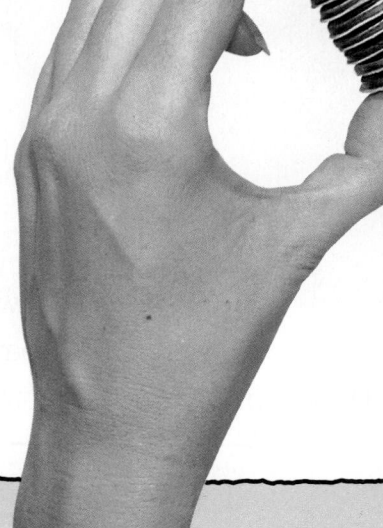

3 Take 6 ½ feet of thin plastic-coated copper wire. Coil it tightly around an iron nail as many times as you can.

4 Attach one end of the copper wire to the bottom coin and the other to the top washer.

WHY IT WORKS

The salt and vinegar start a chemical reaction. Negatively charged particles flow through the coins to the washers, around the wire coil, and back to the battery. The electric current creates a magnetic field that affects a compass needle (see pages 134-135).

5 Test your battery by bringing the nail close to a small compass. The nail should make the compass needle spin.

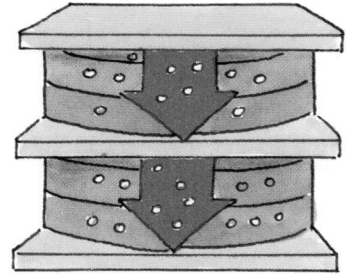

FURTHER IDEAS
Find a juicy lemon. Push one copper and one zinc nail into it. Touch both nails with your tongue. You will feel a tingle from the flow of current in the lemon "battery."

SIMPLE CIRCUITS

The path an electric current takes is called a circuit. Electric current flows from the power supply, to the lightbulb, and back to the power supply. As long as there are no gaps in the circuit, the electric current will flow.

MAKE A CIRCUIT

1 Ask an adult to open up a coat hanger. Bend it into a wavy shape. Push the ends of the wire into a cardboard base. Hold each end in place with clay.

2 Make a loop out of thin wire. Connect it to a long piece of insulated wire. Thread this through a plastic straw to form a handle. Slip the loop onto the wavy wire.

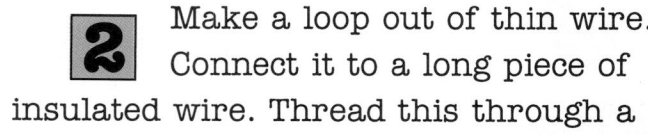

3 Attach a 6-volt lightbulb and 6-volt battery to the base. Wire the battery and bulb to the wavy wire as shown (right).

4 Connect the other end of the bulb to the loop. The wire needs to be long enough to reach both ends of the wavy wire.

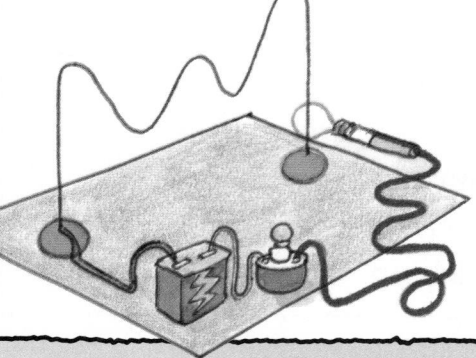

120

5 Check that the bulb lights when you touch the loop to the wavy wire. Now try and move the loop along the path of the wavy wire without letting the two touch!

WHY IT WORKS

Current electricity only flows if there is a complete circuit back to the battery. The gap in this circuit is between the loop and the wavy wire. The wires will touch if your hand is not steady. The gap is closed, the circuit is completed, and the bulb lights up.

FURTHER IDEAS
Try replacing the bulb in this circuit with a small electric buzzer. When you touch the wavy wire, the buzzer will buzz. You could make the game harder by making the wavy wire longer or even more wavy.

CONDUCTORS AND INSULATORS

Some materials allow electricity to flow through them easily. These materials are called electrical conductors. Most metals are good conductors. Other materials, like plastic, do not easily let electricity flow through them. These materials, called insulators, are used to prevent electricity from reaching places where it would be dangerous.

TEST FOR ELECTRICAL CONDUCTORS

1 Find a thick cardboard base. Cut out two squares of aluminum foil. Glue them onto the base. Leave a small gap between them (see right).

2 Attach a piece of thin plastic-coated copper wire to one square. Glue it to the board as shown. Repeat for the other square.

3 Connect one of the wires to a 6-volt lightbulb (right). Glue the bulb to the base.

4 Connect the other wire to a 6-volt battery. Now connect the battery and bulb to a small plastic-coated copper wire.

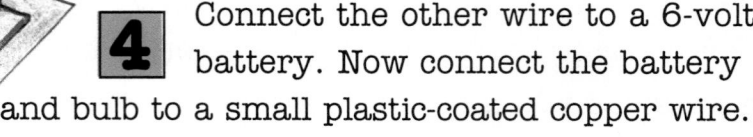

5 Test a range of objects, such as keys, pencils, or erasers by placing them across the two squares.

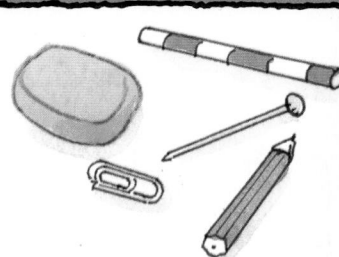

WHY IT WORKS

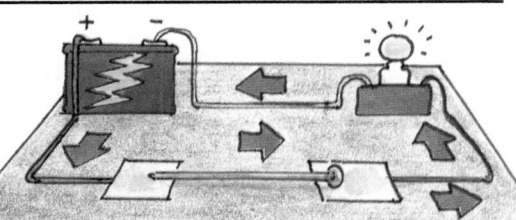

If an object is a conductor, it completes the circuit. The bulb lights up because conductors allow electricity to flow through them. All metals are conductors. Carbon is an unusual non-metal because it also conducts electricity. Pencil "lead" contains carbon in the form of graphite.

FURTHER IDEAS
Make up another circuit without a base. Test water to see if it can conduct electricity. Keep the squares close together in the container. Stir in lots of salt to help the water to conduct. Watch the bulb get brighter as you add more salt.

RESISTANCE

Good conductors of electricity allow electricity to flow easily. A thick wire can conduct more electricity than a thin wire, just like a wide road can carry more cars than a narrow road. The thin wire resists the flow of electricity or has a higher resistance.

MAKE A DIMMER SWITCH

1 Attach a 6-volt battery and 6-volt bulb to a thick cardboard base. Use two long wires and one short one to make a circuit as shown (right).

2 Remove the graphite from a mechanical pencil. Tape or glue together half a dozen graphite rods. Attach the wire from the battery to the bundle.

3 Attach a square of aluminum foil to the wire from the bulb. Check that the circuit is complete and the bulb lights when you touch the square to the graphite.

WHY IT WORKS

Graphite is made of carbon, which is a conductor. As you slide the square along the graphite toward the battery, the electricity travels less distance. This means less resistance, so the bulb gets brighter.

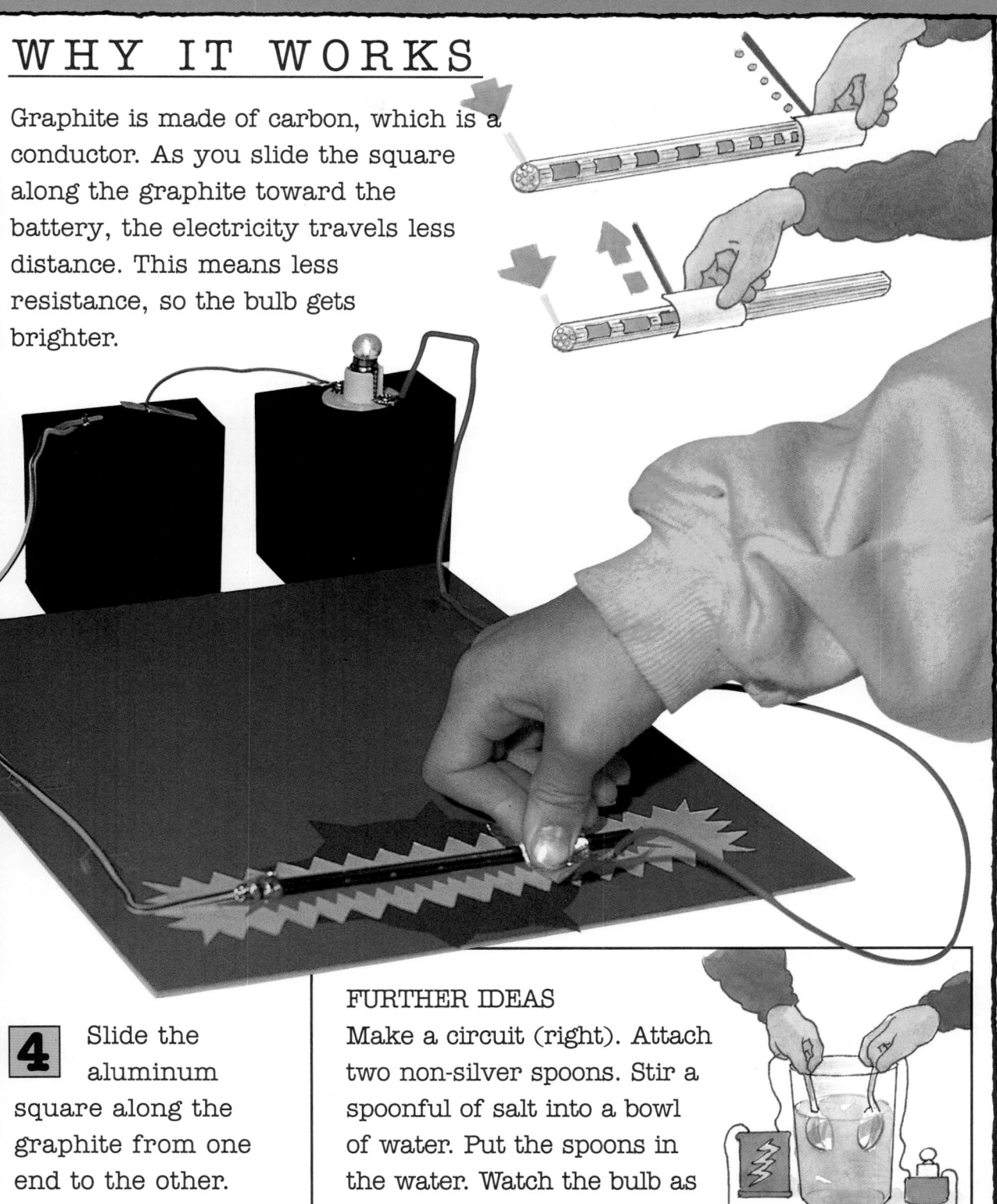

4 Slide the aluminum square along the graphite from one end to the other. Watch the lightbulb.

FURTHER IDEAS
Make a circuit (right). Attach two non-silver spoons. Stir a spoonful of salt into a bowl of water. Put the spoons in the water. Watch the bulb as you move the spoons apart.

OPEN CIRCUITS

Every time you turn on a light you are completing a circuit. As soon as a switch is closed (turned on), the circuit is completed and the electricity operates the bulb or electrical appliance. In 1837, Samuel Morse had the idea of completing and breaking an electrical circuit to send messages.

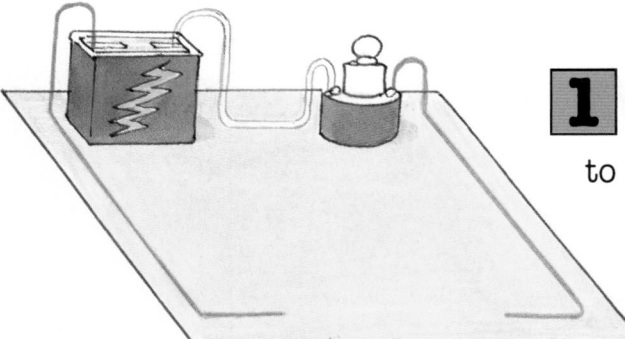

SEND A MESSAGE

1 Make a circuit using a 6-volt battery and 6-volt bulb attached to a thick cardboard base. Leave a gap between the two wires (see left).

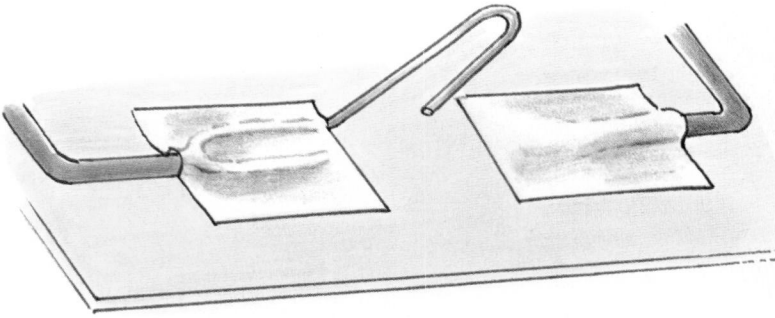

2 Make a switch out of a steel paper clip. Attach it to the end of the wire running from the battery. Tape a square of aluminum foil over the top (see right). Tape another aluminum square over the end of the other wire. Make sure the paper clip reaches this square.

3 Press the paper clip down to touch the square and switch on the bulb. Practice long and short flashes to send a Morse code message.

WHY IT WORKS

Electricity cannot flow when a circuit is open. Closing the switch completes the circuit. The bulb lights immediately because electricity can travel so quickly.

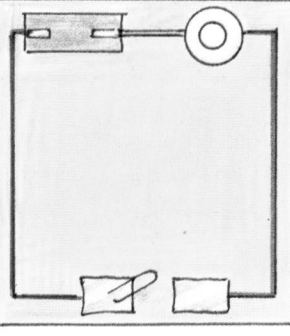 

FURTHER IDEAS

Make a burglar alarm using your circuit board as a base. Tape some pencils or straws along the side edges. Place a second board on top of the pencils leaving the bulb and battery clear. Cover the boards with a mat. When the "intruder" steps on the mat, the switch will be pressed and the burglar alarm will light up.

TURNED ON

Being able to turn a light on or off from two different places can be very useful. If a light can be turned on or off from both the top and the bottom of a staircase then not only is it safer at night but energy is also saved. This kind of switch is called a two-way switch.

MAKE A TWO-WAY SWITCH

1 Fold a piece of cardboard into a wedge shape (shown right). Draw a line down the center. Stick down two pieces of cardboard on each side of the line and draw a staircase.

2 Make a circuit using a 6-volt battery and light-bulb. Push a tack through each piece of cardboard. Attach the wires to them.

3 Push four more tacks into the cardboard (shown below). Connect the upper two with a short piece of wire and repeat for the lower two.

4 Attach a paper clip under each of the first two tacks so that they can turn to touch either the upper or lower tack.

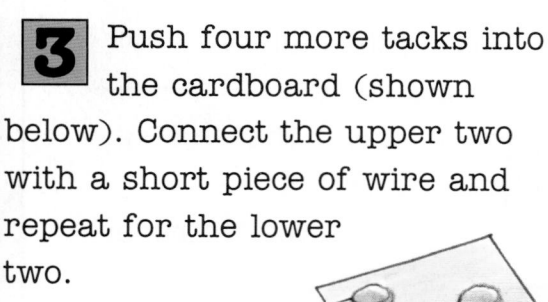

WHY IT WORKS

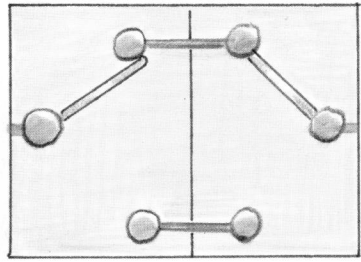 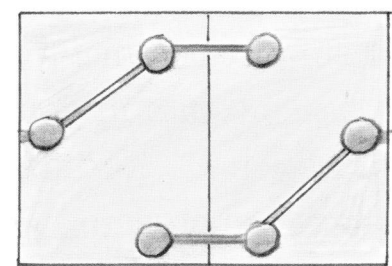 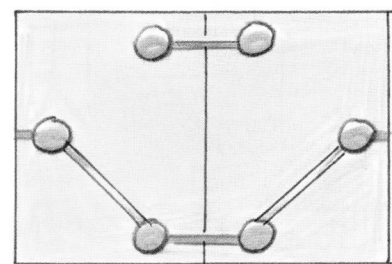

The two-way switch allows two alternative paths for an electric current. Electricity can flow only when both paper clips are touching the same wire. Removing one of the paper clips from the wire breaks the circuit.

5 Turn the switches on and off. Both paper clips must touch one of the two tacks to make a circuit.

FURTHER IDEAS
Make a three-way switch quiz game (see right). When the paper clips point to the same letter, the bulb lights up. When your friend chooses the correct answer (A, B, or C), the bulb lights up.

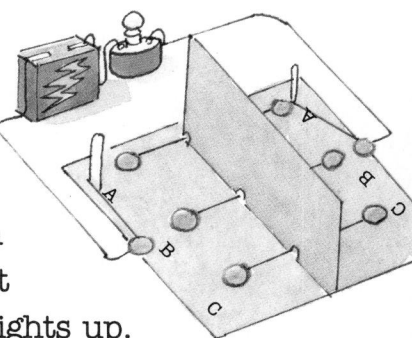

BIGGER CIRCUITS

All the circuits you have built so far have been small and simple, requiring only one piece of wire. Electric circuits in your home consist of many more wires. Finding which wire is connected to which source can be like finding your way through a maze.

MAKE A MAZE

1 Find a large piece of thick cardboard. Cut out ½ inch-wide strips of aluminum foil about the same length as the cardboard.

2 Flatten the aluminum strips, glue them to the cardboard, then make a criss-cross pattern with the strips.

3 Attach a 6 inch-long wire to one side of a 6-volt lightbulb. Then attach a 3.5 ft-long wire to a dowel "pointer," leaving the copper exposed at the end.

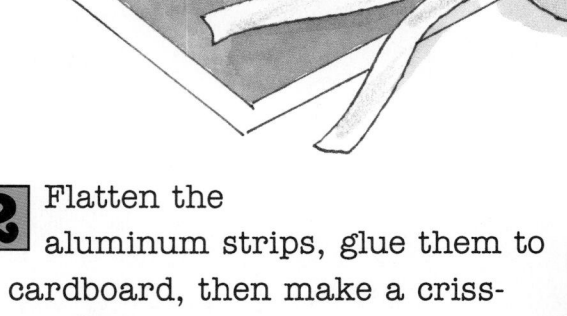

4 Make a circuit (left). Wire the battery to the aluminum at one corner of the board. Test the circuit by touching the pointer to the foil.

5 Cover parts of the aluminum with insulating tape. Copy the pattern shown at the bottom of the page. The gray shaded areas show where the tape should go.

6 Challenge a friend to find a way through the maze keeping the bulb lit. The pointer must touch only the aluminum to complete the circuit.

WHY IT WORKS

When the pointer touches any part of the aluminum connected to the battery, a circuit is created. Electricity can flow and light the bulb. If the pointer touches other parts of the maze, the bulb goes out.

HOUSE LIGHTS

A simple way to arrange more than one lightbulb is in a series, so the electricity flows through one bulb to the next. But if a bulb fails, the circuit is broken, and all the lights go out. In a parallel circuit, each bulb has its own connection to the battery, so if one bulb fails the others are unaffected. House lights work this way.

MAKE A RING CIRCUIT

1 Ask an adult to bend two pieces of wire into two rings, one larger than the other. Use some cardboard as a base for your circuit.

2 Make a circuit out of the two rings and a 6-volt battery (left). Connect the outer ring to one battery terminal, and the inner ring to the other terminal.

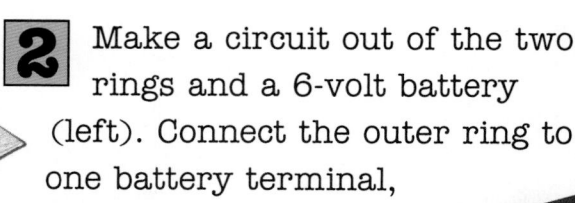

3 Connect two pieces of thin plastic-coated copper wire to the ends of a 6-volt bulb. Check that there is plenty of bare wire showing at the free ends.

132

WHY IT WORKS

Wherever the battery and bulb are placed on the rings, there is always a complete circuit. This type of parallel circuit is called a ring circuit.

4 Attach one of the wires running from the lightbulb to the outer ring, and one to the inner ring. It forms a circuit and the bulb lights up.

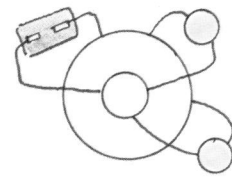 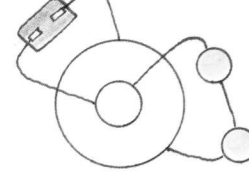

FURTHER IDEAS
Try adding another bulb to your ring circuit. Does one affect the other? Can you find a place on the rings where the circuit does not work?

MOVEMENT FROM ELECTRICITY

Electric motors do all sorts of useful work in the home: They are found in household items such as washing machines, electric heaters, and food processors. The movement produced is usually a spinning motion. The electric motor uses electricity and magnetism to produce movement.

MAKE A SIMPLE MOTOR

1 Wrap four 3.5-foot pieces of wire together to form a loop (see right). Secure the wires with insulation tape.

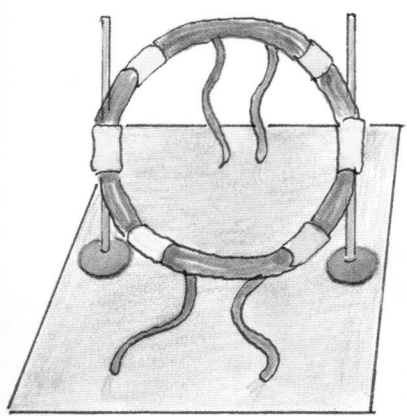

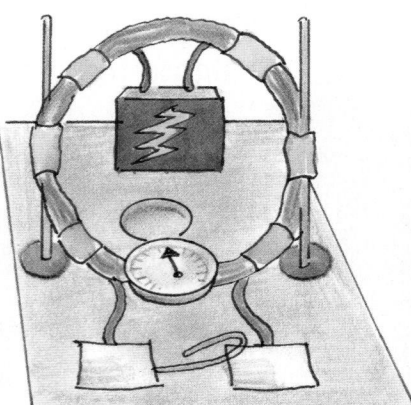

2 On a cardboard base, attach two dowels in an upright position with clay. Tape the wire to the dowels (shown above).

3 Attach the two top wires to a 6-volt battery. Attach the bottom wires to two aluminum squares at the base. Make a switch out of a paper clip.

4 Leave the switch open. Hold a small pocket compass level in the middle of the wire loop. Note the direction the compass points to.

5 Now turn off the switch and watch the effect on the compass. It should spin around until you turn the switch on again.

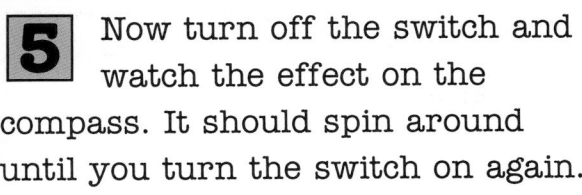

WHY IT WORKS

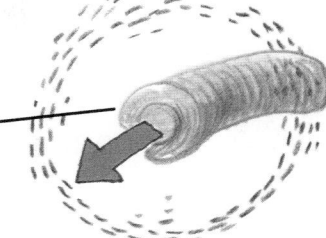

Electric current

Magnetic field

When electricity flows through a wire it creates a magnetic field. When another magnet (the pointer in a compass) is close, the magnets push or pull each other.

FURTHER IDEAS

Coil about three and a half feet of copper wire around an iron nail. Attach the ends of the wire to the terminals of a 6-volt battery. The nail will become an electromagnet which is strong enough to attract steel paper clips.

ELECTROPLATING

An electric current can be used to split chemicals into the elements that they are made of. If an electric current is passed through a liquid called an electrolyte, charged particles will move through it. This is called electrolysis. Cutlery and jewelry are silverplated using electrolysis.

COPPERPLATE A SILVER COIN

1 Fill a clean glass jar with water. This will act as your electrolyte.

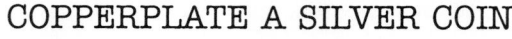

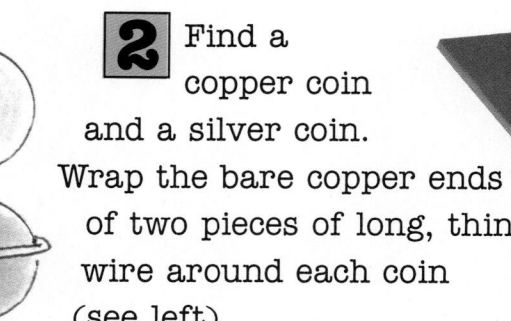

3 Put the coins into the water. Wrap the two wires around a pencil balanced over the top of the jar.

2 Find a copper coin and a silver coin. Wrap the bare copper ends of two pieces of long, thin wire around each coin (see left).

4 Connect the copper coin to the positive (+) terminal of a 6-volt battery, and the silver coin to the negative (-) terminal.

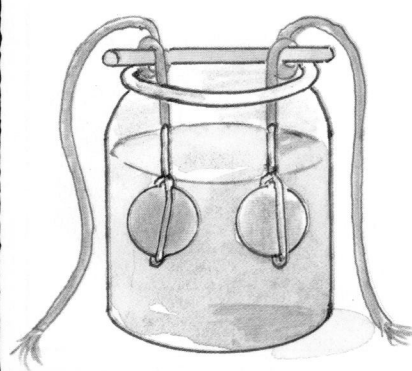

5 Make sure the coins are close but not touching. Leave the circuit set up for five minutes. Take out the two coins and observe.

WHY IT WORKS

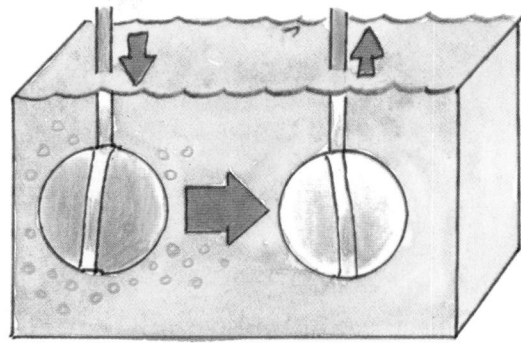

Electric current enters the water through the positive terminal, attached to the copper coin. It carries some of the copper with it. The current carries the copper through the water to the silver coin. The copper is left as a thin layer over the silver coin. The copper can easily be scraped off afterwards. Dispose of the water carefully afterwards as it is poisonous.

FURTHER IDEAS

Try using vinegar with lots of salt stirred into it as the electrolyte instead of water. Using a more powerful battery produces faster and thicker plating.

CONTENTS

Why do things float? 140

Iceberg ahoy! 142

Colorful paper 144

Floating liquids 146

Floating eggs 148

Different depths 150

Unsinkable 152

Port and starboard 154

Jet power 156

Dive deep! 158

Floating underwater 160

Floating on air 162

CHAPTER *Six*

MAKING
THINGS FLOAT
AND SINK

WHY DO THINGS FLOAT?

Wood, cork and ice all float no matter what size or shape they are. However, materials such as modeling clay or steel, sometimes float and sometimes sink. With these materials, it is their shape that decides whether they float or sink.

MAKE A CLAY BOAT

1 Fill a large plastic bowl with water from the tap.

2 Try to float a lump of modeling clay on the surface of the water. Try floating marbles too. Watch them sink.

3 Using your thumbs, press the clay into a boat shape. Hollow out the inside.

4 Draw a sailor on a sheet of cardboard. Color him in and cut out. Fold along the dotted lines as shown so he can sit up.

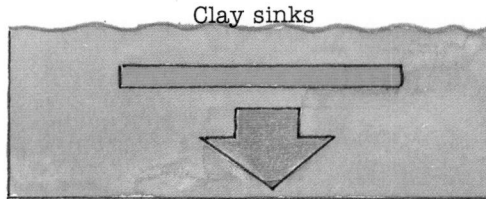

Clay sinks

5 Sit the sailor in the boat. Now float the boat on the water. Put a marble in your boat. It will sink slightly but remains upright.

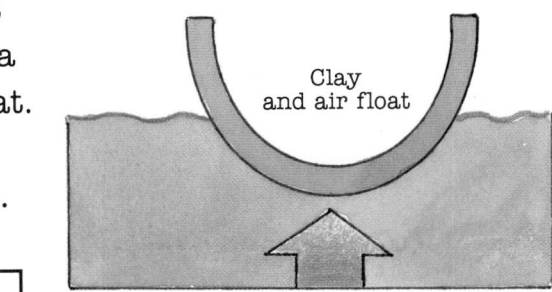

Clay and air float

WHY IT WORKS

One ounce of water takes up more space than one ounce of clay. Because clay is denser than water it sinks. Shaped into a boat, clay fills with air. Air and clays together are less dense than water, so the boat floats.

FURTHER IDEAS
Have a boat-building competition with some friends. Each make a boat using the same amount of clay. Whose boat can hold the most marbles?

ICEBERG AHOY!

When most liquids freeze to solids they become more dense. Water is different. When water freezes it expands (causing burst pipes in winter) and becomes less dense. Ice floats because it is less dense than water. Giant blocks of ice floating in the sea are called icebergs. Ships must take care to avoid icebergs.

WATCH AN ICE-CUBE MELT

1 Add some food coloring to a jar of water. Add enough coloring to turn the water a bright color.

2 Pour the colored water into an ice-cube tray. Put it in a freezer overnight.

3 Fill up a large container with hot tap water. Ask an adult to help you.

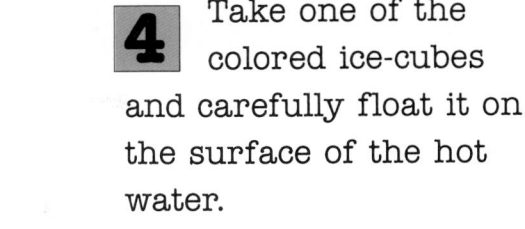

4 Take one of the colored ice-cubes and carefully float it on the surface of the hot water.

5 As the ice becomes water, the color moves around in the warmer water. It sinks to the bottom of the container.

WHY IT WORKS

As the ice melts to water its density increases. This makes it sink to the bottom of the container. There it mixes with the water in the jar and warms up. It becomes less dense and moves back toward the surface.

Melted ice

FURTHER IDEAS
Make a volcano. Fill a jar with hot water. Add coloring. Cover the top of the jar with paper held in place with a rubber band. Put the jar in a bowl of cold water. Pierce the paper. Watch the volcano erupt.

COLORFUL PAPER

It is not only boats and icebergs that float on water. Oil-based liquids that are less dense than water also float on top of water. We sometimes see escaped crude oil floating on the sea in a thin layer that stretches for miles. Such oil slicks can harm the seabed, fish, and birds.

MAKE COLORED PAPER

1 Ask an adult to mix a few drops of oil-based paint with a little turpentine in a paper cup.

2 Place a bowl of water on some old newspapers. Add some of the paint and mix into the water using a stick.

144

3 Carefully lower a sheet of plain paper onto the surface of the water. Let the paper soak up the paint.

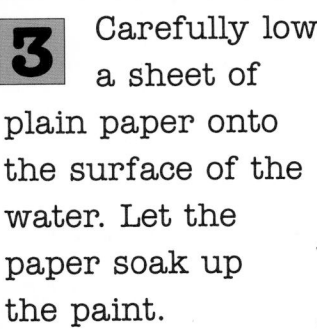

WHY IT WORKS

Oil paints are less dense than water so they float on the surface. For this reason salad oil floats on top of vinegar. You can make the separate layers mix together by shaking them hard.

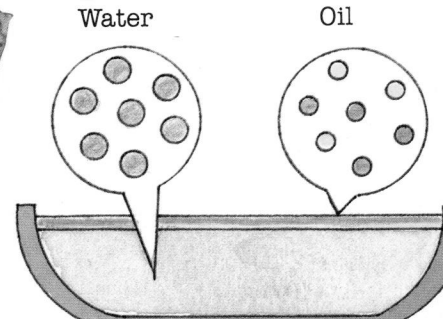

Water   Oil

4 Remove the paper and leave it to dry. Repeat using fresh paper. Stir the water to get different patterns.

FURTHER IDEAS

Try making different patterns by changing the colors of paint. Let the papers dry. Use your favorite patterns for writing paper.

FLOATING LIQUIDS

Many liquids are like water and mix easily with it. But some liquids do not mix with water unless they are forced to. Oils and syrups do not mix well with water. Some liquids are less dense and float on top of water (see pages 144-145). Others are denser so water floats on top of them.

MAKE LAYERS OF FLOATING LIQUIDS

1 Find a clean, empty plastic soda bottle. Ask an adult to cut the top off with a sharp knife.

GET AN ADULT TO DO THIS FOR YOU

2 Slowly pour in some syrup so there is a ³/₄ inch layer in the bottom. Let the syrup settle.

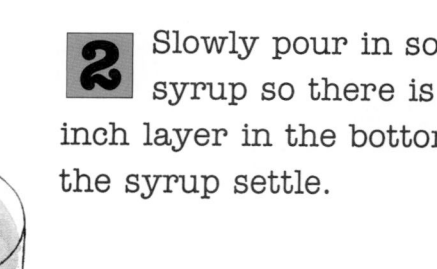

3 Next, slowly pour ³/₄ inch of cooking oil over the layer of syrup.

4 Finally, carefully pour in about ³/₄ inch of water.

5 Examine the three layers. They float on top of each other without mixing. See what happens if you stir gently with a spoon.

WHY IT WORKS

The layers of liquid refuse to mix with each other. The syrup is at the bottom because it is the densest. The oil is the least dense of the three and so floats on the very top.

FURTHER IDEAS
Try floating different objects on your layers of liquid. Experiment with things that you would expect to sink in water.

FLOATING EGGS

How can you tell whether an egg is good or bad without breaking it? Fresh eggs sink if placed in a bowl of fresh water because they are denser than water. But if an egg turns bad, it floats in water. This is because the yolk and white have dried up, which makes it less dense than a good egg.

MAKE AN EGG FLOAT

GET AN ADULT TO DO THIS FOR YOU

1 Find two large containers. Fill one with hot tap water and the other with cold tap water. Get an adult to help.

2 Add a spoonful of table salt to the hot water. Stir in the salt until it has all dissolved.

3 Put a fresh egg into the salty water to see if it floats. If it doesn't, add more salt until it does.

WHY IT WORKS

Salt dissolved in water increases the density of water. Denser liquids are better at keeping objects afloat.

This is why many things that sink in fresh water will float in salted water.

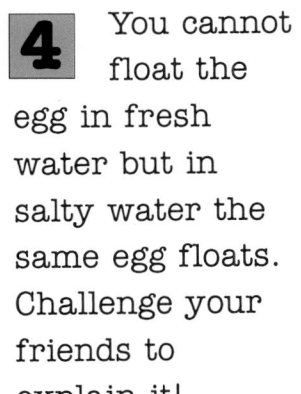

4 You cannot float the egg in fresh water but in salty water the same egg floats. Challenge your friends to explain it!

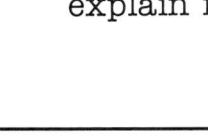

Salted

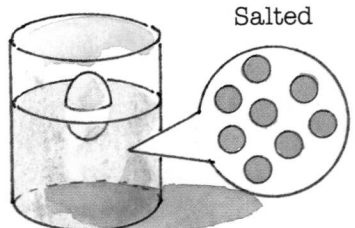

Unsalted

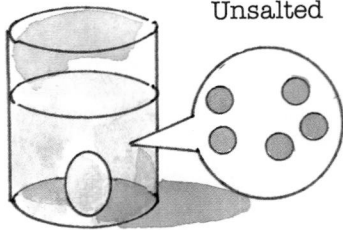

FURTHER IDEAS

See how long it takes for a fresh egg to go bad when not refrigerated. Test it in a vase of fresh water each day. Dispose of the bad egg *carefully* when you've finished.

DIFFERENT DEPTHS

We have seen that each liquid has its own particular density. The denser or "heavier" the liquid, the better it is at making things float in it. Brewers of beer need to know the exact density of beer to ensure the beer tastes just right. A hydrometer is used to test its density.

MAKE A HYDROMETER

1 Pour equal amounts of syrup, cooking oil and hot water into three containers of the same size.

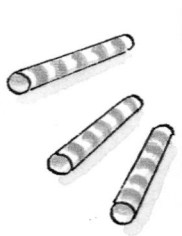 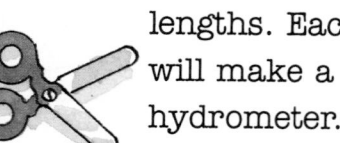

2 Cut a plastic drinking straw into three equal lengths. Each will make a hydrometer.

3 Make three small balls out of clay. Attach one to the end of each straw.

Float your hydrometer in a bowl of water. Add salt or sugar to the water. What effect does this have on the hydrometer?

WHY IT WORKS

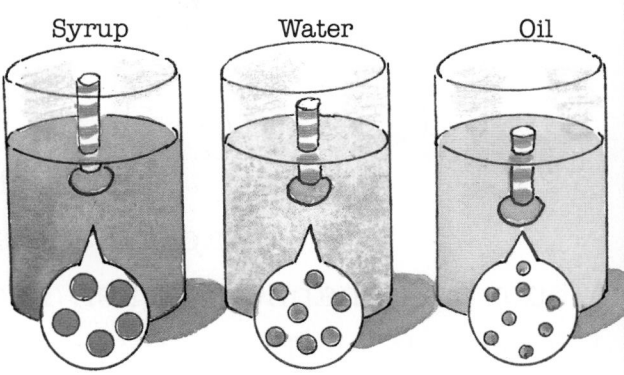

Syrup   Water   Oil

The particles of dense liquids are bigger or closer together. Dense liquids push harder on the hydrometer. The harder the push, the higher up in the liquid the hydrometer floats.

4 Carefully place each hydrometer into the liquids. Compare the different levels at which the hydrometers float.

UNSINKABLE

Boats and ships are always built to be as stable as possible. This means that they do not get pushed over easily by waves in rough seas. Most boats and ships capsize and sink if they are pushed too far. A buoy is a channel marker. Because it is there to warn of danger, it is vital that it never gets pushed over.

MAKE A BUOY

1 Half fill a large container with water.

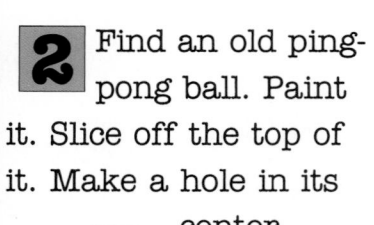

2 Find an old ping-pong ball. Paint it. Slice off the top of it. Make a hole in its center.

GET AN ADULT TO DO THIS FOR YOU

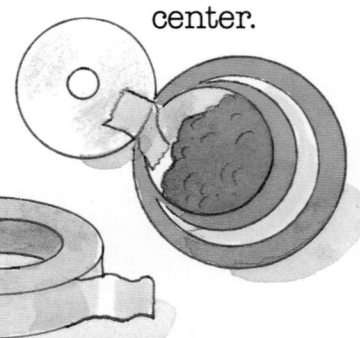

3 Fill the inside of the buoy with clay and tape the top back on.

4 Make a flag out of a triangle of paper and a drinking straw.

5 Stick the flag into the hole in the top of the buoy.

6 Put the buoy in the water. Make some waves. See how difficult it is to push the buoy over.

WHY IT WORKS

The clay acts as "ballast." Ballast is spare weight. The ballast pulls downward into the water and keeps the buoy upright. Boats carry ballast to keep them stable at sea.

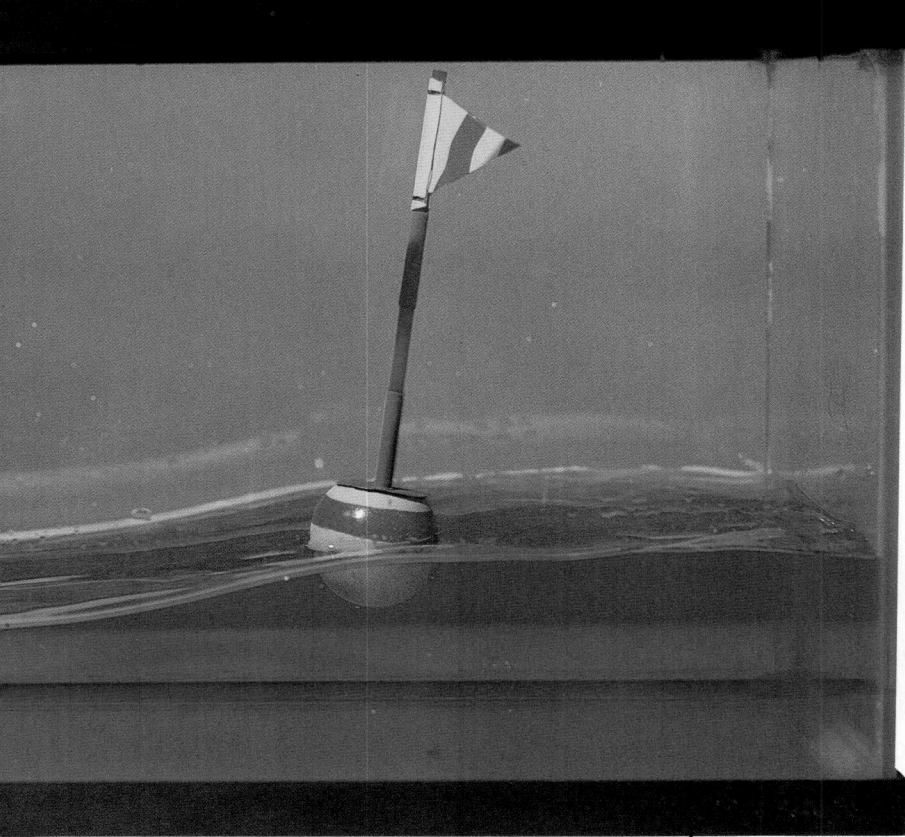

FURTHER IDEAS Compare the stability of your buoy with the boat you made on page 141. Waves lapping over the side of the boat can easily cause it to capsize.

PORT AND STARBOARD

You may have noticed that ships and large boats have steering wheels. Smaller boats have a tiller instead. Both wheel and tiller are used to control a "rudder." The rudder is used to steer the boat.

At sea, sailors say "port" for left and "starboard" for right.

MAKE A BOAT WITH A RUDDER

GET AN ADULT TO HELP YOU WITH THIS

1 Ask an adult to cut a boat shape from a piece of styrofoam. Make two holes as shown.

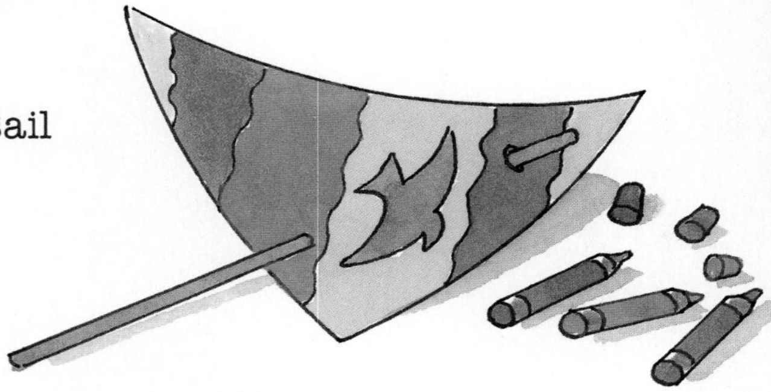

2 Make a brightly colored sail out of thin paper. Push a wooden stick through the sail.

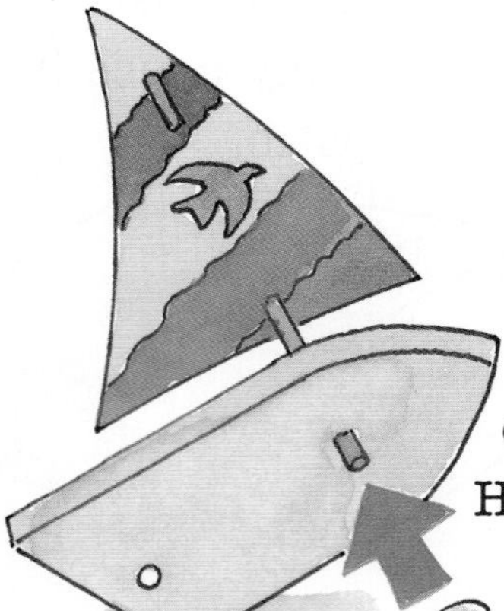

3 Push the stick into the hole at the pointed end of the boat. Hold in place with clay.

4 Cut a rudder out of a waterproof milk carton. Tape it to a drinking straw.

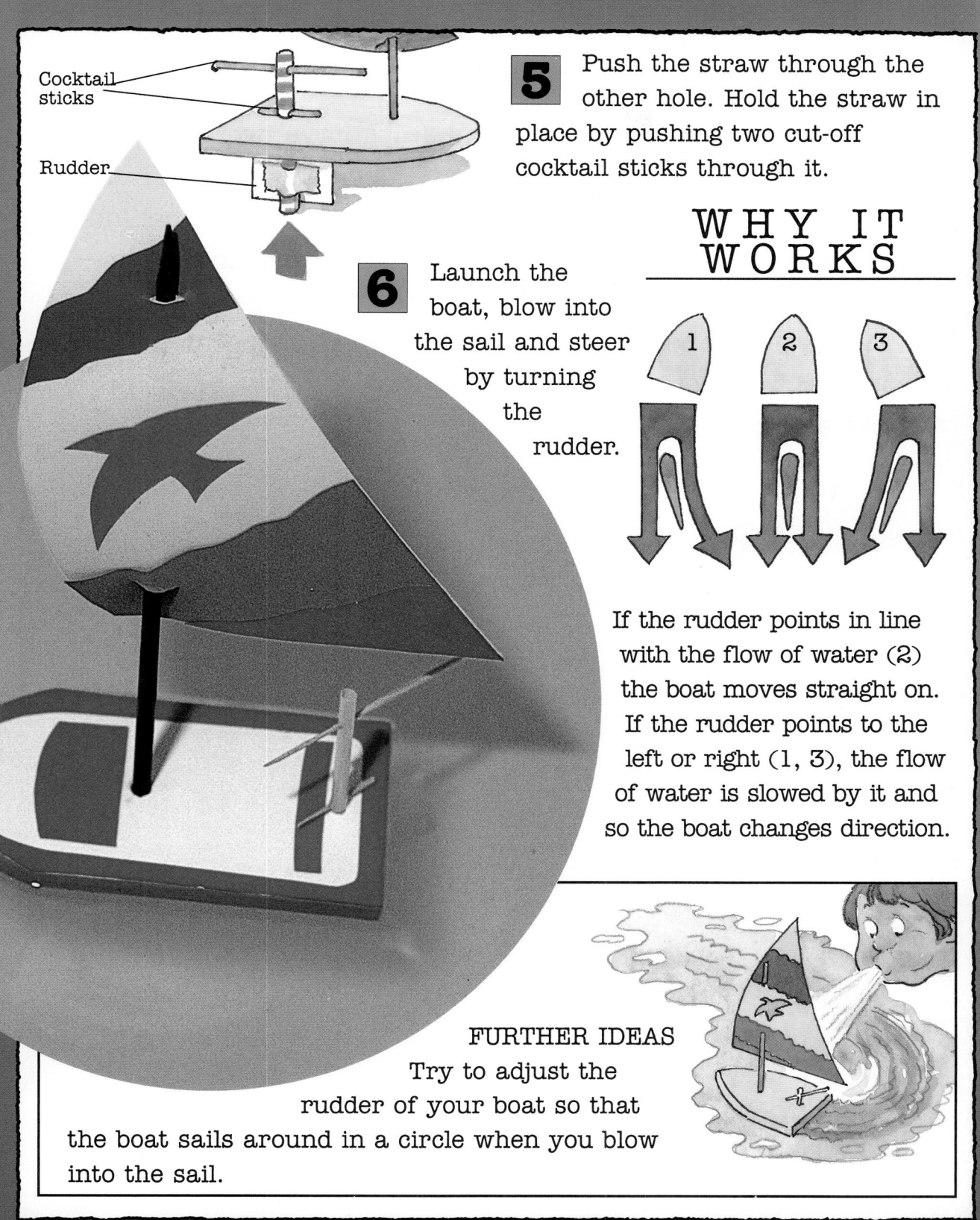

Cocktail sticks

Rudder

5 Push the straw through the other hole. Hold the straw in place by pushing two cut-off cocktail sticks through it.

6 Launch the boat, blow into the sail and steer by turning the rudder.

WHY IT WORKS

1 2 3

If the rudder points in line with the flow of water (2) the boat moves straight on. If the rudder points to the left or right (1, 3), the flow of water is slowed by it and so the boat changes direction.

FURTHER IDEAS
Try to adjust the rudder of your boat so that the boat sails around in a circle when you blow into the sail.

JET POWER

Most boats and ships have propellers which push them along. The propeller cuts through the water, pushing it back behind the vessel. This push against the water "propels", or makes the vessel move forward. A jet-propelled boat can travel at high speeds without a propeller. The "jet", or fast-moving flow of water, pushes the boat along.

MAKE A JET BOAT

1 Decorate an old plastic soda bottle. Weight the bottom of the bottle with clay.

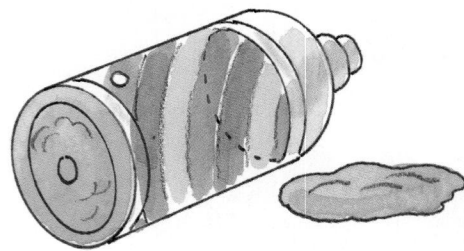

2 Ask an adult to make a hole near the bottom of the bottle (right).

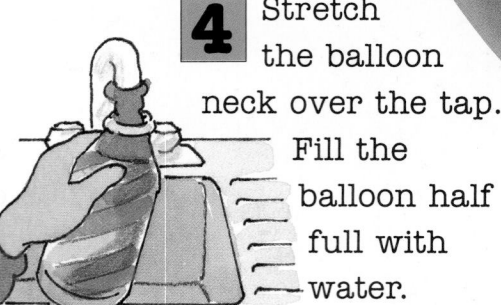

3 Place a balloon inside the bottle. Make sure you do not drop the balloon.

4 Stretch the balloon neck over the tap. Fill the balloon half full with water.

5 Pinch the balloon neck closed. Put clay around the bottle neck to weight the bottle.

6 Still holding the end of the balloon, put the bottle in the bath.

7 Let go of the balloon. Watch the jet of water shoot out and push the boat along.

WHY IT WORKS

Boat moves forward ← | Water out →

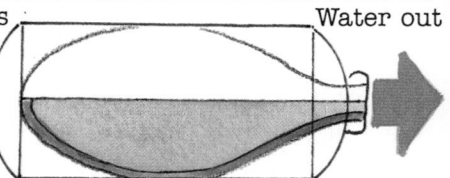

When the water shoots out of the balloon, it pushes against the water in the bath. This pushing force propels the jet boat forward. The quicker the water escapes from the balloon, the faster the boat travels.

FURTHER IDEAS

Cut a boat shape out of cardboard. Make a hole near the stern of the boat. Cut from the stern of the boat to the hole. Float the boat. Drop liquid soap in the hole. The boat will shoot forward.

DIVE DEEP!

Deep under the oceans are some of the last unexplored places on Earth. Deep-sea divers use vessels which can sink to the bottom and then float back to the surface again. Some marine animals such as jellyfish are also able to dive to great depths, then surface again.

MAKE A DIVING JELLYFISH

1 Find a large, clean plastic soda bottle. Fill it up to the top with tap water.

2 Cut both ends off a flexible plastic drinking straw to make a "U" shape.

3 Unbend a paper clip. Bend it into shape (shown at right). Push it into the ends of the straw.

WHY IT WORKS

When you squeeze the bottle, water is pushed into the straw, compressing the air. Water weighs more than air so the jellyfish gets heavier and sinks.

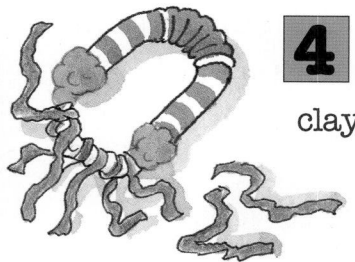

4 Roll out three thin strips of clay. Loop them around the paper clip.

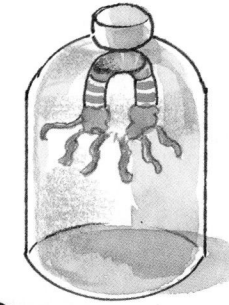

5 This is your jellyfish. Drop it into the bottle and screw the top back on. To make the jellyfish dive, squeeze the bottle.

FURTHER IDEAS
Try making a diver from a small eye-dropper. Fill the dropper almost to the top with water then put it into the bottle of water.

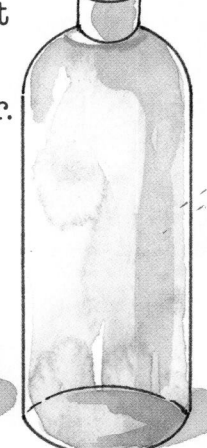

FLOATING UNDERWATER

Submarines are special floating vessels because they can sink and then return to the surface. Ballast tanks control how deep they dive. To make the submarine sink, the tanks are filled with water. To make the submarine rise, the water is pumped out and replaced with air.

FLOATING UNDERWATER

1 Fill an aquarium or large tank with tap water.

GET AN ADULT TO DO THIS FOR YOU

2 Cut four square holes in a plastic soda bottle (left).

3 Put clay around the neck and base of the bottle to weight it.

4 On the other side of the bottle make three holes. Make one large enough to fit a plastic tube.

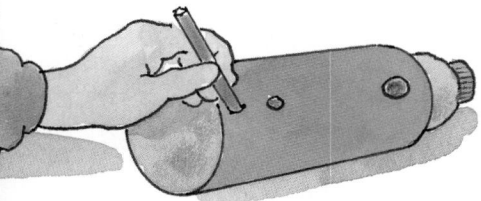

5 Decorate your submarine. Push the end of the tube into the larger of the three holes.

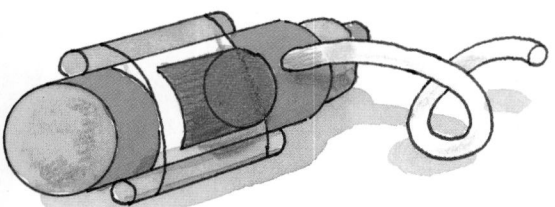

6 Try out your submarine. It will fill with water and sink. Blow into the tube to make it rise.

WHY IT WORKS

The submarine sinks when it fills with water (ballast). When you blow into the tube, the water is forced out and replaced by the air. Air is less dense than water so the submarine surfaces.

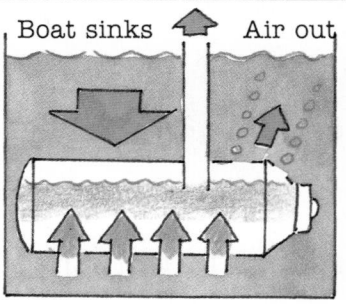

Boat sinks   Air out

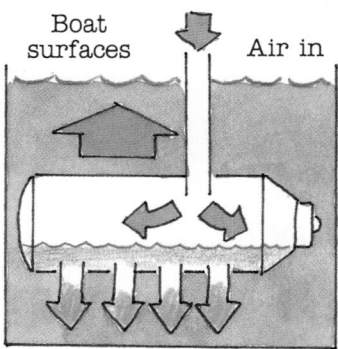

Boat surfaces   Air in

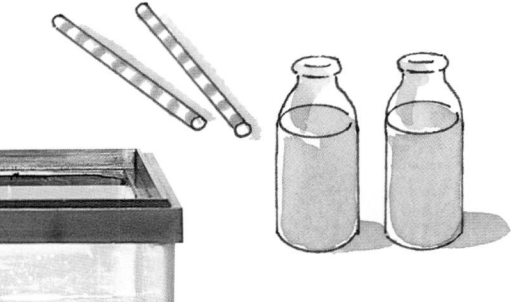

FURTHER IDEAS
Put an empty bottle in the bottom of your aquarium. Let it fill with water. Now blow air into it with a straw to make the bottle rise.

FLOATING ON AIR

The hovercraft is one of the great inventions of the twentieth century. It can travel on water or on land. The engines suck in air and then pump it downward. This creates a cushion of air that keeps the hovercraft from touching the surface over which it is traveling. The passengers enjoy a smooth and bump-free journey.

GET AN ADULT TO DO THIS FOR YOU

MAKE A HOVERCRAFT

1 Ask an adult to cut the top off a plastic soda bottle for you.

2 Wrap some clay around the base of the cut-off bottle top.

3 Make a skirt of paper to go around the clay. Make sure it hangs over it.

4 Blow up a balloon. Pinch the end. Carefully wrap the balloon around the bottle neck without letting it deflate.

5 Find a smooth surface. Place the hovercraft on it and let go of the balloon. Watch your hovercraft glide along.

WHY IT WORKS

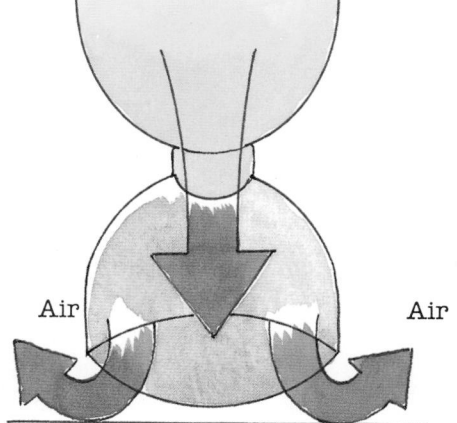

Air   Air

Air from the balloon escapes into the bottle top. The air pressure builds up until it creates a cushion that lifts the bottle slightly. It is the downward force of air that makes the hovercraft hover.

FURTHER IDEAS

Cut a hole in the bottom of a plastic margarine tub. Turn it upside down and fill it with air from a hairdrier. Watch it hover. Fill a paper bag with hot air from a hairdrier. What happens?

CONTENTS

What is a magnet? 166

Long-range force 168

Through and through 170

Chain reaction 172

Magnetic metals 174

Push and pull 176

Useful magnets 178

Very attractive 180

Invisible patterns 182

North and south 184

Hidden magnets 186

Electromagnetism 188

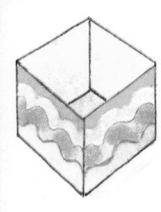

CHAPTER *Seven*

PLAYING WITH MAGNETS

WHAT IS A MAGNET?

People have known about magnets for thousands of years. The first magnets were made out of black rocks called lodestones which are found naturally in the ground. Some metal objects are attracted to this rock. Modern magnets are made from steel. They can be made into almost any shape – horseshoe, bar or ring.

MAKE A FISHING GAME

1 Draw some fish shapes on thin cardboard. Color them in and cut them out. Attach a steel paper clip to each fish.

2 Find a large, clean cardboard box. Decorate the outside so that it looks like the water in a pond.

3 Make two fishing rods. Tie a 30 inch-long piece of string to each stick. Tape a magnet to the end of the string.

4 Using the fishing rods, compete with a friend to see who can "catch" the most fish.

WHY IT WORKS

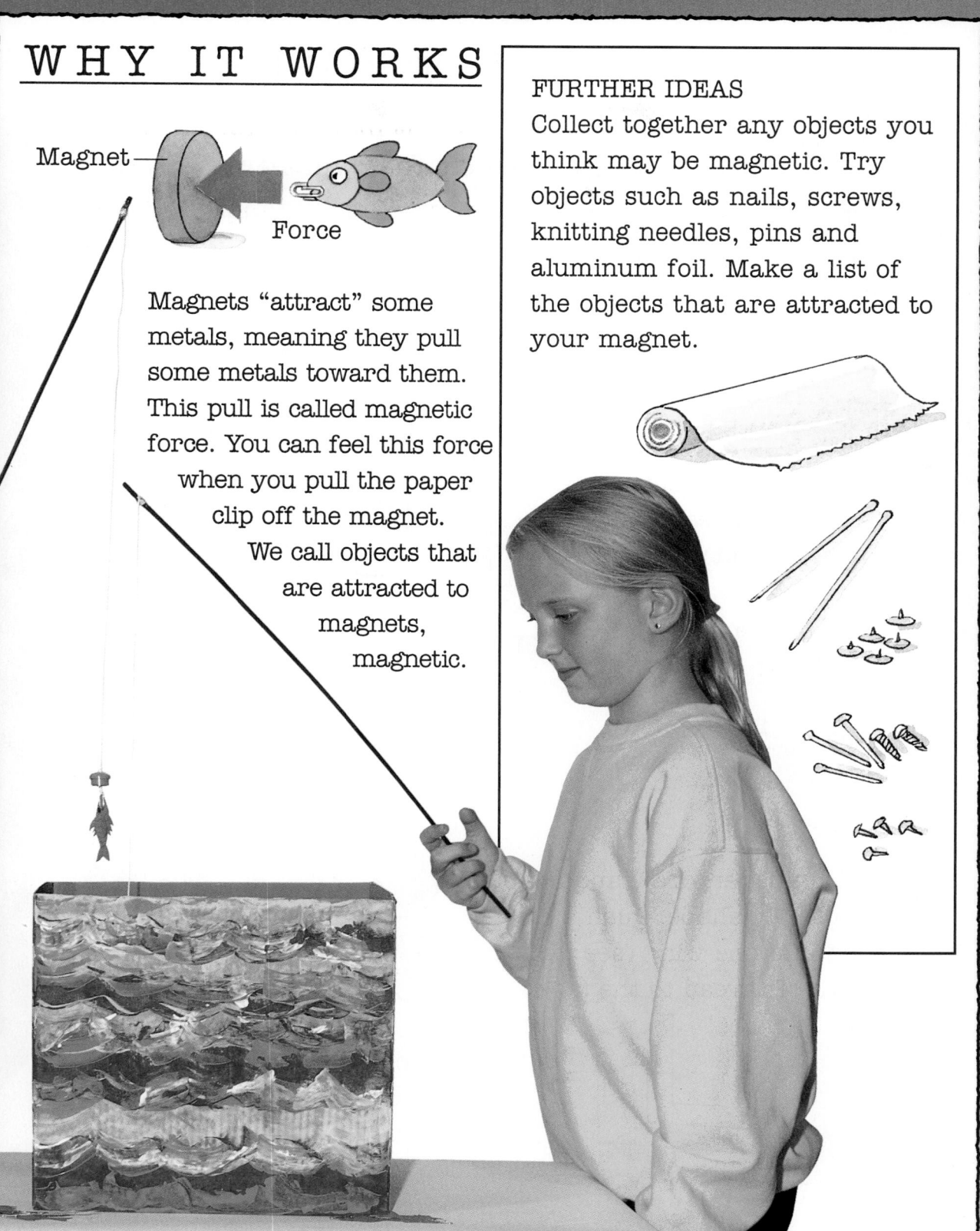

Magnet

Force

Magnets "attract" some metals, meaning they pull some metals toward them. This pull is called magnetic force. You can feel this force when you pull the paper clip off the magnet.

We call objects that are attracted to magnets, magnetic.

FURTHER IDEAS
Collect together any objects you think may be magnetic. Try objects such as nails, screws, knitting needles, pins and aluminum foil. Make a list of the objects that are attracted to your magnet.

LONG-RANGE FORCE

How far away can the magnetic force work? Scientists use magnets that will attract objects from many feet away. Your magnet can attract objects a few inches away. When a magnet and object touch, they "stick" together as if fixed with glue.

MAKE A FLYING BUTTERFLY

1 Find a clean cardboard box. Ask an adult to cut away two opposite sides leaving a "U" shape (shown right).

GET AN ADULT TO HELP YOU WITH THIS

2 Tape a strong bar-shaped magnet along one side of the box (see left).

3 On thin paper, draw and cut out a butterfly shape. Push a thumbtack into one wing (see right). Tie a length of thread to the tack.

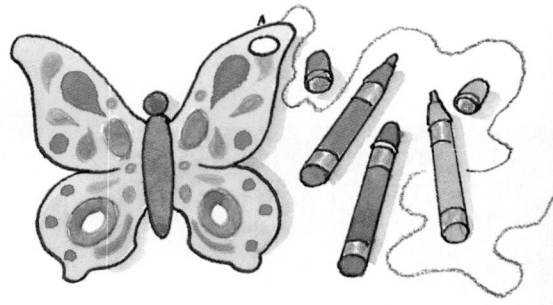

4 Tape the loose end of the thread to the side of the box opposite the magnet. When the thread is pulled taut, the butterfly should almost touch the magnet.

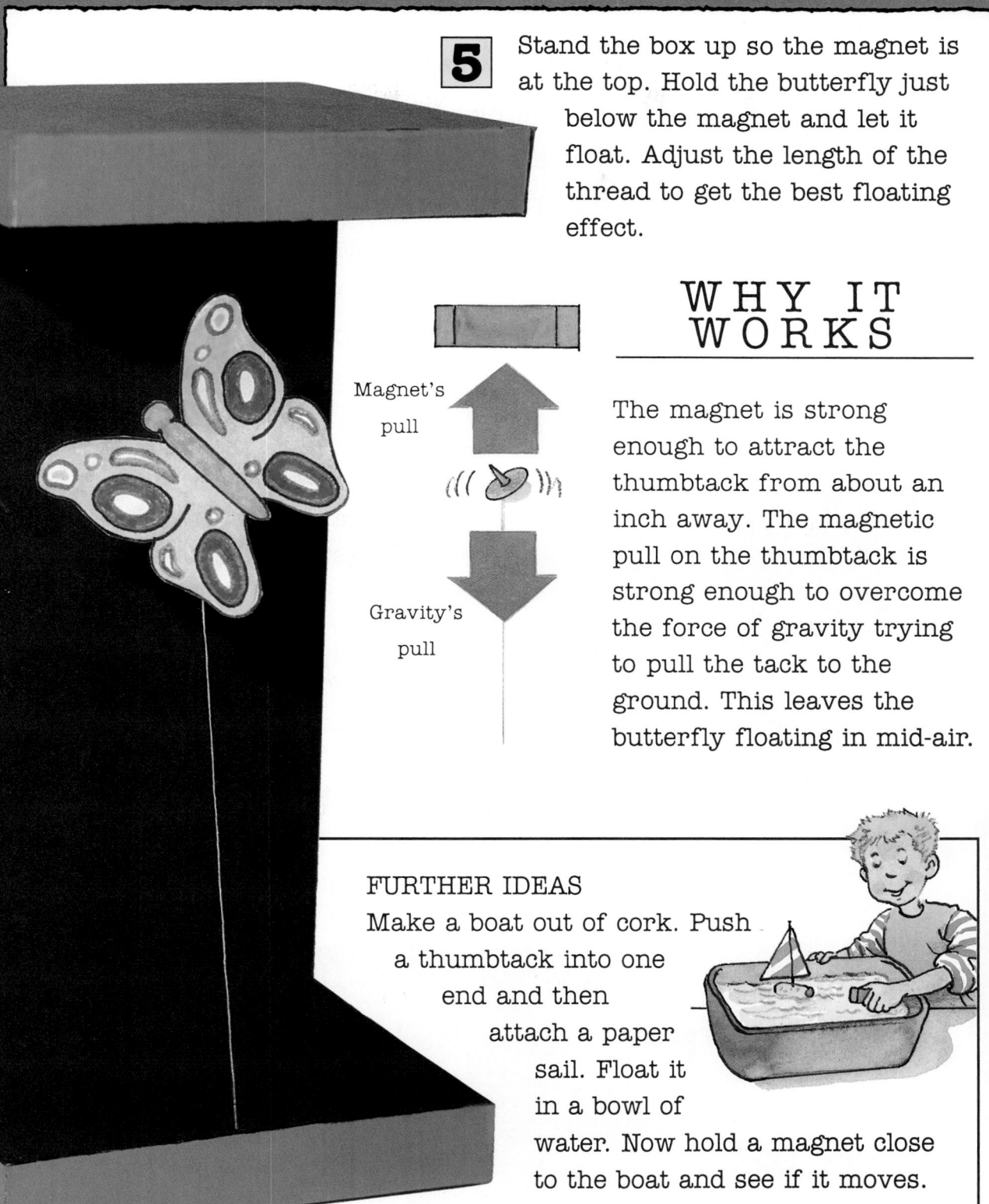

5 Stand the box up so the magnet is at the top. Hold the butterfly just below the magnet and let it float. Adjust the length of the thread to get the best floating effect.

Magnet's pull

Gravity's pull

WHY IT WORKS

The magnet is strong enough to attract the thumbtack from about an inch away. The magnetic pull on the thumbtack is strong enough to overcome the force of gravity trying to pull the tack to the ground. This leaves the butterfly floating in mid-air.

FURTHER IDEAS

Make a boat out of cork. Push a thumbtack into one end and then attach a paper sail. Float it in a bowl of water. Now hold a magnet close to the boat and see if it moves.

THROUGH AND THROUGH

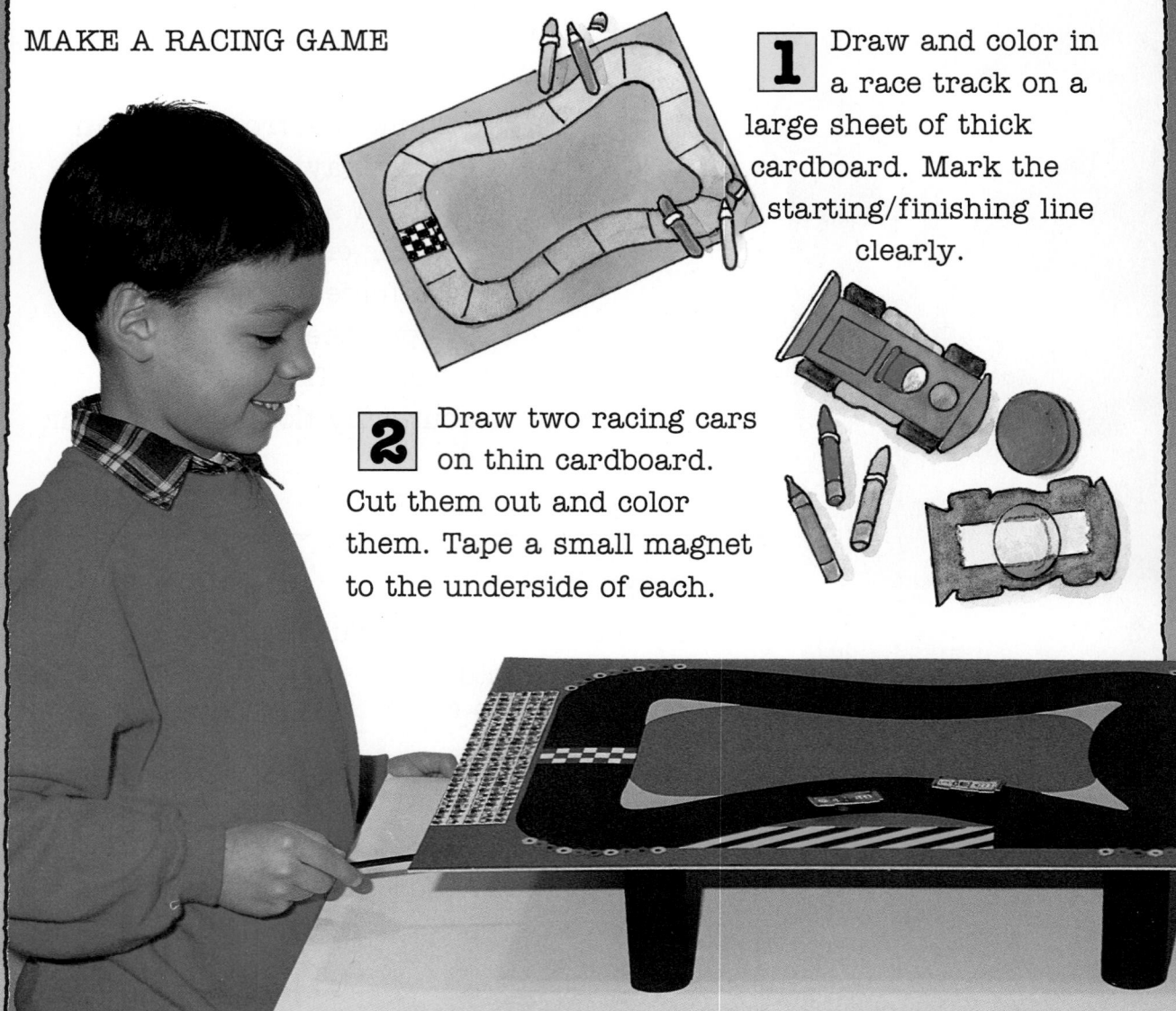

You can stick paper notes to the metal door of a refrigerator with a magnet. The paper and paint cannot block the magnetic force. If the magnetism is strong enough it can work straight through materials as if they were not there. This can be useful for making things move without touching them.

MAKE A RACING GAME

1 Draw and color in a race track on a large sheet of thick cardboard. Mark the starting/finishing line clearly.

2 Draw two racing cars on thin cardboard. Cut them out and color them. Tape a small magnet to the underside of each.

3 Find four cardboard tubes of the same size. Place one under each corner of the race track so it is raised.

4 Find two long, thin sticks. Tape a small magnet to one end of each.

5 You can move your car with the magnet from underneath the race track. Race against a friend, taking care not to mix up each other's cars!

WHY IT WORKS

The magnets under the car and on the stick are attracted to each other. The magnetic force goes through the race track, although the race track does slightly weaken the force.

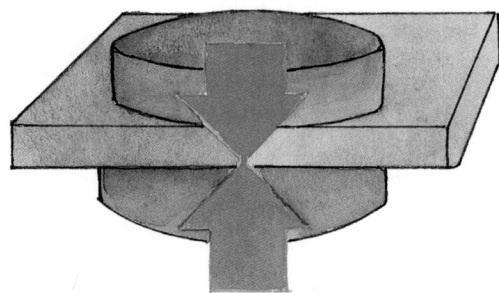

FURTHER IDEAS
Without getting your fingers wet, try to remove a steel paper clip from a glass of water. Move your magnet along the outside of the glass.

CHAIN REACTION

You may have noticed that when magnetic metals touch a magnet they will attract magnetic metals too. We can use this characteristic to build a "chain" of magnetic objects outward from a permanent magnet. Permanent magnets stay magnetic unless they are dropped or get too hot.

MAKE A MAGNETIC SCULPTURE

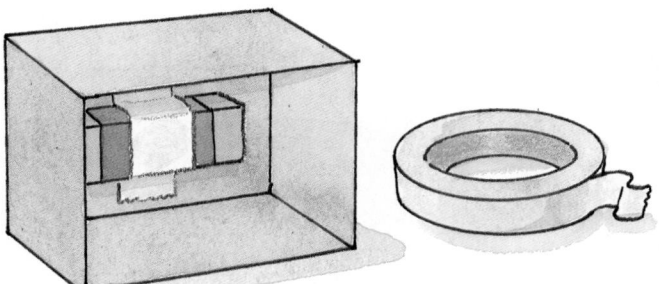

1 Find a small cardboard box. Tape a small magnet to the inside of the bottom of the box. Turn the box upside down.

2 Decorate the box with your own pattern and color it with bright colors.

172

3 Place a few steel paper clips on top of the box above the magnet. Build up a sculpture by adding pins, tacks and nails.

4 Change the shape until you are satisfied with your sculpture. You can reshape it endlessly.

WHY IT WORKS

When a magnetic metal is attracted to a permanent magnet it becomes a magnet too. It can attract other objects but only while it is touching a permanent magnet. This is called "induced" magnetism.

FURTHER IDEAS
Hang a magnet over the edge of a box and tape it into place. Try to form a chain by hanging paper clips from the end of the magnet.

MAGNETIC METALS

There are many different metals, but only three pure metals can be magnetized. These are iron, nickel and cobalt. None of the other pure metals – gold, silver, aluminum – can be made into magnets. But if you mix pure metals together their magnetic characteristics can be altered.

MAKE A COIN TESTER

GET AN ADULT TO HELP YOU WITH THIS

1 Ask an adult to cut a slot at one end of a shoe box (see right). The slot should be just bigger than your largest coin.

2 Cut out a strip of cardboard. Fold into an "L" shape. Tape into place just to the left of the slot.

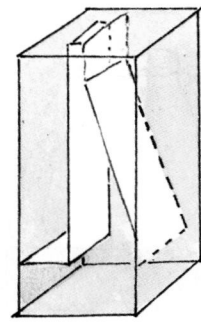

3 Cut another strip of cardboard, creasing it ³⁄₄ inch from the top. Tape this end to the right of the slot. Tape the other end to the side of the box.

4 Cut another strip of cardboard. Fold into the shape shown (right). Make sure it fits into the triangular space between the first pieces.

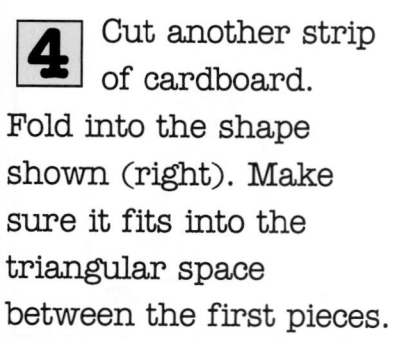

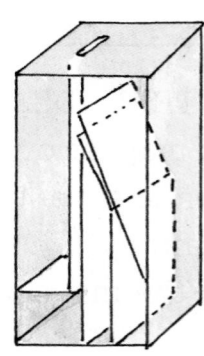

5 Find a strong magnet. Tape it inside the box just to the right of the slot.

6 Drop your coins into the slot. Most will fall to the left side of the box. If you drop iron or steel washers into the slot they will fall to the right side of the box.

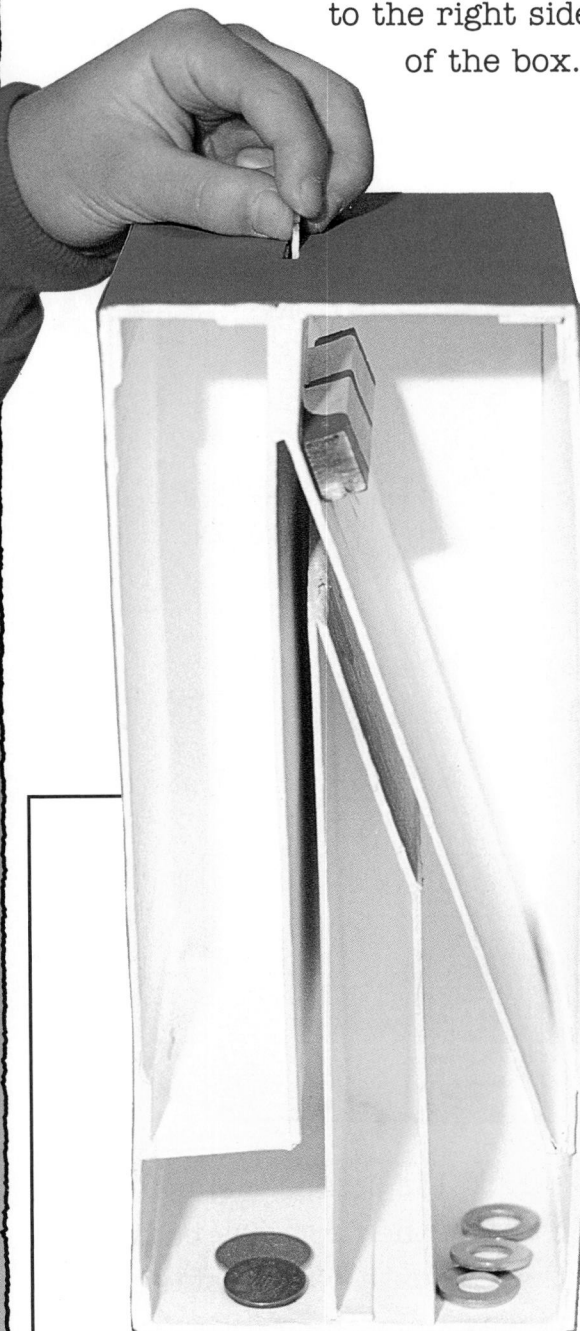

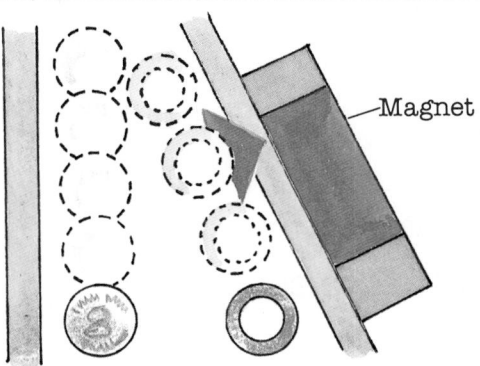

Magnet

Most coins are made from non-magnetic metals such as a copper mix. When you drop them into the box they are not attracted to the magnet and so fall straight down. When you drop iron or steel objects they are attracted by the magnet and are pulled over to the right side of the box.

FURTHER IDEAS
Tableware is often made of stainless steel. Make a ramp out of cardboard and roll spoons or forks down it. Put a magnet under the ramp. See how it affects the path of the tableware. Why not try toy cars as well?

PUSH AND PULL

Magnets have two points where their power is strongest. These are called poles. Every magnet has a north and a south pole. When iron or steel touches a permanent magnet it has poles too (pages 172-173). A good way of testing whether an object is a permanent magnet or not is to see if it will "repel", or push away, another magnet.

MAKE A MAGNET FLOAT

1 Find a cardboard box. Ask an adult to cut away the sides and the middle of the box to leave the shape (shown at right).

GET AN ADULT TO HELP YOU WITH THIS

2 Tape down a strong bar magnet to the base of the box (left).

3 Copy the shape (shown at right) onto a piece of cardboard and cut out. Tape an identical magnet to the cardboard. Fold the cardboard around the magnet.

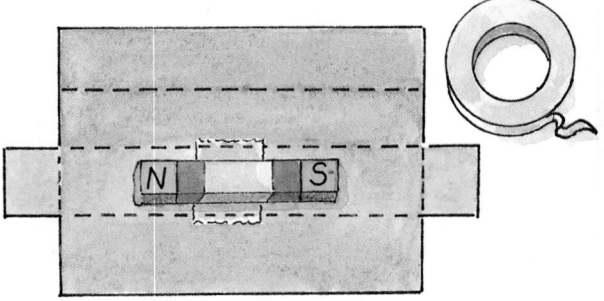

N   S

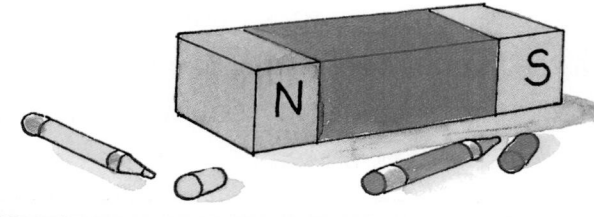

N   S

4 Hold the second magnet on top of the first with both north and south poles facing the same way, tape them together.

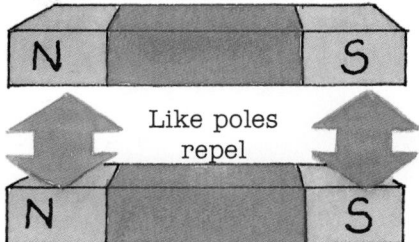

Like poles
repel

5 The top magnet should "float" above the bottom. Try pushing the top magnet.

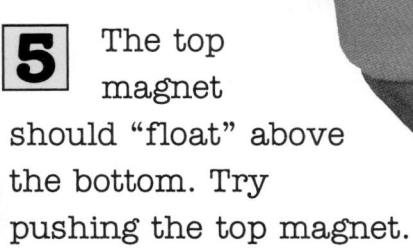

Magnetic poles of the same type repel each other. Gravity is trying to pull the top magnet down, but the two magnets are repelling each other with such force that the top one is held above the bottom. The top magnet would spring away if it wasn't taped in place.

FURTHER IDEAS
Find three horseshoe-shaped magnets. Thread them onto two pencils (shown at right). Line up the poles. See if you can make the magnets float. Try doing the same thing with ring-shaped magnets. Which works best?

USEFUL MAGNETS

Doctors have used magnets to pull tiny bits of iron out of a patient's eye. The advantage of using a magnet is that nothing needs to touch the injured eye. The magnet's ability to attract some materials but not others has been used in many ways. Giant magnets are used to sort out different waste metals.

MAKE A TREASURE HUNT

1 Make a desert island by filling a bowl almost to the top with clean, dry sand.

2 Make a palm tree using part of a large plastic drinking straw as the stem. Attach some green paper leaves to it with tape. Plant it on your island.

3 Make a treasure chest out of colored cardboard. Now find some treasure to put in it. An iron or steel bolt will do.

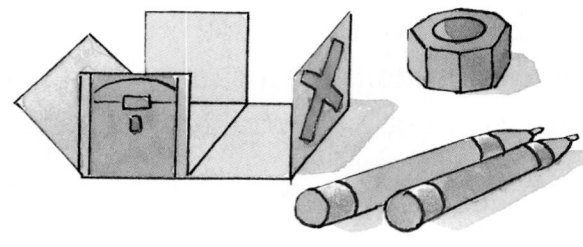

4 Bury the treasure chest in the sand. Make sure it is fairly near to the surface.

5 Search for the treasure using a magnet. You can take turns with a friend to find it.

Magnet

Treasure

WHY IT WORKS

You can hunt for the treasure by moving the magnet over the surface of the sand. When you hold the magnet directly over the steel treasure, the magnet strongly attracts it. The magnetic force goes straight through the sand.

FURTHER IDEAS
Sort out aluminum soda cans that can be recycled by testing each can with a magnet. Aluminum cans are not magnetic.

VERY ATTRACTIVE

Magnets pull magnetic materials such as iron and steel toward them. This pull is called attraction. The stronger the magnet, the stronger its attractive force. Modern household items have many ingenious uses for magnetic attraction. Did you know that a magnet is often used on a refrigerator door to hold it firmly closed?

MAKE A FUNNY FACE

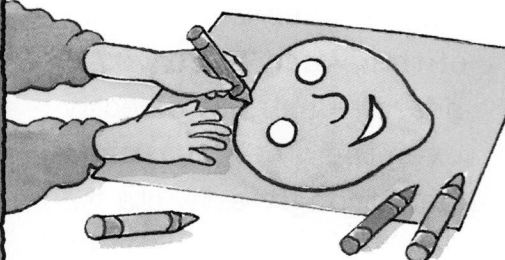

1 Draw the shape of a face on a sheet of thin cardboard. Make the eyes, nose and mouth especially large. Don't draw in any hair or eyebrows.

2 Ask an adult to make some iron filings for you by filing down a nail. Pour the iron filings onto the cardboard in a few places.

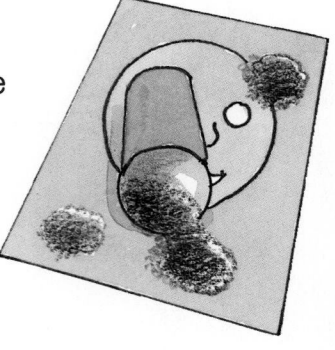

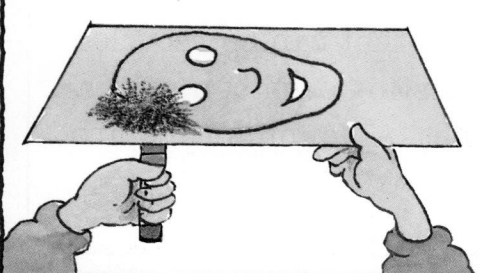

3 Hold the cardboard with one hand and bring a magnet under it with the other. The magnet will attract the iron filings through the cardboard.

4 Arrange the iron filings with the magnet to give your face hair, eyebrows and a beard. Move the magnet away from your funny face.

WHY IT WORKS

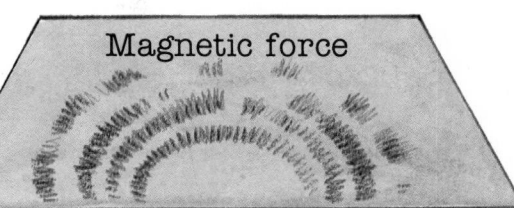

Magnetic force

Magnet

The magnetic force pulls on each tiny piece of iron filing. As you move the magnet under the cardboard the filings are dragged along. When you move the magnet away the iron filings stay in place.

FURTHER IDEAS

Test the strength of your magnet. Use it to move a pin through one page of a book, then through two pages, then three pages and so on until the pages block the magnetic force.

INVISIBLE PATTERNS

Magnetic objects close to a magnet are attracted to it. There is a "field" (space) around the magnet where the magnetic force works. We cannot see this field but can feel its pull on objects. Scientists have discovered that birds use the Earth's magnetic field to guide them on long journeys.

SEE A MAGNETIC FIELD

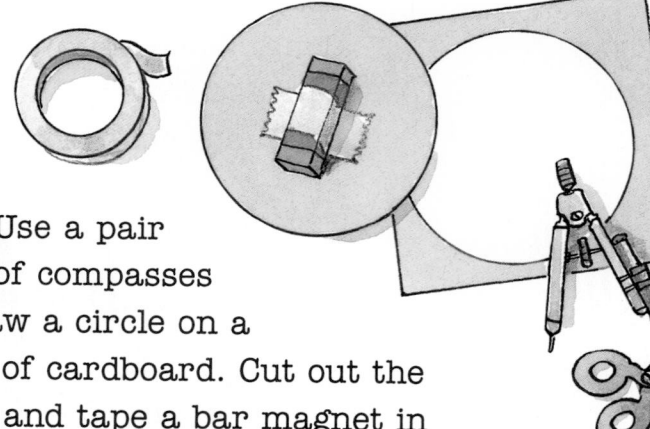

1 Use a pair of compasses to draw a circle on a sheet of cardboard. Cut out the circle and tape a bar magnet in the center.

2 Turn the cardboard over so the magnet is underneath. Evenly sprinkle some iron filings (see page 180) over the surface of the cardboard.

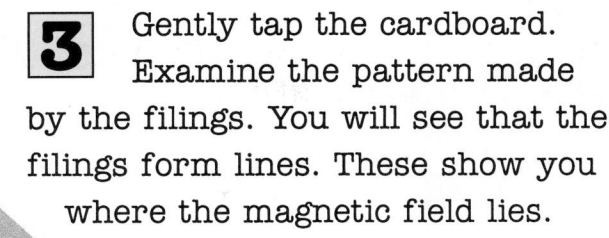

3 Gently tap the cardboard. Examine the pattern made by the filings. You will see that the filings form lines. These show you where the magnetic field lies.

WHY IT WORKS

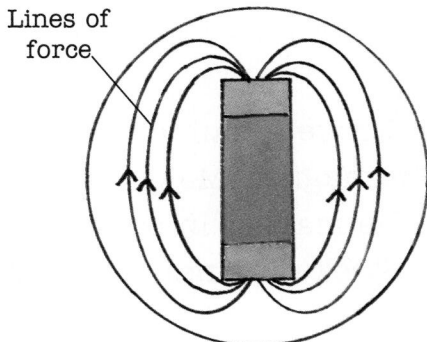

Lines of force

Each filing is attracted to the magnet along invisible lines of force. These make up the magnetic field. The filings are small enough to show the direction in which the field is pulling.

FURTHER IDEAS
Try the experiment again using a horseshoe or ring-shaped magnet. What kind of pattern do the iron filings make?

NORTH AND SOUTH

For centuries travelers have found their way with the help of a compass. Inside a compass is a small magnetic pointer. It spins around but always comes to rest pointing north. From knowing where north is, it is easy to locate south, west and east.

MAKE A COMPASS

1 Stroke a nail with one end of a magnet. Make sure you pass the magnet in one direction only. Stroke the nail about 20 times.

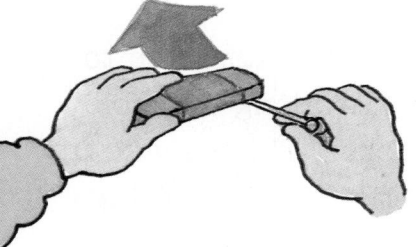

2 Ask an adult to slice a piece of cork. Now tape the magnetized nail to it.

GET AN ADULT TO HELP YOU WITH THIS

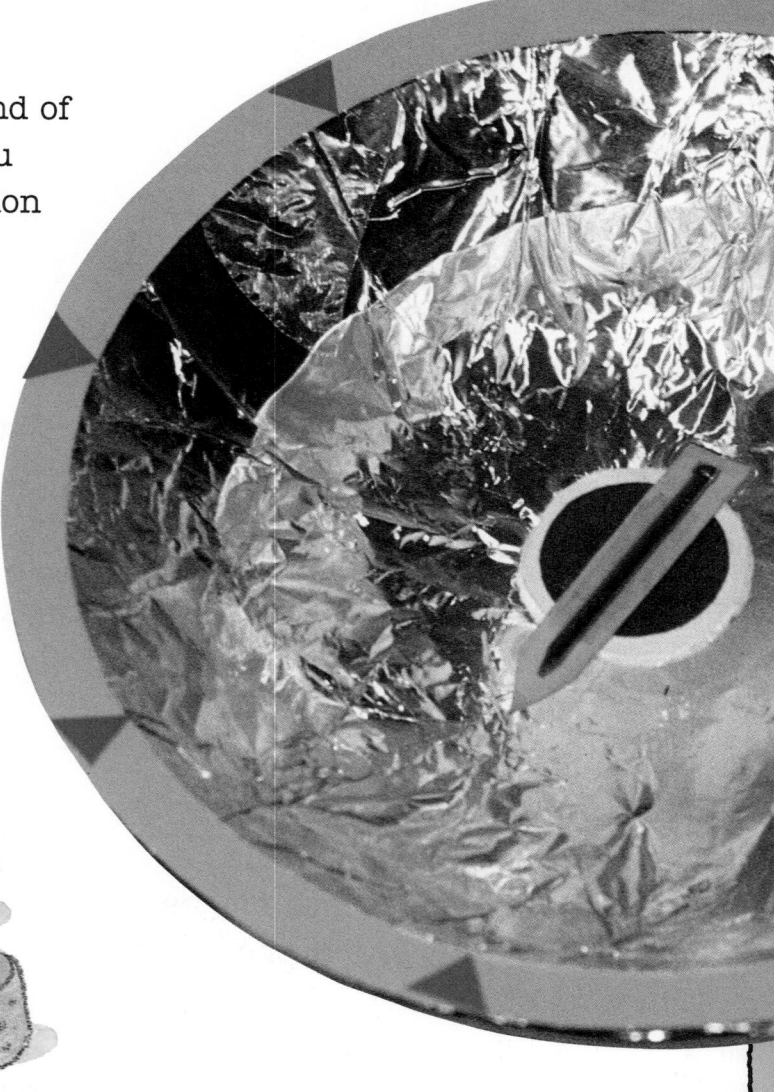

3 Float the cork in a basin of water. Leave until the nail stops moving. Make sure there are no magnetic objects nearby.

WHY IT WORKS

4 The nail will point either north or south. Find out which way it is pointing, then make labels for north, south, west and east.

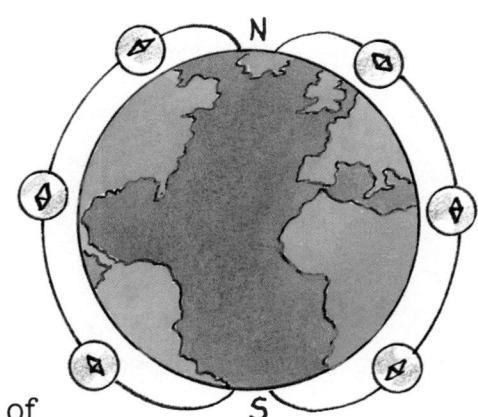

The north pole of a magnet seeks out the north pole of the Earth. It is as if the Earth contained a gigantic magnet. The north pole of the Earth attracts any smaller magnets so that when allowed to, they always point north.

FURTHER IDEAS

Tie a piece of thread around the middle of a bar magnet. Suspend the magnet from the back of a chair. Watch to see if the poles point north-south. What happens when other magnetic objects are close to the magnet?

HIDDEN MAGNETS

You may be surprised how important magnets are in modern machines. Computers use magnetic floppy disks to store huge amounts of information. Tape recorders and video recorders use magnetic tape to store film, sound, and music. These are hidden magnets.

THE AMAZING MAGIC FINGER

1 Magnetize a steel nail by stroking it in one direction with a magnet. Stroke at least 20 times (see page 184).

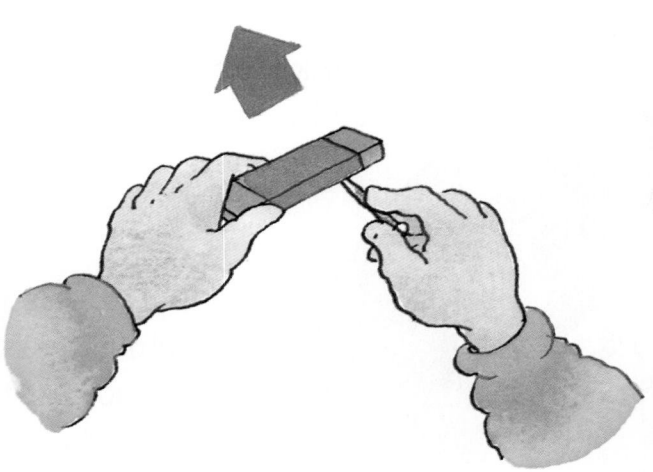

2 Carefully tape the nail to your index finger. Make sure the point cannot hurt anyone.

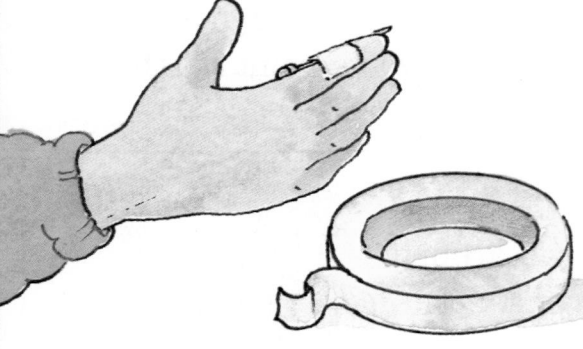

3 Find an old glove that fits your hand snugly. Put it on to hide the magnetized nail.

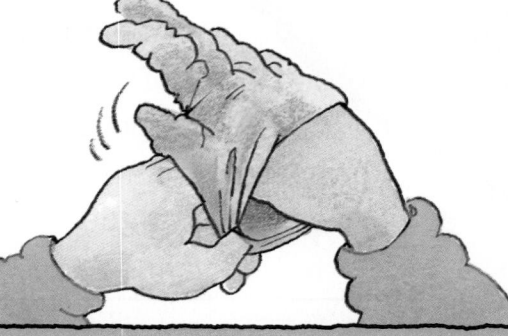

4 Bring your magic finger close to a compass needle. Amaze your friends by making the compass needle swing around.

WHY IT WORKS

Unmagnetized nail

Magnetized nail

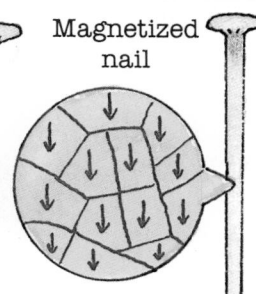

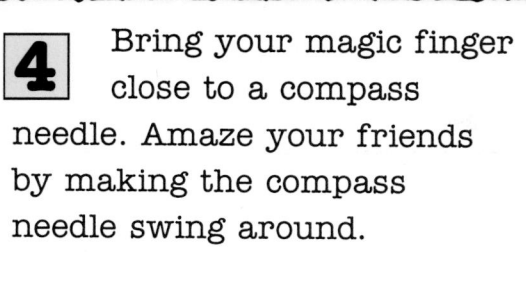

The metal in the nail is made up of millions of tiny crystals. Each can behave like a tiny magnet but they point in different directions.

Stroking the nail with a magnet makes each crystal point the same way. This causes the nail to become magnetized.

FURTHER IDEAS
Use your magic finger for other magic tricks. Impress your friends by balancing a pin or nail right on the end of your finger.

ELECTROMAGNETISM

An electromagnet is a coil of wire around an iron core. You may have seen a crane that has an electromagnet instead of a hook to carry things. Powerful electromagnets can lift heavy iron loads, even whole cars. The load is dropped by switching off the electromagnet.

MAKE AN ELECTROMAGNET

1 Take a cardboard box. Make holes in the center of three sides. Cut two strips of cardboard. Make three holes in each strip (see right).

Holes

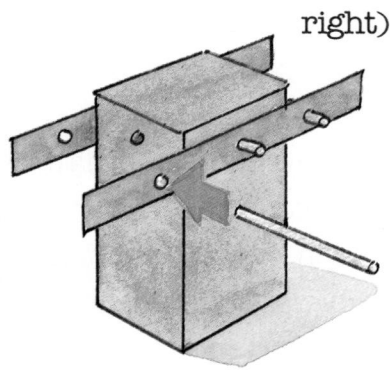

2 Push three pieces of stick through the holes in the strips of cardboard and the box (left). This is your crane arm.

3 Color some smaller boxes to make them look like cars or an iron bar. Glue a steel washer to the top of each one.

4 Take 2 to 3 feet of plastic-coated wire and coil around an iron nail. Connect the wire to the terminals of a battery.

5 Hide the battery in the box. Push the nail and wire through the hole in the front of the crane. Use the electromagnet to pick up paper clips. Switch it off by removing the wire from the battery.

WHY IT WORKS

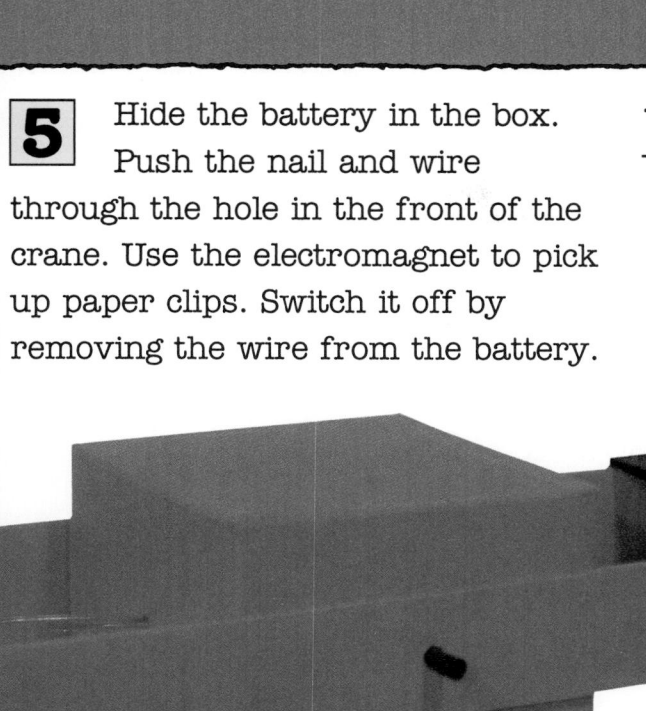

Nail becomes magnetized

Electricity flowing along a wire has a magnetic field around it. The field is made stronger by coiling the wire. The nail inside the coils becomes magnetized by the field. Each part of the iron nail lines up facing the same direction, running from north to south.

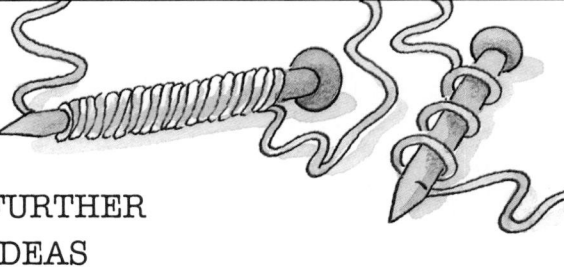

FURTHER IDEAS
Experiment with your electromagnet by changing the number of coils around the nail. What happens when there are fewer coils? What happens when there are more?

CONTENTS

What is a sound? 192

Making a sound 194

Good vibrations 196

The sound drum 198

Listen closely 200

Bouncing sounds 202

Keeping sounds in 204

Vibrating air 206

Different pitches 208

Vibrating strings 210

Tuning up 212

Faraway sounds 214

CHAPTER
Eight

HEARING
SOUNDS

WHAT IS A SOUND?

All sounds are made by something moving. Gently rest your fingertips on your throat as you talk. You can feel your throat vibrating. Vocal cords in your throat move as you speak and make the air in your throat and mouth vibrate. The vibrating air makes sounds.

MAKE A BANGER

1 Take a square sheet of paper and decorate it. Fold it in half diagonally to make a triangle (see right).

Fold

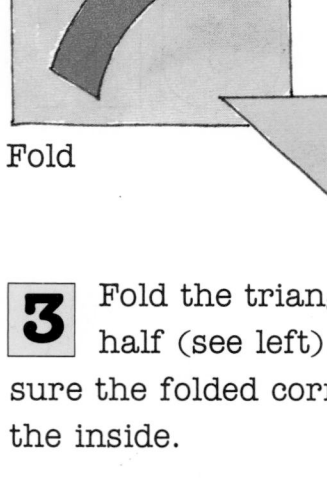

Fold

2 Fold the top right-hand corner downward.

Flap

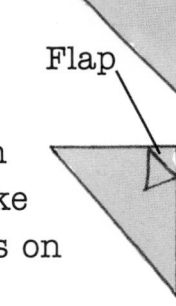

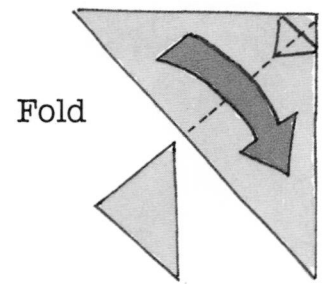

Fold

3 Fold the triangle in half (see left). Make sure the folded corner is on the inside.

4 Make a crease down the middle but do not fold in half.

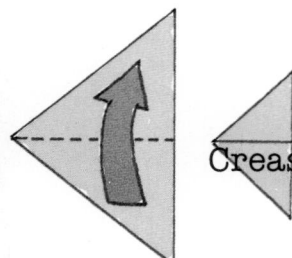

Crease

Fold

5 From the open end of the triangle fold the top layer of paper over along the crease. Flip the triangle over and repeat.

6 Grasp the three pointed ends of the triangle together. Flick your wrist down to make the banger work.

WHY IT WORKS

Flicking your wrist makes the folded paper jump out of place. The paper pushes hard against the air. The pushed air reaches your ears as a "bang."

Air

FURTHER IDEAS
Try making different-sized bangers. Follow the same steps with the largest square of paper you can find. Repeat with the smallest square of paper.

MAKING A SOUND

Sounds travel through the air to reach our ears. On a very windy day, the wind can blow sounds away from you so it is difficult to hear a conversation. If sounds have traveled a long way then they lose some loudness. Sounds made close to us seem louder.

MAKE A BULL ROARER

1 You will need a long cardboard tube, scissors, a ruler, about 19 inches of clothing elastic and 3 to 6 feet of string.

2 Loop the elastic through the tube. Knot the two ends together firmly.

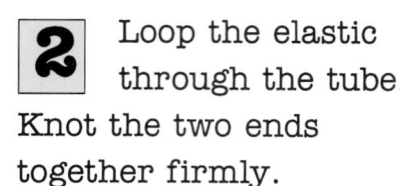

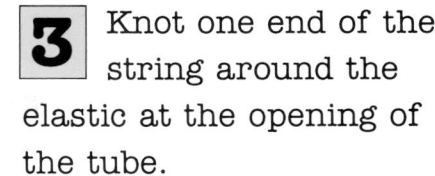

3 Knot one end of the string around the elastic at the opening of the tube.

4 Take the other end of the string in your hand and swing the bull roarer around. Listen to the sound it makes.

WHY IT WORKS

As the tube spins around, air enters and pushes the elastic rapidly backward and forward. Air leaving the tube carries the sounds made from these movements.

Air carrying sound out

Air in

FURTHER IDEAS
Experiment with the bull roarer by using a shorter length of string. If you have room, try a longer length. Listen carefully. How does the difference in length affect the sound?

GOOD VIBRATIONS

Pleasant sounds can come from musical instruments. All musical instruments have parts that move to make vibrations. Vibrations are caused by something moving back and forth very quickly and smoothly. A drum has a head that vibrates when it is hit with a stick. The harder you hit the drum, the bigger the vibrations and the louder the sound.

MAKE A DRUM

1 You will need a large, empty tin can and a clean plastic bag. Carefully cut a circle out of the plastic bag. Make sure it is larger than the can.

2 Stretch the circle of plastic as tightly as you can over the rim of the empty can. Hold it in place with tape.

3 Cut a strip of paper the same width as the can and long enough to go all the way around it. Color it brightly and tape into place.

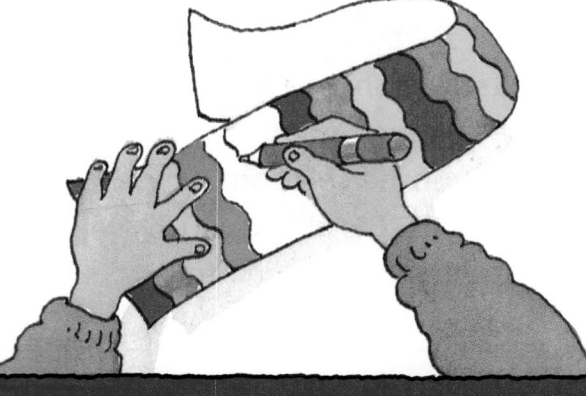

4 Make a pair of drumsticks with wooden dowels. Wrap the tips in cotton and cover with a piece of stocking. Tie into place with string.

5 Test your drum. Hit the drumhead gently in different places and compare the sounds of different vibrations. Try to play a rhythm.

WHY IT WORKS

When you hit the drumhead it vibrates. The air inside the drum vibrates too. These vibrations of air are called sound waves.

FURTHER IDEAS
The movement of the vibrating drumhead is too small to see. Try placing some dried peas on the drum to show the effect of the vibrations.

THE SOUND DRUM

We cannot see sounds but we can see their effects. Sounds travel through the air just like waves in the sea. If the waves are strong enough they can move things in their path. The human ear has an eardrum that moves when hit by sound waves entering the ear.

MAKE A SOUND DRUM

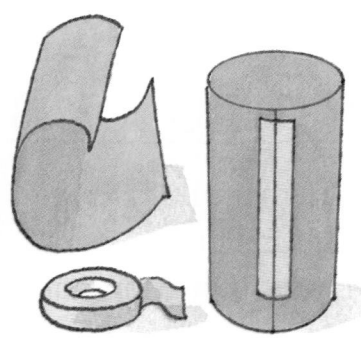

1 Roll a strong sheet of cardboard into a tube. Make sure the cardboard overlaps so that it can be taped together.

2 Cut a circle larger than the end of your tube out of a clean plastic bag. Tape it as tightly as possible over one end of the tube.

3 Cut a cardboard circle the same size. Cut a hole in the middle of it. Tape the circle over the other end of the tube.

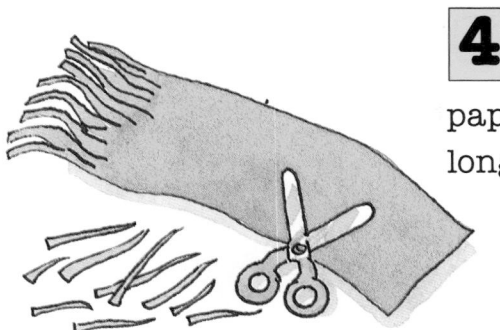

4 Make a target out of a long strip of tissue paper. Cut one end into a long fringe.

5 Point the hole in the bottom of your sound drum toward your target. Tap the plastic drumhead. What happens to your target?

WHY IT WORKS

Tapping the drumhead pushes sound waves through the hole in the bottom of the drum. It also forces rings of air out through the hole, which moves the paper fringe.

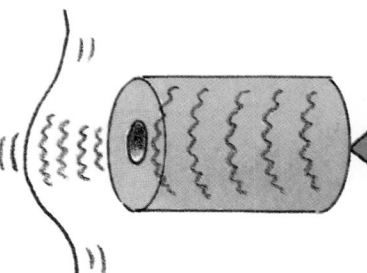

FURTHER IDEAS

You need a partner to help you. Take turns to hit the sound drum and hold the target. What is the farthest distance you can hit the target from?

LISTEN CLOSELY

If you are ill a doctor may use a stethoscope to listen to your heart or lungs. You may have a problem breathing or your heart may not be making the sounds it is supposed to. These sounds are normally too quiet to hear. A stethoscope magnifies them so they can be heard.

MAKE A STETHOSCOPE

1 Cut out two large paper circles. Color them brightly. Make a long cardboard tube. Decorate this too.

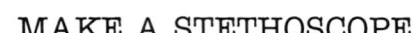

2 Cut a hole in the center of each circle the same size as the tube end. Cut from the hole to the edge of the circle. Tape the edges to form two cones.

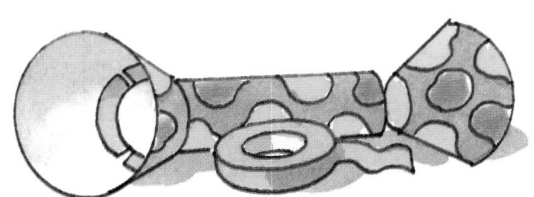

3 Tape one cone shape over each end of the tube. Make the fit as snug as possible.

sound in

4 Now try out your stethoscope. Put your ear to one cone and place the other on a friend's chest.

WHY IT WORKS

As sound waves spread out they become smaller and harder to hear. The first cone stops them from spreading by collecting them together. They move along the tube and out through the second cone into your ear.

FURTHER IDEAS
Use your stethoscope to compare the sound of your heartbeat with your friend's heartbeat. Try to think of other quiet sounds to listen to, such as a friend whispering or a ticking watch.

BOUNCING SOUNDS

Bats have very poor eyesight yet can fly around safely in complete darkness. They can avoid hitting obstacles by bouncing squeaky sounds off them. Bouncing sounds are called echoes. You can hear echoes in places such as large halls or gyms when sounds bounce off the walls.

BOUNCE AN ECHO

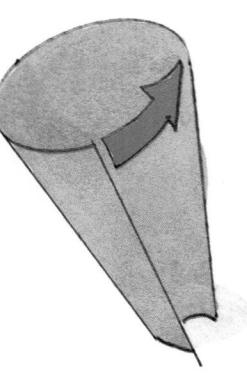

2 One cone is a hearing aid, the other a megaphone to magnify sounds.

1 Cut the shape shown here out of cardboard. Overlap the edges and tape to make a cone. Repeat so you have two large cones.

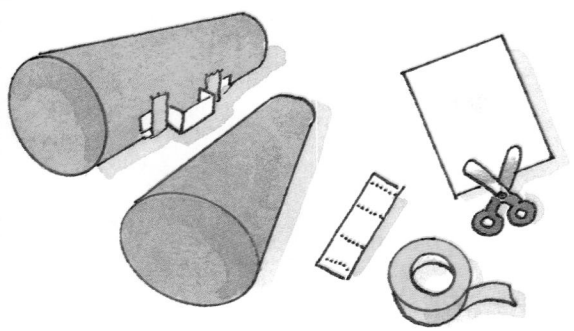

3 Cut out two strips of cardboard. Tape them along the sides of your hearing aid and megaphone to make handles.

Hearing aid

Megaphone

WHY IT WORKS

When a sound wave hits something it can either be absorbed or bounce off. Smooth, flat surfaces bounce sounds best. The sound of your voice bounces off the mirror just as light would.

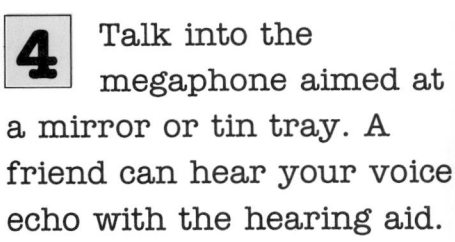

FURTHER IDEAS

Try to bounce sounds off other surfaces. You could compare a cork tile, an egg carton and a wooden block. Which reflects sound waves best?

4 Talk into the megaphone aimed at a mirror or tin tray. A friend can hear your voice echo with the hearing aid.

KEEPING SOUNDS IN

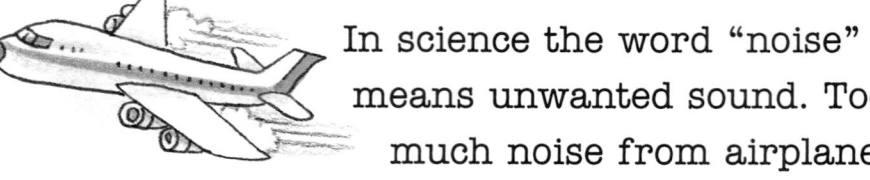

In science the word "noise" means unwanted sound. Too much noise from airplanes or discos is bad for your health. It can keep you from sleeping and even damage your eardrums. A radio studio is soundproofed. Noise is kept out so that it cannot be heard when programs are broadcast.

MAKE A SOUNDPROOF BOX

1 You need a large cardboard box and a shoe box, both with lids. The shoe box must easily fit inside the cardboard box.

2 Decorate the outside of the cardboard box. Use brightly colored paints. When dry, place the shoe box inside the larger box.

3 Pack the space between the boxes with crumpled newspapers. Add a little paper to the inner box.

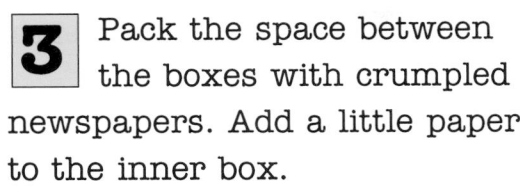

WHY IT WORKS

Sound waves from the alarm cannot escape from the soundproof box. Most sound waves are absorbed by the cardboard and the newspaper. You may hear just a few sound waves leaking out.

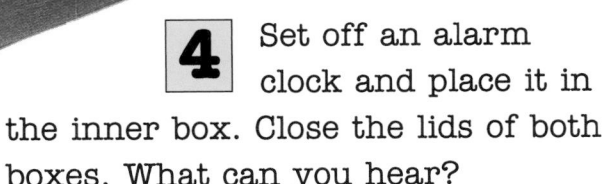
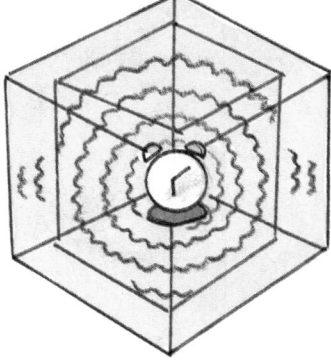

4 Set off an alarm clock and place it in the inner box. Close the lids of both boxes. What can you hear?

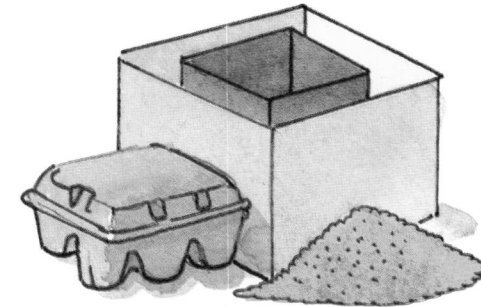

FURTHER IDEAS
Try to improve the soundproofing by replacing the newspaper with egg cartons or sawdust. Make it a fair test by using the same alarm clock each time.

VIBRATING AIR

An orchestra has percussion, wind, and stringed instruments. Wind instruments include flutes, clarinets, and recorders. They are all made out of a tube. When the instrument is played, air inside the tube vibrates and makes sound. Instruments make different sounds because they vary in shape and size.

MAKE A CLARINET

1 Use stiff cardboard to make a cone as shown on page 202. Make sure the small opening at the top is less than half an inch across.

2 Use sharp scissors to cut a "V" shape from the end of a drinking straw.

206

3 Hold the cut end of the straw between your thumb and finger. Pinch the ends together to flatten them.

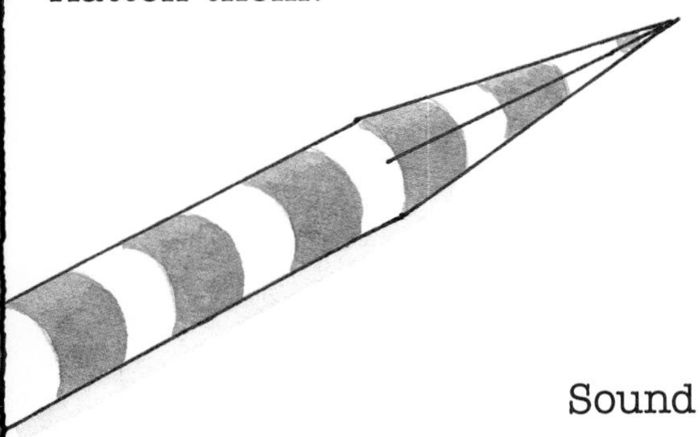

4 Cut off the pinched end of the straw. Push it into the small opening of the cone.

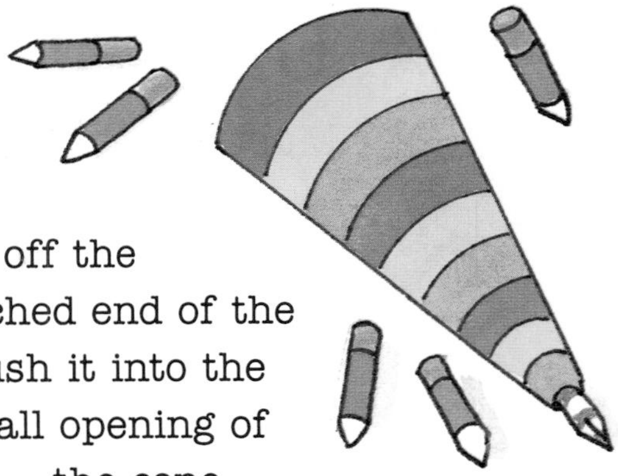

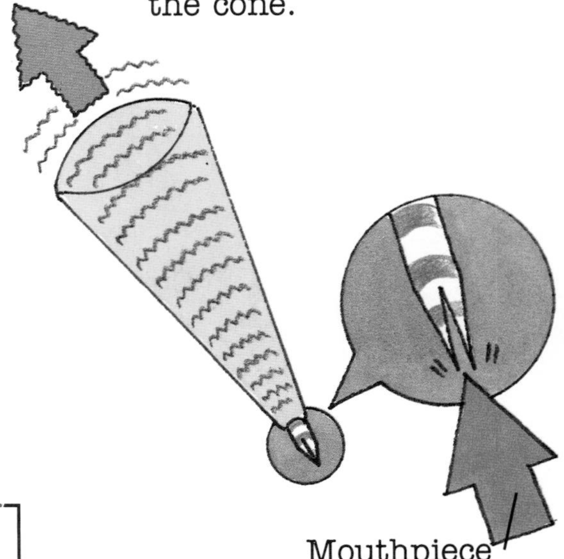

Sound out

5 Try out your clarinet. Put the mouthpiece inside your mouth and blow into the cone. Feel it vibrate as you play a note.

Mouthpiece

FURTHER IDEAS
Make more clarinets using cones of different sizes. Each needs a straw mouthpiece as before. Compare the kinds of notes you get with long and short clarinets. Using your different-sized clarinets, can you and your friends play a tune?

WHY IT WORKS

Blowing through the sharp edges of the straw makes them vibrate. The vibrating straw makes all the air in the cone vibrate and causes sound. We hear these sound waves escaping from the cone.

DIFFERENT PITCHES

Most musical instruments can make a wide range of notes – from low or deep notes that you may be able to feel, to high notes you can only just hear.

Notes differ in pitch. Pitch measures how high or low a note is.

MAKE A XYLOPHONE

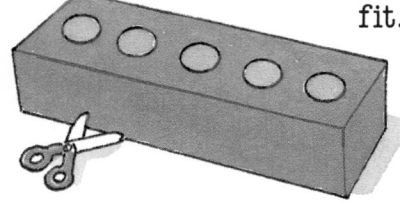

GET AN ADULT TO DO THIS FOR YOU

1 Cut five circles in the lid of a box, big enough for glass bottles to fit.

2 Check that the bottles fit snugly into place. Tape a sheet of cardboard to stand up behind them.

3 Fill each bottle with a different amount of water. Line them up with the fullest at one end and the emptiest at the other.

WHY IT WORKS

Above the water level each bottle contains a tube of air. Hitting the bottles makes the air vibrate. Longer tubes of air (emptier bottles) vibrate more slowly. Slower vibrations make deeper (lower-pitched) sounds.

4 Tap the neck of each bottle with a stick or wooden spoon. Note the different sounds they make. See if you can play a tune.

FURTHER IDEAS
You can make the air in the bottles vibrate another way. Rest your lip on the bottle top and blow.

VIBRATING STRINGS

Stringed instruments include violins, harps, and guitars. Musicians hit or pluck the strings to make them vibrate. Each string is of a different thickness and tautness so each makes a different note. Musicians also change the notes by altering the length of the vibrating string.

MAKE A GUITAR

1 Wash out a large margarine tub. Cut an oval-shaped hole in the lid with a sharp knife or pair of scissors.

GET AN ADULT TO DO THIS FOR YOU

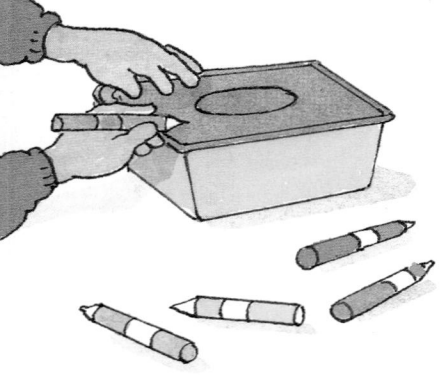

2 Use brightly colored magic markers to decorate the outside of the tub and lid.

3 Wrap six rubber bands of differing thickness lengthwise around the tub. Leave a space between each rubber band.

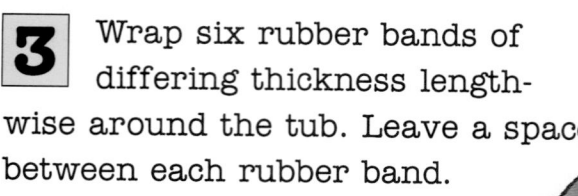

4 Pluck each rubber band with your finger. Compare the sounds made by plucking the ends or middle of each rubber band.

Slower vibrations - lower notes

Faster vibrations - higher notes

WHY IT WORKS

A vibrating rubber band makes the air in the tub vibrate. This makes sound waves which escape through the hole in the lid. Thin rubber bands vibrate much faster than thicker ones. Faster vibrations make higher notes.

FURTHER IDEAS

Place a pencil between the rubber bands and the lid of the tub. This alters the length of the rubber bands and changes the notes they make. Experiment with the pencil in different places along the tub.

TUNING UP

Musicians have to "tune" their instruments. For a stringed instrument this means adjusting each string to just the right tautness to play the correct note. If a string is too slack, it cannot vibrate properly. If it is too taut then the string might snap.

MAKE A SONOMETER

1 You will need a large sheet of thick cardboard. Divide it roughly into thirds. Decorate one side with colored magic markers.

GET AN ADULT TO DO THIS FOR YOU

2 Very carefully use a sharp knife to cut a notch into the sides of two wooden pencils.

3 Find a piece of nylon fishing line about three feet long. Firmly push a thumbtack into one end of the cardboard. Tie one end of the thread to the thumbtack.

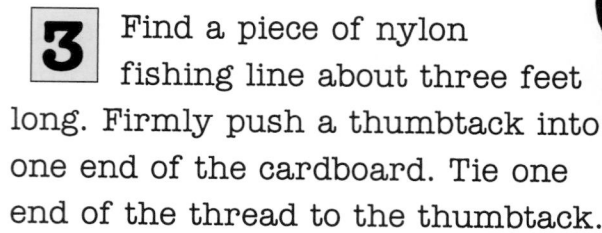

4 Tape the notched pencils into place. Lay the fishing line in the two notches. Tie the other end of the line around a plastic cup weighted down with marbles or stones.

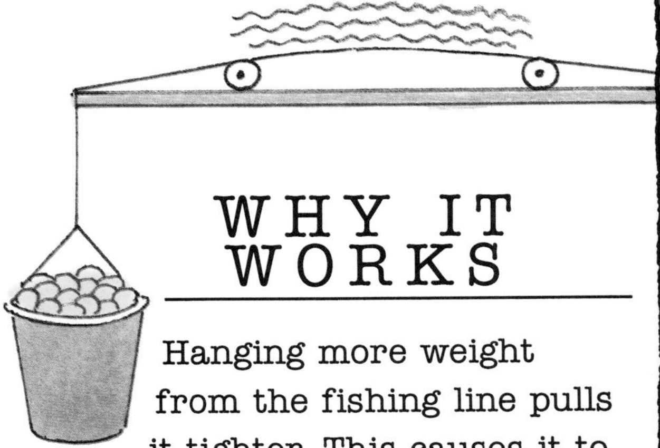

5 Hang the cup over the edge of a table. Pluck the fishing line. Listen to the sound change when you add marbles to the cup.

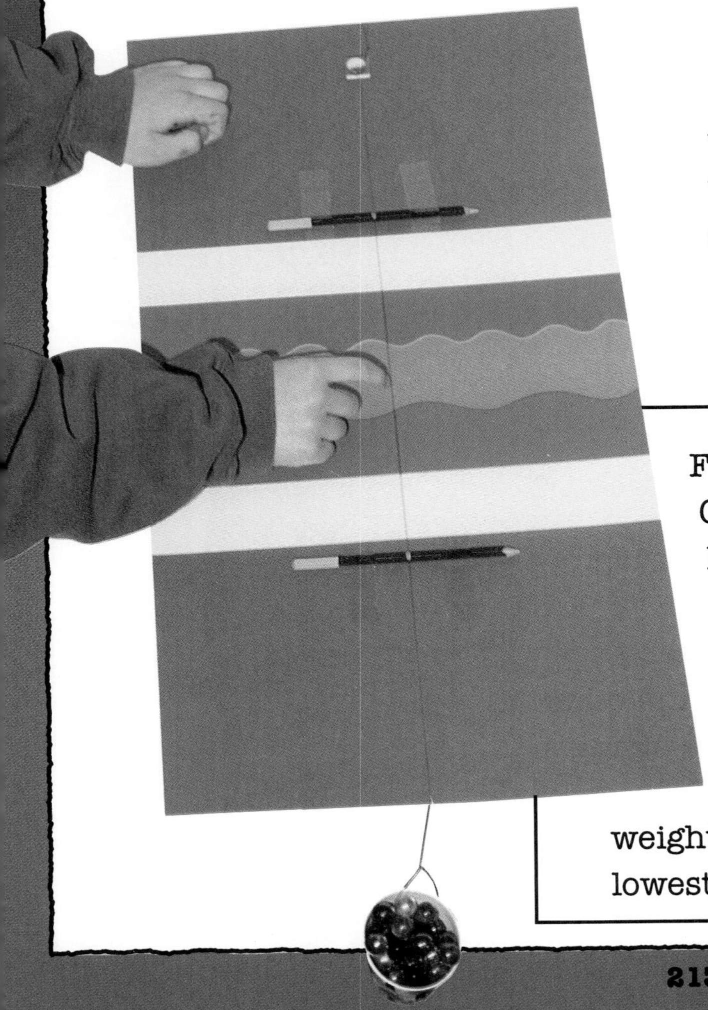

WHY IT WORKS

Hanging more weight from the fishing line pulls it tighter. This causes it to vibrate faster. The faster the vibrations are, the higher the note sounds to us.

FURTHER IDEAS Change the length of fishing line you pluck by moving the pencils closer together or farther apart. Try to predict the length of line and weight to attach to get the highest and lowest possible notes.

FARAWAY SOUNDS

Listening to the ground is an excellent way of listening to faraway sounds. This is because sounds travel faster through the ground than through air. You may have seen a bandit in a cowboy film put his ear to a railway track. Today railway workers use this method to listen for trains. They hear sound trapped in the rails before they see the train.

MAKE A TELEPHONE

1 Find two identical plastic cups. Punch a small hole in the bottom of each with a sharp pencil.

2 Knot one end of a long length of string. Feed the other end through the hole in each cup. Now knot the other end of the string.

GET AN ADULT TO DO THIS FOR YOU

3 Check that the string cannot be easily tugged out of place. Decorate each telephone cup. Use brightly colored magic markers.

WHY IT WORKS

The sounds you make travel along the string as tiny vibrations (you can just feel them if you touch the string). They travel through the plastic cup and the air to reach your ear.

4 With a partner, each take a cup and pull the string taut. Put your cup to your ear. Ask your partner to talk into his or hers. Try to have a conversation.

FURTHER IDEAS

Tie a fork and spoon to a piece of string. Hold the other end of the string to one ear; cover up your other ear. You can "feel" the sound of the jangling utensils. The sounds travel up through the string.

GLOSSARY

Acid
A liquid that turns blue litmus (an indicator) red. Many occur naturally; hydrochloric acid is found in the stomach and helps food digestion.

Alkali
A liquid that turns red litmus (an indicator) blue.

Arch
A shape, roughly semicircular, that is capable of supporting a great deal of weight.

Atom
The smallest complete particle that everything is made up of. Atoms are made up of smaller particles called electrons, protons, and neutrons.

Attract
To pull something toward you.

Ballast
Extra weight carried by vessels. It can be solid or liquid. Ballast helps keep a boat stable. When pumped out, it helps increase buoyancy.

Buoyancy
The ability of a substance to float. Buoyancy depends on the density of the object.

Charge
Electric charge can be either positive or negative. Inside atoms, electrons carry a negative charge and protons carry a positive charge.

Chlorophyll
Chemical pigment that gives green plants their color. It traps the energy contained in sunlight needed for photosynthesis.

Circuit
A complete path around which an electric current can flow.

Compass
An instrument with a magnetized pointer. The pointer always points north because it always lines itself with the Earth's magnetic field.

Compress
To squeeze together into less space.

Conductor
Any material that allows electricity to pass through it.

Convection currents
Circular movements in fluids caused by warm substances rising, cooling, and then falling again.

Crystal
A solid body in which the atoms are arranged in a rigid structure.

Current
A flow of negative charge (electrons) around a circuit.

Density
The weight or heaviness of an object when it takes up a given amount of space.

Drag
The resistance of air or water. A force that holds back moving objects.

Eardrum
A sheet of skin inside your ear. Sounds in the air set it vibrating just like a drumhead. Messages to the brain tell you what the sound is like.

Echo
The reflection or bouncing back of a sound from a surface.

Elastic
An elastic object will recover its original shape after being molded.

Electric motor
A machine that turns electricity into movement by using a magnet.

Electrolyte
A liquid in which a chemical reaction takes place when an electric current flows through it.

Electromagnet
A coil of wire with an iron bar inside it. It becomes a magnet only when electricity is flowing through the coil.

Electroscope
A device used by scientists to measure how much static electricity is contained in an object.

Energy
When a force moves an object, energy is passed to the object (where it may be saved). Heat, light and power are familiar forms of energy.

Filter
A process to purify substances by removing impurities.

Force
A push, pull, or twist that makes an object move or change direction. For example, throwing a ball is exerting force on the ball which makes it move.

Freeze
When a substance turns from a liquid into a solid as its temperature drops.

Frequency
The number of sound vibrations that happen in one second.

Friction
A force that occurs when two surfaces rub against each other. It always slows movement, and brings motion to a stop if no other force is applied to overcome it.

Gravity
The pulling force of the Earth that makes things fall, and gives things weight.

Grip
The action of a surface on another as a result of friction.

Gyroscope
A spinning top that stays upright even if its surroundings are moved.

Hydraulics
The use of liquids, particularly water, in engineering. Hydraulic systems are used for transmitting energy.

GLOSSARY

Hydrometer
Instrument used to measure the density of a liquid by how deeply it sinks into the liquid.

Image
The "picture" of an object usually formed by a lens or photograph.

Indicator
Shows the chemical conditions of a substance by changing color. Litmus turns red for acids, green for alkalis and blue for neutrals.

Induced magnetism
Magnetism caused in magnetic material such as iron or steel, when a permanent magnet is brought very close.

Insulator
Any material that does not let electricity pass through it.

Jet
A fast-moving flow of water or air forced through a small outlet.

Light ray
A very narrow beam of light.

Line of force
A line that shows the magnetic effect around a magnet.

Litmus
An indicator that turns red in acids and blue in alkalis.

Lodestone
A type of rock which is a natural magnet.

Magnetic field
The area around a magnet where the magnetic force works.

Magnetic material
Material that can be made into or attracted to a magnet.

Magnetic pole
Place on a magnet where the magnetic force is strongest. Poles can be north and south.

Magnetize
To turn a magnetic material into a magnet.

Melt
To change from a solid to a liquid when the temperature rises.

Microbe
A microscopic living organism.

Möbius strip
A surface that has only one side. It is made by joining the two ends of a strip that has been twisted around once.

Molecule
Smallest particle of a substance that still has the substance's properties. A molecule may contain several atoms.

Note
A steady sound or tone of the same pitch or frequency.

Oxidize
To combine a substance with oxygen.

Particle
A tiny piece of a substance.

Percussion
Musical instruments played by hitting two things together; for example, a drum and drumstick.

Permanent magnet
A magnet that keeps its magnetism unless it is dropped, knocked, or gets too hot.

Photosynthesis
A chemical process where light energy trapped by chlorophyll combines with water and air to help make a plant grow.

Pigment
The substance added to paints and dyes to give them their color.

Pitch
The highness or lowness of a sound. Pitch depends on the frequency of the vibration causing the sound.

Plastic
When a body can be shaped into a new form, it is said to be plastic. Its properties allow it to be molded and then retain its new shape.

Port
The left side of a boat or ship as you look forward.

Power
The rate at which energy is changed from one form to another. The power of moving car engines is measured in brake horsepower (bhp).

Pressure
The force which presses down on a given area.

Primary color
There are three primary colors of paints and dyes, from which all other colors are made: red, yellow, and blue.

Prism
A transparent wedge, usually of glass, used to split white light into the colors of the rainbow.

Propeller
A rotating object with spiral arms used to drive a boat or other vessel forward.

Pulley
A system of wheels and rope that allows heavy loads to be lifted more easily.

Reflect
When light or sound is bounced back from a surface.

Repel
To push apart. Two south or two north poles repel each other.

Resistance
The ability that a material has to stop or resist the flow of electric current through it.

GLOSSARY

Rigid
When an object is stiff and inflexible, it is said to be rigid. Its structure will not allow it to be bent or formed into any other shape.

Rudder
A flat steering object found under the stern of and underneath a boat.

Saturated
When a substance has been filled to its fullest possible extent.

Shadow
Place of darkness created by an object blocking light.

Sound wave
A regular pattern of vibrations that move through the air or other materials.

Starboard
The right side of a boat or ship as you look forward.

Stethoscope
Instrument used by doctors to hear sounds within the body which are normally too quiet to hear.

Structure
The arrangement of parts to form an entire object.

Temperature
The level of heat that a body has. It is measured in degrees of Celsius, Fahrenheit, and Kelvin.

Terminal
The part of a battery to which wires can be attached.

Tessellation
The ability of shapes to fit together neatly and cover an area without overlapping or leaving any spaces.

Thermal
An ascending current of warm air.

Tiller
The handle used to turn a rudder.

Vibration
A rapid backward and forward movement.

Vocal cord
Flaps of elastic tissue in the human throat which vibrate as air from the lungs is pushed over them, producing the sounds of the human voice.

Volume
The amount of space something takes up.

Weaving
To form a fabric by interlacing fibers. The weft threads are woven through the warp threads, to create the finished cloth.

Woodwind
Wind instruments made from wood or sometimes silver; for example, a clarinet or a flute.

NATURE

for FUN

PROJECTS

Sally Hewitt

COPPER BEECH BOOKS
Brookfield, Connecticut

© Aladdin Books Ltd 2000
Produced by
Aladdin Books Ltd
28 Percy Street
London W1P OLD

First published in the United States
in 2000 by
Copper Beech Books,
an imprint of
The Millbrook Press
2 Old New Milford Road
Brookfield, Connecticut 06804

ISBN 0-7613-0833-4

Editor: Kathy Gemmell

Consultant: Helen Taylor

Designer: Simon Morse

Photography: Roger Vlitos

Illustrators: Tony Kenyon, Stuart Squires – SGA
& Mike Atkinson

Printed in U.A.E.
All rights reserved
Cataloging-in-Publication Data
is on file in the Library of Congress.

Original design concept by David West Children's Books

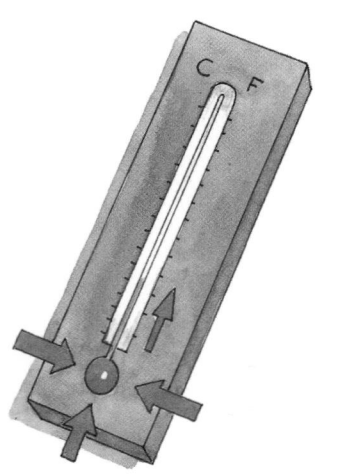

Contents

INTRODUCTION:
How to use this book
224-225

CHAPTER 1:
Weather
226-251

CHAPTER 2:
Rivers, ponds,
and seashore
252-275

CHAPTER 3:
Your backyard
276-301

CHAPTER 4:
Life cycles
302-325

CHAPTER 5:
Woods and meadows
326-349

CHAPTER 6:
All year round
350-373

GLOSSARY
374-377

INDEX
759

Introduction

Nature is all around us all the time. You can have fun learning about the animals and plants around where you live. Discover how to make a

1

wind detector, look at insects skating on a pond, and see what visits your backyard when you're not there.

2

Learn about the life cycle of a butterfly, make leaf rubbings, and build a shelter for a hibernating animal.

3

4

5

6

Look out for numbers like the ones up the side of this page. They will guide you through the step-by-step instructions for the projects and activities, making sure that you do things in the right order.

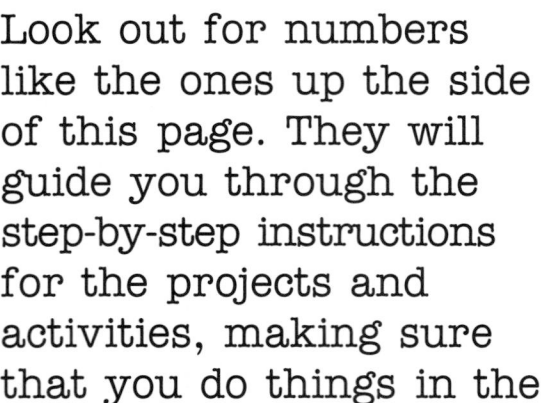

Further facts

Whenever you see this "nature spotters" sign, you will find interesting information, such as how to recognize animal footprints, to help you know and understand more.

Hints and tips

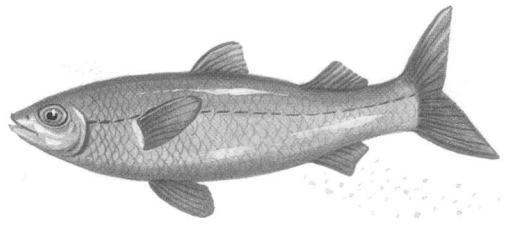

•Try to look at creatures without disturbing them. If you do move them, always return them to the place where you found them.

•When you go for a nature walk, take a waterproof coat and a sun hat, and be ready for all kinds of weather.

•Do not rub your face or eyes when working with plants or soil. Always wash your hands afterward.

Wherever you see this sign, ask an adult to help you. Never use sharp tools or go exploring by yourself.

NEVER LOOK DIRECTLY AT THE SUN

Get an adult to help you

This special warning sign shows where you have to take particular care when doing the project. For example, you should never look straight at the sun. Its powerful rays can damage your eyes and may even cause blindness.

Chapter 1:
WEATHER

Sunshine, pouring rain, blustery wind, and snow are all different kinds of weather. You can have fun learning about the weather. Find out how the seasons change as the earth moves around the sun, and watch for signs of a storm. Take the temperature, make a wind detector, and keep a daily record of the weather where you live.

Contents

CLIMATE 228
Make your own miniclimates.

SEASONS 230
See why the seasons change.

WIND 232
Build your own wind detector.

AIR PRESSURE 234
See how air pressure affects weather.

WATER VAPOR 236
Make your own clouds.

FALLING WATER 238
See how much rain falls each day.

EVAPORATION 240
Measure how fast water disappears.

TEMPERATURE 242
Which is hotter, sun or shade?

THE SUN 244
See how colors affect temperature.

STORMS 246
Find out how far away a storm is.

POLLUTION 248
How does pollution affect weather?

RECORDING THE WEATHER 250
Build your own weather station.

Climate

Some places are hot all year round, while others are cold or rainy. The weather a place has all year is called its climate. Make your own miniclimates and see how they affect how plants grow.

Hot, cold, dry, and wet

1 Collect four plastic tubs, some paper towels, and a pack of seeds that will grow quickly, such as grass or sprouts.

2 Put paper towels in the bottom of the tubs and sprinkle seeds over them. Now put the tubs in places to copy different climates.

4 Put the last tub outside, but don't water it. Now see which of these four miniclimates is the best for growing seeds.

3 Put one of the tubs in the refrigerator. Here it will be cold, dry, and dark, just like a polar climate! Put two tubs on a warm, sunny windowsill. Water only one of these tubs and cover it with a lid.

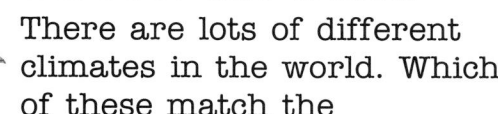

All over the world

There are lots of different climates in the world. Which of these match the miniclimates you made?

Temperate climate

Temperate climates have warm summers, cool winters, and rain during any part of the year.

Desert climate

It hardly ever rains in a desert climate. Many deserts are very hot, but some, like the North and South Poles, are very cold.

Rain forest

It rains nearly every day in a rain forest, and the air is always damp.

Seasons

The climate in some places can change from being hot one month to being cold in another. This is a change of seasons. It happens because the earth is tilted, as you will see from this project.

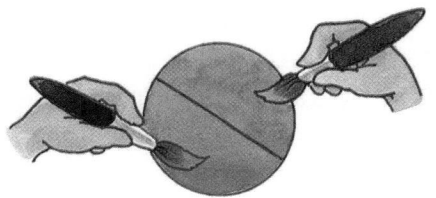

Tilting earth

1 You will need a friend and two balls, one for the sun and one for the earth. Paint one of them yellow to be the sun.

2 Paint a line around the middle of the other ball for the equator – an imaginary line around the earth.

3 Stick corks to the top and bottom for the poles. Now tilt the earth, and you will see that one half is closer to the sun. It will be summer here.

4 Now walk around the sun. Watch the half of the earth that starts off closer to the sun now become farther away. It is now winter in this half.

The seasons

The changing seasons can bring about some dramatic changes to plants and animals.

Spring brings warmer weather after winter. Plants begin to grow, and baby animals are born.

Summer is the hottest time of the year. Trees and flowers are in full bloom.

Fall is colder. Leaves turn brown and start to fall from some trees.

Winter is the coldest season. Animals grow warm winter coats, and snow may fall.

During the summer, the arctic hare has a brown coat. In the winter, this changes to a white coat to help the hare hide in the snow.

Wind

The air around the earth is always moving, sometimes very quickly, causing storms. This moving air is called wind. Build your own detector to measure the strength of the wind.

Wind detector

1 For your wind detector, you will need a long stick, some thin string, tissue paper, writing paper, tinfoil, thin cardboard, thick cardboard, and a hole punch.

Get an adult to help you

2 Cut a strip from each piece of paper and foil. Punch a hole in one end of each strip. Tie the strips along the stick, with the lightest at the top and the heaviest at the bottom.

Tissue paper

Writing paper

Tinfoil

Thin cardboard

Thick cardboard

3 Take your wind detector outside to see how hard the wind is blowing. A breeze will move only the tissue paper. A strong wind will move the heavier cardboard.

The Beaufort Scale

This scale is used by weather experts to measure the strength of wind.

No wind

Smoke moves

Leaves move

Branches move

Crests in water

Wind whistles

Trees bend

It's hard to walk

Shingles blown off

Trees uprooted

Air pressure

Even though you can't feel it, the air above you presses down on you all the time. This is called air pressure. Changes in air pressure usually bring changes in the weather.

Getting heavy

1 Air pressure is measured using a barometer. To make one, you will need a balloon, a glass jar, a drinking straw, a rubber band, a toothpick, scissors, and adhesive tape.

Get an adult to help you

2 Ask an adult to cut the end off the balloon and stretch it tightly over the opening of the jar. Then use the rubber band to hold the balloon firmly in place so it won't slip off.

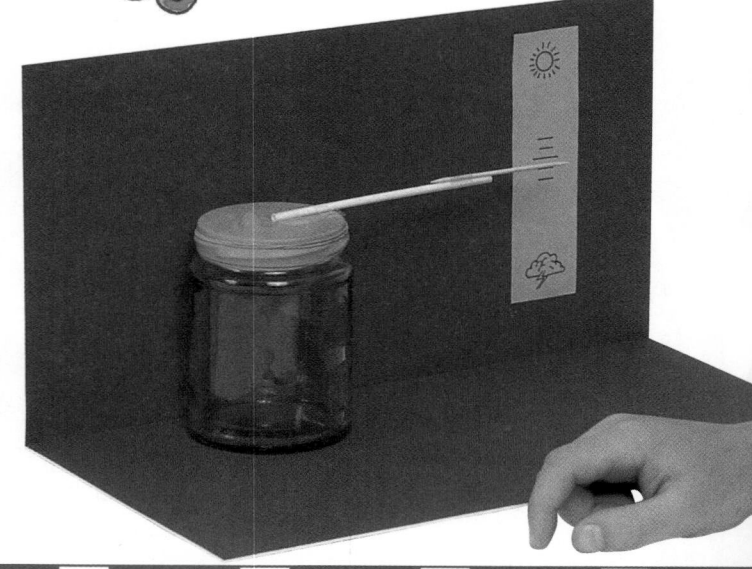

3 Tape the toothpick to one end of the straw. Tape the other end of the straw to the stretched balloon to make a pointer.

4 Because high pressure brings good weather and low pressure bad, draw the sun at the top of a rectangle of cardboard and a cloud at the bottom.

5 Attach the cardboard behind the pointer. Watch your barometer over several days as the changes in air pressure affect the balloon, causing the pointer to rise or fall.

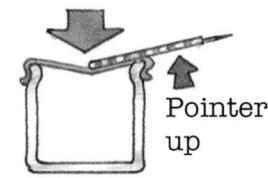

Pointer up

Pointer down

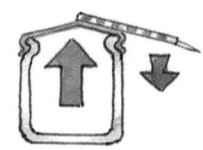

High pressure= Good weather

Low pressure= Bad weather

Barometers

You may have a barometer at home. Its needle shows the air pressure and the kind of weather you can expect.

Compare it with your homemade barometer to see how accurate your homemade one is.

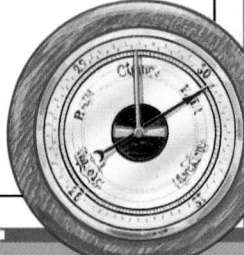

Water vapor

There are tiny droplets of water called water vapor in the air everywhere. Usually, you can't see it but when the air cools, this water vapor turns into larger drops of water and forms clouds.

Making clouds

1 You can make a cloud in a bottle. Fill a clear plastic bottle with hot water.

Get an adult to help you

2 Leave the hot water in the bottle for a few seconds. Now pour half of the water out and put an ice cube in the bottle's opening.

 **3** Watch as the ice cube cools the water vapor in the bottle and creates a misty cloud of water droplets.

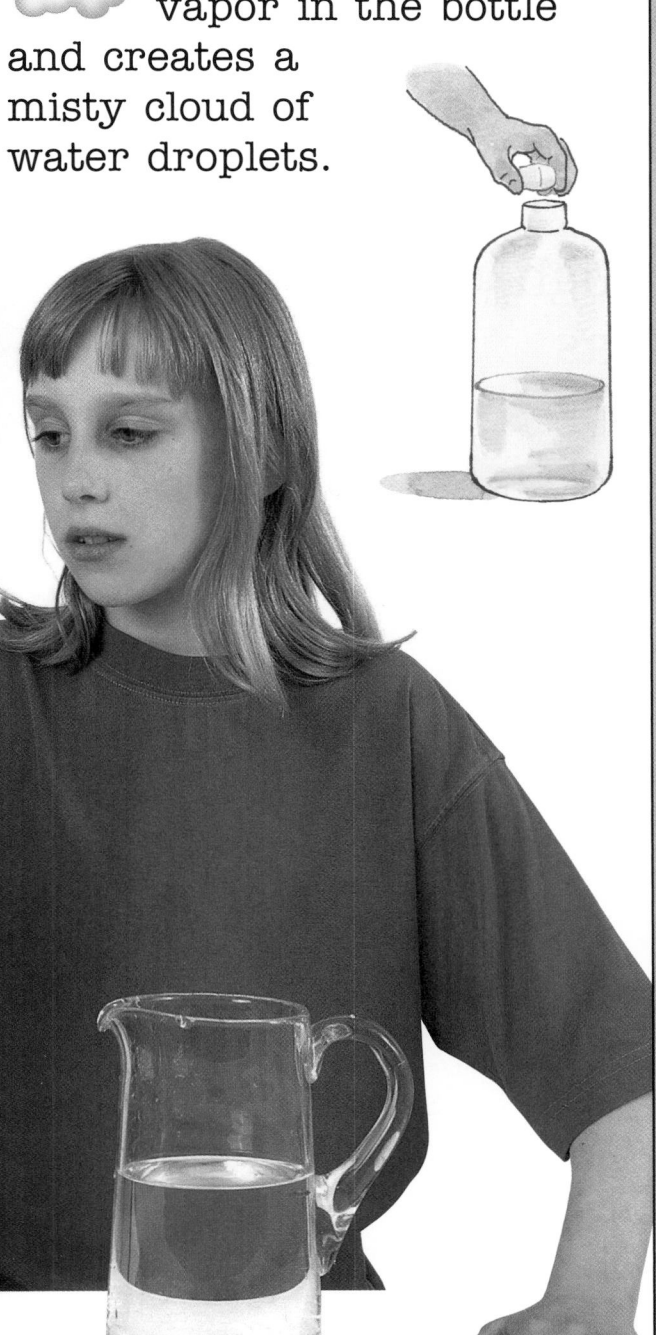

Clouds

Clouds come in lots of shapes and form at different heights. Their shapes and positions can tell us what weather we will have.

Cirrus clouds are high and wispy. They are a warning of bad weather.

White, fluffy **cumulus** clouds can turn into storm clouds.

Cumulonimbus are dark, towering storm clouds.

Stratus are layers of low clouds and can bring rain or snow.

Falling water

The water and ice particles that make up clouds (see pages 236-237) swirl around and bump into each other, becoming bigger. If they become heavy enough, they fall to the ground as rain, hail, or snow.

Collecting rain

Get an adult to help you

1 Make a rain gauge to see how much rain falls where you live. Ask an adult to cut the top off a clear plastic bottle.

2 Turn the top of the bottle upside down and push it back inside the bottle. Tape over the sharp cut edges to make them smoother.

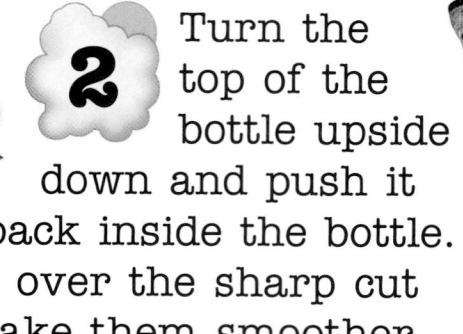

3 Put your rain gauge in an open place outside to catch the rain. Prop it up between four bricks to stop it from being blown over.

4 At the same time each day, pour any rain in your gauge into a measuring cup and check how much has fallen.

Snow and hail

Hail is made from ice crystals in the clouds. They clump together to form small balls of ice that fall to the ground.

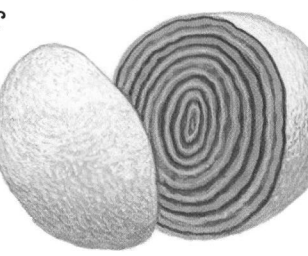

If it's cold enough, the tiny ice crystals can fall. They are called snowflakes, and each one is different.

Evaporation

When the sun shines after a rainfall, puddles of water dry out. The water doesn't disappear, it becomes a gas called water vapor (see pages 236-237). When water does this, we call it evaporation.

Drying puddles

1 Fill an old saucer with water and put it on a sunny windowsill. Mark the edge of the water with a waterproof marker.

2 Mark the edge of the water in the saucer at the same time each day. The marks will show how quickly the water has evaporated into the air.

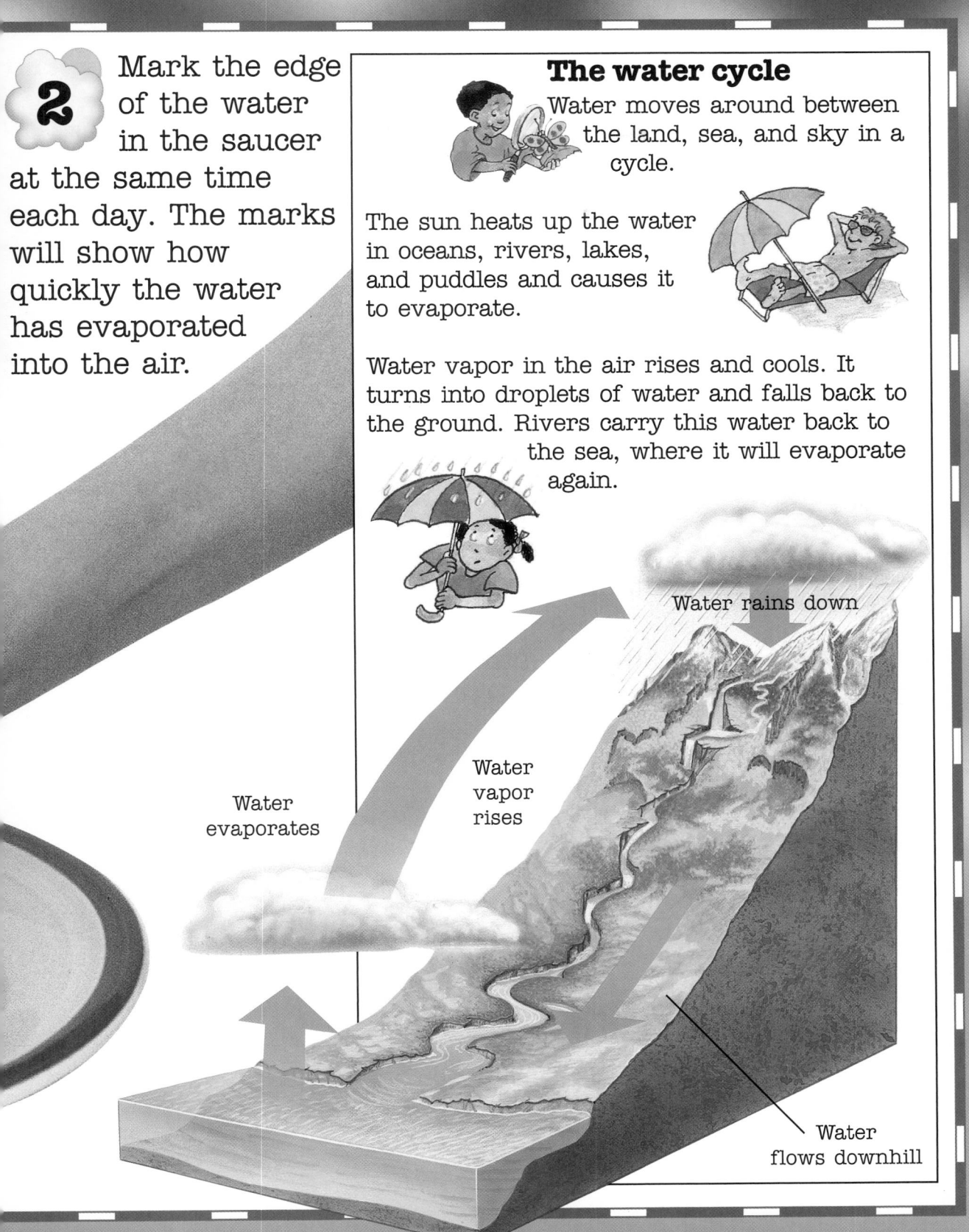

The water cycle

Water moves around between the land, sea, and sky in a cycle.

The sun heats up the water in oceans, rivers, lakes, and puddles and causes it to evaporate.

Water vapor in the air rises and cools. It turns into droplets of water and falls back to the ground. Rivers carry this water back to the sea, where it will evaporate again.

Water rains down

Water vapor rises

Water evaporates

Water flows downhill

Temperature

As the weather changes, you will notice that it gets warmer or colder outside. Temperature is how hot or cold something is, and you can measure it with a thermometer.

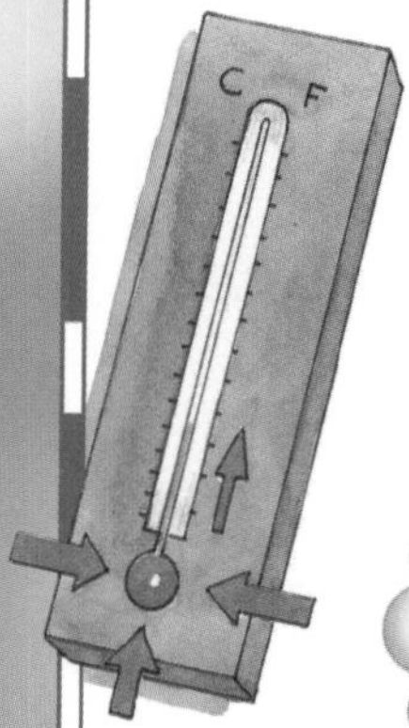

Get an adult to help you

Sun and shade

1 You will need two thermometers. Inside their tubes is a liquid. When this liquid heats up, it expands (gets bigger) and rises up the glass tube.

2 Leave a thermometer in a sunny place. Make a note of the temperature that the liquid inside the thermometer is recording.

BE CAREFUL WITH THERMOMETERS – THE GLASS CAN BREAK!

Degrees

We measure temperature in degrees Fahrenheit, which can be written as °F.

Water boils at 212°F.

212°F

95°F outside feels very hot. Light summer clothes will help you feel cool.

95°F

Room temperature is 68°F, which feels comfortable and warm.

68°F

36°F outside feels cold. You will need to wear a warm coat and hat.

36°F

Water freezes at 32°F.

32°F

3 On the same day, leave a thermometer in a shady place. How does it feel in the shade? Is the temperature higher or lower than in the sun?

The sun

The sun's light and heat are bounced off, or reflected, by shiny things. As a result, they can be used to keep things cool. However, dark things take in heat and warm up, as you will see from this project.

Warm and cool

1 You need tinfoil, a black trash bag, two thermometers, modeling clay, adhesive tape, and two clear plastic bottles filled with cold water.

2 Cover one bottle in tinfoil and the other with the black plastic bag. Hold them in place with adhesive tape.

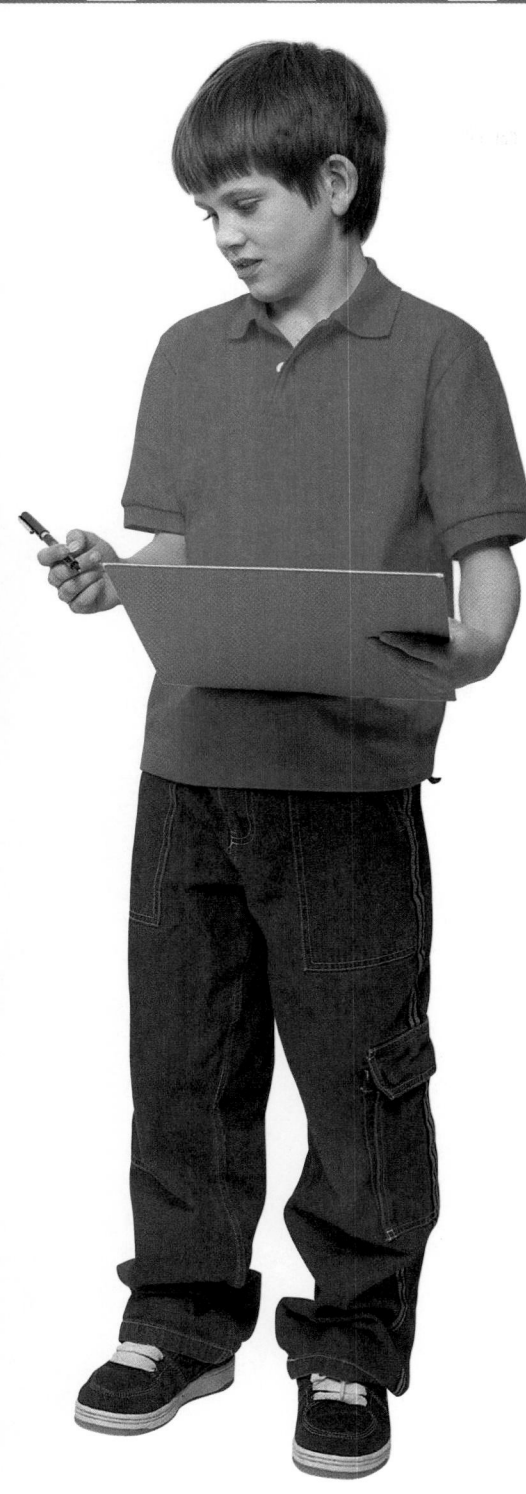

3 Put the thermometers into the bottles and hold them in place with modeling clay. Put the two bottles in the sun for about an hour and then check their temperature. Which bottle is warmer?

Sunglasses

Although the sun gives us heat and light, its rays are strong and can be harmful.

Sunglasses will protect your eyes from these rays in the summer.

NEVER LOOK DIRECTLY AT THE SUN!

Because snow reflects the sun, you may need sunglasses on a bright winter's day, too.

Storms

Storms are violent forms of weather, with strong winds (see pages 232-233), rain, lightning, and thunder. The best place to be during a storm is indoors. But you can still have fun experimenting with storms, even when you're inside.

Thunder and lightning

1 Thunder and lightning happen at the same time. However, because light travels faster than sound, we see the lightning before we hear the thunder. Measure the time between the flash of lightning and the crash of the thunder.

246

2 Figure out how far away the storm is: It takes five seconds for the sound of thunder to travel one mile. A ten second gap means the storm is two miles away.

Whirling winds

Hurricanes are giant whirling storms, hundreds of miles across. They build up over warm, wet seas and cause a lot of damage along coastal areas.

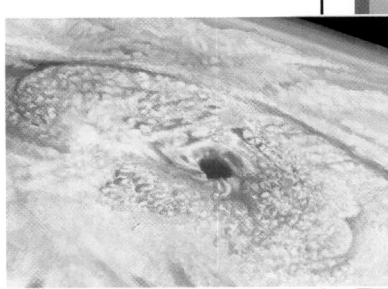

Tornadoes, or whirlwinds, are spirals of whirling air racing across land. They can pick up trucks, uproot trees, and destroy houses in their paths.

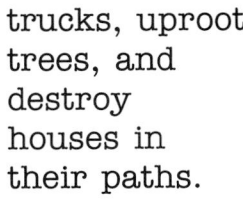

Pollution

The air around us may look clean, but it is full of dirt we can't see. Fumes from traffic, factories, and smoke all pollute the air around us, causing nasty weather, such as acid rain and smog.

Smoke gets in your eye

1 This is a way you can see pollution. Cut out one large and one small square of light colored cloth – old handkerchiefs will do.

Get an adult to help you

2 Glue the small square onto the large square of cloth. Glue it lightly, since you will need to pull it off later.

3 Hang the cloth up outside nearby, but not on, a busy road.

4 After at least a week, pull the small square away and see how clean the cloth is underneath! Pollution in the air has made the rest of the cloth dirty.

Smog and acid rain

Pollution in the air can make rain as acidic as lemon juice! Acid rain damages trees and even wears away stone buildings and statues.

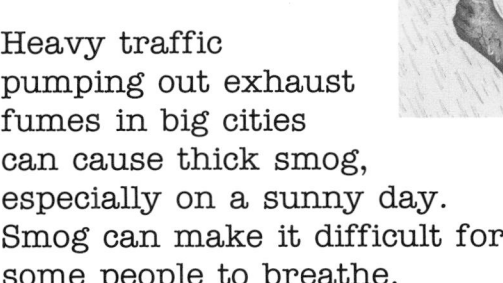

Heavy traffic pumping out exhaust fumes in big cities can cause thick smog, especially on a sunny day. Smog can make it difficult for some people to breathe.

Recording the weather

Use some of the projects in this chapter to create your own weather station. Keep a note of the measurements and see how they compare with the weather forecasts in newspapers or on television.

Keep a daily weather record

1 Hang a thermometer four feet above the ground in the shade. Read it at the same time each day.

2 Your rain gauge will tell you how wet or dry the weather has been.

3 High or low air pressure will help you to tell if the weather is going to be dry or wet.

4 Your wind detector will let you know if it is a good day for flying a kite!

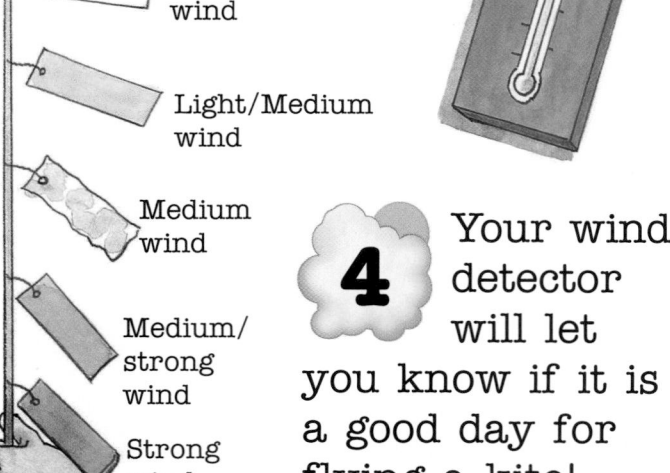

Light wind

Light/Medium wind

Medium wind

Medium/ strong wind

Strong wind

Weather maps

Weather forecasters use little pictures called symbols to make weather maps easy for us to read. Each symbol stands for a certain type of weather.

Dark storm clouds bringing thunder and lightning.

Clouds bringing rain or drizzle.

Clouds broken by patches of sunshine.

Clear skies and sunshine.

The arrow shows where the wind is coming from and how strong it is.

The number in the circle shows the temperature in degrees Fahrenheit.

Chapter 2:
RIVERS, PONDS, AND SEASHORE

Rivers, ponds, and the sea are full
of all kinds of life. You can have
fun learning about the things
that live and grow on, by, or
under the water. Go pond
dipping and look out for insects
skating on the water. Spot
waterbirds, build a dam,
and find out about the
moon and the tides.

Contents

FLOWING WATER 254
See how water flows downhill.

SPEEDY RIVERS 256
Find out how fast a river flows.

POND DIPPING 258
What sort of things live in a pond?

WATER BUGS 260
Take a look at pond creepy crawlies.

BREATHING UNDERWATER 262
How can fish breathe underwater?

MAKE A POND 264
See what visits your own pond.

WATERBIRDS 266
What's so special about waterbirds?

THE TIDE 268
See what happens when the tide goes out.

SEAWEED 270
Examine this sea plant in detail.

ROCK POOLS 272
What lives in these miniworlds?

SHELLFISH 274
How many shells can you collect?

Flowing water

When water from rain, melted snow, lakes, and springs collects together, it becomes a river, carving its way through the earth as it flows downhill. See how a river can change the landscape with this project.

Make a river

1 Watch water flowing downhill by piling up stones of different sizes at one end of a plastic tray to make a hill.

2 Cover the stones with soil. Shape the soil so that you have a hill sloping down to the opposite edge of the tray.

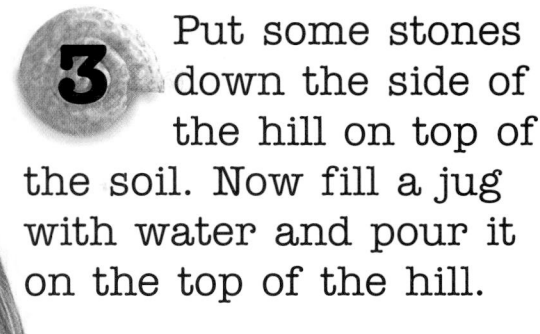

3 Put some stones down the side of the hill on top of the soil. Now fill a jug with water and pour it on the top of the hill.

Fresh and salty water

Rainwater and the water in rivers, lakes, and springs is the water we drink and that plants need to grow. It is called freshwater, which means it is not salty.

Rivers wash salts and minerals from the land into the sea, making it salty. Saltwater is not good to drink!

4 Watch as the water becomes a miniriver, making channels, and carrying soil downhill.

Speedy rivers

Rivers are always on the move. Sometimes they drift slowly along, but at other times they can turn into a rushing torrent. This project will help you to measure the speeds of a river.

Timing sticks

1 Tie different colored string or ribbon tightly onto the end of some short sticks. Take them to a bridge over a river or stream.

DON'T STAND TOO CLOSE TO THE EDGE OF A RIVER!

2 With a friend, try to drop the sticks in the middle and at both sides of the water all at the same time.

3 Time how long it takes for the sticks to appear on the other side of the bridge. Which is the quickest?

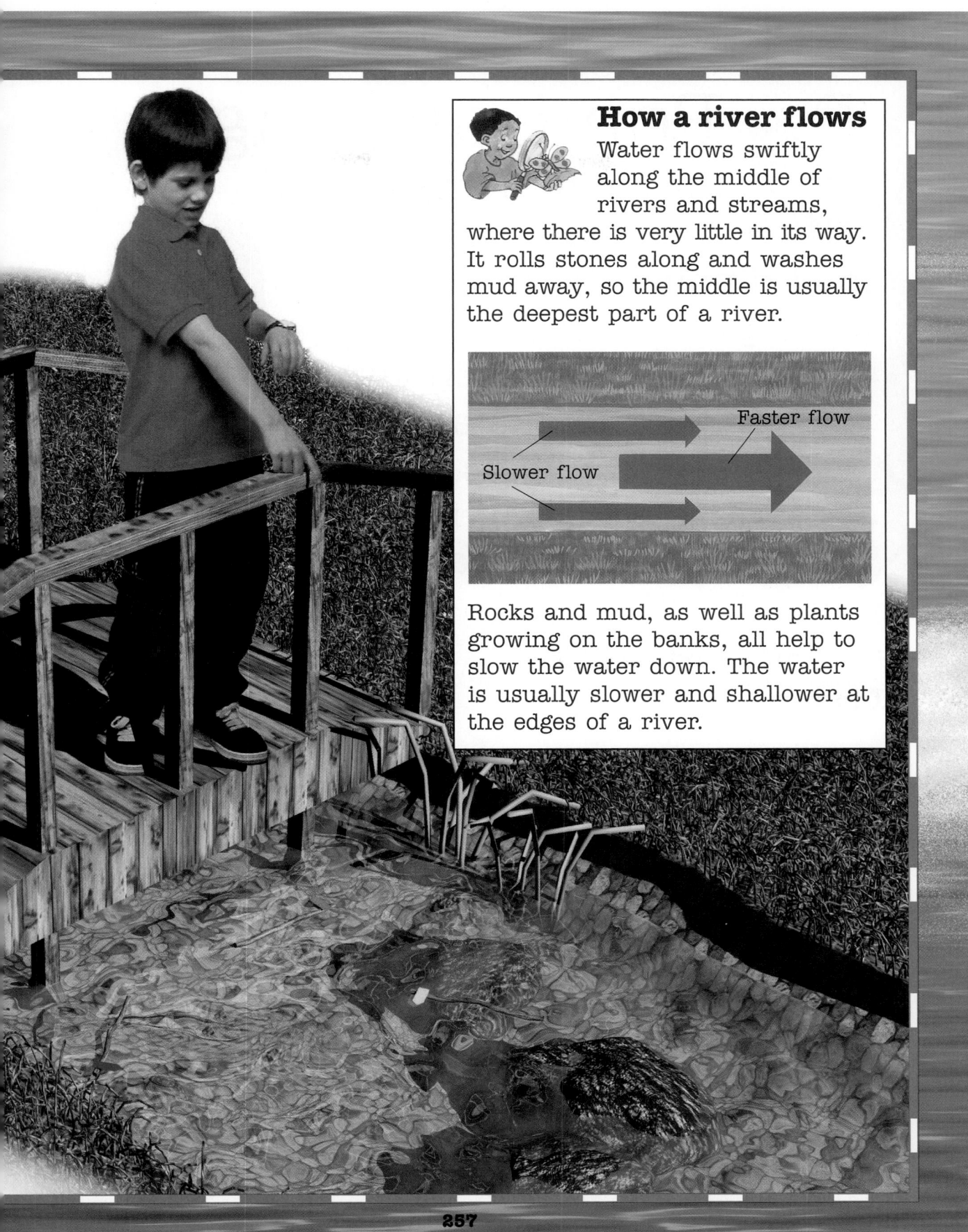

How a river flows

Water flows swiftly along the middle of rivers and streams, where there is very little in its way. It rolls stones along and washes mud away, so the middle is usually the deepest part of a river.

Faster flow

Slower flow

Rocks and mud, as well as plants growing on the banks, all help to slow the water down. The water is usually slower and shallower at the edges of a river.

257

Pond dipping

Spring or summer are the best times to go pond dipping. With just a net and a plastic container, you will find all kinds of plants and animals living in every part of the pond.

DON'T LEAN TOO FAR OVER THE WATER – YOU MIGHT FALL IN!

Dippers

1 Fill a clean plastic container with pond water. Sweep your net in the water near the edge of the pond.

2 Empty the net into the container. With a magnifying glass, examine all the plants and creatures you have caught.

 **3** Now sweep your net nearer the middle of the pond. Have you caught different things?

Pond creatures

Here are just some of the amazing creatures that you might find living in a pond.

Sticklebacks have sharp, spiny fins along their backs.

 **Great pond snails** have rough tongues for eating underwater plants.

Leeches hunt for fish and snails to feed on.

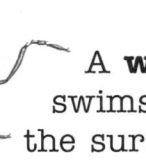 A **water boatman** swims upside down on the surface of the water.

Mosquito larvae hang just below the water breathing air through a tube.

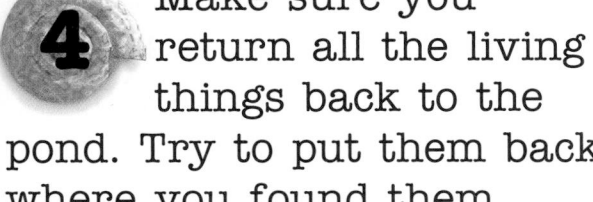 **4** Make sure you return all the living things back to the pond. Try to put them back where you found them.

Water bugs

Creatures live in every part of a pond. They live in the mud, swim in the water, and skate over the surface. Flying insects dart above the water and lay their eggs on the water plants.

Spot the creepy crawlies

1 A water spider spins its web underwater and fills it with bubbles of air. Then it lies in wait for a passing creature to catch and eat.

Dragonfly

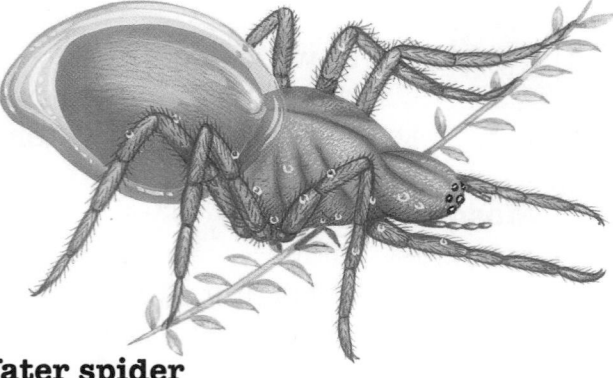

Water spider

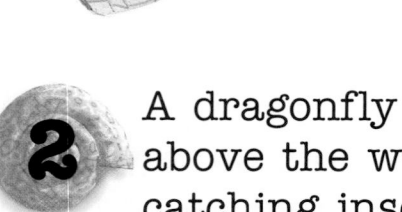

2 A dragonfly darts above the water catching insects with its legs. It has see-through wings and a shiny, colorful body.

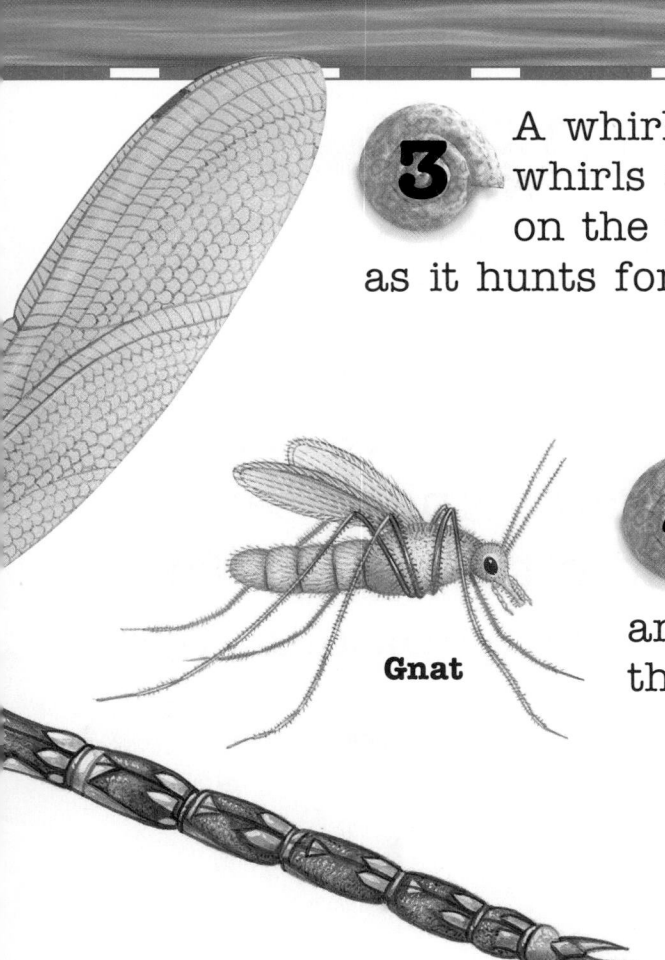

3 A whirligig beetle whirls around on the water as it hunts for food.

Whirligig

Gnat

4 Female gnats suck a tiny amount of blood for a meal from animals or people. They lay their eggs on the water.

Water skin

Fill a glass to the brim with water so that it is almost overflowing. You can see that the water bulges over the top of the glass as if it has a thin skin.

Pollution in the water breaks up this skin. As a result, creatures like pond skaters that live on the surface cannot live in polluted ponds.

5 A pond skater jumps and slides over the skin of the water without breaking it.

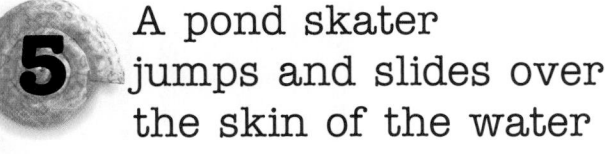

Pond skater

Breathing underwater

Water creatures need to breathe oxygen to live. Some come up to the surface for air, but others stay underwater and breathe the oxygen that is mixed into the water. This project shows you how water plants give off oxygen into the water.

Weedy air

1 You will need pondweed, a funnel, a plastic bottle of water, three lumps of modeling clay, and a see-through container.

2 Put the weed and clay in the bottom of the container and fill with water. Place the funnel on the lumps of clay so that it sits over the pondweed.

3 Carefully place the bottle of water upside down over the funnel. Watch how bubbles of oxygen gradually come from the weed and fill the bottle.

Breathing underwater

Fish do not have lungs; they breathe through special organs called gills. These lie just behind the eyes of a fish.

Water flows into the fish's mouth and passes over the gills. Oxygen in the water is taken into the fish's blood as it flows over its gills.

Lungfish have lungs and gills so that they can breathe both in and out of water. If the water they live in dries up, they can hide in the mud until it rains again.

Make a pond

You have already seen some of the plants and animals that live in ponds. Now build one yourself and see if you can attract some of this wildlife to your own pond.

1 You will need a flat tray, gravel, soil, large stones, and some water plants, such as pondweed.

2 Cover the bottom of the tray with gravel and some soil. Use a big stone to make an island in the middle.

3 Carefully fill the tray with water. Try to use rainwater, as it is best for a pond.

4 Add the plants, fixing them with stones and soil. Or you can plant them in the water in little pots.

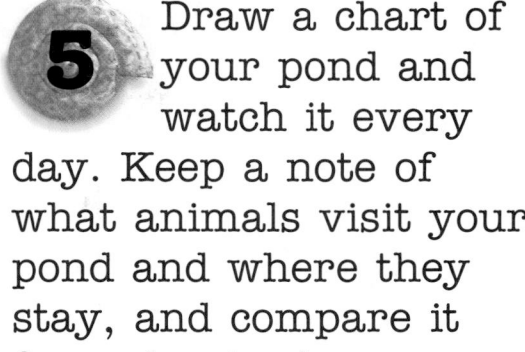

5 Draw a chart of your pond and watch it every day. Keep a note of what animals visit your pond and where they stay, and compare it from day to day.

Frogs

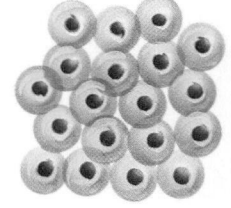

Frogs spend the first part of their lives as tadpoles living underwater. Grown–up frogs live in water and on land.

Frogs lay eggs called frog spawn in the water.

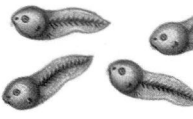

Tadpoles hatch from the eggs and swim underwater.

Tadpoles lose their tails, grow legs, and become little frogs.

Waterbirds

Waterbirds live on rivers, ponds, and the seashore. Watch some waterbirds carefully. In what ways are they like this duck? How are they different?

1 This duck has a flat bill. It uses its bill to filter out seeds, insects, and snails from the water to eat.

2 It also uses its bill to spread oil through its feathers to make them waterproof. Drops of water roll easily off the oil.

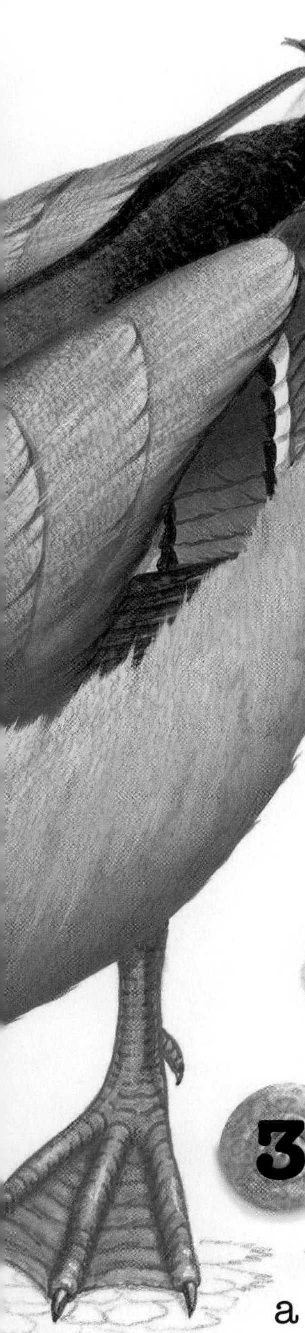

Shapes and sizes

Here are some examples of the different types of waterbirds.

Pelican

A pelican uses its long, strong bill with a pouch like a fishing net to scoop fish out of the water.

Kingfisher

A kingfisher sits on a branch and spots fish to catch in its pointed beak in the water below.

Black-headed gull

A black-headed gull has a hooked bill for catching slippery fish and tearing at food.

Spoonbill

A spoonbill has long, thin legs. It uses these to wade through shallow water, while it picks up food from the bottom with its spoon-shaped bill.

3 Skin stretched between its three toes turn a duck's feet into a kind of paddle. Many waterbirds have webbed feet like these.

The tide

Driftwood

When you go to the beach, you may notice that the edge of the sea moves backward and forward each day. This is called the tide.

Shells

Beachcombing

1 When the sea is at low tide, you will see a mark on the sand where the high tide was. Measure the distance between the low tide and the high tide by pacing it out.

Seaweed

2 Look at the part of the beach you can only see when the tide is low. You should see small piles of sand made by worms as well as bird tracks.

3 As the sea pulls away from the shore, it leaves all kinds of things behind, such as seaweed and bits of pottery. Make a note of some of the things you find by the sea at low tide.

Pottery

Pebbles

High and low tide

The tides are actually caused by the sun and the moon.

Gravity is the force that keeps your feet on the ground and causes things to fall to the ground.

The gravity of the sun and the moon pulls the water in the sea, causing tides.

Seaweed

Seaweeds can be found all along the seashore. They do not have roots like plants that grow on land but have special roots, called holdfasts, that grip onto rocks. This project shows you a good way to study seaweed in close-up.

BE CAREFUL WHEN YOU COLLECT SEAWEED

Floating seaweed

1 Collect some seaweed to take home. Find a see-through vase or jar. Put in the seaweed and use a stone to hold it on the bottom. Now add water.

2 Look at the shape of seaweed when it is held up by water. See how it goes limp and loses its shape out of water.

Types of seaweed

There are three types of seaweed that you can find washed up on the seashore – red, brown, and green.

Carrageen is a red seaweed. You might find some growing in a rock pool.

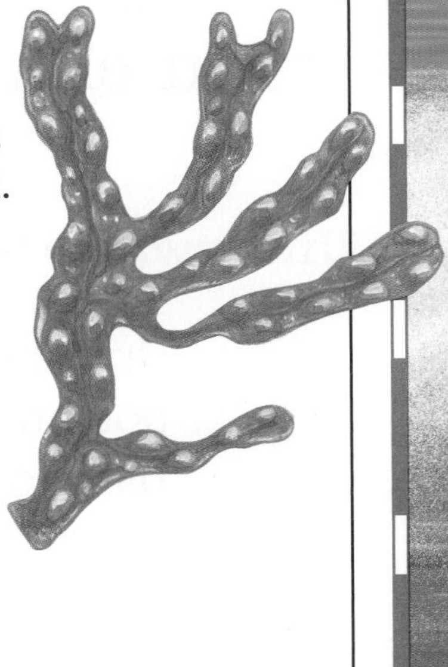

Bladder wrack is a brown seaweed. It has little pockets of air to help it float upright in the water.

Sea lettuce is a green seaweed that looks like the lettuce leaves we eat.

Rock pools

As the tide goes out it leaves behind pools of water among the rocks. Rock pools are places where you can find creatures and plants hiding. Make your own special viewer to see this underwater world clearly.

TAKE CARE ON THE SLIPPERY ROCKS AROUND ROCK POOLS!

Underwater viewer

1 Cut the top and bottom off a plastic bottle and tape over the rough edges to make your underwater viewer.

Get an adult to help you

2 Pull plastic wrap tightly over one end. Put a rubber band around the plastic wrap to stop it from slipping off your viewer.

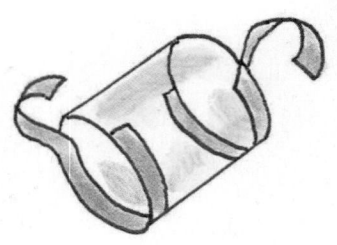

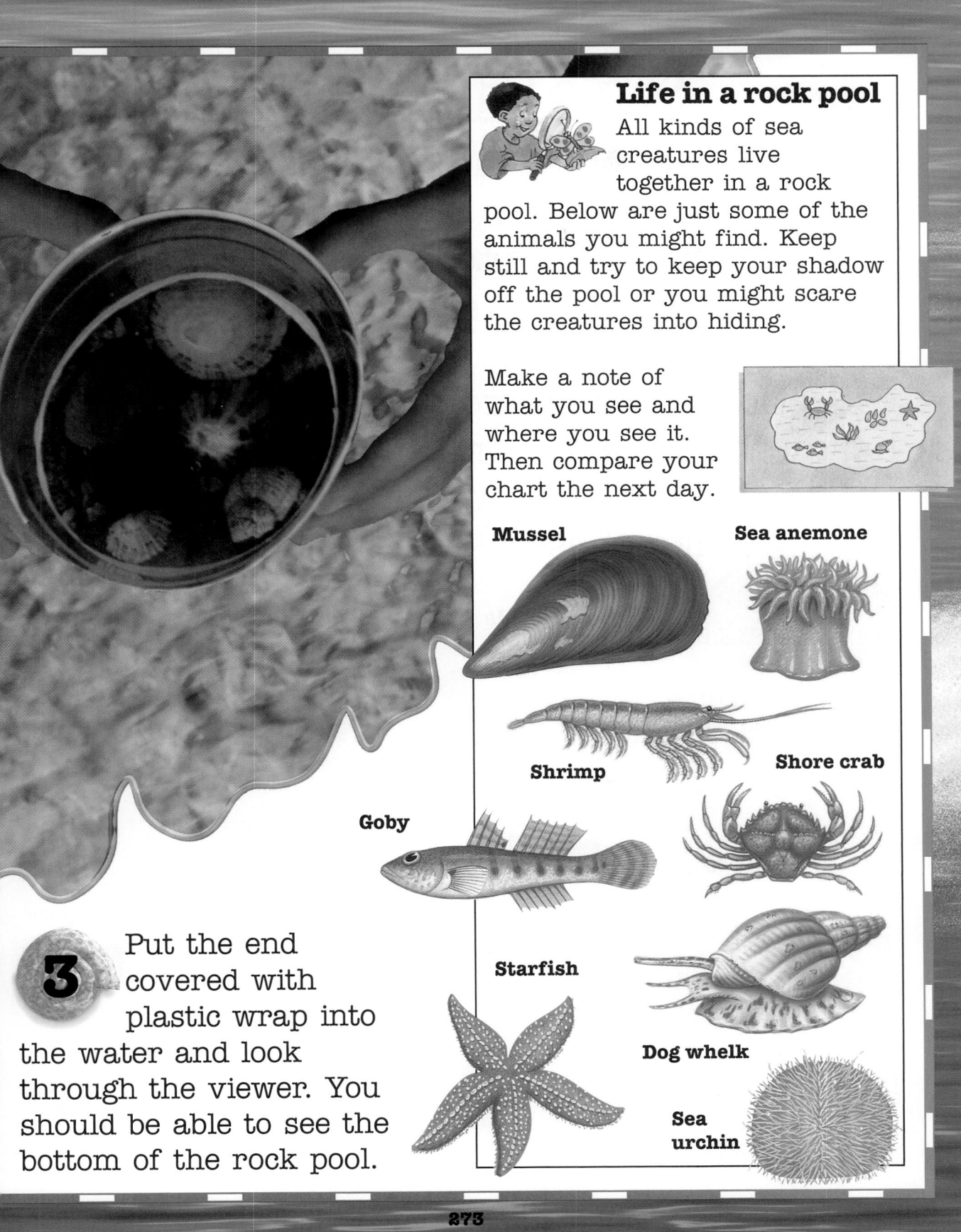

Life in a rock pool

All kinds of sea creatures live together in a rock pool. Below are just some of the animals you might find. Keep still and try to keep your shadow off the pool or you might scare the creatures into hiding.

Make a note of what you see and where you see it. Then compare your chart the next day.

Mussel

Sea anemone

Shrimp

Shore crab

Goby

Starfish

Dog whelk

Sea urchin

3 Put the end covered with plastic wrap into the water and look through the viewer. You should be able to see the bottom of the rock pool.

Shellfish

Shellfish have soft bodies, so they grow a tough shell to protect them. There are many different types of shellfish. Make a collection of shells you find on the beach and sort them into groups like these.

DON'T TAKE SHELLS WITH LIVE CREATURES INSIDE!

Mussels

Scallops

Razor clams

Limpets

4 Scallops, mussels, and razor clams live in shells with hinges. These open up to let the creature feed.

3 Limpets have a single shell to hide under while they cling tightly to a rock.

Collecting shells

1 Arrange your shells into groups depending on each shell's size and shape.

2 These spiral-shaped shells used to be the homes of snail-like animals such as whelks.

Spiral shells

Useful shells

Shellfish have developed some amazing features to feed or protect themselves from creatures who want to eat them.

A **barnacle** waves its legs through a small hole in the top of its shell. It uses these to catch any food which may be floating past.

A **limpet** moves slowly over a rock, scraping off food with its teeth-filled mouth.

A **scallop** escapes from a hungry starfish by flapping its shells open and shut and jet–propelling itself along.

Chapter 3:
YOUR BACKYARD

Look closely and you will find many interesting things in your backyard. Have fun learning about creatures and where to find them. Make a worm garden and watch worms at work in the soil. Plot an ant map and attract birds with a cake. Discover how to find out who visits the yard when you're not there.

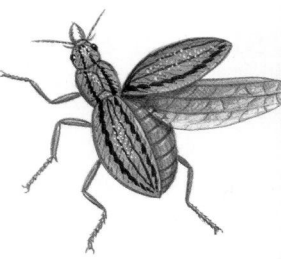

Contents

SOIL **278**
Find out how soil is formed.

ROTTING GARBAGE **280**
See how some garbage disappears.

SEEDS **282**
Grow your own garden.

GREEN GRASS **284**
Find out why grass is green.

PLANTS **286**
Watch plants drink.

FLOWERS **288**
Discover different flower parts.

FEEDING BIRDS **290**
Make a bird cake.

FOOTPRINTS **292**
Find out who visits your backyard.

INSECT VISITORS **294**
Where do insects live?

MINIBEASTS **296**
Build a trap and see what crawls out.

ANTS **298**
Trace ant paths with sugary bread.

WORMS **300**
Make your own worm garden.

Soil

Soil is a very important part of your backyard. It is full of the minerals and water that plants need for growth. Moles, worms, and all kinds of tiny creatures make it their home.

Soil settling

1 Find out what makes up the soil in your backyard. Dig up some soil from the edge of a flower bed and put it in a bucket.

2 Shake some soil in a sieve over the bucket. Sort what is left behind onto some paper. You may find stones, bits of plants, or even creatures that live in the soil.

3 Now put some soil into a screw-top jar. Fill the jar nearly to the top with water and screw on the lid.

4 Shake the soil and water together, then leave the jar to stand.

5 Carefully look at the jar without disturbing it. The soil will settle into layers in the water.

Soil layers

Soil is a mixture of dead plants and animals and tiny pieces of broken-down rock. Different kinds of rock will make sandy, chalky, or sticky clay soil.

Bits of plants

Muddy water

Clay or chalk

Sand

Gravel and stones

Rotting garbage

Dead plants and animals that rot down into the soil help to make it rich and good for new plants to grow in. Not everything rots down quickly. Some garbage stays around for a very long time.

Bags of garbage

1 See what kind of garbage rots away, and what doesn't. Don't throw away banana skins, apple cores, tissues, cans, or potato chip bags - bury them!

NEVER TAKE GARBAGE FROM THE CAN

2 Put some soil into clear plastic bags. Push one piece of garbage into the soil in each bag and seal it.

3 Check the bags every few days, but don't open them. You will see that apple cores rot quickly, but banana skins take a long time. Garbage made of plastic doesn't rot at all.

Natural rotters

There are many different plants and animals that get to work right away on natural garbage like leaves, logs, or dead creatures. They are called decomposers.

Fungi are not really plants. They grow and feed on dead wood.

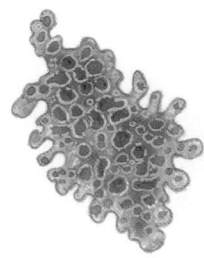

Lichens grow on stone and wood and gradually break them down.

Worms pull leaves and bits of dead plant down into the soil and eat them.

Maggots that hatch from housefly eggs eat the bodies of dead creatures.

Woodlice live in dark, damp places and feed on leaves and wood.

Seeds

Gardeners look after the plants and flowers they want to grow in their yards, and spend a lot of time pulling up weeds that they didn't plant. You can discover what seeds are hiding in the soil, waiting to grow.

Soil gardens

1 Dig up some soil from two different places in the yard, perhaps from under a tree and by a fence. Put the soil from each place in its own plastic tray and label where it came from.

2 Water both trays every other day. After a while, you will see shoots beginning to push up through the soil even though you didn't plant any seeds.

3 Some shoots may become grass or weeds. A seed from a tree may one day grow into a young tree. A rose tree may even grow from a rose hip dropped by a bird.

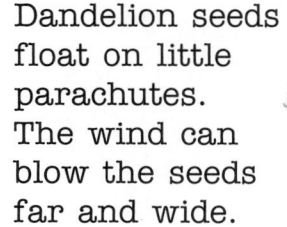

Spreading seeds

Plants have various ways of spreading their seeds to give them a good chance to grow into new, strong plants.

Birds eat juicy fruits, such as cherries. The seeds or pits inside them fall to the ground in the birds' droppings.

Horse chestnut seeds are heavy and fall straight to to the ground. Look for them under a horse chestnut tree.

Dandelion seeds float on little parachutes. The wind can blow the seeds far and wide.

Green grass

Grass in the countryside is food for animals and it can be like a soft, green carpet in the yard. Grass has another job to do, too.

Grass roots hold soil in place in the wind and the rain. Different kinds of grass grow in different soils.

In the dark

1 This project will show you that sunlight is what makes grass green. Find a corner of your lawn.

2 Cover a patch of grass, near the edge of the lawn, with a thick piece of cardboard. Put a stone on it to stop it blowing away.

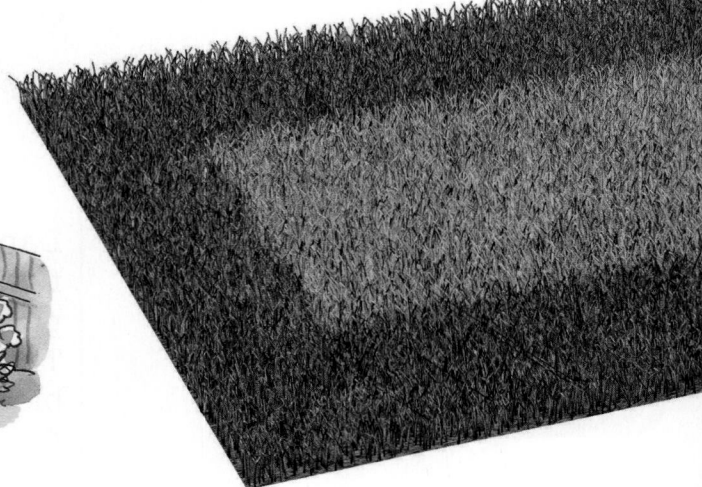

3 Lift up the cardboard after two weeks and see what has happened to the grass. When kept in the dark, grass will turn pale green or yellow and begin to die.

Using sunlight

Like grass, other plants also need sunlight to grow and survive. Plants make their own food using sunlight. This is called photosynthesis.

Photosynthesis

Plants need sunlight to make food using the green color in their leaves, called chlorophyll.

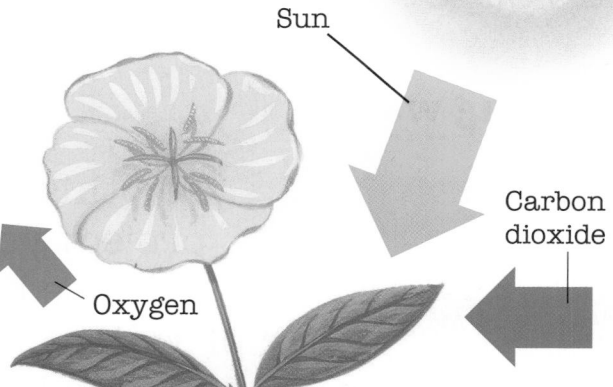

Sun

Carbon dioxide

Oxygen

As part of photosynthesis, plants give out a gas called oxygen.

The green leaves catch the sun's energy. They use the energy to make food from water and a gas called carbon dioxide in the air.

Without sunlight, plants cannot make food and they will die.

Plants

We all have veins to carry blood around our bodies. Plants have veins, too. They carry the water and mineral a plant needs to grow to every part of the plant. Watch how water moves up the stem and into the leaves of a celery stalk.

Drinking water

1 For this project you will need a jar of water, some blue food coloring, and a celery stalk with leaves.

2 Mix the water and blue food coloring together in the jar and put the celery stalk in it. Leave the jar near a window for a few hours.

3 The blue water will slowly rise up the veins in the stalk, then into the leaves, turning them blue.

Get an adult to help you

4 Now slice the stalk across the middle. You will be able to see that the veins in the celery have been stained blue.

Roots

Roots grow downward into the soil to hold the plant in place. They have tiny hairs to suck up the water and minerals that a plant needs from the soil. Water goes into the roots, then up the stem into the leaves, then out into the air.

Carrots and potatoes are swollen roots that store food for the plants.

Water in the soil

Flowers

A plant starts life as a tiny egg. Flowers are the parts of a plant where eggs that become seeds are made. The seeds then grow into new plants. If you look closely at a flower, you will see all the parts it needs for making seeds.

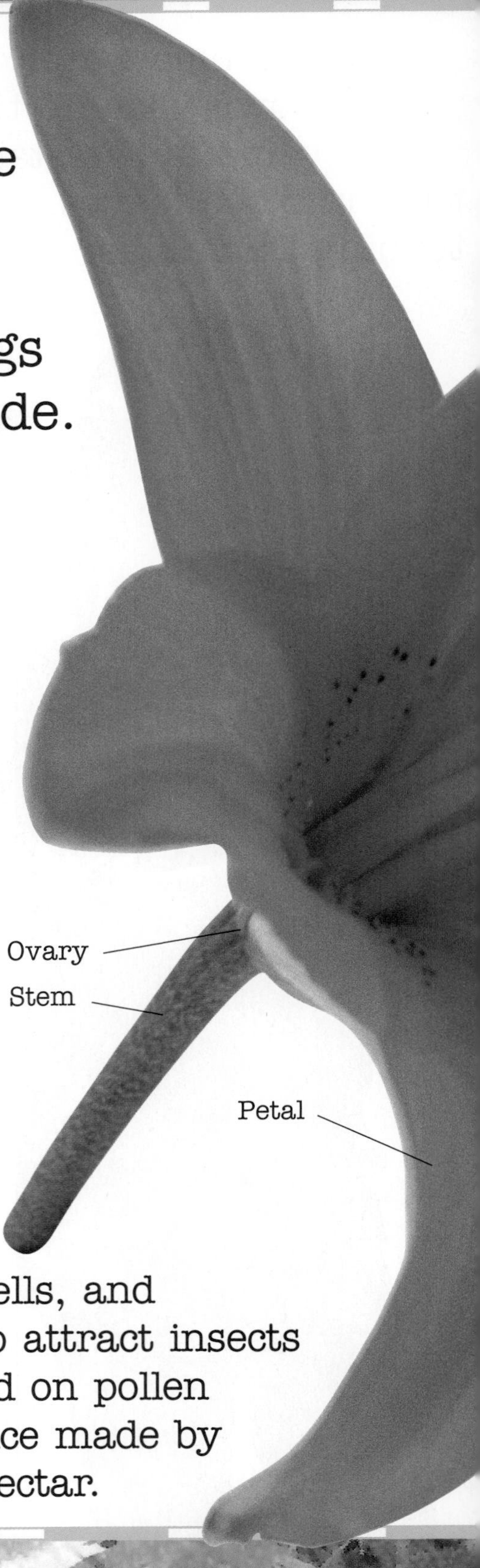

Parts of a flower

1 Stamens grow from the middle of the flower. Yellow powder called pollen is made on the tip of the stamens. Pollen gives some people hayfever.

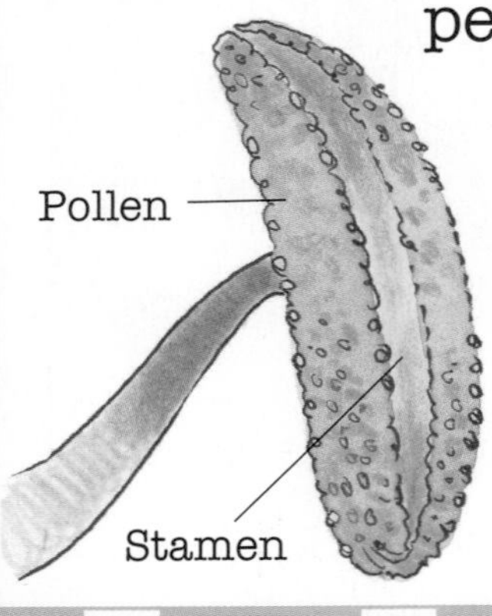

Ovary

Stem

Petal

Pollen

Stamen

2 Petals use colors, smells, and patterns to attract insects and birds that feed on pollen and on a sweet juice made by the plant, called nectar.

Stamen

3 A stigma also grows from the middle of the flower. Pollen grains that land on the stigma grow a tube down to join an egg in the ovary. The egg can then become a seed.

4 The ovary is the case where eggs that become seeds are made.

From stigma

Ovary

Pollen fertilizes an egg to make a seed.

Flower power

Look for flowers of all colors, shapes, sizes, and smells growing in different places in the yard.

Apple blossom

Apple blossoms on an apple tree become fruit in the summer.

Daffodil bulbs can be planted in pots and window boxes.

Daffodil

Honeysuckle grows up walls and fences. It smells very sweet.

Honeysuckle

Stigma

Feeding birds

Birds are visitors to the yard, looking for food and water. In the spring, they may find a sheltered place there to build a nest. You can make sure there is always something for birds to eat and drink.

Winter bird cake

1 In winter, there is less food for birds to find. Use breadcrumbs from a stale loaf, uncooked peanuts, bacon rind, and fat to make a winter bird cake.

2 Line a cake pan or muffin tray with wax paper. Now mix the breadcrumbs, peanuts, and chopped bacon rind together in a bowl.

3 Fat will hold the cake together as well as keep the birds warm when they eat it. Melt the fat in a saucepan over a low heat until it is all liquid.

Get an adult to help you

5 Let the mixture cool. Then turn it out of the tray and put your winter cake outside, out of reach of cats. Put out water, too.

4 Stir the melted fat into the dry mixture and pour it into the cake pan or muffin tray.

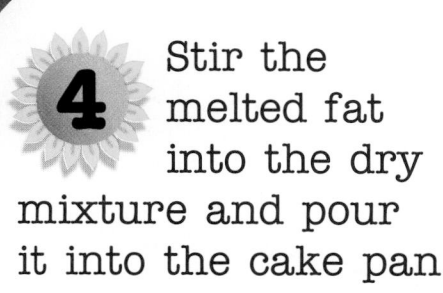

Bird food

Birds will find things to eat all over the yard.

Some birds feed on berries and fruit. Some catch insects in the air.

Caterpillars, snails, and worms make a juicy meal.

Small birds peck for seeds and insects on the ground.

In winter, when the ground is hard and there are no berries, birds will eat your winter cake.

Footprints

Birds are not the only visitors to the backyard who come looking for food and water. Other shy creatures come at night or when there is no one around. Their footprints will let you know who visited.

Hungry visitors

1 Fill a baking tray with damp sand and smooth it over. Put food scraps like brown bread, fruit, vegetables, and nuts on a plate. Pour milk or water into a saucer.

2 Put the food and liquid onto the baking tray and leave it in a quiet part of the yard. Check the tray for footprints in the morning and again in the evening.

3 Make a note of who has left tracks in the sand. Did they come at night or during the day? Look carefully, then smooth over the sand.

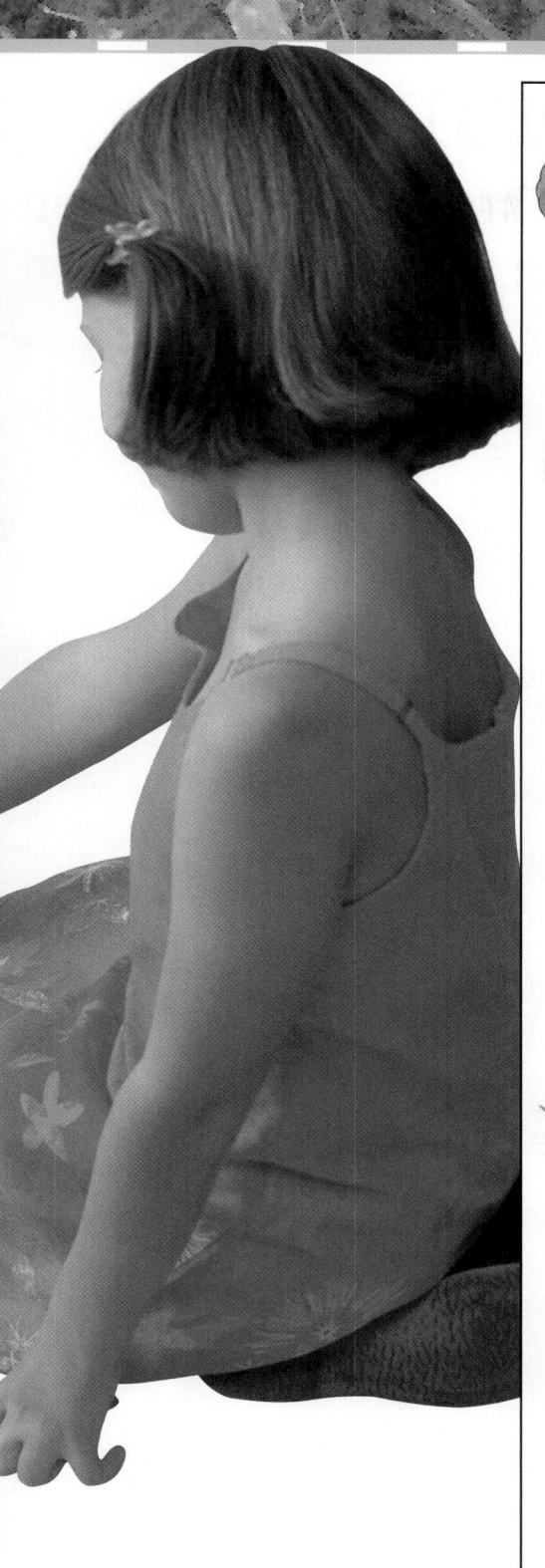

Identifying tracks

You can use these pictures to identify the footprints that have been made in your tray. These pictures are the same size as real animal footprints.

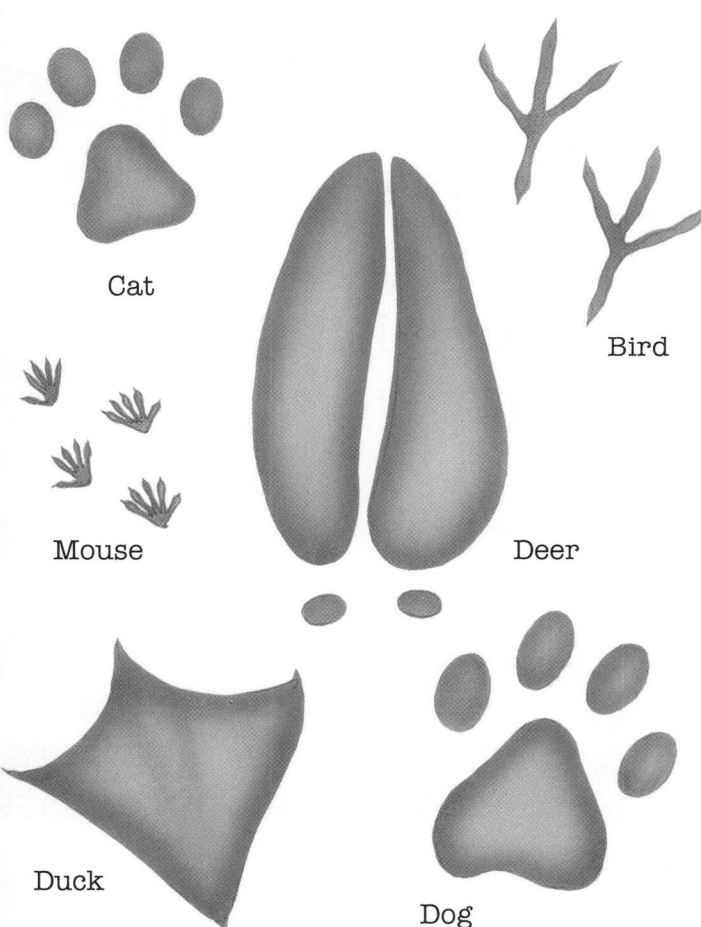

Cat

Bird

Mouse

Deer

Duck

Dog

If you can't see a print to match the ones in your tray, try to find the one that looks most like it. Can you tell if it is a bird or an animal? Is it big or small? Ask an adult to help you work out what any mystery prints are. You could look them up in a field guide.

Insect visitors

Look for insects in the soil, under stones, on plants, resting on walls, hiding in cracks, or swimming in water. Make a chart of the insects that live in or visit the backyard.

Where insects live

Dragonfly

Moth

Spot the insects

1 You will need a sheet of cardboard, a ruler, colored markers, and a magnifying glass.

2 Copy the chart in the picture onto your cardboard. You can add extra columns. Draw a moon if you spot an insect like a moth at night.

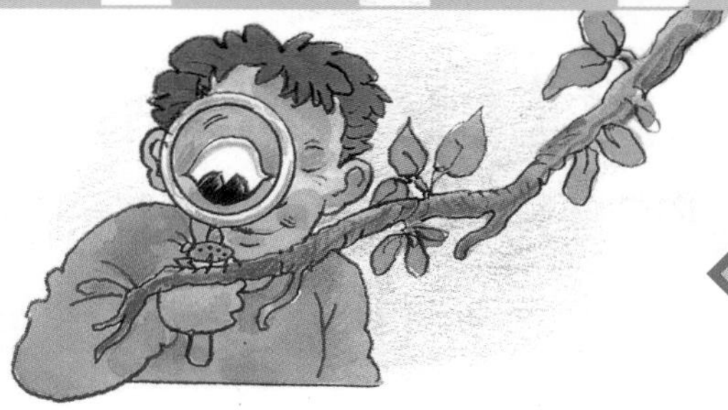

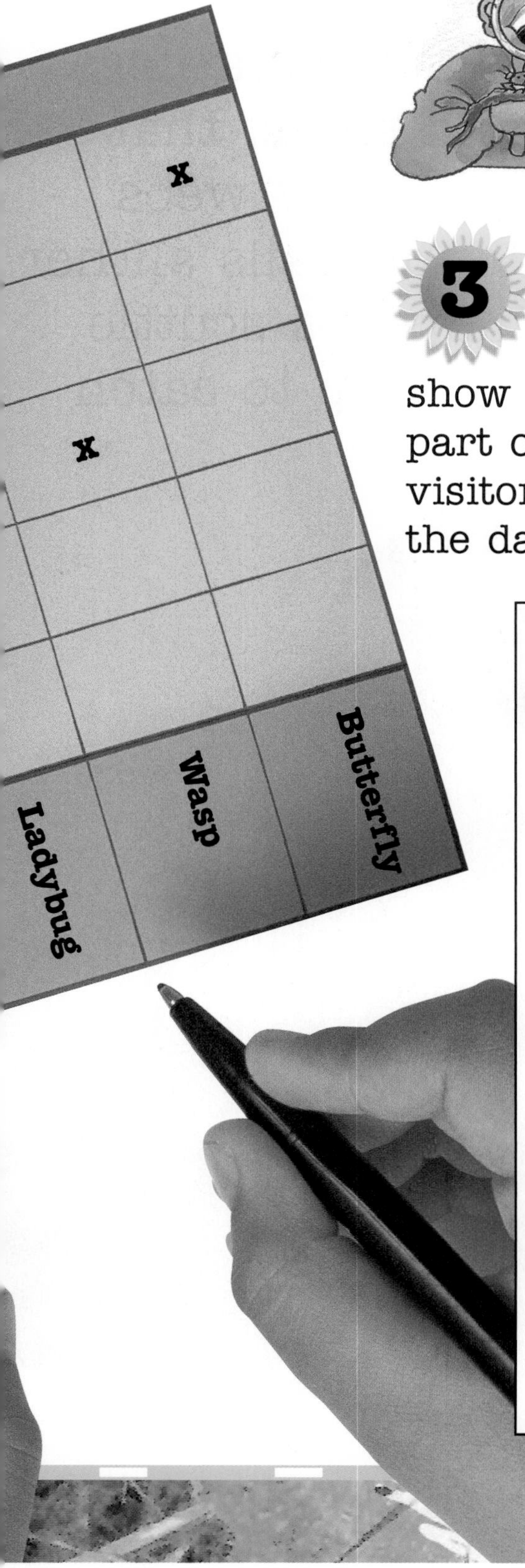

3 Look for insects in the backyard. Mark a cross on the chart to show what they are feeding on. What part of the yard has the most visitors? Do the insects come during the day or at night?

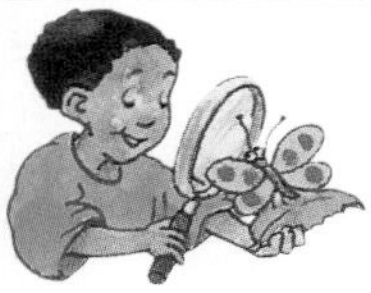

	Ladybug	Wasp	Butterfly
			x
		x	

A bug's parts

Insects all have six legs. They have a skeleton on the outside of their bodies and sensitive feelers called antennae. Many have wings.

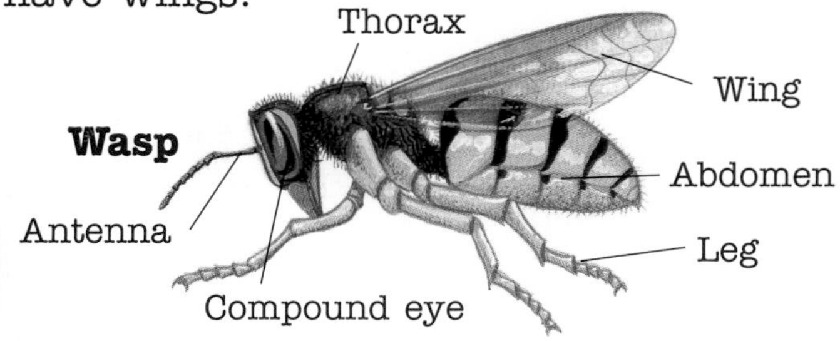

Wasp

Thorax

Wing

Abdomen

Leg

Antenna

Compound eye

Insects can look very different from each other. Beetles have hard, shiny cases to protect their delicate wings. The easiest way to tell if a creature is an insect is to count its legs.

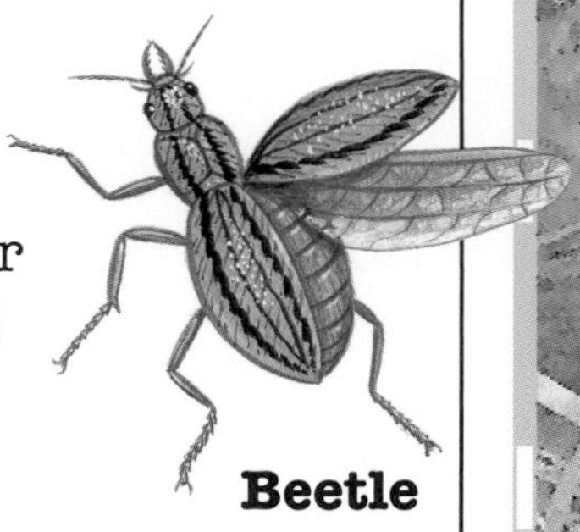

Beetle

Minibeasts

There are many small creatures, such as spiders and slugs, that are not insects. Spiders spin silky webs to catch their food. Slugs and snails slither along on silvery trails. Millipedes scuttle in dark, damp places. Set a trap to catch some minibeasts in your backyard.

Setting a trap

1 Dig a hole in the soil just deep enough to hold a small container. Put in pieces of fruit and a spoonful of cat food or dog food.

2 Cover the trap with a small rock, propping up one end with a stone to leave a small gap.

3 Leave the trap overnight. Lift the rock to see what you have caught. Before you let your minibeasts go, try to find out what they are.

Minibeast spotting

Use a magnifying glass and see if you can spot some of these creatures in your backyard.

A snail hides inside its shell when it is in danger.

Snail

Spiders are not insects because they have eight legs.

Spider

Millipedes, with hundreds of legs, eat leaves and dead plants.

Millipede

Slugs come out to look for food after rain.

Slug

Ants

Ants have six legs, so you know they are insects. Ants often move around in long trails, following the same path. This project will help you find out if there is a busy ants' nest in your backyard.

Ant trails

1 Mix two teaspoons of sugar in a bowl half filled with warm water. Stir until the sugar dissolves.

2 Add small pieces of stale bread and leave them to soak for a few moments. Remove the bread before it gets too soggy and take it into the yard.

Bait

Bait

Nest

Bait

3 Put pieces of bread all over the yard as bait. Ants will find the food and carry it off, moving in a line. If you follow the line, you will find the ants' nest.

Bait

Bait

4 Draw a map of where you put the bread bait. Put in lines to show the paths the ants took to carry their food. The nest should be where all the lines meet.

Ants' nests

Ants live and work together in a nest underground. They build lots of tunnels. A queen ant lays eggs. Worker ants look for food and bring it back home along the tunnels.

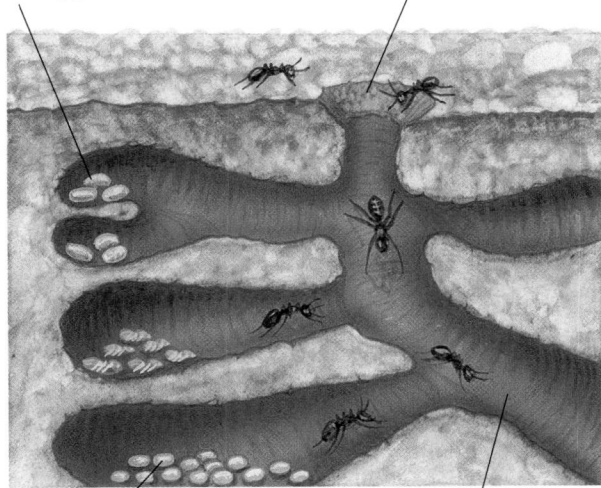

Older eggs

Entrance to nest

Young eggs

Main tunnel

Worms

As worms burrow along under the ground, they eat soil, leaving behind mounds of fine soil called worm casts. You can watch worms pull leaves and dead plants down into the soil to munch.

Worm watching

1 You will need a shoe box, a plastic trash bag, plastic wrap, leaves, tape, dead plants, soil, and worms.

2 Line the box with the plastic trash bag and secure it in place with tape. This will make the box waterproof.

3 Fill the box with damp soil and put in some worms you have dug up from the soil in the yard.

4 Let the worms burrow down into the soil, then sprinkle on the plants and leaves.

5 Cover the box with plastic wrap punched with holes to let in air. How long does it take for the leaves and plants to disappear?

Words on worms

Worms are not garden pests. Gardeners are very happy to have worms in the soil because they help to break it up. Breaking up the soil keeps it full of air, which is good for growing plants. Soil without any worms in it is solid, very heavy to dig, and not as good for growing things.

Chapter 4:
LIFE CYCLES

Animals and plants are alive, so we call them living things. All living things go through a life cycle. You can have fun learning about the different stages that animals and plants go through during their life cycles. You can also see what they need to grow and develop.

Contents

WHEEL OF LIFE 304
Make a life-cycle wheel.

REPRODUCTION 306
Look at who produces eggs.

GROWING UP 308
Make your own life scrapbook.

FOOD FOR GROWTH 310
Find out why we eat the food we do.

PLANTS AND SEEDS 312
Grow your own beans.

GROWING PLANTS 314
Find out what plants need to grow.

GROWING WITHOUT SEEDS 316
Make a potato maze.

BIRD NESTS 318
See what birds use to build nests.

NEWTS AND SNAKES 320
Learn about amphibians and reptiles.

BUTTERFLIES 322
Look at a butterfly's life cycle.

FOOD WEB 324
Build your own food web.

Wheel of life

Life cycles are made up of the stages that all living things go through as they grow and develop. Build a wheel of life to show how a living thing starts its life, then grows into an adult that can start another new life.

Life-cycle wheel

1 You will need two pieces of colored cardboard. Draw around a plate to make two circles and cut them out.

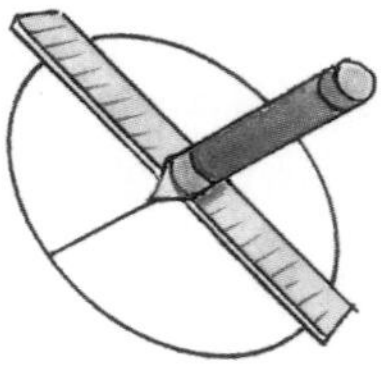

Get an adult to help you

2 Use a ruler to draw lines from top to bottom and side to side of one of the circles. This divides it into quarters. On the other circle, cut out a window. Decorate the rest of the circle.

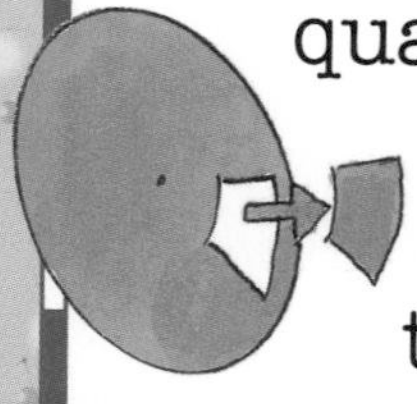

304

3 In each quarter, draw a picture of one stage of the life cycle of a living thing. This wheel shows the life cycle of a flower called a pansy.

•A bee lands on a pansy.

•The bee carries pollen to another pansy.

•The pansy makes seeds, dies, and the seeds fall to the ground.

•A new pansy plant shoots up.

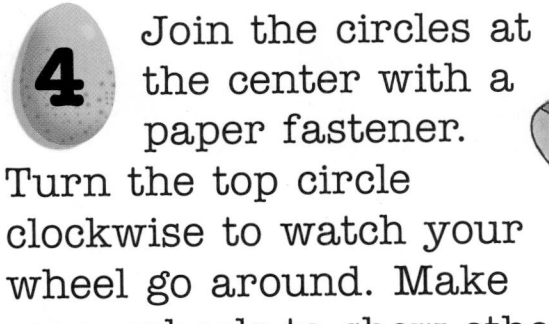

4 Join the circles at the center with a paper fastener. Turn the top circle clockwise to watch your wheel go around. Make more wheels to show other life cycles.

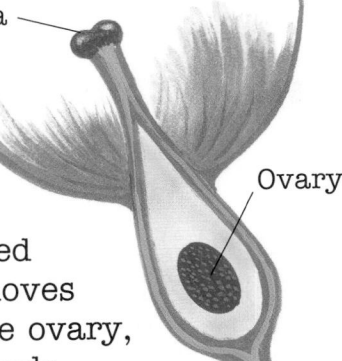

Pollen and seeds

A flower like a pansy makes new seeds when a bee rubs pollen from another pansy onto it.

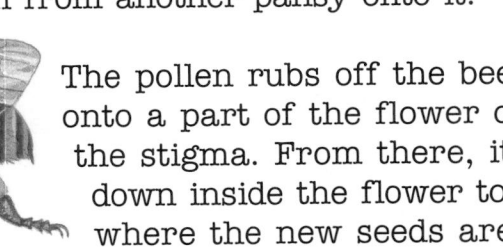

Pollen

The pollen rubs off the bee onto a part of the flower called the stigma. From there, it moves down inside the flower to the ovary, where the new seeds are made.

Stigma

Ovary

Reproduction

For life to go on, living things must reproduce. This means they must make a new baby or plant like themselves. New life usually begins in an egg inside a mother's body. The egg can start to grow when a seed from a male joins it.

WASH YOUR HANDS AFTER TOUCHING RAW EGG

Inside a hen's egg

1 Crack open a hen's egg onto a white plate. Try not to break the yolk. The shell protects the delicate inside.

A red spot inside the yolk is the growing baby chick, called an embryo.

Eggs

Many animals lay eggs. Some time later, the eggs hatch. Other baby creatures grow inside their mothers' bodies.

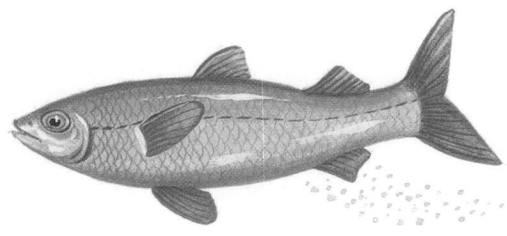

Fish lay a great number of eggs. The eggs float in the water and many are eaten by hungry sea creatures.

Female insects lay tiny eggs and leave them to hatch on their own.

Birds build nests to lay their eggs in. The mother and father birds often take turns to keep the eggs warm and safe.

People and many other animals don't lay eggs. Instead, the egg is inside the mother. When seed, called sperm, from the father joins the egg, a new baby starts to grow. It grows inside the mother until it is ready to be born.

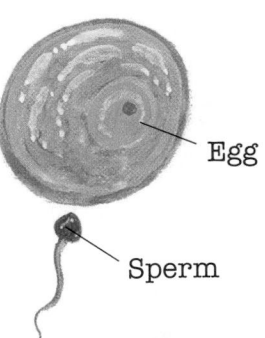

Egg

Sperm

The yellow yolk is food for the embryo.

The egg white is like a cushion around the embryo.

2 Look at the inside of the egg. The egg is full of food for the growing chick. Now cook and eat the egg.

Growing up

It takes many years for a human baby to become an adult. You have grown and changed a great deal since the day you were born. You will stop growing one day but you will never stop changing and learning.

Life scrapbook

1 Stick a picture of you as a baby into a scrapbook. Write down how much you weighed.

2 Ask a friend to draw around your feet on paper. Cut out the shapes and stick them into your scrapbook.

3 Draw around your hands. Do this each year and see how much they grow.

4 Write down how much you weigh. Are you much heavier than when you were born?

Big and small

All animals grow from babies to adults. Some grow much faster than others.

Elephants

An elephant can live for 75 years. A baby stays with its mother for up to ten years.

Mice

After only three weeks, baby mice have to leave their nest to look for their own food.

Parrots

Parrots can live for a very long time. Some have lived to be 80 years old.

Mayflies

Mayflies are born, live their life, and die all in one day. They have one of the shortest lifetimes of any creature.

5 Stick a long piece of paper to a wall. Ask a friend to mark how tall you are. A year later, do the same and see how much you have grown.

Food for growth

You need to eat food from four food groups every day. Proteins help you grow and keep you healthy. Fats keep you warm. Carbohydrates give you energy and keep you going. Fruit and vegetables are full of vitamins.

Lunch boxes

1 Make sure that you pack your lunch box with a healthy meal. Cheese and ham in your sandwiches will give you protein and some fat. Bread will give you carbohydrates.

2 Cheese, yogurt, and butter are all made from milk. They give you protein and some fat. You should also drink plenty of water every day.

Carnivores and herbivores

Animals eat different kinds of food. Animals that eat meat are called carnivores. Animals that just eat plants are called herbivores.

A tiger is a carnivore. It hunts and kills its prey for food.

Sheep are herbivores. They graze on grass.

Ladybugs are carnivores. They feed on tiny bugs called aphids. Aphids suck juice called sap from plants.

3 Fruit and vegetables give you vitamins, minerals, and roughage. Roughage helps your food pass easily through your body.

A giraffe is a herbivore. It stretches its long neck to reach up to eat leaves from tall trees.

4 A lot of salt and sugar is not good for you, so don't pack too many cookies and salty snacks.

Plants and seeds

A bean is a kind of seed that you find inside a bean pod. Plant a bean from a pack and watch it grow into a new bean plant. Look carefully at the different stages the bean goes through.

Plant a bean

1 You will need cotton balls, a glass jar, and beans from a pack.

2 Soak the beans in water overnight to soften their tough skin. Line the jar with cotton. Pour in water until the cotton is damp but not soaking wet.

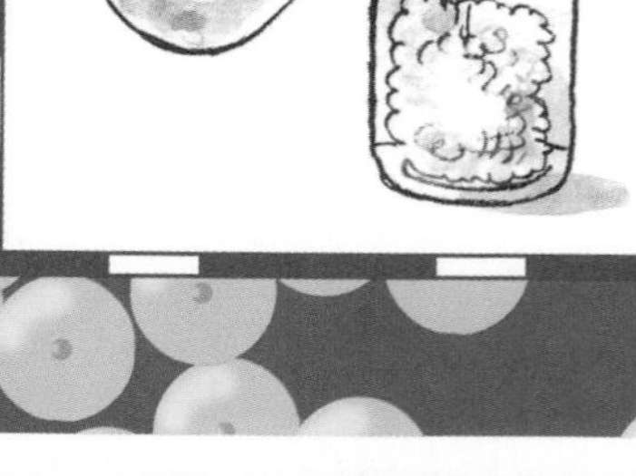

3 Space the beans around the edge of the jar. Put the jar on a windowsill. Dampen the cotton every day.

4 After a few days, the beans will begin to sprout. Make a diary of how they grow. Watch how the roots grow down before the shoots begin to grow up.

Life cycle of a flowering plant

The life cycle of a nasturtium flower follows the same pattern as many other flowering plants.

Spring is the time for seeds under the earth to start growing.

A shoot pushes through the earth toward the light.

In warm weather, flowers bloom. Insects feed on a sweet juice made by the flower, called nectar.

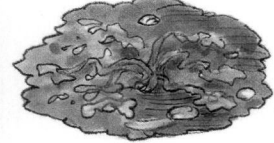

Frost kills the plant, and its seeds fall to the earth where they rest until spring.

Growing plants

Plants need sunlight, water, air, and nutrients from the soil to be able to make their own food and grow. Without even one of these, the plant will not be strong and healthy and may even die. Find out what happens to a plant without sunlight, water, or air.

Happy plants

1 You will need four young plants. Water the first one. Leave it in an airy place in sunlight. Watch how well it grows.

2 Put the second plant next to the first, but don't water it. It will soon start to wilt.

3 Water the third plant, but put a box over it. The green will fade and the plant will begin to die.

Plant survival

Plants have found ways of surviving in all corners of the earth.

Desert plants have long roots. These search for water, which is stored in fleshy stems.

Rain-forest creepers with shiny leaves climb up the tall trees toward the sunlight.

Mountain plants grow close to the ground or in cracks away from cold winds.

4 Spread petroleum jelly on a leaf of the last plant so that air can't get to it. Watch the leaf shrivel after a few days.

3

4

Growing without seeds

Some plants can grow new plants without seeds. A potato is a root that is packed with the food that the new potato plant needs in order to grow. It has little buds called eyes.

A potato maze

1 You can grow a new potato plant from an old potato. You will need a potato with eyes, a shoe box with a lid, cardboard, scissors, and tape.

Get an adult to help you

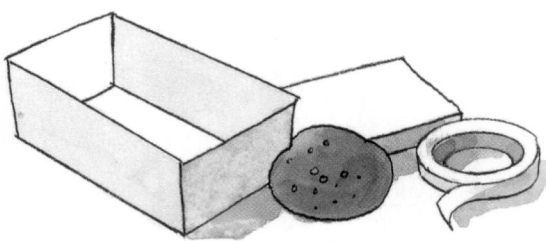

2 Cut three strips of cardboard for the maze and make a hole in one end of the box.

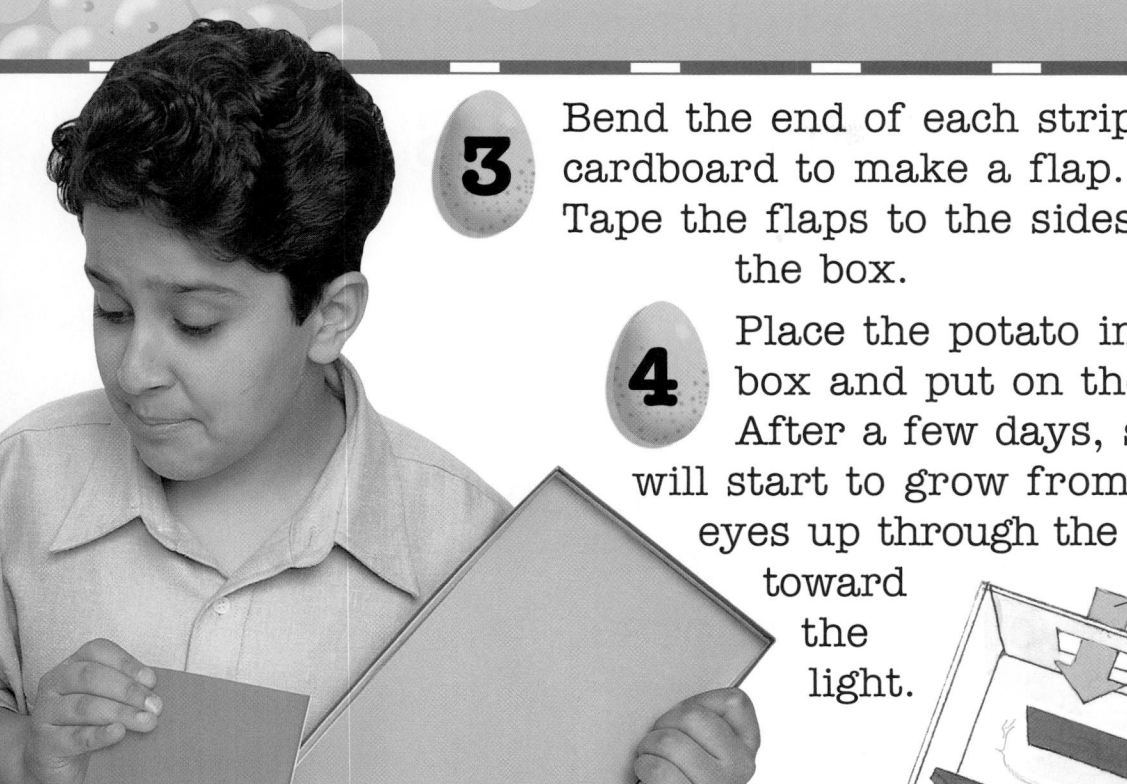

3 Bend the end of each strip of cardboard to make a flap. Tape the flaps to the sides of the box.

4 Place the potato in the box and put on the lid. After a few days, shoots will start to grow from the eyes up through the maze toward the light.

Light

New plants from old plants

New plants can start to grow from parts of old plants.

A new garlic plant will grow from a piece of a garlic bulb.

Strawberry plants grow long stems called runners. New little plants grow along the runners.

You can grow a new African violet plant from a leaf planted in soil.

A piece of a geranium plant will grow roots if you put it in water or plant it.

Shoots will grow from a carrot top if you put it in water.

Bird nests

All birds lay eggs. Most birds build a nest to keep their eggs safe and warm until they hatch. Put out some materials in spring and see which ones a bird will choose to build its nest.

Bird box

1 Ask an adult to make or buy a strong bird box. Mount it securely on a tree where it is safe from cats.

2 Collect materials like straw, cotton balls, dry leaves, hay, feathers, yarn, shredded paper, or even hair from a hairbrush.

3 Spread your materials on the ground around the nesting box. See which ones the birds choose. Birds mostly use natural materials like sticks, leaves, mud, and moss to build their nests.

4 Watch the birds carry the materials into the nesting box. Some may take the nesting materials to build a nest nearby.

Life cycle of a blue tit

Like all birds, a blue tit begins its life inside an egg.

The adult bird keeps the egg warm until it hatches.

The egg hatches into a hungry baby bird called a nestling.

The young bird begins to look for its own food and learns to fly. It is now a fledgling.

It can soon manage without help from its mother and father.

The adult bird finds a mate. The female lays eggs in the spring.

Newts and snakes

Newts, frogs, and toads all belong to a group of animals called amphibians. They lay their eggs, called spawn, in water. Baby amphibians live underwater. As adults, they live in water and on land. Reptiles, like snakes, have scaly skins and lay eggs.

Life cycle of a newt

1 A female newt lays hundreds of eggs on underwater plants. The eggs are surrounded by jelly.

2 Baby newts begin to grow inside the eggs. They feed on the jelly until they hatch out as tadpoles.

3 Newt tadpoles have gills to let them breathe underwater, like fish. They grow lungs to let them breathe air, and they also grow legs.

4 Adult newts live on land. They go back into the water only to keep their skin wet and to lay eggs.

Life cycle of a snake

1 Snakes are reptiles. They lay their eggs on the ground and then leave the eggs to hatch by themselves.

2 Newly hatched snakes are called hatchlings. They look just like tiny adult snakes.

4 Snakes grow and shed their skin all their lives. Adult snakes lay eggs, and a new life cycle begins.

3 As snakes grow, they shed their skin. They grow a new skin, wriggle out of the old skin, and leave it behind in one piece.

Other reptile eggs

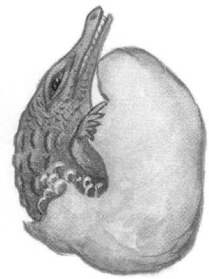

Crocodiles lay their eggs in sand. When they hatch, the mother carries them in her mouth to the water.

Mother turtles bury their eggs in the sand, then swim away. The hatchlings make their own way down to the sea.

321

Butterflies

Some creatures change shape as they become adults. Tadpoles become frogs, and caterpillars become butterflies. This change of shape is called metamorphosis. Find a caterpillar eating leaves. You may be able to follow its metamorphosis into a butterfly.

2 Caterpillars hatch and feed on the leaves where the eggs were laid.

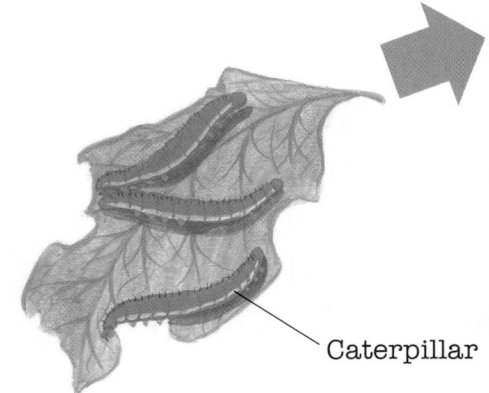

Caterpillar

Life cycle of a butterfly

1 The male butterfly finds a female butterfly to mate with. After mating, the female lays her eggs on a leaf, then flies off.

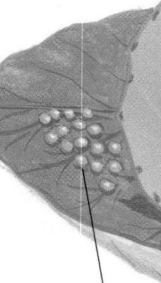

Eggs

3 Each caterpillar hangs by a silk thread and turns into a chrysalis. Inside the chrysalis, amazing changes take place.

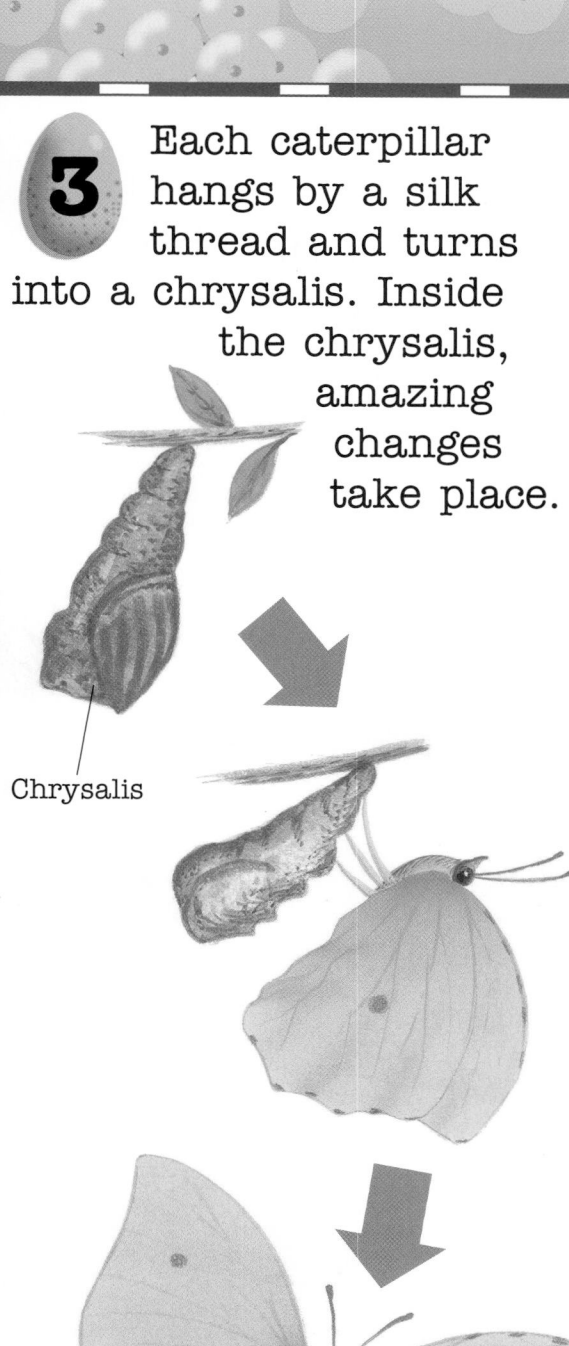

Chrysalis

Dragonfly

A dragonfly is another insect that changes shape.

A male and a female dragonfly mate as they fly through the air.

The female lays her eggs underwater. The eggs hatch into nymphs.

A nymph spends a year underwater. It climbs a reed, splits its skin, and comes out as a dragonfly.

4 A butterfly struggles out of the chrysalis, dries its wings in the sun, and flies away.

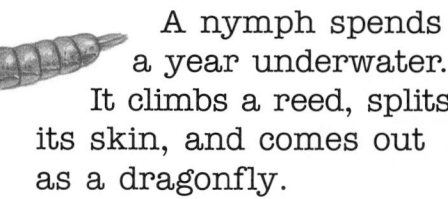

5 Butterflies often live for only a short time. They have an important job to do. They must start a new life cycle.

Food web

All living things depend on the sun. Plants use the sun's energy to make their food. Herbivores eat plants, and carnivores eat the plant eaters. Make a food web to see how life on earth is linked together.

Weave a web

1 Think of animals that live near each other to put in your food web. Draw or cut out pictures of them from magazines.

2 Draw and cut out pictures of air, water, the sun, and some plants. Glue all of your pictures onto folded strips of cardboard.

Get an adult to help you

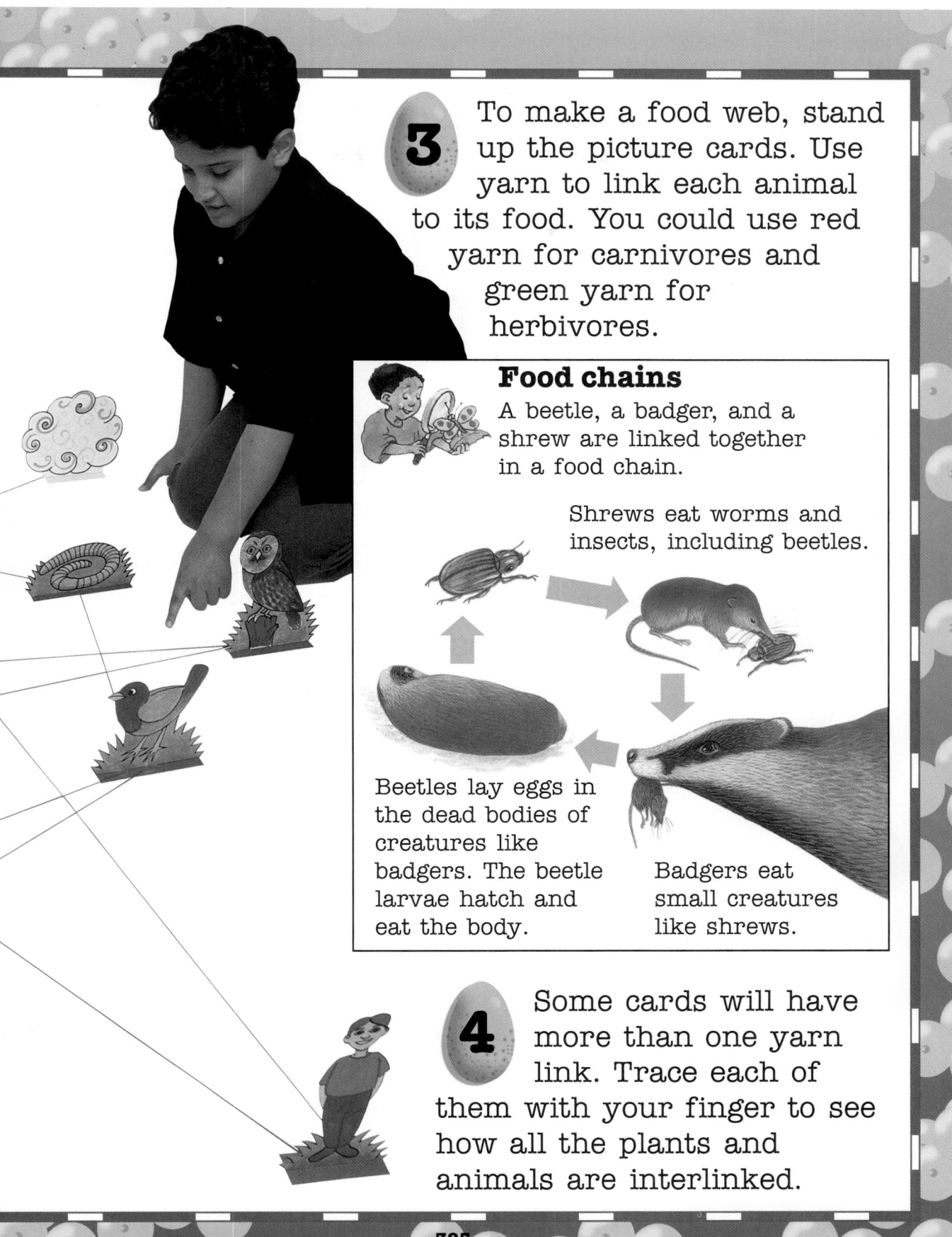

3 To make a food web, stand up the picture cards. Use yarn to link each animal to its food. You could use red yarn for carnivores and green yarn for herbivores.

Food chains

A beetle, a badger, and a shrew are linked together in a food chain.

Shrews eat worms and insects, including beetles.

Beetles lay eggs in the dead bodies of creatures like badgers. The beetle larvae hatch and eat the body.

Badgers eat small creatures like shrews.

4 Some cards will have more than one yarn link. Trace each of them with your finger to see how all the plants and animals are interlinked.

Chapter 5:
WOODS AND MEADOWS

Woods and meadows are places you can visit that are full of many different kinds of wildlife. You can have fun playing a guessing game about where animals live. Learn how to draw meadow flowers and how to look closely at tiny insects. See how to plant a tree and learn how to paint and cut out a camouflaged bird.

Contents

LIFE IN A TREE 328
Look at what lives in a tree.

DIFFERENT WOODLANDS 330
Make rubbings of different leaves.

THE WOODLAND FLOOR 332
See what you can find under a tree.

WOODLAND ANIMALS 334
Look for signs of woodland animals.

WOODLAND BIRDS 336
Learn about cuckoos and other birds.

PLANT A TREE 338
Collect and plant tree seeds.

GRASSES 340
Make a grasses guessing game.

MEADOW FLOWERS 342
Learn about some meadow flowers.

MEADOW INSECTS 344
Sweep meadow grasses for insects.

MEADOW BIRDS 346
Paint a camouflaged bird.

MEADOW ANIMALS 348
Make a meadow mix and match.

Life in a tree

Trees are the biggest plants on the earth. They can live to be very old. All kinds of plants and animals live in the different parts of a tree. Find out which creatures have made their home in a tree near you.

Shake a limb

1 You need a magnifying glass and a large sheet of cardboard. Lay the cardboard under a low branch of a tree.

2 Shake the branch gently. Look through the magnifying glass at the creatures that fall onto the cardboard. Try to find out what each one is.

Tree creatures

Small creatures can find food in every part of a tree. Sometimes, too many insects can kill a tree.

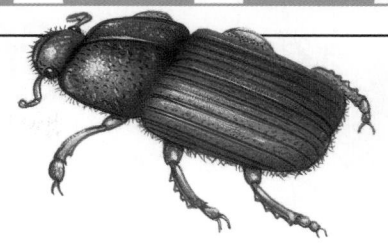

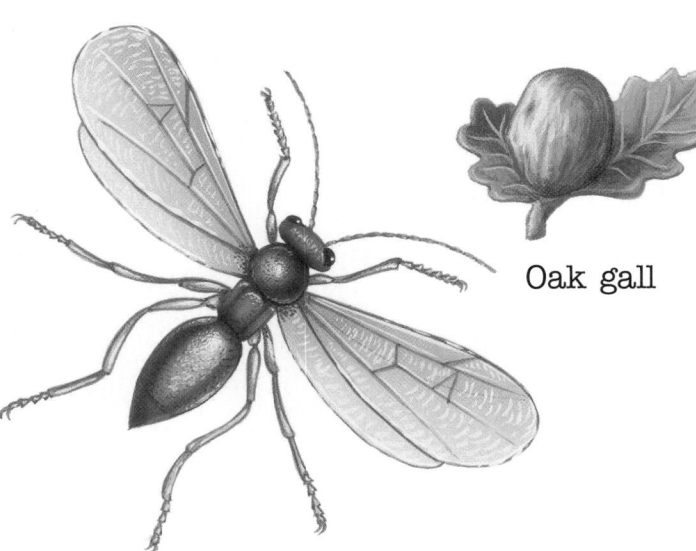

Oak gall

Adult bark beetles feed on buds and new leaves. Their tiny young, called larvae, live in the tree trunk and chew wood.

Gall wasp grubs live inside oak galls. They come out when they have grown into adult gall wasps.

A nut weevil drills a tiny hole and lays its eggs inside a nut such as an acorn. The grubs use the nut for food.

Caterpillars that are the same color as leaves or twigs can be difficult to spot. Holes in the leaves tell you where they have been feeding.

Hole

Acorn

3 Now look up into the branches, in the bark, and around the roots. What other creatures can you see?

PUT CREATURES BACK WHERE YOU FOUND THEM

Different woodlands

Trees grow together to form different kinds of woodland. You can tell what kind of woodland you are in by the shape of the leaves. Deciduous trees have wide, flat leaves. Evergreen trees often have tough, shiny leaves.

Sorting and rubbing leaves

1 Try to visit different kinds of woodland. Pick up leaves from the woodland floor.

2 Sort your leaves into piles of different shapes. Use a book to find out which trees they come from. Are they from deciduous or evergreen trees?

3 Make leaf rubbings by laying paper over each leaf, with the rough side of the leaf facing upward. Rub evenly over the paper with a crayon.

Deciduous and evergreen trees

The leaves on deciduous trees change color in the fall, then fall off the tree in winter. Evergreen trees keep their leaves all year round. Conifers, such as pine trees, are evergreens. They have long, thin leaves called needles.

Sugar maple   Horse chestnut

Sugar maples and horse chestnuts are deciduous trees.

Scots pine   Holly

Scots pines and holly trees are evergreens. Even evergreen trees will shed a few leaves as new ones grow.

The woodland floor

In early spring, before leaves have grown on the trees, the floor in deciduous woods is filled with light. Evergreen woods are always quite dark as the leaves keep out the light. See what you can find on different woodland floors.

Circle a tree

1 To see what lies under a tree, you can circle it. You will need thick string, twigs, a notebook, and a pencil.

2 Press the twigs firmly into the ground around a tree. Loop the string on the ground around the twigs to make a circle.

3 Look carefully at the ground inside the string circle. Draw or make a note of what you see.

Mosses, lichens, and ferns

Mosses, lichens, and ferns are all plants that have no flowers. Look out for them growing on a woodland floor.

Lichens grow on rocks, trees, and soil. They grow very slowly and live for a long time.

Mosses spread over damp ground and on wet logs.

Ferns can grow in many different kinds of soil. Their tightly curled stems open out into green fronds.

DON'T TOUCH DROPPINGS OR FUNGI

4 Use your notes to make a chart of the area under the tree. Draw a circle on a piece of cardboard for the string. Fill in all the things you saw.

Woodland animals

Woodland animals are usually very shy. There are plenty of places to hide in the woods, so they are hard to spot. But you can listen and look for signs that tell you they are not far away.

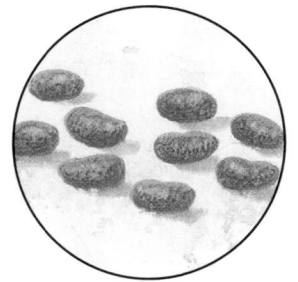

Deer droppings

Spot the signs

1 Look for deer droppings and footprints. A tree with no low-growing leaves might have been browsed (eaten) by a passing deer. In some places, you can spot where a deer has nibbled a ring of bark from a young tree. This can sometimes kill the tree.

Deer browse low-growing leaves into a straight line.

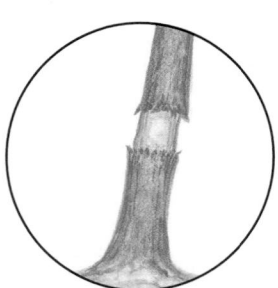

Bark nibbled by deer

2 Badgers look for food at night. They live in holes called sets. See if you can spot bits of plants that they drag into their sets for bedding. Look for badger fur caught on wire.

DO NOT TOUCH BARBED WIRE

Squirrel drey

Squirrel food litter

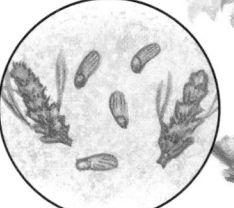

3 Squirrels dart along branches and up and down tree trunks. They build homes called dreys high up in trees. Look under trees for nuts and cones they have dropped.

Hunters and hunted

Foxes and wolves hunt and kill animals that feed on woodland plants. People hunt and eat woodland deer and wild boar.

A red fox has pointed ears and sharp eyes to listen and look for prey.

A boar is a kind of wild pig. It uses its blunt snout to root for food on the woodland floor.

A wood mouse has sharp teeth for nibbling seeds and nuts. It has to watch out for hungry foxes.

Woodland birds

Woods are good places to look for birds. Walk quietly because sudden noises and movements will frighten them away. In spring, birds build nests in hollow trunks or branches. In summer and fall, they find insects, seeds, nuts, and berries to eat. In winter, they find shelter in the trees.

Cuckoo

1 Cuckoos fly south in winter to find food in warmer places. In spring, they fly back north to breed.

2 The mother cuckoo looks for a nest belonging to another bird. She throws out an egg from the nest, lays one of her own in its place, then flies off.

Sights and sounds

Sometimes it is hard to spot birds through the leaves, especially in darker evergreen woods. Look for flashes of color as they fly past, and listen for the noises they make.

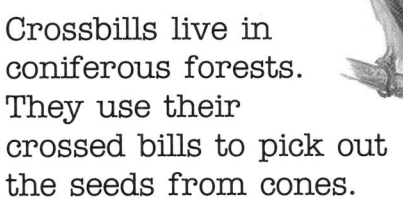

A woodpigeon makes a soft cooing sound. It hops and flies up in the branches, but finds its food on the ground.

Jays are colorful crows and have a harsh cry. They will eat eggs from the nests of smaller birds.

You can hear woodpeckers tapping at tree trunks as they look for insects or drill out a nest hole.

Crossbills live in coniferous forests. They use their crossed bills to pick out the seeds from cones.

3 The cuckoo chick hatches and grows quickly. It pushes the other eggs and smaller chicks out of the nest.

4 The adopted parent birds are kept very busy feeding their big, hungry cuckoo chick.

Plant a tree

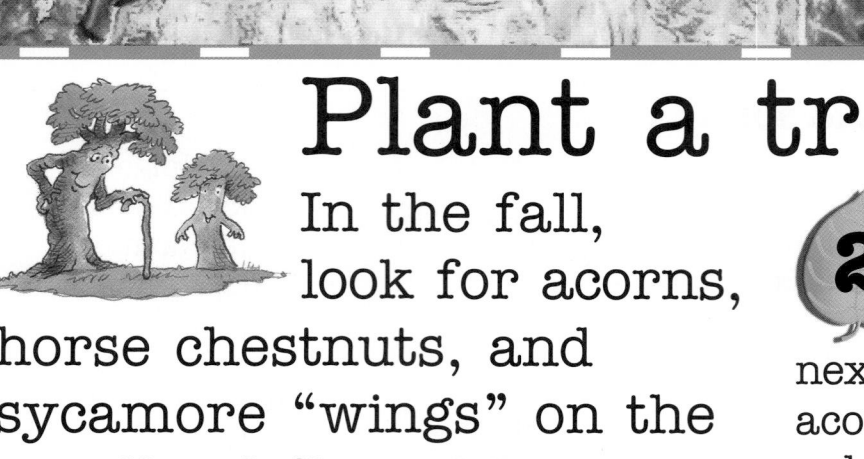

In the fall, look for acorns, horse chestnuts, and sycamore "wings" on the woodland floor. They are all different seeds that will grow into new young trees in the spring. Collect some seeds and try to grow trees from them.

2 Make labels and push them into the soil next to the seeds. An acorn grows into an oak tree and a horse chestnut into a horse chestnut tree.

CHESTNUT

HORSE CHESTNUT

SCOTS PINE

See it grow

1 In the spring, push your seeds into the soil, about 1 inch deep. Trees grow very tall, so leave enough room around each one for roots and branches to spread.

OAK

3 Trees grow slowly, so be patient. Some seeds may not grow at all. Make a chart to record the growth of your first shoot.

Tree rings

Each year, a new layer grows around a tree trunk and makes a ring. By counting the rings inside the trunk of a fallen tree, you can tell the tree's age.

It would take a long time to count the rings of giant trees called sequoias – they can live for over a thousand years.

339

Grasses

The grass in your local park or yard is just one of more than ten thousand different kinds of grasses. Grazing animals like sheep, horses, and cows eat grass. But did you know that you eat grass, too?

Grasses we eat

1 Wheat, rice, corn, and oats are grasses that farmers grow for us to eat. Copy pictures of them onto four pieces of cardboard and label them.

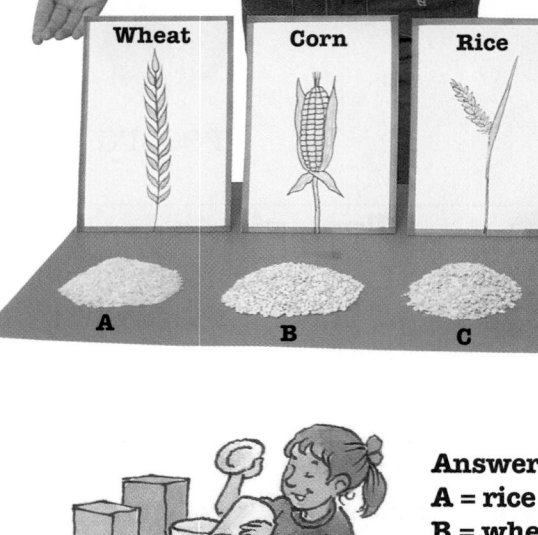

Wheat   Corn   Rice   Oats

A   B   C   D

2 Pour some dry rice, popcorn kernels, flour (or wheat grains), and dry oatmeal in four piles on a piece of cardboard.

Answers:
A = rice
B = wheat grains
C = oats
D = corn kernels

3 Now ask a friend to match each of the four piles to the picture of the crop it came from.

From field to food

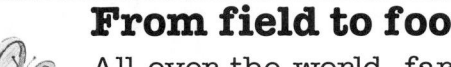

All over the world, farmers grow different kinds of grasses for food. These are called cereal crops. The ripe seeds are the grains. They give us some of our most important food.

Wheat is grown in enormous fields. The grains are ground into flour to make bread and pasta.

Rice is grown underwater in fields called paddies. We cook rice or grind the grains to make breakfast cereals.

Corn gives us corn on the cob, which is good to cook and eat. The grains can be ground into flour.

Oatmeal comes from oats. We use it to make hot cereal and cookies.

Meadow flowers

In the summer, you can see colorful flowers dotted among the tall meadow grasses. They are bright red, blue, purple, and yellow to attract insects. See how many different flowers of each color you can find in a summer meadow.

Flower sketching

1 To sketch flowers, you will need a sketchbook, some colored pencils, and an eraser. Before you start sketching, study the color of the flowers, how many petals each one has, and the shape of their leaves.

Dandelion

Flower

Leaf

Wild flowers

A gardener chooses which flowers to grow in a garden. Meadow flowers grow naturally by spreading their seeds.

The common milkweed grows wild in North America. Soft floss from its seedpods is used for stuffing furniture.

Meadow buttercups have shiny yellow petals. If you hold one under your chin, it makes your skin look yellow like butter.

A thistle has a spiky stem and leaves. Its seeds are on parachutes that blow in the wind.

Look closely at a scabious flower to see that it is made up of a mass of tiny flowers.

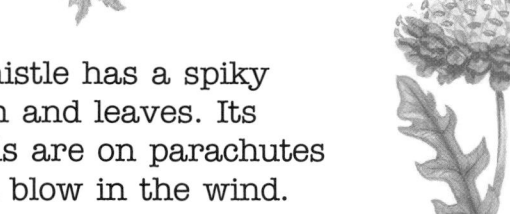

Poppy

Flower

Seed head

2 Copy the flowers as carefully and accurately as you can. You can look up any of the ones you don't know in a flower book later.

DO NOT PICK THE FLOWERS

Meadow insects

There are insects all over a meadow. Butterflies fly among the flowers, beetles scuttle along the ground, and bugs crawl up stems. Insects too small to spot can be swept up in a net.

Insect sweep

1 To look closely at insects, you will need a net with a long handle, a large sheet of paper, and a magnifying glass.

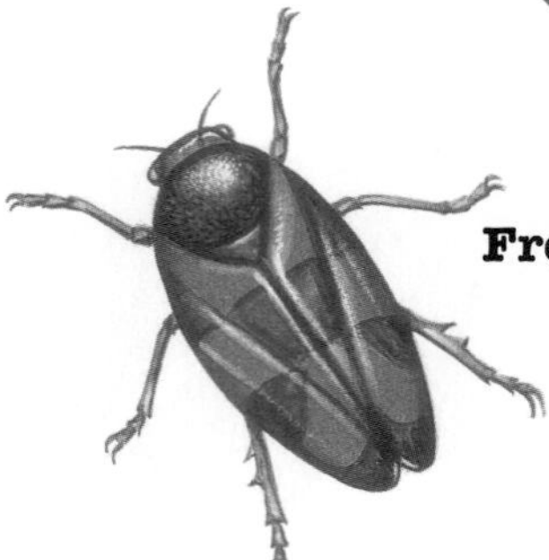

BE CAREFUL OF INSECTS THAT STING

Froghopper

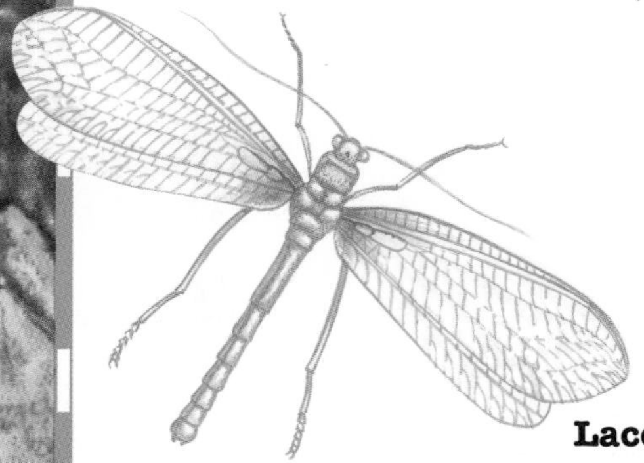

Horsefly

Lacewing

344

2 Sweep the net with a long stroke across the top of meadow grasses. Tip out what you have caught onto the paper.

Brimstone butterfly

Hoverflies

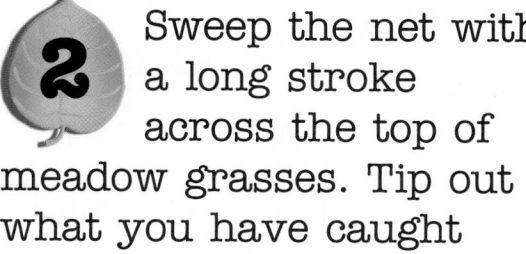

Grasshoppers

If you listen carefully, you are sure to hear grasshoppers chirping in a summer meadow. Grasshoppers call to each other either by rubbing their wings together or by rubbing part of their back legs against their wings. They have long, very strong back legs for hopping through the grass.

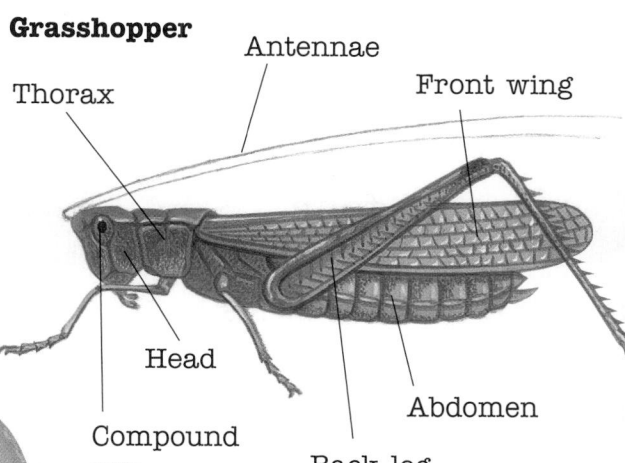

Grasshopper

Thorax
Antennae
Front wing
Head
Compound eye
Back leg
Abdomen

A type of grasshopper called a locust is a pest to farmers in many places. Locusts travel in vast swarms and can eat and destroy whole fields of crops.

3 Look carefully at the insects with your magnifying glass. When you have finished, tip them gently back onto the grass.

Meadow birds

Some birds visit meadows to eat seeds, worms, snails, and insects. Other birds build their nests there. The color of their feathers helps them to hide in the grass. This is called camouflage.

Camouflage a bird

1 You will need four big sheets of cardboard, paints, and scissors. Paint tall grasses onto one sheet of cardboard.

2 When the paint is dry, draw on a bird shape. Cut it out to leave a bird-shaped hole.

3 Paint the other three pieces of cardboard with different coloured splotches, as shown in the main picture. Use clean water for each color.

Birds in the grass

You can watch flocks of birds fly in and feed together in meadows all year round.

Canada geese arrive in flocks and graze on the grass. They make a loud, honking noise.

A skylark disguises where its nest is on the ground by landing away from it and then running to it through the grass.

Crows nest in platforms of sticks in treetops. They feed together in meadows, eating insects and seeds.

Lapwings sometimes arrive to feed in flocks of thousands. They are sometimes called "peewits" because of the sound they make.

4 Put each colored cardboard behind the cardboard with the bird cut out of it. Some colors will camouflage the bird in the grass better than others.

Meadow animals

Grass snakes, moles, rabbits, and foxes are all animals you might see in a meadow. They live in holes underground. Animal droppings or fur around a hole may let you know who lives there.

Match the homes

1 Draw pictures of a grass snake, a mole, a rabbit, and a fox on four pieces of cardboard. Cut them out.

2 Each animal digs a different shaped tunnel or hole. Copy a grass snake nest, a mole nest, a rabbit warren, and a fox lair onto four other pieces of cardboard.

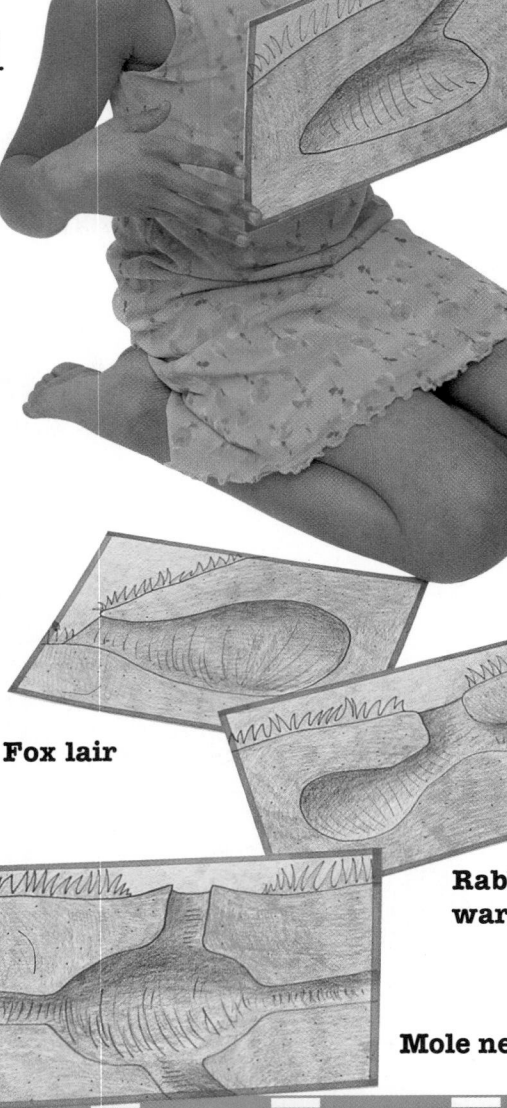

Snake nest

Fox lair

Rabbit warren

Mole nest

348

The harvest mouse

The tiny harvest mouse lives among the grass stalks in fields or meadows.

It hangs onto the stalks with its tail and back legs and uses its front paws to eat the grains.

The mother harvest mouse weaves a round nest made of grass or reed stalks for her babies. In places with hedgerows, she may build a more secure nest by winding stalks of grass around the thicker stalks in the hedge.

3 Hold up each of your tunnel pictures in turn. Ask a friend to match each animal to its home.

Get an adult to help you

Chapter 6:
ALL YEAR ROUND

As the seasons change, you can see differences in the plants and animals around you. Have fun keeping a nature diary, and build a museum of the seasons. Paint summer sunflower pots, make pictures from leaves in the fall, and see how you can help animals keep warm in winter. Listen to the changing noises through the year, and learn about migration.

Contents

NATURE DIARY 352
Make a picture diary each month.

WINDOW BOX 354
Plant an herb window box.

SEASONAL SOUNDS 356
Listen to the sounds of nature.

SUNFLOWERS 358
Paint pots and grow sunflowers.

NECTAR EATERS 360
Which creatures eat nectar?

COLLECTIONS 362
Make a museum of the seasons.

FRUIT SALAD 364
Collect seeded fruits and make a fruit salad.

CHANGING COLOR 366
Make lots of leaf pictures.

LOOKING FOR FOOD 368
Learn about creatures that migrate.

HIBERNATION 370
Build a shelter for a sleeping animal.

ASLEEP IN THE SOIL 372
Grow a plant from a bulb.

Nature diary

Look and listen carefully and you will notice fascinating things happening in nature all year round. You can make a nature diary to keep a record of the things you spot at different times of year, both in the city and in the countryside.

Month by month

1 To make a nature diary, you will need a large pad, pen and pencils, glue, and tape. Make a page for each month like the one in the picture.

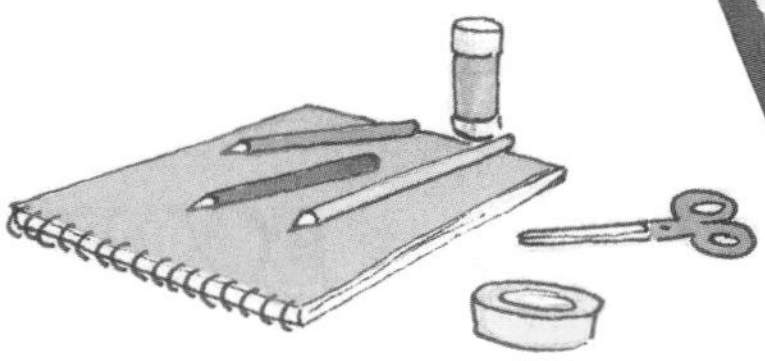

2 Collect leaves and pine needles from the ground. Leave them to dry, then glue them into your diary. Make sure you label them.

Pheasant

DECEMBER
Weather

1
2
3
4
5
6
7
8
9
10
12
13
14
15
16
17
18
19
20
21
22
23
24
25
26
27
28
29
30
31

Scots pine

Fern

Scots pine needles

Oak tree

NOTES:
2nd Dec: - Saw four pheasants pecking in a field.

Puddles frozen

Frost on the grass, bare trees

Keeping records

You can keep records for your nature diary in many different ways. The more ways you use, the more interesting your diary will be.

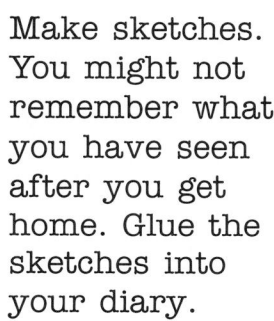

Hang a thermometer outside and record the temperature each day. Write down the different things you spot on hot and cold days.

Make sketches. You might not remember what you have seen after you get home. Glue the sketches into your diary.

If you have a camera, take photographs. You may notice something you didn't spot at first when you see the print.

3 Draw pictures and write notes about interesting things you see. Every day, copy one of the symbols below to show the weather.

Sunny   Cloudy   Rainy   Snowy   Stormy

Window box

You can grow plants all year round even if you don't have a backyard. Try planting herbs in a window box. When they have grown, pinch the leaves to smell the herbs' fragrance.

Indoors and outdoors

1 You will need packets of herb seeds and a window box with compost in it.

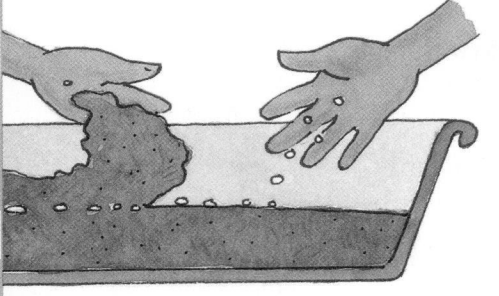

2 Sprinkle the seeds on the compost. Leave space between the different seeds. Lay more compost on top. Put the box on an indoor windowsill or, in spring or summer, outside.

 **4** When the herbs have grown, you can snip off the leaves to use for cooking. Only cut off what you need. The leaves will grow back again.

Herb garden

Herbs from an herb garden can be used for flavoring food, for brewing herbal teas, and for treating illnesses.

 Rosemary tea is good for soothing headaches and upset stomachs.

 The leaves of chives give an onion flavor to salads.

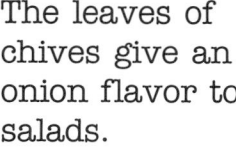 Parsley stalks have a stronger flavor than the leaves.

3 Water the herbs regularly. If they are outside, check that there has been enough rain.

 Basil is grown among other plants to keep insects away. You can add its leaves to tomato dishes.

Seasonal sounds

Go outside and listen carefully. Some sounds you hear are made by people or machines, but others are noises made by nature. Make a note of all the natural sounds you can hear at different times of the year.

Nightingale

Listen closely

1 In the early spring, listen for male birds singing to attract a mate. Later, baby birds cheep noisily for food.

Jay

2 In the summer, insects buzz among the flowers and grasshoppers sing in the grass.

Fly

Grasshopper

Geese

3 In the fall, listen for wings beating as flocks of geese fly south for the winter. In woods, listen for nuts falling into crunchy leaves.

Chestnut

Rough ridges on the grasshopper's back legs rub against the wings to make a chirruping noise.

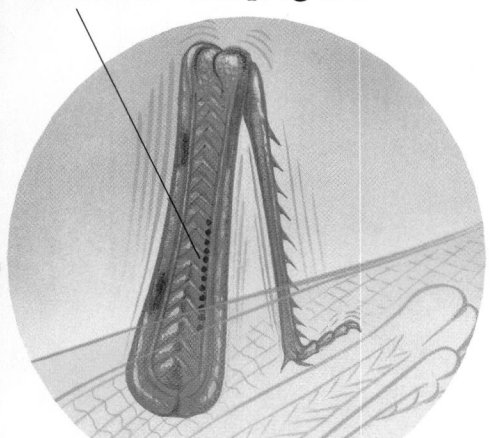

Croaking frogs

In the spring, male frogs gather together in ponds and croak loudly. Each one is trying to attract a female to mate with. They can even croak underwater.

Frog

Air sack

When a frog croaks, a pouch of skin under its chin fills with air and helps the croaking sound to carry over a distance. Some frogs are named after the sounds they make, such as the snoring puddle frog, which is found in parts of Africa.

4 In winter, listen for the harsh caw of crows. They nest in the tops of trees and you can sometimes see them looking for food in trash.

Crow

Sunflowers

Sunflowers are very useful plants. Animals eat the leaves, yellow dye is made from the petals, and oil is pressed from the seeds. Plant a sunflower seed in spring, and by the summer it will have grown taller than you!

Painting and planting

1 You will need a packet of sunflower seeds, soil, three big flower pots, and paints.

2 Paint pictures of sunflowers on the outside of the pots. Plant two or three seeds in each pot. Water them regularly.

3 As the shoots appear, leave the strongest shoot in each pot to grow and pull up the others.

4 Your sunflowers will grow very tall. You can support the stems with sticks.

Follow the sun

Although sunflowers look like bright yellow suns, they are called sunflowers for another reason. In the morning, they face the rising sun. As the sun moves throughout the day, the sunflowers turn their heads to follow it across the sky.

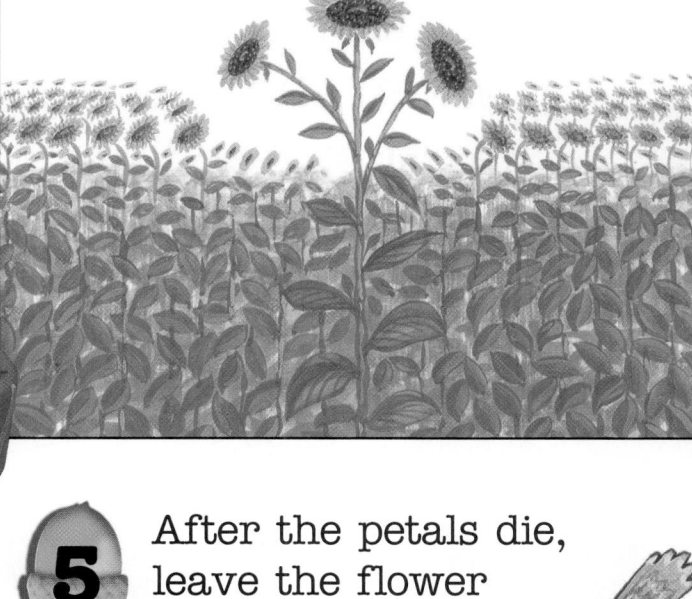

Noon

Morning

Evening

5 After the petals die, leave the flower heads for the birds. They will eat the seeds that form in the middle of the sunflower.

Nectar eaters

Butterflies visit flowers in the daytime. Moths often feed at night. They use long feeding tubes like drinking straws to suck sweet juice called nectar from the flowers. Look for butterflies and moths when the flowers they feed on are in bloom.

Butterfly watching

1 Butterflies are attracted to purple flowers with a strong scent, like buddleia flowers. Buddleia is also called the butterfly bush.

2 Make sketches and take notes of butterflies you see. This will help you look them up later in a field guide.

3 Use binoculars to help you spot butterflies. This will let you see their markings more clearly and will let you watch without disturbing them. You might even see some having a drink from a puddle.

Feeding on flowers

Most butterflies live only for a short time in the summer when the flowers are out. Other creatures that drink nectar, such as hummingbirds, make long journeys to find flowers in bloom all year round.

Honeysuckle smells most strongly at night to attract moths.

Butterflies curl their feeding tubes under their heads when they are not in use.

Tiny Australian honey possums have long tongues to lick nectar from banksia flowers.

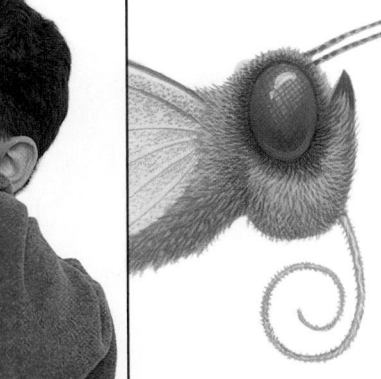

A hummingbird hovers in front of a flower while it sucks nectar with its long tongue.

Collections

Go for a walk at any time of year and you will find all kinds of interesting natural things. Make a collection for each season, or for places you visit like the park or the seashore.

NEVER TAKE EGGS FROM NESTS

Make a minimuseum

1 Find a cardboard box with a good sized base. Cut down the sides to make a frame.

2 Line the box with colored paper. This will be the background for your minimuseum.

Get an adult to help you

Cockleshell

Garden snail shell

Chestnut

Chestnut husk

Maple leaf

Cedar cone

3 Arrange the objects you have collected in the box. Then carefully glue them down. Label each item clearly.

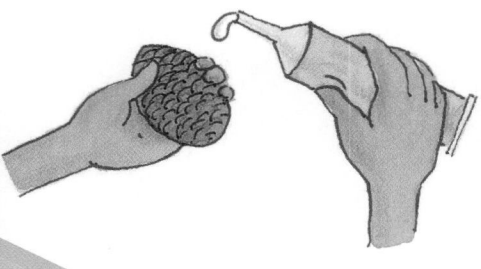

Crow feather

Beech leaf

Flying feathers

Birds are the only creatures that have feathers. Their feathers are shaped for the different jobs they have to do. You can tell which part of a bird's body a feather comes from.

Small covert feathers make the front of the wing smooth.

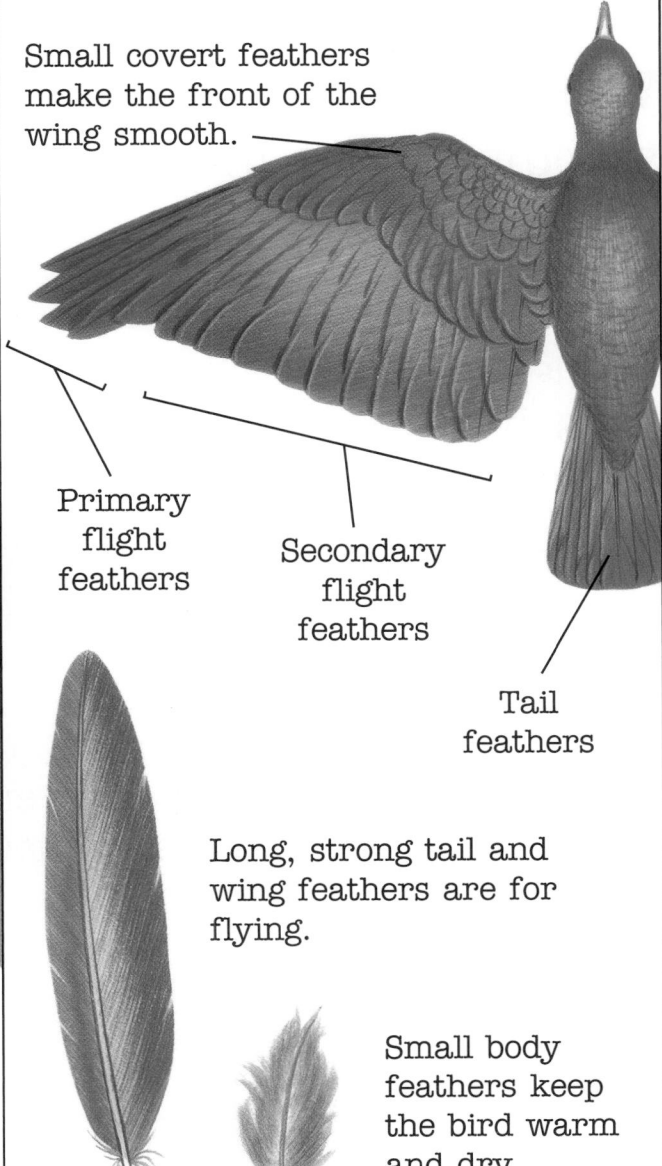

Primary flight feathers

Secondary flight feathers

Tail feathers

Long, strong tail and wing feathers are for flying.

Small body feathers keep the bird warm and dry.

Fruit salad

Fruit is the part of a plant that holds the seeds for a new plant to grow. When a flower dies, a fruit grows in its place. Tiny apples start to grow after the apple blossom dies in the spring. By fall, the apples are juicy and ready to eat.

Chop it up

1 Make a delicious fruit salad with lots of different fruits. First, cut each fruit in half or into quarters.

 **2** Scoop or pick out any seeds you can see. Look carefully at them through a magnifying glass. Remember which seeds come from which fruit.

Get an adult to help you

Wild berries

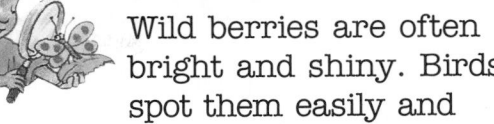 Wild berries are often bright and shiny. Birds spot them easily and swoop down to eat them. The birds then scatter plant seeds in their droppings, letting new plants grow.

In winter, bright red holly berries make a feast for hungry birds when there is little food around.

Mistletoe grows on the branches of other trees. Its white berries are poisonous to people and animals.

Blackberries grow wild on prickly brambles in early fall. Birds, animals, and people like to eat them.

SOME BERRIES ARE POISONOUS. ALWAYS ASK AN ADULT.

3 Ask a friend to match each seed to the fruit it came from.

Changing color

Trees make food using the green color in their leaves, called chlorophyll. In the summer, trees store the food they make. By the fall, the chlorophyll is not needed. It breaks down and turns the leaves red, brown, gold, and orange.

Leaf pictures

1 Collect as many different leaves in the fall as you can. Sort them into different shapes and colors.

2 You will need a clip frame and some colored paper. Cut out a piece of paper the same size as the clip frame and lay it over the base of the frame.

Winter leaves

By winter, most of the fallen leaves will have rotted away. Only leaf skeletons, evergreen leaves, and pine needles remain.

A leaf skeleton forms when the soft part of the leaf rots, leaving the tough stem and the veins.

Holly trees are evergreen. They keep their shiny, prickly leaves all year round.

Pine needles are very thin leaves that can survive the cold. They stay on the trees all winter.

3 Arrange the leaves into a pattern or a picture, then lay the glass on top. The glass will hold the leaves in position.

Get an adult to help you

Looking for food

In spring and summer, animals and birds can usually find plenty of food to eat. Many have to make long journeys to find enough food at other times of year. The journeys they make are called migrations.

Spot migrating birds

1 You can often identify different birds by the way they behave or fly. Before flying off, migrating swallows gather together on telephone wires.

Swallows

Geese

2 Migrating geese fly off together in a V shape. Watch for geese and swallows in the fall. Make picture cards to keep a record of all the migrating birds you spot.

Mexico

South America

Finding the way

Each year, animals, birds, and insects find their way across thousands of miles of land and sea. Whales swim halfway around the world and caribou travel between the Arctic plains and northern forests. Match the colored arrows to the arrows on the globe to see the migration routes.

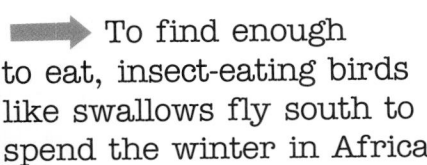

Humpback whales follow the coastline on their journey between cold polar and warm tropical seas.

To find enough to eat, insect-eating birds like swallows fly south to spend the winter in Africa.

Caribou follow the same paths each year. They go south in the fall and back north again in the spring.

North Pole

Europe

Arctic terns have a kind of built-in compass that helps them find their way from the North Pole to the South Pole and back again.

Africa

Monarch butterflies fly south from Canada in huge numbers, to spend the winter in Mexico.

Hibernation

In the winter, when there is very little food around, bears, bats, hedgehogs, and dormice go into a long sleep called hibernation. They hide away in a safe, dry place and sleep until the warm spring weather wakes them up again.

The big sleep

1 Make an animal shelter in the fall. Collect dry sticks and some straw and leaves for warm bedding.

NEVER DISTURB A HIBERNATING ANIMAL

2 In a quiet place outside, make a strong frame with the sticks. Cover it with earth, grass, and leaves and put the bedding inside.

3 Put a soft toy inside to test how safe and dry it is. Don't disturb the shelter. Perhaps an animal will choose to hibernate there.

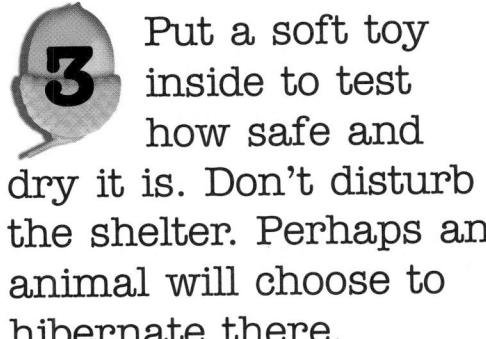

Winter and summer

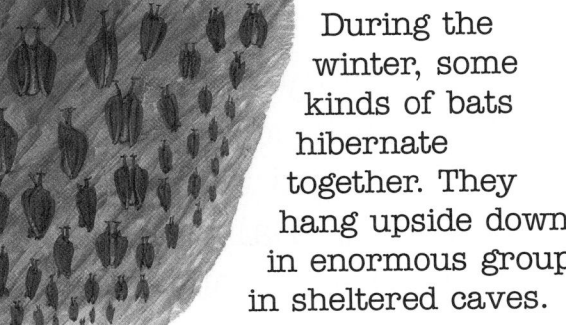

Some animals hibernate together in winter. Some sleep in summer when water is scarce. This summer sleep is called estivation.

During the long winter sleep in her den, a mother bear wakes to give birth to her cubs.

During the winter, some kinds of bats hibernate together. They hang upside down in enormous groups in sheltered caves.

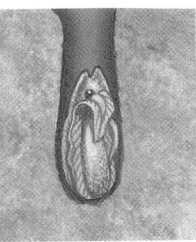

During the summer when their pools dry up, lungfish sleep in the mud. They use their lungs to breathe air.

Asleep in the soil

Just as some animals curl up and sleep all winter, bulbs are asleep, too, buried in the soil. They wait for the warm spring weather to come before they start to grow. See how a hyacinth bulb will not grow in the dark, but starts to grow shoots in the light.

Grow a bulb

1 Start this project in the fall. You will need a hyacinth bulb, a jar, and some toothpicks. Fill the jar nearly to the top with water.

2 Firmly stick four toothpicks in around the middle of the bulb. Balance the bulb in the top of the jar so its base is in the water.

3 Put the bulb in a dark closet. Check it occasionally to make sure it has enough water.

4 Before winter is over, bring the bulb out into the light. It will start to grow and you will soon have a beautifully scented hyacinth flower to enjoy.

Waiting to grow

Eggs, seeds, and tubers, such as potatoes, wait in the sand or earth until the weather is right for them to start to grow. While they are waiting, we say they are dormant.

Potatoes grow to their full size and then lie dormant underground until spring, when a new potato plant starts to grow.

Some mosquitos lay their eggs in mud. The larvae will not hatch until it rains and the mud becomes a pool for them to swim in.

Flower seeds can lie dormant in desert sands for a long time. They only grow when the rain comes.

Glossary

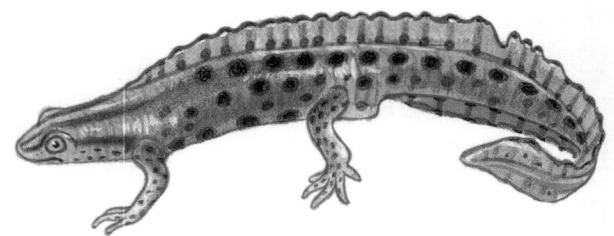

Air pressure
The air around and above you pushes down on you. This is called air pressure. Changes in air pressure usually bring changes in the weather.

Amphibians
Amphibians are animals such as newts that lay their eggs underwater. The young animals live underwater. The adults live both underwater and on land.

Barometer
A barometer is a device that measures air pressure. It can be used to predict the weather.

Bill
A bird's bill is its jaws. Each bird's bill is specially shaped for the kind of food it eats.

Camouflage
Camouflage is when the color and patterns on the coat or feathers of an animal or bird blend in with the background. This helps to keep them safe, as enemies cannot see them.

Carbohydrates
Carbohydrates in food give us energy and help us to keep going. They are found in foods like bread and pasta.

Carnivores
Carnivores are animals that eat meat. They hunt and kill other animals for food.

Cereals
Cereals are types of grasses, such as wheat, oats, rice, and corn, which are grown as crops. Cereals are a very important source of food for people and animals all over the world.

Chlorophyll
Chlorophyll is the green color in plants. Plants use chlorophyll to make food from sunlight.

Climate
The weather an area has throughout the year is called its climate.

Clouds

Clouds form when invisible water vapor in the air cools and turns into visible droplets of water.

Conifers

Conifers are evergreen trees that grow seeds in cones. Pine trees are conifers. They have long, thin leaves called needles.

Deciduous trees

Deciduous trees have large, flat leaves that change color in the fall, then fall off in winter. In the spring, fresh, green leaves grow.

Decomposers

Decomposers are creatures or plants that help dead animals and plants to break down, or decompose, in the soil.

Dormant

When plants are dormant, they are alive but have stopped growing. They wait until the weather is warm enough for them to grow again.

Egg

An egg is where new life starts. People and some animals keep eggs inside their bodies. Birds and fish lay their eggs. A bird's egg contains the food the young bird needs before it hatches.

Estivation

Estivation is a long, summer sleep that some animals have in parts of the world where there is very little water.

Evaporation

When a puddle of water dries up, the water itself does not disappear — it evaporates. This means that it turns into a gas, called water vapor.

Evergreen trees

Evergreen trees keep their leaves all year round. The leaves are often tough and shiny to protect them in cold weather.

Freshwater

Freshwater is the water we drink. Rainwater is fresh and so is most water found in rivers, ponds, and lakes.

Gravity

This is an invisible force that attracts objects to each other. The larger the object, the more gravity it has. The earth's gravity pulls everything down toward the ground.

Herbivores

Herbivores are animals that eat plants or parts of plants, such as nuts and berries. They are often eaten by carnivores.

Herbs

Herbs are plants that have a strong smell and taste in their stems and leaves. We use them for cooking, making herbal teas, and treating illnesses.

Hibernation

In the winter, when there is little food around, some animals save energy by going into a long sleep, called hibernation.

Metamorphosis

Metamorphosis is what happens to an animal that changes shape as it grows, such as a caterpillar changing into a butterfly.

Migration

Migration is the long journey that some creatures make in order to look for food.

Oxygen

Oxygen is an invisible gas in the air. It is very important because it lets all living things breathe and make energy.

Photosynthesis

Photosynthesis is when plants use sunlight, carbon dioxide, water, and the green color in their leaves, called chlorophyll, to make their own food.

Pollen

Pollen is the yellow dust inside a flower. Insects carry pollen from one flower to another.

Pollution

Pollution is when harmful chemicals escape into the air. It can cause nasty weather such as acid rain.

Proteins

Proteins help us grow and keep healthy. They are found in foods like meat and eggs.

Reproduction

For life to continue, all living things must make baby animals or new plants. This is called reproduction. Plants reproduce from seeds or another part of the plant. Animals reproduce when a seed from a male joins an egg from a female and a new life begins.

Reptiles

Reptiles are animals that lay eggs and have scaly, waterproof skin. Some live on land. Others, like crocodiles, live mainly in water.

Roots

Roots hold plants firmly in the ground. Water and minerals from the soil go up through the roots and into the plant.

Seawater

Seawater is salty because it contains minerals and salts that have been washed from the land into the sea.

Seeds

Plants grow from seeds. Inside a seed is a new plant and the food that it needs to begin to grow.

Temperature

Temperature is how warm or cold something is.

Thermometer

A thermometer is an instrument that is used for measuring temperature.

Tides

The sea moves backward and forward each day. These movements are called the tides.

Water vapor

Water vapor is the gas form of water. Most of the time it is invisible, but you can see it when water vapor cools and forms clouds.

Wind

Air that moves from one place to another is called wind. Winds can range from a gentle breeze to a whirling tornado.

GEOGRAPHY
for FUN
PROJECTS

Pam Robson

Copper Beech Books
Brookfield, Connecticut

© Aladdin Books Ltd 2001

Produced by
Aladdin Books Ltd
28 Percy Street
London W1P 0LD

First published in the United States
in 2001 by
Copper Beech Books,
an imprint of
The Millbrook Press
2 Old New Milford Road
Brookfield, Connecticut 06804

ISBN 0–7613–2279–5

Editor: Kathy Gemmell

Designer: Simon Morse

Illustrator: Tony Kenyon

Picture researcher: Brian Hunter Smart

Printed in UAE

Cataloging-in-Publication Data is on
file at the Library of Congress.

The author, Pam Robson, is an experienced teacher.
She has written and advised on many books for children
on geography and science subjects.

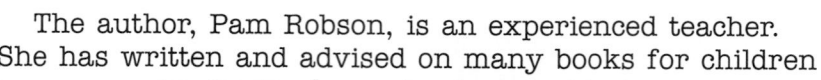

CONTENTS

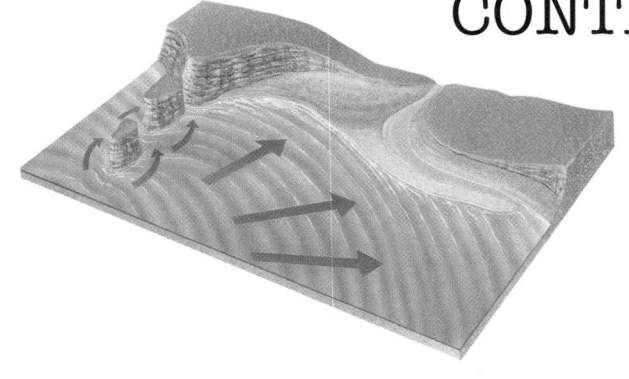

INTRODUCTION:

How to use this book

382-383

CHAPTER 1:

Maps and Plans

384-407

CHAPTER 2:

Mountains and

Our Moving Earth

408-431

CHAPTER 3:

Rivers and Seas

432-457

CHAPTER 4:

Ecosystems

458-483

CHAPTER 5:

People and Places

484-507

CHAPTER 6:

Food and Farming

508-531

GLOSSARY

532-535

INDEX

759

INTRODUCTION

Geography is about people and places and all the changes that take place in the world. It is about understanding how landscapes can be altered over time by natural processes like floods and earthquakes, or by human activity. Geography is about recording these changes. It is about discovering how animals live in harmony with their surroundings, both on the land and at sea, and about studying the effects that pollution can have on an ecosystem. Geography is about the many different ways in which people use the world's resources.

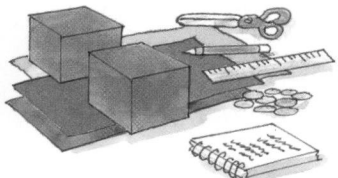

1 Look for numbers like this. Each step for the projects inside the book has been numbered this way. To draw the maps and make the models shown in each project, make sure that you follow the steps in the right order.

FEAUTURE BOXES
● Look for the feature boxes on each double page. They either give further information about the project on the page, or they suggest other interesting activities for you to do.

WHAT'S HAPPENING

● The What's Happening paragraphs explain the geography behind the projects you do or make.

● The Helpful Hints on some pages give you tips for doing the projects.

● Look at the Glossary at the back of this book to find out what important words mean.

● Always use the most up-to-date maps, atlases, websites, and reference books.

● Use the atlas index to find the location of any place you are looking for.

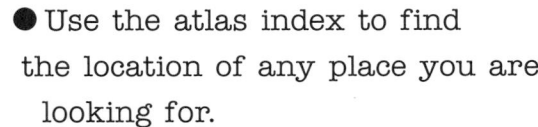

WARNING

● This sign means that you must be careful. Ask an adult to help you when you need to use a sharp tool, a hot liquid, or an electrical appliance. When collecting information for projects, always let an adult know where you are going and what you are doing.

CHAPTER 1

Maps and Plans

There are many different ways to find your way
from place to place. You can follow signposts on
the streets to get to wherever you want to go.

If there are no signposts, you can look at landmarks,
such as a hill or a particular building. Many people use maps
and plans to find their way around.

In this chapter, you will learn how to
make a maze game, discover how to map
mountains, and build a scale model of
your local streets.

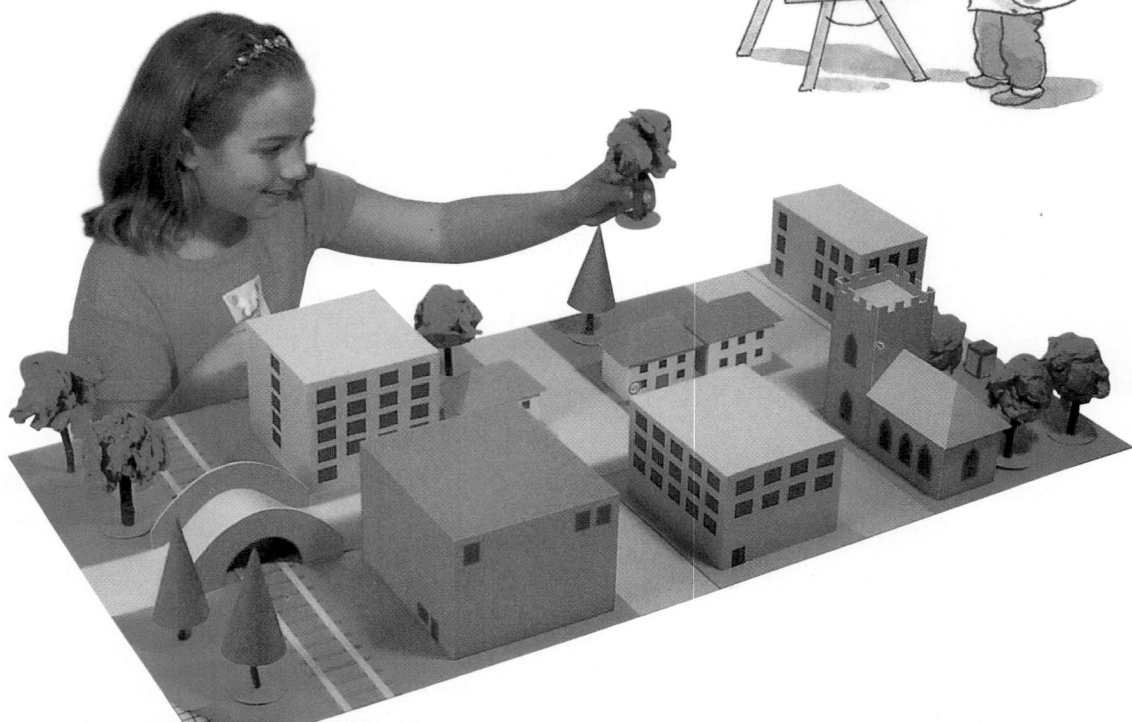

CONTENTS

LEFT AND RIGHT **386**

NORTH OR SOUTH? **388**

BIRD'S-EYE VIEW **390**

BIGGER AND SMALLER **392**

PLANS AND SYMBOLS **394**

READING STREET PLANS **396**

COLORS AND CONTOURS **398**

FIXING POSITION **400**

FINDING THE WAY **402**

PICTURE MAPS **404**

COUNTRIES AND CONTINENTS **406**

LEFT AND RIGHT

Drivers on a trip read road maps or follow signposts to find out when to turn left or right. Hikers use compasses and maps to find their way. All travelers look for landmarks, such as a particular tree, hill, or building, to help them recognize where they are. Inside mazes there are many turnings, but no landmarks or signposts to point the way.

AMAZING MAZE

Make this maze game and help the elephant and giraffe take all the correct turns to reach the water hole.

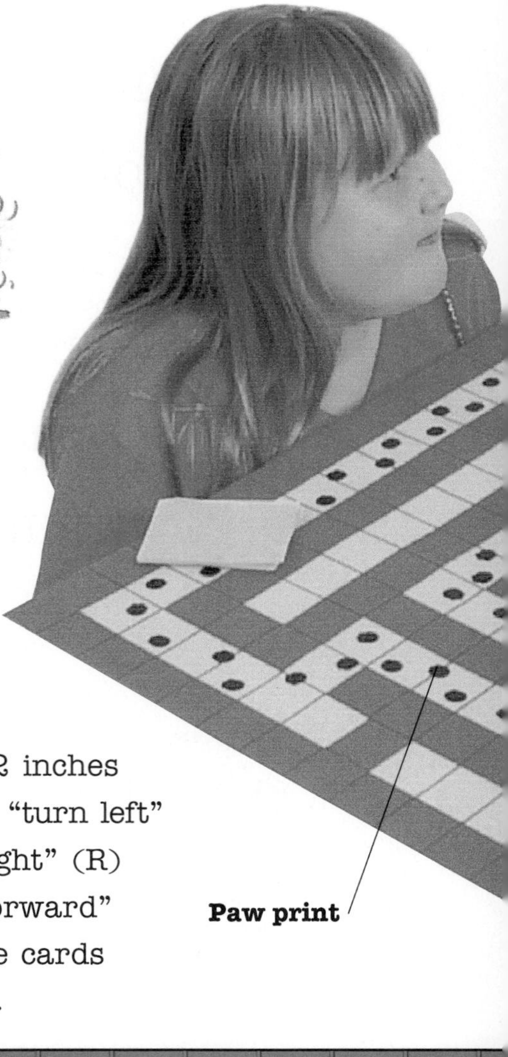

1 Copy the African grassland maze in the photograph on a squared board. Draw the pathways first, then decorate them with paw prints.

 **x 8**

 **x 6**

x 6

2 Cut out twenty pieces of stiff cardboard measuring 2 inches by 3 inches. Design six "turn left" (L) cards, six "turn right" (R) cards, and eight "go forward" (F) cards. Decorate the cards with different animals.

Paw print

3 Make an animal counter for each player by drawing a picture on a circle of stiff cardboard and gluing it on a bottle top. If you have toy animals, you could use them instead. Place the counters at the entrance to the maze.

4 The aim of the game is to reach the water hole first. Stack the cards face down. Take turns picking a card. Turn your counter in the direction of the arrow on the card. If you pick a "go forward" card, you can move to the next junction, but only if you are facing the right way. If you can't move, miss your turn. Replace the cards at the bottom of the pile.

MORE IDEAS

● Play again—in reverse. This time, begin at the water hole. The first one to reach the entrance to the maze is the winner.

● Practice giving directions. Ask a friend to find the way from your school to your home, or from one classroom to another. Write down when to turn left or right and whether there are any landmarks to watch for.

NORTH OR SOUTH?

A long time ago, ships had to sail in sight of land to know where they were. Sailors found their way using landmarks. Then it was discovered that magnetic stones called lodestones pointed toward north when suspended. These were the first compasses. Sailors were then able to sail away from coasts to discover new lands. The first maps had compass faces pointing toward the Orient (the east), which was believed to be the center of the world.

COMPASS FACE

Finding the way with a compass and map is now called orienteering. To do any orienteering, you need to know the points on the compass. Make a compass face to help you remember them.

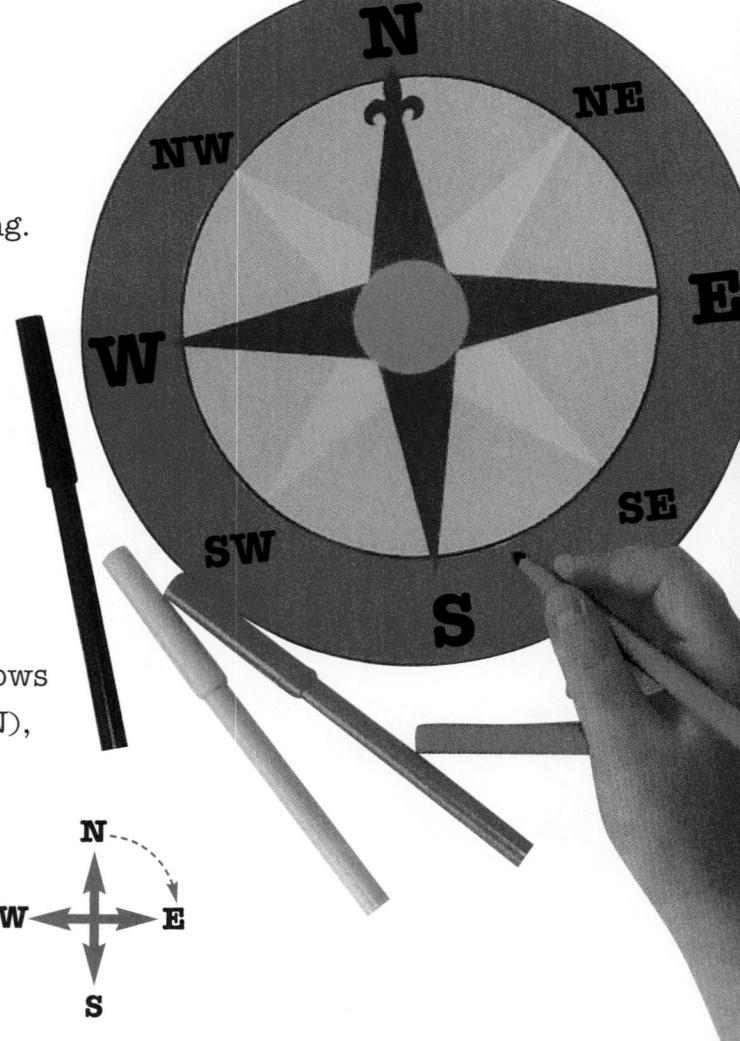

1 Use a ruler to draw a four-point compass face. This shows the four main directions: north (N), east (E), south (S), and west (W). Label them clockwise from the top. Use a protractor to draw more accurately: the clockwise turn between each point is a right angle of 90 degrees.

2 To make an eight-point compass face, draw lines halfway between each of the four main points. Mark these directions NE, SE, SW, NW. Color your compass face. On early maps, north was shown by a fleur-de-lis design like the one shown here. The clockwise turn between each of the eight points is half of a right angle, which is 45 degrees.

HELPFUL HINTS

● Think of a saying to help you remember the clockwise order of north, east, south, and west, such as "Nine, Eight, Seven, Wait."

● Find north by pointing the hour hand of a watch toward the Sun. (Make sure the watch is telling the right time!) Lay the head of a matchstick halfway between the hour hand and twelve, as shown below. The match head will now be pointing south and the other end will be pointing north.

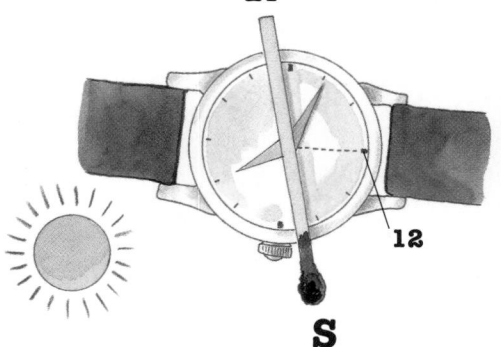

TAKING BEARINGS

● You can figure out the exact position of a landmark by measuring where it is in relation to a fixed position. This is called taking a bearing. Bearings are worked out by measuring angles clockwise from north.

● Choose a landmark that you can see from your yard or school, and work out its bearing. First find north. You can do this using a watch (see left) or by lining up north on a map with north on an orienteering compass. Now measure the clockwise turn from north to the direction of the landmark. This is its bearing.

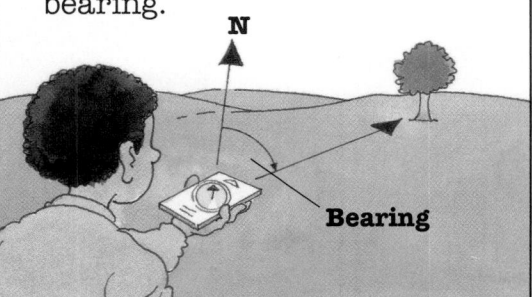

BIRD'S-EYE VIEW

Objects look different when they are viewed from above. A bird in the sky sees everything below in 2D (two dimensions) because objects on the ground look flat. Birds cannot see how high objects are. Someone standing on the ground sees the same objects in 3D (three dimensions). They *can* see how high the objects are. A plan of an object or place is always drawn in 2D. A plan is a bird's-eye view.

3D TO 2D

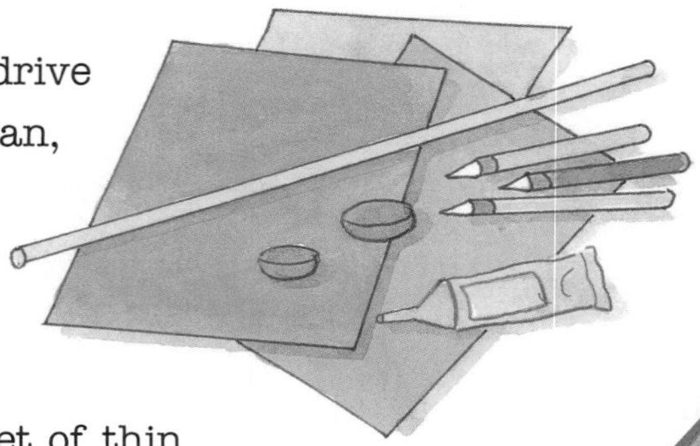

To make a yellow bus drive along this 2-D street plan, you will need two button magnets, a length of dowel, a large sheet of white cardboard, a small sheet of thin yellow cardboard, colored paper, scissors, and glue.

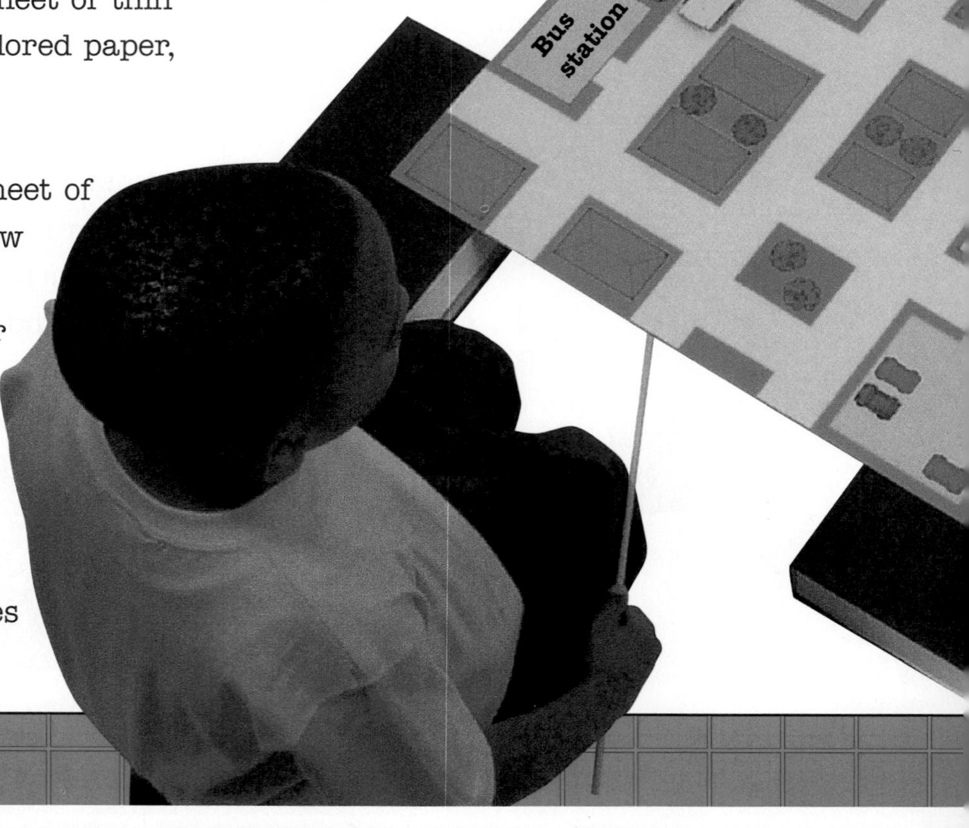

1 On the large sheet of cardboard, draw some streets, or cut them out from paper and paste them on. You can make them up or copy the streets in the photograph. Make sure you leave spaces to put in buildings.

Bus station

2 The 2-D shapes, or symbols, drawn in the left column of the key below show what objects look like from above. Each 2-D shape represents a 3-D object, like a house, a car, or a tree. Draw and color the 2-D shapes onto your plan.

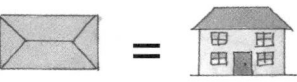 = **House**

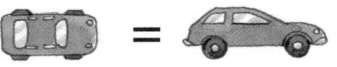 = **Car**

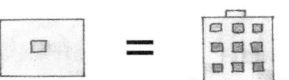 = **Apartment building**

 = **Tree**

3 Support the plan on some thick books to leave a space beneath. Now draw and cut out a 2-D bus from yellow cardboard. Make sure it is the right size to fit your street plan. Glue a button magnet to the bottom of the bus.

4 Glue another magnet to the dowel to make a stick magnet. Place the bus on the plan. Move the stick magnet underneath the plan to make the bus go.

5 Now write a story describing how the bus gets from one place to another on your plan. Put in landmarks and say where the bus turns.

The bus drives out of the bus station and turns left. It drives past the trees on the left and turns right onto Meadow Road. At the apartment building, it turns left onto Main Street, then right onto School Lane. It stops outside the school.

School

MORE IDEAS
● Make sure your street plan has a compass face marked on it. Now write directions for the route of the yellow bus using N, E, S, and W instead of left and right.

BIGGER AND SMALLER

Bees are much smaller than elephants. But a picture of a bee can be larger than the bee really is, while a picture of an elephant can be smaller than a real elephant. In the same way, a plan or map of a place is much smaller than the real place. Drawing something smaller or bigger than it really is, but keeping it exactly the same shape, is called drawing to scale.

1 Choose a large picture of a famous landmark from a magazine. Glue the picture onto a sheet of paper and draw a grid of large squares over it.

2 On graph paper with small squares, count and cut out the same number of squares that you drew on the large grid. Glue your small grid onto cardboard. Now copy the shape of the picture carefully, square by square, onto the smaller grid.

SHRINK THAT PICTURE

To draw a picture to scale, you need graph paper. To reduce the size, use paper with smaller squares, but keep the number of squares the same.

The famous landmark in this picture is the Taj Mahal in India.

PLAYGROUND PLAN

Draw a scale plan of a playground or park close to where you live. You can measure distances by taking paces (steps), so you don't need a tape measure. Tell an adult what you are planning.

● You will need a pencil and some paper.

First find out which way is north (see page 389). Then pace off the size of the area. Write down how many paces you take in each direction. Note where the entrances and exits are. Sketch the position of objects, such as trash cans and benches.

● Use half-inch graph paper to draw out your plan. One pace on the ground can stand for $1/2$ inch on your plan. This means that your scale is $1/2$ inch = 1 pace. Write this on your plan. Draw a compass face. Use 2-D symbols to show the position of objects in the playground.

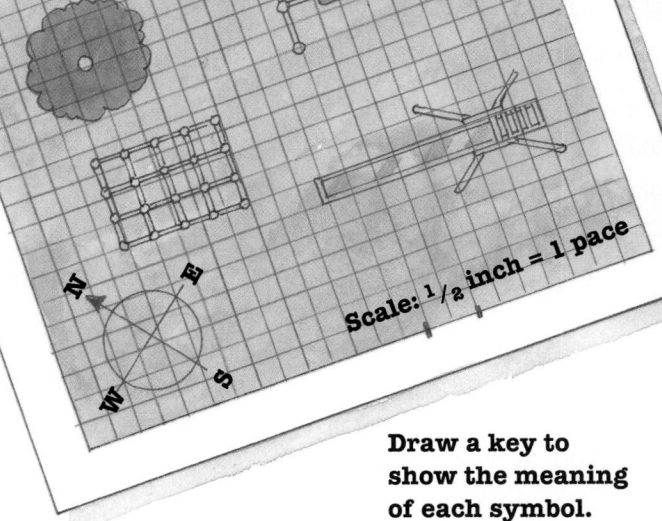

Playground

N E W S

Scale: $1/2$ inch = 1 pace

Draw a key to show the meaning of each symbol.

PLANS AND SYMBOLS

A plan or map needs to be large-scale in order to show important details like paths and houses. Large-scale means that the map shows lots of detail but only a small area. Most countries have large-scale maps showing different parts of the country. The United States Geological Survey (USGS) makes such maps. Street plans are even larger scale than USGS maps—they even show the names of roads and buildings. Buildings often act as landmarks.

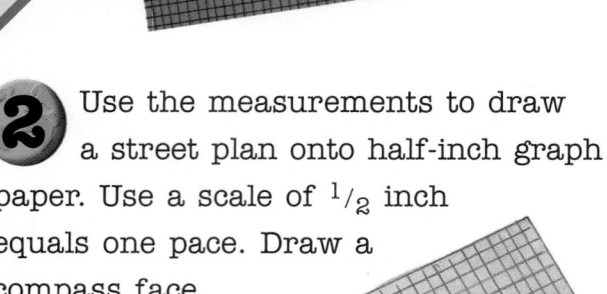

LARGE-SCALE STREET PLAN

Make a large-scale street plan to show the position of the different buildings on a street near your house or school.

1 Ask permission from an adult to carry out a street survey. Always work with a friend, and watch for traffic. Pace off distances between buildings and write down the measurements. Note down the position of each building and what it is used for. Find north (see page 389).

2 Use the measurements to draw a street plan onto half-inch graph paper. Use a scale of $1/2$ inch equals one pace. Draw a compass face.

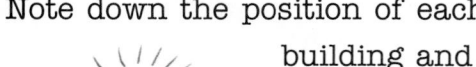

3 Design 2-D symbols for the different buildings and draw them on your plan. Draw a key for the symbols.

KEY TO PLAN

Keys explain the meaning of colors and symbols used on maps and plans. The key below explains the symbols used on the street plan.

 Police station

 Church

 Library

 Post office

 Private house

 Bus stop

 Bridge

 Theater or Movie house

 Public telephone

 Railroad

 Coniferous tree

 Broad-leaved tree

HELPFUL HINTS

● Some symbols are international and are understood worldwide. Look at the key box above or the key on a USGS map of a town or city for ideas for symbols, or you can make up your own.

READING STREET PLANS

Street plans show the 2-D shapes and positions of different buildings and objects, but they cannot show the height of buildings. There are many different kinds of homes. Some people live in apartments, which can be in tall buildings. Others live in houses. A 3-D model of a street can show the height of all the buildings.

HIGH HOPES

From your street plan, you can construct a 3-D model of a real place. Use paper, cardboard, and clean junk materials or natural materials like twigs and pebbles.

1 First, you need more information about the buildings on your street plan. Take photographs or make drawings of them. Count the number of floors in each building.

2 Make your model larger scale than your street plan. Draw a grid on cardboard with larger squares than your plan, but make sure it has exactly the same number of squares. Cut out strips of paper for streets and glue on the model.

3 Draw a 2-D pattern on cardboard for each building. Make sure you know how wide and deep each building is (count the squares it covers on the plan). Score, fold, and glue the pattern. Fold more cardboard for a roof. Draw or glue on doors and windows. Place the buildings on the model.

(1) **Width**

(2) **Depth**

(3) **Number of floors**

4 Shape some pine trees from cones of green paper, as shown. Make broad-leaved trees from crumpled tissue paper. Make tree trunks from twigs. Glue the trunks onto cardboard bases or push them into clay. Position your trees on the model.

MORE IDEAS
● Add smaller objects to your model, like trash cans and telephone booths. Make signposts and traffic lights.
● Does the road have a pedestrian crossing? Make cars and trucks from clay.

HELPFUL HINTS
● Make features like bridges from colored paper and cardboard.
● Finish buildings by painting them. Do any painting before placing the buildings on the model.
● Make sure any entrances face the right way.

COLORS AND CONTOURS

Small-scale maps cover a wider area than large-scale ones, but do not show as much detail. The shape of large areas of land can be shown on small-scale relief maps. Different colors are often used to show the height of the land. On large-scale maps, the height of the land may be shown by lines called contours. Contours are lines joining places that are the same height above sea level.

SINK A MOUNTAIN

Contour lines show the height of the land in 2D. Make a 2-D contour map by taking measurements from a sinking clay mountain.

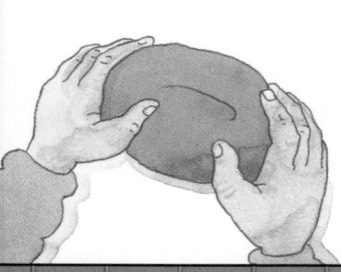

1 You will need some clay, a straight-sided plastic bowl, a pitcher of water, a ruler, and a coffee stirrer.

2 Shape a mountain from clay and put it inside the bowl. Place a ruler upright against the side of the bowl.

3 Pour in one inch of water. Use the coffee stirrer to mark a line around the mountain at the water level. Pour in another inch and mark a line at the new water level. Repeat until the water reaches the summit (top) of the mountain.

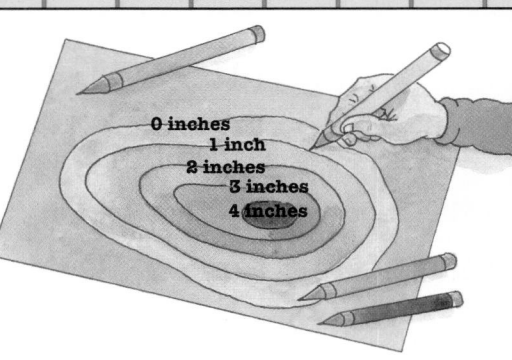

0 inches
1 inch
2 inches
3 inches
4 inches

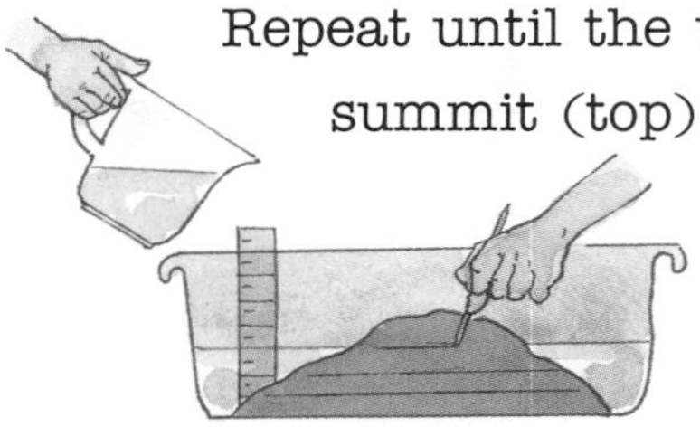

4 Lift the mountain out of the bowl. Look at it from above and observe the pattern of the lines. Draw a contour map, like the one above, of what you see. Write the correct measurements on the contour lines. Color the spaces between the contours in different shades.

RELIEF MAPS

● Look for small-scale relief maps in an atlas. Some relief maps look like 3-D pictures. Hill shading is used so that hills and mountains—like the Dolomites, Apennines, and Alps shown on this map of Italy—look like real hills and mountains. Different colors often show height above sea level. Sometimes crosshatching is used to show the shape of high ground.

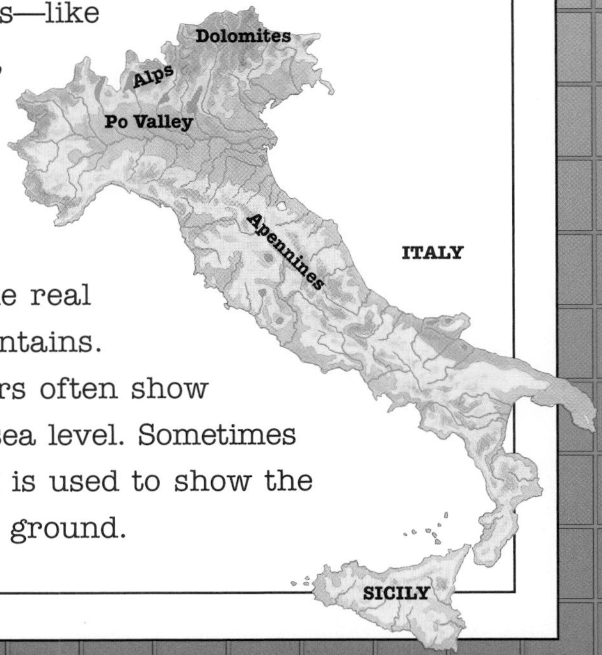

Dolomites
Alps
Po Valley
Apennines
ITALY
SICILY

FIXING POSITION

Describing the position of an object on a page, when there are many objects scattered at random, is tricky. A grid laid over the page makes it much easier. The exact position of every object can then be given using a grid reference, which is the column name followed by the row number.

BIRTHDAY PUZZLE

Send a coded birthday message using a grid. To decode the message, you have to decode the grid references listed in the correct order.

1 Fold a sheet of cardboard in half. Cut a grid of 8 x 11 squares from 1-inch graph paper. Glue it to the front of the cardboard. Cut the board to size if necessary. Leave spaces to write in column names and row numbers.

Leave space for column names along the bottom.

Leave space for row numbers up the left-hand side.

2 Now write each of the letters of the alphabet in a square on the grid. Jumble the letters so you do not read them in order. Draw party objects in the empty squares.

3 From left to right along the bottom of the grid, fill in the column names A to G. Up the left-hand side of the grid, fill in the row numbers 1 to 10. Leave the bottom left square blank.

4 Inside the card, write grid references for each of the letters of the message you want to write. Make sure you write them in the correct order. Use the grid to work out the message below.

A5   B9   A10   A10   B6
E10   F8   C8   F6   A5   A7   B9   B6
B9   D3   B4   E1

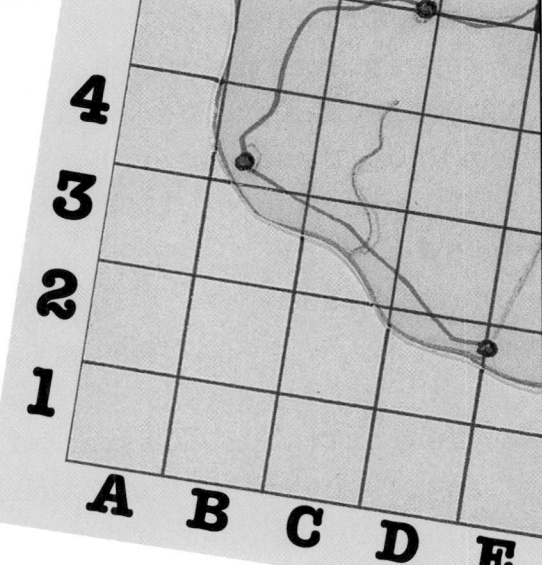

GRID MAPS
● In an atlas, a grid map with numbered spaces can cover a whole region. Each square has a grid reference. This makes it easy to locate a particular place on the map, such as a town or city. On this map, there is a town in square B4.

FINDING THE WAY

A routefinder map is larger scale than a country map. It covers a smaller area, and is divided into squares by a numbered grid. Hikers use routefinder maps because they show paths and landmarks. Routefinder maps are different in different countries.

FINDING THE WAY

On this routefinder map, a grid reference with four figures in it refers to the southwest (SW) corner of a particular square on the map. Can you find the church on this routefinder?

1 The four-figure grid reference for the church is 03, 06. Count along the bottom to 03, then count up to 06, and you are at the SW corner of the square with the church in it.

2 There are two bridges marked on the map. Can you find them? One bridge is in square 02, 05. The other bridge is in square 07, 08. Remember to count along the bottom first, and then up to the correct square.

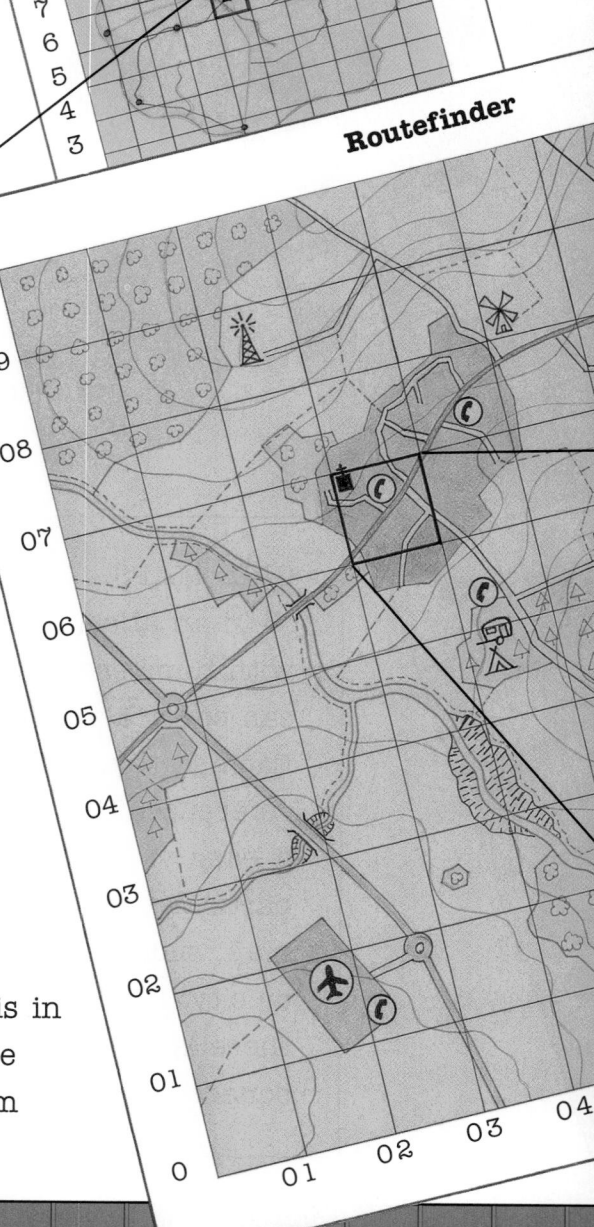

Country map

Routefinder

3 Imagine a magnifying glass placed over square 03, 06. Now imagine that square divided up again by a grid of 100 smaller squares. This lets you see much more detail on that section of the map. It is now a street plan. You can now give a six-figure grid reference, which describes the exact position of a landmark inside the 100 squares on the grid.

MORE IDEAS

● Can you think what kind of map a cyclist needs? Like a hiker, who needs to know where the best footpaths are, a cyclist needs to locate good bicycle routes.

● Look at the street plan. Which feature is next to the police station, at grid reference 034, 066?

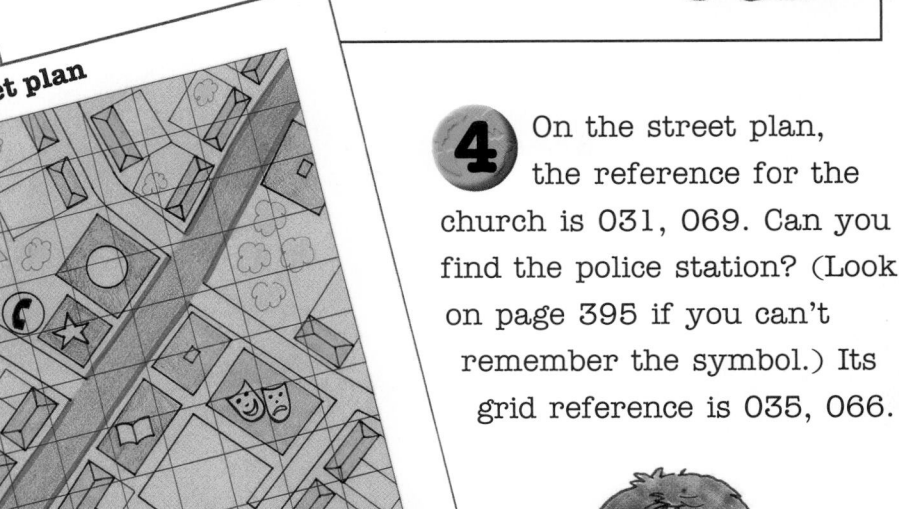

Street plan

4 On the street plan, the reference for the church is 031, 069. Can you find the police station? (Look on page 395 if you can't remember the symbol.) Its grid reference is 035, 066.

PICTURE MAPS

Maps are designed differently to highlight particular features of a place. Relief maps show the shape of the land. Political maps show countries, their capital cities, and their borders. Thematic maps tell us interesting facts about different regions. They give information about weather and climate, farming, and wildlife. Maps like this need a key. Picture maps can tell a story without a key because pictures are used instead of symbols.

PICTURE THIS

Make a picture map of your favorite place. It may be a town, a city, or a country that you have visited on vacation.

1 If you have chosen a country, copy its shape from an atlas. For a city, draw a map of the region. Draw and color pictures of the things you like about the place you have chosen. You can also stick on photographs or pictures from magazines.

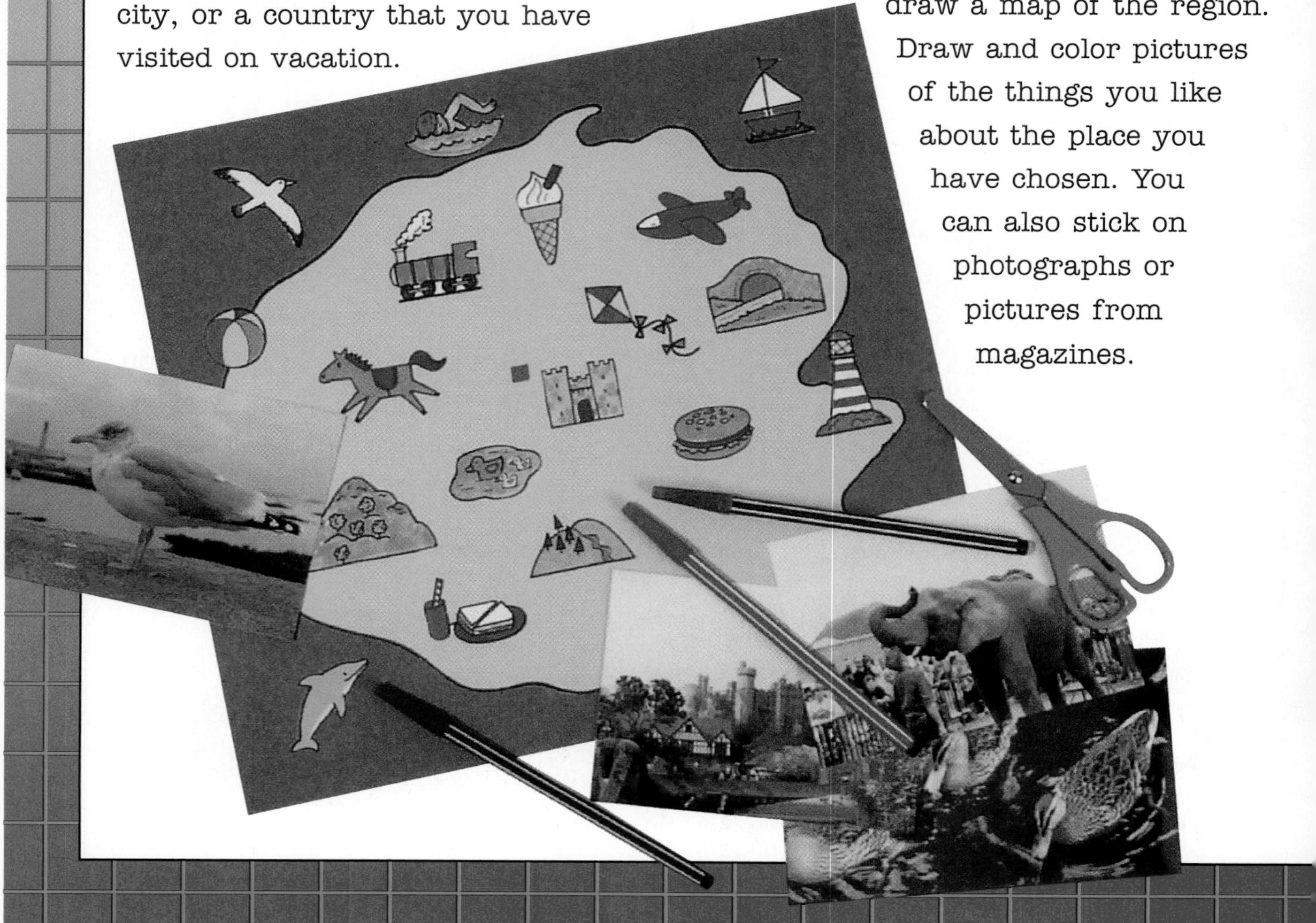

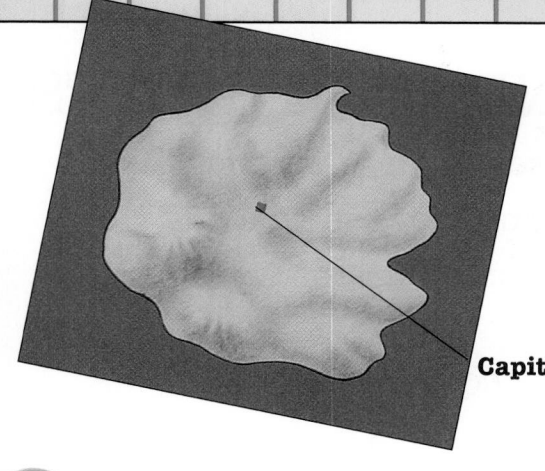

Capital city

3 Political maps of districts use colors to show different counties or regions. Is your favorite place in an urban area (a town) or a rural area (the countryside)?

2 Try to find a relief map of your favorite place in an atlas. Do you remember whether it is flat or mountainous? A relief map like this one shows the shape of the land as a 3-D picture. Other relief maps have contours showing height above sea level.

WEATHER MAPS

● Weather maps use symbols that can be understood anywhere in the world because they are like pictures.

● Look at weather maps on TV. What kind of weather did you have on vacation? Was it sunny or rainy?

● Make weather pictures for your vacation map. What kind of climate does your vacation place usually have?

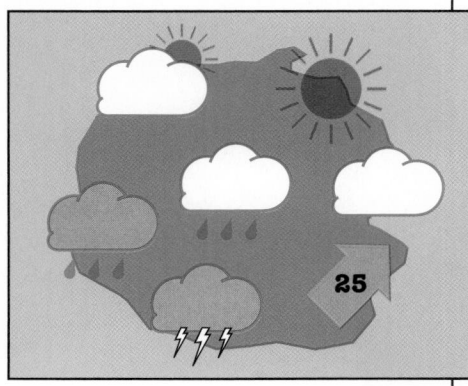

4 One kind of thematic picture map is a farming map, which shows where food is grown. Foods that come from your favorite place might be sold in supermarkets on the other side of the world.

COUNTRIES AND CONTINENTS

The world is divided into seven large landmasses called continents. Each country of the world is part of a continent. The United States is a country on the continent of North America. Egypt is a country on the continent of Africa. France is a country on the continent of Europe.

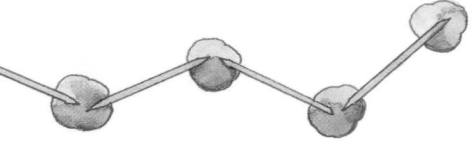

1 Find Italy in an atlas. Look closely at its shape. Do you think it looks like a boot? Copy or trace the shape of Italy onto the piece of cardboard. Color it in, then use clay to stick coffee stirrers around the edge for your coastline. Break the stirrers to get the right shape.

2 Copy Italy's flag and glue it onto your map. Show the position of Rome, the capital city. Now glue on pictures of things you know about Italy. Look at other kinds of maps to help you. You can even glue on some dried pasta!

COUNTRY MAP

To make this collage map of the country of Italy, you will need an atlas, a piece of cardboard, colored paper, glue, scissors, colored pencils, clay, and some coffee stirrers.

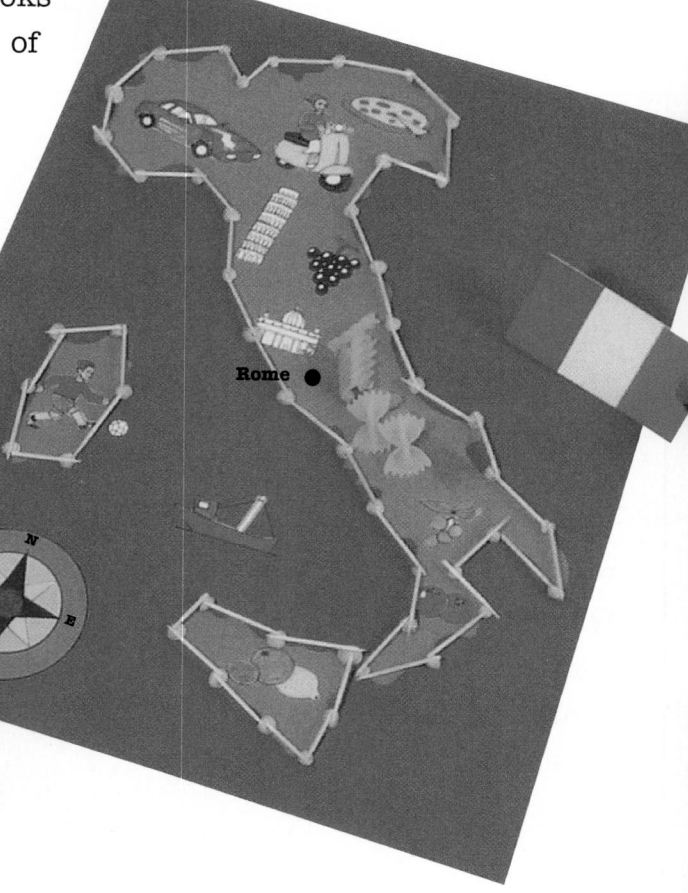

Rome ●

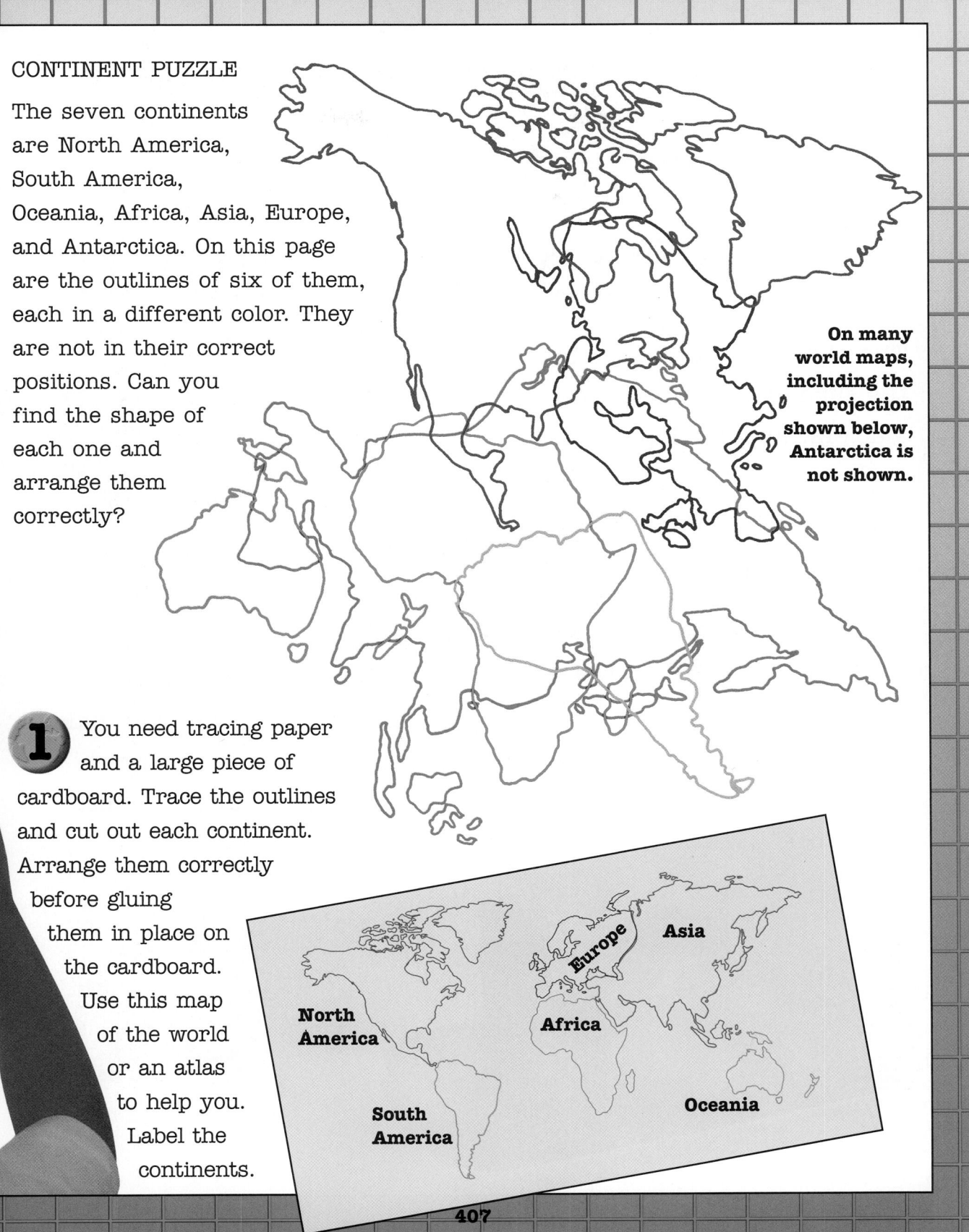

CONTINENT PUZZLE

The seven continents
are North America,
South America,
Oceania, Africa, Asia, Europe,
and Antarctica. On this page
are the outlines of six of them,
each in a different color. They
are not in their correct
positions. Can you
find the shape of
each one and
arrange them
correctly?

On many
world maps,
including the
projection
shown below,
Antarctica is
not shown.

1 You need tracing paper
and a large piece of
cardboard. Trace the outlines
and cut out each continent.
Arrange them correctly
before gluing
them in place on
the cardboard.
Use this map
of the world
or an atlas
to help you.
Label the
continents.

North
America

Europe

Asia

Africa

South
America

Oceania

CHAPTER 2

Mountains and Our Moving Earth

The shape of the land is being changed all the time by volcanic eruptions, slow-moving glaciers, and earthquakes. The hot, liquid rock deep inside the Earth causes tectonic plates to move and, eventually, collide.

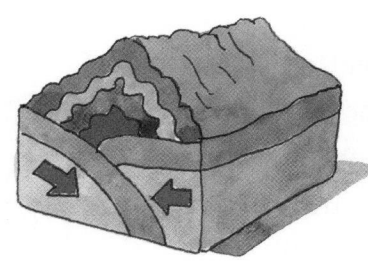

When they collide, rocks are forced upward, and mountains are formed. Ice, wind, and rivers all cause rock to erode, or wear away, which slowly changes the shape of mountains. In this chapter, you will make a continents jigsaw puzzle, construct a rift valley model, and even build your own glacier.

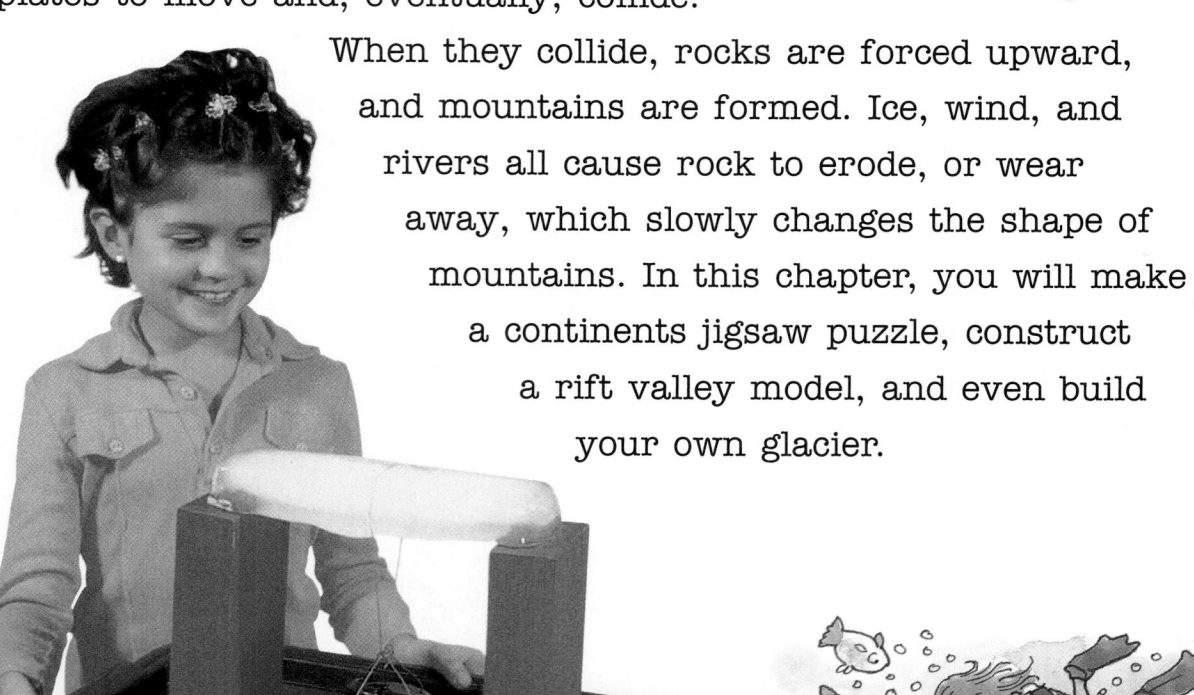

CONTENTS

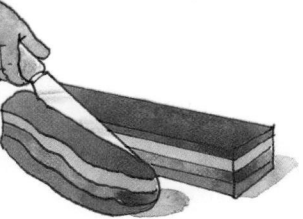

INSIDE THE EARTH **410**

MOVING PLATES **412**

SHAPING MOUNTAINS **414**

FAULTS AND EARTHQUAKES **416**

VOLCANOES **418**

ROCKS AND MINERALS **420**

MOUNTAINS AND MAPS **422**

HOW HIGH? **424**

ICE AND SNOW **426**

RAIN SHADOW **428**

EROSION AND WEATHERING **430**

INSIDE THE EARTH

At the center of Earth is a hard inner core of metallic rock. It is surrounded by an outer core of hot, liquid rock, called magma. Next is a thick layer called the mantle, made up mainly of hard rock with some parts of magma. The magma causes rock in Earth's thin top layer, called the crust, to move around.

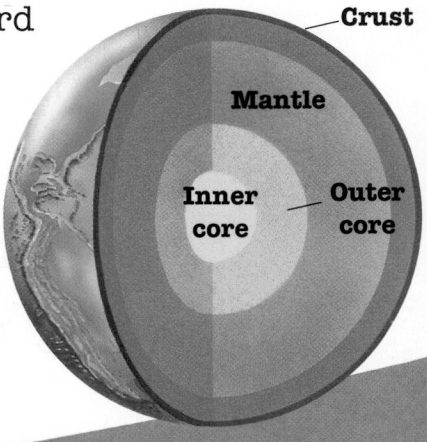

Crust

Mantle

Inner core

Outer core

CUT THROUGH THE WORLD

Make a colorful diagram, called a cross section, of Earth's insides. A cross section is like a 2-D (two-dimensional) slice cut through Earth's core.

The inner core of hard rock is very hot.

Earth is like an egg, with a thin shell called the crust.

1 You will need four sheets of colored paper and a large sheet of cardboard. Use a compass to draw a dark-colored circle with a radius of 5 inches, a red circle with a radius of $4\frac{1}{2}$ inches, an orange circle with a radius of 3 inches, and a yellow circle with a radius of $1\frac{1}{2}$ inches. Cut out the circles.

Radius

2 Glue the 5-inch circle to the cardboard. Line up all the centers of the circles. Now glue the $4\frac{1}{2}$-inch circle on top of the 5-inch circle. Glue the 3-inch circle on top of the $4\frac{1}{2}$-inch circle. Glue the $1\frac{1}{2}$-inch circle down last. Label each layer and decorate each one using pencils of the same color.

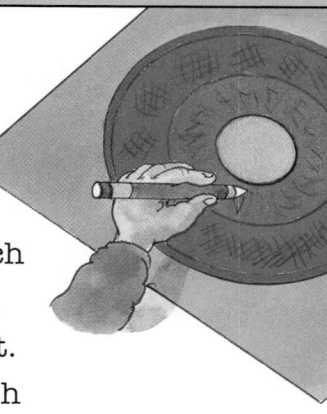

The mantle, made up of hard rock and magma, is 1,900 miles thick.

The outer core is made up of liquid magma.

GOING DOWN

● The deepest hole ever drilled into the Earth's crust is in Russia and is 8 miles deep. This is nearly 3 miles deeper than Mount Everest, the world's highest mountain, is high.

● The thickness of the Earth's crust varies. Beneath the oceans, it is around 3 miles thick. Beneath continents, it can be 22 miles thick. Beneath high mountains, the crust is even thicker.

Ocean

Continental crust

Oceanic crust

Mantle

MOVING PLATES

Earth's thin crust is made up of several pieces, called tectonic plates, that move around on top of magma in the mantle. When plates collide, mountain ranges form. When they slide past each other, there is an earthquake. When they separate or move beneath the mantle, a volcano erupts. Once, all the continents were joined in a huge landmass called Pangaea. Plate movement over millions of years caused them to drift to their present positions.

JIGSAW WORLD

Some of the continent shapes you see on maps can still be fitted together like a jigsaw to make part of Pangaea.

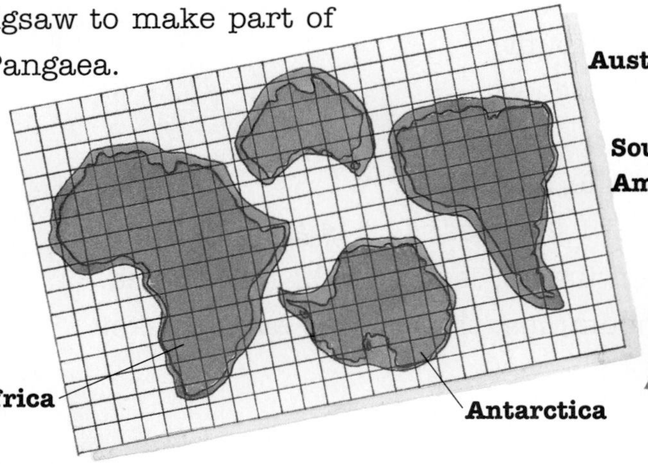

Australia

South America

Africa

Antarctica

1 Each shape above shows a continent or part of a continent. Count the squares in the orange part of each shape, then copy the outline onto graph paper with large squares. This will give you continents of the same shape, but bigger.

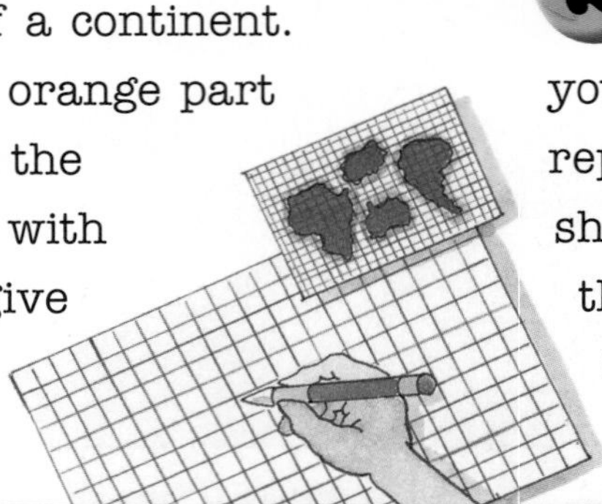

2 Now copy the blue outline around each of your enlarged continents. This represents the continental shelf—the part of the seabed that the continent sits on. Continental shelves are the shallowest parts of the sea.

3 Glue the shapes onto a sheet of stiff cardboard and color them in. Make sure you color the continental shelves blue. Then carefully cut out each shape.

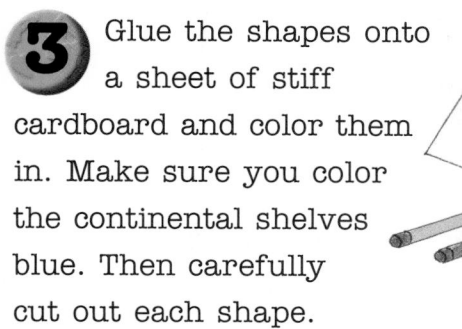

4 Piece together your jigsaw on a large tray. Look carefully at the red area on the big globe below to see what the finished jigsaw should look like.

COLLISION COURSE
● Some tectonic plates have drifted apart, but others have moved closer together. The subcontinent of India (in red below) was once farther south. It gradually moved northward until it collided with Asia. The mountains called the Himalayas were formed as the continental plates collided.

5 million years ago

135 million years ago

India

200 million years ago

● The plates that make up the oceanic crust also move. Here, under the ocean, the rocks are much younger. As the plates pull apart, magma rises from the mantle and solidifies to form new rock.

Pangaea, 220 million years ago

SHAPING MOUNTAINS

Within Earth's crust, there are layers of different rock. These layers are called strata. When moving tectonic plates collide, rock strata are forced upward and shaped into mountains with sharp peaks. These are called fold mountains. The peaks of the Himalayas are fold mountains. So are the Andes, in South America, which are several ranges of mountains formed by plate movements.

FOLDING MOUNTAINS

To make a model showing how rock strata are pushed upward to make high mountains, you will need some colored clay and a knife.

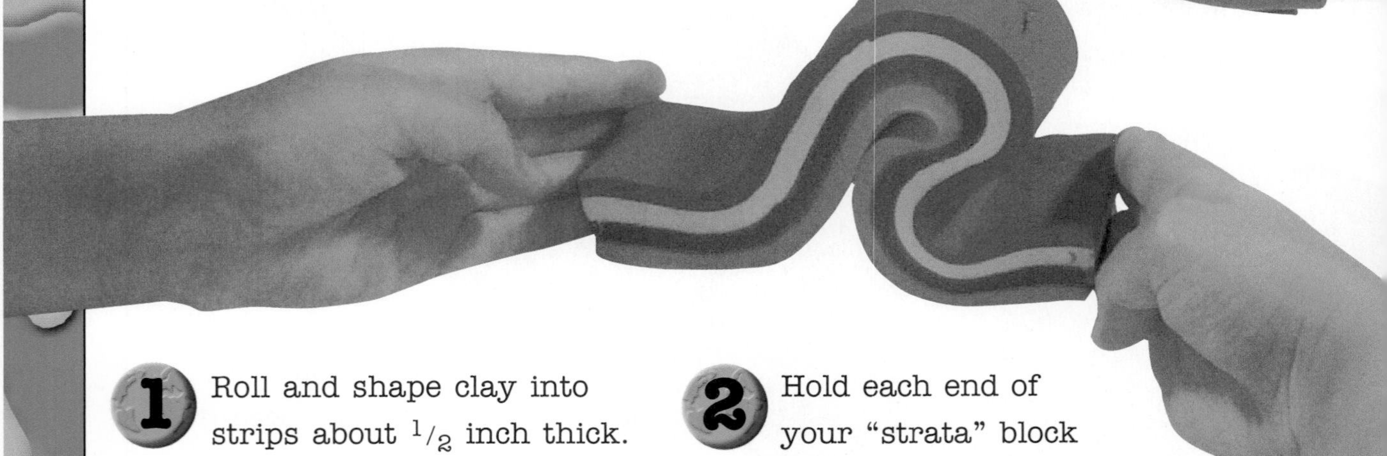

1 Roll and shape clay into strips about $1/2$ inch thick. Place the strips on top of each other and cut them to form a block of layers that look like rock strata.

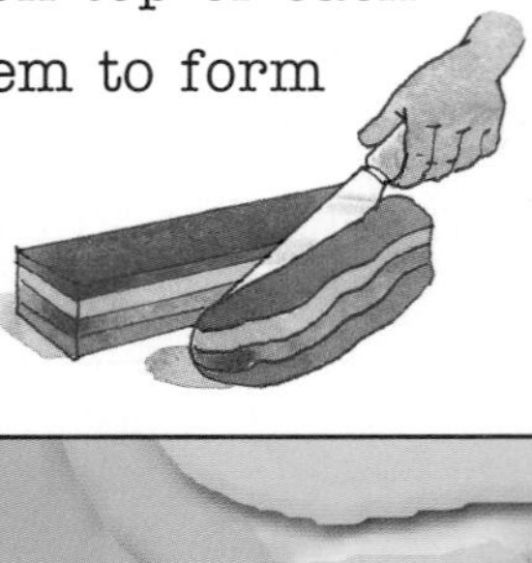

2 Hold each end of your "strata" block and gently push inward. Watch the mountains fold. Make another block and repeat. See how many different mountain shapes you can make this way.

WHAT'S HAPPENING

● The force of plates colliding makes rock strata at the plate edges buckle in different ways. Sometimes rock material from one plate is squeezed against the other plate. It crumples to form more mountains.

Fold mountains form as rock buckles under pressure.

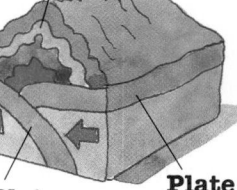

Plate   Plate

CONE-SHAPED MOUNTAINS

● Not all mountains are fold mountains. Many steep-sided mountains start as volcanoes. Over time, the lava cools and hardens into a cone shape (see page 418).

Layers of cooled lava

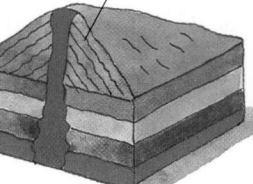

TRENCHES AND SEAMOUNTS

● Most oceans were formed after the breakup of Pangaea. The oceanic crust is still widening. As it collides with a continental plate, it slips below it, and a trench forms. Many tectonic plate edges lie beneath the oceans. The Marianas Trench beneath the Pacific Ocean is the deepest trench in the world, over 6 miles deep in places. Look it up in an atlas.

● As heat from inside Earth rises, huge ridges push up underwater. These undersea mountains, called seamounts, are mostly cone-shaped.

Seamounts

The ocean bed is known as the abyssal plain.

Trench

FAULTS AND EARTHQUAKES

As tectonic plates move around, rocks split and form cracks called faults. The land moves where there is a fault. Mountains with flat tops, called block mountains, form when the rock is forced up. Wide rift valleys form when the rock slips down between two faults. There is a large rift valley in East Africa. Earthquakes happen when rocks crack and move suddenly at a fault. In some parts of the world, such as Japan, this happens regularly.

BLOCK AND RIFT MODEL

To make this model, you will need a cardboard box, thin cardboard, flour, cold water, newspaper, a craft knife, tape, glue, sand, paints, and colored paper.

1 Carefully copy the shape of the model shown here onto the sides of the box. Ask an adult to help you cut around the outline with a craft knife.

2 Cover the top of the box with the cardboard. Use tape to hold it in place.

3 Mix cold water and flour to make a paste. Crumple sheets of newspaper and dip them in the paste. Lay the crumpled newspaper on the model to give the land some shape.

4 When the model is dry, paint it with a mixture of sand and paint. This will give it a textured surface. Glue strips of colored paper to the sides, as shown, to make strata.

WHAT'S HAPPENING

● Pressure pushing up from under the ground forces land upward to create block mountains. A rift valley forms if the land between two parallel faults slips downward.

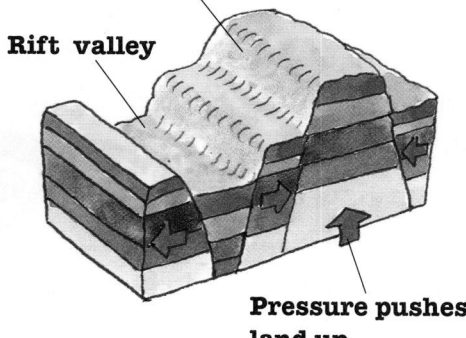

Block mountain

Rift valley

Pressure pushes land up.

EARTHQUAKES

● Earthquakes often happen at plate edges where two plates push against each other. Rocks can stand this pressure for many years, but eventually the strain becomes too great and the rocks snap into a new position. Vibrations caused by the sudden movement spread out from a point underground, called the focus, and make the ground shake.

Plates push against each other, and stress builds.

The rocks snap into place, causing an earthquake.

Epicenter

Damage is worst at the epicenter, directly above the focus.

● The Richter scale measures energy released by an earthquake on a number scale from one to nine.

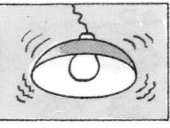

Small earthquake = up to 4.5

Moderate earthquake = 4.5 - 5.5

Major earthquake = 6.5 - 7.5

Great earthquake = more than 7.5

VOLCANOES

Volcanoes are found mainly on the edges of tectonic plates. They are vents or "chimneys" in Earth's crust, through which magma from Earth's mantle erupts to the surface. On the surface, the magma cools to form lava. The lava flows in streams from the vents. Over thousands of years, the surfaces around the vents build up until mountains are formed. A volcano's shape depends on the kind of lava that erupts from it.

LOVELY LAVA

There are different kinds of lava, which flow at different speeds. Lava can be viscous (thick and sticky) like molasses or very runny.

1 Use different lavalike liquids to find out which kind travels fastest down a slope. You will need a metal tray, pancake syrup, cooking oil, and molasses.

2 Place a spoonful of each liquid at one end of the tray. Tilt the tray. Use a watch that shows seconds to time how long each liquid takes to reach the bottom of the tray. Write down the times.

3 Now see how the times differ if you warm or cool the liquids. Ask an adult to help you put the containers in hot water for a while. Then repeat step 2, noting the new flow times. Now put the containers in cool water and repeat the project.

VOLCANOES IN ACTION

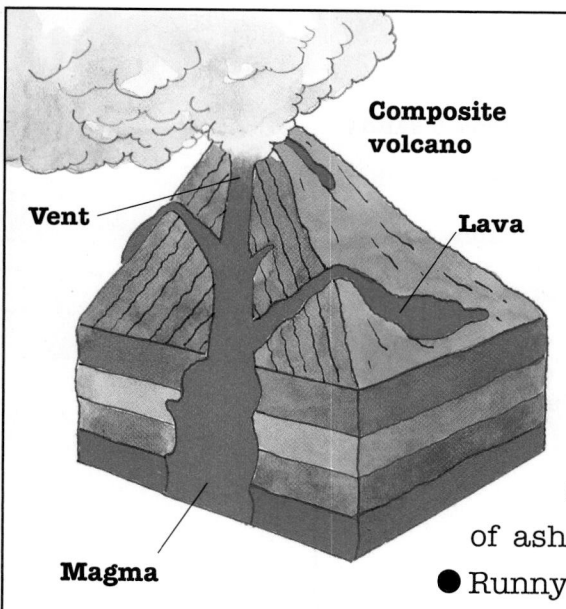

Composite volcano

Vent

Lava

Magma

● Viscous, cooler lava flows more slowly than hot, runny lava. Composite volcanoes have steep sides because they are formed by repeated and frequent flows of stiff, viscous lava. Volcanic eruptions from cones like these are extremely violent.

● Cinder volcanoes are also steep-sided, but are formed by layers of ash and cinder rather than lava.

● Runny lava erupts more gently, then spreads out. Shield and fissure volcanoes form this way.

GEYSERS

● Underground water is sometimes heated by hot magma, and geysers of hot water shoot up out of the ground. These are used as sources of geothermal energy in countries like Iceland.

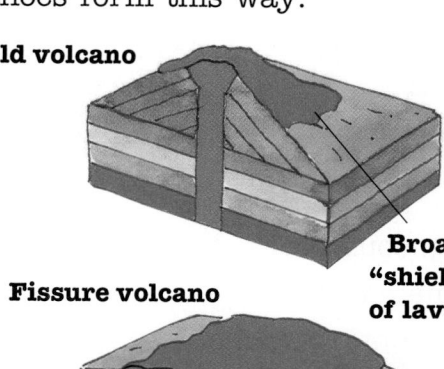

Shield volcano

Broad "shield" of lava

Fissure volcano

Crack in Earth's crust

ROCKS AND MINERALS

The oldest rocks, called igneous rocks, contain crystals. Once igneous rocks have been broken down and changed by the weather, they become sedimentary, or secondhand, rocks. Fossils can be found in the layers, or strata, of sedimentary rocks. Under certain conditions, sedimentary rock can change into another, harder kind of rock, called metamorphic rock.

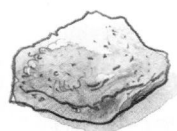

Granite (igneous)

Sandstone (sedimentary)

Marble (metamorphic)

SEDIMENT

To create your own sedimentary layers, you will need some gravel, sand, and mud, a jar with a lid, and some water.

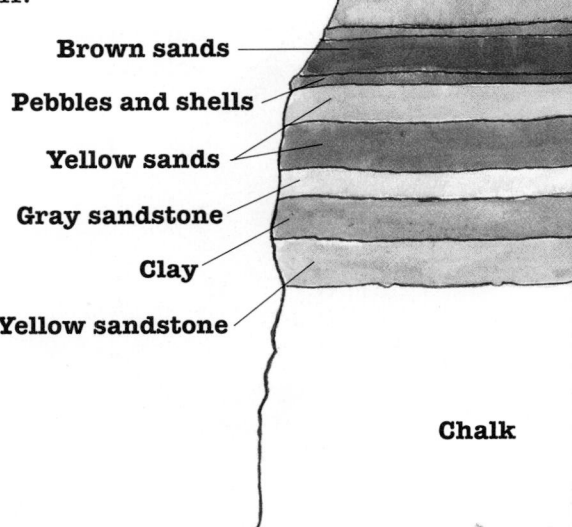

Soil and grass

Clay

Brown sands

Pebbles and shells

Yellow sands

Gray sandstone

Clay

Yellow sandstone

Chalk

● Igneous rocks, like granite, are being formed all the time inside the Earth. Sedimentary rocks, like sandstone, are worn-down igneous rocks. Immense heat and pressure can transform a sedimentary rock, like limestone, into a metamorphic rock, like marble.

1 Put equal amounts of sand, gravel, and mud in layers inside the jar. Cover the layers with water.

2 Screw on the lid tightly, then shake the contents of the jar. Leave it to settle for a few days. Layers of sediment will form.

3 Look closely at the layers. The material with the largest grains settles to the bottom of the jar. Smaller-grained material comes to the top. Make drawings of your "strata" and label them, as in the drawing opposite.

WHERE MINERALS COME FROM

● Rocks are made of minerals. Diamonds are minerals. They are the hardest material known and are used to make cutting tools.

● A scale called Mohs' scale is used to grade the hardness of minerals. Diamonds are at the top of the scale at 10. A mineral at one level can cut minerals in any lower level. Topaz, at 8, is two places below diamond.

Topaz

Diamond

● Diamonds form when magma pushes up volcanic vents and solidifies under great heat and pressure. As it cools, crystals of pure carbon form inside the rock. These carbon crystals are diamonds. Slow cooling makes the largest crystals. As the rock breaks down, some diamond crystals come to the surface.

Some crystals are washed down to the sea.

Volcanic vent

MOUNTAINS AND MAPS

To design maps, cartographers (mapmakers) need exact measurements of the land. Surveyors measure and calculate land height using an instrument called a theodolite. This means that maps can be drawn to scale and can show the exact shape of the land. Mountain heights are always measured from sea level.

1 Ask an adult to help you score the cardboard diagonally using a ruler and craft knife. Cut it in half to make two right-angled triangles. Use only one half.

30° 60° 90°

MOUNTAIN MEASURE

To make and use a theodolite, you need a tape measure, a rectangle of stiff cardboard, a small cardboard tube, thread, tape, a ruler, a craft knife, and string with a key attached.

2 Cut the cardboard tube in half to make two viewers for your theodolite. To make "sights," tape two pieces of thread across the viewing end of each tube, as shown here. Make sure they cross in the center.

3 Tape a viewer to each end of the long side of the triangle. Make a hole at the top of the short side. Push the free end of the string with the key on it through the hole, then knot it so that the key hangs down. This is your plumb line.

HELPFUL HINTS
● Test your theodolite by trying it out on something you already know the height of. You may need to walk backward or forward until you can line up the viewers with the top of the object being measured.

4 Now look through the viewers and line up the center of the sights with the top of a tree. Move forward or backward until the plumb line hangs straight down along the short side of the triangle.

(b)

(a)

5 Ask a friend to measure the distance between you and the foot of the tree (a). The height of the tree is that distance added to your own height (b).

SPOT HEIGHTS AND CONTOURS
● On a contour map, lines join points at the same height above sea level. Where contour lines are very close together, it means the land rises steeply. The highest point on a hill or mountain cannot be shown by contour lines. Instead, a spot height is written on the map showing the exact height at that point. Look in an atlas to find the exact height of Mount Everest.

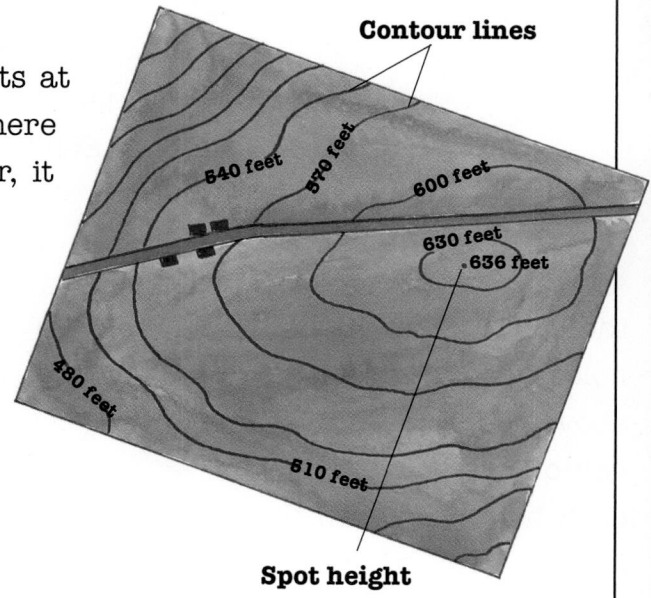

Contour lines

540 feet

570 feet

600 feet

630 feet

.636 feet

480 feet

510 feet

Spot height

HOW HIGH?

Altitude means height above sea level. At high altitudes, the air is thin because there is less oxygen in the Earth's atmosphere at that level. People born in high places have a large heart and lungs, and wide nostrils to breathe in more oxygen. The weight of air pressing down on Earth, called air pressure, is low at high altitudes. In the same way, water pressure is low near the surface (the top) of the sea.

Ben Nevis—4,406 feet

PRESSURE BOTTLE

Make a fountain to show water pressure at work. Air pressure works the same way. You need an empty plastic bottle, a tray, a funnel, clay, paper, a compass, glue, and colored pencils.

1 Look in an atlas to find out the heights of three high mountains. Chart the heights on a picture graph, as shown. Glue the chart around the plastic bottle, leaving a gap down one side.

2 Use a compass to make three holes in the bottle. Position the holes vertically (one above the other) in the gap on the bottle. Make each hole level with the highest point of one of the mountains on your chart.

3 Before filling the plastic bottle with water, cover all three holes with clay. Make sure each hole is completely watertight.

4 Stand the bottle on a tray. Use a funnel to fill the bottle to the top with water. Carefully remove the three pieces of clay and watch what happens.

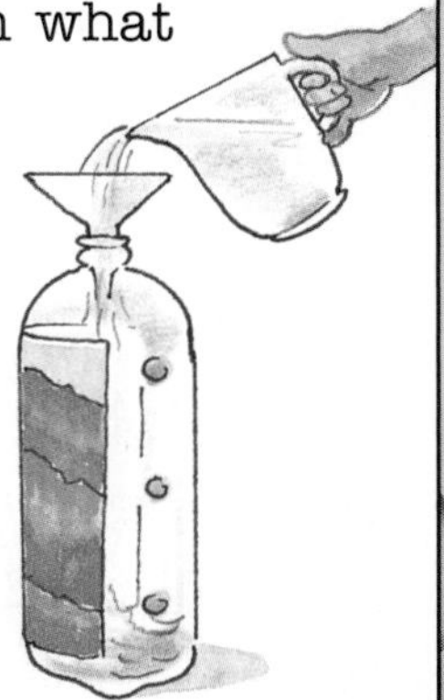

CLEAR AIR
● Astronomers prefer to place telescopes at the tops of mountains because of the thinner, clearer air there. There are few clouds at high altitudes, which makes it much

easier to see the stars and planets.

WHAT'S HAPPENING
● You will notice that the fountain of water at the top does not spurt as far as the two beneath. This is because water pressure is lower at the top than at the bottom. There is more water pushing down on the water at the bottom of the bottle than on the water at the top. In the same way, air pressure is lower at the top of a mountain than at the bottom.

ICE AND SNOW

The higher you go, the colder the climate. Snow is found on mountain peaks, even close to the equator. The level above which snow lies permanently is called the snow line. At the North Pole and South Pole, the snow line is at sea level. Ice forms beneath heavy snow, and rivers of ice called glaciers move slowly down mountainsides carving U-shaped valleys.

HOT WIRE

To show how ice can slide over rocky surfaces, as a glacier does, you will need an ice tray, a freezer, two supports, wire, a large tray, and weights.

1 Fill a rectangular ice tray with water and freeze it. Remove your long ice cube from the dish and position it across the supports, like a bridge, on a large tray.

2 Ask an adult to help you make a wire sling to hold the weights, as shown. Loop a length of wire around the ice cube, and attach its ends to the sling. The sling should hang straight down but not touch the tray.

3 Watch the wire as the heavy weights drag it slowly through the ice. The wire cuts through the ice, but the ice remains in one piece. Eventually, the wire will pass through the ice completely.

WHAT'S HAPPENING

● The pressure of the weighted wire melts the ice, letting the wire pass through it. But above the wire there is no pressure, so the ice freezes again. Below glaciers, the same thing happens as moving ice meets a large rock. The ice melts, flows around the rock, and freezes again on the other side. Melting and refreezing helps the ice slide over large obstacles.

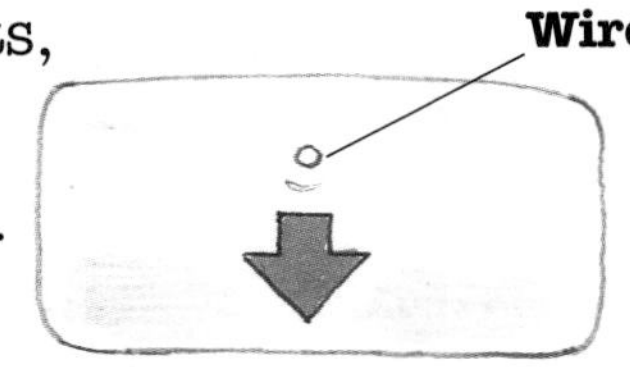

Wire

MOVING ICE AND SNOW

● Glaciers can move around large rocks, but they pick up loose pieces of rock and carry them down mountainsides. These rocks wear away the ground beneath to form U-shaped valleys and also bowl-shaped hollows near mountain peaks, called corries, or cirques.

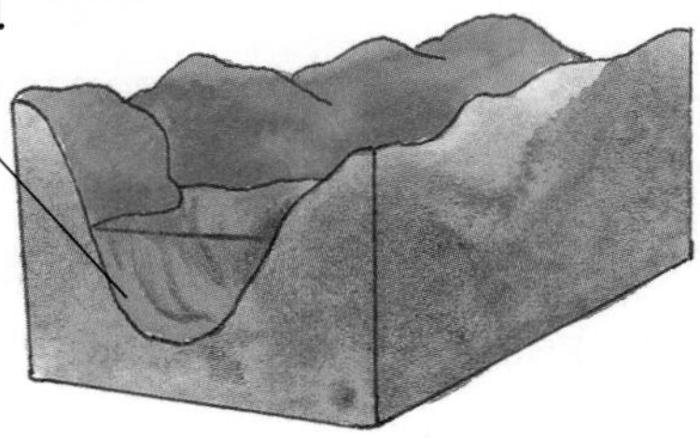

The fjords in Norway were formed by glaciers.

U-shaped valley

● When heavy snow slides down a mountainside, it is called an avalanche. Avalanches often happen when the ground warms slightly and the first snowfall does not freeze hard. A loud noise, or skiers, can set off an avalanche. Whole villages can be buried under the snow.

Loose snow

RAIN SHADOW

Rain falls when warm, moist winds blow from the sea, reach land, then are forced to rise and cool over high mountaintops. Moisture in cooling air near mountain peaks condenses (turns into tiny droplets) to form clouds. When the clouds can hold no more moisture, rain falls. This is called orographic, or relief, rainfall. The far side of the mountain, called the lee side, remains dry, with no rainfall. It is said to be in the rain shadow of the mountain.

WHERE DID ALL THE RAIN GO?

Choose a very rainy day to observe the rain shadow beside a wall. You will need waterproof clothing, three containers (all the same shape and size), and a ruler.

Altitude increases

1 Wearing rain boots, position one container right beside a wall, and the other two containers at varying distances from it. As soon as the rain stops, bring the containers indoors. Be careful not to mix them up!

2 Measure the amount of water in each container. You should find that the container that was nearest the wall has the least water in it. The wall creates a rain shadow. Look at the ground near the wall. Does it seem drier than elsewhere?

Pollution in the atmosphere

Acid rain

Warm air rises and condenses into clouds.

Rain shadow

Rainfall

Mountain range

ACID RAIN

● When rain falls, gases in the air are dissolved. This makes all rainwater naturally slightly acidic. When rain falls on limestone rock, its natural acidity dissolves the rock. But pollution in the air can increase the amount of acidity in rainfall. This harmful acid rain can destroy trees (above) and eat away stonework.

3 Now make a rain-shadow collage showing what you have discovered. Draw a mountain instead of the wall. Copy and color the picture shown here, then glue on cotton clouds. Make sure you label the rain-shadow side of the mountain.

EROSION AND WEATHERING

Over time, land is worn away by rivers and seas, and also by weather. This is called erosion. The eroded material is carried away and left somewhere else. This is called deposition. Erosion and deposition always happen together. On mountain slopes, ice, wind, frost, and rain wear away the rock. Water collects in cracks, freezes, and causes the rock to break. Loose banks of stones may slide down slopes, forming screes.

CRACKING UP

Using balls of modeling clay rolled in plastic wrap, you can carry out an experiment that shows why and how mountain rocks are eroded by frost and ice.

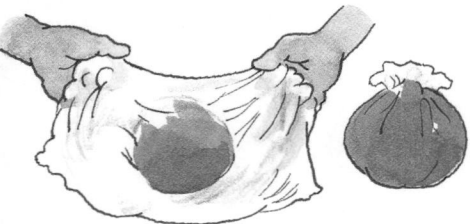

2 Freeze one of the balls of clay. Leave it in the freezer for 24 hours, then remove it. Let it thaw out completely. Then remove the plastic wrap. What differences do you notice between the two balls of clay? Look at the cracks in the thawed clay.

1 Roll two balls from damp modeling clay in the palm of your hands. Spray the outside of the clay with water. Then wrap each ball separately in plastic wrap.

MUDSLIDES

● The clearing of trees from land is called deforestation. Mountainsides erode more quickly after people have chopped down trees. Soil on bare slopes is easily washed away by rain because tree roots no longer hold the soil in place. Heavy rain on eroded slopes can cause mudslides that destroy roads and bury whole towns.

WHAT'S HAPPENING

● Eventually your frozen clay will shatter. The experiment has reproduced what happens, again and again, to rocks frozen by ice and frost on a mountain. Imagine rocks frozen many, many times over centuries. Eventually, those rocks crack, and stones roll down the slopes to form screes.

● The clay shatters because ice fills more space than water, so ice in a crack pushes against the sides and opens the crack even farther. Test this by filling a plastic bottle three-quarters full and freezing it. The ice will fill the bottle—or even break out of it!

3 Spray the thawed clay again. Cover it again with plastic wrap and refreeze. Remove after 24 hours and carry out another observation. Repeat this two or three times, and note the changes each time.

CHAPTER 3
Rivers and Seas

In this chapter, you can find out where rivers are formed, and how they cut their way through the land, forming valleys, waterfalls, and lakes on their way. Ocean tides and waves also change the shape of the land along the coastlines. Water can have tremendous power, and people have been using this power for hundreds of years. In the beginning, it was used to turn grindstones; now we can harness its power to create electricity. You can build your own water wheel, make a river valley model, and grow some stalactites as you learn about rivers and seas.

CONTENTS

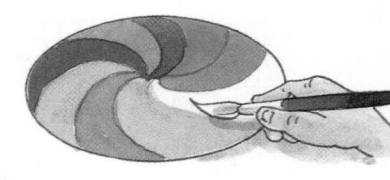

THE SAME WATER **434**

FROM SOURCE TO MOUTH **436**

UNDERGROUND WATER **438**

DOWNRIVER **440**

RIVER POLLUTION **442**

TOO WET, TOO DRY? **444**

THE POWER OF WATER **446**

ON THE BEACH **448**

WAVES AND WIND **450**

OUT AT SEA **452**

UNDER THE SEA **454**

POLLUTION AT SEA **456**

THE SAME WATER

Almost three-quarters of the Earth's surface is water. Most of it is in our oceans or frozen in glaciers (see page 427). In warm weather, water evaporates from rivers and seas, which means it changes into an invisible gas called water vapor. When water vapor cools, it condenses, becomes water again, and falls as rain. This is called the water cycle. The amount of water around us stays the same—it just keeps moving through the water cycle.

WATER CYCLE

Make a model to show the water cycle in action. You will need two large plastic bottles, a narrow cardboard box, a craft knife, cardboard, a wire coat hanger, glue, sticky tape, paint, an aluminum foil tray, ice cubes, and hot water. Ask an adult to help you with the cutting, shaping of hooks, and pouring hot water.

1 Draw the outline of a tree-covered mountain slope on one side of the box. Cut around the shape. Paint the outside of the box.

2 Cut a plastic bottle in half lengthwise. Glue one half inside the box to make a river valley. Slide the foil "sea" tray into the box beneath the narrow end of the bottle.

3 Cut the neck off another large plastic bottle. Cut cloud shapes from cardboard and glue them to one side of the bottle.

OCEAN DEPTHS
● The largest ocean in the world is the Pacific Ocean. An iron ball dropped into the deepest part, which is over 6 miles deep, would take an hour to reach the ocean floor.

N. America
Pacific Ocean
Australia

4 Make hooks from a coat hanger and tape them to the other side of the box, as shown. Rest the bottle on the hooks with its open end facing outward. It should dip at a slight angle.

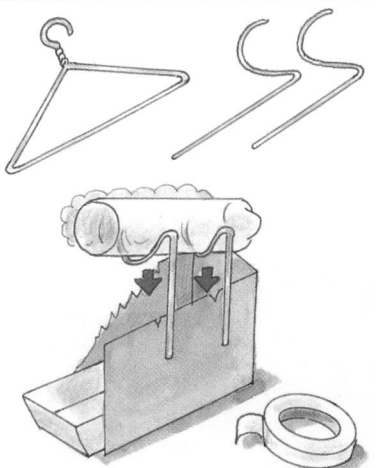

WHAT'S HAPPENING

● Your model demonstrates what happens in the real water cycle, shown here.

5 Put ice cubes into the suspended bottle. Pour hot water into the foil tray. Watch the water vapor rise to make "rain" fall from the cloud.

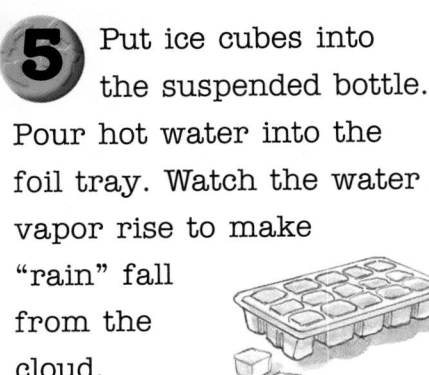

3. The wind blows the clouds toward high land, where the moist air rises and cools even more.

2. As it rises, the water vapor cools and condenses to form tiny droplets, which form clouds.

4. The clouds burst and rain falls into rivers, which flow back to the sea.

1. Heat from the Sun evaporates water from seas and rivers.

5. Some rainwater seeps through the land.

FROM SOURCE TO MOUTH

Rivers begin in the mountains. Some start from a melting glacier or lake. Others start as underground springs. Mountain streams are fast-flowing. They erode (carve out) deep V-shaped valleys. As they reach lower land, closer to the sea, rivers flow more slowly. Here, they erode U-shaped valleys as they curve across wide, flat areas of land called floodplains. The natural loop-like curves shaped by a river are called meanders.

MEANDERING AROUND

To show how water likes to meander, you will need sand, a shallow tray, a ruler, a plastic plant trough, wooden blocks, and a pitcher of water.

1 Scoop dry sand into the tray until it is full. Use the ruler, as shown here, to level the surface and remove any extra sand. Make sure the surface is even.

2 Arrange the blocks so that they are higher than the edge of the plant trough. Position the sand-filled tray with one end on the blocks and the other on the edge of the plant trough. Make sure the tray is sloping gently down toward the trough.

3 Gently pour water onto the sand, so that it flows evenly down the slope. Keep pouring steadily. Watch as your "river" changes its course.

WHAT'S HAPPENING

● All rivers make meanders. Meanders curve more as rivers flow over flat floodplains.

● Water flows faster on outside curves and this erodes the river bank. Where the river flow is slower, on inside curves, material that has been carried down the river is deposited (laid down).

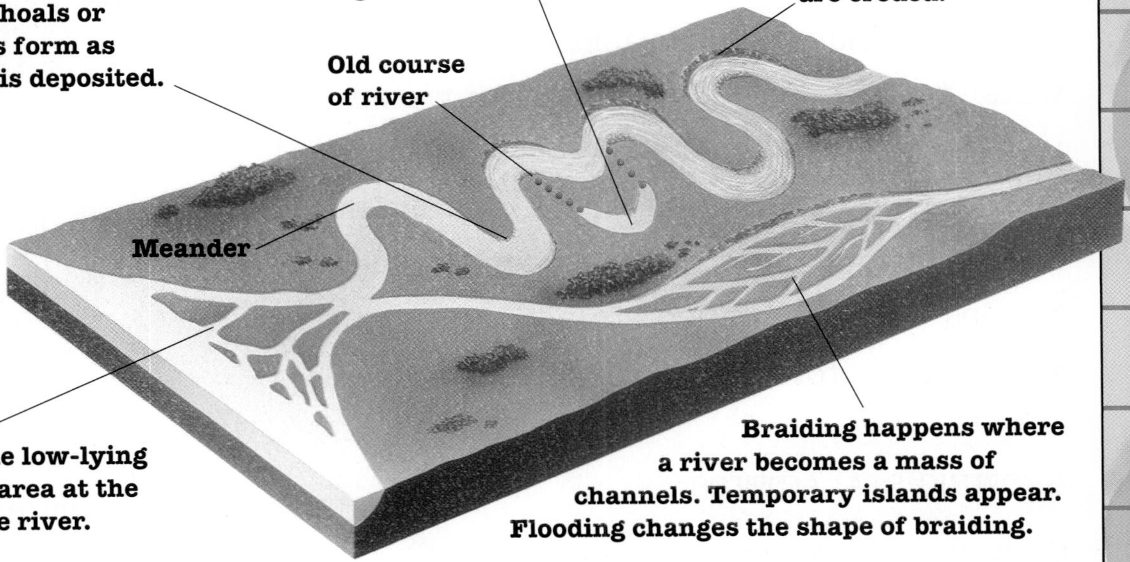

Flow is faster and deeper on outside curves. Cliffs form as river banks are eroded.

If a meander becomes too tightly curved, the river flows across the neck of the curve, leaving an oxbow lake.

Flow is slower and shallower on inside curves. Shoals or sand bars form as material is deposited.

Old course of river

Meander

A delta is the low-lying fan-shaped area at the mouth of the river.

Braiding happens where a river becomes a mass of channels. Temporary islands appear. Flooding changes the shape of braiding.

Lip

WATERFALLS

● Where rivers flow over bands of rock that are too hard to be eroded, a waterfall forms. These can be a few feet high, forming rapids, or hundreds of feet high. On high waterfalls, the water spills over the rock at the lip. A deep pool, called a plunge pool, is eroded by rocks and pebbles that swirl around at the base of a high waterfall.

Plunge pool

UNDERGROUND WATER

Water not carried away by rivers becomes ground water. It seeps through cracks and pores (tiny holes) in rocks and collects underground. Rock that soaks up water like a sponge, like sandstone, is called porous rock. Other rock, like limestone, has many cracks and joints for water to seep through. When rainwater, which is slightly acidic, soaks through limestone, it dissolves minerals in the rock and eventually carves out an underground cave. Inside, "icicles" of rock, called stalactites and stalagmites, form from dissolved minerals.

GROWING STALACTITES

Grow some stalactites using a saturated solution of baking soda (see step 1), two jars, a dish, two paper clips, and some yarn.

1 Fill each jar with warm water. Add baking soda to the water and stir. Keep adding soda until no more can be dissolved. This is a saturated solution.

2 Place the jars slightly apart, in a very warm place, with a dish between them. Fasten a paper clip to each end of the yarn. Lower a paper clip into each jar, as shown, so that the yarn hangs over the dish.

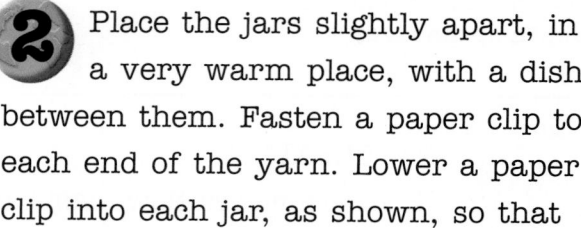

3 Now watch the slow growth of a stalactite in the center of the yarn—it will take about a week for a good stalactite to form. Keep a note of how much it grows each day.

WHAT'S HAPPENING

● The soda solution seeps upward, then collects and drips from the center of the yarn. As the water in the solution evaporates, the soda deposit remains and a stalactite grows down from the yarn.

● Stalactites hang down from cave ceilings. Stalagmites build up from the ground. If you leave it long enough, a stalagmite will grow from the water that drips onto the dish.

FLOODING

● Rainwater can seep only so far into the ground. The level at which it stops, where the rock is saturated (can absorb no more water), is called the water table.

● Limestone is permeable rock— it lets rainwater soak through its cracks until the ground beneath is saturated.

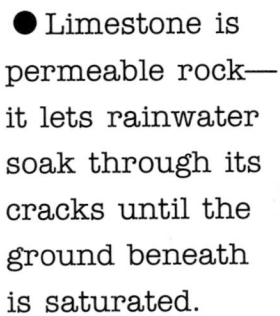

Limestone

Water table

In frequent heavy rain, limestone areas are likely to flood as the water seeps through the rock and raises the level of the water table.

● Heavy rain in mountains is carried downstream in rivers, so floods often happen on floodplains. People build defenses, called levees, to protect their homes.

Floodplain

Major flood level

Flood level

Average river level

Levee

DOWNRIVER

Settlements are often built close to rivers. In the desert area of North Africa, the Nile River provides water for farmers, who grow crops along its banks. The Nile begins as two tributaries, the Blue Nile and the White Nile, which join, then flow northward into the Mediterranean Sea. The Nile is the world's longest river. It is over 4,000 miles long, which is farther than the distance from New York to London.

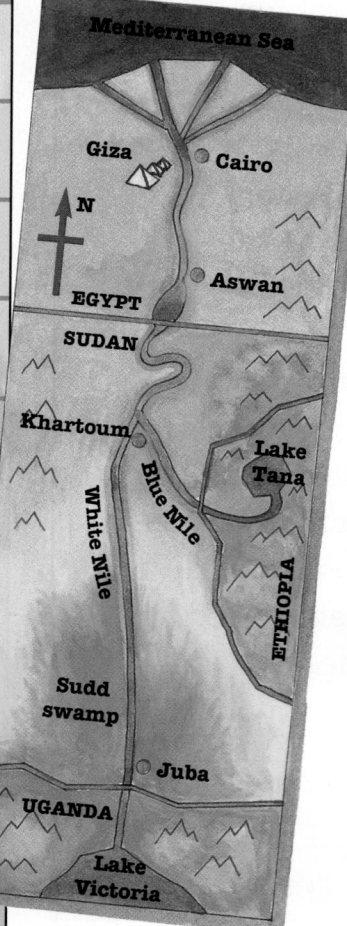

NILE MODEL

A linear map (left) shows important landmarks along a river valley. To make a model of the Nile using this linear map, use a large board, flour, water, newspaper, cardboard, sand, paint, and bottle tops.

Use bottle tops for towns and cities.

1 Find the Nile in an atlas. See if you can spot all the landmarks shown on the linear map. The linear map has no scale. This means that it gives the names of places, but does not show true distance.

2 To make your model, first draw the shape of the Nile onto the board. Then paint it blue. Paint the fertile fields along the river banks green.

3 To make mountains, mix flour and cold water into a thick paste. Tear newspaper into small pieces and soak these in the paste to make papier-mâché. Position small mounds of papier-mâché on the board and shape them into peaks.

Mix sand with yellow paint for the desert.

Make pyramids from cardboard.

When your papier-mâché peaks are dry, paint them.

4 When the painted model is dry, use bottle tops and cardboard to mark the positions of any landmarks, like towns and pyramids. Look at the linear map to find their names, then write neat labels for them.

CROSSING RIVERS

● The first bridge was probably a fallen tree laid across a stream. Now, engineers decide which kind of bridge to build by studying the weight it has to carry and the width of the river.

Weight on bridge
Weight spread

Suspension bridges are used to span wide rivers or bays. They are supported by cables made from strong steel wires twisted together.

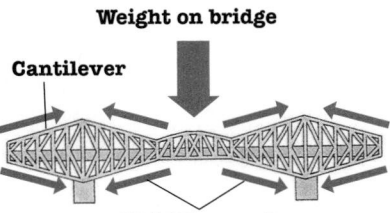

Weight on bridge

Cantilever

Weight spread

A **cantilever bridge** is a balanced structure. Separate cantilevers are joined by short spans of steel.

An **arched bridge** is a very strong structure, as it spreads weight outward and downward around the whole length of each arch.

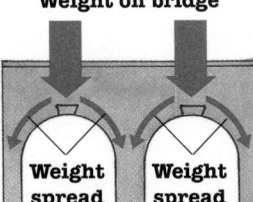

Weight on bridge

Weight spread   Weight spread

RIVER POLLUTION

At its source in the mountains, a stream is sparkling and clear, but farther downstream, human activities cause pollution that reduces the oxygen in the water. Fresh water can become so polluted that plants and animals die. Pesticides sprayed on crops are washed into rivers by the rain. Trash is often dumped in rivers. Waste materials from factories and mines are piped into rivers.

MUDDY FILTER

Our drinking water comes from the water in the water cycle. It is filtered and purified before it reaches our faucets. You can make a water filter using a plastic bottle, sand, water, soil, a paper coffee filter, and a pitcher.

1 Ask an adult to cut the top from the plastic bottle about 4 inches from the lid. Place the top upside down, inside the bottle. Tap it firmly into place.

2 Position the filter paper inside the bottle top. Spoon a layer of sand into the filter. Pour enough water onto the sand to make it wet.

442

3 Mix soil and water in the pitcher. Slowly pour the muddy mixture onto the wet sand inside the filter. Watch the water pass through the sand and collect in the bottom of the bottle.

4 Now study the water in the bottom of the bottle. It will look cleaner, but beware, it is not fit to drink! Our drinking water is filtered many times before it comes out of the faucet. Compare your filtered water with tap water to see the difference.

POLLUTION DISASTERS

● The Rhine is the longest and dirtiest river in Europe. In 1986, after a fire at the Sandoz factory in Switzerland, more than 30 tons of chemicals entered the Rhine (see right). For 125 miles downstream, all living things in the river died. In January 2000, pollution of the Tisza River in Hungary killed most of the fish within hours.

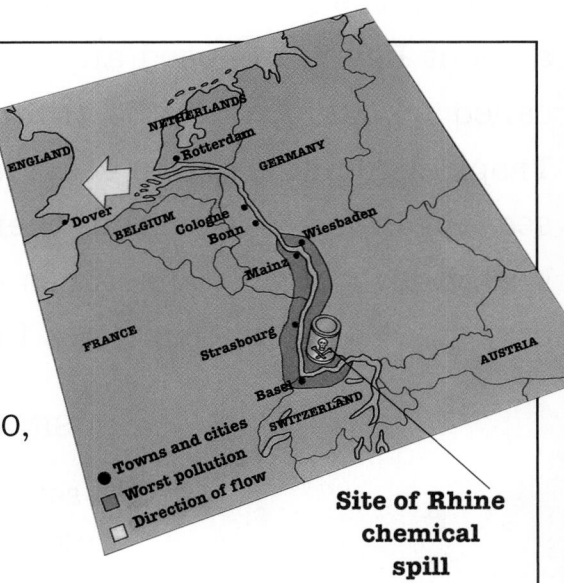

● Towns and cities
□ Worst pollution
□ Direction of flow

Site of Rhine chemical spill

OXYGEN IN WATER

● Water creatures need oxygen to survive. Much oxygen is released from water plants during photosynthesis, which is the way that plants make food using sunlight. You can test this by putting some Canadian pondweed in a bowl of water. Stand it in the Sun and watch bubbles of oxygen appear.

TOO WET, TOO DRY?

In arid (dry) parts of the world, rain may not fall for months. Rivers stop flowing and soil becomes too dry to grow crops. Farmers need to irrigate their land, which means they supply water to the fields, often through ditches. The ancient Egyptians used an irrigation device called a *shaduf*, which is still used today. Tropical countries have a dry and a wet season. In the wet season, there are sudden, heavy downpours. Sometimes there are floods and drought in the same year.

RAISING WATER

To see how a *shaduf* works, you need a craft knife, corrugated cardboard, tape, a clean yogurt cup, string, a wooden spoon, and clay.

1 Ask an adult to help you cut and fold a strip of corrugated cardboard as shown below. Cut a slot at each end, wide enough for the handle of your wooden spoon.

Fold

2 Tie a long piece of string around the yogurt cup under the rim, as shown, then over the top to make a big loop.

3 Knot another piece of string onto the loop on the cup and tie the other end to the wooden spoon, as shown. Tape a large lump of clay to the spoon.

4 Slot and tape the spoon into the base, toward the clay end, as shown. You may have to add more clay when the bucket is full of water, so that it swings up easily.

5 Place your *shaduf* beside a full sink or basin. Lower the bucket. When it is full, you should be able to raise it very easily by the string. You can now pour the water into another basin.

WHAT'S HAPPENING

● A *shaduf* works as a lever. The clay weight makes it easy to lift the full bucket. In Egypt, water is raised from the Nile and poured into channels to irrigate the fields.

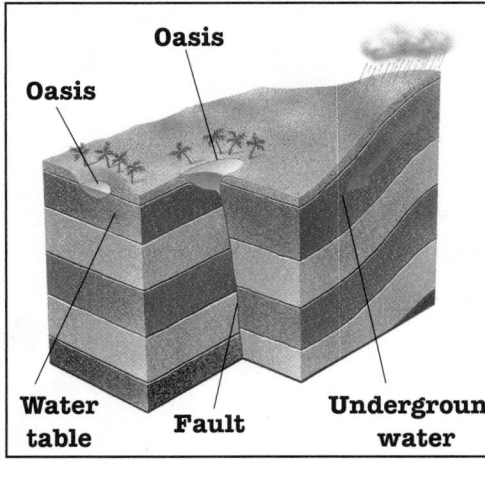

OASIS

● Underground water can seep hundreds of miles through the water table, from distant mountains to low-lying areas. An oasis is where the water table emerges at the surface. This can happen at a hollow in the sand or at a fault, where rock has moved suddenly and a spring appears.

Oasis

Oasis

Oasis

Water table

Fault

Underground water

THE POWER OF WATER

Water power is a clean, renewable source of energy. It has been used for hundreds of years to do work. Water wheels once turned grindstones. Now, water turbines are harnessed to generators that make electricity. This is called hydroelectric power. Huge dams have been built across rivers to provide electricity for cities and towns. However, large dams cause damage to the surrounding land and many people now believe that small dams are better.

WATER WHEEL

To make a water wheel, you will need two large plastic lids, glue, craft sticks, a tray, a craft knife, a plastic bottle, paint, a pushpin, doweling, cardboard, a pitcher, a compass, and water.

1 Ask an adult to pierce a hole in the top of each of the two lids. Glue them together as shown. Now glue craft sticks around the edge of the lids to make paddles.

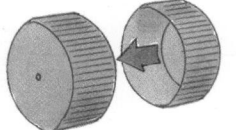

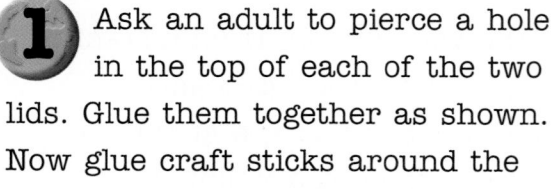

2 Ask an adult to cut V-shapes in the cardboard. Score and fold the cardboard and position around the tray, as shown, to make a support.

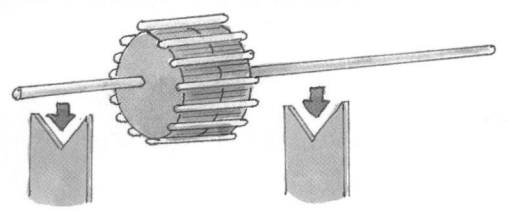

3 Push the doweling through the holes in your wheel, so that one end sticks out farther than the other. Rest it inside the V-shaped notches, as shown.

4 Use a compass to draw a flywheel on cardboard. Cut it out and color brightly. Push a pushpin through the center of the flywheel and into the long end of the doweling.

5 Ask an adult to cut sections from the bottle and glue them together, as shown. Make another support, this time with U-shaped notches and one end higher than the other. Glue on the plastic.

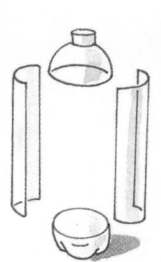

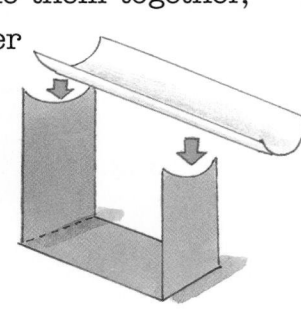

6 Arrange the parts as shown in the photograph. Carefully pour water from the pitcher into the plastic channel. Watch the wheels turn.

WHAT'S HAPPENING

● The energy of the falling water turns the wheel, which spins the flywheel. Raise the pitcher higher, and the added energy in the water will make the wheel turn faster.

● Your flywheel represents a turbine, which drives a generator.

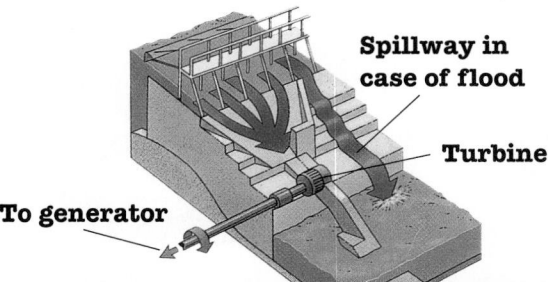

Spillway in case of flood

Turbine

To generator

TIDAL POWER

● Energy from the sea is also used to make electricity. The tide comes in and goes out twice daily. Power stations built across estuaries use turbines that spin in two directions, to harness the tide's energy both as it comes in and as it goes out.

ON THE BEACH

The sea's tides and crashing waves change the shape of our coasts. Tides are caused mainly by the pull of the Moon as it circles the Earth. The pull makes oceans on each side of the globe bulge a little (a high tide) and then fall back (a low tide) every 12 hours or so. Pounding waves and the material they carry cause erosion and deposition. These work together to break down and build up our beaches and cliffs, sometimes forming rocky arches and stacks.

MAKE A COASTLINE

Build a model coastline with a sandy beach to show how waves can gradually wash away the sand from our beaches and form stacks.

1 You will need a long waterproof tray, a pitcher, modeling clay, sand, water, and cardboard. First, shape some tall clay rock stacks and press them firmly in place toward one end of the tray, as shown here.

2 Fill about half the tray with sand, making sure the clay stacks are completely covered. Gently pour water into the rest of the tray.

WHAT'S HAPPENING

● When a part of a wave hits shallower water, it slows down and the rest of the wave bends. When waves reach a headland, they slow, swing around the headland, and hit its sides. This gradually wears it away, leaving a stack or arch.

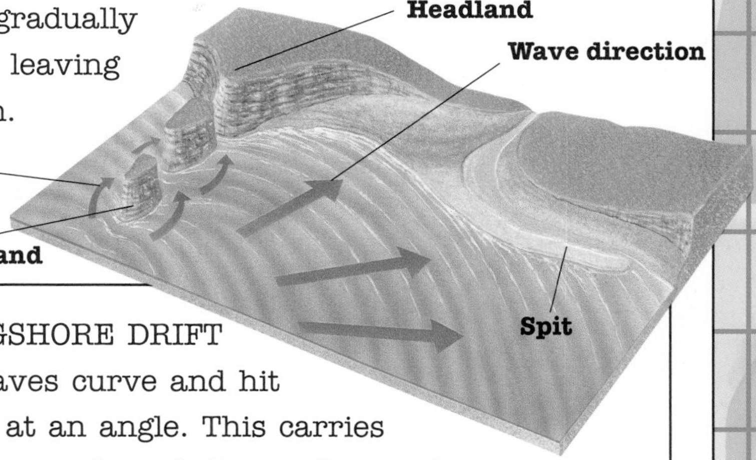

Headland

Wave direction

Waves bend

Stack formed from old headland

Spit

LONGSHORE DRIFT

● Waves curve and hit bays at an angle. This carries pebbles and sand diagonally up the beach. The wave backwash pulls the pebbles and sand back down the slope at right angles to the beach, gradually moving them along in a series of zigzag patterns. This is called longshore drift. Sand banks and spits are formed this way.

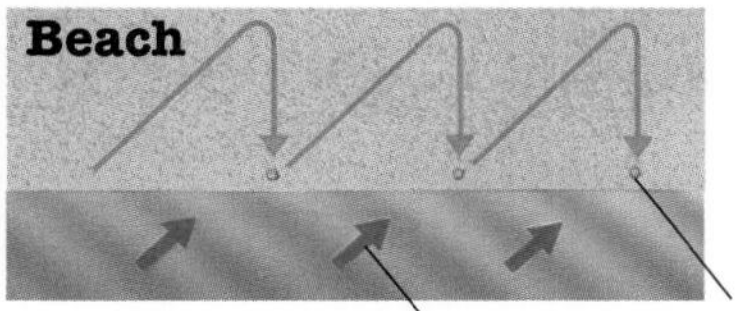

Beach

Sand particle

Wave direction

PEBBLES

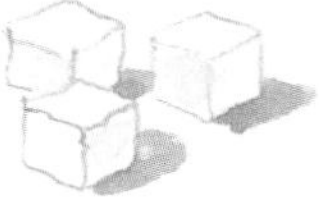

● Pebbles are rocks worn smooth by attrition (rubbing against each other) in rivers or seas. They may be flat or rounded, but are always smooth. Shake sugar lumps in a jar. Watch the edges of the cubes rub against each other until they are smooth, like pebbles.

3 Move the cardboard back and forth to make waves. Gradually, the movement of the waves will wash away, or erode, the sand and expose the stacks. You may even see an arch forming between stacks.

WAVES AND WIND

Waves are started by the wind, way out at sea. It whips the water surface into ripples, which build up into waves as the wind gets stronger. The waves get bigger and bigger as they travel through the sea. Although the waves travel great distances, the water in them stays in the same place, moving up and down, until the wave hits a coast. A huge wave called a tsunami can form if there is an underwater earthquake.

TESTING THE WIND

The stronger the wind, the bigger the wave. Test wind strength by building an anemometer. You will need cardboard, a ping-pong ball, a compass, a pen, a ruler, a craft knife, a pushpin, and glue.

1 Use the compass to draw a curve onto the cardboard. Mark off equal spaces, making a scale for comparing wind speeds.

2 Ask an adult to cut a strip of cardboard with a window, so that you can see the scale. Glue the ping-pong ball to one end.

3 Pin the other end of the strip onto your cardboard scale on the spot where the compass made a small hole. Make sure it can swing freely. Hold your anemometer in a windy spot and see how far the strip is blown.

WAVE MOVEMENT

● If you throw a stone into a pond, ripples form on the surface. A boat will move up and down on the ripples, but not forward or backward. Waves at sea are the same as ripples—they don't move the water forward, only up and down.

● Beneath the waves, water particles move up and down in circles. This causes waves to turn over or break at the surface. When a wave reaches shore, it cannot circulate as well in the shallow water, so it piles up, taller and taller, until it spills over and breaks.

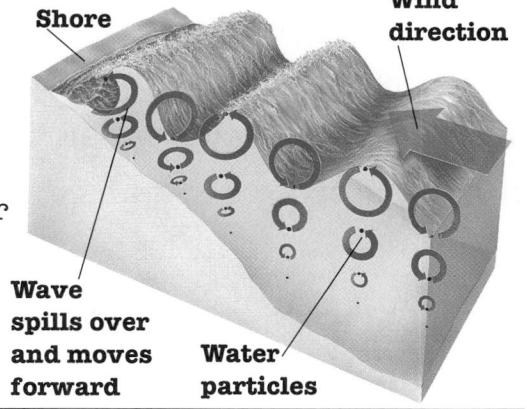

Shore

Wind direction

Wave spills over and moves forward

Water particles

BEAUFORT SCALE

● Storms at sea can drown fishermen and sailors. The Beaufort wind scale (right) was designed for sailors in 1805 by Admiral Sir Francis Beaufort. It ranges from 0 to 12, from calm to hurricane. Force 8 is a gale, force 10 is a stormy sea. Sailors and fishermen listen to the radio for gale warnings before going out to sea.

No wind

Smoke moves

Branches move

Crests on water

Trees bend

Hard to walk

Trees uprooted

Devastation

OUT AT SEA

Water in the world's oceans is moved around by ocean currents. Near the surface, these currents are caused by prevailing winds, which means winds that occur frequently in certain places. The shape of the land and the ocean floor affect deeper ocean currents. The sea water's temperature and density (the heaviness of a certain amount of water) also affect currents. Very salty water, found in hot, subtropical oceans, is more dense than less salty water, found in cold, polar oceans.

FLOATING FISH

To show that salt makes water more dense, you will need a transparent bowl, salt, a spoon, water, a potato, a pitcher, scissors, plastic lids, and food coloring.

1 Make a solution of salt by adding salt to a pitcher of water until no more will dissolve (about 12 big spoonfuls). Make a note of the amount of water you use. Pour the salt solution into the bowl.

2 Measure out the same amount of water. Add food coloring. Then carefully and slowly pour the colored water, over the back of a spoon, on top of the salt solution in the bowl.

3 Ask an adult to cut a slice of potato about ¹/₂ inch thick. Cut out two fins from the plastic lids and attach them to the potato body of your fish. Place the fish in the water and watch what it does.

WHAT'S HAPPENING

● The fish will sink, then float at the level of the salt water. This is because the density of the fish is less than the density of the salt water, but more than the density of the fresh water.

Fresh water

Salt water

OCEAN CURRENTS

● Currents move in circular patterns and are sometimes called gyres. In the northern hemisphere, they spin clockwise. In the southern hemisphere, they spin counterclockwise. Some currents are warm and some cold. Ocean currents warm or cool the air above them and this has a major effect on the Earth's weather.

Icy arctic currents meet warm currents from the south

Warm currents

Cold currents

EL NIÑO

● El Niño is an unusually warm current that affects the Pacific Ocean every few years, around Christmastime. It can affect weather all over the world, and is thought to have been responsible for severe droughts in southern Africa, floods in California, and hurricanes in the Atlantic.

Warm water of El Niño moves toward South America

UNDER THE SEA

The gently sloping part of the seabed around the continents is called the continental shelf. It is covered by shallow seas, but is really part of the continent. Sands and gravel in the continental shelf are rich in minerals. A large part of the world's oil and gas deposits are also found under the sea. Oil and gas are fossil fuels, formed over millions of years in layers of sedimentary rock (see page 420). They are found where silt or sand settled on the seabed and buried plant or animal remains. The world's fossil fuels are nonrenewable, which means they will eventually run out.

1. Dead sea plants and animals are buried in sediment that hardens into porous rock.

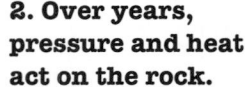

2. Over years, pressure and heat act on the rock.

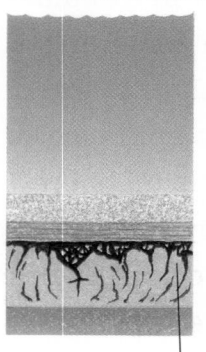

They convert the dead plants and animals into oil and gas.

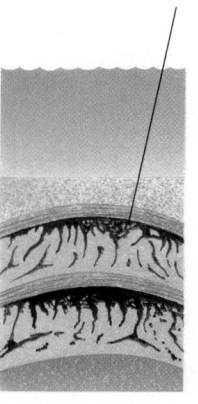

3. Underground pressure forces the oil and gas upward through the porous rock.

FOSSIL FUEL MODEL

Make a model that shows how fossil fuels are formed. You will need glue, cardboard, scissors, sand, and paint.

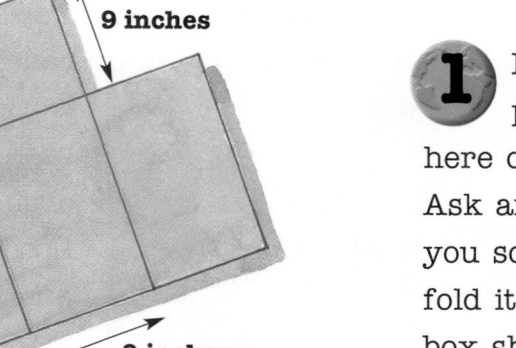

9 inches

13 inches

9 inches

1 Draw the pattern shown here on cardboard. Ask an adult to help you score, cut, and fold it into a long box shape.

2 Paint your box with the layers of sea, rock, gas, and oil shown below. Spread on some glue, then sprinkle on sand to create a realistic effect. Draw and cut out a model oil rig and glue it in position over the oil.

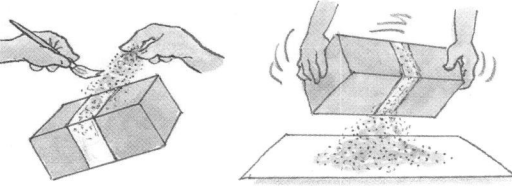

6. Oil rigs drill down to the reservoirs and pump up the oil.

4. The oil and gas reach nonporous rock, which they can't pass through.

5. The trapped oil (black) and gas (green) form underground pockets called reservoirs.

GLOBAL WARMING

● Burning nonrenewable fossil fuels releases polluting gases such as carbon dioxide into the air. World temperatures are thought to be rising because these gases, known as greenhouse gases, are trapping too much heat inside the Earth's atmosphere. This environmental problem is called global warming.

Heat trapped

Greenhouse gases

Heat from the Sun

● Too much global warming will melt the polar icecaps and cause sea levels around the world to rise, flooding low-lying coastal areas. The problem could be reduced if cleaner, renewable sources of energy, like water and wind, were used instead of fossil fuels.

POLLUTION AT SEA

The population of the world is now more than six billion. More people means more trash. Our oceans are now becoming dumping grounds. Polluted water is destroying the food chains of the sea. Oil tanker disasters devastate vast areas of our seas and coasts and kill or harm many thousands of birds, sea mammals, and fish. Scientists use various ways of dealing with the oil spillages. One is to disperse (break up) the oil using chemicals.

OILY WATER

Make some "slick" pictures to see how oil floats and how it can be broken up. You will need a bowl, plastic cups, oil-based paints, turpentine, water, paper, a stick, and dish detergent.

1 Ask an adult to help you mix a few drops of oil-based paint with a little turpentine in a cup. Mix several different colors.

 Fill the bowl with water. Pour in your paints and stir with a stick to make an oily "slick."

3 Lower a sheet of paper onto the water. Let it soak up the paint, then remove and leave it to dry. Stir the water, then repeat to get different oily patterns.

4 Now squeeze a little dish detergent onto the oily paint, move the stick through it, and watch the "slick" disperse.

WHAT'S HAPPENING

● Oil is less dense than water, which means it floats on top of the water. The detergent splits the oily layer into tiny droplets, which can then sink to mix with the water below.

OIL DISASTERS

● When the oil tanker *Erika* sank off the coast of France in 1999, over 18,000 sea birds with feathers coated in oil were picked up from the oil-covered beaches. In 1989, the *Exxon Valdez* (right) hit rocks off Alaska, spilling nearly 40,000 tons of oil. It polluted 1,200 miles of coastline, killing up to 300,000 sea birds, 5,000 rare sea otters, and many seals and fish.

Exxon Valdez

ALASKA

Damaged shoreline

Sea bird habitat

Sea otter habitat

CORAL REEF DESTRUCTION

● Coral reefs are underwater ridges formed by tiny creatures called polyps. They are only found in warm, tropical seas and are home to an amazing variety of marine life. Coral reefs need crystal-clear water to survive. One-tenth of the world's coral reefs have now been so badly damaged by pollution that they will never recover.

CHAPTER 4
Ecosystems

An ecosystem can be as small as an oak tree, or as large as a forest. Weather and climate play a part in every ecosystem. But not only natural factors have an impact. Human progress is forcing wildlife to adapt to  change as the homes of many animals are being destroyed.

Plants and animals in a food chain depend upon each other for survival. The loss of even one species can cause damage to the entire food chain. In this chapter, you can play an ecosystem card game, make a minirainforest, and build a model food web. Learn about ecosystems so that you can help wildlife survive and flourish!

CONTENTS

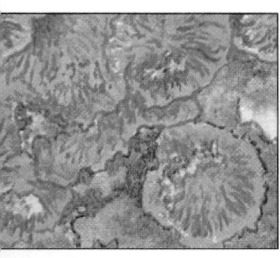

WHAT IS AN ECOSYSTEM? **460**

WHO EATS WHAT? **462**

AN OAK TREE **464**

GLOBAL ECOSYSTEMS **466**

CONIFEROUS FORESTS **468**

TROPICAL RAINFORESTS **470**

HOT DESERTS **472**

COLD DESERTS **474**

FRESHWATER ECOSYSTEMS **476**

ON THE SEASHORE **478**

SALTWATER ECOSYSTEMS **480**

WILDLIFE GARDEN **482**

WHAT IS AN ECOSYSTEM?

The natural home of a plant or animal is called its habitat. Each habitat supports a different community (group) of living things. An ecosystem is made up of any given habitat and its community. The living things in an ecosystem interact with each other. They also interact with the nonliving parts of their environment (surroundings), such as water or weather. Ecosystems can be large or small. A pond or even a tree is a small ecosystem. Our planet is one huge ecosystem. The study of ecosystems is called ecology.

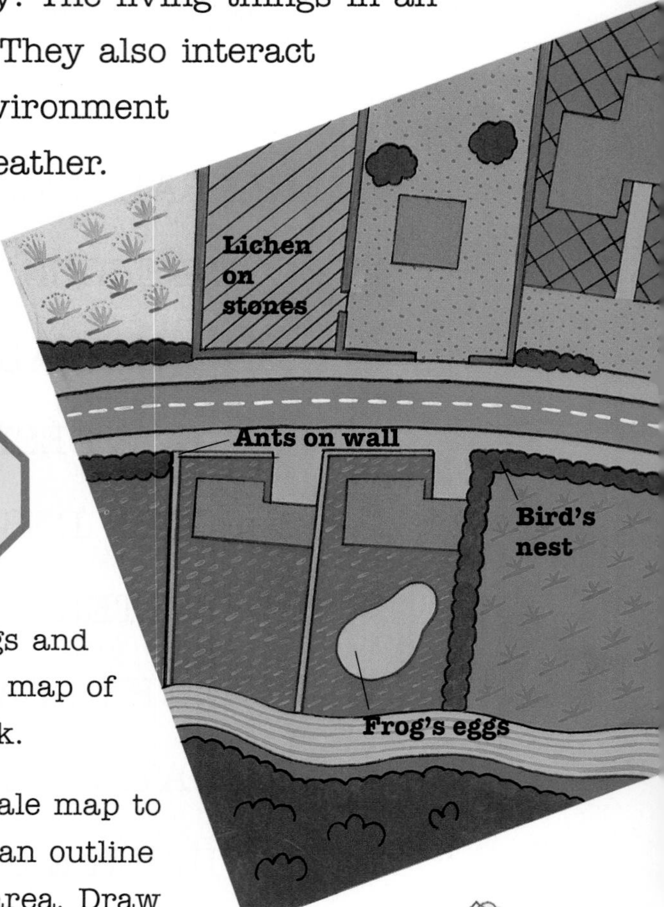

Lichen on stones

Ants on wall

Bird's nest

Frog's eggs

LOCAL ECOSYSTEMS

Make a local ecosystems map.
If you can, choose an area with buildings and open spaces. You will need a large-scale map of the area, colored pencils, and a notebook.

1 Use the large-scale map to sketch or trace an outline map of your chosen area. Draw in the roads and buildings. Ask an adult to walk around the area with you.

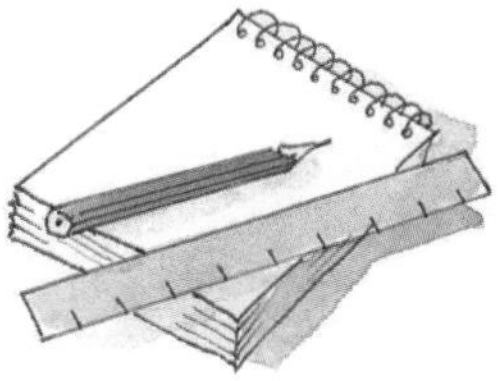

2 Make notes or take photos of different ecosystems. There are often small ecosystems within larger ones. Look for living things interacting with nonliving things, such as insects on a wall.

3 Mark on the map the locations of all the ecosystems you have observed, using different patterns or symbols for each ecosystem. Draw the symbols with pencil first, then color them in.

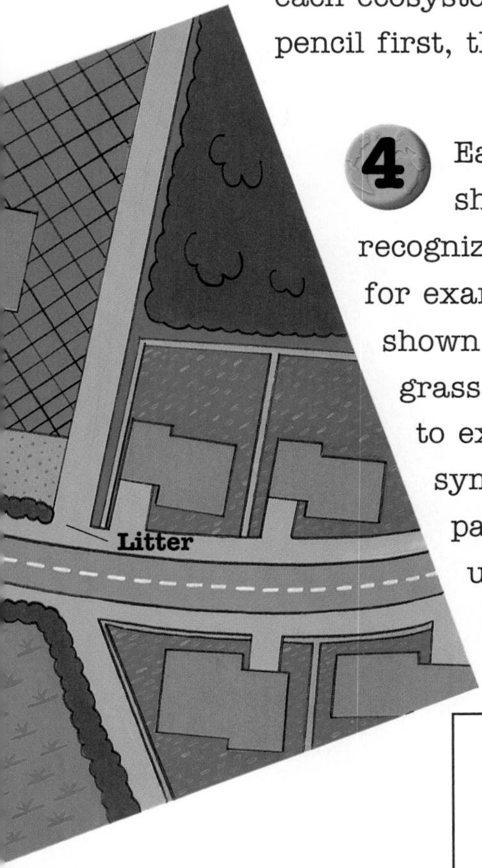

4 Each ecosystem should be easy to recognize. A meadow, for example, could be shown by a tuft of grass. Design a key to explain the symbols and patterns you have used. Print names beside each one.

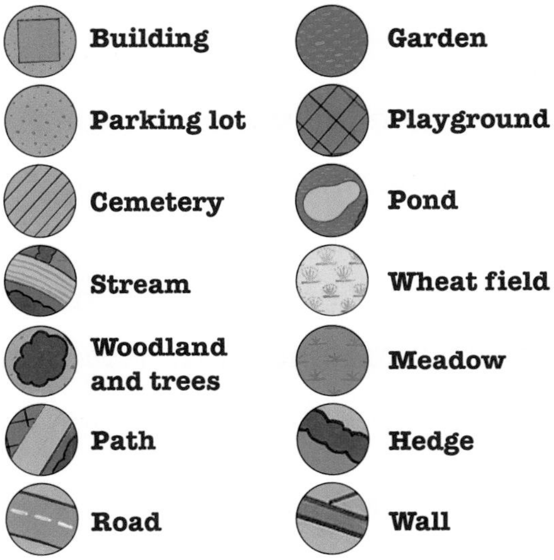

Building
Parking lot
Cemetery
Stream
Woodland and trees
Path
Road

Garden
Playground
Pond
Wheat field
Meadow
Hedge
Wall

Litter

5 Now add to your map any other details you have observed. Depending upon the season, you may have noticed a bird's nest or a fox's lair. Or you may have noticed parts of an ecosystem damaged by litter pollution.

LIVING AND NONLIVING 
● An ecosystem is a jigsaw puzzle of living and nonliving parts. The Sun and weather play a part in every ecosystem. Each part is vital. They are interdependent— if one piece is lost, the whole ecosystem breaks down. Make a list of the living and nonliving parts of your ecosystems.

Ecosystem	Living parts	Nonliving parts
Pond	Frogs, dragonflies, water lilies, pondweed	Water, stones, air, sunshine

461

WHO EATS WHAT?

All living things in an ecosystem depend upon each other for food. They are linked together in a food web. In a healthy ecosystem, there must be a balance between the number of living things that exist there. This balance is called the food pyramid. Usually, there are far fewer carnivores (meat eaters) than herbivores (plant eaters). The carnivores keep the number of herbivores under control. Most natural ecosystems, on land and in water, get their energy from the Sun. The Sun's energy is passed through the food pyramid.

FOOD PYRAMID

4. Large carnivores eat herbivores and small carnivores. So they are both secondary and tertiary (third-level) consumers.

3. Small carnivores eat herbivores. They are secondary (second-level) consumers.

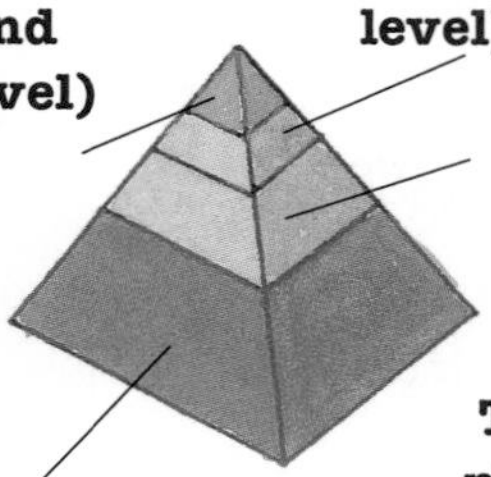

1. Plants are producers—they produce their own food using energy from the Sun.

2. Herbivores are primary (first-level) consumers. They eat green plants directly. They are prey to large and small carnivores.

Person

Bird of prey

Rabbit

Sheep

Plants

Air

FOOD WEB

Food webs show all the members of an ecosystem community and how they interact with each other. Make your own food web to show who eats what.

Sun's energy

1 Cut out pictures of living things found in a wood. Draw and cut out a picture of the Sun, water, and a cloud (for air). Glue your pictures onto folded strips of cardboard.

2 Stand the cards up. Use ribbon and tape to attach each animal to its food. Use red ribbon for carnivores and green ribbon for herbivores. Trace each ribbon with your finger to see how all the plants and animals are interlinked.

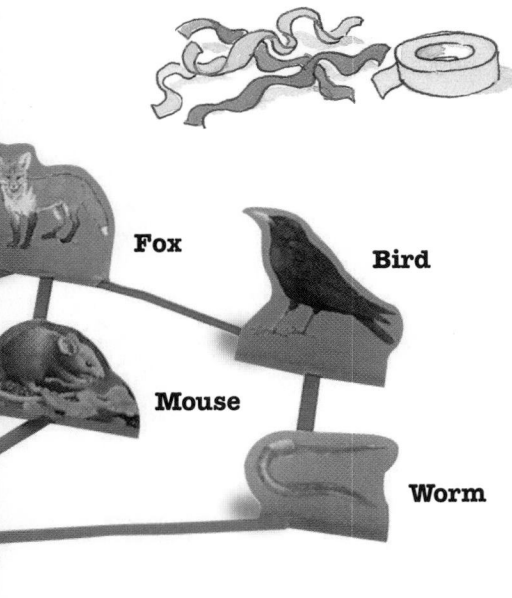

Fox

Bird

Mouse

Worm

Water

ENERGY FROM THE SUN

● Each chain of links in a food web, joining plants to herbivores and carnivores, is called a food chain. Most food chains start with the Sun.

● Chlorophyll, the green color in leaves, uses the Sun's energy to make food. Sunlight turns molecules of water and a gas called carbon dioxide into sugar inside the leaf. This process is called photosynthesis.

Sugar

● In this simple food chain, a cabbage makes food using sunshine. The Sun's energy passes to the caterpillar when it eats a cabbage leaf. A bird then eats the caterpillar. When the bird dies, decomposers —small creatures and plants such as insect larvae and fungi—break down its body into the soil. This enriches the soil, which plants then use to help them grow.

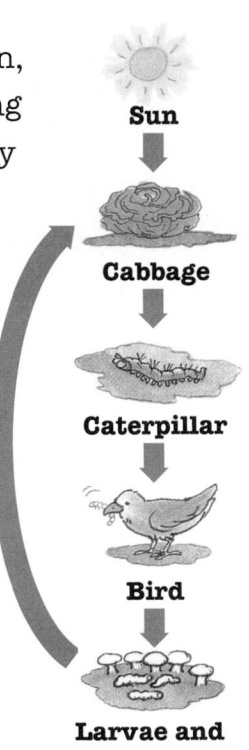

Sun

Cabbage

Caterpillar

Bird

Larvae and fungi

AN OAK TREE

An oak tree supports a small ecosystem. The tree is broad-leaved and deciduous, which means it loses its leaves in winter. The oak is a rich habitat for animals and birds, which find food and building materials on and around the tree. At ground level, there are worms, insects, leaf litter, dead wood, flowers, grasses, and fungi. From the ground beneath the tree to the canopy—the top of the tree—a variety of living things can be observed.

WHAT'S IN A TREE?

Make a seasonal diary for the ecosystem of an oak tree. You will need paper, string, twigs, an old umbrella, and colored pencils.

1 Hang the open umbrella from a lower branch on the tree. Shake the branch lightly. Describe or sketch any minibeasts that fall into your umbrella trap. Record your findings, then return the minibeasts to their habitat.

Spring

Date/time	Weather	
April 12th 11 A.M.		
April 15th 1 P.M.		**Squirrel**—gray
April 16th 4 P.M.		**Worm castings**—lots on ground under tree
April 18th 10 A.M.		**Green woodpecker**—green body, red on head—making a drumming noise on tree trunk
		Wood ants—running up tree trunk / **Primrose**—pale yellow flowers, 5 petals, short stems, thick, dark leaves

2 Ask an adult to help you press some twigs firmly into the ground around the tree. Use string to make a circle on the ground around the twigs. Write down, sketch, or photograph anything you see inside the circle, such as worm castings, old acorn shells, and leaves.

3 Look for small mammals and birds, such as crows, magpies, or even a sparrow hawk, in the tree. Are any birds nesting? If there is a hole in the trunk, there may be a woodpecker's nest. Listen for bird songs.

Wood louse—gray; body like armor

Jay—blue, black, and white feathers

Titmouse

4 Write headings, for time, date, and weather. Write in your observations and stick in sketches, photographs, and even bark rubbings. Add labels to build up a complete picture of an oak tree ecosystem.

ON AND UNDER OAKS

● As seasons change, the oak tree menu changes for the wildlife in and around it. In the fall, large birds and mammals eat acorns. In spring, jays and magpies eat eggs stolen from nests. Titmice eat caterpillars on leaves and buds.

● Nature recycles its waste. Under a tree, you will find decomposers that feed and grow on dead plants and animals, breaking them down into the soil (see below). Decomposed matter does not hold energy, but provides the soil with nutrients (goodness).

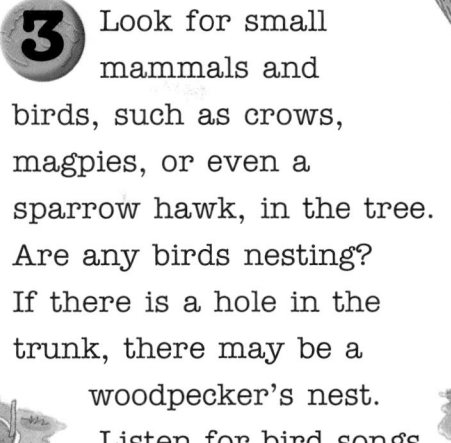

Fungi grow on dead logs and leaves.

Ants, beetles, and other small creatures eat droppings and fungi.

Bacteria break down anything that remains.

GLOBAL ECOSYSTEMS

The world is split into large ecosystems called biomes. Biomes are named after the main type of vegetation (plant life) that grows there. They are shaped by climate—how hot, cold, wet, or dry a place is. Tropical forests have lots of rain and sunshine. Deserts are hot and dry. The tundra (cold desert) is freezing. Mountaintops are also cold. Temperate areas have a warm, moist climate and are rarely very hot or very cold. Each place has its own food web, with wildlife that has adapted to the climate there.

Tundra
Coniferous forest
Temperate grasslands
Temperate forest
Mountains
Desert

Scrub

Savanna

Seasonal tropical forest

Tropical rainforest

Climate depends upon latitude (how far north or south of the Equator a place is), and altitude (height above sea level).

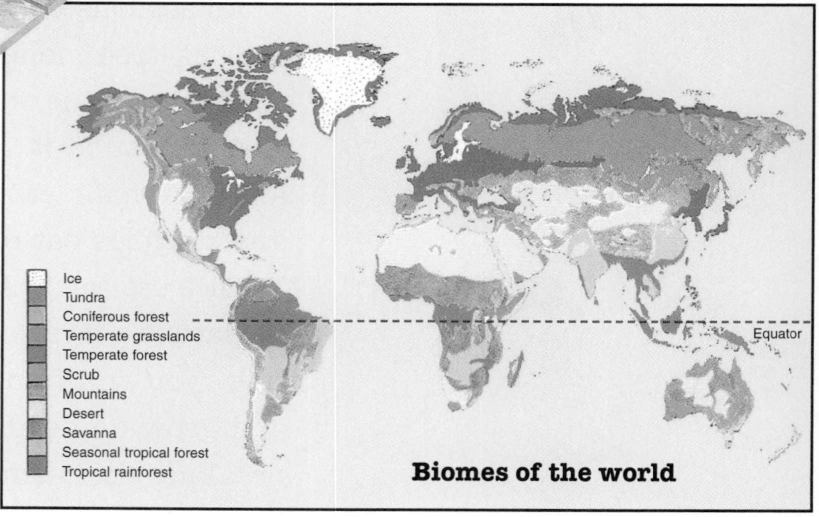

Ice
Tundra
Coniferous forest
Temperate grasslands
Temperate forest
Scrub
Mountains
Desert
Savanna
Seasonal tropical forest
Tropical rainforest

Equator

Biomes of the world

ISLANDS

● Islands often have unique ecosystems. The Galapagos Islands, off the coast of Ecuador, are home to some of the world's rarest creatures, such as giant tortoises and sea lizards (right).

BIOME CARD GAME

To make this game, you will need thin cardboard, scissors, and colored pencils. Each set of cards shows a food chain in a different biome.

1 Cut out 30 pieces of cardboard. Copy the pictures on the cards shown here, until you have two sets of each food chain and six Sun cards. Number and label each set, as shown.

Sun (all sets)
x 6

Temperate forest set

x 2

Tropical rainforest set

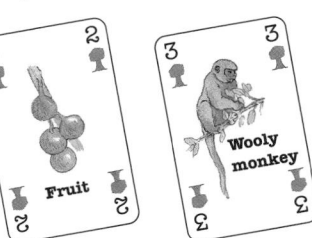
x 2

Tundra set

x 2

Desert set

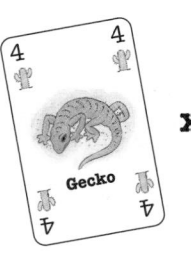
x 2

2 Two or more can play. The aim is to collect four cards belonging to the same set. All sets must include a Sun card (1). Each player begins with four cards. Take turns to pick a card from the pile. Either keep that card or replace it at the bottom of the pile. The first person to collect a whole food chain is the winner.

ADDING MORE CARDS
● Find out about more food chains, in these or other biomes, and make cards for them. Make sure you always have a plant, a herbivore, and a carnivore. Make up a symbol for each new biome.

467

CONIFEROUS FORESTS

Coniferous trees (pines) are softwoods. They grow quickly and lose their needle-like leaves throughout the year. They grow best in the cold north, in Canada and northern Europe. Sunshine rarely reaches the forest floor. Ecosystems in coniferous forests are not nearly as rich as in broad-leaved forests, because few plants grow with so little light. The diversity (variety) of wildlife is not as great, as there are fewer plants for animals and birds to eat. There are not many natural coniferous forests left today – most are now planted by foresters.

Dry

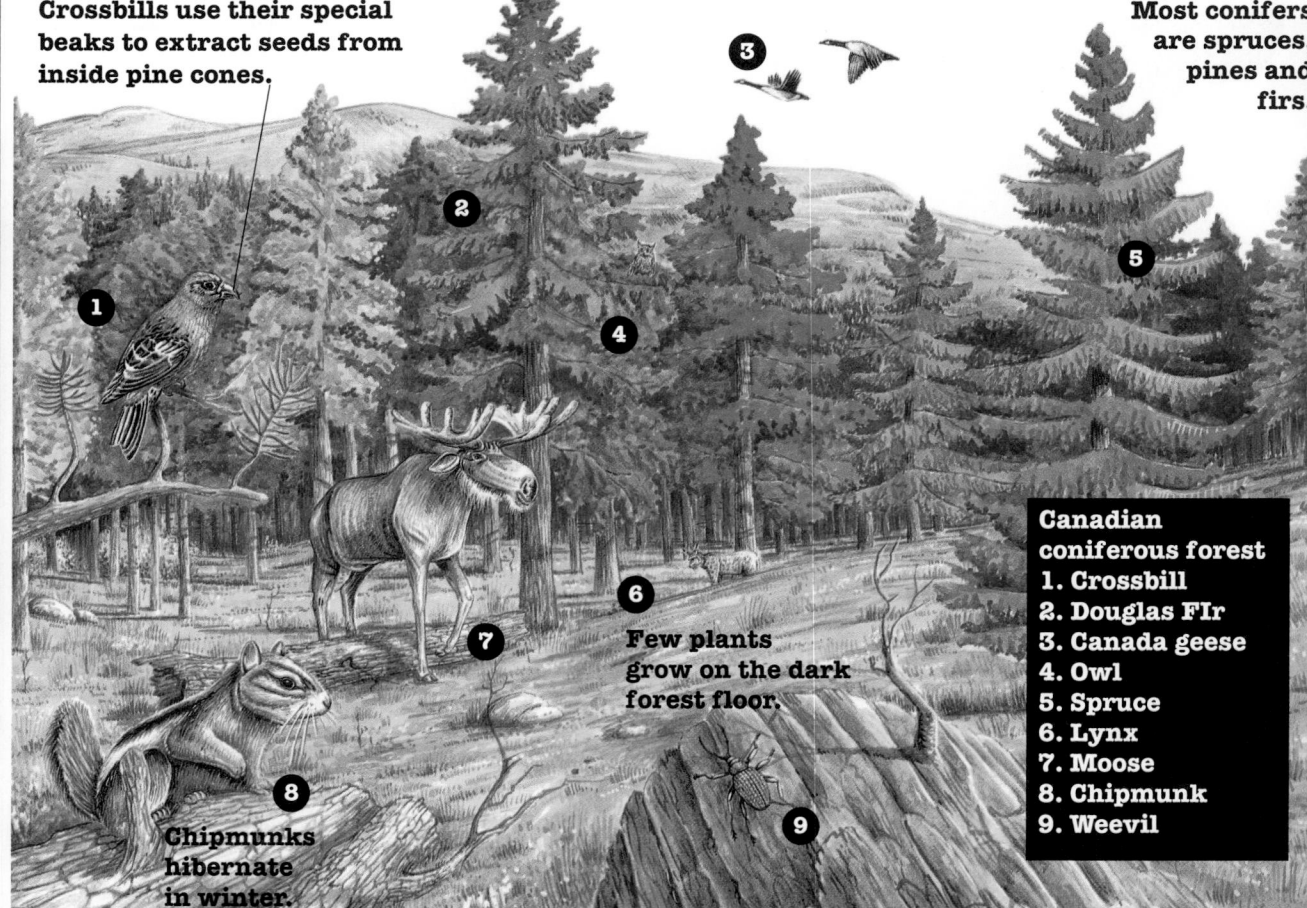

Crossbills use their special beaks to extract seeds from inside pine cones.

Most conifers are spruces, pines and firs.

Few plants grow on the dark forest floor.

Chipmunks hibernate in winter.

Canadian coniferous forest
1. Crossbill
2. Douglas FIr
3. Canada geese
4. Owl
5. Spruce
6. Lynx
7. Moose
8. Chipmunk
9. Weevil

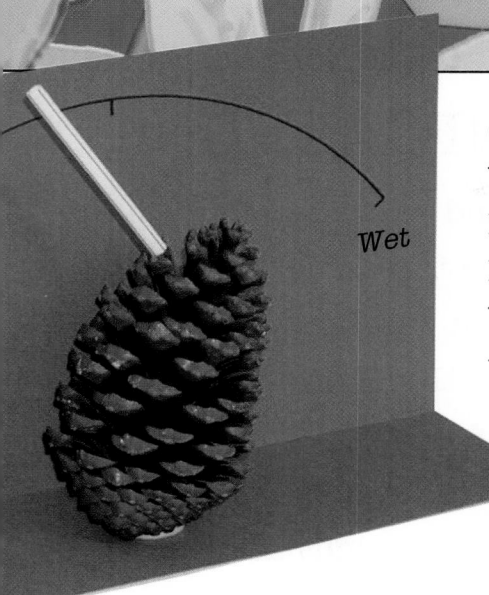

Wet

CONE GAUGE

Use a pine cone to make a hygrometer. This measures the humidity of (moisture in) the air. You will need a pine cone, a thumbtack, a plastic drinking straw, a sheet of card stock, modeling clay and a pen.

1 Stick a thumbtack into one of the middle scales of the cone. Push a straw over the thumbtack's end.

2 Fold the card stock. Position the cone on it using clay, as shown above. Place it outside, sheltered from rain. Wait for the straw to move in moist air. Then draw a wet/dry scale on the card stock (remove the cone to do this, then put it back when you've finished).

WHAT'S HAPPENING

Pine cones hold the seeds of conifers. They close when the air is moist and it is about to rain, to protect the seeds inside. The outside scales absorb the moisture in the air, swell up and bend.

SUSTAINABLE FORESTRY

● In many parts of the world, the wildlife-rich natural vegetation has been cut down and replaced by coniferous plantations. The conifers are then cut down to make paper and furniture. Now foresters practise sustainable forestry. This means they cut down only part of the coniferous plantation at a time so that ecosystems can survive.

TROPICAL RAINFORESTS

Many of the world's plant and animal species live in tropical rainforests, where the climate is always warm and moist. The Amazon rainforest in South America is like a huge apartment building, with different species living at each level. At the bottom is the dark forest floor, then the herb layer, shrub layer, understory, canopy, and, at the top, the emergent layer. Hardwood trees grow tall and straight as they struggle to reach the sunlight. They are so tall that they have roots above the ground.

Emergent layer—the tallest trees push through the canopy to reach the Sun.

Understory—younger trees strive to reach the sunlight.

Herb layer—ferns and herbs grow. Tapirs and insects live here.

Canopy—treetops are bound together by creepers and climbing plants. Home to orchids, birds, monkeys, snakes, and lizards.

Shrub layer—young trees grow from seedlings. Woody plants with large leaves and colorful flowers grow here.

Forest floor—rotting leaf litter covers the poor soil. Few plants grow here, except along rivers, where some sunshine gets through.

MINIRAINFOREST

To create a minirainforest, you will need a small fish tank with a lid (or use plastic wrap), soil, charcoal, gravel, and suitable plants, such as ferns, mosses, orchids, and African violets.

1 Line the bottom of the tank with a layer of charcoal and gravel. Cover with a layer of soil. Make the soil damp before arranging your plants.

2 Arrange the plants before planting. Do not put them too close together as they will need room to grow.

3 Place the lid (or plastic wrap) over the tank and put in a warm spot, but not in direct sunlight. Water every few weeks. The lid will keep the soil moist.

WHAT'S HAPPENING

● Rainforests play a big part in controlling the world's climate. Without trees, there would be less rainfall. Leaves transpire, which means they lose water through tiny holes. Transpiration helps make the air moist. The leaves on the plants in your tank will transpire and keep the air and soil moist.

● Thunderstorms are frequent in rainforests as the warm, moist air rises quickly and cools.

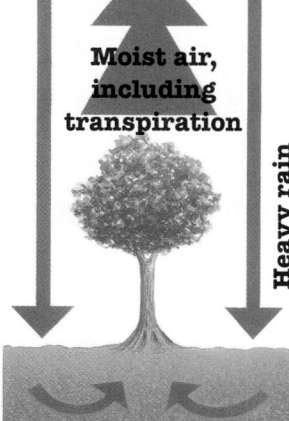

Fast-rising moist air condenses into droplets, which form high thunderclouds.

Cool air

Moist air, including transpiration

Warm air

Heavy rain

Soil is kept moist

EPIPHYTES

● Epiphytes are rainforest plants that grow on other plants. Some grow in the low, darker parts of the forest. Others, like orchids, like the sunshine of the canopy.

DEFORESTATION

● Half the world's rainforests have been destroyed. Some people cut down trees to farm the land for food. Others cut down trees to sell the lumber.

HOT DESERTS

Living things struggle to survive in hot, dry deserts. Many have learned some very strange habits, just to stay alive. The spadefoot toad, found in the Sonoran Desert of Arizona, hibernates underground for most of the year. When the annual midsummer rain approaches, it emerges to mate and lay its eggs in pools of rainwater. Within days, the eggs hatch and become tadpoles, then toads. Then the toads disappear underground again. Desert plants have to survive for long periods without rain. Many survive as seeds. Cacti have shallow roots, close to the surface, ready to catch any rain that falls.

PLANT A DESERT GARDEN

To create a desert garden, you will need a shallow clay bowl, sand and soil, pebbles or gravel, protective gloves, and some small cactus plants. Ask at your local plant nursery for advice on which cacti to buy.

1 Mix together the sand and soil. Fill the bowl three-quarters full with the soil mixture.

2 Put on protective gloves, then plant your cacti. After planting, cover the surface of the soil with pebbles or gravel.

DESERT ANIMALS AND PEOPLES

Gila monster

● Desert animals have had to adapt to hot, dry conditions. In North America, a poisonous lizard called the Gila monster stores fat in its thick tail. It can live on this fat for months without eating. Birds called roadrunners save energy by running instead of flying. Ground squirrels in the Kalahari Desert in southern Africa use their plumed tails as sunshades.

● For thousands of years, the only people living in the Great Australian Desert were Aboriginal nomads—people who regularly move from place to place. Now, most Australian Aborigines live in towns and cities. Bedouins have lived in the deserts of North Africa and Syria for centuries. A few still live as nomads, traveling from oasis to oasis.

Bedouins

HELPFUL HINTS

● Place your desert garden in a sunny position.
● Cacti have sharp spikes, so handle them with care. Use thick leather or suede gloves to protect your hands when handling cacti.

● Do not water your garden too often. Cacti need only a small amount of water. Too much water will cause the stems to rot and will leave a black mark.

COLD DESERTS

Cold deserts, called tundra, are places where the ground is frozen for much of the year. Alpine tundra is found at high altitudes, above the tree line. In the Arctic, there are no trees, only grasses, mosses, and lichens. Lichens are fungi that contain algae. They appear as crusty patches or shrubby growths on rocks. Shrubby lichens can only survive in clean air. They are an important part of tundra ecosystems, and are threatened by pollution, which can be carried a great distance by winds and water.

North of the tundra is the Arctic icecap.

Below the surface is permafrost, which is ground that is frozen all year round.

The tundra has rocky mounds, called pingoes, and long lakes.

Below the tundra is a belt of coniferous forest, called the taiga.

LOOKING FOR LICHENS

One way to check pollution in your area is to look for lichens. The nature and color of any lichens will indicate air quality. If you find only green algae, the air is probably heavily polluted.

1 Ask an adult to come with you to look at local lichens. Look on walls, stones, trees, and gravestones. Record the color and location of any lichens you see. Sketch their appearance. Check the scale opposite to help you identify the lichens.

474

2 Mark your lichen findings on the ecosystems map you made on page 460. Make up a key to show the type of lichen found. Write down the date on which you found them.

Polluted

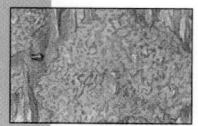
GREEN ALGAE
Found in heavily polluted areas. Probably no lichens.

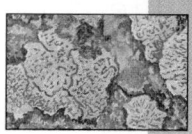
GRAY-GREEN CRUSTY LICHENS
Often found on gravestones. High-level air pollution.

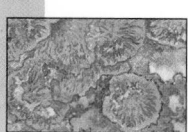
ORANGE CRUSTY LICHENS
Also found on gravestones. Medium-level air pollution.

LEAFY LICHENS
Found on walls and trees. Low-level air pollution.

SHRUBBY LICHENS
Found on rocks and trees. Clean air.

Clean

Lichens can live for 4,000 years. They can survive all climatic conditions. There are 25,000 known species. They grow slowly, only half an inch a year.

SYMBIOSIS AND CAMOUFLAGE

● Symbiosis is a partnership between two living things, from which both benefit. The fungi and algae that make up lichens are symbiotic. The fungi absorb water and minerals, then the algae use these to turn

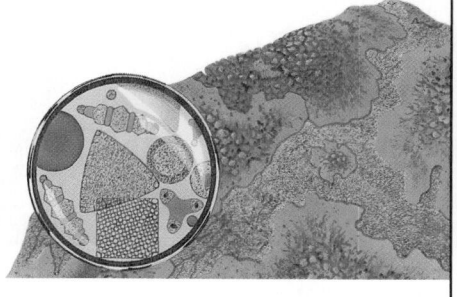

sunshine into food by photosynthesis (see page 463). Both the fungi and algae gain from living together.

● Camouflage is the ability of certain animals to blend in with their natural surroundings and so hide from predators. But predators also use camouflage to hide from their prey.

Arctic fox in summer

Arctic fox in winter

FRESHWATER ECOSYSTEMS

In ponds and lakes, where the water is still, plant life is rich. Rivers and streams have running water, so there is less plant life.

Large predators like perch eat smaller fish. Too many predators in a pond destroy the ecosystem because the secondary consumers are all eaten up. Without secondary consumers to control numbers, the primary consumers increase and eat all the plant life. Without plant life, the pond ecosystem breaks down completely.

ZONE 3: DEEP WATER

ZONE 2: SHALLOW WATER OR SWAMP

Great reedmace

Arrowhead

Water lily

Water crowfoot

Milfoil

POND ZONES

Pond animals move around, but plants remain in one place. Make a pond chart, dividing it into zones according to the plants found there. Be careful near water. Always tell an adult what you are doing.

1 Make sketches and take notes about the plants in and around the pond. Look first at the bank, then at the shallow water, or swampy area around the edge, then at the deep water. Here, you will only be able to see the tops of the plants. Some plants live completely under the water.

ZONE 1: BANKSIDE

Meadow sweet

Marsh marigold

Great pond sedge

Water iris

2 Sketch a cross section of the pond and divide it into zones, as shown here. Zone 1 is the bankside, Zone 2 is the shallow water or swamp area, and Zone 3 is the deep water. Underwater plants, called submerged aquatics, go in the deep water zone. Fill in details about each plant. Use a field guide to help you identify any plants not shown here.

POND LIFE

● Birds that live and feed near fresh water have adapted special feet and beaks. The heron has a long, thin beak with which to catch fish or frogs. It has long legs so it can stand for a long time in deep water waiting for prey.

Flamingo

Avocet

Heron

● Everything in a pond food web depends on plant life, even if you cannot see any plants. Big fish eat small fish, which eat dragonfly larvae, which eat tiny creatures, which feed on microscopic plants.

Dragonfly

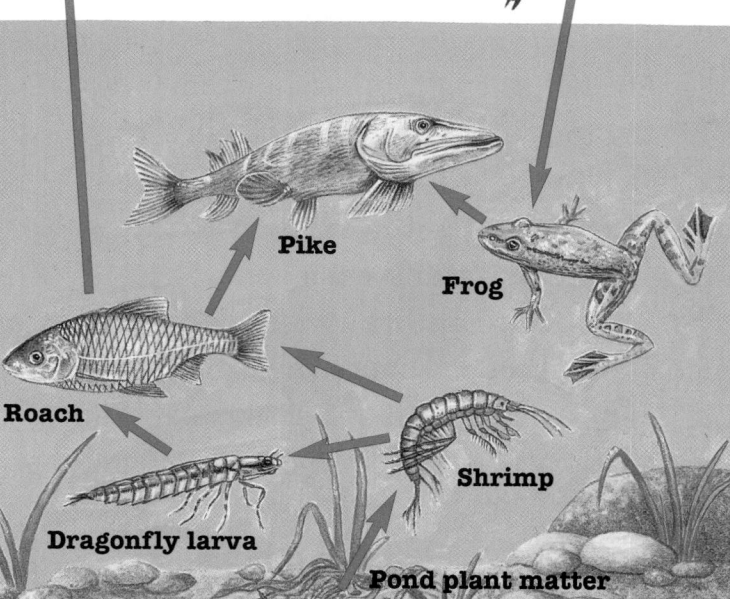

Pike

Frog

Roach

Shrimp

Dragonfly larva

Pond plant matter

ON THE SEASHORE

There are sandy, pebble, and rocky beaches. Each provides a different habitat, but all are affected by the same tidal movements. There are two high and two low tides every day. Very high tides, called spring tides, happen twice a month. Between high-water spring tide marks and low-water spring tide marks, there are five seashore zones. In these zones, plants and animals have adapted to produce a variety of ecosystems. Different seaweeds and shells are found in each zone.

BEACHCOMBER

Next time you go to a beach, carry out a beach ecosystem survey. Tell an adult where you are going and ask a friend to come with you. Always check the times of high tides. Carry out your study at low tide. Select a quiet stretch of beach to study.

Splash zone
Upper shore
High tide mark
Middle shore
Lower shore

1 Stretch a length of string from the top of the beach to the edge of the water. Hold each end in place with a pebble. Mark the string with a pen where you think each zone ends. The five zones are lower shore, middle shore, upper shore, high tide mark, and splash zone.

2 List the differences you notice between the zones. Collect shells, pebbles, and small pieces of seaweed and driftwood. Note carefully which zone you found them in. Record the date, time, and weather conditions.

JETSAM

● Storms at sea often carry jetsam (trash from ships) onto beaches. Ropes, bottles, and cans are found among

seaweed and shells after bad weather. Containers holding dangerous chemicals have been found on beaches. They can gradually alter ecosystems.

SAND DUNES

● Grasses have long roots that hold the sand down in ridges. This prevents the sand from blowing away. Grasses are often planted in sand dunes to stop the sand from blowing any farther.

ROCK POOLS

● Rock pools are left behind when the tide goes out. Plants and animals that live in rock pools cannot survive out of water. In rock pools you may find sea anemones, crabs, sea urchins, starfish, seaweeds, and shrimp. Small fish are also found in pools. Always replace rocks that you move.

3 Map the area of beach you have surveyed onto a sheet of cardboard. Draw in the zones created by high- and low-water marks. Glue on and label everything you have collected.

Rock pool

SALTWATER ECOSYSTEMS

The ocean is the largest habitat on Earth. But sea animals depend upon plants for their food, just as land animals do. The most important marine plants, called phytoplankton, are so small that they can only be seen with a microscope. Phytoplankton are the primary producers in the food chains of the sea. They grow near the surface, where sunlight causes photosynthesis to happen. Microscopic animals called zooplankton then feed on phytoplankton, and larger animals eat the zooplankton.

OCEAN FOOD WEB

Phytoplankton are single-celled algae. If you get a chance, look at a sample of sea water under a microscope, and you will see the pretty patterns on phytoplankton.

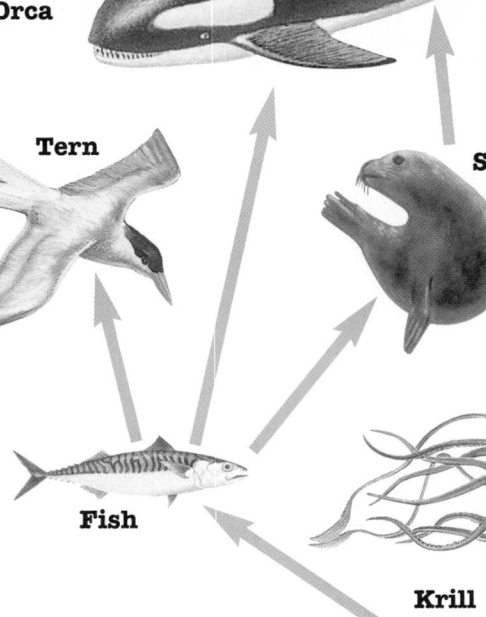

Orca

Tern

Seal

Fish

Squid

Krill

Zooplankton

Phytoplankton

SALTY FACTS

Blue whale

● A food web of the sea includes some of the smallest and largest living things in the world—the blue whale and krill. Krill are tiny shrimplike forms of zooplankton, found in the seas of the Antarctic. Amazingly, they are the only food the blue whale eats. The blue whale can be over 90 feet long. It strains the krill from the ocean through the baleen inside its mouth, which acts like a strainer.

Krill

1. Corals grow around a volcanic island.

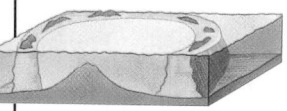

2. The volcano erodes and a lagoon forms.

● In tropical seas, there are low islands called coral reefs that are formed by tiny creatures called polyps. The jellylike polyps build up hard skeletons of calcium carbonate. When they die, the skeletons are left as coral. New polyps grow on top of the dead ones. Coral needs warmth and light, so it grows only near the ocean's surface.

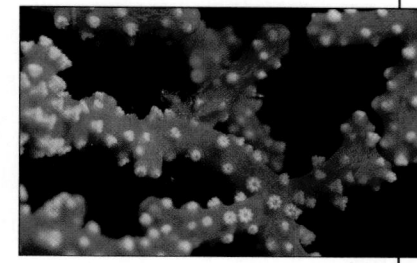

3. The volcano sinks completely. The reef remains, with small, sandy islands on top.

● Coastal mangrove swamp forests are types of tropical forest. Mangrove trees have adapted to survive in the salty water in mud estuaries of tropical rivers. They have special roots that keep the leaves above the water and allow the plant to obtain more oxygen. Mangroves are the habitat of many species, such as fiddler crabs, and are breeding grounds for reef fish.

WILDLIFE GARDEN

As your contribution toward preserving healthy ecosystems, you could make a wildlife garden. Even if you do not have your own garden, you can encourage wildlife by cultivating plants in a windowbox or on a balcony. Plant flowers with strong colors and scents that will attract insects such as bees and butterflies. Peacock butterflies like to lay their eggs beneath nettle leaves. These pages will give you some ideas on how to create a wildlife garden.

A SPACE FOR WILDLIFE

Diversity is the key to a successful wildlife garden. Diversity means providing many different habitats—shady areas, sunny spots, and open spaces. This will attract many creatures. You could make a habitat pile, from logs, to attract insects. Make a bird table so birds can feed safely. You could even build a pond.

HELPFUL HINTS

● Choose the east- or west-facing side of a tree trunk for a birdhouse. A south-facing nest may harm fledglings because they will become too warm.

● A log pile will encourage minibeasts into your wildlife garden. It will also encourage small birds like wrens which feed on insects.

● Leave an area of garden with long grass—this will also encourage minibeasts.

BIRD FEEDER

Make environmentally friendly pine cone bird feeders. You need some long pine cones, a ball of string, a spoon, unsweetened peanut butter, birdseed, waxed paper, and a baking tray.

1 First, cut a length of string for each pine cone. Loop and tie the string to one end of each cone.

2 Use a spoon to smear peanut butter all over each pine cone. Make sure it covers every part of the cone. Press firmly into all the spaces.

3 Sprinkle birdseed onto the waxed paper on the baking tray. Roll the cones in the birdseed until they are all well covered. The birdseed will stick to the peanut butter. Shake off any loose seed.

4 Birds like to feed where they are safe from predators like cats. Position your pine cone bird feeders away from shrubbery, trees, and fences. A tree stump or bird table in the center of an open space is a safe site.

CONTRACT WITH NATURE

● As houses and roads are built, animals and plants are losing their natural habitats. Even common birds like sparrows are disappearing. Remind yourself to do what you can to encourage wildlife by making a contract with nature.

Contract with nature

I ....

Promise ....

....

....

....

Signed ....

CHAPTER 5
People and Places

Some places in the world are very
crowded, and there are others where
hardly any people live. Find out why
people live in certain places rather than others, and how
the place we live affects our lifestyle. See how people build
different kinds of houses in different parts of the world.

People change their surroundings when they
chop down trees or build roads and houses.
In this chapter, you will map your life
journey so far, make
your own windmill,
and learn how to
make paper!

CONTENTS

SETTLEMENTS **486**

SHORT JOURNEYS **488**

LONG JOURNEYS **490**

WORLD WEATHER **492**

HOMES **494**

A CROWDED WORLD **496**

RAW MATERIALS **498**

JOBS AND RESOURCES **500**

ENERGY **502**

COUNTRY PROFILE—KENYA **504**

LANDMARKS **506**

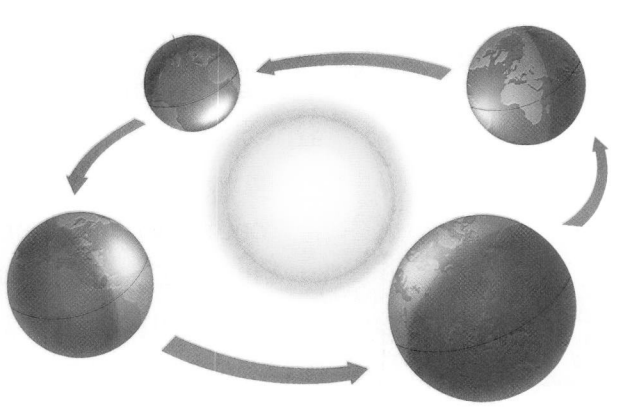

SETTLEMENTS

A settlement is a place where people live. It can be very small, with only a few houses, or as large as a city, where millions of people live. A city has lots of stores and offices and provides services, such as hospitals and schools, for its people. A long time ago, people built settlements close to rivers, because they provided water and were the best way to transport goods. New Orleans grew up at a good location on the Mississippi River.

Street map

Continent map

A house is built by a river for water and easy transportation.

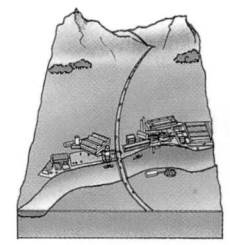

Roads are built and a town forms as more people settle.

The town expands into a city, with services, factories, and many roads.

WHERE YOU LIVE

Make a "nest" of four maps, each on a different scale, to show the first four lines of your address.

Paola Zaghini
14 Appian Way
Rome
Italy
Europe
The Northern Hemisphere
The World
The Galaxy
The U

1 Use a large-scale map to find the street you live on.

2 Find the location of your village, town, or city in an atlas. Is there a river nearby? Now find your country. What shape is it? Does it have a coastline? Find the name of the continent in which you live.

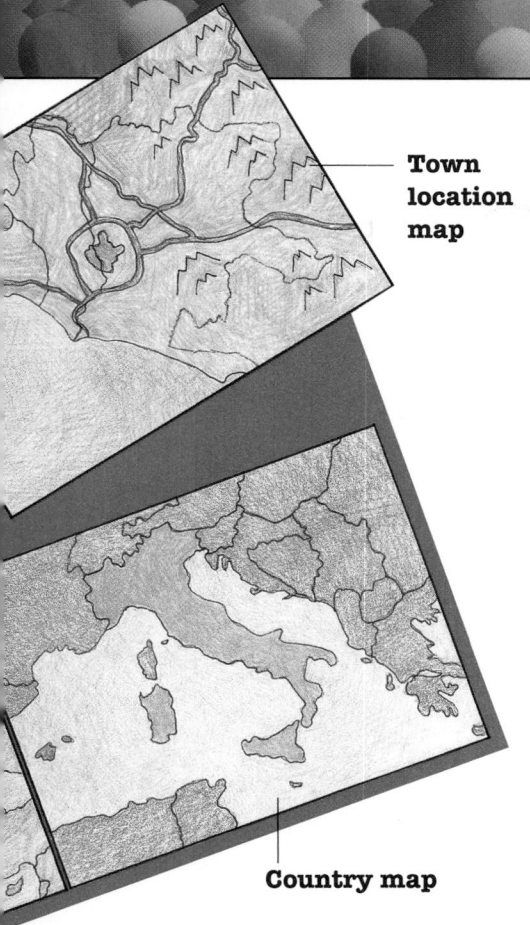

Town location map

Country map

3 Now draw four maps, as shown. Make sure you put in natural features, like rivers. Glue the maps onto cardboard and label them.

HELPFUL HINTS

● The scale on each map is different. A street map is large-scale; a continent map is small-scale. To get the scale right, trace from the atlas.

● Practice using scale by doing map "nests" for places you hear about in the news.

TYPES OF SETTLEMENT

● The area around a settlement is its location. A village is a rural location, which means it is surrounded by countryside. A town or city is an urban location—a built-up area, with many buildings and services.

CITY
Large urban location. Services include stores, offices, factories, places of worship, schools, hospitals, museums, theaters, restaurants, post offices, galleries, roads, and public transportation.

TOWN
Smaller than a city, but with similar services (in big towns). Small towns usually have one main shopping area.

VILLAGE
Up to 2,000 people. Services may include stores, a post office, a school, and public transportation.

HAMLET
Fewer than 50 people. Few services.

FARM or HOMESTEAD
One family. No services, except for electricity and telephone (in developed countries).

● Settlements built on the outskirts of cities are called suburbs. Suburbs sometimes stretch to join up with towns or villages nearby. Together, a city and its suburbs make a metropolitan area.

SHORT JOURNEYS

People make journeys every day. Each time you leave your house—to go to school, to a friend's house, or to the store—you are making a journey. There are different ways to travel a short distance—on foot or by bicycle, car, train, or bus. It usually takes longer to walk, but it is good exercise. People drive to supermarkets to shop. Parents often drive their children to school. Many people commute (travel to work each day) by car, bus, or train.

JOURNEY TIMES

Carry out a survey with a group of friends to find out how you all travel to school. Present your information on a chart. You will need cardboard, scissors, paper, glue, and colored pencils.

Brian
3 mi
20 mins

Tony
2 mi
15 mins

Lisa
2 ¹/₂ mi
20 mins

Tasmin
¹/₄ mi
5 mins

Jin Soo
1 ¹/₂ mi
15 mins

1 First, write out a list of questions to ask. Do you travel to school by car, bus, or train? Do you walk or bicycle? How far from school do you live? How long does your journey take? Record all of your friends' answers on a sheet of paper.

2 Cut out a strip of colored cardboard for each friend. Cut one end of each cardboard strip into an arrow shape.

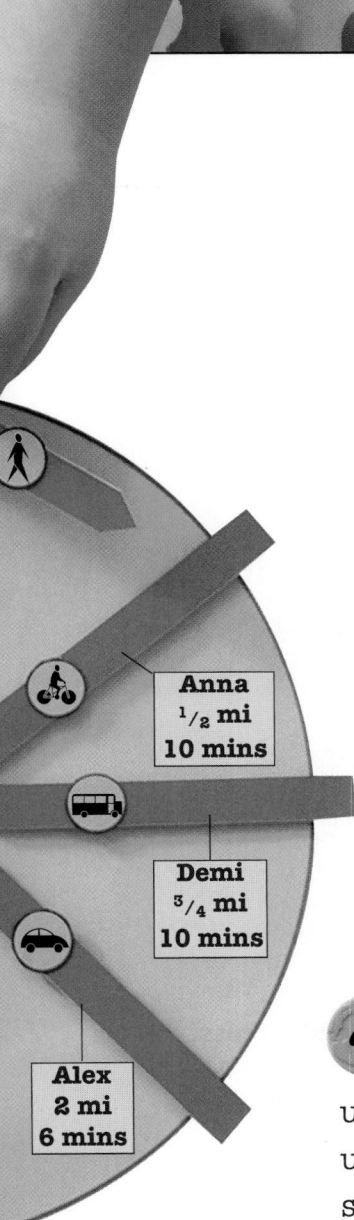

Anna
$^1/_2$ **mi**
10 mins

Demi
$^3/_4$ **mi**
10 mins

Alex
2 mi
6 mins

PEDESTRIANS

● People who walk along sidewalks and footpaths are called pedestrians. In Britain, some children walk to school in a "walking bus." Parents lead the "bus" and collect children along the route.

● Children in some parts of the world have to walk many miles each day to get to school.

3 Draw a symbol of your school in the center of a large cardboard circle. Arrange the arrows around the school. Draw transportation symbols, as shown here. Glue the correct symbol onto each arrow. Write labels on small slips of paper to show how far each person travels and how long it takes.

Car

Bus

Bicycle

Walk

4 Now rearrange the arrows to show how each person travels home from school. Do they use the same forms of transportation as they used in the morning? Make new arrows, symbols, and labels for any changes.

SERVICES CHART

● Redo the chart to show the services you visit from home, such as stores and the library. Put your home at the center of the circle and arrange the arrows to show which form of transportation you use to get to each service. Write labels to show distances and journey times.

LONG JOURNEYS

In earlier times, large numbers of people moved from one region to another, seeking better living conditions and opportunities. But traveling was hard, and people moved short distances. Today, we live in a global community, in which many people can travel long distances quickly and easily. The result is that people from many different countries now live in cities like New York or London, yet keep their ties to family members in their countries of origin.

A MOVING STORY

Make a "family map" to show all the places that you and your family have links with. You need a large map of the world, a pencil, tracing paper, colored yarn, scissors, and pushpins.

1 Do some research about your family tree. Ask questions and look in family albums. Where were you born? Where were your parents and grandparents born? If you have a stepfamily, include them in your research too.

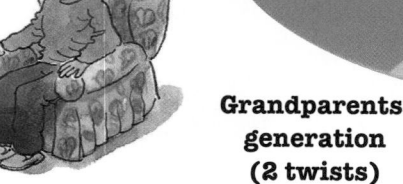

Grandparents' generation (2 twists)

2 Trace the part of the world map you need. It may be just one country if your family has always lived there. Color it and label the continents, countries, or towns. Mark your birthplace in pencil. Draw an arrow from there to the place you lived next, then to the place after that, and so on.

3 Cut lengths of yarn. Choose a different color for each generation of your family. Pin one end of your color of yarn to the place where you were born. Follow the arrows with the yarn, pinning it at each new place.

Parents'
generation
(1 twist)

4 To show the "life journey" taken by your parents and grandparents, twist different colors of yarn around your first strand. Add a twist for each generation. Place and pin the twists as you did for your own life journey. Write labels to show the dates your family moved from place to place.

MIGRATION

● People move for many different reasons, both within their own country and to other countries. Some move to live near family members who have already migrated.

● Some families move from the countryside to large cities to look for work. Most people in developed countries now live in urban areas.

● Some people escape the pollution and litter of cities to live in the countryside. Sometimes, they commute (travel every day) to work in the city.

● People who are forced to leave their own country, because they are living in danger, are called refugees. They seek refuge (a place to feel safe) in other countries. There are many thousands of refugees in the world today. Some escape from war or cruelty, and others flee from natural disasters, such as earthquakes or floods.

WORLD WEATHER

Climate—the usual pattern of weather in a place—affects the way people live. Climate depends mainly on latitude, which is how far north or south of the equator a place is (see below). Countries in tropical latitudes, close to the equator, have a hot, wet climate. Countries in temperate latitudes (between the tropics and the poles) have a mild climate. Altitude, which means height above sea level, also affects climate. Places at high altitudes are always cool, no matter where in the world they are.

LATITUDE AND LONGITUDE

● Numbered lines on maps and globes show latitude (horizontal lines) and longitude (vertical lines). Latitude is measured north or south of the equator, the zero degree (0°) line of latitude. The tropics lie between 0° and 23°N and 23°S. Temperate regions lie between the tropics and 60°N and 60°S. Longitude is measured in degrees east or west of the prime meridian, which runs through London, England.

Prime meridian
60°N
Temperate region
23°N
Tropics
Equator, 0°

CHART IT

Make a chart to show the climate in cities in different parts of the world. You will need an atlas, tracing paper, pencils, a ruler, scissors, and glue.

Aswan
24°N, 32°E
Aswan is in Egypt, on the bank of the Nile River. The climate is very hot and dry—it hardly ever rains there. July is the hottest month.

Bogota
4°N, 74°W

1 Look in the atlas index to find the country and continent in which each city is located. Trace country maps from the atlas and mark the location of each city you have chosen. Glue the maps onto your chart. Find the latitude and longitude for each city from the numbers on the atlas map grids.

Write labels about each place. Does it get a lot of rain? Which is the hottest month?

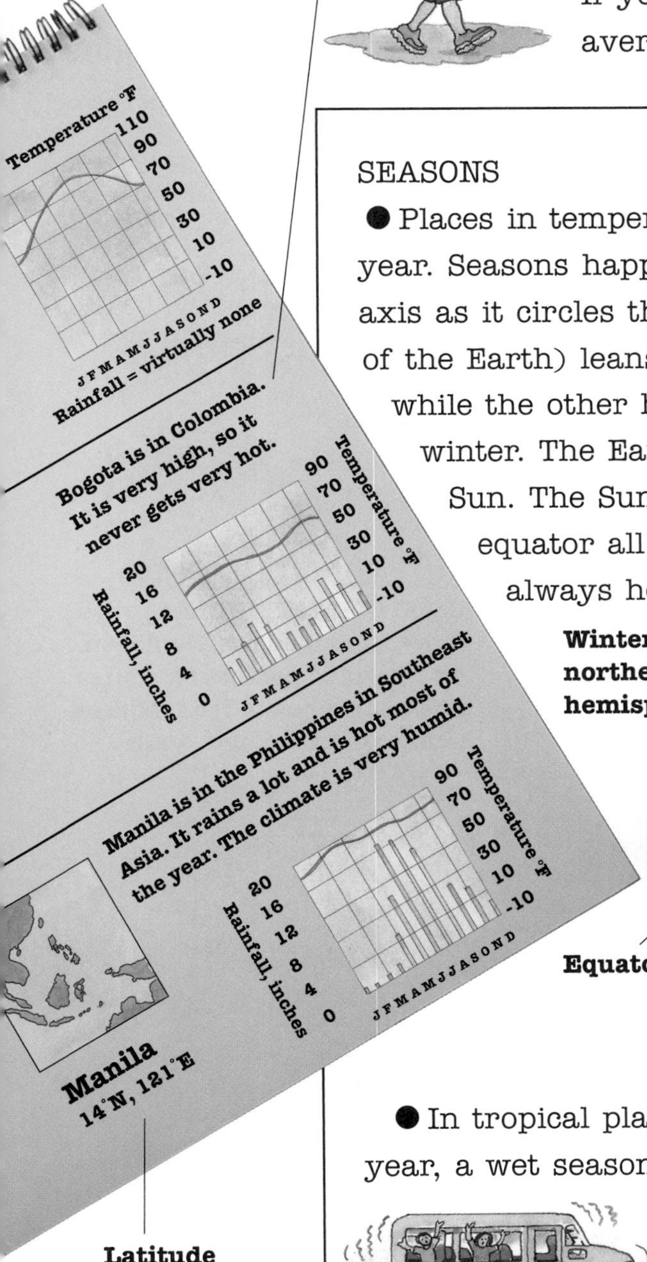

2 Find monthly temperature and rainfall averages from the atlas. Put these in graphs, then glue the graphs on your chart. If you cannot find monthly rainfall, write in average yearly rainfall.

Temperature °F
110
90
70
50
30
10
-10

J F M A M J J A S O N D
Rainfall = virtually none

Bogota is in Colombia. It is very high, so it never gets very hot.

Temperature °F
90
70
50
30
10
-10

Rainfall, inches
20
16
12
8
4
0

J F M A M J J A S O N D

Manila is in the Philippines in Southeast Asia. It rains a lot and is hot most of the year. The climate is very humid.

Temperature °F
90
70
50
30
10
-10

Rainfall, inches
20
16
12
8
4
0

J F M A M J J A S O N D

Manila
14°N, 121°E

Latitude and longitude

SEASONS

● Places in temperate regions have four seasons a year. Seasons happen because the Earth tilts on its axis as it circles the Sun. As one hemisphere (half of the Earth) leans toward the Sun, it has summer, while the other hemisphere leans away, and has winter. The Earth takes a full year to circle the Sun. The Sun shines almost directly over the equator all year, so it is always hot there.

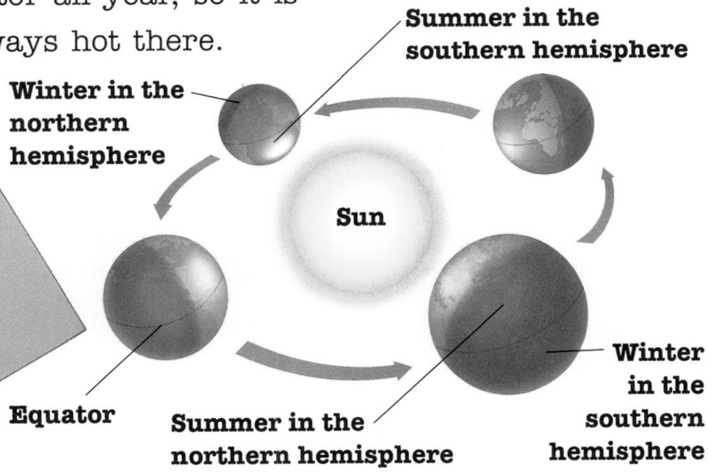

Summer in the southern hemisphere

Winter in the northern hemisphere

Sun

Equator

Summer in the northern hemisphere

Winter in the southern hemisphere

● In tropical places, there are only two seasons each year, a wet season and a dry season. Floods often occur in the wet season. In rural parts of developing countries, this makes travel hard.

HOMES

Climate and location—whether a place is urban or rural—determine what kinds of homes people build. In places with a cold climate, houses often have basements and double-glazed windows. In hot countries, homes must provide shade from the Sun. In areas with high rainfall, roofs must be sloped to let water run off easily. Urban locations in every climate usually have apartment houses, where many people can live in a small area.

TEMPERATE CLIMATE HOMES
Brick, stone, or wood, with big windows to let in light. Sloping roofs let rain run off easily.

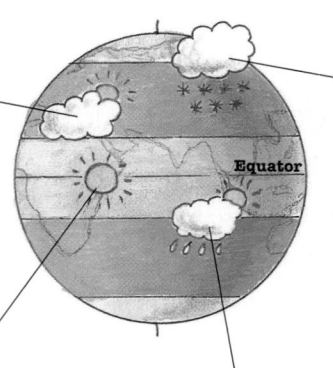

Equator

COLD CLIMATE HOMES
Sloping, ridged roofs with an overhang to protect balconies and people below from sliding snow. Often wooden walls.

HOT, DRY CLIMATE HOMES
Often rectangular, with a flat roof. Small windows and thick walls keep out the Sun.

HOT, WET CLIMATE HOMES
Often wooden walls, raised on platforms to allow cool air to circulate. Roofs often made from corrugated iron.

PLAY THE HOUSE GAME
Learn about climates and homes by making this card game for two players. You will need cardboard and colored pencils.

Temperate climate set

Cold climate set

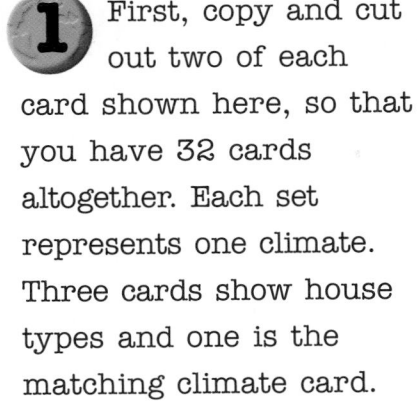

1 First, copy and cut out two of each card shown here, so that you have 32 cards altogether. Each set represents one climate. Three cards show house types and one is the matching climate card.

Hot, wet climate set

Hot, dry climate set

2 Deal four cards each. Lay the remaining cards face down in a pile. The first player picks up the top card then throws a card away. Lay the unwanted cards face up in a pile. The next player can pick up the top card from either pile. The winner is the first to collect one full set.

SHANTY TOWNS

● In developing countries, many very poor people live in shanty towns on the outskirts of large cities. Most have moved near the city to find work. They live in makeshift shanties built of cardboard, corrugated metal, or plywood. The shanty towns have no running water or electricity.

A CROWDED WORLD

As population increases and more people need homes, many parts of the world are becoming overcrowded. A quarter of the world's population now lives in cities and the cities are gradually spreading into vast metropolitan areas. Some cities and countries are more crowded than others. France, for example, has the same population as Britain, but because France is bigger, it is less crowded. We say its population density is lower than Britain's. Population density is the average number of people per square kilometer (km^2) of land.

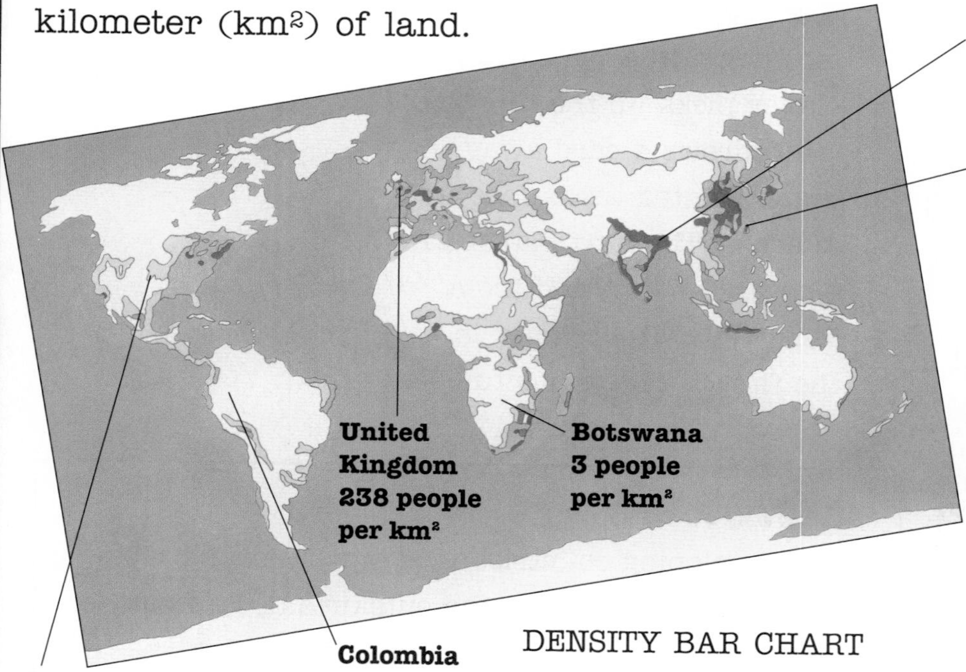

Bangladesh
847 people per km^2

Taiwan
606 people per km^2

United Kingdom 238 people per km^2

Botswana 3 people per km^2

U.S.A. 29 people per km^2

Colombia 32 people per km^2

Population density per km^2	
200+	40-100
100-200	10-40
	under 10

DENSITY BAR CHART

Make a population density bar chart. You will need a long cardboard tube, cardboard, a ruler, scissors, and paint. Use the map above or an atlas to find out population densities in the countries you want to show.

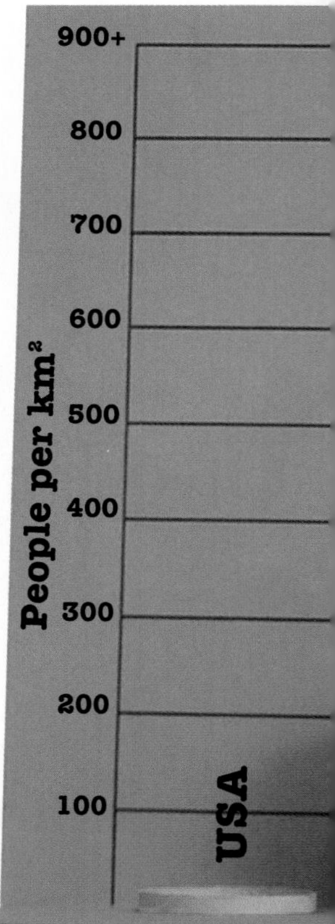

People per km^2

900+
800
700
600
500
400
300
200
100

USA

1. Choose a scale for your "bars," such as 5 cm (2 in) = 100 people per km². Measure and cut lengths of cardboard roll for each country. Paint and label each "bar."

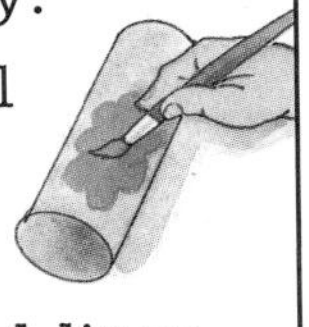

2. Draw and label grid lines across the cardboard, starting about 20 cm (8 in) from the bottom. Fold the bottom to make a base. Glue the "bars" in place.

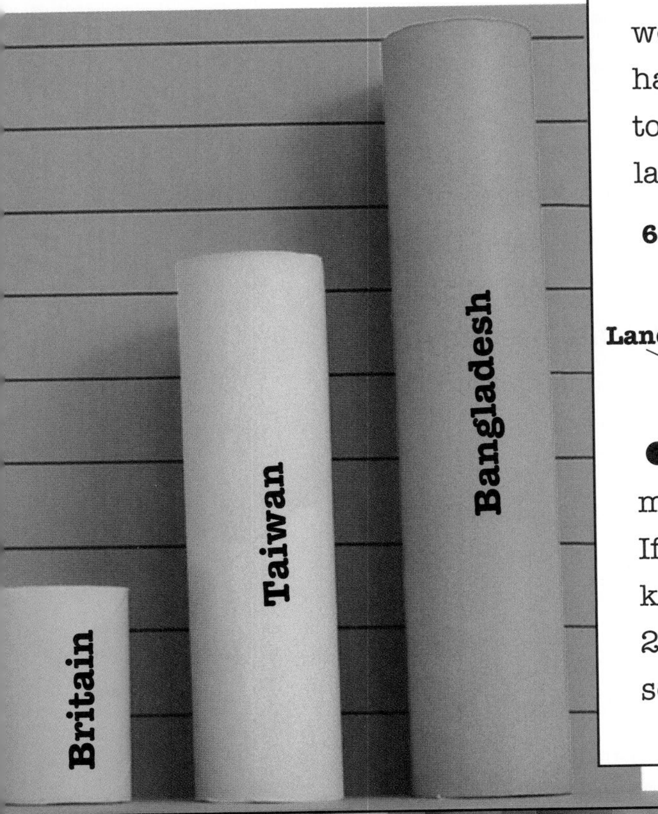

Britain

Taiwan

Bangladesh

POPULATION GROWTH

● The population of the world has greatly increased over the last 50 years. In 1999, the United Nations declared that the world's six billionth baby had been born in Bosnia.

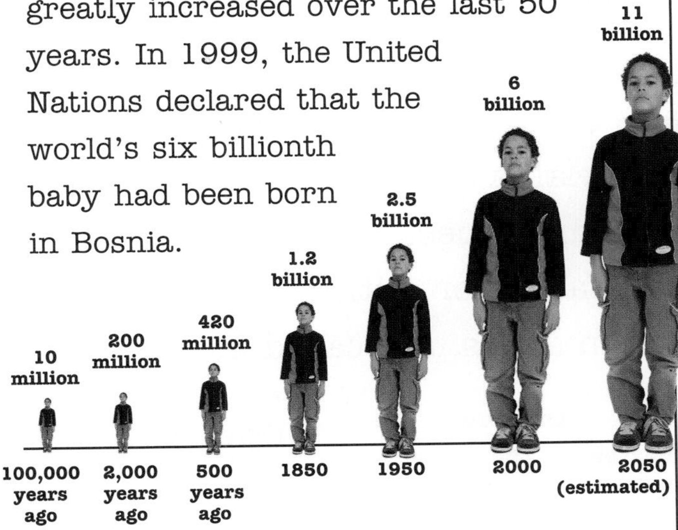

11 billion

6 billion

2.5 billion

1.2 billion

420 million

200 million

10 million

| 100,000 years ago | 2,000 years ago | 500 years ago | 1850 | 1950 | 2000 | 2050 (estimated) |

● As population has grown, people have cleared more and more of the world's forests. Some are cut down to harvest the wood, some to make room to grow crops, and some to provide land for building houses and roads.

6,000 years ago　　**2,000 years ago**　　**Today**

Land　　Forest　　Forest
　　Forest　　Land　　Land

● Population density can also be measured in people per square mile. If you know population per square kilometer, multiply that number by 2.59 to find the population per square mile.

RAW MATERIALS

Everything we use and everything around us is made from material of some kind. Materials that are changed or treated to be made into something else are called raw materials. One important raw material is cotton. The cotton plants need to be picked, cleaned, and processed before being made into fabric for clothes. Finished products, like cotton shirts, are called manufactured goods.

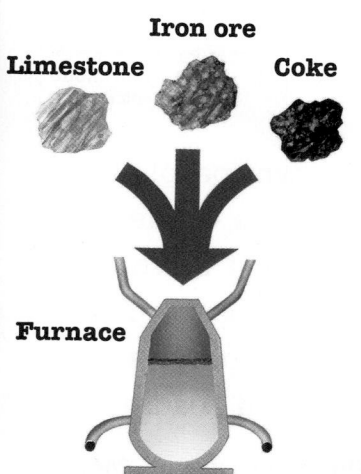

Iron ore

Limestone

Coke

Furnace

Iron

Iron ore is a mineral that is dug from the ground. It is heated in huge furnaces with coke and limestone. The iron separates as a very hot liquid and is poured into molds, where it cools and hardens.

ANIMAL, VEGETABLE, OR MINERAL?

Play this game to learn what different objects are made from. You will need small pictures of objects made from various materials, glue, and cardboard.

1 Draw or cut out pictures of objects from magazines. Glue each picture onto cardboard. Think about the raw materials used to make each one. A leather bag is made from animal hide (skin), so it is grouped as "animal." A book is made from wood pulp, so it is grouped as "vegetable." An iron railing is made from iron ore (see left), so it is classed as "mineral."

2 Write "animal," "vegetable," or "mineral" on the back of each object card. Use these pictures (right) to help you. Anything made from a plant is vegetable. Now quiz your friends. Hold up each card and ask, "Animal, vegetable, or mineral?" The player who gives the right answer keeps the card. The winner is the player with most cards.

 **String—vegetable (sisal or cotton)**

 **Fork—mineral (metal)**

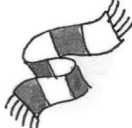 **Scarf—animal (wool)**

 **Apple—vegetable (apple tree)**

 Glass—mineral (sand)

 **Cotton—vegetable (cotton plant)**

 **Pencil—vegetable and mineral (wood and graphite)**

 **Soap—animal or vegetable (animal or vegetable fat)**

 **Plastic spoon—mineral (oil)**

 **Leather shoes—animal (animal hide)**

BRICKS

● Most bricks are made of clay and sand. These raw materials are ground together, then mixed with water and molded into  brick shapes. When the bricks have dried, they are fired in a very hot oven called a kiln to make them hard. The ancient Romans used triangular bricks, but most modern bricks are rectangular.

● To build walls, the finished bricks are laid in layers and stuck together with a cement mixture called mortar.

JOBS AND RESOURCES

People need to work to earn money to pay for food, clothing, and homes. A long time ago, most people worked on the land directly, as hunters or farmers. Then people began to work in manufacturing industries, using the Earth's natural resources—raw materials like wood—to turn into manufactured goods, such as paper. More people were then needed to work selling the manufactured goods. Today, few people work on the land in developed countries. Most work in offices and stores, or in jobs working with people, such as teaching.

PAPER-MAKING

Paper-making uses up one of the Earth's valuable natural resources —trees. The trees are cut down and the wood is turned into pulp, which is made into paper. You can save paper, and trees, by recycling old newspapers to make your own cards and paper.

Paper is rolled into huge sheets, then sold to printers to print newspapers and books.

1 You will need old newspapers, wire mesh, a dishpan, absorbent cloths, a blender, a bucket, thick paper (which you can keep and use again), and water. Tear the newspaper into pieces.

2 Put the pieces in a bucket and cover with water. Soak overnight. Ask an adult to put small amounts of the pulp into the blender and liquefy.

3 Decide on the size of your paper and ask an adult to cut the wire mesh to that size. Pour the liquefied pulp into the dishpan and add water. Stir the mixture. Slide the wire mesh into the mixture.

HIGH-TECH INDUSTRIES
● All over the world, industry is changing rapidly. Many people in India, for example, now work in high-tech industries, such as making computer parts. Many jobs that used to be done using pencil and paper, such as designing buildings, are now done on computers.

4 Lay a cloth flat on some thick paper. Lift the mesh out of the mixture and lay it on the cloth, pulp side down. Press down on the mesh, then lift it, leaving the layer of pulp on the cloth. Place another cloth, then more thick paper on top of the pulp and press. Repeat these layers, as shown.

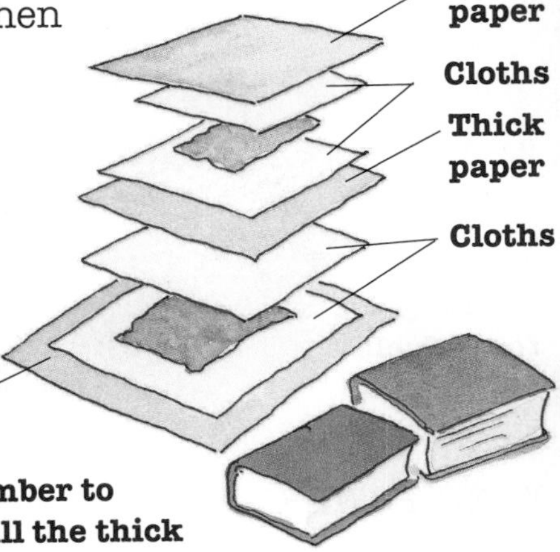

Thick paper

Cloths

Thick paper

Cloths

Thick paper

Remember to keep all the thick paper to use again!

Add colored paper or flowers to the pulp for decoration.

5 Lay some heavy books on top of the last sheet of thick paper. Leave for a few days, then remove the layers. Place your sheets of paper on newspaper to dry. Use your recycled paper to make cards or writing paper.

ENERGY

Most of the energy we use in factories, homes, and cars is created from burning fossil fuels—oil, coal, and natural gas. Fossil fuels cause air pollution when they burn. They give off a gas called carbon dioxide, which gradually builds up in the Earth's atmosphere. Fossil fuels are also nonrenewable, which means they will not last forever. People are looking for other ways to make energy from sources that will not run out, such as the wind, light from the Sun, and running or falling water.

Burning fossil fuels (oil, coal, and gas) releases carbon dioxide gas.

Carbon dioxide builds up in the atmosphere.

Too much carbon dioxide in the atmosphere traps too much heat from the Sun. The Earth gets too warm, making ice melt and sea levels rise. This is called the greenhouse effect.

Burning fossil fuels

WIND POWER

Harness the power of the wind with a windmill. You will need thin paper, a length of dowel, a straight pin, a small bead, scissors, and a ruler.

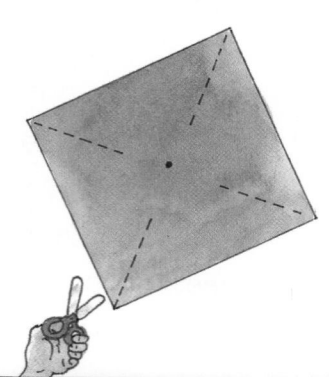

1 Cut out a square from the paper. Mark the center. Draw lines from each corner, almost to the center, as shown here. Cut along the lines.

2 Fold each corner into the center, as shown. Fix in place with a pin. Slide the bead onto the pin, behind the windmill.

3 Push the pin into the dowel, with the bead between the windmill and the dowel. Make sure the point of the pin does not stick out. Now stand in the wind and watch your windmill spin around as it captures the energy of the wind.

SOLAR POWER

● Solar energy comes directly from the Sun. Solar power stations (below) or solar panels attached to homes can capture energy from the Sun to provide heat and hot water. In hot deserts it is easy to catch the Sun's energy. It is more difficult in temperate countries that have lots of cloud and rain.

Solar panels

WIND POWER

● Wind turbines are set up in exposed places. The blades may spin through an area more than 200 feet across. The wind turns the turbine blades just as it spins your windmill. The turbines are connected to generators, which produce electricity. Wind energy is renewable and clean, but some say the turbines spoil the scenery.

COUNTRY PROFILE—KENYA

A country is a specific area of land, defined by humans, that is controlled by a single government. There are about 200 countries in the world.

Studying a country helps you see how different parts of geography fit together—how places and people affect each other. Kenya is a country in the continent of Africa. Its capital city is Nairobi. The zero degree (0°) line of latitude runs through Kenya, which means it is right on the equator, the hottest part of the world.

PROJECT KENYA

Make a travel poster about Kenya and its people. You will need colored pencils, an atlas, and a large sheet of paper. First, look at a globe or an atlas to locate Africa.

1 Write a list of the things that you need to find out about the country. What kind of climate does Kenya have? Does it have seasons? Are there any mountains? How high are they? Is there a coastline? Use the atlas, go to the library, or use the internet to find the information you need.

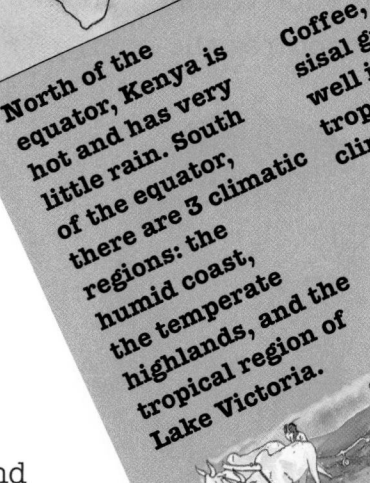

Kenyans mostly speak Kiswahili, but English is also spoken.

Kenya is close to Uganda, Ethiopia, and Tanzania.

North of the equator, Kenya is hot and has very little rain. South of the equator, there are 3 climatic regions: the humid coast, the temperate highlands, and the tropical region of Lake Victoria.

Coffee, tea, and sisal grow well in the tropical climate.

The rainy seasons are: October—December and April—June.

Mount Kenya is part of a chain of volcanic ridges.

TOURISM

● Tourism is one of Kenya's biggest industries. Hundreds of thousands of people visit every year and tourist activities provide jobs for thousands of local people. Many people come to visit the beautiful coastline, but most come to go on safari in one of the country's many national parks, such as Amboseli and the Masai Mara Game Reserve. The national parks are home to wild animals, such as lions, zebras, and elephants.

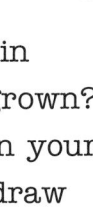

2 There are many different tribal groups in Kenya, but most people are Kikuyu. Do some research to find out more about the Kenyan people. What languages do they speak? What kinds of houses do they live in? What are the main industries? What crops are grown? What do people eat? On your large sheet of paper, draw pictures and write labels for all the things you have found out about Kenya and its people.

LANDMARKS

Tourists visit landmarks all over the world. Some are specially built by humans, as monuments to a great event or person. The Taj Mahal in India was built by Shah Jehan in the seventeenth century as a tomb for his wife. Others are historic buildings or structures—such as Tower Bridge in London—which are famous for their design or for something that happened there in the past. Many landmarks are natural wonders, like waterfalls or mountains. Postcards often show landmarks.

Uluru, or Ayer's Rock, Australia

Taj Mahal, Agra, India

Tower Bridge, London, England

WHERE AM I?

Learn about landmarks in this game. You will need small pictures of different landmarks, cardboard, scissors, glue, and an atlas.

1 Collect postcards or cut out pictures from old magazines. Glue them onto pieces of cardboard.

2 Look in the atlas to find the location of every landmark. On the back of each card, write a few clues about the landmark, such as the capital of the country it is in.

3 Two or more players can play. One person is the tourist and holds up each picture in turn, asking "Where am I?" Players must guess the name of the country or city from the picture. Give clues if nobody gets it on the first try. Whoever gets the answer keeps the card. The winner is the player who collects the most cards.

CHANGING NAMES

● Names are like labels. But names on maps are often changed. Landmarks, streets, towns, and sometimes whole countries are given new names. Zaire, a country in Africa, was renamed the Democratic Republic of Congo. Czechoslovakia, in Eastern Europe, divided into two countries, the Czech Republic and Slovakia. The city of Constantinople is now Istanbul and Bombay is Mumbai.

● Settlements in different places often have the same name. There is a city called Birmingham in England and another one in Alabama, U.S.A. There is a Boston, England and a Boston, Massachusetts, U.S.A. Names can be clues to the past. Many people who

migrated and settled in other countries named their new homes with familiar names from their home countries.

CHAPTER 6
Food and Farming

Once, people had to hunt for food. Then they learned how to collect and grow grass seed and to herd animals, and farming had begun. Now, the population of the world is growing fast, so more and more food is needed. Some farmers are changing their methods so that they can produce more crops. Learning about where food comes from will help you understand the importance of farming all over the world. In this chapter you will construct your own terraced slope, play "farminoes," and do an experiment to see how bananas help each other to ripen.

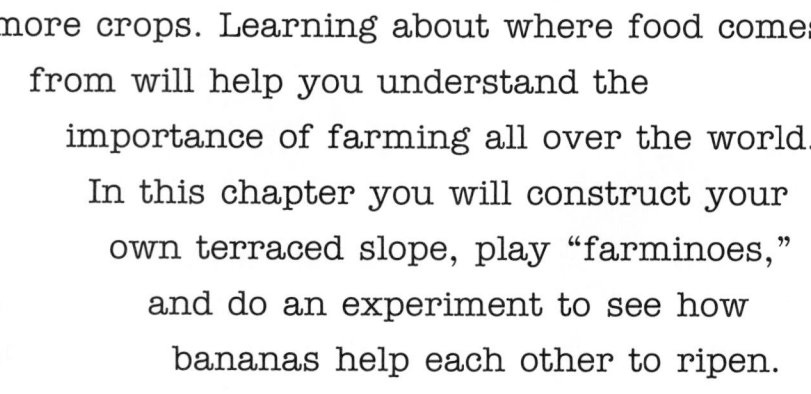

CONTENTS

POPULATION AND FOOD **510**

ALL YEAR ROUND **512**

PRODUCING FOOD **514**

FARM TO TABLE **516**

SUSTAINABLE FARMING **518**

LAND USE **520**

TROPICAL FARMING **522**

NOT ENOUGH FOOD **524**

GLOBAL MARKET **526**

FOOD ON THE MOVE **528**

HEALTHY EATING **530**

POPULATION AND FOOD

In 1999, the population of the world reached 6 billion. Every person needs food to survive, so food supply has to increase as the number of people increases. The supply of food depends mainly on farmers. However, only certain parts of the Earth's surface are suitable for farming. Countries with the most people to feed—in parts of Africa, South America, and Asia—are also among the poorest areas of the world. Here, many farmers can produce only enough food for their own families.

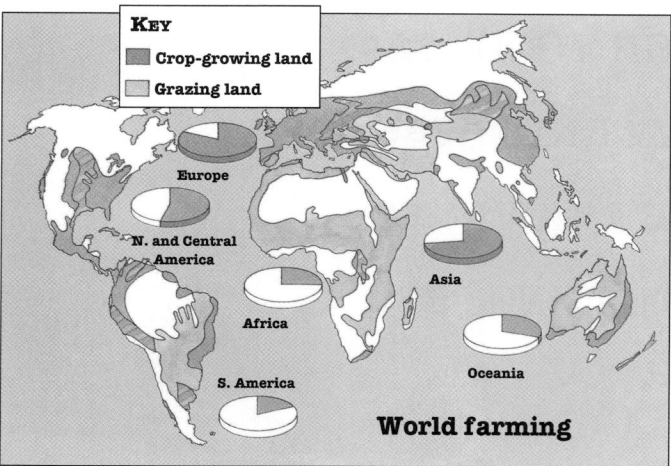

World farming

KEY
- Crop-growing land
- Grazing land

Europe
N. and Central America
Asia
Africa
S. America
Oceania

This map and the pie charts show roughly how much land in each continent is used for productive crop farming. Grassland areas are used for grazing livestock. The white areas are not used or are not suitable for farming.

UPS AND DOWNS OF FARMING

Farmers need good weather and rich soil or their crops will fail. Crops are also destroyed by disease and natural disasters. Make a game to show the ups and downs of farming.

1 Measure and rule a large grid of 10 x 10 squares on cardboard. Number the squares from 1 to 100, starting at the bottom left. Draw and color chutes and ladders onto the board, as shown on page 511.

2 Now use the key to help you design and draw symbols showing farming "ups"—things that help a food crop—and "downs"—things that destroy a food crop. Draw a "down" symbol at the top of each chute, and an "up" symbol at the bottom of each ladder.

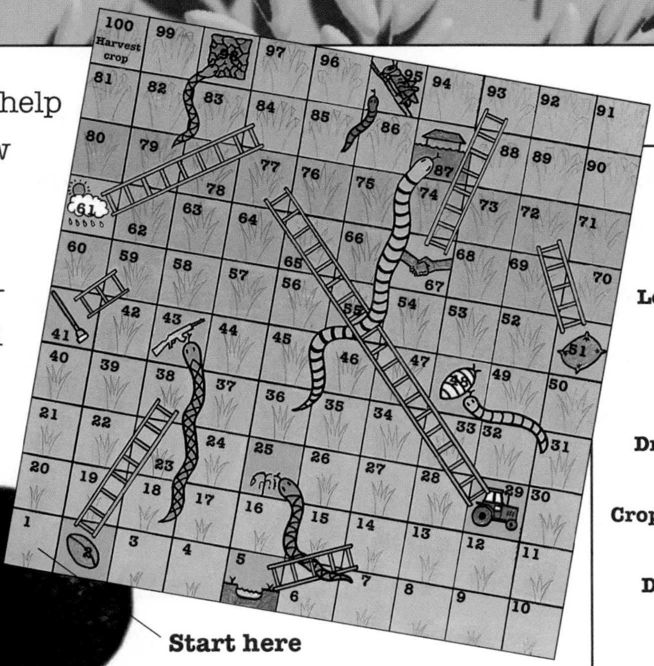

Start here

3 To play, you need a die and a counter for each player. Take turns throwing the die, then move along the numbered squares. If you land at the bottom of a ladder, "climb" to the top. If you land at the top of a chute, "slide" to the bottom. The winner is the first to 100.

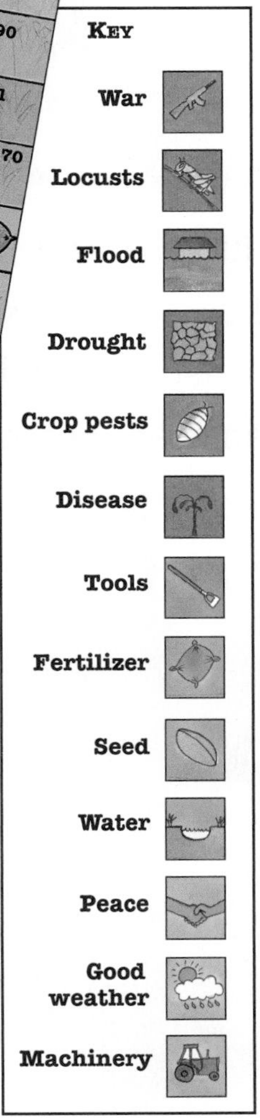

KEY

War

Locusts

Flood

Drought

Crop pests

Disease

Tools

Fertilizer

Seed

Water

Peace

Good weather

Machinery

STAPLE DIETS
● The food crop that grows best and is eaten most in any one country is called its staple diet. Most staple diets are cereal crops, like wheat. In developed countries, where food is plentiful, some people eat a staple diet of fast food, such as burgers.

Wheat, grown in temperate regions, is used to make bread and pasta.

Rice is the staple diet in many developing countries.

Maize, or corn, is the staple diet in parts of Africa and S. America. In the U.S., it is used mainly to feed livestock.

ALL YEAR ROUND

All farmers must prepare the soil, fertilize, plow, sow seed, nurture (look after), and harvest their crops. When these tasks are done depends upon climate and weather. In temperate climates, which are neither too hot nor too cold, farmers rely on the right kind of weather for each season. In spring, when seeds are sown, they hope for sunshine and showers. At harvest time, in late summer, they hope for dry weather with lots of sunshine. Farmers in the developed world use machinery to plant and harvest in large fields.

Plowing

A plow is a farm tool that turns over and breaks up the soil before seed is planted in the spring. Modern plows, such as the moldboard (left), are pulled by a tractor. They have metal blades that cut into the soil.

Sowing

In many developing countries, seed is still sown by hand. In developed countries, farmers use mechanical planters, or seed drills, pulled by tractors.

Growing and harvesting

Crops need rich soil, sunshine, and moisture to grow well. When they are ripe, the crops can be harvested quickly by combine harvesters. These machines combine the cutting and threshing (sorting grain from straw).

Grain

Threshing drum

Driver's cabin

Wheat

Straw

CLOUD-WATCHER

Clouds are made up of tiny water droplets. Rain falls when the droplets become too big. Farmers use clouds to forecast the weather. Make a chart to record the daily weather where you are.

1 Record the clouds each day for a week. What do they look like? Is any rain falling from them? Is the rain a drizzle or a downpour?

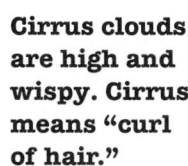

Cirrus clouds are high and wispy. Cirrus means "curl of hair."

Cumulus clouds are either small and fluffy, or they tower into tall, billowing storm clouds. Cumulus means "heap."

Stratus clouds form a low, gray blanket. Stratus means "layer."

2 Note the temperature each day. Place a thermometer outdoors, out of direct sunlight. Always take your readings at the same time each day.

Weather chart		
Date	Temp.	Cloud & rain
March 5th	50°F	rain all day
March 6th	48°F	drizzle
March 7th	51°F	no rain
March 8th	50°F	heavy rain
March 9th	55°F	clear sky, no rain
March 10th	53°F	no rain
March 11th	55°F	no rain

HELPFUL HINTS

● How many sayings about weather do you know? Keep a record to see if the ones you know are true or not.

SOIL

● When wind and rain erode (wear away) rock, they break it down into rock particles. These particles mix with humus to form soil. Humus is the decomposed (rotted) bodies of dead plants and animals. It binds the soil particles together and holds moisture.

Humus is found in topsoil and is rich in nutrients (goodness). Crops need nutrients to grow. Minibeasts like worms live here.

Subsoil contains more rock particles than humus. In rich soil, rainwater and roots should be able to reach into the subsoil.

Broken rocks lie between the subsoil and the bedrock. Groundwater can only seep as far as the bedrock. Very few roots reach here.

PRODUCING FOOD

The kind of farming practiced in temperate regions depends upon soil type and the condition of the land. Arable farming (the growing of crops) is done on low-lying land where the soil is rich. Sheep farming is done in hilly regions. Dairy farming is done on low-lying, rich grassland. Raising animals for food is called livestock farming. Poultry farmers raise birds, like chickens, for food. Mixed farming combines growing crops and raising animals. Truck farmers grow fruits and vegetables for sale in nearby cities.

FARMINOES

Learn about farms by playing "farminoes." You will need paper, cardboard, glue, scissors, and colored pencils.

1 Draw 28 domino shapes onto paper, then copy the farminoes shown below.

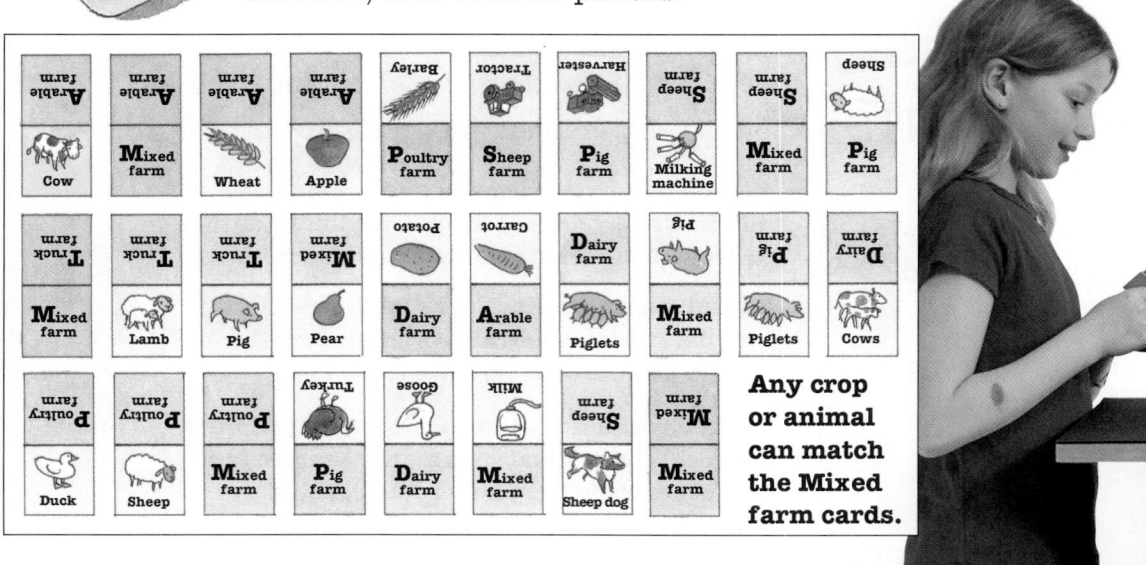

Arable farm	Arable farm	Arable farm	Arable farm	Barley	Tractor	Harvester	Sheep farm	Sheep farm	Sheep
Cow	Mixed farm	Wheat	Apple	Poultry farm	Sheep farm	Pig farm	Milking machine	Mixed farm	Pig farm
Truck farm	Truck farm	Truck farm	Mixed farm	Potato	Carrot	Dairy farm	Pig	Pig farm	Dairy farm
Mixed farm	Lamb	Pig	Pear	Dairy farm	Arable farm	Piglets	Mixed farm	Piglets	Cows
Poultry farm	Poultry farm	Poultry farm	Turkey	Goose	Milk	Sheep farm	Mixed farm		
Duck	Sheep	Mixed farm	Pig farm	Dairy farm	Mixed farm	Sheep dog	Mixed farm		

Any crop or animal can match the Mixed farm cards.

514

2 Ask an adult to help you glue your farminoes onto cardboard, then cut them out.

3 Divide the farminoes equally. Up to four people can play. The first player puts down a farmino, picture side up. The next player must match the crop or animal with the farm type, or the farm type with the crop or animal, as shown here. Take turns matching farminoes. If you cannot play, miss a turn. The winner is the first to have no farminoes left.

FACTORY FARMING

● On factory farms, egg-laying hens live side by side in cages with little room to move. Each hen lays more than 200 eggs a year, but many hens become sick and anxious. Some people prefer to buy free-range eggs, which are laid by hens that have more space to move around.

FOOD MOUNTAINS

● In developed countries, many farmers produce more food than they can sell, due to modern machines and intensive farming methods. The surplus (leftover) food is stored in huge "mountains." In developing countries, farmers cannot produce enough food. Many can only grow enough for their own families, so some people starve. Sometimes, the surplus food is used to help emergency food aid programs in areas where people are starving.

FARM TO TABLE

Farmers work directly with the earth, and are called primary producers. Many farm products, such as eggs, livestock, grains, and vegetables are processed by secondary producers to make other useful things. The products that come from corn (maize) include breakfast cereals and corn syrup, which is used to sweeten soft drinks. Wheat kernels are ground to a fine powder called flour, which is used to make bread. Fruits can be made into juices.

Wheat kernel

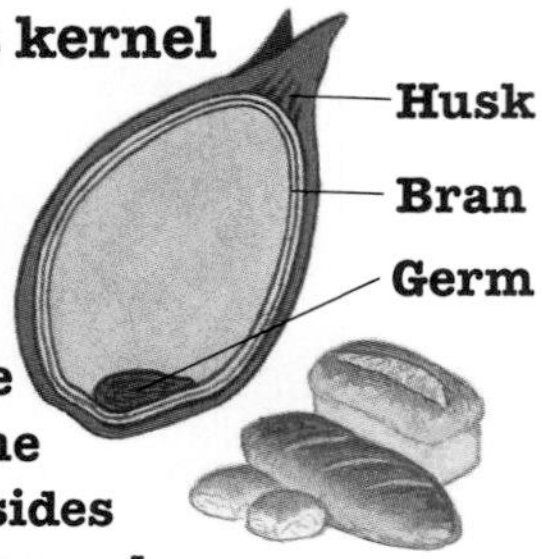

— Husk
— Bran
— Germ

White flour is made from the soft insides of the kernel.

FARMING PAIRS

Pair up farm crops and farm animals with the products made from them. You will need cardboard, paper, scissors, glue, and colored pencils.

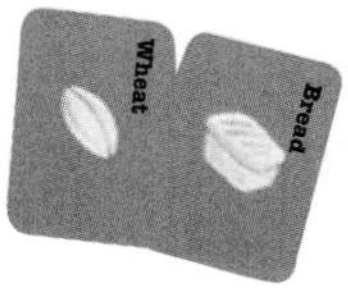

1 Cut out 20 cards from the cardboard. Copy the pictures on the key opposite onto a sheet of paper. Cut each picture out and glue it onto one of your cards. Write the name of each crop or product on the card, as shown. Place the cards upside down in a pile.

2 Two can play. Deal five cards each. Take turns picking a card from the pile. If you can make a pair, lay it in front of you. The first to collect five matching pairs is the winner.

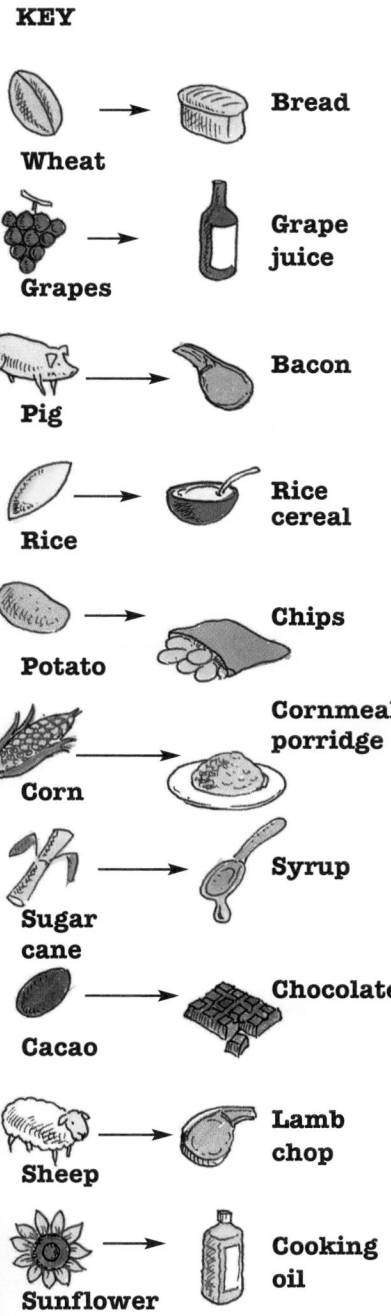

Wheat → Bread

Grapes → Grape juice

Pig → Bacon

Rice → Rice cereal

Potato → Chips

Corn → Cornmeal porridge

Sugar cane → Syrup

Cacao → Chocolate

Sheep → Lamb chop

Sunflower → Cooking oil

You can add more cards to the game by drawing other farm products and the things they are made into.

CATTLE

● Cattle are herbivores, which means they eat plants. They can graze over a large area, finding enough to eat even on poor grazing land. Products that come from cows include leather, milk, beef, and beef fat.

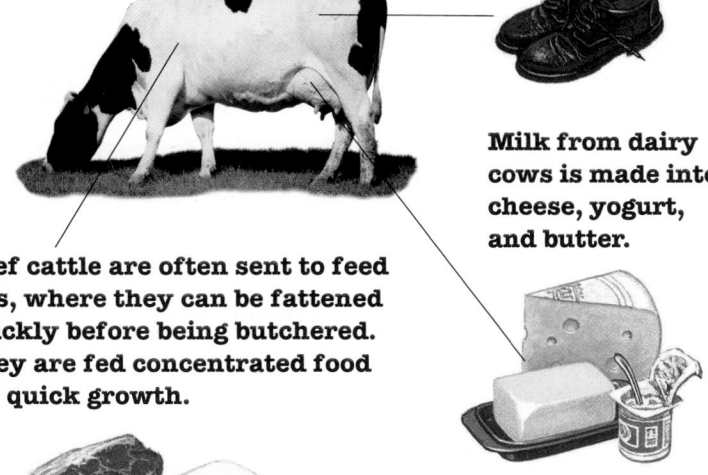

Cow hide is turned into leather for bags, jackets, and shoes.

Milk from dairy cows is made into cheese, yogurt, and butter.

Beef cattle are often sent to feed lots, where they can be fattened quickly before being butchered. They are fed concentrated food for quick growth.

Beef fat is used in cooking and is added to processed foods.

● Livestock can suffer from various diseases. In parts of Africa, the tsetse fly carries a parasite that feeds on the blood of cattle. BSE, or "mad cow disease," spread through several European countries in the 1990s. Thousands of cows were slaughtered (killed), and some people who ate infected meat died. Foot-and-mouth is a highly infectious disease that affects livestock, but is not dangerous to humans. In 1967 and 2001, there were outbreaks in Europe. Thousands of sheep and cattle were slaughtered and burned.

SUSTAINABLE FARMING

Farmers must be able to produce crops year after year. To do this, the soil must remain healthy and fertile. This is called sustainable farming. Modern farming methods and machinery have greatly increased the world's food supply, necessary to feed the growing population. Chemical pesticides and fertilizers are used to produce as many crops as possible. Farmers must make sure that their methods are sustainable—that the crops they plant and chemicals they use do not destroy the goodness in the soil. Some prefer organic farming—using natural fertilizers.

Pesticide

MINIBEAST DETECTIVE

Minibeasts play a large role in keeping soil healthy. To see them, you need some soil, a large sieve, a fine sieve, a large jar, a magnifying glass, paper towels, and an adjustable lamp.

1 First, remove any sticks and stones from the soil sample. Return any worms you find to the soil outside. Then strain the sample into a bowl through the large sieve. Make sure you wash your hands after you have touched the soil.

2 Now pour the soil into the fine sieve and balance it above the jar, as shown above. Position the jar beneath the lamp and wait. After a while, you will see some tiny minibeasts appear in the bottom of the jar.

3 Leave the jar for a few hours, then tip the contents onto the paper towels. Examine the minibeasts closely with a magnifying glass. Use a reference book to identify them, then return them to the soil outside.

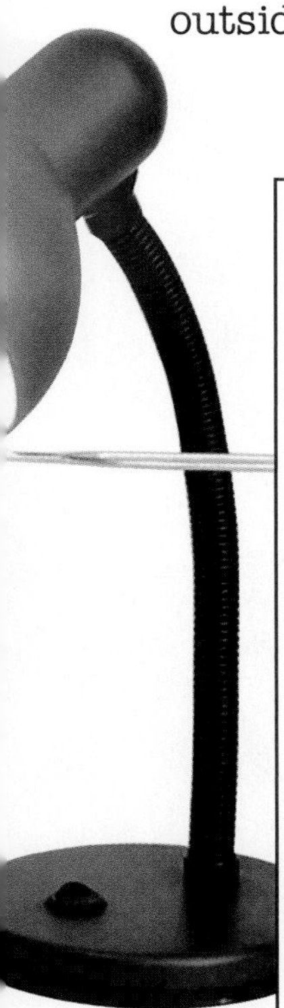

WHAT'S HAPPENING

● Tiny creatures in soil prefer cool, damp conditions beneath the ground. The heat from the lamp warms the soil, and the minibeasts try to escape from the heat into the jar below. These small creatures are vital to the soil. They help maintain its goodness by breaking down dead matter and adding nutrients.

KEEPING SOIL HEALTHY

● Each crop adds or removes different nutrients from the soil. For example, corn takes nitrogen out of the soil, while crops called legumes—peas or beans—put nitrogen back into the soil. To keep the soil healthy, many farmers change the crops grown in a field from one year to the next. This is called crop rotation.

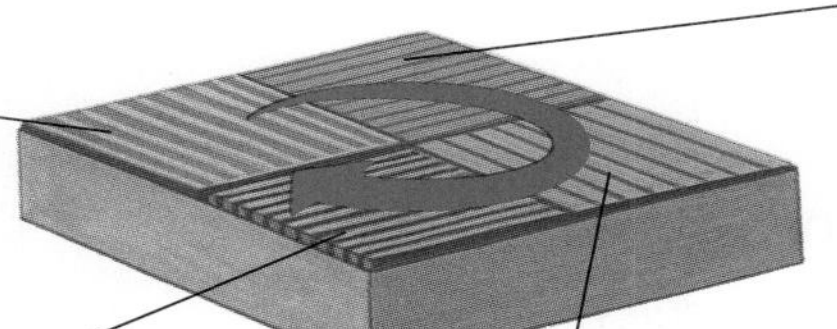

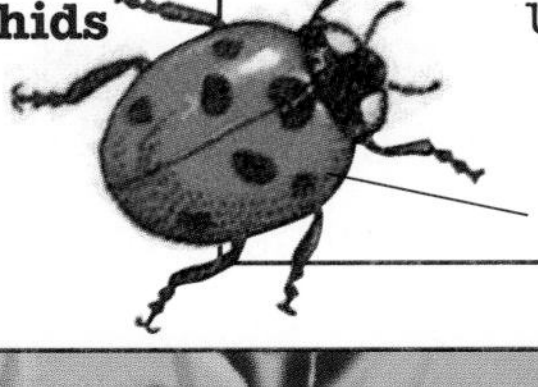

Field 1:
1st year: Corn
2nd year: Peas
3rd year: Wheat
4th year: Potatoes

Field 2:
1st year: Peas
2nd year: Wheat
3rd year: Potatoes
4th year: Corn

Field 3:
1st year: Wheat, 2nd year: Potatoes
3rd year: Corn, 4th year: Peas

Field 4:
1st year: Potatoes, 2nd year: Corn
3rd year: Peas, 4th year: Wheat

● Some farmers use insects to help keep the soil healthy. Ladybugs eat aphids, which eat crops. Relationships like this exist within every natural food web. Planting onions between crops can also deter pests without having to use chemical pesticides. Many people prefer to eat food that has been grown this way, called organic food.

Aphids

Ladybug

LAND USE

Farming has greatly changed the way land is used. Every farm was once natural countryside. Most farming 100 years ago was done on small farms. Today's arable farms often cover huge areas with a single crop, called a monoculture. This is known as intensive farming. Intensive farming can produce more crops than a small farm can, and the crops or products can be sold more cheaply. Machinery and methods have improved so much that far fewer people need to work on the land. But monocultures have changed the environment, too. Wild animals and plants that adapted to small farms, living in meadows and windbreaks, can't find enough food in monocultures.

Wheat

Fruit trees **Poultry**

Soybeans

Cattle

Fruit trees

Corn

Some farmers leave uncultivated areas on the edges of fields for wildlife.

WHAT GROWS WHERE?

Make a map to show how land is used for different kinds of farming. You can include small farms and monocultures. You will need paper and some colored pencils.

1 Look at the different kinds of farm shown earlier in this chapter. If there are farms near your home, think about what kinds of farm they are. What crops are growing? Are there any monocultures? Is there any livestock?

2 Choose which farms you want to show on your map. Draw an outline of fields onto the paper.

3 Color your map and design a key. Use different colors to show the type of farming that is being done in each field. Draw symbols for each of the landmarks or buildings on your map.

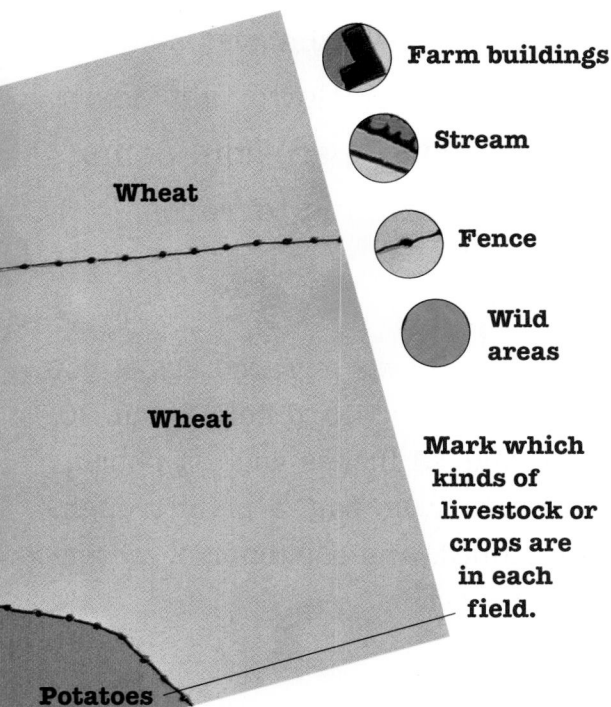

Farm buildings

Stream

Fence

Wild areas

Mark which kinds of livestock or crops are in each field.

Wheat

Wheat

Potatoes

HELPFUL HINTS

● Look at a large-scale map to see if there is any farmland near your house or town. If there is, ask an adult to visit the area with you to look at the kind of farming that is done there.

HABITAT DESTRUCTION

● As natural countryside is plowed up, the wildflowers that grow there are gradually disappearing. The insects that feed on the flowers are going too, which means that birds that feed on the insects are becoming rare. Many songbird species that used to be common on farmland are now endangered.

● Trees and windbreaks help keep the soil in place. Many have been ripped out to make larger fields and, over the years, wind and rain have eroded (worn away) the soil. This has created dustbowls in some areas, where no plants can grow.

● Land around or on farms is often used for recreation. People using the countryside need to follow certain rules to protect the area for farming, wildlife, and for other people to use.

Never leave litter. It can be dangerous for animals.

Keep dogs on a leash so that they do not chase livestock.

TROPICAL FARMING

Many developing countries have tropical climates. In tropical regions, there is a wet season and a dry season, but it is hot all year round. In some places, it is possible to have two harvests in one year. Crops that grow well in tropical climates include coffee, tea, and rice. In the wet season, rainfall is heavy and frequent. On hills, rainwater flows fast down slopes and washes the soil away. This is called soil erosion. Some farmers have learned how to farm slopes by building terraces, like a series of steps.

ON THE TERRACES

To construct your own terraced slope, you will need a deep cardboard box, about 20 inches long and 12 inches wide, a pencil, a craft knife, a trash bag, a plant trough, soil, small stones, and a pitcher of water.

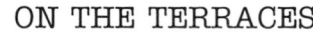

1 Ask an adult to help you cut the cardboard box with the craft knife, so that the sides slope, as shown here. Cut a V-shape in the front. Line the inside of the box with the trash bag.

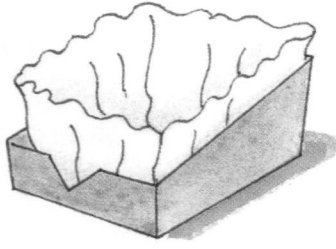

2 Cover the bottom of the lined box with soil. Pile up the soil, so that it is much higher at the back of the box. Position the trough in front, as shown here. Pour water down the slope and watch how easily the soil washes away.

3 Now flatten the soil into flat "steps." Push small stones into the front of each "step," as shown in the photograph. Now pour water down the slope. Note how the soil stays in place instead of washing away.

WHAT'S HAPPENING

● The steps keep the water from flowing too quickly, taking the soil with it. On real terraces, each step is held back by a wall or by plants with strong roots. Ancient Romans planted grapevines and olive trees on terraces. Today, in many parts of Asia, rice is grown on terraced hillsides.

SOIL DEPTH

Humus layer

Temperate   **Tropical**

● In temperate regions, there is usually a deep layer of humus, which contains all the nutrients in the soil. In tropical regions, the nutrients are quickly taken up by plants, which grow well in the hot, moist conditions. Once the nutrients are used up, the humus layer is thin and the soil is no longer any good for growing crops.

SLASH-AND-BURN

Cassava

● Farmers in tropical areas burn trees and bushes to clear ground for planting crops such as cassava. This is called slash-and-burn, or shifting agriculture, because the farmer has to keep on clearing new land. The ashes from the burned wood are full of nutrients, but new crops use up the nutrients quickly. Soon the soil becomes infertile. The farmer then has to start again and burn another area of forest.

NOT ENOUGH FOOD

Although world food production has increased rapidly in the last 50 years, the population has increased even faster. Millions do not have enough to eat and live close to starvation. Millions more are not able to include some important kinds of food in their diet. One big reason for the lack of food is that farmers wear out the soil as they try to produce more and more food from the same land. Natural disasters such as droughts and floods also destroy crops. Many farmers in developing countries do not have the money to buy machinery and tools to improve their farming conditions.

SALTY SOIL

In some areas, the soil can become too salty to grow crops. You can show how this happens in a simple experiment. You will need a tray, soil, salt, and water.

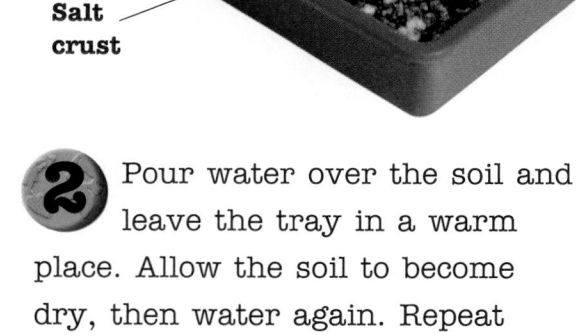

Salt crust

1 Cover the bottom of the tray with about ¹/₂ in. of salt. Cover the salt with a layer of soil about 2 in. deep. Press down firmly.

2 Pour water over the soil and leave the tray in a warm place. Allow the soil to become dry, then water again. Repeat this a few times.

3 Salt crystals will begin to appear on the top of the soil. After about two weeks, a hard crust of salt will form.

WHAT'S HAPPENING

● When there is too much water, the ground becomes waterlogged. In hot sun, surface water evaporates (dries off) quickly and ground water, which contains salts dissolved from rocks, comes up to the surface. This water also evaporates, and the salt left behind forms salt pans. In the Indus valley in Pakistan (left), floods are frequent, and the soil becomes too salty for crops to grow. Each year, there are 100,000 fewer acres to farm.

SUBSISTENCE FARMING

● Farmers who can only grow enough food for their own families are called subsistence farmers. There is a lot of subsistence farming in developing countries. All the planting and harvesting is done by hand.

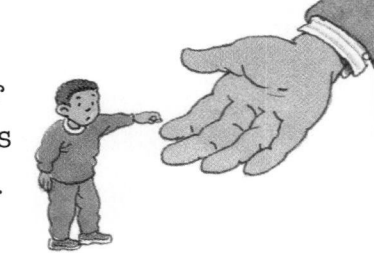

In good years, subsistence farmers may grow enough to sell a few crops at local markets. In drought years, when the rains fail, crops wither, and aid agencies must provide food to prevent the farmers and their families from starving.

Hot, dry winds

Dried-up river

Wilted crops

DROUGHT

● A drought happens when the yearly rains in an area are not heavy enough. Crops and grass for cattle shrivel in the heat. Rivers dry up, and people must walk miles to find water. To help areas that suffer drought frequently, scientists are developing fast-growing seeds that survive on low rainfall.

GLOBAL MARKET

Supermarket shelves hold food crops and products from all over the world. Many are grown in plantations, which are vast monocultures with rows of bushes or trees. Pesticides are used so that as many crops as possible can be produced. In tropical regions, huge plantations of tea (below), sugar cane, pineapples, and coffee are common. In temperate regions, fruit is often grown on plantations. Plantations employ many people to pick and pack the crops.

WHERE DOES IT COME FROM?

Make a map showing where crop products come from. You will need food labels, a map, pencils, cardboard, colored pencils, yarn, pushpins, scissors, and glue.

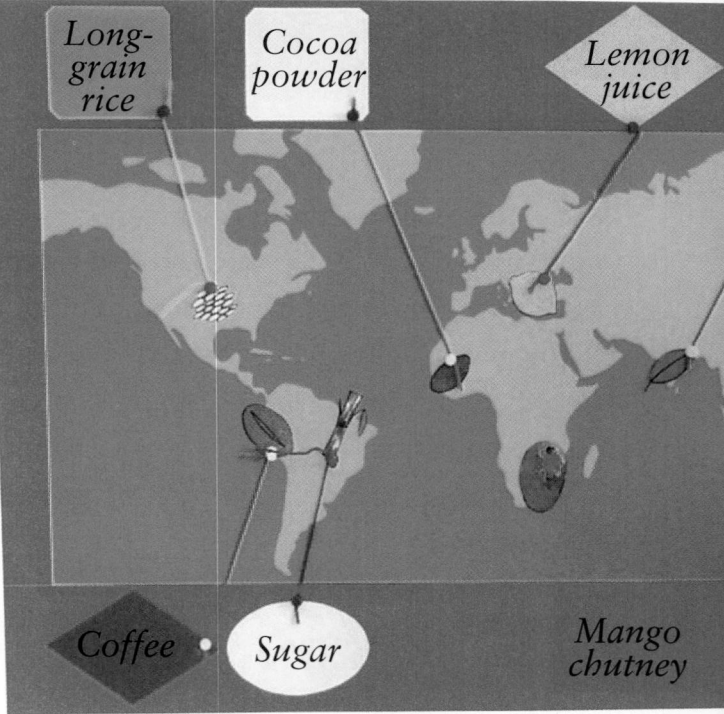

Long-grain rice

Cocoa powder

Lemon juice

Coffee • Sugar

Mango chutney

1 Collect labels from products that come from different countries. Coffee, for example, is grown in Colombia and Kenya. Write down the names of the foods and the names of the countries they come from.

2 Copy a large map of the world. Glue your map onto cardboard, leaving a wide border.

3 Draw and cut out symbols for the food crops you have chosen. Glue the symbols in the correct places on the map. Design and color a key, as shown here.

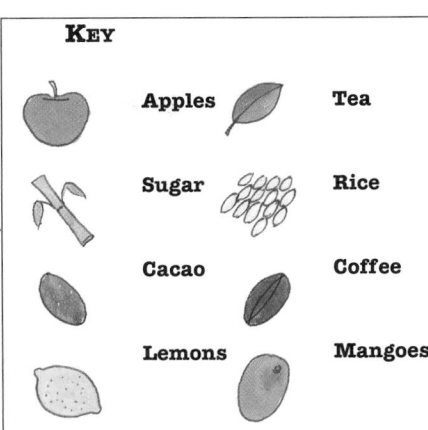

KEY

Apples   Tea

Sugar   Rice

Cacao   Coffee

Lemons   Mangoes

4 Glue your product labels onto the border. Link each one to the correct food crop on the map using lengths of colored yarn and pushpins.

Tea

CASH CROPS

● Crops grown on plantations in tropical countries and sold all over the world are called cash crops. They are grown especially for export, which means to be sold in other countries. Many countries depend on the money from their cash crops. They suffer greatly if world prices for their crops go down, but gain money to improve farming methods if prices are high.

PLANTATION WORKERS

● Workers employed to cultivate cash crops are often poorly paid, but many prefer the work to subsistence farming.

In some countries, a "Fair trade" logo appears on products that come from plantations that pay a decent wage to their workers.

FOOD ON THE MOVE

The banana is a perishable fruit, which means it can rot quickly and lose its value. The banana plant is a huge herb that is so big it is often mistaken for a tree. Huge areas of tropical forest have been cut down so that bananas can be planted as cash crops. Before bananas reach stores, they have a long journey. Look at banana labels to see the many countries in which they are grown. The first bananas grew wild in India. Banana plants were then taken across the world to Central America, where there are now many banana plantations.

1. A stem of bananas can hold 200 bananas, arranged in "hands." Each banana is called a "finger." Workers use a sharp machete, or knife, to cut each stem of green, unripe bananas from the banana plant.

GOING BANANAS

Do an experiment to see how bananas help each other to ripen. You need two unripe bananas, a ripe banana, and two plastic bags.

1 Place one unripe banana in a plastic bag beside the ripe banana. Put the other unripe banana in the second bag.

2 After a few days, compare the bananas. The banana in the bag next to the ripe banana will have ripened faster than the banana in the bag by itself.

WHAT'S HAPPENING

● Bananas naturally produce a gas called ethylene, which makes other bananas ripen. So a ripe banana will make a green banana ripe if they are placed side by side. Just before green bananas reach supermarkets, ethylene gas is used to ripen them quickly.

2. The bananas are loaded into rail trucks, or hung on cables, to be transported for packing. They are washed, cut from their stems, and packed in cartons, then taken to be loaded onto ships.

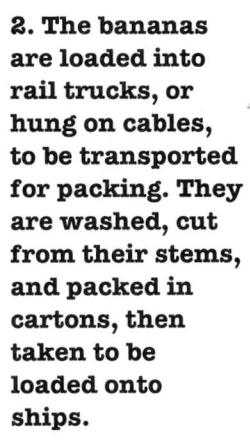

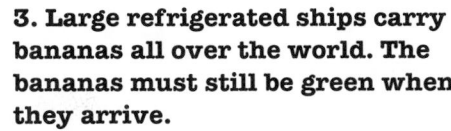

3. Large refrigerated ships carry bananas all over the world. The bananas must still be green when they arrive.

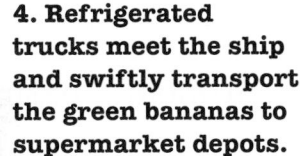

4. Refrigerated trucks meet the ship and swiftly transport the green bananas to supermarket depots.

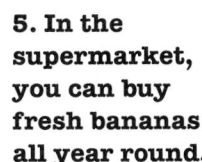

5. In the supermarket, you can buy fresh bananas all year round.

IMPORTED FOOD

● A long time ago, fruit and vegetables from temperate regions were only on sale after harvest time. Now, shoppers can buy fresh carrots or apples at any time of year. Perishable foods from all over the world are on sale in supermarkets because they can be transported long distances at great speed. Look closely at the labels on fresh fruit and vegetables. Make a note of where they come from, as shown here.

Celery from California

Zucchini from Texas

Chili peppers from Mexico

Grapefruit from Florida

Pears from Oregon

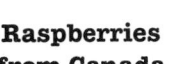

Raspberries from Canada

Apples from South Africa

Cabbage from New York

Mushrooms from Pennsylvania

Asparagus from Michigan

HEALTHY EATING

Food provides us with energy. Most people in developed countries are able to gain enough energy to live healthily by eating a balanced diet, which means eating a variety of foods. In developing countries, it is often more difficult to eat a balanced diet, because farmers are not able to produce enough food for everyone. Farmers and scientists are always trying to develop new farming methods and improve seeds so that more food can be grown, especially in poor soil and poor growing conditions.

A balanced diet includes many kinds of food.

The diet in a developing country may include food from only one or two food groups.

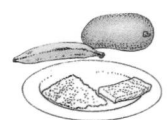

FOOD VALUES

● The body needs four main groups of nutrients to stay healthy, as well as minerals and water. The four groups are carbohydrates, proteins, vitamins, and fats.

Carbohydrates are energy-giving starches in foods such as bread and potatoes; and sugars in foods such as cookies.

Proteins, in meat, eggs, and fish, help growth and repair of the body.

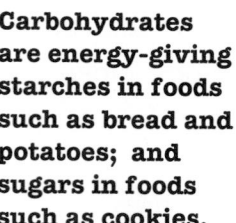

Vitamins are needed to maintain good health. Fruit and vegetables are especially high in certain vitamins.

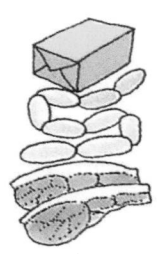

Fats, in butter and meat, also give the body energy.

WEEKLY FOOD INTAKE

Keep a record of the food you eat every day for a week to find out how balanced your diet is. You will need a notebook, a ruler, and a pencil.

1 Use the ruler to draw five columns in your food intake chart. Write headings for the day and time in the first column, then the four food groups: carbohydrates, proteins, vitamins, and fats, in the other columns.

2 Every time you have a meal, make a note of what you eat. Write each piece of food in the correct column in your chart. Remember to include any snacks, such as chips or fruit, that you eat between mealtimes.

Weekly food intake

Day/time	Carbos	Proteins	Vitamins	Fats
Monday 7 A.M.	Toast	Eggs	Orange juice	Butter
10.45 A.M.	Chips			
12.30 P.M.	Rice	Chicken	Salad Apple	
4 P.M.	Bread			Peanut butter

3 Check your chart each day. For a balanced diet, you should have entries in each column. The more energy you use, the more carbohydrates and fats you need to eat.

IMPROVING FARMING

● To improve and vary crops, scientists cross one successful crop plant with another to produce a new plant, called a hybrid, that has the best qualities of both plants.

● Over the last 100 years, wider use of machinery and intensive research into seeds, pest control, and soil have greatly improved food production. But farmers with no money and poor growing conditions still struggle. Scientists continue to develop drought-resistant and disease-resistant seeds to help reduce famine in developing countries.

● Genetically modified (GM) crops are now being developed and tested. They may reduce the need for pesticides and some already give high crop yields (production).

● Hydroponics is a method of growing crops without soil. It is especially useful for testing what conditions plants need to grow best. The plant roots are immersed in a mixture of water, nutrients, and sand or gravel.

Nutrient solution

GLOSSARY

acid rain
Rainfall that damages forests because it contains too much acid, caused by air pollution.

altitude
Height above sea level.

arable farming
Crop farming.

atlas
A book of maps.

attrition
The wearing down of pieces of rock carried by wind, water, or ice.

Beaufort scale
A scale from 0 to 12 classifying wind strength.

biome
A large ecosystem, usually named after the type of vegetation that grows there.

camouflage
The use of color or pattern that enables an animal or plant to merge with its surroundings.

carnivore
A meat eater.

cash crops
Crops that are grown especially to be sold in other countries.

climate
The average weather an area has over the year.

compass
An instrument showing the direction of magnetic north.

condensation
The change that occurs when water vapor (a gas) becomes water (a liquid) as a result of cooling.

consumer
An animal or plant that eats other living things.

crystals
Solids with particles arranged in a regular order, forming flat sides or faces.

decomposer
An organism that breaks down dead plant and animal matter, releasing minerals into the soil.

deforestation
The clearing of forest.

deposition
The laying down of eroded material carried by wind, water, or ice.

developed countries
Countries with lots of industries where most people have a high standard of living.

developing countries
Countries with few industries where many people live in poverty.

ecology
The study of ecosystems.

ecosystem
One community in one habitat and its nonliving environment.

environment
The surroundings of a habitat.

equator
An imaginary line around the center of the world. The zero degree (0°) line of latitude.

erosion
The wearing down of the land by natural forces such as waves, wind, and rain.

evaporation
When heat causes water to become water vapor (a gas). The opposite of condensation.

food web
The way in which living things in a habitat rely on each other for food.

fossil fuels
Fuels like coal, oil, and natural gas, formed from remains of living things.

fossil
Evidence of ancient life that is found in sedimentary rocks.

generation
The period of about 20 years that separates parents and children.

geothermal energy
Natural heat from inside the Earth; a renewable source of energy.

geysers
Hot springs that throw up columns of heated water at regular intervals.

global warming
A rise in world temperatures as too much heat is trapped in Earth's atmosphere due to high levels of carbon dioxide caused by burning fossil fuels.

habitat
The natural home of a plant or animal.

hemisphere
Half of the planet Earth. Summer in the northern hemisphere (north of the equator) is winter in the southern hemisphere (south of the equator).

herbivore
A plant eater.

hydroelectric power
Electrical energy that is obtained from generators operated by water turbines.

igneous rocks
New rocks formed either from magma inside the Earth or from lava that has cooled on the surface.

intensive farming
A modern farming practice that uses machinery on large farms to produce large crops cheaply.

irrigation
Any system designed to carry water to the land so that crops will grow.

large-scale maps
Maps that show lots of detail but only small areas of land.

latitude
Distance in degrees north or south of the equator. Lines of latitude are parallel to the equator.

lichen
An organism composed of two living things, algae and fungi.

livestock
Animals that are farmed.

lodestone
A type of rock with magnetic properties that was used as a compass by sailors long ago.

longitude
Distance in degrees east or west of the prime meridian, which is zero degrees (0°) longitude.

magma
Hot, molten (liquid) rock formed deep inside Earth. Called lava when it erupts on the surface.

meander
A bend in a river.

metamorphic rocks
Igneous or sedimentary rocks that have been changed through great heat and pressure inside the Earth.

metropolitan area
Towns and cities joined into one big urban area.

minerals
Substances that make up rocks. In most minerals, particles are arranged in a regular order, forming crystals.

mixed farming
Farming that combines rearing livestock with growing crops.

monoculture
An area in which only one main crop is grown.

oasis
A source of water in hot desert areas, where the water table reaches the surface.

organic farming
Producing crops without using chemical pesticides or fertilizers.

oxbow lake
A lake left where a river cuts through the narrow neck of a meander.

permeable rock
Rock, like limestone, which allows water to soak through cracks and joints.

photosynthesis
The process that plants use to make food, using sunlight and chlorophyll (the green color in leaves).

plantation
A monoculture farm, especially in tropical countries, where cash crops are grown on a large scale.

population density
The average number of people living in each square kilometer or other unit of area.

porous rock
Rock, like sandstone, which allows water to soak through pores or air holes.

predator
An animal that hunts and eats other animals.

prey
An animal hunted and eaten by a predator.

prime meridian
An imaginary line that circles the Earth, north to south, at 0° longitude.

producer
A green plant that makes food through photosynthesis.

refugee
A person seeking shelter from danger by moving to another country.

Richter scale
A scale to measure the strength of earthquakes.

rural
Located in the country.

scale
Representation of size on a map.

sediment
Matter carried by water or wind and deposited on land.

sedimentary rocks
Rocks formed from sediments.

settlement
A place where people live.

small-scale maps
Maps that show little detail but large areas of land.

stalactite
A growth of calcium carbonate that hangs from the roof of a cave in limestone rock.

stalagmite
A column of calcium carbonate that grows upward from the floor of an underground cave in limestone rock.

staple diet
The most common food eaten by people in a region or country.

strata
Layers of rock.

subsistence farming
Small-scale farming, where farmers only grow enough to feed one family.

sustainable farming
Looking after soil and the environment so that the same land can be farmed year after year.

symbiosis
A partnership that benefits two different species.

tectonic plates
Large blocks of Earth's crust that float on the liquid magma beneath.

temperate regions
The parts of the world where temperatures are moderate, and where there is often a marked difference between the seasons.

tributary
Small stream or river that joins a main river.

tropical regions
The parts of the world, near the equator, where the climate is hot all year round. Tropical regions have a wet season and a dry season.

urban
Located in a town or city.

vegetation
Plant life, especially of a particular region.

water table
The level of ground water below which the rock is completely saturated.

MATH
for fun
PROJECTS

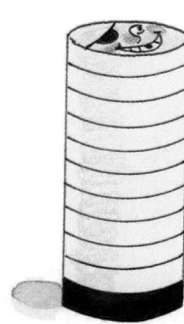

© Aladdin Books Ltd 1999
Designed and produced by
Aladdin Books Ltd
28 Percy Street
London W1P OLD

First published in
the United States
in 1999 by
Copper Beech Books,
an imprint of
The Millbrook Press
2 Old New Milford Road
Brookfield, Connecticut 06804

Project Editor: Sally Hewitt
Editor: Liz White
Design: David West Children's Book Design
Designer: Simon Morse
Photography: Roger Vlitos
Illustrator: Tony Kenyon

Printed in Italy
5 4 3 2 1

ISBN 0-7613-0789-3

MATH
for fun
PROJECTS

Andrew King

Copper Beech Books
Brookfield, Connecticut

CONTENTS

Chapter One
Exploring Numbers **544**

Chapter Two
Making Fractions **570**

Chapter Three
Discovering Patterns **596**

Chapter Four
Getting the Facts **622**

Chapter Five
Exploring Shapes **648**

Chapter Six
Plotting Points and Position **674**

Chapter Seven
Measuring Sizes **700**

Chapter Eight
Measuring Weight and Time **726**

Tables 746

Glossary 754

Index 759

INTRODUCTION

It's amazing what you can do once you have begun to master math! Have you ever wondered how to write computer games, or plan a journey into space? Would you like to be able to find hidden treasure, find your way through mazes, or plan winning strategies? How could you measure the lines, curves, and shapes that surround you?

If you were told that nine-tenths of an iceberg is hidden underwater, could you imagine what that looks like? An understanding of math can reveal how all these things are possible.

Math for Fun Projects introduces you to some of the fascinating feats that math enables you to perform.

You can play Go Fishing to learn about angles, or slice up pizza and learn about fractions. You could use percentages to make a dazzling carpet, or amaze your friends with your x-ray vision using arithmetic.

Through different games and projects you will learn about percentages, symmetry, algebra, setting and sorting, weighing and measuring, and many other mathematical skills. Use the helpful tables at the back of the book to help you if you get stuck.

Follow the STEP-BY-STEP INSTRUCTIONS to help you with the activities.

Use HELPFUL HINTS for tips and clues about the experiments and games.

Look at MORE IDEAS for information about other projects for you to try.

1 Yellow squares mean this is an easy activity.

2 Blue squares mean this is a medium activity.

3 Pink squares mean this is a more difficult activity. You will have to think hard!

CONTENTS

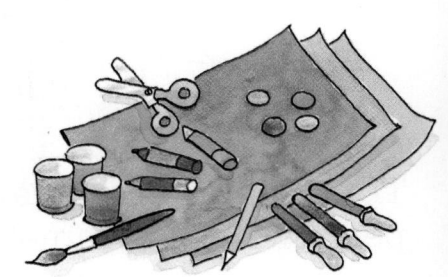

NUMBER FACTS **546**

SUMMING UP **548**

COUNTING DOWN **550**

VALUE YOUR DIGITS! **552**

PLACE YOUR DIGITS **554**

BIG, BIGGER, BIGGEST **556**

SIGN OF THE TIMES **558**

DO THE OPPOSITE **560**

HARD TIMES! **562**

BIG TIME OPERATOR **564**

GAMES GALORE! **566**

PROBLEMS, PROBLEMS... **568**

Chapter One

Exploring Numbers

NUMBER FACTS

When you were younger, you probably learned different ways of **adding** up two numbers to make 10. Being able to remember number facts quickly, like 6+4=10 and also 2+8=10, can be helpful in solving many **arithmetic** problems.

X-RAY VISION!
If you know your number facts to 7 you will be able to do this trick and pretend that you have x-ray vision! For this trick you will need a die. You could make one.

1 Cover a cube with colored paper. Stick on shapes for the "number" spots, or you could draw them on.

2 Throw the die a few times. Each time it comes to rest, make a note of the number that is on the top of the die and the number hidden underneath.

3 Do you notice a pattern? If you can see a pattern you are ready to do the trick! Say to your audience, "I have x-ray vision and I can see through the die to the hidden number!"

HELPFUL HINTS

● The secret to this game is that the opposite sides of the die always add up to **equal** 7. If you see a 3 at the top of the die then the hidden face must be 4 because...

$$3+4=7$$

It is a bit like trying to solve a problem like this: 3+?=7.

MORE IDEAS

● This is like the x-ray vision trick. It uses the same pattern. Can you work it out? You need two dice. Place one on top of the other. The top face and the hidden faces in the middle and underneath will add up to... you've got it — 14! That's because 7+7=14. You can say, "I know what all three hidden numbers add up to!"

● What is it here? If you can solve the sum 3+?=14, you can find out.

SUMMING UP

We often use the word sum to describe any arithmetic problem. The sum is the total of a list of numbers that have been added together.

FIFTEEN!

Fifteen is quite a tricky game. You need to be good at adding up single digit numbers in your head. Make a game board like this with colored cardboard and you are ready to start.

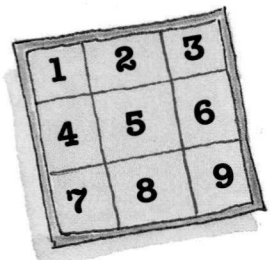

1 To make two sets of pieces, cut out five circles of colored cardboard and five more of a different color.

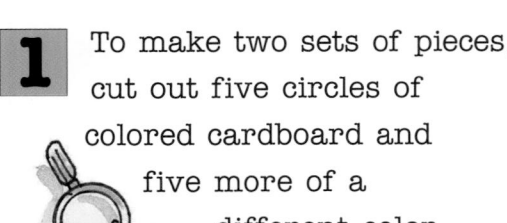

2 Cut a line from the edge to the center of each circle. Slide one cut edge behind the other and stick it in place to make a cone.

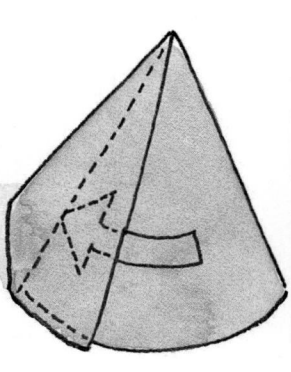

← Cut along the dashed line.

3 Each player chooses a set of pieces and takes turns to cover one square at a time. The winner of the game is the first person to make a total of 15. If you go over 15, you are "bust" and lose.

HELPFUL HINTS

● If you choose one of the larger numbers to start with, be careful, it is easy to go bust!

● Try and make 15 yourself, but remember, your opponent is also trying to make 15. Can you stop them at the same time?

MORE IDEAS

● Is it better to go first or second in this game? Can you figure out a way to make sure that you win every time?

TWENTY-ONE OR BUST!

● This is another exciting game a little bit like Fifteen. You will need a deck of cards. (The ace counts as 1 or 11. The face cards – Jacks, Queens, and Kings – are worth 10.) Draw two cards from the deck. You can then decide to take another card, or "stay." The object of the game is to get as close to 21 as possible without going over.

COUNTING DOWN

Can you count backward? That's easy! Can you count backward in 2s... from any number? Start on 20. Try 105. What about 1,005? Now try counting backward in 3s! Counting backward is one way of **subtracting,** or taking away.

THE BLACK SPOT!
Some people say that this is an ancient pirate game. You will need to do a lot of backward counting to make sure that you don't lose and walk the plank! Play this with a friend.

1 Find ten white checkers and one black checker for the black spot. Draw pirate faces onto circles of cardboard and stick a face onto each white checker. Stack all the pieces in a column with the black spot at the bottom.

2 Decide who is going first. Each player takes turns to remove either one, two, or three pieces. The object of the game is to make your opponent pick the black spot, so they have to walk the plank!

HELPFUL HINTS

● One way of getting better at this game is to search for winning patterns. If you were the winner, try to remember how you started. What did your opponent do next?

MORE IDEAS

● Is it better to go first or second in this game? How would the way you play the game change if another piece was added to the stack? How would the way you play the game change if you could only remove one or two pieces each turn?

SWEET SIXTEEN

● Another great game like The Black Spot is Sweet Sixteen. It can be played with a calculator. Start with 16 on the display and take turns to subtract 1, 2, or 3. If you manage to leave your opponent with 1 on the display then you have won the game.

VALUE YOUR DIGITS!

Numbers are made up of digits like words are made up of letters. But where a digit is placed in a number affects its value. A two digit number is made up of tens and ones. The 2 in 25 has a value of 20 (two tens), the 5 has a value of 5 (five ones).

DRAW A NUMBER

1 You can design your own numbers to show the value of the digits. You will need some graph paper and some pens, pencils, paint... or whatever you like to help with your design.

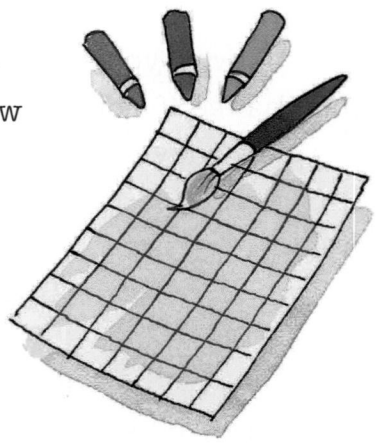

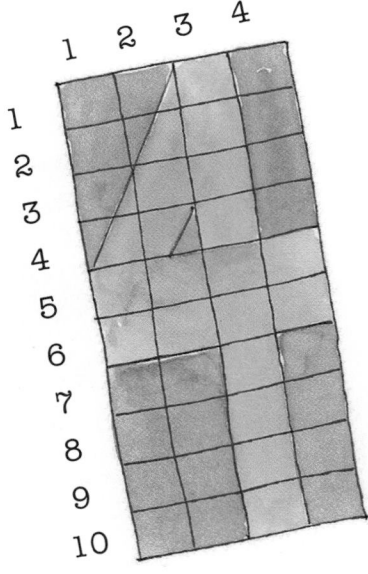

2 Choose a two digit number — what about 46? Draw a rectangle of 40 small squares for the 4 digit and a rectangle of 6 small squares for the 6. Design each digit inside its rectangle.

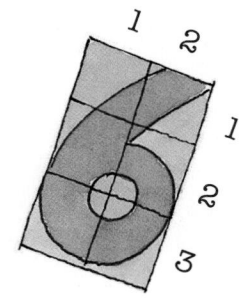

3 Decorate your digits with interesting colors and patterns. Now you can see the value of each digit in your two digit number at a glance.

5 →

8

HELPFUL HINTS

● For a number like 40 there are many rectangles that you could draw. You could choose a rectangle with two sides of 4 and two sides of 10, because 4x10=40 squares. You can draw any rectangle where the side lengths can be multiplied to make 40 squares. Sides of 5 and 8 are also possible because 5x8=40 squares.

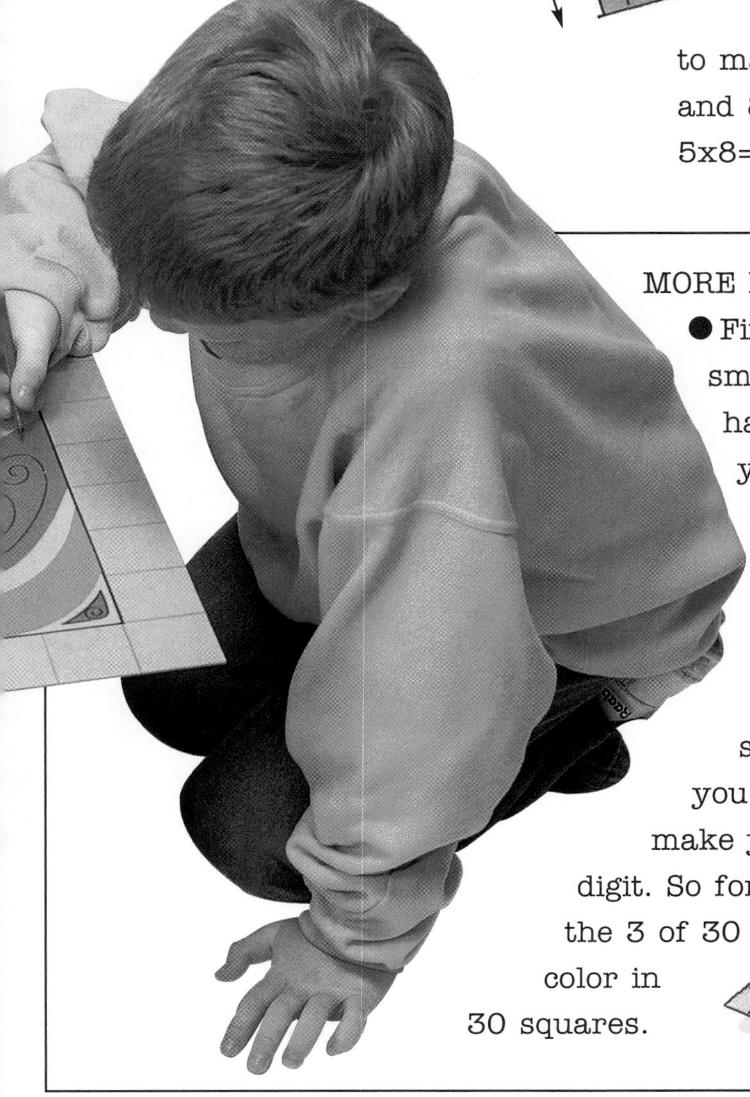

MORE IDEAS

● Find some more paper with very small squares. Instead of just having a rectangular area for your digit, cut out the correct number of squares in any shape and design your digit inside the shape.

● You could color in the number of squares you need to make your digit. So for the 3 of 30 color in 30 squares.

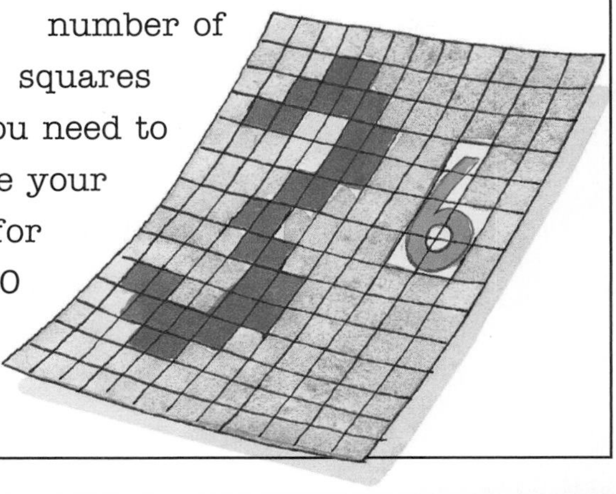

PLACE YOUR DIGITS

Numbers can have any amount of digits! 841 is a three digit number. The first digit shows how many hundreds there are. The 8 has the value of eight hundred. If you rearrange the digits like this — 481 — the 8 has the value of eighty. What value does the 8 have in the number 418?

THREE CARD TRICK
You can play this game with one or two friends.

1 Using colored cardboard make a score card like the one on this page. Now make a set of cards, draw on the digits 1 to 9. Everyone takes three cards.

2 Rearrange your cards. What is the largest number you can make? The player who has the largest number scores a point.

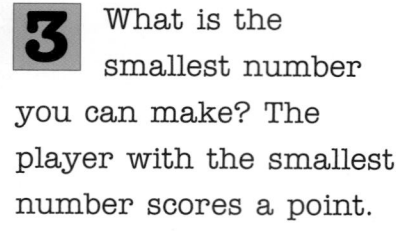

3 What is the smallest number you can make? The player with the smallest number scores a point.

4 On the scorecard write down as many different numbers as you can make with your three cards. Score a point for each number.

5 Place the numbers in order from the smallest to the largest. Score an extra bonus point for doing this correctly. Could this player have scored more points?

HELPFUL HINTS

● When comparing numbers with the same amount of digits to find which is larger, look at the digits on the left side of the number first. The larger the digit the larger the number. If the digit is the same then compare the next one. Repeat this until you find the larger number.

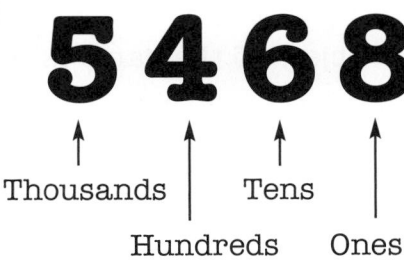

5 4 6 8

↑ Thousands ↑ Hundreds ↑ Tens ↑ Ones

3 CARD TRICK

Digit	5	2	6	points
Largest Number	652			1
Smallest Number	256			1
Different Numbers	625			1
	562			1
	256			1
	652			1
Smallest to Largest	256			
	562			
	625			1
	652			
Total Points				7

MORE IDEAS
● The 5 in 5,468 has a value of five thousand. How many different numbers can you make with these four digits?

555

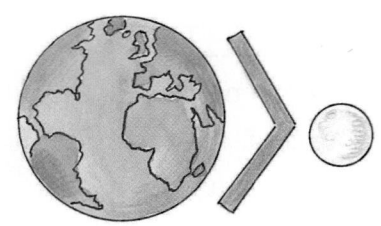

BIG, BIGGER, BIGGEST

Mathematicians use signs to show when a number is smaller or bigger than another number. They are called **inequality signs** and they look like this < or like this >. Whatever is on the open side is larger. For example 10>5.

HI SCORE!

You can play Hi Score on your own or with lots of friends. The object of the game is to make the number on the right of the scorecard as large as you can. This three digit number is your Hi Score.

1 Copy this Hi Score game board. You could make it with colored cardboard and magic marker. Put your name and your friends' names in as the players.

2 Take turns to throw a die. Think carefully about where to place the digit you have thrown. You can't change it later.

3 Each line on the scorecard is a mathematical sentence. You only score if the sentence is true! If your digits were like this 621>451>233 you would score 233. If the numbers were not in the correct order like this 631>423>551 you would score nothing!

HELPFUL HINTS

● The most important digit is the one you put in the hundreds place. If you roll a 6 where would be the best place to put it?

● The number on the open side of the inequality sign, is always the larger one.

BIGGER > smaller

IH

MORE IDEAS

● Invent a game called Lo Score. What will your board look like? Can you write out the rules to go with it? What number would be best to put in the hundreds place of the first column?

SIGN OF THE TIMES

Multiplying numbers is a quick way of adding the same number many times.

That's why some people say "times" to mean multiplication. The multiplication sign looks like this x. If we want to figure out what six 2s are, we don't need to write 2+2+2+2+2+2. We can write 6x2 instead.

MOUNTAIN MULTIPLICATION
Climb the mountain to find the number at the peak.

1 Cut out a triangle of cardboard and draw four "rocks" along the bottom, three rocks in the next row and two rocks in the third row. Cut out some "snow" and stick it on the peak.

3 Add poster putty to the back of each circle and stick the first four onto the bottom row. To find the next number up the mountain, multiply the two numbers below it.

2 Stick two triangles on the back for support and make trees for the sides. Cut out ten small circles of paper and write the numbers 2, 1, 2, 3 on the first four circles.

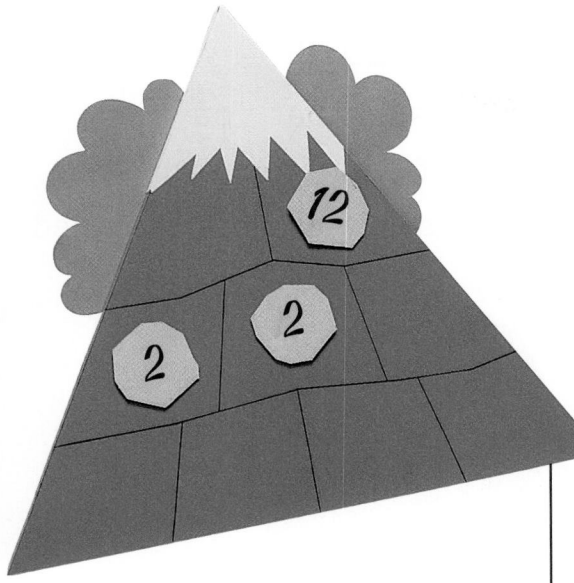

HELPFUL HINTS

● To find the number that is missing underneath the 12 (left), it is helpful to think about it as a multiplication problem like this...

$$2 \times ? = 12$$

4 The number above the 2 and 1 will be 2 because 2x1=2. Figure out what all three numbers are on the next row.

5 Write them on the circles and stick them on. Keep repeating this, until you reach the top.

MORE IDEAS

● Can you figure out all the numbers that cover the mountain (above left) if you only have some of the numbers half way up the slope?

● Make your own mountain problem and get your friends to reach the top.

● Put 13 at the peak. Fill in the numbers on the mountain. What do you notice?

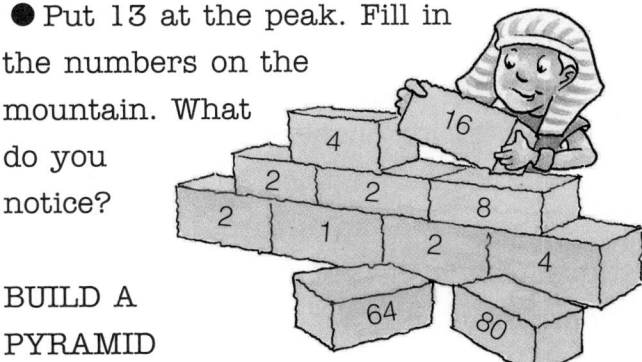

BUILD A PYRAMID

● Put some small numbers on four blocks. These are the base of your pyramid. Multiply the numbers as you did on the mountain and stick the answers on the next layer of blocks. Find the number at the top of the pyramid.

DO THE OPPOSITE

Have your parents ever said that you always do the opposite of what they tell you? When this happens in mathematics, it is called the inverse. The inverse of adding 3 is taking away 3. Do you know the inverse of multiplying by 2? Yes! **Dividing** by 2. What is the inverse of dividing by 4?

WHAT'S THAT NUMBER?

1 Cut some cardboard into small strips about as big as the one in the picture. Fold each strip to make three sections. Shade in the middle section lightly with a colored pencil.

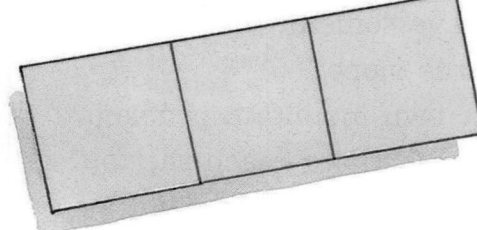

2 Next, choose a multiplication problem such as 3x8=24. The numbers 3 and 8 are the **factors.** The answer, 24, is the **product.**

3 Write the product in the middle square and the factors on either side. Make a pile of about 20 cards like this with different multiplication problems on each.

4 The first player picks up a card and folds one of the factors behind. The second player tries to figure out what the hidden number is. If they are correct, they win the card. Keep going until one player has all the cards.

8 24

60 180 3

MORE IDEAS
● You could play the same game with more difficult numbers.

HANDS DOWN
● This is another good game that you can play using factors and products. Instead of folding over a factor, cover one of the numbers with your hand. You could cover either the product or one of the factors on each side. Can your friends guess what number is hidden?

561

HARD TIMES!

Being able to remember
multiplication facts
quickly is very useful when trying to
solve number problems. You can try to
memorize the tables from the chart at
the back of the book. But, here are
some games that make learning your
times tables much more fun!

CARD TRICKS
This is a game for two or more players.
You will need a deck of cards with all
the face cards removed.

1 Place the cards face
down on the table. Choose a
multiplication table, for example,
the four times table.

2 Now, take
turns to look at two
cards. Is the product of the
two numbers on the cards
in the four times table?

3 If it is, keep the pair and take
another turn. If not, turn the cards
back over, it's the next player's turn. The
winner is the player with the most pairs.

4 You could
keep the cards
2 and 6 and have
another turn.
Could you keep
the 3 and 7?

CHICKEN RACE
The object of this game is to make the biggest score you can.

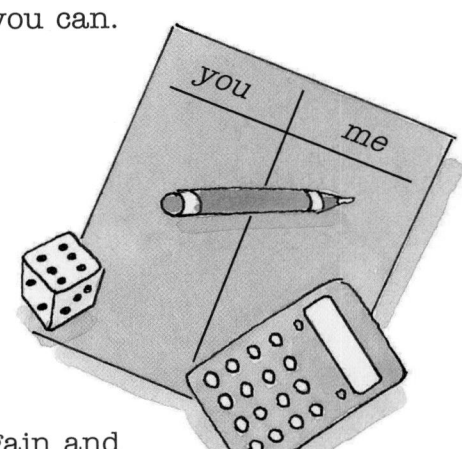

1 You will need a die, a calculator, and a pencil and paper to draw out the chart. The first player throws the die and makes a note of the number.

2 Throw the die again and multiply the two numbers together. Keep throwing the die, multiplying the number on the die with your total. You must decide when to stop because... if a 1 is thrown, you get 0 for that turn! Use a calculator to check that your multiplication is correct.

Dare you keep throwing the die... or are you chicken?!

SCORING
CHICKEN RACE
You could note your scores like this —

But things
  could
  go wrong...

3
    x4
12
    x2
24
    x5
120   stay!

4
    x2
8
    x1 no
       score!

BIG TIME OPERATOR

If you have tried the other activities in this book, you will know more about addition, subtraction, multiplication, division, inverses, sums, factors, and products than when you started! Are you skillful enough to use what you know to solve some of these number explosion problems?

NUMBER EXPLOSIONS

1 How many ways can you make 10? You have probably already thought of quite a few ways of making 10 by adding a couple of single digit numbers. But can you think of more interesting ways of making 10?

2 x 4 + 2 →

1 + 8 + 1 →

10

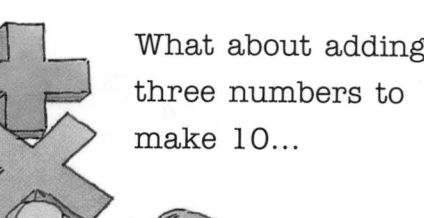

What about adding three numbers to make 10...

2 Use bright colored cardboard to design a huge explosion like the one in the picture and put 10 or any number you choose in the middle.

How about adding a number then subtracting another?

$1 + 12 - 3$

Try starting from 1,000. Can you add, divide, subtract then multiply a number to make 10?

HELPFUL HINTS

● It is easy to be a big time operator and use all the operations if you remember some simple facts about the operations:

addition is the inverse of subtraction
multiplication is the inverse of division

● What happens when you add or subtract 0?
● What happens when you divide or multiply by 1?
● What happens if you multiply or divide by 0?

FURTHER IDEAS

● How can you use the numbers 1, 2, 3, and 4 once each to make 10? One easy way is to add them all together 1+2+3+4=10.
● Use different operations and find other ways to make 10.

1+2+3+4 → 10

GAMES GALORE!

How many board games do you know? Which is your favorite? For some of the games in the book you need to use addition, subtraction, multiplication, and division. Some games use dice, spinners, cards, and pieces. Can you invent your own game?

DESIGN YOUR OWN GAME

1 You might need pencils, pens, cardboard, something to make the pieces with — it all depends on the game you want to make. How creative can you be?

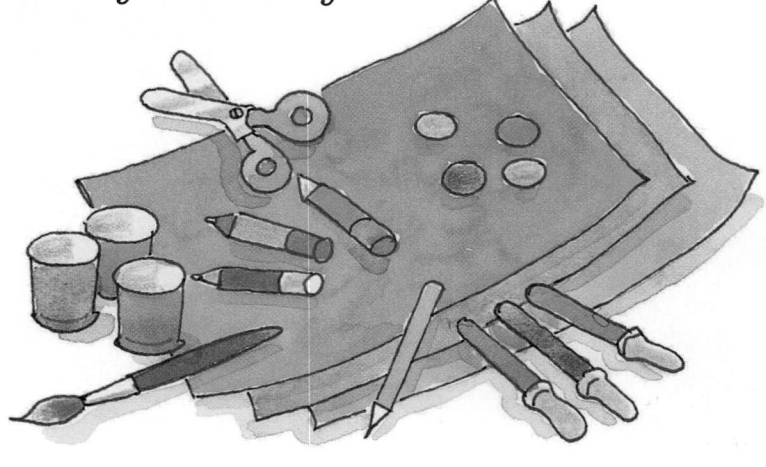

2 You might want to make a counting game. The game might need some cards that give the players different directions like "Go to Jail!" or "Start Again."

3 Decide who the game is going to be for: yourself, some adults, a friend, or a little brother or sister... don't make it too hard if it's for your little brother or sister!

4 Now give your game a theme — it could be animals or sports — what about space?

5 Now write down the rules. What do you have to do to win? Can you think of an exciting name?

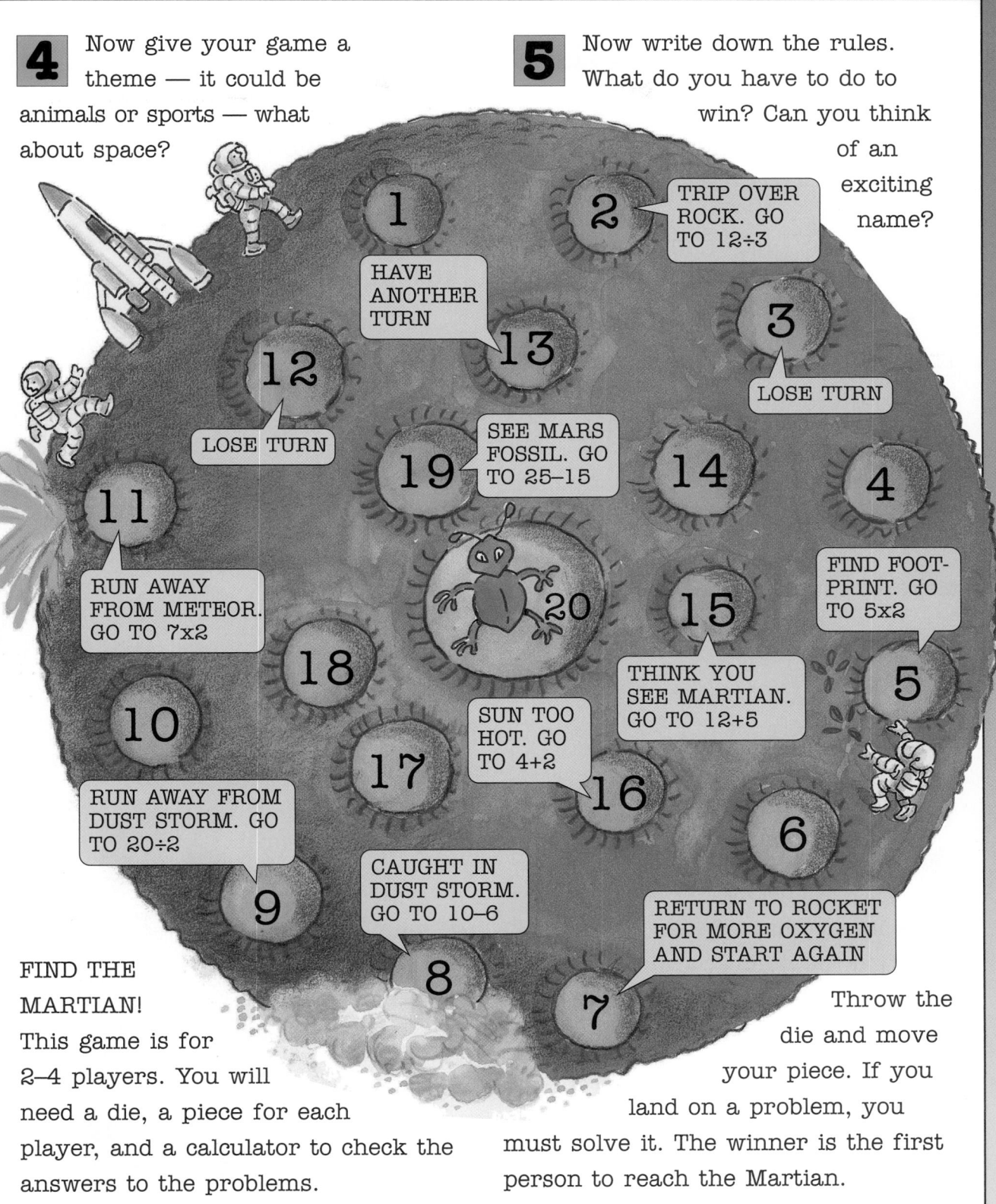

1

2 — TRIP OVER ROCK. GO TO 12÷3

13 — HAVE ANOTHER TURN

3

LOSE TURN

12 — LOSE TURN

19 — SEE MARS FOSSIL. GO TO 25−15

14

4

11 — RUN AWAY FROM METEOR. GO TO 7x2

20

15 — THINK YOU SEE MARTIAN. GO TO 12+5

FIND FOOT-PRINT. GO TO 5x2

5

18

16 — SUN TOO HOT. GO TO 4+2

10

17

6

RUN AWAY FROM DUST STORM. GO TO 20÷2

9

CAUGHT IN DUST STORM. GO TO 10−6

8

7 — RETURN TO ROCKET FOR MORE OXYGEN AND START AGAIN

FIND THE MARTIAN!
This game is for 2–4 players. You will need a die, a piece for each player, and a calculator to check the answers to the problems.

Throw the die and move your piece. If you land on a problem, you must solve it. The winner is the first person to reach the Martian.

567

PROBLEMS, PROBLEMS...

When you have a problem to solve, like finding out how many hairs you have on your head, the best way to tackle it is to make a careful guess, or an estimate, of the answer. Then, while you are tackling the problem, keep a note of any calculations you make. This will help you to check back if you make a mistake.

A NOVEL IDEA

1 Try to work out how many pages there are in a very thick book without looking at the page numbers!

Make an estimate. What do you think... 100, 325, 809?

3 You can look at the page numbers to check your answer.
Can you think of a better way of solving the problem?

2 You could count the number of pages in one chapter. Next find the number of chapters. Now multiply the number of pages in a chapter by the number of chapters. This will give you an answer.

PARTY ANIMALS

1 If you have a party for your friends you will need to make some calculations. How many friends will be coming? Will you go to the zoo?

2 What will it cost? How much allowance do you have? Is it enough? What do you need to buy? Do you need a loan from your parents?

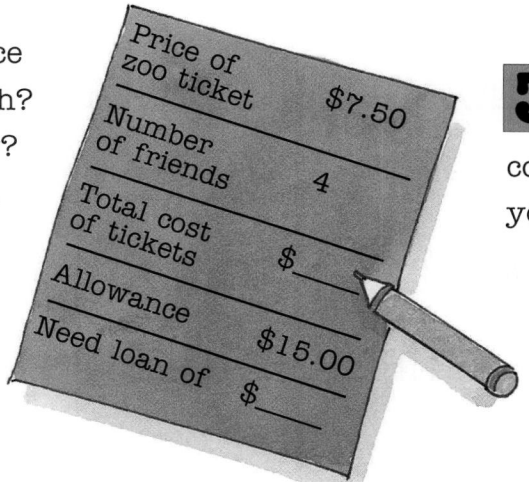

Price of zoo ticket	$7.50
Number of friends	4
Total cost of tickets	$
Allowance	
Need loan of	$15.00

3 Keep a careful note of the costs and how much you have spent.

GO FOR BROKE

Imagine you have just won a million dollars — but you have to spend it within one week! What would you spend it on?

1 Find some catalogs and magazines and decide how you are going to spend the money.

2 You need to prove that you have spent all the money in one week. How are you going to show that you have spent all that money?

RECEIPT
SPORTS CAR
$30,000

CONTENTS

WHAT IS A FRACTION? **572**

ADDING FRACTIONS **574**

FAIR SHARES **576**

DECIMAL FRACTIONS **578**

LARGER OR SMALLER? **580**

ADDING DECIMALS **582**

PERCENTAGES **584**

ESTIMATING PERCENTAGES **586**

MAKING 100% **588**

RATIOS **590**

MORE MIXING **592**

PERFECTLY PROPORTIONED **594**

Chapter Two

Making Fractions

WHAT IS A FRACTION?

A **fraction** is a part of a whole thing like a cake, an apple, or a school class. If a cake has had a slice cut out of it, it is not whole. The slice is a part, or a fraction, of the whole cake. If an apple is cut up, it

is not a whole. The pieces are fractions of the whole.

APPLE GETS THE CHOP

1 This apple has been cut into two equal pieces. It has been cut in **half**. A half is a fraction and we write it like this $1/2$.

2 This apple has been cut into four equal pieces. It has been cut into quarters. A quarter is a fraction too. We write it like this $1/4$.

PIZZA SLICES

1 Trace around a plate on construction paper to make two circles. Decorate both circles like a pizza and cut them out.

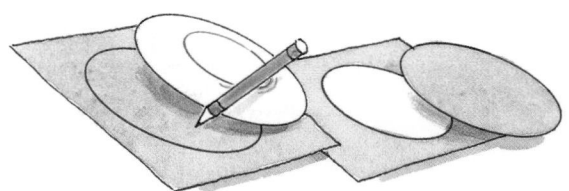

2 Fold one pizza exactly in half. Cut along the fold to make two halves.

3 Repeat step 2 for the second pizza. Now fold each half exactly in half and cut along the folds to make four quarters.

4 How many ways can you fit your pizza slices together to make a whole?

MORE IDEAS

● Try to put three quarters and one half together. You will get one pizza with a quarter left over. You can write this as $1\frac{1}{4}$ or as a fraction $\frac{5}{4}$. Fractions bigger than a whole are called **improper fractions.**

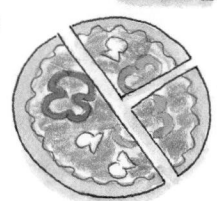

ADDING FRACTIONS

Fractions can be added like any other number. To make a whole pizza (see page 573,) you needed to add the fractions of the pizza together. There are many different ways of adding fractions together to make a whole.

BUILD A FRACTION WALL

1 These children are building a fraction wall using blocks of different sizes.

You can make a small fraction wall from colored cardboard.

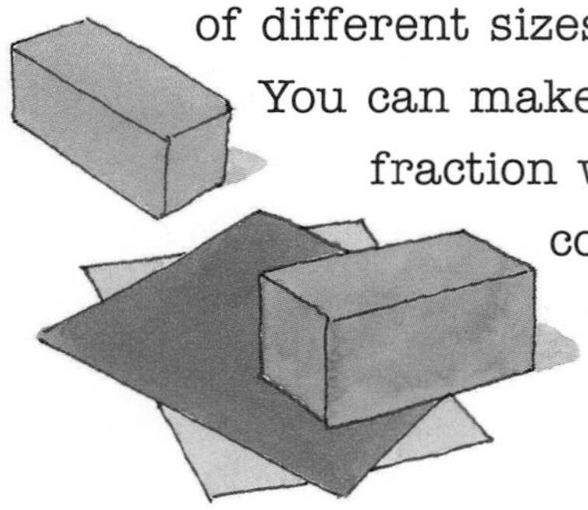

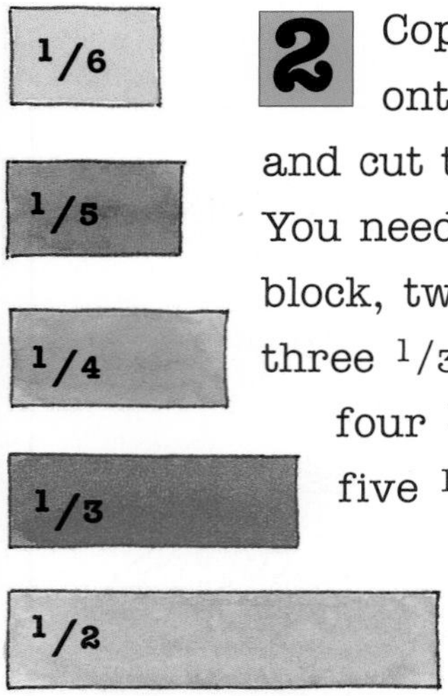

2 Copy these shapes onto the cardboard and cut them all out. You need one whole block, two 1/2 blocks, three 1/3 blocks, four 1/4 blocks, five 1/5 blocks, and six 1/6 blocks.

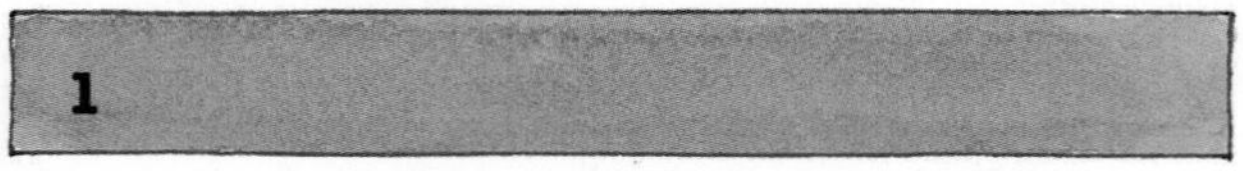

1/6

1/5

1/4

1/3

1/2

1

Remember that each layer of the wall must be exactly equal to a whole block.

3 You can use these blocks to build your own wall. Start with the whole block on the bottom and build your wall using a mixture of fractions.

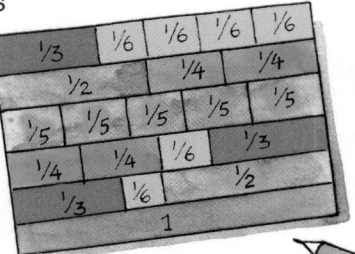

HELPFUL HINTS

● Match all the layers against the whole block. If they fit exactly the sum is correct.

MORE IDEAS

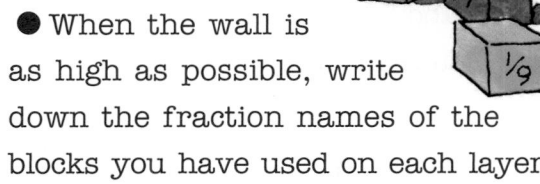

● When the wall is as high as possible, write down the fraction names of the blocks you have used on each layer.

● Extend your wall by making other fraction blocks. How about a ninth — $1/9$?

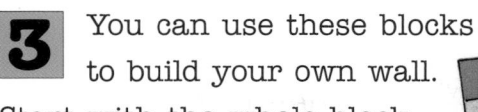

FAIR SHARES

A fraction can also be part of a group of things. Have you ever been asked to share some candy with your brother or sister? When you have divided the candy equally with another person you have divided the candy in half. A half is a fraction of the whole group of candy.

GRAB!

This is a fun fraction game for two, three, or four players. You will need about 50 small pieces or you could use dried beans.

1 Put the pieces in a container. The first player grabs a handful of beans.

2 Try to divide the handful into two equal groups or halves. If you can, you score two points.

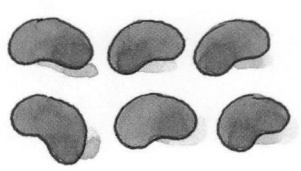

= 2 points.

3 Can you divide the beans into four equal groups, or quarters? If you can, score four more points.

= 4 points.

4 If you can complete steps 1, 2, and 3 you can go on to the bonus round! If you can divide your beans into three equal groups, or thirds, score a bonus of three points.

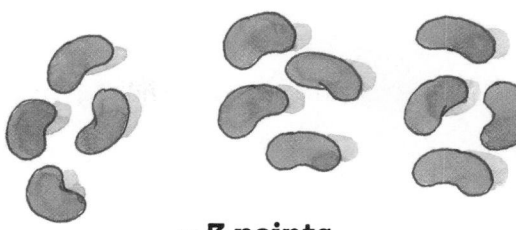

= **3 points.**

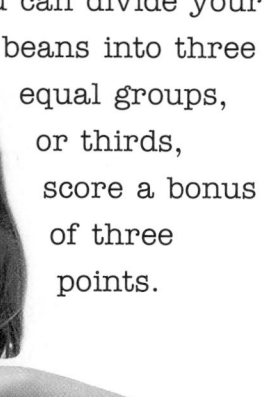

5 When you have taken a turn, put the beans back and the next player takes a turn.

MORE IDEAS

● Is 17 a good number to grab? What about 16? What about 12? Which would earn you the highest score?

● Keep playing the game. Note down the numbers that score the most points. Can you discover the numbers that are best for sharing into equal groups?

DECIMAL FRACTIONS

Decimals are another way of writing fractions. You have probably seen a lot of decimal numbers before without realizing! If you have watched any sporting events on television, the distances jumped or thrown are usually shown as a decimal number.

9.83

A decimal number is one with a **decimal point.** The point separates the whole numbers on the left from the numbers less than 1 on the right.

1 There are ten tenths between 0 and 1. The object of this game is to point to the correct place on the number line.

POINT IT OUT
Try this guessing game with your friends.

0 0.1 0.2 0.3 0.4 0.5 0.6 0.7 0.8 0.9 1.0

2 Copy this game board onto a rectangle of cardboard. Fold the top of the cardboard over so the numbers and marker lines can be hidden.

3 The first player covers the side showing the tenths and asks the second player to find a decimal from 0.1 to 0.9. It could be 0.4 for example. The second player has to estimate where it might be on the number line.

4 Uncover the line and see if they managed to point it out!

MORE IDEAS

● If you have a calculator, find out what happens if you try to show a half on the display.

The buttons you need to press to do this are 1÷2=. You will see 0.5 on the display. Do the same with a quarter, 1÷4=. You will see 0.25.

Try other fractions and see what happens.

● What happens if you try 1÷5? What fraction is this?

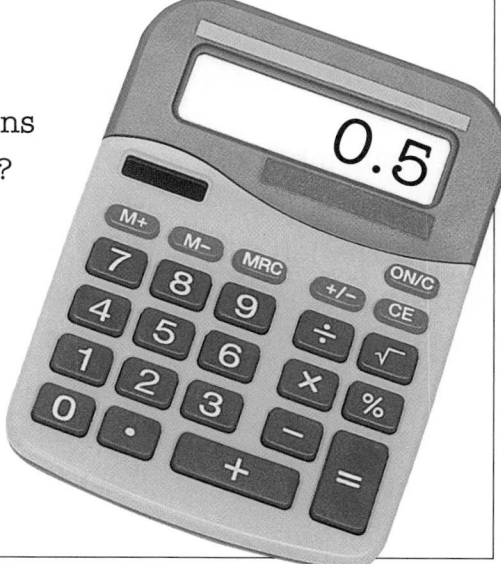

LARGER OR SMALLER?

How do you decide if one decimal number is larger than another? With whole numbers like 134 and 273 you can compare the size of the digits starting on the left. 273 is bigger than 134 because the 2 digit is worth more than the 1 digit. You can compare decimal numbers like 23.75 and 14.28 in the same way.

DIABOLICAL DECIMALS

1 The object of this game is to make the largest number. If you win draw a happy face. First draw a chart like this one. The first player throws the die and decides where to place the digit.

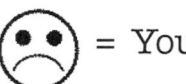 = You win

 = You lose

2 Remember to put a big digit on the left. Where would you put a 5? Be careful, you might throw a 6 next turn!

3 The second player throws and also decides where to place their digit. This continues until the four digit number is completed.

Player ___ John ___

Tens	Ones	Tenths	Hundredths	Score
				☹
5	3	4	1	
6		3	2	

It's Emma's turn to throw. Who do you think will win this game?

HELPFUL HINTS

● To find out who has won compare the digits on the left. If they are the same move to the next digits to their right. If they still match repeat the process until you have found out who has made the larger number.

Player _____ Emma

Tens	Ones	Tenths	Hundredths	Score
6	4	3	3	😊
	4		1	

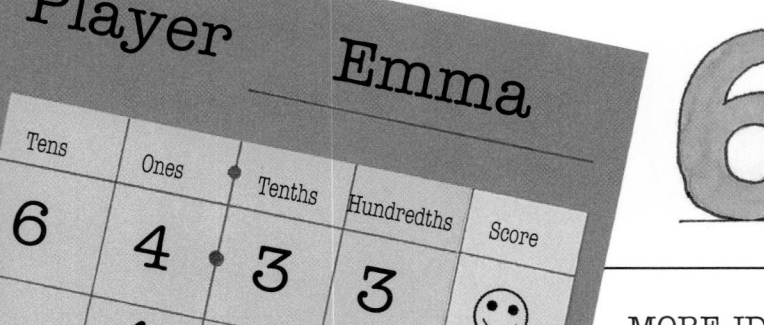

MORE IDEAS

● There are some interesting variations to Diabolical decimals that you can play.

● The winner could be the player who makes the smallest number.

● You can also play a game in teams of two. Take turns to throw the die and try to get your numbers as close together as possible. The winning team is the one with the smallest difference between their pairs of numbers. Use a calculator to check.

Team 1
4 3.6 2 😊
4 2.5 1

Team 2
6 2.6 5 ☹
6 5.6 3

581

ADDING DECIMALS

Adding decimal numbers is as easy as adding whole numbers. The key to making it easy is remembering to add digits from the same position in the number system. In other words, adding tens to tens, ones to ones, tenths to tenths, and hundredths to hundredths.

> If the answer to 23 + 34 = 57 then 2.3 + 3.4 = 5.7

SPLOTCH IT!
This game is all about adding up tenths. Tenths are shown by the first digit to the right of the decimal point. Remember, ten tenths make 1.

1 Make a set of splotch cards. Cut out a stack of 20 splotches from some colored cardboard.

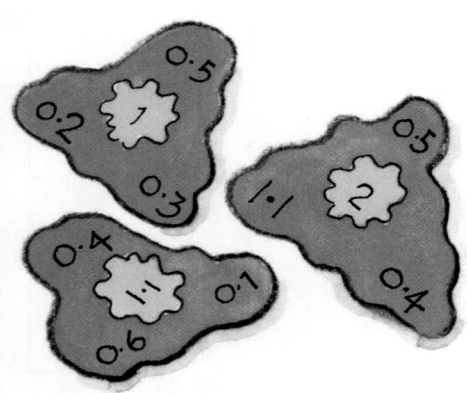

2 Write in the numbers. Make sure the numbers on the edges of the splotch all add up to the total in the center.

3 Take turns to hold up a splotch card with one of the corners covered.

● To make sure you are putting the correct totals in the center of your cards it might be a good idea to use a calculator to check the answer. Remember to press the decimal point!

4 Can your opponent work out what the hidden number is? You could solve it like this 0.5 + 0.4 + ? = 2

MORE IDEAS

● You could change this game around by covering the total in the middle. Are you still as good?

● See if you can figure out what is in the middle of this card. You could try to solve it like this 0.6+0.3+1.1=?.

PERCENTAGES

Percentages are a way of showing fractions as a part of one hundred. A half of a hundred is fifty. We call fifty out of a hundred, fifty percent. The symbol mathematicians use for percent looks like this %. Twenty-five is a quarter of a hundred, so a quarter can be written as 25%. A **tenth** of a hundred is 10. How do you think a tenth would be written as a percentage?

PERCENTAGE PATTERNS
Take a look at this hundred square. Each one of the small squares represents 1%.

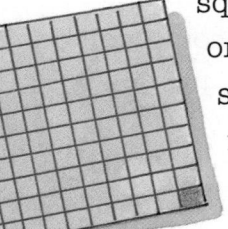

1 If half of the hundred square is filled in, 50 squares will be covered, or 50%.

2 We could show 50% like this, but there are many fun ways to show it on a hundred square!

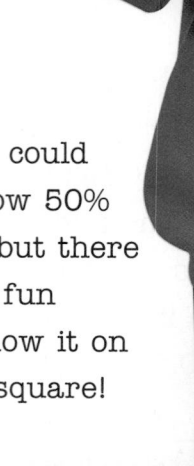

584

3 Find some graph paper and see if you can design an unusual pattern that covers exactly 50% of the hundred square.

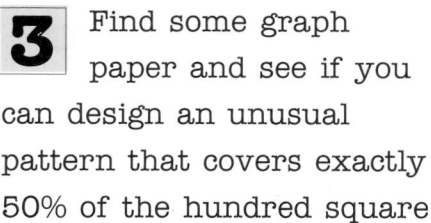

HELPFUL HINTS

● For 50% of the hundred square to be covered you must color 50 small squares. When you plan your design mark the squares lightly with a pencil. It is easier to make a change if you have miscounted!

MORE IDEAS

● Try some different percentage amounts to cover your hundred square. What about a design that shows 30% of the square? How about 51%?

● Make your design as interesting as you can.

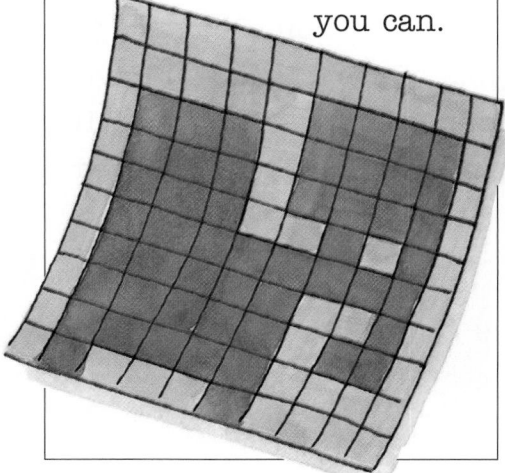

ESTIMATING PERCENTAGES

Making an **estimate** is like making a careful guess. People make estimates using percentages.

If a teacher says "about fifty percent of the class have done their homework" she estimates that about half the class have done it!

$$\frac{Amount}{Whole} \times 100 = Percentage$$

HOW SQUARE ARE YOUR EYES?
This hundred square represents the whole day, 24 hours. You can make your own one to find out how you spend your time.

1 You will need a plain piece of square paper and some coloring pens to fill in your own grid.
First, fold the paper in half and keep folding in strips. Unfold the paper and fold in the other direction. Open out the paper and you will find that you have made squares. Mark out a big square of 10x10 small squares to make a hundred square grid.

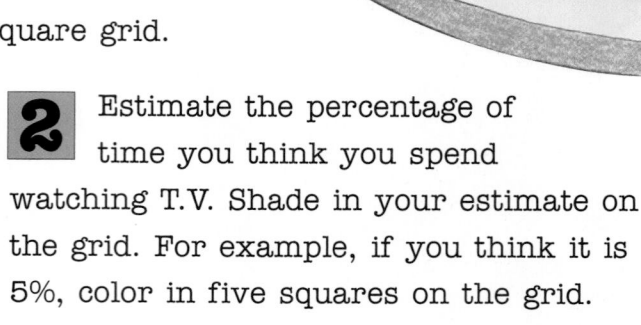

At School

Sleeping

Eating

2 Estimate the percentage of time you think you spend watching T.V. Shade in your estimate on the grid. For example, if you think it is 5%, color in five squares on the grid.

3 Next, estimate the percentage of the day spent doing other things like eating, sleeping, playing, and working. Shade in the amounts on your hundred square.

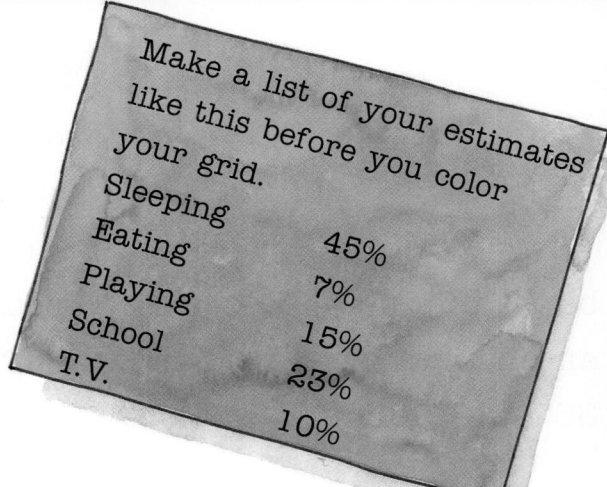

Make a list of your estimates like this before you color your grid.

Sleeping	45%
Eating	7%
Playing	15%
School	23%
T.V.	10%

Watching T.V.

Playing

HELPFUL HINTS

● Make sure your whole hundred square gets covered. There shouldn't be any gaps — you are always doing something, even if it is sleeping!

● Use a different bright color for each activity.

4 Compare your finished hundred square with the one in this picture. Have you estimated that you are sleepier or more wide awake?!

MORE IDEAS

● How good is your estimate?

● Find an older friend or an adult who is really good at math. Ask them to calculate the real percentages of how you spend your day!

● How does your estimate compare?

MAKING 100%

Have you ever heard of anything being described as 100% pure or 100% genuine? 100% means everything, the whole. The whole doesn't have to be made up of 100 separate pieces. Do you remember that 50% is another way of describing a half? 50% of 80 is 40. 50% of 36 is 18. What is 50% of 90?

MAGIC CARPETS
Some traditional carpet designs from around the world use many colors and patterns.

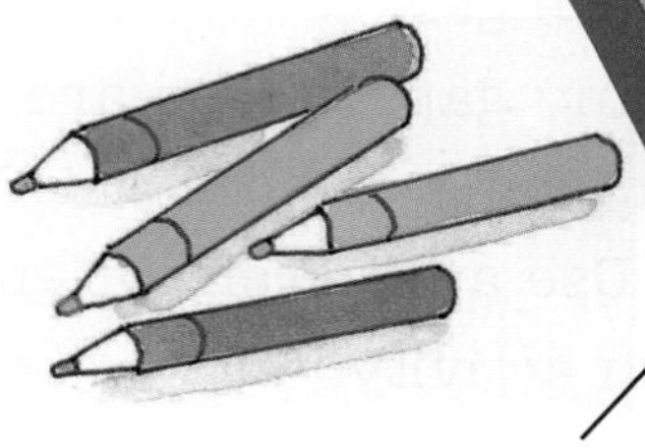

40 squares

1 You can copy the grids onto the page but it is easier to find some graph paper. Draw three carpets
1st carpet - 60 squares
2nd carpet - 40 squares
3rd carpet - 80 squares

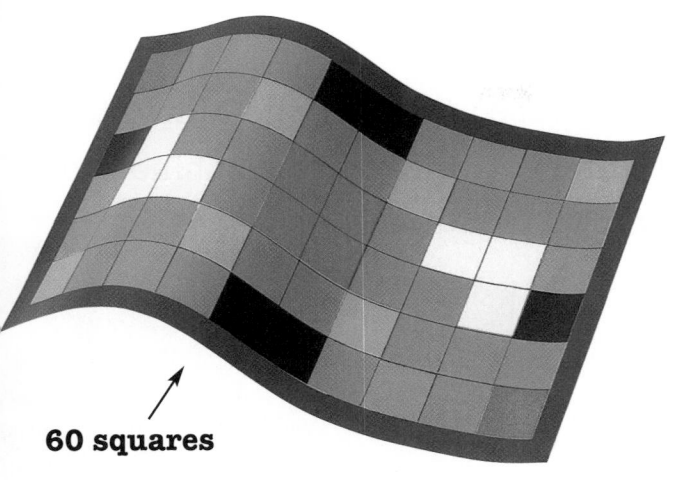

60 squares

2 Design your own carpet pattern using six colors. Your design must be 50% blue, 10% red, 10% yellow, 10% green, 10% black, 10% white. Check the percentages that have been used for the carpets in this picture.

HELPFUL HINTS

● If you are stuck, find out what 50% of your carpet is.

● For the first carpet of 60 squares, 50% is half the total — which is 30 squares!

● To find 10% divide the total, 60 by 10. This gives the answer 6. So, 30 squares will be blue, 6 red, 6 yellow, 6 green, 6 black, and 6 white.

80 squares

MORE IDEAS

● Design some more carpets. This time make them more intricate by dividing some squares in half.

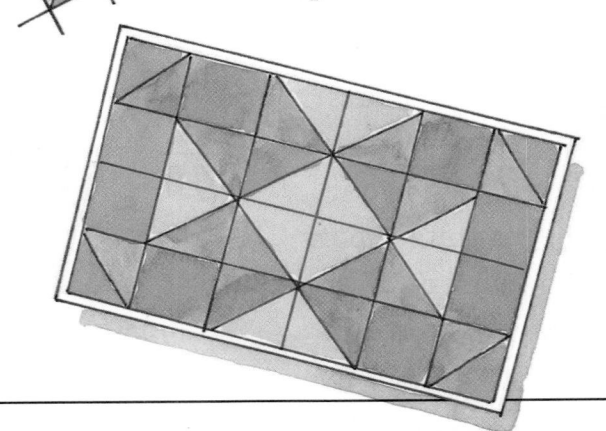

RATIOS

Ratios can be used to show the amounts in which different things are combined to make a whole. Paints are very often made up of mixtures of the primary colors — red, blue, and yellow. To get an exact shade they are mixed according to a particular ratio. Two parts red to one part blue makes purple. The parts can be measured with teaspoons. You would write it like this 2:1 red blue.

MIXING IT

1 You can make your own color chart by some careful mixing. Choose two colors.

2 Make a chart showing where you will paint your different tints. Show the ratio of different paints you will use.

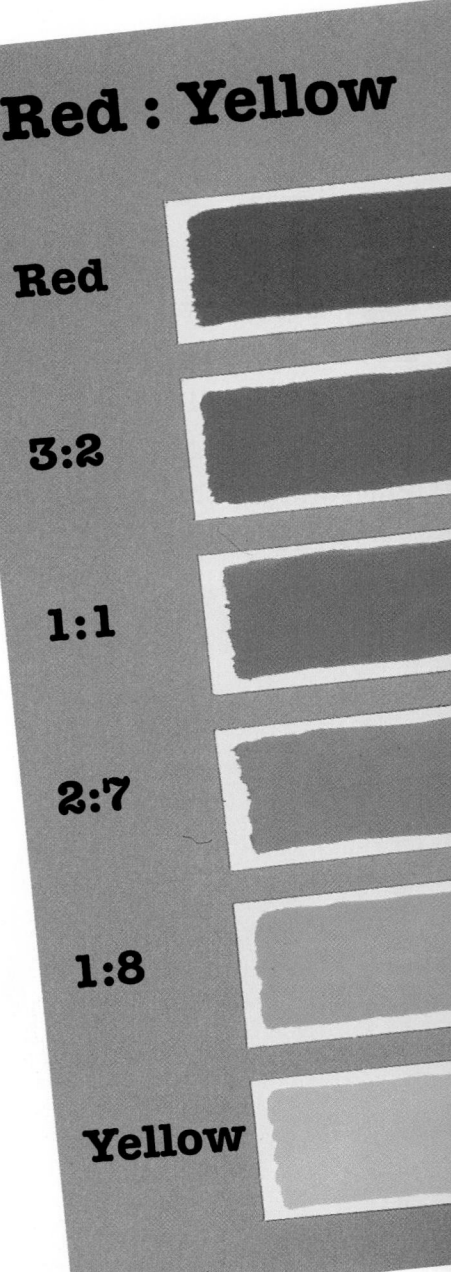

Red : Yellow

Red

3:2

1:1

2:7

1:8

Yellow

3 If you are mixing paints in the ratio of 3:2 use a small spoon to measure out three parts red to two parts yellow and mix carefully.

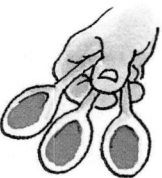 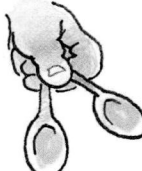

4 Paint a small sample of the different mixtures into each area to complete your reference chart.

HELPFUL HINTS

● When you are mixing the colors make sure the amount you use for each part is always the same! The easiest way to make sure you are accurate is to use a teaspoon that you can level off with a piece of cardboard.

● When you have used one mixture make sure you wash your brush carefully, otherwise you will finish up with muddy looking colors that all look the same!

MORE IDEAS

● Find different ways of mixing the three primary colors together.

● What does 1 red : 4 yellow : 1 blue look like?

● Which is your favorite color? What is the ratio of the three colors?

● Try to work out the ratios of the color of your favorite crayon. Use different ratios until you can find a match.

MORE MIXING

Ratios can also show how more than two quantities can be mixed. You probably use ratios a lot without realizing it. If you wanted to record how flour, butter, and sugar were combined to make some cookies it could be written like this 3:2:2 three parts flour, two parts butter, and two parts sugar. The parts could be measured with cups or spoons. You could do the same for mixing drinks.

SHAKEN NOT STIRRED
You can make some fantastic fruit drinks by mixing ingredients carefully!

1 Try starting with orange juice, apple juice, and seltzer. A delicious combination is five parts apple, two parts orange, and three parts seltzer. You can make the drink like this.

2 First find a small container, like an eggcup, and a large glass. Fill the eggcup, or the measurer you have chosen, five times with apple juice and tip it into the glass.

3 Now add two eggcups of the orange juice.

Apple	Orange	Seltzer	Good/Bad?
5	2	3	Excellent

HELPFUL HINTS

● Remember to keep a careful note of the number of parts you have mixed together and the mixtures you liked. You might want to note this in a table.

4 Last of all pour in three eggcups of seltzer. Stir it and taste. Mmmmm....

5 What do you think? Now try your own mixture.

MORE IDEAS

● What about trying other ingredients to make that perfect drink? You could try some other fruit juices, lemonade can be nice, or what about a little vinegar!

● Make sure you ask an adult if you want to try these or any other ingredients in your drink.

PERFECTLY PROPORTIONED

Many things in nature, including people, grow in a very precise way. For example, the size of everyone's head has a particular relationship, or proportion, to their height. If you measure around your head and multiply that length by three, the answer you get will be roughly the same as your height.

ARE YOU SIX FEET TALL?
You may not believe it but you are about six feet tall! In fact, nearly everyone is! Using ratios you can prove that most people are about six feet tall.

1 Find a long strip of cardboard or paper and ask an adult to stand next to it. Have the adult take off a shoe. Place the heel of the shoe on the floor, toe pointing upward against the cardboard.

2 Mark where the end of the toe is with a pen then move the shoe up so that the heel is where your mark is.

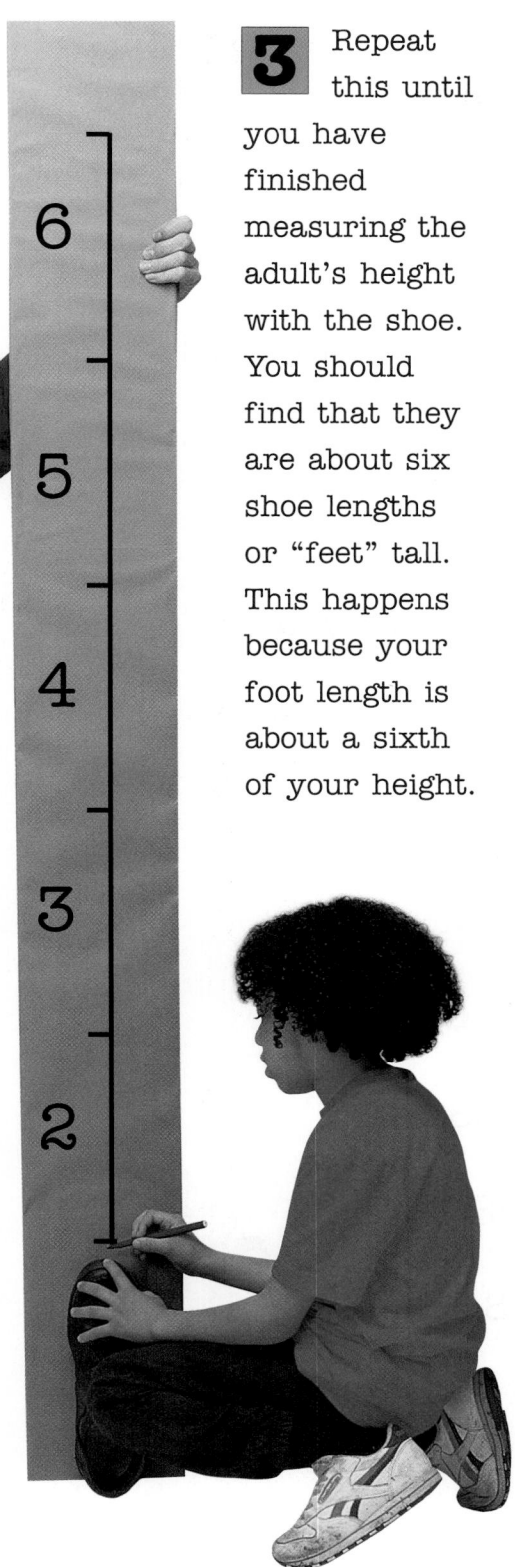

3 Repeat this until you have finished measuring the adult's height with the shoe. You should find that they are about six shoe lengths or "feet" tall. This happens because your foot length is about a sixth of your height.

HELPFUL HINTS

● The proportions of younger growing bodies are not usually the same as an adult's. You can try this with your friends but it might be more reliable to test it on an adult.

MORE IDEAS

● Another fascinating body ratio is sometimes known as Pythagoras's navel. This ratio compares a person's height with the height of the navel from the ground.

● It is usually in the ratio of 1:1.6

● This is a very special ratio called the Golden Mean. It is often found in nature and was considered by the ancient Greeks to have divine properties.

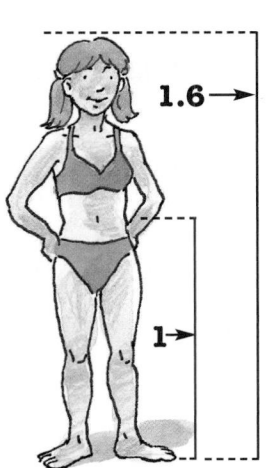

● Measure your height, then the height of your navel from the floor. Divide the first height by the second. How close to 1.6 is the result? Is your body of divine proportion?

CONTENTS

NUMBER PATTERNS **598**

PATTERNS IN MULTIPLICATION **600**

TRIANGULAR NUMBERS **602**

LETTERS AND NUMBERS **604**

OPERATIONS AND FUNCTIONS **606**

THINK OF A NUMBER **608**

NUMBER CODES **610**

KNOW YOUR NUMBERS **612**

MORE MYSTERY **614**

MAN-MADE PATTERNS **616**

NATURAL PATTERNS **618**

NATURAL NUMBERS **620**

Chapter Three

Discovering Patterns

NUMBER PATTERNS

You can find patterns everywhere in numbers. Even numbers can be divided in two without leaving any remainder.

Squared numbers are made by multiplying the same number by itself, 3x3=9. There are many other strange and beautiful **number patterns**, some of which you will find out about in this book!

KEYPAD CRISIS

Play this with a friend.

1 Oh no! You have been locked out of your spaceship and you need to get back inside! You need to press numbers on the keypads to let you back in, but some of the numbers are missing.

2 Luckily all the numbers are laid out in patterns. But what are they?

3 Some keypads have more than one number pattern. How many can you find?

4 Look along the rows of numbers, up and down, and from corner to corner. You may be able to find more than one number pattern on the keypad. One player closes their eyes and the second player covers one number on each keypad.

HELPFUL HINTS

● Some patterns are easy to follow. You can often figure them out by counting forward or counting backward. Which numbers come next in these sequences?

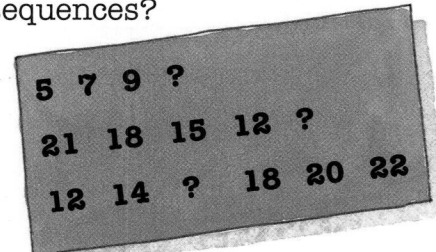

5 7 9 ?

21 18 15 12 ?

12 14 ? 18 20 22

● To find the missing number you needed to spot the number pattern.

● In these sequences there was a pattern of odd numbers, one which counted down in threes, and one of even numbers counting up in twos.

MORE IDEAS

● You can make the keypad game more fun by hiding three or more numbers on each keypad.

● Try drawing your own keypad and making your own number patterns. If you are designing a pad to play against an adult, see how difficult you can make it!

5 The first player opens their eyes and tries to figure out which number has been hidden.

599

PATTERNS IN MULTIPLICATION

Knowing multiplication facts is very helpful when you are trying to solve some number problems.

There are number patterns in multiplication that can help you remember your tables. You can also use your tables to make beautiful patterns.

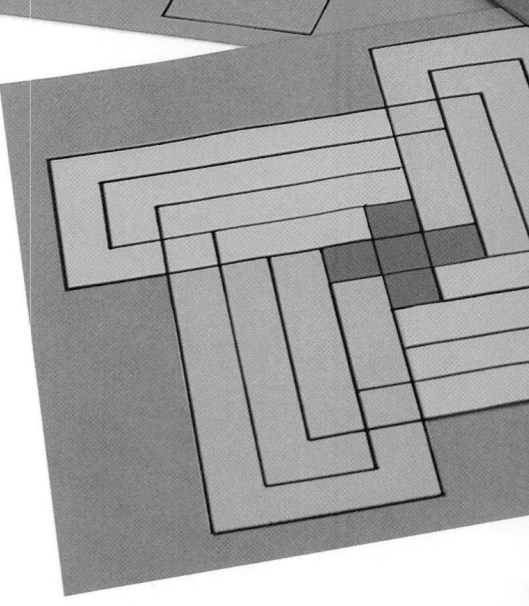

SPIROLATERALS

1 You can make spirals with multiplication tables called spirolaterals. It helps to have some graph paper, but if you are careful with a ruler and a pencil, that will work too. Choose a multiplication table.

2 How about the six times table? Add up the digits in each number. Have you noticed a pattern?

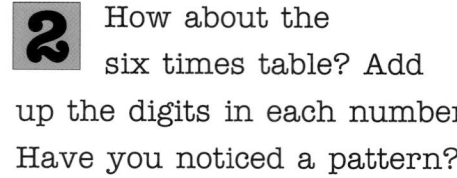

6	12	18	24	30	36	42	48
6	1+2	1+8	2+4	3+0	3+6	4+2	4+8
6	3	9	6	3	9	6	3

because 4+8=12
1+2=3

3 If you get a two-digit number when you add the digits together, keep adding them until you get a single-digit number.

4 Draw the first line 6 squares long then make a **right-angled** turn. The length of the next line is 3. Turn in the same direction again. The next is 9. Keep following the pattern until the lines start to retrace themselves. You could color in the patterns with colored pencils.

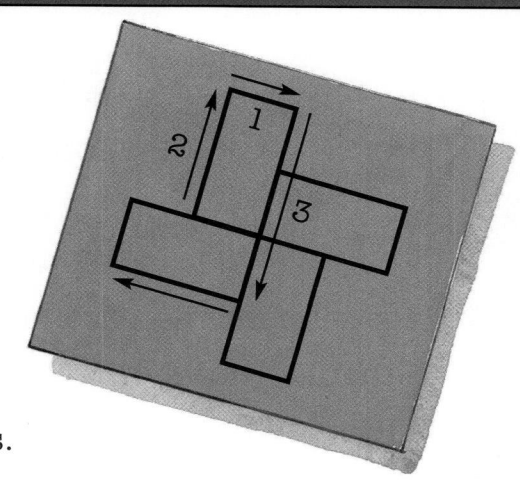

5 Try doing the same with other multiplication tables. Do any look like these?

MORE IDEAS

● Tear the corner off a piece of cardboard. Draw a straight line from the corner to the torn edge. Cut along the line. Mark the top corner with an "x," mark points from the tip at 1, 2, and 3 in. along the edge you have cut. On a plain piece of paper draw a line 2 in. long. Place the cardboard along the line with corner "x" at one end. Draw a line 1 in. long back down the edge of the cardboard (using the measurements). Then rest your piece of cardboard along the line you have drawn with the marked corner at the end. Draw back 3 in. along the measured edge. Repeat these three steps over and over until you have made a pattern like the one on the left.

TRIANGULAR NUMBERS

Look at this number pattern

1   3   6   10   15...

What do you think comes next? This sequence is part of a special pattern called triangular numbers. To find out why they are called triangular numbers see page 748. It is made by adding consecutive numbers like this:

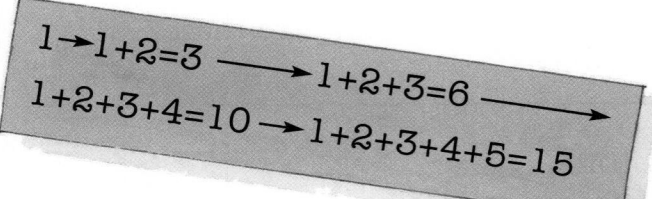

$$1 \rightarrow 1+2=3 \longrightarrow 1+2+3=6 \longrightarrow$$
$$1+2+3+4=10 \rightarrow 1+2+3+4+5=15$$

Use this pattern to advise the government of Metropolis!

HIGHWAY MADNESS

1 The government of Metropolis has decided to build highways to link their seven cities. Because they are worried about the environment, they make a rule that every city must be linked directly to every other city by only one road.

How many roads need to be built?

2 Start by drawing two cities. How many roads need to be built to link them? Now draw three cities. How many roads would need to be built now?

3 Without drawing out the highway system, predict how many highways would need to be built for the seven cities in Metropolis.

4 Now mark them out and join them all with roads. Has the government of Metropolis made a good policy decision? What advice would you give to the government?

HELPFUL HINTS

● First find out how many roads need to be built with a smaller number of cities – say 3, 4, and 5. Look at the pattern of the triangular numbers on page 748. Three cities need three roads (1+2=3). Four cities need six roads (1+2+3=6). You can use the triangular pattern to figure out how many roads five cities would need.

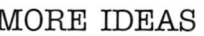

1,2,3, 4,5...

MORE IDEAS

● Another interesting puzzle like Highway Madness is the handshakes problem.

If you have eight people in a room and they all want to greet each other by shaking hands, how many handshakes will there be?

● You could start by figuring out how many handshakes you would need for a smaller group – as you did with the roads in Highway Madness.

LETTERS AND NUMBERS

In mathematics letters are sometimes used to represent numbers. This branch of mathematics is called **algebra**. It is a useful way of solving problems when you don't have any numbers to help or you are not sure what the numbers might be. Sometimes the numbers can be found out, then they can be substituted into a formula. In other words, they are swapped over for some of the letters.

NAME NUMBERS

1 If a=1, b=2, c=3, and d=4, what do x, y, and z equal?

ANDREW is worth 65 points because
A=1   N=14   D=4   R=18   E=5   W=23
1 + 14 + 4 + 18 + 5 + 23 = 65

2 How many points is your name worth?

Think about the names of friends. Whose name do you think is worth the most points? Is it the name with the most letters?

NICOLA = 54

3 Do you have a "twin?" – someone whose name scores the same number of points as yours?

SIMON = 70

HELPFUL HINTS

● When you are figuring out how much your name is worth, it is helpful to set all the letters of the alphabet out in a table so you can quickly look up their value.

● When you are adding up a lot of numbers, it is easy to make a mistake. Check what you have done. A calculator can be useful.

MORE IDEAS

● The title of this page is "Letters and Numbers." It is worth 210 points. Can you make a sentence that is worth 200 points? How close can you get?

Can you score 300 points using a 17-letter sentence?

OPERATIONS AND FUNCTIONS

A function is when +, −, x, ÷, or other operations are used to change numbers. A **function** is a little like a machine in a factory that processes, or changes, something into something else.

NUMBER CRUNCHERS

1 You are the new engineer in the factory. You can see how the machine below works because the machine's functions are clearly labeled on the outside. When the 3 goes in, a 7 comes out because the function inside is x2 and then +1.

2 Unfortunately not all the machines are as clearly labeled. But you discover that if you put a number in a machine, it still gets crunched and changed.

Test the machine a few more times. What would happen if you put a number 6 in? What about 23? Try some other numbers and see what happens.

3 Try finding out the function for this number cruncher!

Which functions do you think were used in the big machine to turn the 2 into a 4? Can you think of any other way of doing it?

HELPFUL HINTS

● If you get stuck, try out a few operations in the machines and see what happens when you put a number in. Look for a pattern.

● If you are really stuck here are some clues:

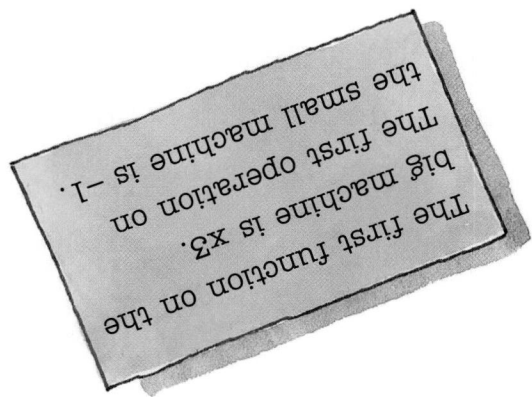

The first function on the big machine is ×3.
The first operation on the small machine is −1.

MORE IDEAS

● Make up your own number cruncher machines. You could have more than two operations in each machine! Figure out some inputs and outputs, then see if a friend can solve your puzzle!

5 THINK OF A NUMBER

In algebra, when letters are used in calculations they could mean anything! But we can still work with them. If we do not know what a number is we could call it "n." Here is a trick that will work with any number. Try it out on your friends.

n

+6

×3

-18

NUMBER RECYCLING PLANT

1 This is a way of calculating with any number and changing it using lots of different operations – adding, multiplying, dividing, and subtracting – and always arriving at the same result!

2 Your friends may need a calculator and a pencil and paper to help them.

Divide by the number you first thought of.

3 Now say to your friends, "This truly remarkable trick can magically transform any number into a beautiful single one! Yes, it is true!"

- Make sure you remember the number you started with. It helps to keep a note of your calculations.
- This could be recorded in a table:

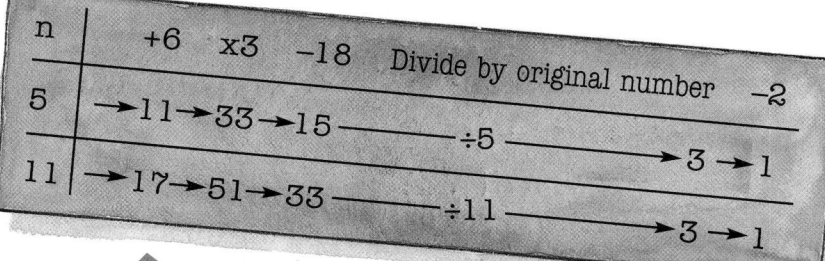

n	+6	x3	−18	Divide by original number	−2
5	→11→33→15			÷5	3 →1
11	→17→51→33			÷11	3 →1

- Can you see now how the trick works?

MORE IDEAS

- If you divide any number by itself, the answer is always 1. $7÷7=1$, $5÷5=1$, $59÷59=1$, and $123÷123=1$. Try doing the same with another number.
- Now you know how the magic works, try to make your own trick using many different functions that can turn numbers into ones.
- What happens when you divide or multiply a number by 0? Could you use this in your trick?

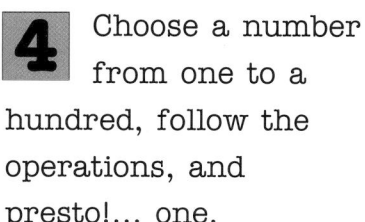

4 Choose a number from one to a hundred, follow the operations, and presto!... one.

NUMBER CODES

We are so used to counting with the numerals 0123456789 and using the decimal system that they seem timeless, as though they have always been there. But they haven't! Different cultures have used a variety of counting systems and numbers.

Some of these can still be seen in regular use. Have you seen any Roman numerals? Letters are used to represent the numbers.

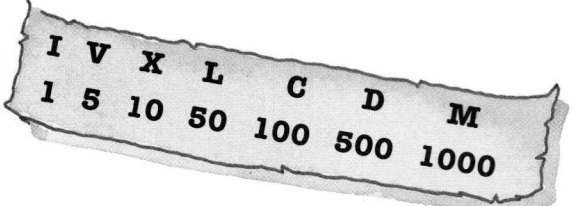

I	V	X	L	C	D	M
1	5	10	50	100	500	1000

The Mayan people lived over 2,000 years ago. Their number system used twenties and ones. We need to decode the system to know what the symbols represent.

= 0

= 1

= 2

= 3

= 4

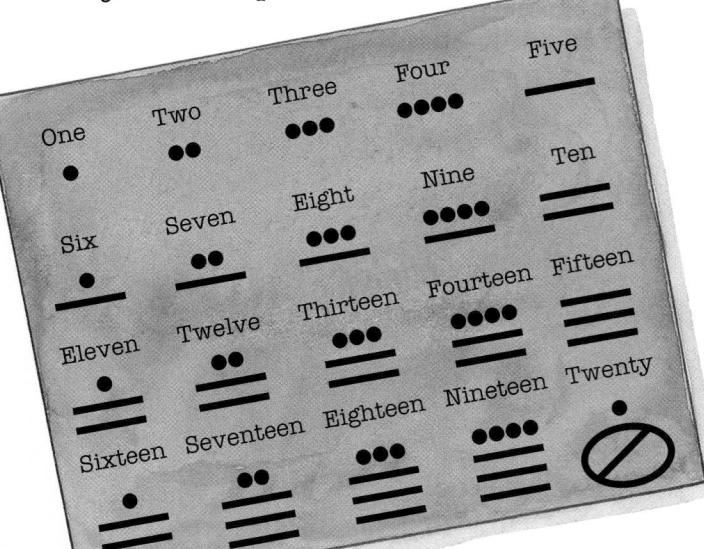

One
Two
Three
Four
Five
Six
Seven
Eight
Nine
Ten
Eleven
Twelve
Thirteen
Fourteen
Fifteen
Sixteen
Seventeen
Eighteen
Nineteen
Twenty

A number like 57 would be written like this...

because

2x20=40

+17=57

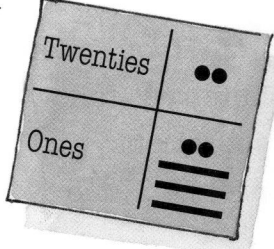

Twenties	••
Ones	••

NUMBER DISCOVERY

1 Imagine that you have been exploring uncharted land. You stumble across a stone tablet. There are some strange markings – they look like numbers.

This number is 28

=5   =6

You eventually figure out what each symbol means.

=7   =8

=9

2 What number do you think this is?

3 How would you write down 82? What about 56? Try 170!

Answer is 7 1 5

The system of counting was based on fives from 1 – 19 and then in groups of twenty.

This symbol represented a zero.

MORE IDEAS

- Make up some problems with the numbers and see if your friends can solve them.
- Can you make up your own number codes?
- Find out about other counting systems. The Babylonian system is amazing!

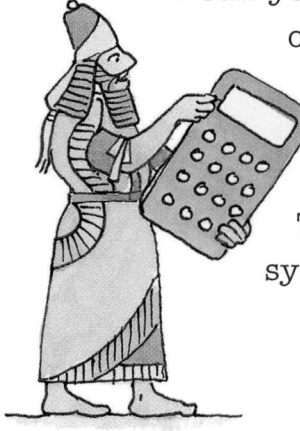

KNOW YOUR NUMBERS

The more you know about numbers the more patterns, links, and connections you will be able to make between them. What do you know about the number **25**? It is a square number, because **5x5=25**. It is a quarter of **100**. My uncle is **25** years old. It is an odd number. List everything you know about another number. How many connections can you make?

A solo spot for me. Odd and on my own. Who am I?

I had 10 subtracted and then I was multiplied by 2. That made 12. Who am I?

I can be divided by 12, 9, 6, 4, 3, and 2. If I am multiplied by 10 the answer is the same as the degrees in a whole turn. I am an even number. The product of my digits is 18. Who am I?

I was multiplied by 3 and then 3 was added. That made 30. Who am I?

The number of squares on a chessboard. 2 multiplied by itself six times. Who am I?

MYSTERY NUMBERS

1 The more you know about numbers the easier it will be for you to solve these number riddles. What are the mystery numbers and how are they all connected?

The sum of the first five odd numbers. An odd two digit number. Who am I?

The sum of my digits is said to be unlucky. I am not quite half a century. Who am I?

Add the sides of a square to the faces on a die and multiply by 10. Who am I?

I was divided by 9 and when 8 was subtracted, I was cut down to the size of just 1. Who am I?

The legs on most animals, tables, and chairs. Who am I?

HELPFUL HINTS

● With some of the mystery numbers you can work backward to find the answer by using the inverse or opposite operation. The inverse of ×3 is ÷3.

The inverse of +6 is −6.

● For the problem "I was multiplied by 3 and then 3 was added. That made 30. Who am I?" you can begin from the 30. Work backward by subtracting 3, which makes 27 and then dividing by 3, which gives 9... the answer!

MORE IDEAS

● Make up your own mystery numbers! Think up your clues carefully and try them out on your friends. Remember to check your clues first!

MORE MYSTERY

To solve some problems you have to try to keep in mind a number of clues at the same time – simultaneously. In fact these are sometimes called simultaneous equations. They can be solved algebraically, but many simple ones can also be solved through trial and error. Try these!

COMBINATION CRACKERS

You have been on the trail of cunning criminals who have stolen some valuable jewels! A tattered, smudged piece of paper has been secretly passed to you with some clues that enable you to unlock the case holding the treasure.

1 The case has a four-digit combination lock and you only have a matter of minutes before the thieves return.

These are the clues...

The third digit is three more than the first.

The second digit is two more than the fourth.

All the digits add up to 17.

The second digit is three.

HELPFUL HINTS

- Stuck?! Then try to solve the problem using algebra. If the digits are a, b, c, and d, we know that b=d+2 and that b=3. So if b=3 then 3=d+2 and therefore d=1.

- Use algebra to find out what a and c are. When the numbers you have chosen match all the clues then you have cracked the code and unlocked the case!

Answer is 5 3 8 1

MORE IDEAS

- If you found the first puzzle easy try this one!

You need to escape on a high-powered motorcycle, but it is chained up by, would you believe it, a four-digit combination lock. These are your clues for unlocking it...

- Why don't you find your own chain or case and make up your own clues!

The motorcycle answer is 3 1 6 4

> The first number is one less than the fourth.
>
> The sum of all the digits is fourteen.
>
> The third number is twice as big as the first.
>
> The fourth number is two less than the third.

MAN-MADE PATTERNS

People love patterns. Patterns can be seen all over the world on buildings, on furniture, clothes, and even on bodies. Have you seen any ancient Celtic knot patterns or those created by Islamic artists across the Middle East and North Africa? Perhaps you know of others. These designs illustrate many beautiful mathematical patterns.

SHONGO PATTERNS

This intricate pattern comes from Africa and is drawn by children on the ground in mud, clay, or sand.

1 The pattern is drawn in one continuous line. Your pencil should never be lifted from the paper. You can cross lines, but you should never go along the same line twice.

2 These are the first three patterns in the sequence. Try to draw them.

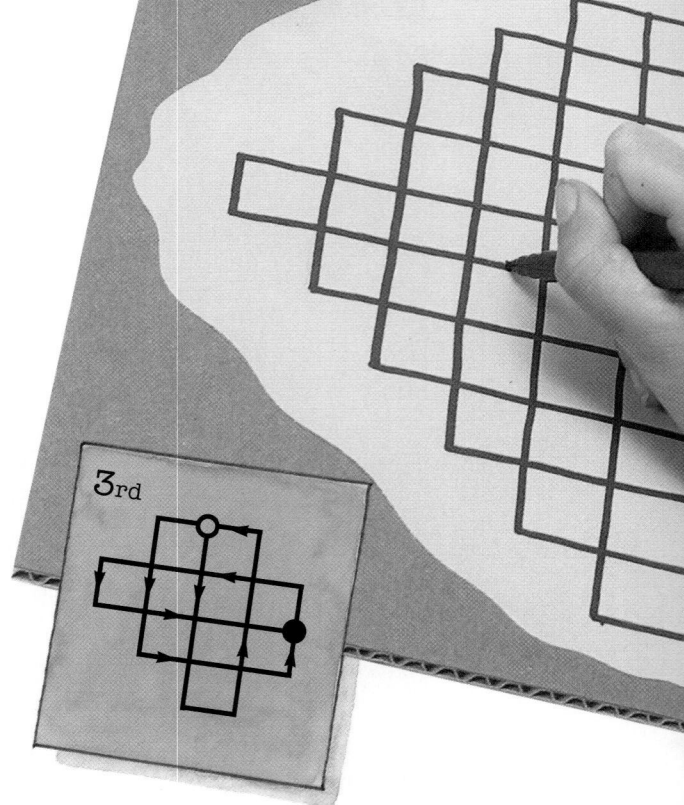

3 When you have drawn the first three try to draw the fourth. What about the fifth? Remember, your pencil should never leave the paper.

4 What patterns do you notice as you draw the shapes?

How long is the starting line on each of the new shapes? Count the squares covered by each shape. Can you see any number patterns?

Describe as much as you can about the 100th shongo pattern without any drawing.

HELPFUL HINTS

● If you find it hard to get a sense of the pattern, trace over the shapes following the arrows on the lines carefully.

● It is a good idea to start drawing the patterns on graph paper. As you become more confident draw the shapes freehand on blank paper.

● After a little practice, you will be surprised how quickly they can be drawn.

● When you are looking for patterns, it is a good idea to note what you see in a table.

Shape	1st	2nd	3rd	4th
Perimeter	8	12	16	

MORE IDEAS

● This beautiful pattern comes from an ancient Celtic gravestone.

● Find some patterns from other cultures and try to draw them.

● What similarities or differences are there between the patterns you have found and the shongo pattern?

NATURAL PATTERNS

Nature is full of patterns. Next time you look at a plant or tree in your yard or park look at the curves, **angles**, and spirals that are formed. These patterns can be represented by numbers.

SPIRALS

You can draw many of these patterns by following a series of simple instructions.

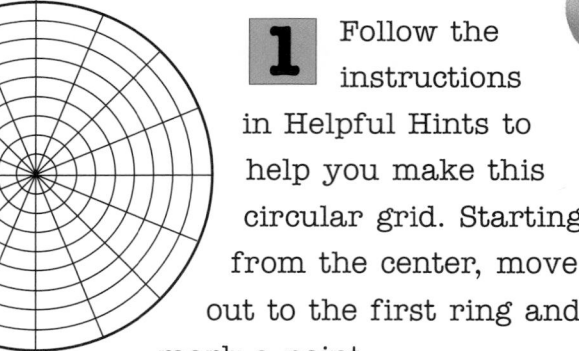

1 Follow the instructions in Helpful Hints to help you make this circular grid. Starting from the center, move out to the first ring and mark a point.

2 Lift your pen and move one section of the grid clockwise and out to the next circle and mark the point. Join the points.

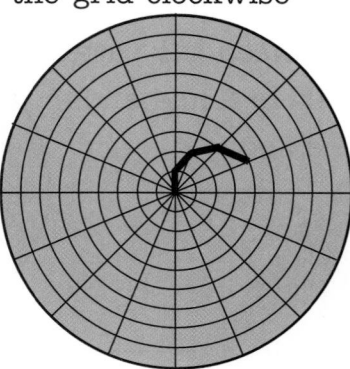

Keep moving out and clockwise one circle at a time, marking points and joining them.

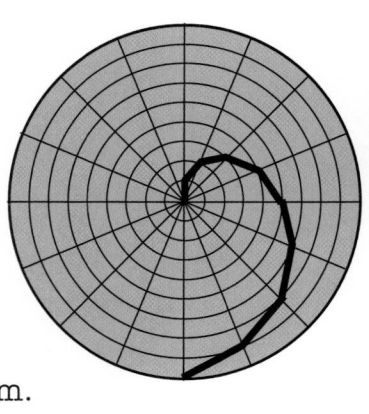

618

3 When you reach the outside circle, you will have made a curve.

HELPFUL HINTS

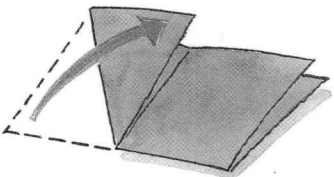

● Find a piece of graph paper. Keep your compass point in the middle and draw 10 circles a half inch apart. Fold the paper in half and fold each side over and then over again.

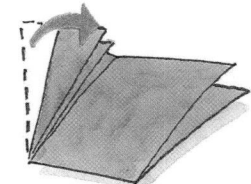

MORE IDEAS

● Make another curve starting from the same center point. This time turn counterclockwise. You have drawn a beautiful leaf. Make lots of curves in a pattern on the same grid.

● Try other patterns. What happens if you move out two circles at a time?

● Try moving out one circle and turning two sectors.

● Other patterns can be made by following the grid lines and coloring in bright colors rather than just joining the points.

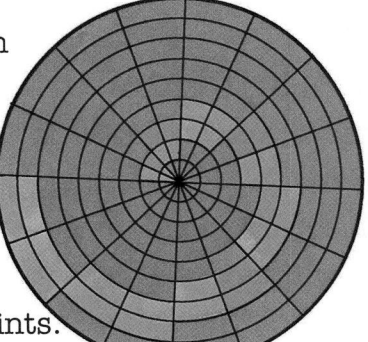

NATURAL NUMBERS

Nature can change simple number patterns into beautiful shapes. The Fibonacci sequence can be found everywhere in nature. Artists and architects have also used it in designs. It begins like this **1 1 2 3 5 8 13 21 34...** Can you see what the pattern is? The next number in the sequence is created by adding the previous two numbers, so the next number will be 21+34=55.

FIBONACCI FACTS

Did you know that the number of clockwise spirals on a sunflower head is 55 and the counterclockwise spirals is 34? Count them and check! Pineapples have 8 seeds arranged in a clockwise spiral and 13 in a counterclockwise spiral.

CURVE STITCHING

Other beautiful patterns can be made by adding numbers. For this project you will need a thick piece of cardboard. Draw out a cross on it.

1 On each arm of the cross mark five points 1 in. apart. Mark the points on each arm with the numbers 1, 2, 3, 4, and 5. Pierce each point with a thick needle. Get an adult to help you with this.

2 Thread a needle with a long piece of yarn. Choose your favorite color. In one quarter, stitch together the points that add up to 6, for example 1 and 5. When you have done one quarter, move on to the next with a different color yarn.

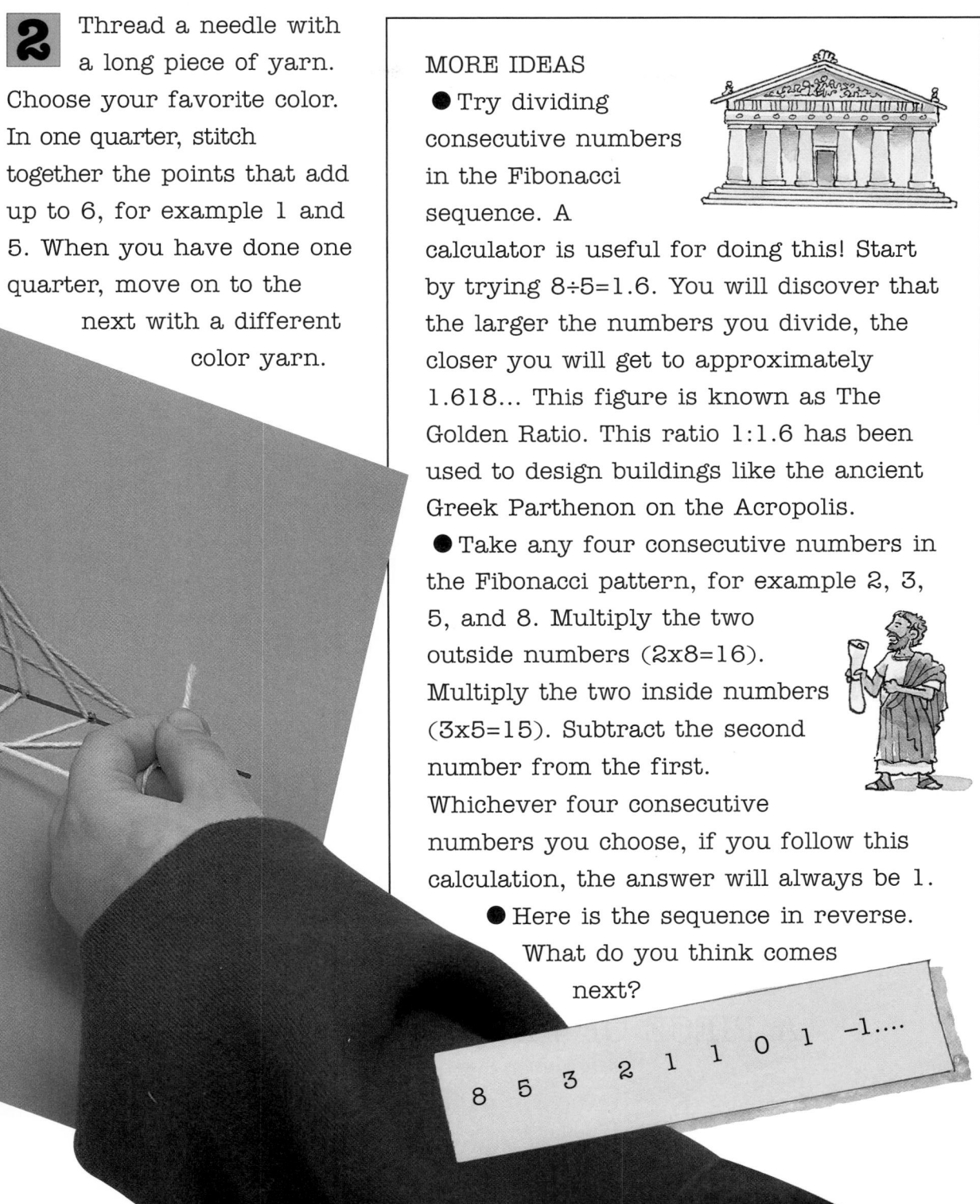

MORE IDEAS

● Try dividing consecutive numbers in the Fibonacci sequence. A calculator is useful for doing this! Start by trying 8÷5=1.6. You will discover that the larger the numbers you divide, the closer you will get to approximately 1.618... This figure is known as The Golden Ratio. This ratio 1:1.6 has been used to design buildings like the ancient Greek Parthenon on the Acropolis.

● Take any four consecutive numbers in the Fibonacci pattern, for example 2, 3, 5, and 8. Multiply the two outside numbers (2x8=16). Multiply the two inside numbers (3x5=15). Subtract the second number from the first. Whichever four consecutive numbers you choose, if you follow this calculation, the answer will always be 1.

● Here is the sequence in reverse. What do you think comes next?

8 5 3 2 1 1 0 1 −1....

CONTENTS

SORTING AND SETS **624**

CARROLL DIAGRAMS **626**

VENN DIAGRAMS **628**

THINKING LOGICALLY **630**

PLAY TO WIN! **632**

THE RIGHT PLACE **634**

DEFINITELY MAYBE **636**

TAKE A CHANCE **638**

SPIN THE SPINNER **640**

GRAPHS AND CHARTS **642**

DATASTREAMS **644**

A PIECE OF PIE! **646**

Chapter Four

Getting the Facts

SORTING AND SETS

When your mom or dad says "clean your room!" they are really just trying to help you with your mathematics! When you clean up, you may group and order your toys so they can be found more easily. Each group of toys is called a **set**. Every toy is called an **element**.

THESE SHOES ARE
MADE FOR WALKING
You can do this with a
brother, sister, or friend.

1 How many shoes are there in the house? Ask an adult if you can collect them all together and put them in one big pile.

2 This is the set of all shoes in the house. Each shoe is an element of the set. How many shoes are there in the set? Let's hope it is an even number!

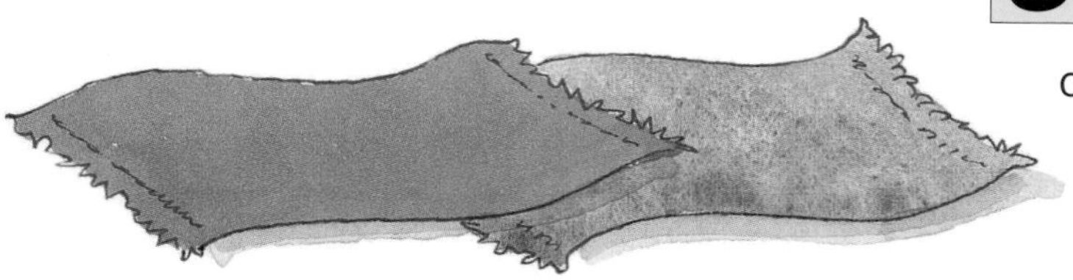

3 Find two colored towels. Sort the shoes into two sets on the towels: adult's shoes and children's shoes. Each of these groups is called a subset.

4 Can you sort them in any other way?

Dress shoes and everyday shoes.

Indoor and outdoor shoes.

Uncomfortable and comfortable shoes.

Left foot and right foot shoes.

Shoes that are smaller than your foot and shoes that are larger.

5 Sort them into sets that belong to each person in the house.

6 And last of all, can you sort them so that they go back to the right place in the house?

HELPFUL HINTS

● To help you play these sorting games choose one shoe. Take turns to think of different words or phrases to describe the shoe.

● How many can you think of? Three... five... how about ten?

MORE IDEAS

● Try sorting out your pens and pencils into different groups.

● You could sort your pencils into those that need to be sharpened and those that are sharp. What other ways could they be sorted to help you find them more easily?

CARROLL DIAGRAMS

A set of elements have at least one thing, or **property**, in common. If you have a set of fruit you can say that any element in the set is either "an apple" or "not an apple." Carroll diagrams are a way of sorting information like this.

PICK 'N' MIX

Have you ever opened a large box of candy and then spent a long time looking for your favorite... or avoided the one with the chewy center that you hate! A Carroll diagram can help you to sort out the yummy from the yucky. First decide on something about the candy you really like... perhaps you like toffee... perhaps you hate chocolate.

1 In a Carroll diagram we call the headings **categories**. In this diagram toffee and chocolate will be the categories. Draw your diagram like the one at the top of page 627.

A candy that has toffee and chocolate would go here.

	Chocolate	Not chocolate
Toffee		
Not toffee		

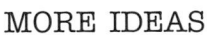

One that has chocolate but no toffee would go here.

Where would you put a candy that has no chocolate and no toffee?

2 Sort out your candy. In which part of the diagram are your favorite candy? Where are your least favorite?

HELPFUL HINTS
● Most candy boxes give a guide to their contents on the side. Keep it handy. It might stop you from making a terrible mistake!

MORE IDEAS
● What else can you sort using Carroll diagrams? How about the laundry? (Ask an adult.)
● Try categories like "shirt" and "not shirt," and "adult" and "not adult."

VENN DIAGRAMS

The elements of a set don't always fall into two easy groups. An element might be a part of different sets at the same time. Venn diagrams are a useful way of showing this.

DOUBLE TROUBLE!
This is a game that uses a Venn diagram. Pick a subject for your set. What about animals?

1 Draw two overlapping circles as below, or make them from colored cardboard. Label each circle as a different subset.

Set
1pt.

3pts.

Subsets
2pts.

2 You might choose prehistoric and carnivorous animals. Each circle is a subset of the whole (universal) set of animals.

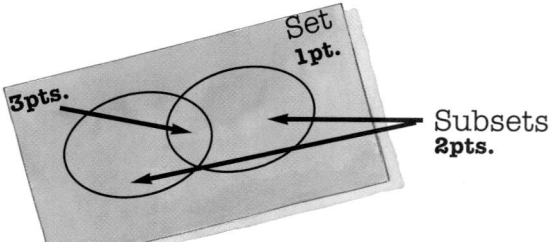

3 Think of any animal. Write it on a piece of cardboard and place it where it belongs on the diagram. A Stegosaur scores two points, a cow scores one point.

4 What about a carnivorous (meat-eating) animal? A lion scores two points.

5 If you can think of an animal that is carnivorous and prehistoric it would go in the striped intersection and score three points!

HELPFUL HINTS

● It might be useful to find books with animal facts and dinosaur facts to help you play this game.

MORE IDEAS

● You could make up your own game using other sets. How about the set of musical instruments. The two overlapping subsets could be electrical instruments and stringed instruments!

● Harder, but great fun, is to think up three overlapping sets. Try this one. How would you change the scoring system?

Carnivorous animals

Animals with fur

Animals that live in water

6 Have five turns each and see who can get the highest score.

THINKING LOGICALLY

When you woke up this morning you solved quite a tricky problem – getting dressed! You had to think logically. What did you do first? What did you do next? Did you put your clothes on in the correct order and on the right parts of your body?!

THE SHOWMAN, HIS TIGER, A DUCK, AND THE SACK OF CORN

How good are you at thinking logically? This is an old problem. You need to help the showman cross a river with his tiger, duck, and sack of corn.

1 There is a boat but it is so small that it can only hold the showman and one of the others.

2 The showman can't leave the tiger with the duck as the duck will be eaten. He can't leave the duck with the corn for fear of losing all the corn. How does he get across?

3 Find some toys and pretend they are the showman, tiger, duck, and corn. Make a river with blue paper.

4 Put all the toys on one side of the river. What would happen if the showman took the tiger over first? Is it a better plan to take the corn? Would it be a good idea to take the duck?

CORN

5 When you think you have figured out how it could be done, make up a short story with the toys and tell it to your friends.

HELPFUL HINTS

● Have you worked out the first thing that the showman should transport across the river?

● It couldn't be the tiger, because the duck would be left on its own with the tasty corn!

● He couldn't take the corn because the tiger would be all alone with the juicy duck!! So, the first thing that needs to go is the... duck.

● What happens next? One last clue: The showman can bring something back across the river with him if he needs to.

MORE IDEAS

● The Towers of Hanoi is an ancient logic problem. You need to move the pile of disks from the red square to the green square. Only one disk may be moved at a time. A larger disk can never be placed on a smaller disk. You could play this game with three coins of different sizes. What is the smallest number of moves it takes to do it?

PLAY TO WIN!

Have you ever played Tic-tac-toe? Can anyone beat you? If you play cleverly, you can make sure that you never lose! To play this game well you need to use logic. There are many games that depend on skill and strategy (planning). Chess and Checkers are good games; perhaps you could also find out about Othello or Go.

DIAMONDS

Diamonds is an ancient game of skill for two players that some believe was played by Arabian princes.

1 First you need to make a square board divided into 16 squares. Cut out 20 counters, you could make them diamond-shaped.

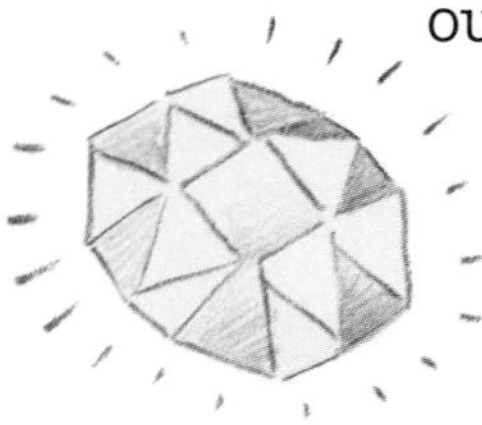

2 When you play Tic-tac-toe you need to get a line of three to win. But in Diamonds you lose if three diamonds are placed in a line. The line might be vertical, horizontal, diagonal, even if there is a gap in the line.

3 Each player has 10 diamonds. Take turns to place a diamond on a square.

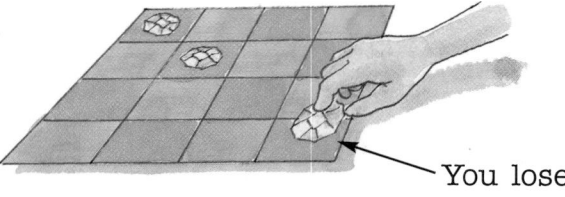

You lose

HELPFUL HINTS

● Before you put a diamond on the board look carefully! Check each row and don't forget the diagonal lines.

4 The winner takes all the diamonds on the board! Start the game again and play with your new set of diamonds. The game ends when one person has won all the diamonds.

MORE IDEAS

● What is the greatest number of diamonds you could fit on the board without getting three in a straight line? It is easy to place 6. Can you fit on any more?

● It is fun to try this game on a 64-square chessboard. You can play with up to six players!

THE RIGHT PLACE

Finding the right place to send, store, or find things can be a tricky business. Look at the address on some letters that have been sent to you.

Your address might have a house number, street name, the town you live in, state, zip code, and perhaps country, – lots of information to make sure that the letter reaches the right person.

AMAZING MONSTER MOUNTAINS
Use colored cardboard, pens, and glue to make the monsters and mountain in the picture.

1 Are you brave enough to help them find their home on the mountain?

2 Here are some clues to help you.

- All the monsters on the right of the mountain have round, green bodies. The other monsters have red bodies.

- Monsters at the bottom of the mountain have short, green hair. All the other monsters have blue, curly hair.

- The monsters all have two eyes except the one at the peak that has three.

- All of the monsters on the mountain have triangular noses, two feet, and two arms.

3 Some of the places on the mountain are still empty. You might have to make some more monsters and put them in their homes.

HELPFUL HINTS

- When you are deciding where to put your monster check against all the clues one at a time. Then go through the clues and make a list of the different things you need to include in your drawing. Your list might look something like this:

green body
blue, curly hair
two eyes

MORE IDEAS

- You can make more great monster mountain puzzles with your friends. Draw a mountain, or trace the one on the page. Add more features like a cave or some trees.
- Next, make up some clues, then draw the monsters. Make sure they match the clues you have given!

DEFINITELY MAYBE

Do you think it will rain tomorrow? If you take a card from a deck what are the chances you will draw an ace? When mathematicians study questions like these they are studying the likelihood or probability of something happening.

FLIPPER

When you flip a coin into the air what might happen when it lands? Two things could happen. It might show a head or a tail. The likelihood of getting a tail is one chance in two, or you could say a half.

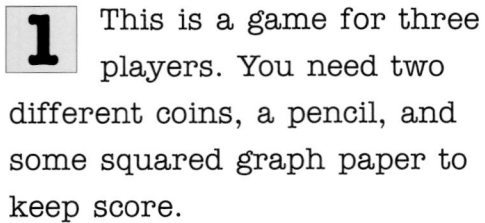

1 This is a game for three players. You need two different coins, a pencil, and some squared graph paper to keep score.

2 The first player gets a point if you can see two heads after the coins have been flipped. The second player gets a point if you can see a head and a tail.

The third player gets a point if there are two tails.

3 Take turns to be the coin flipper and keep score of the points.

4 Flip the coins about 20 times each. Who is winning? Is this a fair game? Which team would you rather be if you started the game again?

HELPFUL HINTS

● It makes it easier to understand this game if you use two different coins when you are flipping. You can find out which team has the best chance of winning by looking at all the possible things that could happen – the possible outcomes. There are four possibilities:

Coin 1   **Coin 2**

● There is only one chance in four of getting two heads and only one chance in four of getting two tails, but there are two chances in four of getting one of each!

● What are you going to choose next time?

MORE IDEAS

● Try playing Flipper with four coins. Which would be the best "team" to choose? All heads? How about two heads and two tails? Do you think three tails and a head would be best? Experiment, find out, then challenge your friends to a game!

● Why is "heads I win, tails you lose" an unfair way to decide who wins when you flip a coin?

TAKE A CHANCE

There are many games that use a mixture of luck, skill, and strategy. Backgammon is an exciting game to play, so is Monopoly. Good players are those that know how to make the best decision whatever the throw of the die or draw of the cards.

Can you work out the best way to play Sweaty palms?

SWEATY PALMS

1 You need some dried beans and three or more players for this game – in fact the more players you have the better! Each player secretly holds one or two beans in his or her hand.

2 Next, everyone tries to guess the total being held by the whole group. The person who makes the best guess is the winner!

3 How many beans do you think these four players are holding? Is 3 a good guess? Are some guesses better than others?

4 Play the game a few times. Do some numbers come up more often than others? What are your chances of making a correct guess?

HELPFUL HINTS

● Be careful when you make your guess.

● Remember that each player must hold one or two beans. If everyone is holding one what is the total being held? If everyone is holding two what is the total being held now?

MORE IDEAS

● To get really good at Sweaty palms look at all the different ways the numbers could be made in a game with four players. How many ways are there of making 4? What about 8? Can you figure out how many ways there are of making the other possible numbers: 5, 6, and 7?

● The number that can be made the most different ways is the best choice!

SPIN THE SPINNER

Many games of chance depend on the roll of a die or a spin of a disk. Can you think of some? When a die is rolled there are six possible outcomes – either a 1, 2, 3, 4, 5, or 6.

SIX-A-SIDE SOCCER SPIN

1 Have you ever played five-a-side soccer? This is a game of six-a-side with spinners! You need to make one spinner for every person playing. You will need cardboard, scissors, and some pens or pencils. Each player must choose a team from the grid below.

2 Pick a team from the grid below. Each team has its own numbers.

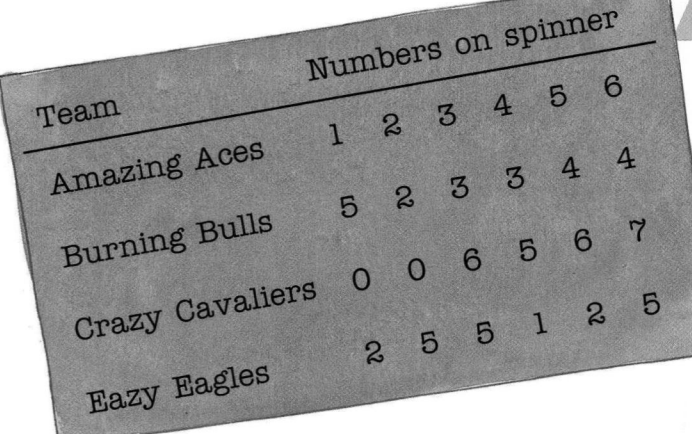

Team	Numbers on spinner					
Amazing Aces	1	2	3	4	5	6
Burning Bulls	5	2	3	3	4	4
Crazy Cavaliers	0	0	6	5	6	7
Eazy Eagles	2	5	5	1	2	5

3 Cut the cardboard into a six-sided regular hexagon like this. Draw and decorate your team's spinner with the numbers and colors and push a sharp pencil through the center.

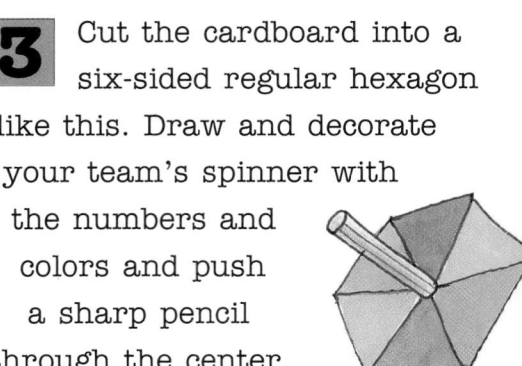

4 To play a match against another team, spin the spinner. The spinner that comes to rest on the highest number wins the match.

5 If your team is the Cavaliers and four of you are playing then you might keep a scorecard like this:

Cavaliers	6-4	Eagles
Cavaliers	3-7	Aces
Cavaliers		Bulls

HELPFUL HINTS

● You can find out which teams are the best by working out all the possible outcomes when two of the spinners are spun. You could make a color chart to compare the Cavaliers and the Aces:

7	C	C	C	C	C	C
6	C	C	C	C	C	D
5	C	C	C	C	D	A
6	C	C	C	C	C	D
0	A	A	A	A	A	A
0	A	A	A	A	A	A
	1	2	3	4	5	6

Cavaliers (vertical axis)   Aces (horizontal axis)

6 Play ten matches against each team. Don't count the draws. Which team did you choose? Why did you think it had the best chance of winning? If you played again, would you choose the same team?

● There are 36 possible outcomes. There are 20 possibilities that the Cavaliers could win (red), 3 of a draw (yellow), and 13 for the Aces to win (blue). So, the Cavaliers have a better team.

GRAPHS AND CHARTS

Graphs and charts are used by mathematicians to make information clearer or make certain facts stand out. If you were collecting information to find your friends' favorite cartoon character you might begin by keeping a check list. But you can show this information more clearly in a bar graph.

THE TOP TEN CHART

You could use a bar graph to help plan the music for a party. You would need to find out the type of music that everyone would want to dance to. What information do you need to help you decide? What are your friends' favorite pop stars? First, draw out a tally table like the one on the left.

1 Now ask your friends to name three pop stars they like. Write down each name mentioned and put a check by it each time that name gets a vote.

12
11
10
9
8
7
6
5
4
3
2
1

Pop Star A   Pop Star B

2 Next, draw out a bar graph using the information you collected in your check list. Each pop star gets one colored square for each vote. You can use your graph to find out which pop music is favorite!

Pop Star C

Pop Star D

Pop Star E

HELPFUL HINTS

● You might find it easier to use graph paper when you are filling in your bar graph. Make sure the paper is long enough to fit in the pop star with the most checks. If you don't plan carefully you might run out of room at the top of the graph!

MORE IDEAS

● Another graph like a bar graph is a pictogram. Instead of coloring in a block, draw a small picture of each item that gets a vote. You could use a pictogram to plan the food at your party. Collect information about what everyone likes to eat and try to chart the information in a pictogram.

DATASTREAMS

Some information gathered in experiments is continuous! When you are young your growth is continuous – it doesn't stop. If you measured your height every year you could make a graph of the data. It may look like there are sudden big jumps in the graph but in fact you did grow continuously over the year.

UPS AND DOWNS

Have you ever taken part in an important event like a school play? Throughout the day you might sometimes feel happy and at other times sad. A datastream is a good way of showing this.

1 Look at this graph. It shows the feelings of someone taking part in a school play, from when she wakes up in the morning to when the performance finishes.

2 The graph has been written on (or annotated) to describe why she felt happy or sad at different times.

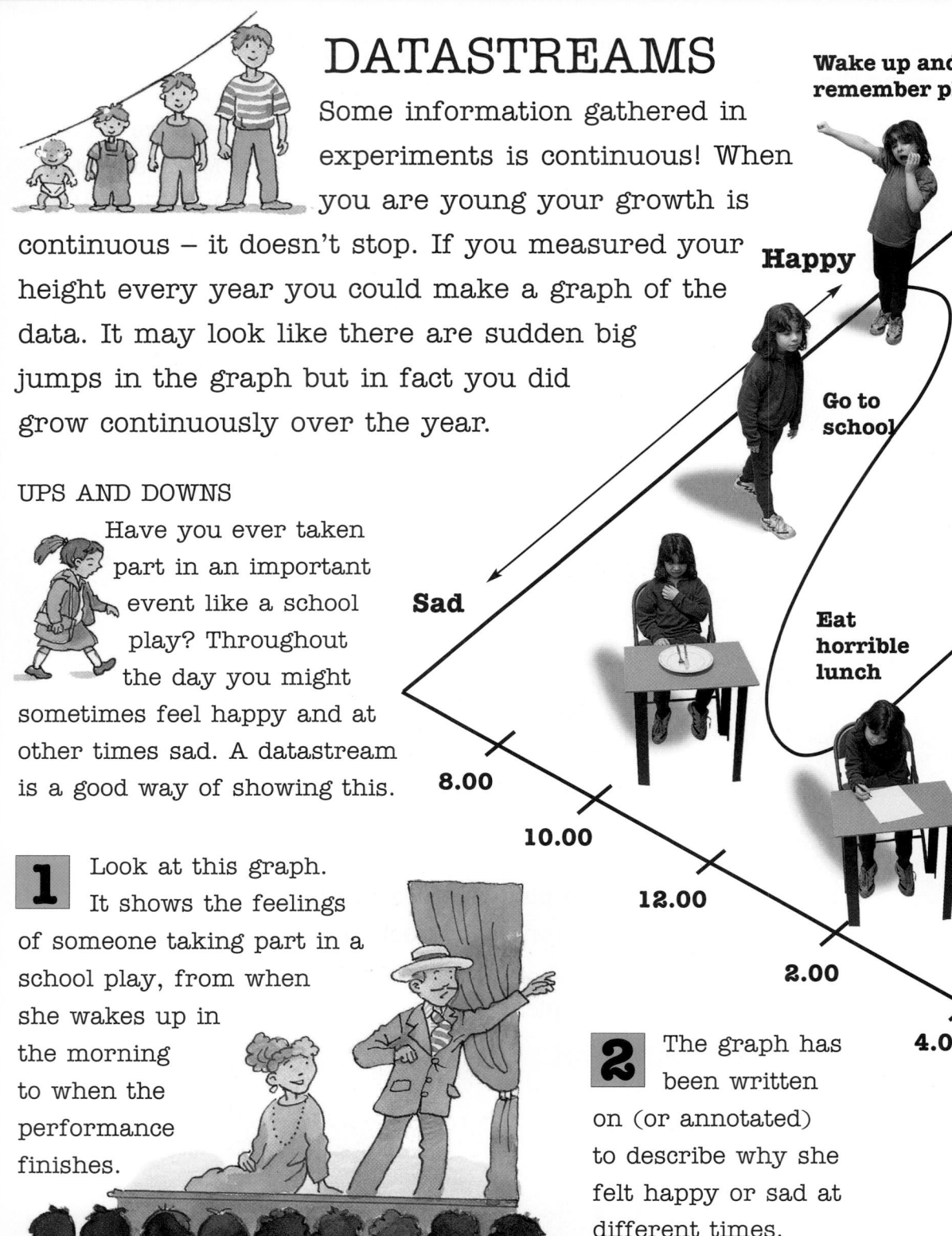

Wake up and remember play

Happy

Go to school

Sad

Eat horrible lunch

8.00

10.00

12.00

2.00

4.00

Finish work before play

3 Choose your own special event and draw out a graph like this one.

Prepare costume for play

Play starts

Audience claps

Forget my lines

4 Next, annotate the graph to help describe why you felt either happy or sad at different times in the day.

.00

8.00

HELPFUL HINTS

● You could start the graph by drawing a horizontal line across the page.

● Mark a point on the left and, next to it, the time you woke up. Now draw a vertical line straight up.

● Write in the time on the horizontal line. You might find it easier

to think about how you felt at the time you woke up, then mark a point; how you felt when you got to school, then mark a point. Mark points throughout the day and finally join up the points to make a curve.

MORE IDEAS

● Sometimes when you take part in an exciting event you might not feel just happy or sad. You could feel a mixture of both feelings – at the end of the play you could feel happy that everyone thought you had done well, but sad that the play had finished. How could you show that on the graph?

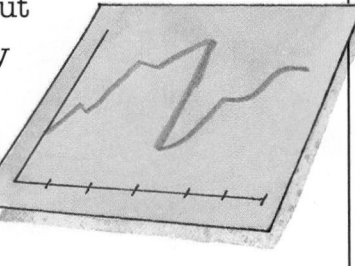

A PIECE OF PIE!

Many types of graphs and charts are used to show information clearly. Pie charts are usually circle-shaped. They are used to show fractions of a whole. Why do you think it is called a pie chart? This pie chart shows how children traveled to their school. Which part of the pie is the largest? It is easy to see that most children walked to school.

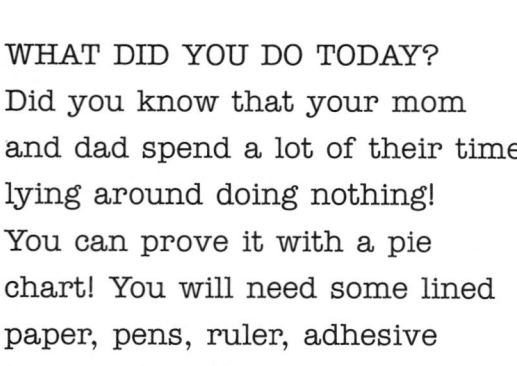

WHAT DID YOU DO TODAY?
Did you know that your mom and dad spend a lot of their time lying around doing nothing! You can prove it with a pie chart! You will need some lined paper, pens, ruler, adhesive tape, and some scissors.

1 First you need to gather some information. Ask your mom or dad how much time every day they spend on eating, the amount of time at work, time spent watching T.V., the amount of time traveling, and the amount of time sleeping.

2 Next, cut out a long bar from the lined paper about 5 inches wide stretching over 24 lines. Each line represents one hour of the day.

3 If two hours are spent traveling, color in two bars. Use a different color for each activity. When you have filled in the 24 bars loop the strip over into a circle and stick the ends together. Rest the circle on some paper, draw around it, and mark off the points for each activity. Draw a line from the points to the center and color in the different sections.

HELPFUL HINTS

● When you are collecting your information the time doesn't need to be exact. Measurements to the nearest hour or half hour will do.

MORE IDEAS

● You can use pie charts to find the amount of time a T.V. channel gives to different types of programs. Look at a T.V. guide and choose a channel. How much time is given to news, cartoons, movies, or other categories? Turn the information into a pie chart.

CONTENTS

SQUARES AND RECTANGLES **650**

TESSELLATIONS **652**

THE THIRD DIMENSION **654**

TRIANGLES **656**

MORE TRIANGLES **658**

PYRAMIDS **660**

CIRCLES **662**

STRETCHING CIRCLES **664**

CENTERS, SECTORS, AND CONES **666**

POLYGONS **668**

TANGRAMS **670**

POLYHEDRA **672**

Chapter Five

Exploring Shapes

SQUARES AND RECTANGLES

What do you know about squares? They have four corners and four sides, but do you know what is special about them? The sides are all the same length and the angles at the corners are all the same. Rectangles' corners are all the same angle and their opposite sides are the same length.

THE BLACK HOLE

1 Two players must try to cover a piece of paper with rectangles, without falling down the black hole! You need paper, colored pencils, and a ruler.

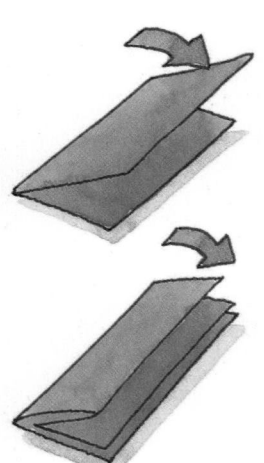

2 To make the grid for the game, fold a piece of paper in half lengthways as shown in the picture. Repeat this three more times. Unfold the paper and do the same, folding from top to bottom.

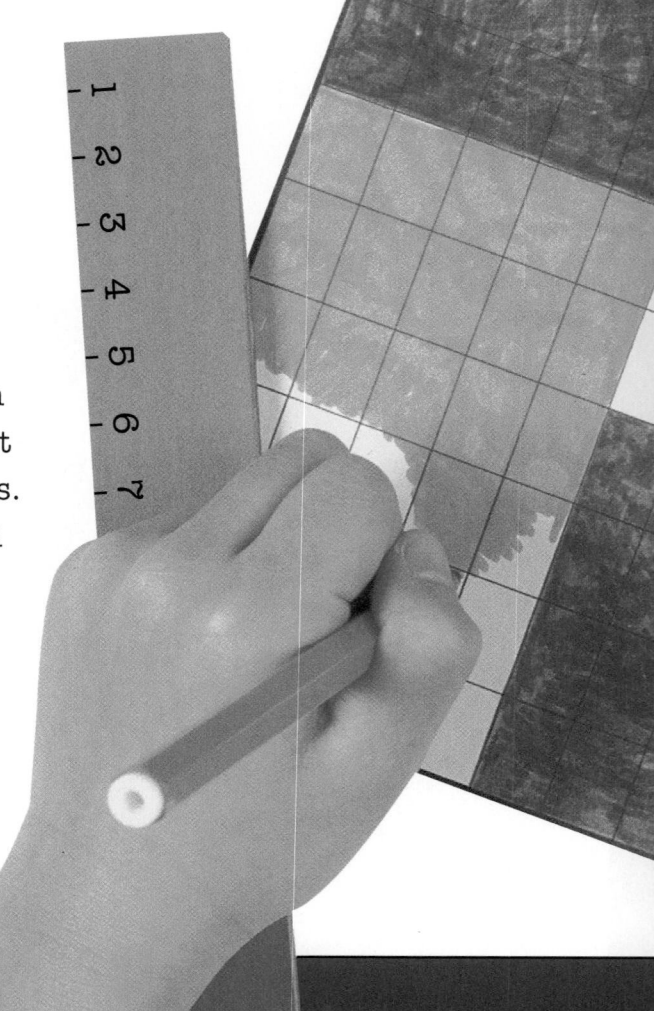

3 Unfold the paper and draw lines along the folds to make your grid. Choose any square and draw the black hole.

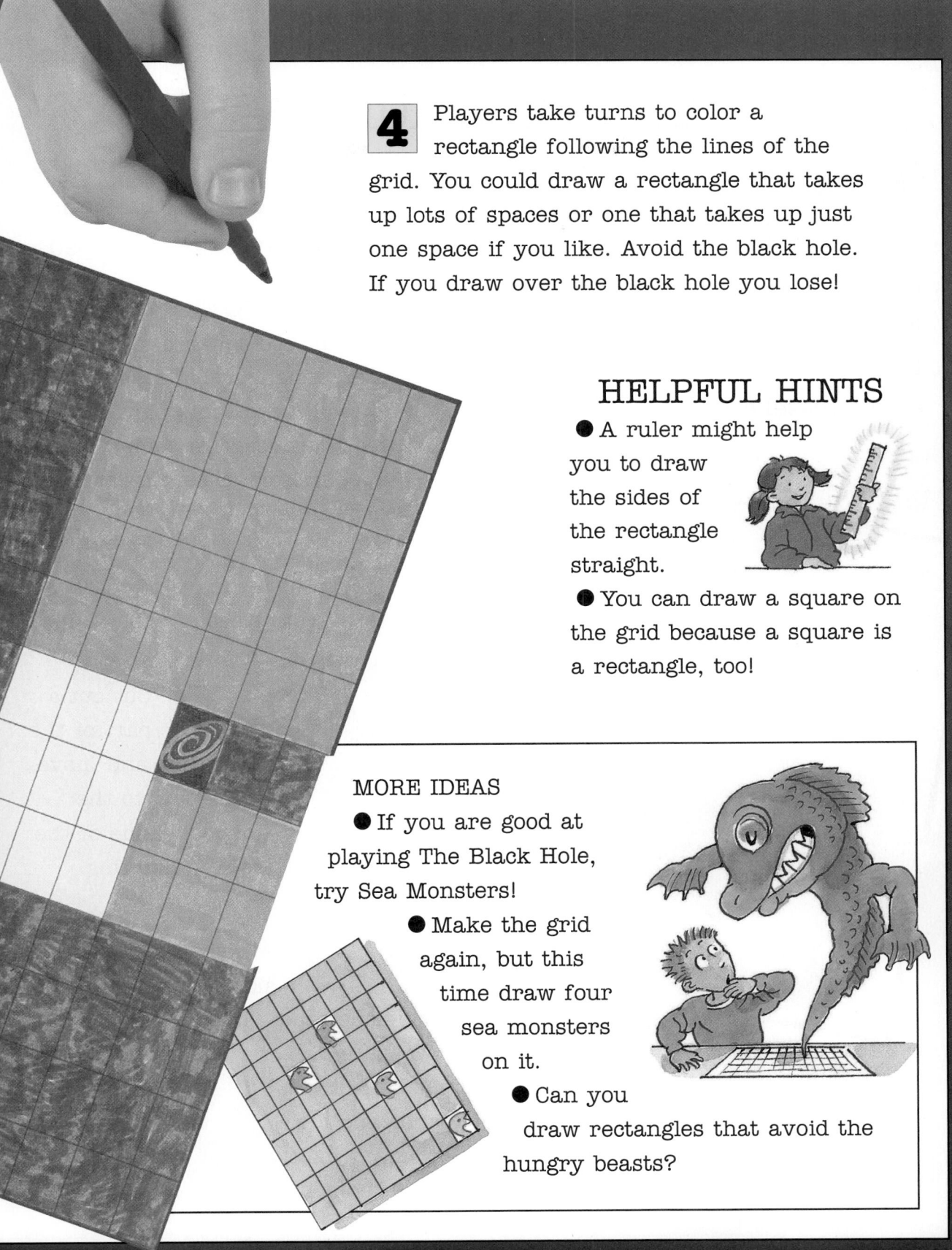

4 Players take turns to color a rectangle following the lines of the grid. You could draw a rectangle that takes up lots of spaces or one that takes up just one space if you like. Avoid the black hole. If you draw over the black hole you lose!

HELPFUL HINTS

● A ruler might help you to draw the sides of the rectangle straight.

● You can draw a square on the grid because a square is a rectangle, too!

MORE IDEAS

● If you are good at playing The Black Hole, try Sea Monsters!

● Make the grid again, but this time draw four sea monsters on it.

● Can you draw rectangles that avoid the hungry beasts?

TESSELLATIONS

Do you have any tiles in your house? There might be some in the kitchen or bathroom, on the walls, or on the floor. The tiles are often square shaped because they fit together easily, leaving no gaps. When a shape fits together like this we say the shape tessellates.

TESSELLATING TILES

You can use squares to make interesting tessellating shapes. You will need some paper, thick cardboard, a compass, tape, scissors, a pencil, and colored markers.

1 Cut a square of cardboard with sides of about 2 in.

2 Cut out a part of the square and move the part to the opposite side of the square like this.

3 Attach it to the other side of the square with some tape. Place your new tile in the middle of the paper and draw around it lightly with a pencil.

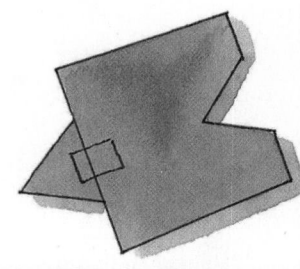

4 Pick up the tile and place it so it fits in with the first outline. There shouldn't be any gaps! Keep repeating this across the page until it is covered.

5 Outline the tiles with a thick marker and decorate the tiles with a bright pattern.

HELPFUL HINTS

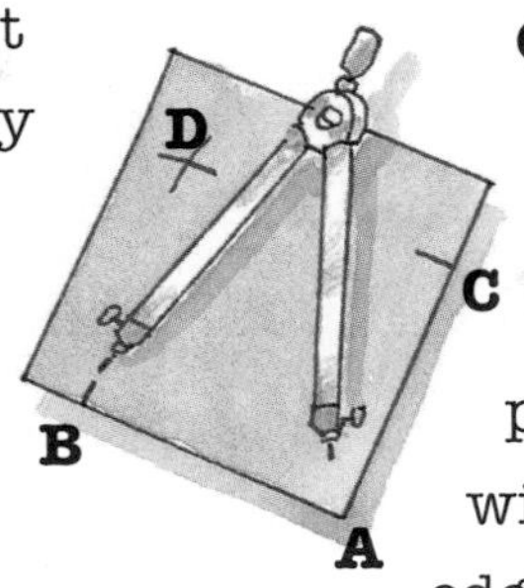

● You can make a square with a compass. Open the arms about 2 in. apart. Place the point at the corner of the page (A) and make a mark with the compass along the two edges of the paper (B and C). Place the compass point on B and mark an arc, do the same on C. Where the arcs cross mark D. Use the ruler to join A, B, C, and D and cut out your square.

MORE IDEAS

● Try making more complex tile patterns by cutting out more than one part of the square.

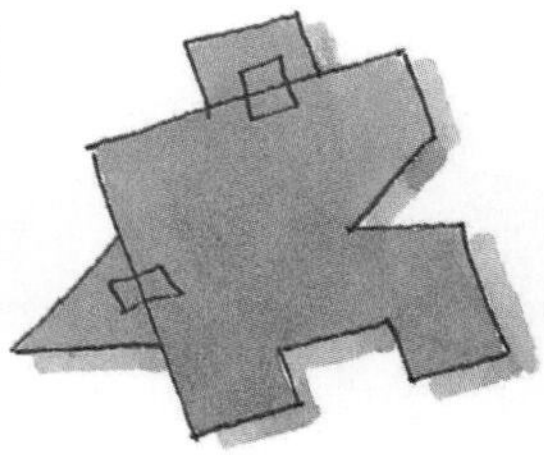

● Make sure you move the part you have cut to line up exactly on the opposite side of the square.

THE THIRD DIMENSION

Shapes that are flat, like squares and rectangles, have two **dimensions**, length and width. Three-dimensional shapes, like cereal boxes and cans, also have height. Some boxes can be opened out and flattened. When this is done you can see the two-dimensional shapes, called faces, it is made from. The flat unfolded shape is the **net** of the box.

FISHING NETS

Find a die. How many faces does it have? What shape are they? There are six square faces. We call this shape a cube. If you could unfold the cube to make a net what would it look like?

1 Make six equal squares from cardboard — these will be the six faces of the cube. Draw a fishing net and fish on each of the faces.

2 Arrange the squares with one or more of their sides together to make a net for a cube. If your net were folded, would it make a cube?

3 Tape the squares on the plain sides and try folding the net into a cube. Does it work? If it does, unfold it again and draw a picture of the arrangement of the squares.

4 Can you find another way of arranging the squares into a net that makes a cube?

HELPFUL HINTS

● A quick way of making a large square is to take the corner of a piece of thin cardboard and bend it over until it reaches the opposite side like this.

● Make a mark where it meets the edge then fold the small piece over so that a straight line is made across the cardboard. Cut along the line to make the square.

Same length

Cut along line

MORE IDEAS

● Draw some nets that you know can be folded to make a cube. Now draw some nets that you know will not make a cube.

● Challenge your friends to figure out just by looking at the nets whether they will make a cube.

5 There are lots of different nets that make a cube. How many can you find?

TRIANGLES

I'm sure you know what a triangle is but did you know how amazing they are? You can use them to make many shapes with any number of straight sides. Take these triangles for a "walk" and see what shapes you can make!

WALKING TRIANGLES

1 Draw a triangle with a ruler on a piece of cardboard. Cut it out carefully. Mark one of the corners with a marker on the front and back.

2 Put your triangle on a piece of paper. The marked corner stays fixed — it does not ever move from that spot. Draw around the triangle.

3 Now, flip over the triangle, keeping the marked point fixed and the edge of the outline touching the cardboard like this. Draw around the triangle again.

4 Keep repeating this until the triangles you have drawn are about to overlap. Draw around the edge of your shape with a ruler and color in the triangles carefully to make some beautiful patterns.

HELPFUL HINTS

● When you draw around your triangle, do it lightly and quickly with a pencil. If you make a mistake, it is easy to erase it later. Remember, you will be going over the lines later with markers and a ruler.

MORE IDEAS

● Don't stop drawing the triangles when they are about to overlap. Keep walking the triangle! What happens to the shape that you make? Go on, get carried away!

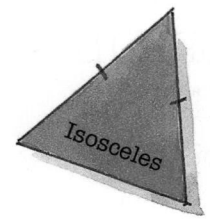

MORE TRIANGLES

Did you know there are different types of triangles?

An isosceles triangle has two sides of equal length — the marks show that sides are equal.

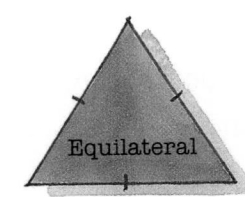

All the sides of an equilateral triangle are the same length.

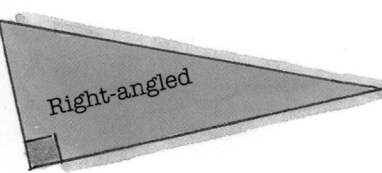

A right-angled triangle has one corner that looks like the corner of a square.

A scalene triangle has no equal sides.

TROTTO!

1 Trotto can be played by two, three, or four players. To play, make 12 cards. On each card draw a triangle, make sure you draw three of each type. Draw in the marks on the equilateral, isosceles, and right-angled triangles.

2 Find a die and cover each face with blank stickers. Write "miss turn" twice, "scalene," "isosceles," "equilateral," "right-angled" on the faces.

3 Deal out the cards. Place them on the floor face up. Take turns to throw the die. If it shows one of your triangles turn it over and pass the die to the next player.

HELPFUL HINTS

● Equilateral triangle: Draw a line and open the compass to the length of the line. Put the compass point on one end of the line and draw an arc. Put the point on the other end of the line and draw another arc. Draw a line

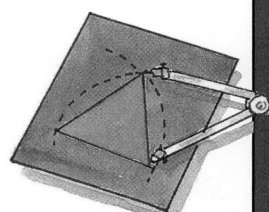

from where the two arcs cross to each end of the line.

● Isosceles triangle: Draw a short line. Open the compass so it is longer than the line. Draw two arcs as you did above. Draw a line from where the arcs cross to each end of the line.

● Right-angled: Make a right angle measurer by folding any sized scrap of cardboard roughly in half. Fold it again so the folded edge meets itself neatly. Draw along the straight edges of your measurer then join the ends of the line with a ruler.

4 The winner is the first player to turn over all their cards!

● Scalene: Easy! Just draw a triangle with no equal sides.

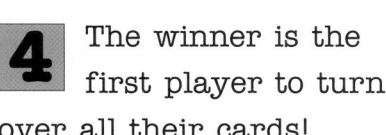

PYRAMIDS

A tetrahedron might sound like an alien from outer space, but it's not! It is a three-dimensional shape, a pyramid with four faces. What makes a tetrahedron special is that all four faces are triangles. It is also called a triangular-based pyramid. You have probably seen other pyramid shapes, like those in Egypt. Square-based pyramids have four triangular faces and one square face.

PYRAMID
SKELETONS!
Dare you attempt
the pyramid
skeleton challenge?

1 If you feel brave enough you will need some straws, scissors, and modeling clay.

2 Cut six straws to about 4 in. long.

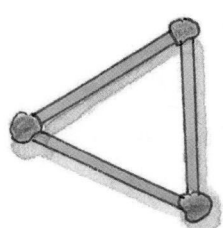

3 Join three straws in a triangle with the modeling clay.

4 Now stick a straw in each of the three corners and bend them over until they meet at the top. Secure them with some more modeling clay.

HELPFUL HINTS

● You don't need to measure each straw with a ruler to get the same length. A quick way of doing it is to cut one to the length you want, then use that straw as a measure against the other straws.

5 You have made the skeleton of a tetrahedron. Can you make the skeleton of a square-based pyramid with eight straws?

MORE IDEAS

● Try making a star skeleton. You will need 36 straws of the same length. Don't make the straws too long otherwise the skeleton might become weak. Make a cube from 12 of the straws.

● On each of the faces make a pyramid with four more straws. In no time you will have made a beautiful star!

CIRCLES

Trace around a plate on some paper and cut it out. You can find the center of the **circle** by folding it in half twice. The center is where the folds meet. Draw a line along the fold that crosses the center of a circle. This line is called the **diameter**. The length of the circle's edge is called the **circumference**.

Diameter

DRAWING DAISIES

1 You can make beautiful flower shapes by drawing circles! All you need is a compass, paper, markers, and pencils.

2 Draw a circle in the middle of a piece of paper. Pick up the compass but don't move the arms! Place the point anywhere on the circumference and draw another circle.

3 Put the point of the compass on one of the places where the two circles meet and draw the third circle.

4 Draw a fourth circle where the edge of two of the circles meet like this. Keep drawing circles until you have made a lovely pattern.

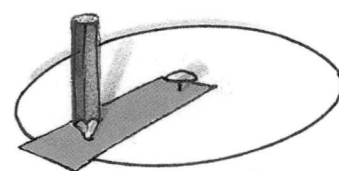

HELPFUL HINTS

● You don't have to have a compass to make these patterns. It is easy to make your own circle drawer!

● You will need a piece of cardboard, scissors, a push pin, and a pencil. Cut out a strip of cardboard. Make a hole with the pin at each end of the cardboard. Leave the pin in the cardboard and push the pencil through the other hole. Now you can draw lots of circles!

5 Now you can decorate your flower with beautiful colors and make a fabulous display!

MORE IDEAS

● Try drawing different patterns. First draw a circle then place the point of the compass on the edge 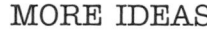 and draw another circle. Draw a third circle where the two meet. Now mark all the points on the edge of the shape where two circles meet and draw three more circles. Repeat this as many times as you like. Do you notice a tessellating pattern?

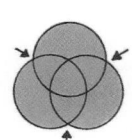

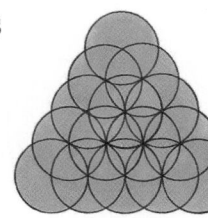

STRETCHING CIRCLES

Shapes can be changed by making them bigger, smaller, and in many other ways, too. One interesting way of changing circles is to stretch them. When a circle is stretched it becomes oval or an ellipse.

MAKING FACES

1 To make faces you need more than your own face and a mirror! Find an old photograph or a picture of a face from a magazine. Make sure the face fills as much of the picture as possible.

2 Place a compass point at the center of the face and lightly draw as large a circle as possible. Cut out the circle.

3 Turn it upside down and cut lines across the circle from one side of the face to the other about six or seven times like this. You could make your cuts straight or wiggly.

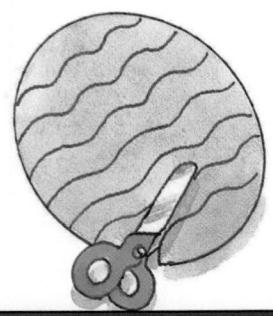

4 Turn the strips face up and put them back into a circle. Now stretch them out leaving the same space between each piece and make a funny face! Stick it onto cardboard.

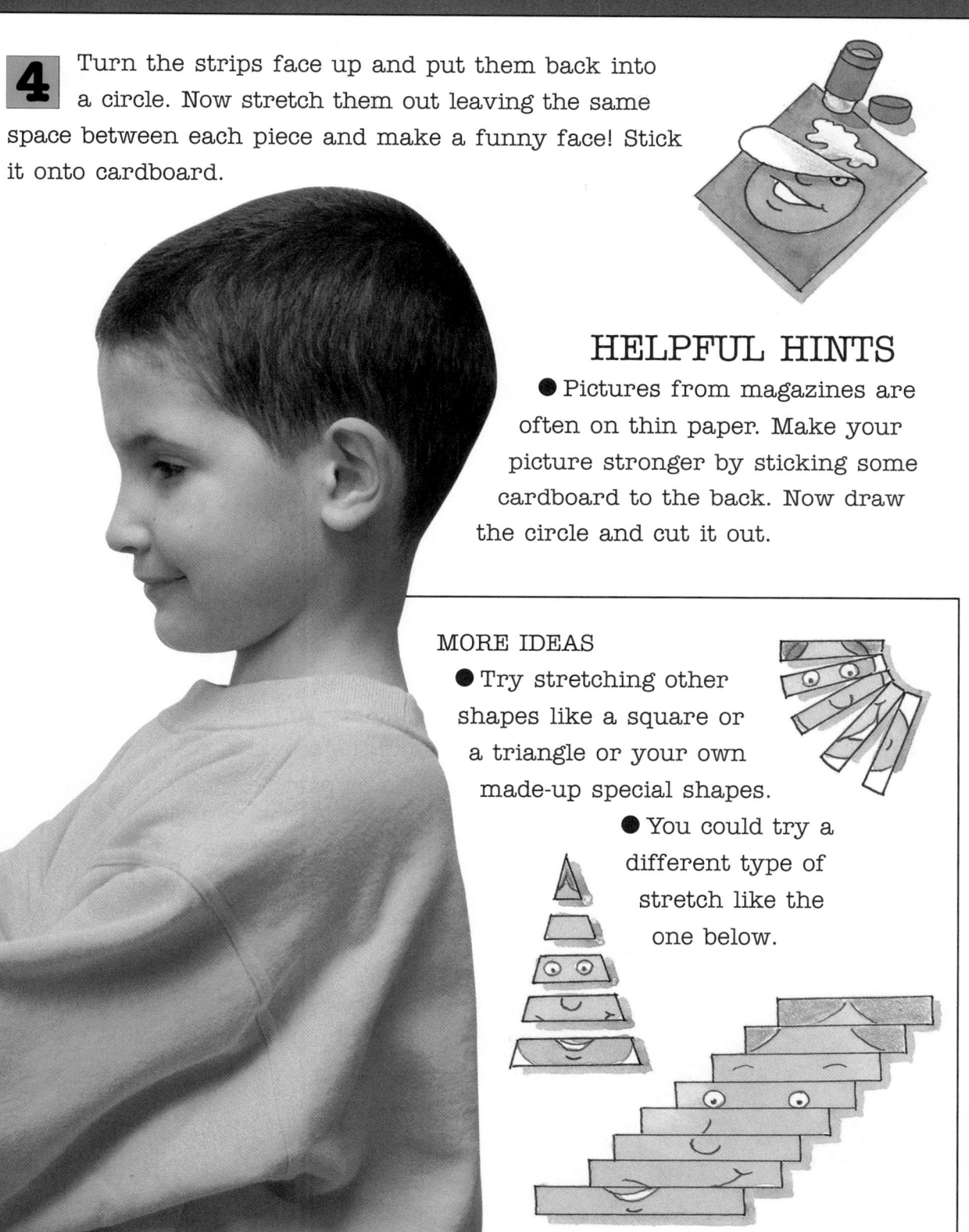

HELPFUL HINTS

● Pictures from magazines are often on thin paper. Make your picture stronger by sticking some cardboard to the back. Now draw the circle and cut it out.

MORE IDEAS

● Try stretching other shapes like a square or a triangle or your own made-up special shapes.

● You could try a different type of stretch like the one below.

CENTERS, SECTORS, AND CONES

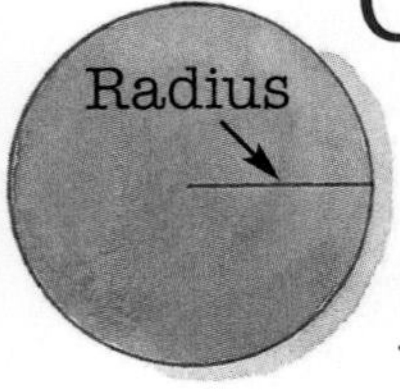

Radius

When you draw a circle with a compass, the compass point is the center of the circle. The distance between the center and the edge of a circle is called the **radius**. If you draw a line from the center to the edge of the circle it will always be the same length. If two lines are drawn it looks as though a wedge of cake has been cut. This wedge is called a sector.

HATS

It is a lot of fun designing party hats! To make your hats you will need plenty of colored cardboard, markers, scissors, tape, a compass, streamers, and shapes to decorate your hats.

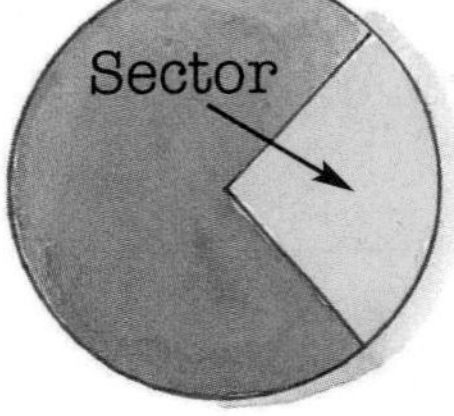

Sector

1 Draw a large circle on some cardboard with your compass. Now draw the radius. Draw another radius. You could make the sector either wide or narrow.

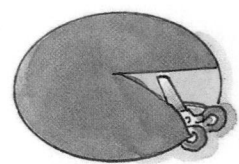

2 Cut out the circle and the sector and carefully stick the edges of the larger sector together like this. You have now made a **cone**!

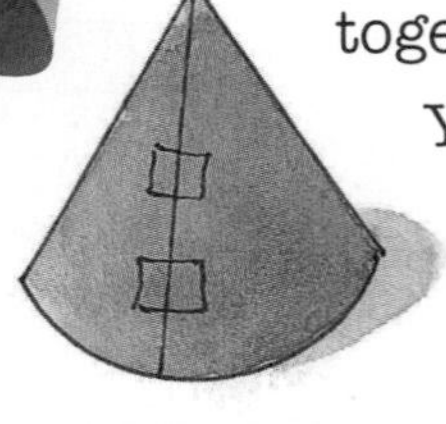

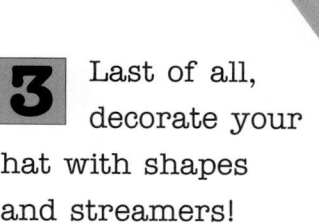

HELPFUL HINTS

● To help the hats stay on your friends' heads make a small hole on the inside of the hat on each side close to the ears. Thread some elastic through the hole. Tie a knot, to stop the elastic from slipping back through the hole, and do the same on the other side.

3 Last of all, decorate your hat with shapes and streamers!

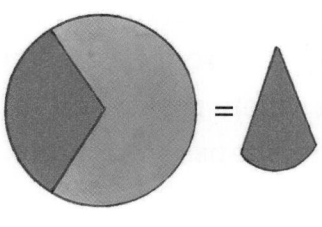

MORE IDEAS

● Experiment by cutting out different sizes of sectors from the circles. How does it change the shape of the cone?

● Cutting out a large sector will make the hat more pointed. If you cut out a small sector the hat will stay quite flat.

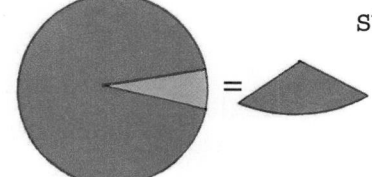

POLYGONS

A polygon is a flat two-dimensional shape with three or more straight sides. Some have special names. A pentagon has five sides. Hexagons have six sides. Heptagons have seven sides. Octagons have eight sides.

FEELY SHAPES
If you don't know the names of shapes, how well can you describe them?

1 Three or more players can play Feely Shapes. You will need some cardboard, scissors, pencils, a ruler, paper, and a bag to hide the shapes you make.

2 Draw some shapes on the cardboard. The lines must be straight but can be any length and the corners can be any angle.

Now cut them out and put them in the bag.

3 One of the players chooses a shape inside the bag. They must keep it hidden and describe it to the other players without looking at it!

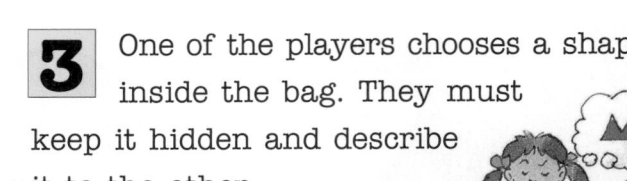

4 The other players try and draw the shape that is being described. When the other players have finished their sketches, take the shape out of the bag.

HELPFUL HINTS

● With some practice you can become very good at describing polygons.

● Try to describe the number of straight sides. Do they feel long or short?

● What do the corners of the shape feel like? Are they very pointed?

MORE IDEAS

● Try playing the same game again, but this time include shapes with curved edges, like circles and ellipses, or your own made-up shape!

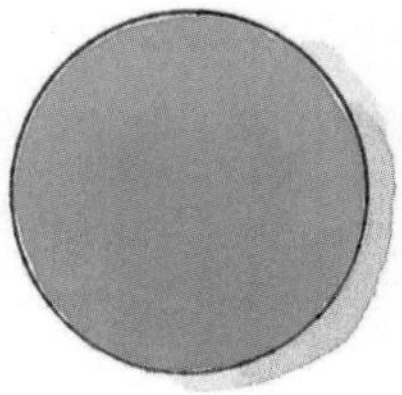

5 The winner is the player that has made the best drawing of the polygon.

TANGRAMS

A tangram is an ancient Chinese shape puzzle, a little like a jigsaw. Some people think tangrams are about 2,500 years old! It is made up of five triangles, a square, and a parallelogram, which is another four-sided shape.

CATS AND DRAGONS

To make the tangram shapes you need a square of thin cardboard, markers, a ruler, and a pair of scissors.

1 Draw a grid of 16 squares on the cardboard like this. Copy the tangram shapes from below with a marker and ruler.

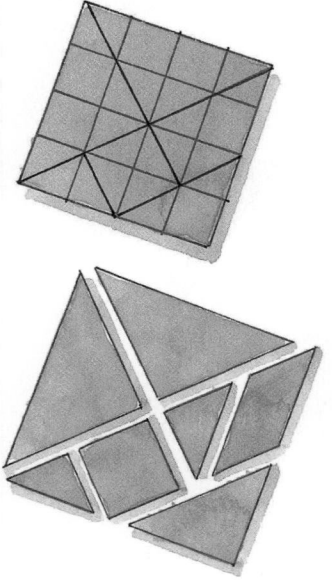

2 Cut out the seven shapes and mix them up. Can you put them back together to make a square? Challenge your friends and see if they can make a square!

3 Perhaps you found that easy! But can you arrange all seven shapes to make a rectangle?

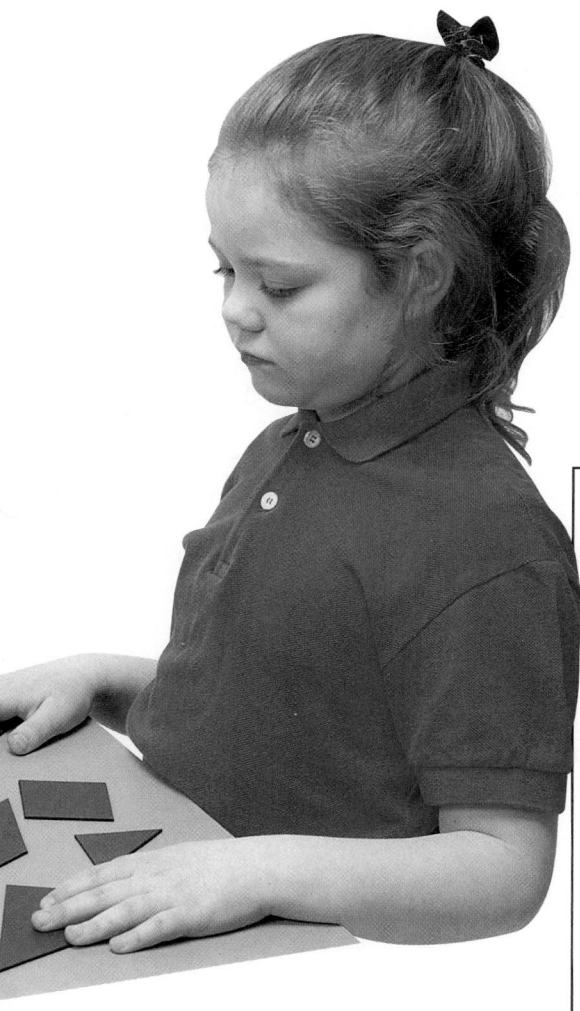

4 Try making a cat shape with the tangram pieces. Remember, you must use all seven pieces.

HELPFUL HINTS

● You can make the grid for the tangram by folding the square piece of thin cardboard in half. Fold it in half again in the same direction. Unfold the square and repeat the folding from top to bottom. Your cardboard is now ready for you to copy the tangram shapes.

MORE IDEAS

● Why not make up your own tangram puzzle? Each puzzle must use all seven pieces.

● First arrange your pieces carefully on some paper. Draw around the outline lightly in pencil.

● Go over the outline again using a ruler and a marker to make it clearer. Last of all, give your puzzle a name like "the dragon" and challenge a friend to match the tangram shapes to your puzzle.

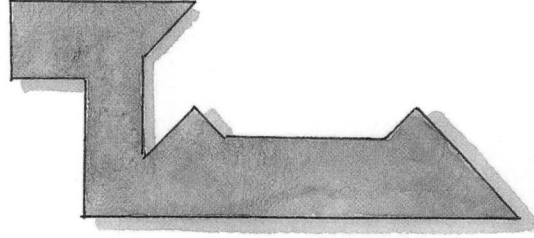

POLYHEDRA

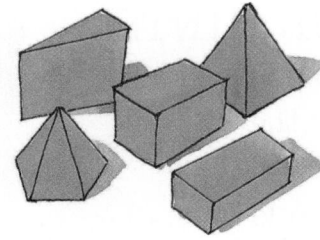

A polyhedron is a three-dimensional shape. It can have any number of faces. A tetrahedron has four triangular faces and a cube has six square faces. How many faces do you think an octahedron has? That's right, eight faces!

BUILD IT!

If you look carefully around your home, you can find lots of different shapes: a box of cereal, a cylinder from the inside of a toilet paper roll, a ball, a die, or cube. Perhaps you have some wooden building blocks.

1 To play Build It! you need two of each shape. Collect about five pairs of identical shapes. If you want to, you could paint them all the same color, but check with an adult first.

2 Now sit back-to-back with a friend. Build a model with all your shapes but make sure your friend can't see!

3 Try to describe how your model is built as clearly as you can. Can your friend match your model exactly?

4 When you have both finished describing and building the model, stand up and look at how well you both did! Do the models match?

HELPFUL HINTS

● It helps to describe the position of each shape. You might say...

the cube is on top of
or
to the right of
or
underneath
or
next to
or
touching the corner of

How else can you help your partner?

MORE IDEAS

● Collect some more three-dimensional shapes and play this fun memory game. Put all the shapes on a table and let your friends have a look. Now have your friends turn away while you remove one of the shapes. Change the position of the remaining shapes then shout "ready!" Your friends now have to try and guess which shape you have taken!

CONTENTS

COMPASS POINTS **676**

MAP REFERENCES **678**

COORDINATES **680**

WHICH WAY? **682**

QUARTER TURNS **684**

ROTATING TILES **686**

ANGLES **688**

DEGREES OF TURN **690**

MORE TURNS **692**

MIRROR, MIRROR... **694**

REFLECTIVE SYMMETRY **696**

ROTATIONAL SYMMETRY **698**

Chapter Six

Plotting Points and Position

COMPASS POINTS

For years sailors and explorers have found their way by following the points on a compass. The magnetic needle always points to the north so you can work out the other directions, south, west, and east. Sometimes, other points are shown in between north, south, east, and west. Halfway between north and west is — you've guessed it, northwest!

PIRATE'S TREASURE!

1 This is a good party game. You must direct the pirate to the treasure! You will need a

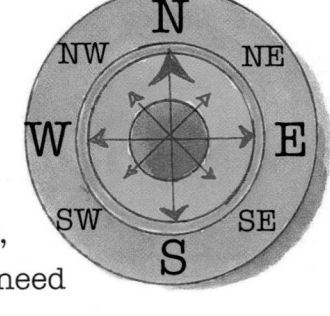

blindfold, a big box of candy for the treasure, a large sheet of paper, and markers.

2 First, you need to make your compass. See Helpful Hints for tips on how to do this.

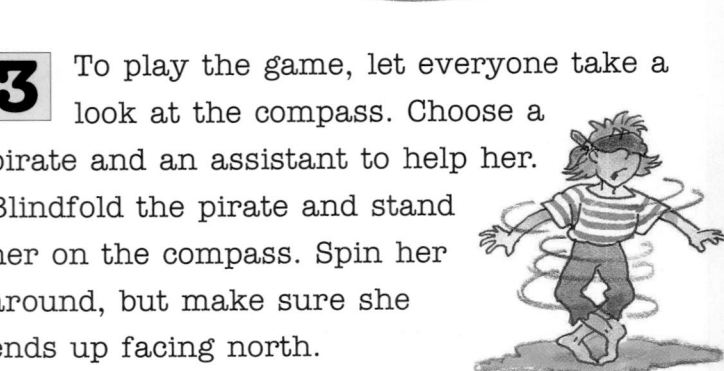

3 To play the game, let everyone take a look at the compass. Choose a pirate and an assistant to help her. Blindfold the pirate and stand her on the compass. Spin her around, but make sure she ends up facing north.

4 Hide the treasure somewhere in the room. Then the assistant must direct the pirate to the treasure. He might give directions like, "Turn east and take two steps forward. Now turn northeast and move four steps ..." How long does it take to find the treasure?

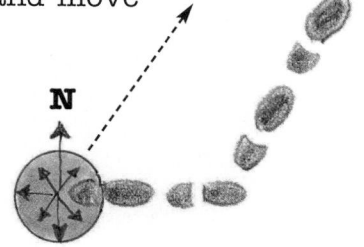

HELPFUL HINTS

● One way to remember where the different points of the compass are is to compare them to a clock face. If north is at 12 o'clock, then east is at 3 o'clock, south is at 6 o'clock, and west is at 9 o'clock.

● Another way is to make up a phrase for the letters N, E, S, and W, the initials of the main points on the compass as you move around clockwise. **N**eptune **E**ats **S**ea **W**eed is one. Can you think of another?

● You can make your own compass by folding a piece of paper into quarters. Now fold in half again to make a triangular shape like this. Unfold the paper. Now you can draw in all the compass points and decorate it to look like a real pirate's compass!

MAP REFERENCES

Finding somewhere on a map could be quite a problem, but luckily map makers make it easier for us. They draw a grid of criss-crossing lines over the map and in between each line is usually a letter or a number. Each part of the map can now be found by a reference or address.

CUP CRAZY
Can you use map references to find some candy?

1 You will need markers, a ruler, candy, cardboard, and 16 plastic cups. You could paint them so you can't see through them.

2 Draw out a grid of 16 squares on the cardboard and place a cup upside down on each square. Label the squares A, B, C, and D along the bottom and label the numbers 1, 2, 3, and 4 up the sides.

3 Secretly hide a piece of candy under one of the cups and ask your friend to guess where it is. They have to guess using a reference, for example, C2. You reply either "hot" if they have guessed correctly, "warm" if they are just one cup away, or "cold" if they are farther away.

4 How quickly can you find the candy?

HELPFUL HINTS

● It is a good habit to get used to saying the letter reference first and then the number as this is the usual way that map references are used.

A2 or C4

MORE IDEAS

● You could play the same game but with even more cups!

● How many can you find? Make sure you ask an adult first before you borrow them for the game. They don't have to be laid out in a square — what about a rectangular grid?

● You could also play the game by hiding more than one candy; try two or three.

COORDINATES

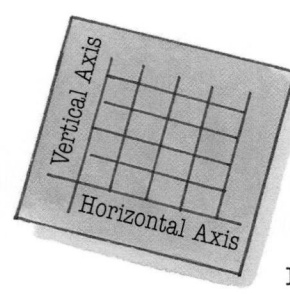

Coordinates are used to plot points on a graph. On a flat, two-dimensional graph a pair of numbers, for example (5,1), is used to show a position. The first number shows how far to move along the **horizontal axis** and the second number shows how far up the **vertical axis** the point is.

CONNECTIONS

1 Connections is a game for two players where you use coordinates to score points. You will need some cardboard, a ruler, markers, two dice, and two different sets of colored counters.

2 Make a game board like the one above. Make all the lines about 1 inch apart. Put a 0 where the lines meet then 1-6 on each axis.

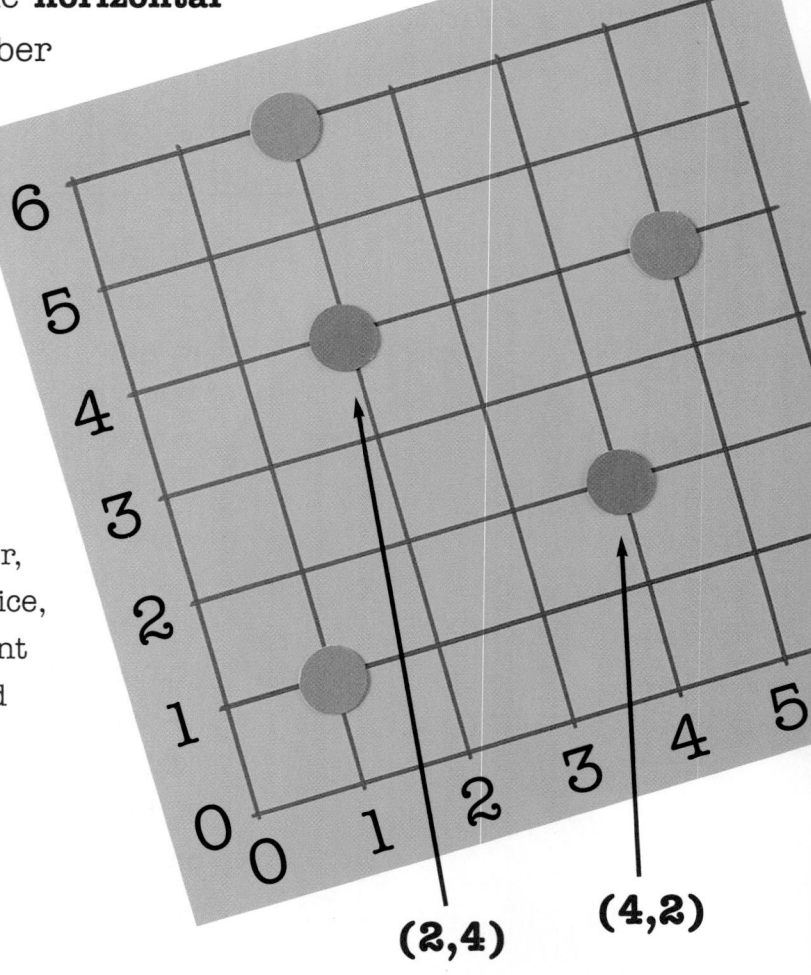

(2,4)   (4,2)

3 The first player throws the two dice. If a 4 and a 2 are thrown, you can choose to place a counter on either (2,4) or (4,2).

4 Now the second player must throw the dice and place their counter in an empty position.

2 points

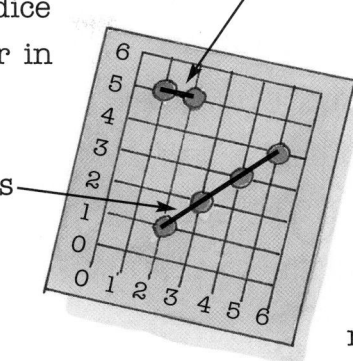

4 points

5 Every time you can place a counter, score one point. If you make a line of two counters, score two points. A line of three scores three points and so on.

6 Keep a record of your scores on a chart. The player with the highest score after 12 turns wins.

HELPFUL HINTS
● If you find it difficult to remember which coordinate comes first, you might find it helpful to think of it as "along the hall," for the first number and "up the stairs" for the second!

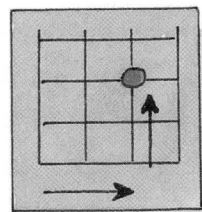

MORE IDEAS
● X Marks the Spot is a great coordinates game. You can play with the Connections grid.
● The first player secretly decides the coordinates of their hidden point, (2,2) for example, writes it on some paper, and puts it in an envelope.

● The other player guesses where it is — let's say they guess (4,4).
● Now the first player gives a clue by saying how many straight line spaces away their secret X point is. You can't count diagonal lines. In this example it is four spaces away.
● How quickly can you find where X marks the spot?

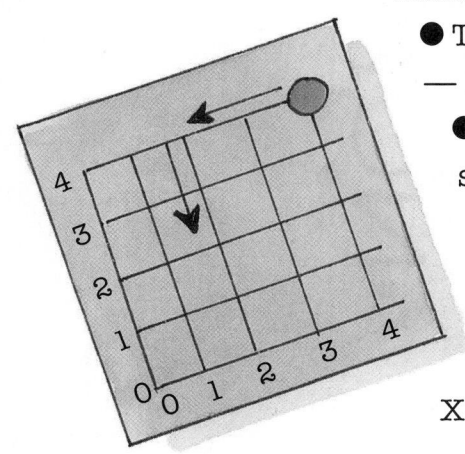

WHICH WAY?

Have you ever been lost in a maze? Mazes are full of right and left turns, and a lot of dead ends. The secret of escape is knowing which direction to take!

MINOTAUR MAZES

In Greek legend, a beast called the Minotaur lived in a maze. The maze was so complex no one ever escaped!

1 You can make your own Minotaur Mazes. You will need a large piece of plain paper, play dough, paint, and pencils.

2 Roll the play dough out into long, thin sausages. These will be the walls of your maze.

3 Place the thin rolls on the paper with some right and left turns like this.

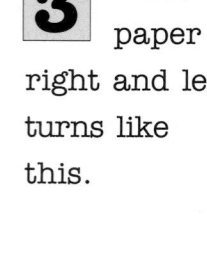

4 Make sure you leave an entrance to the maze and an exit. How difficult can you make the maze?

5 When you are happy with your maze, paint over the paper and play dough walls.

HELPFUL HINTS

● When you paint over the paper and play dough don't make the mixture too wet. It can leak under the play dough so it becomes difficult to see where the walls are.

MORE IDEAS
● The Celtic people also loved mazes. Many of their designs were curved like this one.
● Can you make a maze with curves to fit inside a circle?

6 Let the paint dry then remove the play dough. Draw around the edges of the walls to make them stand out clearly and challenge a friend to escape through your Minotaur Maze!

QUARTER TURNS

When people talk about turns they often mean a quarter turn to the left or a quarter turn to the right. A quarter turn is a little like the turn between the edges on the corner of a square.

WRAPPING PAPER PRINTS

This is a great way of using turns to make wrapping paper. You will need some large potatoes, paint, a ruler, a pencil, a knife (ask an adult first), and as big a sheet of paper as you can find.

1 Cut the potato in half like this. With a dark pencil make a design on the base of the cut potato.

2 Ask an adult to help you to use the knife to cut away the potato.

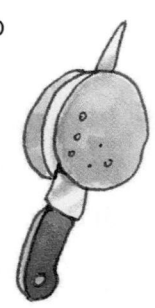

Leave the design standing out.

3 On the top of the potato make a "V" shape to show the direction of your potato printing block. Now you are ready to print!

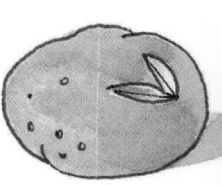

4 Choose a color and cover your block design with paint. Start at the top left of your sheet, making sure the "V" arrow is pointing directly toward you, then gently press the potato onto the sheet.

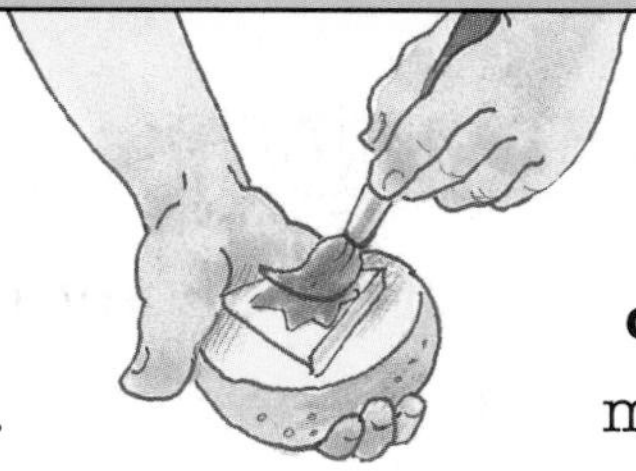

5 Now turn the potato a quarter turn **clockwise** like this and make another print in the next square.

6 Keep repeating the pattern of turns until you cover the whole sheet.

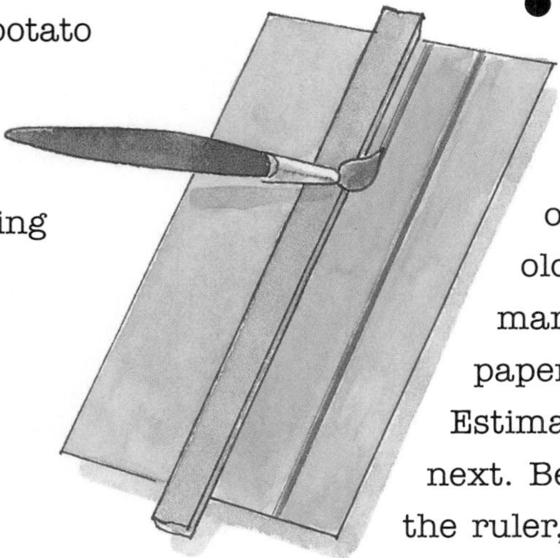

HELPFUL HINTS

● The pattern may look better if you space the prints evenly. You can make guidelines as part of the pattern by using an old ruler and a paintbrush or markers. Rest the ruler on the paper and paint or draw a line. Estimate where to put the ruler next. Be careful how you pick up the ruler, it might smear the paint on the paper!

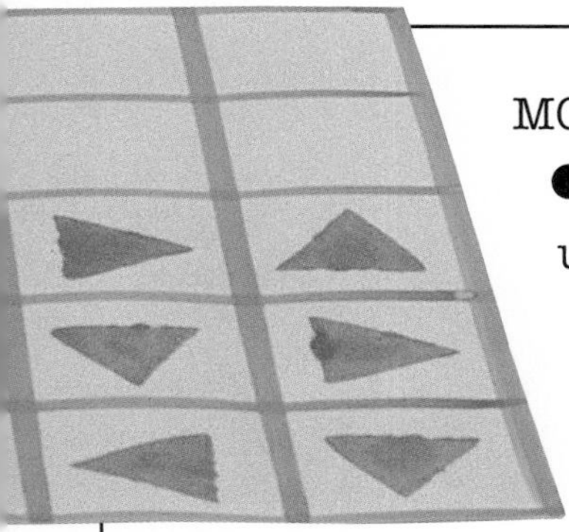

MORE IDEAS

● You could make the pattern more interesting by using two colors.

● Why not try using different potato block designs to create more unusual patterns.

ROTATING TILES

People from many countries around the world love using tile patterns in their homes and on buildings. Some of the swirling patterns look very complicated, but are quite easy to make if you follow the pattern of turns carefully.

BLOCKS

1 You will need a block of wood about 2 inches long and 2 inches wide, scissors, a pencil, a ruler, thick string, strong glue, paint, and paper.

2 Mark the top of the block with an arrow so you will be able to see which way it is pointing when you are making prints.

3 On the other side make two marks on each edge of the block evenly spaced 1 inch apart.

4 Next, cut some short lengths of string and stick them on the block. Make sure that the beginning and end of the string lead from one of the marks on the block to another.

5 Cover the string in paint and press firmly onto the paper. Pick the block up carefully, rotate it a quarter turn clockwise, and repeat the print in the next square. Keep repeating this until the grid is full.

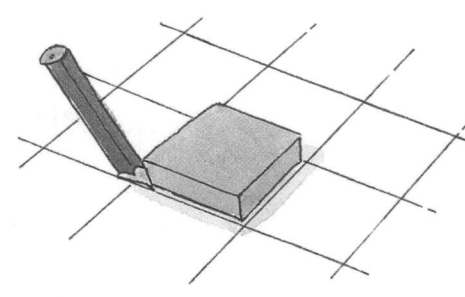

HELPFUL HINTS

● To make your block printing as accurate as possible you might find it best to begin by drawing out the square tile pattern. Using your block, trace around the outline then move the block to the first outline and keep repeating.

MORE IDEAS

● Make some more designs, but this time glue the string in straight lines from one mark to another like this. Sticking the string in straight and curved lines also produces some interesting effects. Try experimenting with different designs and different patterns of turns (or rotations).

ANGLES

A quarter turn is also called a right angle. A square has four right angles and so does a rectangle. A right angle can be measured as having 90 **degrees**. Angles of less than 90 degrees are called acute. Those of more than 90 degrees are called obtuse angles.

ANGLING

1 Are you good at angling? To play this game you need to make 18 game cards. Draw angles on the back, make sure you draw six of each angle (acute, obtuse, and right). Why not draw a fish on the back? Helpful Hints gives advice on how to draw the angles.

2 The object of the game is to win as many cards as possible by collecting matching angles.

3 Shuffle the cards and lay them out flat in the "pond." The first player turns over three cards.

4 If they are all the same type of angle, you win the cards. If they are not all the same, turn them back over, try to remember where they are, and the next player has their turn. The player with the most cards at the end wins.

HELPFUL HINTS

● Start by making a right-angle tester. Find a scrap of cardboard and fold it in half and half again. Make sure when you make the second fold that the folded edges meet and are straight.

● Right Angles: Draw a straight line with the ruler. Sit your tester straight on the line and then mark the right angle against the side of your tester. Mark the corner with a small square.

● Acute Angles:
Make sure the angle between the two lines is less than a right angle. Rest the tester on one of the straight lines. If it covers all of the angle then the angle is acute.

● Obtuse Angles: When you use the tester you will be able to see some of the obtuse angle.

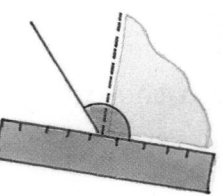

MORE IDEAS
● Half a turn is 180 degrees (see page 690). Angles greater than half a turn are called reflex angles. They look bent back on themselves! Make six reflex angles and add them to the pond.

Reflex angle

DEGREES OF TURN

Do you remember that the angle between two lines can be measured in degrees. There are 360 degrees in one whole turn. Half a turn is 180 degrees and a quarter turn is 90 degrees.

1 Pull the arms of a compass about 2 inches apart and draw a circle on some cardboard. Draw a smaller circle about half the size inside it then cut out the large circle.

2 Choose a different color cardboard, make a circle with the compass arms at 1.5 inches apart, and cut that out, too.

3 Lightly mark the center of both circles and draw a straight line from the edge to the center of the circles. Now, cut along each line.

WHAT'S THAT ANGLE?
How good are you at estimating angles quickly? To play this game you need to make an angle measurer.

690

4 Copy the degree measurement marks around the circle you have drawn on the larger circle from this example.

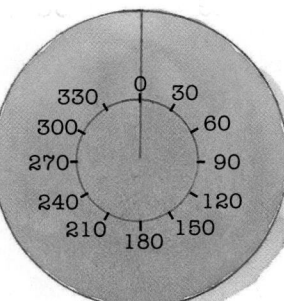

5 Slide the two circles of cardboard into each other so they overlap and the numbers are hidden. Ask your friend to find an angle. They put their finger on the angle measurer, estimating where it is.

6 Turn the smaller circle around to the finger and see if they have guessed correctly!

HELPFUL HINTS

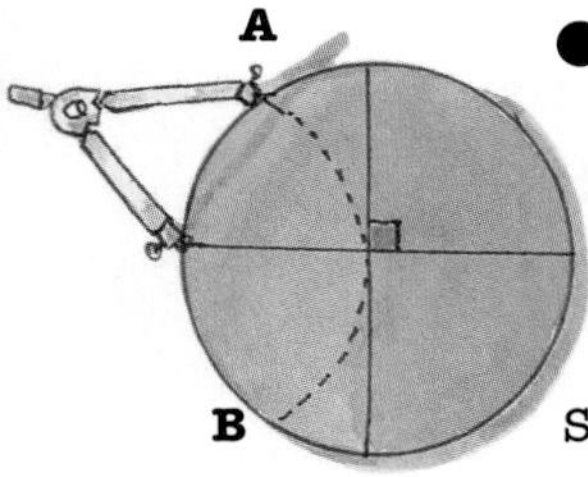

A

B

● To mark the degrees accurately on your circle follow these steps.

● After you have drawn the smaller inside circle don't move the compass arms. Draw a cross on it. Place the compass point where the cross meets the edge of the circle and make two marks on either side of the circle (**A** and **B**).

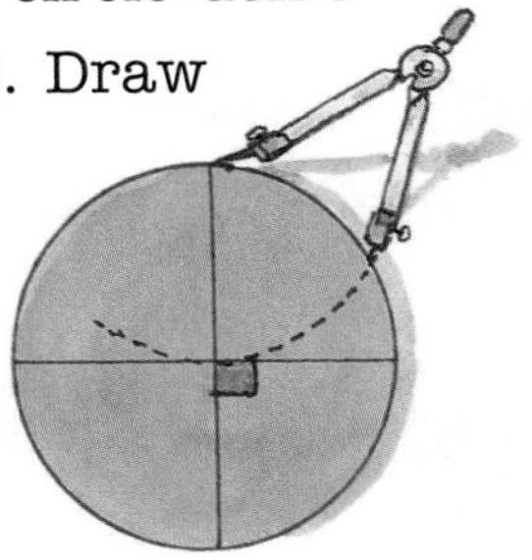

● Repeat this on the other three points where the cross meets the circle. Draw a line from each mark through the center of the circle to the other side.

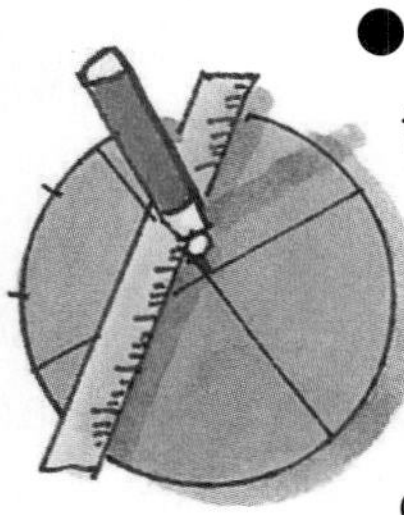

691

90° MORE TURNS

If you have looked at the activities on the last few pages, you will know that the angle of turn between two lines is measured in degrees. Mathematicians usually write degrees as a little circle in the air next to the number like this, 90°.

TREASURE TROVE

1 This is a great game for 2 or 3 players. Draw out the Treasure Trove grid onto some cardboard, using the hints on page 691 to help mark the angles accurately. Decorate it with bright colors.

2 Now make two sets of 20 cards. For the first set you need to mark the cards 0, 1, 2, or 3. For the second set mark the cards 0 to 9.

3 Find a treasure, like some candy, to place on each sector of the board. Now, you are ready to play!

4 The players take turns to draw one card from the first pile and two from the second. This gives a degree measurement. If it is 248° for example, they would pick up the treasure between 240° and 270°. The player who collects the most treasure wins.

HELPFUL HINTS

● If the first card you draw is a 0, it looks as if you have drawn a strange-looking number like 062°! You can ignore the 0, so the degree you have picked would be 62°.

MORE IDEAS

● You could play the same sort of game, but this time design your circle like a pizza! Cut out the 12 sectors of the circle and instead of winning the treasure in the sector you take away that part of the pizza!

30°
60°
90°
120°

MIRROR, MIRROR...

Look at your reflection in a mirror, it is exactly the same as you, except it is back to front. When a shape is reflected it might look very different or exactly the same, it depends on where you put the mirror. If it looks the same, the mirror is on a **line of symmetry.**

HALVE IT!
You might be able to draw a face, but can you draw just half?

1 Draw a straight line down the center of a piece of paper. This is your line of symmetry where you will place a mirror after you have finished drawing.

2 Draw half the face on just one side of the line.

3 It might help to fold the paper in half along the line you have drawn so you don't accidentally draw on the wrong side.

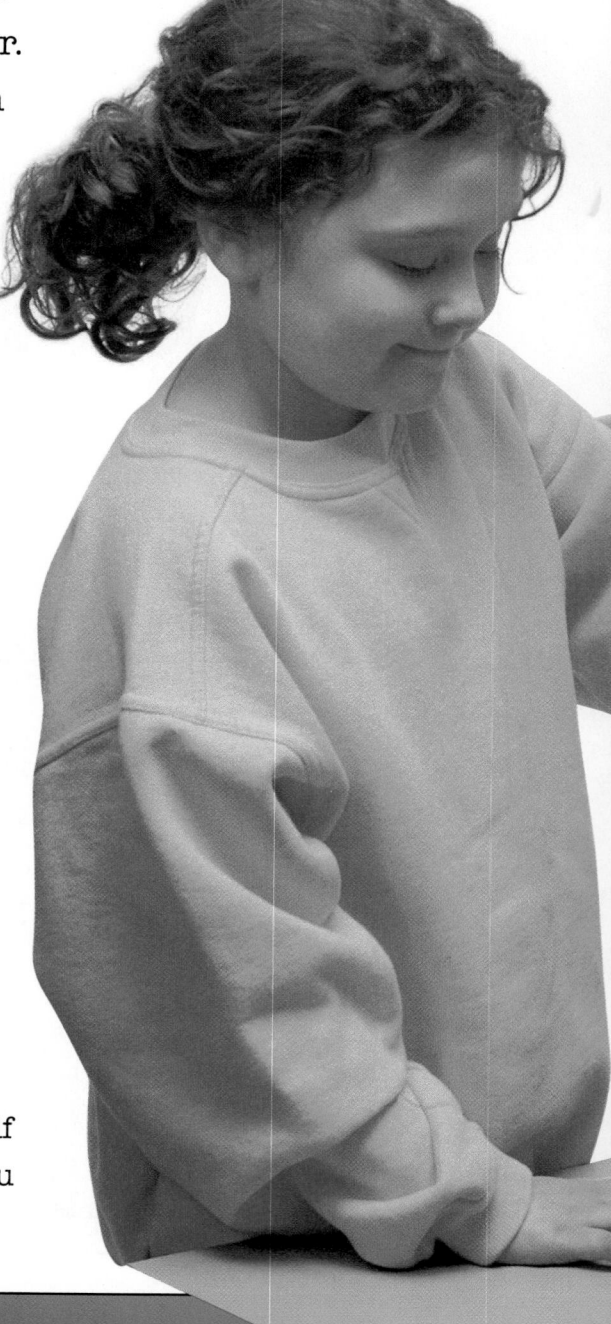

4 When you have finished your picture, put a mirror along the line of symmetry and look into it. You will see a face with two sides that are exactly the same, making a whole symmetrical face.

HELPFUL HINTS

● Before you start to draw the face, look at your own face in a mirror. Hold a large book up across half your face like this.

How many eyes can you see? Ears? How much of your mouth can you see? What about your nose?

MORE IDEAS

● A famous Italian inventor and artist named Leonardo da Vinci used to keep a diary. He wanted to keep his thoughts secret so he wrote it in mirror writing, back to front! It was hard to read.

● Can you write your name in mirror writing? Try it and check by holding it up to a mirror.

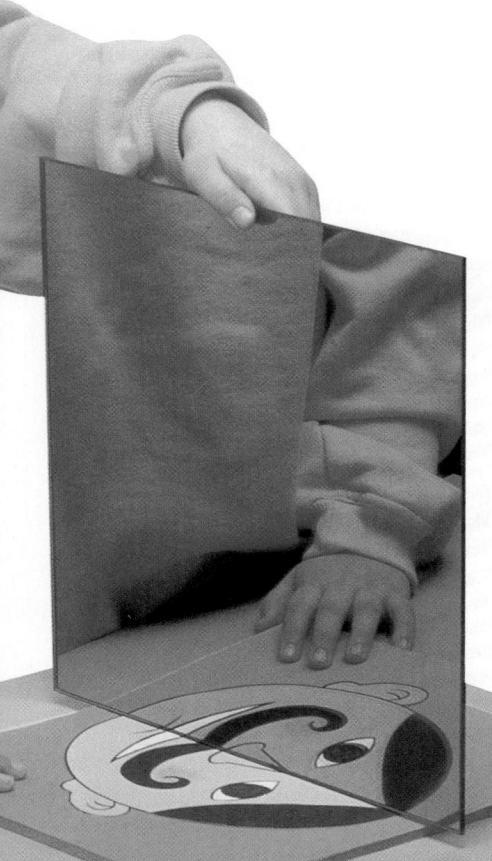

REFLECTIVE SYMMETRY

Some shapes have more than one line of symmetry. This means you can put the mirror in more than one place and the shape will still look the same. A square has four lines of symmetry, a rectangle has two.

BUNTING BONANZA!

Have you ever seen bunting at a fair or a party? There are usually long lines of repeating symmetrical patterns. Often each shape in the pattern is a reflection of the one before it.

1 It is fun making these patterns — you could make one to decorate the border of a bulletin board or frame one of your pictures.

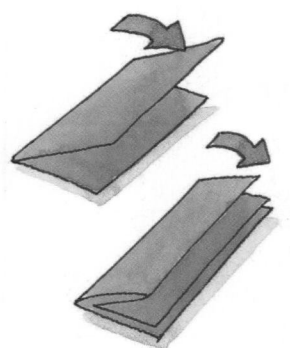

2 Fold a piece of paper in half twice like this. If you have a long piece of paper, you can make more folds.

3 With the paper still folded cut off a square from one end. Draw a shape in pencil on the paper — what about the outline of a person?

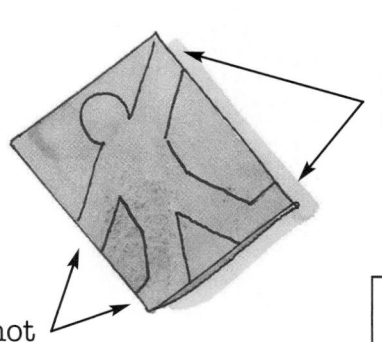

Do not cut here

Do not cut here

HELPFUL HINTS

● When you draw your design, you need to make sure that it touches both sides of the square where the folds are. If you don't, when you cut out the shape all the bunting will fall into pieces!

4 Now cut out the shape while it is still folded. Get an adult to help you with this. Don't cut the sides where the shape meets the edges. Then unfold the paper, lots of perfect mirror images of your original shape will appear!

MORE IDEAS

● This is a great way of using reflective symmetry to make place mats for a party. Draw around a large plate and cut it out. Fold it in half and again and once more like this. Now, use the scissors to cut out small parts. When you have finished, unfold the shape and admire your handiwork!

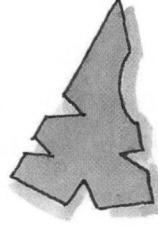

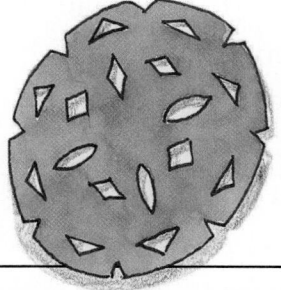

ROTATIONAL SYMMETRY

If a shape is moved around a central point and still looks the same when it is in its new position, we say it has **rotational symmetry**. A square has rotational symmetry of order 4 because it can be rotated four times into a different position but still appears to be the same.

IN A SPIN

You can make some amazing shapes with rotational symmetry.

1 Draw a shape on some cardboard no bigger than your hand. It might have curves or straight lines or a mixture of both. Don't make it too complicated, it might be difficult to cut out!

2 Cut out the shape and pierce it roughly in the middle with a push pin. You might need an adult to help you with this.

3 Put the shape in the middle of some paper and draw around it lightly. Rotate it around the push pin a quarter turn so it is facing to the right and draw around it again. Repeat this with the shape facing you then with it facing to the left.

4 Lift the shape and the push pin off the paper and use a thick marker to draw around the edge of the new shape you have created. This new shape has rotational symmetry of order 4. You will find that it can be rotated to four different positions and still look the same.

HELPFUL HINTS

● When you are rotating the shape on the paper, put a thick wad of newspaper underneath, otherwise the pin might make a hole in the table!

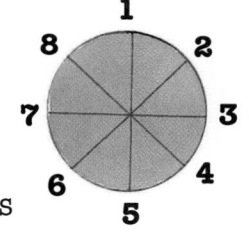

MORE IDEAS

● It is easy to make shapes with rotational symmetry of order 8. Imagine the eight points of a compass like this.

● Make a new small shape and rotate it to face each of the eight points of the compass. Draw around the edge, or perimeter, and then cut it out and mount it as you did before.

Original shape

5 Cut out the shape, turn it over so you can't see the pencil lines, and stick it on a sheet of colored paper to make it look good.

699

CONTENTS

LENGTH OF A LINE **702**

MEASURING CURVES **704**

VITAL STATISTICS **706**

AREA **708**

MEASURING AREA **710**

CALCULATING AREA **712**

PERIMETER **714**

AREA AND PERIMETER **716**

TO THE MAX **718**

VOLUME **720**

CAPACITY **722**

VOLUME OR CAPACITY? **724**

Chapter Seven

Measuring Sizes

LENGTH OF A LINE

How tall are you? How high can you reach? To answer questions like these we need to measure length. People used to measure length by counting up the number of hand lengths... but everyone's hands are slightly different. Now most people use a **standard measurement** like feet to measure length.

MAKE A DERBY
Can your horse be first past the winning post?

1 Find a piece of cardboard. Fold it in half lengthwise and cut it along the fold. Do the same again with another piece of cardboard and stick the four parts together to make one long strip.

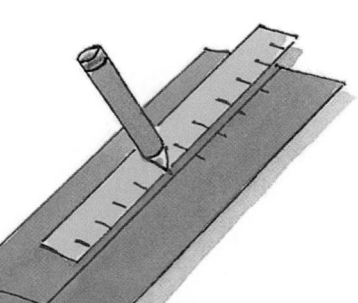

2 Starting from the bottom of the cardboard, use a ruler with inches to draw a straight line up the middle.

3 Mark in all the inch spaces on the line from one inch at the bottom to 12 inches, which makes one foot, at the top.

4 Now you can decorate it to look like a race course. Make a winning post from some cardboard and stand it at one end. Cut out two cardboard shapes of horses and riders and decorate them brightly.

HELPFUL HINTS

● To make a neat seam, turn over the cardboard. Place the strips next to each other, but not overlapping. Cover the seam with some tape. Now turn it over... a perfect finish!

5 Cut out a rectangle of thick cardboard for each horse to stand on. To make the horse stand up, attach it to the base with two pieces of play dough.

MORE IDEAS

● You can make the game even more fun by making some danger cards!

● If somebody throws a 1, they must pick up a card. The message might say "Horse frightened by mouse, miss a turn" or how about "High fence, go back 4in!"

6 Place your horses at the start and take turns to roll the die and move your horse forward. The first past the post wins!

MEASURING CURVES

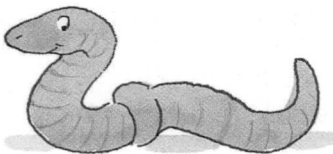

The difficult thing with rulers is that they are always straight. Unfortunately, most of the world isn't. In fact, it is wonderful how wiggly and bendy the world is. Without bumps and curves the world would be a far less interesting place! So, how can you go about measuring them?

WIGGLY WORMS

How good are your friends at guessing the right length of straight lines? What about wiggly lines? Make some wiggly worms to find out!

1 Find some string or thick colored cord and measure out some different lengths against a ruler. You could cut lengths of 2, 4, 6, and 8 inches.

2 Stick the lengths of string in a wiggly line on pieces of cardboard. These will be your worms. Now draw around each worm on the cards and decorate each worm to look really slimy!

3 Write the length of each worm on the back of the cards so you don't forget.

4 in.

8 in.

4 Challenge your friends to guess the length of each worm. The person that makes the nearest guess is the winner!

HELPFUL HINTS

● If some of your friends find it hard to make a good guess, you could show them how to use a "rule of thumb" to help. Strangely enough, with this "rule of thumb" you use your little finger! Most little fingers are about .25 in. wide so you can use it to move along the back of the worm to estimate its length.

MORE IDEAS

● Why don't you try estimating the length of edges! If you have got some old vegetables, cut them in half and draw around the edge on a piece of paper. Guess how long each edge is and write it down.

● You can find out how long the edge really is by using some string to match along the edge of the outline and mark off the length. Next, straighten the string and measure its length against a ruler and check to see how close you really were!

VITAL STATISTICS

"You have grown so tall!" Whenever you meet someone who hasn't seen you for a while it's usually the first thing they say. Sometimes, people call measurements of the body the vital statistics. You need to know yours to find clothes that will fit and comfortable shoes.

SKELETONS

You can make a skeleton to show your vital statistics!

1 Find some cardboard and cut it up into long strips.

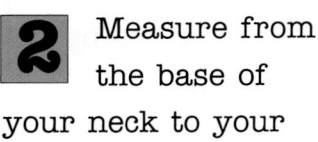

2 Measure from the base of your neck to your hips with a tape measure. Tape some strips together to match the measurement. This will be the backbone. Write this on the strip so you don't forget.

3 Now measure the width of your hips. Cut a strip to match and attach it to the other strip with a butterfly pin. Put the pin through both pieces of paper and bend the arms back. Ask an adult to help you with this.

4 Measure other parts of your body and pin them all on to make your skeleton! How many parts can you include? What about your fingers and toes?

HELPFUL HINTS

● You could draw a stick figure first to show the parts of your body you are going to measure. As you measure each part, write it down on the stick figure picture.

● You can then cut all the strips of cardboard to the right length and join them together. You could make some strips thicker to make your skeleton more realistic.

● You can add a skull to your skeleton by measuring around your head with a tape measure. Make a strip to match the length, loop it over, and stick it together.

● Do the same again, measuring around your head from top to bottom. Loop the strip around and stick it to the first skull loop.

● Make a bright face from pieces of cardboard and stick this onto the head with tape.

AREA

Have you ever had new tiles put into your bathroom or kitchen? We call the space you want to cover, the **area**. Often the tiles are square shaped and this is how the size of an area is measured — in squares.

TILE FLIPPING

To win this game you need to capture the area covered by the tiles by flipping all the squares over to your color.

1 Find two pieces of different colored cardboard the same size. Stick them together back to back. Draw a square grid on the cardboard with lines about 1 in. apart. The squares will be your tiles.

2 Cut out 16 tiles. Now you are ready to play the game.

3 Turn the tiles so that eight are showing red and eight are green. Arrange them in a square.

4 The first player is the green team. He rolls a die. If a 3 is rolled, then three cards are turned over from red to green.

HELPFUL HINTS
● When you stick the cardboard together make sure you cover the whole sheet with a thin layer of glue. If you don't, some of the tiles might fall apart when they are cut into squares.

5 Now it is the red player's turn. He has one throw and turns back the number of cards shown on the die from green to red.

MORE IDEAS
● To play Tile Flipping you arranged the 16 square tiles to make a bigger square shape. What other numbers of tiles can you find that can be arranged to make a square? You could try four tiles, but there are others, too. These are special numbers that are called square numbers!

6 The die is then passed back and the battle to win all sixteen squares continues until one of the players captures them all!

MEASURING AREA

Like measuring length, not everything in the world comes in straight lines or simple squares that are easy to count and measure. Most areas that need measuring come in all sorts of unusual shapes.

BIG FOOT?
What do you think covers the greatest area, your foot or your hand? Take a quick look at them and press one against the other.

1 Draw a grid of squares on a piece of paper with your ruler. Helpful Hints tells you how to do this if you are stuck.

2 Place one of your feet on the grid and get a friend to draw around it with a bright marker. Color in the shape of the foot so you can see it clearly.

3 Do the same again on another grid with your hand.

4 To find the area of the foot, count all the whole squares inside the print.

but not one like this.

5 Next, count all the squares that are more than half covered by the print. You would count a square like this...

6 What is the total area covered by your foot? Now count the squares covered by your hand. Which is the largest?

HELPFUL HINTS

● To make the grid of squares, line your ruler up with the edge of the paper and draw a straight line. Move the ruler along the paper so that the edge is now resting on the line you have just drawn. Draw a new line and repeat this across the page. Do the same moving across the page in the other direction like this to make the squares.

MORE IDEAS

● Why don't you find out the area covered by your mom or dad's foot?

● Make a guess and then find out. But watch out, they may have smelly feet!

CALCULATING AREA

You can't always find the area of something by counting squares! Sometimes, it is easier to calculate area by using multiplication tables. If you need to find the area of a rectangle all you need to do is multiply the length by the width. So, for a rectangle that has sides of 2 in. and 4 in. the area is 2 in. x 4 in. = 8 **square inches**!

AREA ARITHMETIC
To be good at this game your friends will need good estimation skills and a good memory for number facts.

1 Plan some rectangles to draw on a piece of scrap paper.

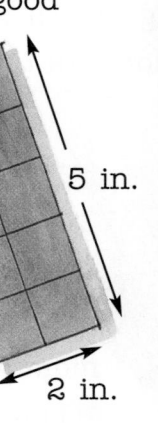

5 in.

2 in.

2 The first one might be 2 in. long and 5 in. wide, so the area would be 2 in. x 5 in. = 10 square inches.

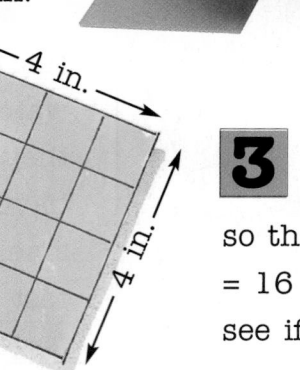

4 in.

4 in.

3 The second might be 4 in. long and 4 in. wide, so the area would be 4 in. x 4 in. = 16 square inches. It is easy to see if you mark off the squares.

4 Make about ten different rectangles and draw them on cardboard. Don't mark in the individual squares. Mark each rectangle with a letter. Write the answers on a piece of paper and hide it from your friend.

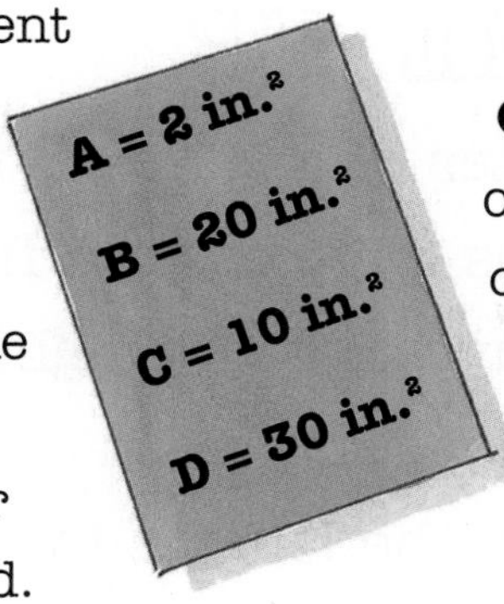

A = 2 in.²
B = 20 in.²
C = 10 in.²
D = 30 in.²

HELPFUL HINTS

● To make it easier for some of your friends to play, you could draw a square inch on the corner of each card to help them with their estimates.

1 square inch ────→

5 Now, challenge your friends to estimate the area of each of the rectangles. The person who estimates most accurately wins!

MORE IDEAS

● Have you noticed that some rectangles look different but have the same area?

● A rectangle with sides of 3 in. and 6 in. and one with sides 9 in. and 2 in. long both have the same area because 3 in. x 6 in. = 18 square inches and 2 in. x 9 in. = 18 square inches.

● Make up a new quiz. This time make all the rectangles different shapes but the same area. Do you think your friends will notice your trick?

PERIMETER

The perimeter of a shape is the line that goes around its edge. It is quite easy to figure out the perimeter of some shapes with straight edges. You can measure the length of each edge with a ruler then add up the lengths to find the total. The lengths of each side of this triangle are 3 in., 4 in., and 5 in. The total length is 3 in. + 4 in. + 5 in. = 12 in.

STRING SHAPES
This is a fun way of making lots of strange and unusual shapes that all have the same perimeter length.

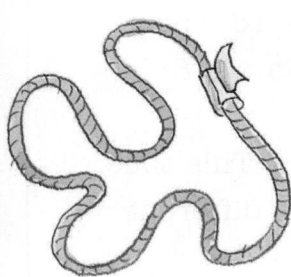

1 Measure out a piece of string about three feet long. Join the ends of the string with a piece of tape like this.

2 Find a large piece of paper and put the string on it. Now, arrange the string to make an interesting shape. Make sure the string doesn't loop over itself.

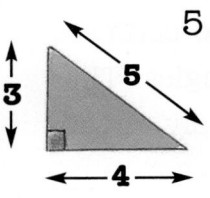

3 Now, draw close to the outside edge of the string lightly with a pencil. Take the string away and paint the area on the inside of the perimeter your favorite color.

4 Now, paint the outside a different color. Wait until the paint dries and then go over the perimeter again with a thick black marker to make it stand out.

5 Try making a new shape with the same piece of string — something that looks completely different. The perimeter will still be the same!

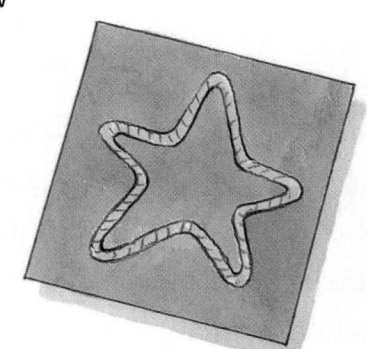

6 Whatever shape you have made with the string, the perimeter will always be three feet!

HELPFUL HINTS

● To make it easier to draw around the string on the paper without it moving, you could stick down parts of it with some play dough.

MORE IDEAS

● Can you make all the letters of your name in turn with the three-foot piece of string as the perimeter?

● You could make each letter on a separate piece of paper then decorate them to make them look colorful.

AREA AND PERIMETER

The perimeter goes all the way around a shape. The inside of the shape is called the area. Some shapes have the same area but the length of the perimeter may be longer or shorter, it doesn't always stay the same.

SQUARE SHUFFLING
Can you shuffle eight squares to make the longest possible perimeter?

1 When you have made eight square cards try an arrangement. One side of each square must touch one side of at least one other square.

2 If you arranged the cards like this, the perimeter would be 14 sides long.

3 What is the longest perimeter you can make?

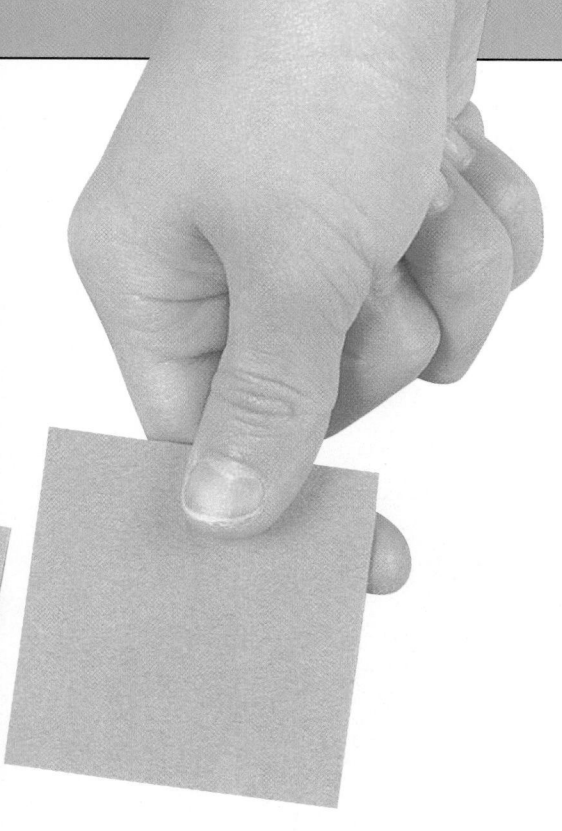

4 If you think you have found the longest perimeter try to find the shortest!

HELPFUL HINTS

● A quick way of making a square from a piece of cardboard is to gently fold over one of the corners to touch the side edge and then make a mark where it meets. Then fold over the end to that mark and make a sharp crease like this. Cut along the crease and you have a square.

Cut along crease

MORE IDEAS

● You can make the longest perimeter in lots of different ways. Here is one way of doing it.

● Did you find any others? Can you see how arrangements of squares that give the longest perimeter are similar? They all spread out the squares so that as many edges as possible of each square are part of the perimeter.

● Now you know this rule, can you quickly find a shape with twelve squares with the longest perimeter possible? It should have a perimeter 26 sides long. What would be the longest perimeter you could make if you used 24 squares?

TO THE MAX

One problem mathematicians often face is how to get the maximum out of something. Knowing how to find the maximum amount of area when the perimeter has to stay the same is very useful for solving lots of practical problems.

THE FARMER'S FENCE
Can you help the farmer to fix his fences so that he can make as much space for his chickens as possible?

1 The farmer is poor and can only afford 16 panels of fencing. The fences will only join together in a straight line or at right angles.

2 The farmer decides to make a plan. You could use old burned matches, **but make sure you ask an adult first.**

3 He started by laying out the fences like this. The area inside the perimeter of the fence is ten squares.

He tries again. This time the area is worse! Only nine squares.

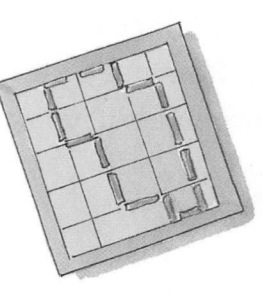

4 Can you find a better way of arranging the perimeter fencing to make the greatest possible area for the farmer's chickens?

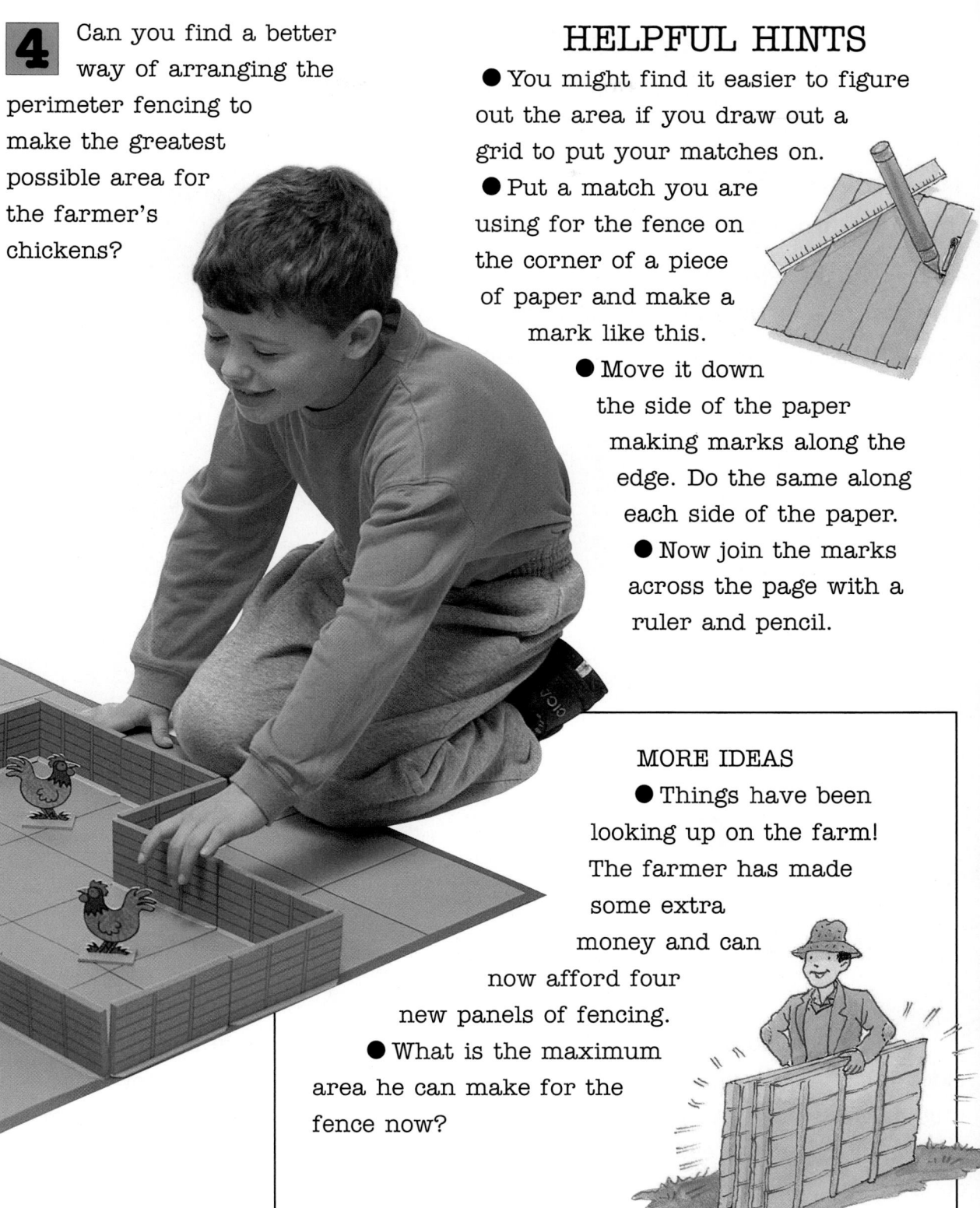

HELPFUL HINTS

● You might find it easier to figure out the area if you draw out a grid to put your matches on.

● Put a match you are using for the fence on the corner of a piece of paper and make a mark like this.

● Move it down the side of the paper making marks along the edge. Do the same along each side of the paper.

● Now join the marks across the page with a ruler and pencil.

MORE IDEAS

● Things have been looking up on the farm! The farmer has made some extra money and can now afford four new panels of fencing.

● What is the maximum area he can make for the fence now?

VOLUME

You might have heard your mom or dad suggest that you "turn the volume down and play quietly!" When mathematicians use the word **volume** they are not talking about the amount of sound that is made. The volume of a shape is the amount of space it takes up. It is often measured in **cubed inches**.

1 in.

MAKIN' AND SHAPIN'
Can you shape a cube of play dough into amazing monsters?

1 First of all, try making one cubed inch. Draw a square inch on a piece of paper as above.

2 Roll some play dough into a ball. Use two rulers to squash the sides until it fits the square. Keep doing this to all the sides until you have made a cube. You might have to add more dough or take some away to make each side of the cube fit the square.

3 Now you have made a cubed inch it doesn't matter what you do to it, squash it, pinch it or push a hole through it — it will always be one cubed inch.

4 But one cubed inch is a little small. Draw out a square 5 in. by 5 in. This makes an area of 5 in. x 5 in. = 25 square inches.

5 When you have made this larger cube it will be 5 in. x 5 in. x 5 in. = 125 cubed inches. You can make some amazing monsters with a volume of this size!

HELPFUL HINTS

● Remember that the volume will only stay the same size if you keep all the play dough together.

● If you start to take pieces off the volume will be smaller. If you add pieces on it will become larger.

MORE IDEAS

● It is amazing how large the volume of some small shapes can be.

● To find the volume of a cube you have to multiply the length of the edge by itself and then once more. So, the volume of a cube that has edges 2 in. long would be 2 in. x 2 in. x 2 in. = 8 cubed inches. What is the volume of a cube with edges of 10 in.? What about 99 in.? You may need a calculator to figure out this one.

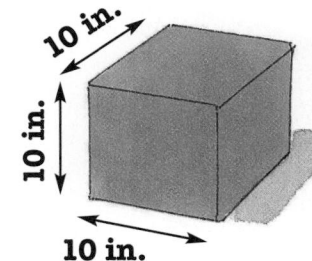

10 in.
10 in.
10 in.

CAPACITY

A ten-gallon hat was meant to have the **capacity** to hold ten gallons of water! Capacity is the way we measure the amount of substance a container will hold.

FILL IT UP!

How good are you at estimating the amount of water you need to fill up different containers?

1 Ask an adult if you can borrow some different empty containers like bottles and cups from the kitchen. Now find an old bottle top and get a large jug of water.

2 How many full bottle tops of water do you think it will take to fill up the cup for example?

Container	Estimate	Actual
Cup	24	
Egg cup	9	
Bottle	300	

3 Write down all the different containers on a score card and make an estimate of the number of full bottle tops you think each one will hold.

4 Now try filling the cup carefully. How many can it take before the water spills over the top? Write the total down on the scorecard. The person who makes the best estimate is the winner.

HELPFUL HINTS

● This can be quite a wet and messy game! It is a good idea to do the filling or pouring over a sink. If it is easier on a table put a towel down and place the containers on it to save everyone from getting soaked!

MORE IDEAS

● Ask an adult if you can borrow a measuring jug from the kitchen.

● You can play a similar game with cups. Fill a cup up to the brim and tip all the water into the jug. If you look on the side of the jug, you can see the measuring marks. These might be in fluid ounces, marked fl.oz., pints, marked pt., or gallons, marked gal. See if you can estimate how far up the measuring jug the water from a different size cup will go when you pour it in. How accurate can you make your estimates?

VOLUME OR CAPACITY?

Volume and capacity are similar. Volume is the amount of space occupied by an object and capacity refers to the amount of substance a container can hold. The capacity of a bottle holding 16 fl. oz. does not change, but if you gulp some of the drink the volume of liquid is less.

WATER MUSIC

Some musical instruments make use of different volumes of air to make different notes. You can make your own bottle orchestra.

1 Ask an adult if you can borrow a glass bottle and a measuring jug. Tap the bottle with a pencil and listen to the sound it makes.

2 Try pouring in different volumes of water. Perhaps 8 fl. oz. first.

3 Tap the outside of the bottle with a pencil. How has the sound changed? Yes! it is a higher note. Try 16 fl. oz., then 24 fl. oz. How is the sound affected now?

4 Try gathering some other glass bottles and make each have a different note. Can you make up a tune?

HELPFUL HINTS

● It is easier if you use bottles that are exactly the same. When you have found the amount of water in the bottle that gives you the note you want you can keep a record of what you have done by tipping all the water back into the measuring jug and writing down the amount.

● Take a look at the number of fluid ounces you used and write it down, so when you play your composition for bottles and orchestra you will know exactly how much to pour into each container!

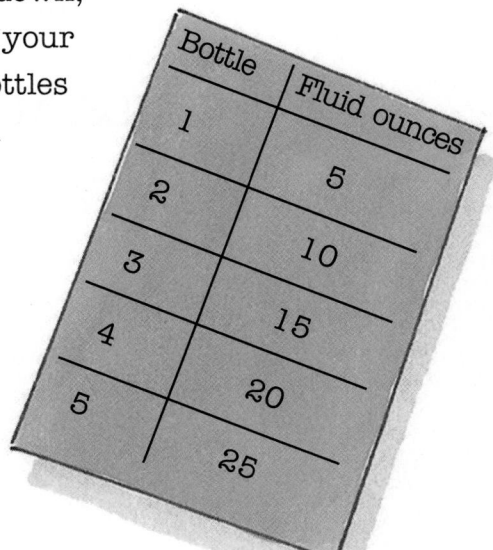

Bottle	Fluid ounces
1	5
2	10
3	15
4	20
5	25

CONTENTS

WEIGHT **728**

POUNDS **730**

OUNCES **732**

TIME **734**

MEASURING TIME **736**

JUST A MINUTE **738**

WHAT DID YOU DO TODAY? **740**

DIGITAL CLOCKS **742**

SECONDS, MINUTES, HOURS... **744**

Chapter Eight

Measuring Weight and Time

WEIGHT

How heavy is an elephant?
How about a mouse?
How heavy is the lump
of cheese in your refrigerator? We can
measure how heavy things are by weighing
them. Sometimes, the weight of an object
is called its **mass**, and we can
measure it in ounces (oz.) or
pounds (lb.).

SLIMMING SNAKES
Did you know the weight
of an object never changes,
no matter what shape it is?
Make these snakes and find
out for yourself.

2 Roll the play
dough with your
hands to make a short,
fat snake.

1 Choose your favorite
play dough color.
Measure 5 ounces on
a **scale** and roll the play
dough into a ball.

3 Put it back on a scale
and weigh it again. How
much does it weigh now? Yes!
Exactly the same... 5 ounces.

4 Keep rolling out the snake. How thin can you make it?

5 Every so often, weigh it again on the scale. It always weighs the same!

HELPFUL HINTS

● Remember that you must not let any part of your snake break off, otherwise the weight will change. This is quite tricky when the snake gets very skinny!

MORE IDEAS

● Weigh out another 5 oz. of play dough and make another animal, perhaps a dog. Although it looks very different from the snake, they both weigh exactly the same.

● Now make the body of an elephant with your new piece of play dough. Measure out another 3 oz. of dough of a different color or colors. Use this for the legs, ears, tail, and trunk. What do you think the elephant will weigh? That's right, it will weigh 8 ounces because 5 oz. + 3 oz. = 8 oz.

6 It doesn't matter how fat or thin you make the snake, the weight never changes.

POUNDS

Most heavy things in the house, like your mom or dad, are weighed in pounds. Can you find out how many pounds they weigh? How many pounds do you weigh?

HOW MANY?

You can play this guessing game with your friends. Do you know how many ounces make one pound? It's sixteen! This can be written in figures like this...

16 oz. = 1 lb.

1 First, decide what you are going to weigh. You need to estimate how many of each item it will take to make 1 pound. Make scorecards for each of your friends and write down your estimates.

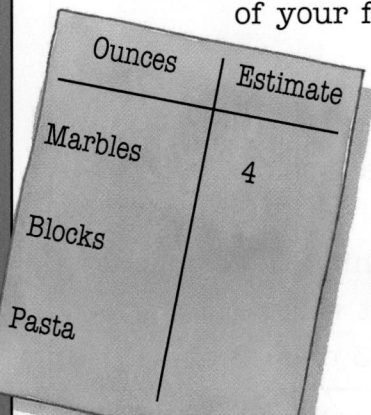

Ounces	Estimate
Marbles	4
Blocks	
Pasta	

2 Now collect the objects to weigh and the scale you are going to measure with.

3 If you are estimating the number of marbles needed to make 1 pound, then take turns with your friends to keep adding one more marble at a time... and watch the weight slowly rise!

4 When the scale shows 1 lb., stop and count the number of marbles on the scale. The player that made the best guess is the winner!

HELPFUL HINTS

● If you are measuring with a bathroom scale, you will need a lightweight container to hold the things you are weighing.

● To be good at this game, it helps to get a feeling for a pound. Take a look in your kitchen cabinet. Sugar, rice, and other foods are often sold in weights of 1 lb. Make sure you ask an adult before you start looking!

MORE IDEAS

● Now that you are good at estimating the numbers of different things that make 1 lb., you can play Combo Crazy! Choose any two of the objects you have been weighing. Can you combine some pasta and marbles to make 1 lb.? How close can you get to a pound?

OUNCES

Which is heavier: an ounce of feathers or an ounce of nails? They are both the same! The feathers take up more space, but they weigh the same.

If something is large, it doesn't mean that it is always heavier than something small. If you remember this, it will help you to play human scale.

HUMAN SCALE

1 Choose about ten things from around the house. What about a cushion, a cup, a book... perhaps you can think of some other interesting items. Write the name of each object on a piece of paper.

2 Now you need to be a human scale! Which do you think is the heaviest object? Put it on the right-hand side of the table.

3 Which do you think is the lightest? Place that on the left. Can you put everything else in order, from lightest to heaviest?

4 Now you can find out how good you are as a human scale! Start with what you think is the lightest object and weigh it on a scale. How many ounces does it weigh?

Shoe 7 oz.

Cushion 6 oz.

Cup 5 oz.

5 Write the weight on a card and put it next to the card of the object.

6 Do the same for all the other objects. How good were you at getting everything in order?

HELPFUL HINTS

● There are lots of different scales you could use. Some are easier to understand than others. You could ask an adult to help.

● If you use a kitchen scale, you can choose light and heavy objects. When using a bathroom scale, choose heavier objects only.

MORE IDEAS

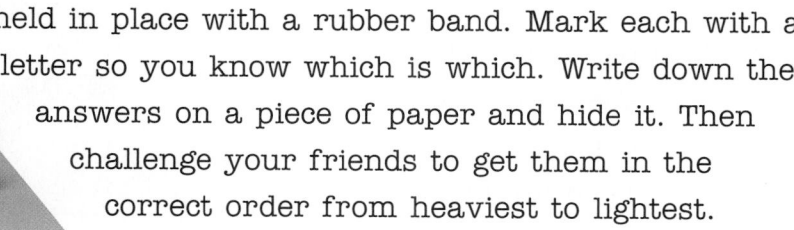

● You can play another game like this with old containers. Measure 2 oz., 3 oz., 4 oz., 5 oz., 6 oz., and 8 oz. of rice into six containers. Cover each with a paper napkin that can be held in place with a rubber band. Mark each with a letter so you know which is which. Write down the answers on a piece of paper and hide it. Then challenge your friends to get them in the correct order from heaviest to lightest.

TIME

Who is the fastest? How long does it take to travel into town? Since the beginning of time people have been trying to measure time! In the past people used other ways of measuring time. They looked at shadows made by the sun on sun dials, and at night they watched the speed at which candles melted to measure time.

DRIP, DROP, TICK, TOCK
One way you can measure time is by using a water clock. You can make your own water clock to measure exactly one minute.

1 Find a large glass jar and stick a white strip of paper to the side like this.

2 Find an old dishwashing liquid bottle with a cap, and carefully cut off the bottom half. You will need an adult to help you with this.

3 Make sure you have a clock with a second hand ready.

4 Put some play dough at the neck of the bottle. Make a small hole in it. Make sure the cap is screwed on tightly. Fill the bottle with water from the bottom.

5 Hold it over the jar. When you are ready, take off the cap so the water starts to trickle into the jar. After one minute, mark on the paper the level the water has reached in the jar.

6 If the water is still running through after two minutes, make another mark. When it has finished, you have made a water clock that you can fill with water and use as a timer.

MORE IDEAS
- You can play dress-up races using your water clock as a timer!
- See if you can find an old hat, shirt, pants, and some of your mom or dad's shoes. Can you or your friends put them on before the water trickles through up to the minute mark?

MEASURING TIME

How many different watches or clocks are there in your house? What do they have in common? Clocks usually have a short hour hand and a long minute hand. Some may have a second hand, too. We measure time in seconds, minutes, and hours.

TIME FLIES

You can play this game with a friend. The object is to start your clock at 6 o'clock and be the first to reach 9 o'clock.

1 To make your clock, draw around a large plate on some cardboard and cut it out. Copy the hours from this example onto your circle.

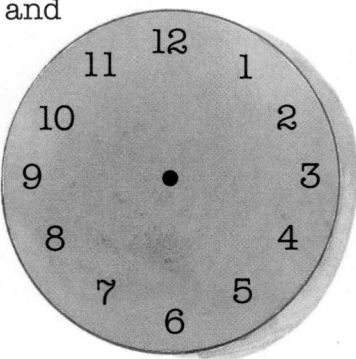

2 To make the hands, cut out two strips of cardboard. Make one longer than the other. Use a paper fastener to push through the hands and the center of the clock face. Set the hands to 6 o'clock.

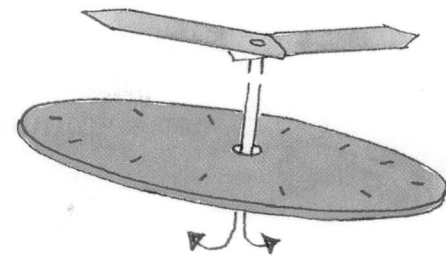

3 Think up activities that take 5, 10, 20, or 30 minutes. Make 25 cards and write the different activities and times on them.

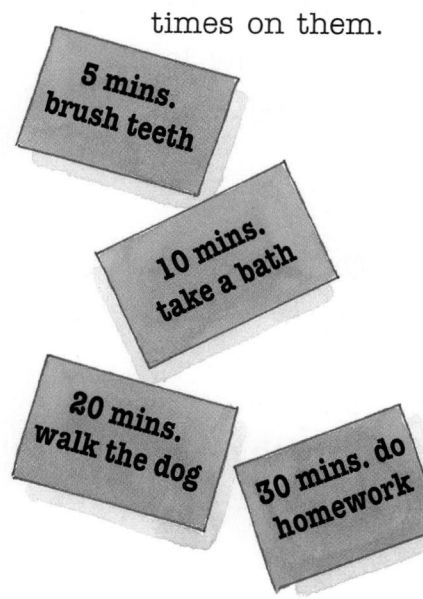

5 mins. brush teeth

10 mins. take a bath

20 mins. walk the dog

30 mins. do homework

4 Take turns to take a card from the pile. Move your clock hands around the amount of minutes shown on the card. The first to reach 9 o'clock wins the game.

JUST A MINUTE

"Just a minute…" "Wait a minute." People use sayings like these all the time, but why does a minute never seem the same length as the minute you are thinking of?

A minute is the same as sixty seconds — that's easy to remember! But it doesn't always help us to feel how long a minute is!

TIME UP

This is a good game to help you feel how long a minute is.
You can play the game with two or more friends. You will need a watch with a second hand.

1 The player in charge of the watch says "Go!" The other players have to guess when they think a minute is over.

2 When you think a minute has passed, you must raise your hand high in the air.

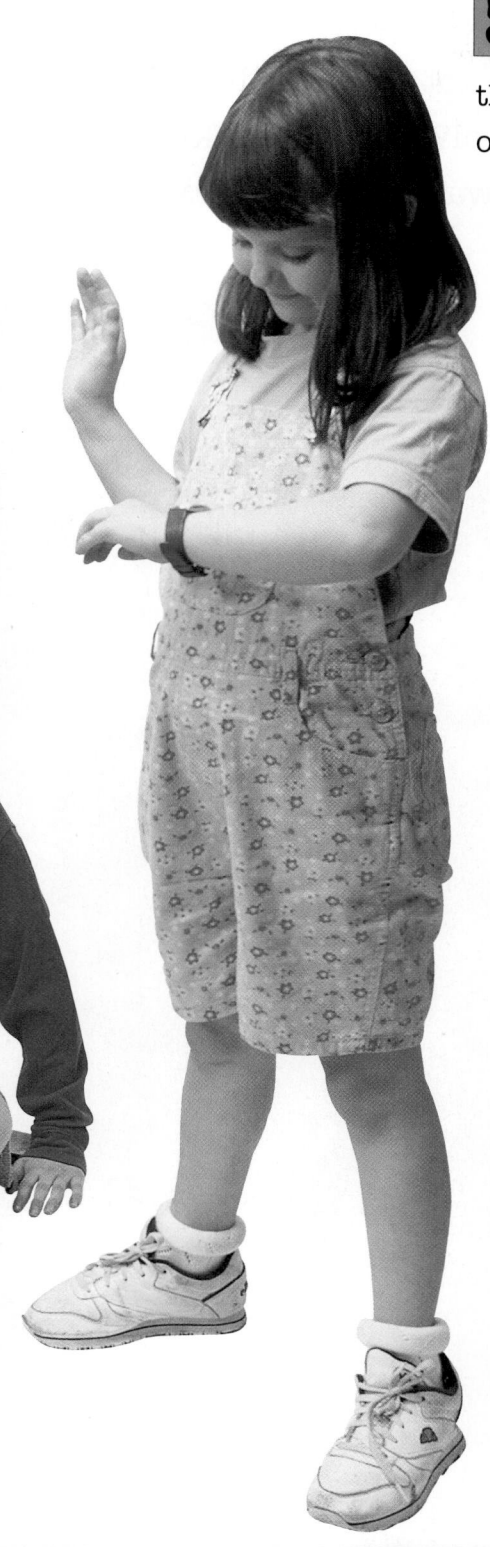

3 When the minute is over, the person with the watch shouts "Time is over." The people who have not already raised their hands are out.

4 The winner is the last person to raise a hand before the minute is over.

HELPFUL HINTS

● The second hand on a clock is the one that moves the quickest. When the hand has moved around a full circle, one minute has passed.

● Sometimes, it is easiest to start timing the minute when the second hand reaches the 12, and then stop when it comes around to the 12 again.

● It may be hard to count out a minute in your head. It can help if you add a long word, like "elephant," in between each number you count. If you count "one elephant, two elephant, three elephant" this might help you to count seconds more accurately.

WHAT DID YOU DO TODAY?

Why do parents always want to know what you've been doing at school? Don't they know that after a hard day all you want to do is play! Some people keep a note of the activities they do each day in a book called a diary.

ACTIVITY WALLCHART

You could chart what you do each day in a diary and turn it into a colorful wallchart. You will need some cardboard, paper, scissors, pens, and a ruler.

7am	4pm	1am
8am	5pm	2am
9am	6pm	3am
10am	7pm	4am
11am	8pm	5am
12 noon	9pm	6am
1pm	10pm	
2pm	11pm	
3pm	12 midnight	

1 Draw out a diary like the one above to show each of the 24 hours in one day.

2 As you go through your day, fill out your diary with the activities you do during each hour.

3 Make about 35 small cards and choose some activities. Then write the activities on the cards. You might want to write "sleep" on ten of them, "watch t.v." on five, "play" on five, "meal" on five, and "school" on ten. Can you think of any others?

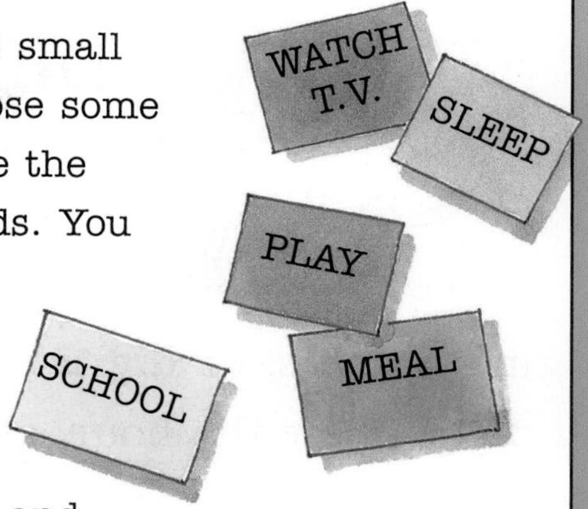

WATCH T.V.

SLEEP

PLAY

SCHOOL

MEAL

4 Find a large piece of cardboard for your wallchart and draw on it 24 smaller squares — one square for each hour of your diary. Label each square with the hour time. Stick the chart onto your wall. Check with an adult first.

5 Now go through your diary and for each hour stick the correct activity card onto your wallchart.

6 When you have finished your 24 hours, you can see how much time you spent sleeping that day. How much time did you spend at school? How about playing?

DIGITAL CLOCKS

Some clocks and watches don't have a face and hands. The time is shown in numbers, or **digits**. Usually the first two digits show the hour, and the last two the minutes. These are called digital clocks.

STOP THE CLOCK

1 Can you arrange some matchsticks to make a time as close to the deadline as possible? Ask an adult before you use the matchsticks.

2 You could draw a guide for your matchsticks like this.

3 You could begin by just trying to make some different times with your matchsticks. This is how you can make eleven minutes before eight, or 07:49.

06.00

17

4 Make one pile of cards and write numbers on them from 17 to 21.

5 Make another pile of cards and write some times on them, for example 06.00.

6 You and a friend must each pick a card from the first pile. This will show you how many sticks you can use to make the time.

7 Now choose one time card. You must both try to arrange your sticks as near to this time as possible. The person nearest wins.

HELPFUL HINTS

● If you find it hard to remember what the digits on a clock look like, then use a calculator to remind you — the numbers look the same.

MORE IDEAS

● You could even use the 24-hour clock. A time like one o'clock in the afternoon is shown as `13:00` hours and ten o'clock at night is `22:00` hours.

SECONDS, MINUTES, HOURS...

How long does it take you to get to school? One minute, 15 minutes? You might say it took 900 seconds, but that would seem a little strange! There are many different measurements of time. When we describe how long something takes, we try to use a measurement that others find easy to understand and that isn't overly exact.

HOW OLD ARE YOU?
No! not years old. That's too easy. How many hours old are you? There is a way that you can find out. You will need a calculator to help you.

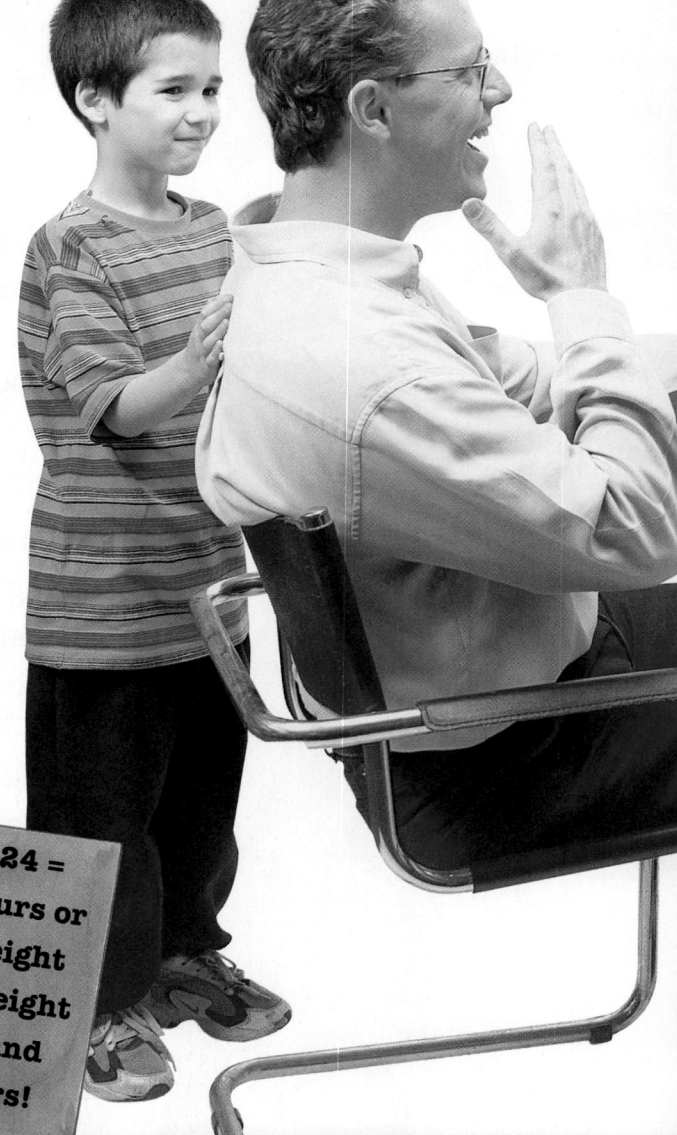

1 Multiply your age by the number of days in a year. If you are 9 it would look like this.

9 x 365 = 3,285 days

2 Now multiply the answer 3,285, by the number of hours in a day.

3,285 x 24 = 78,840 hours or Seventy-eight thousand, eight hundred and forty hours!

3 Make a birthday card for your mom, dad, brother, or sister, with their age in hours on the front. Find out how many years old they will be next birthday.

35 years old
in hours
---
35 years x
365 days x
24 hours =

306,600 hours

4 Then all you have to do is follow the same calculation. Multiply the number of years by 365, and then the answer to that by 24.

HAPPY
BIRTHDAY
DAD
YOU ARE

306,600

HOURS
OLD TODAY

5 Thank goodness you are only making a card and not a cake for their birthday with all those candles!

MORE IDEAS
● If you want to sound very clever, you can estimate the number of minutes old someone is. A quick way to do this, is to halve the person's age and add a million on the end! So, if your friend is 10 years old, then a good estimate is that they are 5 million minutes old.

8 years old
in minutes is
8 ÷ 2 = 4
add six zeros =

4,000,000
minutes old

TIMES TABLES

1x1=1	1x4=4	1x7=7	1x10=10
2x1=2	2x4=8	2x7=14	2x10=20
3x1=3	3x4=12	3x7=21	3x10=30
4x1=4	4x4=16	4x7=28	4x10=40
5x1=5	5x4=20	5x7=35	5x10=50
6x1=6	6x4=24	6x7=42	6x10=60
7x1=7	7x4=28	7x7=49	7x10=70
8x1=8	8x4=32	8x7=56	8x10=80
9x1=9	9x4=36	9x7=63	9x10=90
10x1=10	10x4=40	10x7=70	10x10=100
11x1=11	11x4=44	11x7=77	11x10=110
12x1=12	12x4=48	12x7=84	12x10=120
1x2=2	1x5=5	1x8=8	1x11=11
2x2=4	2x5=10	2x8=16	2x11=22
3x2=6	3x5=15	3x8=24	3x11=33
4x2=8	4x5=20	4x8=32	4x11=44
5x2=10	5x5=25	5x8=40	5x11=55
6x2=12	6x5=30	6x8=48	6x11=66
7x2=14	7x5=35	7x8=56	7x11=77
8x2=16	8x5=40	8x8=64	8x11=88
9x2=18	9x5=45	9x8=72	9x11=99
10x2=20	10x5=50	10x8=80	10x11=110
11x2=22	11x5=55	11x8=88	11x11=121
12x2=24	12x5=60	12x8=96	12x11=132
1x3=3	1x6=6	1x9=9	1x12=12
2x3=6	2x6=12	2x9=18	2x12=24
3x3=9	3x6=18	3x9=27	3x12=36
4x3=12	4x6=24	4x9=36	4x12=48
5x3=15	5x6=30	5x9=45	5x12=60
6x3=18	6x6=36	6x9=54	6x12=72
7x3=21	7x6=42	7x9=63	7x12=84
8x3=24	8x6=48	8x9=72	8x12=96
9x3=27	9x6=54	9x9=81	9x12=108
10x3=30	10x6=60	10x9=90	10x12=120
11x3=33	11x6=66	11x9=99	11x12=132
12x3=36	12x6=72	12x9=108	12x12=144

FRACTION WALL

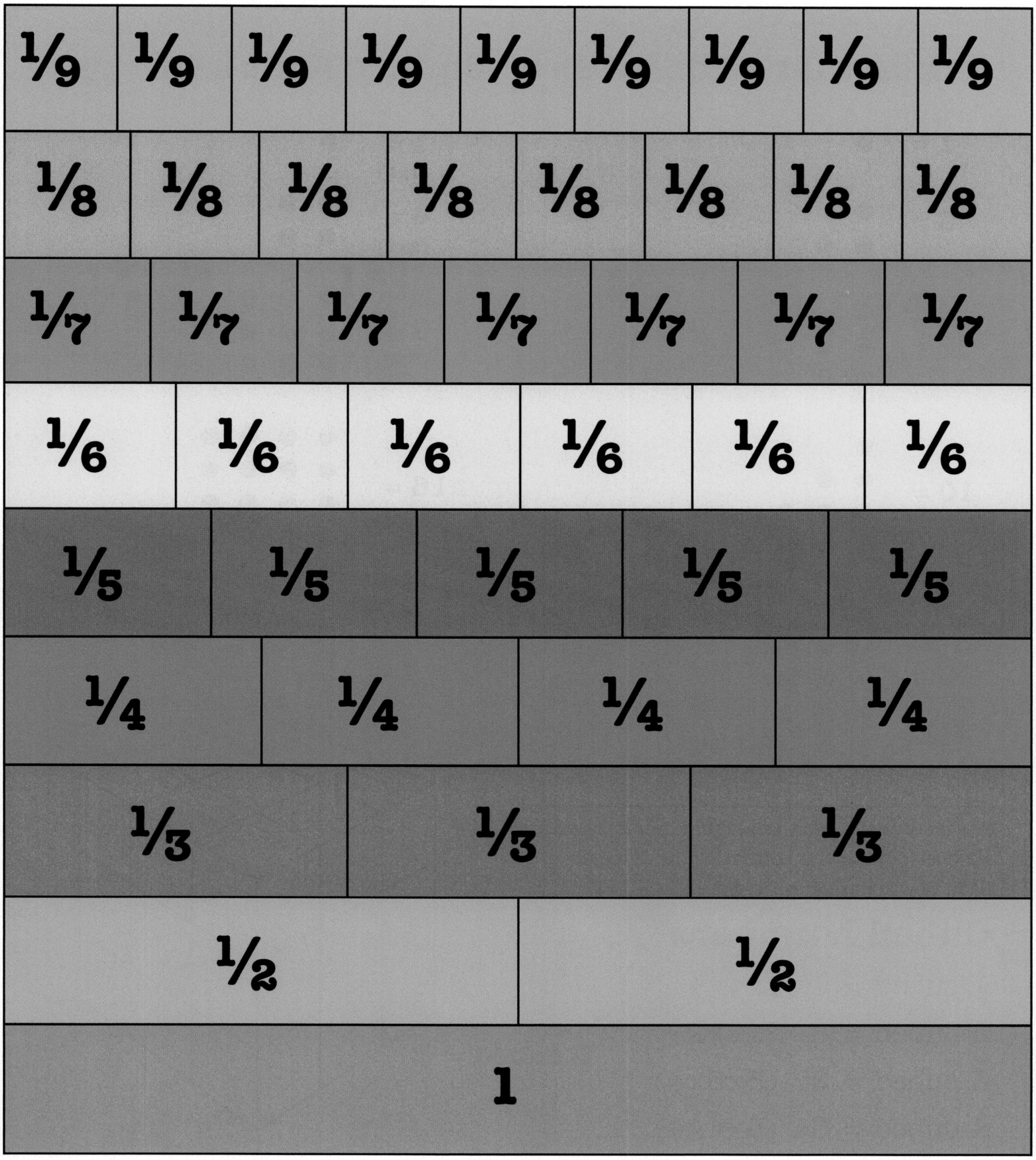

| ⅑ | ⅑ | ⅑ | ⅑ | ⅑ | ⅑ | ⅑ | ⅑ | ⅑ |

| ⅛ | ⅛ | ⅛ | ⅛ | ⅛ | ⅛ | ⅛ | ⅛ |

| ⅐ | ⅐ | ⅐ | ⅐ | ⅐ | ⅐ | ⅐ |

| ⅙ | ⅙ | ⅙ | ⅙ | ⅙ | ⅙ |

| ⅕ | ⅕ | ⅕ | ⅕ | ⅕ |

| ¼ | ¼ | ¼ | ¼ |

| ⅓ | ⅓ | ⅓ |

| ½ | ½ |

| 1 |

COMMON PATTERNS

Triangular Numbers

1 = ●

3 = ●
    ● ●

6 = ●
    ● ●
    ● ● ●

10 = ●
     ● ●
     ● ● ●
     ● ● ● ●

15 = ●
     ● ●
     ● ● ●
     ● ● ● ●
     ● ● ● ● ●

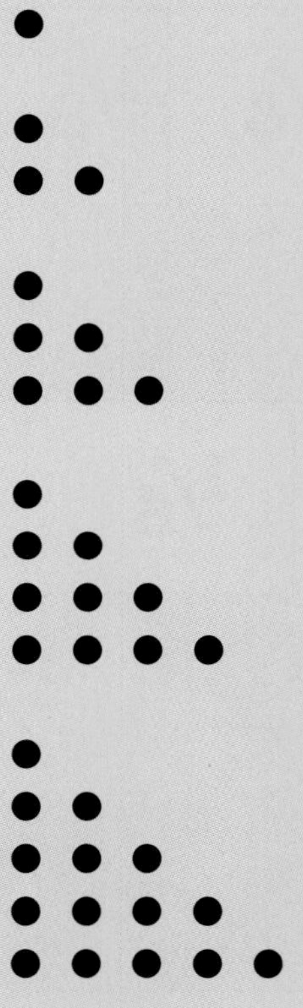

To find out the next triangular number, add another row to the bottom of the triangle. Each row has one more dot.

Square Numbers

1 = ●
(1x1)

4 = ● ●
(2x2) ● ●

9 = ● ● ●
(3x3) ● ● ●
     ● ● ●

16 = ● ● ● ●
(4x4) ● ● ● ●
     ● ● ● ●
     ● ● ● ●

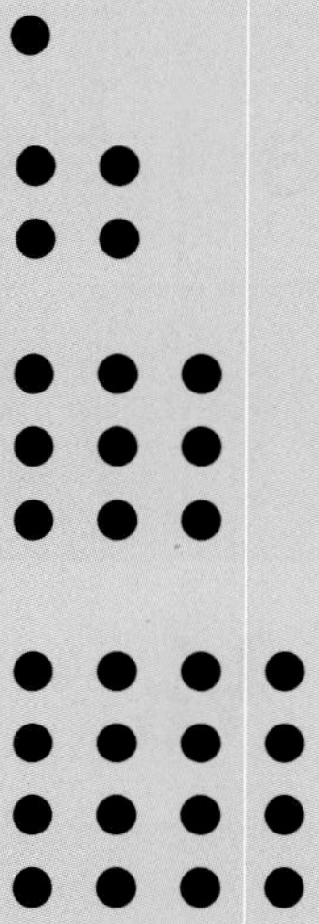

Cubed Numbers

1 cubed = 1 (1x1x1)

2 cubed = 8 (2x2x2)

3 cubed = 27 (3x3x3)

4 cubed = 64 (4x4x4)

3 cubed =

COMMON GRAPHS

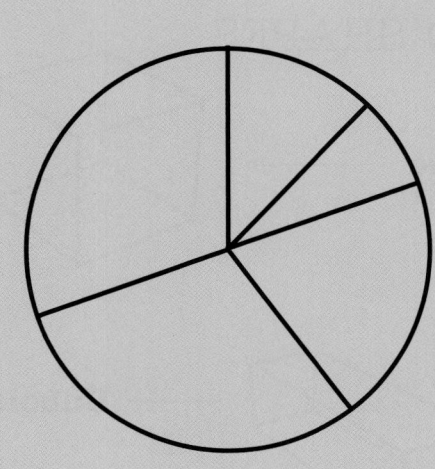

Pie Chart

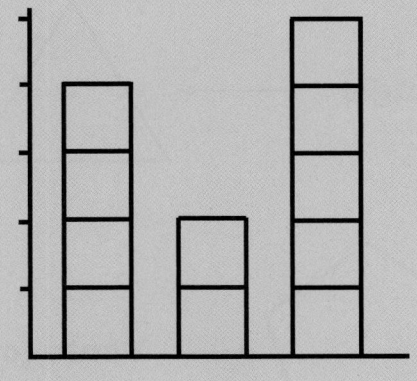

Bar Graph

Pictogram

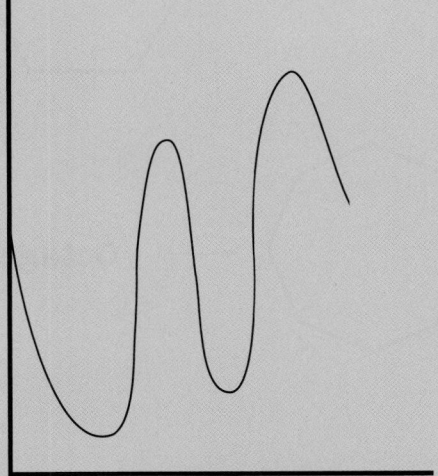

Line Graph

COMMON SHAPES

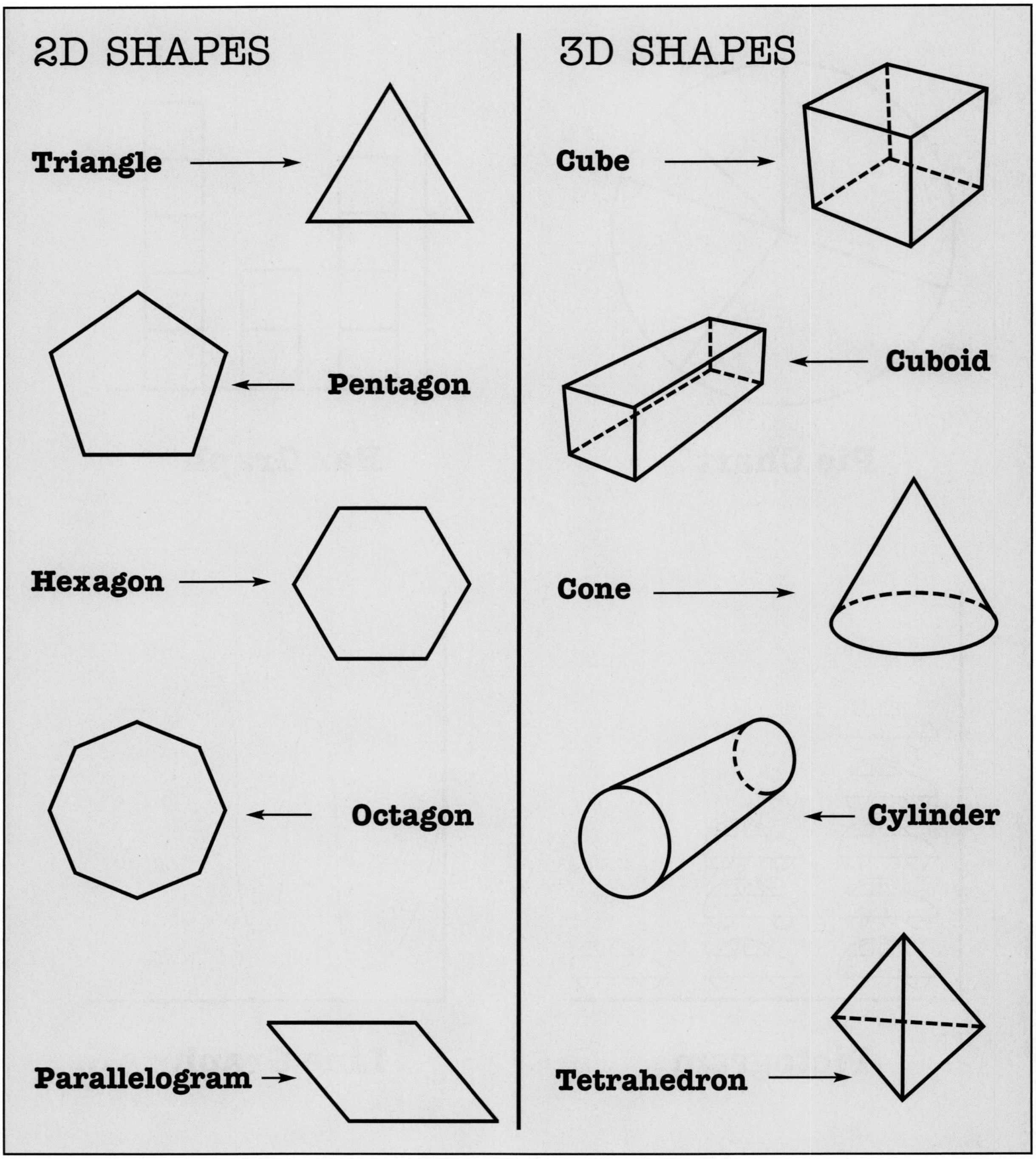

2D SHAPES

Triangle ⟶

Pentagon ⟵

Hexagon ⟶

Octagon ⟵

Parallelogram →

3D SHAPES

Cube ⟶

Cuboid ⟵

Cone ⟶

Cylinder ⟵

Tetrahedron ⟶

ANGLES AND COMPASSES

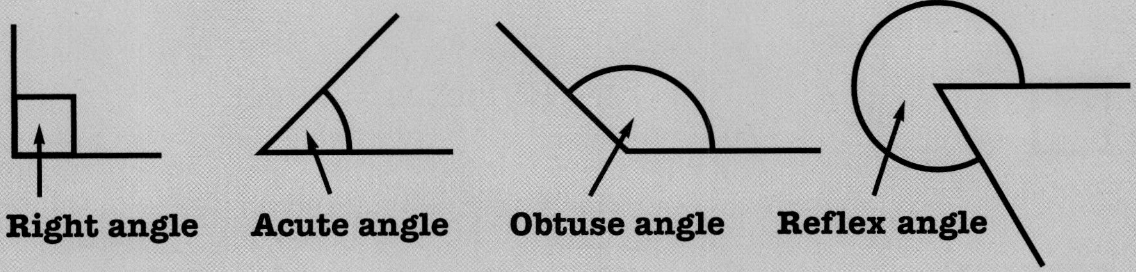

Right angle   **Acute angle**   **Obtuse angle**   **Reflex angle**

Compass bearings

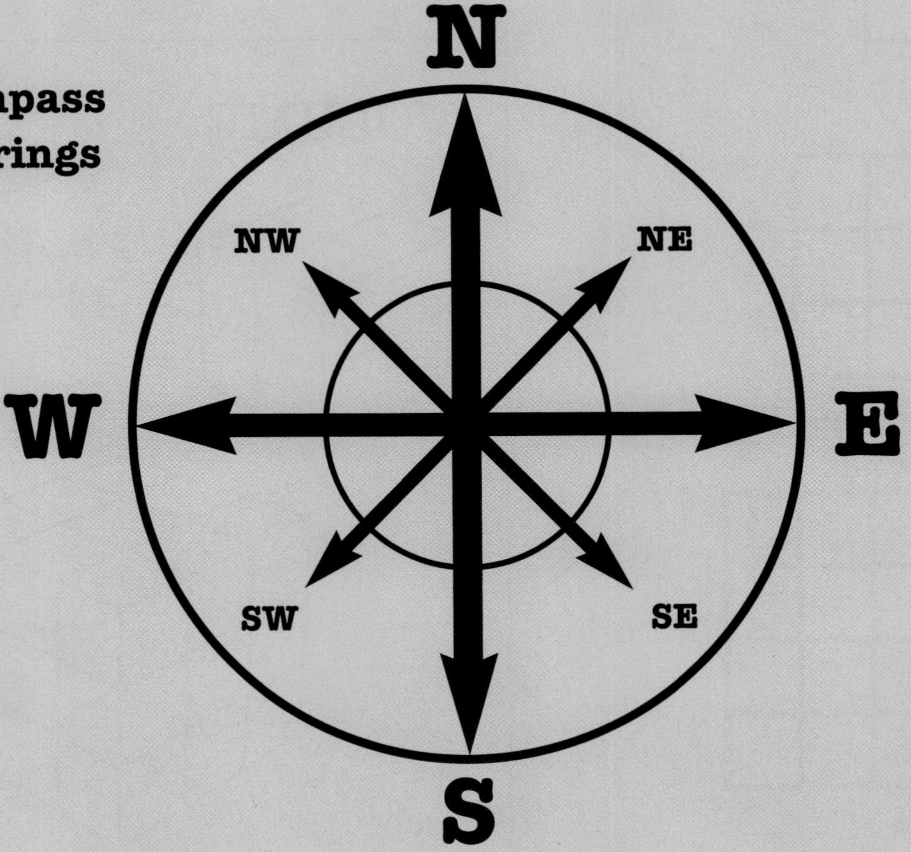

N

NW   NE

W   E

SW   SE

S

COMMON
MEASUREMENTS

AREA

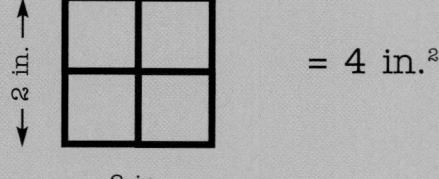

= 1 in.^{2}

= 4 in.^{2}

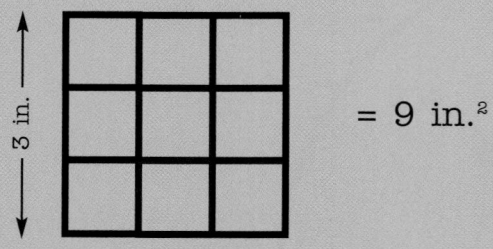

= 9 in.^{2}

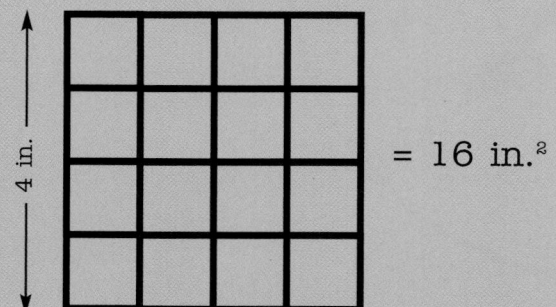

= 16 in.^{2}

LENGTH

12 inches = 1 foot

3 feet = 1 yard

1,760 yards = 1 mile

VOLUME

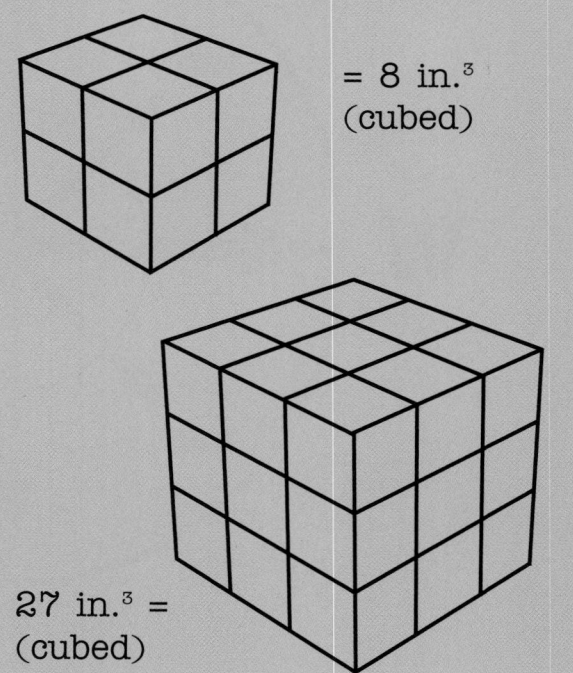

= 8 in.^{3}
(cubed)

27 in.^{3} =
(cubed)

TIME AND WEIGHT

Time

60 seconds = 1 minute

60 minutes = 1 hour

24 hours = 1 day

Weight

16 ounces = 1 pound

2000 pounds = 1 ton

24-hour clock

GLOSSARY

Addition
When you use addition, two or more numbers are put together to find their total. The addition sign looks like this +, so 6+4=10.

Algebra
In problem solving, letters are sometimes used to represent numbers or other amounts such as height or weight. This is useful when there are no numbers to help you or you are not sure what the numbers or amounts might be. This kind of mathematics is called algebra.

Angles
Where two straight lines meet, they make an angle. We can measure these in degrees. An angle of 90 degrees is called a right angle.

Area
Area is the size of a space inside a flat shape. We can measure area by counting the number of squares that cover a shape.

Arithmetic
Arithmetic is the art of calculating with numbers. You use arithmetic when you solve number problems using addition, subtraction, multiplication, and division.

Capacity
Capacity is the way we measure the amount that something will hold. A jug that holds a pint of water has the capacity of one pint.

Category
If you were sorting animals into sets, first you would have to decide on the categories you wanted to use. One category could be animals that eat meat, so a lion and a dog would both belong to this category.

Circle
A circle is a round shape with one curved edge. The distance from the center of the circle to any point on its edge is always exactly the same.

Circumference
The circumference is the length all the way around the edge of a circle.

Clockwise
When you turn clockwise it means you turn in the same direction as the hands of a clock. If you turn counterclockwise, you turn in the opposite direction to the hands of a clock.

Cone
A cone is a solid shape. The base it stands on is a circle. Its curved surface goes up to a point at the top.

GLOSSARY

Coordinates

Coordinates are two numbers that show where a point is in a space, for example, on a map or on a graph. The numbers (2,4) might show the position two places along and four places up a grid.

Cubed inches

A cubed inch is the volume of a cube measuring 1 in. long, 1 in. wide, and 1 in. high. One cubed inch is also written 1 in.³.

Decimal

We use a decimal number system. That means that we count in ones and groups of tens.

Decimal point

A decimal point separates the digits worth 1 or more on the left from digits less than 1 on the right. A decimal number looks like this 426.25.

Degrees

Angles can be measured in degrees. Mathematicians use the sign ° for degrees. A full turn is 360°. A quarter turn is 90°. A half turn is 180°. A three-quarter turn is 270°.

Diameter

The diameter is a line that cuts a circle exactly in half. It goes from the edge of the circle, through the center, and to the edge on the other side.

Digit

Numbers are made up of digits. There are two digits in the number 25: a 2 and a 5. There are three digits in the number 683: a 6, an 8, and a 3.

Dimension

We use dimensions to measure shapes. Flat shapes like circles or squares are 2D because they have two dimensions. We can measure how long and how wide they are. Solid shapes like cones and cubes are 3D because they have three dimensions. We can measure how long, how wide, and how high they are.

Division

Division is the opposite or inverse of multiplication. You could use division to find out how many 2s there are in 12. The division sign looks like this ÷ , so 12÷2=6.

Element

Each item that is in a set is called an element, so in a set of shoes, one shoe is an element of that set.

GLOSSARY

Equals

The equals sign looks like this =. Whatever is on one side of the equals sign has to be the same amount as on the other side. Both sides must balance, so 7−1=3+1+2.

Estimate

An estimate is a careful guess. You could estimate how many petals you think there are on a daisy. When you have made an estimate, you could check it by counting the petals.

Factor

In multiplication, the numbers that you multiply together are the factors, so 6 and 2 are factors of 12.

Fraction

A fraction is part of a whole. A slice of pizza is a fraction of the whole pizza. A fraction looks like this: $3/4$. The top number tells us how many parts of the whole there are in the fraction. The bottom number tells us how many parts the whole has been divided into.

Function

A function is a rule or a set of rules that are followed. A function could be "double the number and take 1 away," so the number 3 becomes 5 and the number 4 becomes 7.

Graph

A graph is a way of showing information so that it is quick and easy to understand and use. Pie charts, bar graphs, pictograms, and line graphs are all different types of graphs.

Half

A half is a fraction. We write it like this: $1/2$. You get two halves when you divide something into two equal parts.

Horizontal axis

The horizontal axis is the line going across the bottom of a graph.

Improper fraction

Fractions bigger than a whole are called improper fractions. $5/4$ is an improper fraction because the number on the top is larger than the number on the bottom.

Inequality sign

The inequality sign shows that one number is bigger or smaller than another. It looks like this < or like this >. Whatever is on the open side is larger, so 10>5.

GLOSSARY

Line of symmetry

A line of symmetry cuts a shape in half so both halves look exactly the same.

Mass

Mass describes how much there is of something. Mass is sometimes used as another word for weight. It is often measured in ounces.

Multiplication

Multiplication is a way of adding the same number many times. The sign looks like this x. Six 2s can be written like this 2+2+2+2+2+2 or like this 6x2, so 6x2=12.

Net

A net is a flat shape made when the sides of a solid shape, like a cube, are opened out. When the net is folded and the sides are joined together it makes a solid shape again.

Number patterns

Number patterns are formed when something is repeated again and again. For example, a number pattern can be made when a group of numbers are repeated like this – 2, 3, 4, 2, 3, 4, 2, 3, 4. Doing something to a number, such as adding 3 again and again, makes another kind of number pattern like this – 1, 4, 7, 10.

Percentage

A percentage is a part of a hundred. A percent sign looks like this: %. 1% means 1 out of a hundred. 25% means 25 out of a hundred.

Product

The product is the number you get when you multiply other numbers together, so 12 is the product of 6x2.

Property

Items in a set all have properties or things that can describe them. One property of an apple is that it is a fruit. Another property is that it has a round shape. An apple can belong to a set of apples, or a set of things with a round shape, or to a set of fruit.

Radius

The radius is the distance from the center to the edge of a circle. Any straight line drawn from the center to the edge of a circle is called a radial line.

Ratio

A ratio is a way of comparing the amount of different things in a whole. If you mix two teaspoons of yellow paint to one teaspoon of red paint to make orange, you have used the ratio of 2:1 in your mixture.

GLOSSARY

Right angle

A right angle is a quarter turn or 90°. The corners of squares and rectangles are all right angles.

Rotational symmetry

A shape has rotational symmetry if it looks exactly the same when it has been moved around a central point.

Scale

A scale is a machine we use for measuring how much things weigh. A kitchen scale measures light-weight things such as an apple, and a bathroom scale can measure heavy things like your mom and dad.

Set

When mathematicians put things into groups, each group is called a set. All the things in the set have something the same about them.

Square inches

A square inch is the area of a square with sides of one inch long. Four square inches can be written 4 in.² and would fit into a square with sides of two inches long.

Standard measurements

The units of measurement we use, like inches, must always be the same or we cannot be sure how big anything is. Some standard units commonly used today are pints, fluid ounces, and feet.

Subtraction

Subtraction is the opposite of addition. When you subtract you take one number away from another to find their difference. The subtraction sign is sometimes known as minus and looks like this –, so 10 - 4=6.

Tenth

If you divide something into ten equal parts, one of those parts is a tenth. A tenth can look like this: $1/10$. The number after a decimal point shows you tenths. So the digit 6, in the number 1.6, is 6 tenths.

Vertical axis

The vertical axis is the line going up the side of a graph.

Volume

The volume of a shape is the amount of space it takes up. You would take up much less space than an elephant. Volume is usually measured in cubic inches.

INDEX

acid rain 248, 249, 376,
  429, 532
acids 32, 33, 53, 90, 91,
  216
acorns 329, 338
acute (math) 688, 689, 751
addition (math) 546, 547,
  558, 564, 565, 566, 574,
  582, 608, 614, 754
air 141, 159, 161, 163,
  229, 232, 234, 236, 241,
  248, 259, 260, 262, 271,
  285, 287, 291, 301, 314,
  315, 320, 323, 324, 357,
  371, 374, 376, 377
  floating on 162-163
air pressure 234, 235, 250,
  374, 424, 425
algae 474, 475, 480
algebra (math) 604, 608,
  614, 615, 754
alkalis 33, 90, 91, 216
altitude 424, 425, 428, 466,
  474, 492, 532
alum, potash of 38, 39
amber 116, 117
amphibians 320, 374
angles (math) 618, 650,
  668, 688, 689, 690, 691,
  692, 751, 754
antenna 295, 345
ants 276, 298, 299
aphids 311
arable farming 514, 532
arches 43, 58, 59, 216
area (math) 708, 710, 711,
  712, 713, 716, 718, 719,
  721, 752, 754
arithmetic (math) 546, 548,
  754

astronauts 64
atlases 399, 401, 404, 405,
  406, 407, 415, 440, 492,
  493, 504, 532
atmosphere 424, 429, 455,
  502
atoms 114, 216
attraction see *magnetism*
attrition 449, 532
avalanches 427

backyard 224, 276-301,
  354
badgers 325, 335
baking soda 92, 93
balance 66, 67, 69
  balancing man 66-67
ballast 153, 160, 161, 216
balloons 46, 47
banger 192-193
bar graphs (math) 642,
  643, 749
bark 329, 334
barometers 234, 235, 374
bats 202
batteries 118, 128, 133,
  135, 137
beaches 448, 449,   478
beans 312, 313
Beaufort Scale 233, 451,
  532
bees 295, 305
beetles 295, 325, 329, 344
berries 291, 336, 365, 376
bills 266, 267, 374
biomes 466, 467, 532
birds 182, 266, 267, 269,
  276, 283, 290, 291, 292,
  293, 307, 318, 319, 326,
  336, 337, 346, 347, 356,

361, 363, 365, 368, 369,
  374, 375, 461, 463, 464,
  468, 470, 473, 477, 482,
  483
blotting paper 91, 106
boats and ships 152-157
bottle fountain 98-99
bridges 58-59, 397, 402,
  441
bugs 295, 311, 344
buildings 386, 390, 394,
  395, 396, 397
building sites 78
bulbs 289, 317, 372, 373
bull roarer 194-195
buoy 152-153
buoyancy 140, 141, 142,
  216
butterflies 224, 295, 322,
  323, 344, 345, 360, 361,
  369, 376

cameras 14, 15, 20
  pinhole camera 14-15
camouflage 326, 346, 347,
  374, 475, 532
candles 89, 108-109
cannon 84
capacity (math) 722, 724,
  754
capsizing 152, 153
carbohydrates 310,
  374
carbon dioxide 92-93, 111,
  285, 376
carnivores 311, 324, 325,
  374, 376, 462, 463, 467,
  532
Carroll diagrams (math)
  626, 627

INDEX

cash crops 527, 528, 532

categories (math) 626, 754

caterpillars 291, 322, 323, 329, 376

cattle 517, 525

cereal crops 511

cereals 341, 374

charts (math) 562, 563, 580, 590, 591, 641, 642, 646, 681, 740, 741, 749

chlorophyll 11, 216, 219, 285, 366, 374, 376

chrysalis 323

circles (math) 558, 573, 618, 619, 647, 662, 663, 664, 665, 666, 667, 669, 690, 691, 736, 754

circuits 120, 121, 123, 125, 126, 128, 130, 216
    parallel 132
    ring 132-133

circumference (math) 662, 754

cities 486, 487, 490, 491, 492, 495, 496, 504, 505, 507

climate 228, 229, 230, 374, 404, 405, 426, 466, 470, 471, 492, 493, 494, 495, 504, 512, 532

clockwise (math) 677, 685, 687, 754

clouds 235, 236, 237, 238, 251, 353, 375, 377, 425, 428, 429, 435

coasts 448, 450, 455, 456, 457

coins 42-43
    tester 174-175

colored paper 144-145

colors
    changes 32-33
    mixing 24-25
    primary 28, 219
    separating 28-29
    splitting 106-107

communities 460, 462

compasses 184-185, 187, 216, 386, 388, 389, 391, 393, 394, 532

compasses (math) 676, 677, 690, 691, 699, 751

compression 159, 216

computers 186

condensation 428, 434, 435, 532

conductors 122, 123, 124, 125, 216

cones (math) 666, 667, 750, 754

coniferous forests 337, 466, 468, 469, 474

conifers 331, 375

consumers 462, 476, 532

continental shelf 412, 413, 454

continents 406, 407, 411, 412, 486, 487, 490, 504, 510

contours 398, 399, 405, 423

convection currents 97, 216

coordinates (math) 680, 681, 755

core 410, 411

corn 340, 341, 374

countryside 284, 352

cranes 74, 188

crocodiles 321, 377

crop rotation 519

crust 410, 411, 412, 413,

414, 415, 418, 419

crystals 38, 39, 40-41, 216, 420, 421, 532

cubed inches (math) 720, 721, 752, 755

cubes (math) 654, 655, 661, 672, 673, 720, 721, 748, 750, 752

currents 452, 453

curves (math) 619, 645, 669, 698, 704

cutlery 136

cylinders (math) 672, 750

dairy farming 514

darkness 12

datastreams (math) 644

daylight 12

deciduous trees 330, 331, 332, 375

decimal point (math) 578, 580, 582, 755

decimals (math) 578, 580, 582, 610, 755

decomposers 281, 375, 463, 465, 532

deer 293, 334, 335

deforestation 431, 471, 532

degrees (math) 688, 689, 690, 691, 692, 693, 755

deltas 437

density 141, 143, 145, 147, 148, 149, 161, 216, 452, 453, 457
    testing 150-151

deposition 430, 437, 448, 532

depth, illusion of 27

deserts 229, 315, 441, 466, 467, 472, 473, 474

INDEX

developed countries 491, 500, 511, 515, 530, 532

developing countries 493, 495, 511, 512, 515, 522, 524, 525, 530, 531, 532

diameter (math) 662, 755

diamonds 421

digits (math) 552, 553, 554, 555, 556, 557, 564, 580, 581, 582, 600, 613, 614, 615, 742, 743, 755

dimensions 390, 391, 393, 395, 396, 397, 398, 399, 405

dimensions (math) 654, 672, 673, 680, 755

dimmer switches 124

diseases 510, 511, 517, 531

diving 158-159

division (math) 560, 564, 565, 566, 576, 577, 589, 609, 612, 613, 621, 755

dormant 373, 375

drag 76, 77, 217

dragonfly 260, 294, 323

drinking water 442, 443

droppings 283, 333, 334, 348, 365

droughts 444, 453, 511, 524, 525, 531

drums 196-197, 198-199

dyes 28, 30-31
  tie-dye handkerchief 30-31
  vegetable 31

ear 198

eardrums 198, 204, 217

Earth 12, 13, 226, 230, 231, 232, 315, 324, 328, 376
  magnetic field of 185

earthquakes 412, 416, 417, 450, 491

echoes 202-203, 217

eclipses 12

ecology 460, 532

ecosystems 460, 461, 462, 464, 466, 469, 474, 476, 478, 480, 482, 532

eggs 42-43, 148-149, 260, 261, 265, 281, 288, 289, 299, 306, 307, 318, 319, 320, 321, 322, 323, 325, 329, 336, 337, 373, 375, 377
  spinning eggs 81

elasticity 50-51

electricity 114-137
  currents 118-121, 129, 137
  static 116, 117, 118

electrolysis 136

electrolytes 136, 137, 217

electromagnets 188-189

electroplating 136-137

electroscopes 116-117, 217

elements (math) 624, 626, 628, 755

ellipses (math) 664, 669

El Niño 453

embryo 306, 307

energy 73, 81, 217

engines 82

environment 460, 532

equator 492, 493, 504, 532

equals (math) 547, 658, 659, 756

equilateral (math) 658, 659

erosion 430, 431, 436, 437, 448, 513, 521, 522, 533

estimates (math) 568, 579, 586, 587, 712, 713, 722, 723, 730, 731, 745, 756

estivation 371, 375

evaporation 240, 241, 375, 434, 435, 439, 533

evergreen trees 330, 331, 332, 367, 375

expansion 89, 97, 98, 99, 142

fabrics 54, 55

factors (math) 560, 561, 564, 756

Fahrenheit 243, 251

fall 231, 331, 336, 338, 350, 357, 364, 365, 366, 368, 369, 370, 372, 375

faults 416

feathers 266, 318, 346, 363, 374

ferns 333, 353

fertilizers 511, 518

fibers 54, 55

filtering 100-101

fish 259, 263, 267, 307, 320, 375

fishing game 166-167

fledgling 319

flick book 20-21

floating magnet 176-177

floodplains 436, 437, 439

floods 437, 439, 444, 447, 453, 455, 491, 493, 511, 524, 525

flour 340, 341

flowers 90, 94-95, 231, 278, 282, 288, 289, 305, 313, 326, 333, 342, 343, 344, 356, 359, 360, 361, 364,

INDEX

373

flying butterfly 168-169

food chains 463, 467, 480

food coloring 92, 94, 98, 107, 108

food mountains 515

food webs 462, 463, 466, 477, 480, 481, 519, 533

footpaths 394, 402, 403

footprints 224, 292, 293, 334

force 62-85, 157, 217

force meter 62-63

fossil fuels 454, 455, 502, 533

fossils 420, 533

fountain 98-99

fractions (math) 572, 573, 574, 575, 576, 584, 646, 747, 756

freezing 89, 217

freshwater 255, 376

frogs 265, 320, 322, 357

friction 70, 71, 217

fruit 283, 289, 292, 296, 310, 311, 364, 365

functions (math) 606, 607, 609, 756

fungi 463, 464, 465, 474, 475

funny face 180-181

gearwheels 82-83

gemstones 38

generations 490, 491, 533

geothermal energy 419, 533

geysers 419, 533

gills 263, 320

glaciers 426, 427, 434, 436

glass 46, 50

global warming 455, 533

grains 340, 341

graphite 124, 125

graphs (math) 552, 588, 600, 619, 636, 642, 643, 644, 645, 646, 680, 749, 756

grasses 228, 283, 284, 285, 311, 340, 341, 342, 345, 346, 347, 349, 353, 356, 371, 374

grasshoppers 345, 356, 357

gravity 62-63, 64-65, 66, 67, 69, 169, 177, 217, 269, 376

greenhouse effect 502

grids 392, 396, 400, 401, 402, 403

grids (math) 586, 587, 618, 619, 650, 678, 679, 681, 687, 710, 711

grip 70, 71, 72, 73, 217

groups (math) 577, 625, 628

grubs 329

gypsum 48, 49

gyroscopes 80-81, 217

habitats 457, 460, 464, 478, 480, 481, 482, 483, 521, 533

hail 238, 239

halves (math) 572, 573, 576, 579, 584, 588, 689, 690, 696, 697, 745, 756

harvests 512, 522, 525, 529

hatching 307, 319, 321, 323, 325, 337, 373, 375

hatchling 321

hearing aid 202-203

heartbeats 200, 201

hemispheres 453, 493, 533

herbivores 311, 324, 325, 376, 462, 463, 467, 517, 533

herbs 354, 355, 376

hibernation 224, 370, 371, 376

high-tech industries 501

holdfasts 270

holly 331, 367

horizontal axis (math) 680, 756

horse chestnuts 283, 331, 338

hovercraft 162-163

hurricanes 247, 451, 453

hydraulic force 74-75, 217

hydroelectric power 446, 533

hydrometer 150-151

ice 88-89, 140, 142-143, 236, 237, 238, 239

icebergs 142

ice-cubes 142-143

igneous rock 420, 533

images 14-15, 17, 21, 27, 218

improper fractions (math) 573, 756

indicators 33, 90-91, 218

industries 500, 501, 505

inequality signs (math) 556, 557, 756

ink 106, 107

invisible ink 104-105

insects 224, 252, 260, 266, 291, 294, 295, 296, 297, 298, 307, 313, 323, 326, 329, 336, 342, 344, 345, 346, 347, 355, 356, 369,

INDEX

460, 463, 464, 470, 482

insulators 122, 130-131, 218

intensive farming 515, 520, 533

inverses (math) 560, 564, 565, 613

iron 102, 103, 174, 175, 176
  filings 180, 181, 182, 183
  oxide 102, 103

irrigation 444, 445, 533

isosceles (math) 658, 659

Jack-in-the-box 50-51

jets 156, 157, 218
  jet-propelled boat 156-157

jobs 500, 501, 505

journeys 488, 489, 490, 491

kaleidoscope 16-17

ladybugs 295, 311

lakes 241, 254, 255, 376, 436

landmarks 386, 387, 388, 389, 391, 392, 394, 402, 403, 440, 506, 507

large-scale maps 394, 398, 402, 533

larvae 325, 329, 373

latitude 466, 492, 504, 533

lava 415, 418, 419, 533

leaves 224, 231, 233, 281, 285, 286, 287, 297, 300, 301, 311, 315, 317, 319, 322, 370, 371, 375, 376

legs 295, 297, 320, 345, 349, 357

lemon juice 104

lichens 281, 333, 460, 467, 474, 475, 533

life cycles 224, 302-325

light
  energy 10
  rays 12, 15, 16, 17, 19, 218
  splitting 22-23
  white 22, 23, 25

lightbulbs 120, 132

limestone 438, 439

linear maps 440

line of symmetry (math) 696, 757

liquids
  floating 146-147
  frozen 142
  layers of 146-147

litmus paper 33, 218

livestock 510, 511, 514, 516, 517, 520, 521, 533

locations 486, 487, 494, 506

lodestones 166, 218, 388, 534

longitude 492, 534

longshore drift 449

loudness 194, 196

lungs 263, 320, 371

machinery 511, 512, 518, 520, 524

magma 410, 411, 412, 413, 418, 419, 421, 534

magnets 135, 166-189, 390, 391
  bar 166, 185
  hidden 186
  horseshoe-shaped 166, 177, 183
  household uses of 180

permanent 172, 173, 176, 219

ring-shaped 166, 177, 183

magnetism
  and animals 182
  attraction 167, 168, 169, 180
  induced 173, 218
  magnetic fields 119, 135, 182, 183, 189, 218
  magnetic force 167, 168, 170, 171, 181, 182, 183, 218
  magnetic materials 167, 174, 180, 218
  magnetic poles 176, 177, 218
  magnetic sculpture 172-173
  repulsion 117, 176, 177

magnetizing objects 186-187, 218

mantle 410, 411, 412, 413, 418

maps 251, 276, 422, 486, 487, 490, 492

mass (math) 728, 757

mating 323, 357

mazes 130

meadows 326, 342-349

meanders 436, 437, 534

measurements 393, 394, 398, 399

megaphone 202-203

melting 89, 218

metals 122
  aluminum 179
  non-magnetic 175
  pure 174

INDEX

steel 166, 175, 176
  nails 186-187
  wool 102, 103
metamorphic rocks 420, 534
metamorphosis 322, 376
metropolitan areas 487,
  496, 534
mice 293, 309, 335, 349
microbalance 68-69
microbes 110, 218
migration 350, 368, 369,
  376, 491, 507
milk 52, 53
millipedes 296, 297
minerals 255, 278, 286,
  287, 311, 377, 420, 421,
  438, 498, 499, 534
minibeasts 464, 482, 513,
  518, 519
mirror images 17
mixed farming 514, 534
Möbius strips 36-37, 218
molecules 218
moles 278, 348
monocultures 520, 526, 534
moon 12, 252, 269, 294
Morse, Samuel 126
mosaics 57
mosquito 259, 373
mosses 319, 333
moths 294, 360, 361
motors 134
mountains 398, 399, 405,
  411, 413, 414, 415, 422,
  423, 434, 436, 439, 441,
  442, 445, 466, 504, 506
multiplication (math) 553,
  558, 559, 561, 562, 564,
  565, 566, 568, 594, 598,
  600, 601, 609, 612, 621,

712, 721, 744, 745, 757
muscles 63
musical instruments 196-
  197, 206-213
  clarinet 206-207
  guitar 210-211
  stringed 210-212
  tuning 212
  wind 206, 207

navigation 182, 184
nectar 288, 313, 360, 361
needles 331, 352, 367, 375
nests 290, 298, 299, 307,
  309, 318, 319, 336, 337,
  346, 347, 348, 349, 362
nets (math) 654, 655, 757
Newton, Sir Isaac 62, 85
newtons 62
newts 320, 374
nomads 473
north poles 185
notes 208, 210, 212, 213,
  219
number patterns (math)
  547, 598, 599, 757
nuts 292, 329, 335, 336,
  357, 376

oaks 329, 338, 353
oasis 445, 534
oats 340, 341, 374
obtuse (math) 688, 689,
  751
oceans 411, 413, 415, 434,
  435, 452
oil disasters 457
oils 144, 145, 146, 147
orchestras 206
organic farming 518, 519,

534
orienteering 388, 389
ovaries 288, 289, 305
oxbow lakes 437, 534
oxidization 102, 103, 105,
  219
oxygen 105, 108, 109, 262,
  263, 285, 376

paints and inks 28, 29
Pangaea 412, 413, 415
paper 36, 44, 45, 46, 47,
  50
papier-mâché 46-47
parallelogram (math) 670,
  750
percentages (math) 584,
  585, 586, 587, 588, 589,
  757
perimeter (math) 699, 714,
  715, 716, 717, 718, 719
periscope 18-19
perishable food 528, 529
permeable rock 439, 534
pesticides 442, 518, 519,
  526, 531
pests 301, 345
petals 288, 342, 343, 358,
  359
pheasants 352, 353
photosynthesis 11, 219,
  285, 376, 443, 463, 475,
  480, 534
phytoplankton 480
pictograms (math) 643, 749
pie charts (math) 646, 647,
  749
pigments 31, 219
pines 331, 352, 367, 375
plantations 526, 527, 528,

INDEX

534

plants 10, 11, 224, 225, 228, 231, 255, 257, 258, 259, 260, 262, 264, 265, 270, 272, 278, 279, 280, 281, 282, 283, 285, 286, 287, 288, 294, 297, 300, 301, 302, 305, 306, 311, 312, 313, 314, 315, 316, 317, 320, 324, 325, 328, 333, 335, 350, 354, 358, 364, 373, 375, 376, 377

plastics 44, 45, 52, 53, 122, 219

political maps 404, 405

pollen 288, 289, 305, 376

pollution 248, 249, 261, 376, 429, 442, 443, 455, 456, 457, 461, 474, 475, 491, 502

polygons (math) 668, 669

polyhedron (math) 672

ponds 224, 252, 258, 259, 260, 261, 264, 265, 266, 357, 376, 451, 460, 461, 476, 477, 482

pondweed 262, 263, 264

population 496, 497, 510, 518, 524

population density 496, 497, 534

porous rock 438, 454, 534

port and starboard 154, 219

predators 475, 476, 483, 534

prey 462, 475, 477, 534

prime meridian 492, 534

prisms 22, 219

producers 462, 480, 535

products 516, 517, 526, 527

products (math) 560, 561,

564, 757

propellers 156, 219

properties (math) 595, 626, 757

proportions (math) 594, 595

protein 310, 377

pulleys 78-79, 219

quarters (math) 572, 573, 576, 579, 584, 684, 685, 690, 698

racing game 170-171

radius (math) 666, 757

rain 226, 229, 237, 238, 239, 240, 246, 250, 251, 254, 263, 264, 284, 297, 353, 355, 373, 376, 444

rainbows 22-23, 25

rainfall 428, 429, 471

rain forests 229, 315, 466, 467, 470, 471

rain shadow 428, 429

rainwater 435, 438, 439

ratios (math) 590, 591, 592, 594, 595, 757

red cabbage 32, 33, 90, 91

reflection 16-17, 19, 23, 202-203, 219

reflective symmetry (math) 696, 697

reflex (math) 689, 751

refugees 491, 535

relief maps 399, 404, 405

reproduction 306-307, 357

reptiles 320, 321, 377

repulsion *see magnetism*

rice 340, 341, 374

Richter scale 417, 535

right angles (math) 601,

658, 659, 688, 689, 718, 751, 758

rivers 241, 252, 254, 255, 256, 257, 266, 376

roads 386, 394, 397, 486, 497

rock pools 271, 272, 273

roots 270, 284, 287, 313, 315, 316, 317, 329, 377

rotational symmetry (math) 698, 699, 758

rudders 154-155, 220

rural areas 405, 487, 494, 535

rust race 102-103

salt 101

salts 255, 311, 377, 525

saltwater 255

scalene (math) 658, 659

scales 392, 393, 535

scales (math) 728, 731, 732, 758

scots pine 331, 338, 352, 353

screes 430, 431

seashore 252, 266, 270, 271, 362

sea level 398, 399, 405

seasons 226, 230, 231, 350, 356, 362, 493, 504, 512, 522

seaweed 268, 269, 270, 271

sectors (math) 666, 667

sediment 420, 421, 535

sedimentary rocks 420, 454, 535

seeds 228, 266, 282, 283, 288, 289, 291, 305, 306, 307, 312, 313, 316, 335, 336, 337, 338, 339, 341,

INDEX

343, 346, 347, 354, 358, 359, 364, 365, 373, 375, 377, 511, 512, 525, 530, 531

services 486, 487, 489

sets, badger 335

sets (math) 548, 549, 624, 626, 628, 629, 633, 758

settlements 486, 487, 507, 535

shadows 13, 220

shaduf 444, 445

shapes 36-59, 66

shellfish 274, 275

shells 268, 274, 275, 306, 362

shoots 283, 313, 317, 359, 372

shrews 325

simultaneous equations (math) 614

skins 320, 321, 323, 357, 377

slugs 296, 297

small-scale maps 398, 399, 535

smog 248, 249

snails 259, 266, 291, 296, 297, 346

snakes 320, 321, 348

snow 226, 231, 237, 238, 239, 245, 254, 353

soil 225, 254, 255, 264, 265, 276, 278, 279, 280, 282, 284, 287, 294, 296, 300, 301, 314, 333, 338, 358, 372, 375, 512, 513, 514, 518, 519, 522, 523, 524, 525, 530, 531

solutions 38, 40, 41

sonometer 212-213

sounds
  absorbing 203
  bouncing 202-203
  distance of 194, 195, 199
  low and high 208, 209, 211, 213
  magnifying 200
  noise 204
  pitch 208, 219
  reflecting 203, 219
  travel of 194, 198, 214-215

sound drum 198-199

soundproof box 204-205

sound waves 197, 198, 201, 203, 205, 207, 211, 220

spawn 265, 320

sperm 307

spiders 296, 297

spinning tops 80-81

spring 231, 258, 290, 313, 318, 319, 332, 336, 338, 354, 356, 358, 364, 368, 369, 370, 372, 373

springs 50, 51

square inches (math) 712, 713, 720, 721, 752, 758

squirrels 335

stability 152, 153

stalactites 40-41, 438, 439, 535

stalagmites 438, 439, 535

stamen 288

standard measurements (math) 702, 758

staple diets 511, 535

starboard 220

stethoscope 200-201, 220

Sticklebacks 259

stigma 289, 305

storms 226, 232, 237, 246, 247, 251, 353

strata 414, 415, 420, 421, 535

street plans 394-395, 396, 403

strength 42, 43, 44, 45, 59, 62-85

submarine 160-161

subsistence farming 525, 527, 535

subtraction (math) 550, 551, 564, 565, 566, 621, 758

sugars 311

summer 231, 245, 258, 289, 336, 342, 345, 350, 354, 356, 358, 361, 366, 368, 371, 375

sun 225, 226, 230, 231, 235, 240, 241, 243, 244, 245, 269, 285, 323, 324, 359, 389, 461, 462, 463, 467, 502, 503

sundial 12-13

sunlight 10, 11, 12, 13, 22

surfaces 71

sustainable farming 518, 535

sustainable forestry 469

switches 126, 128-129

sycamore 338

symbiosis 475, 535

symbols 391, 393, 394, 395, 403, 404, 405

symbols (math) 584, 610, 611

INDEX

tables (math) 562, 593, 600, 601, 609, 617, 642, 712, 746, 747, 748, 749, 750, 751, 752, 753

tadpoles 265, 320, 322

tectonic plates 412, 413, 414, 415, 416, 417, 418, 535

telephone 214-215

television pictures 24

temperate regions 229, 466, 493, 511, 512, 514, 523, 526, 529, 535

temperature 98, 220, 226, 242, 243, 245, 251, 353, 377

tenths (math) 579, 581, 582, 758

terraces 522, 523

tessellation 56, 57, 220

tessellation (math) 652

tetrahedron (math) 660, 661, 672, 750

thematic maps 404, 405

thermals 96, 220

thermometers 98, 242, 243, 244, 245, 250, 353, 377

thorax 295, 345

threads 54, 55

thunder and lightning 246, 251

tidal power 447

tides 252, 268, 269, 272, 377, 447, 448, 478

tillers 154-155, 220

time (math) 734, 735, 736, 737, 742, 743, 753

triangles (math) 656, 657, 658, 659, 660, 665, 670, 672, 714, 748, 750

triangular numbers (math) 602, 603, 748

tourism 505, 506

towns 486, 487, 507

tractors 72, 73

transpiration 471

treasure hunt 178-179

trees 231, 233, 247, 249, 282, 283, 311, 315, 318, 326, 328, 329, 330, 331, 332, 333, 334, 335, 336, 337, 338, 339, 347, 353, 357, 366, 367, 375, 386, 391, 395, 397, 464, 465, 468, 470, 471, 474, 475, 481, 483

triangle puzzle 56-57

tributaries 440, 535

tropical regions 522, 523, 526, 535

trucks 74

tundra 466, 467, 474

two-way switch 128-129

underwater floating 160-161

United States Geological Survey 394, 395

urban areas 405, 487, 491, 494, 535

valleys 416, 417, 426, 427, 436, 440

vegetation 466, 469, 535

Venn diagrams (math) 628

vertical axis (math) 680, 758

vibrations 192, 196, 197, 206, 207, 209, 210, 211, 212, 213, 215, 220

vinegar 52, 53, 91, 92, 93

vitamins 310, 311

vocal cords 192, 220

volcano 92-93

volcanoes 412, 415, 418, 419, 481

Volta, Alessandro 118

volts 118

volume (math) 720, 721, 724, 752, 758

warp 55

wasps 295, 329

water 88, 89, 90, 94, 95, 96, 97, 98, 99, 100, 101, 102, 103, 106, 107, 110, 141, 142, 159

watercress, growing of 10-11

water cycles 434-435

water pressure 424-425

water tables 439, 445, 535

water vapor 236, 237, 240, 241, 375, 377, 434, 435

waves 448, 449, 450, 451

weather 226, 251, 313, 353, 370, 372, 373, 374, 375

weaving 54-55, 220

weeds 282

weft 55

weight 59, 63, 68, 77, 79

weight (math) 728, 729, 730, 731, 732, 733, 753

wheat 340, 341, 374

wheels 72, 82

INDEX

width (math) 654, 707, 712

winches 79

wind 224, 226, 232, 233, 246, 247, 250, 251, 283, 284, 315, 343, 377, 435, 450, 452, 474, 502

wings 260, 295, 323, 345, 357, 363

winter 229, 231, 245, 290, 291, 331, 336, 350, 357, 365, 367, 369, 370, 371, 372, 373, 375, 376

woodland 330-339

worms 269, 276, 278, 281, 291, 300, 301, 325, 346

xylophone 208-209

yeast 110-111

zooplankton 480, 481

ENGLISH

Irregular verbs......20-21
Spelling rules............52
Commonly misspelled
  words......................53
Punctuation review
 54-55
MLA bibliography
  rules..............370-371
APA bibliography
  rules..............372-373
Punctuation
  review............374-375
Avoiding logic errors in
  writing....................60
Glossary of
  terms 1386-1388

FOREIGN LANGUAGE

French for the
  traveler 133-139
French-English
  dictionary......140-144
English-French
  dictionary......145-151
German for the
  traveler..........163-169
German-English
  dictionary......170-175

English-German
  dictionary......176-181
Spanish for the
  traveler..........198-203
Spanish-English
  dictionary......204-209
English-Spanish
  dictionary......210-215
Latin-English
  dictionary 231-238
English-Latin
  dictionary 238-244

MATHEMATICS

Rules for
  exponents 244
Fraction and decimal
  equivalents............272
Scientific notation and
  calculators 283
Basic math facts 318
Math symbols..........319
Math formulas
 320-321
Equivalents and
  conversions............367
Calculus functions ..373
Greek alphabet
  (calculus)..............377

Limit values............377
Formulas and
  theorems 1145-1148

SCIENCE

Mitosis 203
Meiosis...................205
Atomic masses 230
Periodic
  table 234-235
Equations for laws
  of motion and
  gravity 248
SI units............476-477
Human organ
  systems 494-495
Periodic
  table 504
Equations of
  motion 536

SOCIAL SCIENCES

ABCs of studying....572
Ways to improve test
  scores....................588
Interview tips..........660
Constitutional
  amendments..........456